www.wadsworth.com

wadsworth.com is the World Wide Web site for Wadsworth and is your direct source to dozens of online resources.

At *wadsworth.com* you can find out about supplements, demonstration software, and student resources. You can also send email to many of our authors and preview new publications and exciting new technologies.

wadsworth.com
Changing the way the world learns®

2003-2004 EDITION

American Government and Politics Today

Steffen W. Schmidt

Mack C. Shelley

Barbara A. Bardes

THOMSON

WADSWORTH

Australia • Canada • Mexico • Singapore • Spain
United Kingdom • United States

THOMSON

★

WADSWORTH

Publisher: Clark Baxter
Acquiring Editor: David Tatom
Senior Development Editor: Sharon Adams Poore
Assistant Editor: Julie Yardley
Marketing Manager: Janise Fry
Project Editor: Hal Humphrey
Print Buyer: Barbara Britton
Permissions Editor: Joohee Lee
Production and Design: Bill Stryker

Photo Researcher: Anne Sheroff
Copy Editor: Pat Lewis
Illustrator: Bill Stryker
Cover Designer: Bill Stryker
Cover Images: Background flag image by Frank Walsh/Photonica;
girl with flag by Ethan Miller/Reuters/Getty Images
Text and Cover Printer: Transcontinental
Compositor: Parkwood Composition Service

Printed in Canada

2 3 4 5 6 7 06 05 04 03

For more information about our products, contact us at:
Thomson Learning Academic Resource Center
1-800-423-0563
For permission to use material from this text, contact us by:
Phone: 1-800-730-2214
Fax: 1-800-730-2215
Web: http://www.thomsonrights.com

Library of Congress ISSN: 1079–0071
ISBN: 0–534–59256–2

Wadsworth/Thomson Learning
10 Davis Drive
Belmont, CA 94002-3098
USA

Asia
Thomson Learning
5 Shenton Way #01-01
UIC Building
Singapore 068808

Australia
Nelson Thomson Learning
102 Dodds Street
South Melbourne, Victoria 3205
Australia

Canada
Nelson Thomson Learning
1120 Birchmount Road
Toronto, Ontario M1K 5G4
Canada

Europe/Middle East/Africa
Thomson Learning
High Holborn House
50/51 Bedford Row
London WC1R 4LR
United Kingdom

Latin America
Thomson Learning
Seneca, 53
Colonia Polanco
11560 Mexico D.F.
Mexico

Spain
Paraninfo Thomson Learning
Calle/Magallanes, 25
28015 Madrid, Spain

Contents in Brief

Contents

CHAPTER 2
The Constitution 31

CHAPTER 3
Federalism 79

CHAPTER 5
Civil Rights: Equal Protection 145

CHAPTER 8
Interest Groups 229

CHAPTER 9
Political Parties 259

CHAPTER 10
Campaigns, Nominations, and Elections 291

CHAPTER 11
The Media and Cyberpolitics 331

CHAPTER 13
The Presidency 391

CHAPTER 15
The Judiciary 451

Features of Special Interest

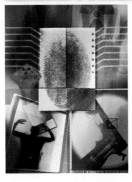

Preface

As always, we have made major additions to this new edition of *American Government and Politics Today*. Regrettably, many of those changes and additions were made necessary by the turmoil, confusion, and political responses brought about by the terrorist attacks on the World Trade Center and the Pentagon on September 11, 2001. Fortunately, though, this nation, its people, and its government rose to the occasion. Though the world will never be the same, for most Americans daily life has more or less returned to normal. Nonetheless, major issues remain. How far should our government go in protecting this nation from future attacks? Should some of our civil liberties be compromised in order to ferret out those who support, or actually are, terrorists? How much can this nation actually protect itself further? We discuss many of these issues in a new feature entitled *America's Security.*

There are, of course, other lasting problems that resulted from these horrifying attacks on the United States. In 2000, federal government officials estimated a $10 trillion budget surplus over the following decade. In fact, the federal government began running budget deficits anew in 2001 as it responded to terrorism with increased spending on homeland security and the military.

Some say that the terrorists did not just attack America, but attacked everything for which America stands. If true, then we have good news: in the long run, the terrorists will lose. What this nation has stood for, stands for, and will always stand for shall never change: individual freedom and liberty, tolerance and openness, initiative, and hard work and serious play.

2002 Election Results Included and Analyzed

Our combined teaching experience has been that students respond to up-to-date information about political events. Consequently, we have included all relevant results of the November 2002 elections. In addition, we have analyzed these results in terms of how they will affect our political processes at the national, state, and local levels. While we have updated all of the text to be consistent with these election results, in particular we have added the features listed below. Throughout the text, all materials referring to the 2002 elections are accompanied by a special logo.

- ■ *The Effect of the Elections on the Balance of Power* (Chapter 1).
- ■ *Trends in Federalism* (Chapter 2).
- ■ *Political Leadership by Women* (Chapter 5).
- ■ *The Accuracy of the 2002 Polls* (Chapter 7).
- ■ *Interest Groups: The Candidates of Choice* (Chapter 8).
- ■ *Partisan Trends in the 2002 Elections* (Chapter 9).
- ■ *The Role of the Media in the 2002 Elections* (Chapter 11).
- ■ *Congressional Characteristics after the 2002 Elections* (Chapter 12).
- ■ *Party Control of Congress after the 2002 Elections* (Chapter 12).

The Interactive Focus of this Text

Whether it be the problems that face the president, voter participation, or terrorism, we constantly strive to involve the student reader in the analysis. We make sure that the reader comes to understand that politics is not an abstract process but a very human enterprise, one involving interaction among individuals from all walks of life. We emphasize how different outcomes can affect students' civil rights and liberties, employment opportunities, and economic welfare.

Throughout the text, we encourage the reader to think critically. Virtually all of the features included in this text end with serious questions designed to pique the student's interest. A feature titled *Which Side Are You On?* directly challenges the reader to find a connection between controversial issues facing the nation and the reader's personal life. We further encourage interacting with the political system by ending each chapter with a feature titled *Making a Difference* and online exercises (to be discussed shortly) that students can perform to access and analyze political information. In addition, we offer a free, student-oriented supplement called *Thinking Globally, Acting Locally.* This supplement is designed to help students get involved and become active citizens.

Enclosed Free *American Government and Politics Today* Interactive CD-ROM

Every new copy of the 2003–2004 Edition of *American Government and Politics Today* is automatically packaged with a free CD-ROM. Brand new to the book, this interactive CD-ROM features the complete text in electronic format, as well as the following integrated features: animated figures, simulations, video clips, MicroCase® exercises, Internet activities, InfoTrac® exercises, participation exercises, public opinion data, hot links, and additional resources such as speeches, inaugural addresses, court cases, the *Federalist Papers,* and more. Each chapter in the text ends with a section titled *Your CD-ROM Resources* that lists the added resources on the CD for easy reference.

The Most Complete Web Connection

Not only has the political world been changing rapidly, but so, too, has the way in which information throughout the world is disseminated. We continue to make sure that our text leads the industry in terms of its integration with the Web. For this edition, you will find the following Web-based resources:

■ **The Wadsworth American Government Resource Center—at** **http://politicalscience.wadsworth.com/amgov.** The American Government Resource Center provides a rich array of tools that help students understand the American political process. These materials are organized around nineteen core American government topics, each of which features a set of eight student activities designed to inspire and motivate active citizenship. These activities include simulations, participation activities, MicroCase exercises, an InfoTrac College Edition reader, related links, Internet activities, source readings, issues in the news, current events quizzes, and video studies.

■ **A text-specific site for this book**—accessible through the Wadsworth American Government Resource Center's site or directly at **http://politicalscience.wadsworth.com/schmidt.** *American Government and Politics Today* includes tutorial quizzing, InfoTrac exercises, Internet activities, and related links unique to this book.

■ **InfoTrac® College Edition**—an online search engine that will take the student to exactly where he or she needs to go to find relevant information, including full-text articles in important political science journals and other sources. A special icon in the margin indicates that InfoTrac will provide information and links relating to the particular topic being discussed in the text.

■ **E-mocracy**—a section at the end of each chapter that lists and briefly describes important Web sites relating to topics covered in the chapter and takes the student through specific exercises on how to use Web resources for a better understanding of American government.

■ **American Government Internet Activities**—a free booklet that takes the student on a grand tour of numerous Web sites, each related to a specific major topic in American government studies. The student is asked to perform exercises on the Web for each topic covered.

■ **Online testing**—which allows instructors to provide and grade examinations online, using *ExamView*.

■ **WebTutor on WebCT or Blackboard**—a content-rich, easy-to-use, Web-based study aid for students that includes presentations of concepts, flashcards with audio clips, Web links, tutorials, discussion questions, and more.

Special Pedagogical Aids and High-Interest Features

The 2003–2004 Edition of *American Government and Politics Today* contains numerous pedagogical aids and high-interest features to assist both students and instructors in the learning/teaching process. The following list summarizes the special elements that can be found in each chapter:

■ *Chapter Outline*—a preview of the contents of the chapter.

■ *What If . . .* —a discussion of a hypothetical situation that begins with a "Background" section and concludes with "For Critical Analysis" questions.

■ *Margin Definitions*—for all important terms.

■ *Did You Know . . . ?*—margin features presenting various facts and figures that add relevance, humor, and some fun to the learning process.

■ *Which Side Are You On?*—a special feature designed to elicit student responses to controversial issues.

■ *America's Security*—a new feature that examines the many ways in which a newly security-conscious America is dealing with terrorist threats.

■ *Global View*—a feature that looks at specific developments, events, or government structures in other nations of the world.

■ *Politics and . . .* —a feature that examines the influence of politics on a variety of issues, including *Politics and the Media, Politics and Religion,* and *Politics and Education.*

■ *Why Is It Important Today?*—a concluding section in each chapter that discusses how the challenges in American government affect every citizen today.

■ *Making a Difference*—a chapter-ending feature showing the student some specific ways in which she or he can become actively involved in American politics.

■ *Key Terms*—a chapter-ending list, with page numbers, of all terms in the chapter that were boldfaced and defined in the margins.

■ *Chapter Summary*—a point-by-point summary of the chapter text.

■ *Selected Print and Media Resources*—offers suggested scholarly readings as well as popular books and films relevant to chapter topics.

■ *Your CD-ROM Resources*—a section concluding each chapter that lists additional resources on the enclosed CD-ROM for easy reference.

■ *E-mocracy*—a feature that discusses politics and the Internet and suggests Web sites and Internet activities related to the chapter's topics.

Appendices

Because we know that this book serves as a reference, we have included important documents for the student of American government to have close at hand. A fully annotated copy of the U.S. Constitution appears at the end of Chapter 2, as an appendix to that chapter. In addition, we have included the following appendices:

■ The Declaration of Independence.

■ How to Read Case Citations and Find Court Decisions.

■ Presidents of the United States.

■ *Federalist Papers* No. 10, No. 51, and No. 78.

■ Justices of the U.S. Supreme Court since 1900.

■ Party Control of Congress since 1900.

■ Spanish Equivalents for Important Terms in American Government.

A Complete Supplements Package

We are proud to be the authors of a text that has the most complete, accessible, and fully integrated supplements package on the market. Together, the text and the supplements listed below constitute a total learning/teaching package for you and your students. For further information on any of these supplements, contact your Wadsworth/Thomson Learning sales representative.

Supplements for Instructors

■ *Instructor's Resource CD-ROM*—Includes the Instructor's Manual, Test Bank, Exam View, PowerPoint slides containing the figures from the text, and the Video Case Study Instructor's Manual.

■ *Instructor's Manual.*

■ *Online Instructor's Manual* (password protected).

■ *Multimedia Manager for Political Science: A Microsoft PowerPoint Link Tool.*

■ *My Course 2.0.*

■ *Test Bank.*

■ *ExamView.*

■ *American Government Transparency Acetates Package*, 2003 Edition.

- *Political Science Video Library.*

- *CNN Today: American Government*, Volumes I , II, III, and IV (VHS videos).

- *Video Case Studies in American Government.*

- *Video Case Studies Instructor's Manual.*

Supplements for Students

- *Study Guide.*

- *WebTutor on WebCT* or *Blackboard.*

- *American Government: An Introduction Using* MicroCase ExplorIT, *Seventh Edition.*

- *America at Odds* CD-ROM.

- *American Government Internet Activities*, Third Edition.

- *Readings in American Government*, Fourth Edition.

- *Supplemental government texts for California and Texas.*

- *An Introduction to Critical Thinking and Writing in American Politics.*

- *Handbook of Selected Court Cases.*

- *Thinking Globally, Acting Locally.*

- *Handbook of Selected Legislation and Other Documents.*

- *College Survival Guide: Hints and References to Aid College Students*, Fourth Edition.

- *InfoTrac® College Edition.*

- *InfoTrac® College Edition Student Guide for Political Science.*

For Users of the Previous Edition

As usual, we thank you for your past support of our work. We have made numerous changes to this text for the 2003–2004 Edition, many of which we list below. We have rewritten much of the text, added numerous new features, and updated it to reflect the results of the 2002 elections.

New Special Features

- *America's Security.*

- *Politics and . . . .*

- *Elections 2002.*

New *What If . . .* Features

- "What If . . . The States Were Responsible for Homeland Defense?" (Chapter 3).

- "What If . . . You Had to Carry a National Identification Card?" (Chapter 4).

- "What If . . . The Supreme Court Banned Affirmative Action?" (Chapter 6).

- "What If . . . Exit Polls Were Banned?" (Chapter 7).

- "What If . . . Every Lobbying Contact Had to Be Recorded?" (Chapter 8).

■ "What If . . . The Legislative and Executive Branches Were Always Controlled by the Same Party?" (Chapter 9).

■ "What If . . . We Had a National Election System?" (Chapter 10).

■ "What If . . . There Were No Executive Privilege?" (Chapter 13).

■ "What If . . . Bureaucrats Were Really Held Accountable?" (Chapter 14).

New *America's Security* Features

■ Networks and Netwars (Chapter 1).

■ Big Brother Can Recognize You—Biometrics Is Now a Reality (Chapter 2).

■ Chipping Away at State Police Power (Chapter 3).

■ Military Tribunals for Suspected Terrorists (Chapter 4).

■ Should We Shut the Immigration Door? (Chapter 5).

■ Polling in Times of National Crisis (Chapter 7).

■ Interest Groups and Aviation Security (Chapter 8).

■ Party Politics in the Aftermath of 9/11 (Chapter 9).

■ Was the Airline Bailout Necessary? (Chapter 12).

■ The President's Role in Wartime (Chapter 13).

■ Placing Curbs on Information Disclosure (Chapter 14).

■ Does National Security Require Secret Courts (Chapter 15).

■ Policymaking in the Face of Terrorism (Chapter 16).

■ Nuclear Proliferation and Terrorists (Chapter 17).

Significant Changes within Chapters

Each chapter contains new features, updated information and tabular data, and, whenever feasible, the most current information available on the problems facing the nation. The effects of emerging technology, including the Internet, are emphasized throughout. Here we list other significant changes made to each chapter.

■ Chapter 1—has been revised to include new developments that are changing the focus of American politics and government, including the war on terrorism and the changing ethnic face of America. The discussion of ideology has also been expanded, and the chapter now includes a description of "teledemocracy" as a new type of direct democracy in the Internet age.

■ Chapter 2—explores new scholarly research regarding the system of checks and balances established by the framers of the Constitution.

■ Chapter 3—provides a more detailed discussion of federal grants to the states and the trend toward states' rights.

■ Chapters 4, 5, and 6—have been extensively revised and updated to include discussions of recent court cases involving church-state issues, free speech on the Internet and on college campuses, the death penalty, the Americans with Disabilities Act, and affirmative action. In addition, these chapters now include detailed discussions of how the war on terrorism is affecting Americans' civil liberties, immigrants' rights, and constitutional protections generally.

■ Chapter 7—has been significantly revised to streamline the sections discussing technology and opinion polls and public opinion and the political process. The subsection on political culture was also extensively revised to include the crisis following the 2000 elections and the public's response to the events of September 11, 2001.

- Chapter 8—includes a new section discussing interest groups and campaign finance.

- Chapter 10—includes a discussion of the Bipartisan Campaign Reform Act of 2002 and the efforts to reform the election process in the wake of election irregularities in 2000.

- Chapter 11—includes numerous updates. In addition, the section on bias in the media was completely rewritten to incorporate new scholarly literature on this topic.

- Chapter 13—explores the challenges facing President George W. Bush during his first years in office, particularly with respect to the war on terrorism.

- Chapter 17—examines how the threat of terrorism has affected U.S. foreign policy. This chapter also discusses various "hot spots" around the world and their influence on U.S. policy.

New Print Supplements

- A new edition of *Readings in American Government.*

- A new edition of transparency acetates.

- A new edition of the *Instructor's Manual.*

- A new edition of the *Test Bank.*

- *InfoTrac College Edition Student Guide for Political Science.*

New Multimedia Supplements

- *American Government and Politics Today* Interactive CD-ROM.

- *WebTutor* on *WebCT* or *Blackboard.*

- *American Government: An Introduction Using* MicroCase ExplorIT, Seventh Edition.

- *ExamView.*

- Political Science Video Library.

- New Web resources.

- New CNN videos.

- My Course 2.0.

- *Instructor's Resource* CD-ROM.

- *Video Case Studies in American Government.*

- *Multimedia Manager for Political Science: A Microsoft PowerPoint Link Tool.*

Acknowledgments

Since we started this project a number of years ago, a sizable cadre of individuals has helped us in various phases of the undertaking. The following academic reviewers offered numerous constructive criticisms, comments, and suggestions during the preparation of all previous editions:

Danny M. Adkison
Oklahoma State University

Sharon Z. Alter
William Rainey Harper College, Illinois

William Arp III
Louisiana State University

Kevin Bailey
North Harris Community College, Texas

Evelyn Ballard
Houston Community College

Orlando N. Bama,
McLennan Community College, Texas

Dr. Charles T. Barber
University of Southern Indiana, Evansville,

Clyde W. Barrow
Texas A&M University

David S. Bell
Eastern Washington University

David C. Benford, Jr.
Tarrant County Junior College

John A. Braithwaite
Coastline College

Lynn R. Brink
North Lake College, Irving, Texas

Barbara L. Brown
Southern Illinois University at Carbondale

Richard G. Buckner
Santa Fe Community College

Kenyon D. Bunch
Fort Lewis College, Durango, Colorado

Ralph Bunch
Portland State University, Oregon

Carol Cassell
University of Alabama

Frank T. Colon
Lehigh University, Pennsylvania

Frank J. Coppa
Union County College, Cranford, New Jersey

Robert E. Craig
University of New Hampshire

Doris Daniels
Nassau Community College, New York

Carolyn Grafton Davis
North Harris County College, Texas

Paul B. Davis
Truckee Meadows Community College, Nevada

Richard D. Davis
Brigham Young University

Ron Deaton
Prince George's Community College, Maryland

Marshall L. DeRosa
Louisiana State University, Baton Rouge

Michael Dinneen
Tulsa Junior College, Oklahoma

Gavan Duffy
University of Texas at Austin

Gregory Edwards
Amarillo College, Texas

George C. Edwards III
Texas A&M University

Mark C. Ellickson
Southwestern Missouri State University,
Springfield

Larry Elowitz
Georgia College

John W. Epperson
Simpson College, Indianola, Indiana

Daniel W. Fleitas
University of North Carolina at Charlotte

Elizabeth N. Flores
Del Mar College, Texas

Joel L. Franke
Blinn College, Brenham, Texas

Barry D. Friedman
North Georgia College

Robert S. Getz
SUNY–Brockport, New York

Kristina Gilbert
Riverside Community College, California

William A. Giles
Mississippi State University

Donald Gregory
Stephen F. Austin State University

Forest Grieves
University of Montana

Dale Grimnitz
Normandale Community College,

Bloomington, Minnesota

Stefan D. Haag
Austin Community College, Texas

Willie Hamilton
Mount San Jacinto College, California

Jean Wahl Harris
University of Scranton, Pennsylvania

David N. Hartman
Rancho Santiago College,
Santa Ana, California

Robert M. Herman
Moorpark College, California

Richard J. Herzog
Stephen F. Austin State University,
Nacogdoches, Texas

Paul Holder
McClennan Community College, Waco, Texas

Michael Hoover
Seminole Community College,
Sanford, Florida

J. C. Horton
San Antonio College, Texas

Robert Jackson
Washington State University

Willoughby Jarrell
Kennesaw College, Georgia

Loch K. Johnson
University of Georgia

Donald L. Jordan
United States Air Force Academy, Colorado

John D. Kay
Santa Barbara City College, California

Charles W. Kegley
University of South Carolina

Bruce L. Kessler
Shippensburg University, Pennsylvania

Jason F. Kirksey
Oklahoma State University

Nancy B. Kral
Tomball College, Texas

Dale Krane
Mississippi State University

Samuel Krislov
University of Minnesota

William W. Lamkin
Glendale Community College

Harry D. Lawrence
Southwest Texas Junior College, Uvaide, Texas

Ray Leal
Southwest Texas State University, San Marcos

Sue Lee
Center for Telecommunications, Dallas
County Community College District

Carl Lieberman
University of Akron, Ohio

Orma Linford
Kansas State University

James J. Lopach
University of Montana

Eileen Lynch
Brookhaven College, Texas

James D. McElyea
Tulsa Junior College, Oklahoma

Thomas J. McGaghie
Kellogg Community College, Michigan

William P. McLauchlan
Purdue University, Indiana

William W. Maddox
University of Florida

S. J. Makielski, Jr.
Loyola University, New Orleans

Jarol B. Manheim
George Washington University

J. David Martin
Midwestern State University, Texas

Bruce B. Mason
Arizona State University

Thomas Louis Masterson
Butte College, California

Steve J. Mazurana
University of Northern Colorado

Stanley Melnick
Valencia Community College, Florida

Robert Mittrick
Luzurne County Community College,
Pennsylvania

Helen Molanphy
Richland College, Texas

James Morrow
Tulsa Community College

Keith Nicholls
University of Alabama

Stephen Osofsky
Nassau Community College, New York

John P. Pelissero
Loyola University of Chicago

Neil A. Pinney
Western Michigan University

George E. Pippin
Jones County Community College, Mississippi

Walter V. Powell
Slippery Rock University, Pennsylvania

Michael A. Preda
Midwestern State University, Texas

Mark E. Priewe
University of Texas at San Antonio

Charles Prysby
University of North Carolina

Donald R. Ranish
Antelope Valley College, California

John D. Rausch
Fairmont State University, West Virginia

George E. Pippin
Jones County Junior College, Mississippi

Renford Reese
California State Polytechnic University—
Pomona

Curt Reichel
University of Wisconsin

Russell D. Renka
Southeast Missouri State University

Paul Rozycki
Charles Stewart Mott Community College,
Flint, Michigan

Bhim Sandhu
West Chester University, Pennsylvania

Pauline Schloesser
Texas Southern University

Eleanor A. Schwab
South Dakota State University

Len Shipman
Mount San Antonio College, California

Scott Shrewsbury
Mankato State University, Minnesota

Alton J. Slane
Muhlenberg College, Pennsylvania

Joseph L. Smith
Grand Valley State University, Michigan

Michael W. Sonnlietner
Portland Community College, Oregon

Gilbert K. St. Clair
University of New Mexico

Carol Stix
Pace University, Pleasantville, New York

Gerald S. Strom
University of Illinois at Chicago

John R. Todd
North Texas State University

Ron Velton
Grayson County College, Texas

Albert C. Waite
Central Texas College

Benjamin Walter
Vanderbilt University, Tennessee

B. Oliver Walter
University of Wyoming

Mark J. Wattier
Murray State University, Kentucky

Thomas L. Wells
Old Dominion University, Virginia

Jean B. White
Weber State College, Utah

Allan Wiese
Mankato State University, Minnesota

Lance Widman
El Camino College, California

J. David Woodard
Clemson University, South Carolina

Robert D. Wrinkle
Pan American University, Texas

The 2003–2004 Edition of this text is the result of our working closely with reviewers who each offered us penetrating criticisms, comments, and suggestions for how to improve the text. Although we haven't been able to take account of all requests, each of the reviewers listed below will see many of his or her suggestions taken to heart.

Hugh M. Arnold
Clayton College and State University, Georgia

Shari Garber Bax
Central Missouri State University

Victoria A. Farrar-Myers
University of Texas at Arlington

Justin Halpern
Northeastern State University, Oklahoma

Regina Swopes
Northeastern Illinois University

Albert C. Waite
Central Texas College

In preparing this edition of *American Politics and Government Today*, we were the beneficiaries of the expert guidance of a skilled and dedicated team of publishers and editors. We would like, first of all, to thank Susan Badger, the president of Wadsworth Publishing Company, for the support she has shown for this project. We have benefited greatly from the supervision and encouragement given by David Tatom, editorial director. Sharon Adams Poore, our senior developmental editor, also deserves our thanks for her efforts in coordinating reviews and in many other aspects of project development. We are also indebted to Diana Long and Julie Iannacchino, editorial assistants, for their contributions to this project.

We are grateful to Bill Stryker, our production manager, for a remarkable design and for making it possible to get the text out on time. In addition, our gratitude goes to all of those who worked on the various supplements offered with this text and to Melinda Newfarmer, who coordinates the Web site and the CD-ROM. We would also like to thank Janise Fry, marketing manager, for her tremendous efforts in marketing the text.

Many other people helped during the research and editorial stages of this edition as well. Erin Wait skillfully coordinated the authors' efforts and provided editorial and research assistance from the outset of the project through its final stages. Pat Lewis's copyediting and Judy Kiviat's and Suzie DeFazio's proofreading abilities contributed greatly to the book. We also thank Sherri Downing-Alfonso and Roxie Lee for their proofreading and other assistance, which helped us to meet our ambitious publishing schedule, and Sue Jasin of K&M Consulting for her contributions to the smooth running of the project.

Any errors, of course, remain our own. We welcome comments from instructors and students alike. Suggestions that we have received on previous editions have helped us to improve this text and to adapt it to the changing needs of instructors and students.

Steffen Schmidt   Mack Shelley   Barbara Bardes

About the Authors

Steffen W. Schmidt

Steffen W. Schmidt is a professor of political science at Iowa State University. He grew up in Colombia, South America, and studied in Colombia, Switzerland, and France. He obtained his Ph.D. from Columbia University, New York, in public law and government.

Schmidt has published six books and over seventy articles in scholarly journals. He is also the recipient of numerous prestigious teaching prizes, including the Amoco Award for Lifetime Career Achievement in Teaching and the Teacher of the Year award. He is a pioneer in the use of Web-based and real-time video courses and is a member of the American Political Science Association's section on Computers and Multimedia. He is on the editorial board of the *Political Science Educator*.

Schmidt has a political talk show on WOI radio, where he is known as Dr. Politics. The show has been broadcast live from various U.S. and international venues.

Schmidt likes to snow ski, ride hunter jumper horses, and race sailboats.

Mack C. Shelley II

Mack C. Shelley II is a professor of political science and statistics at Iowa State University. After receiving his Bachelor's degree from American University in Washington, D.C., he went on to graduate studies at the University of Wisconsin at Madison, where he received a Master's degree and a Ph.D. He taught for two years at Mississippi State University prior to arriving at Iowa State in 1979.

Shelley has published numerous articles, books, and monographs on public policy In1993, he was elected co-editor of the *Policy Studies Journal*. His published books include *The Permanent Majority: The Conservative Coalition in the United States Congress; Biotechnology and the Research Enterprise: A Guide to the Literature* (with William F. Woodman and Brian J. Reichel); and *American Public Policy: The Contemporary Agenda* (with Steven G. Koven and Bert E. Swanson).

In his spare time, Shelley has been known to participate in softball, bowling (he was on two championship faculty teams), and horseback riding. When his son was given a pool table for his fourteenth birthday, he took up that game as a pastime.

Barbara A. Bardes

Barbara A. Bardes is a professor of political science and Dean of Raymond Walters College at the University of Cincinnati. She received her Bachelor of Arts degree and Master of Arts degree from Kent State University, and her Ph.D. from the University of Cincinnati. She held a faculty position at Loyola University in Chicago for many years before returning to Cincinnati, her home town, as a college administrator.

Bardes has written articles on public opinion and foreign policy, and on women and politics. She has authored *Thinking about Public Policy; Declarations of Independence: Women and Political Power in Nineteenth Century American Novels;* and *Public Opinion: Measuring the American Mind* (with Robert W. Oldendick).

Bardes's home is located in a very small hamlet in Kentucky called Rabbit Hash, famous for its 150-year-old General Store. Her hobbies include travel, gardening, needlework, and antique collecting.

PART ONE

The American System

WHAT IF...
Americans Had to Pass a Test to Vote?

BACKGROUND

If an immigrant wants to become an American citizen, he or she must meet a number of requirements. These requirements include understanding the English language and passing a test on the Constitution and U.S. history.

In contrast, if a citizen wants to register to vote, generally all he or she must do is to find the local government registration office, sign a card or a short document, and present some form of identification to show that the voter lives in that state. Under federal law, the forms for voter registration must be made available at a number of locations, including driver's license bureaus and welfare offices. Registering to vote is obviously much simpler than becoming a citizen.

WHAT IF AMERICANS HAD TO PASS A TEST TO VOTE?

Many studies have shown that Americans actually have very little knowledge about their government or their political representatives. Although voting turnout has declined over the last fifty years, far more people vote than know the names of their congressional representatives or which political party controls Congress.

Furthermore, Americans know very little about what their representatives are empowered to do. When asked about the powers of Congress or the contents of the Constitution, Americans do not have much knowledge. True, Americans do pay attention to political campaigns and make decisions about candidates and issues as elections come closer. Yet requiring Americans to pass a test on their political system before being entitled to vote might produce more informed voters.

WHAT SHOULD A TEST COVER?

If the national government, for example, would require that all voters pass a test before they could vote for a national office such as the presidency or a seat in Congress, what should the test cover? It could be argued that the test should stress basic facts, such as the functions of the branches of government or the length of terms of senators and representatives. Perhaps questions on the way that laws are passed or how government regulations are created might be more appropriate. The test that persons must take to become naturalized citizens includes such questions. Some might suggest that it is most important for voters to know something about the office for which they are casting a vote and about the individuals who are seeking their support.

IS A TEST FOR VOTERS LEGAL?

At the present time, it is illegal for a government to require voters to pass literacy tests. Such tests were used as a tool in the southern states to keep African Americans from voting from the period after the Civil War until the civil rights movement of the 1960s. The Voting Rights Act of 1965 outlawed such tests for any voter who had completed the sixth grade in school. A new literacy or history test could be required by an act of Congress, however.

IS A TEST FOR VOTERS DEMOCRATIC?

The question of whether a test for voters is democratic is much more important than whether such a test could be made legal. The theory of democratic government holds that each member of society has an equal vote and an equal voice in making political decisions. In fact, many of the "checks and balances" in the U.S. Constitution were approved by the founders because they knew that many of the voters in their new nation were not well educated. The lack of an education has never been a reason for denying individuals the right to vote, because that right is considered a fundamental tenet of the system rather than a privilege to be earned.

The idea of requiring a test for voters would raise a host of other issues. For example, inevitably questions would arise about who would write the test and who would grade it. Clearly, a required test for voters could be used, again, as a political tool to keep some groups from voting while encouraging others—one of the oldest political maneuvers in the world.

FOR CRITICAL ANALYSIS

1. What kinds of information do you think would be most important for voters to know before voting in a presidential election?
2. If a test for voting were approved, what might be the political impact of such a test on the composition of the electorate?

Worth events and domestic crises create political changes that affect the way all of us live. All of us have experienced sometimes small, sometimes dramatic changes in our lives since terrorists attacked the United States on September 11, 2001. Note, though, that changes in American politics and government have not always required such a terrible tragedy. The American political landscape has been changing, for better or for worse, since the colonists first set foot on this continent. One thing is for sure, though: in all times of crises, Americans have looked to their government for solutions—and the government has acted. In that respect, the reaction of federal, state, and local governments after 9/11 was not unprecedented. Certainly, most Americans, whatever their political views, were thankful that "someone" was in charge during the hours, days, and even months following the terrorist attacks of 9/11. Most crises have not required a military response, but the American public generally supported President George W. Bush's decision to destroy the al Qaeda[1] terrorist network in Afghanistan, along with the Taliban government that harbored it.

In the name of the war on terrorism, government has restricted some of our rights and liberties. Now more than ever, we need an informed citizenry who can evaluate whether legislation of this type has gone too far. Perhaps, as we suggest in the *What If . . .* feature that opens this chapter, if citizens had to pass a test to vote we might indeed have a citizenry better able to evaluate these new restrictions.

In this chapter, we will discuss some of the questions and principles that are fundamental to the construction of any political system. Part of the excitement of the American political system is that these questions and principles continue to be debated in the United States as we attempt to balance forces of change and stability.

Change versus Stability

People and governments need stability as well as change. Agreement on the rules of the road, on the structure of government, and especially on the processes by which change is made gives people the confidence they need to plan for their own futures. If governments change capriciously or suddenly, no individual or family can be sure that their plans are safe.

---

[1] *Al Qaeda* is an Arabic word meaning "the Base." It is transliterated into English using different spellings, including *al Qaida* and *al-Qa'idah*.

Afghan girls watch a U.S. soldier of the 101st Airborne Division during a search for weapons stockpiles and al Qaeda members in July 2002. Remnants of the Taliban and al Qaeda were suspected of taking shelter in the mountains of southeast Afghanistan, near the Pakistan border. (AP Photo/Scott Nelson)

Due to our electoral system, Americans have the opportunity to maintain or to change the balance of power in their national government every two years. In the 2002 elections, the overwhelming majority of members of Congress were returned safely to their seats. In the 2004 presidential elections, the voters will decide whether to leave the executive reins of government in the hands of President George W. Bush or vote in a new leader.

ELECTIONS 2002   The Effect of the Elections on the Balance of Power

Typically, the party of the president loses seats in Congress during the midterm elections. The Democrats had high hopes for narrowing the Republican hold on the House of Representatives, which was a slim 15 out of 435 seats, and for expanding their hold on power in the Senate. But the 2002 elections defied this trend. The Republicans gained seats in both chambers, giving President George W. Bush solid congressional support to pursue his agenda in 2003 and 2004.

In addition, many scholars predict that Republican control of Congress will assure conservative appointments to the federal judiciary, including to the Supreme Court. When Democrats controlled the Senate Judiciary Committee, they frequently blocked Bush's conservative nominees, as you will read in Chapter 15. Now Bush may resubmit some of those nominees, who are more likely to be approved in a Republican-controlled Senate.

The willingness of Americans to respond to new challenges and, when necessary, to demand changes in the way the government works is at the core of our democratic nation. Change—even revolutionary change—is a tribute to the success of a political system. As Abraham Lincoln put it, "This country with all its institutions, belongs to the people who inhabit it. Whenever they shall grow weary of the existing government, they can exercise their Constitutional right of amending it, or the revolutionary right to dismember or overthrow it."[2]

In the chapters that follow, we will look more closely at the **institutions** of our government and how they have changed over the decades. We will examine how the political processes of the nation work to accomplish those changes. To begin, we will look at why political institutions and processes are necessary in any society and what purposes they serve.

Institution
A long-standing, identifiable structure or association that performs certain functions for society.

What Is Politics?

Why do nations and people struggle so hard to establish a form of government and continue to expend so much effort in politics to keep that government functioning? Politics and forms of government are probably as old as human society. There are many definitions of politics, but all try to explain how human beings regulate conflict within their society. As soon as humans began to live in groups, particularly groups that were larger than their immediate families, they found that they needed to establish rules about behavior, property, the privileges of individuals and groups, and how people would survive together. **Politics** can best be understood as the process of resolving conflicts and deciding, as Harold Lasswell put it, "who gets what, when, and how."[3]

Politics
A process that regulates conflict within a society; according to Harold Lasswell, "who gets what, when, and how" in a society.

---

[2] First Inaugural Address, March 4, 1861.

[3] Harold Lasswell, *Politics: Who Gets What, When and How* (New York: McGraw-Hill, 1936).

The Evolution of Politics

In the early versions of human society, the tribe or village, politics was relatively informal. Tribal elders or hereditary chiefs were probably vested with the power to decide who married whom, who was able to build a hut on the best piece of land, and which young people succeeded them into the positions of leadership. Other societies were "democratic" from the very beginning, giving their members some role in the choice of leadership and rules. Early human societies rarely had the concept of property, so few rules were needed to decide who owned which piece of property or who inherited that piece. The concepts of property and inheritance are much more modern. As society became more complex and humans became settled farmers rather than hunters and gatherers, resolving problems associated with property, inheritance, sales and exchanges, kinship, and rules of behavior became more important. Politics developed into the process by which some of these questions were answered.

Resolution of Conflicts

Inevitably, conflicts arise in society, because members of a group are distinct individuals with unique needs, values, and perspectives. Political processes may be required to help resolve at least three different kinds of conflicts that may arise in a society:

1. People may differ over their beliefs, either religious or personal, or over basic issues of right and wrong. This kind of debate has arisen in recent years over the desirability and validity of state-sanctioned same-sex marriages. The issue of whether individuals should have the right to commit physician-assisted suicide has also aroused this type of debate.

2. People within a society may differ greatly in their perception of what the society's goals should be. For example, Americans disagree about whether the national government has the right to prohibit the medical use of marijuana once a state's citizens have voted on its legality. The debate over this issue is similar to the one over assisted suicide.

3. People also may differ over how the government spends its resources. At any given time, the resources of the government (obtained from society) are limited. Therefore, Americans may disagree over which groups will receive more and which will receive less. For example, if the government spends more on senior citizens by increasing Medicare and Social Security payments, by necessity, the government will spend less on younger people.

The Need for Government and Power

If *politics* refers to conflict and conflict resolution, **government** refers to the institutions, or permanent structures, that have the power to enforce rules that impose order and stability on society. In early human societies, such as families and small tribes, there was no need for formal structures of government. Decisions were made by acknowledged leaders in those societies. In families, all members may meet together to decide values and priorities. When a community makes decisions through informal rules, politics exists—but not government. In most contemporary societies, these activities continue in many forms. For example, when a church decides to build a new building or hire a new minister, that decision may be made politically, but there is in fact no government. Politics can be found in schools, social groups, and any other organized group. When a society reaches a certain level of complexity, however, it becomes necessary to establish a permanent or semipermanent group of individuals to act for the whole, to become the government.

DID YOU KNOW . . .
That the word *politikos* (pertaining to citizen or civic affairs) was used by the Greeks thousands of years ago and that the English word *politics* entered the language around 1529**?**

Government
The institutions, or permanent structures, that have the power to enforce rules that impose order and stability on society.

Governments range in size from the volunteer city council and one or two employees of a small town to the massive and complex structures of the U.S. government or those of any other large, modern nation. Generally, governments not only make the rules but also implement them through the use of police, judges, and other government officials. (Today, the pervasive accessibility of the Internet has created a host of difficulties for governments' policing efforts—see this chapter's *America's Security* feature.)

Authority and Legitimacy

In addition to instituting and carrying out laws regulating individual behavior, such as traffic laws and criminal laws, most modern governments also attempt to carry out public policies that are intended to fulfill specific national or state goals. For example, a state may decide that its goal is to reduce teen-age consumption of alcohol and the driving accidents caused by such behavior. To do that, the state may institute extremely strong penalties for drinking, along with a statewide education program for teen-agers and younger children about the dangers of drinking and driving. The U.S. government has implemented a series of environmental laws meant to improve air and water quality. These laws require citizens to follow certain rules, such as using unleaded gasoline. Federal air-quality regulations have also forced car manufacturers to produce more fuel-efficient vehicles and, in some urban areas, require citizens to take their vehicles through pollution-inspection stations to see if their cars meet government standards.

Why do citizens obey these laws and subject themselves to these regulations? One reason citizens obey government is that it has the **authority** to make such laws. By authority, we mean the ultimate right to enforce compliance with decisions. Americans also believe the laws should be obeyed because they possess **legitimacy**—that is, they are appropriate and rightful. The laws have been made according to the correct and accepted political process by representatives of the people. Therefore, the people accept the laws as legitimate and having political authority.

The Question of Power

Another and perhaps more basic answer as to why we comply with the laws and rules of the government is that we understand that government has the **power** to enforce the law. We obey environmental laws and pay taxes in part because we acknowledge the legitimacy of the law. We also know that the government has the power to coerce our compliance with the law. Governments differ in the degree to which they must

Authority
The features of a leader or an institution that compel obedience, usually because of ascribed legitimacy. For most societies, government is the ultimate authority.

Legitimacy
A status conferred by the people on the government's officials, acts, and institutions through their belief that the government's actions are an appropriate use of power by a legally constituted governmental authority following correct decision-making policies. These actions are regarded as rightful and entitled to compliance and obedience on the part of citizens.

Power
The ability to cause others to modify their behavior and to conform to what the power holder wants.

Osama Bin Laden is pictured here in a televised broadcast in October 2001. Bin Laden's al Qaeda terrorist network is a nonstate organization dispersed worldwide and capable of thwarting government's traditional policing efforts. (AP Photo/Al Jazeera)

America's Security

Networks and Netwars

The terrorist attacks on the United States on 9/11 were not masterminded by a traditional governmental institution. Nor were they carried out impulsively. Rather, as we belatedly found out, they were masterminded by a nongovernmental, quasi-hierarchical terrorist organization, al Qaeda, which had planned the attacks over many months. Carrying out those terrorist acts would probably have been impossible before the advent of, and access to, worldwide instantaneous communications via the Internet. Traditional governments today must confront terrorist and criminal networks, such as al Qaeda, that are engaged in what some political scientists call "netwars."*

IN FUTURE WARS, THE BATTLE MAY NOT BE BETWEEN ARMIES

Throughout world history, sovereign states have sent forth armies to wage battles against their enemies. Although today's terrorist groups may possess biological and chemical weapons of mass destruction, and even eventually nuclear bombs, they do not rely on traditional armies. The 9/11 terrorist

*See especially David Ronfeldt and John Arquilla, *Networks and Netwars: The Future of Terror, Crime, and Militancy* (Santa Monica, Calif.: Rand Corp., 2001).

attacks did not require the use of tanks and regular armed forces. Rather, the attack on America came from a worldwide network, although its purported leader, Osama Bin Laden, apparently was based in Afghanistan. Bin Laden's al Qaeda is a new type of *nonstate* enemy operating in small, dispersed units connected via the Internet. These units can disrupt traditional governments and civil society and then melt into the landscape and disappear for a while, only to reemerge intact with the capability of creating more terror.

THE EDGE GOES TO NONSTATE ACTORS, UNLESS . . .

Traditional governments are hierarchically structured. They are based on traditional pyramids of power and organization. In contrast, today's terrorist groups consist of many networked nonstate organizations and usually operate using a more horizontal type of organizational structure in which there are many nodes of power and information.

Some have suggested that to fight successfully against these nonstate terrorist networks, traditional nations must restructure their organizations, at least partially, along the same lines as their new enemies. In other words, the traditional nations will need to organize themselves into multi-organizational networks. As one analyst has noted, "The network appears to be the next form of organization—long after tribes, hierarchies, and markets—to come into its own to redefine societies, and in so doing, the nature of conflict and cooperation." †

AMERICA'S FUNDAMENTAL SECURITY CHALLENGE

Even before 9/11, the challenge posed by these new networks had been recognized. In 2000, for example, the State Department had issued a study about patterns of global terrorism, and

†*Ibid.*, p. 2.

the Interagency Working Group had published *International Crime Threat Assessment.* The National Intelligence Council also recognized the problem in its *Global Trends 2015* report. Our military leaders today are aware that they must fight fire with fire by cracking and attacking terrorists' networks worldwide. Such a sustained attack appears to involve a loss of some of our privacy rights, however, particularly with respect to government "snooping" throughout the Internet.

On the positive side, our authorities can work more closely with nongovernmental organizations (so-called NGOs) and other nonstate groups that are helping to build a civil society through networking. These groups can be viewed as our civil-society net warrior allies. One typical example is the International Campaign to Ban Land Mines. This NGO has no central headquarters or bureaucracy. Rather, it is based on open communications among a network of national campaigns, all coordinated on behalf of a common goal. This civil-society network even includes some governmental officials. Human rights groups and other groups that wish to spread democratic values worldwide are also developing network-based organizations.

FOR CRITICAL ANALYSIS

If terrorist groups are really a part of worldwide networks, why has the U.S. government been so concerned with certain traditional state governments, such as those in Iran, Iraq, and North Korea?

To find out more about this topic, use the term "totalitarianism" in the Subject guide.

Compliance
The act of accepting and carrying out authorities' decisions.

Totalitarian Regime
A form of government that controls all aspects of the political and social life of a nation. All power resides with the government. The citizens have no power to choose the leadership or policies of the country.

Oligarchy
Rule by a few members of the elite, who generally make decisions to benefit their own group.

Elite
An upper socioeconomic class that controls political and economic affairs.

Aristocracy
Rule by the best suited, through virtue, talent, or education; in later usage, rule by the upper class.

Anarchy
The condition of having no government and no laws. Each member of the society governs himself or herself.

Democracy
A system of government in which ultimate political authority is vested in the people. Derived from the Greek words *demos* ("the people") and *kratos* ("authority").

Direct Democracy
A system of government in which political decisions are made by the people directly, rather than by their elected representatives; probably possible only in small political communities.

Legislature
A governmental body primarily responsible for the making of laws.

rely on coercion to gain **compliance** from their citizens. In authoritarian nations, the use of force is far more common than in democratic nations, where most citizens comply with the law because they accept the authority of the government and its officials. In authoritarian or **totalitarian regimes,** the will of the government is imposed frequently and is upheld by the use of force.

The concept of power also involves the ability of one individual or a group of individuals to influence the actions of another individual or group. We frequently speak of the power of the president to convince Congress to pass laws, or the power of a certain interest group, such as the National Rifle Association, to influence legislation. We also speak frequently of the power of money to influence political decisions. These uses of power are informal and involve using rewards, rather than the threat of coercion, to ensure compliance. More often than not, political power in the government is a matter of influence and persuasion rather than coercion.

Who Governs?

One of the most fundamental questions of politics has to do with which person or groups of people control society through the government. Who possesses the power to make decisions about who gets what and how the benefits of the society are distributed among the people?

Sources of Political Power

At one extreme is a society governed by a totalitarian regime. In such a political system, a small group of leaders or a single individual—a dictator—makes all political decisions for the society. Every aspect of political, social, and economic life is controlled by the government. The power of the ruler is total (thus, the term *totalitarianism*).

Many of our terms for describing the distribution of political power are derived from the ancient Greeks, who were the first Western people to study politics systematically. A society in which political decisions were controlled by a small group was called an **oligarchy,** meaning rule by a few members of the **elite,** who generally benefited themselves. Another form of rule by the few was known as **aristocracy,** meaning rule by the most virtuous, the most talented, or the best suited to the position. Later in European history, aristocracy meant rule by the titled or the upper classes. In contrast to such a top-down form of control was the form known as **anarchy,** or the condition of no government. Anarchy exists when each individual makes his or her own rules for behavior, and there are no laws and no government.

The Greek term for rule by the people was **democracy.** Although most Greek philosophers were not convinced that democracy was the best form of government, they understood and debated the possibility of such a political system. Within the limits of their culture, some of the Greek city-states operated as democracies.

Direct Democracy as a Model

From the ancient Greek city-states comes a model for governance that has framed the modern debate over whether the people can make decisions about their own government and laws. The Athenian system of government is usually considered the model for **direct democracy** because the citizens of that community debated and voted directly on all laws, even those put forward by the ruling council of the city. The most important feature of Athenian democracy was that the **legislature** was composed of all of the citizens. Women, foreigners, and slaves, however, were excluded because they were not citizens. The outstanding feature of this early form of government was that it required a high level of participation from every citizen; that participation was seen as benefiting the individual and the city-state. The

Athenians recognized that although a high level of participation might lead to instability in government, citizens, if informed about the issues, could be trusted to make decisions about the laws governing their community.

Direct Democracy Today.   Direct democracy also has been practiced in some Swiss cantons and, in the United States, in New England town meetings and in some midwestern township meetings. At New England town meetings, which can include all of the voters who live in the town, important decisions are made for the community—such as levying taxes, hiring city officials, and deciding local ordinances—by majority vote. Some states provide a modern adaptation of direct democracy for their citizens; in most states, representative democracy is supplemented by the **initiative** or the **referendum**—a process by which the people may vote directly on laws or constitutional amendments. The **recall** process, which is available in over one-third of the states, allows the people to vote to remove an official from state office.

Teledemocracy.   Because of the Internet, Americans have more access to political information than ever before. Voters can now go online to examine the record of any candidate for any office. Constituents can badger their congressional representatives and state legislators by sending them e-mails. Individuals can easily and relatively inexpensively form political interest groups using the Internet. They can even contribute to a particular politician's campaign via the Internet.

   Therefore, to some extent, we are gradually progressing toward a type of teledemocracy in which citizens and their political representatives communicate with each other easily and frequently online. Should we take a further step and create a direct democracy in which citizens cast online votes on important policy issues as they arise? This would be the extreme version of teledemocracy and much more akin to the Athenian direct democracy model. Actually, in 2000, Colorado offered its citizens the opportunity of voting online.[4] Some advocates of teledemocracy believe that voting online will transform politics as we know it.[5] (See this chapter's *Which Side Are You On?* feature on the next page for a further discussion of this topic.)

---

[4] Dave Brady, "Netting Voters," *The Industry Standard,* June 26, 2000, p. 119.
[5] Ted Becker and Crista D. Slaton, *The Future of Teledemocracy* (Westport, Conn.: Praeger, 2000).

To find out more about this subject, use the term "direct democracy" in Keywords.

Initiative
A procedure by which voters can propose a law or a constitutional amendment.

Referendum
An act of referring legislative (statutory) or constitutional measures to the voters for approval or disapproval.

Recall
A procedure allowing the people to vote to dismiss an elected official from state office before his or her term has expired.

This town meeting in Vermont allows every citizen of the town to vote directly and in person for elected officials, for proposed policies, and, in some cases, for the town budget. To be effective, such a form of direct democracy requires that the citizens stay informed about local politics, attend town meetings, and devote time to discussion and decision making. (AP Photo/Toby Talbot)

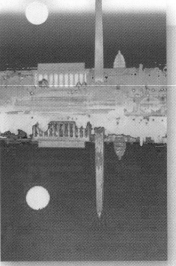

Which Side Are You On?
Should Politicians Be Forced to Follow the Results of Electronic Voting on Policy Issues?

In the ultimate in electronic democracy, or teledemocracy, the entire nation would be able to express its views on important policy issues via voting on the Internet. Even without such an extensive teledemocracy in place, the public can, through opinion polls, express its support or disdain for a particular policy. There is no law, though, that forces Congress to respond to the public's views on issues.

A notable example of congressional unresponsiveness to public opinion was the impeachment of President Bill Clinton (1993–2001). Virtually every opinion poll found that the majority of Americans did not believe that Clinton should be impeached and removed from office. Nonetheless, congressional Republicans continued with impeachment proceedings. This is just one example of what some political scientists argue is a widening gulf between policy decisions and the preferences of the American people.* As other examples, consider that during much of the 1990s, the public, through opinion polls, voiced a desire for legislation to reform campaign financing and regulate tobacco. Congress was unresponsive, nonetheless.

*See especially Lawrence R. Jacobs and Robert Y. Shapiro, *Politicians Don't Pander: Political Manipulation and the Loss of Democratic Responsiveness* (Chicago: University of Chicago Press, 2000).

Americans are becoming more comfortable with turning to the Internet to express their opinions, known as teledemocracy. Some states are even allowing voting on the Internet. Shown here, an elderly couple receives assistance with casting their votes via the Internet. What problems might arise with Internet voting? (AP Photo/Matt York)

MAKING THE CONNECTION STICK

Today's politicians clearly watch public opinion polls but not for the purpose of deciding what policies would best coincide with the public's wishes. Rather, they check the polls to figure out how to change the "spin" of their political messages to their constituents. In so doing, they attempt to obtain public support for the policies that they and their most generous supporters favor, which are not necessarily the policies that the public appears most to favor.

To lessen this disconnect between public opinion and policy actions, we could institute a set of rules based on the outcome of electronic voting on important policy issues. We could, for example, require (through a constitutional amendment) that whenever two-thirds of the nation's eligible voters televoted in favor of or against a particular policy issue, Congress would have to work in the direction of that overwhelming public opinion.

DOES TELEDEMOCRACY PRESENT TOO MANY PROBLEMS?

In spite of the apparent widening disparity between public opinion and congressional policy actions, not everyone believes that teledemocracy would correct the situation. First, not everyone is connected to the Internet, especially not everyone from poor families. We certainly would not want to have congressional actions based on electronic voting that was not representative. Second, some believe that we elect our representatives to act as our stewards—in our best interests as a nation, not necessarily in our best interests as individuals. Although policies made by our representatives may often not benefit us individually, in the end, they may make us a better nation.

WHAT'S YOUR POSITION?

To what extent do you believe that members of Congress should be forced to respond to strong public opinion when they make policy? Is the threat of not being reelected a strong enough incentive for senators and representatives to want to satisfy their constituents' desires?

GOING ONLINE

The Teledemocracy Action News + Network, or TAN+N, is the Web site of the Global Democracy Movement. It provides news and links about teledemocracy and e-voting in the United States and around the world. Visit its Web site at **http://frontpage.auburn.edu/tann**. For information on how public opinion polls influence policy decisions today, visit the following Web sites: **http://www.publicagenda.org**, **http://www.pollingreport.com**, and **http://people-press.org**.

The Dangers of Direct Democracy

Although they were aware of the Athenian model, the framers of the U.S. Constitution—for the most part—were opposed to such a system. For many centuries preceding this country's establishment, any form of democracy was considered to be dangerous and to lead to instability. But in the eighteenth and nineteenth centuries, the idea of government based on the **consent of the people** gained increasing popularity. Such a government was the main aspiration of the American Revolution, the French Revolution in 1789, and many subsequent ones. The masses, however, were considered to be too uneducated to govern themselves, too prone to the influence of demagogues (political leaders who manipulate popular prejudices), and too likely to abrogate minority rights.

James Madison defended the new scheme of government set forth in the U.S. Constitution, while warning of the problems inherent in a "pure democracy":

> A common passion or interest will, in almost every case, be felt by a majority of the whole . . . and there is nothing to check the inducements to sacrifice the weaker party or an obnoxious individual. Hence it is that such democracies have ever been spectacles of turbulence and contention, and have ever been found incompatible with personal security or the rights of property; and have in general been as short in their lives as they have been violent in their deaths.[6]

Like many other politicians of his time, Madison feared that pure, or direct, democracy would deteriorate into mob rule. What would keep the majority of the people, if given direct decision-making power, from abusing the rights of minority groups?

Representative Democracy

The framers of the U.S. Constitution chose to craft a **republic,** meaning a government in which the power rests with the people, who elect representatives to govern them and to make the laws and policies. To eighteenth-century Americans, the idea of a republic also meant a government based on common beliefs and virtues that would be fostered within small communities. The rulers were to be amateurs—good citizens—who would take turns representing their fellow citizens, in a way similar to the Greek model.[7]

To allow for change while ensuring a measure of stability, the U.S. Constitution created a form of republican government known as a **representative democracy.** The people hold the ultimate power over the government through the election process, but policy decisions are all made by elected officials. Even this distance between the people and the government was not sufficient. Other provisions in the Constitution made sure that the Senate and the president would be selected by political elites rather than by the people, although later changes to the Constitution allowed the voters to elect members of the Senate directly. This modified form of democratic government came to be widely accepted throughout the Western world as a compromise between the desire for democratic control and the needs of the modern state. The *Making a Difference* feature at the end of the chapter suggests some ways for you to explore how representative democracies work.

Principles of Democratic Government.   All representative democracies rest on the rule of the people as expressed through the election of government officials. In the 1790s, only free white males were able to vote, and in some states they had to be property owners as well. Women did not receive the right to vote in national elections in the United States until 1920, and the right to vote was not really secured by African Americans until the 1960s. Today, **universal suffrage** is the rule.

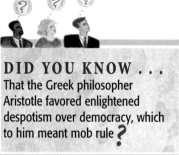

DID YOU KNOW . . .
That the Greek philosopher Aristotle favored enlightened despotism over democracy, which to him meant mob rule **?**

Consent of the People
The idea that governments and laws derive their legitimacy from the consent of the governed.

Republic
A form of government in which sovereignty rests with the people, who elect agents to represent them in lawmaking and other decisions.

Representative Democracy
A form of government in which representatives elected by the people make and enforce laws and policies.

Universal Suffrage
The right of all adults to vote for their representatives.

---

[6] James Madison, in Alexander Hamilton, James Madison, and John Jay, *The Federalist Papers,* No. 10 (New York: Mentor Books, 1964), p. 81. See Appendix D of this textbook.
[7] See Chapter 2 for a discussion of the founders' ideas.

Volunteers register voters in the Spanish Harlem section of New York City. By setting up a table in the neighborhood, the election officials make registration more convenient for voters as well as less threatening. Both political parties often conduct voter-registration drives in the months before general elections. (Lisa Quinones, Black Star)

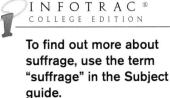

INFOTRAC®
COLLEGE EDITION

To find out more about suffrage, use the term "suffrage" in the Subject guide.

Majority
More than 50 percent.

Majority Rule
A basic principle of democracy asserting that the greatest number of citizens in any political unit should select officials and determine policies.

Limited Government
A form of government based on the principle that the powers of government should be clearly limited either through a written document or through wide public understanding; characterized by institutional checks to ensure that government serves the public rather than private interests.

Granting every person the right to participate in the election of officials recognizes the equal voting power of each citizen. This emphasis on the equality of every individual before the law is central to the American system. Because everyone's vote counts equally, the only way to make fair decisions is by some form of **majority** will. But to ensure that **majority rule** does not become oppressive, modern democracies also provide guarantees of minority rights. If certain democratic principles did not protect minorities, the majority might violate the fundamental rights of members of certain groups, especially groups that are unpopular or dissimilar to the majority population. In the past, the majority has imposed such limitations on African Americans, Native Americans, and Japanese Americans, to name only a few.

One way to guarantee the continued existence of a representative democracy is to hold free, competitive elections. Thus, the minority always has the opportunity to win elective office. For such elections to be totally open, freedom of the press and speech must be preserved so that opposition candidates may present their criticisms of the government.

Constitutional Democracy.   Another key feature of Western representative democracy is that it is based on the principle of **limited government.** The powers of the government are clearly limited, either through a written document or through widely shared beliefs. The U.S. Constitution sets down the fundamental structure of the government and the limits to its activities. Such limits are intended to prevent political decisions based on the whims or ambitions of individuals in government rather than on constitutional principles.

Do We Have a Democracy?

The sheer size and complexity of American society seem to make it unsuitable for direct democracy on a national scale. Some scholars suggest that even representative democracy is difficult to achieve in any modern state. They point to the low level of turnout for presidential elections and the even lower turnout for local ones. Polling data have shown that many Americans are neither particularly interested in politics nor well informed. Few are able to name the persons running for Congress in their districts, and even fewer can discuss the candidates' positions. Members of Congress claim to represent their constituents, but few constituents follow the issues, much less communicate their views to their representatives. For the average citizen, the national government is too remote, too powerful, and too bureaucratic to be influenced by one vote.

Democracy for the Few

If ordinary citizens are not really making policy decisions with their votes, who is? One answer suggests that elites really govern the United States. Proponents of **elite theory** see society much as Alexander Hamilton did, when he said,

> All communities divide themselves into the few and the many. The first are the rich and the wellborn, the other the mass of the people. . . . The people are turbulent and changing; they seldom judge or determine right. Give therefore to the first class a distinct, permanent share in the government. They will check the unsteadiness of the second, and as they cannot receive any advantage by a change, they therefore will ever maintain good government.

Elite theory describes an American mass population that is uninterested in politics and that is willing to let leaders make the decisions. Some versions of elite theory posit a small, cohesive elite class that makes almost all the important decisions regarding the nation,[8] whereas others suggest that voters choose among competing elites. New members of the elite are recruited through the educational system so that the brightest children of the masses allegedly have the opportunity to join the elite stratum.

In such a political system, the primary goal of the government is stability, because elites do not want any change in their status. Major social and economic change takes place only if elites see their resources threatened. This selfish interest of the elites does not mean, however, that they are necessarily undemocratic or always antiprogressive. Whereas some policies, such as favorable tax-avoidance laws, may be perceived as elitist in nature, other policies benefit many members of the public. Indeed, political scientists Thomas Dye and Harmon Ziegler propose that American elites are more devoted to democratic principles and rights than are most members of the mass public.[9]

---

[8] Michael Parenti, *Democracy for the Few,* 7th ed. (Belmont, Calif.: Wadsworth, 2001).
[9] Thomas Dye and Harmon Ziegler, *The Irony of Democracy: An Uncommon Introduction to American Politics,* 11th ed. (Orlando, Fla.: Harcourt Brace, 1999).

DID YOU KNOW . . .
That the phrase "In God We Trust" was made the national motto on July 30, 1956, but had appeared on U.S. coins as early as 1864 ?

Elite Theory
A perspective holding that society is ruled by a small number of people who exercise power in their self-interest.

Elites may have far more power and influence on the political system than do voters from the lower and middle classes. Because they share an educational background from selective schools, a higher income level, and common lifestyles with government policymakers, they are more likely to see government policymakers on a social basis and to form friendships with elected officials.
(Rob Nelson, Stock Boston)

Many observers contend that economic and social developments in the last several years have strengthened the perception that America is governed by an elite, privileged group. Wealthy citizens have educational opportunities that poorer individuals believe they cannot afford. Moreover, as you will read in Chapter 10, political campaigns are expensive, and campaign costs have increased steadily each year. Today, candidates for political office, unless they can raise campaign funds from wealthy supporters or interest groups, have to drop out of the race—or not enter it in the first place. Some predict that if present trends continue, we will indeed have a "democracy for the few."

Democracy for Groups

A different school of thought looks at the characteristics of the American electorate and finds that our form of democracy is based on group interests. Even if the average citizen cannot keep up with political issues or cast a deciding vote in any election, the individual's interests will be protected by groups that represent her or him.

Pluralism
A theory that views politics as a conflict among interest groups. Political decision making is characterized by bargaining and compromise.

Pluralism.   Theorists who subscribe to **pluralism** as a way of understanding American politics believe that people are naturally social and inclined to form associations. In the pluralists' view, politics is the struggle among groups to gain benefits for their members. Given the structures of the American political system, group conflicts tend to be settled by compromise and accommodation so that each interest is satisfied to some extent.

Pluralists see public policy as resulting from group interactions carried out within Congress and the executive branch. Because there are a multitude of interests, no one group can dominate the political process. Furthermore, because most individuals have more than one interest, conflict among groups does not divide the nation into hostile camps.

There are a number of flaws in some of the basic assumptions of this theory. Among these are the relatively low number of people who formally join interest groups, the real disadvantages of pluralism for poor citizens, and the belief that group decision making always reflects the best interests of the nation.

Hyperpluralism
A situation that arises when interest groups become so powerful that they dominate the political decision-making structures, rendering any consideration of the greater public interest impossible.

Hyperpluralism.   With these flaws in mind, critics see a danger that groups may become so powerful that all policies become compromises crafted to satisfy the interests of the largest groups. The interests of the public as a whole, then, cannot be considered. Critics of pluralism have suggested that a democratic system can be virtually paralyzed by the struggle between interest groups. This struggle results in a condition sometimes called **hyperpluralism,** meaning that groups and their needs control the government and decision making rather than the government's acting for the good of the nation.

Both pluralism and elite theory attempt to explain the real workings of American democracy. Neither approach is complete, nor can either be proved. Viewing the United States as run by elites reminds us that the founders themselves were not great defenders of the mass public. In contrast, the pluralist view underscores both the advantages and the disadvantages of Americans' inclination to join, to organize, and to pursue benefits for themselves. It points out all of the places within the American political system in which interest groups find it comfortable to work. With this knowledge, the system can be adjusted to keep interest groups within the limits of the public good.

Ideas and Politics: Political Culture

Political Culture
The collection of beliefs and attitudes toward government and the political process held by a community or nation.

The writers of the American constitution believed that the structures they had created would provide for both democracy and a stable political system. They also believed that the nation would be sustained by its **political culture**—a concept defined as a patterned set of ideas, values, and ways of thinking about government and politics. In fact, one of the roles that the founders assigned to women in the early years of the republic was to be the guardians of the political culture and the teachers of fundamental beliefs to generations of children.

Political Socialization and the Dominant Culture

There is considerable consensus among American citizens about certain concepts basic to the U.S. political system. Given that the vast majority of Americans are descendants of immigrants having diverse cultural and political backgrounds, how can we account for this consensus? Primarily, it is the result of **political socialization—** the process by which such beliefs and values are transmitted to new immigrants and to our children. The nation depends on several different agents to transmit the precepts of our national culture to children and newcomers to our nation.

The most obvious source of political socialization is the family. Parents teach their children about the value of participating in the political system through their example and through their approval. One of the primary functions of the public education system in the United States is to teach the values of the political culture to students through history courses, through discussions of political issues, and through the rituals of pledging allegiance to the flag and celebrating national holidays. Traditionally, political parties also have played a role in political socialization as a way to bring new voters to their ranks. We will look at the political socialization process more closely in Chapter 7.

Before we discuss some of the most fundamental concepts of the American political culture, it is important to note that these values can be considered those of the **dominant culture.** The dominant culture in the United States has its roots in Western European civilization. From that civilization, American politics has inherited a bias toward individualism, private property, Judeo-Christian ethics, and, to some extent, the male domination of societal decisions. As the descendants of more recent immigrant groups, especially those from Asian and Islamic nations, become part of the American mainstream, there will be more challenges to the dominant culture. Other cultural heritages honor community or family over individualism and sometimes place far less emphasis on materialism. Additionally, changes in our own society have brought about the breakdown of some values, such as the sanctity of the family structure, and the acceptance of others, such as women pursuing careers in the workplace.

Political Socialization
The process through which individuals learn a set of political attitudes and form opinions about social issues. The family and the educational system are two of the most important forces in the political socialization process.

Dominant Culture
The values, customs, language, and ideals established by the group or groups in a society that traditionally have controlled politics and government institutions in that society.

Certain groups within the United States insist on maintaining their own cultural beliefs and practices. The Amish, pictured here, are descended from German religious sects and live in close communities in Pennsylvania, Ohio, Indiana, and Illinois, as well as in other states. The more conservative Amish groups do not use modern conveniences, such as automobiles or electricity, and have resisted immunizations and mandatory schooling for their children. (Brooks Kraft, Corbis-Sygma)

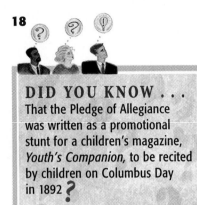

Liberty
The greatest freedom of individuals that is consistent with the freedom of other individuals in the society.

INFOTRAC ®
COLLEGE EDITION

For updates on this issue, use the term "terrorism" in the Subject guide.

Equality
A concept that all people are of equal worth.

After the September 11 terrorist attacks, state governors deployed National Guard troops to commercial airports to give travelers an increased sense of security. How can the government maintain a balance between the need for security and civil liberties? (AP Photo/ Wilfredo Lee)

The Fundamental Values

Some nations are very homogeneous, with most of their citizens having the same ethnic and religious background and sharing a common history. Achieving consensus on the basic values of the political culture is fairly easy in these nations. Because the United States is a nation of immigrants, socializing people into the political culture is an important function of the society. Over the two hundred years of its history, however, the people of the United States have formed a deep commitment to certain values and ideas. Among these are liberty, equality, and property.

Liberty.   The term **liberty** can be defined as the greatest freedom of individuals that is consistent with the freedom of other individuals in the society. In the United States, our civil liberties include religious freedom—both the right to practice whatever religion one chooses and freedom from any state-imposed religion. Our civil liberties also include freedom of speech—the right to express our opinions freely on matters, including government actions. Freedom of speech is perhaps one of our most prized liberties, because a democracy could not endure without it. These and other basic guarantees of liberty are found not in the body of the U.S. Constitution but in the Bill of Rights, the first ten amendments to the Constitution.

The process of ensuring liberty for all Americans did not end with the adoption of the Bill of Rights but has continued throughout our history. Political issues often turn on how a particular liberty should be interpreted or the extent to which it should be limited in the interests of society as a whole. Some of the most emotionally charged issues today, for example, have to do with whether our civil liberties include the liberty to have an abortion or (for terminally ill persons) the right to commit assisted suicide. Today, a major concern is whether civil liberties should be sacrificed to combat terrorism—see this chapter's *Politics and Liberty* feature for a discussion of this issue.

Equality.   The Declaration of Independence states, "All men are created equal." Today, that statement has been amended by the political culture to include groups other than white males—women, African Americans, Native Americans, Asian Americans, and others. The definition of **equality**, however, has been disputed by

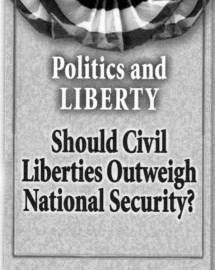

Politics and LIBERTY

Should Civil Liberties Outweigh National Security?

In the wake of the terrorist attacks on September 11, 2001, federal, state, and local governments took steps to strengthen domestic security. For example, the USA Patriot Act,* signed into law in October 2001, allows the federal government to detain noncitizens indefinitely, without a trial or hearing, on the attorney general's finding of "reasonable grounds to believe" the individuals are involved in terrorism. In the weeks following September 11, the federal government detained approximately 1,200 people.

In November 2001, President George W. Bush issued an executive order authorizing noncitizens charged in connection with the terrorist attacks to be tried by military tribunals, in which "it is not practicable to apply . . . the principles of law and the rules of evidence generally recognized in the trial of criminal cases in the United States district

*The title of this act is an acronym for "Uniting and Strengthening America by Providing Appropriate Tools Required to Intercept and Obstruct Terrorism" and often appears in capital letters as the USA PATRIOT Act of 2001.

courts." In addition, wiretapping laws were modified to give agents of the Federal Bureau of Investigation more freedom to track and monitor the activities of suspected terrorists.

Some of these steps infringe on individual civil liberties highly valued in the United States. Yet these and other government actions following the attacks are a relief to many Americans who fear more terrorism. To others, who fear the erosion of civil liberties protected by the Constitution, they are a cause of great concern.

CIVIL LIBERTIES AND AMERICAN DEMOCRACY

In the Declaration of Independence, Thomas Jefferson declared that "men are . . . endowed by their Creator with certain unalienable rights." The protection of these rights against abuses by government was the basis of the American Revolution. The framers of the Constitution and the Bill of Rights hoped to protect the individual from the tyranny of the central government. In their experience, the greatest threat to the common person, both in Great Britain and in the colonies, was the unbridled power wielded by the government. Only by securing the written promises contained in the Bill of Rights, the framers believed, could the people be guaranteed the right to the "pursuit of happiness" for which the Revolution had been fought.

CIVIL LIBERTIES ARE NOT ABSOLUTE

The civil liberties guaranteed by the Bill of Rights are a cornerstone of American democracy. But they are not absolute. The United States Supreme Court has described some of the circumstances under which the government may encroach on civil liberties:

"When clear and present danger of riot, disorder, . . . or other immediate threat to public safety, peace, or other, appears, the power of the State to prevent or punish is obvious."[†] At what point does the exercise of one person's civil liberties create a danger to others?

In the case of *Terminiello v. City of Chicago*,[‡] a man was convicted for inciting an angry crowd to a breach of the peace. His conviction was overturned by the United States Supreme Court on the ground that the city ordinance under which he was convicted violated his First Amendment right to free speech. In his famous dissent, Justice Robert Jackson argued that government could limit certain liberties if doing so would prevent outbreaks of violence. "There is danger that, if the Court does not temper its doctrinaire logic with a little practical wisdom, it will convert the constitutional Bill of Rights into a suicide pact."

Justice Jackson is frequently quoted by those who argue that the rigid protection of civil liberties in the war against terrorism will expose U.S. citizens to further attack. Upholding the Bill of Rights could be suicide, they argue. Others, however, assert that by infringing on constitutionally protected civil liberties, the government itself could become an instrument of terror.

FOR CRITICAL ANALYSIS

What liberties and privacy rights would you be willing to sacrifice in order to achieve protection against terrorist acts?

[†]*Cantwell v. State of Connecticut,* 310 U.S. 296 (1940). (See Appendix B at the end of this text for information on how court decisions are referenced.)
[‡]337 U.S. 1 (1949).

Americans since the Revolution. Does equality mean simply political equality—the right to register to vote, to cast a ballot, and to run for political office? Does equality mean equal opportunity for individuals to develop their talents and skills? If the latter is the meaning of equality, what should the United States do to ensure equal opportunities for the poor and the disabled? As you will read in later chapters of this book, much of America's politics has concerned just such questions. Although most Americans believe strongly that all persons should have the opportunity to fulfill their potential, many disagree about whether it is the government's responsibility to eliminate economic and social differences. Interestingly, the Internet may ultimately provide Americans with a forum in which all are equal—regardless of race, color, ethnic origin, gender, economic status, and the like.

Property. Many Americans probably remember that the "unalienable rights" asserted in the Declaration of Independence are the rights to "life, liberty, and the pursuit of happiness." The inspiration for that phrase, however, came from the writings of an English philosopher, John Locke (1632–1704), who stated that people's rights were to life, liberty, and **property.** In American political culture, the pursuit of happiness and property are considered to be closely related. A capitalist economy is based on private property rights. Indeed, Americans place great value on owning land, acquiring material possessions, and seeking profits through new business ventures.

Property can be seen as giving its owner political power and the liberty to do whatever he or she wants. At the same time, the ownership of property immediately creates inequality in society. The desire to own property, however, is so widespread among all classes of Americans that socialist movements, which advocate the redistribution of wealth and property, have had a difficult time securing a wide following here.

Democracy, liberty, equality, and property—these concepts lie at the core of American political culture. Other concepts—such as majority rule—are closely related to them. These fundamental principles are so deeply ingrained in U.S. culture that most Americans rarely question them. (Note that not all countries' citizens place as much worth on these values as Americans do. See, for example, the country discussed in this chapter's *Global View* feature.)

The Stability of the Culture

Political culture plays an important role in holding society together because the ideas at the core of that culture must persuade people to support and participate in the existing political process. If people begin to doubt the ideas underlying the culture, they will not transmit those beliefs to their children or support existing institutions.

Stability and Ethnic Subgroups. Consider that some subgroups, such as Native Americans and the Amish, have made concerted efforts to preserve their language or cultural practices. Many immigrant groups, including Hispanics, Asian Americans, and Caribbean Americans, maintain their language or cultural values within American cities and states. The question then arises whether these subgroups also subscribe to the values of the American political culture.

Studies of immigrant groups and ethnic subgroups generally have shown that they are as supportive of the concepts of American political culture as other Americans are. For example, when asked if they would rather live in the United States than anywhere else, 95 percent of whites said the United States, as did 87 percent of African American respondents and 92 percent of Hispanics. Some surveys have shown that immigrants are even more enthusiastic about American values than are native-born respondents.

Stability in the Face of Contested Elections. For what seemed to be an agonizingly long period of time after the 2000 presidential elections, there was little, if any, certainty about who would be the next president of the United States. Election challenges in numerous states, but most importantly in Florida, caused the outcome of the elections to be in doubt for almost a month following Election Day 2000. Some commentators said it was the most serious political crisis in our history. Others called it a constitutional crisis. Nonetheless, no more than 17 percent of Americans polled ever described the situation as remotely close to a political or constitutional crisis.[10]

Property
Anything that is or may be subject to ownership. As conceived by the political philosopher John Locke, the right to property is a natural right superior to human law (laws made by government).

---

[10] As reported in *Public Perspective,* March/April 2002, p. 11, summarizing the results of Gallup/CNN/*USA Today* polls conducted between November 11 and December 10, 2000.

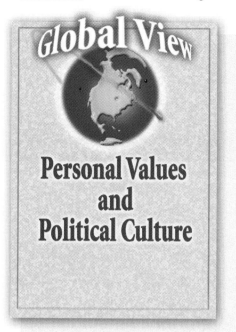

Global View

Personal Values and Political Culture

If you have lived in the United States for most of your life, you have acquired a *political culture* that consists of, at a minimum, a belief in individual freedom and privacy, separation of church and state, and tolerance for other races and religions. Had you grown up in another nation, the political culture you acquired might be quite different.

Several years ago, political scientist Samuel P. Huntington suggested that future wars would not be fought between nations but between civilizations—there would be a *clash of civilizations,* based in part on different political cultures.* In particular, he referred to the gulf between Western and Islamic cultures.

At the time, his hypothesis was widely criticized as too general and too crude. Today, Huntington's critics are quieter, and his supporters are increasing in number. For example, researchers at RoperASW, a public polling organization, presented empirical data supporting the view that people from different societies hold certain personal values very distinct from those of other societies.† Personal values, formed by political and religious cultures, tend to divide rather than unite civilizations, even in this era of unprecedented globalization.

Comparing Saudi Arabia and the United States

The researchers at RoperASW used polling data acquired through extensive interviews conducted year after year to show that the views of Saudi Arabians on key issues relating to polit-

*Samuel P. Huntington, *The Clash of Civilizations and the Remaking of World Order* (New York: Simon & Schuster, 1996).
†Thomas A. W. Miller and Geoffrey D. Feinberg, "Culture Clash," *Public Perspective,* March/April 2002, pp. 6–9.

ical culture were the most distinct from the views of Americans. Saudis and Americans shared only four of their top ten values or principles (family, faith, education, and justice). More significant are the differences found by the poll. Freedom ranks high as a personal value in America, but does not even make the top ten in Saudi Arabia. Obedience is in the top ten in Saudi Arabia, but not in America. Self-esteem is important to Americans while modesty is important to Saudis.

The Culture Gap Is Real

While RoperASW is quick to point out that it did not examine "civilizations," its research results are enlightening. Clearly, the United States and Saudi Arabia have widely different personal and political values. Furthermore, the poll showed that while the views of Saudi Arabians were the most distant from the views of Americans, Saudis did not feel a "cultural kinship" to European, Japanese, Latin American, Chinese, Hindu, or Russian culture, either.‡ If the United States and Saudi Arabia are representative of Western and Islamic societies, respectively, the data show that the culture gap between them is real, not just perceived, and may explain why common ground has been so hard to find.

Differences Do Not Necessarily Mean a Clash of Civilizations

Of course, no one can argue that the personal values in one country are better than the personal values in another. Nor do such differences in culture guarantee that there will be a so-called clash of civilizations. What we do know from studies such as the one just described is that cultural differences are very real. We in America cannot simply assume that everybody, everywhere yearns for the type of open society that we have fostered.

FOR CRITICAL ANALYSIS

Why do you think Americans ended up with a political culture in which individuality and freedom are so highly cherished?

‡*Ibid.,* p. 8.

Saudi women, covered in abayas (the traditional head-to-toe robe and headscarf), must wait at the "ladies only" counter in McDonald's. In Saudi Arabia, modesty ranks among the highest personal values, while individual freedom is ranked low by poll respondents. (AP Photo/ Saleh Rifai)

Americans are so strongly wedded to the existing political culture that they do not worry much even during periods of great uncertainty.

The Changing Face of America

The face of America is changing as its citizens age, become more diverse, and generate new needs for laws and policies. Long a nation of growth, the United States has become a middle-aged nation with a low birthrate and an increasing number of older citizens who want services from the government. The 2000 census showed that between 1990 and 2000, the U.S. population grew 13.2 percent, faster than experts expected. Both the aging of the population and its changing ethnic composition will have significant political consequences.

The Aging of America

As Figure 1–1 shows, the population is aging quickly; the median age (the age at which half the people are older and half are younger) was thirty-five in the year 2000. Even more startling is the fact that almost 13 percent of the population is now sixty-five years old or older. By the year 2050, more than one-fourth of the population will be retired or approaching retirement.

The shrinking of the younger population, not only in the United States but in all developed countries of the world, is a phenomenon not seen since the dying days of the Roman Empire. The implications for society are significant. For one thing, if the current retirement and pension systems, including Social Security, remain in place, a very large proportion of each worker's wages will go to taxes to support benefits for the retired population (see Chapter 16). For another, it means that to increase the younger population, we will need to open the doors to more immigrants—a politically divisive issue. As one scholar notes, the United States is not alone in this problem. All of the countries of the developed world, and China and Brazil as well, now have a birthrate well below the replacement rate of 2.2 live births per woman of reproductive age. In other words, all developed nations will be facing similar changes and issues as their populations continue to age.[11]

Ethnic Change

The ethnic character of the United States is also changing. Whites have a very low birthrate, whereas African Americans and Hispanics have more children per family. As displayed in Figure 1–2, including the effects of immigration, the proportion of

[11] Peter Drucker, "The Next Society," *The Economist,* November 1, 2001, p. 16.

FIGURE 1–1

The Aging of America

The figures clearly show that the portion of the population over age sixty-five will double by 2050.

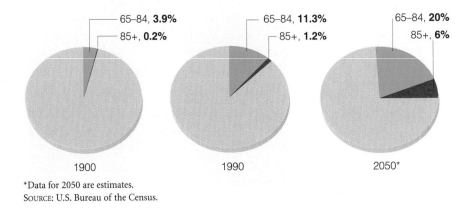

65–84, **3.9%**
85+, **0.2%**

65–84, **11.3%**
85+, **1.2%**

65–84, **20%**
85+, **6%**

1900   1990   2050*

*Data for 2050 are estimates.
Source: U.S. Bureau of the Census.

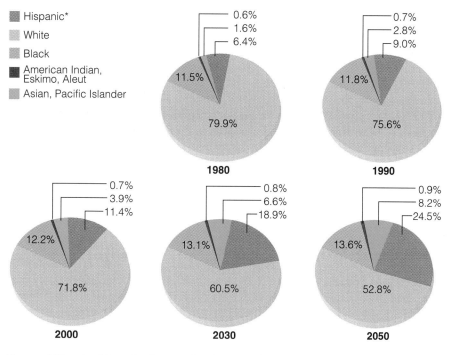

FIGURE 1–2

Distribution of the U.S. Population by Race and Hispanic Origin, 1980 to 2050

By 2050, minorities will constitute about half of the U.S. population.

*Persons of Hispanic origin can be of any race. Data for 2030 and 2050 are estimates.
SOURCE: U.S. Bureau of the Census.

whites has decreased, and the proportions of Hispanics, African Americans, and Asian Americans have increased.

Indeed, in some areas today, such as Los Angeles and other cities and counties across the Southwest, Mexican Americans now constitute a majority of the population. Significantly, in 2001, the Census Bureau announced that in California, the nation's most populous state, whites had become a minority. As a result of this shift in majority-minority status, it is often unclear what diversity means and what integration policies should aim to accomplish. Somewhat ironically, many policies that were originally designed to integrate members of minority groups into the mainstream are now being used to achieve the opposite: to ensure that whites can participate in predominantly nonwhite programs. Notably, because of the difficulties presented by the outmoded and demeaning majority/minority terminology, the San Diego City Council recently decided to ban the term *minority* entirely from city documents.[12]

Other Trends

Other changes in the face of America have more to do with our changing society. More Americans are filling the urban places of the nation in comparison with rural areas. By 2003, more than 75 percent of the population lived in an urban environment. Women continue to increase their participation in the educational system. By the beginning of the new century, as many women as men had completed their high school educations, and the percentage of women who have completed college continues to grow.

Change also continues in the structure of American families, although the traditional two-parent family is still very strong. Just twenty years ago, more than 85 percent of children lived in a two-parent family. Today, 71 percent of children under age eighteen live in two-parent families, and 25 percent live with only one parent. About one-fourth of the children of one-parent families live in poverty.

---

[12]Gregory Rodriguez, "Where the Minorities Rule," *The New York Times,* February 16, 2002, p. 6.

Ideology
A comprehensive and logically ordered set of beliefs about the nature of people and about the institutions and role of government.

Liberalism
A set of beliefs that includes the advocacy of positive government action to improve the welfare of individuals, support for civil rights, and tolerance for political and social change.

Conservatism
A set of beliefs that includes a limited role for the national government in helping individuals, support for traditional values and lifestyles, and a cautious response to change.

To find out more about liberalism, use the term "liberalism" in the Subject guide.

To find out more about conservatism, use the term "conservatism" in the Subject guide.

Other changes also have consequences for social policies. Although the national government has been committed to ending poverty since the mid-1960s, over one-tenth of all Americans still live in households that have incomes below the official poverty line. Although this number is large, it is below the 22 percent figure recorded in 1960. The number of Americans who lack basic skills is also disturbing; recent national surveys have found that about one-fifth of all Americans are barely literate and have difficulty dealing with simple documents.

Each of these trends raises political questions for the society as a whole. These facts challenge voters and their representatives to change policies in order to address these issues—if society can agree on how to do so.

Ideas and Politics: Ideology

An **ideology** is a closely linked set of beliefs about the goal of politics and the most desirable political order. True ideologies are well-organized theories that can guide virtually every decision that an individual or society can make. The major ideologies of our time are usually represented as a continuum from the far left to the far right, according to their views of the role government should play in a society. On the extreme left of the spectrum are those, such as Communists, who believe that the government should exercise central control over the economy and the political system in the interests of promoting total equality and security. Those on the extreme right of the spectrum, such as Libertarians, believe that government should play a minimal role in society and that individuals should have the greatest political and economic freedom possible.

Most Americans, though, do not derive their views on politics from the more extreme ideologies. In fact, the U.S. political spectrum has been dominated for decades by two relatively moderate ideological positions: **liberalism** and **conservatism.**

What Liberals Believe

American liberals believe that the government should take strong positive action to solve the nation's economic and social problems. They believe that it is the obligation of the government to embrace opportunities for the economic and social equality of all individuals. Generally, liberals tend to support social-welfare programs to assist the disadvantaged, to endorse progressive taxation to redistribute income from wealthy classes to the poorer groups in society, and to rely on government regulation to guide the activities of business and the economy. Today, liberals are often identified with policies supporting women's rights, civil rights, affirmative action, and generally more spending on domestic programs and less on national defense.

Often, those holding liberal views tend to identify themselves as Democrats. This does not necessarily mean, though, that all Democrats hold the liberal views just discussed. Rather, it means that, overall, the Democratic Party's positions on policies and issues find more sympathy among liberals than do those of the Republican Party.

What Conservatives Believe

In contrast to liberals, conservatives usually feel that the national government has grown too large, that state and local governments should be able to make their own decisions, and that the private sector needs less interference from the government. They tend to believe that the individual is primarily responsible for his or her own well-being. They are generally less supportive of national government programs to redistribute income, such as welfare, and programs that promote equality, such as affirmative action or assistance to disadvantaged groups.

In the moral sphere, conservatives tend to support more government regulation of social values and moral decisions than do liberals. Thus, conservatives tend to oppose gay rights legislation and to support stronger curbs on pornography. Conservatives usually show less tolerance for different life choices. They are more likely than liberals to accept government attempts to regulate personal behavior and morals.

As with liberals and the Democratic Party, there is a close relationship between conservatives and the Republican Party. Again, however, not all conservatives are Republicans, and not all Republicans subscribe to the conservative views just discussed. It is also worth noting that, while some of the nation's political leaders are strongly ideological, most Americans are not. In fact, election research suggests that only a small percentage of all Americans, perhaps less than 10 percent, can be identified as *ideologues*—those who are strongly committed to an ideology. To some extent, this is because most citizens are not all that interested in many political issues. Additionally, most Americans tend to conceive of politics more in terms of the political parties or economic well-being rather than in terms of a particular ideology.

DID YOU KNOW . . .
That about 14 percent of all legal immigrants to the United States plan to live in the Los Angeles/Long Beach, California, area **?**

American Politics: Why Is It Important Today?

Today, what happens in Washington, D.C., in state capitals, and even in city halls is perhaps more important than it has been at any time since World War II (1939–1945). In the wake of the September 11 terrorist attacks, personal security is on everyone's minds. As we observed earlier in this chapter, during times of crisis, Americans look to their government for action. Security is regarded as primarily the responsibility of government at all levels. Congress and the president responded initially with little political wrangling. They enacted airline security measures and approved attacks on the al Qaeda terrorist network in Afghanistan. Soon after the attacks, however, political conflict reappeared in debates on expanding the war on terrorism to other nations and on elevating the Office of Homeland Security to a cabinet-level department. In this sense, politics plays a direct role in ensuring Americans' safety.

Even on a more mundane basis, what happens in the nation's lawmaking bodies affects our lives every day. The food we eat, the cars we drive, the schools we attend—all are subject to laws and regulations issued by government bodies.

Particularly in these troubled times, American politics has taken on increased importance. Now, more than ever before, American citizens must be able to analyze correctly the many trade-offs involved in current and future policy. They have to become better informed. Whether we should go so far as to require voters to pass a test before being able to vote is an issue we discussed in the first page of this chapter. A radical thought? Yes. Yet its underlying premise is nonetheless worthy of serious discussion.

MAKING A DIFFERENCE | Seeing Democracy in Action

One way to begin to understand the American political system is to observe a legislative body in action. There are thousands of elected legislatures in the United States at all levels of government. You might choose to visit the city council, a school board, the township board of trustees, the state legislature, or the U.S. Congress.

Background Preparation

Before attending a business session of the legislature, try to find out how the members are elected. Look at your state government's Web site. Are the members chosen by the "at-large" method of election so that each member represents the whole community, or are they chosen by specific geographic districts or wards? Some other questions you might want to ask are these: Is there a chairperson or official leader who controls the meetings and who may have more power than the other leaders? What are the responsibilities of this legislature? Are the members paid political officials, or do they volunteer their services? Do the officials serve as full-time or part-time employees?

When You Visit

When you visit the legislature, keep in mind the theory of representative democracy. The legislators or council members are elected to represent their constituents (those who voted them into office). Observe how often the members refer to their constituents or to the special needs of their community or electoral district. Listen carefully for the sources of conflict within a community. If there is a debate, for example, over a zoning proposal that involves the issue of

land use, try to figure out why some members oppose the proposal. Perhaps the greatest sources of conflict in local government are questions of taxation and expenditure. It is important to remember that the council or board is also supposed to be working toward the good of the whole; listen for discussions of the community's priorities.

Arrange for an Interview

If you want to follow up on your visit and learn more about representative government in action, try to get a brief interview with one of the members of the council or board. In general, legislators are very willing to talk to students, particularly students who also are voters. Ask the member how he or she sees the job of representative. How can the wishes of the constituents be identified? How does the representative balance the needs of the ward or district with the good of the whole community? You also might ask the member how he or she keeps in touch with constituents and informs them of the activities of the council or board. You can write to many legislators via e-mail. You might ask how much e-mail they receive and who actually answers it.

Watch C-SPAN

For a different view of democracy in action, watch the activities of the House of Representatives or Senate on one of the C-SPAN channels on cable television. These public television channels show speeches and actions on the floor of both chambers, broadcast committee hearings when possible, and televise interviews with government officials and the journalists who

cover government and politics. If you watch the action on the floor of the House, for example, notice how few members actually are present. Is the member addressing her or his colleagues, or the voters back home? Why do you think members use large charts and graphs? Most observers of Congress believe that members dress differently and use a different speaking style since the proceedings have been televised.

Think about the advantages and disadvantages of representative democracy. Do you think the average citizen would take the time to consider all of the issues that representatives must debate? Do you think that, on the whole, the elected representatives act responsibly for their constituents?

Checking Out Local Government

To find out when and where local legislative bodies meet, look up the number of the city hall or county building in the telephone directory, and call the clerk of council. You might also check cable television listings. In many communities, city council meetings and county board meetings can be seen on public access channels. For information on the structure of your local government, contact the local chapter of the League of Women Voters.

Many cities and almost all state governments have Internet Web sites to investigate. Take a look at some of these, and consider the usefulness of the information provided there to the average citizen.

Key Terms

anarchy 10	elite theory 15	liberty 18	property 20
aristocracy 10	equality 18	limited government 14	recall 11
authority 8	government 7	majority 14	referendum 11
compliance 10	hyperpluralism 16	majority rule 14	representative democracy 13
consent of the people 13	ideology 24	oligarchy 10	republic 13
conservatism 24	initiative 11	pluralism 16	totalitarian regime 10
democracy 10	institution 6	political culture 16	universal suffrage 13
direct democracy 10	legislature 10	political socialization 17	
dominant culture 17	legitimacy 8	politics 6	
elite 10	liberalism 24	power 8	

Chapter Summary

1 The willingness of Americans to debate new initiatives and to demand changes in the way the government works is at the core of the nation's political system. Americans worked hard to establish this form of government and continue to expend effort in politics to keep it functioning.

2 *Politics* can be defined as the process of resolving conflicts, or, as defined by Harold Lasswell, the process of determining "who gets what, when, and how" in a society. *Government* can be defined as the institutions, or permanent structures, that have the power to enforce rules that impose order and stability on society. The prerogative of government to make decisions is based on authority, legitimacy, and power. Sources of power include direct democracy, a system of government in which political decisions are made by the people directly.

3 Fearing the problems of a direct democracy, the framers of the Constitution set up a representative, or indirect, democracy. The people control the government through the election of representatives. In principle, decisions are made by majority rule, although the rights of minorities are protected.

4 Some scholars believe that most of the power in our society is held by elite leaders who actively influence political decisions, while the masses are apathetic. The pluralist viewpoint, in contrast, suggests that groups representing the different interests of the people struggle for political power. In pluralist theory, the political process is characterized by bargaining and compromise between groups.

5 The American political system is characterized by a set of cultural beliefs that includes liberty, equality, and property. These beliefs are passed on to each generation of Americans through the process of political socialization.

6 The face of America is changing as the population ages and becomes more ethnically diverse. Other changes—including the urbanization of the population, the growing number of women in the work force, and poverty—are also altering the face of the nation.

7 Americans' ideas about how government should act in their lives vary widely. These views may be included in liberal, conservative, or other ideological positions.

Selected Print and Media Resources

SUGGESTED READINGS

Beem, Christopher. *The Necessity of Politics: Reclaiming Public Life (Morality and Society).* Chicago: University of Chicago Press, 1999. This author argues that simply having a healthy civil society is not enough to keep our democracy alive. He believes that society needs politics, political ideas, and a government to exist.

D'Souza, Dinesh. *What's So Great about America.* Washington, D.C.: Regnery Publishing, 2002. The author argues against those who criticize American political and cultural traditions. He believes that after the September 11 attacks on our country, a clear understanding of the moral basis of Western civilization is needed more than ever.

Gamble, Andrew. *Politics and Fate (Themes for the 21st Century).* Malden, Mass.: Blackwell Publishers, 2000. The author contends that many people have become disenchanted with the traditional view that politics is a means used by societies to exercise control over their fate. In this book, Gamble comes to the defense of politics, explaining why we cannot do without politics and the political processes.

Haskell, John. *Direct Democracy or Representative Government? Dispelling the Populist Myth.* Boulder, Colo.: Westview Press, 2000. The author expresses his concern over how the increased use of citizen initiatives, television, and the Internet make direct democracy increasingly possible in this country. He fears that direct democracy will lead to unstable political majorities that are more impulsive and less deliberative than the representative elected bodies envisioned by the founders.

Lasswell, Harold. *Politics: Who Gets What, When and How.* New York: McGraw-Hill, 1936. This classic work defines the nature of politics.

Tocqueville, Alexis de. *Democracy in America.* Edited by Phillips Bradley. New York: Vintage Books, 1945. Life in the United States is described by a French writer who traveled through the nation in the 1820s.

White, John Kenneth. *The Values Divide: American Politics and Culture in Transition.* Chatham, N.J.: Chatham House, 2002. In this insightful book, a noted political science professor concludes that America is less a place than a "dream." He notes that the American dream is alive and well and that a vast majority of Americans believe that it is possible to achieve it—and that many Americans feel that they have achieved it.

MEDIA RESOURCES

All Things Considered—A daily broadcast of National Public Radio that provides extensive coverage of political, economic, and social news stories.

Lord of the Flies—A 1990 film focusing on what happens to a group of schoolchildren when they are stranded on a desert island after their plane crashes. Is there a need for government and rules? How are these rules created?

Mr. Smith Goes to Washington—A classic movie, produced in 1939, starring Jimmy Stewart as the honest citizen who goes to Congress trying to represent his fellow citizens. The movie dramatizes the clash between representing principles and representing corrupt interests.

2001: A Space Odyssey—One of the classic movies of all time. Produced in 1968, it raises the question of whether artificial intelligence, or a kind of supergovernment (in the form of HAL, a computer), should take control of events because, as HAL says, "This mission is too important for me to allow you to jeopardize it."

Your CD-ROM Resources

In addition to the chapter content containing hot links, the following resources are available on the CD-ROM:

- **Internet Activities**—The medical use of marijuana; the al Qaeda terrorist network.

- **Critical Thinking Exercises**—What should citizens of the United States know? How has September 11th changed your life? Are you a political liberal or conservative?

- **Self-Check on Important Themes**—Can You Answer These?

- **Animated Figures**—Figure 1–1, "The Aging of America," and Figure 1–2, "Distribution of the U.S. Population by Race and Hispanic Origin."

- **Video**—*Desires of the Founders.*

- **Public Opinion Data**—What are Americans thinking about the war on terrorism?

- **InfoTrac Exercise**—"Revitalizing Democracy."

- **Simulation**—You Are There!

- **Participation Exercise**—Support an interest group of great interest to you.

- **MicroCase Exercise**—"By the Numbers: Democracy and Political Theory."

- **Additional Resources**—All court cases, Alexis de Tocqueville, *Democracy in America* (1835), Henry David Thoreau, *Civil Disobedience* (1849), Herbert Croly, *The Promise of American Life* (1909), President John F. Kennedy's Inaugural Address (1961).

e-mocracy

Connecting to American Government and Politics

The Web has become a virtual library, a telephone directory, a contact source, and a vehicle to improve your understanding of American government and politics today. To help you become familiar with Web resources, we conclude each chapter in this book with an *E-Mocracy* feature. The *Logging On* section in each of these features includes Internet addresses, or uniform resource locators (URLs), that will take you to Web sites focusing on topics or issues discussed in the chapter. Realize that Web sites come and go continually, so some of the Web sites that we include in the *Logging On* section may not exist by the time you read this book.

Each *E-Mocracy* feature also includes an Internet activity. These activities are designed to lead you to Web sites that you can explore to learn more about an important political issue. Finally, numerous other resources especially relevant to this text are listed at the end of each of these *E-Mocracy* features.

A word of caution about Internet use: Many students surf the Web for political resources. When doing so, you need to remember to approach these sources with care. For one thing, you should be very careful when giving out information about yourself. You also need to use good judgment because the reliability or intent of any given Web site is often unknown. Some sites are more concerned with accuracy than others, and some sites are updated to include current information while others are not.

Logging On

We have a powerful and interesting Web site for the textbook, which you can access through the Wadsworth American Government Resource Center. Go to

http://politicalscience.wadsworth.com/amgov

You may also want to visit the home page of Dr. Politics—offered by Steffen Schmidt, one of the authors of this book—for some interesting ideas and activities relating to American government and politics. Go to

http://www.public.iastate.edu/~sws/homepage.html

For discussion of current public-policy issues that are facing the American political system, try the resources at the Institute for Philosophy and Public Policy at

http://www.puaf.umd.edu/ippp

Information about the rules and requirements for immigration and citizenship can be found at the Web site of the U.S. Immigration and Naturalization Service:

http://www.ins.usdoj.gov

For a basic "front door" to almost all U.S. government Web sites, click onto the very useful site maintained by the University of Michigan:

http://www.lib.umich.edu/govdocs/govweb.html

For access to federal government offices and agencies, go to the U.S. government's official Web site at

http://www.firstgov.gov

To learn about the activities of one of the nation's oldest liberal political organizations, go to the Web site of the Americans for Democratic Action (ADA) at the following URL:

http://adaction.org

You can gain insight into conservative positions on political issues by going to the Web site of the American Conservative Union at

http://www.conservative.org

Using the Internet for Political Analysis

Imagine that you are not an American citizen. Try to figure out how you can become an American citizen through the process of naturalization. Log on to the Web site of the Immigration and Naturalization Service using the URL given below. Click on "Immigration Services and Benefits" and find the topic "Naturalization."

http://www.ins.usdoj.gov

Read the qualifications or eligibility requirements and decide whether you qualify. Then investigate the test materials given on the Web site to see if you would pass the history test to qualify for naturalization. Finally, look through the materials on the Web site and consider whether an immigrant is likely to (1) have a computer, (2) use the Web site, (3) understand the language, and (4) succeed in finding answers to his or her questions.

BACKGROUND

Our Constitution is the oldest written constitution in the world today. One of the reasons it has endured is that the framers used broad enough language to allow room for interpretation. The United States Supreme Court has become the ultimate decision maker when it comes to deciding what the seven thousand words in our Constitution mean. But society has changed, at least in part, because of changes in technology.

Issues concerning telephone conversations and transmission of ideas over the Internet certainly were not even pipe dreams two hundred years ago. Because the principles in our Constitution are broadly expressed, the Supreme Court has been able to apply those principles to meet the needs of new generations. Because of its flexibility and adaptability, our Constitution is often referred to as a "living Constitution."

WHAT IF CONSTITUTIONAL INTERPRETATION NEVER CHANGED?

Some students of our Constitution believe that the way the Constitution is interpreted and applied should never change. Assume for a moment that whatever was in the minds of the framers some two hundred years ago remained the backbone of present-day views of the supreme law of the land. What kind of legal foundation would we have?

A RESTRICTED VIEW OF THE COMMERCE CLAUSE

Consider first the commerce clause. That clause, which is found in Article I, Section 8, of the Constitution, states that "Congress shall have the power" to "regulate Commerce . . . among the several States." The key to understanding the commerce clause is that it presumably concerns only *interstate* commerce—what goes on between and among the several states. The clause says nothing about Congress regulating activities within states (*intrastate* commerce).

The interpretation of the power of the national government to regulate all commerce has clearly changed since the framers first penned the above words. Over time, the Supreme Court has interpreted the commerce clause to mean that Congress has the power to regulate not only interstate commerce, but also any intrastate commerce that has a "substantial effect" on interstate commerce.

If the Supreme Court had not interpreted the commerce clause so expansively, clearly our government would be different today. Many of the regulatory activities of the national government would not exist. Indeed, the national government would be a fraction of its size (but perhaps the state and local governments would be larger).

CIVIL RIGHTS AND LIBERTIES

The first ten amendments to the Constitution, the Bill of Rights, lay out the basic rights that all citizens shall enjoy. Many of the crucial issues with respect to our personal rights and liberties were not even conceived of two hundred years ago.

Consider the Fourth Amendment right to be free of unreasonable searches and seizures. Originally, searches and seizures had to do with physical elements, items that could be touched or seen. In today's wired world, however, searches and seizures can take the form of police surveillance via electronic means. Over time, the Supreme Court has held that unless certain requirements are met, electronic surveillance constitutes an unreasonable search, in violation of the Fourth Amendment. If the original interpretations of this amendment were still followed, we would probably have much less protection against electronic surveillance.

Consider privacy rights. The framers did not mention a right to privacy in the Bill of Rights. Rather, modern-day interpretations have concluded that a right to privacy is implied by several of the first ten amendments to the Constitution. Further, consider such issues as abortion and assisted suicide. It is almost impossible to imagine how the Constitution as interpreted two hundred years ago could apply to these issues.

Finally, consider that the Declaration of Independence promised equality. Yet the Constitution *implicitly* acknowledged the institution of slavery and gave full political rights only to property-owning white males. The majority of Americans, including women and Native Americans, had no such rights. Had we stayed with the meaning of the Constitution as it was originally understood, certainly most of the political and civil rights enjoyed by the majority of American citizens today would not exist.

FOR CRITICAL ANALYSIS

1. What is the alternative to a "living Constitution"?
2. Why was privacy not as significant an issue two hundred years ago as it is today?

> We the People of the United States, in Order to form a more perfect Union, establish Justice, insure domestic Tranquility, provide for the common defence, promote the general Welfare, and secure the Blessings of Liberty to ourselves and our Posterity, do ordain and establish this Constitution for the United States of America.

Every schoolchild in America has at one time or another been exposed to these famous words from the Preamble to the U.S. Constitution. The document itself is remarkable. The U.S. Constitution, compared with others in the states and in the world, is relatively short. Because amending it is difficult (as you will see later in this chapter), it also has relatively few amendments. Perhaps even more remarkable is the fact that it has remained largely intact for over two hundred years. In large part, this is because the principles set forth in the Constitution are sufficiently broad that they can be adapted to meet the needs of a changing society—as you learned in this chapter's *What If . . .* feature.

How and why this Constitution was created is a story that has been told and retold. It is worth repeating, because the historical and political context in which this country's governmental machinery was formed is essential to understanding American government and politics today. The Constitution did not result just from creative thinking. Many of its provisions were grounded in contemporary political philosophy. The delegates to the Constitutional Convention in 1787 brought with them two important sets of influences: their political culture and their political experience. In the years between the first settlements in the New World and the writing of the Constitution, Americans had developed a political philosophy about how people should be governed and had tried out numerous forms of government. These experiences gave the founders the tools with which they constructed the Constitution.

Initial Colonizing Efforts

The first English outpost in North America was set up by Sir Walter Raleigh in the 1580s for the purpose of harassing the Spanish treasure fleets. The group, known as the Roanoke Island Colony, stands as one of history's great mysteries: After a three-year absence to resupply the colony, Raleigh's captain, John White, returned in 1590 to find signs that the colony's residents apparently had moved north to Chesapeake Bay. White was unable to search further, and no evidence of the fate of the "lost colony"

The first British settlers who landed on the North American continent faced severe tests of endurance. This woodcut depicts a cold existence for the settlers in the late 1500s and early 1600s. (The Granger Collection)

Representative Assembly
A legislature composed of individuals who represent the population.

has ever been found. Local legends in North Carolina maintain that the lost colonists survived and intermarried with the Native Americans, and that their descendants live in the region today. Recent climatological studies may have shed some light on the mystery, however. Scientists at the University of Arkansas concluded, based on the rings of ancient cypress trees still growing in the swamps of that area, that the most extreme drought during the trees' eight-hundred-year history coincided with the attempted settlement on Roanoke Island and lasted for three years.[1]

In 1607, the English government sent over a group of farmers to establish a trading post, Jamestown, in what is now Virginia. The Virginia Company of London was the first to establish a permanent English colony in the Americas. The king of England gave the backers of this colony a charter granting them "full power and authority" to make laws "for the good and welfare" of the settlement. The colonists at Jamestown instituted a **representative assembly,** setting a precedent in government that was to be observed in later colonial adventures.

Jamestown was not a commercial success. Of the 105 men who landed, 67 died within the first year. But 800 new arrivals in 1609 added to their numbers. By the spring of the next year, frontier hazards had cut their numbers to 60. Of the 6,000 people who left England for Virginia between 1607 and 1623, 4,800 perished. The historian Charles Andrews has called this the "starving time for Virginia."[2] The climatological researchers just mentioned suggest that this "starving time" may have been brought about by another severe drought in the Jamestown area, which lasted from 1607 to 1612.

Separatists, the *Mayflower,* and the Compact

The first New England colony was established in 1620. A group of mostly extreme Separatists, who wished to break with the Church of England, came over on the ship *Mayflower* to the New World, landing at Plymouth (Massachusetts). Before going onshore, the adult males—women were not considered to have any political status—drew up the Mayflower Compact, which was signed by forty-one of the forty-four men aboard the ship on November 21, 1620. The reason for the compact was obvious. This group was outside the jurisdiction of the Virginia Company of London, which

[1] D. W. Stahle *et al.,* "The Lost Colony and Jamestown Droughts," *Science,* April 24, 1998.
[2] Charles M. Andrews, *The Colonial Period of American History,* Vol. 1 (New Haven, Conn.: Yale University Press, 1934), p. 110.

The signing of the compact aboard the *Mayflower.* In 1620, the Mayflower Compact was signed by almost all of the men aboard the ship *Mayflower,* just before disembarking at Plymouth, Massachusetts. It stated, "We . . . covenant and combine ourselves together into a civil body politick . . . ; and by vertue hearof to enact, constitute, and frame such just and equal laws . . . as shall be thought [necessary] for the generall good of the Colonie." (The Granger Collection)

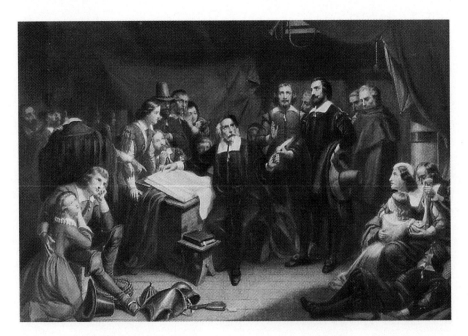

had chartered their settlement in Virginia, not Massachusetts. The Separatist leaders feared that some of the *Mayflower* passengers might conclude that they were no longer under any obligations of civil obedience. Therefore, some form of public authority was imperative. As William Bradford (one of the Separatist leaders) recalled in his accounts, there were "discontented and mutinous speeches that some of the strangers amongst them had let fall from them in the ship; That when they came a shore they would use their owne libertie; for none had power to command them."[3]

The compact was not a constitution. It was a political statement in which the signers agreed to create and submit to the authority of a government, pending the receipt of a royal charter. The Mayflower Compact's historical and political significance is twofold: it depended on the consent of the affected individuals, and it served as a prototype for similar compacts in American history. According to Samuel Eliot Morison, the compact proved the determination of the English immigrants to live under the rule of law, based on the *consent of the people*.[4]

More Colonies, More Government

Another outpost in New England was set up by the Massachusetts Bay Colony in 1630. Then followed Rhode Island, Connecticut, New Hampshire, and others. By 1732, the last of the thirteen colonies, Georgia, was established. During the colonial period, Americans developed a concept of limited government, which followed from the establishment of the first colonies under Crown charters. Theoretically, London governed the colonies. In practice, owing partly to the colonies' distance from London, the colonists exercised a large measure of self-government. The colonists were able to make their own laws, as in the Fundamental Orders of Connecticut in 1639. The Massachusetts Body of Liberties in 1641 supported the protection of individual rights and was made a part of colonial law. In 1682, the Pennsylvania Frame of Government was passed. Along with the Pennsylvania Charter of Privileges of 1701, it established the rationale for our modern Constitution and Bill of Rights. All of this legislation enabled the colonists to acquire crucial political experience. After independence was declared in 1776, the states quickly set up their own constitutions.

British Restrictions and Colonial Grievances

The conflict between Britain and the American colonies, which ultimately led to the Revolutionary War, began in the 1760s when the British government decided to raise revenues by imposing taxes on the American colonies. Policy advisers to Britain's young King George III, who ascended the throne in 1760, decided that it was only logical to require the American colonists to help pay the costs of Britain's defending them during the French and Indian War (1756–1763). The colonists, who had grown accustomed to a large degree of self-government and independence from the British Crown, viewed the matter differently.

In 1764, the Sugar Act was passed. Many colonists were unwilling to pay the required tax. Further regulatory legislation was to come. In 1765, the British Parliament passed the Stamp Act, providing for internal taxation, or, as the colonists' Stamp Act Congress assembled in 1765 called it, "taxation without representation." The colonists boycotted the purchase of English commodities in return. The success

---

[3]John Camp, *Out of the Wilderness: The Emergence of an American Identity in Colonial New England* (Middleton, Conn.: Wesleyan University Press, 1990).

[4]See Morison's "The Mayflower Compact" in Daniel J. Boorstin, ed., *An American Primer* (Chicago: University of Chicago Press, 1966), p. 18.

DID YOU KNOW . . .
That the *Mayflower* was about 90 feet long from stem to stern, had three masts, and weighed about 180 tons **?**

MILESTONES IN EARLY U.S. POLITICAL HISTORY
1585 English outpost set up on Roanoke Island.
1607 Jamestown established; Virginia Company lands settlers.
1620 Mayflower Compact signed.
1630 Massachusetts Bay Colony set up.
1639 Fundamental Orders of Connecticut adopted.
1641 Massachusetts Body of Liberties adopted.
1682 Pennsylvania Frame of Government passed.
1701 Pennsylvania Charter of Privileges written.
1732 Last of the thirteen colonies established.
1756 French and Indian War declared.
1765 Stamp Act; Stamp Act Congress meets.
1774 First Continental Congress.
1775 Second Continental Congress; Revolutionary War begins.
1776 Declaration of Independence signed.
1777 Articles of Confederation drafted.
1781 Last state signs Articles of Confederation.
1783 "Critical period" in U.S. history begins; weak national government until 1789.
1786 Shays' Rebellion.
1787 Constitutional Convention.
1788 Ratification of Constitution.
1791 Ratification of Bill of Rights.

of the boycott (the Stamp Act was repealed a year later) generated a feeling of unity within the colonies. The British, however, continued to try to raise revenues in the colonies. When duties on glass, lead, paint, and other items were passed in 1767, the colonists again boycotted English goods. The colonists' fury over taxation climaxed in the Boston Tea Party: colonists dressed as Mohawk Indians dumped almost 350 chests of British tea into Boston Harbor as a gesture of tax protest. In retaliation, the British Parliament passed the Coercive Acts (the "Intolerable Acts") in 1774, which closed Boston Harbor and placed the government of Boston under direct British control. The colonists were outraged—and they responded.

The Colonial Response: The Continental Congresses

New York, Pennsylvania, and Rhode Island proposed the convening of a colonial congress. The Massachusetts House of Representatives requested that all colonies hold conventions to select delegates to be sent to Philadelphia for such a congress.

The First Continental Congress

First Continental Congress
The first gathering of delegates from twelve of the thirteen colonies, held in 1774.

The **First Continental Congress** was held at Carpenter's Hall on September 5, 1774. It was a gathering of delegates from twelve of the thirteen colonies (delegates from Georgia did not attend until 1775). At that meeting, there was little talk of independence. The Congress passed a resolution requesting that the colonies send a petition to King George III expressing their grievances. Resolutions were also passed requiring that the colonies raise their own troops and boycott British trade. The British government condemned the Congress's actions, treating them as open acts of rebellion.

The delegates to the First Continental Congress declared that in every county and city, a committee was to be formed whose mission was to spy on the conduct of friends and neighbors and to report to the press any violators of the trade ban. The formation of these committees was an act of cooperation among the colonies, which represented a step toward the creation of a national government.

The Second Continental Congress

Second Continental Congress
The 1775 congress of the colonies that established an army.

By the time the **Second Continental Congress** met in May 1775 (this time all of the colonies were represented), fighting already had broken out between the British and the colonists. One of the main actions of the Second Congress was to establish an army. It did this by declaring the militia that had gathered around Boston an army and naming George Washington as commander in chief. The participants in that Congress still attempted to reach a peaceful settlement with the British Parliament. One declaration of the Congress stated explicitly that "we have not raised armies with ambitious designs of separating from Great Britain, and establishing independent states." But by the beginning of 1776, military encounters had become increasingly frequent.

King George III (1738–1820) was king of Great Britain and Ireland from 1760 until his death on January 29, 1820. Under George III, the first attempt to tax the American colonies was made. Ultimately, the American colonies, exasperated at renewed attempts at taxation, proclaimed their independence on July 4, 1776. (National Portrait Gallery)

Public debate was acrimonious. Then Thomas Paine's *Common Sense* appeared in Philadelphia bookstores. The pamphlet was a colonial best seller. (To do relatively as well today, a book would have to sell between eight and ten million copies in its first year of publication.) Many agreed that Paine did make common sense when he argued that

> a government of our own is our natural right: and when a man seriously reflects on the precariousness [instability, unpredictability] of human affairs, he will become convinced, that it is infinitely wiser and safer, to form a constitution of our own in a cool and deliberate manner, while we have it in our power, than to trust such an interesting event to time and chance.[5]

---

[5] *The Political Writings of Thomas Paine*, Vol. 1 (Boston: J. P. Mendum Investigator Office, 1870), p. 46.

Students of Paine's pamphlet point out that his arguments were not new—they were common in tavern debates throughout the land. Rather, it was the near poetry of his words—which were at the same time as plain as the alphabet—that struck his readers.

Declaring Independence

On April 6, 1776, the Second Continental Congress voted for free trade at all American ports for all countries except Great Britain. This act could be interpreted as an implicit declaration of independence. The next month, the Congress suggested that each of the colonies establish state governments unconnected to Britain. Finally, in July, the colonists declared their independence from Great Britain.

The Resolution of Independence

On July 2, the Resolution of Independence was adopted by the Second Continental Congress:

> RESOLVED, That these United Colonies are, and of right ought to be free and independent States, that they are absolved from allegiance to the British Crown, and that all political connection between them and the state of Great Britain is, and ought to be, totally dissolved.

The actual Resolution of Independence was not legally significant. On the one hand, it was not judicially enforceable, for it established no legal rights or duties. On the other hand, the colonies were already, in their own judgment, self-governing and independent of Britain. Rather, the Resolution of Independence and the subsequent Declaration of Independence were necessary to establish the legitimacy of the new nation in the eyes of foreign governments, as well as in the eyes of the colonists themselves. What the new nation needed most were supplies for its armies and a commitment of foreign military aid. Unless it appeared in the eyes of the world as a political entity separate and independent from Britain, no foreign government would enter into a contract with its leaders.

July 4, 1776—The Declaration of Independence

By June 1776, Thomas Jefferson already was writing drafts of the Declaration of Independence in the second-floor parlor of a bricklayer's house in Philadelphia. On adoption of the Resolution of Independence, Jefferson had argued that a declaration clearly putting forth the causes that compelled the colonies to separate from Britain was necessary. The Second Congress assigned the task to him, and he completed his work on the declaration, which enumerated the colonists' major grievances against Britain. Some of his work was amended to gain unanimous acceptance (for example, his condemnation of the slave trade was eliminated to satisfy Georgia and North Carolina), but the bulk of it was passed intact on July 4, 1776. On July 19, the modified draft became "the unanimous declaration of the thirteen United States of America." On August 2, it was signed by the members of the Second Continental Congress.

Famous Worldwide. The Declaration of Independence has become one of the world's most famous and significant documents. The words opening the second paragraph of the Declaration indicate why this is so:

> We hold these Truths to be self-evident, that all Men are created equal, that they are endowed by their Creator with certain unalienable Rights, that among these are Life, Liberty, and the Pursuit of Happiness—That to secure these Rights, Governments are instituted among Men, deriving their just Powers from the Consent of the Governed, that whenever any Form of Government becomes destructive of these Ends, it is the Right of the People to alter or abolish it, and to institute new Government.

"You know, the idea of taxation with representation doesn't appeal to me very much either."

Drawing by Handelsman;
© 1970 The New Yorker Magazine, Inc.

Members of the Second Continental Congress adopted the Declaration of Independence on July 4, 1776. Minor changes were made in the document in the following two weeks. On July 19, the modified draft became the "unanimous declaration of the thirteen United States of America." On August 2, the members of the Second Continental Congress signed it. The first official printed version carried only the signatures of the Congress's president, John Hancock, and its secretary, Charles Thompson. (Photo Researchers, Van Bucher)

Natural Rights

Rights held to be inherent in natural law, not dependent on governments. John Locke stated that natural law, being superior to human law, specifies certain rights of "life, liberty, and property." These rights, altered to become "life, liberty, and the pursuit of happiness," are asserted in the Declaration of Independence.

Social Contract

A voluntary agreement among individuals to secure their rights and welfare by creating a government and abiding by its rules.

Natural Rights and a Social Contract. The assumption that people have **natural rights** ("unalienable Rights"), including the rights to "Life, Liberty, and the Pursuit of Happiness," was a revolutionary concept at that time. Its use by Jefferson reveals the influence of the English philosopher John Locke (1632–1704), whose writings were familiar to educated American colonists, including Jefferson.[6] In his *Two Treatises on Government*, published in 1690, Locke had argued that all people possess certain natural rights, including the rights to life, liberty, and property, and that the primary purpose of government was to protect these rights. Furthermore, government was established by the people through a **social contract**—an agreement among the people to form a government and abide by its rules. As you read earlier, such contracts, or compacts, were not new to Americans. The Mayflower Compact was the first of several documents that established governments or governing rules based on the consent of the governed.

After setting forth these basic principles of government, the Declaration of Independence goes on to justify the colonists' revolt against Britain. Much of the remainder of the document is a list of what "He" (King George III) had done to deprive the colonists of their rights. (See Appendix A at the end of this book for the complete text of the Declaration of Independence.)

Once it had fulfilled its purpose of legitimating the American Revolution, the Declaration of Independence was all but forgotten for many years. According to scholar Pauline Maier, the Declaration did not become enshrined as what she calls "American Scripture" until the nineteenth century.[7]

The Rise of Republicanism

Although the colonists had formally declared independence from Britain, the fight to gain actual independence continued for five more years—until the British General Cornwallis surrendered at Yorktown in 1781. In 1783, after Britain formally recognized the independent status of the United States in the Treaty of Paris, Washington disbanded the army. During these years of military struggles, the states faced the additional challenge of creating a system of self-government for an independent United States.

---

[6] Not all scholars believe that Jefferson was truly influenced by Locke. For example, Jay Fliegelman states that "Jefferson's fascination with Homer, Ossian, Patrick Henry, and the violin is of greater significance than his indebtedness to Locke." Jay Fliegelman, *Declaring Independence: Jefferson, Natural Language, and the Culture of Performance* (Stanford, Calif.: Stanford University Press, 1993).

[7] See Pauline Maier, *American Scripture: Making the Declaration of Independence* (New York: Knopf, 1997).

Some colonists in the middle and lower southern colonies had demanded that independence be preceded by the formation of a strong central government. But the anti-Royalists in New England and Virginia, who called themselves Republicans, were against a strong central government. They opposed monarchy, executive authority, and virtually any form of restraint on the power of local groups. These so-called Republicans were a major political force from 1776 to 1780. Indeed, they almost prevented victory over the British by their unwillingness to cooperate with any central authority.

During this time, all of the states adopted written constitutions. Eleven of the constitutions were completely new. Two of them—those of Connecticut and Rhode Island—were old royal charters with minor modifications. Republican sentiment led to increased power for the legislatures. In Pennsylvania and Georgia, **unicameral** (one-body) **legislatures** were unchecked by executive or judicial authority. Basically, the Republicans attempted to maintain the politics of 1776. In almost all states, the legislature was predominant.

The Articles of Confederation: Our First Form of Government

The fear of a powerful central government led to the passage of the Articles of Confederation. The term **confederation** is important; it means a voluntary association of *independent* **states,** in which the member states agree to only limited restraints on their freedom of action. As a result, confederations seldom have an effective executive authority.

In June 1776, the Second Continental Congress began the process of drafting what would become the Articles of Confederation. The final form of the Articles was achieved by November 15, 1777. It was not until March 1, 1781, however, that the last state, Maryland, agreed to ratify what was called the Articles of Confederation and Perpetual Union. Well before the final ratification of the Articles, however, many of them were implemented: the Continental Congress and the thirteen states conducted American military, economic, and political affairs according to the standards and the form specified by the Articles.[8]

Under the Articles, the thirteen original colonies, now states, established on March 1, 1781, a government of the states—the Congress of the Confederation. The Congress was a unicameral assembly of so-called ambassadors from each state, with each state possessing a single vote. Each year, the Congress would choose one of its members as its president, but the Articles did not provide for a president of the United States. The Congress was authorized in Article X to appoint an executive committee of the states "to execute in the recess of Congress, such of the powers of Congress as the United States, in Congress assembled, by the consent of nine [of the thirteen] states, shall from time to time think expedient to vest with them." The Congress was also allowed to appoint other committees and civil officers necessary for managing the general affairs of the United States. In addition, the Congress could regulate foreign affairs and establish coinage and weights and measures. But it lacked an independent source of revenue and the necessary executive machinery to enforce its decisions throughout the land. Article II of the Articles of Confederation guaranteed that each state would retain its sovereignty. Figure 2–1 illustrates the structure of the government under the Articles of Confederation; Table 2–1 on page 40 summarizes the powers—and the lack of powers—of Congress under that system.

---

[8] Robert W. Hoffert, *A Politics of Tensions: The Articles of Confederation and American Political Ideas* (Niwot, Colo.: University Press of Colorado, 1992).

Unicameral Legislature
A legislature with only one legislative body, as compared with a bicameral (two-house) legislature, such as the U.S. Congress. Nebraska is the only state in the Union with a unicameral legislature.

Confederation
A political system in which states or regional governments retain ultimate authority except for those powers they expressly delegate to a central government. A voluntary association of independent states, in which the member states agree to limited restraints on their freedom of action.

State
A group of people occupying a specific area and organized under one government; may be either a nation or a subunit of a nation.

FIGURE 2–1

The Confederal Government Structure under the Articles of Confederation

Congress
Congress had one house. Each state had two to seven members, but only one vote. The exercise of most powers required approval of at least nine states. Amendments to the Articles required the consent of all the states.

Committee of the States
A committee of representatives from all the states was empowered to act in the name of Congress between sessions.

Officers
Congress appointed officers to do some of the executive work.

The States

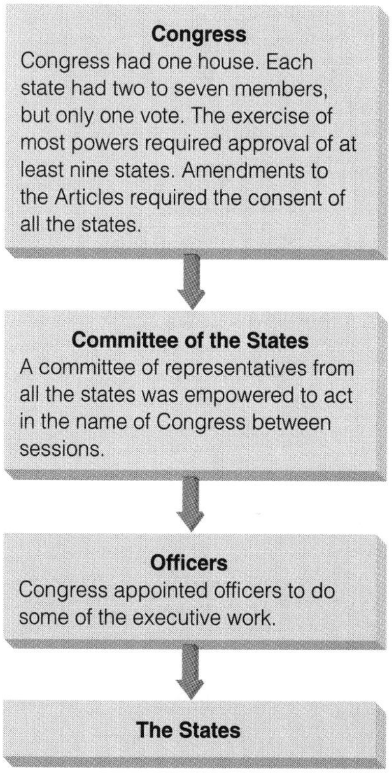

TABLE 2–1

Powers of the Congress of the Confederation

CONGRESS HAD POWER TO	CONGRESS LACKED POWER TO
▪ Declare war and make peace. ▪ Enter into treaties and alliances. ▪ Establish and control armed forces. ▪ Requisition men and money from states. ▪ Regulate coinage. ▪ Borrow money and issue bills of credit. ▪ Fix uniform standards of weight and measurement. ▪ Create admiralty courts. ▪ Create a postal system. ▪ Regulate Indian affairs. ▪ Guarantee citizens of each state the rights and privileges of citizens in the several states when in another state. ▪ Adjudicate disputes between states upon state petition.	▪ Provide for effective treaty-making power and control foreign relations; it could not compel states to respect treaties. ▪ Compel states to meet military quotas; it could not draft soldiers. ▪ Regulate interstate and foreign commerce; it left each state free to set up its own tariff system. ▪ Collect taxes directly from the people; it had to rely on states to collect and forward taxes. ▪ Compel states to pay their share of government costs. ▪ Provide and maintain a sound monetary system or issue paper money; this was left up to the states, and monies in circulation differed tremendously in value.

Accomplishments under the Articles

Although the Articles of Confederation had many defects, there were also some accomplishments during the eight years of their existence. Certain states' claims to western lands were settled. Maryland had objected to the claims of Massachusetts, New York, Connecticut, Virginia, the Carolinas, and Georgia. It was only after these states consented to give up their land claims to the United States as a whole that Maryland signed the Articles of Confederation. Another accomplishment under the Articles was the passage of the Northwest Ordinance of 1787, which established a basic pattern of government for new territories north of the Ohio River.

Weaknesses of the Articles

Although Congress had the legal right to declare war and to conduct foreign policy, it did not have the right to demand revenues from the states. It could only *ask* for them. Additionally, the actions of Congress required the consent of nine states. Any amendments to the Articles required the unanimous consent of the Congress and confirmation by every state legislature. Furthermore, the Articles did not create a national system of courts.

Basically, the functioning of the government under the Articles depended on the goodwill of the states. Article III of the Articles simply established a "league of friendship" among the states—no national government was intended.

Probably the most fundamental weakness of the Articles, and the most basic cause of their eventual replacement by the Constitution, concerned the lack of power to raise money for the militia. The Articles lacked any language giving Congress coercive power to raise money (by levying taxes) to provide adequate support for the military forces controlled by Congress. When states refused to send money to support the government (not one state met the financial requests made by Congress under the Articles), Congress resorted to selling off western lands to speculators or issuing bonds that sold for less than their face value. Due to a lack of resources, the Continental Congress was forced to disband the army, even in the face of serious Spanish and British military threats.

Shays' Rebellion and the Need for Revision of the Articles

Because of the weaknesses of the Articles of Confederation, the central government could do little to maintain peace and order in the new nation. The states bickered among themselves and increasingly taxed each other's goods. At times they prevented trade altogether. By 1784, the country faced a serious economic depression. Banks were calling in old loans and refusing to give new ones. People who could not pay their debts were often thrown into prison.

By 1786, in Concord, Massachusetts, the scene of one of the first battles of the Revolution, there were three times as many people in prison for debt as there were for all other crimes combined. In Worcester County, Massachusetts, the ratio was even higher—twenty to one. Most of the prisoners were small farmers who could not pay their debts owing to the disorganized state of the economy.

In August 1786, mobs of musket-bearing farmers led by former revolutionary captain Daniel Shays seized county courthouses and disrupted the trials of the debtors in Springfield, Massachusetts. Shays and his men then launched an attack on the federal arsenal at Springfield, but they were repulsed. Shays' Rebellion demonstrated that the central government could not protect the citizenry from armed rebellion or provide adequately for the public welfare. The rebellion spurred the nation's political leaders to action. As John Jay wrote to Thomas Jefferson,

> Changes are Necessary, but what they ought to be, what they will be, and how and when to be produced, are arduous Questions. I feel for the Cause of Liberty. . . . If it should not take Root in this Soil[,] Little Pains will be taken to cultivate it in any other.[9]

DID YOU KNOW . . .
That the 1776 constitution of New Jersey granted the vote to "all free inhabitants," including women, but the number of women who turned out to vote resulted in male protests and a new law limiting the right to vote to "free white male citizens"**?**

Drafting the Constitution

The Virginia legislature called for a meeting of all the states to be held at Annapolis, Maryland, on September 11, 1786—ostensibly to discuss commercial problems only. It was evident to those in attendance (including Alexander Hamilton and James Madison) that the national government had serious weaknesses that had to be addressed if it were to survive. Among the important problems to be solved were the relationship between the states and the central government, the powers of the national legislature, the need for executive leadership, and the establishment of policies for economic stability.

At this Annapolis meeting, a call was issued to all of the states for a general convention to meet in Philadelphia in May 1787 "to consider the exigencies of the union." When the Republicans, who favored a weak central government, realized that the Philadelphia meeting would in fact take place, they approved the convention in February 1787. They made it explicit, however, that the convention was "for the sole and express purpose of revising the Articles of Confederation." Those in favor of a stronger national government—the Federalists, as they were to be called—had different ideas.

The designated date for the opening of the convention at Philadelphia, now known as the Constitutional Convention, was May 14, 1787. Because few of the delegates had actually arrived in Philadelphia by that time, however, it was not formally opened in the East Room of the Pennsylvania State House until May 25.[10] Fifty-five

---

[9] Excerpt from a letter from John Jay to Thomas Jefferson written in October 1786, as reproduced in Winthrop D. Jordan *et al., The United States,* combined ed., 6th ed. (Englewood Cliffs, N.J.: Prentice Hall, 1987), p. 135.

[10] The State House was later named Independence Hall. This was the same room in which the Declaration of Independence had been signed eleven years earlier.

of the seventy-four delegates chosen for the convention actually attended the convention. (Of those fifty-five, only about forty played active roles at the convention.) Rhode Island was the only state that refused to send delegates.

Who Were the Delegates?

Who were the fifty-five delegates to the Constitutional Convention? They certainly did not represent a cross section of eighteenth-century American society. Indeed, most were members of the upper class. Consider the following facts:

1. Thirty-three were members of the legal profession.
2. Three were physicians.
3. Almost 50 percent were college graduates.
4. Seven were former chief executives of their respective states.
5. Six were owners of large plantations.
6. Eight were important businesspersons.

They were also relatively young by today's standards: James Madison was thirty-six, Alexander Hamilton was only thirty-two, and Jonathan Dyton of New Jersey was twenty-six. The venerable Benjamin Franklin, however, was eighty-one and had to be carried in on a portable chair borne by four prisoners from a local jail. Not counting Franklin, the average age was just over forty-two.

The Working Environment

The conditions under which the delegates worked for 115 days were far from ideal and were made even worse by the necessity of maintaining total secrecy. The framers of the Constitution felt that if public debate were started on particular positions, delegates would have a more difficult time compromising or backing down to reach agreement. Consequently, the windows were usually shut in the East Room of the State House. Summer quickly arrived, and the air became heavy, humid, and hot by noon of each day. Also, when the windows were open, flies swarmed into the room. The delegates did, however, have a nearby tavern and inn to which they retired each evening. The Indian Queen became the informal headquarters of the delegates.

Factions among the Delegates

We know much about the proceedings at the convention because James Madison kept a daily, detailed personal journal. A majority of the delegates were strong nationalists—they wanted a central government with real power, unlike the central government under the Articles of Confederation. George Washington and Benjamin Franklin preferred limited national authority based on a separation of powers. They were apparently willing to accept any type of national government, however, as long as the other delegates approved it. A few advocates of a strong central government, led by Gouverneur Morris of Pennsylvania and John Rutledge of South Carolina, distrusted the ability of the common people to engage in self-government.

Among the nationalists were several monarchists, including Alexander Hamilton, who was chiefly responsible for the Annapolis Convention's call for the Constitutional Convention. In a long speech on June 18, he presented his views: "I have no scruple in declaring . . . that the British government is the best in the world and that I doubt much whether anything short of it will do in America."

Another important group of nationalists were of a more democratic stripe. Led by James Madison of Virginia and James Wilson of Pennsylvania, these democratic nationalists wanted a central government founded on popular support.

Still another faction consisted of nationalists who were less democratic in nature and who would support a central government only if it were founded on very nar-

Elbridge Gerry (1744–1814), from Massachusetts, was a patriot during the Revolution. He was a signatory of the Declaration of Independence and later became governor of Massachusetts (1810–1812). He became James Madison's new vice president when Madison was reelected in December 1812. (The Library of Congress)

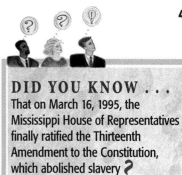

rowly defined republican principles. This group was made up of a relatively small number of delegates, including Edmund Randolph and George Mason of Virginia, Elbridge Gerry of Massachusetts, and Luther Martin and John Francis Mercer of Maryland.

Most of the other delegates from Maryland, New Hampshire, Connecticut, New Jersey, and Delaware were concerned about only one thing—claims to western lands. As long as those lands became the common property of all of the states, they were willing to support a central government.

Finally, there was a group of delegates who were totally against a national authority. Two of the three delegates from New York quit the convention when they saw the nationalist direction of its proceedings.

Politicking and Compromises

The debates at the convention started on the first day. James Madison had spent months reviewing European political theory. When his Virginia delegation arrived ahead of most of the others, it got to work immediately. By the time George Washington opened the convention, Governor Edmund Randolph of Virginia was prepared to present fifteen resolutions. In retrospect, this was a masterful stroke on the part of the Virginia delegation. It set the agenda for the remainder of the convention—even though, in principle, the delegates had been sent to Philadelphia for the sole purpose of amending the Articles of Confederation. They had not been sent to write a new constitution.

The Virginia Plan. Randolph's fifteen resolutions proposed an entirely new national government under a constitution. It was, however, a plan that favored the large states, including Virginia. Basically, it called for the following:

1. A **bicameral** (two-house) **legislature,** with the lower chamber chosen by the people and the smaller upper chamber chosen by the lower chamber from nominees selected by state legislatures. The number of representatives would be proportional to a state's population, thus favoring the large states. The legislature could void any state laws.
2. The creation of an unspecified national executive, elected by the legislature.
3. The creation of a national judiciary appointed by the legislature.

It did not take long for the smaller states to realize they would fare poorly under the Virginia plan, which would enable Virginia, Massachusetts, and Pennsylvania to form a majority in the national legislature. The debate on the plan dragged on for a number of weeks. It was time for the small states to come up with their own plan.

INFOTRAC ®
COLLEGE EDITION

To find out more about James Madison, use the term "Madison, James" in the Subject guide.

Bicameral Legislature
A legislature made up of two chambers, or parts. The U.S. Congress, composed of the House of Representatives and the Senate, is a bicameral legislature.

George Washington presided over the Constitutional Convention of 1787. Although the convention was supposed to have started on May 14, 1787, few of the delegates had actually arrived in Philadelphia by that date. It formally opened in the East Room of the Pennsylvania State House (later named Independence Hall) on May 25. Only Rhode Island did not send any delegates. (The Granger Collection)

Supremacy Doctrine
A doctrine that asserts the superiority of national law over state or regional laws. This principle is rooted in Article VI of the Constitution, which provides that the Constitution, the laws passed by the national government under its constitutional powers, and all treaties constitute the supreme law of the land.

Great Compromise
The compromise between the New Jersey and the Virginia plans that created one chamber of the Congress based on population and one chamber representing each state equally; also called the Connecticut Compromise.

The New Jersey Plan.   On June 15, lawyer William Paterson of New Jersey offered an alternative plan. After all, argued Paterson, under the Articles of Confederation all states had equality; therefore, the convention had no power to change this arrangement. He proposed the following:

1. The fundamental principle of the Articles of Confederation—one state, one vote—would be retained.
2. Congress would be able to regulate trade and impose taxes.
3. All acts of Congress would be the supreme law of the land.
4. Several people would be elected by Congress to form an executive office.
5. The executive office would appoint a Supreme Court.

Basically, the New Jersey plan was simply an amendment of the Articles of Confederation. Its only notable feature was its reference to the **supremacy doctrine,** which was later included in the Constitution.

The "Great Compromise."   The delegates were at an impasse. Most wanted a strong national government and were unwilling even to consider the New Jersey plan. But when the Virginia plan was brought up again, the small states threatened to leave. It was not until July 16 that the **Great Compromise** was achieved. Roger Sherman of Connecticut proposed the following:

1. A bicameral legislature in which the House of Representatives would be apportioned according to the number of free inhabitants in each state, plus three-fifths of the slaves.
2. An upper house, the Senate, which would have two members from each state elected by the state legislatures.

This plan, also called the Connecticut Compromise because of the role of the Connecticut delegates in the proposal, broke the deadlock. It did exact a political price, however, because it permitted each state to have equal representation in the Senate. Having two senators represent each state in effect diluted the voting power of citizens living in more heavily populated states and gave the smaller states disproportionate political powers. But the Connecticut Compromise resolved the large-state/small-state controversy. In addition, the Senate acted as part of a checks-and-balances system against the House, which many feared would be dominated by, and responsive to, the masses.

The Three-Fifths Compromise.   The Great Compromise also settled another major issue—how to deal with slaves in the representational scheme. Slavery was legal everywhere except in Massachusetts, but it was concentrated in the South. The South wanted slaves to be counted equally in determining representation in Congress. Delegates from the northern states objected. Sherman's three-fifths compromise solved the issue, satisfying those northerners who felt that slaves should not be counted at all and those southerners who wanted them to be counted as free whites. Actually, Sherman's Connecticut plan spoke of three-fifths of "all other persons" (and that is the language in the Constitution itself). It is not hard to figure out, though, who those other persons were.

The slavery issue was not completely eliminated by the three-fifths compromise. Many delegates were opposed to slavery and wanted it banned entirely in the United States. Charles Pinckney of South Carolina led strong southern opposition to the idea of a ban on slavery. Finally, the delegates agreed that Congress could limit the importation of slaves after 1808. The compromise meant that the issue of slavery itself was never addressed. The South won twenty years of unrestricted slave trade and a requirement that escaped slaves in free states be returned to their owners in slave states. (See this chapter's *Which Side Are You On?* feature for a further discussion of the founders' views on the slavery question.)

Which Side Are You On?
Should the Founders Have Banned Slavery Outright?

One of the most hotly debated issues at the Constitutional Convention concerned slavery. As we discussed elsewhere, the three-fifths compromise was the result of that debate. There was also another compromise: the importation of slaves would not be banned until after 1808. The debate over slavery, or, more specifically, over how the founders dealt with it, continues to this day. Some contend that those delegates who opposed slavery should have made greater efforts to ban it completely.*

DID THE FOUNDERS HAVE NO OTHER CHOICE?

Supporters of the slavery compromise and the resulting Constitution argue that the founders had no choice. The South was an important part of the economy, and the southern states had over 600,000 slaves. The delegates from North Carolina, South Carolina, and Georgia apparently would never have agreed to the Constitution if slavery had been threatened—meaning that these states would not have remained part of the Union. Furthermore, as James Madison said, "Great as the evil is, a dismemberment of the Union would be worse. . . . If those states should disunite from the other states, . . . they might solicit and obtain aid from foreign powers."† Benjamin Franklin, then president of the Pennsylvania Society for the Abolition of Slavery, also feared that without a slavery compromise, delegates from the South would abandon the convention.

RIGHT OR WRONG, ETHICS SHOULD PREVAIL

Critics of the founders' actions nonetheless believe that any compromise with respect to slavery implicitly acknowledged the validity of the institution of slavery. According to these critics, the delegates who opposed slavery had a moral commitment to make greater efforts to ban the institution. Not surprisingly, many of the delegates' contemporaries considered the compromise to be a "betrayal" of the Declaration of Independence's principle of equality among all men.

*See Paul Finkelman's criticism of the founders' actions with respect to the slavery issue in *Slavery and the Founders: Race and Liberty in the Age of Jefferson,* 2d ed. (Armonk, N.Y.: M. E. Sharpe, 2000).
†Speech before the Virginia ratifying convention on June 17, 1788, as cited in Bruno Leone, ed., *The Creation of the Constitution* (San Diego: Greenhaven Press, 1995), p. 159.

An American slave market as depicted in a painting from the nineteenth century. The writers of the Constitution did not ban slavery in the United States but did agree to limit the importation of new slaves after 1808. Nowhere are the words *slavery* or *slaves* used in the Constitution. Instead, the Constitution uses such language as "no person held in service" and "all other persons." (Kean Archives)

WHAT'S YOUR POSITION?

Had you been an antislavery state's delegate to the Constitutional Convention, would you have taken a firm stand against the institution of slavery? Under what circumstances, if any, would you have compromised?

GOING ONLINE

To learn more about the founders' discussion of the slavery issue, go to the following Web sites: **http://www.yale. edu/lawweb/avalon/debates/debcont.htm** (click on "August 8" for James Madison's notes on the discussion of whether slaves should count as part of a state's population for purposes of representation, as well as about banning the slave trade); and **http://www.yale.edu/lawweb/ avalon/federal/fed.htm** (click on "No. 42" to access *Federalist Paper* No. 42, which indicates how difficult it was for the founders simply to ban the slave trade in 1808).

DID YOU KNOW ...

That during the four centuries of slave trading, an estimated ten million to eleven million Africans were transported to the Americas?

Separation of Powers
The principle of dividing governmental powers among the executive, the legislative, and the judicial branches of government.

Madisonian Model
A structure of government proposed by James Madison in which the powers of the government are separated into three branches: executive, legislative, and judicial.

Checks and Balances
A major principle of the American government system whereby each branch of the government exercises a check on the actions of the others.

James Madison (1751–1836) contributed to the colonial cause by bringing to it a deep understanding of government and political philosophy. These resources first proved valuable in 1776, when he helped to draft the constitution for the new state of Virginia. Madison was prominent in disestablishing the Anglican Church when he was a representative of his county in the Virginia legislature from 1784 to 1786. At the Annapolis Convention, he supported New Jersey's motion to hold a federal constitutional convention the following year. Madison earned the title "master builder of the Constitution" because of his persuasive logic during the Constitutional Convention. His contributions to *The Federalist Papers* showed him to be a brilliant political thinker and writer. (Kean Archives)

Other Issues.   The agrarian South and the mercantile North were in conflict. The South was worried that the northern majority in Congress would pass legislation unfavorable to its economic interests. Because the South depended on exports of its agricultural products, it feared the imposition of export taxes. In return for acceding to the northern demand that Congress be given the power to regulate commerce among the states and with other nations, the South obtained a promise that export taxes would not be imposed. Even today, such taxes are prohibited. The United States is among the few countries that do not tax their exports.

There were other disagreements. The delegates could not decide whether to establish only a Supreme Court or to create lower courts as well. They deferred the issue by mandating a Supreme Court and allowing Congress to establish lower courts. They also disagreed over whether the president or the Senate would choose the Supreme Court justices. A compromise was reached with the agreement that the president would nominate the justices and the Senate would confirm the nominations.

These compromises, as well as others, resulted from the recognition that if one group of states refused to ratify the Constitution, it was doomed.

Working toward Final Agreement

The Connecticut Compromise was reached by mid-July. The makeup of the executive branch and the judiciary, however, was left unsettled. The remaining work of the convention was turned over to a five-man Committee of Detail, which presented a rough draft of the Constitution on August 6. It made the executive and judicial branches subordinate to the legislative branch.

The Madisonian Model—Separation of Powers.   The major issue of **separation of powers** had not yet been resolved. The delegates were concerned with structuring the government to prevent the imposition of tyranny—either by the majority or by a minority. It was Madison who proposed a governmental scheme—sometimes called the **Madisonian model**—to achieve this: the executive, legislative, and judicial powers of government were to be separated so that no one branch had enough power to dominate the others. The separation of powers was by function, as well as by personnel, with Congress passing laws, the president enforcing and administering laws, and the courts interpreting laws in individual circumstances.

Each of the three branches of government would be independent of the others, but they would have to cooperate to govern. According to Madison, in *Federalist Paper* No. 51 (see Appendix D), "the great security against a gradual concentration of the several powers in the same department consists in giving to those who administer each department the necessary constitutional means and personal motives to resist encroachments of the others."

The Madisonian Model—Checks and Balances.   The "constitutional means" Madison referred to is a system of **checks and balances** through which each branch of the government can check the actions of the other branches. For example, Congress can enact laws, but the president has veto power over congressional acts. The Supreme Court has the power to declare acts of Congress and of the executive branch unconstitutional, but the president appoints the justices of the Supreme Court, with the advice and consent of the Senate. (The Supreme Court's power to declare acts unconstitutional was not mentioned in the Constitution, although arguably the framers assumed that the Court would have this power—see the discussion of judicial review later in this chapter.) Figure 2–2 outlines these checks and balances.

Madison's ideas of separation of powers and checks and balances were not new. Indeed, the influential French political thinker Baron de Montesquieu (1689–1755) had explored these concepts in his book *The Spirit of the Laws,* published in 1748.

FIGURE 2-2

Checks and Balances

The major checks and balances among the three branches are illustrated here. Some of these checks are not mentioned in the Constitution, such as judicial review—the power of the courts to declare federal or state acts unconstitutional—or the president's ability to refuse to enforce judicial decisions or congressional legislation. Checks and balances can be thought of as a confrontation of powers or responsibilities. Each branch checks the action of another; two branches in conflict have powers that can result in balances or stalemates, requiring one branch to give in or both to reach a compromise.

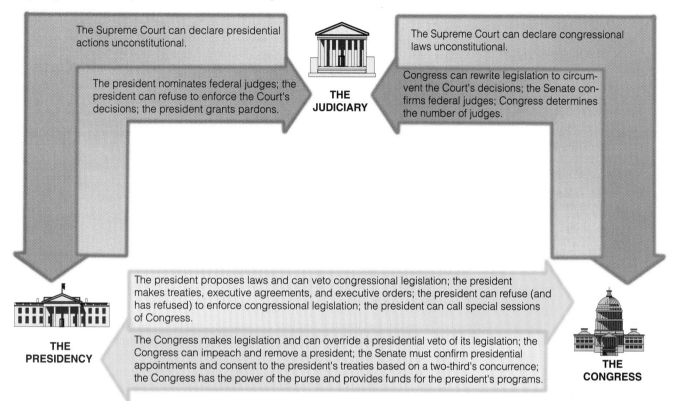

Montesquieu not only discussed the "three sorts of powers" (executive, legislative, and judicial) that were necessarily exercised by any government but also gave examples of how, in some nations, certain checks on these powers had arisen and had been effective in preventing tyranny.

In the years since the Constitution was ratified, the checks and balances built into it have evolved into a sometimes complex give-and-take among the branches of government. Generally, as political scientist Regina Swopes has noted, for nearly every check that one branch has over another, the branch that has been checked has found a way of getting around it. For example, suppose that the president checks Congress by vetoing a bill. Congress can override the presidential veto by a two-thirds vote. Additionally, Congress holds the "power of the purse." If it disagrees with a program endorsed by the executive branch, it can simply refuse to appropriate the funds necessary to operate that program. Similarly, the president can impose a countercheck on Congress if the Senate refuses to confirm a presidential appointment, such as a judicial appointment. The president can simply wait until Congress is in recess and then make what is called a "recess appointment," which does not require the Senate's approval.

The Executive.   Some delegates favored a plural executive made up of representatives from the various regions. This was abandoned in favor of a single chief executive. Some argued that Congress should choose the executive. To make the presidency completely independent of the proposed Congress, however, an **electoral college** was

Electoral College
A group of persons called electors selected by the voters in each state and Washington, D.C.; this group officially elects the president and vice president of the United States. The number of electors in each state is equal to the number of each state's representatives in both chambers of Congress. The Twenty-third Amendment to the Constitution permits Washington, D.C., to have as many electors as a state of comparable population.

INFOTRAC ®
COLLEGE EDITION

To find out more about the Constitution, use the term "United States Constitution" in the Subject guide, and then go to subdivision "history."

Federal System

A system of government in which power is divided by a written constitution between a central government and regional, or subdivisional, governments. Each level must have some domain in which its policies are dominant and some genuine political or constitutional guarantee of its authority.

Ratification

Formal approval.

Federalist

The name given to one who was in favor of the adoption of the U.S. Constitution and the creation of a federal union with a strong central government.

Anti-Federalist

An individual who opposed the ratification of the new Constitution in 1787. The Anti-Federalists were opposed to a strong central government.

adopted, probably at James Wilson's suggestion. To be sure, the electoral college created a cumbersome presidential election process (see Chapter 10). It could even result in a candidate who came in second in the popular vote becoming president by being the top vote getter in the electoral college. The electoral college insulated the president, however, from direct popular control. The seven-year single term that some of the delegates had proposed was replaced by a four-year term and the possibility of reelection.

The Final Document

On September 17, 1787, the Constitution was approved by thirty-nine delegates. Of the fifty-five who had attended originally, only forty-two remained. Three delegates refused to sign the Constitution. Others disapproved of at least parts of it but signed anyway to begin the ratification debate.

The Constitution that was to be ratified established the following fundamental principles:

1. Popular sovereignty, or control by the people.
2. A republican government in which the people choose representatives to make decisions for them.
3. Limited government with written laws, in contrast to the powerful monarchical British government against which the colonists had rebelled.
4. Separation of powers, with checks and balances among branches to prevent any one branch from gaining too much power.
5. A federal system that allows for states' rights, because the states feared too much centralized control.

You will read about federalism in detail in Chapter 3. Suffice it to say here that in the **federal system** established by the founders, sovereign powers—ruling powers—are divided between the states and the national government. The Constitution expressly delegated certain powers to the national government. For example, the national government was given the power to regulate commerce among the states. The Constitution also declared that the president is the nation's chief executive and the commander in chief of the armed forces. Additionally, the Constitution made it clear that laws made by the national government take priority over conflicting state laws. At the same time, the Constitution provided for numerous states' rights, including the right to control commerce within state borders and to exercise those governing powers that were not delegated to the national government.

The federal system created by the founders was a novel form of government at that time—no other country in the world had such a system. It was invented by the founders as a compromise solution to the controversy over whether the states or the central government should have ultimate sovereignty. As you will read in Chapter 3, the debate over where the line should be drawn between states' rights and the powers of the national government has characterized American politics ever since. The founders did not go into detail with respect to where this line should be drawn, thus leaving it up to scholars and court judges to divine the founders' intentions. (Similar questions now face many European nations as they decide whether they should create a federal form of government for the European Union. See this chapter's *Global View* for a discussion of this issue.)

The Difficult Road to Ratification

The founders knew that **ratification** of the Constitution was far from certain. Indeed, because it was almost guaranteed that many state legislatures would not ratify it, the delegates agreed that each state should hold a special convention. Elected delegates to these conventions would discuss and vote on the Constitution. Further departing from the Articles of Confederation, the delegates agreed that as soon as nine states (rather than all thirteen) approved the Constitution, it would take effect, and Congress could begin to organize the new government.

The Federalists Push for Ratification

The two opposing forces in the battle over ratification were the Federalists and the Anti-Federalists. The **Federalists**—those in favor of a strong central government and the new Constitution—had an advantage over their opponents, called the **Anti-Federalists,** who wanted to prevent the Constitution as drafted from being ratified. In the first place, the Federalists had assumed a positive name, leaving their opposition the negative label of *Anti*-Federalist.[11] More important, the Federalists had attended the Constitutional Convention and knew of all the deliberations that had taken place. Their opponents had no such knowledge, because those deliberations had not been open to the public. Thus, the Anti-Federalists were at a disadvantage in terms of information about the document. The Federalists also had time, power, and money on their side. Communications were slow. Those who had access to the best communications were Federalists—mostly wealthy bankers, lawyers, plantation owners, and merchants living in urban areas, where communication was better. The Federalist campaign was organized relatively quickly and effectively to elect Federalists as delegates to the state ratifying conventions.

The Anti-Federalists, however, had at least one strong point in their favor: they stood for the status quo. In general, the greater burden is placed on those advocating change.

The Federalist Papers. In New York, opponents of the Constitution were quick to attack it. Alexander Hamilton answered their attacks in newspaper columns over the signature "Caesar." When the Caesar letters had little effect, Hamilton switched to the pseudonym Publius and secured two collaborators—John Jay and James Madison. In a very short time, those three political figures wrote a series of eighty-five essays in defense of the Constitution and of a republican form of government. These widely read essays appeared in New York newspapers from October 1787 to August 1788 and were reprinted in the newspapers of other states. Although we do not know for certain who wrote every one, it is apparent that Hamilton was responsible for about two-thirds of the essays. These included the most important ones interpreting the Constitution, explaining the various powers of the three branches, and presenting a theory of judicial review. Madison's *Federalist Paper* No. 10 (see Appendix D), however, is considered a classic in political theory; it deals with the nature of groups—or factions, as he called them. In spite of the rapidity with which *The Federalist Papers* were written, they are considered by many to be perhaps the best example of political theorizing ever produced in the United States.[12]

The Anti-Federalist Response. The Anti-Federalists used such pseudonyms as Montezuma and Philadelphiensis in their replies. Many of their attacks against the Constitution were also brilliant. They claimed that it was a document written by aristocrats and would lead to aristocratic tyranny. More important, the Anti-Federalists believed that the Constitution would create an overbearing and overburdening central government hostile to personal liberty. (The Constitution said nothing about freedom

---

[11] There is some irony here. At the Constitutional Convention, those opposed to a strong central government pushed for a federal system because such a system would allow the states to retain some of their sovereign rights (see Chapter 3). The label Anti-Federalists thus contradicted their essential views.

[12] Some scholars believe that *The Federalist Papers* played only a minor role in securing ratification of the Constitution. Even if this is true, they still have lasting value as an authoritative explanation of the Constitution.

Global View

Should the EU Create a Federal Form of Government?

Today, the European Union (EU) consists of fifteen nations. Numerous other countries have applied for membership in the union. In 2000, the European University Institute in Florence, Italy, at the request of the European Commission, drafted a model constitution for the EU that essentially would establish a federal form of government. The preamble of the model constitution states, among other things, that "[t]his Constitution shall prevail over other European and national law, including Treaties of the Union, should conflict arise."* This is similar to the U.S. constitutional provision that if a state or local law conflicts with a national law, the national law will take precedence.

Just as delegates to the Constitutional Convention in the United States were reluctant to forfeit state sovereign powers, so are European nations. At the time of the Constitutional Convention, the independent status of the states was relatively new. In contrast, most European nations have been in existence for centuries, making it even more difficult for them to part with any sovereign powers. Many other controversial issues also remain. Some believe that signatory member states should have the right to leave the EU at any time. In the United States, a civil war was fought over that issue.

FOR CRITICAL ANALYSIS

Why should an existing EU member nation agree to give up any of its sovereignty?

*As cited in "Our Constitution for Europe," The Economist, October 28, 2000, p. 18.

INFOTRAC®
COLLEGE EDITION

To find out more about this subject, use the term "Anti-Federalists" in Keywords.

of the press, freedom of religion, or any other individual liberty.) They wanted to include a list of guaranteed liberties, or a bill of rights. Finally, the Anti-Federalists decried the weakened power of the states.

The Anti-Federalists cannot be dismissed as a bunch of unpatriotic extremists. They included such patriots as Patrick Henry and Samuel Adams. They were arguing what had been the most prevalent view of the time. This view derived from the French political philosopher Montesquieu, who, as mentioned earlier, was an influential political theorist at that time. Montesquieu believed that liberty was safe only in relatively small societies governed by direct democracy or by a large legislature with small districts. The Madisonian view favoring a large republic, particularly expressed in *Federalist Papers* No. 10 and No. 51 (see Appendix D), was actually the more *un*popular view of the time. Madison was probably convincing because citizens were already persuaded that a strong national government was necessary to combat foreign enemies and to prevent domestic insurrections. Still, some researchers believe it was mainly the bitter experiences with the Articles of Confederation, rather than Madison's arguments, that created the setting for the ratification of the Constitution.[13]

The March to the Finish

The struggle for ratification continued. Strong majorities were procured in Delaware, Pennsylvania, New Jersey, Georgia, and Connecticut. After a bitter struggle in Massachusetts, that state ratified the Constitution by a narrow margin on February 6, 1788. By the spring, Maryland and South Carolina had ratified by sizable majorities. Then on June 21 of that year, New Hampshire became the ninth state to ratify the Constitution. Although the Constitution was formally in effect, this meant little without Virginia and New York—the latter did not ratify for yet another month (see Table 2–2). (Was the Constitution actually favored by a majority of citizens at the time? See the feature *Politics and the Constitution* for a discussion of this issue.)

---

[13] Of particular interest is the view of the Anti-Federalist position contained in Herbert J. Storing, *What the Anti-Federalists Were For* (Chicago: University of Chicago Press, 1981). Storing also edited seven volumes of the Anti-Federalist writings, *The Complete Anti-Federalist* (Chicago: University of Chicago Press, 1981). See also Josephine F. Pacheco, *Antifederalism: The Legacy of George Mason* (Fairfax, Va.: George Mason University Press, 1992).

TABLE 2–2

Ratification of the Constitution

STATE	DATE	VOTE FOR–AGAINST
Delaware	Dec. 7, 1787	30–0
Pennsylvania	Dec. 12, 1787	43–23
New Jersey	Dec. 18, 1787	38–0
Georgia	Jan. 2, 1788	26–0
Connecticut	Jan. 9, 1788	128–40
Massachusetts	Feb. 6, 1788	187–168
Maryland	Apr. 28, 1788	63–11
South Carolina	May 23, 1788	149–73
New Hampshire	June 21, 1788	57–46
Virginia	June 25, 1788	89–79
New York	July 26, 1788	30–27
North Carolina	Nov. 21, 1789*	194–77
Rhode Island	May 29, 1790	34–32

*Ratification was originally defeated on August 4, 1788, by a vote of 84–184.

Politics and THE CONSTITUTION

Did the Majority of Americans Support the Constitution?

In 1913, historian Charles Beard published *An Economic Interpretation of the Constitution of the United States.** This book launched a debate that has continued ever since—the debate over whether the Constitution was supported by a majority of Americans.

BEARD'S THESIS

Beard's central thesis was that the Constitution had been produced primarily by wealthy property owners who desired a stronger government able to protect their property rights. Beard also claimed that the Constitution had been imposed by undemocratic methods to prevent democratic majorities from exercising real power. He pointed out that there was never any popular vote on whether to hold a constitutional convention in the first place. Furthermore, even if such a vote had

*Charles A. Beard, *An Economic Interpretation of the Constitution of the United States* (New York: Macmillan, 1913; New York: Free Press, 1986).

been taken, state laws generally restricted voting rights to property-owning white males, meaning that most people in the country (white males without property, women, Native Americans, and slaves) were not eligible to vote. Finally, Beard pointed out that even the word *democracy* was distasteful to the founders. The term was often used by conservatives to smear their opponents.

STATE RATIFYING CONVENTIONS

As for the various state ratifying conventions, the delegates had been selected by only 150,000 of the approximately four million citizens of that time. That does not seem very democratic—at least not by today's standards. Some historians have suggested that if a Gallup poll could have been taken at that time, the Anti-Federalists would probably have outnumbered the Federalists.[†]

Certainly, some of the delegates to state ratifying conventions from poor, agrarian areas feared that an elite group of Federalists would run the country just as oppressively as the British had governed the colonies. Amos Singletary, a delegate to the Massachusetts ratifying convention, contended that those who urged the adoption of the Constitution "expect to get all the power and all the money into their own hands, and then they will swallow up all us little folks . . . just as the whale swallowed Jonah."[‡] Others who were similarly situated, though,

[†]Jim Powell, "James Madison—Checks and Balances to Limit Government Power," *The Freeman,* March 1996, p. 178.
[‡]As quoted in Bruno Leone, ed., *The Creation of the Constitution* (San Diego: Greenhaven Press, 1995), p. 215.

felt differently. Jonathan Smith, who was also a delegate to the Massachusetts ratifying convention, regarded a strong national government as a "cure for disorder"—referring to the disorder caused by the rebellion of Daniel Shays and his followers.[§]

SUPPORT WAS PROBABLY WIDESPREAD

Much has been made of the various machinations used by the Federalists to ensure the Constitution's ratification (and they did resort to a variety of devious tactics, including purchasing at least one printing press to prevent the publication of Anti-Federalist sentiments). Yet the perception that a strong central government was necessary to keep order and protect the public welfare appears to have been fairly pervasive among all classes—rich and poor alike.

FOR CRITICAL ANALYSIS

Massachusetts delegate Jonathan Smith posited an example to make his point that the Constitution should be ratified: "Suppose two or three of you had been at the pains to break up a piece of rough land, and sow it with wheat; would you let it lie waste because you could not agree on what sort of a fence to make?" What light, if any, does this sentiment shed on the American political process generally?

[§]*Ibid.,* p. 217.

The Bill of Rights

The U.S. Constitution would not have been ratified in several important states if the Federalists had not assured the states that amendments to the Constitution would be passed to protect individual liberties against incursions by the national government. Many of the recommendations of the state ratifying conventions included specific rights that were considered later by James Madison as he labored to draft what became the Bill of Rights.

A "Bill of Limits"

Although called the Bill of Rights, essentially the first ten amendments to the Constitution were a "bill of limits," because the amendments limited the powers of the national government in regard to the rights and liberties of individuals. (For the past several decades, the courts have held that the guarantees set forth in the Bill of Rights imply another right—the right to privacy. Does the increasing use of camera and biometric surveillance in public places infringe too greatly on this right to privacy? For a discussion of this question, see this chapter's *America's Security* feature.)

Ironically, a year earlier Madison had told Jefferson, "I have never thought the omission [of the Bill of Rights] a material defect" of the Constitution. But Jefferson's enthusiasm for a bill of rights apparently influenced Madison, as did his desire to gain popular support for his election to Congress. He promised in his campaign letter to voters that, once elected, he would force Congress to "prepare and recommend to the states for ratification, the most satisfactory provisions for all essential rights."

Madison had to cull through more than two hundred state recommendations.[14] It was no small task, and in retrospect he chose remarkably well. One of the rights appropriate for constitutional protection that he left out was equal protection under the laws—but that was not commonly regarded as a basic right at that time. It was not until 1868 that an amendment guaranteeing that no state shall deny equal protection to any person was ratified. (The Supreme Court has applied this guarantee to certain actions of the federal government as well.)

The final number of amendments that Madison and a specially appointed committee came up with was seventeen. Congress tightened the language somewhat and eliminated five of the amendments. Of the remaining twelve, two—dealing with the apportionment of representatives and the compensation of the members of Congress—were not ratified immediately by the states. Eventually, Supreme Court decisions led to legislative reforms relating to apportionment. The amendment relating to compensation of members of Congress was ratified 203 years later—in 1992!

No Explicit Limits on State Government Powers

On December 15, 1791, the national Bill of Rights was adopted when Virginia agreed to ratify the ten amendments. On ratification, the Bill of Rights became part of the U.S. Constitution. The basic structure of American government had already been established. Now the fundamental rights and liberties of individuals were protected, at least in theory, at the national level. The proposed amendment that Madison characterized as "the most valuable amendment in the whole lot"—which would have prohibited the states from infringing on the freedoms of conscience, press, and jury trial—had been eliminated by the Senate. Thus, the Bill of Rights as adopted did not limit state power, and individual citizens had to rely on the guarantees contained in the particular state constitution or state bill of rights. The country had to wait until the violence of the Civil War before significant limitations on state power in the form of the Fourteenth Amendment became part of the national Constitution.

Altering the Constitution: The Formal Amendment Process

The U.S. Constitution consists of 7,000 words. It is shorter than every state constitution except that of Vermont, which has 6,880 words. One of the reasons the federal Constitution is short is that the founders intended it to be only a framework for gov-

---

[14] For details on these recommendations, including their sources, see Leonard W. Levy, *Origins of the Bill of Rights* (New Haven, Conn.: Yale University Press, 1999).

America's Security

Big Brother Can Recognize You— Biometrics Is Now a Reality

Although the Constitution does not specifically mention the right to privacy, it has been inferred from other amendments in the Bill of Rights, as you discovered in this chapter's opening *What If . . .* feature. Given the increased security concerns that are evident everywhere since 9/11, privacy rights have taken on an even greater significance.

FIRST, IT'S CAMERAS

The Washington, D.C., police force responded to the terrorists' targeting of the Pentagon and the White House, plus the anthrax scare, by opening the Joint Operations Command Center of the Synchronized Operations Command

Complex (SOCC). Within this center are fifty officials who monitor a wall of forty video screens. They show images of travelers, drivers, residents, and pedestrians in the nation's capital. Such monitors are also in public schools in that area and will be expanded to include subways and parks.

Virtually everyone agrees that privacy has been curtailed. As the associate director of the American Civil Liberties Union, Barry Steinhardt, observed: "Technology is giving government what amounts to Superman's vision." The public seems to be relatively unconcerned, though. A Harris poll taken one week after the terrorist attacks in New York and Washington, D.C., found that 63 percent of those polled favored expanded camera surveillance on the streets and in public places.

NEXT, IT'S BIOMETRICS

Standard video cameras are only recorders: they do not "recognize" us or send information about us to a third party. Biometric technology, however, goes one step further. This technology allows the camera to identify anyone who comes into view by scanning her or his physical characteristics and then matching the results of the scan with information in a large database. Using biometrics, videos taken at terrorist

training camps could be fed into a computer, which would log features of the faces. This information would then be distributed to U.S. airports, embassies, and other strategic locations.

Already, airports in Great Britain and Iceland utilize face-recognition biometrics to protect against terrorism. A computer linked to surveillance cameras in key airports in these countries profiles individuals based on as many as eighty different facial structures, such as cheekbone formation, the nose bridge, and the space between the eyes. These facial "signatures," once noted, are compared to facial structures of known criminals and terrorists. So far, privacy concerns in the United States have limited the use of biometrics. After all, facial-recognition cameras would circumvent the anonymity that is important to many Americans.

Nonetheless, biometric technology is now being used at some U.S. airports. For example, in 2002, the Fresno, California, municipal airport started testing a facial-recognition system. Each passenger is asked to step in front of a six-foot tube of brushed aluminum while a camera snaps a series of photographs. These photographs are compared to a database of known terrorists. If a terrorist match occurs, a siren sounds. Airports in Dallas, Boston, and Providence, Rhode Island, started installing similar technology at about the same time. The systems being tested break down the human face into twenty-six points of bone structure. These points are converted into numbers and compared to headshots in the database. The systems are not infallible. About 20 percent of the time, the facial-scanning system failed to get a good photograph.

Surveillance cameras at the Portland, Maine, airport captured suspected September 11th hijackers Mohamed Atta (right) and Abdulaziz Alomari just hours before they boarded planes in Boston that they crashed into the World Trade Center. Face-recognition technology may have thwarted their efforts. Would any rights be endangered with such a system? (AP Photo)

FOR CRITICAL ANALYSIS

Suppose that facial-recognition systems were installed nationwide. How serious might the problem of "false positives" be each day?

This debate in the Vermont State Senate Chamber resulted in a resolution sent to Congress to further protect the U.S. flag. Congress subsequently passed a compromise resolution that requires Congress to ensure that Americans show proper respect for the flag. What might have prevented Congress from taking the time to pass the necessary constitutional amendment? (AP Photo/ Toby Talbot)

erning, to be interpreted by succeeding generations. One of the reasons it has remained short is that the formal amending procedure does not allow for changes to be made easily. Article V of the Constitution outlines the ways in which amendments may be proposed and ratified (see Figure 2–3).

Two formal methods of proposing an amendment to the Constitution are available: (1) a two-thirds vote in each chamber of Congress or (2) a national convention that is called by Congress at the request of two-thirds of the state legislatures (the second method has never been used).

Ratification can occur by one of two methods: (1) by a positive vote in three-fourths of the legislatures of the various states or (2) by special conventions called in the states for the specific purpose of ratifying the proposed amendment and a positive vote in three-fourths of them. The second method has been used only once, to repeal Prohibition. That situation was exceptional because it involved an amendment (the Twenty-first) to repeal an amendment (the Eighteenth, which had created Prohibition). State conventions were necessary for repeal of the Eighteenth Amendment because the "pro-dry" legislatures in the most conservative states would never have passed the repeal. (Note that Congress determines the method of ratification to be used by all states for each proposed constitutional amendment.)

Many Amendments Proposed, Few Accepted

Congress has considered more than eleven thousand amendments to the Constitution. Only thirty-three have been submitted to the states after having been approved by the required two-thirds vote in each chamber of Congress, and only twenty-seven have been ratified—see Table 2–3. (The full, annotated text of the U.S. Constitution, including its amendments, is presented in a special appendix to this chapter.) It should be clear that the amendment process is much more difficult than a graphic depiction such as Figure 2–3 can indicate. Because of competing social and economic interests, the requirement that two-thirds of both the House and Senate approve the amendments is difficult to achieve. Thirty-four senators, representing only seventeen sparsely populated states, could block any amendment. For example, the Republican-controlled House approved the Balanced Budget Amendment within the first one hundred days of the 104th Congress in 1995, but it was defeated in the Senate by one vote.

After approval by Congress, the process becomes even more arduous. Three-fourths of the state legislatures must approve the amendment. Only those amendments that have wide popular support across parties and in all regions of the country are likely to be approved.

FIGURE 2–3

The Formal Constitutional Amending Procedure

There are two ways of proposing amendments to the U.S. Constitution and two ways of ratifying proposed amendments. Among the four possibilities, the usual route has been proposal by Congress and ratification by state legislatures.

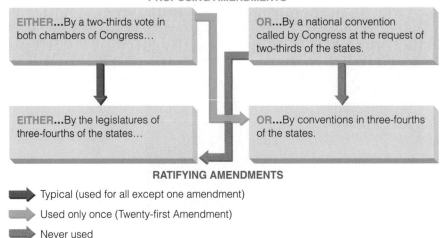

PROPOSING AMENDMENTS

EITHER...By a two-thirds vote in both chambers of Congress...

OR...By a national convention called by Congress at the request of two-thirds of the states.

EITHER...By the legislatures of three-fourths of the states...

OR...By conventions in three-fourths of the states.

RATIFYING AMENDMENTS

➡ Typical (used for all except one amendment)

➡ Used only once (Twenty-first Amendment)

➡ Never used

TABLE 2–3

Amendments to the Constitution

AMENDMENTS	SUBJECT	YEAR ADOPTED	TIME REQUIRED FOR RATIFICATION
1st–10th	The Bill of Rights	1791	2 years, 2 months, 20 days
11th	Immunity of states from certain suits	1795	11 months, 3 days
12th	Changes in electoral college procedure	1804	6 months, 3 days
13th	Prohibition of slavery	1865	10 months, 3 days
14th	Citizenship, due process, and equal protection	1868	2 years, 26 days
15th	No denial of vote because of race, color, or previous condition of servitude	1870	11 months, 8 days
16th	Power of Congress to tax income	1913	3 years, 6 months, 22 days
17th	Direct election of U.S. senators	1913	10 months, 26 days
18th	National (liquor) prohibition	1919	1 year, 29 days
19th	Women's right to vote	1920	1 year, 2 months, 14 days
20th	Change of dates for congressional and presidential terms	1933	10 months, 21 days
21st	Repeal of the Eighteenth Amendment	1933	9 months, 15 days
22d	Limit on presidential tenure	1951	3 years, 11 months, 3 days
23d	District of Columbia electoral vote	1961	9 months, 13 days
24th	Prohibition of tax payment as a qualification to vote in federal elections	1964	1 year, 4 months, 9 days
25th	Procedures for determining presidential disability and presidential succession and for filling a vice presidential vacancy	1967	1 year, 7 months, 4 days
26th	Prohibition of setting minimum voting age above eighteen in any election	1971	3 months, 7 days
27th	Prohibition of Congress's voting itself a raise that takes effect before the next election	1992	203 years

Why was the amendment process made so difficult? The framers feared that a simple amendment process could lead to a tyranny of the majority, which could pass amendments to oppress disfavored individuals and groups. The cumbersome amendment process does not seem to stem the number of amendments that are proposed each year in Congress, however, particularly in recent years.

Limits on Ratification

A reading of Article V of the Constitution reveals that the framers of the Constitution specified no time limit on the ratification process. The Supreme Court has held that Congress can specify a time for ratification as long as it is "reasonable." Since 1919, most proposed amendments have included a requirement that ratification be obtained within seven years. This was the case with the proposed Equal Rights Amendment. When three-fourths of the states had not ratified in that time, however, Congress extended the limit for an additional three years and three months. That extension expired on June 30, 1982, and the amendment still had not been ratified. Another proposed amendment, which would have guaranteed congressional representation to the District of Columbia, fell far short of the thirty-eight state ratifications needed before its August 22, 1985, deadline.

On May 7, 1992, the Michigan state legislature became the thirty-eighth state to ratify the Twenty-seventh Amendment (on congressional compensation)—one of the two "lost" amendments of the twelve that originally were sent to the states in 1789. Because most of the amendments proposed in recent years have been given a time limit of only seven years by Congress, it was questionable for awhile whether the amendment would take effect even if the necessary number of states ratified it. Is 203 years too long a lapse of time between the proposal and the final ratification of an amendment? It apparently was not, because the amendment was certified as legitimate by archivist Don Wilson of the National Archives on May 18, 1992.

INFOTRAC®
COLLEGE EDITION

To find out more about the amendment process, use the term "United States Constitution" in the Subject guide, and then go to subdivision "amendments."

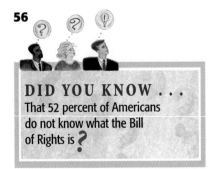

The National Convention Provision

The Constitution provides that a national convention requested by the legislatures of two-thirds of the states can propose a constitutional amendment. Congress has received approximately 400 convention applications since the Constitution was ratified; every state has applied at least once. Less than 20 applications were submitted during the Constitution's first 100 years, but more than 150 have been filed in the last two decades. No national convention has been held since 1787, and many national political and judicial leaders are uneasy about the prospect of convening a body that conceivably could do as the Constitutional Convention did—create a new form of government. The state legislative bodies that originate national convention applications, however, appear not to be uncomfortable with such a constitutional modification process; more than 230 state constitutional conventions have been held.

Informal Methods of Constitutional Change

Formal amendments are one way of changing our Constitution, and, as is obvious by their small number, they have not been resorted to very frequently. If we discount the first ten amendments (the Bill of Rights), which were adopted soon after the ratification of the Constitution, there have been only seventeen formal alterations of the Constitution in the more than two hundred years of its existence.

But looking at the sparse number of formal constitutional changes gives us an incomplete view. The brevity and ambiguity of the original document have permitted great changes in the Constitution by way of varying interpretations over time. As the United States grew, both in population and territory, new social and political realities emerged. Congress, presidents, and the courts found it necessary to interpret the Constitution's provisions in light of these new realities. The Constitution has proved to be a remarkably flexible document, adapting itself time and again to new events and concerns.

Congressional Legislation

The Constitution gives Congress broad powers to carry out its duties as the nation's legislative body. For example, Article I, Section 8, of the Constitution gives Congress the power to regulate foreign and interstate commerce. Although there is no clear definition of foreign commerce or interstate commerce in the Constitution, Congress has cited the *commerce clause* as the basis for passing thousands of laws that have defined the meaning of foreign and interstate commerce. Similarly, Article III, Section 1, states that the national judiciary shall consist of one supreme court and "such inferior courts, as Congress may from time to time ordain and establish." Through a series of acts, Congress has used this broad provision to establish the federal court system of today.

Presidential Actions

Even though the Constitution does not expressly authorize the president to propose bills or even budgets to Congress,[15] presidents since the time of Woodrow Wilson (who served as president from 1913 to 1921) have proposed hundreds of bills to Congress each year. Presidents have also relied on their Article II authority as commander in chief of the nation's armed forces to send American troops abroad into combat, although the

---

[15] Note, though, that the Constitution, in Article II, Section 3, does state that the president "shall from time to time . . . recommend to [Congress's] consideration such measures as he shall judge necessary and expedient." Some scholars interpret this phrase to mean that the president has the constitutional authority to propose bills and budgets to Congress for consideration.

Constitution provides that Congress has the power to declare war. Presidents have also conducted foreign affairs by the use of **executive agreements,** which are legally binding documents made between the president and a foreign head of state. The Constitution does not mention such agreements.

Judicial Review

Another way of changing the Constitution—or of making it more flexible—is through the power of judicial review. **Judicial review** refers to the power of U.S. courts to invalidate actions undertaken by the legislative and executive branches of government. A state court, for example, may rule that a statute enacted by the state legislature is unconstitutional. Federal courts (and ultimately, the United States Supreme Court) may rule unconstitutional not only acts of Congress and decisions of the national executive branch but also state statutes, state executive actions, and even provisions of state constitutions.

Not a Novel Concept.   The Constitution does not specifically mention the power of judicial review. Those in attendance at the Constitutional Convention, however, probably expected that the courts would have some authority to review the legality of acts by the executive and legislative branches, because, under the common law tradition inherited from England, courts traditionally exercised this authority. Indeed, Alexander Hamilton, in *Federalist Paper* No. 78 (see Appendix D), explicitly outlined the concept of judicial review. Whether the power of judicial review can be justified constitutionally is a question that has been subject to some debate, particularly in recent years. For now, suffice it to say that in 1803, the Supreme Court claimed this power for itself in *Marbury v. Madison,*[16] in which the Court ruled that a particular provision of an act of Congress was unconstitutional.

Allows Court to Adapt the Constitution.   Through the process of judicial review, the Supreme Court adapts the Constitution to modern situations. Electronic technology, for example, did not exist when the Constitution was ratified. Nonetheless, the Supreme Court has used the Fourth Amendment guarantees against unreasonable searches and seizures to place limits on the use of wiretapping and other electronic eavesdropping methods by government officials. At some point, the Court may need to decide whether certain new antiterrorism laws passed by Congress or state legislatures violate the Fourth Amendment—or other constitutional provisions. Additionally, the Supreme Court has changed its interpretation of the Constitution in accordance with changing times. It ruled in 1896 that "separate-but-equal" public facilities for African Americans were constitutional; but by 1954 the times had changed, and the Supreme Court reversed that decision.[17] Woodrow Wilson summarized the Supreme Court's work when he described it as "a constitutional convention in continuous session." Basically, the law is what the Supreme Court says it is at any point in time.

Interpretation, Custom, and Usage

The Constitution has also been changed through its interpretation by both Congress and the president. Originally, the president had a staff consisting of personal secretaries and a few others. Today, because Congress delegates specific tasks to the president and the chief executive assumes political leadership, the executive office staff alone has increased to several thousand persons. The executive branch provides legislative leadership far beyond the intentions of the Constitution.

Executive Agreement
A binding international agreement made between chiefs of state that does not require legislative sanction.

Judicial Review
The power of the Supreme Court or any court to declare unconstitutional federal or state laws and other acts of government.

INFOTRAC®
COLLEGE EDITION

To find out more about this topic, use the term "judicial review" in the Subject guide.

---

[16] 5 U.S. 137 (1803). See Chapter 15 for a further discussion of the *Marbury v. Madison* case.
[17] *Brown v. Board of Education of Topeka,* 347 U.S. 483 (1954).

Citizens protest the availability of pornography on the Internet. How should the First Amendment's guarantee of freedom of speech be applied to materials available on the World Wide Web? (Wally McNamee/Black Star)

Changes in the ways of doing political business have also altered the Constitution. The Constitution does not mention political parties, yet these informal, "extraconstitutional" organizations make the nominations for offices, run the campaigns, organize the members of Congress, and in fact change the election system from time to time. The emergence and evolution of the party system, for example, have changed the way of electing the president. The Constitution calls for the electoral college to choose the president. Today, the people vote for electors who are pledged to the candidate of their party, effectively choosing the president themselves. Perhaps most strikingly, the Constitution has been adapted from serving the needs of a small, rural republic with no international prestige to providing a framework of government for an industrial giant with vast geographic, natural, and human resources.

The Constitution: Why Is It Important Today?

Our Constitution is a flexible one. If it were not, as we pointed out in this chapter's opening *What If . . .* feature, it would not have lasted for over two hundred years. It is now the longest-lived written constitution in the world. It is also the most imitated constitution in the world. There is a good reason why our Constitution has lasted so long and been imitated so much—Americans enjoy more rights and liberties than perhaps do the residents of any other country today.

Nevertheless, just because our Constitution has endured for over two hundred years does not mean that we can take it for granted. In other words, citizens nationwide have to be ever vigilant to make sure that our government does not chip away at our rights and liberties. As we have already pointed out, the individual protections afforded by the Constitution cannot be thrown aside even though we face an increased threat of terrorism. What is the trade-off involved here? How much privacy and personal freedom should we give up in order to obtain more security? This question is one that you and every other American must consider.

Benjamin Franklin is said to have answered a question from a curious citizen about what kind of government the constitutional convention had given the United States by saying, "A republic, if you can keep it." Many countries have a constitution that includes the rights of free speech, religion, and assembly. There is, however, a big difference between what is written and what is reality. The U.S. Constitution is not just a group of words conveying beautiful concepts. It is a true governing document—but to remain effective it must be supported by the American people *and* enforced by the government.

Ultimately we, the people, decide how many of our liberties will endure. Indeed, as the noted American jurist Judge Learned Hand once stated, "Liberty lies in the hearts of men and women; when it dies there, no constitution . . . can ever do much to help it."

MAKING A DIFFERENCE | How Can You Affect the U.S. Constitution?

The Constitution is an enduring document that has survived more than two hundred years of turbulent history. It is also a changing document, however. Twenty-seven amendments have been added to the original Constitution. How can you, as an individual, actively help to rewrite the Constitution?

Consider how one person decided to affect the Constitution. Shirley Breeze, head of the Missouri Women's Network, decided to bring the Equal Rights Amendment (ERA) back to life after its "death" in 1982. She spearheaded a movement that gained significant support. Today, bills to ratify the ERA have been introduced not only in Missouri but also in other states that did not ratify it earlier, including Illinois, Virginia, and Oklahoma.

At the time of this writing, national coalitions of interest groups are supporting or opposing a number of proposed amendments. Two hotly debated proposed amendments concern prayer in the schools and abortion rights. If you are interested in either of these issues and would like to make a difference, the contacts given in the following subsections will help you get started.

There is also another way that you can affect the Constitution—by protecting your existing rights and liberties under the Constitution. In the wake of the 9/11 attacks, a number of new laws have been enacted that many believe go too far in curbing our constitutional rights. If you agree and want to join with others who are concerned over this issue, a good starting point would be to visit the Web site of the American Civil Liberties Union (ACLU) at **http://www.aclu.org**. The mission of the ACLU has long been to make sure our constitutional rights are not infringed.

School Prayer Amendment

The proposed school prayer amendment, or Religious Freedom Amendment, would allow for student-sponsored prayer in public schools.

Supporters of the amendment claim that it is necessary to correct Supreme Court rulings that have strayed from the meaning of the First Amendment's provisions on freedom of religion. To learn more about the arguments in favor of the school prayer amendment, contact:

Christian Coalition of America
499 So. Capitol Street SW
Suite 615
Washington, DC 20003
202-479-6900
http://www.cc.org

Critics of the amendment claim that the amendment would allow students to impose their religious beliefs on classmates by holding prayers at mandatory school events. For information on this position, contact:

American Civil Liberties Union
125 Broad Street, 18th Floor
New York, NY 10004
212-549-2500
http://www.aclu.org

Abortion

One of the organizations whose primary goal is to secure the passage of the Human Life Amendment is:

American Life League
P.O. Box 1350
Stafford, VA 22555
540-659-4171
http://www.all.org

The Human Life Amendment would recognize in law the "personhood" of the unborn, secure human rights protections for an unborn child from the time of fertilization, and prohibit abortion under any circumstances.

A political action and information organization working on behalf of "pro-choice" issues—that is, the right of women to have control over reproduction—is:

National Abortion and
Reproductive Rights
Action League (NARAL)
1156 15th St., Suite 700
Washington, DC 20005
202-973-3000
http://www.naral.org

Key Terms

Anti-Federalist 48

bicameral legislature 43

checks and balances 46

confederation 39

electoral college 47

executive agreement 57

federal system 48

Federalist 48

First Continental Congress 36

Great Compromise 44

judicial review 57

Madisonian model 46

natural rights 38

ratification 48

representative assembly 34

Second Continental Congress 36

separation of powers 46

social contract 38

state 39

supremacy doctrine 44

unicameral legislature 39

Chapter Summary

1 An early effort by England to establish North American colonies was unsuccessful. The first permanent English colonies were established at Jamestown in 1607 and Plymouth in 1620. The Mayflower Compact created the first formal government for the British colonists. By the mid-1700s, other British colonies had been established along the Atlantic seaboard from Georgia to Maine.

2 In 1763, the British tried to reassert control over their increasingly independent-minded colonies through a series of taxes and legislative acts. The colonists responded with boycotts of British products and protests. Representatives of the colonies formed the First Continental Congress in 1774. The delegates sent a petition to the British king expressing their grievances. The Second Continental Congress established an army in 1775 to defend colonists against any attacks by British soldiers.

3 On July 4, 1776, the Second Continental Congress approved the Declaration of Independence. Perhaps the most revolutionary aspects of the Declaration were its assumptions that people have natural rights to life, liberty, and the pursuit of happiness; that governments derive their power from the consent of the governed; and that people have a right to overthrow oppressive governments. During the Revolutionary War, all of the colonies adopted written constitutions that severely curtailed the power of executives, thus giving their legislatures predominant powers. By the end of the Revolutionary War, the states had signed the Articles of Confederation, creating a weak central government with few powers. The Articles proved to be unworkable because the national government had no way to assure compliance by the states with such measures as securing tax revenues.

4 General dissatisfaction with the Articles of Confederation prompted delegates to call a convention at Philadelphia in 1787. Although the delegates originally convened with the idea of amending the Articles, the discussions soon focused on creating a constitution for a new form of government. The Virginia plan and the New Jersey plan were offered but did not garner widespread support. A compromise offered by the state of Connecticut helped to break the large-state/small-state disputes dividing the delegates. The final version of the Constitution provided for the separation of powers, checks and balances, and a federal form of government.

5 Fears of a strong central government prompted the addition of the Bill of Rights to the Constitution. The Bill of Rights secured for Americans a wide variety of freedoms, including the freedoms of religion, speech, and assembly. It was initially applied only to the federal government, but amendments to the Constitution following the Civil War made it clear that the Bill of Rights also applied to the states.

6 An amendment to the Constitution may be proposed either by a two-thirds vote in each house of Congress or by a national convention called by Congress at the request of two-thirds of the state legislatures. Ratification can occur either by a positive vote in three-fourths of the legislatures of the various states or by special conventions called in the states for the specific purpose of ratifying the proposed amendment and a positive vote in three-fourths of these state conventions. Informal methods of constitutional change include congressional legislation, presidential actions, judicial review, and changing interpretations of the Constitution.

Selected Print and Media Resources

SUGGESTED READINGS

Finkelman, Paul. *Slavery and the Founders: Race and Liberty in the Age of Jefferson,* 2d ed. Armonk, N.Y.: M. E. Sharpe, 2000. This controversial and provocative book provides a critical account of the founders' attitudes toward slavery and the legal status of slaves in the early years of the nation.

Hamilton, Alexander, James Madison, and John Jay. *The Federalist Papers.* Cambridge, Mass.: Harvard University Press, 1961. The complete set of columns from the *New York Packet* defending the new Constitution is presented.

Levy, Leonard W. *Origins of the Bill of Rights.* New Haven, Conn.: Yale University Press, 1999. The author presents an exciting history of the debates surrounding the origins of the Bill of Rights and the important role played by James Madison in getting Congress to act on the amendments.

Orwell, George. *1984.* New York: Knopf, 1992. This is a classic novel about a society in which the totalitarian government ("Big Brother") watches over all. Originally published in 1949, this book is especially relevant today in view of the increased surveillance of the public in the interests of security against terrorism.

Sheldon, Charles H., and Stephen L. Wasby. *Essentials of the American Constitution.* Boulder, Colo.: Westview Press, 2001. The authors present a readable and readily understandable analysis of the concepts set forth in our founding document.

MEDIA RESOURCES

In the Beginning—A Bill Moyers program that features discussions with three prominent historians about the roots of the Constitution and its impact on our society.

John Locke—A video exploring the character and principal views of John Locke.

Where America Began—A video tour of American colonial history, including Jamestown, Williamsburg, and Yorktown.

Your CD-ROM Resources

In addition to the chapter content containing hot links, the following resources are available on the CD-ROM:

- **Internet Activities**—The Mayflower Compact, *Common Sense.*
- **Critical Thinking Exercises**—Debate with King George III, All Men are Created Equal, Leaks at the Philadelphia Convention.
- **Self-Check on Important Themes**—Can You Answer These?
- **Public Opinion Data**—Do Americans support Constitutional amendments on school prayer and abortion rights?

- **Video**—*The Constitution and Impeachment.*
- **InfoTrac Exercise**—"Commonplace or an Anachronism?"
- **Simulation**—You Are There!
- **Participation Exercise**—Participate in a newsgroup.
- **MicroCase Exercise**—"By the Numbers: The Constitution."
- **Additional Resources**—All court cases, *Common Sense,* The Mayflower Compact, Robert Yates's "Letters of Brutus," Articles of Confederation.

e-mocracy

The Internet and Our Constitution

Today, you can find online many important documents from the founding period, including descriptions of events leading up to the American Revolution, the Articles of Confederation, notes on the Constitutional Convention, the Federalists' writings, and the Anti-Federalists' responses.

You are able to access the Internet and explore a variety of opinions on every topic imaginable because you enjoy the freedoms—including freedom of speech—guaranteed by our Constitution. Even today, more than two hundred years after the U.S. Bill of Rights was ratified, citizens in some countries do not enjoy the right to free speech. Nor can they surf the Web freely, as U.S. citizens do.

For example, the Chinese government employs a number of methods to control Internet use. One method is to use filtering software to block electronic pathways to any objectionable sites, including the sites of Western news organizations. Another method is to prohibit Internet users from sending or discussing information that has not been publicly released by the government. Still another method is to monitor the online activities of Internet

users. None of these methods is foolproof, however. Indeed, some observers claim that the Internet, by exposing citizens in politically oppressive nations to a variety of views on politics and culture, will eventually transform those nations.

We should note that such restrictions also can exist in the United States. For example, there have been persistent efforts by Congress and many courts to limit access to Web sites deemed pornographic. Free speech advocates have attacked these restrictions as unconstitutional, as you will read in Chapter 4.

Logging On

For U.S. founding documents, including the Declaration of Independence, scanned originals of the U.S. Constitution, and *The Federalist Papers,* go to Emory University School of Law's Web site at

http://www.law.emory.edu/FEDERAL

The University of Oklahoma Law Center has a number of U.S. historical documents online, including many of those discussed in this chapter. Go to

http://www.law.ou.edu/hist

The National Constitution Center provides information on the Constitution—including its history, current debates over constitutional provisions, and news articles—at the following site:

http://www.constitutioncenter.org

A study aid for the U.S. Constitution is available at the following Web site, which provides links to many different views for each segment of the Constitution:

http://tcnbp/index.htm

To look at state constitutions, go to

http://www.findlaw.com/casecode/state.html

Using the Internet for Political Analysis

As noted in this chapter, the U.S. Constitution is one of the most concise in the world. It clearly reflects the basic values of the framers in its emphasis on republican government, liberty, and limited government. Take a look at some modern constitutions by clicking on some of the countries listed at the following site:

http://www.uni-wuerzburg.de/law/home.html

Choose at least two constitutions from non-Western nations—that is, from nations in Africa, Asia, the Middle East, or Central or South America. Compare these constitutions to that of the United States in terms of guarantees of the people's rights and liberties, the power of the central government, and the relationship between religion and the government.

The Preamble

We the People of the United States, in Order to form a more perfect Union, establish Justice, insure domestic Tranquility, provide for the common defence, promote the general Welfare, and secure the Blessings of Liberty to ourselves and our Posterity, do ordain and establish this Constitution for the United States of America.

The Preamble declares that "We the People" are the authority for the Constitution (unlike the Articles of Confederation, which derived their authority from the states). The Preamble also sets out the purposes of the Constitution.

Article I. (Legislative Branch)

The first part of the Constitution is called Article 1; it deals with the organization and powers of the lawmaking branch of the national government, the Congress.

Section 1. Legislative Powers

All legislative Powers herein granted shall be vested in a Congress of the United States, which shall consist of a Senate and House of Representatives.

Section 2. House of Representatives

Clause 1: Composition and Election of Members. The House of Representatives shall be composed of Members chosen every second Year by the People of the several States, and the Electors in each State shall have the Qualifications requisite for Electors of the most numerous Branch of the State Legislature.

Each state has the power to decide who may vote for members of Congress. Within each state, those who may vote for state legislators may also vote for members of the House of Representatives (and, under the Seventeenth Amendment, for U.S. senators). When the Constitution was written, nearly all states limited voting rights to white male property owners or taxpayers at least twenty-one years old. Subsequent amendments granted voting power to African American men, all women, and eighteen-year-olds.

Clause 2: Qualifications. No Person shall be a Representative who shall not have attained to the Age of twenty five Years, and been seven Years a Citizen of the United States, and who shall not, when elected, be an Inhabitant of that State in which he shall be chosen.

Each member of the House must (1) be at least twenty-five years old, (2) have been a U.S. citizen for at least seven years, and (3) be a resident of the state in which she or he is elected.

Clause 3: Apportionment of Representatives and Direct Taxes. Representatives [and direct Taxes][1] shall be apportioned among the several States which may be included within this Union, according to their respective Numbers [which shall be determined by adding to the whole Number of free Persons, including those bound to Service for a Term of Years, and excluding Indians not taxed, three fifths of all other Persons].[2] The actual Enumeration shall be made within three Years after the first Meeting of the Congress of the United States, and within every subsequent Term of ten Years, in such Manner as they shall by Law direct. The Number of Representatives shall not exceed one for every thirty Thousand, but each State shall have at Least one Representative; and until such enumeration shall be made, the

---

*The spelling, capitalization, and punctuation of the original have been retained here. Brackets indicate passages that have been altered by amendments to the Constitution.

[1]Modified by the Sixteenth Amendment.
[2]Modified by the Fourteenth Amendment.

State of New Hampshire shall be entitled to chuse three, Massachusetts eight, Rhode Island and Providence Plantations one, Connecticut five, New York six, New Jersey four, Pennsylvania eight, Delaware one, Maryland six, Virginia ten, North Carolina five, South Carolina five, and Georgia three.

A state's representation in the House is based on the size of its population. Population is counted in each decade's census, after which Congress reapportions House seats. Since early in the twentieth century, the number of seats has been limited to 435.

Clause 4: Vacancies. When vacancies happen in the Representation from any State, the Executive Authority thereof shall issue Writs of Election to fill such Vacancies.

The "Executive Authority" is the state's governor. When a vacancy occurs in the House, the governor calls a special election to fill it.

Clause 5: Officers and Impeachment. The House of Representatives shall chuse their Speaker and other Officers; and shall have the sole Power of Impeachment.

The power to impeach is the power to accuse. In this case, it is the power to accuse members of the executive or judicial branch of wrongdoing or abuse of power. Once a bill of impeachment is issued, the Senate holds the trial.

Section 3. The Senate

Clause 1: Term and Number of Members. The Senate of the United States shall be composed of two Senators from each State [chosen by the Legislature thereof],[3] for six Years; and each Senator shall have one Vote.

Every state has two senators, each of whom serves for six years and has one vote in the upper chamber. Since the Seventeenth Amendment in 1913, all senators have been elected directly by voters of the state during the regular election.

Clause 2: Classification of Senators. Immediately after they shall be assembled in Consequence of the first Election, they shall be divided as equally as may be into three Classes. The Seats of the Senators of the first Class shall be vacated at the Expiration of the second Year, of the second Class at the Expiration of the fourth Year, and of the third Class at the Expiration of the sixth Year, so that one third may be chosen every second Year; [and if Vacancies happen by Resignation, or otherwise, during the Recess of the Legislature of any State, the Executive thereof may make temporary Appointments until the next Meeting of the Legislature, which shall then fill such Vacancies].[4]

---

[3]Repealed by the Seventeenth Amendment.
[4]Modified by the Seventeenth Amendment.

One-third of the Senate's seats are open to election every two years (unlike the House, all of whose members are elected simultaneously).

Clause 3: Qualifications. No Person shall be a Senator who shall not have attained to the Age of thirty Years, and been nine Years a Citizen of the United States, and who shall not, when elected, be an Inhabitant of that State for which he shall be chosen.

Every senator must be at least thirty years old, a citizen of the United States for a minimum of nine years, and a resident of the state in which he or she is elected.

Clause 4: The Role of the Vice President. The Vice President of the United States shall be President of the Senate, but shall have no Vote, unless they be equally divided.

The vice president presides over meetings of the Senate but cannot vote unless there is a tie. The Constitution gives no other official duties to the vice president.

Clause 5: Other Officers. The Senate shall chuse their other Officers, and also a President pro tempore, in the Absence of the Vice President, or when he shall exercise the Office of President of the United States.

The Senate votes for one of its members to preside when the vice president is absent. This person is usually called the president pro tempore because of the temporary situation of the position.

Clause 6: Impeachment Trials. The Senate shall have the sole Power to try all Impeachments. When sitting for that Purpose, they shall be on Oath or Affirmation. When the President of the United States is tried, the Chief Justice shall preside: And no Person shall be convicted without the Concurrence of two thirds of the Members present.

The Senate conducts trials of officials that the House impeaches. The Senate sits as a jury, with the vice president presiding if the president is not on trial.

Clause 7: Penalties for Conviction. Judgment in Cases of Impeachment shall not extend further than to removal from Office, and disqualification to hold and enjoy any Office of honor, Trust, or Profit under the United States: but the Party convicted shall nevertheless be liable and subject to Indictment, Trial, Judgment, and Punishment, according to Law.

On conviction of impeachment charges, the Senate can only force an official to leave office and prevent him or her from holding another office in the federal government. The individual, however, can still be tried in a regular court.

Section 4. Congressional Elections: Times, Manner, and Places

Clause 1: Elections. The Times, Places and Manner of holding Elections for Senators and Representatives, shall be prescribed in each State by the Legislature thereof; but the Congress may at any time by Law make or alter such Regulations, except as to the Places of chusing Senators.

Congress set the Tuesday after the first Monday in November in even-numbered years as the date for congressional elections. In states with more than one seat in the House, Congress requires that representatives be elected from districts within each state. Under the Seventeenth Amendment, senators are elected at the same places as other officials.

Clause 2: Sessions of Congress. [The Congress shall assemble at least once in every Year, and such Meeting shall be on the first Monday in December, unless they shall by Law appoint a different Day.][5]

Congress has to meet every year at least once. The regular session now begins at noon on January 3 of each year, subsequent to the Twentieth Amendment, unless Congress passes a law to fix a different date. Congress stays in session until its members vote to adjourn. Additionally, the president may call a special session.

Section 5. Powers and Duties of the Houses

Clause 1: Admitting Members and Quorum. Each House shall be the Judge of the Elections, Returns, and Qualifications of its own Members, and a Majority of each shall constitute a Quorum to do Business; but a smaller Number may adjourn from day to day, and may be authorized to compel the Attendance of absent Members, in such Manner, and under such Penalties as each House may provide.

Each chamber may exclude or refuse to seat a member-elect.

The quorum rule requires that 218 members of the House and 51 members of the Senate be present in order to conduct business. This rule is normally not enforced in the handling of routine matters.

Clause 2: Rules and Discipline of Members. Each House may determine the Rules of its Proceedings, punish its Members for disorderly Behaviour, and, with the Concurrence of two thirds, expel a Member.

The House and the Senate may adopt their own rules to guide their proceedings. Each may also discipline its members for conduct that is deemed unacceptable. No member may be expelled without a two-thirds majority vote in favor of expulsion.

Clause 3: Keeping a Record. Each House shall keep a Journal of its Proceedings, and from time to time publish the same, excepting such Parts as may in their Judgment require

Secrecy; and the Yeas and Nays of the Members of either House on any question shall, at the Desire of one fifth of those Present, be entered on the Journal.

The journals of the two chambers are published at the end of each session of Congress.

Clause 4: Adjournment. Neither House, during the Session of Congress, shall, without the Consent of the other, adjourn for more than three days, nor to any other Place than that in which the two Houses shall be sitting.

Congress has the power to determine when and where to meet, provided, however, that both chambers meet in the same city. Neither chamber may recess in excess of three days without the consent of the other.

Section 6. Rights of Members

Clause 1: Compensation and Privileges. The Senators and Representatives shall receive a Compensation for their services, to be ascertained by Law, and paid out of the Treasury of the United States. They shall in all Cases, except Treason, Felony and Breach of the Peace, be privileged from Arrest during their Attendance at the Session of their respective Houses, and in going to and returning from the same; and for any Speech or Debate in either House, they shall not be questioned in any other Place.

Congressional salaries are to be paid by the U.S. Treasury rather than by the members' respective states. The original salaries were $6 per day; in 1857 they were $3,000 per year. Both representatives and senators currently are paid $150,000 each year.

Treason is defined in Article III, Section 3. A felony is any serious crime. A breach of the peace is any indictable offense less than treason or a felony. Members cannot be arrested for things they say during speeches and debates in Congress. This immunity applies to the Capitol Building itself and not to their private lives.

Clause 2: Restrictions. No Senator or Representative shall, during the Time for which he was elected, be appointed to any civil Office under the Authority of the United States, which shall have been created, or the Emoluments whereof shall have been encreased during such time; and no Person holding any Office under the United States, shall be a Member of either House during his Continuance in Office.

During the term for which a member was elected, he or she cannot concurrently accept another federal government position.

Section 7. Legislative Powers: Bills and Resolutions

Clause 1: Revenue Bills. All Bills for raising Revenue shall originate in the House of Representatives; but the Senate may propose or concur with Amendments as on other Bills.

---

[5]Changed by the Twentieth Amendment.

All tax and appropriation bills for raising money have to originate in the House of Representatives. The Senate, though, often amends such bills and may even substitute an entirely different bill.

Clause 2: The Presidential Veto.   Every Bill which shall have passed the House of Representatives and the Senate, shall, before it becomes a Law, be presented to the President of the United States; If he approve he shall sign it, but if not he shall return it, with his Objections to the House in which it shall have originated, who shall enter the Objections at large on their Journal, and proceed to reconsider it. If after such Reconsideration two thirds of that House shall agree to pass the Bill, it shall be sent together with the Objections, to the other House, by which it shall likewise be reconsidered, and if approved by two thirds of that House, it shall become a Law. But in all such Cases the Votes of both Houses shall be determined by Yeas and Nays, and the Names of the Persons voting for and against the Bill shall be entered on the Journal of each House respectively. If any Bill shall not be returned by the President within ten Days (Sundays excepted) after it shall have been presented to him, the Same shall be a Law, in like Manner as if he had signed it, unless the Congress by their Adjournment prevent its Return in which Case it shall not be a Law.

When Congress sends the president a bill, he or she can sign it (in which case it becomes law) or send it back to the chamber in which it originated. If it is sent back, a two-thirds majority of each chamber must pass it again for it to become law. If the president neither signs it nor sends it back within ten days, it becomes law anyway, unless Congress adjourns in the meantime.

Clause 3: Actions on Other Matters.   Every Order, Resolution, or Vote to which the Concurrence of the Senate and House of Representatives may be necessary (except on a question of Adjournment) shall be presented to the President of the United States; and before the Same shall take Effect, shall be approved by him, or being disapproved by him, shall be repassed by two thirds of the Senate and House of Representatives, according to the Rules and Limitations prescribed in the Case of a Bill.

The president must either sign or veto everything that Congress passes, except votes to adjourn and resolutions not having the force of law.

Section 8. The Powers of Congress

Clause 1: Taxing.   The Congress shall have Power To lay and collect Taxes, Duties, Imposts and Excises, to pay the Debts and provide for the common Defence and general Welfare of the United States; but all Duties, Imposts and Excises shall be uniform throughout the United States;

Duties are taxes on imports and exports. Impost is a generic term for tax. Excises are taxes on the manufacture, sale, or use of goods.

Clause 2: Borrowing.   To borrow Money on the credit of the United States;

Congress has the power to borrow money, which is normally carried out through the sale of U.S. treasury bonds on which interest is paid. Note that the Constitution places no limit on the amount of government borrowing.

Clause 3: Regulation of Commerce.   To regulate Commerce with foreign Nations, and among the several States, and with the Indian Tribes;

This is the commerce clause, which gives to the Congress the power to regulate interstate and foreign trade. Much of the activity of Congress is based on this clause.

Clause 4: Naturalization and Bankruptcy.   To establish an uniform Rule of Naturalization, and uniform Laws on the subject of Bankruptcies throughout the United States;

Only Congress may determine how aliens can become citizens of the United States. Congress may make laws with respect to bankruptcy.

Clause 5: Money and Standards.   To coin Money, regulate the Value thereof, and of foreign Coin, and fix the Standard of Weights and Measures;

Congress mints coins and prints and circulates paper money. Congress can establish uniform measures of time, distance, weight, and so on. In 1838, Congress adopted the English system of weights and measurements as our national standard.

Clause 6: Punishing Counterfeiters.   To provide for the Punishment of counterfeiting the Securities and current Coin of the United States;

Congress has the power to punish those who copy American money and pass it off as real. Currently, the fine is up to $5,000 and/or imprisonment for up to fifteen years.

Clause 7: Roads and Post Offices.   To establish Post Offices and post Roads;

Post roads include all routes over which mail is carried—highways, railways, waterways, and airways.

Clause 8: Patents and Copyrights.   To promote the Progress of Science and useful Arts, by securing for limited Times to Authors and Inventors the exclusive Right to their respective Writings and Discoveries;

Authors' and composers' works are protected by copyrights established by copyright law, which currently is the 1978 Copyright Act. Copyrights are valid for the life of the author or composer plus fifty years. Inventors' works are protected by patents, which vary in length of protection from three and a half to seventeen years. A patent gives a person the exclusive right to control the manufacture or sale of her or his invention.

Clause 9: Lower Courts. To constitute Tribunals inferior to the supreme Court;

Congress has the authority to set up all federal courts, except the Supreme Court, and to decide what cases those courts will hear.

Clause 10: Punishment for Piracy. To define and punish Piracies and Felonies committed on the high Seas, and Offences against the Law of Nations;

Congress has the authority to prohibit the commission of certain acts outside U.S. territory and to punish certain violations of international law.

Clause 11: Declaration of War. To declare War, grant Letters of Marque and Reprisal, and make Rules concerning Captures on Land and Water;

Only Congress can declare war, although the president, as commander in chief, can make war without Congress's formal declaration. Letters of marque and reprisal authorized private parties to capture and destroy enemy ships in wartime. Since the middle of the nineteenth century, international law has prohibited letters of marque and reprisal, and the United States has honored the ban.

Clause 12: The Army. To raise and support Armies, but no Appropriation of Money to that Use shall be for a longer Term than two Years;

Congress has the power to create an army; the money used to pay for it must be appropriated for no more than two-year intervals. This latter restriction gives ultimate control of the army to civilians.

Clause 13: Creation of a Navy. To provide and maintain a Navy;

This clause allows for the maintenance of a navy. In 1947, Congress created the U.S. Air Force.

Clause 14: Regulation of the Armed Forces. To make Rules for the Government and Regulation of the land and naval Forces;

Congress sets the rules for the military mainly by way of the Uniform Code of Military Justice, which was enacted in 1950 by Congress.

Clause 15: The Militia. To provide for calling forth the Militia to execute the Laws of the Union, suppress Insurrections and repel Invasions;

The militia is known today as the National Guard. Both Congress and the president have the authority to call the National Guard into federal service.

Clause 16: How the Militia Is Organized. To provide for organizing, arming, and disciplining the Militia, and for governing such Part of them as may be employed in the Service of the United States, reserving to the States respectively, the Appointment of the Officers, and the Authority of training the Militia according to the discipline prescribed by Congress;

This clause gives Congress the power to "federalize" state militia (National Guard). When called into such service, the National Guard is subject to the same rules that Congress has set forth for the regular armed services.

Clause 17: Creation of the District of Columbia. To exercise exclusive Legislation in all Cases whatsoever, over such District (not exceeding ten Miles square) as may, by Cession of particular States, and the Acceptance of Congress, become the Seat of the Government of the United States, and to exercise like Authority over all Places purchased by the Consent of the Legislature of the State in which the Same shall be, for the Erection of Forts, Magazines, Arsenals, dock-Yards, and other needful Buildings;—And

Congress established the District of Columbia as the national capital in 1791. Virginia and Maryland had granted land for the District, but Virginia's grant was returned because it was believed it would not be needed. Today, the District covers sixty-nine square miles.

Clause 18: The Elastic Clause. To make all Laws which shall be necessary and proper for carrying into Execution the foregoing Powers, and all other Powers vested by this Constitution in the Government of the United States, or in any Department or Officer thereof.

This clause—the necessary and proper clause, or the elastic clause—grants no specific powers, and thus it can be stretched to fit different circumstances. It has allowed Congress to adapt the government to changing needs and times.

Section 9. The Powers Denied to Congress

Clause 1: Question of Slavery. The Migration or Importation of such Persons as any of the States now existing shall think proper to admit, shall not be prohibited by the Congress prior to the Year one thousand eight hundred and eight, but a Tax or duty may be imposed on such Importation, not exceeding ten dollars for each Person.

"Persons" referred to slaves. Congress outlawed the slave trade in 1808.

Clause 2: Habeas Corpus. The privilege of the Writ of Habeas Corpus shall not be suspended, unless when in Cases of Rebellion or Invasion the public Safety may require it.

A writ of habeas corpus is a court order directing a sheriff or other public officer who is detaining another person to "produce the body" of the detainee so the court can assess the legality of the detention.

Clause 3: Special Bills. No Bill of Attainder or ex post facto Law shall be passed.

A bill of attainder is a law that inflicts punishment without a trial. An ex post facto law is a law that inflicts punishment for an act that was not illegal when it was committed.

Clause 4: Direct Taxes. [No Capitation, or other direct, Tax shall be laid, unless in Proportion to the Census or Enumeration herein before directed to be taken.][6]

A capitation is a tax on a person. A direct tax is a tax paid directly to the government, such as a property tax. This clause was intended to prevent Congress from levying a tax on slaves per person and thereby taxing slavery out of existence.

Clause 5: Export Taxes. No Tax or Duty shall be laid on Articles exported from any State.

Congress may not tax any goods sold from one state to another or from one state to a foreign country. (Congress does have the power to tax goods that are bought from other countries, however.)

Clause 6: Interstate Commerce. No Preference shall be given by any Regulation of Commerce or Revenue to the Ports of one State over those of another: nor shall Vessels bound to, or from, one State, be obliged to enter, clear, or pay Duties in another.

Congress may not treat different ports within the United States differently in terms of taxing and commerce powers. Congress may not tax goods sent from one state to another. Finally, Congress may not give one state's port a legal advantage over those of another state.

Clause 7: Treasury Withdrawals. No Money shall be drawn from the Treasury, but in Consequence of Appropriations made by Law; and a regular Statement and Account of the Receipts and Expenditures of all public Money shall be published from time to time.

Federal funds can be spent only as Congress authorizes. This is a significant check on the president's power.

Clause 8: Titles of Nobility. No Title of Nobility shall be granted by the United States: And no Person holding any

Office of Profit or Trust under them, shall, without the Consent of the Congress, accept of any present, Emolument, Office, or Title, of any kind whatever, from any King, Prince, or foreign State.

No person in the United States may hold a title of nobility, such as duke or duchess. This clause also discourages bribery of American officials by foreign governments.

Section 10. Those Powers Denied to the States

Clause 1: Treaties and Coinage. No State shall enter into any Treaty, Alliance, or Confederation; grant Letters of Marque and Reprisal; coin Money; emit Bills of Credit; make any Thing but gold and silver Coin a Tender in Payment of Debts; pass any Bill of Attainder, ex post facto Law, or Law impairing the Obligation of Contracts, or grant any Title of Nobility.

Prohibiting state laws "impairing the Obligation of Contracts" was intended to protect creditors. (Shays' Rebellion—an attempt to prevent courts from giving effect to creditors' legal actions against debtors—occurred only one year before the Constitution was written.)

Clause 2: Duties and Imposts. No State shall, without the Consent of the Congress, lay any Imports or Duties on Imports or Exports, except what may be absolutely necessary for executing its inspection Laws; and the net Produce of all Duties and Imposts, laid by any State on Imports or Exports, shall be for the Use of the Treasury of the United States; and all such Laws shall be subject to the Revision and Controul of the Congress.

Only Congress can tax imports. Further, the states cannot tax exports.

Clause 3: War. No State shall, without the Consent of Congress, lay any Duty of Tonnage, keep Troops, or Ships of War in time of Peace, enter into any Agreement or Compact with another State, or with a foreign Power or engage in War, unless actually invaded, or in such imminent Danger as will not admit of delay.

A duty of tonnage is a tax on ships according to their cargo capacity. No states may effectively tax ships according to their cargo unless Congress agrees. Additionally, this clause forbids any state to keep troops or warships during peacetime or to make a compact with another state or foreign nation unless Congress so agrees. States can, in contrast, maintain a militia, but its use has to be limited to internal disorders that occur within a state—unless, of course, the militia is called into federal service.

Article II. (Executive Branch)

Section 1. The Nature and Scope of Presidential Power

Clause 1: Four-Year Term. The executive Power shall be vested in a President of the United States of America. He shall

---

[6]Modified by the Sixteenth Amendment.

hold his Office during the Term of four Years, and, together with the Vice President, chosen for the same Term, be elected, as follows.

The president has the power to carry out laws made by Congress, called the executive power. He or she serves in office for a four-year term after election. The Twenty-second Amendment limits the number of times a person may be elected president.

Clause 2: Choosing Electors from Each State. Each State shall appoint, in such Manner as the Legislature thereof may direct, a Number of Electors, equal to the whole Number of Senators and Representatives to which the State may be entitled in the Congress; but no Senator or Representative, or Person holding an Office of Trust or Profit under the United States, shall be appointed an Elector.

The "Electors" are known more commonly as the "electoral college." The president is elected by electors—that is, representatives chosen by the people—rather than by the people directly.

Clause 3: The Former System of Elections. [The Electors shall meet in their respective States, and vote by Ballot for two Persons, of whom one at least shall not be an Inhabitant of the same State with themselves. And they shall make a List of all the Persons voted for, and of the Number of Votes for each; which List they shall sign and certify, and transmit sealed to the Seat of the Government of the United States, directed to the President of the Senate. The President of the Senate shall, in the Presence of the Senate and House of Representatives, open all the Certificates, and the Votes shall then be counted. The Person having the greatest Number of Votes shall be the President, if such Number be a Majority of the whole Number of Electors appointed; and if there be more than one who have such Majority, and have an equal Number of Votes, then the House of Representatives shall immediately chuse by Ballot one of them for President; and if no Person have a Majority, then from the five highest on the List the said House shall in like Manner chuse the President. But in chusing the President, the Votes shall be taken by States, the Representation from each State having one Vote; A quorum for this Purpose shall consist of a Member or Members from two thirds of the States, and a Majority of all the States shall be necessary to a Choice. In every Case, after the Choice of the President, the Person having the greater Number of Votes of the Electors shall be the Vice President. But if there should remain two or more who have equal Votes, the Senate shall chuse from them by Ballot the Vice President.][7]

The original method of selecting the president and vice president was replaced by the Twelfth Amendment. Apparently, the framers did not anticipate the rise of political parties and the development of primaries and conventions.

Clause 4: The Time of Elections. The Congress may determine the Time of chusing the Electors, and the Day on which they shall give their Votes; which Day shall be the same throughout the United States.

Congress set the Tuesday after the first Monday in November every fourth year as the date for choosing electors. The electors cast their votes on the Monday after the second Wednesday in December of that year.

Clause 5: Qualifications for President. No person except a natural born Citizen, or a Citizen of the United States, at the time of the Adoption of this Constitution, shall be eligible to the Office of President; neither shall any Person be eligible to that Office who shall not have attained to the Age of thirty five Years, and been fourteen Years a Resident within the United States.

The president must be a natural-born citizen, be at least thirty-five years of age when taking office, and have been a resident within the United States for at least fourteen years.

Clause 6: Succession of the Vice President. [In Case of the Removal of the President from Office, or of his Death, Resignation or Inability to discharge the Powers and Duties of the said Office, the same shall devolve on the Vice President, and the Congress may by Law provide for the Case of Removal, Death, Resignation or Inability, both of the President and Vice President, declaring what Officer shall then act as President, and such Officer shall act accordingly, until the Disability be removed, or a President shall be elected.][8]

This former section provided for the method by which the vice president was to succeed to the presidency, but its wording is ambiguous. It was replaced by the Twenty-fifth Amendment.

Clause 7: The President's Salary. The President shall, at stated Times, receive for his Services, a Compensation, which shall neither be encreased nor diminished during the Period for which he shall have been elected, and he shall not receive within that Period any other Emolument from the United States, or any of them.

The president maintains the same salary during each four-year term. Moreover, she or he may not receive additional cash payments from the government. Originally set at $25,000 per year, the salary is currently $200,000 a year plus a $50,000 taxable expense account.

Clause 8: The Oath of Office. Before he enter on the Execution of his Office, he shall take the following Oath or Affirmation: "I do solemnly swear (or affirm) that I will faith-

---

[7]Changed by the Twelfth Amendment.

[8]Modified by the Twenty-fifth Amendment.

fully execute the Office of President of the United States, and will to the best of my Ability, preserve, protect and defend the Constitution of the United States."

The president is "sworn in" prior to beginning the duties of the office. Currently, the taking of the oath of office occurs on January 20, following the November election. The ceremony is called the inauguration. The oath of office is administered by the chief justice of the United States Supreme Court.

Section 2. Powers of the President
Clause 1: Commander in Chief. The President shall be Commander in Chief of the Army and Navy of the United States, and of the Militia of the several States, when called into the actual Service of the United States; he may require the Opinion, in writing, of the principal Officer in each of the executive Departments, upon any Subject relating to the Duties of their respective Offices, and he shall have Power to grant Reprieves and Pardons for Offences against the United States, except in Cases of Impeachment.

The armed forces are placed under civilian control because the president is a civilian, but still commander in chief of the military. The president may ask for the help of the heads of each of the executive departments (thereby creating the cabinet). The cabinet members are chosen by the president with the consent of the Senate, but they can be removed without Senate approval.
The president's clemency powers extend only to federal cases. In those cases, he or she may grant a full or conditional pardon, or reduce a prison term or fine.

Clause 2: Treaties and Appointment. He shall have Power, by and with the Advice and Consent of the Senate, to make Treaties, provided two thirds of the Senators present concur; and he shall nominate, and by and with the Advice and Consent of the Senate, shall appoint Ambassadors, other public Ministers and Consuls, Judges of the supreme Court, and all other Officers of the United States, whose Appointments are not herein otherwise provided for, and which shall be established by Law; but the Congress may by Law vest the Appointment of such inferior Officers, as they think proper, in the President alone, in the Courts of Law, or in the Heads of Departments.

Many of the major powers of the president are identified in this clause, including the power to make treaties with foreign governments (with the approval of the Senate by a two-thirds vote) and the power to appoint ambassadors, Supreme Court justices, and other government officials. Most such appointments require Senate approval.

Clause 3: Vacancies. The President shall have Power to fill up all Vacancies that may happen during the Recess of the Senate, by granting Commissions which shall expire at the end of their next Session.

The president has the power to appoint temporary officials to fill vacant federal offices without Senate approval if Congress is not in session. Such appointments expire automatically at the end of Congress's next term.

Section 3. Duties of the President
He shall from time to time give to the Congress Information of the State of the Union, and recommend to their Consideration such Measures as he shall judge necessary and expedient; he may, on extraordinary Occasions, convene both Houses, or either of them, and in Case of Disagreement between them, with Respect to the Time of Adjournment, he may adjourn them to such Time as he shall think proper; he shall receive Ambassadors and other public Ministers; he shall take Care that the Laws be faithfully executed, and shall Commission all the Officers of the United States.

Annually, the president reports on the state of the union to Congress, recommends legislative measures, and proposes a federal budget. The State of the Union speech is a statement not only to Congress but also to the American people. After it is given, the president proposes a federal budget and presents an economic report. At any time he or she so chooses, the president may send special messages to Congress while it is in session. The president has the power to call special sessions, to adjourn Congress when its two houses do not agree for that purpose, to receive diplomatic representatives of other governments, and to ensure the proper execution of all federal laws. The president further has the ability to empower federal officers to hold their positions and to perform their duties.

Section 4. Impeachment
The President, Vice President and all civil Officers of the United States, shall be removed from Office on Impeachment for, and Conviction of, Treason, Bribery, or other high Crimes and Misdemeanors.

Treason denotes giving aid to the nation's enemies. The definition of high crimes and misdemeanors is usually given as serious abuses of political power. In either case, the president or vice president may be accused by the House (called an impeachment) and then removed from office if convicted by the Senate. (Note that impeachment does not mean removal, but rather the condition of being accused of treason or high crimes and misdemeanors.)

Article III. (Judicial Branch)

Section 1. Judicial Powers, Courts, and Judges
The judicial Power of the United States, shall be vested in one supreme Court, and in such inferior Courts as the Congress may from time to time ordain and establish. The Judges, both of the supreme and inferior Courts, shall hold their Offices during good Behaviour, and shall, at stated Times, receive for their Services a Compensation, which shall not be diminished during their Continuance in Office.

The Supreme Court is vested with judicial power, as are the lower federal courts that Congress creates. Federal judges serve in their offices for life unless they are impeached and convicted by Congress. The payment of federal judges may not be reduced during their time in office.

Section 2. Jurisdiction

Clause 1: Cases under Federal Jurisdiction. The judicial Power shall extend to all Cases, in Law and Equity, arising under this Constitution, the Laws of the United States, and Treaties made, or which shall be made, under their Authority;—to all Cases affecting Ambassadors, other public Ministers and Consuls;—to all Cases of admiralty and maritime Jurisdiction;—to Controversies to which the United States shall be a Party;—to Controversies between two or more States; [—between a State and Citizens of another State;—][9] between Citizens of different States;—between Citizens of the same State claiming Lands under Grants of different States, [and between a State, or the Citizens thereof, and foreign States, Citizens or Subjects.][10]

The federal courts take on cases that concern the meaning of the U.S. Constitution, all federal laws, and treaties. They also can take on cases involving citizens of different states and citizens of foreign nations.

Clause 2: Cases for the Supreme Court. In all Cases affecting Ambassadors, other public Ministers and Consuls, and those in which a State shall be a Party, the supreme Court shall have original Jurisdiction. In all the other Cases before mentioned, the supreme Court shall have appellate Jurisdiction, both as to Law and Fact, with such Exceptions, and under such Regulations as the Congress shall make.

In a limited number of situations, the Supreme Court acts as a trial court and has original jurisdiction. These cases involve a representative from another country or involve a state. In all other situations, the cases must first be tried in the lower courts and then can be appealed to the Supreme Court. Congress may, however, make exceptions. Today the Supreme Court acts as a trial court of first instance on rare occasions.

Clause 3: The Conduct of Trials. The Trial of all Crimes, except in Cases of Impeachment, shall be by Jury; and such Trial shall be held in the State where the said Crimes shall have been committed; but when not committed within any State, the Trial shall be at such Place or Places as the Congress may by Law have directed.

Any person accused of a federal crime is granted the right to a trial by jury in a federal court in that state in which the crime was committed. Trials of impeachment are an exception.

---

[9]Modified by the Eleventh Amendment.
[10]Modified by the Eleventh Amendment.

Section 3. Treason

Clause 1: The Definition of Treason. Treason against the United States, shall consist only in levying War against them, or, in adhering to their Enemies, giving them Aid and Comfort. No Person shall be convicted of Treason unless on the Testimony of two Witnesses to the same overt Act, or on Confession in open Court.

Treason is the making of war against the United States or giving aid to its enemies.

Clause 2: Punishment. The Congress shall have Power to declare the Punishment of Treason, but no Attainder of Treason shall work Corruption of Blood, or Forfeiture except during the Life of the Person attainted.

Congress has provided that the punishment for treason ranges from a minimum of five years in prison and/or a $10,000 fine to a maximum of death. "No Attainder of Treason shall work Corruption of Blood" prohibits punishment of the traitor's heirs.

Article IV. (Relations among the States)

Section 1. Full Faith and Credit

Full Faith and Credit shall be given in each State to the public Acts, Records, and judicial Proceedings of every other State. And the Congress may by general Laws prescribe the Manner in which such Acts, Records and Proceedings shall be proved, and the Effect thereof.

All states are required to respect one another's laws, records, and lawful decisions. There are exceptions, however. A state does not have to enforce another state's criminal code. Nor does it have to recognize another state's grant of a divorce if the person obtaining the divorce did not establish legal residence in the state in which it was given.

Section 2. Treatment of Citizens

Clause 1: Privileges and Immunities. The Citizens of each State shall be entitled to all Privileges and Immunities of Citizens in the several States.

A citizen of a state has the same rights and privileges as the citizens of another state in which he or she happens to be.

Clause 2: Extradition. A Person charged in any State with Treason, Felony, or other Crime, who shall flee from Justice, and be found in another State, shall on Demand of the executive Authority of the State from which he fled, be delivered up, to be removed to the State having Jurisdiction of the Crime.

Any person accused of a crime who flees to another state must be returned to the state in which the crime occurred.

Clause 3: Fugitive Slaves. [No Person held to Service or Labour in one State, under the Laws thereof, escaping into another, shall, in Consequence of any Law or Regulation therein, be discharged from such Service or Labour, but shall be delivered up on Claim of the Party to whom such Service or Labour may be due.][11]

This clause was struck down by the Thirteenth Amendment, which abolished slavery in 1865.

Section 3. Admission of States
Clause 1: The Process. New States may be admitted by the Congress into this Union; but no new State shall be formed or erected within the Jurisdiction of any other State; nor any State be formed by the Junction of two or more States, or Parts of States, without the Consent of the Legislatures of the States concerned as well as of the Congress.

Only Congress has the power to admit new states to the union. No state may be created by taking territory from an existing state unless the state's legislature so consents.

Clause 2: Public Land. The Congress shall have Power to dispose of and make all needful Rules and Regulations respecting the Territory or other Property belonging to the United States; and nothing in this Constitution shall be so construed as to Prejudice any Claims of the United States, or of any particular State.

The federal government has the exclusive right to administer federal government public lands.

Section 4. Republican Form of Government
The United States shall guarantee to every State in this Union a Republican Form of Government, and shall protect each of them against Invasion; and on Application of the Legislature, or of the Executive (when the Legislature cannot be convened) against domestic Violence.

Each state is promised a form of government in which the people elect their representatives. The federal government is bound to protect states against any attack by foreigners or during times of trouble within a state.

Article V. (Methods of Amendment)
The Congress, whenever two thirds of both Houses shall deem it necessary, shall propose Amendments to this Constitution, or on the Application of the Legislatures of two thirds of the several States, shall call a Convention for proposing Amendments, which, in either Case, shall be valid to all Intents and Purposes, as Part of this Constitution, when ratified by the Legislatures of three fourths of the several States, or by Conventions in three fourths thereof, as the one or the other Mode of Ratification may be proposed by the Congress; Provided that no Amendment which may be made prior to the Year One thousand eight hundred and eight shall in any Manner affect the first and fourth Clauses in the Ninth Section of the First Article; and that no State, without its Consent, shall be deprived of its equal Suffrage in the Senate.

Amendments may be proposed in either of two ways: a two-thirds vote of each chamber (Congress) or at the request of two-thirds of the states. Ratification of amendments may be carried out in two ways: by the legislatures of three-fourths of the states or by the voters in three-fourths of the states. No state may be denied equal representation in the Senate.

Article VI. (National Supremacy)
Clause 1: Existing Obligations. All Debts contracted and Engagements entered into, before the Adoption of this Constitution shall be as valid against the United States under this Constitution, as under the Confederation.

During the Revolutionary War and the years of the Confederation, Congress borrowed large sums. This clause pledged that the new federal government would assume those financial obligations.

Clause 2: Supreme Law of the Land. This Constitution, and the Laws of the United States which shall be made in Pursuance thereof; and all Treaties made, or which shall be made, under the Authority of the United States, shall be the supreme Law of the Land; and the Judges in every State shall be bound thereby, any Thing in the Constitution or Laws of any State to the Contrary notwithstanding.

This is typically called the supremacy clause; it declares that federal law takes precedence over all forms of state law. No government, at the local or state level, may make or enforce any law that conflicts with any provision of the Constitution, acts of Congress, treaties, or other rules and regulations issued by the president and his or her subordinates in the executive branch of the federal government.

Clause 3: Oath of Office. The Senators and Representatives before mentioned, and the Members of the several State Legislatures, and all executive and judicial Officers, both of the United States and of the several States, shall be bound by Oath or Affirmation, to support this Constitution; but no religious Test shall ever be required as a Qualification to any Office or public Trust under the United States.

Every federal and state official must take an oath of office promising to support the U.S. Constitution. Religion may not be used as a qualification to serve in any federal office.

Article VII. (Ratification)
The Ratification of the Conventions of nine States shall be sufficient for the Establishment of this Constitution between the States so ratifying the Same.

---

[11]Repealed by the Thirteenth Amendment.

Nine states were required to ratify the Constitution. Delaware was the first and New Hampshire the ninth.

Done in Convention by the Unanimous Consent of the States present the Seventeenth Day of September in the Year of our Lord one thousand seven hundred and Eighty seven and of the Independence of the United States of America the Twelfth. In witness whereof we have hereunto subscribed our Names, Articles in addition to, and amendment of the Constitution of the United States of America, proposed by Congress and ratified by the Legislatures of the several states, pursuant to the Fifth Article of the original Constitution.

Go. WASHINGTON
Presid't. and deputy from Virginia

Attest
WILLIAM JACKSON
Secretary

DELAWARE
Geo. Read
Gunning Bedford jun
John Dickinson
Richard Bassett
Jaco. Broom

MASSACHUSETTS
Nathaniel Gorham
Rufus King

CONNECTICUT
Wm. Saml. Johnson
Roger Sherman

NEW YORK
Alexander Hamilton

NEW JERSEY
Wh. Livingston
David Brearley
Wm. Paterson
Jona. Dayton

PENNSYLVANIA
B. Franklin
Thomas Mifflin
Robt. Morris
Geo. Clymer
Thos. FitzSimons
Jared Ingersoll
James Wilson
Gouv. Morris

NEW HAMPSHIRE
John Langdon
Nicholas Gilman

MARYLAND
James McHenry
Dan of St. Thos. Jenifer
Danl. Carroll

VIRGINIA
John Blair
James Madison Jr.

NORTH CAROLINA
Wm. Blount
Richd. Dobbs Spaight
Hu. Williamson

SOUTH CAROLINA
J. Rutledge
Charles Cotesworth Pinckney
Charles Pinckney
Pierce Butler

GEORGIA
William Few
Abr. Baldwin

Amendments to the Constitution of the United States

The Bill of Rights[12]

Amendment I.
Religion, Speech, Assembly, and Petition

Congress shall make no law respecting an establishment of religion, or prohibiting the free exercise thereof; or abridging the freedom of speech, or of the press; or the right of the people peaceably to assemble, and to petition the Government for a redress of grievances.

Congress may not create an official church or enact laws limiting the freedom of religion, speech, the press, assembly, and petition. These guarantees, like the others in the Bill of Rights (the first ten amendments), are not absolute—each may be exercised only with regard to the rights of other persons.

Amendment II.
Militia and the Right to Bear Arms

A well regulated Militia, being necessary to the security of a free State, the right of the people to keep and bear Arms, shall not be infringed.

To protect itself, each state has the right to maintain a volunteer armed force. States and the federal government regulate the possession and use of firearms by individuals.

Amendment III.
The Quartering of Soldiers

No Soldier shall, in time of peace be quartered in any house, without the consent of the Owner, nor in time of war, but in a manner to be prescribed by law.

Before the Revolutionary War, it had been common British practice to quarter soldiers in colonists' homes. Military troops do not have the power to take over private houses during peacetime.

Amendment IV.
Searches and Seizures

The right of the people to be secure in their persons, houses, papers, and effects, against unreasonable searches and seizures, shall not be violated, and no Warrants shall issue, but upon probable cause, supported by Oath or affirmation, and partic-

ularly describing the place to be searched, and the persons or things to be seized.

Here the word warrant *means "justification" and refers to a document issued by a magistrate or judge indicating the name, address, and possible offense committed. Anyone asking for the warrant, such as a police officer, must be able to convince the magistrate or judge that an offense probably has been committed.*

Amendment V.
Grand Juries, Self-incrimination, Double Jeopardy, Due Process, and Eminent Domain

No person shall be held to answer for a capital, or otherwise infamous crime, unless on a presentment or indictment of a Grand Jury, except in cases arising in the land or naval forces, or in the Militia, when in actual service in time of War or public danger; nor shall any person be subject for the same offence to be twice put in jeopardy of life or limb; nor shall be compelled in any criminal case to be a witness against himself, nor be deprived of life, liberty, or property, without due process of law; nor shall private property be taken for public use, without just compensation.

There are two types of juries. A grand jury considers physical evidence and the testimony of witnesses, and decides whether there is sufficient reason to bring a case to trial. A petit jury hears the case at trial and decides it. "For the same offence to be twice put in jeopardy of life or limb" means to be tried twice for the same crime. A person may not be tried for the same crime twice or forced to give evidence against herself or himself. No person's right to life, liberty, or property may be taken away except by lawful means, called the due process of law. Private property taken for use in public purposes must be paid for by the government.

Amendment VI.
Criminal Court Procedures

In all criminal prosecutions, the accused shall enjoy the right to a speedy and public trial, by an impartial jury of the State and district wherein the crime shall have been committed, which district shall have been previously ascertained by law, and to be informed of the nature and cause of the accusation; to be confronted with the witnesses against him; to have compulsory process for obtaining witnesses in his favor, and to have the Assistance of Counsel for his defence.

Any person accused of a crime has the right to a fair and public trial by a jury in the state in which the crime took place. The charges against that person must be so indicated. Any accused person has the right to a lawyer to defend him or her and to question those who testify against him or her, as well as the right to call people to speak in his or her favor at trial.

---

[12]On September 25, 1789, Congress transmitted to the state legislatures twelve proposed amendments, two of which, having to do with congressional representation and congressional pay, were not adopted. The remaining ten amendments became the Bill of Rights. In 1992, the amendment concerning congressional pay was adopted as the Twenty-seventh Amendment.

Amendment VII.
Trial by Jury in Civil Cases

In Suits at common law, where the value in controversy shall exceed twenty dollars, the right of trial by jury shall be preserved, and no fact tried by jury, shall be otherwise re-examined in any Court of the United States, than according to the rules of the common law.

A jury trial may be requested by either party in a dispute in any case involving more than $20. If both parties agree to a trial by a judge without a jury, the right to a jury trial may be put aside.

Amendment VIII.
Bail, Cruel and Unusual Punishment

Excessive bail shall not be required, nor excessive fines imposed, nor cruel and unusual punishments inflicted.

Bail is that amount of money that a person accused of a crime may be required to deposit with the court as a guarantee that she or he will appear in court when requested. The amount of bail required or the fine imposed as punishment for a crime must be reasonable compared with the seriousness of the crime involved. Any punishment judged to be too harsh or too severe for a crime shall be prohibited.

Amendment IX.
The Rights Retained by the People

The enumeration in the Constitution, of certain rights, shall not be construed to deny or disparage others retained by the people.

Many civil rights that are not explicitly enumerated in the Constitution are still held by the people.

Amendment X.
Reserved Powers of the States

The powers not delegated to the United States by the Constitution, nor prohibited by it to the States, are reserved to the States respectively, or to the people.

Those powers not delegated by the Constitution to the federal government or expressly denied to the states belong to the states and to the people. This clause in essence allows the states to pass laws under its "police powers."

Amendment XI
(Ratified on February 7, 1795).
Suits against States

The Judicial power of the United States shall not be construed to extend to any suit in law or equity, commenced or prosecuted against one of the United States by Citizens of another State, or by Citizens or Subjects of any Foreign State.

This amendment has been interpreted to mean that a state cannot be sued in federal court by one of its citizens, by a citizen of another state, or by a foreign country.

Amendment XII
(Ratified on June 15, 1804).
Election of the President

The Electors shall meet in their respective states, and vote by ballot for President and Vice-President, one of whom, at least, shall not be an inhabitant of the same State with themselves; they shall name in their ballots the person voted for as President, and in distinct ballots the person voted for as Vice-President, and they shall make distinct lists of all persons voted for as President, and of all persons voted for as Vice-President, and of the number of votes for each, which lists they shall sign and certify, and transmit sealed to the seat of the government of the United States, directed to the President of the Senate;—The President of the Senate shall, in the presence of the Senate and House of Representatives, open all the certificates and the votes shall then be counted;—The person having the greatest number of votes for President, shall be the President, if such number be a majority of the whole number of Electors appointed; and if no person have such majority, then from the persons having the highest numbers not exceeding three on the list of those voted for as President, the House of Representatives shall choose immediately, by ballot, the President. But in choosing the President, the votes shall be taken by States, the representation from each State having one vote; a quorum for this purpose shall consist of a member or members from two-thirds of the States, and a majority of all States shall be necessary to a choice. [And if the House of Representatives shall not choose a President whenever the right of choice shall devolve upon them, before the fourth day of March next following, then the Vice-President shall act as President, as in the case of the death or other constitutional disability of the President.][13]—The person having the greatest number of votes as Vice-President, shall be the Vice-President, if such number be a majority of the whole number of Electors appointed, and if no person have a majority, then from the two highest numbers on the list, the Senate shall choose the Vice-President; a quorum for the purpose shall consist of two-thirds of the whole number of Senators, and a majority of the whole number shall be necessary to a choice. But no person constitutionally ineligible to the office of President shall be eligible to that of Vice-President of the United States.

The original procedure set out for the election of president and vice president in Article II, Section 1, resulted in a tie in 1800 between Thomas Jefferson and Aaron Burr. It was not until the next year that the House of Representatives chose Jefferson to be president. This amendment changed the procedure by providing for separate ballots for president and vice president.

Amendment XIII
(Ratified on December 6, 1865).
Prohibition of Slavery

Section 1.

Neither slavery nor involuntary servitude, except as a punishment for crime whereof the party shall have been duly con-

---

[13]Changed by the Twentieth Amendment.

victed, shall exist within the United States, or any place subject to their jurisdiction.

Some slaves had been freed during the Civil War. This amendment freed the others and abolished slavery.

Section 2.

Congress shall have power to enforce this article by appropriate legislation.

Amendment XIV
(Ratified on July 9, 1868).
Citizenship, Due Process, and Equal Protection of the Laws

Section 1.

All persons born or naturalized in the United States, and subject to the jurisdiction thereof, are citizens of the United States and of the State wherein they reside. No State shall make or enforce any law which shall abridge the privileges or immunities of citizens of the United States; nor shall any State deprive any person of life, liberty, or property, without due process of law; nor deny to any person within its jurisdiction the equal protection of the laws.

Under this provision, states cannot make or enforce laws that take away rights given to all citizens by the federal government. States cannot act unfairly or arbitrarily toward, or discriminate against, any person.

Section 2.

Representatives shall be apportioned among the several States according to their respective numbers, counting the whole number of persons in each State, excluding Indians not taxed. But when the right to vote at any election for the choice of electors for President and Vice President of the United States, Representatives in Congress, the Executive and Judicial officers of a State, or the members of the Legislature thereof, is denied to any of the male inhabitants of such State, being [twenty-one][14] years of age, and citizens of the United States, or in any way abridged, except for participation in rebellion, or other crime, the basis of representation therein shall be reduced in the proportion which the number of such male citizens shall bear to the whole number of male citizens twenty-one years of age in such State.

Section 3.

No person shall be a Senator or Representative in Congress, or elector of President and Vice President, or hold any office, civil or military, under the United States, or under any State, who having previously taken an oath, as a member of Congress, or as an officer of the United States, or as a member of any State legislature, or as an executive or judicial officer of any State, to support the Constitution of the United States, shall have engaged in insurrection or rebellion against the same, or given aid or comfort to the enemies thereof. But Congress may by a vote of two-thirds of each House, remove such disability.

This provision forbade former state or federal government officials who had acted in support of the Confederacy during the Civil War to hold office again. It limited the president's power to pardon those persons. Congress removed this "disability" in 1898.

Section 4.

The validity of the public debt of the United States, authorized by law, including debts incurred for payment of pensions and bounties for services in suppressing insurrection or rebellion, shall not be questioned. But neither the United States nor any State shall assume or pay any debt or obligation incurred in aid of insurrection or rebellion against the United States, or any claim for the loss or emancipation of any slave, but all such debts, obligations and claims shall be held illegal and void.

Section 5.

The Congress shall have power to enforce, by appropriate legislation, the provisions of this article.

Amendment XV
(Ratified on February 3, 1870).
The Right to Vote

Section 1.

The right of citizens of the United States to vote shall not be denied or abridged by the United States or by any State on account of race, color, or previous condition of servitude.

No citizen can be refused the right to vote simply because of race or color or because that person was once a slave.

Section 2.

The Congress shall have power to enforce this article by appropriate legislation.

Amendment XVI
(Ratified on February 3, 1913).
Income Taxes

The Congress shall have power to lay and collect taxes on incomes, from whatever source derived, without apportionment among the several States, and without regard to any census or enumeration.

This amendment allows Congress to tax income without sharing the revenue so obtained with the states according to their population.

Amendment XVII
(Ratified on April 8, 1913).
The Popular Election of Senators

The Senate of the United States shall be composed of two Senators from each State, elected by the people thereof, for six

---

[14]Changed by the Twenty-sixth Amendment.

years; and each Senator shall have one vote. The electors in each State shall have the qualifications requisite for electors of the most numerous branch of the State legislatures.

When vacancies happen in the representation of any State in the Senate, the executive authority of such State shall issue writs of election to fill such vacancies: *Provided,* That the legislature of any State may empower the executive thereof to make temporary appointments until the people fill the vacancies by election as the legislature may direct.

This amendment shall not be so construed as to affect the election or term of any Senator chosen before it becomes valid as part of the Constitution.

This amendment modified portions of Article I, Section 3, that related to election of senators. Senators are now elected by the voters in each state directly. When a vacancy occurs, either the state may fill the vacancy by a special election, or the governor of the state involved may appoint someone to fill the seat until the next election.

Amendment XVIII
(Ratified on January 16, 1919).
Prohibition

Section 1.
After one year from the ratification of this article the manufacture, sale, or transportation of intoxicating liquors within, the importation thereof into, or the exportation thereof from the United States and all territory subject to the jurisdiction thereof for beverage purposes is hereby prohibited.

Section 2.
The Congress and the several States shall have concurrent power to enforce this article by appropriate legislation.

Section 3.
This article shall be inoperative unless it shall have been ratified as an amendment to the Constitution by the legislatures of the several States, as provided in the Constitution, within seven years from the date of the submission hereof to the States by the Congress.[15]

This amendment made it illegal to manufacture, sell, and transport alcoholic beverages in the United States. It was repealed by the Twenty-first Amendment.

Amendment XIX
(Ratified on August 18, 1920).
Women's Right to Vote.

The right of citizens of the United States to vote shall not be denied or abridged by the United States or by any State on account of sex.

Congress shall have power to enforce this article by appropriate legislation.

Women were given the right to vote by this amendment, and Congress was given the power to enforce this right.

Amendment XX
(Ratified on January 23, 1933).
The Lame Duck Amendment

Section 1.
The terms of the President and Vice President shall end at noon on the 20th day of January, and the terms of Senators and Representatives at noon on the 3d day of January, of the years in which such terms would have ended if this article had not been ratified; and the terms of their successors shall then begin.

This amendment modified Article I, Section 4, Clause 2, and other provisions relating to the president in the Twelfth Amendment. The taking of the oath of office was moved from March 4 to January 20.

Section 2.
The Congress shall assemble at least once in every year, and such meeting shall begin at noon on the 3d day of January, unless they shall by law appoint a different day.

Congress changed the beginning of its term to January 3. The reason the Twentieth Amendment is called the Lame Duck Amendment is because it shortens the time between when a member of Congress is defeated for reelection and when he or she leaves office.

Section 3.
If, at the time fixed for the beginning of the term of the President, the President elect shall have died, the Vice President elect shall become President. If a President shall not have been chosen before the time fixed for the beginning of his term, or if the President elect shall have failed to qualify, then the Vice President elect shall act as President until a President shall have qualified; and the Congress may by law provide for the case wherein neither a President elect nor a Vice President elect shall have qualified, declaring who shall then act as President, or the manner in which one who is to act shall be selected, and such person shall act accordingly until a President or Vice President shall have qualified.

This part of the amendment deals with problem areas left ambiguous by Article II and the Twelfth Amendment. If the president dies before January 20 or fails to qualify for office, the presidency is to be filled in the order given in this section.

Section 4.
The Congress may by law provide for the case of the death of any of the persons from whom the House of Representatives may choose a President whenever the rights of choice shall have devolved upon them, and for the case of the death of any

---

[15]The Eighteenth Amendment was repealed by the Twenty-first Amendment.

of the persons from whom the Senate may choose a Vice President whenever the right of choice shall have devolved upon them.

Congress has never created legislation subsequent to this section.

Section 5.
Sections 1 and 2 shall take effect on the 15th day of October following the ratification of this article.

Section 6.
This article shall be inoperative unless it shall have been ratified as an amendment to the Constitution by the legislatures of three-fourths of the several States within seven years from the date of its submission.

Amendment XXI
(Ratified on December 5, 1933).
The Repeal of Prohibition

Section 1.
The eighteenth article of amendment to the Constitution of the United States is hereby repealed.

Section 2.
The transportation or importation into any State, Territory, or possession of the United States for delivery or use therein of intoxicating liquors, in violation of the laws thereof, is hereby prohibited.

Section 3.
This article shall be inoperative unless it shall have been ratified as an amendment to the Constitution by conventions in the several States, as provided in the Constitution, within seven years from the date of the submission hereof to the States by the Congress.

The amendment repealed the Eighteenth Amendment but did not make alcoholic beverages legal everywhere. Rather, they remained illegal in any state that so designated them. Many such "dry" states existed for a number of years after 1933. Today, there are still "dry" counties within the United States, in which alcoholic beverages are illegal.

Amendment XXII
(Ratified on February 27, 1951).
Limitation of Presidential Terms

Section 1.
No person shall be elected to the office of the President more than twice, and no person who has held the office of President, or acted as President, for more than two years of a term to which some other person was elected President shall be elected to the office of President more than once. But this Article shall not apply to any person holding the office of President when this Article was proposed by the Congress, and shall not prevent

any person who may be holding the office of President, or acting as President, during the term within which this Article becomes operative from holding the office of President or acting as President during the remainder of such term.

Section 2.
This article shall be inoperative unless it shall have been ratified as an amendment to the Constitution by the legislatures of three-fourths of the several States within seven years from the date of its submission to the States by the Congress.

No president may serve more than two elected terms. If, however, a president has succeeded to the office after the halfway point of a term in which another president was originally elected, then that president may serve for more than eight years, but not to exceed ten years.

Amendment XXIII
(Ratified on March 29, 1961).
Presidential Electors for
the District of Columbia

Section 1.
The District constituting the seat of Government of the United States shall appoint in such manner as the Congress may direct:

A number of electors of President and Vice President equal to the whole number of Senators and Representatives in Congress to which the District would be entitled if it were a State, but in no event more than the least populous State; they shall be in addition to those appointed by the States, but they shall be considered, for the purposes of the election of President and Vice President, to be electors appointed by a State; and they shall meet in the District and perform such duties as provided by the twelfth article of amendment.

Section 2.
The Congress shall have power to enforce this article by appropriate legislation.

Citizens living in the District of Columbia have the right to vote in elections for president and vice president. The District of Columbia has three presidential electors, whereas before this amendment it had none.

Amendment XXIV
(Ratified on January 23, 1964).
The Anti–Poll Tax Amendment

Section 1.
The right of citizens of the United States to vote in any primary or other election for President or Vice President, for electors for President or Vice President, or for Senator or Representative in Congress, shall not be denied or abridged by the United States, or any State by reason of failure to pay any poll tax or other tax.

Section 2.

The Congress shall have power to enforce this article by appropriate legislation.

No government shall require a person to pay a poll tax in order to vote in any federal election.

Amendment XXV
(Ratified on February 10, 1967).
Presidential Disability and Vice Presidential Vacancies

Section 1.

In case of the removal of the President from office or of his death or resignation, the Vice President shall become President.

Whenever a president dies or resigns from office, the vice president becomes president.

Section 2.

Whenever there is a vacancy in the office of the Vice President, the President shall nominate a Vice President who shall take office upon confirmation by a majority vote of both Houses of Congress.

Whenever the office of the vice presidency becomes vacant, the president may appoint someone to fill this office, provided Congress consents.

Section 3.

Whenever the President transmits to the President pro tempore of the Senate and the Speaker of the House of Representatives his written declaration that he is unable to discharge the powers and duties of his office, and until he transmits to them a written declaration to the contrary, such powers and duties shall be discharged by the Vice President as Acting President.

Whenever the president believes she or he is unable to carry out the duties of the office, she or he shall so indicate to Congress in writing. The vice president then acts as president until the president declares that she or he is again able to properly carry out the duties of the office.

Section 4.

Whenever the Vice President and a majority of either the principal officers of the executive departments or of such other body as Congress may by law provide, transmit to the President pro tempore of the Senate and the Speaker of the House of Representatives their written declaration that the President is unable to discharge the powers and duties of his office, the Vice President shall immediately assume the powers and duties of the office as Acting President.

Thereafter, when the President transmits to the President pro tempore of the Senate and the Speaker of the House of Representatives his written declaration that no inability exists, he shall resume the powers and duties of his office unless the Vice President and a majority of either the principal officers of the executive department or of such other body as Congress may by law provide, transmit within four days to the President pro tempore of the Senate and the Speaker of the House of Representatives their written declaration that the President is unable to discharge the powers and duties of his office. Thereupon Congress shall decide the issue, assembling within forty-eight hours for that purpose if not in session. If the Congress, within twenty-one days after receipt of the latter written declaration, or, if Congress is not in session, within twenty-one days after Congress is required to assemble, determines by two-thirds vote of both Houses that the President is unable to discharge the powers and duties of his office, the Vice President shall continue to discharge the same as Acting President; otherwise, the President shall resume the powers and duties of his office.

Whenever the vice president and a majority of the members of the cabinet believe that the president cannot carry out his or her duties, they shall so indicate in writing to Congress. The vice president shall then act as president. When the president believes that she or he is able to carry out her or his duties again, she or he shall so indicate to Congress. If, though, the vice president and a majority of the cabinet do not agree, Congress must decide by a two thirds vote within three weeks who shall act as president.

Amendment XXVI
(Ratified on July 1, 1971).
The Eighteen-Year-Old Vote

Section 1.

The right of citizens of the United States, who are eighteen years of age or older, to vote shall not be denied or abridged by the United States or by any State on account of age.

No one over eighteen years of age can be denied the right to vote in federal or state elections by virtue of age.

Section 2.

The Congress shall have power to enforce this article by appropriate legislation.

Amendment XXVII
(Ratified on May 7, 1992).
Congressional Pay

No law varying the compensation for the services of the Senators and Representatives shall take effect, until an election of representatives shall have intervened.

This amendment allows the voters to have some control over increases in salaries for congressional members. Originally submitted to the states for ratification in 1789, it was not ratified until 203 years later, in 1992.

The States Were Responsible for Homeland Defense ?

BACKGROUND

The Constitution drafted by the founders created a federal form of government, in which sovereign powers are *shared* by the national government and the state governments. Although the Constitution expressly delegated certain powers to the national government and reserved all other powers to the states, the precise nature of the powers to be exercised by the national government and the state governments, respectively, has long been subject to debate.

During various times in our history, state governments have claimed significant powers. Today, in the wake of the terrorist attacks of September 11, 2001, an important question relating to *federalism*, the topic of this chapter, is the role of state governments in defending against future terrorist attacks.

WHAT IF THE STATES WERE RESPONSIBLE FOR HOMELAND DEFENSE?

Some maintain that state and local governments should play a significant role in defending the homeland against terrorist attacks. Indeed, since the September 11 attacks, the debate over how to protect critical infrastructure and the public, and who will pay for that protection, has dominated state legislative houses and governors' mansions. Oklahoma governor Frank Keating wrote in an August 2001 article for the *Journal of Homeland Security* that policymakers should "recognize that in virtually every possible terrorism scenario, first responders will be local."

Certainly, this was the case after the September 11 attacks. New York City police officers and firefighters were the first on the scene at the World Trade Center. Many of the ongoing tasks involving crowd control, cleanup, and the securing of key facilities against further attack were borne by state and local personnel, as well as by the National Guard under state command.

REVIVING THE STATE GUARDS

If state governments were responsible for homeland defense, they would need to create special forces, or units, to handle the work. Reviving the state guards, or militias, is one possibility. John R. Brinkerhoff, a retired U.S. Army colonel and former associate director for national preparedness of the Federal Emergency Management Agency, argues that restoring state militias under the command of state governors should be a critical component of homeland security. According to Brinkerhoff, "The revitalized state guards should be under the command of the respective governors and be dedicated to homeland defense duties within their respective states. They should be supported by the states but subsidized by the federal government at least to the extent of making military uniforms, arms, field gear, vehicles, radios, and other supplies and equipment available."

Although Article I, Section 10, of the Constitution prohibits the states from keeping troops or warships during peacetime, the Constitution does allow states to maintain militias—as long as their use is limited to internal disorders. State militias can be federalized, according to Article I, Section 8, "to execute the Laws of the Union, suppress Insurrections and repel Invasions." The 1916 National Defense Act federalized all organized militias as the National Guard of the United States. As the National Guard took on an increasingly federal role during World War I (1914–1918) and World War II (1939–1945), most states were left without a militia.

At different times during the twentieth century, various states revived their state militias as organized, volunteer forces under the authority of state governors. (Note that these militias should not be confused with private military groups that refer to themselves as "militias.") Today, twenty-five states have official state militias, or guards. Since the 1990s, state emergencies requiring a rapid local response have increasingly involved terrorist attacks, including the Oklahoma City bombing in 1995 and the terrorist attacks on September 11, 2001. The threat of coordinated terrorist attacks may revive the constitutional debate over dual roles for state militia and the branches of the federal military.

FOR CRITICAL ANALYSIS

1. Do you think that the federal government is better equipped than the states to defend the United States against terrorist attacks, or should the states be given a more comprehensive role in homeland defense?

2. Should the states create revitalized state guards, as allowed by the U.S. Constitution, which would be dedicated to homeland defense duties?

In the United States, rights and powers are reserved to the states by the Tenth Amendment. It may appear that since September 11, 2001, the federal government, sometimes called the national or central government, predominates. Nevertheless, that might be a temporary exaggeration, for there are 87,900 separate governmental units in this nation, as you can see in Table 3–1.

Visitors from France or Spain are often awestruck by the complexity of our system of government. Consider that a criminal action can be defined by state law, by national law, or by both. Thus, a criminal suspect can be prosecuted in the state court system or in the federal court system (or both). Often, economic regulation over exactly the same matter exists at the local level, the state level, and the national level—generating multiple forms to be completed, multiple procedures to be followed, and multiple laws to be obeyed. Numerous programs are funded by the national government but administered by state and local governments.

There are various ways of ordering relations between central governments and local units. *Federalism* is one of these ways. Understanding federalism and how it differs from other forms of government is important in understanding the American political system. Indeed, many political issues today, including the one discussed in this chapter's opening *What If . . .*, would not arise if we did not have a federal form of government in which governmental authority is divided between the central government and various subunits.

Three Systems of Government

There are about two hundred independent nations in the world today. Each of these nations has its own system of government. Generally, though, there are three ways of ordering relations between central governments and local units: (1) a unitary system, (2) a confederal system, and (3) a federal system. The most popular, both historically and today, is the unitary system.

A Unitary System

A **unitary system** of government is the easiest to define. Unitary systems allow ultimate governmental authority to rest in the hands of the national, or central, government. Consider a typical unitary system—France. There are departments and municipalities

Unitary System
A centralized governmental system in which local or subdivisional governments exercise only those powers given to them by the central government.

DID YOU KNOW . . .
That in Florida, Michigan, Mississippi, North Carolina, North Dakota, Virginia, and West Virginia, male-female cohabitation is against the law and punishable by a short jail term, a fine up to $500, or both?

TABLE 3–1

With more than 87,900 separate governmental units in the United States today, it is no wonder that intergovernmental relations in the United States are so complicated. Actually, the number of school districts has decreased over time, but the number of special districts created for single purposes, such as flood control, has increased from only about 8,000 during World War II to nearly 35,000 today.

Federal government		1
State governments		50
Local governments		87,849
Counties	3,034	
Municipalities	19,431	
(mainly cities or towns)		
Townships	16,506	
(less extensive powers)		
Special districts	35,356	
(water, sewer, and so on)		
School districts	13,522	
TOTAL		87,900

SOURCE: U.S. Census Bureau, *Preliminary Report, 2002 Census of Governments*.

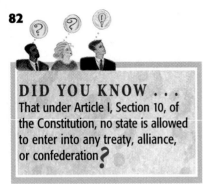

Confederal System

A system of government consisting of a
league of independent states, each having
essentially sovereign powers. The central
government created by such a league has
only limited powers over the states.

in France. Within the departments and the municipalities are separate government
entities with elected and appointed officials. So far, the French system appears to be
very similar to the U.S. system, but the similarity is only superficial. Under the unitary
French system, the decisions of the governments of the departments and municipalities can be overruled by the national government. The national government also can
cut off the funding of many departmental and municipal government activities.
Moreover, in a unitary system such as that in France, all questions related to education,
police, the use of land, and welfare are handled by the national government.[1] Great
Britain, Sweden, Israel, Egypt, Ghana, and the Philippines also have unitary systems of
government, as do most countries today.

A Confederal System

You were introduced to the elements of a **confederal system** of government in
Chapter 2, when we examined the Articles of Confederation. A confederation is the
opposite of a unitary governing system. It is a league of independent states in which a
central government or administration handles only those matters of common concern expressly delegated to it by the member states. The central governmental unit has
no ability to make laws directly applicable to individuals unless the member states
explicitly support such laws. The United States under the Articles of Confederation
and the Confederate States during the American Civil War were confederations.

There are few, if any, confederations in the world today that resemble those that
existed in the United States. Switzerland is a confederation of twenty-three sovereign
cantons. Countries also have formed organizations with one another for limited purposes, such as the military/peacekeeping roles of the North Atlantic Treaty Organization
and the United Nations. These organizations, however, are not true confederations.

A Federal System

The federal system lies between the unitary and confederal forms of government. As
mentioned in Chapter 2, in a *federal system*, authority is divided, usually by a written constitution, between a central government and regional, or subdivisional, governments
(often called constituent governments). The central government and the constituent governments both act directly on the people through laws and through the actions of elected
and appointed governmental officials. Within each government's sphere of authority,
each is supreme, in theory. Thus, a federal system differs sharply from a unitary one in
which the central is supreme and the constituent governments derive their
authority from it. Australia, Canada, Mexico, India, Brazil, and Germany are examples of
nations with federal systems. See Figure 3–1 for a comparison of the three systems.

Why Federalism?

Why did the United States develop in a federal direction? We look here at that question as well as at some of the arguments for and against a federal form of government.

A Practical Solution

As you saw in Chapter 2, the historical basis of the federal system was laid down in
Philadelphia at the Constitutional Convention, where strong national government
advocates opposed equally strong states' rights advocates. This dichotomy continued
through to the ratifying conventions in the several states. The resulting federal system was a compromise. The supporters of the new Constitution were political prag-
matists—they realized that without a federal arrangement, there would be no

---

[1]Recent legislation has altered somewhat the unitary character of the French political system.

ratification of the new Constitution. The appeal of federalism was that it retained state traditions and local power while establishing a strong national government capable of handling common problems.

Even if the colonial leaders had agreed on the desirability of a unitary system, the problems of size and regional isolation would have made such a system difficult operationally. At the time of the Constitutional Convention, the thirteen colonies taken together were larger geographically than England or France. Slow travel and communication, combined with geographic spread, contributed to the isolation of many regions within the colonies. For example, it could take up to several weeks for all of the colonies to be informed about one particular political decision.

Other Arguments for Federalism

The arguments for federalism in the United States and elsewhere involve a complex set of factors, some of which we already have noted. First, for big countries, such as the United States, India, and Canada, federalism allows many functions to be "farmed out" by the central government to the states or provinces. The lower levels of government, accepting these responsibilities, thereby can become the focus of political dissatisfaction rather than the national authorities. Second, even with modern transportation and communications systems, the sheer geographic or population size of some nations makes it impractical to locate all political authority in one place. Finally, federalism brings government closer to the people. It allows more direct access to, and influence on, government agencies and policies, rather than leaving the population restive and dissatisfied with a remote, faceless, all-powerful central authority.

Benefits for the United States. In the United States, federalism historically has yielded many benefits. State governments long have been a training ground for future national leaders. Some presidents made their political mark as state governors. The states themselves have been testing grounds for new government initiatives. As United States Supreme Court justice Louis Brandeis once observed:

> It is one of the happy incidents of the federal system that a single courageous state may, if its citizens choose, serve as a laboratory and try novel social and economic experiments without risk to the rest of the country.[2]

Examples of programs pioneered at the state level include unemployment compensation, which began in Wisconsin, and air-pollution control, which was initiated in

---

[2] *New State Ice Co. v. Liebmann,* 285 U.S. 262 (1932).

FIGURE 3–1

The Flow of Power in Three Systems of Government

In a unitary system, the flow of power is from the central government to the local and state governments. In a confederal system, the flow of power is in the opposite direction—from the state and local governments to the central government. In a federal system, the flow of power, in principle, goes both ways.

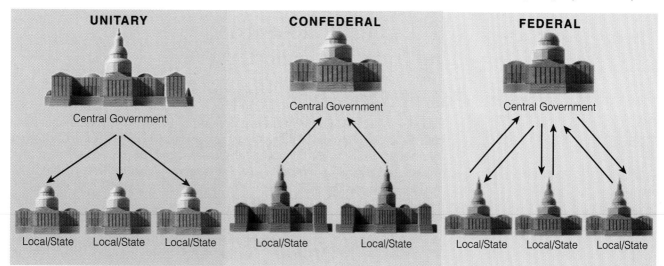

UNITARY — Central Government — Local/State, Local/State, Local/State

CONFEDERAL — Central Government — Local/State, Local/State

FEDERAL — Central Government — Local/State, Local/State, Local/State

California. Currently, states are experimenting with policies ranging from educational reforms to the medical use of marijuana. Since the passage of the 1996 welfare reform legislation, which gave more control over welfare programs to state governments (see Chapter 16), states have also been experimenting with different methods of delivering welfare assistance.

Federalism Allows for Many Political Subcultures.   Additionally, the American way of life always has been characterized by a number of political subcultures, which divide along the lines of race and ethnic origin, wealth, education, and, more recently, age, degree of religious fundamentalism, and sexual preference. The existence of diverse political subcultures would appear to be at odds with a political authority concentrated solely in a central government. Had the United States developed into a unitary system, the various political subcultures certainly would have been less able to influence government behavior (relative to their own regions and interests) than they have been, and continue to be, in our federal system.

Arguments against Federalism

Not everyone thinks federalism is such a good idea. Some see it as a way for powerful state and local interests to block progress and impede national plans. Others see dangers in the expansion of national powers at the expense of the states. President Ronald Reagan (1981–1989) said, "The Founding Fathers saw the federalist system as constructed something like a masonry wall. The States are the bricks, the national government is the mortar. . . . Unfortunately, over the years, many people have increasingly come to believe that Washington is the whole wall."[3]

Smaller political units are more likely to be dominated by a single political group, and the dominant groups in some cities and states have resisted implementing equal rights for all minority groups. (This was essentially the argument that James Madison put forth in *Federalist Paper* No. 10, which you can read in Appendix D of this text.) Others point out, however, that the dominant factions in other states have been more progressive than the national government in many areas, such as the environment.

Critics of federalism also argue that too many Americans suffer as a result of the inequalities across the states. As you will read later in this chapter, individual states differ markedly with respect to educational spending and achievement, crime and crime prevention, and even the safety of their buildings (see this chapter's *America's Security* feature). Not surprisingly, these critics argue for increased federal legislation and oversight. This might involve creating national educational standards, national building code standards, national expenditure minimums for crime control, and so on.

The Constitutional Basis for American Federalism

No mention of the designation "federal system" can be found in the U.S. Constitution. Nor is it possible to find a systematic division of governmental authority between the national and state governments in that document. Rather, the Constitution sets out different types of powers. These powers can be classified as (1) the powers of the national government, (2) the powers of the states, and (3) prohibited powers. The Constitution also makes it clear that if a state or local law conflicts with a national law, the national law will prevail.

Air pollution in Los Angeles, California. In our federal system of government, states have often been the testing grounds for programs later adopted by the federal government for nationwide implementation. Air-pollution control, for example, was initiated in California to cope with the threatening conditions produced by the large population in the area and the famous congestion of automobile traffic. (Ron Watts, Black Star)

---

[3] Text of the address by the president to the National Conference of State Legislatures, Atlanta, Georgia (Washington, D.C.: The White House, Office of the Press Secretary, July 30, 1981), as quoted in Edward Millican, *One United People: The Federalist Papers and the National Idea* (Lexington, Ky.: The University Press of Kentucky, 1990).

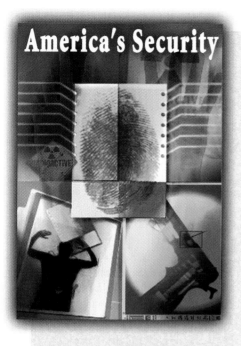
America's Security

Chipping Away at State Police Power

THE POST–WORLD-TRADE-CENTER-COLLAPSE WORLD

Within months after the collapse of the World Trade Center towers on September 11, 2001, federal employees investigating that collapse called for the adoption of new national standards for the construction of public and governmental buildings. Their goal—obviously laudable—was and continues to be to make large buildings more resistant to what happened after two jets crashed into New York City's financial center. Indeed, on March 6, 2002, the director of the National Institute of Standards and Technology, Arden Bement, Jr., stated during congressional hearings that it is "imperative" for the United States "to learn from the worst-ever building disaster in human history, and take aggressive remedial action to minimize future losses."

Actually, there was a precedent for a call by the federal government for a change in nationwide building standards. After the 1971 earthquake in the San Fernando Valley of Los Angeles, the federal government recommended several measures to the western states to make buildings more resistant to earthquake damage. Many western states adopted some modified form of those recommendations.

AN ECONOMIC TRADE-OFF IS INVOLVED

Although it is well and good for the federal government to argue in favor of building skyscrapers that are less vul-nerable to terrorist attacks, doing so would be costly. To achieve greater structural stability, any new skyscraper would have to have more columns and stronger connections between steel supports. The first change would not only increase the cost per square foot of the skyscraper, but would also reduce the amount of office space that the owners could offer for rent. In any event, improving the structural integrity of future buildings will add to their cost.

WHO IS TO DECIDE?

In principle, the federal government has no direct control over skyscraper building codes. Congress could, of course, pass a uniform skyscraper building code act, but then someone would challenge its constitutionality on the ground that it violates the Tenth Amendment. Our federal form of government continues to allow for non-uniformity in state police power. The question now is whether the nation can afford this nonuniformity in light of the threat to America's security.

FOR CRITICAL ANALYSIS

What groups might be against increasing the structural integrity of new buildings? Why?

The Tenth Amendment reserves to the states or to the people all powers not granted to the national government. The states have used these reserve powers to dictate building codes, among other things. This action falls under the states' police power to enact laws to promote the safety and welfare of those who live within their borders. Building codes throughout the United States are not uniform. They depend on local and state politics, unions that control construction workers, earthquake potential, flood potential, and the like. Some building codes are very strict; others are relatively loose. Throughout the history of the United States, the federal government has rarely interfered with state police power with respect to how buildings should be built. No federal agency can enforce local building codes.

Powers of the National Government

The powers delegated to the national government include both expressed and implied powers, as well as the special category of inherent powers. Most of the powers expressly delegated to the national government are found in Article I, Section 8, of the Constitution. These **enumerated powers** include coining money, setting standards for weights and measures, making uniform naturalization laws, admitting new states, establishing post offices, and declaring war. Another important enumerated power is the power to regulate commerce among the states—a topic we deal with later in this chapter.

Enumerated Powers
Powers specifically granted to the national government by the Constitution. The first seventeen clauses of Article I, Section 8, specify most of the enumerated powers of Congress.

The Necessary and Proper Clause.   The implied powers of the national government are also based on Article I, Section 8, which states that the Congress shall have the power

> [t]o make all Laws which shall be necessary and proper for carrying into Execution the foregoing Powers, and all other Powers vested by this Constitution in the Government of the United States, or in any Department or Officer thereof.

Elastic Clause, or Necessary and Proper Clause

The clause in Article I, Section 8, that grants Congress the power to do whatever is necessary to execute its specifically delegated powers.

This clause is sometimes called the **elastic clause,** or the **necessary and proper clause,** because it provides flexibility to our constitutional system. It gives Congress all of those powers that can be reasonably inferred but that are not expressly stated in the brief wording of the Constitution. The clause was first used in the Supreme Court decision of *McCulloch v. Maryland*[4] (discussed later in this chapter) to develop the concept of implied powers. Through this concept, the national government has succeeded in strengthening the scope of its authority to meet the numerous problems that the framers of the Constitution did not, and could not, anticipate.

Inherent Powers.   A special category of national powers that is not implied by the necessary and proper clause consists of what have been labeled the inherent powers of the national government. These powers derive from the fact that the United States is a sovereign power among nations, and as such, its national government must be the only government that deals with other nations. Under international law, it is assumed that all nation-states, regardless of their size or power, have an *inherent* right to ensure their own survival. To do this, each nation must have the ability to act in its own interest among and with the community of nations—by, for instance, making treaties, waging war, seeking trade, and acquiring territory. Note that no specific clause in the Constitution says anything about the acquisition of additional land. Nonetheless, through the federal government's inherent powers, we made the Louisiana Purchase in 1803 and then went on to acquire Florida, Texas, Oregon, Alaska, Hawaii, and numerous other lands. The United States grew from a mere thirteen states to fifty states, plus several "territories."

The national government has these inherent powers whether or not they have been enumerated in the Constitution. Some constitutional scholars categorize inherent powers as a third type of power, completely distinct from the delegated powers (both expressed and implied) of the national government.

Powers of the State Governments

The Tenth Amendment states that the powers not delegated to the United States by the Constitution, nor prohibited by it to the states, are reserved to the states, or to the people. These are the reserved powers that the national government cannot deny to the states. Because these powers are not expressly listed—and because they are not limited to powers that are expressly listed—there is sometimes a question as to whether a certain power is delegated to the national government or reserved to the states. State powers have been held to include each state's right to regulate commerce within its borders and to provide for a state militia. States also have the reserved power to make laws on all matters not prohibited to the states by the national or state constitutions and not expressly, or by implication, delegated to the national government. The states also have **police power**—the authority to legislate for the protection of the health, morals, safety, and welfare of the people. Their police power enables states to pass laws governing such activities as crimes, marriage, contracts, education, traffic laws, and land use.

Police Power

The authority to legislate for the protection of the health, morals, safety, and welfare of the people. In the United States, most police power is a reserved power of the states.

The ambiguity of the Tenth Amendment has allowed the reserved powers of the states to be defined differently at different times in our history. When there is widespread support for increased regulation by the national government, the Tenth

---

[4]4 Wheaton 316 (1819).

Amendment tends to recede into the background. When the tide turns the other way (in favor of states' rights), as it has in recent years, the Tenth Amendment is resurrected to justify arguments supporting increased states' rights.

Concurrent Powers

In certain areas, the states share **concurrent powers** with the national government. Most concurrent powers are not specifically stated in the Constitution; they are only implied. An example of a concurrent power is the power to tax. The types of taxation are divided between the levels of government. States may not levy a tariff (a set of taxes on imported goods); the federal government may not tax real estate; and neither may tax the facilities of the other. If the state governments did not have the power to tax, they would not be able to function other than on a ceremonial basis. Other concurrent powers include the power to borrow money, to establish courts, and to charter banks and corporations. Concurrent powers are normally limited to the geographic area of the state and to those functions not delegated by the Constitution exclusively to the national government—such as the coinage of money and the negotiation of treaties.

Prohibited Powers

The Constitution prohibits or denies a number of powers to the national government. For example, the national government has expressly been denied the power to impose taxes on goods sold to other countries (exports). Moreover, any power not delegated expressly or implicitly to the federal government by the Constitution is prohibited to it. For example, the national government cannot create a national public school system. The states are also denied certain powers. For example, no state is allowed to enter into a treaty on its own with another country.

The Supremacy Clause

The supremacy of the national constitution over subnational laws and actions can be found in the **supremacy clause** of the Constitution. The supremacy clause (Article VI, Clause 2) states the following:

> This Constitution, and the Laws of the United States which shall be made in Pursuance thereof; and all Treaties made . . . under the Authority of the United States, shall be the supreme Law of the Land; and the Judges in every State shall be bound thereby, any Thing in the Constitution or Laws of any State to the Contrary notwithstanding.

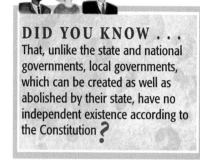

DID YOU KNOW . . .
That, unlike the state and national governments, local governments, which can be created as well as abolished by their state, have no independent existence according to the Constitution **?**

Concurrent Powers
Powers held jointly by the national and state governments.

Supremacy Clause
The constitutional provision that makes the Constitution and federal laws superior to all conflicting state and local laws.

A local New York police officer questions a truck driver on the Queensboro Bridge shortly after the attacks on the World Trade Center on September 11, 2002. Because homeland security is a massive job, cooperation among all levels of government is needed. (AP Photo/Ed Bailey)

Interstate compacts have long been used as a way to address issues that affect more than one state. An interstate compact between New York and New Jersey in 1921 created the Port Authority of New York and New Jersey to develop and maintain harbor facilities in that area, including the Port Authority Bus Terminal shown here. Today, there are over two hundred interstate compacts. (Robert Brenner, PhotoEdit)

Horizontal Federalism
Activities, problems, and policies that require state governments to interact with one another.

In other words, states cannot use their reserved or concurrent powers to thwart national policies. All national and state officers, as well as judges, must be bound by oath to support the Constitution. Hence, any legitimate exercise of national governmental power supersedes any conflicting state action.[5] Of course, deciding whether a conflict actually exists is a judicial matter, as you will soon read when we discuss the case of *McCulloch v. Maryland*.

National government legislation in a concurrent area is said to *preempt* (take precedence over) conflicting state or local laws or regulations in that area. One of the ways in which the national government has extended its powers, particularly during the twentieth century, is through the preemption of state and local laws by national legislation. Consider that in the first decade of the twentieth century, fewer than 20 national laws preempted laws and regulations issued by state and local governments. By the beginning of the twenty-first century, this number had risen to nearly 120.

Some political scientists believe that national supremacy is critical for the longevity and smooth functioning of a federal system. Nonetheless, the application of this principle has been a continuous source of conflict. Indeed, as you will see, the most extreme result of this conflict was the Civil War.

Vertical Checks and Balances

Recall from Chapter 2 that one of the concerns of the founders was to prevent the national government from becoming too powerful. For that reason, they divided the government into three branches—legislative, executive, judicial. They also created a system of checks and balances that allowed each branch to check the actions of the other branches. The federal form of government created by the founders also involves checks and balances. These are sometimes called "vertical" checks and balances because they involve relationships between the states and the national government.

For example, the reserved powers of the states act as a check on the national government. Additionally, the states' interests are represented in the national legislature (Congress), and the citizens of the various states determine who will head the executive branch (the presidency). The founders also made it impossible for the central government to change the Constitution without the states' consent, as you read in Chapter 2. Finally, national programs and policies are administered by the states, which gives the states considerable control over the ultimate shape of those programs and policies.

The national government, in turn, can check state policies by exercising its constitutional powers under the clauses just discussed, as well as under the commerce clause (to be discussed later). Furthermore, the national government can influence state policies indirectly through federal grants, as you will learn later in this chapter.

Interstate Relations

So far we have examined only the relationship between central and state governmental units. The states, however, have numerous commercial, social, and other dealings among themselves. These interstate relations make up what can be called **horizontal federalism**. The national Constitution imposes certain "rules of the road" on horizontal federalism, which have had the effect of preventing any one state from setting itself apart from the other states. The three most important clauses relating to horizontal federalism in the Constitution, all taken from the Articles of Confederation, require each state to do the following:

---

[5]An excellent example of this is President Dwight Eisenhower's disciplining of Arkansas governor Orval Faubus in 1957 by federalizing the National Guard to enforce the court-ordered desegregation of Little Rock High School.

1. Give full faith and credit to every other state's public acts, records, and judicial proceedings (Article IV, Section 1).
2. Extend to every other state's citizens the privileges and immunities of its own citizens (Article IV, Section 2).
3. Agree to return persons who are fleeing from justice in another state back to their home state when requested to do so (Article IV, Section 2).

Following these constitutional mandates is not always easy for the states. For example, one question that has arisen in recent years is whether states will be constitutionally obligated to recognize same-sex marriages performed in other states. For a discussion of this issue, see this chapter's feature entitled *Politics and Gender* on the following page.

Additionally, states may enter into agreements called **interstate compacts**—if consented to by Congress. In reality, congressional consent is necessary only if such a compact increases the power of the contracting states relative to other states (or to the national government). Typical examples of interstate compacts are the establishment of the Port Authority of New York and New Jersey by an interstate compact between those two states in 1921 and the regulation of the production of crude oil and natural gas by the Interstate Oil and Gas Compact of 1935.

Interstate Compact
An agreement between two or more states. Agreements on minor matters are made without congressional consent, but any compact that tends to increase the power of the contracting states relative to other states or relative to the national government generally requires the consent of Congress. Such compacts serve as a means by which states can solve regional problems.

Defining Constitutional Powers—The Early Years

Recall from Chapter 2 that constitutional language, to be effective and to endure, must have some degree of ambiguity. Certainly, the powers delegated to the national government and the powers reserved to the states contain elements of ambiguity, thus leaving the door open for different interpretations of federalism. Disputes over the boundaries of national versus state powers have characterized this nation from the beginning. In the early 1800s, the most significant disputes arose over differing interpretations of the implied powers of the national government under the necessary and proper clause and the respective powers of the national government and the states in regard to commerce.

Although political bodies at all levels of government play important roles in the process of settling such disputes, ultimately it is the Supreme Court that casts the final vote. As might be expected, the character of the referee will have an impact on the ultimate outcome of any boundary dispute. From 1801 to 1835, the Supreme Court was headed by Chief Justice John Marshall, a Federalist who advocated a strong central government. We look here at two cases decided by the Marshall Court: *McCulloch v. Maryland*[6] and *Gibbons v. Ogden*.[7] Both cases are considered milestones in the movement toward national government supremacy.

McCulloch v. Maryland (1819)

The U.S. Constitution says nothing about establishing a national bank. Nonetheless, at different times Congress chartered two banks—the First and Second Banks of the United States—and provided part of their initial capital; they were thus national banks. The government of Maryland imposed a tax on the Second Bank's Baltimore branch in an attempt to put that branch out of business. The branch's cashier, James William McCulloch, refused to pay the Maryland tax. When Maryland took McCulloch to its state court, the state of Maryland won. The national government appealed the case to the Supreme Court.

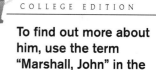
---

[6]4 Wheaton 316 (1819).
[7]9 Wheaton 1 (1824).

DID YOU KNOW ...
That the Liberty Bell cracked when it was rung at the funeral of John Marshall in 1835?

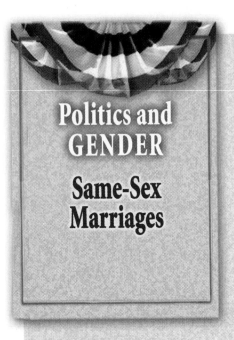

Politics and GENDER

Same-Sex Marriages

The Constitution, under Article IV, Section 1, requires that each state give full faith and credit to every other state's public acts. If you are legally married under the laws of Nevada, the other forty-nine states have to recognize that marriage. What if you live in a state that recognizes same-sex marriages? Does that mean that all other states must recognize such marriages and give each partner to the marriage the same privileges and benefits accorded to partners in opposite-sex marriages?

HAWAII TAKES THE LEAD

In 1993, the Hawaii Supreme Court ruled that banning same-sex marriages might violate the equal protection clause of the Hawaii constitution. The court stated that unless Hawaii could offer a "compelling" reason to maintain this discriminatory practice, it must be abandoned. The Hawaii Supreme Court then sent the case back to the trial court to determine if the state did indeed have such a compelling reason. In 1996, the trial court ruled that the state had failed to meet this burden and therefore the ban on same-sex marriages violated the state constitution.

This court ruling had an immediate impact on the American public—and on Congress. Congress quickly passed the Defense of Marriage Act of 1996, which allowed state governments to ignore same-sex marriages performed in other states. Somewhat ironically, the Hawaii court decisions that gave rise to these concerns largely came to naught. In 1998, the residents of that state voted for a state constitutional amendment that allows the Hawaii legislature to ban same-sex marriages. Subsequent events in Vermont, however, reignited the controversy over same-sex marriages.

ENTER VERMONT

In 1999, the Vermont Supreme Court ruled that same-sex couples should be entitled to the same benefits of marriage as opposite-sex couples. The court said that it was up to the Vermont legislature to implement the decision. According to the court, the legislature could either allow gay cou-

ples to marry or allow them to register as "domestic partners," as long as they would have all the same rights and benefits that married couples have.

Subsequently, in April 2000, the Vermont legislature passed a law permitting gay and lesbian couples to form "civil unions." Partners forming civil unions would be entitled to receive some three hundred state benefits available to married couples, including the rights to inherit a partner's property, to decide on medical treatment for an incapacitated partner, and to arrange for burial procedures. Vermont civil unions, however, would not be recognized by the federal government and thus would not entitle partners in those unions to any federal benefits, such as spousal Social Security benefits, associated with marriage.

Whether the Vermont law will stand is not certain. In the spring of 2001, the Vermont House of Representatives passed a bill that would repeal the law. The final outcome of this action is not yet known, and it probably will hinge on how the United States Supreme Court eventually rules on the issue. In the meantime, the question remains: If a state law allows for same-sex marriages, are other states obligated to recognize those marriages under the "full faith and credit" clause of the Constitution? According to the Defense of Marriage Act, they will not be. Nevertheless, we can be sure that someone, somewhere will challenge the constitutionality of the Defense of Marriage Act. Until the Supreme Court rules on the issue, we do not know whether horizontal federalism will apply to this issue.

FOR CRITICAL ANALYSIS

Opinion polls routinely show that the majority of Americans are against same-sex marriages.* Should such polls influence legislators on this issue?

*Public Perspective, January/February 2000, pp. 22–31.

For a while there was a form of same-sex marriage allowed in Hawaii. Currently, Vermont legally sanctifies same-sex unions. Other states do not, however, and this creates certain legal problems. For example, Connecticut refused to grant a divorce to a same-sex couple that had been legally married in Vermont. What other legal issues might arise when same-sex couples legally married in Vermont move to other states? (AP Photo/Honolulu Star Bulletin, Ken Ige)

One of the issues before the Court was whether the national government had the implied power, under the necessary and proper clause, to charter a bank and contribute capital to it. The other important question before the Court was the following: If the bank was constitutional, could a state tax it? In other words, was a state action that conflicted with a national government action invalid under the supremacy clause?

Chief Justice John Marshall held that if establishing such a national bank aided the national government in the exercise of its designated powers, then the authority to set up such a bank could be implied. Having established this doctrine of implied powers, Marshall then answered the other important question before the Court and established the doctrine of national supremacy. Marshall stated that no state could use its taxing power to tax an arm of the national government. If it could, "the declaration that the Constitution . . . shall be the supreme law of the land, is [an] empty and unmeaning [statement]."

Marshall's decision enabled the national government to grow and to meet problems that the Constitution's framers were unable to foresee. Today, practically every expressed power of the national government has been expanded in one way or another by use of the necessary and proper clause.

Gibbons v. Ogden (1824)

One of the more important parts of the Constitution included in Article I, Section 8, is the so-called **commerce clause,** in which Congress is given the power "[t]o regulate Commerce with foreign Nations, and among the several States, and with the Indian Tribes." The meaning of this clause was at issue in *Gibbons v. Ogden.*

There were actually several issues before the Court in this case. The first issue had to do with how the term *commerce* should be defined. New York's highest court had defined the term narrowly to mean only the shipment of goods, or the interchange of commodities, *not* navigation or the transport of people. The second issue was whether the national government's power to regulate interstate commerce extended to commerce within a state (*intra*state commerce) or was limited strictly to commerce among the states (*inter*state commerce). The third issue was whether the power to regulate interstate commerce was a concurrent power (as the New York court had concluded) or an exclusive national power.

Marshall defined *commerce* as *all* commercial intercourse—all business dealings—including navigation and the transport of people. Marshall also held that the commerce power of the national government could be exercised in state jurisdictions, even though it cannot reach *solely* intrastate commerce. Finally, Marshall emphasized that the power to regulate interstate commerce was an *exclusive* national power.

Marshall's expansive interpretation of the commerce clause in *Gibbons v. Ogden* allowed the national government to exercise increasing authority over all areas of economic affairs throughout the land. Congress did not immediately exploit this broad grant of power. In the 1930s and subsequent decades, however, the commerce clause became the primary constitutional basis for national government regulation—as you will read later in this chapter.

States' Rights and the Resort to Civil War

We usually think of the Civil War simply as the fight to free the slaves, but that issue was closely intertwined with another one. Also at the heart of the controversy that led to the Civil War was the issue of national government supremacy versus the rights of the separate states. Essentially, the Civil War brought to an ultimate and violent climax the ideological debate that had been outlined by the Federalist and Anti-Federalist parties even before the Constitution was ratified.

John Marshall (1755–1835) was the fourth chief justice of the Supreme Court. When Marshall took over, the Court had little power and almost no influence over the other two branches of government. Some scholars have declared that Marshall is the true architect of the American constitutional system, because he single-handedly gave new power to the Constitution. Early in his career, he was an attorney and was elected to the first of four terms in the Virginia Assembly. He was instrumental in the fight to ratify the Constitution in Virginia. Prior to being named to the Supreme Court, he won a seat in Congress in 1799 and in 1800 became secretary of state to John Adams. (The Library of Congress)

Commerce Clause

The section of the Constitution in which Congress is given the power to regulate trade among the states and with foreign countries.

INFOTRAC ®
COLLEGE EDITION

To find out more about the war, use the term "United States Civil War" in the Subject guide.

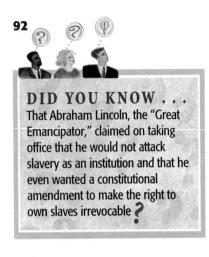

The Shift Back to States' Rights

As we have seen, while John Marshall was chief justice of the Supreme Court, he did much to increase the power of the national government and to reduce that of the states. During the Jacksonian era (1829–1837), however, a shift back to states' rights began. The question of the regulation of commerce became one of the major issues in federal-state relations. The business community preferred state regulation (or, better yet, no regulation) of commerce.

When Congress passed a tariff in 1828, the state of South Carolina attempted to nullify the tariff (render it void), claiming that in cases of conflict between a state and the national government, the state should have the ultimate authority over its citizens.

Over the next three decades, the North and South became even more sharply divided—over tariffs that mostly benefited northern industries and over the slavery issue. On December 20, 1860, South Carolina formally repealed its ratification of the Constitution and withdrew from the Union. On February 4, 1861, representatives from six southern states met at Montgomery, Alabama, to form a new government called the Confederate States of America.

War and the Growth of the National Government

The ultimate defeat of the South in 1865 permanently ended any idea that a state within the Union can successfully claim the right to secede, or withdraw, from the Union. Ironically, the Civil War—brought about in large part because of the South's desire for increased states' rights—resulted in the opposite: an increase in the political power of the national government.

The Civil War was not fought over just the question of slavery. Rather, the supremacy of the national government was at issue. Had the South won, presumably any state or states would have the right to secede from the Union. (The Library of Congress)

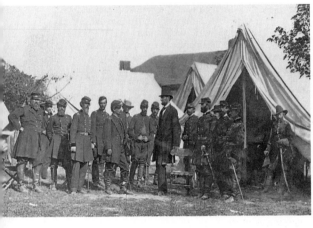

Thousands of new employees were hired to run the Union war effort and to deal with the social and economic problems that had to be handled in the aftermath of war. A billion-dollar ($1.3 billion, which is over $11.5 billion in today's dollars) national government budget was passed for the first time in 1865 to cover the increased government expenditures. The first (temporary) income tax was imposed on citizens to help pay for the war. Both the increased national government spending and the nationally imposed income tax were precursors to the expanded future role of the national government in the American federal system.[8] Civil liberties were curtailed in the Union and in the Confederacy in the name of the wartime emergency. The distribution of pensions and widow's benefits also boosted the national government's social role. The North's victory set the nation on the path to a modern industrial economy and society.

The Continuing Dispute over the Division of Power

Although the outcome of the Civil War firmly established the supremacy of the national government and put to rest the idea that a state could secede from the Union, the war by no means ended the debate over the division of powers between the national government and the states. In fact, many current political issues raise questions relating to states' rights and federalism. (For a discussion of one such issue, see this chapter's *Which Side Are You On?* feature.)

The debate over the division of powers in our federal system can be viewed as progressing through at least two general stages since the Civil War: dual federalism and cooperative federalism.

INFOTRAC ®
COLLEGE EDITION

To find out more about this issue, use the term "state rights" in the Subject guide.

---

[8]The future of the national government's powerful role was cemented with the passage of the Sixteenth Amendment (ratified in 1913), which authorized the federal income tax.

Which Side Are You On?
Should States Have the Right to Permit Assisted Suicide?

Do terminally ill patients have the right to end their own lives through physician-assisted suicide? During the 1990s, this issue reached the forefront when the laws of two states—Washington and New York—banning assisted suicide were ruled unconstitutional by two federal appellate courts. In 1997, however, the United States Supreme Court upheld the laws. The Court concluded that the liberty protected by the Constitution does not include a right to commit suicide.* In effect, the Court's ruling left the decision in the hands of the states.

Since then, one state—Oregon—has legalized assisted suicide. By a voter initiative, the citizens of Oregon adopted the Death with Dignity Act, which became effective in 1997. The act allows terminally ill people, with the assistance of physicians, to end their lives. The Oregon law, which remains in effect, has generated significant controversy. Among other things, it has led to a clash between Oregon's law and federal policy.

THE BUSH ADMINISTRATION ATTACKS THE LAW

In November 2001, Attorney General John Ashcroft, head of the U.S. Department of Justice, attempted to override Oregon's law. He issued a "directive" that prohibited physicians from prescribing lethal doses of federally controlled drugs for persons suffering from terminal illness. His reasoning was that under the Controlled Substances Act of 1970, federally controlled drugs may be used only for a "legitimate medical purpose"—and taking the life of a terminally ill patient did not qualify as a legitimate medical purpose. The state of Oregon then sued the Justice Department, claiming that Ashcroft could not prevent the state from implementing the law.

The federal court judge hearing the case, Judge Robert E. Jones, ruled in April 2002 that the federal government does not have the authority to prohibit doctors from dispensing

lethal drugs used in doctor-assisted suicide.† The Justice Department appealed the ruling to a federal appellate court.

SHOULD THE FEDERAL GOVERNMENT OVERRIDE STATES' RIGHTS?

Supporters of the Oregon law point out that the law has been overwhelmingly approved by Oregon's citizens. Ashcroft's November 2001 directive thus directly counters the wishes of Oregon's citizens. Furthermore, claim the opponents of the directive, the Controlled Substances Act was passed as part of the war on drugs. Certainly, members of Congress, when passing the act, did not intend for it to apply to drugs used for the purpose of achieving "death with dignity." In effect, claims this group, Ashcroft, through the directive, attempted to impose his own opposition to physician-assisted suicide at the expense of states' rights.

Supporters of the law say that, if need be, they will take the case all the way to the United States Supreme Court. They point out that the law has not been abused. From the time the act became effective in October 1997 through the beginning of 2002, only ninety-one people in Oregon had ended their lives under the care of physicians with the use of federally controlled drugs.

WHAT'S YOUR POSITION?

Should the states or the federal government have the final word on whether physician-assisted suicide is legal?

GOING ONLINE

There is no dearth of online sites to visit concerning the often-heated debate over the right to die. The Hemlock Society promotes "death with dignity." You can obtain more information at **http://www.hemlock.org**. At the other end of the spectrum is the American Foundation for Suicide Prevention, which argues vigorously against assisted suicide. To examine its arguments, go to **http://www.afsp.org**.

*Washington v. Glucksberg, 521 U.S. 702 (1997).

†State of Oregon v. Ashcroft, 192 F.Supp.2d 1077 (D. Or. 2002).

Dual Federalism

During the decades following the Civil War, the prevailing doctrine was that of **dual federalism**—a doctrine that emphasizes a distinction between federal and state spheres of government authority. Various images have been used to describe different configurations of federalism over time. Dual federalism is commonly depicted as a layer cake, because the state governments and the national government are viewed as separate entities, like separate layers in a cake.

Dual Federalism
A system of government in which the states and the national government each remain supreme within their own spheres. The doctrine looks on nation and state as coequal sovereign powers. It holds that acts of states within their reserved powers are legitimate limitations on the powers of the national government.

I N F O T R A C ®
COLLEGE EDITION

To find out more about the New Deal, use the term "New Deal, 1933–1939" in the Subject guide.

Cooperative Federalism
The theory that the states and the national government should cooperate in solving problems.

Picket-Fence Federalism
A model of federalism in which specific programs and policies (depicted as vertical pickets in a picket fence) involve all levels of government—national, state, and local (depicted by the horizontal boards in a picket fence).

Generally, in the decades following the Civil War the states exercised their police power to regulate affairs within their borders, such as intrastate commerce, and the national government stayed out of purely local affairs. The courts tended to support the states' rights to exercise their police power and concurrent powers in regard to the regulation of intrastate activities. For example, in 1918, the Supreme Court ruled that a 1916 federal law banning child labor was unconstitutional because it attempted to regulate a local problem.[9] In the 1930s, however, the doctrine of dual federalism receded into the background as the nation attempted to deal with the Great Depression.

Cooperative Federalism

Franklin D. Roosevelt was inaugurated on March 4, 1933, as the thirty-second president of the United States. In the previous year, nearly 1,500 banks had failed (and 4,000 more would fail in 1933). Thirty-two thousand businesses closed down, and one-fourth of the labor force was unemployed. The national government had been expected to do something about the disastrous state of the economy. But for the first three years of the Great Depression, the national government did very little. That changed with the new Democratic administration's energetic intervention in the economy. FDR's "New Deal" included numerous government spending and welfare programs, in addition to voluminous regulations relating to economic activity.

Some political scientists have described the era since 1937 as characterized by **cooperative federalism**, in which the states and the national government cooperate in solving complex common problems. The New Deal programs of Franklin Roosevelt, for example, often involved joint action between the national government and the states. The pattern of national-state relationships during these years gave rise to a new metaphor for federalism—that of a marble cake.

The 1960s and 1970s saw an even greater expansion of the national government's role in domestic policy, and today, few activities are beyond the reach of the regulatory arm of the national government. The evolving pattern of national-state-local government relationships during the 1960s and 1970s gave rise to yet another metaphor—**picket-fence federalism**, a concept devised by political scientist Terry Sanford. The horizontal boards in the fence represent the different levels of government (national, state, and local), while the vertical pickets represent the various programs and policies in which each level of government is involved. Officials at each level of government work together to promote and develop the policy represented by each picket.

---

[9] *Hammer v. Dagenhart,* 247 U.S. 251 (1918). This decision was overruled in *United States v. Darby,* 312 U.S. 100 (1940).

In the 1800s, very young children worked in coal mines. Today, child-labor laws prohibit employers from hiring such young workers. Some argue that even in the absence of child-labor laws, few, if any, children would still be working in the mines, because the United States is a much richer country than it was a hundred years ago. Presumably, today's parents, no longer at subsistence income levels, would opt to have their children go to school. (The Library of Congress)

Federal Grants-in-Aid

Even before the Constitution was adopted, the national government gave grants to the states in the form of land to finance education. Some of you may even be going to a "land-grant" state university. The national government also provided land grants for canals, railroads, and roads. In 1808, Congress gave cash grants-in-aid to states to pay for the state militias. In the twentieth century, the federal grants-in-aid program increased significantly, especially during Roosevelt's administration during the Great Depression and again during the 1960s, when the dollar amount of grants-in-aids quadrupled. They were used for improvements in education, pollution control, recreation, and highways. With this increase in grants, however, came a bewildering number of restrictions and regulations.

By 1985, **categorical grants-in-aid** amounted to more than $100 billion a year. They were spread out across four hundred separate programs, but the largest five accounted for over 50 percent of the revenues spent. These five programs involved Medicaid, highway construction, unemployment benefits, housing assistance, and welfare programs to assist mothers with dependent children and the disabled. For fiscal year 2003, the national government gave an estimated $238 billion back to the states through grants-in-aid. The shift toward a greater role for the central government in the United States can be clearly seen in Figure 3–2, which shows the increase in central government spending as a percentage of total government spending.

The main reason that federal grants to the states have increased so much is that for state officials they appear to be "free." After all, state officials do not have to tax their constituents more if the federal government pays for a new bridge, a museum improvement, or a new highway. State governors in particular like federal grants for this reason. In addition, given the way federalism works in the United States, federal dollars sent to one congressional district have to be matched by other federal dollars sent to many other congressional districts.

Feeling the Pressure—The Strings Attached to Federal Grants. No dollars sent to the states are completely free of "strings," however; all funds come with requirements that must be met by the states. Often, through the use of grants, the national government has been able to exercise substantial control over matters that traditionally fell under the purview of state governments. When the federal government gives federal

DID YOU KNOW . . .
That part of the $4.2 million federal block grants received by four Native American tribes since 1997 goes toward the building of "smoke shops"—stores that sell discounted cigarettes and pipe tobacco **?**

Categorical Grants-in-Aid
Federal grants-in-aid to states or local governments that are for very specific programs or projects.

FIGURE 3–2

The Shift toward Central Government Spending

Before the Great Depression, local governments accounted for 60 percent of all government spending, with the federal government accounting for only 17 percent. By 2003, federal government spending was over 65 percent, local governments accounted for only 15.6 percent, and the remainder was spent by state governments.

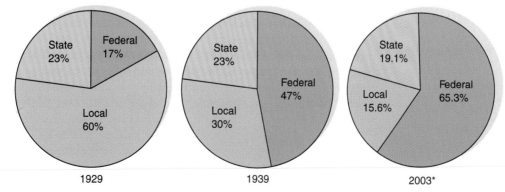

*Estimated.
Source: U.S. Deparment of Commerce, Bureau of the Census, *Government Finance* (Washington, D.C.: U.S. Government Printing Office, 2002).

This housing development in Minnesota was one of the many projects sponsored by the New Deal's Works Progress Administration (WPA) in the 1930s. The federal government's efforts to alleviate unemployment (in this case, among construction workers) during the Great Depression signaled a shift from dual federalism to cooperative federalism. (Minnesota Historical Society)

funds for highway improvements, for example, it may condition the funds on the state's cooperation in a federal policy. This is exactly what the federal government did in the 1980s and 1990s to force the states to raise their minimum drinking age to twenty-one.

Block Grants. Block grants lessen the restrictions on grants-in-aid given to state and local governments by grouping a number of categorical grants under one broad purpose. Governors and mayors generally prefer block grants because they give the states more flexibility in how the money is spent.

Out of the numerous block grants that were proposed from 1966 until the election of Ronald Reagan in 1980, only five were actually legislated. At the Reagan administration's urging, Congress increased the number to nine. By the beginning of the 1990s, such block grants accounted for slightly over 10 percent of all federal aid programs.

One major set of block grants concerns aid to state welfare programs. The Personal Responsibility and Work Opportunity Reconciliation Act of 1996 ended the existing program and substituted for it a welfare block grant to each state. Each grant has an annual cap. According to some, this is one of the more successful block grant programs.

Although state governments desire block grants, Congress generally prefers categorical grants because the expenditures can be targeted according to congressional priorities. These priorities include programs, such as those for disadvantaged groups and individuals, that significantly benefit many voters.

Federal Mandates. For years, the federal government has passed legislation requiring that states improve environmental conditions and the civil rights of certain groups. Since the 1970s, the national government has enacted literally hundreds of **federal mandates** requiring the states to take some action in areas ranging from the way voters are registered to ocean-dumping restrictions to the education of persons with disabilities. The Unfunded Mandates Reform Act of 1995 requires the Congressional Budget Office to identify areas in which implementing mandates costs state and local governments more than $50 million. Nonetheless, the federal government routinely continues to pass mandates that cost more than that for the states and local governments to implement. Consider a recent federal mandate involving the *expansion* of eligibility for Medicaid, the federally subsidized, but state-operated health-care program for low-income Americans. Some researchers believe that this mandate alone will cost the states $70 billion a year during the first half of the 2000s.

Block Grants
Federal programs that provide funds to state and local governments for general functional areas, such as criminal justice or mental-health programs.

Federal Mandate
A requirement in federal legislation that forces states and municipalities to comply with certain rules.

INFOTRAC ®
COLLEGE EDITION

To find out more about this topic, use the term "federal mandates" in Keywords.

ELECTIONS 2002 Trends in Federalism

One of the salient features of President Bush's conservatism is his belief that the states, and not the federal government, should manage large social programs, such as health insurance, education, and welfare. As you will read shortly, a number of judicial decisions in the last five years have bolstered states' rights. Some observers believe that more conservative judges, nominated by Bush and approved by the Republican-controlled Senate, may continue this trend, but this is not certain. The Bush administration has also attacked the states on some issues, such as state-approved assisted suicide laws and medical marijuana laws.

Federalism and the Supreme Court

The United States Supreme Court, which normally has the final say on constitutional issues, necessarily plays a significant role in determining the line between federal and state powers. Consider the decisions rendered by Chief Justice John Marshall in the cases discussed earlier in this chapter. Since the 1930s, Marshall's broad interpretation of the commerce clause has made it possible for the national government to justify its regulation of virtually any activity, even when an activity would appear to be purely local in character.

Since the 1990s, however, the Supreme Court has been reining in the national government's powers under the commerce clause somewhat. The Court has also given increased emphasis to state powers under the Tenth and Eleventh Amendments to the Constitution.

Reining in the Commerce Power

In a widely publicized 1995 case, *United States v. Lopez*,[10] the Supreme Court held that Congress had exceeded its constitutional authority under the commerce clause when it passed the Gun-Free School Zones Act in 1990. The Court stated that the act,

---

[10] 514 U.S. 549 (1995).

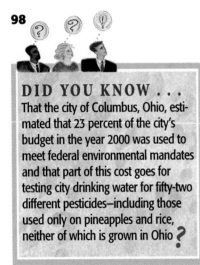

which banned the possession of guns within one thousand feet of any school, was unconstitutional because it attempted to regulate an area that had "nothing to do with commerce, or any sort of economic enterprise." This marked the first time in sixty years that the Supreme Court had placed a limit on the national government's authority under the commerce clause.

In 2000, in *United States v. Morrison*,[11] the Court held that Congress had over-reached its authority under the commerce clause when it passed the Violence against Women Act in 1994. The Court invalidated a key section of the act that provided a federal remedy for gender-motivated violence, such as rape. The Court noted that in enacting this law Congress had extensively documented that violence against women had an adverse "aggregate" effect on interstate commerce: it deterred potential victims from traveling, from engaging in employment, and from transacting business in interstate commerce. It also diminished national productivity and increased medical and other costs. Nonetheless, the Court held that evidence of an aggregate effect on commerce was not enough to justify national regulation of noneconomic, violent criminal conduct.

State Sovereignty and the Eleventh Amendment

In its 1999–2000 term, the Supreme Court issued a series of decisions that bolstered the authority of state governments under the Eleventh Amendment to the Constitution. As interpreted by the Court, that amendment precludes lawsuits against state governments for violations of rights established by federal laws unless the states consent to be sued. For example, in a 1999 case, *Alden v. Maine*,[12] the Court held that Maine state employees could not sue the state of Maine for violating the overtime pay requirements of a federal act. According to the Court, state immunity from such lawsuits "is a fundamental aspect of the sovereignty which [the states] enjoyed before the ratification of the Constitution, and which they retain today."

In 2000, in *Kimel v. Florida Board of Regents*,[13] the Court held that the Eleventh Amendment precluded employees of a state university from suing the state to enforce a federal statute prohibiting age-based discrimination. This decision means that although private-sector employees are protected under this federal law, state employees are not.

Tenth Amendment Issues

In 1992, the United States Supreme Court held that requirements imposed on the state of New York under a federal act regulating low-level radioactive waste were inconsistent with the Tenth Amendment and thus unconstitutional. According to the Court, the act's "take title" provision, which required states to accept ownership of waste or regulate waste according to Congress's instructions, exceeded the enumerated powers of Congress. Although Congress can regulate the handling of such waste, "it may not conscript state governments as its agents" in an attempt to enforce a program of federal regulation.[14]

In 1997, the Court revisited this Tenth Amendment issue. In *Printz v. United States*,[15] the Court struck down the provisions of the federal Brady Handgun Violence Prevention Act of 1993 that required state employees to check the backgrounds of prospective handgun purchasers. Said the Court:

---

[11]529 U.S. 598 (2000).
[12]527 U.S. 706 (1999).
[13]528 U.S. 62 (2000).
[14]*New York v. United States,* 505 U.S. 144 (1992).
[15]521 U.S. 898 (1997).

[T]he federal government may neither issue directives requiring the States to address particular problems, nor command the States' officers, or those of their political subdivisions, to administer or enforce a federal regulatory program.

The Court held that the provisions violated "the very principle of separate state sovereignty," which was "one of the Constitution's structural protections of liberty."

Federalism: Why Is It Important Today?

The fact that we have a federal form of government can touch your personal life in significant ways. For example, consider the federal-state conflict over the right to die, an issue we examined in this chapter. If you or one of your loved ones ends up suffering from a terminal illness, a pressing issue for you may be whether the state in which you live has a law allowing physician-assisted suicide and whether the federal government has allowed that law to stand.

Our federal form of government also means diversity—because different state and local governments have different laws, policies, and the like. For example, there is no one uniform body of national laws with respect to criminal sanctions. For wrongdoers, the amount of time spent in prison often depends as much on where the crime was committed as on the crime itself. Consider that the sentences received for three separate crimes differ significantly from one region of the country to another (see Figure 3–3). Even at the county level, there are great differences in criminal sentencing—just another reason why federalism is important. Consider the state of Georgia. Cocaine dealers sentenced in Henry and Butts Counties receive, on average, a sentence of nearly eighteen years in prison, while their counterparts in Fulton, Dekalb, Douglas, and Clayton Counties usually get six years or less.[16]

Where you live will also determine your monthly welfare payment if you ever find yourself in need. The average welfare payment in Alaska is around $950 per month, whereas the average payments in Alabama, Mississippi, Louisiana, and Tennessee are all under $200 per month. Where you live also determines how much is spent per year for your child's education in the public schools. This amount ranges from over $10,000 per child in New Jersey to under $5,000 per child in Alabama, Mississippi, and Utah. In contrast, in a unitary system of government, government spending per year per pupil is the same throughout the country. Generally, the diversity offered by a federal system means that you can "vote with your feet"—you can move to a state where more money is spent on education, welfare payments are higher, or politicians are "tougher on crime."

---

[16]Bill Rankin, "Special Report: Unequal Justice," *The Atlanta Journal-Constitution* (January 25, 1998), p. A1.

FIGURE 3–3

Regional Sentencing Differences

As this table shows, punishment for crimes can vary significantly, depending on the region of the country in which the crime is prosecuted.

CRIME	MEAN PRISON SENTENCE IN SOUTH (IN MONTHS)	MEAN PRISON SENTENCE OUTSIDE SOUTH (IN MONTHS)
Rape	183	142
Robbery	130	96
Burglary	84	53

SOURCE: Bureau of Justice Statistics, *State Court Sentencing of Convicted Felons*, 1996 (Washington, D.C.: U.S. Department of Justice, 2000), 56–57, Tables 5.2 and 5.3.

MAKING A DIFFERENCE | Writing Letters to the Editor

Just about every day an issue concerning federalism is discussed in the media. Advocates of decentralization—a shift of power from federal to state or local governments—argue that we must recognize the rights of states to design their own destinies and master their own fates. Advocates of centralization—more power to the national government—see the shift toward decentralization as undermining the national purpose, common interests, and responsibilities that bind us together in pursuit of national goals.

Issues Relating to Federalism

In this chapter, you have read about several issues that face the American people—issues that likely would not exist if we did not have a federal form of government.

A big question is how much the national government should do for the people. Is it within the power of the national government to decide what the law should be on abortion? Before 1973, each state set its own laws without interference from the national government. Who should be responsible

for the homeless? Should the national government subsidize state and local efforts to help them?

Express Your Views

You may have valid, important points to make on these or other issues. One of the best ways to make your point is by writing an effective letter to the editor of your local newspaper (or even to a national newspaper such as the *New York Times*). First, you should familiarize yourself with the kinds of letters that are accepted by the newspapers to which you want to write. Then follow these rules for writing an effective letter:

1. Use a computer, and double-space the lines. If possible, use a spelling checker and grammar checker.

2. Your lead topic sentence should be short, to the point, and powerful.

3. Keep your thoughts on target—choose only one topic to discuss in your letter. Make sure it is newsworthy and timely.

4. Make sure your letter is concise; never let your letter exceed a page and a half in length (double-spaced).

5. If you know that facts were misstated or left out in current news stories about your topic, supply the facts. The public wants to know.

6. Don't be afraid to express moral judgments. You can go a long way by appealing to the readers' sense of justice.

7. Personalize the letter by bringing in your own experiences, if possible.

8. Sign your letter, and give your address (including your e-mail address, if you have one) and your telephone number.

9. Send your letter to the editorial office of the newspaper or magazine of your choice. Virtually all publications now have e-mail addresses and home pages on the Web. The Web sites usually give information on where you can send mail.

10. With appropriate changes, you can send your letter to other newspapers and magazines as well. Make sure, however, that the letters are not exactly the same. If your letter is not published, try again. Eventually, one will be.

Key Terms

block grants 96

categorical grants-in-aid 95

commerce clause 91

concurrent powers 87

confederal system 82

cooperative federalism 94

dual federalism 93

elastic clause 86

enumerated powers 85

federal mandate 96

horizontal federalism 88

interstate compact 89

necessary and proper clause 86

picket-fence federalism 94

police power 86

supremacy clause 87

unitary system 81

Chapter Summary

1 There are three basic models for ordering relations between central governments and local units: (a) a unitary system (in which ultimate power is held by the national government), (b) a confederal system (in which ultimate power is retained by the states), and (c) a federal system (in which governmental powers are divided between the national government and the states). A major reason for the creation of a federal system in the United States is that it reflected a compromise between the views of the Federalists (who wanted a strong national government) and those of the Anti-Federalists (who wanted the states to retain their sovereignty), thus making ratification of the Constitution possible.

2 The Constitution expressly delegated certain powers to the national government in Article I, Section 8. In addition to these expressed powers, the national government has implied and inherent powers. Implied powers are those that are reasonably necessary to carry out the powers expressly delegated to the national government. Inherent powers are those held by the national government by virtue of its being a sovereign state with the right to preserve itself.

3 The Tenth Amendment to the Constitution states that powers not delegated to the United States by the Constitution, nor prohibited by it to the states, are reserved to the states, or to the people. In certain areas, the Constitution provides for concurrent powers, such as the power to tax, which are powers that are held jointly by the national and state governments. The Constitution also denies certain powers to both the national government and the states.

4 The supremacy clause of the Constitution states that the Constitution, congressional laws, and national treaties are the supreme law of the land. States cannot use their reserved or concurrent powers to override national policies. Vertical checks and balances allow the states to influence the national government and vice versa.

5 The three most important clauses in the Constitution relating to interstate relations, or horizontal federalism, require that (a) each state give full faith and credit to every other state's public acts, records, and judicial proceedings; (b) each state extend to every other state's citizens the privileges and immunities of its own citizens; and (c) each state agree to return persons who are fleeing from justice to another state back to their home state when requested to do so.

6 Two landmark Supreme Court cases expanded the constitutional powers of the national government. Chief Justice John Marshall's expansive interpretation of the necessary and proper clause of the Constitution in *McCulloch v. Maryland* (1819) enhanced the implied power of the national government. Marshall's broad interpretation of the commerce clause in *Gibbons v. Ogden* (1824) further extended the constitutional regulatory powers of the national government.

7 At the heart of the controversy that led to the Civil War was the issue of national government supremacy versus the rights of the separate states. Ultimately, the effect of the South's desire for increased states' rights and the subsequent Civil War was an increase in the political power of the national government.

8 Since the Civil War, federalism has evolved through at least two general phases: dual federalism and cooperative federalism. In dual federalism, each of the states and the federal government remain supreme within their own spheres. The era since the Great Depression has sometimes been labeled one of cooperative federalism, in which states and the national government cooperate in solving complex common problems.

9 Categorical grants-in-aid from the federal government to state governments help finance numerous projects, such as Medicaid, highway construction, unemployment benefits, and welfare programs. By attaching special conditions to the receipt of federal grants, the national government can effect policy changes in areas typically governed by the states. Block grants, which group a number of categorical grants under one broad purpose, usually have fewer strings attached, thus giving state and local governments more flexibility with respect to how the funds are used. Federal mandates—laws requiring states to implement certain policies, such as policies to protect the environment—have generated controversy because they are often so costly.

10 The United States Supreme Court plays a significant role in determining the line between state and federal powers. Since the 1990s, the Court has been reining in somewhat the national government's powers under the commerce clause and has given increased emphasis to state powers under the Tenth and Eleventh Amendments to the Constitution.

Selected Print and Media Resources

SUGGESTED READINGS

Hamilton, Alexander, James Madison, and John Jay. *The Federalist Papers.* Cambridge, Mass.: Harvard University Press, 1961. These essays remain an authoritative exposition of the founders' views of federalism.

Johnson, Walter. *Soul by Soul: Life inside the Antebellum Slave Market.* Cambridge, Mass.: Harvard University Press, 1999. Slavery, the abolitionist movement, and states' rights principles were intertwined forces leading to the Civil War. In this book, readers are taken inside the New Orleans slave market, the largest in the nation, and shown how 100,000 men, women, and children were packaged, priced, and sold.

Warren, Robert Penn. *All the King's Men,* rev. ed. Chicago: Harcourt Brace, 2001. This book is a fictionalized account of Governor Huey Long of Louisiana, one of the nation's "most astounding politicians."

Yarbrough, Tinsley E. *The Rehnquist Court and the Constitution.* New York: Oxford University Press, 2000. In this portrait of today's Supreme Court, the author focuses on developing issues, including the Court's use of long-dormant federal principles to curb the national government's authority over the states.

MEDIA RESOURCES

All the King's Men—A classic film about power, demagoguery, and populism in the 1930s in Louisiana, which was run by "the Kingfish," Huey Long. This film certainly can serve as a starting point for a discussion of state power.

Can the States Do It Better?—A film in which various experts explore the debate over how much power the national government should have and use documentary film footage and other resources to illustrate historical instances of this debate.

Your CD-ROM Resources

In addition to the chapter content containing hot links, the following resources are available on the CD-ROM:

- **Internet Activities**—"Grand-Place Europe," the evolution of federalism.

- **Critical Thinking Exercises**—Prevention and preparation for future terrorist attacks, criticism of federalism.

- **Self-Check on Important Themes**—Can You Answer These?

- **Animated Figure**—Figure 3–1, "The Flow of Power in Three Systems of Government."

- **Videos**—*Unitary and Confederal Systems, Dual to Cooperative Federalism.*

- **Public Opinion Data**—Trust in the American government.

- **InfoTrac Exercise**—"Shrinking Federal Powers."

- **Simulation**—You Are There!

- **Participation Exercise**—Write a letter to the editor expressing your views on welfare reform.

- **MicroCase Exercise**—"By The Numbers: Federalism."

- **Additional Resources:**

  1. All court cases
  2. Thomas Jefferson, *The Kentucky Resolution* (sometimes known as *The Kentucky Resolve)* (1798)
  3. Daniel Webster, *Reply to Hayne* (1830)
  4. Robert Toombs, *Justification of States' Rights and Secession* (1861)
  5. Theodore Roosevelt, *The New Nationalism* (1910)
  6. Ronald Reagan's Inaugural Address (1981)

e-mocracy

Your Federal, State, and Local Governments Are Available at a Click of Your Mouse

Although we are not yet voting online, your access to federal, state, and local government offices has improved dramatically since the Internet has entered just about everybody's life. Some bureaucrats now talk about *e-government.* Instead of waiting in line to renew car registrations, residents of Scottsdale, Arizona, can renew online since the state got help from IBM. In Colorado, heating and air-conditioning contractors can obtain permits from a Web site run by NetClerk, Inc. In many jurisdictions, all parking tickets can be handled with a credit card and a computer connected to the Internet.

The number of government services available online is growing rapidly, particularly given the marketing efforts of such companies as EzGov, Inc., and an online customer relationship management company called Siebel Systems. Government spending on Internet projects was only $1.5 billion in 2000; it should be well over $6 billion in 2005. In 2002, over 25 million online applications or filings to federal, state, and local governments were made. By 2006, that number should reach 350 million. In that same year, it is expected that almost $30 billion in taxes and fees will be collected online. Government is truly at your fingertips today.

Logging On

You can learn how some communities have benefited from implementing online government through EzGov, Inc., by reading some of the comments at EzGov's Web site. Go to

http://www.ezgov.com/ gov_partner_flash.jsp

Federalism is an important aspect of our democracy. To learn more about the establishment of our federal form of government and about some of today's issues relating to federalism, visit some of the Web sites listed in the remainder of this *Logging On* section.

To learn the founders' views on federalism, you can access *The Federalist Papers* online at

http://www.law.emory.edu/FEDERAL

The following site has links to U.S. state constitutions, *The Federalist Papers,* and international federations, such as the European Union:

http://www.constitution.org/cs_feder.htm

Project Vote Smart's Web site on current issues in American government offers a number of articles on federalism/states' rights. Go to

http://www.vote-smart.org/issues/ FEDERALISM_STATES_RIGHTS

The following Web site of the Council of State Governments is a good source for information on state responses to federalism issues:

http://www.statesnews.org

You can find a directory of numerous federalism links at

http://www.gmu.edu

The Brookings Institution's policy analyses and recommendations on a variety of issues, including federalism, can be accessed at

http://www.brook.edu

For a libertarian approach to issues relating to federalism, go to the Cato Institute's Web page at

http://www.cato.org

Using the Internet for Political Analysis

Today, the federal government and the many state and local governments interact in a variety of ways. These governments are connected by a web of financial support, legal regulations, and shared resources. The federal government has created a Web site where state and local governments can go to get information about working with the federal government and its agencies. Go to

http://www.firstgov.gov

Click on "Governments," the link to online services for governments. Under "State and Local Employees," click on "More." This page provides multiple links to government information on topics ranging from health, public safety, and education to bioterrorism and disaster preparedness. Choose a category and follow the links to the Web sites for various federal and state agencies. If you were a state government employee, would you find this Web site helpful? In what ways does the Internet help support a federal form of government?

Now follow the links to the "Citizen Gateway" and "Business Gateway" and compare how citizens and businesses can interact with the federal government over the Internet. Do you think it is helpful or confusing to citizens and businesses to have governments at the local, state, and federal levels to turn to with a problem or concern?

PART TWO

Civil Rights and Liberties

CHAPTER 4
Civil Liberties

Civil Liberties and the
Fear of Government
•
Extending the Bill of Rights
to State Governments
•
Freedom of Religion
•
Freedom of Expression
•
Freedom of the Press
•
The Right to Assemble and
to Petition the Government
•
More Liberties under Scrutiny:
Matters of Privacy
•
The Great Balancing Act:
The Rights of the Accused
versus the Rights of Society

BACKGROUND

Numerous countries require their citizens to carry national identification cards. In Spain, this document is compulsory for anyone over fourteen years of age. Spaniards carry their national ID card the same way we carry our driver's licenses. Most other countries in the European Union have mandatory state-issued identity card systems as well. Argentina requires its citizens to obtain a national ID card when they are eight years old. In Kenya, the government introduced national ID cards in 1996.

Clearly, the precedent is there if the United States wishes to proceed with a national identification system. Traditionally, Americans have been opposed to a national ID card, but that changed immediately after 9/11. Almost 70 percent of adults polled were in favor of a national ID system.*

WHAT IF YOU HAD TO CARRY A NATIONAL ID CARD?

We could have a system that would require every resident of the United States at a certain age to obtain a national ID card. On what basis would a card be issued? A birth certificate? A driver's license? According to Joseph Atick, head of a New Jersey biometric information system manufacturer, "ID documents in the United States aren't worth the plastic they are printed on." Birth certificates are easily forged today, and fake driver's licenses are readily available on the Internet at numerous sites.

PERHAPS BIOMETRIC IDENTIFICATION SHOULD BE REQUIRED

An effective, but not 100 percent foolproof, national ID system might use some form of biometric identification involving facial or fingerprint scans. The ID card then could include retinal scans, palm prints, or standard thumbprints. After all, banks and other check-cashing facilities are already using thumbprints.

One problem with incorporating biometric information into cards is that they would be expensive. Such a system could take up to five years to implement and would cost billions of dollars.

USING SMART CARDS

A typical ID system uses "dumb" cards that can provide only the information actually printed on the cards. So-called smart cards, in contrast, contain a magnetic stripe, a computer chip, or some other technology that links each card to a central database. Such cards are used as debit cards in Europe already. U.S. passports are, in effect, smart cards because they contain a magnetic stripe. When you reenter the United States, your U.S. passport is swiped through a card-reading machine. The information is then linked to a central database. The same could be done with any national ID card system.

If we had a national ID system using smart cards, border-crossing guards, gun dealers, and airline employees could use card readers in order to monitor the criminal record and other identifying information of persons with whom they are dealing. Required background checks for the purchase of firearms would be relatively inexpensive for the individual gun dealer or federal official instituting a check. (This ignores, of course, the multibillion-dollar cost of initiating and implementing such a system.)

We could also institute, along with a national ID system, background checks before an ID card is issued. All such information would be kept in a central database.

IS A NATIONAL ID SYSTEM IN OUR FUTURE?

Political winds remain turbulent with respect to support for a national ID system. President George W. Bush has not overtly favored it. In contrast, Senator Dick Durbin (D., Ill.) proposed federal funding for developing such a system in 2002. He wants to give state motor vehicle authorities access to computer databases maintained by the Social Security Administration, law enforcement agencies, and especially the Immigration and Naturalization Service.

Durbin's concept mirrors that of many other supporters of such a system. Nonetheless, others simply want to improve current driver's licenses by making them harder to forge and allowing background checks.

Opponents of a national ID system have stood firm: they oppose it because of privacy problems. They believe that the long-term erosion of privacy rights will far outweigh any benefits a national ID card might offer in our nation's fight against global terrorism.

FOR CRITICAL ANALYSIS

1. If you were convinced that a national ID system would help prevent future terrorism, would you support such a system despite its possible abuse?

2. How might a potential terrorist thwart any national ID system?

*Business Week, November 5, 2001, p. 86. Five months later, though, a USA Today/CNN/Gallup Poll reported that only 50 percent favored a national ID system.

Most Americans believe that they have more individual freedom than virtually any other people on earth. For the most part, this opinion is accurate. The freedoms and rights that we take for granted are relatively unknown in some parts of the world. Citizens in many other nations also have few privacy rights—rights that in the United States are among our most prized. Indeed, if the United States suddenly had the same rules, laws, and procedures governing constitutional rights and liberties as some other countries, American jails would be filled overnight with transgressors. Certainly, few people would be discussing the possible erosion of privacy rights, as we do in the chapter-opening *What If . . .*, because very likely such rights would not exist.

Civil Liberties and the Fear of Government

Remember from Chapter 2 that to obtain ratification of the Constitution by the necessary nine states, the Federalists had to deal with Americans' fears of a too-powerful national government. The Bill of Rights was the result. These first ten amendments to the U.S. Constitution were adopted by Congress on September 25, 1789, and ratified by three-fourths of the states by December 15, 1791. Linked directly to the strong prerevolutionary sentiment for natural rights was the notion that a right was first and foremost a *limitation* on any government's ruling power. Thus, when we speak of **civil liberties** in the United States, we are referring mostly to the specific limitations on government outlined in the Bill of Rights (although there are such limitations in the Constitution's main text itself, including the prohibition against *ex post facto* laws and others found in Section 9 of Article I).

As you read through these chapters, bear in mind that the Bill of Rights, like the rest of the Constitution, is relatively brief. The framers set forth broad guidelines, leaving it up to the courts to interpret these constitutional mandates and apply them to specific situations. Thus, judicial interpretations shape the true nature of the civil liberties and rights that we possess. Because judicial interpretations change over time, so do our liberties and rights. As you will read in the following pages, there have been numerous conflicts over the meaning of such simple phrases as *freedom of religion* and *freedom of the press*. To understand what freedoms we actually have, we need to examine how the courts—and particularly the Supreme Court—have resolved some of those conflicts. One important conflict has to do with whether the national Bill of Rights limited state governments as well as the national government.

Extending the Bill of Rights to State Governments

Most citizens do not realize that, as originally intended, the Bill of Rights limited only the powers of the national government. At the time the Bill of Rights was ratified, there was little concern over the potential of state governments to curb civil liberties. For one thing, state governments were closer to home and easier to control. For another, most state constitutions already had bills of rights. Rather, the fear was of the potential tyranny of the national government. The Bill of Rights begins with the words, "Congress shall make no law . . . ." It says nothing about *states* making laws that might abridge citizens' civil liberties. In 1833, in *Barron v. Baltimore*,[1] the United States Supreme Court held that the Bill of Rights did not apply to state laws.

The Fourteenth Amendment

State bills of rights were similar to the national one, but there were some differences. Furthermore, each state's judicial system interpreted the rights differently. Citizens in different states, therefore, effectively had different sets of civil rights. It was not until

Civil Liberties
Those personal freedoms that are protected for all individuals and that generally deal with individual freedom. Civil liberties typically involve restraining the government's actions against individuals.

---

[1]7 Peters 243 (1833).

after the Fourteenth Amendment was ratified in 1868 that civil liberties guaranteed by the national Constitution began to be applied to the states. Section 1 of that amendment provides, in part, as follows:

> No State shall . . . deprive any person of life, liberty, or property, without due process of law.

There was no question that the Fourteenth Amendment applied to state governments. For decades, however, the courts were reluctant to define the liberties spelled out in the national Bill of Rights as constituting "due process of law," which was protected under the Fourteenth Amendment. It was not until 1925, in *Gitlow v. New York*,[2] that the United States Supreme Court held that the Fourteenth Amendment protected the freedom of speech guaranteed by the First Amendment to the Constitution.

Incorporation of the Fourteenth Amendment

Incorporation Theory
The view that most of the protections of the Bill of Rights are applied against state governments through the Fourteenth Amendment's due process clause.

Only gradually, and never completely, did the Supreme Court accept the **incorporation theory**—the view that most of the protections of the Bill of Rights are incorporated into the Fourteenth Amendment's protection against state government actions. Table 4–1 shows the rights that the Court has incorporated into the Fourteenth Amendment and the case in which it first applied each protection. As you can see in that table, in the fifteen years following the *Gitlow* decision, the Supreme Court incorporated into the Fourteenth Amendment the other basic freedoms (of the press, assembly, the right to petition, and religion) guaranteed by the First Amendment. These and the later Supreme Court decisions listed in Table 4–1 have bound the fifty states to accept for their respective citizens most of the rights and freedoms that are set forth in the U.S. Bill of Rights. We now look at some of those rights and freedoms, beginning with the freedom of religion.

INFOTRAC ®
COLLEGE EDITION

To find out more about this issue, use the term "freedom of religion" in the Subject guide.

Freedom of Religion

In the United States, freedom of religion consists of two principal precepts as they are presented in the First Amendment. The first has to do with the separation of church and state, and the second guarantees the free exercise of religion.

[2]268 U.S. 652 (1925).

TABLE 4–1

Incorporating the Bill of Rights into the Fourteenth Amendment

YEAR	ISSUE	AMENDMENT INVOLVED	COURT CASE
1925	Freedom of speech	I	*Gitlow v. New York,* 268 U.S. 652.
1931	Freedom of the press	I	*Near v. Minnesota,* 283 U.S. 697.
1932	Right to a lawyer in capital punishment cases	VI	*Powell v. Alabama,* 287 U.S. 45.
1937	Freedom of assembly and right to petition	I	*De Jonge v. Oregon,* 299 U.S. 353.
1940	Freedom of religion	I	*Cantwell v. Connecticut,* 310 U.S. 296.
1947	Separation of church and state	I	*Everson v. Board of Education,* 330 U.S. 1.
1948	Right to a public trial	VI	*In re Oliver,* 333 U.S. 257.
1949	No unreasonable searches and seizures	IV	*Wolf v. Colorado,* 338 U.S. 25.
1961	Exclusionary rule	IV	*Mapp v. Ohio,* 367 U.S. 643.
1962	No cruel and unusual punishment	VIII	*Robinson v. California,* 370 U.S. 660.
1963	Right to a lawyer in all criminal felony cases	VI	*Gideon v. Wainwright,* 372 U.S. 335.
1964	No compulsory self-incrimination	V	*Malloy v. Hogan,* 378 U.S. 1.
1965	Right to privacy	I, III, IV, V, IX	*Griswold v. Connecticut,* 381 U.S. 479.
1966	Right to an impartial jury	VI	*Parker v. Gladden,* 385 U.S. 363.
1967	Right to a speedy trial	VI	*Klopfer v. North Carolina,* 386 U.S. 213.
1969	No double jeopardy	V	*Benton v. Maryland,* 395 U.S. 784.

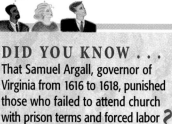

The Separation of Church and State—The Establishment Clause

The First Amendment to the Constitution states, in part, that "Congress shall make no law respecting an establishment of religion." In the words of Thomas Jefferson, the **establishment clause** was designed to create a "wall of separation of Church and State." Perhaps Jefferson was thinking about the religious intolerance that characterized the first colonies. Although many of the American colonies were founded by groups in pursuit of religious freedom, nonetheless they were quite intolerant of religious beliefs that did not conform to those held by the majority of citizens within their own communities. Jefferson undoubtedly was also aware that state religions were the rule; among the original thirteen American colonies, nine of them had official religions.

As interpreted by the Supreme Court, the establishment clause in the First Amendment means at least the following:

> Neither a state nor the federal government can set up a church. Neither can pass laws which aid one religion, aid all religions, or prefer one religion over another. Neither can force nor influence a person to go to or to remain away from church against his will or force him to profess a belief or disbelief in any religion. No person can be punished for entertaining or professing religious beliefs or disbeliefs, for church attendance or nonattendance. No tax in any amount, large or small, can be levied to support any religious activities or institutions, whatever they may be called, or whatever form they may adopt to teach or practice religion. Neither a state nor the federal government can, openly or secretly, participate in the affairs of any religious organizations or groups and vice versa.[3]

The establishment clause covers all conflicts about such matters as the legality of state and local government aid to religious organizations and schools, allowing or requiring school prayers, the teaching of evolution versus fundamentalist theories of creation, the posting of the Ten Commandments in schools or public places, and discrimination against religious groups in publicly operated institutions. (The establishment clause's mandate that government can neither promote nor discriminate against religious beliefs raises particularly knotty questions at Christmas time, when holiday displays may include religious symbols—see this chapter's *Politics and Religion* feature on the following page for a discussion of this issue.)

Aid to Church-Related Schools. Throughout the United States, all property owners except religious, educational, fraternal, literary, scientific, and similar nonprofit institutions must pay property taxes. A large part of the proceeds of such taxes goes to support public schools. But not all school-age children attend public schools. Fully 12 percent attend private schools, of which 85 percent have religious affiliations. Numerous cases have reached the Supreme Court in which the Court has tried to draw a fine line between permissible public aid to students in church-related schools and impermissible public aid to religion. These issues have arisen most often at the elementary and secondary levels.

In 1971, in *Lemon v. Kurtzman,*[4] the Court ruled that direct state aid could not be used to subsidize religious instruction. The Court in the *Lemon* case gave its most general statement on the constitutionality of government aid to religious schools, stating that the aid had to be secular in aim, that it could not have the primary effect of advancing or inhibiting religion, and that the government must avoid "an excessive government entanglement with religion." All laws under the establishment clause are now subject to the three-part *Lemon* test. How the test is applied, however, has varied over the years.

DID YOU KNOW...
That Samuel Argall, governor of Virginia from 1616 to 1618, punished those who failed to attend church with prison terms and forced labor ?

Establishment Clause
The part of the First Amendment prohibiting the establishment of a church officially supported by the national government. It is applied to questions of state and local government aid to religious organizations and schools, questions of the legality of allowing or requiring school prayers, and questions of the teaching of evolution versus fundamentalist theories of creation.

---

[3] *Everson v. Board of Education,* 330 U.S. 1 (1947).
[4] 403 U.S. 602 (1971).

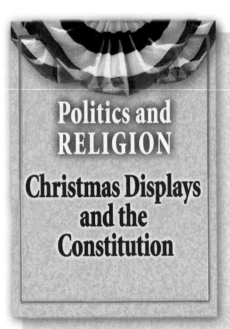

Politics and RELIGION

Christmas Displays and the Constitution

The thorny issue of whether religious displays on public property violate the establishment clause often arises during the holiday season. Time and again, the courts have wrestled with this issue, but it has never been resolved in a way that satisfies everyone. In a 1984 case, the United States Supreme Court decided that a city's official Christmas display, which included a crèche (Nativity scene), did not violate the establishment clause because the crèche was just one part of a larger holiday display that featured secular symbols, such as reindeer and candy canes.*

*Lynch v. Donnelly, 465 U.S. 668 (1984).

In a later case, the Court held that the presence of a crèche inside a county courthouse violated the establishment clause because it was not in close proximity to nonreligious symbols, including a Christmas tree, which were located outside, on the building's steps. The presence of a menorah (a nine-branched candelabrum used in celebrating Hanukkah) on the building's steps, however, did not violate the establishment clause because the menorah was situated in close proximity to the Christmas tree.† The courts have applied this reasoning in cases involving similar issues, but challenges continue to emerge that seem to defy rational analysis, as do their solutions.

RED POINSETTIAS—NO; WHITE POINSETTIAS—YES

One of the latest disputes relating to acceptable displays of religious symbols in public areas concerned the Ramsey County courthouse and the St. Paul City Hall. During the Christmas season of 2001, St. Paul put together a world peace exhibit displaying doves, many different flags, and a large Vision of Peace statue. The display also included red poinsettias. A city resident complained because she believed that a red poinsettia was a Christian sym-

†County of Allegheny v. American Civil Liberties Union, 492 U.S. 573 (1989).

bol. A compromise was reached: red poinsettias were removed, but white ones were allowed to remain.

MAKING CHRISTMAS DISAPPEAR

Rather than broadening traditional Christmas displays to accommodate other traditions and religions, there appears to be a trend toward eliminating references to Christmas in public places. Pittsburgh now refers to "Sparkle Days" to avoid using the word *Christmas.* In numerous school districts, pupils are not allowed to wear red and green scarves during the holiday season. In some cities, mayors have requested that their employees avoid saying "Merry Christmas" or "Happy Hanukkah" to one another, at least while on the job. Some schools have even eliminated the celebration of any holidays to avoid offending anyone.

FOR CRITICAL ANALYSIS

Does the separation of church and state imply that no public-supported institution should celebrate a religious holiday?

In a number of cases, the Supreme Court has held that state programs helping church-related schools are unconstitutional. The Court has also denied state reimbursements to religious schools for field trips and for developing achievement tests. In a series of other cases, however, the Supreme Court has allowed states to use tax funds for lunches, textbooks, diagnostic services for speech and hearing problems, standardized tests, and transportation for students attending church-operated elementary and secondary schools. In 2000, in *Mitchell v. Helms,*[5] the Court held that the use of public funds to provide all schools, including parochial schools, with computers and Internet links did not violate the Constitution.

A Change in the Court's Position.   Generally, today's Supreme Court has shown a greater willingness to allow the use of public funds for programs in religious schools than was true at times in the past. Consider that in 1985, in *Aguilar v. Felton,*[6] the Supreme Court ruled that state programs providing special educational services for disadvantaged students attending religious schools violated the establishment clause.

[5] 530 U.S. 793 (2000).
[6] 473 U.S. 402 (1985).

In 1997, however, when the Supreme Court revisited this decision, the Court reversed its position. In *Agostini v. Felton,*[7] the Court held that *Aguilar* was "no longer good law." What had happened between 1985 and 1997 to cause the Court to change its mind? Justice Sandra Day O'Connor answered this question in the *Agostini* opinion: what had changed since *Aguilar,* she stated, was "our understanding" of the establishment clause. Notably, between 1985 and 1997, the Court's make-up had changed considerably. In fact, six of the nine justices who participated in the 1997 decision were appointed after the 1985 *Aguilar* decision.

School Vouchers. Questions concerning the use of public funds for church-related schools are likely to continue as state legislators search for new ways to improve the educational system in this country. An issue that has come to the forefront in recent years has to do with school vouchers. In a voucher system, educational vouchers (state-issued credits) can be used to "purchase" education at any school, public or private.

School districts in Florida, Ohio, and Wisconsin have all been experimenting with voucher systems. In 2000, a federal appellate court reviewed a case involving Ohio's voucher program. Under that program, some $10 million in public funds is spent annually to send 4,300 Cleveland students to fifty-one private schools, all but five of which are Catholic schools. The case presented a straightforward constitutional question: Is it a violation of the principle of separation of church and state for public tax money to be used to pay for religious education? The federal appellate court held that the Ohio program violated the establishment clause,[8] and the case was appealed to the United States Supreme Court. In 2002, the Supreme Court held that the Cleveland voucher program was constitutional. The Court concluded, by a five-to-four vote, that Cleveland's use of taxpayer-paid school vouchers to send children to private schools was constitutional even though more than 95 percent of the students use the vouchers to attend Catholic or other religious schools. The Court's majority reasoned that the program did not unconstitutionally entangle church and state because families theoretically could use the vouchers for their children to attend religious schools, secular private academies, suburban public schools, or charter schools, even though few public schools had agreed to accept vouchers. The Court's decision raised a further question that will need to be decided—whether religious and private schools that accept government vouchers must comply with disability and civil rights laws as public schools currently are required to do.

The Issue of School Prayer—*Engel v. Vitale.* Do the states have the right to promote religion in general, without making any attempt to establish a particular religion? That is the question in the issue of school prayer and was the precise question presented in 1962 in *Engel v. Vitale,*[9] the so-called Regents' Prayer case in New York. The State Board of Regents of New York had suggested that a prayer be spoken aloud in the public schools at the beginning of each day. The recommended prayer was as follows:

> Almighty God, we acknowledge our dependence upon Thee,
> And we beg Thy blessings upon us, our parents, our teachers, and our Country.

Such a prayer was implemented in many New York public schools.

The parents of a number of students challenged the action of the regents, maintaining that it violated the establishment clause of the First Amendment. At trial, the parents lost. The Supreme Court, however, ruled that the regents' action was unconstitutional because "the constitutional prohibition against laws respecting an establishment of a religion must mean at least that in this country it is no part of the business of government to compose official prayers for any group of the American people to

---

[7] 521 U.S. 203 (1997).
[8] *Simmons-Harris v. Zelman,* 234 F.3d 945 (6th Cir. 2000).
[9] 370 U.S. 421 (1962).

Children pray in school. Such in-school prayer is in violation of Supreme Court rulings based on the First Amendment. A Supreme Court ruling does not necessarily carry with it a mechanism for enforcement everywhere in the United States, however. (Bruce Flynn, Picture Group)

INFOTRAC®
COLLEGE EDITION

To find out more about this debate, use the term "prayer public schools" in the Subject guide.

recite as part of a religious program carried on by any government." The Court's conclusion was based in part on the "historical fact that governmentally established religions and religious persecutions go hand in hand." In *Abington School District v. Schempp*[10] (1963), the Supreme Court outlawed daily readings of the Bible and recitation of the Lord's Prayer in public schools.

The Debate over School Prayer Continues. Although the Supreme Court has ruled repeatedly against officially sponsored prayer and Bible-reading sessions in public schools, other means for bringing some form of religious expression into public education have been attempted. In 1983, the Tennessee legislature passed a bill requiring public school classes to begin each day with a minute of silence. Alabama also had a similar law. In *Wallace v. Jaffree*[11] (1985), the Supreme Court struck down as unconstitutional the Alabama law authorizing one minute of silence for prayer or meditation in all public schools. Applying the three-part *Lemon* test, the Court concluded that the law violated the establishment clause because it was "an endorsement of religion lacking any clearly secular purpose."

Since then, the lower courts have interpreted the Supreme Court's decision to mean that states can require a moment of silence in the schools as long as they make it clear that the purpose of the law is secular, not religious. For example, in 1997, a federal appellate court held that Georgia's "Moment of Quiet Reflection in Schools Act" did not violate the establishment clause because the act clearly stated that the moment of silence was "not intended to be and shall not be conducted as a religious service or exercise but shall be considered as an opportunity for a moment of silent reflection on the anticipated activities of the day."[12] Similarly, in 2001, a federal appellate court upheld a Virginia law requiring public schools to observe a moment of silence at the beginning of the day. The Virginia law states that schools must pause for a minute of silence so that students may meditate, pray, or sit quietly.[13]

Some states, particularly in the South, are not happy with the idea that a school is not permitted to open the day with a moment of prayer. Indeed, despite the Supreme Court's ruling on this issue, South Carolina state legislators have proposed a bill to transform the moment of silence that begins each school day into a moment of prayer. Generally, since the terrorist attacks of September 11, 2001, there has been an upsurge of support for prayer in the schools. Very likely, this issue will be with us for some time.

Controversy over the Pledge of Allegiance. In 2002, the U.S. Circuit Court of Appeals for the Ninth Circuit stunned the nation with its controversial ruling that the words "under God" in the Pledge of Allegiance violated the establishment clause of the First Amendment. The Supreme Court had already ruled in 1943 that students cannot be forced to recite the Pledge of Allegiance. The plaintiff in the 2002 case, an atheist and the father of an eight-year-old daughter attending a public school, argued that his daughter's constitutional rights were violated when she was forced to "watch and listen" as her teacher led her classmates "in a ritual proclaiming that there is a God."[14] The ruling brought harsh criticism from President George W. Bush, who promised that the Justice Department would fight to overturn the ruling, as well as from members of Congress and the public at large.

Prayer outside the Classroom. The courts have also dealt with cases involving prayer in public schools outside the classroom, particularly prayer during graduation ceremonies. In 1992, in *Lee v. Weisman*,[15] the Supreme Court held that it was unconstitutional for a school to invite a rabbi to deliver a nonsectarian prayer at graduation.

[10] 374 U.S. 203 (1963).
[11] 472 U.S. 38 (1985).
[12] *Brown v. Gwinnett County School District,* 112 F.3d 1464 (11th Cir. 1997).
[13] *Brown v. Gilmore,* 258 F.3d 265 (4th Cir. 2001).
[14] *Newdow v. U.S. Congress,* 292 F.3d 597.
[15] 505 U.S. 577 (1992).

The Court said nothing about *students* organizing and leading prayers at graduation ceremonies and other school events, however, and these issues continue to come before the courts. A particularly contentious question in the last few years involves student-initiated prayers before sporting events, such as football games. In 1999, a federal appellate court held that while school prayer at graduation did not violate the establishment clause, students could not use a school's public address system to lead prayers at sporting events.[16] In 2000, the Supreme Court affirmed this decision.[17]

In spite of the Court's ruling, students in a number of schools in Texas continue to pray over public address systems at sporting events. In other areas, the Court's ruling is skirted by avoiding the use of the public address system. For example, in a school in North Carolina, a pregame prayer was broadcast over a local radio station and heard by fans who took radios to the game for that purpose.

The Ten Commandments.   A related church-state issue has to do with whether the Ten Commandments may be displayed in public schools—or on any public property. In recent years, a number of states have considered legislation that would allow or require schools to post the Ten Commandments in school buildings. Supporters of the "Hang Ten" movement claim that schoolchildren are not being taught the fundamental religious and family values that frame the American way of life. They believe that posting the commandments in classrooms will not harm anyone, and it may help. They further argue that the Ten Commandments are more than just religious documents. The commandments are also secular in nature because they constitute a part of the official and permanent history of American government. Therefore, displaying the Ten Commandments on public property should not violate the establishment clause.

---

[16] *Doe v. Santa Fe Independent School District,* 168 F.3d 806 (5th Cir. 1999).
[17] *Santa Fe Independent School District v. Doe,* 530 U.S. 290 (2000).

President George W. Bush joins students in saying the Pledge of Allegiance. The Supreme Court ruled in 1943 that students cannot be forced to recite the Pledge of Allegiance. Some controversy remains regarding the words "under God" in the Pledge, however, as demonstrated by a 2002 Circuit Court decision. Do you agree with the U.S. Circuit Court of Appeals for the Ninth Circuit that inserting the words "under God" in the Pledge, even if students are not forced to recite it, violates the establishment clause of the First Amendment? (AP Photo/Doug Mills)

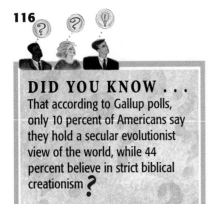

Opponents of such laws claim that they mark an unconstitutional government entanglement with the religious life of citizens. They point out that the Supreme Court made this clear in its 1980 decision in *Stone v. Graham*.[18] In that case, the Court held that a Kentucky law requiring that the Ten Commandments be posted in every public school classroom in the state violated the establishment clause. Despite the Supreme Court's ruling, however, the movement to "Hang Ten" continues. To date, the Supreme Court has declined to revisit its 1980 decision.[19]

Forbidding the Teaching of Evolution. For many decades, certain religious groups, particularly in the southern states, have opposed the teaching of evolution in the schools. To these groups, evolutionary theory directly counters their religious belief that human beings did not evolve but were created fully formed, as described in the biblical story of the creation. State and local attempts to forbid the teaching of evolution, however, have not passed constitutional muster in the eyes of the United States Supreme Court. For example, in 1968 the Supreme Court held, in *Epperson v. Arkansas*,[20] that an Arkansas law prohibiting the teaching of evolution violated the establishment clause, because it imposed religious beliefs on students. The Louisiana legislature passed a law requiring the teaching of the biblical story of the creation alongside the teaching of evolution. In 1987, in *Edwards v. Aguillard*,[21] the Supreme Court declared that this law was unconstitutional, in part because it had as its primary purpose the promotion of a particular religious belief.

Subsequently, a Louisiana school board required teachers in its district to recite disclaimers that evolution lessons are "not intended to influence or dissuade the Biblical version of Creation or any other concept." In 2000, a federal appellate court held that the disclaimer violated the establishment clause because it was aimed at the "protection and maintenance of a particular religious viewpoint."[22]

Nonetheless, state and local groups around the country, particularly in the so-called Bible Belt, continue their efforts against the teaching of evolution. The Tennessee legislature recently considered a bill that would allow a school to fire any teacher who presents evolution as fact. A proposed amendment to the bill would also protect teachers who want to teach the biblical theories of the creation along with evolution. Alabama has approved a disclaimer to be inserted in biology textbooks, indicating that evolution is "a controversial theory some scientists present as a scientific explanation for the origin of living things." A school district in Georgia adopted a policy that creationism could be taught along with evolution. No doubt, these laws and policies will be challenged on constitutional grounds.

Religious Speech. Another controversy in the area of church-state relations has to do with religious speech in public schools or universities. For example, in *Rosenberger v. University of Virginia*,[23] the issue concerned whether the University of Virginia violated the establishment clause when it refused to fund a Christian group's newsletter but granted funds to more than one hundred other student organizations. The Supreme Court ruled that the university's policy unconstitutionally discriminated against religious speech. The Court pointed out that the money came from student fees, not general taxes, and was used for the "neutral" payment of bills for student groups. Justice David Souter, who dissented from the majority's conclusion, saw

[18] 449 U.S. 39 (1980).

[19] In 2002, the Supreme Court declined to review a case [*Indiana Civil Liberties Union v. O'Bannon*, 259 F.3d 766 (7th Cir. 2001)] in which a federal appellate court held that Indiana could not erect a six-foot-high stone tablet containing the Ten Commandments, even though it was part of a historical display and the Bill of Rights was inscribed on the other side of the tablet.

[20] 393 U.S. 97 (1968).

[21] 482 U.S. 578 (1987).

[22] *Freiler v. Tangipahoa Parish Board of Education*, 201 F.3d 602 (5th Cir. 2000).

[23] 515 U.S. 819 (1995).

nothing neutral about the Court's decision. He stated, "The Court today, for the first time, approves direct funding of core religious activities by an arm of the state."

More recently, the Supreme Court reviewed a case involving a similar claim of discrimination against a religious group, the Good News Club. The club, which is sponsored by a Christian evangelical group, offers religious instruction to young school-children. The club sued the school board of a public school in Milford, New York, when the board refused to allow the club to meet on school property after the school day ended. The club argued that the school board's refusal to allow the club to meet on school property, when other groups, such as the Girl Scouts and the 4-H Club, were permitted to do so, amounted to discrimination on the basis of religion. Ultimately, the Supreme Court agreed, ruling that the Milford school board's decision violated the establishment clause.[24]

The Free Exercise Clause

The First Amendment constrains Congress from prohibiting the free exercise of religion. Does this **free exercise clause** mean that no type of religious practice can be prohibited or restricted by government? Certainly, a person can hold any religious belief that he or she wants; or a person can have no religious belief. When, however, religious *practices* work against public policy and the public welfare, the government can act. For example, regardless of a child's or parent's religious beliefs, the government can require certain types of vaccinations. Additionally, public school students can be required to study from textbooks chosen by school authorities.

The extent to which government can regulate religious practices always has been subject to controversy. For example, in 1990, in *Oregon v. Smith*,[25] the Supreme Court ruled that the state of Oregon could deny unemployment benefits to two drug counselors who had been fired for using peyote, an illegal drug, in their religious services. The counselors had argued that using peyote was part of the practice of a Native American religion. Many criticized the decision as going too far in the direction of regulating religious practices.

In 1993, Congress responded to the public's criticism by passing the Religious Freedom Restoration Act (RFRA). One of the specific purposes of the act was to overturn the Supreme Court's decision in *Oregon v. Smith*. The act required national, state, and local governments to "accommodate religious conduct" unless the government could show that there was a *compelling* reason not to do so. Moreover, if the government did regulate a religious practice, it had to use the least restrictive means possible.

Many people felt that the RFRA went too far in the other direction—it accommodated practices that were contrary to the public policies of state governments. Proponents of states' rights complained that the act intruded into an area traditionally governed by state laws, not the national government. In 1997, in *City of Boerne v. Flores*,[26] the Supreme Court agreed and held that Congress had exceeded its constitutional authority when it passed the RFRA. According to the Court, the act's "sweeping coverage ensures its intrusion at every level of government, displacing laws and prohibiting official actions of almost every description and regardless of subject matter."

Freedom of Expression

Perhaps the most frequently invoked freedom that Americans have is the right to free speech and a free press without government interference. Each of us has the right to have our say, and all of us have the right to hear what others say. For the most part,

DID YOU KNOW . . .
That when President Ronald Reagan gave a speech on the glories of freedom of the press during a 1983 visit to Japan, he demanded that the entire speech be "off the record"?

Free Exercise Clause
The provision of the First Amendment guaranteeing the free exercise of religion.

---

[24] *Good News Club v. Milford Central School,* 533 U.S. 98 (2001).
[25] 494 U.S. 872 (1990).
[26] 521 U.S. 507 (1997).

Americans can criticize public officials and their actions without fear of reprisal or imprisonment by any branch of our government.

Permitted Restrictions on Expression

At various times, restrictions on expression have been permitted. A description of several such restrictions follows.

Clear and Present Danger.   When a person's remarks present a clear and present danger to the peace or public order, they can be curtailed constitutionally. Justice Oliver Wendell Holmes used this reasoning in 1919 when examining the case of a socialist who had been convicted for violating the Espionage Act. Holmes stated:

> The question in every case is whether the words are used in such circumstances and are of such a nature as to create a *clear and present danger* that they will bring about the substantive evils that Congress has a right to prevent. It is a question of proximity and degree. [Emphasis added.][27]

> **Clear and Present Danger Test**
> The test proposed by Justice Holmes for determining when government may restrict free speech. Restrictions are permissible, he argued, only when speech presents a "clear and present danger" to the public order.

Thus, according to the **clear and present danger test**, expression may be restricted if evidence exists that such expression would cause a condition, actual or imminent, that Congress has the power to prevent. Commenting on this test, Justice Louis D. Brandeis in 1920 said, "Correctly applied, it will reserve the right of free speech . . . from suppression by tyrannists, well-meaning majorities, and from abuse by irresponsible, fanatical minorities."[28]

> **Bad-Tendency Rule**
> A rule stating that speech or other First Amendment freedoms may be curtailed if there is a possibility that such expression might lead to some "evil."

Modifications to the Clear and Present Danger Rule.   Later, in a series of decisions, the United States Supreme Court modified the clear and present danger rule. In *Gitlow v. New York*,[29] the Court enunciated the **bad-tendency rule.** According to this rule, speech or other First Amendment freedoms may be curtailed if there is a possibility that such expression might lead to some "evil." In the *Gitlow* case, a member of a left-wing group was convicted of violating New York State's criminal anarchy statute when he published and distributed a pamphlet urging the violent overthrow of the U.S. government. In its majority opinion, the Supreme Court held that although the First Amendment afforded protection against state incursions on freedom of expression, Gitlow could be punished legally in this particular instance because his expression would tend to bring about evils that the state had a right to prevent.

The Supreme Court again modified the clear and present danger test in a 1951 case, *Dennis v. United States*.[30] At the time, there was considerable tension between the United States and the Soviet Union, the pro-Communist government that ruled Russia and surrounding republics from 1917 until 1991. Twelve members of the American Communist Party were convicted of violating a statute that made it a crime to conspire to teach, advocate, or organize the violent overthrow of any government in the United States. The Supreme Court affirmed the convictions, significantly modifying the clear and present danger test in the process. The Court applied a "grave and probable danger rule." Under this rule, "the gravity of the 'evil' discounted by its improbability justifies such invasion of free speech as is necessary to avoid the danger." This rule gave much less protection to free speech than did the clear and present danger test.

Some claim that the United States did not achieve true freedom of political speech until 1969. In that year, in *Brandenburg v. Ohio*,[31] the Supreme Court overturned the conviction of a Ku Klux Klan leader for violating a state statute. The statute prohibited anyone from advocating "the duty, necessity, or propriety of sabotage, violence,

---

[27] *Schenck v. United States,* 249 U.S. 47 (1919).
[28] *Schaefer v. United States,* 251 U.S. 466 (1920).
[29] 268 U.S. 652 (1925).
[30] 341 U.S. 494 (1951).
[31] 395 U.S. 444 (1969).

or unlawful methods of terrorism as a means of accomplishing industrial or political reform." The Court held that the guarantee of free speech does not permit a state "to forbid or proscribe advocacy of the use of force or of law violation except where such advocacy is directed to inciting or producing imminent lawless actions and is likely to incite or produce such action." The "incitement test" enunciated by the Court in this case is a difficult one for prosecutors to meet. As a result, the Court's decision significantly broadened the protection given to advocacy speech.

No Prior Restraint. Restraining an activity before that activity has actually occurred is referred to as **prior restraint**. It involves censorship, as opposed to subsequent punishment. Prior restraint of expression would require, for example, a permit before a speech could be made, a newspaper published, or a movie or TV show exhibited. Most, if not all, Supreme Court justices have been especially critical of any governmental action that imposes prior restraint on expression. The Court clearly expressed this attitude in *Nebraska Press Association v. Stuart*,[32] a case decided in 1976:

> A prior restraint on expression comes to this Court with a "heavy presumption" against its constitutionality. . . . The government thus carries a heavy burden of showing justification for the enforcement of such a restraint.

One of the most famous cases concerning prior restraint was *New York Times v. United States*[33] (1971), the so-called Pentagon Papers case. The *Times* and the *Washington Post* were about to publish the Pentagon Papers, an elaborate secret history of the U.S. government's involvement in the Vietnam War (1964–1975). The secret documents had been obtained illegally by a disillusioned former Pentagon official. The government wanted a court order to bar publication of the documents, arguing that national security was being threatened and that the documents had been stolen. The newspapers argued that the public had a right to know the information contained in the papers and that the press had the right to inform the public. The Supreme Court ruled six to three in favor of the newspapers' right to publish the information. This case affirmed the no prior restraint doctrine.

Typically, prior restraints have been associated with the press. Recently, though, the California Supreme Court issued a ruling that, according to some commentators, amounts to prior restraint in the workplace. The case involved several Hispanic employees who claimed that their supervisor's insults and racist comments had created a hostile work environment. The lower court agreed and awarded damages to the employees. In upholding the ruling, the California Supreme Court took the bold step of issuing a list of offensive words that can no longer be used in any workplace in the state, even among Hispanic Americans themselves. Three justices harshly dissented from the majority opinion, referring to it as "the exception that swallowed the First Amendment."[34] Several media commentators and legal scholars were also astonished at what they referred to as the court's "assault on the First Amendment."[35]

The Protection of Symbolic Speech

Not all expression is in words or in writing. Gestures, movements, articles of clothing, and other forms of expressive conduct are considered **symbolic speech**. Such speech is given substantial protection today by our courts. For example, in a landmark decision issued in 1969, *Tinker v. Des Moines School District*,[36] the Supreme Court held that the wearing of black armbands by students in protest against the

Prior Restraint
Restraining an action before the activity has actually occurred. It involves censorship, as opposed to subsequent punishment.

Symbolic Speech
Nonverbal expression of beliefs, which is given substantial protection by the courts.

These protesters are burning an American flag as a symbolic expression of their opposition to government policy. Would a constitutional amendment to prohibit such actions place unacceptable limitations on symbolic speech? (Les Stone, Sygma)

---

[32] 427 U.S. 539 (1976). See also *Near v. Minnesota*, 283 U.S. 697 (1931).
[33] 403 U.S. 713 (1971).
[34] *Aguilar v. Avis Rent A Car System*, 21 Cal.4th 121 (1999).
[35] See, for example, Greg Mitchell, "California Court Upholds Hate Speech Gag," *The National Law Journal*, August 16, 1999, p. A6; and John Leo, "Watch What You Say," *U.S. News & World Report*, March 20, 2000, p. 18.
[36] 393 U.S. 503 (1969).

Vietnam War was a form of speech protected by the First Amendment. The case arose after a school administrator in Des Moines, Iowa, issued a regulation prohibiting students in the Des Moines School District from wearing the armbands. The Supreme Court reasoned that the school district was unable to show that the wearing of the armbands had disrupted normal school activities. Furthermore, the school district's policy was discriminatory, as it banned only certain forms of symbolic speech (the black armbands) and not others (such as lapel crosses and fraternity rings).

In 1989, in *Texas v. Johnson,*[37] the Supreme Court ruled that state laws that prohibited the burning of the American flag as part of a peaceful protest also violated the freedom of expression protected by the First Amendment. Congress responded by passing the Flag Protection Act of 1989, which was ruled unconstitutional by the Supreme Court in June 1990.[38] Congress and President George H. W. Bush immediately pledged to work for a constitutional amendment to "protect our flag"—an effort that has yet to be successful.

In *R.A.V. v. City of St. Paul, Minnesota*[39] (1992), the Supreme Court ruled that a city statute banning bias-motivated disorderly conduct (in this case, the placing of a burning cross in another's front yard as a gesture of hate) was an unconstitutional restriction of speech. Freedom of speech can also apply to group-sponsored events. In 1995, the Supreme Court held that forcing the organizers of Boston's St. Patrick's Day parade to include gays and lesbians violated the organizers' freedom of speech.[40]

The Protection of Commercial Speech

Commercial Speech
Advertising statements, which increasingly have been given First Amendment protection.

Commercial speech is usually defined as advertising statements. Can advertisers use their First Amendment rights to prevent restrictions on the content of commercial advertising? Until the 1970s, the Supreme Court held that such speech was not protected at all by the First Amendment. By the mid-1970s, however, more and more commercial speech was brought under First Amendment protection. According to Justice Harry A. Blackmun, "Advertising, however tasteless and excessive it sometimes may seem, is nonetheless dissemination of information as to who is producing and selling what product for what reason and at what price."[41] Generally, the Supreme Court will consider a restriction on commercial speech valid as long as it (1) seeks to implement a substantial government interest, (2) directly advances that interest, and (3) goes no further than necessary to accomplish its objective.

Unprotected Speech: Obscenity

Numerous state and federal statutes make it a crime to disseminate obscene materials. Generally, the courts have not been willing to extend constitutional protections of free speech to what they consider obscene materials. But what is obscenity? Justice Potter Stewart once stated, in *Jacobellis v. Ohio,*[42] a 1964 case, that even though he could not define obscenity, "I know it when I see it." The problem, of course, is that even if it were agreed on, the definition of obscenity changes with the times. Victorians deeply disapproved of the "loose" morals of the Elizabethan Age. The works of Mark Twain and Edgar Rice Burroughs have at times been considered obscene (after all, Tarzan and Jane were not legally wedded).

Definitional Problems.   The Supreme Court has grappled from time to time with the problem of specifying an operationally effective definition of obscenity. In 1973,

---

[37] 488 U.S. 884 (1989).
[38] *United States v. Eichman,* 496 U.S. 310 (1990).
[39] 505 U.S. 377 (1992).
[40] *Hurley v. Irish-American Gay, Lesbian and Bisexual Group of Boston,* 515 U.S. 557 (1995).
[41] *Virginia State Board of Pharmacy v. Virginia Citizens Consumer Council, Inc.,* 425 U.S. 748 (1976).
[42] 378 U.S. 184 (1964).

in *Miller v. California*,[43] Chief Justice Warren Burger created a formal list of requirements that currently must be met for material to be legally obscene. Material is obscene if (1) the average person finds that it violates contemporary community standards; (2) the work taken as a whole appeals to a prurient interest in sex; (3) the work shows patently offensive sexual conduct; and (4) the work lacks serious redeeming literary, artistic, political, or scientific merit. The problem, of course, is that one person's prurient interest is another person's medical interest or artistic pleasure. The Court went on to state that the definition of prurient interest would be determined by the community's standards. The Court avoided presenting a definition of obscenity, leaving this determination to local and state authorities. Consequently, the *Miller* case has had widely inconsistent applications.

Protecting Children. In regard to child pornography, the Supreme Court has upheld state laws making it illegal to sell materials showing sexual performances by minors. In 1990, in *Osborne v. Ohio*,[44] the Court ruled that states can outlaw the possession of child pornography in the home. The Court reasoned that the ban on private possession is justified because owning the material perpetuates commercial demand for it and for the exploitation of the children involved. At the federal level, the Child Protection Act of 1984 made it a crime to receive knowingly through the mails sexually explicit depictions of children.

Pornography on the Internet. A significant problem facing Americans and their lawmakers today is how to control obscenity and child pornography that are disseminated via the Internet. In 1996, Congress first attempted to protect minors from pornographic materials on the Internet by passing the Communications Decency Act (CDA). The act made it a crime to make available to minors online any "obscene or indecent" message that "depicts or describes, in terms patently offensive as measured by contemporary community standards, sexual or excretory activities or organs." The act was immediately challenged in court as an unconstitutional infringement on free speech.

When the case eventually came before the Supreme Court, the Court agreed that the act imposed unconstitutional restraints on free speech. In the eyes of the Court, the terms *indecent* and *patently offensive* covered large amounts of nonpornographic material with serious educational or other value. Moreover, said the Court, "the 'community standards' criterion as applied to the Internet means that any communication available to a nationwide audience will be judged by the standards of the community most likely to be offended by the message." The Court therefore invalidated the law.[45]

Later attempts by Congress to curb pornography on the Internet have also been held unconstitutional by the courts. For example, the Children's Online Privacy Protection Act of 1998 imposed criminal penalties on those who distribute material that is "harmful to minors" without using some kind of age-verification system to separate adult and minor users. The act has been tied up in the courts since its passage. In 2000, Congress enacted the Children's Internet Protection Act, which requires public schools and libraries to block adult content from access by children by installing filtering software. This act has also been challenged in court as unconstitutional on the ground that it blocks access to too much information, including information of educational value. (For a discussion of another act challenged as unconstitutional, see this chapter's *Which Side Are You On?* feature on page 122.)

Unprotected Speech: Slander

Can you say anything you want about someone else? Not really. Individuals are protected from **defamation of character,** which is defined as wrongfully hurting a person's

---

[43] 413 U.S. 5 (1973).
[44] 495 U.S. 103 (1990).
[45] *Reno v. American Civil Liberties Union*, 521 U.S. 844 (1997).

I N F O T R A C ®
COLLEGE EDITION

For updates on this topic, use the term "Internet censorship" in Keywords.

Defamation of Character
Wrongfully hurting a person's good reputation. The law has imposed a general duty on all persons to refrain from making false, defamatory statements about others.

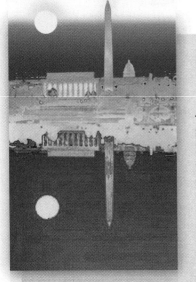

Which Side Are You On?
Should Virtual Pornography Be a Crime?

The history of legislation involving pornography is long, complicated, and often inconsistent. One area of law in the field of pornography, however, that seems to be well settled involves child pornography. Whether it be photos on paper, moving images on video, or both of these transmitted on the Internet, federal and state laws are quite clear about the illegality of involving minors in lewd and lascivious visual products. A new controversy has arisen in this area nonetheless. It involves the depiction of "fake" minors engaged in sexual acts in still photos and movies.

"VIRTUALLY REAL" PORNOGRAPHY

Current software programs allow digital images to be created that are extremely lifelike. Indeed, most Hollywood movies today use some digital images, often without the viewer knowing that the images are "fake." When this technology is applied to pornography, the results are amazingly real. If a computer programmer, using just a computer, creates a lifelike set of child actors and uses commands on the computer to have them engage in sexual acts, is this a violation of child pornography laws?

At issue here is whether "child" pornography that does not involve children violates the law. After all, the main purpose underlying child pornography laws is to protect children, and in particular those who are involved in actual child pornography. If no children are actually involved, have child pornography laws been violated?

CONGRESS AND THE COURTS TAKE A STAND, BUT THE CONTROVERSY IS FAR FROM OVER

In 1996, Congress passed the Child Pornography Prevention Act. This act bans the distribution and possession of computer-generated images that appear to depict minors engaging in lewd and lascivious behavior. Those who believe that the act is unconstitutional say that it creates, for the first time in our history, a "thought crime." They see a basic tension between the act and the First Amendment to the U.S. Constitution. In contrast, those who support the act argue that the availability of child pornography on the Web, whether it be virtual or real, encourages the abuse of children. As Professor Eric M. Freedman of Hofstra Law School stated, the 1996 law "proceeds on the premise that the underlying idea is so pathological that it should be banned from public discourse."*

To date, cases challenging the law's constitutionality have come before four federal appellate courts, which have rendered conflicting decisions on the issue. The Supreme Court agreed to review one of those decisions, in which the federal appellate court struck down the 1996 law on the ground that it was unconstitutionally vague and overbroad. The federal appellate court concluded that the government can place significant restraints on free speech rights only if the restraints are necessary to promote a compelling government interest. In the court's eyes, the government has a compelling interest only in protecting children from actual, not "fake," child pornography.[†]

The United States Supreme Court held in 2002, in *Ashcroft v. Free Speech Coalition,*[‡] that the Child Pornography Prevention Act (CPPA) is overbroad and unconstitutional, and that its limits on freedom of speech were unjustified. The Court pointed out that pictures of teenagers engaging in sexual activity have been a theme in art and literature for centuries. Thus, according to the court, the CPPA lacks "the required link between its prohibitions and the affront to community standards prohibited by the obscenity definition." The Court held further that virtual child pornography is not "intrinsically related" to the sexual abuse of children and rejected government arguments that the CPPA is necessary because pedophiles may use virtual child pornography to seduce children. As the Court wrote, "the mere tendency of speech to encourage unlawful acts is not a sufficient reason for banning it, absent some showing of a direct connection between the speech and imminent illegal conduct."

WHAT'S YOUR POSITION?

Do you believe that there is a significant distinction between actual and virtual pornography? Explain.

GOING ONLINE

The Department of Justice maintains a Web site in its Criminal Division devoted to the issue of child exploitation and obscenity. To learn more about the law on this issue, visit **http://www.usdoj.gov/criminal/ceos/index.html** and click on any of the numerous links, or use the site's search function.

*As quoted in Adam Liptak, "When Is a Fake Too Real? That's Virtually Uncertain," *The New York Times,* January 28, 2001, p. 3.
[†]*Free Speech Coalition v. Reno,* 198 F.3d 1083 (9th Cir. 1999).
[‡]122 S.Ct. 1389 (2002).

good reputation. The law has imposed a general duty on all persons to refrain from making false, defamatory statements about others. Breaching this duty orally involves the wrongdoing called **slander.** (Breaching it in writing involves the wrongdoing called *libel,* which is discussed later.)

Legally, slander is the public uttering of a false statement that harms the good reputation of another. Slanderous public uttering means that the defamatory statements are made to, or within the hearing of, persons other than the defamed party. If one person calls another dishonest, manipulative, and incompetent when no one else is around, that does not constitute slander. The message is not communicated to a third party. If, however, a third party accidentally overhears defamatory statements, the courts have generally held that this constitutes a public uttering and therefore slander, which is prohibited.

Fighting Words and Hecklers' Veto

The Supreme Court has prohibited types of speech that tend to incite an immediate breach of peace. For example, public speakers may not use **fighting words.** These may include racial, religious, or ethnic slurs that are so inflammatory that they will provoke the "average" listener to fight. At least one court has held that throwing a burning cross into a person's yard, a form of symbolic speech, constitutes fighting words.[46] Members of a crowd listening to a speech are prohibited from exercising a **hecklers' veto.** The boisterous and disruptive behavior of hecklers poses the threat of disruption or violence, so hecklers are vetoing the essential rights of the speaker.

Campus Speech

In recent years, students have been facing free speech challenges on campuses. One issue has to do with whether a student should have to subsidize, through student activity fees, organizations that promote causes that the student finds objectionable.

Student Activity Fees.   In 2000, this issue came before the Supreme Court in a case brought by several University of Wisconsin students against the university's board of regents. The students argued that their mandatory student activity fees—which helped to fund liberal causes with which they disagreed, including gay rights—violated their First Amendment rights of free speech, free association, and free exercise of religion. They contended that they should have the right to choose whether to fund organizations that promoted political and ideological views that were offensive to their personal beliefs. To the surprise of many, the Supreme Court rejected the students' claim and ruled in favor of the university. The Court stated that "the university may determine that its mission is well served if students have the means to engage in dynamic discussions of philosophical, religious, scientific, social and political subjects in their extracurricular life. If the university reaches this conclusion, it is entitled to impose a mandatory fee to sustain an open dialogue to these ends."[47]

Campus Speech and Behavior Codes.   Another free speech issue relates to campus speech and behavior codes. Some state universities have issued codes that challenge the boundaries of the protection of free speech provided by the First Amendment. These codes are designed to prohibit so-called hate speech—abusive speech attacking persons on the basis of their ethnicity, race, or other criteria. For example, a University of Michigan code banned "any behavior, verbal or physical, that stigmatizes or victimizes an individual on the basis of race, ethnicity, religion, sex, sexual orientation, creed, national origin, ancestry, age, marital status, handicap" or

Slander
 The public uttering of a false statement that harms the good reputation of another. The statement must be made to, or within the hearing of, persons other than the defamed party.

Fighting Words
 Words that, when uttered by a public speaker, are so inflammatory that they could provoke the average listener to violence; the words are usually of a racial, religious, or ethnic type.

Hecklers' Veto
 Boisterous and generally disruptive behavior by listeners to public speakers that, in effect, vetoes the public speakers' right to speak.

---

[46] *O'Mara v. Commonwealth,* 33 Va.App. 525 (2000).
[47] *Board of Regents of the University of Wisconsin System v. Southworth,* 529 U.S. 217 (2000).

Vietnam-veteran status. A federal court found that the code violated students' First Amendment rights.[48]

Although the courts generally have held, as in the University of Michigan case, that campus speech codes are unconstitutional restrictions on the right to free speech, such codes continue to exist. For example, the University of North Dakota's code of conduct prohibits speech "intentionally producing psychological discomfort." The University of Minnesota bans speech that shows "insensitivity to the experiences of women." West Virginia University bans speech exhibiting "feelings" about gays that evolve into "attitudes." The University of Connecticut bans "inconsiderate jokes," while Colby College in Waterville, Maine, bans any speech that causes a loss of "self-esteem or a vague sense of danger."[49]

Defenders of such constraints on speech argue that they are necessary not only to prevent violence but also to promote equality among different cultural, ethnic, and racial groups on campus and greater sensitivity to the needs and feelings of others. Critics worry that campus censorship is fostering the idea that only "good" speech (as defined by the liberal agenda) should be protected by the First Amendment, while "bad" speech (speech opposing that agenda) should be punished.

Hate Speech on the Internet

Campus speech codes raise a controversial issue: whether rights to free speech can (or should) be traded off to reduce violence in America. This issue extends to hate speech transmitted on the Internet as well, which is a growing concern for many Americans. Those who know how to navigate the online world can find information on virtually any topic, from how to build bombs to how to produce anthrax to how to wage war against the government. Here again, the issue is whether free speech on the Internet should be restrained in the interests of protecting against violence.

Generally, it is doubtful that much can be done to constrain speech on the Internet simply because the U.S. government cannot exercise authority over what citizens in other nations do—and the Internet is an international vehicle for the transmission of opinion. Notably, numerous Web sites have sprung up in recent years to "counter" hate speech on the Web. For example, a number of Web sites give suggestions to parents who wish to keep their children from accessing such materials online.

Freedom of the Press

Freedom of the press can be regarded as a special instance of freedom of speech. Of course, at the time of the framing of the Constitution, the press meant only newspapers, magazines, and perhaps pamphlets. As technology has modified the ways in which we disseminate information, the laws touching on freedom of the press have been modified. What can and cannot be printed still occupies an important place in constitutional law, however.

Defamation in Writing

Libel

A written defamation of a person's character, reputation, business, or property rights. To a limited degree, the First Amendment protects the press from libel actions.

Libel is defamation in writing (or in pictures, signs, or films, or any other communication that has the potentially harmful qualities of written or printed words). As with slander, libel occurs only if the defamatory statements are observed by a third party. If one person writes another a private letter wrongfully accusing him or her of embezzling funds, that does not constitute libel. It is interesting that the courts have generally held that dictating a letter to a secretary constitutes communication of the

---

[48] *Doe v. University of Michigan,* 721 F.Supp. 852 (1989).

[49] For other examples, see Alan Charles Kors and Harvey Silverglate, *The Shadow University* (New York: HarperCollins, 1999).

letter's contents to a third party, and therefore, if defamation has occurred, the wrongdoer can be sued.

Newspapers are often involved in libel suits. *New York Times Co. v. Sullivan*[50] (1964) explored an important question regarding libelous statements made about **public figures**—public officials and employees who exercise substantial governmental power, as well as any persons who are generally in the public limelight. The Supreme Court held that only when a statement was made with **actual malice**—that is, with either knowledge of its falsity or a reckless disregard of the truth—against a public official could damages be obtained.

The standard set by the Court in the *New York Times* case has since been applied to public figures generally. Statements made about public figures, especially when they are made via a public medium, are usually related to matters of general public interest; they are made about people who substantially affect all of us. Furthermore, public figures generally have some access to a public medium for answering disparaging falsehoods about themselves, whereas private individuals do not. For these reasons, public figures have a greater burden of proof (they must prove that the statements were made with actual malice) in defamation cases than do private individuals.

A Free Press versus a Fair Trial: Gag Orders

Another major issue relating to freedom of the press concerns media coverage of criminal trials. The Sixth Amendment to the Constitution guarantees the right of criminal suspects to a fair trial. In other words, the accused have rights. The First Amendment guarantees freedom of the press. What if the two rights appear to be in conflict? Which one prevails?

Jurors certainly may be influenced by reading news stories about the trial in which they are participating. In the 1970s, judges increasingly issued **gag orders,** which restricted the publication of news about a trial in progress or even a pretrial hearing. In a landmark 1976 case, *Nebraska Press Association v. Stuart,*[51] the Supreme Court unanimously ruled that a Nebraska judge's gag order had violated the First Amendment's guarantee of freedom of the press. Chief Justice Warren Burger indicated that even pervasive adverse pretrial publicity did not necessarily lead to an unfair trial and that prior restraints on publication were not justified. Some justices even went so far as to indicate that gag orders are never justified.

In spite of the *Nebraska Press Association* ruling, the Court has upheld certain types of gag orders. In *Gannett Co. v. De Pasquale*[52] (1979), for example, the highest court held that if a judge found a reasonable probability that news publicity would harm a defendant's right to a fair trial, the court could impose a gag rule: "Members of the public have no constitutional right under the Sixth and Fourteenth Amendments to *attend* criminal trials."

The *Nebraska* and *Gannett* cases, however, involved pretrial hearings. Could a judge impose a gag order on an entire trial, including pretrial hearings? In *Richmond Newspapers, Inc. v. Virginia*[53] (1980), the Court ruled that actual trials must be open to the public except under unusual circumstances.

Films, Radio, and TV

As was noted, only in a few cases has the Supreme Court upheld prior restraint of published materials. The Court's reluctance to accept prior restraint is less evident with respect to motion pictures. In the first half of the twentieth century, films were routinely submitted to local censorship boards. In 1968, the Supreme Court ruled that

Public Figures
Public officials, movie stars, and generally all persons who become known to the public because of their positions or activities.

Actual Malice
Actual malice in libel cases generally consists of intentionally publishing any written or printed statement that is injurious to the character of another with either knowledge of the statement's falsity or a reckless disregard for the truth.

INFOTRAC®
COLLEGE EDITION

To find out more about libel, use the term "libel" in the Subject guide.

Gag Order
An order issued by a judge restricting the publication of news about a trial in progress or a pretrial hearing in order to protect the accused's right to a fair trial.

[50] 376 U.S. 254 (1964).
[51] 427 U.S. 539 (1976).
[52] 443 U.S. 368 (1979).
[53] 448 U.S. 555 (1980).

Radio "shock jock" Howard Stern apparently offended the sensitivities of the Federal Communications Commission (FCC). That regulatory body fined Stern's radio station owner hundreds of thousands of dollars for Stern's purportedly obscene outbursts on radio. The extent to which the FCC can regulate speech over the air involves the First Amendment. What is considered permissible and acceptable on radio and TV today probably would have been considered "obscene" three decades ago. (Bill Swersey, Getty Images)

a film can be banned only under a law that provides for a prompt hearing at which the film is shown to be obscene. Today, few local censorship boards exist. Instead, the film industry regulates itself primarily through the industry's rating system.

Radio and television broadcasting has the most limited First Amendment protection. Broadcasting initially received less protection than the printed media because, at that time, the number of airwave frequencies was limited.

In 1934, the national government established the Federal Communications Commission (FCC) to regulate electromagnetic wave frequencies. No one has a right to use the airwaves without a license granted by the FCC. The FCC grants licenses for limited periods and imposes numerous regulations on broadcasting. One of these regulations, called the **equal time rule**, requires any station that gives or sells airtime to a political candidate to make an equal amount of time available for purchase to all competing candidates. Another rule, sometimes referred to as the **personal attack rule**, provides that if a radio or television station is used to attack the honesty or integrity of a person, the station must see to it that the person attacked is afforded the fullest opportunity to respond. The FCC can also impose sanctions on radio or TV stations that broadcast "filthy words," even if the words are not legally obscene.

The Right to Assemble and to Petition the Government

The First Amendment prohibits Congress from making any law that abridges "the right of the people peaceably to assemble, and to petition the Government for a redress of grievances." Inherent in such a right is the ability of private citizens to communicate their ideas on public issues to government officials, as well as to other individuals. The Supreme Court has often put this freedom on a par with the freedom of speech and the freedom of the press. Nonetheless, it has allowed municipalities to require permits for parades, sound trucks, and demonstrations, so that public officials may control traffic or prevent demonstrations from turning into riots.

This became a major issue in 1977 when the American Nazi Party wanted to march through the largely Jewish suburb of Skokie, Illinois. The American Civil Liberties Union defended the Nazis' right to march (in spite of its opposition to the Nazi philosophy). The Supreme Court let stand a lower court's ruling that the city of

Equal Time Rule
A Federal Communications Commission regulation that requires broadcasting stations that give or sell air time to political candidates to make equal amounts of time available to all competing candidates.

Personal Attack Rule
A Federal Communications Commission regulation that requires broadcasting stations, if the stations are used to attack the honesty or integrity of persons, to allow the persons attacked the fullest opportunity to respond.

With their right to assemble and demonstrate protected by the Constitution, members of the modern Ku Klux Klan march in Wilmington, North Carolina. The police escort is charged with making sure that neither the marchers nor the observers provoke any violence. (Paul Miller, Stock Boston)

Skokie had violated the Nazis' First Amendment guarantees by denying them a permit to march.[54]

An issue that has surfaced in recent years is whether communities can prevent gang members from gathering together on the streets without violating their right of assembly or associated rights. Although some actions taken by cities to prevent gang members from gathering together or "loitering" in public places have passed constitutional muster, others have not. For example, in a 1997 case, the California Supreme Court upheld a lower court's order preventing gang members from appearing in public together.[55] In 1999, the United States Supreme Court held that Chicago's "antiloitering" ordinance violated the constitutional right to due process of law because, among other things, it left too much power to the police to determine what constituted "loitering."[56]

A question for Americans today is whether individuals should have the right to "assemble" online for the purpose of advocating violence against certain groups (such as physicians who perform abortions) or advocating values that are opposed to our democracy (such as terrorism). Recall from the *America's Security* feature in Chapter 1 that while some online advocacy groups promote interests consistent with American political values, other groups have as their goal the destruction of those values. Whether First Amendment freedoms should be sacrificed (by the government's monitoring of Internet communications, for example) in the interests of national security is a question that will no doubt be debated for some time to come.

More Liberties under Scrutiny: Matters of Privacy

No explicit reference is made anywhere in the Constitution to a person's right to privacy. Until relatively recently, the courts did not take a very positive approach toward the right to privacy. For example, during Prohibition, suspected bootleggers' telephones

---

[54] *Smith v. Collin,* 439 U.S. 916 (1978).
[55] *Gallo v. Acuna,* 14 Cal.4th 1090 (1997).
[56] *City of Chicago v. Morales,* 527 U.S. 41 (1999).

were routinely tapped, and the information obtained was used as a legal basis for prosecution. In *Olmstead v. United States*[57] (1928), the Supreme Court upheld such an invasion of privacy. Justice Louis Brandeis, a champion of personal freedoms, strongly dissented from the majority decision in this case. He argued that the framers of the Constitution gave every citizen the right to be left alone. He called such a right "the most comprehensive of rights and the right most valued by civilized men."

In the 1960s, the highest court began to modify the majority view. In 1965, in *Griswold v. Connecticut*,[58] the Supreme Court overthrew a Connecticut law that effectively prohibited the use of contraceptives, holding that the law violated the right to privacy. Justice William O. Douglas formulated a unique way of reading this right into the Bill of Rights. He claimed that the First, Third, Fourth, Fifth, and Ninth Amendments created "penumbras, formed by emanations from those guarantees that help give them life and substance," and he went on to talk about zones of privacy that are guaranteed by these rights. When we read the Ninth Amendment, we can see the foundation for his reasoning: "The enumeration in the Constitution, of certain rights, shall not be construed to deny or disparage others retained by the people." In other words, just because the Constitution, including its amendments, does not specifically talk about the right to privacy does not mean that this right is denied to the people.

Some of today's most controversial issues relate to privacy rights. One issue has to do with the erosion of privacy rights in an information age. Other issues have to do with abortion and the "right to die." Since the terrorist attacks of September 11, 2001, Americans have faced another crucial question regarding privacy rights: To what extent should Americans sacrifice privacy rights in the interests of national security?

Privacy Rights in an Information Age

An important privacy issue, created in part by new technology, is the amassing of information on individuals by government agencies and private businesses, such as marketing firms. The average American citizen has personal information filed away in dozens of agencies—such as the Social Security Administration and the Internal Revenue Service. Because of the threat of indiscriminate use of private information by nonauthorized individuals, Congress passed the Privacy Act in 1974. This was the first law regulating the use of federal government information about private individuals. Under the Privacy Act, every citizen has the right to obtain copies of personal records collected by federal agencies and to correct inaccuracies in such records.

The ease with which personal information can be obtained by using the Internet for marketing and other purposes has led to unique challenges with regard to privacy rights. Some fear that privacy rights with respect to personal information may soon be a thing of the past. Whether privacy rights can survive in an information age is a question that Americans and their leaders continue to confront.

Privacy Rights and Abortion

Historically, abortion was not a criminal offense before the "quickening" of the fetus (the first movement of the fetus in the uterus, usually between the sixteenth and eighteenth weeks of pregnancy). During the last half of the nineteenth century, however, state laws became more severe. By 1973, performance of an abortion was a criminal offense in most states.

---

[57] 277 U.S. 438 (1928). This decision was overruled later in *Katz v. United States,* 389 U.S. 347 (1967).
[58] 381 U.S. 479 (1965).

Roe v. Wade. In *Roe v. Wade*[59] (1973), the United States Supreme Court accepted the argument that the laws against abortion violated "Jane Roe's" right to privacy under the Constitution. The Court did not answer the question about when life begins. It simply said that "the right to privacy is broad enough to encompass a woman's decision whether or not to terminate her pregnancy." The Court held that during the first trimester (three months) of pregnancy, abortion was an issue solely between a woman and her doctor. The state could not limit abortions except to require that they be performed by licensed physicians. During the second trimester, to protect the health of the mother, the state was allowed to specify the conditions under which an abortion could be performed. During the final trimester, the state could regulate or even outlaw abortions except when necessary to preserve the life or health of the mother.

After *Roe*, the Supreme Court issued decisions in a number of cases defining and redefining the boundaries of state regulation of abortion. During the 1980s, the Court twice struck down laws that required a woman who wished to have an abortion to undergo counseling designed to discourage abortions. In the late 1980s and early 1990s, however, the Court took a more conservative approach. Although the Court did not explicitly overturn the *Roe* decision, it upheld state laws that place restrictions on abortion rights. For example, in *Webster v. Reproductive Health Services*[60] (1989), the Court upheld a Missouri statute that, among other things, banned the use of public hospitals or other taxpayer-supported facilities for performing abortions. And, in *Planned Parenthood v. Casey*[61] (1992), the Court upheld a Pennsylvania law that required preabortion counseling, a waiting period of twenty-four hours, and, for girls under the age of eighteen, parental or judicial permission. As a result, abortions are now more difficult to obtain in some states than others.

---

[59] 410 U.S. 113 (1973). Jane Roe was not the real name of the woman in this case. It is a common legal pseudonym used to protect a person's privacy.
[60] 492 U.S. 490 (1989).
[61] 505 U.S. 833 (1992).

Pro-life groups increased their demonstrations against abortion facilities in the 1990s and early 2000s. The clash between the pro-abortion and the pro-life forces has resulted in several deaths. The Supreme Court has imposed restrictions on what pro-life groups can do in their demonstrations around abortion clinics. (Christopher Brown, Stock Boston)

The Controversy Continues.   Abortion continues to be a divisive issue. Antiabortion forces continue to push for laws banning abortion, to endorse political candidates who support their views, and to organize protests. Because of several episodes of violence attending protests at abortion clinics, in 1994 Congress passed the Freedom of Access to Clinic Entrances Act. The act prohibits protesters from blocking entrances to such clinics. The Supreme Court ruled in 1993 that abortion protesters can be prosecuted under laws governing racketeering,[62] and in 1998 a federal court in Illinois convicted antiabortion protesters under these laws. In 1997, the Supreme Court upheld the constitutionality of prohibiting protesters from entering a fifteen-foot "buffer zone" around abortion clinics and from giving unwanted counseling to those entering the clinics.[63]

In 2000, the Supreme Court again visited the abortion issue when it reviewed a challenge to a Nebraska law banning "partial-birth" abortions. Over thirty other states also ban the controversial procedure. In a partial-birth abortion, which is used during the second trimester of pregnancy, the fetus is brought feet first through the birth canal and aborted by inserting a suction tube into the skull—which remains in the womb—and removing the contents. Abortion rights activists claim that the procedure is among the safest ways to perform an abortion in the second trimester. Opponents argue that it ends the life of a child that might be able to live outside the womb. The Supreme Court invalidated the Nebraska law, thereby upholding the basic premise of *Roe v. Wade*—the right to choose.[64] The Court's ruling will almost certainly affect the validity of similar laws in other states.

In another decision in the same year, the Court upheld a Colorado law requiring demonstrators to stay at least eight feet away from people entering and leaving clinics unless people consented to be approached. The Court concluded that the law's restrictions on speech-related conduct did not violate the free speech rights of abortion protesters.[65]

To find out more about this subject, use the term "abortion" in the Subject guide.

Privacy Rights and the "Right to Die"

The 1976 case involving Karen Ann Quinlan was one of the first publicized right-to-die cases.[66] The parents of Quinlan, a young woman who had been in a coma for nearly a year and who had been kept alive during that time by a respirator, wanted her respirator removed. In 1976, the New Jersey Supreme Court ruled that the right to privacy includes the right of a patient to refuse treatment and that patients unable to speak can exercise that right through a family member or guardian. In 1990, the Supreme Court took up the issue. In *Cruzan v. Director, Missouri Department of Health*,[67] the Court stated that a patient's life-sustaining treatment can be withdrawn at the request of a family member only if there is "clear and convincing evidence" that the patient did *not* want such treatment.

Since the 1976 *Quinlan* decision, most states have enacted laws permitting people to designate their wishes concerning life-sustaining procedures in "living wills" or durable health-care powers of attorney. These laws and the Supreme Court's *Cruzan* decision largely have resolved this aspect of the right-to-die controversy.

In the 1990s, however, another issue surfaced: Do privacy rights include the right of terminally ill people to end their lives through physician-assisted suicide? Until 1996, the courts consistently upheld state laws that prohibited this practice, either through specific statutes or under their general homicide statutes. In 1996, after two

[62] *National Organization of Women v. Joseph Scheidler*, 509 U.S. 951 (1993).
[63] *Schenck v. ProChoice Network*, 519 U.S. 357 (1997).
[64] *Stenberg v. Carhart*, 530 U.S. 914 (2000).
[65] *Hill v. Colorado*, 530 U.S. 703 (2000).
[66] *In re Quinlan*, 70 N.J. 10 (1976).
[67] 497 U.S. 261 (1990).

federal appellate courts ruled that state laws banning assisted suicide (in Washington and New York) were unconstitutional, the issue reached the Supreme Court. In 1997, in *Washington v. Glucksberg,*[68] the Court stated, clearly and categorically, that the liberty interest protected by the Constitution does not include a right to commit suicide, with or without assistance. To hold otherwise, said the Court, would be "to reverse centuries of legal doctrine and practice, and strike down the considered policy choice of almost every state."

In effect, the Supreme Court left the decision in the hands of the states. Since then, assisted suicide has been allowed in only one state—Oregon. Even in that state, however, it is uncertain whether physicians will be able to prescribe lethal drugs for terminal patients. As discussed in Chapter 3, this is a point of controversy between the federal government (which controls prescription drugs) and the state government.

Privacy Rights versus Security Issues

As former Supreme Court Justice Thurgood Marshall once said, "Grave threats to liberty often come in times of urgency, when constitutional rights seem too extravagant to endure." Certainly, being attacked by terrorists and living under the threat of future terrorist actions have created a "time of urgency." Not surprisingly, anti-terrorist legislation since the attacks on September 11, 2001, has eroded certain basic rights, in particular the Fourth Amendment protections against unreasonable searches and seizures. Current legislation allows the government to conduct "roving" wiretaps. Previously, only specific telephone numbers, cellphone numbers, or computer terminals could be tapped.

Now a specific person under suspicion can be monitored electronically no matter what form of electronic communication he or she uses. Such roving wiretaps go against the Supreme Court's interpretation of the Fourth Amendment, which requires a judicial warrant to describe the *place* to be searched, not just the person. One of the goals of the framers was to avoid *general* searches. Further, once a judge approves an application for a roving wiretap, when, how, and where the monitoring occurs will be left to the FBI's discretion. As an unavoidable result, a third party will have access to the conversations and e-mails of hundreds of people, who falsely believe them to be private.

The United States is not the only country that faces the question of how to balance civil liberties and security issues. For a discussion of how some other nations have dealt with this challenge, see this chapter's *Global View* on page 132.

The Great Balancing Act: The Rights of the Accused versus the Rights of Society

The United States has one of the highest violent crime rates in the world. It is not surprising, therefore, that many citizens have extremely strong opinions about the rights of those accused of criminal offenses. When an accused person, especially one who has confessed to some criminal act, is set free because of an apparent legal "technicality," many people may feel that the rights of the accused are being given more weight than the rights of society and of potential or actual victims. Why, then, give criminal suspects rights? The answer is partly to avoid convicting innocent people, but mostly because all criminal suspects have the right to due process of law and fair treatment.

The courts and the police must constantly engage in a balancing act of competing rights. At the basis of all discussions about the appropriate balance is, of course, the U.S.

[68] 521 U.S. 702 (1997).

How Other Countries Deal with the Threat of Terrorism

Americans are just waking up to what it means to live with the threat of terrorism, but other countries have been living with this threat for many years.

Britain Reacts

Great Britain has faced troubles in Northern Ireland for more than three decades. The British Terrorism Act was aimed at giving police the power to track down and neutralize terrorists in Northern Ireland. After 9/11, nonetheless, the British government passed the Anti-Terrorism, Crime, and Security Act giving the police more powers to investigate, arrest, and detain terrorist suspects.

The act also created new offenses. It permits the British judicial system to deal with terrorist acts and their planning no matter where in the world they are carried out. The act also allows foreign nationals suspected of terrorism to be detained indefinitely without charge or trial, simply based on a certificate signed by the home secretary (a position similar to that of the attorney general of the United States). In other words, there is no presumption of innocence in cases dealing with foreign suspects, who can be held for six months in a high-security jail. A special immigration commission investigates their cases. There is no right to appeal to the normal courts.

Germany Reacts, Too

Because of its Nazi past and its struggle with left-wing terrorism in the 1970s, Germany is quite tough on political extremists. Germans have to carry identity cards (the subject of this chapter's opening *What If . . .*). The government is nonetheless tolerant toward most groups that have a religious basis, even Islamic fundamentalists.

Fewer Individual Rights in France and Japan

The further south you go in Europe, the fewer civil liberties you have. In France, for example, if you do not have an appropriate identity card when checked on the street by a police officer, you can end up in the local police station, especially if you appear to be foreign. Any criminal investigation, especially one involving suspected terrorists, can include numerous phone taps, and police can put suspects behind bars without a charge for up to four years.

Japan suffered domestic terrorism in a nerve-gas attack by a religious sect in 1995. As a result, and especially after 9/11, Japanese police currently have wide powers for arrest and interrogation. Every Japanese resident has to register his or her address with the local authorities. The government has much more expansive powers to seize assets of suspected terrorists and criminals than do police in America.

FOR CRITICAL ANALYSIS

Britain has a strong tradition of civil liberties. Do you think that the British laws to curb terrorism infringe too strongly on those liberties?

Bill of Rights. The Fourth, Fifth, Sixth, and Eighth Amendments deal specifically with the rights of criminal defendants. (You will learn about some of your rights under the Fourth Amendment in the *Making a Difference* feature at the end of this chapter.)

Rights of the Accused

The basic rights of criminal defendants are outlined below. When appropriate, the specific constitutional provision or amendment on which a right is based also is given.

Limits on the Conduct of Police Officers and Prosecutors
- No unreasonable or unwarranted searches and seizures (Amend. IV).
- No arrest except on probable cause (Amend. IV).
- No coerced confessions or illegal interrogation (Amend. V).
- No entrapment.
- Upon questioning, a suspect must be informed of her or his rights.

Defendant's Pretrial Rights
- Writ of *habeas corpus* (Article I, Section 9).
- Prompt arraignment (Amend. VI).
- Legal counsel (Amend. VI).
- Reasonable bail (Amend. VIII).
- To be informed of charges (Amend. VI).
- To remain silent (Amend. V).

Writ of *Habeas Corpus*
Habeas corpus means, literally, "you have the body." A writ of *habeas corpus* is an order that requires jailers to bring a person before a court or judge and explain why the person is being held in prison.

Trial Rights

- Speedy and public trial before a jury (Amend. VI).
- Impartial jury selected from a cross section of the community (Amend. VI).
- Trial atmosphere free of prejudice, fear, and outside interference.
- No compulsory self-incrimination (Amend. V).
- Adequate counsel (Amend. VI).
- No cruel and unusual punishment (Amend. VIII).
- Appeal of convictions.
- No double jeopardy (Amend. V).

Some worry that the Bush administration's plan to prosecute suspected terrorists in military tribunals instead of regular criminal courts represents a threat to the constitutional rights of accused persons. For a discussion of this issue, see this chapter's *America's Security* feature on the next page.

Extending the Rights of the Accused

During the 1960s, the Supreme Court, under Chief Justice Earl Warren, significantly expanded the rights of accused persons. In a case decided in 1963, *Gideon v. Wainwright*,[69] the Court held that if a person is accused of a felony and cannot afford an attorney, an attorney must be made available to the accused person at the government's expense. Although the Sixth Amendment to the Constitution provides for the right to counsel, the Supreme Court had established a precedent twenty-one years earlier in *Betts v. Brady*,[70] when it held that only criminal defendants in capital cases automatically had a right to legal counsel.

Miranda v. Arizona. In 1966, the Court issued its decision in *Miranda v. Arizona*.[71] The case involved Ernesto Miranda, who was arrested and charged with the kidnapping and rape of a young woman. After two hours of questioning, Miranda confessed

---

[69] 372 U.S. 335 (1963).
[70] 316 U.S. 455 (1942).
[71] 384 U.S. 436 (1966).

This man is being read his *Miranda* rights by the arresting officer. These rights, which concern minimum procedural safeguards, were established in the 1966 case *Miranda v. Arizona*. Also known as the *Miranda* warnings, they require that arrested persons be informed prior to questioning (1) that they have the right to remain silent, (2) that anything they say may be used as evidence against them, and (3) that they have the right to the presence of an attorney. (Elana Rooraid, PhotoEdit)

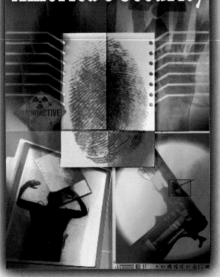

America's Security

Military Tribunals for Suspected Terrorists

About two months after 9/11, Attorney General John Ashcroft and Vice President Dick Cheney announced that suspected terrorists would be prosecuted in American military tribunals. There was an immediate outcry against this violation of constitutional safeguards. Nonetheless, President George W. Bush called military trials "absolutely the right thing to do."

THE USE OF MILITARY TRIBUNALS IN AMERICA'S PAST

During times of crisis, particularly war, the United States has routinely used military tribunals. In one such tribunal during the Revolutionary War, the British secret agent John Andre was convicted of collaborating with traitor Benedict Arnold and was hanged.

During the Civil War, the Union Army conducted over four thousand trials by military tribunals. Many male residents of a coal-producing region in northeastern Pennsylvania were convicted of

draft resistance by a military tribunal and were sent to a prisoner-of-war camp. In the last days of the Civil War, several nonmilitary personnel were hanged after being convicted by military tribunals of spying for the South.

In 1942, during World War II, German agents who had traveled by submarine to Florida, Long Island, and New York were convicted and sentenced to death by military tribunals.

REDUCED RIGHTS OF THE ACCUSED

In November 2001, President Bush promulgated an executive order setting up military tribunals for noncitizens. Under that order, the administration had the complete freedom to set the terms of the prosecution. The defendant was to have far fewer rights than any military defendant facing a court-martial.

In March 2002, in response to significant public criticism of the proposed tribunals, the Pentagon made public a revised set of rules that allow suspected terrorists to have the presumption of innocence; the right to choose counsel and to see evidence; a trial in public; and the right to remain silent. The prosecution in military tribunals must prove that the defendant is guilty beyond a reasonable doubt. The military judges can convict a defendant by a two-thirds majority vote unless there is a decision to impose the death penalty. For the death penalty to be imposed, the judges' decision must be unanimous.

Defendants in such trials, however, do not have the right to a jury trial. Additionally, hearsay can be accepted as evidence. Finally, there can be no

civilian review of the judge's decision. The only right to appeal is to a panel of other military judges. This can hardly be called an independent review.

THE REASONING BEHIND MILITARY TRIBUNALS

The Bush administration argued that, in view of these "extraordinary times," secret military tribunals were necessary to safeguard evidence that could be used to prevent future terrorist attacks on Americans and their country. The administration further argued that members of juries in the normal courtroom setting would feel threatened if they sentenced a terrorist to prison or death. Moreover, the government does not want to give terrorist leaders and supporters a forum for expressing their anti-American views.

Consider also that in a normal criminal trial, much evidence can be thrown out based on the exclusionary rule—which is used to keep evidence that is gathered illegally from being admitted in court. By this standard, a nuclear suitcase bomb device found in a defendant's house could be excluded as evidence if police obtained it without a search warrant. The administration does not think that people bent on destroying this country should have such constitutional rights.

FOR CRITICAL ANALYSIS

Under what circumstances would you argue that foreign terrorist suspects should have the same constitutional rights that criminal suspects have in our normal criminal justice system?

and was later convicted. Miranda's lawyer appealed his conviction, arguing that the police had never informed Miranda that he had a right to remain silent and a right to be represented by counsel. The Court, in ruling in Miranda's favor, enunciated the *Miranda* rights that are now familiar to virtually all Americans:

> Prior to any questioning, the person must be warned that he has a right to remain silent, that any statement he does make may be used against him, and that he has a right to the presence of an attorney, either retained or appointed.

Two years after the Supreme Court's *Miranda* decision, Congress passed the Omnibus Crime Control and Safe Streets Act of 1968. Section 3501 of the act reinstated a rule that had been in effect for 180 years before *Miranda*—namely, that statements by defendants can be used against them as long as the statements were voluntarily made. The Justice Department immediately disavowed Section 3501 as unconstitutional and has continued to hold this position. As a result, Section 3501, although it was never repealed, has never been enforced. In 2000, after a federal appellate court stunned the nation by holding that the all-but-forgotten provision was enforceable, the Supreme Court held that the *Miranda* warnings were constitutionally based and could not be overruled by a legislative act.[72]

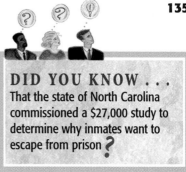

Exceptions to the *Miranda* Rule. As part of a continuing attempt to balance the rights of accused persons against the rights of society, the Supreme Court has made a number of exceptions to the *Miranda* rule. In 1984, for example, the Court recognized a "public safety" exception to the rule. The need to protect the public warranted the admissibility of statements made by the defendant (in this case, indicating where he placed the gun) as evidence in a trial, even though the defendant had not been informed of his *Miranda* rights.[73]

In 1985, the Court further held that a confession need not be excluded even though the police failed to inform a suspect in custody that his attorney had tried to reach him by telephone.[74] In an important 1991 decision, the Court stated that a suspect's conviction will not be automatically overturned if the suspect was coerced into making a confession. If the other evidence admitted at trial is strong enough to justify the conviction, then the fact that the confession was obtained illegally can be, in effect, ignored.[75] In yet another case, in 1994, the Supreme Court ruled that a suspect must unequivocally and assertively state his or her right to counsel in order to stop police questioning. Saying, "Maybe I should talk to a lawyer" during an interrogation after being taken into custody is not enough.

---

[72] *Dickerson v. United States,* 530 U.S. 428 (2000).

[73] *New York v. Quarles,* 467 U.S. 649 (1984).

[74] *Moran v. Burbine,* 475 U.S. 412 (1985).

[75] *Arizona v. Fulminante,* 499 U.S. 279 (1991).

More and more state and local governments have adopted so-called Megan's laws, laws that inform citizens when criminal sexual offenders move into their neighborhood. Do such laws violate the rights of individuals who have "paid their debt to society," or do they rightfully forewarn a community of potential danger? (A. Ramey, PhotoEdit)

The Court held that police officers are not required to decipher the suspect's intentions in such situations.[76]

Videotaped Interrogations.   In view of the numerous exceptions, there are no guarantees that the *Miranda* rule will survive indefinitely. Increasingly, though, law enforcement personnel are using digital cameras to record interrogations. According to some scholars, the taping of *all* custodial interrogations would satisfy the Fifth Amendment's prohibition against coercion and in the process render the *Miranda* warnings unnecessary.

The Exclusionary Rule

Exclusionary Rule
A policy forbidding the admission at trial of illegally seized evidence.

At least since 1914, judicial policy has prohibited the admission of illegally seized evidence at trials in federal courts. This is the so-called **exclusionary rule.** Improperly obtained evidence, no matter how telling, cannot be used by prosecutors. This includes evidence obtained by police in violation of a suspect's *Miranda* rights or of the Fourth Amendment. The Fourth Amendment protects against unreasonable searches and seizures and provides that a judge may issue a search warrant to a police officer only on probable cause (a demonstration of facts that permit a reasonable belief that a crime has been committed). The question that must be determined by the courts is what constitutes an "unreasonable" search and seizure.

The reasoning behind the exclusionary rule is that it forces police officers to gather evidence properly, in which case their due diligence will be rewarded by a conviction. The exclusionary rule has always had critics who argue that it permits guilty persons to be freed because of innocent errors.

This rule was first extended to state court proceedings in a 1961 Supreme Court decision, *Mapp v. Ohio.*[77] In this case, the Court overturned the conviction of Dollree Mapp for the possession of obscene materials. Police found pornographic books in her apartment after searching it without a search warrant and despite her refusal to let them in.

Over the last several decades, however, the Supreme Court has diminished the scope of the exclusionary rule by creating some exceptions to its applicability. For example, in 1984 the Supreme Court held that illegally obtained evidence could be admitted at trial if law enforcement personnel could prove that they would have obtained the evidence legally anyway.[78] In another case decided in the same year, the Court held that a police officer who used a technically incorrect search warrant form to obtain evidence had acted in good faith and therefore the evidence was admissible at trial. The Court thus created the "good faith" exception to the exclusionary rule.[79]

The Death Penalty

Capital punishment remains one of the most debated aspects of our criminal justice system. Those in favor of the death penalty maintain that it serves as a deterrent to serious crime and satisfies society's need for justice and fair play. Those opposed to the death penalty do not believe it has any deterrent value and hold that it constitutes a barbaric act in an otherwise civilized society.

Cruel and Unusual Punishment?   The Eighth Amendment prohibits cruel and unusual punishment. Throughout history, "cruel and unusual" referred to punishments

---

[76] *Davis v. United States,* 512 U.S. 452 (1994).
[77] 367 U.S. 643 (1961).
[78] *Nix v. Williams,* 467 U.S. 431 (1984).
[79] *Massachusetts v. Sheppard,* 468 U.S. 981 (1984).

that were more serious than the crimes—the phrase referred to torture and to executions that prolonged the agony of dying. The Supreme Court never interpreted "cruel and unusual" to prohibit all forms of capital punishment in all circumstances. Indeed, a number of states had imposed the death penalty for a variety of crimes and allowed juries to decide when the condemned could be sentenced to death. Many believed, however, and in 1972 the Supreme Court agreed, in *Furman v. Georgia*,[80] that the imposition of the death penalty was random and arbitrary.

The Supreme Court's 1972 decision stated that the death penalty, as then applied, violated the Eighth and Fourteenth Amendments. The Court ruled that capital punishment is not necessarily cruel and unusual if the criminal has killed or attempted to kill someone. In its opinion, the Court invited the states to enact more precise laws so that the death penalty would be applied more consistently. By 1976, twenty-five states had adopted a two-stage, or *bifurcated,* procedure for capital cases. In the first stage, a jury determines the guilt or innocence of the defendant for a crime that has been determined by statute to be punishable by death. If the defendant is found guilty, the jury reconvenes in the second stage and considers all relevant evidence to decide whether the death sentence is, in fact, warranted.

In *Gregg v. Georgia*,[81] the Supreme Court ruled in favor of Georgia's bifurcated process, holding that the state's legislative guidelines had removed the ability of a jury to "wantonly and freakishly impose the death penalty." The Court upheld similar procedures in Texas and Florida, establishing a "road map" for all states to follow that would assure them protection from lawsuits based on Eighth Amendment grounds. On January 17, 1977, Gary Mark Gilmore became the first American to be executed (by Utah) under the new laws.

The Death Penalty Today. Today, thirty-eight states (see Figure 4–1) and the federal government have capital punishment laws based on the guidelines established by the *Gregg* case. Between 1977 and 2001, there were 749 executions. (Note that state governments are responsible for almost all executions in this country. The executions of Timothy McVeigh and Juan Raul Garza in 2001 marked the first death sentences carried out by the federal government since 1963.) Currently, there are about 3,700 prisoners on death row across the nation.

[80] 408 U.S. 238 (1972).
[81] 428 U.S. 153 (1976).

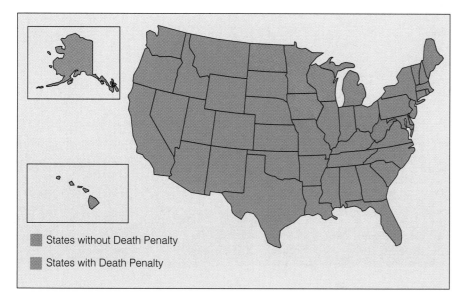

States without Death Penalty

States with Death Penalty

FIGURE 4–1

States That Allow the Death Penalty

Today, as shown in this figure, thirty-eight states have laws permitting capital punishment. Lethal injection is the sole method of execution in twenty of these states. In sixteen states, the laws provide for either lethal injection or some other method (including gas, firing squad, or—in one state—hanging), depending on the prisoner's wishes or other circumstances. In two states (Alabama and Nebraska), electrocution is the sole method of execution.

DID YOU KNOW . . .
That at one time, New York had a law that imposed the death penalty on anyone who jumped off a building ?

The number of executions per year reached a high in 1998 at ninety-eight and then began to fall. In 2001, sixty-six death-row inmates were executed. Some believe that the declining number of executions reflects the waning support among Americans for the imposition of the death penalty. In 1994, polls indicated that 80 percent of Americans supported the death penalty. Recent polls, however, suggest that this number has dropped to between 50 and 60 percent, depending on the poll.

The number of executions may decline even further due to the Supreme Court's 2002 ruling in *Ring v. Arizona*.[82] The Court held that only juries, not judges, could impose the death penalty, thus invalidating the laws of five states that allow judges to make this decision. The ruling means that the death sentences of 168 death-row inmates will have to be reconsidered by the relevant courts. The sentences of many of these inmates will likely be commuted to life in prison.

Time Limits for Death-Row Appeals.   In 1996, Congress passed the Anti-Terrorism and Effective Death Penalty Act. The law sharply limited federal court access for all defendants convicted in state courts. It also imposed a severe time limit on death-row appeals. The law required federal judges to hear these appeals and issue their opinions within a specified time period. Many are concerned that the shortened appeals process increases the possibility that innocent persons may be put to death. Since 1973, ninety-eight prisoners have been freed from death row after new evidence suggested that they were wrongfully convicted. On average, it takes about seven years to exonerate someone on death row. In recent years, however, the time between conviction and execution has been shortened from an average of ten to twelve years to an average of six to eight years.

---

[82] 122 S.Ct. 2428 (2002).

People gather outside a Virginia penitentiary to keep vigil. They are protesting against the execution of a convict. (William Campbell/Corbis Sygma)

Civil Liberties:
Why Are They Important Today?

In the past, every time there was a crisis, civil liberties were jeopardized because of fears of disloyalties among the populace. During World War II, we removed more than 110,000 Americans of Japanese descent from their homes on the West Coast and sent them to special "internment camps" because we were afraid that they would not remain loyal to the United States. The fear was that they would be potential spies for Japan, our enemy. In the 1950s, when we worried that the Soviet Union's Communist doctrine would spread to our shores, the "Red scare" ensued.[83] Various "witch hunts" attempted to expose Communists and their sympathizers within the American movie industry, educational sector, and elsewhere.

Today, we are in another time of crisis, and our civil liberties are indeed being threatened, as we have pointed out throughout this chapter. You may think that you could never be affected by a reduction in this nation's civil liberties, but consider this: You could mistakenly be identified as a member or a supporter of a subversive group. Your privacy rights might be violated on a continuing basis through a general wiretap on all of your land-based, cell-based, and e-mail communications. If you are in the United States on a visa, even if you have permanent residency, you could be picked up and held, sometimes without the possibility of communicating with others, if you are suspected of having something to do with terrorism.

On a broader basis, most Americans take their civil liberties—as generally outlined in the Bill of Rights—for granted. Americans traveling to other countries often are surprised by the visible presence of armed military in the streets and the stringent security measures taken in public places such as airports. (Of course, such measures have become increasingly common in the United States as well since the terrorist attacks of September 11, 2001.) Citizens in other countries often have to be careful of what they say and to whom they say it, because there may be serious repercussions for openly criticizing their government or for being too friendly with foreign visitors, such as Americans. When you go abroad, you need to be careful too, about being active politically. You can be jailed, or worse, in other countries for allegedly or actually engaging in antigovernment activities. An example is Lori Berenson, an American traveler in Peru who in 1995 was sentenced to jail until 2016 for allegedly supporting terrorist acts against the Peruvian government. The same thing, of course, can happen to foreign visitors in the United States. After September 11, over 1,100 foreign nationals were detained.

---

[83] Communists were called "Reds" after the Russian Revolution in 1917 because of their choice of red as the color for the Soviet Union's flag and because the revolutionary army was called the "Red Army."

MAKING A DIFFERENCE | Your Civil Liberties: Searches and Seizures

What happens if you are stopped by members of the police force? Your civil liberties protect you from having to provide information other than your name and address. Indeed, you are not really required to produce identification, although it is a good idea to show this to the officers. Normally, even if you have not been placed under arrest, the officers have the right to frisk you for weapons, and you must let them proceed. The officers cannot, however, check your person or your clothing further if, in their judgment, no weapon-like object is produced.

Searches of Your Person

The officers may search you only if they have a search warrant or probable cause that they will likely find incriminating evidence if the search is conducted. If the officers do not have probable cause or a warrant, physically resisting their attempt to search you normally is unwise; it is usually best simply to refuse orally to give permission for the search, preferably in the presence of a witness. Also, it is usually advisable to tell the officer as little as possible about yourself and the situation that is under investigation. Being polite and courteous, though firm, is better than acting out of anger or frustration and making the officers irritable. If you are arrested, it is best to keep quiet until you can speak with a lawyer.

Searches of Your Car

If you are in your car and are stopped by the police, the same fundamental rules apply. Always be ready to show your driver's license and car registration quickly. You may be asked to get out of the car. The officers may use a flashlight to peer inside if it is too dark to see otherwise. None of this constitutes a search. A true search requires either a warrant or probable cause. No officer has the legal right to search your car simply to find out if you may have committed a crime. Police officers can conduct searches that are incident to lawful arrests, however.

Searches of Your Home

If you are in your residence and a police officer with a search warrant appears, you should examine the warrant before granting entry. A warrant that is correctly made out will state the exact place or persons to be searched, a description of the object sought, and the date of the warrant (which should be no more than ten days old), and it will bear the signature of a judge or magistrate. If the search warrant is in order, you should not make any statement. If you believe the warrant to be invalid, you should make it clear orally that you have not consented to the search, preferably in the presence of a witness. If the warrant later is proved

to be invalid, normally any evidence obtained will be considered illegal.

Officers who attempt to enter your home without a search warrant can do so only if they are pursuing a suspected felon into the house. Rarely is it advisable to give permission for a warrantless search. You, as the resident, must be the one to give permission if any evidence obtained is to be considered legal. The landlord, manager, or head of a college dormitory cannot give legal permission. A roommate, however, can give permission for a search of his or her room, which may allow the police to search areas where you have personal belongings.

If you find yourself a guest in a location that is being legally searched, you may be legally searched also. But unless you have been placed under arrest, you cannot be compelled to go to the police station or into a squad car.

If you would like to find out more about your rights and obligations under the laws of searches and seizures, you might wish to contact the following organization:

The American Civil Liberties Union
125 Broad St., 18th Floor
New York, NY 10004
212-549-2500
http://www.aclu.org

Key Terms

Chapter Summary

1 To deal with Americans' fears of a too-powerful national government, after the adoption of the U.S. Constitution, Congress proposed a Bill of Rights. These ten amendments to the Constitution were ratified by the states by the end of 1791. The amendments set forth civil liberties—that is, they are limitations on the government.

2 Originally, the Bill of Rights limited only the power of the national government, not that of the states. Gradually, however, the Supreme Court accepted the selective incorporation theory under which no state can violate most provisions of the Bill of Rights.

3 The First Amendment protects against government interference with the freedom of religion by requiring a separation of church and state (under the establishment clause) and by guaranteeing the free exercise of religion. Controversial issues relating to the establishment clause include aid to church-related schools, school prayer, the teaching of evolution versus creationism, school vouchers, the posting of the Ten Commandments in public places, and discrimination against religious speech. The government can interfere with the free exercise of religion only when religious practices work against public policy or the public welfare.

4 The First Amendment protects against government interference with the freedom of speech, which includes symbolic speech (expressive conduct). Restrictions are permitted when expression presents a clear and present danger to the peace or public order, or when expression has a bad tendency (that is, when it might lead to some "evil"). Expression may be restrained before it occurs, but such prior restraint has a "heavy presumption" against its constitutionality. Commercial speech (advertising) by businesses has received limited First Amendment protection. Speech that has not received First Amendment protection includes expression judged to be obscene, although online obscenity and pornography have posed serious challenges for lawmakers and the courts. Other unprotected speech includes utterances considered to be slanderous and speech constituting fighting words or a hecklers' veto.

5 The First Amendment protects against government interference with the freedom of the press, which can be regarded as a special instance of freedom of speech. Speech by the press that does not receive protection includes libelous statements made with actual malice. Publication of news about a criminal trial may be restricted by a gag order in some circumstances.

6 The First Amendment protects the right to assemble peaceably and to petition the government. Permits may be required for parades, sound trucks, and demonstrations to maintain the public order, and a permit may be denied to protect the public safety.

7 Under the Ninth Amendment, rights not specifically mentioned in the Constitution are not denied to the people. Among these unspecified rights is a right to privacy, which has been implied through the First, Third, Fourth, Fifth, and Ninth Amendments. A major privacy issue today is how best to protect privacy rights in cyberspace. Questions concerning whether an individual's privacy rights include a right to have an abortion or a "right to die" also continue to elicit controversy. Another major challenge today concerns the extent to which Americans may forfeit privacy rights to control terrorism.

8 The Constitution includes protections for the rights of persons accused of crimes. Under the Fourth Amendment, no one may be subject to an unreasonable search or seizure or arrested except on probable cause. Under the Fifth Amendment, an accused person has the right to remain silent. Under the Sixth Amendment, an accused person must be informed of the reason for his or her arrest. The accused also has the right to adequate counsel, even if he or she cannot afford an attorney, and the right to a prompt arraignment and a speedy and public trial before an impartial jury selected from a cross section of the community.

9 In *Miranda v. Arizona* (1966), the Supreme Court held that criminal suspects, prior to interrogation by law enforcement personnel, must be informed of certain constitutional rights, including the right to remain silent and the right to counsel.

10 The exclusionary rule forbids the admission in court of illegally seized evidence. There is a "good faith exception" to the exclusionary rule: illegally seized evidence need not be thrown out owing to, for example, a technical defect in a search warrant. Under the Eighth Amendment, cruel and unusual punishment is prohibited. Whether the death penalty is cruel and unusual punishment continues to be debated.

Selected Print and Media Resources

SUGGESTED READINGS

Bradbury, Ray. *Fahrenheit 451.* New York: Ballantine Books, 1995. This haunting novel, first published in 1951, takes us into a world where the trivial is exalted and books are burned (the title refers to the temperature at which paper burns). It depicts a society in which all freedom of thought and expression has been lost, and censorship reigns.

Epps, Garrett. *To an Unknown God: Religious Freedom on Trial.* New York: St. Martin's Press, 2001. The author chronicles the journey through the courts of *Oregon v. Smith,* a case decided by the Supreme Court in 1990. The author regards this case as one of the Supreme Court's most momentous decisions concerning religious freedom in the last fifty years.

Etzioni, Amitai. *The Limits of Privacy*. New York: Basic Books, 1999. The author acknowledges that no society can long remain free without privacy, yet he believes that American communities have other goals that outweigh privacy concerns. His underlying theme is that society must balance individual rights against the common good, and this may require sacrificing some privacy rights.

Gottlieb, Roger S. *Joining Hands: Politics and Religion Together for Social Change*. Boulder, Colo.: Westview Press, 2002. In this exploration of the political role of religion and the spiritual component of politics, the author argues that religious belief and spiritual practice are integral to the politics of social change in the United States.

Heffernan, William C., and John Kleinig, eds. *From Social Justice to Criminal Justice*. New York: Oxford University Press, 2000. In the United States, economically deprived persons come into contact with the criminal justice system in disproportionate numbers. The essays in this collection explore some of the more troubling moral and ethical questions stemming from this situation.

Lewis, Anthony. *Gideon's Trumpet*. New York: Vintage, 1964. This classic work discusses the background and facts of *Gideon v.*

Wainwright, the 1963 Supreme Court case in which the Court held that the state must make an attorney available for any person accused of a felony who cannot afford a lawyer.

MEDIA RESOURCES

The Chamber—A movie, based on John Grisham's novel by the same name, about a young lawyer who defends a man (his grandfather) who has been sentenced to death and faces imminent execution.

Execution at Midnight—A video presenting the arguments and evidence on both sides of the controversial death-penalty issue.

May It Please the Court: The First Amendment—A set of audiocassette recordings and written transcripts of the oral arguments made before the Supreme Court in sixteen key First Amendment cases. Participants in the recording include nationally known attorneys and several Supreme Court justices.

The People versus Larry Flynt—An R-rated 1996 film that clearly articulates the conflict between freedom of the press and how a community defines pornography.

Your CD-ROM Resources

In addition to the chapter content containing hot links, the following resources are available on the CD-ROM:

- **Internet Activities**—Flag burning, libel and slander.
- **Critical Thinking Exercises**—*Zelman v. Simmons-Harris, Roe v. Wade*
- **Self-Check on Important Themes**—Can You Answer These?
- **Video**—*Abortion.*
- **Public Opinion Data**—Do Americans want national ID cards?
- **InfoTrac Exercise**—"Defending the Faiths."
- **Simulation**—You Are There!

- **Participation Exercise**—Express your views on a current issue.
- **MicroCase Exercise**—"By the Numbers: Civil Liberties in Other Nations."
- **Additional Resources:**
  1. All court cases
  2. John Locke, *On Liberty*
  3. Thomas Jefferson, *Virginia Statute of Religious Liberty*
  4. Sedition Act of 1798 and Espionage Act of 1918

e-mocracy

Understanding Your Civil Liberties

Today, the online world offers opportunities for Americans to easily access information concerning the nature of their civil liberties, how they originated, and how they may be threatened by various government actions. Several of the Web sites in the *Logging On* section of Chapter 2 present documents that set forth and explain the civil liberties guaranteed by the Constitution. In the *Logging On* section that follows, we list other Web sites that include resources from which you may gain insights into the nature of these liberties.

Logging On

At Project Vote Smart's Web site, you can find discussions of major issues, including those involving civil liberties, abortion, and crime. Go to

http://www.vote-smart.org/issues

The American Civil Liberties Union (ACLU), the nation's leading civil liberties organization, provides an extensive array of information and links concerning civil rights issues at

http://www.aclu.org

The Liberty Counsel describes itself as "a nonprofit religious civil liberties education and legal defense organization

established to preserve religious freedom." The URL for its Web site is

http://www.lc.org

Summaries and the full text of Supreme Court constitutional law decisions, plus a virtual tour of the Supreme Court, are available at

http://oyez.nwu.edu

If you want to read historic Supreme Court decisions, you can find them, listed by name, at

http://supct.law.cornell.edu/supct

The Center for Democracy and Technology (CDT) focuses on how developments in communications technology are affecting the constitutional liberties of Americans. You can access the CDT's site at

http://www.cdt.org

For a report by the American Library Association's Intellectual Freedom Committee concerning the use of filtering software and other issues relating to free speech on the Internet, go to

http://www.ala.org/alaorg/oif/
ifc2002ac.html

You can find current information on privacy issues relating to the Internet at the Electronic Privacy Information Center's Web site. Go to

http://www.epic.org/privacy

For the history of flag protection and the First Amendment, as well as the status of the proposed flag amendment in Congress, go to

http://www.freedomforum.org/packages/
first/Flag/timeline.htm

Using the Internet for Political Analysis

As you read in this chapter, governments, including the federal, state, and local governments, are restrained from interfering with cetain individual freedoms. The Bill of Rights contained in the U.S. Constitution and the bills of rights contained in the various state constitutions all protect the individual from certain government actions. Nonetheless, governments frequently take action against individual liberties. Various groups monitor these government infringements on civil liberties. One of the most well-known groups is the American Civil Liberties Union (ACLU).

Point your browser to the URL for the ACLU:

http://www.aclu.org

On the home page, you will find a list of features and issues related to civil liberties. Click on one of the feature articles and read about the issue it raises and the ACLU's stand on it. Do you think this is an important civil liberty to defend? Do you agree with the ACLU's position on the issue? Click on links to other issues on the site that interest you. Is there anything concerning the issue that surprises you, or have you learned about a government law or action that you had never heard about before?

WHAT IF...
Medical Care Was a Civil Right?

WHAT IF MEDICAL CARE WAS A CIVIL RIGHT?

The United States is the only industrialized country in the world that relies heavily on the free market for medical care. That is, the quality of the health care an American receives often depends on that person's ability—through personal wealth or an insurance plan—to pay for it. As you will read in this chapter, our civil rights are largely rooted in the Fourteenth Amendment's guarantee of equal treatment under the law for all Americans. If medical care was a civil right, the government would be obligated to make sure that all Americans, rich and poor alike, had equal access to medical care.

If medical care was a civil right, we would probably have a public health system much like our public school system. Anytime we felt we had a medical "need," we could see a physician. No money would change hands. This does not mean, however, that medical care would be "free." Taxpayers would share the burden of medical costs, just as taxpayers pay for the costs of our public school system.

THE SINGLE-PAYER SYSTEM

Most countries that consider medical care a right use the "single-payer" system, in which the single payer is the government. Under this system, after a patient visits a physician or receives treatment, the bill is sent to the government.

If we adopted a single-payer system of national medical insurance, millions of uninsured Americans would be covered. Furthermore, private health-insurance companies would go out of business, because they would be unnecessary. Indeed, health-insurance companies and health maintenance organizations (HMOs) that "manage" medical care for their customers are the target of much anger and frustration. Contrary to what one would expect, the recent rise in the ranks of the health-care uninsured has not been among the nation's poor, many of whom are covered by government programs. The fastest-growing group of uninsured persons consists of members of the middle class (those with an annual income ranging from $33,400 to $66,800).

WOULD THE QUALITY OF HEALTH CARE DECLINE?

Given the benefits of a national insurance program, why doesn't the United States adopt one? Part of the answer might be found in Canada's experience with its single-payer system. As you might imagine, when something is considered to be "free," the quantity demanded of that product or service increases. Even with tax rates much higher than those in the United States, the Canadian government finds it impossible to pay for all of the health care its citizens want. In recent years, the Canadian government has had to close hospitals and limit the amount of care that medical professionals can give. As a result, hospitals have had to turn away patients or have not given them the quality of care they require.

FOR CRITICAL ANALYSIS

1. Why do you think many physicians' associations are opposed to a single-payer health-care system?
2. Suppose that the United States had a medical system modeled on our public school system. Consumers would be able to choose between receiving public medical care or paying extra for private medical care, just as some families opt to pay more so that their children can attend private schools. Would this type of medical system be fairer than the present system? Why or why not?

The topic of this chapter's opening *What If . . .* feature—the right to receive medical care—certainly was not an issue in the early years of this nation. In spite of the words set forth in the Declaration of Independence that "all Men are created equal," the concept of equal treatment under the law was a distant dream. In fact, the majority of the population in those years had few rights. As you learned in Chapter 2, the framers of the Constitution permitted slavery to continue. Slaves thus were excluded from the political process. Women also were excluded for the most part, as were Native Americans, African Americans who were not slaves, and even white men who did not own property. Indeed, it has taken this nation more than two hundred years to approach even a semblance of equality among all Americans.

Equality is at the heart of the concept of civil rights. Generally, the term **civil rights** refers to the rights of all Americans to equal treatment under the law, as provided for by the Fourteenth Amendment to the Constitution. Although the terms *civil rights* and *civil liberties* are sometimes used interchangeably, scholars tend to make a distinction between the two. As you learned in Chapter 4, civil liberties are basically *limitations* on government; they specify what the government *cannot* do. Civil rights, in contrast, specify what the government *must* do—to ensure equal protection and freedom from discrimination.

Essentially, the history of civil rights in America is the story of the struggle of various groups to be free from discriminatory treatment. In this chapter, we look at two movements that had significant consequences for the history of civil rights in America: the civil rights movement of the 1950s and 1960s and the women's movement, which began in the mid-1800s and continues today. Each of these movements resulted in legislation that secured important basic rights for all Americans—the right to vote and the right to equal protection under the laws. In the next chapter, we explore a question with serious implications for today's voters and policymakers: What should be the government's responsibility when equal protection under the law is not enough to ensure truly equal opportunities for Americans?

Note that numerous minorities in this nation have suffered—and some continue to suffer—from discrimination. Hispanics, Native Americans, Asian Americans, Arab Americans from Middle Eastern countries, and persons from India have all had to struggle for equal treatment, as have people from various island nations and other countries. The fact that these groups are not singled out for special attention in the following pages should not be construed to mean that their struggle for equality is any less significant than the struggles of those groups that we do discuss.

Civil Rights
Generally, all rights rooted in the Fourteenth Amendment's guarantee of equal protection under the law.

This portrait is of Dred Scott (1795–1858), an American slave who was born in South Hampton County, Virginia, and who later moved with his owner to the state of Illinois, where slavery was illegal. He was the nominal plaintiff in a test case that sought to obtain his freedom on the ground that he lived in the free state of Illinois. Although the Supreme Court ruled against him, he was soon emancipated and became a hotel porter in St. Louis. (Missouri Historical Society)

African Americans and the Consequences of Slavery in the United States

Article I, Section 2, of the U.S. Constitution states that congressional representatives are to be apportioned among the states according to their respective numbers. These numbers were to be obtained by adding to the total number of free persons "three fifths of all other Persons." The "other persons" were, of course, slaves. A slave was thus equal to three-fifths of a white person. As Abraham Lincoln stated sarcastically, "All men are created equal, except Negroes." Before 1863, the Constitution thus protected slavery and made equality impossible in the sense we use the word today. African American leader Frederick Douglass pointed out that "Liberty and Slavery—opposite as Heaven and Hell—are both in the Constitution."

The constitutionality of slavery was confirmed just a few years before the outbreak of the Civil War in the famous *Dred Scott v. Sanford*[1] case of 1857. The Supreme Court held that slaves were not citizens of the United States, nor were they entitled

---

[1] 19 Howard 393 (1857).

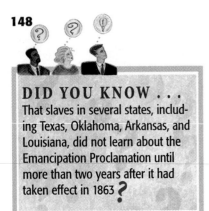

to the rights and privileges of citizenship. The Court also ruled that the Missouri Compromise, which banned slavery in the territories north of 36°30′ latitude (the southern border of Missouri), was unconstitutional. The *Dred Scott* decision had grave consequences. Most observers contend that the ruling contributed to making the Civil War inevitable.

Ending Constitutional Servitude

With the emancipation of the slaves by President Lincoln's Emancipation Proclamation in 1863 and the passage of the Thirteenth, Fourteenth, and Fifteenth Amendments during the Reconstruction period following the Civil War, constitutional inequality was ended.

The Thirteenth Amendment (1865) states that neither slavery nor involuntary servitude shall exist within the United States. The Fourteenth Amendment (1868) tells us that *all* persons born or naturalized in the United States are citizens of the United States. It states, furthermore, that "[n]o State shall make or enforce any law which shall abridge the privileges or immunities of citizens of the United States; nor shall any State deprive any person of life, liberty, or property, without due process of law; nor deny to any person within its jurisdiction the equal protection of the laws." Note the use of the terms *citizen* and *person* in this amendment. *Citizens* have political rights, such as the right to vote and run for political office. Citizens also have certain privileges or immunities (see Chapter 3). All *persons,* however, including legal *and* illegal immigrants, have a right to due process of law and equal protection under the law.

The Fifteenth Amendment (1870) seems equally impressive: "The right of citizens of the United States to vote shall not be denied or abridged by the United States or by any State on account of race, color, or previous condition of servitude." Pressure was brought to bear on Congress to include in the Fourteenth and Fifteenth Amendments a prohibition against discrimination based on sex, but with no success.

As we shall see, the words of these amendments had little immediate effect. Although slavery was legally and constitutionally ended, African American political and social inequality has continued to the present time. In the following sections, we discuss several landmarks in the struggle of African Americans to overcome this inequality.

The Civil Rights Acts of 1865 to 1875

At the end of the Civil War, President Lincoln's Republican Party controlled the national government and most state governments, and the so-called Radical Republicans, with their strong antislavery stance, controlled that party. The Radical Republicans pushed through the Thirteenth, Fourteenth, and Fifteenth Amendments to the Constitution (the "Civil War amendments"). From 1865 to 1875, they succeeded in getting Congress to pass a series of civil rights acts that were aimed at enforcing these amendments. Even Republicans who were not necessarily sympathetic to a strong antislavery position wanted to undercut Democratic domination of the South. What better way to do so than to guarantee African American suffrage?

The first Civil Rights Act in the Reconstruction period that followed the Civil War was passed in 1866 over the veto of President Andrew Johnson. That act extended citizenship to anyone born in the United States and gave African Americans full equality before the law. The act further authorized the president to enforce the law with national armed forces. Many considered the law to be unconstitutional, but such problems disappeared in 1868 with the adoption of the Fourteenth Amendment.

Among the more important of the six other civil rights acts passed in the nineteenth century was the Enforcement Act of May 31, 1870, which set out specific criminal sanctions for interfering with the right to vote as protected by the Fifteenth Amendment and by the Civil Rights Act of 1866. Equally important was the Civil

Rights Act of April 20, 1872, known as the Anti–Ku Klux Klan Act. This act made it a federal crime for anyone to use law or custom to deprive an individual of his or her rights, privileges, and immunities secured by the Constitution or by any federal law. Section 2 of that act imposed detailed penalties or damages for violation of the act.

The last of these early civil rights acts, known as the Second Civil Rights Act, was passed on March 1, 1875. It declared that everyone is entitled to full and equal enjoyment of public accommodations, theaters, and other places of public amusement, and it imposed penalties for violators. This act, however, was virtually nullified by the *Civil Rights Cases* of 1883 discussed below.

The Ineffectiveness of the Civil Rights Laws

The civil rights acts of the 1870s are of special interest because they were an indication that congressional power or authority applied both to official, or government, action and to private action. The theory behind the acts was that if a state government failed to act, Congress could act in its absence. Thus, Congress could legislate directly against private individuals who were violating the constitutional rights of other individuals when state officials failed to protect those rights. At the time, this was a novel theory. It was not implemented in practice until the 1960s.

These Reconstruction statutes, or civil rights acts, ultimately did little to secure equality for African Americans in their civil rights, however. Both the *Civil Rights Cases* and the case of *Plessy v. Ferguson* effectively nullified these acts. Additionally, various voting barriers were erected that prevented African Americans from exercising their right to vote.

The *Civil Rights* Cases. The Supreme Court invalidated the 1875 Civil Rights Act when it held, in the *Civil Rights Cases*[2] of 1883, that the enforcement clause of the Fourteenth Amendment (which states that "[n]o State shall make or enforce any law which shall abridge the privileges or immunities of citizens") was limited to correcting actions by states in their *official* acts; thus, the discriminatory acts of *private* citizens were not illegal. ("Individual invasion of individual rights is not the subject

---

[2] 109 U.S. 3 (1883).

Abraham Lincoln reads the Emancipation Proclamation on July 22, 1862. The Emancipation Proclamation did not abolish slavery (that was done by the Thirteenth Amendment, in 1865), but it ensured that slavery would be abolished if and when the North won the Civil War. After the Battle of Antietam on September 17, 1862, Lincoln publicly announced the Emancipation Proclamation and declared that all slaves residing in states that were still in rebellion against the United States on January 1, 1863, would be freed once those states came under the military control of the Union Army. (The Granger Collection)

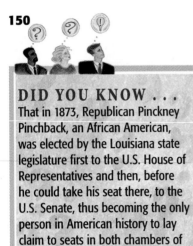

DID YOU KNOW . . .

That in 1873, Republican Pinckney Pinchback, an African American, was elected by the Louisiana state legislature first to the U.S. House of Representatives and then, before he could take his seat there, to the U.S. Senate, thus becoming the only person in American history to lay claim to seats in both chambers of Congress simultaneously?

Separate-but-Equal Doctrine
The doctrine holding that segregation in schools and public accommodations does not imply that one race is superior to another, and that separate-but-equal facilities do not violate the equal protection clause.

White Primary
A state primary election that restricts voting to whites only; outlawed by the Supreme Court in 1944.

Jim Crow laws required the segregation of the races, particularly in public facilities such as this theater. The name "Jim Crow" came from a nineteenth-century vaudeville character who was called Jim (a common name) Crow (for a black-colored bird). Thus, the name "Jim Crow" was applied to laws and practices affecting African Americans. (From the Dorothy Sterling Collection of the Amistad Research Center)

matter of the Amendment.") The 1883 Supreme Court decision met with widespread approval throughout most of the United States.

In a dissenting opinion, Justice John Marshall Harlan contended that the Thirteenth Amendment gave Congress broad powers to enact laws to ensure the rights of former slaves. According to Justice Harlan, the freedom conferred by that amendment included the freedom from all "badges of slavery."

Twenty years after the Civil War, the nation was all too willing to forget about the Civil War amendments and the civil rights legislation of the 1860s and 1870s. The other civil rights laws that the Court specifically did not invalidate became dead letters in the statute books, although they were never repealed by Congress. At the same time, many former proslavery secessionists had regained political power in the southern states. In the last decades of the nineteenth century, these racists enacted the Jim Crow laws, which will be discussed next in relation to the separate-but-equal doctrine.

Plessy v. Ferguson: **Separate but Equal.** A key decision during this period concerned Homer Plessy, a Louisiana resident who was one-eighth African American. In 1892, he boarded a train in New Orleans. The conductor made him leave the car, which was restricted to whites, and directed him to a car for nonwhites. At that time, Louisiana had a statute providing for separate railway cars for whites and African Americans.

Plessy went to court, claiming that such a statute was contrary to the Fourteenth Amendment's equal protection clause. In 1896, the United States Supreme Court rejected Plessy's contention. The Court concluded that the Fourteenth Amendment "could not have been intended to abolish distinctions based upon color, or to enforce social . . . equality." The Court indicated that segregation alone did not violate the Constitution: "Laws permitting, and even requiring, their separation in places where they are liable to be brought into contact do not necessarily imply the inferiority of either race to the other."[3] So was born the **separate-but-equal doctrine.**

The only justice to vote against this decision was John Marshall Harlan, a former slaveholder. He stated in his dissent, "Our Constitution is color-blind, and neither knows nor tolerates classes among citizens." Justice Harlan also predicted that the separate-but-equal doctrine would "in time prove to be . . . as pernicious [destructive] as the decision . . . in the Dred Scott Case."

For more than half a century, the separate-but-equal doctrine was accepted as consistent with the equal protection clause in the Fourteenth Amendment. In practical terms, the separate-but-equal doctrine effectively nullified that clause. *Plessy v. Ferguson* became the judicial cornerstone of racial discrimination throughout the United States. Even though *Plessy* upheld segregated facilities in railway cars only, it was assumed that the Supreme Court was upholding segregation everywhere as long as the separate facilities were equal. The result was a system of racial segregation, particularly in the South, that required separate drinking fountains; separate seats in theaters, restaurants, and hotels; separate public toilets; and separate waiting rooms for the two races—collectively known as Jim Crow laws. "Separate" was indeed the rule, but "equal" was never enforced, nor was it a reality.

Voting Barriers. The brief enfranchisement of African Americans ended after 1877, when the federal troops that occupied the South during the Reconstruction era were withdrawn. Southern politicians regained control of state governments and, using everything except race as a formal criterion, passed laws that effectively deprived African Americans of the right to vote. By using the ruse that political party primaries were private, southern whites were allowed to exclude African Americans. The **white primary** was upheld by the Supreme Court until 1944 when, in *Smith v. Allwright,*[4] the Court found it to be a violation of the Fifteenth Amendment.

---

[3] *Plessy v. Ferguson,* 163 U.S. 537 (1896).
[4] 321 U.S. 649 (1944).

Another barrier to African American voting was the **grandfather clause**, which restricted the voting franchise to those who could prove that their grandfathers had voted before 1867. **Poll taxes** required the payment of a fee to vote; thus, poor African Americans—as well as poor whites—who could not afford to pay the tax were excluded from voting. Not until the Twenty-fourth Amendment to the Constitution was ratified in 1964 was the poll tax eliminated as a precondition to voting. **Literacy tests** also were used to deny the vote to African Americans. Such tests asked potential voters to read, recite, or interpret complicated texts, such as a section of the state constitution, to the satisfaction of local registrars.

The End of the Separate-but-Equal Doctrine

A successful attack on the separate-but-equal doctrine began with a series of lawsuits in the 1930s to admit African Americans to state professional schools. By 1950, the Supreme Court had ruled that African Americans who were admitted to a state university could not be assigned to separate sections of classrooms, libraries, and cafeterias.

In 1951, Oliver Brown decided that his eight-year-old daughter, Linda Carol Brown, should not have to go to an all-nonwhite elementary school twenty-one blocks from her home, when there was a white school only seven blocks away. The National Association for the Advancement of Colored People (NAACP), formed in 1909, decided to help Oliver Brown. The outcome would have a monumental impact on American society. Actually, Brown's suit was one of a series of cases, first argued in 1952, that contested state laws permitting or requiring the establishment of separate school facilities based on race. Following the death of Chief Justice Frederick M. Vinson and his replacement by Earl Warren in 1953, the Supreme Court asked for rearguments.

Brown v. Board of Education of Topeka. The 1954 unanimous decision in *Brown v. Board of Education of Topeka*[5] established that public school segregation of races violates the equal protection clause of the Fourteenth Amendment. Concluding that separate schools are inherently unequal, Chief Justice Warren stated that "to separate [African Americans] from others of similar age and qualifications solely because of their race generates a feeling of inferiority as to their status in the community that may affect their hearts and minds in a way unlikely ever to be undone." Warren said that separation implied inferiority, whereas the majority opinion in *Plessy v. Ferguson* had said the opposite.

"With All Deliberate Speed." The following year, in *Brown v. Board of Education*[6] (sometimes called the second *Brown* decision), the Court asked for rearguments concerning the way in which compliance with the 1954 decision should be undertaken. The Supreme Court declared that the lower courts needed to ensure that African Americans would be admitted to schools on a nondiscriminatory basis "with all deliberate speed." The high court told lower federal courts that they had to take an activist role in society. The district courts were to consider devices in their desegregation orders that might include "the school transportation system, personnel, [and] revision of school districts and attendance areas into compact units to achieve a system of determining admission to the public schools on a nonracial basis."

Reactions to School Integration

One unlooked-for effect of the "all deliberate speed" decision was that the term *deliberate* was used as a loophole by some officials, who were able to delay desegregation by showing that they were indeed acting with all deliberate speed but still were

---

[5]347 U.S. 483 (1954).
[6]349 U.S. 294 (1955).

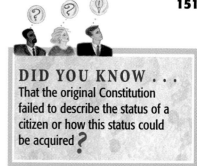

DID YOU KNOW . . .
That the original Constitution failed to describe the status of a citizen or how this status could be acquired **?**

Grandfather Clause
A device used by southern states to exempt whites from state taxes and literacy laws originally intended to disenfranchise African American voters. It restricted the voting franchise to those who could prove that their grandfathers had voted before 1867.

Poll Tax
A special tax that must be paid as a qualification for voting. The Twenty-fourth Amendment to the Constitution outlawed the poll tax in national elections, and in 1966 the Supreme Court declared it unconstitutional in all elections.

Literacy Test
A test administered as a precondition for voting, often used to prevent African Americans from exercising their right to vote.

INFOTRAC®
COLLEGE EDITION

To find out more about segregation, use the term "segregation" in the Subject guide.

unable to desegregate. Another reaction to court-ordered desegregation was "white flight." In some school districts, the public school population became 100 percent nonwhite when white parents sent their children to newly established private schools, sometimes known as "segregation academies."

The white South did not let the Supreme Court ruling go unchallenged. Arkansas's Governor Orval Faubus used the state's National Guard to block the integration of Central High School in Little Rock in September 1957. The federal court demanded that the troops be withdrawn. Finally, President Dwight Eisenhower had to federalize the Arkansas National Guard and send it to quell the violence. Central High became integrated.

The universities in the South, however, remained segregated. When James Meredith, an African American student, attempted to enroll at the University of Mississippi in Oxford in 1962, violence flared there, as it had in Little Rock. Two men were killed, and a number of people were injured in campus rioting. President John Kennedy sent federal marshals and ordered federal troops to maintain peace and protect Meredith. One year later, George Wallace, governor of Alabama, promised "to stand in the schoolhouse door" to prevent two African American students from enrolling at the University of Alabama in Tuscaloosa. Wallace was forced to back down when Kennedy federalized the Alabama National Guard.

An Integrationist Attempt at a Cure: Busing

In most parts of the United States, residential concentrations by race have made it difficult to achieve racial balance in schools. Although it is true that a number of school boards in northern districts created segregated schools by drawing school district lines arbitrarily, the residential concentration of African Americans and other minorities in well-defined geographic locations has contributed to the difficulty of achieving racial balance. This concentration results in *de facto* **segregation.**

Court-Ordered Busing.   The obvious solution to both *de facto* and *de jure* **segregation** seemed to be transporting some African American schoolchildren to white schools and some white schoolchildren to African American schools. Increasingly, the courts ordered school districts to engage in such **busing** across neighborhoods. Busing led to violence in some northern cities, such as in south

De Facto Segregation
Racial segregation that occurs because of past social and economic conditions and residential patterns.

De Jure Segregation
Racial segregation that occurs because of laws or administrative decisions by public agencies.

Busing
The transportation of public school students from areas where they live to schools in other areas to eliminate school segregation based on residential patterns.

For a number of years after the *Brown* decision, whites reacted aggressively, particularly with respect to the attempt to desegregate the school system in Little Rock, Arkansas. After the local school board secured approval of the federal courts for desegregation, Governor Orval Faubus sent in the state's National Guard to prevent a handful of African American students from entering Little Rock Central High School on September 2, 1957. On September 24, President Dwight Eisenhower sent in five hundred soldiers, many of whom remained there for the rest of the school year to preserve order.
(Burt Glinn, Magnum)

Boston, where African American students were bused into blue-collar Irish Catholic neighborhoods. Indeed, busing was unpopular with many groups. In the mid-1970s, almost 50 percent of African Americans interviewed were opposed to busing, and approximately three-fourths of the whites interviewed held the same opinion. Nonetheless, through the next decade, the Supreme Court fairly consistently upheld busing plans in the cases it decided.

Changing Directions. In an apparent reversal of previous decisions, the Supreme Court in June 1986 let stand (did not accept for review) a lower federal court's decision that allowed the Norfolk, Virginia, public school system to end fifteen years of court-ordered busing of elementary schoolchildren.[7] The Norfolk school board supported the decision because of a drop in enrollment from 32,500 whites attending public schools in 1970, when busing was ordered, to fewer than 14,000 in 1985. In 1991, in *Board of Education v. Dowell,*[8] the Supreme Court instructed a lower court administering a desegregation decree that if school racial concentration was a product of residential segregation that resulted from "private decision making and economics," its effects may be ignored entirely.

In *Freeman v. Pitts,*[9] decided in 1992, the Supreme Court also stressed the importance of "local control over the education of children." In *Freeman,* a Georgia school district, which had once been segregated by law and was operating under a federal court–administered desegregation decree, was allowed to regain partial control over its schools, even though it was judged to have not complied with certain aspects of the decree. In 1995, the Supreme Court ruled in *Missouri v. Jenkins*[10] that the state of Missouri could stop spending money to attract a multiracial student body in urban school districts through major educational improvements. This decision dealt a potentially fatal blow to the use of magnet schools for racial integration.

The End of Integration? By the late 1990s and early 2000s, the federal courts had become increasingly unwilling to uphold race-conscious policies designed to further

---

[7] *Riddick v. School Board of City of Norfolk,* 627 F.Supp. 814 (E.D.Va. 1984).
[8] 498 U.S. 237 (1991).
[9] 503 U.S. 467 (1992).
[10] 515 U.S. 70 (1995).

DID YOU KNOW . . .
That by September 1961, more than 3,600 students had been arrested for participating in civil rights demonstrations and that 141 students and 58 faculty members had been expelled by colleges and universities for their part in civil rights protests ?

INFOTRAC®
COLLEGE EDITION

To find out more about busing, use the term "school busing" in the Subject guide.

To remedy *de facto* segregation, the courts often imposed busing requirements on school districts. Busing meant transporting children from white neighborhoods to nonwhite schools, and vice versa. Busing has been one of the most controversial domestic policies in the history of this country. Initially, bused students had to be escorted by police because of potential violence. This scene was photographed in Boston in the 1970s. (AP Photo)

school integration and diversity—outcomes that are not mandated by the Constitution. For example, in one case a school district in Montgomery County, Maryland, had refused to allow a white boy to transfer to its magnet program due to the impact his admission would have on the program's "diversity profile." In 1999, a federal appellate court held that the school district's decision not to admit the boy violated the equal protection clause of the Constitution. The Supreme Court declined to review the case, thus letting the decision stand.[11] In another case, a man sued the Charlotte-Mecklenburg Board of Education in North Carolina after his white daughter was denied admission to a magnet school because of her race. In 2001, a federal appellate court held that the school district had achieved the goal of integration,[12] meaning that race-based admission quotas could no longer be constitutionally imposed.

The Resurgence of Minority Schools.   Today, schools around the country are again becoming segregated, in large part because of *de facto* segregation. The rapid decline in the relative proportion of whites who live in large cities and high minority birthrates have increased the minority presence in those urban areas. Today, one out of every three African American and Hispanic students goes to a school with more than 90 percent minority enrollment. In the largest U.S. cities, fifteen out of sixteen African American and Hispanic students go to schools with almost no whites.

Generally, Americans are now taking another look at what desegregation means. The attempt to integrate the schools, particularly through busing, has largely failed to improve educational resources and achievement for African American children. In a recent Gallup poll, only 26 percent of the respondents thought that minority students would be helped by stepping up integration efforts; 60 percent believed that a better alternative would be to increase funding to minority schools. A full 82 percent of those polled felt that students should be allowed to attend local schools, no matter what their racial composition.

Clearly, the goal of racially balanced schools envisioned in the 1954 *Brown v. Board of Education of Topeka* decision is now giving way to the goal of better-educated children, even if that means educating them in schools in which the students are of the same race or in which race is not considered. Indeed, some school districts today, such as those in Cambridge, Massachusetts, are trying a different approach to desegregation: assigning students to schools based on income factors instead of race. This approach is based on the assumption that poverty is a better indicator of poor academic achievement than race.

The Civil Rights Movement

The *Brown* decision applied only to public schools. Not much else in the structure of existing segregation was affected. In December 1955, a forty-three-year-old African American woman, Rosa Parks, boarded a public bus in Montgomery, Alabama. When the bus became crowded and several white people stepped aboard, Parks was asked to move to the rear of the bus, the "colored" section. She refused, was arrested, and was fined $10; but that was not the end of the matter. For an entire year, African Americans boycotted the Montgomery bus line. The protest was headed by a twenty-seven-year-old Baptist minister, Dr. Martin Luther King, Jr. During the protest period, he went to jail, and his house was bombed. In the face of overwhelming odds, however, King won. In 1956, a federal district court issued an injunction prohibiting the segregation of buses in Montgomery. The era of civil rights protests had begun.

---

[11] *Eisenberg v. Montgomery County Public Schools,* 197 F.3d 123 (4th Cir. 1999).
[12] *Belk v. Charlotte-Mecklenburg Board of Education,* 269 F.3d 305 (4th Cir. 2001).

Rosa Parks was born on February 4, 1913, in Tuskegee, Alabama. She was active in the Montgomery Voters' League and the NAACP League Council. After the successful boycott of the Montgomery bus system, which was sparked by her actions, she was fired from her job and moved to Detroit. In 1987, she founded the Rosa Raymond Parks Institute for Self-Development, offering guidance to disadvantaged African Americans. (AP Photo/Paul Warner)

King's Philosophy of Nonviolence

The following year, in 1957, King formed the Southern Christian Leadership Conference (SCLC). King's philosophy of nonviolent civil disobedience was influenced, in part, by the life and teachings of Mahatma Gandhi (1869–1948). Gandhi had led Indian resistance to the British colonial system from 1919 to 1947. He used tactics such as demonstrations and marches, as well as purposeful, public disobedience to unjust laws, while remaining nonviolent. King's followers successfully used these methods to gain wider public acceptance of their cause.

Nonviolent Demonstrations. For the next decade, African Americans and sympathetic whites engaged in sit-ins, freedom rides, and freedom marches. In the beginning, such demonstrations were often met with violence, but the contrasting image of nonviolent African Americans and violent, hostile whites created strong public support for the civil rights movement. When African Americans in Greensboro, North Carolina, were refused service at a Woolworth's lunch counter, they organized a sit-in that was aided day after day by sympathetic whites and other African Americans. Enraged customers threw ketchup on the protesters. Some spat in their faces. The sit-in movement continued to grow, however. Within six months of the first sit-in the Greensboro Woolworth's, hundreds of lunch counters throughout the South were serving African Americans.

The sit-in technique was also successfully used to integrate interstate buses and their terminals, as well as railroads engaged in interstate transportation. Although buses and railroads that were engaged in interstate transportation were prohibited by law from segregating African Americans from whites, they stopped doing so only after the sit-in protests.

The Birmingham Protest. The civil rights movement gathered momentum in the 1960s. One of the most famous of the violence-plagued protests occurred in Birmingham, Alabama, in the spring of 1963, when Police Commissioner Eugene "Bull" Connor unleashed police dogs and used electric cattle prods against the protesters. The object of the protest had been to provoke a reaction by local officials so that the federal government would act. People throughout the country viewed the event on national television with indignation and horror. King himself was thrown in jail, and it was during this period that he wrote his famous "Letter from a Birmingham Jail."[13]

The media coverage of the Birmingham protest and the violent response it elicited played a key role in the process of ending Jim Crow conditions in the United States. The ultimate result was the most important civil rights act in the nation's history, the Civil Rights Act of 1964 (to be discussed shortly).

King's March on Washington. In August 1963, King organized the massive March on Washington for Jobs and Freedom. Before nearly a quarter-million white and African American spectators and millions watching on television, King told the world his dream:

I have a dream that my four little children will one day live in a nation where they will not be judged by the color of their skin but by the content of their character.... When we let freedom ring, when we let it ring from every village and every hamlet, from every state and every city, we will be able to speed up that day when all God's children, black men and white men, Jews and Gentiles, Protestants and Catholics, will be able to join hands and sing in the words of that old Negro Spiritual, "Free at last! Free at last! Thank God almighty, we are free at last!"

King's dream was not to be realized immediately, however. Eighteen days after his famous speech, four African American girls attending Bible class in the basement room of the Sixteenth Street Baptist Church in Birmingham, Alabama, were killed by a bomb explosion.[14]

Dr. Martin Luther King, Jr., acknowledges the crowd at the August 1963 March on Washington for Jobs and Freedom. Nearly a quarter-million African Americans and sympathetic whites participated in the march. The march is best remembered for King's eloquent "I have a dream" speech and the assembled multitude singing "We Shall Overcome," the anthem of the civil rights movement. (AP Photo)

Another Approach—Black Power

Not all African Americans agreed with King's philosophy of nonviolence or with the idea that King's strong Christian church background should represent the core spirituality of African Americans. Indeed, Black Muslims and other African American separatists advocated a more militant stance against the politics of cultural assimilation. During the 1950s and 1960s, when King was spearheading nonviolent protests

---

[13] A copy of this letter is included in Andrew Carroll, ed., *Letters of a Nation: A Collection of Extraordinary American Letters* (New York: Kodansha America, 1997), pp. 208–226.

[14] Two of the perpetrators of the church bombing were not convicted until nearly forty years later: Thomas Blanton, Jr., in 2001 and Bobby Frank Cherry in 2002.

Malcolm X strongly opposed the philosophy of nonviolence espoused by Martin Luther King, Jr., and urged African Americans to "fight back" against white supremacy. Subsequently, several books and a movie by Spike Lee added to the revival of Malcolm X as a symbol of African American identity. (AP Photo)

and demonstrations to achieve civil rights for African Americans, black power leaders insisted that African Americans should "fight back" instead of turning the other cheek. Indeed, some would argue that without the fear generated by black militants, a "moderate" like King would not have garnered such widespread support from white America.

Malcolm Little (who became Malcolm X when he joined the Black Muslims in 1952) and other leaders in the black power movement believed that African Americans fell into two groups: the "Uncle Toms," who peaceably accommodated the white establishment, and the "New Negroes," who took pride in their color and culture and who preferred and demanded racial separation as well as power. Malcolm X was assassinated in 1965, but he became an important reference point for a new generation of African Americans and a symbol of African American identity.

DID YOU KNOW . . .
That during the Mississippi Summer Project in 1964, organized by students to register African American voters, there were 1,000 arrests, 35 shooting incidents, 30 buildings bombed, 25 churches burned, 80 people beaten, and at least 6 murders **?**

Modern Civil Rights Legislation

Police-dog attacks, cattle prods, high-pressure water hoses, beatings, bombings, the March on Washington, and black militancy—all of these events and developments led to an environment in which Congress felt compelled to act on behalf of African Americans. The second era of civil rights acts, sometimes referred to as the second Reconstruction period, was under way.

The Civil Rights Act of 1957 established a Civil Rights Commission and a new Civil Rights Division within the Justice Department. The Civil Rights Act of 1960 provided that whenever a pattern or practice of discrimination was documented, the Justice Department could bring suit, even against a state. The act also set penalties for obstructing a federal court order by threat of force and for illegally using and transporting explosives. But the 1960 Civil Rights Act, as well as that of 1957, had little substantive impact.

The same cannot be said about the Civil Rights Acts of 1964 and 1968 or the Voting Rights Act of 1965 (discussed next). With those acts, Congress assumed a leading role in the enforcement of the constitutional notion of equality for *all* Americans, as provided by the Fourteenth and Fifteenth Amendments.

The Civil Rights Act of 1964

As the civil rights movement mounted in intensity, equality before the law came to be "an idea whose time has come," in the words of conservative Senate Minority Leader Everett Dirksen. The Civil Rights Act of 1964, the most far-reaching bill on civil rights in modern times, forbade discrimination on the basis of race, color, religion, gender, and national origin. The major provisions of the act were as follows:

1. It outlawed arbitrary discrimination in voter registration.
2. It barred discrimination in public accommodations, such as hotels and restaurants, whose operations affect interstate commerce.
3. It authorized the federal government to sue to desegregate public schools and facilities.
4. It expanded the power of the Civil Rights Commission and extended its life.
5. It provided for the withholding of federal funds from programs administered in a discriminatory manner.
6. It established the right to equality of opportunity in employment.

Several factors led to the passage of the 1964 act. As noted earlier, there had been a dramatic change in the climate of public opinion owing to violence perpetrated against protesting African Americans and whites in the South. Second, the assassination of President John Kennedy in 1963 had, according to some, a significant effect on the national conscience. Many believed the civil rights program to be the legislative tribute

Filibuster
In the Senate, unlimited debate to halt action on a particular bill.

Cloture
A method invoked to close off debate and to bring the matter under consideration to a vote in the Senate.

Equal Employment Opportunity Commission (EEOC)
A commission established by the 1964 Civil Rights Act to (1) end discrimination based on race, color, religion, gender, or national origin in conditions of employment and (2) promote voluntary action programs by employers, unions, and community organizations to foster equal job opportunities.

Subpoena
A legal writ requiring a person's appearance in court to give testimony.

that Congress paid to the martyred Kennedy. Congress passed the act only after the longest **filibuster** in the history of the Senate (eighty-three days) and only after **cloture** was imposed for the first time to cut off a civil rights filibuster.

Title VII of the Civil Rights Act of 1964 is the cornerstone of employment-discrimination law. It prohibits discrimination in employment based on race, color, religion, gender, or national origin. Under Title VII, executive orders were issued that banned employment discrimination by firms that received any federal funding. The 1964 Civil Rights Act created a five-member commission, the **Equal Employment Opportunity Commission (EEOC)**, to administer Title VII.

The EEOC can issue interpretive guidelines and regulations, but these do not have the force of law. Rather, they give notice of the commission's enforcement policy. The EEOC also has investigatory powers. It has broad authority to require the production of documentary evidence, to hold hearings, and to **subpoena** and examine witnesses under oath.

The Voting Rights Act of 1965

As late as 1960, only 29.1 percent of African Americans of voting age were registered in the southern states, in stark contrast to 61.1 percent of whites. In 1965, Martin Luther King, Jr., took action to change all that. Selma, the seat of Dallas County, Alabama, was chosen as the site to dramatize the voting-rights problem. In Dallas County, only 2 percent of eligible African Americans had registered to vote by the beginning of 1965. King organized a fifty-mile march from Selma to the state capital in Montgomery, where marchers would attempt to register to vote. He didn't get very far. Acting on orders of Governor George Wallace to disband the marchers, state troopers did so with a vengeance—with tear gas, clubs, and whips.

Once again the national government was required to intervene to force compliance with the law. President Lyndon Johnson federalized the National Guard, and the march continued. During the march, the president went on television to address a special joint session of Congress urging passage of new legislation to ensure African Americans the right to vote. The events during the Selma march and Johnson's dramatic speech, in which he invoked the slogan of the civil rights movement ("We shall overcome"), were credited for the swift passage of the Voting Rights Act of 1965.

The Voting Rights Act of 1965 had two major provisions. The first one outlawed discriminatory voter-registration tests. The second major section authorized federal registration of persons and federally administered voting procedures in any political subdivision or state that discriminated electorally against a particular group. In part, the act provided that certain political subdivisions could not change their voting procedures and election laws without federal approval. The act targeted counties, mostly in the South, in which less than 50 percent of the eligible population was registered to vote. Federal voter registrars were sent to these areas to register African Americans who had been restricted by local registrars. Within one week after the act was passed, forty-five federal examiners were sent to the South. A massive voter-registration drive covered the country.

The Civil Rights Act of 1968 and Other Housing-Reform Legislation

Martin Luther King, Jr., was assassinated on April 4, 1968. Nine days after King's death, President Johnson signed the Civil Rights Act of 1968, which forbade discrimination in most housing and provided penalties for those attempting to interfere with individual civil rights (giving protection to civil rights workers, among others). Subsequent legislation added enforcement provisions to the federal government's rules pertaining to discriminatory mortgage-lending practices. Today, all lenders must report to the federal government the race, gender, and income of all mortgage-loan seekers, along with the final decision on their loan applications.

Increased Political Participation by African Americans

As a result of the Voting Rights Act of 1965, its amendments, and the large-scale voter-registration drives in the South, the number of African Americans registered to vote climbed dramatically. By 1980, 55.8 percent of African Americans of voting age in the South were registered. In recent elections, the percentage of voting-age African Americans who have registered to vote is just slightly less than the percentage of voting-age whites who have registered to vote.

Today, there are more than 8,500 African American elected officials in the United States. There are thirty-four African Americans in the 108th Congress. In 1984, the Reverend Jesse Jackson became the first African American candidate to compete seriously for the presidential nomination. In 1989, Virginia became the first state to elect an African American governor. General Colin Powell became the first African American to be appointed chairman of the Joint Chiefs of Staff (in 1989) and, after retiring from the service, secretary of state (in 2001). In 1991, Clarence Thomas became a justice of the Supreme Court, replacing Thurgood Marshall, the first African American justice.

The movement of African American citizens into high elected office has thus been sure, if exceedingly slow. Black candidates continue to face an uphill fight to gain top political offices, such as governorships and U.S. Senate seats. Notably, recent polling data show that most Americans do not consider race a significant factor with regard to presidential candidates. In 1958, when the Gallup poll first asked whether respondents would be willing to vote for an African American as president, only 38 percent of the public said yes. By 2002, this percentage had reached 95 percent.

Political Participation by Other Minorities

As mentioned earlier, the civil rights movement focused primarily on the rights of African Americans. Yet the legislation resulting from the movement ultimately has benefited virtually all minority groups. The Civil Rights Act of 1964, for example, prohibits discrimination against any person because of race, color, or national origin. Subsequent amendments to the Voting Rights Act of 1965 extended its protections to other minorities, including Hispanic Americans, Asian Americans, Native Americans, and Native Alaskans. To further protect the voting rights of minorities, the act now provides that states must make bilingual ballots available in counties where 5 percent or more of the population speaks a language other than English.

The political participation of other minority groups in the United States has also been increasing. Hispanics are gaining political power in several states. The growing political presence of the Hispanic population was highlighted in 2002 by a historic event: the two top Democratic candidates for the Texas gubernatorial nomination, Tony Sanchez and Dan Morales, held one of their debates in Spanish. Today, over 5 percent of the legislative seats in Arizona, California, Colorado, Florida, New Mexico, and Texas are held by legislators of Hispanic ancestry. At the national level, the percentage of Hispanics in Congress is somewhat lower—they constitute about 3 percent of that institution's members. There is also a Native American in Congress—Senator Ben Nighthorse Campbell (R., Colo.), who was elected to the Senate in 1992 after having served in the House from 1987 to 1992.

Even though political participation by minorities has increased dramatically since the 1960s, the number of political offices held by members of minority groups remains disproportionately low compared to their numbers in the overall population. This will likely change in the future due to the continued influx of immigrants, particularly from Mexico. Collectively, Hispanics, African Americans, Native

Americans, and Asian Americans are now a majority of the populations in California, Hawaii, and New Mexico. It is estimated that by 2010 minority populations will collectively outnumber whites in Texas and New York as well.

Lingering Social and Economic Disparities

According to Joyce Ladner of the Brookings Institution, one of the problems with the race-based civil rights agenda of the 1950s and 1960s is that it did not envision remedies for cross-racial problems. How, for example, should the nation address problems, such as poverty and urban violence, that affect underclasses in all racial groups? In 1967, when Martin Luther King, Jr., proposed a Poor People's Campaign, he recognized that a civil rights coalition based entirely on race would not be sufficient to address the problem of poverty among whites as well as blacks. During his 1984 and 1988 presidential campaigns, African American leader Jesse Jackson also acknowledged the inadequacy of a race-based model of civil rights when he attempted to form a "Rainbow Coalition" of minorities, women, and other underrepresented groups, including the poor.[15]

Some contend that government intervention is necessary to eliminate the social and economic disparities that persist within the American population. Others believe that the most effective means of addressing these issues is through coalitions of government groups, private businesses, community-based groups, and individuals. Indeed, a number of civil rights activists today are pursuing the latter strategy. (See this chapter's *Politics and Diversity* feature for a discussion of how artistic expression is sometimes used to portray a more ethnically diverse America than exists in reality.)

---

[15] Joyce A. Ladner, "A New Civil Rights Agenda," *The Brookings Review*, Vol. 18, No. 2 (Spring 2000), pp. 26–28.

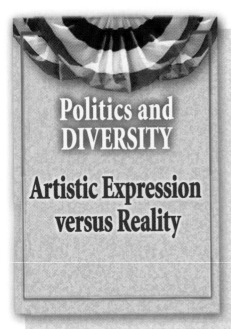

Politics and DIVERSITY

Artistic Expression versus Reality

Immediately after the terrorist attacks on the World Trade Center towers, New York's firefighters rushed to the scene from all over the city and the suburbs. As they attempted to help people escape the buildings, 343 of these firefighters died when the towers collapsed.

Not surprisingly, the city wished to commemorate those who died while attempting to save others. A now-famous news photo of three firefighters at Ground Zero raising an American flag that had been found in the rubble was to be the basis of a nineteen-foot-high bronze statue. There was only one problem—the proposed statue, if it was to be faithful to the photo, would be of three *white* firefighters. Because twelve of the firefighters who died were black and twelve were Hispanic, the city decided to make a multiethnic representation. Fire department spokesperson Frank Gribbon explained that "given that those who died were of all races and all ethnicities and that the statue was to be symbolic of those sacrifices, ultimately a decision was made

to honor no one in particular but everyone who made the supreme sacrifice."

The director of the studio that created the statue pointed out that it was not meant to be an exact replica. Perhaps more disturbing to some was the true ethnic composition of New York City's 11,500 firefighters: only 2.7 percent were black, and only 3.9 percent were Hispanic. Actually, New York City had more black and Hispanic firefighters in the 1970s than it has today.

FOR CRITICAL ANALYSIS

Do you agree with the decision made by New York City officials to alter the historical record for the sake of symbolism in this case? What other alternatives might city officials have considered besides altering, for the memorial, the event depicted in the photo?

Finally, even today, race consciousness continues to divide African Americans and white Americans. Whether we are talking about college attendance, media stereotyping, racial profiling, or academic achievement, the black experience is different from the white experience. As a result, African Americans view the nation and many specific issues differently than their white counterparts do.[16] In survey after survey, when blacks are asked whether they have achieved racial equality, few believe that they have. In contrast, whites are five times more likely than blacks to believe that racial equality has been achieved.[17] In spite of the civil rights movement and civil rights legislation, African Americans continue to feel a sense of injustice in matters of race, and this feeling is often not apparent to, or appreciated by, the majority of white America.

Immigration and the Civil Rights Agenda

Time and again, this nation has been challenged and changed—and culturally enriched—by immigrant groups. All of these immigrants have faced the challenges involved in living in a new and different political and cultural environment. Most of them have had to overcome language barriers, and many have had to deal with discrimination in one form or another because of their color, their inability to speak English fluently, or their customs. The civil rights legislation passed during and since the 1960s has done much to counter the effects of prejudice against immigrant groups by ensuring that they obtain equal rights under the law.

One of the questions facing Americans and their political leaders today concerns the effect of immigration on American politics and government. Another issue has to do with the impact of immigration and interracial marriages on the traditional civil rights agenda. (Still another issue is whether immigrants from countries where some citizens are known to support terrorism should be allowed to enter this country at all. See this chapter's *America's Security* feature on page 162 for a discussion of this question.)

INFOTRAC®
COLLEGE EDITION

For updates and more information about this topic, use the term "immigration" in the Subject guide.

---

[16] Lawerence D. Bobo, et al., "Through the Eyes of Black America," *Public Perspective,* May/June 2001, p. 13.
[17] *Ibid.,* p. 15, Figure 2.

In Los Angeles, Mexican Americans celebrate Cinco de Mayo. Is the United States a nation of many ethnic cultures existing separately, or is it a melting pot of diverse cultures? (David Young-Wolff, PhotoEdit)

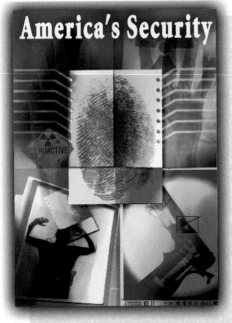

America's Security

Soon after the attacks on the World Trade Center and the Pentagon, many political leaders, perhaps at the behest of their constituents, looked at our immigration policies in view of security issues. After all, the purported terrorists were from other countries (mainly Saudi Arabia). The most vocal critics of our immigration policy literally want to shut America's door to immigrants. That the terrorist attacks occurred while the American economy was suffering from a recession did not, of course, help matters. Anti-immigrant forces

Should We Shut the Immigration Door?

often have used high unemployment as a reason to restrict immigration. The 9/11 events simply provided these critics with an additional argument to support their views.

STUDENT VISAS— THEN AND NOW

Several of the 9/11 hijackers were in this country legally on student visas. Indeed, newly approved student visas for two of the hijackers arrived at their flight school in Florida two months *after* the attacks, emphasizing how inefficient, understaffed, and underfunded the Immigration and Naturalization Service (INS) has been for years. The State Department's inspector general pointed out that one consulate in a "suspect" country had an annual travel budget of only $300 to perform background checks on over 100,000 visa applicants.

According to those who support reduced immigration in the interests of furthering America's security, all visa applicants from "suspect" areas of the world should be subject to stricter scrutiny. Supporters of reduced immigration often have the goal of scrutinizing more closely travelers from any

nations in which anti-American groups like al Qaeda have found supporters. Those countries would include, for example, Somalia, Pakistan, Bosnia, the Philippines, and Indonesia, as well as Saudi Arabia.

PROPOSED SECURITY GUIDELINES

The INS gives out over 500,000 student visas each year. Many of these visas are given to individuals coming from countries where some residents are known to support terrorism. Under proposed new security guidelines, U.S. immigration authorities will have to conduct additional checks on these students. Universities will have to report to the INS whether students who requested visas actually enroll in course work at their campuses. After all, many of the 9/11 hijackers never showed up for classes despite having received valid student visas.

FOR CRITICAL ANALYSIS

Would it ever be possible to close off the borders of the United States entirely? What practical constraints are there on such an action?

The Continued Influx of Immigrants

Today, immigration rates are the highest they have been since their peak in the early twentieth century. Currently, about one million people a year immigrate to this country, and those who were born on foreign soil now constitute nearly 10 percent of the U.S. population—twice the percentage of thirty years ago.

Since 1977, four out of five immigrants have come from Latin America or Asia. Hispanics are now overtaking African Americans as the nation's largest minority. If current immigration rates continue, by the year 2050 minority groups collectively will constitute the "majority" of Americans. If Hispanics, African Americans, and perhaps Asians were to form coalitions, they could increase their political strength dramatically and would have the numerical strength to make significant changes. According to Ben Wattenberg of the American Enterprise Institute, in the future the "old guard" white majority will no longer dominate American politics.

The Problem of Racial Classifications

One of the challenges facing the government today is that the lines separating racial groups are becoming increasingly blurred. About 25 percent of Hispanics marry persons outside their group, as do nearly one-third of the Asians living in America; and many African Americans have both a black and a white heritage. A few years ago, golf professional Tiger Woods emphasized the growing problem of racial identity. When Oprah Winfrey asked Woods about his ethnic status, he said he was not a black but a "Cablinasian"—a combination of Caucasian, black, Indian, and Asian.

The blurring of racial distinctions is significant for the civil rights agenda because the U.S. Census Bureau and other federal and state agencies traditionally have used racial classifications to determine who is eligible for certain benefits. Since 1977, for example, the federal government has identified Americans using the following racial categories: black, white, American Indian, Alaskan native, and Asian/Pacific islander. "Hispanic" is a separate category. Yet how can these classifications be applied to the millions of Americans with mixed ethnic and racial backgrounds? In the 2000 census, the government tried to address this problem by allowing respondents to check more than one racial box. Some contend that the government should go even further and drop racial categories from the census entirely.

DID YOU KNOW...
That in 1916, four years before the Nineteenth Amendment gave women the right to vote, Jeannette Rankin became the first woman to be elected to the U.S. House of Representatives **?**

Women's Struggle for Equal Rights

Like African Americans and other minorities, women also have had to struggle for equality. During the first phase of this struggle, the primary goal of women was to obtain the right to vote. Some women had hoped that the founders would provide such a right in the Constitution. In 1776, Abigail Adams wrote to her husband, John Adams, the following words in reference to new laws that would be necessary if a Declaration of Independence was issued:

> I desire you would remember the ladies.... If particular care and attention is not paid to the ladies, we are determined to foment a rebellion and will not hold ourselves bound by any laws in which we have no voice or representation.[18]

Despite this request, the founders did not include in the Constitution a provision guaranteeing women the right to vote. Nor did it deny to women—or to any others—this right. Rather, the founders left it up to the states to decide such issues, and, as stated earlier, by and large, the states limited the franchise to adult white males who owned property. That only property owners could vote apparently did not seem unusual to the founders. The prevailing view seems to have been that "the people who own the country ought to govern it," as John Jay phrased it.

Early Women's Political Movements

The first political cause in which women became actively engaged was the slavery abolition movement. Yet even male abolitionists felt that women should not take an active role on the subject in public. When the World Antislavery Convention was held in London in 1840, women delegates were barred from active participation. Partly in response to this rebuff, two American delegates, Lucretia Mott and Elizabeth Cady Stanton, returned from that meeting with plans to work for women's rights in the United States.

In 1848, Mott and Stanton organized the first women's rights convention in Seneca Falls, New York. The three hundred people who attended approved a Declaration of Sentiments: "We hold these truths to be self-evident: that all men *and women* are created equal." In the following twelve years, groups of feminists held seven conventions in different cities in the Midwest and East. With the outbreak of the Civil War, however, advocates of women's rights were urged to put their support behind the war effort, and most agreed.

Elizabeth Cady Stanton (1815–1902) was a social reformer and a women's suffrage leader. At her wedding to Henry B. Stanton in 1840, she insisted on dropping the word *obey* from the marriage vows. She wrote *The History of Women's Suffrage,* which was published in 1886. (Corbis, Bettmann)

---

[18] As quoted in Carroll, ed., *Letters of a Nation,* p. 60.

Susan B. Anthony (1820–1906) was a leader of the women's suffrage movement who was also active in the antialcohol and antislavery movements. In 1869, with Elizabeth Cady Stanton, she founded the National Woman Suffrage Association. In 1888, she organized the International Council of Women and, in 1904, the International Women's Suffrage Alliance, in Berlin. (Corbis/Bettmann)

Suffrage
The right to vote; the franchise.

The Suffrage Issue and the Fifteenth Amendment.   "The right of citizens of the United States to vote shall not be denied or abridged by the United States or by any State on account of race, color, or previous condition of servitude." So reads Section 1 of the Fifteenth Amendment to the Constitution, which was ratified in 1870. The campaign for the passage of this amendment split the women's **suffrage** movement. Militant feminists wanted to add "sex" to "race, color, or previous condition of servitude." Other feminists, along with many men, opposed this view; they wanted to separate African American suffrage and women's suffrage to ensure the passage of the amendment. So, although the African American community supported the women's suffrage movement, it became separate from the racial equality movement. Still, some women attempted to vote in the years following the Civil War. One, Virginia Louisa Minor, was arrested and convicted in 1872. She appealed to the Supreme Court, but the Court upheld her conviction.[19]

Women's Suffrage Associations.   Susan B. Anthony and Elizabeth Cady Stanton formed the National Woman Suffrage Association in 1869. According to their view, women's suffrage was a means to achieve major improvements in the economic and social situation of women in the United States. In other words, the vote was to be used to obtain a larger goal. Lucy Stone, however, felt that the vote was the only major issue. Members of the American Woman Suffrage Association, founded by Stone and others, traveled to each state, addressed state legislatures, wrote, published, and argued their convictions. They achieved only limited success. In 1890, the two organizations quit battling and joined forces. The National American Woman Suffrage Association had only one goal—the enfranchisement of women—but it made little progress.

By the early 1900s, small radical splinter groups were formed, such as the Congressional Union, headed by Alice Paul. This organization worked solely for the passage of an amendment to the U.S. Constitution. Willing to use "unorthodox" means to achieve its goal, this group and others took to the streets; parades, hunger strikes, arrests, and jailings ensued. Finally, in 1920, seventy-two years after the Seneca Falls convention, the Nineteenth Amendment was passed: "The right of citizens of the United States to vote shall not be denied or abridged by the United States or by any State on account of sex." Women were thus enfranchised. Although today it may seem that the United States was slow to give women the vote, it was really not too far behind the rest of the world (see Table 5–1).

The Modern Women's Movement

After gaining the right to vote in 1920, women engaged in little organized political activity until the 1960s. The civil rights movement of that decade resulted in a growing awareness of rights for all groups, including women. Additionally, the publication of Betty Friedan's *The Feminine Mystique* in 1963 focused national attention on the unequal status of women in American life.

---

[19] *Minor v. Happersett,* 21 Wall. 162 (1874). The Supreme Court reasoned that the right to vote was a privilege of state, not federal, citizenship. The Court did not consider privileges of state citizenship to be protected by the Fourteenth Amendment.

TABLE 5–1

Years, by Country, in Which Women Gained the Right to Vote

1893: New Zealand	**1919:** Germany	**1945:** Italy	**1953:** Mexico
1902: Australia	**1920:** United States	**1945:** Japan	**1956:** Egypt
1913: Norway	**1930:** South Africa	**1947:** Argentina	**1963:** Kenya
1918: Britain	**1932:** Brazil	**1950:** India	**1971:** Switzerland
1918: Canada	**1944:** France	**1952:** Greece	**1984:** Yemen

SOURCE: Center for the American Woman and Politics.

In 1966, Friedan and others who were dissatisfied with the lack of aggressive action against gender discrimination by the then-largest women's organizations—the National Federation of Business and Professional Women's Clubs and the League of Women Voters—formed the National Organization for Women (NOW). NOW immediately adopted a blanket resolution designed "to bring women into full participation in the mainstream of American society *now*, exercising all the privileges and responsibilities thereof in truly equal partnership with men."

NOW has been in the forefront of what is often called the *feminist movement*. Historian Nancy Cott contends that the word *feminism* first began to be used around 1910. At that time, **feminism** meant, as it does today, political, social, and economic equality for women—a radical notion that gained little support among members of the suffrage movement. It is difficult to measure the support for feminism today because the term means different things to different people. When the dictionary definition of a feminist—"someone who supports political, economic, and social equality for women"—was read to respondents in a survey, however, 67 percent labeled themselves as feminists.[20]

The initial focus of the modern women's movement was not on expanding the political rights of women. Rather, leaders of NOW and other liberal women's rights advocates sought to eradicate gender inequality through a constitutional amendment.

The Equal Rights Amendment. The proposed Equal Rights Amendment (ERA), which was first introduced in Congress in 1923 by leaders of the National Women's Party, states as follows: "Equality of rights under the law shall not be denied or abridged by the United States or by any state on account of sex." For years the amendment was not even given a hearing in Congress, but finally it was approved by both chambers and sent to the state legislatures for ratification on March 22, 1972.

As was noted in Chapter 2, any constitutional amendment must be ratified by the legislatures (or conventions) in three-fourths of the states before it can become law. Since the early 1900s, most proposed amendments have required that ratification occur within seven years of Congress's adoption of the amendment. The necessary thirty-eight states failed to ratify the ERA within the seven-year period specified by Congress, even though it was supported by numerous national party platforms, six presidents, and both chambers of Congress. To date, efforts to reintroduce the amendment have not succeeded.

During the national debate over the ratification of the ERA, a women's countermovement emerged. Many women perceived the goals pursued by NOW and other liberal women's organizations as a threat to their way of life. At the head of the countermovement was Republican Phyllis Schlafly and her conservative organization, Eagle Forum. Eagle Forum's "Stop-ERA" campaign found significant support among fundamentalist religious groups and various other conservative organizations. The campaign was effective in blocking the ratification of the ERA.

Challenging Gender Discrimination in the Courts. When the ERA failed to be ratified, women's rights organizations began to refocus their efforts. Although NOW continued to press for the ERA, other groups challenged discriminatory statutes and policies in the federal courts, contending that **gender discrimination** violated the Fourteenth Amendment's equal protection clause. Since the 1970s, the Supreme Court has tended to scrutinize gender classifications closely and has invalidated a number of such statutes and policies. For example, in 1977 the Court held that police and firefighting units cannot establish arbitrary rules, such as height and weight requirements, that tend to preclude women from joining those occupations.[21] In

DID YOU KNOW...
That a Gallup poll taken in early 2000 found that 15 percent of the women polled described themselves as homemakers, but not one man described himself as such?

Feminism
The movement that supports political, economic, and social equality for women.

Gender Discrimination
Any practice, policy, or procedure that denies equality of treatment to an individual or to a group because of gender.

---

[20] Nancy E. McGlen and Karen O'Connor, *Women, Politics, and American Society,* 2d ed. (Upper Saddle River, N.J.: Prentice Hall, 1998), p. 11.
[21] *Dothard v. Rawlinson,* 433 U.S. 321 (1977).

A female cadet begins her training at the Virginia Military Institute. In 1996, the Supreme Court ruled that the institute's policy of accepting only males violated the equal protection clause of the Constitution. (A. R. Alonso, Sygma)

1983, the Court ruled that insurance companies cannot charge different rates for women and men.[22]

A question that the Court has not ruled on is whether women should be allowed to participate in military combat. Generally, the Supreme Court has left this decision up to Congress and the Department of Defense. Although recently women have been allowed to serve as combat pilots and on naval warships, to date they have not been allowed to join infantry combat units. In regard to military training institutes, however, the Supreme Court held in 1996 that the state-financed Virginia Military Institute's policy of accepting only males violated the equal protection clause.[23]

Expanding Women's Political Opportunities.   Following the failure of the ERA, in addition to fighting discrimination in the courts, the women's movement began to work for increased representation in government. Several women's political organizations that are active today concentrate their efforts on getting women elected to political offices. These organizations include the National Women's Political Caucus, the Coalition for Women's Appointments, the Feminist Majority Foundation, and the National Education for Women's Leadership (the NEW Leadership).

A variety of women's political action committees, or PACs (see Chapter 8), have also been created and are now important sources of financial support for women candidates. The largest of these PACs is EMILY's List (EMILY stands for "Early Money Is Like Yeast—It Makes the Dough Rise"). This PAC supports Democratic women candidates for congressional offices and governorships. Founded in 1985, EMILY's List now has about 68,000 members who contribute funds to be used for political campaigns.

Women in Politics Today

The efforts of women's rights advocates and organizations have helped to increase the number of women holding political offices in all areas of government.

---

[22] *Arizona v. Norris,* 463 U.S. 1073 (1983).

[23] *United States v. Virginia,* 518 U.S. 515 (1996).

Women in Congress. Although the men's club atmosphere still prevails in Congress, the number of women holding congressional seats has increased significantly in recent years. Elections during the 1990s brought more women to Congress than either the Senate or the House had seen before. Additionally, in 2001, for the first time, a woman was elected to a leadership post in Congress. Nancy Pelosi, a congressional representative from California, was elected as the Democrats' minority whip in the U.S. House of Representatives.

DID YOU KNOW . . .
That a student complained to University of Oregon officials that the university's motto, *Mens Agitat Molem* (which roughly translated from the Latin means "Mind over Matter"), was sexist and suggested that it be changed to *Mens and Womens Agitat Molem* **?**

ELECTIONS 2002 Political Leadership by Women

Although the number of women in Congress did not increase after the 2002 elections, this campaign cycle did see a number of firsts for women in politics. There were governor's races in thirty-six states, and women competed for the top state job in twenty of them. Although several were defeated in primaries, the general election saw ten women run as their party's candidate for governor, and six of these women won. Eleven women competed for seats in the United States Senate, and a record number (126) ran in the general election for seats in the House of Representatives. Congresswoman Nancy Pelosi, the first woman to rise to a major party leadership position in the House, was elected Democratic minority leader when Richard Gephardt stepped down from that post.

Women in the Executive and Judicial Branches. Although no woman has yet been nominated for president by a major political party, in 1984 a woman, Geraldine Ferraro, became the Democratic nominee for vice president. Another woman, Elizabeth Dole, made a serious run at the Republican presidential nomination in the 2000 campaigns. Notably, a recent Gallup poll found that 92 percent of Americans said that they would vote for a qualified woman for president if she was nominated by their party.

An increasing number of women are also being appointed to cabinet posts. Franklin Roosevelt appointed the first woman to a cabinet post—Frances Perkins, who was secretary of labor from 1933 to 1945. Gerald Ford (1974–1977) appointed a woman as secretary of housing and urban development, and each subsequent president has appointed at least two women to head cabinet departments. President Bill Clinton appointed four women to his cabinet, more than any previous president. One of Clinton's appointees, Madeleine Albright, was appointed to the important cabinet post of secretary of state. President George W. Bush appointed three women to cabinet positions and two women to other significant federal offices.

Increasingly, women are sitting on federal judicial benches as well. President Ronald Reagan was credited with a historic first when he appointed Sandra Day O'Connor to the Supreme Court in 1981. President Clinton, during his first term, appointed another woman, Ruth Bader Ginsburg, to the Court.

Women in State and Local Government. Women have had more success in gaining political offices in state legislatures and local governments. Several women have been elected to governorships, and about one-fourth of all state legislative seats are now held by women. In some states, including Washington, Colorado, and Nevada, over one-third of these seats are held by women. Additionally, Chicago, Houston, San Francisco, and Minneapolis have had female mayors, as have 17 percent of U.S. cities with populations of more than thirty thousand.

Continuing Disproportionate Leadership. For all their achievements in the political arena, however, the number of women holding political offices remains disproportionately low compared to their participation as voters. In recent elections, the

House Minority Whip Nancy Pelosi (D., Calif.) holds a whip she received from outgoing House Minority Whip David Bonior (D., Mich.). In 2001, Pelosi became the first woman elected to a leadership post in Congress. In 2002, she was elected Democratic minority leader. (AP Photo/ Joe Marquette)

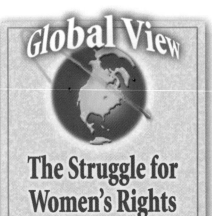

Global View

The Struggle for Women's Rights around the World

Although the last several decades have seen women's rights emerge as a global issue, progress has been slow. Only 72 of the 535 members of the U.S. Congress are women. Small numbers of women in the French Parliament have led to calls in France for legislation that guarantees that equal numbers of men and women will be elected. The struggle for women's rights in countries where cultural or legal practices perpetuate the inequality of women is even more difficult.

The Problem of Violence

Most people consider the right to be free from violence as one of the most basic human rights. Women's rights advocates point out that this right is threatened in societies that do not accept the premise that men and women are equal. In some parts of India, for example, a wife is considered the property of her husband, and he can do with her as he pleases. This has led to the practice of dowry killing. (A dowry is a sum of money given to a husband by the bride's family.) In a number of cases, husbands, dissatisfied with the size of dowries, have killed their wives in order to remarry for a "better deal"—a crime that is rarely prosecuted.

The Situation in Afghanistan

As the United States prepared to drive the Taliban government from power in Afghanistan in 2001, a startling documentary, "Behind the Veil," was aired repeatedly on CNN. A courageous female reporter had secretly filmed Afghan women being beaten in the streets, killed in public for trivial offenses, and generally subjugated in extreme ways. For the first time ever, women's rights became a major issue in our foreign policy. Americans learned that Afghan girls were barred from schools, and by law women were not allowed to work. Women who had lost their husbands during Afghanistan's civil wars were forced into begging and prostitution. Women had no access to medical care, and any woman found with an unrelated man could be (and many were) executed by stoning. The Taliban's so-called morals squad routinely beat women who laughed aloud in public.

FOR CRITICAL ANALYSIS

The United States was critical of the Taliban's treatment of women. Is it fair or appropriate for one country to judge the cultural practices of another? Why or why not?

---

absolute turnout of female voters nationally has been slightly higher than that of male voters. (For a discussion of the political status of women in other countries, see this chapter's *Global View* feature.)

Gender-Based Discrimination in the Workplace

Traditional cultural beliefs concerning the proper role of women in society continue to be evident not only in the political arena but also in the workplace. Since the 1960s, however, women have gained substantial protection against discrimination through laws mandating equal employment opportunities and equal pay.

Title VII of the Civil Rights Act of 1964

Title VII of the Civil Rights Act of 1964 prohibits gender discrimination in the employment context and has been used to strike down employment policies that discriminate against employees on the basis of gender. Even so-called protective policies have been held to violate Title VII if they have a discriminatory effect. In 1991, for example, the Supreme Court held that a fetal protection policy established by Johnson Controls, Inc., the country's largest producer of automobile batteries, violated Title VII. The policy required all women of childbearing age working in jobs that entailed periodic exposure to lead or other hazardous materials to prove that they were infertile or to transfer to other positions. Women who agreed to transfer

often had to accept cuts in pay and reduced job responsibilities. The Court concluded that women who are "as capable of doing their jobs as their male counterparts may not be forced to choose between having a child and having a job."[24]

In 1978, Congress amended Title VII to expand the definition of gender discrimination to include discrimination based on pregnancy. Women affected by pregnancy, childbirth, or related medical conditions must be treated—for all employment-related purposes, including the receipt of benefits under employee-benefit programs—the same as other persons not so affected but similar in ability to work.

Sexual Harassment

The Supreme Court has also held that Title VII's prohibition of gender-based discrimination extends to **sexual harassment** in the workplace. Sexual harassment occurs when job opportunities, promotions, salary increases, and so on are given in return for sexual favors. A special form of sexual harassment, called hostile-environment harassment, occurs when an employee is subjected to sexual conduct or comments that interfere with the employee's job performance or are so pervasive or severe as to create an intimidating, hostile, or offensive environment.

Definitional Problems. One of the questions faced by employers and employees—as well as the courts—is how to determine the point at which offensive conduct in the workplace is so "pervasive or severe" as to create a hostile working environment. In 1993, in *Harris v. Forklift Systems, Inc.,*[25] the Supreme Court attempted to give some guidelines on this issue, as well as on another question: Must a worker claiming to be a victim of hostile-environment harassment establish that the offensive conduct gave rise to serious emotional or psychological effects? Justice O'Connor answered both questions by stating, "So long as the environment would reasonably be perceived, and is perceived, as hostile or abusive, there is no need for it also to be psychologically injurious."

The Court's More Recent Decisions Concerning Harassment. In 1998, in *Faragher v. City of Boca Raton,*[26] the Court addressed another important question: Should an employer be held liable for its supervisor's sexual harassment of an employee even though the employer was unaware of the harrassment? The Court ruled that the employer in this case was liable but stated that the employer might have avoided such liability if it had taken reasonable care to prevent harassing behavior—which the employer had not done. In another case, *Burlington Industries v. Ellerth,*[27] the Court similarly held that an employer was liable for sexual harassment caused by a supervisor's actions even though the employee had suffered no tangible job consequences as a result of those actions. Again, the Court emphasized that a key factor in holding the employer liable was whether the employer had exercised reasonable care to prevent and promptly correct any sexually harassing behavior.

In another 1998 case, *Oncale v. Sundowner Offshore Services, Inc.,*[28] the Supreme Court addressed a further issue: Should Title VII protection be extended to cover situations in which individuals are harassed by members of the same sex? The Court answered this question in the affirmative.

Wage Discrimination

By the year 2010, women will constitute a majority of U.S. workers. Although Title VII and other legislation since the 1960s have mandated equal employment opportunities for men and women, women continue to earn less, on average, than men do.

DID YOU KNOW . . .
That a female worker at the sewer plant in Palmer, Massachusetts, filed a sexual-harassment complaint against the city after finding a sexually explicit magazine in the plant superintendent's drawer while looking for billing information ?

Sexual Harassment
Unwanted physical or verbal conduct or abuse of a sexual nature that interferes with a recipient's job performance, creates a hostile environment, or carries with it an implicit or explicit threat of adverse employment consequences.

INFOTRAC®
COLLEGE EDITION

For updates and more information about this issue, use the term "sexual harassment" in the Subject guide.

---

[24] *United Automobile Workers v. Johnson Controls, Inc.,* 499 U.S. 187 (1991).
[25] 510 U.S. 17 (1993).
[26] 524 U.S. 725 (1998).
[27] 524 U.S. 742 (1998).
[28] 523 U.S. 75 (1998).

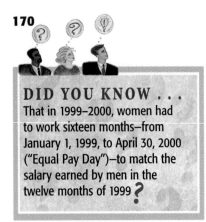

The Equal Pay Act of 1963. The issue of wage discrimination was first addressed during World War II (1939–1945), when the War Labor Board issued an "equal pay for women" policy. In implementing the policy, the board often evaluated jobs for their comparability and required equal pay for comparable jobs. The board's authority ended with the war. Supported by the next three presidential administrations, the Equal Pay Act was finally enacted in 1963 as an amendment to the Fair Labor Standards Act of 1938.

Basically, the Equal Pay Act requires employers to pay equal pay for substantially equal work. In other words, males cannot legally be paid more than females who perform essentially the same job. The Equal Pay Act did not address the fact that certain types of jobs traditionally held by women pay lower wages than the jobs usually held by men. For example, more women than men are salesclerks and nurses, whereas more men than women are construction workers and truck drivers. Even if all clerks performing substantially similar jobs for a company earned the same salaries, they would still be earning less than the company's truck drivers.

When Congress passed the Equal Pay Act in 1963, a woman, on average, made 59 cents for every dollar earned by a man. Figures recently released by the U.S. Department of Labor suggest that women now earn 76 cents for every dollar that men earn. In some areas, the wage gap is widening. According to the results of a General Accounting Office survey reported in 2002, female managers in ten industries made less money relative to male managers in 2000 than they did in 1995. In the entertainment industry, for example, in 2000 female managers earned 62 cents for every dollar earned by male managers—down from 83 cents in 1995.[29]

The Glass Ceiling. Although increased numbers of women are holding jobs in professions or business enterprises that were once dominated by men, few women hold top positions in their firms. Less than 12 percent of the Fortune 500 companies in America—America's leading corporations—have a woman as one of their five highest-paid executives. In all, according to Census Bureau statistics, men still hold 93 percent of the top corporate management positions in this country. Because the barriers faced by women in the corporate world are subtle and not easily pinpointed, they have been referred to as the "glass ceiling."

In the last decade, however, gender has become less of an issue in the workplace. Women are now breaking through the glass ceiling in far greater numbers than before. In fact, the latest government statistics show that in the last several years more women than men have been promoted to executive positions.

Civil Rights: Why Are They Important Today?

Civil rights have come a long way for all groups of Americans during the last fifty years. No longer is "a woman's place in the home." No longer is there legal segregation in public schools, colleges, and universities. No longer are minorities without protections in the workplace. Today, equal rights for minority groups are mandated by federal laws and, in many states by state laws as well. Americans feel that they enjoy a level of civil rights equal to or greater than that enjoyed in the rest of the world. (Some people claim, however, that the idea of a civil right can be taken to an extreme and that the expansion of civil rights has circumvented reasonable approaches to handling social problems—see this chapter's *Which Side Are You On?* feature for a further discussion of this issue.)

---

[29] The results of this survey are online at **http://www.gao.gov/audit.htm**. To view a copy of the results, enter "GAO-02-156" in the search box.

Which Side Are You On?
Do We Have Too Many Rights?

When the framers presented the final form of the Constitution to the states for ratification, many had reservations because the document did not provide sufficient protections for individual rights. Hence, we ended up with the Bill of Rights. Initially, individual rights expanded only gradually, but in the last half of the twentieth century, they expanded dramatically. The underlying goal of the "rights movement" is to protect our freedoms, particularly from the potentially crushing weight of federal, state, and local governments.

THE RIGHTS MOVEMENT
MAY HAVE GONE PAST COMMON SENSE

Today, some argue that the rights movement has created a sense of entitlement at the expense of personal responsibility. When people feel their rights have been violated, they call a lawyer. For example, in one case, a playground slide in Oologah, Oklahoma, a local landmark donated to the city in 1935, became the subject of a lawsuit. Parents sued the city when their child, left unattended, suffered minor injuries on the slide. The city dismantled the slide and sold it. To avoid future lawsuits, other cities have removed playground equipment such as seesaws and merry-go-rounds, and New York City routinely cuts tree limbs near its playgrounds to keep children from climbing the trees.

Patients have the right not to be misdiagnosed by their doctors. But the result is a health-care system in which doctors order expensive tests and follow-up visits that raise the cost of health care. Health-insurance premiums are then driven up, leaving millions of Americans uninsured—Americans who, many argue, have the right to affordable medical care.

Parents have the right to know that the equipment they buy for their children is safe. But where do the rights of parents end and the responsibility of manufacturers begin? This line is so blurred in our litigious society that collapsible strollers now come with the warning, "Remove child before folding." To some, the effort to protect individual rights has all but eclipsed the longstanding goal of society to be governed by laws and policies that defend reasonable conduct.[*]

THERE CAN NEVER BE TOO
MANY INDIVIDUAL RIGHTS

What has made America great, according to others, is that individuals can stand up to government. The expansion of the Bill of Rights has given Americans a better sense of individuality and self-esteem. Those in favor of expanding individual rights even further believe that the positions of women and minorities in today's society have improved only because of this expansion of individual rights.

Although too many lawsuits may be a by-product of these expanded rights, in their view, what is most important is the *net* effect. In other words, if we subtract the cost of "too many" rights from the benefits of all of these individual rights, we can see that, on net, American society is better off.

Moreover, is it possible to do an "accounting" when a feeling of empowerment is involved? When teachers, members of minority groups, women, and even juveniles know that they have recourse to the courts when their rights are trampled on, they feel stronger. That is what empowerment is all about. The result can be a more productive society overall and a society in which individuals know that others have to respect their rights—or pay the consequences.

WHAT'S YOUR POSITION?

Do expanded individual rights potentially reduce individual responsibility? Who benefits the most from expanded rights?

GOING ONLINE

For links to articles that are concerned with how the emphasis on civil rights can conflict with other social values, go to **http://www.rightsreform.net/links** and to **http://www.ourcommongood.com**. For a site whose mission is to promote the continued pursuit of social and economic justice, visit the Web site of Civilrights.org at **http://www.civilrights.org**.

[*]See, for example, Philip K. Howard, *The Lost Art of Drawing the Line: How Fairness Went Too Far* (New York: Random House, 2001).

Clearly, however, we still have some distance to go in the struggle for equal rights. Women still suffer from wage discrimination and face a "glass ceiling" in their efforts to advance to executive positions. Women, as well as African Americans and other minority groups, continue to be disproportionately represented in government offices. Young people face unequal educational opportunities. Not everyone has the ability to pay for medical care, as we pointed out in this chapter's opening *What If . . .*

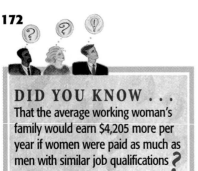

feature. Some contend that what we need today is a new civil rights agenda that puts less emphasis on race, ethnic origin, and gender and more on social and economic needs. Already, a new generation of civil rights activists is focusing simply on the challenge of improving the plight of the poor, without regard to race, ethnic origin, or gender.

One of the reasons a new civil rights agenda may be necessary is that the old concepts of majority versus minority are no longer applicable to the changing face of America. Consider that whites now constitute less than 50 percent of the population in California, Hawaii, and New Mexico, as mentioned earlier in this chapter. Consider also that intermarriage has broken down the old racial classifications. How does one classify, in terms of ethnicity or race, an individual who is part Chinese, part Thai, part black, and part white? How does one classify another individual who is part Mexican, part Anglo, and part black? In the color spectrum of a rainbow, there is no bright line separating one color from another. The same can be said with respect to the ethnic spectrum in the United States.

MAKING A DIFFERENCE | Citizenship and Immigrants' Rights

A great debate has taken place in recent years over the issue of immigrants' rights. The questions have included whether illegal immigrants can become citizens, whether employers are liable for hiring illegal immigrants, and whether the economy can absorb so many new workers.

What You Can Do

You can become involved in this national controversy over immigration and citizenship policy in a number of ways. You can pay attention to the often contradictory policies that are proposed in Congress to deal with the problem. If you feel deeply enough about this issue, you might wish to join action organizations that lobby through influencing public opinion or by exerting direct pressure on Congress and the executive branch. You can also lobby your local government to enact laws allowing aliens fleeing persecution to live in your community.

Immigrants' Rights Organizations

Many organizations are concerned with the way in which illegal immigrants are treated by federal and state police and immigration officials. Such groups want to maintain the nation's commitment to relatively free entry to people of all racial, ethnic, religious, political, and economic backgrounds. Their goals are fair immigration rules, greater protection for resident illegal aliens, and a more pluralistic and tolerant culture. The following groups are generally in favor of the right to immigrate and immigrants' rights:

National Network for Immigrant and Refugee Rights
310 Eighth St., Suite 303
Oakland, CA 94607
510-465-1984
http://www.nnirr.org

National Immigrants' Rights Project
American Civil Liberties Union
125 Broad St.
New York, NY 10004
212-549-2660
http://www.aclu.org/issues/ immigrant/hmir.html

Groups that usually support stricter enforcement of existing immigration laws or a more homogeneous culture include the following:

Federation for American Immigration Reform
1666 Connecticut Ave. N.W.
Suite 400
Washington, DC 20009
202-328-7004
http://www.fairus.org

U.S. English
1747 Pennsylvania Ave. N.W.
Suite 1100
Washington, DC 20006
202-833-0100
http://www.us-english.org

Key Terms

busing 152

civil rights 147

cloture 158

de facto segregation 152

de jure segregation 152

Equal Employment
   Opportunity Commission
   (EEOC) 158

feminism 165

filibuster 158

gender discrimination 165

grandfather clause 151

literacy test 151

poll tax 151

separate-but-equal
   doctrine 150

sexual harassment 169

subpoena 158

suffrage 164

white primary 150

Chapter Summary

1 The civil rights movement started with the struggle by African Americans for equality. Before the Civil War, most African Americans were slaves, and slavery was protected by the Constitution and the Supreme Court. African Americans were not considered citizens or entitled to the rights and privileges of citizenship. In 1863 and during the years after the Civil War, the Emancipation Proclamation and the Thirteenth, Fourteenth, and Fifteenth Amendments (the "Civil War amendments") legally and constitutionally ended slavery. From 1865 to 1875, to enforce the Civil War amendments, Congress passed a number of laws (civil rights acts). African Americans gained citizenship, the right to vote, equality before the law, and protection from deprivation of these rights.

2 Politically and socially, African American inequality continued. The *Civil Rights Cases* (1883) and *Plessy v. Ferguson* (1896) effectively nullified the civil rights acts of 1865 to 1875. In the *Civil Rights Cases,* the Supreme Court held that the Fourteenth Amendment did not apply to private invasions of individual rights. In *Plessy,* the Court upheld the separate-but-equal doctrine, declaring that segregation did not violate the Constitution. African Americans were excluded from the voting process through poll taxes, grandfather clauses, white primaries, and literacy tests.

3 Legal segregation was declared unconstitutional by the Supreme Court in *Brown v. Board of Education of Topeka* (1954), in which the Court stated that separation implied inferiority. In *Brown v. Board of Education* (1955), the Supreme Court ordered federal courts to ensure that public schools were desegregated "with all deliberate speed." Segregationists resisted with legal tactics, violence, and "white flight." Integrationists responded with court orders, federal marshals, and busing. Also in 1955, the modern civil rights movement began with a boycott of segregated public transportation in Montgomery, Alabama. Of particular impact was the Civil Rights Act of 1964. The act bans discrimination on the basis of race, color, religion, gender, or national origin in employment and public accommodations. The act created the Equal Employment Opportunity Commission to administer the legislation's provisions.

4 The Voting Rights Act of 1965 outlawed discriminatory voter-registration tests and authorized federal registration of persons and federally administered procedures in any state or political subdivision evidencing electoral discrimination or low registration rates. Subsequent amendments to this act extended its protections to other minorities. As a result of the Voting Rights Act, its amendments, and federal registration drives, African American political participation increased dramatically.

5 The protective legislation passed during and since the 1960s applies not only to African Americans but to other ethnic groups as well. Other minorities have also been increasingly represented in national and state politics, although they have yet to gain representation proportionate to their numbers in the U.S. population. Lingering social and economic disparities have led to a new civil rights agenda—one focusing less on racial differences and more on economic differences.

6 America has always been a land of immigrants and continues to be so. Today, more than one million immigrants from other nations enter the United States each year, and about 10 percent of the U.S. population consists of foreign-born persons. The civil rights legislation of the 1960s and later has helped immigrants to overcome some of the effects of prejudice and discrimination against them. One of the pressing issues facing today's political leaders is whether U.S. immigration policy should be changed.

7 In the early history of the United States, women were considered citizens, but by and large they had no political rights. After the first women's rights convention in 1848, the women's movement gained momentum. Women's organizations continued to work toward the goal of the enfranchisement of women. Progress was slow, and it was not until 1920, when the Nineteenth Amendment was ratified, that women finally obtained the right to vote.

8 The modern women's movement began in the 1960s in the wake of the civil rights movement. The National Organization for Women (NOW) was formed in 1966 to bring about complete equality for women in all walks of life. When the efforts to secure the ratification of the Equal Rights Amendment failed, the women's movement began to focus on litigation and increased political representation of women to further the goal of gender equality. Although women have found it difficult to gain positions of political leadership, their numbers in

Congress and in state and local government bodies increased significantly in the 1990s and early 2000s.

9 Women continue to struggle against gender discrimination in the employment context. Federal government efforts to eliminate gender discrimination in the workplace include Title VII of the Civil Rights Act of 1964, which prohibits, among other things, gender-based discrimination. The Supreme Court has upheld the right of women to be free from sexual harassment on the job, but defining what constitutes sexual harassment, particularly hostile-environment sexual harassment, continues to be a problem. Wage discrimination also continues to be a problem for women, as does the "glass ceiling" that prevents them from rising to the top of their business or professional firms.

Selected Print and Media Resources

SUGGESTED READINGS

Horowitz, David. *Uncivil Wars: The Controversy over Reparations for Slavery.* San Francisco: Encounter Books, 2001. Should African Americans receive reparations (payments) for their suffering in the past due to government policies, just as Japanese Americans and others have received such reparations? The author explores this question and provides a counterargument to the growing movement supporting reparations.

Keyssar, Alexander. *The Right to Vote: The Contested History of Democracy in the United States.* New York: Basic Books, 2001. Keyssar explores in detail the evolution of voting rights in the United States and offers some interesting insights along the way into why voting rights were expanded in some eras and contracted in others.

Patterson, James T. *Brown v. Board of Education: A Civil Rights Milestone and Its Troubled Legacy.* New York: Oxford University Press, 2001. The author, a distinguished historian on the faculty of Brown University, offers a candid look at the controversy over the 1954 *Brown v. Board of Education* decision and its consequences for American society.

Walker, Alice. *The Color Purple.* Chicago: Harcourt Brace, 1992. This Pulitzer Prize–winning novel, which was originally published in 1982, is about a black woman's struggle for justice, dignity, and empowerment. The book is rich in themes that concern women's issues.

Woodward, C. Vann. *The Strange Career of Jim Crow.* New York: Oxford University Press, 1957. This is the classic study of segregation in the southern United States.

MEDIA RESOURCES

Beyond the Glass Ceiling—A CNN–produced program showing the difficulties women face in trying to rise to the top in corporate America.

Dr. Martin Luther King: A Historical Perspective—One of the best documentaries on the civil rights movement, focusing on the life and times of Martin Luther King, Jr.

Frederick Douglass—A documentary about the man who escaped slavery to become a world-famous orator, journalist, diplomat, abolitionist, and civil rights advocate in the mid-1800s.

I Have a Dream—Another film on Martin Luther King, Jr., this one focusing on the 1963 march on Washington and King's "I have a dream" speech, which some consider to be one of the greatest speeches of all time.

Malcolm X—A 1992 film, directed by Spike Lee and starring Denzel Washington, that depicts the life of the controversial "black power" leader Malcolm X. Malcolm X, who was assassinated on February 21, 1965, clearly had a different vision from that of Martin Luther King, Jr., regarding how to achieve civil rights, respect, and equality for black Americans.

Separate but Equal—A video focusing on Thurgood Marshall, the lawyer (and later Supreme Court justice) who took the struggle for equal rights to the Supreme Court, and on the rise and demise of segregation in America.

Your CD-ROM Resources

In addition to the chapter content containing hot links, the following resources are available on the CD-ROM:

- **Internet Activities**—Jim Crow laws, equal pay for women.

- **Critical Thinking Exercises**—National health insurance system, immigration, struggles for African Americans and women.

- **Self-Check on Important Themes**—Can You Answer These?

- **Video**—*Affirmative Action.*

- **Public Opinion Data**—Race relations in the U.S.

- **InfoTrac Exercise**—"At Least You're Not Black: Asian Americans in U.S. Race Relations."

- **Simulation**—You Are There!

- **Participation Exercise**—Write your senator or representative regarding a bill that would have a significant impact on civil rights if passed.

- **MicroCase Exercise**—"By the Numbers: 'Life Chances' for Whites and African Americans."

- **Additional Resources**—All court cases, Elizabeth Cady Stanton, *The Seneca Falls Declaration* (1848), Standing Bear, *This Land Was Owned by Our Tribe* (1879), Civil Rights Act of 1964, Voting Rights Act of 1965, Civil Rights Act of 1968.

e-mocracy

Colorblind on the Web

Experts at Forrester Research, Inc., have concluded that the Web offers Americans new ways to build friendships and personal relationships. Among other things, young Americans enjoy the "colorblind" nature of the Web. There is no way to know if e-mail recipients or persons in a chat room are black, white, brown, or some other color. There is no way to tell if they are rich or poor or if they speak with a southern accent or even a stutter. Of course, it is too early to proclaim that the Internet will do away with judgments based on appearance altogether, but the Forrester researchers have found that the "Net-powered" generation has a higher comfort level with diversity than its elders do. Once people have established an online relationship, they are less likely to let prejudices concerning race, age, or appearance affect that relationship.

Logging On

There are an incredible number of resources on the World Wide Web relating to civil rights—and particularly the problem of discrimination. One of the most active and visible civil rights organizations today is the American Civil Liberties Union. You can access its Web site at

http://www.aclu.org

An extensive collection of information on Martin Luther King, Jr., is offered by the Martin Luther King Papers Project at Stanford University. Go to

http://www.stanford.edu/group/King

To learn more about the Equal Employment Opportunity Commission (EEOC) or to find out how to file a complaint with that agency, go to

http://www.eeoc.gov

The National Association for the Advancement of Colored People (NAACP) is online at

http://www.naacp.org

For information on the League of Latin American Citizens (LULAC), go to

http://www.lulac.org

The URL for the Feminist Majority Foundation, which provides information on empowerment and equality for women, is

http://www.feminist.org

To contact the National Organization for Women (NOW) or check out the resources and links it offers, go to

http://www.now.org

You can find an extensive array of political information and news concerning the African American community at

http://www.bigvote.org

The National Immigration Forum "embraces and upholds America's tradition as a nation of immigrants." You can access this organization's Web site at

http://www.immigrationforum.org

Using the Internet for Political Analysis

Sometimes, given all of the laws that have been passed and court cases decided, it may seem that all of the basic issues concerning equality for American citizens have been resolved. To test that assumption, take a look at one of the Web sites listed here and identify at least two or three issues of equal treatment that remain unresolved.

Latino Issues Forum, at

http://www.lif.org

NAACP Online, at

http://www.naacp.org

Feminist Majority Online, at

http://www.feminist.org

CHAPTER 6

Civil Rights: Beyond Equal Protection

Affirmative Action
•
Bilingual Education
•
Special Protection
for Older Americans
•
Securing Rights
for Persons with Disabilities
•
The Rights and Status
of Gay Males and Lesbians
•
The Rights and
Status of Juveniles

The Supreme Court Banned Affirmative Action ?

BACKGROUND

By the 1970s, affirmative action in the form of racial quotas and preferences had become widespread in college admissions, government construction contracts, and elsewhere. The Supreme Court ruled in 1978 in *Regents of the University of California v. Bakke* that although race could not be the sole criterion for determining admissions, it could be one of several factors.

In the latter half of the 1990s, the federal courts began to chip away at racial preferences, at least in college admissions. In 1996, Californians voted to outlaw racial preferences by all state-sponsored institutions, including state universities and colleges. Two years later, the state of Washington did likewise. In 2002, a federal appeals court outlawed the University of Georgia's use of racial preferences.

WHAT IF THE SUPREME COURT BANNED AFFIRMATIVE ACTION?

What if the Supreme Court rules that any type of affirmative action program is unconstitutional? Preferences favoring one group or class of people necessarily involve discriminating against another group or class. Would a complete ban on affirmative action unleash a national firestorm? Would colleges and universities, particularly the Ivy League schools, become overwhelmingly white? Although we have no way of knowing for certain what might result on a national basis, we do know what happened in California.

POST–PROPOSITION 209 CALIFORNIA

After Californians passed Proposition 209 in 1996 outlawing state programs that discriminated against—or gave preference to—individuals based on their race, some things did change for the University of California system. Since 1996, the percentages of blacks and Hispanics have dropped at the Berkeley and Los Angeles campuses. In contrast, they have risen at other University of California campuses. (It should be noted, too, that the number of Asian students has increased at the Berkeley and Los Angeles campuses.)

Perhaps alarmed at having fewer black and Hispanic students at the two major University of California campuses, the president of that system quietly put into effect a "top 4 percent plan." Under this plan, the top 4 percent of students from certain low-performing and predominantly minority high schools are automatically accepted at the Berkeley and Los Angeles campuses. Since 1996, Texas has had a similar plan, but using a much higher percentage.

AFFIRMATIVE ACTION HAS BECOME MORE DIFFICULT TO IMPLEMENT, ANYWAY

If the Supreme Court banned affirmative action, some minorities might actually benefit. Most affirmative action programs originally targeted African Americans. Later, Hispanics were targeted. But America has numerous other minority groups, including Chinese Americans, Japanese Americans, and Pacific Islanders. There are also numerous multiracial Americans, many of whom cannot easily be pigeonholed into a "legal" minority group. Banning all affirmative action might increase the chances that these noncategorized minorities would get into colleges and universities, obtain government construction contracts, and the like.

Some argue that extending "minority" status for affirmative action purposes to all minorities and women is a better approach than banning affirmative action entirely. The problem with this solution is that two-thirds of the American population would be classed as minorities.

AN END TO RACIAL CLASSIFICATION?

Proponents of banning affirmative action believe that doing so would lead to an end to racial classification. After all, before preferences can be given under any affirmative action rule, a minority class has to be identified. Typically, this has been done based on race—Hispanic, African American, and so on. Such racial classifications force those who participate to be identified by their group rather than by their individual character. Those in favor of banning affirmative action claim that just as racial classification was unacceptable when it was used to *exclude* certain individuals from various programs, it should be unacceptable when it is used to *include* certain individuals in those programs.

FOR CRITICAL ANALYSIS

1. Affirmative action has been justified in part by the need to create more diversity in the American workplace and educational institutions. Is this argument as strong today as it would have been a hundred years ago? Why or why not?

2. Is it possible that the abolition of affirmative action at prestigious universities could lead to higher graduation rates for minority students at those institutions?

This chapter's opening *What If . . .* touched on an issue that has long challenged Americans: How can the goal of equality best be achieved? More specifically, does equality mean equality of opportunity or equality of outcome? If social benefits, such as access to higher educational facilities, are based on merit (talent, skills, and achievement), equality of opportunity will exist, because all students have the opportunity to make it to the top of their classes. Yet some degree of inequality will certainly result, because some students have more talents and skills than others.

Remember from the previous chapter that the Civil Rights Act of 1964 prohibited discrimination against any person on the basis of race, color, national origin, religion, or gender. The act also established the right to equal opportunity in employment. A basic problem remained, however: minority groups and women, because of past discrimination, often lacked the education and skills to compete effectively in the marketplace. In 1965, the federal government attempted to remedy this problem by implementing the concept of affirmative action. **Affirmative action** policies attempt to "level the playing field" by giving special preferences in educational admissions and employment decisions to groups that have been discriminated against in the past. These policies go beyond a strict interpretation of the equal protection clause of the Fourteenth Amendment. So do a number of other laws and programs established by the government during and since the 1960s.

In this chapter, we explore the controversy engendered by affirmative action policies and bilingual education programs. We then look at the gains that have been made by older Americans, persons with disabilities, and gay men and lesbians in their struggle for equal treatment. We conclude the chapter with a discussion of the rights and status of children in American society.

Affirmative Action
A policy in educational admissions or job hiring that gives special consideration or compensatory treatment to traditionally disadvantaged groups in an effort to overcome present effects of past discrimination.

Affirmative Action

In 1965, President Lyndon Johnson ordered that affirmative action policies be undertaken to remedy the effects of past discrimination. All government agencies, including those of state and local governments, were required to implement such policies. Additionally, affirmative action requirements were imposed on companies that sell goods or services to the federal government and on institutions that receive federal funds. Affirmative action policies were also required whenever an employer had been ordered to develop such a plan by a court or by the Equal Employment Opportunity Commission because of evidence of past discrimination. Finally, labor unions that had been found to discriminate against women or minorities in the past were required to establish and follow affirmative action plans.

Affirmative action programs have been controversial because they sometimes result in discrimination against majority groups, such as white males (or discrimination against other minority groups that may not be given preferential treatment under a particular affirmative action program). At issue in the current debate over affirmative action programs is whether such programs, because of their inherently discriminatory nature, violate the equal protection clause of the Fourteenth Amendment to the Constitution.

The *Bakke* Case

The first Supreme Court case addressing the constitutionality of affirmative action programs examined a program implemented by the University of California at Davis. Allan Bakke, a Vietnam War veteran and engineer who had been turned down for medical school at the Davis campus of the University of California, discovered that his academic record was better than those of some of the minority applicants who had been admitted to the program. He sued the University of California regents,

On the University of Michigan campus, students react to a federal appeals court decision in 2002 to uphold the use of race in admissions to the university's law school. Proponents of affirmative action call themselves members of the "new civil rights movement" and have formed a group called the Fight for Equality By Any Means Necessary (BAMN). (AP Photo/Danny Moloshok)

Reverse Discrimination
The charge that affirmative action programs requiring preferential treatment or quotas discriminate against those who do not have minority status.

Citizens in California demonstrate their opposition to Proposition 209, the ballot initiative that ended all state-sponsored affirmative action programs in the state. Why are affirmative action programs more controversial today than they were a decade or so ago? (Mark Richards, PhotoEdit)

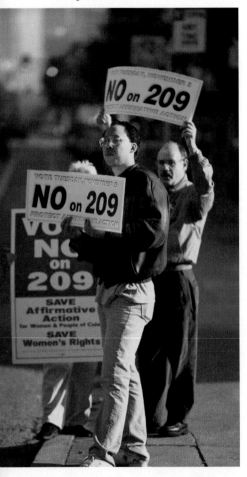

alleging **reverse discrimination**. The UC–Davis Medical School had held sixteen places out of one hundred for educationally "disadvantaged students" each year, and the administrators at that campus admitted to using race as a criterion for admission for these particular minority slots. At trial in 1974, Bakke said that his exclusion from medical school violated his rights under the Fourteenth Amendment's provision for equal protection of the laws. The trial court agreed. On appeal, the California Supreme Court agreed also. Finally, the regents of the university appealed to the United States Supreme Court.

In 1978, the Supreme Court handed down its decision in *Regents of the University of California v. Bakke.*[1] The Court did not actually rule against affirmative action programs. Rather, it held that Bakke must be admitted to the UC–Davis Medical School because its admissions policy had used race as the sole criterion for the sixteen "minority" positions. Justice Lewis Powell, speaking for the Court, indicated that while race can be considered "as a factor" among others in admissions (and presumably hiring) decisions, race cannot be the sole factor. So affirmative action programs, but not specific quota systems, were upheld as constitutional.

Further Limitations on Affirmative Action

A number of cases decided during the 1980s and 1990s placed further limits on affirmative action programs. In a landmark decision in 1995, *Adarand Constructors, Inc. v. Peña,*[2] the Supreme Court held that any federal, state, or local affirmative action program that uses racial or ethnic classifications as the basis for making decisions is subject to "strict scrutiny" by the courts. Under a strict-scrutiny analysis, to be constitutional, a discriminatory law or action must be narrowly tailored to meet a *compelling* government interest. In effect, the Court's opinion in *Adarand* means that an affirmative action program cannot make use of quotas or preferences for unqualified persons, and once it has succeeded in achieving that compelling government interest, the program must be changed or dropped.

In 1996, a federal appellate court went even further. In *Hopwood v. State of Texas,*[3] two white law school applicants sued the University of Texas School of Law in Austin, alleging that they were denied admission because of the school's affirmative action program. The program allowed admissions officials to take race and other factors into consideration when determining which students would be admitted. The federal appellate court held that the program violated the equal protection clause because it discriminated in favor of minority applicants. Significantly, the court directly challenged the *Bakke* decision by stating that the use of race even as a means of achieving diversity on college campuses "undercuts the Fourteenth Amendment." The Supreme Court declined to hear the case, thus letting the lower court's decision stand.

State Ballot Initiatives

As mentioned in the chapter-opening *What If . . .* feature, a ballot initiative known as Proposition 209, passed by California voters in 1996, amended that state's constitution to end all state-sponsored affirmative action programs. The law was immediately challenged in court by civil rights groups and others. These groups claimed that the law violated the Fourteenth Amendment by denying racial minorities and women the equal protection of the laws. In 1997, however, a federal appellate court upheld the constitutionality of the amendment. Thus, affirmative action is now illegal in California in all state-sponsored institutions, including state agencies and educational institutions. In 1998, Washington voters also approved a law banning affirmative action in that state.

---

[1] 438 U.S. 265 (1978).
[2] 515 U.S. 200 (1995).
[3] 84 F.3d 720 (5th Cir. 1996).

Will Affirmative Action Survive?

Many groups contend that the time has come for a "colorblind" society in which business firms, government agencies, and educational institutions do not make decisions on the basis of racial and ethnic differences. Nevertheless, affirmative action continues to receive widespread support. The Clinton administration (1993–2001) was in favor of retaining such policies, although perhaps with some modifications. The Bush administration has not advocated continuing affirmative action, but neither has it argued against these policies. As already indicated, the Supreme Court has not yet issued a blanket decision on the matter.

Bilingual Education

The continuous influx of immigrants into this country presents an ongoing challenge—how to overcome language barriers. About half of the states have responded to this challenge by passing "English-only" laws, making English the official language of those states (for a further discussion of these laws and whether they should be upheld, see this chapter's *Which Side Are You On?* feature on the following page). Language issues have been particularly challenging for the schools. Throughout our history, educators have been faced with the question of how best to educate children who do not speak English or do not speak it very well.

Early Language Policies

In the nineteenth century, the language of instruction was not a significant political issue. Children were taught in a wide variety of languages, depending on the wishes of the parents in a particular school district. Some schools provided instruction in German, which was the nation's most common second language at that time. Other schools taught children in Polish, Dutch, or Italian. Some midwestern districts established special "dual-language" schools in which students were taught for half a day in English and half a day in German.

By the beginning of the twentieth century, this open language policy began to change as waves of new immigrants from Europe arrived in the United States. Political leaders in some states began to fear the political effects of what some perceived to be

---

INFOTRAC®
COLLEGE EDITION

For updates and more information about this topic, use the term "affirmative action" in the Subject guide.

Which Side Are You On?
Should English-Only Laws Be Upheld?

Contrary to popular belief, English is not the official language of the United States. In fact, there is no official language. English is nonetheless the language of choice in most transactions conducted in this country, as well as in literature, on television, and so on.

Through the years, the states have been able to pass different forms of English-only laws as they have seen fit. Some of these laws have been challenged as unconstitutional and discriminatory. Some state and federal appellate courts have agreed; others have not.

In 2001, the United States Supreme Court reviewed a case involving this issue. The Alabama State Department of Safety had implemented a policy requiring that all driver's tests be administered in English. Prior to 1991, the state had administered the written part of the driver's examination in twelve languages, including Spanish, Cambodian, Japanese, and Thai. In 1991, the department required English-only exams and banned the use of interpreters and translation dictionaries. A group of non-English-speaking residents of Alabama claimed that the agency's policy discriminated against them in violation of the Civil Rights Act of 1964. The Supreme Court did not agree and held that the plaintiffs had no right to sue the Alabama agency for the discriminatory effects of its policy.*

ENGLISH-ONLY LAWS ARE BENEFICIAL

Proponents of English-only laws argue that one reason America became great was that its immigrants quickly learned English and were assimilated. They view English-

*Alexander v. Sandoval, 532 U.S. 275 (2001).

only laws as a counter to policies that allow and indeed encourage the use of other languages. Those who support the Alabama English-only rule for driver's license exams argue that it makes sense because, after all, drivers in Alabama must be able to read road signs, all of which are in English.

ENGLISH-ONLY LAWS ARE CLEARLY DISCRIMINATORY

Those who argue against English-only laws point out that they affect non-English-speaking residents in a discriminatory way. That is to say, even if the laws are not intentionally discriminatory, their effect, or impact, is discriminatory. Therefore, such laws, at a minimum, violate provisions of the Civil Rights Act of 1964. Moreover, opponents of English-only laws point out that those who speak English poorly need time to assimilate and to learn the language. During this assimilation period, English-only laws prevent such individuals from having full access to the workplace, government benefits, and the like.

WHAT'S YOUR POSITION?

Do you think that English-only laws are discriminatory and should be banned? Or can they serve a useful purpose? Generally, who gains and who loses in states that pass English-only laws?

GOING ONLINE

To learn more about arguments in favor of English-only laws, visit the Web sites of U.S. English (at **http://www. us-english.org**) and English First (at **http://www. englishfirst.org**). The American Civil Liberties Union presents arguments against English-only laws at **http://www.aclu.org/library/pbp6.html**.

DID YOU KNOW . . .
That about one-third of the world's nations have official language provisions in their constitutions **?**

a growing "babel of tongues." By 1915, thirteen states had passed laws requiring basic subjects, such as math, geography, and science, be taught in English. Anti-German sentiment during World War I (1914–1918) led to further fears of the effects of educating students in a foreign language (particularly German). By the end of the war, thirty-seven states had passed laws restricting foreign-language instruction.

Although most of these restrictive laws were subsequently repealed or struck down by the courts, English-only instruction became the norm throughout the country. Increased immigration from Mexico and Latin American countries during the 1950s, however, caused many educators to be concerned about the language problems facing these immigrants. Spanish had effectively become America's second language, yet local school districts in some parts of the Southwest prohibited children from speaking Spanish, even on school playgrounds. In the 1960s, bilingual education programs began to be implemented as a solution to the language problems facing immigrants.

Accommodating Diversity with Bilingual Education

Bilingual education programs teach children in their native language while also teaching them English. To some extent, today's bilingual education programs are the result of the government policies favoring multiculturalism that grew out of the civil rights movement. Multiculturalism involves the belief that the government should accommodate the needs of different cultural groups and should protect and encourage ethnic and cultural differences.

Children attending classes taught in English were frequently encouraged by their teachers as well as their parents to speak English as much as possible, both at school and at home. Children who did so felt distanced from their grandparents and family members who spoke no English and, as a result, felt cut off from their ethnic backgrounds. Bilingual education was premised on the hope that, over time, Hispanic children would become truly bilingual without having to sacrifice their close family relationships and cultural heritage.

Congress authorized bilingual education programs in 1968 when it passed the Bilingual Education Act, which was intended primarily to help Hispanic children learn English. In a 1974 case, *Lau v. Nichols*,[4] the Supreme Court bolstered the claim that children have a right to bilingual education. In that case, the Court ordered a California school district to provide special programs for Chinese students with language difficulties if a substantial number of these children attended school in the district. Today, most bilingual education programs are for Hispanic American children, particularly in areas of the country, such as California and Texas, where there are large numbers of Hispanic residents.

The Current Controversy over Bilingual Education

The bilingual programs established in the 1960s and subsequently have increasingly been coming under attack. Indeed, in 1998 California residents passed a ballot initiative that called for the end of bilingual education programs in that state. The law allowed schools to implement "English-immersion" programs instead. In these programs, students are given intensive instruction in English for a limited period of time and then placed in regular classrooms.

---

[4]414 U.S. 563 (1974).

Children are taught in Spanish and English at the J. F. Oyster Bilingual Elementary School in Washington, D.C. Proponents of bilingual education argue that such instruction helps students acquire English more quickly than English-only programs and builds greater literacy in both the first language and in English. Evidence in California seems to point in the other direction, however. After that state's bilingual program was terminated, achievement in formerly bilingual schools actually improved. Why might this have occurred? (AP Photo/Evan Vucci)

The law was immediately challenged in court on the ground that it unconstitutionally discriminated against non-English-speaking groups. A federal district court, however, concluded that the new law did not violate the equal protection clause and allowed the law to stand, thus ending bilingual education efforts in California.

Special Protection for Older Americans

Americans are getting older. In colonial times, about half the population was under the age of sixteen. In 1990, fewer than one in four Americans was under the age of sixteen, and half the population was thirty-three or older. By the year 2050, at least half could be thirty-nine or older.

Today, about 35 million Americans (nearly 13 percent of the population) are aged sixty-five or older. As can be seen in Figure 6–1, by the year 2020, this figure is projected to reach about 54 million. By 2040, the portion of the population over age sixty-five will more than double.

Senior citizens face a variety of problems unique to their group. One problem that seems to endure, despite government legislation designed to prevent it, is age discrimination in employment. Others include health care and income security. Since the 1930s, the government has established programs, such as Social Security and Medicare, designed to protect the health and welfare of older Americans. Although we touch on these public benefits in this section, they are explored more fully in Chapter 16.

Age Discrimination in Employment

Age discrimination is potentially the most widespread form of discrimination, because anyone—regardless of race, color, national origin, or gender—could be a victim at some point in life. The unstated policies of some companies not to hire or to demote or dismiss people they feel are "too old" have made it difficult for some older workers to succeed in their jobs or continue with their careers. Additionally, older workers have fallen victim at times to cost-cutting efforts by employers. To reduce operational costs,

To find out more about this topic, use the term "age discrimination" in the Subject guide.

FIGURE 6–1

Population Projections: Persons Aged 65 or Older (in Millions)

As shown here, the number of Americans who will be sixty-five years of age or older will grow dramatically during the next decade. The number will more than double between 2005 and 2040. The political power of these older Americans will grow as their numbers increase.

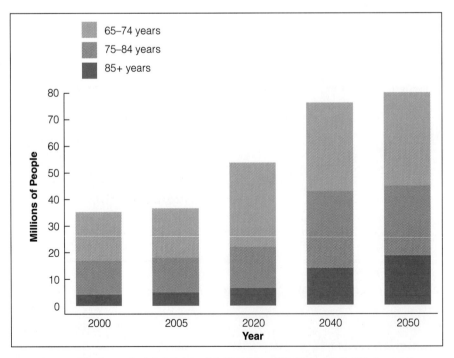

SOURCE: Bureau of the Census, *Statistical Abstract of the United States* (Washington, D.C.: U.S. Government Printing Office, 2002), p. 17.

companies may replace older, higher-salaried workers with younger, lower-salaried workers.

The Age Discrimination in Employment Act of 1967. In an attempt to protect older employees from such discriminatory practices, Congress passed the Age Discrimination in Employment Act (ADEA) in 1967. The act, which applies to employers, employment agencies, and labor organizations and covers individuals over the age of forty, prohibits discrimination against individuals on the basis of age unless age is shown to be a bona fide occupational qualification reasonably necessary to the normal operation of the particular business.

Specifically, it is against the law to discriminate by age in wages, benefits, hours worked, or availability of overtime. Employers and unions may not discriminate in providing fringe benefits, such as education or training programs, career development, sick leave, and vacations. It is a violation of the act to publish notices or advertisements indicating an age-preference limitation or discrimination based on age. Even advertisements that imply a preference for youthful workers over older workers are in violation of the law. Requesting age on an application is not illegal but may be closely scrutinized in light of the employer's hiring practices.

To succeed in a suit for age discrimination, an employee must prove that the employer's action, such as a decision to fire the employee, was motivated, at least in part, by age bias. Proof that qualified older employees are generally discharged before younger employees or that co-workers continually made unflattering age-related comments about the discharged worker may be enough. In 1996, the Supreme Court held that even if an older worker is replaced by a younger worker falling under the protection of the ADEA—that is, by a younger worker who is also over the age of forty—the older worker is entitled to bring a suit under the ADEA. The Court stated that the issue in all ADEA cases is whether age discrimination has in fact occurred, regardless of the age of the replacement worker.[5]

As discussed in Chapter 3 in the context of federalism, in 2000 the Supreme Court limited the applicability of the ADEA in its decision in *Kimel v. Florida Board of Regents*.[6] The Court held that the sovereign immunity granted the states by the Eleventh Amendment to the Constitution precluded suits against a state by private parties alleging violations of the ADEA. Victims of age discrimination can bring actions under state statutes, however, and most states have laws protecting their citizens from age discrimination.

Mandatory Retirement. The ADEA, as initially passed, did not address one of the major problems facing older workers—**mandatory retirement** rules, which required employees to retire when they reached a certain age. Mandatory retirement rules often meant that competent, well-trained employees who wanted to continue working were unable to do so. In 1978, in an amendment to the ADEA, Congress prohibited mandatory retirement rules with respect to most employees under the age of seventy. Many states had already passed similar statutes. In 1986, Congress outlawed mandatory retirement rules entirely for all but a few selected occupations, such as firefighting.

Age, Political Participation, and Public Benefits

If we use voter participation as a measure of political involvement, it is clear that political participation increases with age. Generally, the over-sixty-five age group ranks first in voter registration and in actual turnout on election day. Usually, the voting rate in the over-sixty-five category is at least twice that of the youngest voting group (those under twenty-one years of age).

DID YOU KNOW . . .
That in 1922, at age eighty-seven, Rebecca Latimer Felton was the first and oldest woman to serve in the U.S. Senate—although she was appointed as a token gesture and was allowed to serve only one day **?**

Mandatory Retirement
Forced retirement when a person reaches a certain age.

---

[5] *O'Connor v. Consolidated Coil Caterers Corp.*, 517 U.S. 308 (1996).
[6] 528 U.S. 62 (2000).

Older Americans work for their interests through a number of large and effective political associations. The largest group is the AARP, formerly known as the American Association of Retired Persons, whose members are limited to those aged fifty and older. Founded in 1958, it has a current membership of more than 35 million. The AARP and the National Retired Teachers' Association have united in a powerful joint effort to ensure beneficial treatment for older Americans by lobbying for legislation at the federal and state levels. They use the same staff in Washington and provide almost the same services to their members, including low-priced group insurance and travel programs.

Because of their voting and lobbying power, Americans over the age of sixty-five receive a disproportionate share of government spending. Almost half of the entire federal budget is spent on Medicare and Social Security. Medicare costs recently have risen at about twice the rate of inflation for the economy as a whole. Many programs, such as Medicare and Social Security, have been tied legislatively to external factors so that spending on them has become, to a large degree, uncontrollable and automatic. Indeed, there is growing concern over whether the government is allocating too many resources to seniors and not enough to the welfare of younger Americans.

Securing Rights for Persons with Disabilities

Like older Americans, persons with disabilities did not fall under the protective umbrella of the Civil Rights Act of 1964. Remember from Chapter 5 that the 1964 act prohibited discrimination against any person on the basis of race, color, national origin, religion, or gender. As just noted, Congress addressed the problem of age discrimination in 1967. By the 1970s, Congress also began to pass legislation to protect Americans with disabilities. In 1973, Congress passed the Rehabilitation Act, which prohibited discrimination against persons with disabilities in programs receiving federal aid. A 1978 amendment to the act established the Architectural and Transportation Barriers Compliance Board. Regulations for ramps, elevators, and the like in all federal buildings were implemented. Congress passed the Education for All Handicapped Children Act in 1975. It guarantees that all children with disabilities will receive an "appropriate" education. The most significant federal legislation with respect to the rights of persons with disabilities, however, is the Americans with Disabilities Act (ADA), which Congress passed in 1990.

The Americans with Disabilities Act of 1990

The ADA requires that all public buildings and public services be accessible to persons with disabilities. The act also mandates that employers must reasonably accommodate the needs of workers or potential workers with disabilities. Physical access means ramps; handrails; wheelchair-accessible restrooms, counters, drinking fountains, telephones, and doorways; and more accessible mass transit. In addition, other steps must be taken to comply with the act. Car-rental companies must provide cars with hand controls for disabled drivers. Telephone companies are required to have operators to pass on messages from speech-impaired persons who use telephones with keyboards.

The ADA requires employers to "reasonably accommodate" the needs of persons with disabilities unless to do so would cause the employer to suffer an "undue hardship." The ADA defines persons with disabilities as persons who have physical or mental impairments that "substantially limit" their everyday activities. Health conditions that have been considered disabilities under federal law include blindness, alcoholism, heart disease, cancer, muscular dystrophy, cerebral palsy, paraplegia, diabetes,

President George H. W. Bush signs the 1990 Americans with Disabilities Act. The act requires corporations and public institutions to implement access for disabled Americans and requires employers to accommodate workers with disabilities. (Ron Sachs, Sygma)

acquired immune deficiency syndrome (AIDS), and the human immunodeficiency virus (HIV) that causes AIDS.

The ADA does not require that *unqualified* applicants with disabilities be hired or retained. If a job applicant or an employee with a disability, with reasonable accommodation, can perform essential job functions, however, then the employer must make the accommodation. Required accommodations may include installing ramps for a wheelchair, establishing more flexible working hours, creating or modifying job assignments, and creating or improving training materials and procedures.

Interpreting and Applying the ADA

The ADA has been controversial, not because of its goal—preventing discrimination against persons with disabilities—but because of the difficulties in interpreting and applying the act's provisions. For example, what constitutes a physical or mental impairment? At what point does such an impairment "substantially limit" a "major life activity," and what constitutes a major life activity? Finally, what exactly is required to "reasonably accommodate" persons with disabilities, and at what point does accommodation constitute an "undue hardship" for employers?

The courts have had to address these questions, and the outcome of any particular case is not always predictable. For example, in one case an employee came to work toting a loaded gun. The employer, who, like all employers, was required by law to maintain a safe workplace for employees, fired the employee on the spot. The employee took the employer to court, and the jury concluded that the employee's behavior was the result of a mental impairment. Therefore, the employer should not have fired him but accommodated his disability in some way, such as by giving him a leave of absence.

Uncertainty about how the act will be applied creates special problems for employers, business owners, and organizations that must comply with the act's requirements. Despite the ADA's shortcomings, however, many persons suffering from disabilities have benefited from the act, as well as from the changing social attitudes toward them that the act has helped to foster. And a significant number of people with disabilities take advantage of the act's protective provisions. As you can see in Figure 6–2, about one-fifth of the complaints filed with the Equal Employment Opportunity Commission in 2001 were for disability-based discrimination.

INFOTRAC®
COLLEGE EDITION

For updates and more information about this issue, use the term "Americans with Disabilities Act" in the Subject guide.

FIGURE 6–2

Charges Filed with the EEOC in 2001 Alleging Discrimination

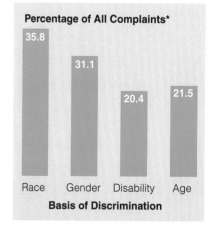

Percentage of All Complaints*

Basis of Discrimination	
Race	35.8
Gender	31.1
Disability	20.4
Age	21.5

*Percents sum to more than 100 percent because some complaints allege more than one form of discrimination.

SOURCE: Equal Employment Opportunity Commission, 2002.

Limiting the Scope and Applicability of the ADA

Beginning in 1999, the Supreme Court has issued a series of decisions that effectively limit the scope of the ADA. In 1999, for example, the Court held in *Sutton v. United Airlines, Inc.*[7] that a condition (in this case, severe myopia, or near-sightedness) that can be corrected with medication or a corrective device (in this case, corrective lenses) is not considered a disability under the ADA. In other words, the determination of whether a person is substantially limited in a major life activity is based on how the person functions when taking medication or using corrective devices, not on how the person functions without these measures. Since then, the courts have held that plaintiffs with bipolar disorder, epilepsy, diabetes, and other conditions do not fall under the ADA's protections if the conditions can be corrected with medication or corrective devices—even though the plaintiffs contended that they were discriminated against because of their conditions.

In a 2002 decision, the Court further limited the scope of the ADA by its broad interpretation of what constitutes a substantially limiting impairment of a major life activity. The case before the Court raised the question of whether carpal tunnel syndrome constituted a disability under the ADA. The Court unanimously held that it did not. The Court stated that although an employee with carpal tunnel syndrome could not perform the manual tasks associated with her job, the injury did not constitute a disability under the ADA because it did not "substantially limit" the major life activity of performing manual tasks.[8] In other words, someone suffering from severe carpal tunnel syndrome must be impaired to the extent that it prevents or severely restricts activities that are of central importance to most people's daily lives, not just work-related tasks.

The Supreme Court has also limited the applicability of the ADA by holding that lawsuits under the ADA cannot be brought against state government employers.[9] In a 2001 case, the Court concluded—as it did with respect to the ADEA, as mentioned earlier—that states, as sovereigns, are immune from lawsuits brought against them by private parties under the federal ADA.

---

[7] 527 U.S. 471 (1999).
[8] *Toyota Manufacturing, Kentucky, Inc. v. Williams,* 534 U.S. 184 (2002).
[9] *Board of Trustees of the University of Alabama v. Garret,* 531 U.S. 356 (2001).

The disabled have emerged as a significant political force. Persons with disabilities have held numerous demonstrations, demanding to have their rights upheld in the work force and in society. (Mark Richards, PhotoEdit)

The Rights and Status of Gay Males and Lesbians

On June 27, 1969, patrons of the Stonewall Inn, a New York City bar popular with gay men and lesbians, responded to a police raid by throwing beer cans and bottles because they were angry at what they felt was unrelenting police harassment. In the ensuing riot, which lasted two nights, hundreds of gay men and lesbians fought with police. Before Stonewall, the stigma attached to homosexuality and the resulting fear of exposure had tended to keep most gay men and lesbians quiescent. In the months immediately after Stonewall, however, "gay power" graffiti began to appear in New York City. The Gay Liberation Front and the Gay Activist Alliance were formed, and similar groups sprang up in other parts of the country. Thus, Stonewall has been called "the shot heard round the homosexual world."

Growth in the Gay Male and Lesbian Rights Movement

The Stonewall incident marked the beginning of the movement for gay and lesbian rights. Since then, gay men and lesbians have formed thousands of organizations to exert pressure on legislatures, the media, schools, churches, and other organizations to recognize their right to equal treatment. One of the largest gay rights groups today is the Human Rights Campaign Fund, whose goal is to see federal gay rights laws passed. Another major group is the National Gay and Lesbian Task Force, which works toward the repeal of state sodomy laws (laws prohibiting certain forms of sexual activity, including homosexual relationships). The American Civil Liberties Union also actively promotes laws protecting gay men and lesbians, as do several other liberal civil rights organizations.

To a great extent, lesbian and gay groups have succeeded in changing public opinion—and state and local laws—relating to their status and rights. Nevertheless, they continue to struggle against age-old biases against homosexuality, often rooted in deeply held religious beliefs, and the rights of gay men and lesbians remain an extremely divisive issue in American society. These biases were clearly illustrated in a widely publicized case involving the Boy Scouts of America. The case arose after a Boy Scout troop in New Jersey refused to allow gay activist James Dale to be a Scout leader. In 2000, the case came before the Supreme Court, which held that, as a private organization, the Boy Scouts had the right to determine the requirements for becoming a Scout leader.[10]

State and Local Laws against Gay Men and Lesbians

Prior to the Stonewall incident in 1969, forty-nine states had sodomy laws (Illinois, which had repealed its sodomy law in 1962, was the only exception). During the 1970s and 1980s, more than half of these laws were either repealed or struck down by the courts.

The trend toward repealing state antigay laws ended in 1986 with the Supreme Court's decision in *Bowers v. Hardwick*.[11] In that case, the Court upheld, by a five-to-four vote, a Georgia law that made homosexual conduct between two adults a crime. Justice Byron White, writing for the majority, stated that "we are quite unwilling" to "announce . . . a fundamental right to engage in homosexual sodomy." Since this decision, however, courts in some states have invalidated state sodomy statutes on the ground that they violate rights guaranteed by state constitutions. For example, in

---

[10] *Boy Scouts of America v. Dale,* 530 U.S. 640 (2000).
[11] 478 U.S. 186 (1986).

1998 the Supreme Court of Georgia held that the state's sodomy statute violated the right of privacy as guaranteed by the Georgia constitution's due process clause.[12] Today, sodomy statutes have been repealed or invalidated in all but eighteen states.

In a 1996 case, *Romer v. Evans*,[13] the Supreme Court issued a decision that had a significant impact on the rights of gay men and lesbians. The case involved a Colorado state constitutional amendment that invalidated all existing state and local laws protecting homosexuals from discrimination. The Supreme Court held that the amendment violated the equal protection clause of the Constitution because it denied to homosexuals in Colorado—but to no other Colorado residents—"the right to seek specific protection of the law." The Court stated that the equal protection clause simply does not permit Colorado to make homosexuals "unequal to everyone else."

Today, twelve states[14] and more than 230 cities and counties have special laws protecting lesbians and gay men against discrimination in employment, housing, public accommodations, and credit. Several laws at the national level have also been changed in the past two decades. Among other things, the government has lifted a ban on hiring gay men and lesbians and voided a 1952 law prohibiting gay men and lesbians from immigrating to the United States. Currently, Congress is considering a bill that would bar workplace discrimination based on sexual orientation.

The Gay Community and Politics

Politicians at the national level have not overlooked the potential significance of homosexual issues in American politics. While conservative politicians generally have been critical of efforts to secure gay and lesbian rights, liberals, by and large, have been speaking out for gay rights in the last two decades. In 1980, the Democratic platform included a gay plank for the first time. Walter Mondale, former vice president of the United States and the Democratic Party nominee for president in 1984, addressed a gay convention and openly bid for the political support of gay and lesbian groups. The gay community also supported Jesse Jackson's 1988 bid for the presidency and Jackson's Rainbow Coalition.

President Bill Clinton long embraced much of the gay rights agenda and became the first sitting president to address a gay rights organization. In 1997, in a speech intentionally reminiscent of Harry Truman's 1947 speech to an African American civil rights organization, Clinton pledged his support for equal rights for gay and lesbian Americans at a fund-raiser sponsored by the Human Rights Campaign Fund. In 2000, George W. Bush became the first Republican presidential candidate to meet with a large group of openly gay leaders to discuss their issues. Although Bush asserted that he would continue to oppose gay marriage and adoption, he also said that being openly gay would not disqualify a person from serving in a prominent position in his administration.

While to date eleven openly gay men and lesbians have been elected to the U.S. House of Representatives, none has succeeded yet in gaining a seat in the U.S. Senate. Gay rights groups continue to work for more political representation in Congress, however. In the 2002 campaigns, gay and lesbian rights groups supported at least 15 candidates for the Senate and 168 candidates for the House.

Gay Men and Lesbians in the Military

The U.S. Department of Defense traditionally has viewed homosexuality as incompatible with military service. Supporters of gay and lesbian rights have attacked this

---

[12] *Powell v. State*, 270 Ga. 327 (1998).

[13] 517 U.S. 620 (1996).

[14] California, Connecticut, Hawaii, Maryland, Massachusetts, Minnesota, Nevada, New Hampshire, New Jersey, Rhode Island, Vermont, and Wisconsin. Maine also had a law protecting gay and lesbian rights until February 1998, when the law was repealed in a referendum.

policy in recent years, and in 1993 the policy was modified. In that year, President Clinton announced that a new policy, generally characterized as "don't ask, don't tell," would be in effect. Enlistees would not be asked about their sexual orientation, and gay men and lesbians would be allowed to serve in the military so long as they did not declare that they were gay or lesbian, or commit homosexual acts. Military officials endorsed the new policy, after opposing it initially, but supporters of gay rights were not enthusiastic. Clinton had promised during his presidential campaign to repeal outright the long-standing ban.

Several gay men and lesbians who have been discharged from military service have protested their discharges by bringing suit against the Defense Department. In one case, a former Navy lieutenant, Paul Thomasson, was dismissed from the service in 1995 after stating "I am gay" in a letter to his commanding admiral. In 1996, a federal appellate court reviewed the case and concluded that the courts should defer, as they traditionally have, to the other branches of government, especially in military policy. A dissenting judge wrote that Thomasson was being punished for "nothing more than an expression of his state of mind."[15]

A widely publicized 1998 case involved the Navy's dismissal of a naval officer, Timothy McVeigh,[16] on the ground that he had entered "gay" on a profile page for his account with America Online (AOL). Naval officers claimed that this amounted to a public declaration of McVeigh's gay status and thus justified his discharge. McVeigh argued that it was not a public declaration. Furthermore, contended McVeigh, the Navy had violated a 1986 federal privacy law governing electronic communications by obtaining information from AOL without a warrant or a court order. In 1998, a federal court judge agreed and ordered the Navy to reinstate McVeigh.[17]

At issue in these cases are the constitutional rights to free speech, privacy, and the equal protection of the laws. Because the lower courts are in disagreement, it is likely that the Supreme Court will rule on the matter in the future.

Same-Sex Marriages

Perhaps one of the most sensitive political issues with respect to the rights of gay and lesbian couples is whether they should be allowed to marry, just as heterosexual couples are. Recall from Chapter 3's *Politics and Gender* feature that the controversy over this issue was fueled in 1993 when the Hawaii Supreme Court ruled that denying marriage licenses to gay couples might violate the equal protection clause of the Hawaii constitution. The court stated that unless Hawaii could offer a "compelling" reason to maintain this discriminatory practice, it must be abandoned. The Hawaii Supreme Court then sent the case back to the trial court to determine if the state did indeed have such a compelling reason. In 1996, the trial court ruled that the state had failed to meet this burden, and therefore the ban on same-sex marriages violated the state constitution.

In the wake of these events, other states began to worry about whether they would have to treat persons who were legally married in Hawaii as married couples in their states as well. Opponents of gay rights pushed for state laws banning same-sex marriages, and a number of states enacted such laws. At the federal level, Congress passed the Defense of Marriage Act of 1996, which bans federal recognition of lesbian and gay couples and allows state governments to ignore same-sex marriages performed in other states. Ironically, the Hawaii court decisions that gave rise to these concerns have largely come to naught. In 1998, the residents in that state voted for a state constitutional amendment that allows the Hawaii legislature to ban same-sex marriages.

The controversy over gay marriages was fueled again by developments in the state of Vermont. In 1999, the Vermont Supreme Court ruled that gay couples are entitled

---

[15] *Thomasson v. Perry,* 80 F.3d 915 (4th Cir. 1996).

[16] This is not the Timothy McVeigh who was convicted for the 1995 bombing of the Alfred P. Murrah Federal Building in Oklahoma City.

[17] *McVeigh v. Cohen,* 983 F.Supp. 215 (D.C. 1998).

Gay men and lesbians demonstrate in New York City's Bryant Park in favor of same-sex marriages. They want the state of New York to legalize such marriages. (Ilkka Uimonen, Sygma)

to the same benefits of marriage as opposite-sex couples. Subsequently, in April 2000, the Vermont legislature passed a law permitting gay and lesbian couples to form "civil unions." The law entitled partners forming civil unions to receive some three hundred state benefits available to married couples, including the rights to inherit a partner's property and to decide on medical treatment for an incapacitated partner. It did not, however, entitle those partners to receive any benefits allowed to married couples under federal law, such as spousal Social Security benefits. Many felt that the Vermont legislature did not go far enough—it should have allowed full legal marriage rights to same-sex couples. (For a discussion of one nation that has taken this step, see this chapter's *Global View* feature.) As mentioned in Chapter 3, the Vermont legislature is currently considering a bill that would repeal the 2000 law, so the future of civil unions in that state is still unclear.

Child Custody and Adoption

Gay men and lesbians have also faced difficulties in obtaining child-custody and adoption rights. Courts around the country, when deciding which of two parents should have custody, have wrestled with how much weight, if any, should be given to a parent's sexual orientation. For some time, the courts were split fairly evenly on this issue. In about half the states, courts held that a parent's sexual orientation should not be a significant factor in determining child custody. Courts in other states, however, tended to give more weight to sexual orientation. In one case, a court even went so far as to award custody to a father because the child's mother was a lesbian, even though the father had served eight years in prison for killing his first wife. Today, however, courts in the majority of states no longer deny custody or visitation rights to persons solely on the basis of their sexual orientation.

The last decade has also seen a sharp climb in the number of gay men and lesbians who are adopting children. To date, twenty-two states have allowed lesbians and gay men to adopt children through state-operated or private adoption agencies.

INFOTRAC®
COLLEGE EDITION

For updates and more information about gay rights, use the term "gay liberation movement" in the Subject guide.

Same-Sex Marriages Legalized in the Netherlands

The issue of gay marriage has definitely become global. In 1998, the Netherlands legalized "registered partnerships." Then, in 2000, the Dutch legislature passed a law allowing same-sex couples to legally marry and have the same rights and privileges as heterosexual married couples.

On the Stroke of Midnight

On April 1, 2001, four same-sex Dutch couples were married at Amsterdam City Hall. The event was watched by hundreds of journalists and gay activists. These couples were able to legally marry because the new Dutch law no longer defines marriage as a union between a man and a woman. A partner in a same-sex marriage in the Netherlands can take the other partner's last name. Same-sex marriage partners can also adopt children, if the children are Dutch.

Will Other Nations Respect Dutch Law?

Inevitably, as same-sex couples marry in the Netherlands and move to other countries, legal problems will surface. In particular, the Dutch law raises a question similar to that faced by states in the United States with respect to other states' laws: Will other nations recognize a same-sex marriage performed in the Netherlands? Traditionally, a marriage performed in one country has been recognized in other countries, particularly within the European Union. Given the controversy over gay marriages worldwide, one can expect conflicts among nations over this issue in the future.

FOR CRITICAL ANALYSIS

What benefits to society might accrue from the passage of same-sex marriage laws similar to those in the Netherlands? Which groups might oppose such laws?

This couple was among four gay couples who married in Amsterdam's City Hall on April 1, 2001, the day a new law in the Netherlands allowing such marriages took effect. (AP Photo/ Peter Dejong)

The Rights and Status of Juveniles

Approximately 76 million Americans—almost 30 percent of the total population—are under twenty-one years of age. The definition of *children* ranges from persons under age sixteen to persons under age twenty-one. However defined, children in the United States have fewer rights and protections than any other major group in society.

The reason for this lack of rights is the common presumption of society and its lawmakers that children are basically protected by their parents. This is not to say that children are the exclusive property of the parents. Rather, an overwhelming case in favor of *not* allowing parents to control the actions of their children must be presented before children can be given authorization to act without parental consent (or before the state can be given authorization to act on children's behalf without regard to their parents' wishes).

Supreme Court decisions affecting children's rights began a process of slow evolution with *Brown v. Board of Education of Topeka*, the landmark civil rights case of 1954 discussed in Chapter 5. In *Brown*, the Court granted children the status of

rights-bearing persons. In 1967, in *In re Gault*,[18] the Court expressly held that children have a constitutional right to be represented by counsel at the government's expense in a criminal action. Five years later, the Court acknowledged that "children are 'persons' within the meaning of the Bill of Rights. We have held so over and over again."[19] In 1976, the Court recognized a girl's right to have an abortion without consulting her parents.[20] (More recently, however, the Court has allowed state laws to dictate whether the child must obtain consent.)

Voting Rights and the Young

The Twenty-sixth Amendment to the Constitution, ratified on July 1, 1971, reads as follows:

> The right of citizens of the United States, who are eighteen years of age or older, to vote shall not be denied or abridged by the United States or by any State on account of age.

Before this amendment was ratified, the age at which citizens could vote was twenty-one in most states. Why did the Twenty-sixth Amendment specify age eighteen? Why not seventeen or sixteen? And why did it take until 1971 to allow those between the ages of eighteen and twenty-one to vote?

There are no easy answers to such questions. One cannot argue simply that those under twenty-one, or those under eighteen for that matter, are "incompetent." Incompetent at what? Certainly, one could find a significant number of seventeen-year-olds who can understand the political issues presented to them as well as can many adults eligible to vote. One of the arguments used for granting suffrage to eighteen-year-olds was that, because they could be drafted to fight in the country's wars, they had a stake in public policy. At the time, the example of the Vietnam War (1964–1975) was paramount.

Have eighteen- to twenty-year-olds used their right to vote? Yes and no. In 1972, immediately after the passage of the Twenty-sixth Amendment, 58 percent of eighteen- to twenty-year-olds were registered to vote, and 48.4 percent reported that they had voted. But by the 1996 presidential elections, of the 10.7 million Americans in the eighteen-to-twenty voting-age bracket, 45.6 percent were registered, and 31.2 percent reported that they had voted. The 2000 presidential elections showed similar results. In contrast, voter turnout among Americans aged sixty-five or older is very high, usually between 60 and 70 percent.

The Rights of Children in Civil and Criminal Proceedings

Children today have limited rights in civil and criminal proceedings in our judicial system. Different procedural rules and judicial safeguards apply in civil and criminal laws. **Civil law** relates in part to contracts among private individuals or companies. **Criminal law** relates to crimes against society that are defined by society acting through its legislatures.

Civil Rights of Juveniles.   The civil rights of children are defined exclusively by state law with respect to private contract negotiations, rights, and remedies. The legal definition of **majority** varies from eighteen to twenty-one years of age, depending on the state. As a rule, an individual who is legally a minor cannot be held responsible for contracts that he or she forms with others. In most states, only contracts entered into for so-called **necessaries** (things necessary for subsistence, as determined by the courts) can be enforced against minors. Also, when minors engage in negligent behav-

Civil Law
The law regulating conduct between private persons over noncriminal matters. Under civil law, the government provides the forum for the settlement of disputes between private parties in such matters as contracts, domestic relations, and business relations.

Criminal Law
The law that defines crimes and provides punishment for violations. In criminal cases, the government is the prosecutor because crimes are against the public order.

Majority
Full age; the age at which a person is entitled by law to the right to manage her or his own affairs and to the full enjoyment of civil rights.

Necessaries
In contract law, necessaries include whatever is reasonably necessary for suitable subsistence as measured by age, state, condition in life, and so on.

---

[18] 387 U.S. 1 (1967).
[19] *Wisconsin v. Yoder*, 406 U.S. 205 (1972).
[20] *Planned Parenthood of Central Missouri v. Danforth*, 428 U.S. 52 (1976).

ior, typically their parents are liable. If, for example, a minor destroys a neighbor's fence, the neighbor may bring suit against the child's parent but not against the child.

Civil law also encompasses the area of child custody. Child-custody rulings have traditionally given little weight to the wishes of the child. Courts have maintained the right to act on behalf of the child's "best interests" but have sometimes been constrained from doing so by the "greater" rights possessed by adults. For instance, a widely publicized Michigan Supreme Court ruling awarded legal custody of a two-and-a-half-year-old Michigan resident to an Iowa couple, the child's biological parents. A Michigan couple, who had cared for the child since shortly after its birth and who had petitioned to adopt the child, lost out in the custody battle. The court clearly said that the law had allowed it to consider only the parents' rights and not the child's best interests.

Children's rights and their ability to articulate their rights for themselves in custody matters were strengthened, however, by several well-publicized rulings involving older children. In one case, for example, an eleven-year-old Florida boy filed suit in his own name, assisted by his own privately retained legal counsel, to terminate his relationship with his biological parents and to have the court affirm his right to be adopted by foster parents. The court granted his request, although it did not agree procedurally with the method by which the boy initiated the suit.[21] The news media characterized the case as the first instance in which a minor child had "divorced" himself from his parents.

Criminal Rights of Juveniles.   One of the main requirements for an act to be criminal is intent. The law has given children certain defenses against criminal prosecution because of their presumed inability to have criminal intent. Under the **common law,** children up to seven years of age were considered incapable of committing a crime because they did not have the moral sense to understand that they were doing wrong. Children between the ages of seven and fourteen were also presumed to be incapable of committing a crime, but this presumption could be challenged by showing that the child understood the wrongful nature of the act. Today, states vary in

Common Law
Judge-made law that originated in England from decisions shaped according to prevailing customs. Decisions were applied to similar situations and thus gradually became common to the nation.

---

[21]*Kingsley v. Kingsley,* 623 So.2d 780 (Fla.App. 1993).

This juvenile is being arrested in the same way that an adult would be, but he does not have the rights under criminal law of an adult. Juveniles normally receive less severe punishment than adults do for similar crimes, however. (Bart Bartholomew, Black Star)

their approaches. Most states retain the common law approach, although age limits vary from state to state. Other states have simply set a minimum age for criminal responsibility.

All states have juvenile court systems that handle children below the age of criminal responsibility who commit delinquent acts. The aim of juvenile courts is allegedly to reform rather than to punish. In states that retain the common law approach, children who are above the minimum age but are still juveniles can be turned over to the criminal courts if the juvenile court determines that they should be treated as adults. Children still do not have the right to trial by jury or to post bail. Also, in most states parents can still commit their minor children to state mental institutions without allowing the child a hearing.

Although minors still do not usually have the full rights of adults in criminal proceedings, they have certain advantages. In felony, manslaughter, murder, armed robbery, and assault cases, traditionally juveniles were not tried as adults. They were often sentenced to probation or "reform" school for a relatively few years regardless of the seriousness of their crimes. Today, however, most states allow juveniles to be tried as adults (often at the discretion of the judge) for certain crimes, such as murder. When they are tried as adults, they are treated to due process of law and tried for the crime, rather than being given the paternalistic treatment reserved for the juvenile delinquent. Juveniles who are tried as adults may also face adult penalties, including the death penalty. Currently, about seventy people are on the nation's death rows for crimes that they committed when they were sixteen or seventeen.

Approaches to Dealing with Crime by Juveniles.   What to do about crime committed by juveniles is a pressing problem for today's political leaders. One approach to the problem is to treat juveniles as adults, which more and more judges seem to be doing. There appears to be widespread public support for this approach, as well as for lowering the age at which juveniles should receive adult treatment in criminal proceedings. Polling data show that two-thirds of U.S. adults think that juveniles under the age of thirteen who commit murder should be tried as adults. Another approach is to hold parents responsible for the crimes of their minor children (a minority of the states do so under so-called parental-responsibility laws). These are contradictory approaches, to be sure. Yet they perhaps reflect the divided opinion in our society concerning the rights of children versus the rights of parents.

In the wake of school shootings and other crimes committed in the schools, many districts have implemented what are called zero-tolerance policies. These policies have become controversial in recent years because, according to some, they are enforced without regard to the particular circumstances surrounding an incident. (See this chapter's *Politics and Juveniles* feature for a further discussion of this issue.)

Civil Rights Issues: Why Are They Important Today?

Fifty years ago, the laws protecting several of the groups discussed in this chapter were largely nonexistent. The reason we now have laws protecting older Americans, persons with disabilities, and gay males and lesbians is that these and other groups pressured the government to enact such laws. If no one had taken action on these issues, you can be sure that these groups would still have few, if any, legal protections. Certainly, they would not enjoy the degree of equal protection under the laws that they enjoy today.

That said, it is clear that the struggle for equality is far from over. Civil rights are very important in our society today, particularly for those who continue to face dis-

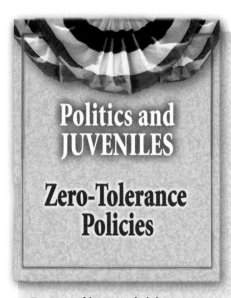

Politics and JUVENILES

Zero-Tolerance Policies

Because of increased violence among America's youth, both in and out of school, an increasingly large number of school districts have implemented zero-tolerance rules.

THE GUN-FREE SCHOOL ZONES ACT PUT THE WHEELS IN MOTION

Zero tolerance throughout the nation's schools began with the Gun-Free School Zones Act of 1990. Under the act, a student who brings a firearm to school must be expelled for one year. State and local authorities have expanded the principle to require mandatory expulsion for threats of violence, disobedience, defiance of authority, disruptive behavior, profanity, and possession of drugs or alcohol. Obviously, enforcement varies from school district to school district.

The federal government estimates that almost 100,000 students each year are expelled under zero-tolerance rules. In the Chicago public schools alone, about 2,500 students are expelled each year and another 13,000 are suspended.

ZERO-TOLERANCE POLICIES SOMETIMES LEAD TO THE ABSURD

Since the implementation of zero-tolerance policies, numerous students have been suspended for trivial actions. A Massachusetts girl was expelled for bringing a plastic knife with her lunch. A Pennsylvania boy was suspended for having a soft plastic toy axe as part of his Halloween fire-fighter costume. A high school honors student in Richmond, Virginia, was expelled for five days when he defended himself against an attacker. Two Chicago eighth graders were arrested and suspended for bringing bags of colored powder to school. The bags contained Kool-Aid. It was only after the children's attorneys forced the authorities to test the substance that the charges were dropped.

THE COURTS WILL NOT INTERVENE

Benjamin Ratner, a conscientious eighth grader at a middle school in Virginia, took a knife away from a schoolmate who said she was considering suicide. He was suspended for four months because he was caught holding the knife. The school has a zero-tolerance policy.

The Ratners sued the school district. A federal court ruled that the courts have no say about zero-tolerance policies. The judge, however, praised Ben's common sense. The court pointed out that there is only one way to change zero-tolerance policies: the state legislatures must make new laws.

FOR CRITICAL ANALYSIS

School-ground killings make the news, but they constitute less than 0.6 percent of all youth homicides. Do these statistics justify the loosening of zero-tolerance policies? Why or why not?

crimination because of their race, color, national origin, religion, disability, age, gender, or sexual preferences. How equality can best be attained continues to generate controversy. The debate over affirmative action is illustrative. Is it time to go beyond affirmative action programs based on race, ethnicity, and gender to programs based on other criteria, such as economic disadvantage? Should affirmative action be banned entirely—a possibility we looked at in the chapter-opening *What If . . .* feature? However this controversy is decided, you can be sure that the decision will have a significant effect on American society.

In spite of laws protecting against age discrimination, older Americans continue to struggle against this form of discrimination in the workplace—largely because it is difficult to prove, to a court's satisfaction, that age discrimination has actually occurred. Similarly, persons with disabilities face ongoing challenges. One challenge is not knowing, for certain, whether a particular physical or mental impairment will qualify as a disability under the Americans with Disabilities Act. The answer often depends on how a specific court decides the issue. Meanwhile, gay males and lesbians continue to face discrimination in all walks of life. Whether same-sex couples should be permitted to marry and have the right to adopt children are issues that remain divisive in our society. Finally, some contend that we do far too little to ensure the welfare and protect the rights of children in our society.

MAKING A DIFFERENCE | Dealing with Discrimination

When you apply for a job, you may be subjected to a variety of possibly discriminatory practices—based on your race, color, gender, religion, age, national origin, sexual preference, or disability. You may also be subjected to a battery of tests, some of which you may feel are discriminatory. At both the state and federal levels, the government continues to examine the fairness and validity of criteria used in job-applicant screening.

Taking the First Steps

If you believe that you have been discriminated against by a potential employer, you may wish to consider the following steps:

1. Evaluate your own capabilities, and determine if you are truly qualified for the position.
2. Analyze the reasons that you were turned down. Do you feel that others would agree with you that you have been the object of discrimination, or would they uphold your employer's claim?
3. If you still believe that you have been unfairly treated, you have

recourse to several agencies and services.

You should first speak to the personnel director of the company and politely explain that you feel you have not been adequately evaluated. If asked, explain your concerns clearly. If necessary, go into explicit detail, and indicate that you feel you may have been discriminated against.

Contacting State Agencies

If a second evaluation is not forthcoming, contact the local branch of your state employment agency. If you still do not obtain adequate help, contact one or more of the following state agencies, usually found by looking in your telephone directory under "State Government" listings.

1. If a government entity is involved, a state ombudsperson or citizen aide who will mediate may be available.
2. You may wish to contact the state civil rights commission, which will at least give you advice even if it does not wish to take up your case.

3. The state attorney general's office will normally have a division dealing with discrimination and civil rights.
4. There may be a special commission or department specifically set up to help you, such as a women's status commission or a commission on Hispanics or Asian Americans. If you are a woman or a member of such a minority group, contact these commissions.

Contacting National Organizations

Finally, at the national level, you can contact the American Civil Liberties Union, 125 Broad St., New York, N.Y. 10004-2400, 212-549-2500, or check

http://www.aclu.org

You can also contact the most appropriate federal agency: the Equal Employment Opportunity Commission, 1801 L St. N.W., Washington, DC 20507, 202-663-4900, or go to

http://www.eeoc.gov

Key Terms

affirmative action 179	common law 195	majority 194	necessaries 194
civil law 194	criminal law 194	mandatory retirement 185	reverse discrimination 180

Chapter Summary

1 Affirmative action programs have been controversial because they can lead to reverse discrimination against majority groups or even other minority groups. In an early case on the issue, *Regents of the University of California v. Bakke* (1978), the Supreme Court held that using race as the sole criterion for admission to a university is improper. Since *Bakke* a number of Supreme Court decisions have further limited affirmative action programs. Recent Supreme Court decisions, particularly

Adarand Constructors, Inc. v. Peña, and decisions by the lower courts that the Supreme Court has let stand, such as *Hopwood v. State of Texas*, have led some observers to conclude that it will be difficult in the future for any affirmative action program to pass constitutional muster. California voters banned state-sponsored affirmative action in that state in a 1996 ballot initiative known as Proposition 209, which was upheld as constitutional by a federal appellate court. In 1998, voters in the state of Washington ended affirmative action in that state. Whether affirmative action programs will survive the current backlash against them remains to be seen.

2   Bilingual education programs, like affirmative action, have come under attack in recent years. The major criticism against bilingual education programs is that they impede children's ability to learn English quickly and succeed academically.

3   Problems associated with aging and retirement are becoming increasingly important as the number of older persons in the United States increases. The Age Discrimination in Employment Act of 1967 prohibits job-related discrimination against individuals over the age of forty on the basis of age, unless age is shown to be a bona fide occupational qualification reasonably necessary to the normal operation of the business. Amendments to the act prohibit mandatory retirement except in a few selected professions. As a group, older people contribute significantly to American political life, ranking first in voter registration and turnout and being well represented in Congress. Through a variety of organizations, older Americans lobby effectively at both the federal and state levels.

4   In 1973, Congress passed the Rehabilitation Act, which prohibits discrimination against persons with disabilities in programs receiving federal aid. Regulations implementing the act provide for ramps, elevators, and the like in all federal buildings. The Education for All Handicapped Children Act (1975) provides that all children with disabilities should receive an "appropriate" education. The Americans with Disabilities Act of 1990 prohibits job discrimination against persons with physical and mental disabilities, requiring that positive steps be taken to comply with the act. The act also requires expanded access to public facilities, including transportation, and to services offered by such private concerns as car-rental and telephone companies.

5   Gay and lesbian rights groups, which first began to form in 1969, now number in the thousands. These groups work to promote laws protecting gay men and lesbians from discrimination and to repeal antigay laws. Since 1969, sodomy laws have been repealed or struck down by the courts in all but eighteen states. Twelve states and more than 230 cities and counties now have laws prohibiting discrimination based on sexual orientation. Gay men and lesbians are no longer barred from federal employment or from immigrating to this country, and Congress is currently considering a bill that would ban employment discrimination against gay men and lesbians. Since 1980, liberal Democrats at the national level have supported gay and lesbian rights and sought electoral support from these groups. The military's "don't ask, don't tell" policy has fueled extensive controversy, as have same-sex marriages and child-custody issues.

6   Although children form a large group of Americans, they have the fewest rights and protections, in part because it is commonly presumed that parents protect their children. The Twenty-sixth Amendment grants the right to vote to those aged eighteen or older. In most states, only contracts entered into for necessaries can be enforced against minors. When minors engage in negligent acts, their parents may be held liable. Minors have some defense against criminal prosecution because of their presumed inability to have criminal intent at certain ages. For those below the age of criminal responsibility, there are state juvenile courts. When minors are tried as adults, they are entitled to the procedural protections afforded to adults and are subject to adult penalties, including the death penalty.

Selected Print and Media Resources

SUGGESTED READINGS

Leone, Bruno, *et al.*, eds. *Child Welfare: Opposing Viewpoints.* San Diego, Calif.: Greenhaven Press, 1998. This "issues" book presents opposing viewpoints on various aspects of child welfare.

Murdoch, Joyce, and Deb Price. *Courting Justice: Gay Men and Lesbians v. the Supreme Court.* New York: Basic Books, 2001. The authors present an extremely thorough analysis of gay-rights cases that have come before the United States Supreme Court in the last fifty years. In the process, they also portray the heroic quest for justice by the petitioners, who frequently lost everything in the effort.

Roemer, John E. *Equality of Opportunity.* Cambridge, Mass.: Harvard University Press, 1998. Roemer examines the two positions in the affirmative action debate and concludes that both emphasize equal opportunity; they differ over whether equal opportunity should be required before or after the competition (such as for jobs) starts.

Sowell, Thomas. *The Quest for Cosmic Justice.* New York: Free Press, 1999. Sowell takes issue with the idea of social ("cosmic") justice—the liberal notion that people can right all wrongs through such programs as affirmative action and equal pay acts. He claims that such concepts undermine the principles of liberty and justice on which this nation was founded.

Spann, Girardeau A. *The Law of Affirmative Action: Twenty-Five Years of Supreme Court Decisions on Race and Remedies.* New York: New York University Press, 2000. The author examines every major United States Supreme Court decision on racial affirmative action and seeks to explain the Court's position on the issue in recent years.

Steele, Shelby. *A Dream Deferred: The Second Betrayal of Black Freedom in America.* New York: HarperCollins, 1998. The author, a distinguished black intellectual, contends that affirmative action (a "second betrayal" of black Americans) is less an attempt to create true equality between the races than an attempt by liberals to rid the country of guilt for slavery and segregation (the first betrayal).

MEDIA RESOURCES

Affirmative Action: The History of an Idea—This program explores the historical roots of affirmative action and the current debate over its usefulness.

Cocoon—A 1985 film fantasy about a group of Florida retirees who have found their fountain of youth in the form of friendly extraterrestrials.

G. I. Jane—A 1997 film about a woman who is out to prove that she can survive Navy SEAL training that is so rigorous that many (60 percent) of the men do not make it.

Shot by a Kid—A film documenting the relationship among children, guns, and violence in four major cities of the United States.

Your CD-ROM Resources

In addition to the chapter content containing hot links, the following resources are available on the CD-ROM:

- **Internet Activities**—Implementing the Americans with Disabilities Act, Zero tolerance policies.
- **Critical Thinking Exercises**—Bilingual education, voting.
- **Self-Check on Important Themes**—Can You Answer These?
- **Animated Figures**—Figure 6–1, "Population Projections: Persons Aged 65 or Older," Figure 6–2, "Charges Filed with the EEOC Alleging Discrimination."
- **Videos**—*The Bakke Case, Proposition 209.*

- **Public Opinion Data**—Find contrasting views on several topics.
- **InfoTrac Exercise**—"Affirmative Action: Don't Mend It or End It—Bend It."
- **Simulation**—You Are There!
- **Participation Exercise**—Participate in a NewsGroup on homosexuality.
- **MicroCase Exercise**—"By the Numbers: Government Spending on Entitlement Programs."
- **Additional Resources**—All court cases, The Americans with Disabilities Act (1990), Dewey, *Democracy and Education* (1916).

e-mocracy

Civil Rights Information Online

Today, thanks to the Internet, information on civil rights issues is literally at your fingertips. By simply accessing the American Civil Liberties Union's Web site (the URL for this organization is given below, in the *Logging On* section), you can learn about the major civil rights issues facing Americans today. A host of other Web sites offer data on the extent to which groups discussed in this chapter are protected under state and federal laws. You can also find numerous advocacy sites that indicate what you can do to help promote the rights of a certain group.

Logging On

For information on, and arguments in support of, affirmative action and the rights of the groups discussed in this chapter, a good source is the American Civil Liberties Union's Web site. Go to:

http://www.aclu.org

The National Organization for Women (NOW) offers online information and updates on the status of women's rights, including affirmative action cases involving women. Go to

http://www.now.org

An excellent source for information on discrimination based on age and disability is the Equal Employment Opportunity Commission's Web site at

http://www.eeoc.gov

You can find information on the Americans with Disabilities Act (ADA) of 1990, including the act's text, at

http://www.jan.wvu.edu/links/adalinks.htm

You can access the Web site of the Human Rights Campaign Fund, the nation's largest gay and lesbian political organization, at

http://www.hrc.org

If you are interested in children's rights and welfare, a good starting place is the Web site of the Child Welfare Institute. Go to

http://www.gocwi.org

Using the Internet for Political Analysis

Imagine that you are the owner of a new franchise business and are hiring your first employees. Several of the applicants are over the age of sixty-five, and one of them tells you that she has impaired hearing but has a good hearing aid to assist her.

Using one of the Web sites given below, look up Labor and Employment Law and develop some guidelines for your hiring practices that will not violate laws prohibiting discrimination against older Americans and workers with disabilities. Consider the information that you find on the Web. To what extent would you rely on this information when you write an employment manual? What other resources might you also check?

FindLaw, at

http://www.findlaw.com

Legal Resource Guide, at

http://www.ilrg.com

PART THREE

People and Politics

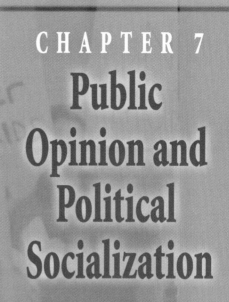

BACKGROUND

The media love to project the winner of an election before the actual votes are counted. To do so, they use the results of exit polls. These polls are conducted at selected precincts in each state. Trained interviewers visit each of the selected precincts and take a systematic sample of voters at different times during the day. Sampled voters are asked to fill out a written questionnaire indicating their age, ethnic group, income, gender, political party, and how they voted. The media can make projections based on exit polls within one hour after the voting booths close. Because of inaccurate projections during the 2000 presidential elections, however, many politicians and citizens alike have suggested that exit polls be banned.

WHAT IF EXIT POLLS WERE BANNED?

On November 7, 2000, the television networks declared Al Gore the winning presidential candidate in the state of Florida before all the polls across the country had closed. Indeed, the networks called Gore the winner in Florida before all the polls in that state had closed. Not surprisingly, the networks (plus the Associated Press) were strongly criticized. More important, though, is the contention that the networks' premature statements about election outcomes caused voters from the apparent losing party to stay home. If exit polls were banned, it would be very difficult for the media to make predictions (right or wrong) about the winners.

PERHAPS MORE VOTER TURNOUT, PARTICULARLY IN THE WEST

Because the results of exit polls from the East are known relatively early in the afternoon on the West Coast, many voters in the western states might consider staying home if they know that their candidate has won or lost by a large margin. Thus, a ban on exit polls might increase voter participation in the western states.

We must realize, though, that a ban on exit polls would not prevent the networks from reporting actual election results. Therefore, the news media might still report *partial* election results in time to influence voters' behavior on the West Coast. Certainly, though, the networks could not "declare" a winner of any presidential race in the early evening, East Coast time.

THE PRESS AND THE FIRST AMENDMENT

The media's behavior during election night would obviously be different if exit polls were banned. They would have less information to analyze and therefore fewer "hot stories" to broadcast about projected election results. Given that all congressional representatives and one-third of the U.S. senators are up for election every two years, not being able to discuss those races in detail on the evening of election day would reduce TV viewership.

There is a First Amendment issue here, too. The U.S. Constitution does not, in general, allow the government to restrict what the news media can or cannot do. Hence, it is difficult to see how a law preventing the news media from projecting the winners in an election would be held constitutional. Some states have already attempted to limit reporters' access to voters at polling places, but the courts have declared most of these laws unconstitutional. According to election director Carin Dessauer of CNN Interactive, exit polling is "an indispensable tool that helps us pursue certain angles of the story and provide better coverage. Primarily, it provides valuable information to use on our site when all polls close." CNN Interactive has a policy of not releasing the results of exit polls in a state until after the voting booths in that state have closed.

Other Web sites do not have the same policy. Therefore, as a practical matter, how could predictions made on the Internet be squelched? Even if the federal government passed a law banning such predictions based on exit polls, computer servers for such sites could be located in another country, out of the reach of the federal government.

FOR CRITICAL ANALYSIS

1. If exit polls were banned, could members of the news media still project winners? If so, how?
2. Political scientists and politicians glean much valuable information from detailed statistics derived from exit polls. Is there a way to allow exit polling and the collection of such data without influencing election projections?

M
ost observers of the American political scene believe that the ability of Americans to freely express their opinions constitutes the bedrock of our representative system. Americans have numerous vehicles for expressing their opinions. They can vote in elections. They can send letters to the editors of numerous newspapers. They can send letters and e-mails to their political representatives. They can organize and participate in marches and protests. They can respond to opinion polls, including the exit polls discussed in the chapter-opening *What If . . .* feature. Public opinion clearly plays an important role in our political system, just as it does in any democracy.

President George W. Bush found out how important public opinion was when he announced that the administration was going to try terrorist defendants in military tribunals where the defendants would have few rights. Public opinion was so negative that Bush felt forced to announce new rules for the tribunals that gave defendants more rights. (See the *America's Security* feature in Chapter 4 for a further discussion of the rights of defendants in the proposed military tribunals.) In contrast, Bush's war on terrorism received widespread support from Americans. The public showed this support in media articles, talk shows, responses to public opinion polls on the issue, e-mails to the White House, and other ways. This support bolstered the Bush administration's authority during a time of crisis. Indeed, Bush's approval ratings of slightly over 90 percent were the highest ever recorded in the history of the Gallup poll, which is conducted by one of the major polling organizations.

There is no doubt that public opinion can be powerful. Political scientists often point to two presidential decisions to illustrate this power. In 1968, President Lyndon Johnson decided not to run for reelection because of the intense and negative public reaction to the war in Vietnam. In 1974, President Richard Nixon resigned in the wake of a scandal when it was obvious that public opinion no longer supported him. The extent to which public opinion affects policymaking is not always so clear, however. For example, suppose that public opinion strongly supports a certain policy. If political leaders adopt that position, is it because they are responding to public opinion or to their own views on the issue? In addition, political leaders can themselves, to some extent, shape public opinion. For these and other reasons, scholars must deal with many uncertainties when analyzing the impact of public opinion on policymaking.

INFOTRAC®
COLLEGE EDITION

To find out more about exit polls, use the term "exit polls" in the Subject guide.

Public support for a president's policies is important in a democratic system. Although President George W. Bush received average public approval ratings during his first year in office, his approval ratings soared during his second year, as demonstrated by this public appearance in Iowa in 2002. What factors might explain this difference? (AP Photo/ Doug Mills)

Defining Public Opinion

There is no one public opinion, because there are many different "publics." In a nation of over 286 million people, there may be innumerable gradations of opinion on an issue. What we do is describe the distribution of opinions among the public about a particular question. Thus, we define **public opinion** as the aggregate of individual attitudes or beliefs shared by some portion of the adult population.

Typically, public opinion is distributed among several different positions, and the distribution of opinion can tell us how divided the public is on an issue and whether compromise is possible. When a large proportion of the American public appears to express the same view on an issue, we say that a **consensus** exists, at least at the moment the poll was taken. Figure 7–1 shows the pattern of opinion that might be called consensual. Issues on which the public holds widely differing attitudes result in **divisive opinion** (see Figure 7–2). Figure 7–3 shows a distribution of opinion indicating that most Americans either have no information about the issue or are not interested enough in the issue to formulate a position. Politicians may feel that the lack of public knowledge of an issue gives them more room to maneuver, or they may be wary of taking any action for fear that opinion will crystallize after a crisis.

An interesting question arises as to when *private* opinion becomes *public* opinion. Everyone probably has a private opinion about the competence of the president, as well as private opinions about more personal concerns, such as the state of a neighbor's lawn. We say that private opinion becomes public opinion when the opinion is publicly expressed and concerns public issues. When someone's private opinion becomes so strong that the individual is willing to go to the polls to vote for or against a candidate or an issue—or is willing to participate in a demonstration, discuss the issue at work, speak out on television or radio, or participate in the political process in any one of a dozen other ways—then the opinion becomes public opinion.

Public Opinion
The aggregate of individual attitudes or beliefs shared by some portion of the adult population. There is no one public opinion, because there are many different "publics."

Consensus
General agreement among the citizenry on an issue.

Divisive Opinion
Public opinion that is polarized between two quite different positions.

INFOTRAC®
COLLEGE EDITION

To find out more about this topic, use the term "public opinion" in the Subject guide.

FIGURE 7–1

Consensus Opinion

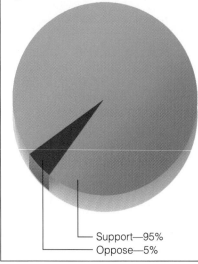

Question: If the United States can identify the groups or nations responsible for the attacks of 9/11, would you support or oppose taking military action against them?

Support—95%
Oppose—5%

SOURCE: Survey by ABC News/*Washington Post*, September 13, 2001.

FIGURE 7–2

Divisive Opinion

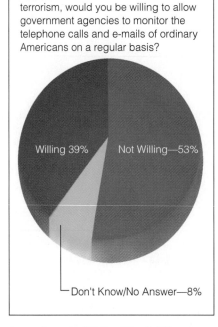

Question: In order to reduce the threat of terrorism, would you be willing to allow government agencies to monitor the telephone calls and e-mails of ordinary Americans on a regular basis?

Willing 39%   Not Willing—53%

Don't Know/No Answer—8%

SOURCE: Survey by CBS News/*New York Times*, September 13–14, 2001.

FIGURE 7–3

Nonopinion

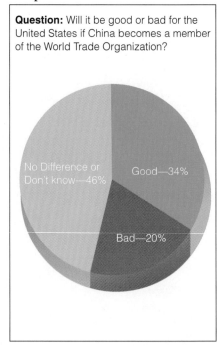

Question: Will it be good or bad for the United States if China becomes a member of the World Trade Organization?

No Difference or Don't know—46%   Good—34%

Bad—20%

SOURCE: Pew Research Center for the People and the Press, survey conducted February 9–14, 2000.

Measuring Public Opinion

In a democracy, people express their opinions in a variety of ways, as mentioned in this chapter's introduction. One of the most common means of gathering and measuring public opinion on specific issues is, of course, through the use of **opinion polls**.

The History of Opinion Polls

During the 1800s, certain American newspapers and magazines spiced up their political coverage by doing face-to-face straw polls (unofficial polls indicating the trend of political opinion) or mail surveys of their readers' opinions. In the early twentieth century, the magazine *Literary Digest* further developed the technique of opinion polls by mailing large numbers of questionnaires to individuals, many of whom were its own subscribers. From 1916 to 1936, more than 70 percent of the magazine's election predictions were accurate.

Literary Digest's polling activities suffered a setback in 1936, however, when the magazine predicted, based on more than two million returned questionnaires, that Republican candidate Alfred Landon would win over Democratic candidate Franklin D. Roosevelt. Landon won in only two states. A major problem with the *Digest*'s polling technique was its continuing use of nonrepresentative respondents. In 1936, at the bottom of the Great Depression, the magazine's subscribers were, for one thing, considerably more affluent than the average American.

Several newcomers to the public opinion poll industry accurately predicted Roosevelt's landslide victory. The organizations of these newcomers are still active in the poll-taking industry today: the Gallup poll of George Gallup and the Roper poll founded by Elmo Roper. Gallup and Roper, along with Archibald Crossley, developed the modern polling techniques of market research. Using personal interviews with small samples of selected voters (less than a few thousand), they showed that they could predict with accuracy the behavior of the total voting population.

By the 1950s, improved methods of sampling and a whole new science of survey research had been developed. Survey research centers sprang up throughout the United States, particularly at universities. Some of these survey groups are the American Institute of Public Opinion at Princeton, New Jersey; the National Opinion Research Center at the University of Chicago; and the Survey Research Center at the University of Michigan.

Sampling Techniques

How can interviewing fewer than two thousand voters tell us what tens of millions of voters will do? Clearly, it is necessary that the sample of individuals be representative of all voters in the population. Consider an analogy. Let's say we have a large jar containing ten thousand pennies of various dates, and we want to know how many pennies were minted within certain decades (1950–1959, 1960–1969, and so on).

Representative Sampling. One way to estimate the distribution of the dates on the pennies—without examining all ten thousand—is to take a representative sample. This sample would be obtained by mixing the pennies up well and then removing a handful of them—perhaps one hundred pennies. The distribution of dates might be as follows:

- *1950–1959: 5 percent.*
- *1960–1969: 5 percent.*
- *1970–1979: 20 percent.*
- *1980–1989: 30 percent.*
- *1990–present: 40 percent.*

DID YOU KNOW . . .
That James Madison and others argued in *The Federalist Papers* that because public opinion is potentially dangerous, it should be diffused through a large republic with separation of government powers ?

Opinion Poll
A method of systematically questioning a small, selected sample of respondents who are deemed representative of the total population. Opinion polls are widely used by government, business, university scholars, political candidates, and voluntary groups to provide reasonably accurate data on public attitudes, beliefs, expectations, and behavior.

INFOTRAC®
COLLEGE EDITION

To find out more about polls, use the term "public opinion polls" in the Subject guide.

If the pennies are very well mixed within the jar, and if you take a large enough sample, the resulting distribution will probably approach the actual distribution of the dates of all ten thousand coins.

The Principle of Randomness.   The most important principle in sampling, or poll taking, is randomness. Every penny or every person should have a known chance, and especially an *equal chance,* of being sampled. If this happens, then a small sample should be representative of the whole group, both in demographic characteristics (age, religion, race, living area, and the like) and in opinions. The ideal way to sample the voting population of the United States would be to put all voter names into a jar—or a computer—and randomly sample, say, two thousand of them. Because this is too costly and inefficient, pollsters have developed other ways to obtain good samples. One of the most interesting techniques is simply to choose a random selection of telephone numbers and interview the respective households. This technique produces a relatively accurate sample at a low cost.

To ensure that the random samples include respondents from relevant segments of the population—rural, urban, Northeast, South, and so on—most survey organizations randomly choose, say, urban areas that they will consider as representative of all urban areas. Then they randomly select their respondents within those areas. A generally less accurate technique is known as *quota sampling.* For this type of poll, survey researchers decide how many persons of certain types they need in the survey—such as minorities, women, or farmers—and then send out interviewers to find the necessary number of these types. This method is often not only less accurate, but it also may be biased if, say, the interviewer refuses to go into certain neighborhoods or will not interview after dark.

Generally, the national survey organizations take great care to select their samples randomly, because their reputations rest on the accuracy of their results. Usually, the Gallup or Roper polls interview about 1,500 individuals, and their results have a very high probability of being correct—within a margin of 3 percentage points. The accuracy with which the Gallup poll has predicted national election results is reflected in Table 7–1.

Problems with Polls

Public opinion polls are snapshots of the opinions and preferences of the people at a specific moment in time and as expressed in response to a specific question. Given that definition, it is fairly easy to understand situations in which the polls are wrong. For example, opinion polls leading up to the 1980 presidential election showed President Jimmy Carter defeating challenger Ronald Reagan. Only a few analysts noted the large number of "undecided" respondents to poll questions a week before the election. Those voters shifted massively to Reagan at the last minute, and Reagan won the election.

The famous photo of Harry Truman showing the front page that declared his defeat in the 1948 presidential elections is another tribute to the weakness of polling. Again, the poll that predicted his defeat was taken more than a week before election day.

Sampling Errors.   Polls may also report erroneous results because the pool of respondents was not chosen in a scientific manner. That is, the form of sampling and the number of people sampled may be too

President Harry Truman holds up the front page of the *Chicago Daily Tribune* issue that predicted his defeat on the basis of a Gallup poll. The poll had indicated that Truman would lose the 1948 contest for his reelection by a margin of 55.5 to 44.5 percent. Gallup's poll was completed more than a week before the election, so it missed the undecided voters. Truman won the election with 49.9 percent of the vote. (Corbis, UPI/Bettmann)

TABLE 7–1

Gallup Poll Accuracy Record

YEAR	GALLUP FINAL SURVEY		ELECTION RESULTS		DEVIATION
2002	51.0%	Republican	52.8%	Republican	−1.8
2000	50.0	BUSH	48.0	BUSH	+2.0
1998	49.1	Democratic	53.2	Republican	−4.1
1996	52.0	CLINTON	49.0	CLINTON	+3.0
1994	58.0	Republican	51.0	Republican	+7.0
1992	49.0	CLINTON	43.2	CLINTON	+5.8
1990	54.0	Democratic	54.1	Democratic	−0.1
1988	56.0	BUSH	53.9	BUSH	+2.1
1984	59.0	REAGAN	59.1	REAGAN	−0.1
1982	55.0	Democratic	56.1	Democratic	−1.1
1980	47.0	REAGAN	50.8	REAGAN	−3.8
1978	55.0	Democratic	54.6	Democratic	+0.4
1976	48.0	CARTER	50.0	CARTER	−2.0
1974	60.0	Democratic	58.9	Democratic	+1.1
1972	62.0	NIXON	61.8	NIXON	+0.2
1970	53.0	Democratic	54.3	Democratic	−1.3
1968	43.0	NIXON	43.5	NIXON	−0.5
1966	52.5	Democratic	51.9	Democratic	+0.6
1964	64.0	JOHNSON	61.3	JOHNSON	+2.7
1962	55.5	Democratic	52.7	Democratic	+2.8
1960	51.0	KENNEDY	50.1	KENNEDY	+0.9
1958	57.0	Democratic	56.5	Democratic	+0.5
1956	59.5	EISENHOWER	57.8	EISENHOWER	+1.7
1954	51.5	Democratic	52.7	Democratic	−1.2
1952	51.0	EISENHOWER	55.4	EISENHOWER	−4.4
1950	51.0	Democratic	50.3	Democratic	+0.7
1948	44.5	TRUMAN	49.9	TRUMAN	−5.4
1946	58.0	Republican	54.3	Republican	+3.7
1944	51.5	ROOSEVELT	53.3	ROOSEVELT	−1.8
1942	52.0	Democratic	48.0	Democratic	+4.0
1940	52.0	ROOSEVELT	55.0	ROOSEVELT	−3.0
1938	54.0	Democratic	50.8	Democratic	+3.2
1936	55.7	ROOSEVELT	62.5	ROOSEVELT	−6.8

Note: No congressional poll done in 1986.

SOURCES: *The Gallup Poll Monthly,* November 1992; *Time,* November 21, 1994; *The Wall Street Journal,* November 6, 1996; and authors' update.

Sampling Error
The difference between a sample's results and the true result if the entire population had been interviewed.

small to overcome **sampling error**, which is the difference between the sample results and the true result if the entire population had been interviewed. The sample would be biased, for example, if the poll interviewed people by telephone and did not correct for the fact that more women than men answer the telephone and that some populations (college students and very poor individuals, for example) cannot be found so easily by telephone. Unscientific mail-in polls, telephone call-in polls, and polls completed by the workers in a campaign office are usually biased and do not give an accurate picture of the public's views. Because of these and other problems with polls, some have suggested that polling be regulated by the government (see this chapter's *Which Side Are You On?* feature).

As poll takers get close to election day, they become even more concerned about their sample of respondents. Some pollsters continue to interview eligible voters, meaning those over eighteen and registered to vote. Many others use a series of questions in the poll and other weighting methods to try to identify "likely voters" so that they can be more accurate in their election-eve predictions. When a poll changes its method from reporting the views of eligible voters to reporting those of likely voters, the results are likely to change dramatically.

Which Side Are You On?
Should Polling Be Regulated?

Public opinion polling was once confined to the work of universities and a handful of very large and well-respected polling firms, such as Gallup and Roper. Now, anyone can open a polling shop on the Web or in his or her basement using telephones and a few computers. Currently, polling is, for the most part, completely unregulated. Interviewers are not necessarily trained and certainly not licensed. Polling organizations may be private or public, but they are not regulated in terms of their contracts, operations, or disclosure of results. The media giants that commission polls to obtain results to be reported on the air or in print see polling as part of their news-gathering operation and, therefore, as protected by the First Amendment's guarantee of freedom of the press.

WHY REGULATE POLLS?

What are the concerns that might lead to regulation? The media have agreed among themselves not to release their predictions of election outcomes before the polls close in California, but they do release many other pieces of information from the exit polls during the day. Some of that information may influence voter turnout or votes. As we asked in the chapter-opening *What If . . .* feature, should the media be prohibited from releasing any data until the next day? Polls are often paid for by campaign cash, including the taxpayers' matching funds in the presi-

dential race. Should those polls be public? Additionally, polling can be used to influence voters, particularly through "push polling" (see this chapter's *Politics and Polls* feature on page 212). Should the use of polls to influence voters be prohibited? Should questions used by pollsters be censored or regulated by a government agency?

ARE POLLS REALLY ALL THAT POWERFUL?

If you think that polls are or can be too powerful, influencing voters and policy decisions, then more regulations might be appropriate. At the same time, polls have no legal power; they are simply the report of what those who were polled have to say. If polls are seen as having very little power, regulation would seem unwarranted.

WHAT'S YOUR POSITION?

Would regulating public opinion polls be a true restriction on free speech and deprive the public of the opportunity to debate information that should be freely available?

GOING ONLINE

If you are interested in reading more about the issues that surround polling, especially in an election year, check out *USA Today's* Web site at **http://www.usatoday.com** and search "polling." If you would like to read more about the polling industry's view on regulation and see examples of its voluntary standards, go to the Web site for the American Association for Public Opinion Research at **http://www.aapor.org**.

Poll Questions.   Finally, it makes sense to expect that the results of a poll will depend on the questions that are asked. Depending on what question is asked, voters could be said either to support a particular proposal or to oppose it. One of the problems with many polls is the yes/no answer format. For example, suppose that a poll question asks, "Are you in favor of abortion?" A respondent who is in favor of abortion in some circumstances but not in others has no way of indicating this view because "yes" and "no" are the only possible answers. Furthermore, respondents' answers are also influenced by the order in which questions are asked, by the possible answers they are allowed to choose, and, in some cases, by their interaction with the interviewer. To some extent, people try to please the interviewer. They answer questions about which they have no information and avoid some answers to try to measure up to the interviewer's expectations. (In some foreign nations, respondents may avoid certain types of answers for political reasons—see this chapter's *Global View* feature for a discussion of this issue.)

Push Polls.   Most recently, some campaigns have been using "push polls," in which the respondents are given misleading information in the questions asked to get them to vote against a candidate. Obviously, the answers given are likely to be influenced by such techniques. For a further discussion of push polls, see this chapter's *Politics and Polls* feature on the next page.

"One final question: Do you now own or have you ever owned a fur coat?"
Drawing by Mick Stevens. *The New Yorker.*

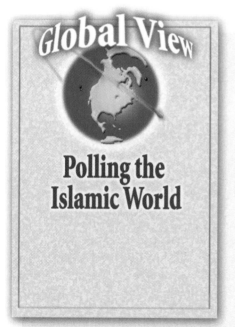

Global View

Polling the Islamic World

While Americans—and, indeed, most Westerners—take polling for granted, polling is relatively uncommon in the Islamic world. The Gallup organization recently polled 10,000 people in nine predominantly Islamic countries.* We look here at some of the problems the pollsters faced in evaluating the responses and at some of the views expressed by the respondents.

*Indonesia, Iran, Jordan, Kuwait, Lebanon, Morocco, Pakistan, Saudi Arabia, and Turkey.

Measurement Issues

Many factors influence how survey respondents react to certain questions. In the Western world, respondents to surveys generally express their views freely in response to the survey questions. In contrast, as the Gallup organization noted in its poll of citizens of Islamic nations, the views expressed by the respondents might reflect the "official position" taken by their governments rather than the respondents' own opinions.

According to Frank Newport, editor in chief of the Gallup poll, the responses to the polling questions reflected, at least in part, the official government stance of the countries in which the surveys were conducted. Nonetheless, concluded Newport, this fact does not make the responses less valid. After all, said Newport, "Everyone's attitudes must come from some source—usually a combination of early socialization, family, peers, media exposure, and even genetic tendencies. There is no doubt that official government policies and communications can affect them."†

†Frank Newport, "Measurement Issues in the Nine-Country Gallup Poll of the Islamic World," Gallup Poll Release, March 13, 2002.

Some Results of the Poll

In general, the polling results showed that residents of Islamic nations have negative views of Western culture. When asked whether the Western value system was having a positive or negative influence on the Islamic value system, a sizable majority responded that the influence was negative. Respondents also felt that Western nations do not treat minorities in their own countries fairly and that Westerners have immoral lifestyles and weak family values. In spite of these negative views of the West, the majority of those interviewed in the nine Islamic countries indicated that the terrorist attacks on 9/11 were morally unjustifiable. When asked how relations between the Islamic nations and the Western world might be improved, a commonly voiced opinion was that the West should show more respect for the Arab/Islamic world and its religion.

FOR CRITICAL ANALYSIS

All opinions have origins somewhere. Does it matter if a person's opinion derives from the government or from friends and colleagues?

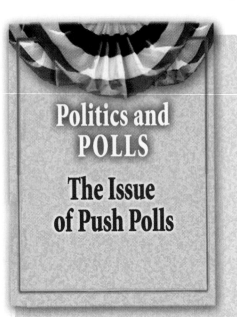

Politics and POLLS

The Issue of Push Polls

The notion that candidates can use polls to "push" the respondents into voting for the candidate sponsoring the poll is relatively new to politics. Nonetheless, this type of polling is increasingly being used in political campaigns.

WHAT IS A PUSH POLL?

The National Council on Public Polls defines a *push poll* as a technique in which telephone calls are used to canvass vast numbers of potential voters, feeding them false and damaging "information" about a candidate under the guise of taking a poll to see how this "information" affects voter preferences. In fact, the intent is to "push" the voters away from one candidate and towards the opposing candidate.

Push polls are typically used in an effort to reach a high percentage of voters just before the close of an election campaign. Whereas a normal polling interview lasts from a few minutes to over thirty minutes, a push poll typically lasts no longer than sixty seconds, and sometimes only twenty seconds.

THE INCREASING USE OF PUSH POLLS

Designing polling questions so as to influence the respondents' votes has become widespread. Indeed, the practice has spread throughout all levels of U.S. politics—local, state, and federal. In 1996, in a random survey of forty-five candidates, researchers found that thirty-five of them claimed to have been victimized by negative push-polling techniques used by their opponents.* Now even advocacy groups, as well as candidates for political offices, are using push polls.

During the 2000 presidential primaries, Republican presidential hopeful John McCain accused the Bush camp of making more than 200,000 "advocacy" calls, asking voters about their likely choices in the elections. The calls used long questions containing information about McCain's record. The Bush camp said that the information was accurate. In contrast, McCain saw this as negative "push polling."

Push polling continued during the 2002 congressional campaigns. Its use was widespread in campaigns for governorships and other state offices.

FOR CRITICAL ANALYSIS

Is it possible to tell whether a survey question is worded "neutrally" or is worded in a biased manner in an effort to elicit a particular response?

*Karl T. Feld, "When Push Comes to Shove: A Polling Industry Call to Arms," *Public Perspective,* September/October 2001, p. 38.

Because of these problems, you need to be especially careful when evaluating poll results. For some suggestions on how to be a critical consumer of public opinion polls, see the feature *Making a Difference* at the end of this chapter. Some have suggested that during times of crisis, it is particularly important for pollsters to avoid these kinds of problems and try to obtain accurate results. See this chapter's *America's Security* feature for a further discussion of this issue.

ELECTIONS 2002   The Accuracy of the 2002 Polls

As election day approached, pollsters and political analysts began to use the phrase "too close to call" in regard to numerous races. In fact, polling organizations reported results in the week before the November 5 election that were close enough to make the election within the margin of error for each poll. However, the direction of the polls differed dramatically. Some predicted Democratic wins across the nation, while others suggested that momentum in the last few days was shifting to the Republicans. A number of state polls were way off the mark in their predictions. Some pollsters noted that the increase in cellular phones and call blocking may have caused considerable errors in polling, especially for less sophisticated polling operations. The failure of the Voter News Service to deliver exit polling on election night further cast doubt on the whole election polling enterprise.

America's Security

Gary Langer, the director of polling for ABC News, stated that on September 11, 2001, after the terrorist attacks on the World Trade Center and the Pentagon, some pollsters questioned whether it was appropriate to poll public opinion on the events that were happening. One pollster thought it might be too much like attorneys "ambulance chasing." According to Langer, such sentiments are misplaced: "Measuring immediate public opinion at a time of crisis is meaningful and valuable. . . . It captures both personal reactions and policy preferences at a vital moment."*

*Gary Langer, "Touchpoint: Responsible Polling in the Wake of 9/11," *Public Perspective,* March/April 2002, p. 14.

Polling in Times of National Crisis

POLLING RESULTS IN THE WAKE OF 9/11

Within a relatively short time after the 9/11 attacks, independent polling organizations and academic institutions were able to paint a detailed and coherent picture of the public response to the attacks. An understanding of Americans' views on the attacks helped to give both direction and support to the Bush administration's ensuing war on terrorism.

One major polling result was that the American public showed "strong support" for the war in Afghanistan—83 percent of Americans were in favor of the war. This percentage was 30 points higher than the "strong support" for the Persian Gulf War in January 1991.† Public opinion polls also showed that Americans' perception of a threat to the United States had reached a level unseen since the Japanese attacked Pearl Harbor in 1941, thrusting the United States into World War II. Americans saw inaction as a greater risk than military action in the war against terrorism.

THE IMPORTANCE OF "GETTING IT RIGHT"

Moments of crisis often have long-lasting effects. The events of September

†*Ibid.*

11, 2001, probably will be viewed as a touchpoint in history, one that scholars and students will be revisiting for generations. Because of this, it is important to "get it right," as Langer put it, when conducting polls in times of crisis. In other words, pollsters should take great care in constructing and analyzing polls to ensure that the results accurately reflect the public's views.

Langer suggests that when polls are constructed, the questions should be carefully worded so that they are not misleading or weighted in favor of one response versus another. When polling results are analyzed, a context should be provided so that a phrase such as "strong support" takes on meaning. For example, as noted above, "strong support" for the war in Afghanistan, in itself, says little. But when the percentage of respondents supporting that war is compared to the percentage who supported the Persian Gulf War in 1991, the degree of support takes on meaning and significance.

FOR CRITICAL ANALYSIS

In a time of crisis, should the president and other government officials wait until they know the public's opinion on the issue before undertaking any significant action?

Technology and Opinion Polls

Public opinion polling is based on scientific principles, particularly with respect to randomness. Today, technological advances allow numerous polls to be taken over the Internet, but serious questions have been raised about the ability of pollsters to obtain truly random samples using this medium. The same was said not long ago when another technological breakthrough changed public opinion polling—the telephone.

The Advent of Telephone Polling

During the 1970s, telephone polling began to predominate over in-person polling. Obviously, telephone polling is less expensive than sending interviewers to poll respondents in their homes. Additionally, telephone interviewers do not have to

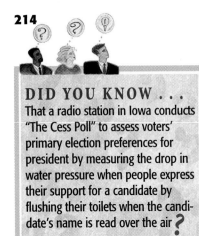

worry about safety problems, particularly in high-crime areas. Finally, telephone interviews can be conducted relatively quickly. They allow politicians or the media to poll one evening and report the results the next day.

Telephone Polling Is No Longer So Useful.   Somewhat ironically, the success of telephone polling has led to its demise. The telemarketing industry in general has become so pervasive that people increasingly refuse to respond to telephone polls. More and more households either use caller ID systems to screen calls or have their calls picked up by an answering machine. Most people can determine within the first thirty seconds of a call whether the call is legitimate or of interest to them, and they hang up if it is not.

Nonresponse Rates Have Skyrocketed.   Nonresponses in telephone polling include unreachable numbers, refusals, answering machines, and call-screening devices. The nonresponse rate has increased to as high as 80 percent for most telephone polls. Such a high nonresponse rate undercuts confidence in the survey results. In most cases, polling only 20 percent of those on the list cannot lead to a random sample. Even more important for politicians is the fact that polling organizations are not required to report their response rates.

Enter Internet Polling

Obviously, Internet polling is not done on a one-on-one basis in that there is no voice communication. In spite of the potential problems, the Harris Poll, a widely respected national polling organization, conducted online polls during the 1998 elections. Its election predictions were accurate in many states. Nonetheless, it made a serious error in one southern gubernatorial election. The Harris group refined its techniques and continued online polling in 2000. This organization believes that because so many individuals respond to its Internet polls, proper weighting of the results will achieve the equivalent of a random-sampled poll.

Public opinion scholars argue that the Harris Poll procedure violates the mathematical basis of random sampling. Nonetheless, according to some scholars, the Internet population is looking more like the rest of America: a slight majority of Internet users are women; 43 percent of African American adults are on the Internet; and 47 percent of Hispanics have Internet access.[1]

"Nonpolls" on the Internet.   Even if organizations such as the Harris group succeed in obtaining the equivalent of a random sample when polling on the Internet, another problem will remain: the proliferation of "nonpolls" on the Internet. Every media outlet that maintains a Web site allows anyone to submit her or his opinion. Numerous organizations and for-profit companies send polls to individuals via e-mail. Mister Poll (**http://www.mrpoll.com**) bills itself as the Internet's largest online polling database. Mister Poll allows you to create your own polls just for fun or to include them on your home page. In general, Mister Poll, like numerous other polling sites, asks a number of questions on various issues and seeks answers from those who log on to its site. Although the Mister Poll Web site states, "None of these polls is scientific," sites such as this one undercut the efforts of legitimate pollsters to use the Internet scientifically.

Will Internet Polling Go the Way of Telephone Polling?   Perhaps the greatest threat to the science of polling, whether polls are conducted via the Internet or otherwise, is simply that Americans are overwhelmed with polling data. They are tired

---

[1] Elena Larsen and Lee Rainie, "Going Online: A Classic Technology Adoption Story," *Public Perspective*, July/August 2001, p. 39.

of pollsters' attempts to poll them, and they are overwhelmed by the deluge of poll results. Although some results may be legitimate and derive from truly scientific work, many are obtained from cheap, quick, and poorly executed polls. How can any American determine which data are legitimate?

If all polls appear equal, will the American public believe any of them? If polls and polling come to be regarded as inaccurate, then the practice of scientific polling may disappear.

How Public Opinion Is Formed: Political Socialization

Most Americans are willing to express opinions on political issues when asked. How do people acquire these opinions and attitudes? Most views that are expressed as political opinions are acquired through a process known as **political socialization**. By this we mean that people acquire their political attitudes, often including their party identification, through relationships with their families, friends, and co-workers. The most important influences in this process are the following: (1) the family, (2) the educational environment and achievement of the individual, (3) peers, (4) religion, (5) economic status and occupation, (6) political events, (7) opinion leaders, (8) the media, and (9) race, gender, and other demographic traits.

Although family and teachers were once seen as the primary agents of political socialization, many scholars today believe the media are displacing these traditional avenues. Busy families and large class sizes have decreased the amount of individual, face-to-face contact young people have with parents and teachers, while time spent with television and the Internet has increased. But the media are agents of socialization by default, not by design.[2] The implications of the increased role of the media in political socialization are under scrutiny by political and social scientists.

Furthermore, scholars question how accurately we can predict political behavior based on old notions of political socialization. It is less likely today than in the past, for example, that the children of conservatives will grow up to be conservatives and that the children of liberals will grow up to be liberals. Indeed, some studies suggest that political socialization within the family is actually taking a "trickle up" direction, as children expose their parents to new media and new sources of political information.[3] Thus, even though the influence of the family on political socialization may be changing, it is still an obvious place to start our examination of this process.

The Importance of the Family

Family plays a vital role in political socialization. Not only do our parents' political attitudes and actions affect our adult opinions, but the family also links us to other socialization forces, such as ethnic identity, social class, educational opportunities, and religious beliefs. How do parents transmit their political attitudes? Studies suggest that the influence of parents is due to two factors: communication and receptivity. Parents communicate their feelings and preferences to children constantly. Because children have such a strong need for parental approval, they are very receptive to their parents' views.[4] The "trickle up" effect, mentioned earlier, is not as effective as this "trickle

DID YOU KNOW . . .
That an error rate of plus or minus three points means that the poll results could be 3 percentage points higher or 3 percentage points lower than the actual distribution of opinion in the public (this means that a poll result of 50 percent for and 50 percent against could represent an actual distribution of 53 percent to 47 percent on the issue)

Political Socialization
The process by which people acquire political beliefs and attitudes.

INFOTRAC®
COLLEGE EDITION

To find out more about this topic, use the term "political socialization" in the Subject guide.

---

[2] See the discussion of the media's influence on politics in Richard Davis and Diana Owens, *New Media and American Politics* (New York: Oxford University Press, 1998).
[3] Michael McDevitt and Steven H. Chaffee, "Second Chance Political Socialization: 'Trickle-up' Effects of Children on Parents," in Thomas J. Johnson *et al.*, eds., *Engaging the Public: How Government and the Media Can Reinvigorate American Democracy* (Lanham, Md.: Rowman & Littlefield Publishers, 1998), pp. 57–66.
[4] Barbara A. Bardes and Robert W. Oldendick, *Public Opinion: Measuring the American Mind*, 2d ed. (Belmont, Calif.: Wadsworth Publishing Co., 2003), p. 73.

down" process because parents are less receptive to children's views and expect greater deference from their children. Nevertheless, studies show that if children are exposed to political ideas at school and in the media, they will share these ideas with their parents, giving the parents what some scholars call a "second chance" at political socialization.

Educational Influence on Political Opinion

From the early days of the republic, schools were perceived to be important transmitters of political information and attitudes. Children in the primary grades learn about their country mostly in patriotic ways. They learn about the Pilgrims, the flag, and some of the nation's presidents. They also learn to celebrate national holidays. Later, in the middle grades, children learn more historical facts and come to understand the structure of government and the functions of the president, judges, and Congress. By high school, students have a more complex understanding of the political system, may identify with a political party, and may take positions on issues.

Generally, education is closely linked to political participation. The more education a person receives, the more likely it is that the person will be interested in politics, be confident in his or her ability to understand political issues, and be an active participant in the political process. Recent polls, however, suggest that younger Americans are not interested in politics. Indeed, as many as one-third of today's college students say that government has no influence on their lives.[5]

Peers and Peer Group Influence

Peer Group
A group consisting of members sharing common relevant social characteristics. These groups play an important part in the socialization process, helping to shape attitudes and beliefs.

Once a child enters school, the child's friends become an important influence on behavior and attitudes. For young children and for adults, friendships and associations in **peer groups** are influential on political attitudes. We must, however, separate the effects of peer group pressure on opinions and attitudes in general from peer group pressure on political opinions. For the most part, associations among peers are nonpolitical. Political attitudes are more likely to be shaped by peer groups when the peer groups are involved directly in political activities.

Individuals who join interest groups based on ethnic identity may find, for example, a common political bond through working for the group's civil liberties and rights. African American activist groups may consist of individuals who join together to support government programs that will aid the African American population. Members of a labor union may feel strong political pressure to support certain pro-labor candidates.

Religious Influence

Religious associations tend to create definite political attitudes, although why this occurs is not clearly understood. Surveys show that Roman Catholic respondents tend to be more liberal on economic issues than are Protestants. Apparently, Jewish respondents are more liberal on all fronts than either Catholics or Protestants. In terms of voting behavior, it has been observed that northern white Protestants are more likely to vote Republican, whereas northern white Roman Catholics more often vote Democratic; everywhere in the United States, Jews mostly vote Democratic.

In the last decade, fundamentalist Christians, sometimes known as evangelical Christians, have played an increasing role in American politics. A recent Pew Research Center for the People and the Press study found that 42 percent of white evangelical Protestants are Republicans as compared to 35 percent only ten years ago. How do we

[5] Adam Clymer, "College Students Not Drawn to Voting or Politics," *The New York Times,* January 12, 2000, p. A14.

know that an individual is an evangelical Christian? Public opinion polls use a combination of questions about religious beliefs to identify those with more fundamentalist ideas. These questions include whether the respondent believes in the Bible as the literal truth and sees himself or herself as "born again." These conservative Christians are significant politically because their views are represented by well-organized and well-financed organizations that try to influence elections across the nation.

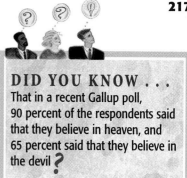

The Influence of Economic Status and Occupation

How wealthy you are and the kind of job you hold are also associated with your political views. Social-class differences emerge on a wide range of issues. Poorer people are more inclined to favor government social-welfare programs but are likely to be conservative on social issues such as abortion. The upper middle class is more likely to hold conservative economic views but to be tolerant of social change. People in lower economic strata also tend to be more isolationist on foreign policy issues and are more likely to identify with the Democratic Party and vote for Democratic candidates. Support for civil liberties and tolerance of different points of view tend to be greater among those with higher social status and lower among those with lower social status. Probably, it is educational differences more than the pattern of life at home or work that account for this.

The Influence of Political Events

People's political attitudes may be shaped by political events and the nation's reactions to them. In the 1960s and 1970s, the war in Vietnam—including revelations about the secret bombing in Cambodia—and the **Watergate break-in** and subsequent presidential cover-up fostered widespread cynicism toward government.

When events produce a long-lasting political impact, **generational effects** result. Voters who grew up in the 1930s during the Great Depression were likely to form lifelong attachments to the Democratic Party, the party of Franklin D. Roosevelt. There was some evidence that the years of economic prosperity under Ronald Reagan during the 1980s may have influenced young adults to identify with the Republican Party. President George W. Bush's immediate and decisive response to the events of 9/11 may have a similar effect. The extent to which the Bush administration's actions during this time of crisis will affect the party identification of young voters, however, remains to be seen.

Generational effects occur only when the event is a true crisis that changes the life of the nation. The Great Depression of the 1930s was one of those events, as was the Vietnam War. Certainly, the terrorist attacks of September 11, 2001, will change the political attitudes of Americans for years to come. Sustained periods of economic prosperity or decline can also influence the youngest generation of voters to feel an attachment to the party in power at the time. Generally, though, events that may seem extremely important in one presidency, such as the historic impeachment and trial of President Bill Clinton in 1998 and 1999, may have very little, if any, impact on voters over the long run.

Watergate Break-in
The 1972 illegal entry into the Democratic National Committee offices by participants in President Richard Nixon's reelection campaign.

Generational Effect
A long-lasting effect of events of a particular time period on the political opinions or preferences of those who came of political age at that time.

Opinion Leaders' Influence

We are all influenced by those with whom we are closely associated or whom we hold in great respect—friends at school, family members and other relatives, teachers, and so on. In a sense, these people are **opinion leaders,** but on an informal level; that is, their influence over us is not necessarily intentional or deliberate. We are also influenced by formal opinion leaders, such as presidents, lobbyists, congresspersons, news commentators, or religious leaders, who have as part of their jobs the task of swaying people's views. Their interest lies in defining the political agenda in such a way that discussions about policy options will take place on their terms.

Opinion Leader
One who is able to influence the opinions of others because of position, expertise, or personality. Such leaders help to shape public opinion.

An event such as the terrorist attacks of September 11, 2001, can influence opinions and attitudes of Americans for many years. The political leadership shown during such a time of crisis is also influential on public opinion. President George W. Bush, shown here at the site of the World Trade Center collapse in New York City, received high public approval ratings for his leadership during the crisis. (AP Photo/Doug Mills)

Media Influence

Media
The technical means of communication with mass audiences.

Clearly, the **media**—newspapers, television, radio, and Internet sources—strongly influence public opinion. This is because the media inform the public about the issues and events of our times and thus have an agenda-setting effect. In other words, to borrow from Bernard Cohen's classic statement on the media and public opinion, the media may not be successful in telling people what to think, but they are "stunningly successful in telling their audience what to think about."[6]

Today, many contend that the media's influence on public opinion has grown to equal that of the family. For example, in her analysis of the role played by the media in American politics,[7] media scholar Doris A. Graber points out that high school students, when asked where they obtain the information on which they base their attitudes, mention the mass media far more than their families, friends, and teachers. This trend, combined with the increasing popularity of such information sources as talk shows and the Internet, may significantly alter the nature of the media's influence on public debate in the future. (See Chapter 11 for a more detailed analysis of the role of the media in American political life.)

The Influence of Demographic Traits

Finally, where you live, what racial group you identify with, and which gender you are can influence your political attitudes. Although regional differences are relatively unimportant today compared to just a few decades ago, there is still a tendency for the South and East to be more Democratic than the West and Midwest. Perhaps more

[6] *The Press and Foreign Policy* (Princeton, N.J.: Princeton University Press, 1963), p. 81.
[7] See Doris A. Graber, *Mass Media and American Politics,* 6th ed. (Chicago: University of Chicago Press, 2001).

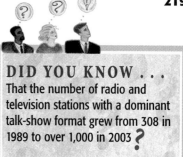

important than region is residence—urban, suburban, or rural. People in big cities tend to be liberal and Democratic because of the greater concentration of minorities and newer ethnic groups. Those who live in smaller communities tend to be conservative and, in many areas, Republican.

African Americans tend to be more liberal than whites on social-welfare issues, civil liberties, and even foreign policy. Since the 1930s, party preference and voting among African Americans have supported the Democrats very heavily.

It is somewhat surprising that a person's chronological age has comparatively little impact on political preferences. Still, young adults are somewhat more liberal than older people on most issues, and they are considerably more progressive than older Americans on such issues as marijuana legalization, pornography, civil disobedience, and racial and gender equality.

The Gender Gap

Until the 1980s, there was little evidence that men's and women's political attitudes were very different. The election of Ronald Reagan in 1980, however, soon came to be associated with a **gender gap.** A May 1983 Gallup poll revealed that more men than women approved of Reagan's job performance. The gender gap has reappeared in subsequent presidential elections, with more women tending to support the Democratic candidate than the Republican one. In the 2000 elections, 54 percent of women voted for Democratic candidate Al Gore, compared with 42 percent of men.

Women also appear to hold different attitudes from their male counterparts on a range of issues other than presidential preferences. They are much more likely than men to oppose capital punishment and the use of force abroad. Studies have also shown that women are more concerned about risks to the environment, more supportive of social welfare, and more supportive of extending civil rights to gay men and lesbians than are men. These differences of opinion appear to be growing and may become an important factor in future elections at national, state, and local levels.[8]

Gender Gap
A term most often used to describe the difference between the percentage of votes a candidate receives from women and the percentage of votes the candidate receives from men. The term came into use after the 1980 presidential elections.

Public Opinion and the Political Process

Public opinion affects the political process in many ways. Politicians, whether in office or in the midst of a campaign, see public opinion as important to their careers. The president, members of Congress, governors, and other elected officials realize that strong support by the public as expressed in opinion polls is a source of power in dealing with other politicians. It is far more difficult for a senator to say no to the president if the president is immensely popular and if polls show approval of the president's policies. Public opinion also helps political candidates identify the most important concerns among the public and may help them shape their campaigns successfully.

Nevertheless, surveys of public opinion are not equivalent to elections in the United States. Although opinion polls may influence political candidates or government officials, elections are the major vehicle through which Americans can bring about changes in their government.

Political Culture and Public Opinion

Americans are divided into a multitude of ethnic, religious, regional, and political subgroups. Given the diversity of American society and the wide range of opinions contained within it, how is it that the political process continues to function without being stalemated by conflict and dissension? One explanation is rooted in the concept of the American political culture, which can be described as a set of attitudes and ideas about

INFOTRAC ®
COLLEGE EDITION

To find out more about this topic, use the term "political culture" in the Subject guide.

---

[8] Jody Newman, "The Gender Story: Women as Voters and Candidates in the 1996 Elections," in *America at the Polls,* 1996 (Storrs, Conn.: Roper Center, 1997), pp. 102–103.

DID YOU KNOW . . .
That when Americans were asked if they think race relations are good or bad in the United States, 68 percent said that they were "bad," but when asked about race relations in their own communities, 75 percent said that they were "good"?

Political Trust
The degree to which individuals express trust in the government and political institutions, usually measured through a specific series of survey questions.

the nation and the government. As discussed in Chapter 1, our political culture is widely shared by Americans of many different backgrounds. To some extent, it consists of symbols, such as the American flag, the Liberty Bell, and the Statue of Liberty. The elements of our political culture also include certain shared beliefs about the most important values in the American political system, including (1) liberty, equality, and property; (2) support for religion; and (3) community service and personal achievement. The structure of the government—particularly federalism, the political parties, the powers of Congress, and popular rule—is also an important value.

Political Culture and Support for Our Political System.   The political culture provides a general environment of support for the political system. If the people share certain beliefs about the system and a reservoir of good feeling exists toward the institutions of government, the nation will be better able to weather periods of crisis. Such was the case after the 2000 presidential elections when, for several weeks, it was not certain who the next president would be and how that determination would be made. At the time, some contended that the nation was facing a true constitutional crisis. Certainly, in many nations of today's world this would be the case. In fact, however, the broad majority of Americans did not feel that the uncertain outcome of the elections had created a constitutional crisis. As mentioned in Chapter 1, polls taken during this time found that, on the contrary, most Americans were confident in our political system's ability to decide the issue peaceably and in a lawful manner.[9]

Political Trust.   The political culture also helps Americans evaluate their government's performance. At times in our history, **political trust** in government has reached relatively high levels. As you can see in Table 7–2, a poll taken two weeks after the 9/11 attacks found that trust in government was higher than it had been for more than three decades. At other times, political trust in government has fallen to low levels. For example, during the 1960s and 1970s, when the Vietnam War was in progress and the Watergate scandal occurred, surveys showed that the overall level of political trust in government had declined steeply. A considerable proportion of Americans seemed to feel that they could not trust government officials and that they could not count on officials to care about the ordinary person. This index of political trust reached an all-time low in the early 1990s but has climbed steadily since then.

Public Opinion about Government

A vital component of public opinion in the United States is the considerable ambivalence with which the public regards many major national institutions. Table 7–3

---

[9] As reported in *Public Perspective*, March/April 2002, p. 11, summarizing the results of Gallup/CNN/USA *Today* polls conducted between November 11 and December 10, 2000.

TABLE 7–2

Trends in Political Trust

QUESTION: HOW MUCH OF THE TIME DO YOU THINK YOU CAN TRUST THE GOVERNMENT IN WASHINGTON TO DO WHAT IS RIGHT—JUST ABOUT ALWAYS, MOST OF THE TIME, OR ONLY SOME OF THE TIME?

	1964	1968	1972	1974	1976	1978	1980	1982	1984	1986	1988	1990	1992	1994	1996	1998	2000	2001
Percentage saying: Always/Most of the time	76	61	53	36	33	29	25	32	46	42	44	27	23	20	25	34	40	64
Some of the time	22	36	45	61	63	67	73	64	51	55	54	73	75	79	71	66	59	35

SOURCES: *New York Times*/CBS News Surveys; the University of Michigan Survey Research Center, National Election Studies; the Pew Research Center for the People and the Press; Council for Excellence in Government; and a *Washington Post* poll conducted September 25–27, 2001.

TABLE 7–3

Confidence in Institutions Trend

QUESTION: I AM GOING TO READ A LIST OF INSTITUTIONS IN AMERICAN SOCIETY. WOULD YOU PLEASE TELL ME HOW MUCH CONFIDENCE YOU, YOURSELF, HAVE IN EACH ONE—A GREAT DEAL, QUITE A LOT, SOME, OR VERY LITTLE?

	PERCENTAGE SAYING "GREAT DEAL" OR "QUITE A LOT"														
	1975	**1977**	**1979**	**1981**	**1983**	**1985**	**1987**	**1989**	**1991**	**1993**	**1995**	**1997**	**1999**	**2001**	**2002**
Church or organized religion	68	65	65	64	62	66	61	52	56	53	57	56	58	60	45
Military	58	57	54	50	53	61	61	63	69	67	64	60	68	66	79
U.S. Supreme Court	49	46	45	46	42	56	52	46	39	43	44	50	49	50	50
Banks and banking	NA	NA	60	46	51	51	51	42	30	38	43	41	43	44	47
Public schools	NA	54	53	42	39	48	50	43	35	39	40	40	36	38	38
Congress	40	40	34	29	28	39	NA	32	18	19	21	22	26	26	29
Newspapers	NA	NA	51	35	38	35	31	NA	32	31	30	35	33	36	35
Big business	34	33	32	20	28	31	NA	NA	22	23	21	28	30	28	20
Television	NA	NA	38	25	25	29	28	NA	24	21	33	34	34	34	35
Organized labor	38	39	36	28	26	28	26	NA	22	26	26	23	28	26	26

NA = Not asked.

SOURCE: Gallup poll, June 28, 2002.

shows trends from 1975 to 2002 in Gallup public opinion polls asking respondents, at regularly spaced intervals, how much confidence they had in the institutions listed. Over the years, military and religious organizations have ranked highest. Note, however, the decline in confidence in churches in 2002 following several sex abuse cases against Catholic priests and what many regarded as a "cover-up" of the abuse by the Catholic hierarchy. Note also the heightened regard for the military after the war in the Persian Gulf in 1991. Not only did the Gulf War give a temporary boost to President George H. W. Bush's popularity, but it also seemed to inspire patriotism and support for the military throughout the nation. Table 7–3 shows that in 1991, the public had more confidence in the military than it did in the church or organized religion, in newspapers, or in any institution of government. In 2002, confidence in the military soared, most likely because Americans recognized the central role to be played by the military in the war on terrorism following the 9/11 terrorist attacks.

The United States Supreme Court, which many people do not see as a particularly political institution, although it is clearly involved in decisions with vitally important consequences for the nation, has scored well over time, as have banks and banking. Less confidence is expressed in newspapers, big business, television, and organized labor, all of which certainly are involved directly or indirectly in the political process. In 1991, following a scandal involving congressional banking practices and other embarrassments, confidence in Congress fell to a record low of 18 percent. Confidence in Congress has yet to return to the levels reported in the 1970s and 1980s.

Although people may not have much confidence in government institutions, they nonetheless turn to government to solve what they perceive to be the major problems facing the country. Table 7–4 on page 222, which is based on Gallup polls conducted from the years 1975 to 2002, shows that the leading problems clearly have changed over time. The public tends to emphasize problems that are immediate. It is not at all unusual to see fairly sudden, and even apparently contradictory, shifts in public perceptions of what government should do. In recent years, education, the economy, and terrorism reached the top of the problems list.

Public Opinion and Policymaking

If public opinion is important for democracy, are policymakers really responsive to public opinion? A study by political scientists Benjamin I. Page and Robert Y. Shapiro

TABLE 7–4

Most Important Problem Trend, 1975 to Present

2002	Terrorism, economy	1988	Economy, budget deficit
2001	Economy, education	1987	Unemployment, economy
2000	Morals, family decline	1986	Unemployment, budget deficit
1999	Crime, violence	1985	Fear of war, unemployment
1998	Crime, violence	1984	Unemployment, fear of war
1997	Crime, violence	1983	Unemployment, high cost of living
1996	Budget deficit	1982	Unemployment, high cost of living
1995	Crime, violence	1981	High cost of living, unemployment
1994	Crime, violence, health care	1980	High cost of living, unemployment
1993	Health care, budget deficit	1979	High cost of living, energy problems
1992	Unemployment, budget deficit	1978	High cost of living, energy problems
1991	Economy	1977	High cost of living, unemployment
1990	War in Middle East	1976	High cost of living, unemployment
1989	War on drugs	1975	High cost of living, unemployment

SOURCES: *New York Times*/CBS News poll, January 1996; *Gallup Report*, 2000; *Gallup Report*, 2002.

suggests that in fact the national government is very responsive to the public's demands for action.[10] In looking at changes in public opinion poll results over time, Page and Shapiro show that when the public supports a policy change, the following occurs: policy changes in a direction consistent with the change in public opinion 43 percent of the time, policy changes in a direction opposite to the change in opinion 22 percent of the time, and policy does not change at all 33 percent of the time. So, overall, the national government could be said to respond to changes in public opinion about two-thirds of the time. Page and Shapiro also show, as should be no surprise, that when public opinion changes more dramatically—say, by 20 percentage points rather than by just 6 or 7 percentage points—government policy is much more likely to follow changing public attitudes.

Setting Limits on Government Action.   Although opinion polls cannot give exact guidance on what the government should do in a specific instance, the opinions measured in polls do set an informal limit on government action. For example, consider the highly controversial issue of abortion. Most Americans are moderates on this issue; they do not approve of abortion as a means of birth control, but they do feel that it should be available under certain circumstances. Yet sizable groups of people express very intense feelings both for and against abortion. Given this distribution of opinion, most elected officials would rather not try to change policy to favor either of the extreme positions. To do so would clearly violate the opinion of the majority of Americans. In this case, as in many others, *public opinion does not make public policy; rather, it restrains officials from taking truly unpopular actions.* If officials do act in the face of public opposition, the consequences of such actions will be determined at the ballot box.

To what degree should public opinion influence policymaking? It would appear that members of the public have different views on this issue than policy leaders do. The results of a recent poll about polls showed that whereas 68 percent of the public feel that public opinion should have a great deal of influence on policy, only 43 percent of policy leaders hold this opinion.[11] Why would a majority of policy leaders *not* want to be strongly influenced by public opinion? One answer to this

---

[10] See the extensive work of Page and Shapiro in Benjamin I. Page and Robert Y. Shapiro, *The Rational Public: Fifty Years of Trends in Americans' Policy Preferences* (Chicago: University of Chicago Press, 1992).

[11] Mollyann Brodie *et al.,* "Polling and Democracy: The Will of the People," *Public Perspective,* July/August 2001, pp. 10–14.

question is that public opinion polls can provide only a limited amount of guidance to policymakers.

The Limits of Polling.   Politicians must make choices. When they do so, their choices necessarily involve trade-offs. Although this term is rarely used in a political setting, it applies nonetheless. Although politicians vote for increased spending to improve education, by necessity there must be less spending on other worthy projects. When politicians vote for increased spending to further the war on terrorism, there must be decreased spending in some other area of the government budget.

Individuals who are polled do not have to make such trade-offs when they respond to questions. Indeed, survey respondents usually are not even given a choice of trade-offs in their policy opinions. Pollsters typically ask respondents whether they want more or less spending in a particular area, such as education. Rarely, though, is a dollar amount assigned. Additionally, broad poll questions often provide little guidance for policymakers. What does it mean if a majority of those polled want "free" medical treatment for everyone in need? Obviously, medical care is never free. Certain individuals may receive medical care free of charge, but society as a whole has to pay for it. In short, polling questions do not reflect the cost of any particular policy choice. Moreover, to make an informed policy choice requires an understanding not only of the policy area but also of the consequences of any given choice. Virtually no public opinion polls make sure that those polled have such information.

Finally, government decisions cannot be made simply by adding up individual desires. Politicians engage in a type of "horse trading." All politicians know that they cannot satisfy every desire of every constituent. Therefore, each politician attempts to maximize the *net* benefits to his or her constituents, while keeping within whatever the government budget happens to be. This process occurs at all levels of government—local, state, and federal.

Public Opinion: Why Is It Important Today?

Public opinion is important today because it can lead to changes in policy. Earlier in this chapter, we described how public opinion put pressure on President George W. Bush to change his policy with respect to military tribunals. We also pointed out that positive public opinion can give a politician greater leeway when making policy, as evidenced by the public's strong support for the war in Afghanistan in 2001 and 2002.

Remember, though, that the relationship between changes in public opinion and changes in public policy is more indirect than direct: the public's preferences provide broad guidelines within which policymakers can operate. In essence, the importance of public opinion lies more in its ability to prevent totally objectionable policies than in its ability to specify particular policy mandates. The result is that any publicly considered policy will at least be tolerable for most people.

Public opinion is only as effective as the polls that measure it, however. No one in America can avoid public opinion polls. One can scarcely glance at the nightly news without seeing the results of the latest poll about some important (or superfluous) issue. Certainly, public opinion polls are important to the political process today. Otherwise, it would be hard to explain why politicians spend so many millions of dollars each year for such expensive information. Both policymakers and the public need to be critical consumers of opinion polls, as discussed in this chapter's *Making a Difference* feature.

MAKING A DIFFERENCE | Be a Critical Consumer of Opinion Polls

Americans are inundated with the results of public opinion polls. The polls, often reported to us through television news, the newspaper, *Time, Newsweek,* or radio, purport to tell us a variety of things: whether the president's popularity is up or down, whether gun control is more popular now than previously, or who is leading the pack for the next presidential nomination.

What must be kept in mind with this blizzard of information is that not all poll results are equally good or equally believable. As a critical consumer, you need to be aware of what makes one set of public opinion poll results valid and other results useless or even dangerously misleading.

Selection of the Sample

How were the people who were interviewed selected? Pay attention only to opinion polls that are based on scientific, or random, samples, in which a known probability was used to select every person who was interviewed. These *probability samples,* as they are also called, can take a number of different forms. The simplest to understand is known as a *random sample,* in which everybody had a known, and possibly an equal, chance of being chosen to be interviewed. As a rule, do not give credence to the results of opinion polls that consist of shopping-mall interviews. The main problem with this kind of opinion taking, which is a special version of a so-called *accidental sample,* is that not everyone had an equal chance of being in the mall when the interview took place. Also, it is almost certain that the

people in the mall are not a reasonable cross section of a community's entire population (shopping malls would tend to attract people who are disproportionately younger, female, mobile, and middle class).

Probability samples are useful (and nonprobability samples are not) for the following reason: when you know the odds that the particular sample would have been chosen randomly from a larger population, you can calculate the range within which the real results for the whole population would fall if everybody had been interviewed. Well-designed probability samples will allow the pollster to say, for example, that he or she is 95 percent sure that 61 percent of the public, plus or minus 4 percentage points, supports national health insurance. It turns out that if you want to become twice as precise about a poll result, you would need to collect a sample four times as large. This tends to make accurate polls quite expensive and difficult to collect. Typically, the Gallup organization seldom interviews more than about 1,500 respondents.

Interview Method

There are other important points to keep in mind when you see opinion poll results. How were people contacted for the poll—by mail, by telephone, in person in their homes, or in some other way (such as via the Internet)? By and large, because of its lower cost, polling firms have turned more and more to telephone interviewing. This method usually can produce highly accurate results. Its disadvantage is that telephone inter-

views typically need to be short and to deal with questions that are fairly easy to answer. Interviews in person are better for getting useful information about why a particular response was given to a question. They take much longer to complete, however, and are not as useful if results must be generated quickly. Results from mailed questionnaires should be taken with a grain of salt. Usually, only a small percentage of people complete them and send them back.

Nonpolls

Be particularly critical of telephone "call-in" polls or "Internet polls." When viewers or listeners of television or radio shows are encouraged to call in their opinions to an 800 telephone number, the call is free, but the polling results are useless. Users of the Internet also have an easy way to make their views known. Only people who are interested in the topic will take the trouble to respond, however, and that group, of course, is not representative of the general public. Polls that use 900 numbers are perhaps even more misleading. The only respondents to those polls are those who care enough about the topic to pay for a call. Both types of polls are likely to be manipulated by interest groups or the campaign staff of a political candidate, who will organize their supporters to make calls and reinforce their own point of view. Remember, when seeing the results of any poll, to take a moment and try to find out how the poll was conducted.

Key Terms

consensus 206	media 218	peer group 216	public opinion 206
divisive opinion 206	opinion leader 217	political socialization 215	sampling error 210
gender gap 219	opinion poll 207	political trust 220	Watergate break-in 217
generational effect 217			

Chapter Summary

1 Public opinion is the aggregate of individual attitudes or beliefs shared by some portion of the adult population. A consensus exists when a large proportion of the American public appears to express the same view on an issue. Divisive opinion exists when the public holds widely different attitudes on an issue. Nonopinion exists when most Americans either have no information about an issue or are not interested enough in the issue to form a position on it.

2 Most descriptions of public opinion are based on the results of opinion polls. The accuracy of polls depends on sampling techniques that include a representative sample of the population being polled and that ensure randomness in the selection of respondents.

3 Problems with polls include sampling errors (which may occur when the pool of respondents is not chosen in a scientific manner), the difficulty of knowing the degree to which responses are influenced by the type and order of questions asked, the frequent use of a yes/no format for answers to the questions, and the interviewer's techniques. Many are concerned about the increasingly widespread use of "push polls" (in which the questions "push" the respondent toward a particular candidate).

4 Advances in technology have changed polling techniques over the years. During the 1970s, telephone polling came to be widely used. Today, largely due to extensive telemarketing by businesses, people often refuse to answer calls, and nonresponse rates in telephone polling have skyrocketed. Because of the difficulty of obtaining a random sample in the online environment, Internet polls are often "nonpolls." Whether Internet polls can overcome this problem remains to be seen.

5 People's opinions are formed through the political socialization process. Important factors in this process are the fam-

ily, educational institutions, peers and peer groups, religion, economic status and occupation, significant political events, opinion leaders, the media, demographic traits, and gender. While the family is usually seen as the most important influence in opinion formation, increasingly the media's ability to influence opinion is coming to equal that of the family.

6 Public opinion affects the political process in many ways. The political culture provides a general environment of support for the political system, allowing the nation to weather periods of crisis, such as the uncertainties following the 2000 elections and the terrorist attacks of September 11, 2001. The political culture also helps Americans to evaluate their government's performance. At times, there have been relatively high levels of political trust in government; at other times, the level of political trust has declined steeply. Similarly, Americans' confidence in government institutions varies over time, depending on a number of circumstances. Generally, though, Americans turn to government to solve what they perceive to be the major problems facing the country. In 2002, Americans ranked terrorism and the economy as the two most significant problems facing the nation.

7 Public opinion also plays an important role in policymaking. Measurement of policy changes relative to changes in public opinion shows that policy leaders respond to changes in public opinion about two-thirds of the time. Although polling data show that a majority of Americans would like policy leaders to be influenced to a great extent by public opinion, politicians cannot always be guided by opinion polls because the respondents do not understand the costs and consequences of policy decisions nor the trade-offs involved in making such decisions. An important function of public opinion is to set limits on government action through public pressure.

Selected Print and Media Resources

SUGGESTED READINGS

Abner, Herbert B. *Polling and the Public: What Every Citizen Should Know.* Washington, D.C.: CQ Press, 2001. This clearly written and often entertaining book explains what polls are, how they are conducted and interpreted, and how the wording and ordering of survey questions, as well as the interviewer's techniques, can significantly affect the respondents' answers.

Bardes, Barbara A., and Robert W. Oldendick. *Public Opinion: Measuring the American Mind,* 2d ed. Belmont, Calif.: Wadsworth Publishing Co., 2003. This examination of public opinion polling looks at the uses of public opinion data and recent technological issues in polling in addition to providing excellent coverage of public opinion on important issues over a period of decades.

Graber, Doris A., ed. *Media Power in Politics,* 4th ed. Washington, D.C.: CQ Press, 2000. This collection of essays on media power includes several excellent articles on the media's role in shaping public opinion.

Jacobsen, Clay. *Circle of Seven.* Nashville, Tenn.: Broadman & Holman, 2000. A gripping novel pitting one man, a television reporter, against a media group that manipulates opinion polls and the media to further its own ends.

Warren, Kenneth F. *In Defense of Public Opinion Polling.* Boulder, Colo.: Westview Press, 2001. The author, himself a pollster, explains how public opinion polls are used by politicians and the media and why they are valuable.

MEDIA RESOURCES

Logan's Run—A 1976 classic sci-fi film about life in a futuristic city that is peopled by clones and in which individuals must die at the age of thirty. The film raises disturbing questions about whether public opinion matters.

Wag the Dog—A 1997 film that provides a very cynical look at the importance of public opinion. The film, which features Dustin Hoffman and Robert DeNiro, follows the efforts of a presidential political consultant who stages a foreign policy crisis to divert public opinion from a sex scandal in the White House.

Vox Populi: Democracy in Crisis—A PBS special focusing on why public confidence in government, which has plummeted during recent decades, still has not recovered.

Your CD-ROM Resources

In addition to the chapter content containing hot links, the following resources are available on the CD-ROM:

- **Internet Activities**—Sampling error, Internet election forecasting.

- **Critical Thinking Exercises**—The Gallop poll, mass media, the gender gap.

- **Self-Check on Important Themes**—Can You Answer These?

- **Animated Figures**—Figure 7–1, "Consensus Opinion," Figure 7–2, "Divisive Opinion," Figure 7–3, "Nonopinion."

- **Videos**—*Probability, Evaluating Polls.*

- **Public Opinion Data**—Find contrasting views on government-regulated polling and the abolition of exit polling.

- **InfoTrac Exercise**—"The Power of the Polls."

- **Simulation**—You Are There!

- **Participation Exercise**—You too can be a pollster! Pick an issue of concern to students at your college or university and create a poll.

- **MicroCase Exercise**—"By the Numbers: Voices on 'Hot-button' Issues."

e-mocracy

Online Polling and Poll Data

News organizations, interest groups, not-for-profit groups, and online e-zines are now using online polling to gather the opinions of their readers and viewers. All the user has to do is log on to the Web site and click on the box indicating the preferred response. People can respond to online polls more easily than to call-in polls, and in most cases, they are free to the user. Realize, though, that online polls are totally nonscientific because the respondents are all self-selected. Essentially, Internet polls are pseudopolls because only those who choose to do so respond, making the polls much more likely to be biased and based on an unrepresentative sample.

At the same time, the Internet is an excellent source for polling reports and data. All of the major polling organizations have Web sites where they include news releases about polls they have conducted. Some sites make the polling data available for free to users; others require that a user pay a subscription fee before accessing the polling archives on the site.

Logging On

Yale University Library, one of the great research institutions, offers access to Social Science Libraries and Information Services. If you want to roam around some library sources of public opinion data, this is an interesting site to visit. Go to

http://www.library.yale.edu/socsci/opinion

According to its home page, the mission of National Election Studies (NES) "is to produce high quality data on voting, public opinion, and political participation that serves the research needs of social scientists, teachers, students, and policymakers concerned with understanding the theoretical and empirical foundations of mass politics in a democratic society." This is a good place to obtain information related to public opinion. Find it at

http://www.umich.edu/~nes

The Polling Report Web site offers polls and their results organized by topic. It is up-to-date and easy to use. Go to

http://www.pollingreport.com

The Gallup organization's Web site offers not only polling data (although a user must pay a subscription fee to obtain access to many polling reports) but also information on how polls are constructed, conducted, and interpreted. Go to

http://www.gallup.com

Another site that features articles and polling data on public opinion is the Web site of the Zogby Poll at

http://www.zogby.com

Using the Internet for Political Analysis

To sharpen your skills in using public opinion data, point your browser to one of the sites noted in the *Logging On* section or to a site maintained by one of the national newspapers. Pick a subject or topic on which the site maintains public opinion polling results (often you must use the Contents button for this). Then try to identify and consider the following types of information: First, how large was the sample, and how big is the "confidence" interval cited in the study? Do you know who commissioned the poll and to whom the results were given? Second, examine at least three questions and responses, and answer the following: How might the wording of the question have influenced the responses? How can you tell if the survey respondents had any information about the question asked? Was the number of respondents who couldn't answer the question substantial? Can you tell if respondents could answer the question without much information? Finally, consider how much a political leader might learn from this poll.

BACKGROUND

The First Amendment to the Constitution gives every citizen the right to "assemble and petition the government" for the resolution of his or her grievances. This right pertains to individuals, to groups, and to organizations, such as large corporations and labor unions.

The problem is, how can we make sure that those who lobby or influence political officials are not using corrupt means to do so? Congress has imposed registration requirements on lobbyists, but recent events suggest that recordings of exactly what lobbyists say to politicians when pressing their cases might put an end to even the appearance of corruption.

WHAT IF EVERY LOBBYING CONTACT HAD TO BE RECORDED?

Citizens, members of Congress, the press, and even the president would love to know exactly what lobbyists say when they meet with political decision makers. For example, when Enron Corporation, a leading energy company based in Houston, Texas, failed in 2001, a scandal erupted regarding the degree of influence Enron executives had exerted on government officials. Many commentators suggested that the Bush administration must have been unduly influenced by Enron executives when it formulated its proposed energy policy. After all, President George W. Bush was a Texan and had received campaign contributions from Enron executives. Further investigation revealed that Enron had contributed to many members of Congress and to the Clinton campaigns. What did Enron executives want from all these politicians?

One way to increase public knowledge of what lobbyists seek and how they influence politicians would be to eliminate the current regulations that require lobbyists to register and instead require that every contact anyone has with an elected or appointed official be recorded. The record could be written notes, an audio or video recording, or notes written on a computer or hand-held device. Voters, paid lobbyists, politicians, and the press could access these records on the Internet.

THE LOSS OF PRIVACY

Requiring that all contacts between lobbyists (of any type) and public officials be recorded would eliminate the privacy and freedom of movement of those involved. Nevertheless, so long as the legislation did not attempt to limit the type or number of contacts, it might not violate the Constitution.

This new requirement, coupled with the new campaign-financing law passed in 2002, would certainly cut down on the social demands placed on members of Congress. No longer would they attend fund-raisers and receptions held by interest groups every evening in Washington. After all, who would pay hundreds of dollars to "rub elbows" with public officials if they could not speak privately with the officials about public matters?

Of course, collecting these millions of reports and archiving them for retrieval would be a logistical nightmare. With modern information technology, however, it would be possible, particularly if the records were collected via the Internet.

Would anyone take the time to read these millions of reports to find out what every public official is discussing and hearing? When environmental groups succeeded in getting the Bush administration to release documents associated with the formulation of its energy policy, it took thirty attorneys and staff members several nights just to comb through the papers for a few relevant e-mails. Would information gained from recordings of conversations with elected officials be used in election campaigns to attack an incumbent? Finally, would disclosing every conversation destroy all trust between officials and their constituents?

FOR CRITICAL ANALYSIS

1. How would recording the conversations of lobbyists be likely to change the tactics they use to influence public officials? Would they find other ways to get their points across?
2. Should individuals have a right to privacy in their conversations with others, including conversations with elected officials?

The structure of American government invites the participation of **interest groups** at various stages of the policymaking process. For example, interest groups played a role in the legislation passed by Congress after the September 11 terrorist attacks. In a show of national unity, the House of Representatives and the Senate voted overwhelmingly to give President George W. Bush authority to use military force in response to the attacks and passed a $40 billion emergency spending bill to pay for the response.

Two weeks after the attacks, life on Capitol Hill returned to the more normal process of dissension and debate. The president's requests for further antiterrorism legislation spurred fast and furious action by interest groups, which quickly sent their **lobbyists** to persuade Congress to adopt their positions on these bills. The airlines, which form a powerful interest group, quickly expressed their need for congressional help. They were gratified by an airline bailout bill to make up for the enormous losses they suffered as a result of the closure of U.S. airspace after the attacks and the drop in the number of passengers in the weeks that followed. After the bill passed, however, lobbyists for the many other industries that were hurt by the attacks began asking for their own assistance packages, including car-rental firms, the hotel industry, and travel and tourism companies.

Perhaps the oddest lobbying efforts were seen during the debate over the aviation security bill. We look at these efforts in this chapter's *America's Security* feature.

Interest Groups: A Natural Phenomenon

Alexis de Tocqueville observed in 1834 that "in no country of the world has the principle of association been more successfully used or applied to a greater multitude of objectives than in America."[1] The French traveler was amazed at the degree to which Americans formed groups to solve civic problems, establish social relationships, and speak for their economic or political interests. Perhaps James Madison, when he wrote *Federalist Paper* No. 10 (see Appendix D), had already judged the character of his country's citizens similarly. He supported the creation of a large republic with several states to encourage the formation of many interests. The multitude of interests, in

---

[1] Alexis de Tocqueville, *Democracy in America*, Vol. 1, edited by Phillips Bradley (New York: Knopf, 1980), p. 191.

Interest Group
An organized group of individuals sharing common objectives who actively attempt to influence policymakers in all three branches of the government and at all levels.

Lobbyist
An organization or individual who attempts to influence the passage, defeat, or contents of legislation and the administrative decisions of government.

Lobbying activity becomes most intense the day a vote is being taken on an important issue. Not surprisingly, lobbyists are often found in the lobbies of Congress. (Dennis Brack, Black Star)

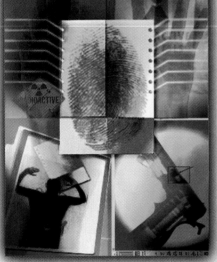

Interest Groups and Aviation Security

In November 2001, President George W. Bush signed into law an aviation security bill. Before this bill passed, baggage and passenger screening at airports had been the responsibility of the airlines and local airport authorities. Generally, an airport would contract with one of a handful of international corporations for security screeners. The job required little education or experience, and workers tended to be very low paid. Background checks for airport security personnel were very limited.

THE DEMAND FOR IMPROVED SECURITY

After 9/11, the president, Congress, and the public demanded that airport security be improved. The Senate favored

Surrounded by members of Congress and representatives of the airline industry, President George W. Bush signs the aviation security bill. In addition to lobbyists for the airline industry, several other interest groups lobbied for changes to the bill before the president signed it. In what ways was the final form of the bill influenced by these lobbying efforts? (AP Photo/ J. Scott Applewhite)

making airport security a federal responsibility and making all screeners federal employees. The Republican majority in the House favored letting the private security firms continue but under federal oversight. A little-known interest group, the Airline Security Association, launched a major lobbying effort to keep private corporations in business. Its lobbyists cited the excellent work of many security agencies and quickly named the "airport screener of the year."

As the debate continued, it became clear that the price of requiring airport screening personnel to be employees of the federal government would be very high, both for the government and for existing employees who wanted to continue their jobs. To be eligible for these new federal jobs, current employees would need to pass background checks and have a high school diploma. One proposed provision would have required that all screeners be U.S. citizens for at least five years. About one-third of then-current screeners, however, did not have high school degrees, and another significant proportion were not U.S. citizens. Groups that represent immigrants and the Hispanic Congressional Caucus opposed these requirements.*

*James C. Benton and Peter Cohn, "White House, Aviation Safety Conferees Grope Their Way toward Compromise," *Congressional Quarterly Weekly*, November 10, 2001, p. 2676.

Unions were also unhappy with the proposed bill because it would have prohibited these new federal employees from striking. Other groups that tried to influence the bill included the airline pilots, the flight attendants, the airlines' trade group, federal employees' unions, and the makers of screening equipment.

THE END RESULT— A COMPROMISE

The end result was a compromise. Aviation security became a federal responsibility, and all passenger and baggage screeners were required to become federal employees within one year. After two years of this system, an airport may ask to go back to private contractors, but only under federal supervision. To keep business happy with this version of the bill, Republicans slipped in some provisions to protect businesses hurt by the terrorist attacks.†

While this debate was going on, Americans continued to cut down on air travel, and airline companies suffered losses. It was clear that the American public wanted assurance that air travel would again be safe, but the interested parties continued to lobby and jockey over this important legislation. Although this activity may have seemed out of place in a national emergency, interest groups representing individuals, businesses, and other kinds of associations have roots deep in American history and culture.

FOR CRITICAL ANALYSIS

Do you think it is appropriate for interest groups to lobby for their positions in times of national emergency? Can you imagine circumstances in which people can be hurt by delays in passing legislation due to intense lobbying?

SAFER SKIES FOR AMERICA

†"Aviation Security," *Congressional Quarterly Weekly*, December 22, 2001, p. 3055.

Madison's view, would work to discourage the formation of an oppressive larger minority or majority interest.

Surely, neither Madison nor de Tocqueville foresaw the formation of more than a hundred thousand associations in the United States. Poll data show that more than two-thirds of all Americans belong to at least one group or association. While the majority of these affiliations could not be classified as "interest groups" in the political sense, Americans do understand the principles of working in groups.

Today, interest groups range from the elementary school parent-teacher association and the local "Stop the Sewer Plant Association" to the statewide association of insurance agents. They include small groups such as local environmental organizations and national groups such as the Boy Scouts of America, the American Civil Liberties Union, the National Education Association, and the American League of Lobbyists.

Interest Groups and Social Movements

Interest groups are often spawned by mass **social movements.** Such movements represent demands by a large segment of the population for change in the political, economic, or social system. Social movements are often the first expression of latent discontent with the contemporary system. They may be the authentic voice of weaker or oppressed groups in society that do not have the means or standing to organize as interest groups. For example, the women's movement of the nineteenth century suffered social disapproval from most mainstream political and social leaders. Because women were unable to vote or take an active part in the political system, it was difficult for women who desired greater freedoms to organize formal groups. After the Civil War, when more women became active in professional life, the first real women's rights group, the National Woman Suffrage Association, came into being.

African Americans found themselves in an even more disadvantaged situation after the end of the Reconstruction period. They were unable to exercise political rights in many southern and border states, and their participation in any form of organization could lead to economic ruin, physical harassment, or even death. The civil rights movement of the 1950s and 1960s was clearly a social movement. Although several formal organizations worked to support the movement—including the Southern Christian Leadership Conference, the National Association for the Advancement of Colored People, and the Urban League—only a social movement could generate the kinds of civil disobedience that took place in hundreds of towns and cities across the country.

Social movements are often precursors of interest groups. They may generate interest groups with specific goals that successfully recruit members through the incentives the group offers. In the case of the women's movement of the 1960s, the National Organization for Women was formed out of a demand to end gender-segregated job advertising in newspapers.

Why So Many?

Whether based in a social movement or created to meet an immediate crisis, interest groups continue to form and act in American society. One reason for the multitude of interest groups is that the right to join a group is protected by the First Amendment to the U.S. Constitution (see Chapter 4). Not only are all people guaranteed the right "peaceably to assemble," but they are also guaranteed the right "to petition the Government for a redress of grievances." This constitutional provision encourages Americans to form groups and to express their opinions to the government or to their elected representatives as members of a group. Group membership makes the individual's opinions appear more powerful and strongly conveys the group's ability to vote for or against a representative.

Alexis de Tocqueville (1805–1859), a French social historian and traveler, commented on Americans' predilection for joining groups. (Corbis/Bettmann)

Social Movement
  A movement that represents the demands of a large segment of the public for political, economic, or social change.

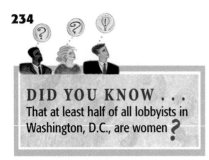

In addition, our federal system of government provides thousands of "pressure points" for interest group activity. Americans can form groups in their neighborhoods or cities and lobby the city council and their state government. They can join statewide groups or national groups and try to influence government policy through the Congress or through one of the executive agencies or cabinet departments. Representatives of giant corporations may seek to influence the president himself at social events or fund-raisers. When attempts to influence government through the executive and legislative branches fail, interest groups turn to the courts, filing suit in state or federal court to achieve their political objectives. Pluralist theorists, as discussed in Chapter 1, point to the openness of the American political structure as a major factor in the power of groups in American politics.

Why Do Americans Join Interest Groups?

One puzzle that has fascinated political scientists is why some people join interest groups, whereas many others do not. Everyone has some interest that could benefit from government action. For many individuals, however, those concerns remain unorganized interests, or **latent interests.**

Latent Interests
Public-policy interests that are not recognized or addressed by a group at a particular time.

According to political theorist Mancur Olson, it simply may not be rational for individuals to join most groups. He introduces the idea of the "collective good." This concept refers to any public benefit that, if available to any member of the community, cannot be denied to any other member, whether or not he or she participated in the effort to gain the good.

Although collective benefits are usually thought of as coming from such public goods as clean air or national defense, benefits are also bestowed by the government on subsets of the public. Price subsidies to dairy farmers and loans to college students are examples. Olson uses economic theory to propose that it is not rational for interested individuals to join groups that work for group benefits. In fact, it is often more rational for the individual to wait for others to procure the benefits and then share them. How many college students, for example, join the American Association of Community Colleges, an organization that lobbies the government for increased financial aid to students? The difficulty interest groups face in recruiting members when the benefits can be obtained without joining is referred to as the **free rider problem.**

Free Rider Problem
The difficulty interest groups face in recruiting members when the benefits they achieve can be gained without joining the group.

If so little incentive exists for individuals to join together, why are there thousands of interest groups lobbying in Washington? According to the logic of collective action, if the contribution of an individual *will* make a difference to the effort, then it is worth it to the individual to join. Thus, smaller groups, which seek benefits for only a small proportion of the population, are more likely to enroll members who will give time and money to the cause. Larger groups, which represent general public interests (the women's movement or the American Civil Liberties Union, for example), will find it relatively more difficult to get individuals to join. People need an incentive—material or otherwise—to join.[2]

Solidary Incentives

Interest groups offer **solidary incentives** for their members. Solidary incentives include companionship, a sense of belonging, and the pleasure of associating with others. Although originally the National Audubon Society was founded to save the snowy egret from extinction, today most members join to learn more about birds and to meet and share their pleasure with other individuals who enjoy bird watching

Solidary Incentive
A reason or motive having to do with the desire to associate with others and to share with others a particular interest or hobby.

---

[2]For further reading on this complex and interesting theory, see Mancur Olson, *The Logic of Collective Action* (Cambridge, Mass.: Harvard University Press, 1965).

as a hobby. Even though the incentive might be solidary for many members, this organization nonetheless also pursues an active political agenda, working to preserve the environment and to protect endangered species. Most members may not play any part in working toward larger, more national goals unless the organization can convince them to take political action or unless some local environmental issue arises.

Material Incentives

For other individuals, interest groups offer direct **material incentives.** A case in point is the AARP (formerly the American Association of Retired Persons), which provides discounts, insurance plans, and organized travel opportunities for its members. Because of its exceptionally low dues ($12.50 annually) and the benefits gained through membership, the AARP has become the largest—and a very powerful—interest group in the United States. The AARP can claim to represent the interests of millions of senior citizens and can show that they actually have joined the group. For most seniors, the material incentives outweigh the membership costs.

Many other interest groups offer indirect material incentives for their members. Such groups as the American Dairy Association or the National Association of Automobile Dealers do not give discounts or freebies to their members, but they do offer indirect benefits and rewards by, for example, protecting the material interests of their members from government policymaking that is injurious to their industry or business.

Purposive Incentives

Interest groups also offer the opportunity for individuals to pursue political, economic, or social goals through joint action. Such **purposive incentives** offer individuals the satisfaction of taking action for the sake of their beliefs or principles. The individuals who belong to groups focusing on the abortion issue or gun control, for example, do so because they feel strongly enough about the issues to support the groups' work with money and time.

Some scholars have argued that many people join interest groups simply for the discounts, magazine subscriptions, and other tangible benefits and are not really interested in the political positions taken by the group. According to William P. Browne, however, research shows that people really do care about the policy stance of an interest group. Members of a group seek people who share the group's views and then ask them to join. As one group leader put it, "Getting members is about scaring the hell out of people."[3] People join the group and then feel that they are doing something about a cause that is important to them.

In view of the many incentives for joining interest groups, why do the majority of Americans not belong to such groups? This question is explored in this chapter's *Which Side Are You On?* feature on the following page.

Types of Interest Groups

Thousands of groups exist to influence government. Among the major types of interest groups are those that represent the main sectors of the economy. In more recent years, a number of "public-interest" organizations have been formed to represent the needs of the general citizenry, including some "single-issue" groups. The interests of

---

[3] William P. Browne, *Groups, Interests, and U.S. Public Policy* (Washington, D.C.: Georgetown University Press, 1998), p. 23.

Material Incentive
A reason or motive having to do with economic benefits or opportunities.

Purposive Incentive
A reason or motive having to do with ethical beliefs or ideological principles.

President George W. Bush addresses the national meeting of the carpenters' union in 2002. He sought the union's support for a bill in Congress that would subsidize costs for insurance against terrorist attacks and, in his view, create jobs. (AP Photo/Ron Edmonds)

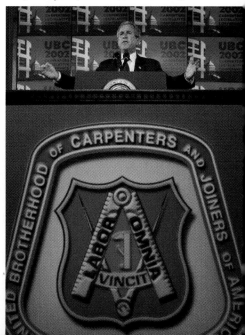

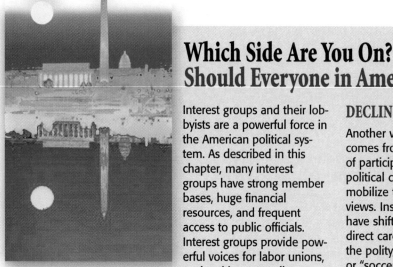

Which Side Are You On?
Should Everyone in America Have a Lobby?

Interest groups and their lobbyists are a powerful force in the American political system. As described in this chapter, many interest groups have strong member bases, huge financial resources, and frequent access to public officials. Interest groups provide powerful voices for labor unions, senior citizens, small-business owners, big corporations, teachers, and many others. The right to form such groups and to present the groups' ideas is guaranteed in the Bill of Rights.

The majority of American citizens, however, do not belong to an interest group. They connect with their elected officials at the ballot box or, on occasion, through a letter or request to the official's staff, but most do not join a political interest group. Are these Americans at a disadvantage when it comes to obtaining representation of their interests?

THE PLIGHT OF THE POOR

What about poor Americans or U.S. residents who are not citizens and cannot vote? Americans who are disadvantaged economically cannot afford to join interest groups; if they are members of the working poor, they may hold two or more jobs just to survive, leaving them no time to participate in interest groups. Other groups in the population—including non-English-speaking groups, resident aliens, single parents, disabled Americans, and younger voters—probably do not have the time or expertise even to find out what group might represent them. Consequently, some scholars suggest that interest groups and lobbyists are the privilege of upper-middle-class Americans and those who belong to unions or other special groups. Should all Americans have access to the same kind of representation? How could every American become part of a group that would lobby for his or her particular interest?

R. Allen Hays examines the plight of poor Americans in his book *Who Speaks for the Poor?** Hays studied groups and individuals who have lobbied for public housing and other issues related to the poor and concludes that the poor depend largely on indirect representation. Most efforts on behalf of the poor come from a policy network of groups—including public housing officials, welfare workers and officials, public-interest groups, and some liberal general interest groups—that speak loudly and persistently for the poor. He concludes that poor Americans themselves remain outside the interest group network and have little direct voice of their own.

DECLINING PARTICIPATION

Another view on which groups have a voice in politics comes from Steven E. Schier, who writes about the decline of participation in national politics.[†] Schier suggests that political campaigns and lobbying campaigns no longer try to mobilize the majority of Americans to vote or express their views. Instead, he argues, campaigns and interest groups have shifted to a strategy of "activation," in which they direct carefully targeted messages to specific groups within the polity, such as "right-to-life" groups or "Hispanic voters" or "soccer moms" or "hardhat Republicans." By targeting such groups and trying to mobilize a large proportion of their members to fight for their own special interests, this strategy gives the appearance of great political activity.

Politicians respond to the activity and act for the special interest. Most of the public, however, is not involved in the debate and is not encouraged to participate. Thus, participation declines, and the public sees politics as defined by special interests. Schier believes that the country would be better off if the majority of Americans engaged in political debate and participated in elections through voting and other activities.

WHICH IS MORE EFFECTIVE—JOINING INTEREST GROUPS OR PARTICIPATING IN ELECTIONS?

The perspectives offered by Hays and Schier raise several questions about the most effective way for Americans to influence their elected officials. Hays's view suggests that Americans' voices may not be heard unless they have interest groups speaking directly for them. Schier, in contrast, puts more faith in the political process. He thinks that the influence of the special interests could be countered if the majority of Americans would vote and actively engage in the political process.

WHAT'S YOUR POSITION?

Should Americans try to obtain better representation by joining interest groups? Or should they simply pay more attention to political issues and participate in elections?

GOING ONLINE

To investigate this issue further, go to the Public Agenda Web site at **http://www.publicagenda.org** and click on one of the issues such as Poverty or Immigration. Review the position paper and public opinion polls given for that topic. Is there any way to know what the affected individuals—the poor or the immigrants—think about the policy? Would this be different if they had interest groups?

---

*R. Allen Hays, *Who Speaks for the Poor?* (New York: Routledge, 2001).

[†]Steven E. Schier, *By Invitation Only: The Rise of Exclusive Politics in the United States* (Pittsburgh, Pa.: University of Pittsburgh Press, 2000).

foreign governments and foreign businesses are also represented in the American political arena. The memberships of some major interest groups are shown in Table 8–1.

Economic Interest Groups

More interest groups are formed to represent economic interests than any other type of interests. The variety of economic interest groups mirrors the complexity of the American economy. The major sectors that seek influence in Washington, D.C.,

INFOTRAC® COLLEGE EDITION

To find out more about these groups, use the term "pressure groups" in the Subject guide.

TABLE 8–1

Characteristics of Selected Interest Groups

Name (Founded)	Members (Individuals or as noted)
Business/Economic	
Business Roundtable (1972)	200 corporations (10 million employees)
The Conference Board, Inc. (1916)	3,000 labor unions, colleges & universities, etc.
National Association of Manufacturers (1895)	14,000 companies
U.S. Chamber of Commerce (1912)	200,000 companies, state & local chambers of commerce, etc.
Civil/Constitutional Rights	
AARP (1958)	35,000,000
American Civil Liberties Union (1920)	300,000
Amnesty International USA (1961)	over 1 million
Handgun Control, Inc. (1974)	500,000
Leadership Conference on Civil Rights, Inc. (1950)	180 national organizations
League of United Latin American Citizens (LULAC) (1929)	115,000
Mexican-American Legal Defense and Educational Fund (1968)	—
National Abortion Rights Action League (1969)	500,000
National Association for the Advancement of Colored People (1909)	over 500,000
National Gay and Lesbian Task Force (1973)	35,000
National Organization for Women, Inc. (1966)	300,000
National Rifle Association of America (1871)	3,400,000
National Urban League (1910)	1,600,000
Community/Grassroots	
The American Society for the Prevention of Cruelty to Animals (1866)	475,000
Association of Community Organizations for Reform Now (ACORN) (1970)	over 120,000
Mothers Against Drunk Driving (1980)	2 million
Environmental	
Environmental Defense Fund (1967)	300,000
Greenpeace USA (1971)	250,000
League of Conservation Voters (1970)	40,000
National Audubon Society (1905)	600,000
National Wildlife Federation (1936)	4,500,000
The Nature Conservancy (1951)	over 1 million
Sierra Club (1892)	700,000
The Wilderness Society (1935)	200,000
World Wildlife Fund (1948)	over 1 million
International Affairs	
Accuracy in Media (1969)	over 16,000
American Israel Public Affairs Committee (1954)	65,000
Human Rights Watch (1978)	—

SOURCE: Foundation for Public Affairs, *Public Interest Profiles 1995–1996* (Washington, D.C.: Congressional Quarterly Press, 1995); and authors' update.

include business, agriculture, labor unions and their members, government workers, and professionals.

Business Interest Groups.   Thousands of business groups and trade associations work to influence government policies that affect their respective sectors. "Umbrella groups" represent certain types of businesses or companies that deal in a particular type of product. The U.S. Chamber of Commerce, for example, is an umbrella group that represents businesses, and the National Association of Manufacturers is an umbrella group that represents only manufacturing concerns. The American Pet Products Manufacturers Association works for the good of manufacturers of pet food, pet toys, and other pet products, as well as for pet shops. This group strongly opposes more regulation of stores that sell animals and restrictions on importing pets. Other major organizations that represent business interests, such as the Better Business Bureaus, take positions on policies but do not actually lobby in Washington, D.C.[4]

Some business groups are decidedly more powerful than others. The U.S. Chamber of Commerce, which has more than 200,000 member companies, can bring constituent influence to bear on every member of Congress. Another powerful lobbying organization is the National Association of Manufacturers. With a staff of more than sixty people in Washington, D.C., the organization can mobilize several dozen well-educated, articulate lobbyists to work the corridors of Congress on issues of concern to its members.

Although business interest groups are likely to agree on anything that reduces government regulation or taxation, they often do not agree on the specifics of policy, and the sector has been troubled by disagreement and fragmentation within its ranks. Business groups and trade associations used to lobby at cross-purposes because they had no way to coordinate their messages. Faced with increasing efforts by organized labor to support Democratic candidates for Congress, business interests agreed in 1996 to form "the Coalition," an informal organization that raises money specifically to help Republican candidates for Congress.[5]

Agricultural Interest Groups.   American farmers and their workers represent less than 2 percent of the U.S. population. In spite of this, farmers' influence on legislation beneficial to their interests has been enormous. Farmers have succeeded in their aims because they have very strong interest groups. They are geographically dispersed and therefore have many representatives and senators to speak for them. The American Farm Bureau Federation, established in 1919, has over 4.9 million members and is usually regarded as conservative. It was instrumental in getting government guarantees of "fair" prices during the Great Depression in the 1930s.[6] Another important agricultural special interest organization is the National Farmers' Union (NFU), which is considered more liberal. As farms have become larger and "agribusiness" has become a way of life, single-issue farm groups have emerged. The American Dairy Association, the Peanut Growers Group, and the National Soybean Association, for example, work to support their respective farmers and associated businesses. In recent years, agricultural interest groups have become active on many new issues. Among other things, they have opposed immigration restrictions and are very involved in international trade issues as they seek new markets. One of the newest agricultural groups is the American Farmland Trust, which supports policies to conserve farmland and protect natural resources.

---

[4] Charles S. Mack, *Business, Politics, and the Practice of Government Relations* (Westport, Conn.: Quorum Books, 1997), p. 14.

[5] H. R. Mahood, *Interest Groups in American National Politics: An Overview* (New York: Prentice Hall, 2000), p. 34.

[6] The Agricultural Adjustment Act of 1933 (declared unconstitutional) was replaced by the 1937 Agricultural Adjustment Act and later changed and amended several times.

As proof of how powerful the agricultural lobby still is in the United States, in May 2002 President George W. Bush signed the Farm Security and Rural Investment Act, the largest agricultural subsidy act in U.S. history.

Labor Interest Groups.   Interest groups representing the **labor movement** date back to at least 1886 when the American Federation of Labor (AFL) was formed. In 1955, the AFL joined forces with the Congress of Industrial Organizations (CIO). Today, the combined AFL-CIO is a large union with a membership exceeding 13 million workers and an active political arm called the Committee on Political Education. Other unions are also active politically. One of the most widely known is the International Brotherhood of Teamsters, which was led by Jimmy Hoffa until his expulsion in 1967 because of alleged ties with organized crime. The Teamsters Union was established initially in 1903 and today has a membership of 1.5 million. The Automobile, Aerospace, and Agricultural Implement Workers of America (formerly the United Automobile Workers), founded in 1935, now has a membership of 760,000. Also very active in labor lobbying is the United Mine Workers union, representing about 130,000 members.

The role of unions in American society has weakened in recent years, as witnessed by a decline in union membership (see Figure 8–1 on page 240). In the age of automation and with the rise of the **service sector**, blue-collar workers in basic industries (autos, steel, and the like) represent a smaller and smaller percentage of the total working population. Because of this decline in the industrial sector of the economy, national unions are looking to nontraditional areas for their membership, including migrant farm workers, service workers, and, most recently, public employees—such as police officers; firefighting personnel; and teachers, including college professors. Indeed, public-sector unions are the fastest-growing labor organizations.

Although the proportion of the work force that belongs to a union has declined over the years, American labor unions have not given up their efforts to support sympathetic

Labor Movement
Generally, the full range of economic and political expression of working-class interests; politically, the organization of working-class interests.

Service Sector
The sector of the economy that provides services—such as food services, insurance, and education—in contrast to the sector of the economy that produces goods.

Members of the Operating Engineers, Laborers, and Carpenters union protest the policies of a construction company, claiming that this particular company's actions are undermining union wages and benefits. Labor unions have wielded considerable political power since the twentieth century. Why has that power declined somewhat in recent years? (AP Photo/The Capital Times, David Sandell)

**Decline in Union Membership,
1948 to Present**

As shown in this figure, the percentage of the total work force that is represented by labor unions has declined precipitously over the last two decades. Note, however, that in contrast to the decline in union membership in the private sector, the percentage of government workers who are unionized has increased significantly.

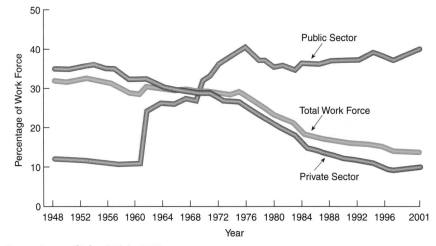

SOURCE: Bureau of Labor Statistics, 2002.

candidates for Congress or for state office. Currently, the AFL-CIO, under the leadership of John J. Sweeney, has a political budget that exceeds $30 million for each two-year political cycle, which it uses to help Democratic candidates nationwide. Although interest groups that favor Republicans continue to help their candidates, the efforts of labor are more sustained and more targeted. Labor offers a candidate (such as Democratic presidential candidate Al Gore in 2000) a corps of volunteers in addition to campaign contributions. A massive turnout by labor union members in critical elections can significantly increase the final vote totals for Democratic candidates.

Public Employee Interest Groups.   The degree of unionization in the private sector has declined since 1965, but this has been partially offset by growth in the unionization of public employees. Figure 8–1 shows the growth in the public-sector work force. With a total work force of more than 7.1 million, these unions are likely to continue expanding.

Both the American Federation of State, County, and Municipal Employees and the American Federation of Teachers are members of the AFL-CIO's Public Employee Department. Originally, the public employee unions started out as social and professional organizations. Over the years, they have become quite militant and are often involved in strikes. Many of these strikes are illegal, because certain public employees do not have the right to strike and essentially sign a contract so stating.

A powerful interest group lobbying on behalf of public employees is the National Education Association (NEA), a nationwide organization of about 2.5 million administrators, teachers, and others connected with education. The NEA lobbies intensively for increased public funding of education. The NEA sponsors regional and national conventions each year and has an extensive program of electronic media broadcasts, surveys, and the like.

Interest Groups of Professionals.   Numerous professional organizations exist, including the American Bar Association, the Association of General Contractors of America, the Institute of Electrical and Electronic Engineers, the Screen Actors Guild, and others. Some professional groups, such as lawyers and doctors, are more influential than others due to their social status. Lawyers have a unique advantage—a large number of members of Congress share their profession. In terms of money spent on lobbying, however, one professional organization stands head and shoulders above the rest—the American Medical Association (AMA). Founded in 1847, it is now affiliated with more than 2,000 local and state medical societies and has a total membership of 300,000. The AMA spent an estimated $3 million in 2000 presidential campaign contributions in its efforts to influence legislation.

Environmental Groups

Environmental interest groups are not new. We have already mentioned the National Audubon Society, which was founded in 1905 to protect the snowy egret from the commercial demand for hat decorations. The patron of the Sierra Club, John Muir, worked for the creation of national parks more than a century ago. But the blossoming of national environmental groups with mass memberships did not occur until the 1970s. Since the first Earth Day, organized in 1972, many interest groups have sprung up to protect the environment in general or unique ecological niches. The groups range from the National Wildlife Federation, with a membership of more than 4.5 million and an emphasis on education, to the fairly elite Environmental Defense Fund, with a membership of 300,000 and a focus on influencing federal policy. Other groups include the Nature Conservancy, which uses members' contributions to buy up threatened natural areas and either give them to state or local governments or manage them itself, and the more radical Greenpeace Society and Earth First.

Public-Interest Groups

Public interest is a difficult term to define because, as we noted earlier, there are many publics in our nation of over 286 million. It is almost impossible for one particular public policy to benefit everybody, which makes it practically impossible to define the public interest. Nonetheless, over the past few decades, a variety of lobbying organizations have been formed "in the public interest."

Public Interest
The best interests of the collective, overall community; the national good, rather than the narrow interests of a self-serving group.

The Coast Guard keeps a Greenpeace boat from getting too close to a tanker near the harbor of Long Beach, California. The environmentalist group was protesting the impact of oil on the world's climate. How effective are such tactics by environmentalist groups in influencing government policy? (AP Photo/Reed Saxon)

Ralph Nader began the movement to create public-interest groups through the publication, in 1965, of his book *Unsafe at Any Speed,* which criticized General Motors for underplaying the dangers of its Corvair automobile. Since that time, he has founded a number of not-for-profit public-interest groups that track business and governmental actions in specific policy arenas. In 2000, he was the presidential candidate for the Green Party. (AP Photo/J. Scott Applewhite)

Nader Organizations.   The best-known and perhaps the most effective public-interest groups are those organized under the leadership of consumer activist Ralph Nader. Nader's rise to the top began after the publication, in 1965, of his book *Unsafe at Any Speed,* a lambasting critique of the purported attempt by General Motors (GM) to keep from the public detrimental information about its rear-engine Corvair. Partly as a result of Nader's book, Congress began to consider testimony in favor of an automobile safety bill. GM made a clumsy attempt to discredit Nader's background. Nader sued, the media exploited the story, and when GM settled out of court for $425,000, Nader became the recognized champion of consumer interests. Since then, Nader has turned over much of his income to the more than sixty public-interest groups that he has formed or sponsored. In 2000, Nader ran for president on the ticket of the Green Party.

Other Public-Interest Groups.   Partly in response to the Nader organizations, numerous conservative public-interest law firms have sprung up that are often pitted against the consumer groups in court. Some of these are the Mountain States Legal Defense Foundation, the Pacific Legal Foundation, the National Right-to-Work Legal Defense Foundation, the Washington Legal Foundation, and the Mid-Atlantic Legal Foundation.

One of the largest public-interest groups is Common Cause, founded in 1968, whose goal is to reorder national priorities toward "the public" and to make governmental institutions more responsive to the needs of the public. Anyone willing to pay dues of $20 a year can become a member. Members are polled regularly to obtain information about local and national issues requiring reassessment. Some of the activities of Common Cause have been (1) helping to ensure the passage of the Twenty-sixth Amendment (giving eighteen-year-olds the right to vote), (2) achieving greater voter registration in all states, (3) supporting the complete withdrawal of all U.S. forces from South Vietnam in the 1970s, and (4) promoting legislation that would limit campaign spending.

Other public-interest groups are active on a wide range of issues. The goal of the League of Women Voters, founded in 1920, is to educate the public on political matters. Although generally nonpartisan, it has lobbied for the Equal Rights Amendment and for government reform. The Consumer Federation of America is an alliance of about two hundred local and national organizations interested in consumer protection. The American Civil Liberties Union dates back to World War I (1914–1918), when, under a different name, it defended draft resisters. It generally enters into legal disputes related to Bill of Rights issues.

Special Interest Groups

Special interest groups, being narrowly focused, may be able to call more attention to their respective causes because they have simple and straightforward goals and because their members tend to care intensely about the issues. Thus, such groups can easily motivate their members to contact legislators or to organize demonstrations in support of their policy goals.

A number of interest groups focus on just one issue. The abortion debate has created various groups opposed to abortion (such as Right to Life) and groups in favor of abortion (such as the National Abortion Rights Action League). Other single-issue groups are the National Rifle Association, the Right to Work Committee (an anti-union group), and the Hudson Valley PAC (a pro-Israel group).

Other groups represent particular groups of Americans who share a common characteristic, such as age or ethnicity. Such interest groups lobby for legislation that may benefit their members in terms of rights or just represent a viewpoint.

The AARP, as mentioned earlier, is one of the most powerful interest groups in Washington, D.C., and, according to some, the strongest lobbying group in the United States. It is certainly the nation's largest interest group, with a membership of over 35 million. The AARP has accomplished much for its members over the years. It played a significant role in the creation of Medicare and Medicaid, as well as in obtaining cost-of-living increases in Social Security payments. Today, though, the AARP is under attack. In part, this is because of the changed circumstances of today's older Americans. Whereas they were once among the poorer groups of our society, today they are, on average, among the country's wealthiest citizens. In other words, they no longer need special legislation to protect their welfare to the extent that they once did. Nonetheless, the AARP continues to pressure Congress for legislation that benefits this group of Americans.

Foreign Governments

Home-grown interests are not the only players in the game. Washington, D.C., is also the center for lobbying by foreign governments as well as private foreign interests. Large research and lobbying staffs are maintained by governments of the largest U.S. trading partners, such as Japan, South Korea, Canada, and the European Union (EU) countries. Even smaller nations, such as those in the Caribbean, engage lobbyists when vital legislation affecting their trade interests is considered. Frequently, these foreign interests hire former representatives or former senators to promote their positions on Capitol Hill.

The job of lobbyists never stops. These Washington lobbyists are scrutinizing news reports to ascertain the positions of members of Congress on policy issues that will have an impact on the interests that the lobbyists represent. While many critics of lobbyists and interest groups argue that they distort the actions of government, the First Amendment prohibits the government from regulating their speech. (Tom McCarthy/PhotoEdit)

What Makes an Interest Group Powerful?

At any time, thousands of interest groups are attempting to influence state legislatures, governors, Congress, and members of the executive branch of the U.S. government. What characteristics make some of those groups more powerful than others and more likely to have influence over government policy? Generally, interest groups attain a reputation for being powerful through their membership size, leadership, financial resources, and cohesiveness.

Size and Resources

No legislator can deny the power of an interest group that includes thousands of his or her own constituents among its members. Labor unions and organizations such as the AARP and the American Automobile Association are able to claim voters in every congressional district. Having a large membership—more than 13 million in the case of the AFL-CIO—carries a great deal of weight with government officials. The AARP now has more than 35 million members and a budget of $435 million for its operations. In addition, the AARP claims to represent all older Americans, close to 20 percent of the population, whether they join the organization or not.

Having a large number of members, even if the individual membership dues are relatively small, provides an organization with a strong financial base. Those funds pay for lobbyists, television advertisements, mailings to members, a Web site, and many other resources that help an interest group make its point to politicians. The business organization with the largest membership is probably the U.S. Chamber of Commerce, which has more than 200,000 members. The Chamber uses its members' dues to pay for staff and lobbyists, as well as a sophisticated communications network so that it can contact members in a timely way. All of the members can receive e-mail and check the Web site to get updates on the latest legislative proposals.

Other organizations may have few members but can nonetheless muster significant financial resources. The pharmaceutical lobby, which represents many of the major drug manufacturers, is one of the most powerful interest groups in Washington due to its financial resources. In 2001, this lobby had 625 registered lobbyists and reported spending more than $197 million in 1999–2000 for lobbying and campaign expenditures. The pharmaceutical companies hired fifteen major lobbying firms in 2001 and counted dozens of former members of Congress among their lobbyists.[7]

Leadership

Money is not the only resource that interest groups need to have. Strong leaders who can develop effective strategies are also important. For example, the election of John Sweeney as the president of the AFL-CIO in 1995 brought a new vision to the American labor movement. Under his leadership, the labor movement became a revitalized force in American politics. During the 2000 election campaigns, American labor leaders adopted another effective strategy when they attempted to attract immigrants as new members of their organizations.

Other interest groups, including some with few financial resources, succeed in part because they are led by individuals with charisma and access to power, such as Jesse Jackson of the Rainbow Coalition. Sometimes, choosing a leader with a particular image can be an effective strategy for an organization. The National Rifle Association had more than organizational skills in mind when it elected actor Charlton Heston as its president. The strategy of using an actor identified with powerful roles as the spokesperson for the organization worked to improve its national image.

Cohesiveness

Regardless of an interest group's size or the amount of money in its coffers, the motivation of an interest group's members is a key factor in determining how powerful it is. If the members of the group hold their beliefs strongly enough to send letters to their representatives, join a march on Washington, or work together to defeat a candidate, that organization is considered powerful. As described earlier, the American labor movement's success in electing Democratic candidates made the labor movement a more powerful lobby. In contrast, although groups that oppose abortion rights have had little success in influencing elections, they are considered powerful because their members are vocal and highly motivated. Other measures of cohesion include the ability of a group to get its members to contact Washington quickly or to give extra money when needed. The U.S. Chamber of Commerce excels at both of these strategies. In comparison, the AARP cannot claim that it can get its 35 million members to contact their congressional representatives, but it does seem to influence the opinions of older Americans and their views of political candidates.

Interest Group Strategies

Interest groups employ a wide range of techniques and strategies to promote their policy goals. Although few groups are successful at persuading Congress and the

---

[7] Leslie Wayne and Melody Petersen, "A Muscular Lobby Rolls Up Its Sleeves," *The New York Times,* November 4, 2001, Sect. 3, pp. 1, 13.

president to endorse their programs completely, many are able to block—or at least weaken—legislation injurious to their members. The key to success for interest groups is the ability to have access to government officials. To achieve this, interest groups and their representatives try to cultivate long-term relationships with legislators and government officials. The best of such relationships are based on mutual respect and cooperation. The interest group provides the official with excellent sources of information and assistance, and the official in turn gives the group opportunities to express its views.

The techniques used by interest groups may be divided into direct and indirect techniques. With **direct techniques,** the interest group and its lobbyists approach the officials personally to press their case. With **indirect techniques,** in contrast, the interest group uses the general public or individuals to influence the government on behalf of the interest group.

Direct Techniques

Lobbying, publicizing ratings of legislative behavior, building coalitions, and providing campaign assistance are the four main direct techniques used by interest groups.

Lobbying Techniques. As might be guessed, the term *lobbying* comes from the activities of private citizens regularly congregating in the lobbies of legislative chambers before a session to petition legislators. In the latter part of the nineteenth century, railroad and industrial groups openly bribed state legislators to pass legislation beneficial to their interests, giving lobbying a well-deserved bad name. Although private individuals still call on political officials to advance their own causes, most lobbyists today are professionals. They are either consultants to a company or interest group or members of a Washington, D.C., law firm that specializes in providing such services. Such firms employ hundreds of former members of Congress and former government officials, including former presidential candidates Bob Dole and Walter Mondale. Lobbyists are valued for their network of contacts in Washington. As Ed Rollins, a former White House aide, put it, "I've got many friends who are all through the agencies and equally important, I don't have many enemies. . . . I tell my clients I can get your case moved to the top of the pile."[8]

Lobbyists engage in an array of activities to influence legislation and government policy. These include, at a minimum, the following:

1. Engaging in private meetings with public officials, including the president's advisers, to make known the interests of the lobbyists' clients. Although acting on behalf of their clients, often lobbyists furnish needed information to senators and representatives (and government agency appointees) that they could not hope to obtain on their own. It is to the lobbyist's advantage to provide accurate information so that the policymaker will rely on this source in the future.
2. Testifying before congressional committees for or against proposed legislation being considered by Congress.
3. Testifying before executive rulemaking agencies—such as the Federal Trade Commission or the Consumer Product Safety Commission—for or against proposed rules.
4. Assisting legislators or bureaucrats in drafting legislation or prospective regulations. Often, lobbyists furnish legal advice on the specific details of legislation.

Direct Technique
An interest group activity that involves interaction with government officials to further the group's goals.

Indirect Technique
A strategy employed by interest groups that uses third parties to influence government officials.

---

[8] As quoted in Mahood, *Interest Groups in American National Politics,* p. 51.

5. Inviting legislators to social occasions, such as cocktail parties, boating expeditions, and other events, including conferences at exotic locations. Most lobbyists feel that contacting legislators in a more relaxed social setting is effective.

6. Providing political information to legislators and other government officials. Often, the lobbyists will have better information than the party leadership about how other legislators are going to vote. In this case, the political information they furnish may be a key to legislative success.

7. Supplying nominations for federal appointments to the executive branch.

The Ratings Game.   Many interest groups attempt to influence the overall behavior of legislators through their rating systems. Each year, the interest group selects legislation that it feels is most important to the organization's goals and then monitors how legislators vote on it. Each legislator is given a score based on the percentage of times that he or she voted in favor of the group's position. The usual scheme ranges from 0 to 100 percent. In the ratings scheme of the Americans for Democratic Action, for example, a rating of 100 means that a member of Congress voted with the group on every issue and is, therefore, very liberal. Ratings are a shorthand way of describing members' voting records for interested citizens. They can also be used to embarrass members. For example, an environmental group identifies the twelve representatives with the worst voting records on environmental issues and labels them "the Dirty Dozen," and a watchdog group describes those representatives who took home the most "pork" for their districts or states as the biggest "Pigs."

Building Alliances.   Another direct technique used by interest groups is to form a coalition with other groups concerned about the same legislation. Often, these groups will set up a paper organization with an innocuous name to represent their joint concerns. In one case, for example, environmental, labor, and consumer groups formed an alliance called the Citizens Trade Campaign to oppose the passage of the North American Free Trade Agreement in 1993. Members of such a coalition share expenses and multiply the influence of their individual groups by combining their efforts. Other advantages of forming a coalition are that it looks as if larger public interests are at stake, and it blurs the specific interests of the individual groups involved. These alliances also are efficient devices for keeping like-minded groups from duplicating one another's lobbying efforts.

Campaign Assistance.   Interest groups have additional strategies to use in their attempts to influence government policies. Groups recognize that the greatest concern of legislators is to be reelected, so they focus on the legislators' campaign needs. Associations with large memberships, such as labor unions or the National Education Association, are able to provide workers for political campaigns, including precinct workers to get out the vote, volunteers to put up posters and pass out literature, and people to staff telephone banks for campaign headquarters.

In many states where certain interest groups have large memberships, candidates vie for the groups' endorsements in the campaign. Gaining those endorsements may be automatic, or it may require that the candidates participate in debates or interviews with the interest groups. Endorsements are important because an interest group usually publicizes its choices in its membership publication and because the candidate can use the endorsement in her or his campaign literature. Traditionally, labor unions such as the AFL-CIO and the Teamsters have endorsed Democratic Party candidates. Republican candidates, however, often try to persuade union locals at least to refrain from any endorsement. Making no endorsement can then be perceived as disapproval of the Democratic Party candidate.

INFOTRAC ®
COLLEGE EDITION

To find out more about this subject, use the term "campaign finance" in Keywords.

ELECTIONS 2002 Interest Groups:
The Candidates of Choice

With control of the Congress clearly in play, interest groups redoubled their efforts in 2002 to elect candidates who would favor their respective positions. Labor unions and environmental groups provided resources and manpower to support Democratic candidates, while business organizations and corporations provided soft money to the Republicans. Some businesses even stuffed the payroll envelopes of their workers with election information and encouraged absentee voting to get their employees to participate. President George W. Bush proved to be a formidable fundraiser, attending events across the country to raise more money for his party. The election results suggested that Democratic campaigners did not devote enough resources to get-out-the-vote efforts, while the Republicans received substantial help from interest groups that believed a Republican controlled Congress would help their sectors of the economy.

Indirect Techniques

Interest groups can also try to influence government policy by working through third parties—who may be constituents or the general public. Indirect techniques mask the interest group's own activities and make the effort appear to be spontaneous. Furthermore, legislators and government officials are often more impressed by contacts from constituents than from an interest group's lobbyist.

Generating Public Pressure. In some instances, interest groups try to produce a "ground swell" of public pressure to influence the government. Such efforts may include advertisements in national magazines and newspapers, mass mailings, television publicity, and demonstrations. The Internet and satellite links make communication efforts even more effective. Interest groups may commission polls to find out what the public's sentiments are and then publicize the results. The intent of this activity is to convince policymakers that public opinion overwhelmingly supports the group's position.

Some corporations and interest groups also engage in a practice that might be called **climate control.** With this strategy, public relations efforts are aimed at improving the public image of the industry or group and are not necessarily related to any specific political issue. Contributions by corporations and groups in support of public television programs, sponsorship of special events, and commercials extolling the virtues of corporate research are some ways of achieving climate control. For example, to improve its image in the wake of litigation against tobacco companies, Philip Morris began advertising its assistance to community agencies, including halfway houses for teen offenders and shelters for battered women. By building a reservoir of favorable public opinion, groups believe that their legislative goals will be less likely to encounter opposition by the public.

Using Constituents as Lobbyists. One of the most effective interest group activities is the use of constituents to lobby for the group's goals. In the "shotgun" approach, the interest group tries to mobilize large numbers of constituents to write, phone, or send e-mails to their legislators or the president. Often, the group provides postcards or form letters for constituents to fill out and mail. These efforts

Climate Control
The use of public relations techniques to create favorable public opinion toward an interest group, industry, or corporation.

are effective on Capitol Hill only when there is an extraordinary number of responses, however, because legislators know that the voters did not initiate the communications on their own.

A more influential variation of this technique uses only important constituents. Known as the "rifle" technique, or the "Utah plant manager's theory," the interest group contacts an influential constituent, such as the manager of a local plant in Utah, to contact the senator from Utah.[9] Because the constituent is seen as being responsible for many jobs or other resources, the legislator is more likely to listen carefully to the constituent's concerns about legislation than to a paid lobbyist.

Interest Groups and Campaign Money

In the last two decades, interest groups and individual companies have found new, very direct ways to contact elected officials through campaign donations. Elected officials, in turn, have become dependent on these donations to run increasingly expensive campaigns. Interest groups and corporations funnel money to political candidates through several devices: **political action committees (PACs)**, **soft money** contributions, and **issue advocacy advertising**. These devices developed as a means of circumventing the campaign-financing reforms of the early 1970s, which limited contributions by individuals and unions to set amounts.

PACs and Political Campaigns

The 1974 and 1976 amendments to the Federal Election Campaign Act of 1971 allow corporations, labor unions, and other interest groups to set up PACs to raise money for candidates, as will be discussed in Chapter 10. For a PAC to be legitimate, the money must be raised from at least fifty volunteer donors and must be given to at least five candidates in the federal election. PACs can contribute up to $5,000 to each candidate in each election. Each corporation or each union is limited to one PAC. As you might imagine, corporate PACs obtain funds from executives in their firms, and unions obtain PAC funds from their members.

The number of PACs has grown significantly since 1977, as has the amount they spend on elections. There were about 1,000 PACs in 1976; today, there are more than 4,500 (see Figure 8–2). Total spending by PACs grew from $19 million in 1973 to almost $900 million in 1999–2000. About 32 percent of all campaign money spent by House candidates in 2000 came from PACs.[10]

Interest groups funnel PAC money to the candidates they think can do the most good for them. Frequently, they make the maximum contribution of $5,000 per election to candidates who face little or no opposition. The summary of PAC contributions given in Figure 8–3 shows that the great bulk of campaign contributions goes to incumbent candidates rather than to challengers. Table 8–2 on page 250 shows the amounts contributed by the top twenty PACs.

As Table 8–2 also shows, some PACs give most of their contributions to candidates of one party. Other PACs, particularly corporate PACs, tend to give money to Democrats in Congress as well as to Republicans, because, with both houses of Congress so closely divided, predicting which party will be in control after an election is almost impossible. Why, you might ask, would business leaders give to Democrats who may be more liberal than themselves? Interest groups see PAC contributions as a

Political Action Committee (PAC)
A committee set up by and representing a corporation, labor union, or special interest group. PACs raise and give campaign donations on behalf of the organizations or groups they represent.

Soft Money
Campaign contributions that evade contribution limits by being given to parties and party committees to help fund general party activities.

Issue Advocacy Advertising
Advertising paid for by interest groups that supports or opposes a candidate or candidate's position on an issue without mentioning voting or elections.

INFOTRAC ®
COLLEGE EDITION

For updates and more information on PACs, use the term "political action committees" in the Subject guide.

---

[9] Kay Lehman Schlozman and John T. Tierney, *Organized Interests and American Democracy* (New York: Harper & Row, 1986), p. 293.
[10] Federal Election Commission, 2002.

FIGURE 8–2

PAC Growth, 1977 to 2000

This figure shows the significant increase in PACs since 1977 as well as the large number of corporate PACs relative to PACs that are sponsored by other types of organizations.

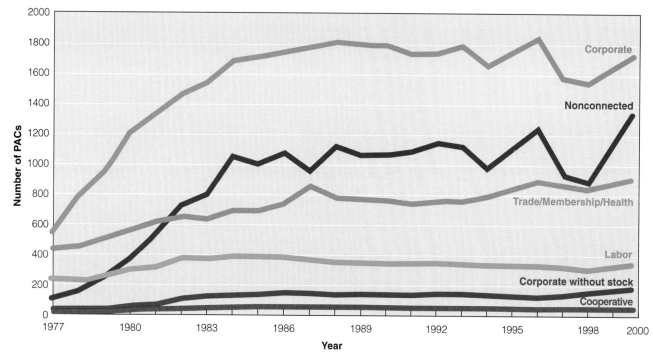

SOURCE: Federal Election Commission, 2002.

FIGURE 8–3

PAC Contributions to Congressional Candidates, 1986 to 2000

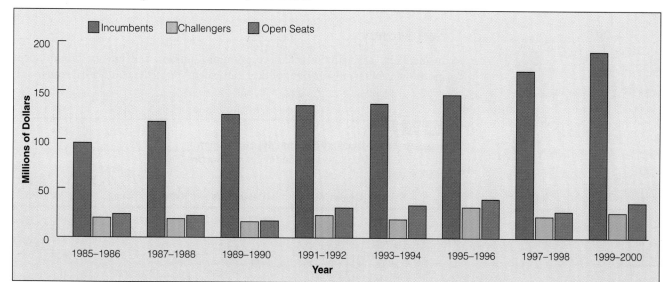

SOURCE: Federal Election Commission, 2002.

TABLE 8–2

The Top Twenty Contributors to Federal Candidates, 2001–2002 Election Cycle*

RANK	PAC NAME	TOTAL	DEM. %	REP. %
1	National Association of Realtors	$3,269,426	48%	52%
2	Laborers Union	$2,537,000	88	12
3	Machinists/Aerospace Workers Union	$2,249,850	99	1
4	Association of Trial Lawyers of America	$2,235,753	87	12
5	National Automobile Dealers Association	$2,221,250	35	65
6	American Medical Association	$2,104,319	43	57
7	Teamsters Union	$1,967,971	84	16
8	American Federation of State, County and Municipal Employees	$1,899,000	96	3
9	International Brotherhood of Electrical Workers	$1,878,800	95	4
10	Carpenters and Joiners Union	$1,789,000	73	27
11	Credit Union National Association	$1,699,773	45	55
12	United Food and Commercial Workers Union	$1,603,044	99	1
13	United Auto Workers	$1,578,250	98	1
14	National Association of Home Builders	$1,534,100	39	61
15	Service Employees International Union	$1,485,309	89	9
16	National Beer Wholesalers Association	$1,435,750	24	76
17	SBC Communications	$1,398,749	40	60
18	American Federation of Teachers	$1,364,315	99	1
19	Ironworkers Union	$1,363,500	88	12
20	AFL-CIO	$1,329,074	94	6

*Includes subsidiaries and affiliated PACs, if any.

SOURCE: Center for Responsive Politics, 2002.

way to ensure *access* to powerful legislators, even though the groups may disagree with the legislators some of the time. PAC contributions are, in a way, an investment in a relationship. As Table 8–3 shows, business contributions go to Democrats as well as to Republicans; in contrast, labor contributions focus overwhelmingly on Democrats.

The campaign-financing regulations clearly limit the amount that a PAC can give to any one candidate, but there is no limit on the amount that a PAC can spend on issue advocacy, either on behalf of a candidate or party or in opposition to one.

Soft Money

In the 1999–2000 election cycle, corporations, unions, and interest groups spent more than $493 million on political campaigns for federal offices through soft

TABLE 8–3

Business-Labor-Ideology Split in PAC, Soft Money, and Individual Donations to Candidates and Parties, 2000

	GRAND TOTAL	DEMOCRATS	REPUBLICANS	DEM. %	REP. %
Business	$1,233,136,672	$517,463,696	$705,847,951	42%	57%
Labor	$90,105,425	$84,833,306	$5,093,944	94	6
Ideological	$75,920,267	$38,476,928	$36,968,464	51	49
Other	$144,991,377	$55,765,191	$86,418,924	38	60
Unknown	$92,861,587	$28,296,243	$62,338,029	30	67

SOURCE: Center for Responsive Politics, 2002.

Drawing by Joseph Farris © 1994 The New Yorker Magazine, Inc.

"A <u>very</u> special interest to see you, Senator."

money, a practice that was outlawed by the campaign-financing reform legislation of 2002. As you will learn in Chapter 10, soft money contributions have included all contributions to campaign funds that are unregulated by federal or state law. In general, such contributions were made to national party committees for certain "party-building" purposes, including voter-registration drives, the national convention, and general overhead. Soft money contributions are permitted at the state level in thirty states but are prohibited in the rest.[11]

The question for the voter is: What has soft money bought? Corporations and interest groups have supplied soft money contributions for several reasons. First, they wished to see candidates elected who would be friendly to their own interests. In addition, they hoped to gain access to the candidate after his or her election. Who could refuse an appointment to a $100,000 donor? Because most industries and trade associations have given soft money to both parties, however, it is not clear that the winners have been as grateful as might have been expected.

Issue Advocacy Advertising

Corporations and interest groups also use television, radio, the Internet, and billboards to advertise their positions on issues and to persuade the public to share their views. For example, in the weeks following the September 11 attacks, Congress considered a provision giving the president special "fast track" authority to make trade deals with other nations. Defeated in Congress during the Clinton administration, the legislation passed the House of Representatives in 2001. Interest groups aired television ads in certain areas

---

[11] Charles S. Mack, *Business, Politics, and the Practice of Government Relations* (Westport, Conn.: Quorum Books, 1997), p. 226.

urging viewers to contact their members of Congress to vote either for or against this legislation. Because of the continuing coverage of the war on terrorism, however, many viewers probably did not even understand the message about trade, and few acted on it. (The "fast track" bill was not signed into law until August 2002.)

What is new in the last ten years is the proliferation of issue advocacy ads during political campaigns. During campaigns, interest groups and trade associations create, pay for, and then air hundreds of advertisements. These ads call attention to the positions or voting patterns of a candidate but do not tell the voter to "vote for" or "vote against" that person. Thus, the advertising is protected as "free speech" under the First Amendment rather than regulated as campaign advertising. Such advertising is often criticized for being deceptive either in its message or in not revealing its true sponsorship. The 2002 campaign-financing reform law includes a provision that prohibits issue advocacy groups from airing commercials supporting or opposing candidates sixty days before the general election and thirty days before a primary election (the 2002 law will be discussed in more detail in Chapter 10).

Regulating Lobbyists

Congress made its first attempt to control lobbyists and lobbying activities through Title III of the Legislative Reorganization Act of 1946, otherwise known as the Federal Regulation of Lobbying Act. The act actually provided for public disclosure more than for regulation, and it neglected to specify which agency would enforce its provisions. The 1946 legislation defined a lobbyist as any person or organization that received money to be used principally to influence legislation before Congress. Such persons and individuals were supposed to "register" their clients and the purposes of their efforts, and report quarterly on their activities.

The legislation was tested in a 1954 Supreme Court case, *United States v. Harriss,*[12] and was found to be constitutional. The Court agreed that the lobbying law did not violate due process, freedom of speech or of the press, or the freedom to petition. The Court narrowly construed the act, however, holding that it applied only to lobbyists who were influencing federal legislation *directly.*

The Results of the 1946 Act

The result of the act was that a minimal number of individuals registered as lobbyists. National interest groups, such as the National Rifle Association and the American Petroleum Institute, could employ hundreds of staff members who were, of course, working on legislation but only register one or two lobbyists who were engaged *principally* in influencing Congress. There were no reporting requirements for lobbying the executive branch, federal agencies, the courts, or congressional staff. Approximately seven thousand individuals and organizations registered annually as lobbyists, although most experts estimated that ten times that number were actually employed in Washington to exert influence on the government.

The Reforms of 1995

The reform-minded Congress of 1995–1996 overhauled the lobbying legislation, fundamentally changing the ground rules for those who seek to influence the federal government. Lobbying legislation, passed in 1995, included the following provisions:

1. A lobbyist is defined as anyone who spends at least 20 percent of his or her time lobbying members of Congress, their staffs, or executive-branch officials.

---

[12] 347 U.S. 612 (1954).

2. Lobbyists must register with the clerk of the House and the secretary of the Senate within forty-five days of being hired or of making their first contact. The registration requirement applies to organizations that spend more than $20,000 in one year or to individuals who are paid more than $5,000 annually for their work.

3. Semiannual reports must disclose the general nature of the lobbying effort, specific issues and bill numbers, the estimated cost of the campaign, and a list of the branches of government contacted. The names of the individuals contacted need not be reported.

4. Representatives of U.S.-owned subsidiaries of foreign-owned firms and lawyers who represent foreign entities also are required to register for the first time.

5. The requirements exempt "grassroots" lobbying efforts and those of tax-exempt organizations, such as religious groups.

DID YOU KNOW . . .
That lobbyists have their own lobbying organization, the American League of Lobbyists ?

Concurrently with the debate on the 1995 law, both the House and the Senate adopted new rules on gifts and travel expenses: the House adopted a flat ban on gifts, and the Senate limited gifts to $50 in value and to no more than $100 in gifts from a single source in a year. There are exceptions for gifts from family members and for home-state products and souvenirs, such as T-shirts and coffee mugs. Both chambers ban all-expenses-paid trips, golf outings, and other such junkets. An exception applies for "widely attended" events, however, or if the member is a primary speaker at an event. These gift rules stopped the broad practice of taking members of Congress to lunch or dinner, but the various exemptions and exceptions have caused much controversy as the Senate and House Ethics Committees have considered individual cases.

Interest Groups and Representative Democracy

The significant role played by interest groups in shaping national policy has caused many to question whether we really have a democracy at all. To be sure, most interest groups have a middle-class or upper-class bias. Members of interest groups can afford to pay the membership fees, are generally fairly well educated, and normally participate in the political process to a greater extent than the "average" American. Furthermore, leaders of interest groups tend to constitute an "elite within an elite" in the sense that they usually are from a higher social class than their members. The most powerful interest groups—those with the most resources and political influence—are primarily business, trade, or professional groups. In contrast, public-interest groups or civil rights groups make up only a small percentage of the interest groups lobbying Congress.

Interest Groups: Elitist or Pluralist?

Remember from Chapter 1 that the elite theory of politics presumes that most Americans are uninterested in politics and are willing to let a small, elite group of citizens make decisions for them. Pluralist theory, in contrast, views politics as a struggle among various interest groups to gain benefits for their members. The pluralist approach views compromise among various competing interests as the essence of political decision making. In reality, neither theory describes American politics very accurately. If interest groups led by elite, upper-class individuals are the dominant voices in Congress, then what we see is a conflict among elite groups—which would support the elitist theory, not a pluralist approach.

Interest-Group Influence

The results of lobbying efforts—congressional legislation—do not always favor the interests of the most powerful groups, however. In part, this is because not all interest groups have an equal influence on government. Each group has a different combination

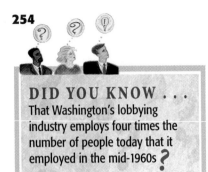

of resources to use in the policymaking process. While some groups are composed of members who have high social status and enormous economic resources, such as the National Association of Manufacturers, other groups derive influence from their large memberships. The AARP, for example, has more members than any other interest group. Its large membership allows it to wield significant power over legislators. Still other groups, such as environmentalists, have causes that can claim strong public support even from people who have no direct stake in the issue. Groups such as the National Rifle Association are well organized and have highly motivated members. This enables them to channel a stream of mail or electronic messages toward Congress with a few days' effort.

Even the most powerful interest groups do not always succeed in their demands. Whereas the U.S. Chamber of Commerce may be accepted as having a justified interest in the question of business taxes, many legislators might feel that the group should not engage in the debate over the future of Social Security. In other words, groups are seen as having a legitimate concern in the issues closest to their interests but not necessarily in broader issues. This may explain why some of the most successful groups are those that focus on very specific issues—such as tobacco farming, funding of abortions, or handgun control—and do not get involved in larger conflicts.

Complicating the question of interest group influence is the fact that many groups' lobbyists are former colleagues, friends, or family members of current members of Congress. Do these lobbyists wield more influence over congressional policymaking than the wishes of constituents?

Interest Groups: Why Are They Important Today?

The role of interest groups in American politics has been in question since the writing of the Constitution. James Madison, among many others, worried about how to control the "mischiefs of faction" while recognizing that the very business of a democracy is to resolve the conflicts between interests. Today, the power of interest groups is probably greater than ever before. PACs sponsored by interest groups are able to raise and spend huge amounts of money to support candidates and parties. Politicians admit that such support buys access, if not influence. Groups use modern technology, and increasingly the Internet, to rally their members. And Congress seems unable to get beyond the adjudication of interests to write policy for the good of all.

In the future, Americans will consider whether to limit the role that interest groups can play in campaigns and elections either by reducing the financial support these groups can give or by eliminating that influence altogether through some public financing scheme. Then, all taxpayers would support campaigns rather than special groups. It is unlikely that there will be any attempt to limit severely the contact that groups have with political decision makers because their right to access is protected by the First Amendment to the Constitution. Lobbyists could, however, be required to report publicly every contact; interest groups could be required to make public the amount that they spend on attempts to influence government; or the government could regulate the use of the media by specialized groups for their own interest.

The existence of interest groups, nonetheless, has great advantages for a democracy. By participating in such groups, individual citizens are empowered to influence government in ways far beyond the ballot. Groups do increase the interest and participation of voters in the system. And, without a doubt, these groups can protect the rights of minorities through their access to all branches of the government. Thus, the future could see a continued expansion of interest groups. No doubt, numerous groups, particularly among segments of society that have been left out of the debate, will take advantage of the Internet to promote their interests at lower cost. In any event, it is unlikely that these political associations will disappear soon.

MAKING A DIFFERENCE | The Gun Control Issue

Is the easy availability of handguns a major cause of crime? Do people have a right to possess firearms to defend home and hearth? These questions are part of a long-term and heated battle between organized profirearm and antifirearm camps. The disagreements run deeply and reflect strong sentiments on both sides. The fight is fueled by the one million gun incidents occurring in the United States each year—the murders, suicides, assaults, accidents, robberies, and injuries in which guns are involved. In 1999, the Columbine High School shootings in Colorado brought the debate to a fever pitch.

Issues in the Debate

Issues in the debate include child-safety features on guns and the regulation of gun dealers who sell firearms at gun shows. Proponents of gun control seek safety locks and more restrictions on gun purchases—if not a ban on them entirely—while decreasing existing arsenals of privately owned weapons. Proponents of firearms claim that firearms are a cherished tradition, a constitutional right, and a vital defense need for individuals. They contend that the problem lies not in the sale and ownership of the weapons themselves but in the criminal use of firearms.

The National Coalition to Ban Handguns favors a total ban, taking the position that handguns "serve no valid purpose, except to kill people." Such a ban is opposed by the National Rifle Association of America (NRA). The NRA, founded in 1871, is currently one of the most powerful single-issue groups on the American political scene, representing the seventy million gun owners in the United States. The NRA claims, among other things, that a gun law won't reduce the number of crimes. It is illogical to assume, according to the NRA, that persons who refuse to obey laws prohibiting rape, murder, and other crimes will obey a gun law.

Guns and Younger Americans

A matter of particular concern to many Americans is the increase in crimes involving guns among younger Americans. Many proponents of gun control insist that controlling the purchase of weapons would reduce the availability of guns to children. In response to these efforts, some states have passed laws that hold adults liable for not locking away their firearms. In addition, a number of cities have sued gun manufacturers for not controlling the flow of their products to unscrupulous dealers who sell guns to criminals and gang members in inner-city areas.

Tougher gun control laws are on the legislative agenda in Congress and in most states. To find out more about the NRA's position, contact that organization at the following address:

The National Rifle Association
11250 Waples Mill Rd.
Fairfax, VA 22030
703-267-1000
http://www.nra.org

If, however, you are concerned with the increase in gun-related crimes and feel that stricter gun laws are necessary, you can get involved through the following organizations:

The Coalition to Stop Gun Violence
1023 15th St. N.W., Suite 600
Washington, DC 20036
202-408-0061
http://www.gunfree.org

Brady Center to
Prevent Gun Violence
1225 Eye St. N.W., Suite 1100
Washington, DC 20005
202-289-7319
http://www.handguncontrol.org

Key Terms

climate control 247	issue advocacy advertising 248	political action committee (PAC) 248	social movement 233
direct technique 245	labor movement 239		soft money 248
free rider problem 234	latent interests 234	public interest 241	solidary incentive 234
indirect technique 245	lobbyist 231	purposive incentive 235	
interest group 231	material incentive 235	service sector 239	

Chapter Summary

1 An interest group is an organization whose members share common objectives and who actively attempt to influence government policy. Interest groups proliferate in the United States because they can influence government at many points in the political structure and because they offer solidary, material, and purposive incentives to their members. Interest groups are often created out of social movements.

2 Major types of interest groups include business, agricultural, labor, public employee, professional, and environmental groups. Other important groups may be considered public-interest groups. In addition, special interest groups and foreign governments lobby the government.

3 Interest groups use direct and indirect techniques to influence government. Direct techniques include testifying before committees and rulemaking agencies, providing information to legislators, rating legislators' voting records, aiding in political campaigns, and building alliances. Indirect techniques to influence government include campaigns to rally public sentiment, letter-writing campaigns, efforts to influence the climate of opinion, and the use of constituents to lobby for the group's interest.

4 Interest groups and corporations use several types of campaign donations to gain access to elected officials and support the election of their preferred candidates. These devices include PAC contributions, soft money, and funding for issue advocacy advertising.

5 The 1946 Legislative Reorganization Act was the first attempt to control lobbyists and their activities through registration requirements. The Supreme Court narrowly construed the act as applying only to lobbyists who directly seek to influence federal legislation.

6 In 1995, Congress approved new legislation requiring anyone who spends 20 percent of his or her time influencing legislation to register. Also, any organization spending $20,000 or more and any individual who is paid more than $5,000 annually for his or her work must register. Semiannual reports must include the name of clients, the bills in which they are interested, and the branches of government contacted. Grassroots lobbying and the lobbying efforts of tax-exempt organizations are exempt from the rules.

Selected Print and Media Resources

SUGGESTED READINGS

Ainsworth, Scott H. *Analyzing Interest Groups: Group Influence on People and Policies.* New York: W. W. Norton, 2002. The author provides an insightful analysis of the role of interest groups in American government and specific examples of how interest groups influence both the public and the policymaking process.

Biersack, Robert, Clyde Wilcox, and Paul Herrnson, eds. *After the Revolution: PACs, Lobbies, and the Republican Congress.* Reading, Mass.: Addison-Wesley, 1999. This collection of essays examines the lobbying tactics of a number of quite different interest groups.

Goldstein, Kenneth M. *Interest Groups, Lobbying, and Participation in America.* Port Chester, N.Y.: Cambridge University Press, 1999. What motivates individuals to participate in interest groups? This volume looks at how leaders of interest groups recruit new members.

Kollman, Ken. *Outside Lobbying: Public Opinion and Interest Group Strategies.* Princeton, N.J.: Princeton University Press, 1998. This volume focuses on how groups rally public support for their positions.

Mack, Charles S. *Business, Politics, and the Practice of Government Relations.* Westport, Conn: Quorum Books, 1997. The author provides an in-depth examination of how businesses practice "government relations," including how corporations plan strategies to get government policies changed and how they lobby public officials.

Mollenkamp, Carrick, Adam Levy, Joseph Menn, and Jeffrey Rothfeder. *The People vs. Big Tobacco: How the States Took on the Cigarette Giants.* New York: Bloomberg Press, 1998. This book is a careful account of the conflicts and legal battles that led to the tobacco settlement.

Rozell, Mark J., and Clyde Wilcox. *Interest Groups in American Campaigns: The New Face of Electioneering.* Washington, D.C.: CQ Press, 1999. This collection of essays provides valuable insights into the close relationships among interest groups, PACs, and political parties during the campaign season.

Schier, Steven E. *By Invitation Only: The Rise of Exclusive Politics in the United States.* Pittsburgh, Pa.: University of Pittsburgh Press, 2000. According to this author, participation in American politics has declined from the high rate of the 1960s to a much lower rate today because politicians and interest groups now target only certain groups to be extremely active in influencing government and getting out their own votes for a specific cause.

Wilson, James Q. *Political Organizations* (with a new introduction to the 1974 edition). Princeton, N.J.: Princeton University Press, 1995. This is one of the classic works on the formation and membership of interest groups in American society. Wilson looks closely at the motivations of a group's members and the relationship of the members to the leaders of a group.

MEDIA RESOURCES

Norma Rae—A 1979 film about an attempt by a northern union organizer to unionize workers in the southern textile industry; stars Sally Field.

Silkwood—A 1979 film focusing on the story of a nuclear plant worker who attempted to investigate safety issues at the plant and ended up losing her job; stars Meryl Streep and Cher.

The West Wing—A popular television series that is widely regarded as being an accurate portrayal of the issues and political pressures faced by a president and his White House staff.

Your CD-ROM Resources

In addition to the chapter content containing hot links, the following resources are available on the CD-ROM:

- **Internet Activities**—Ralph Nader, AARP.

- **Self-Check on Important Themes**—Can You Answer These?

- **Animated Figures**—Figure 8–1, "Decline in Union Membership, 1948 to Present," Figure 8–2, "PAC Growth, 1977 to 2000."

- **Videos**—*The Gun Lobby, Negotiated Rule Making.*

- **Public Opinion Data**—Find contrasting opinions on federal screening in airports, recording lobbyist contacts with legislators, and banning handguns.

- **InfoTrac Exercise**—"The Secrets to Washington's Power Game."

- **Simulation**—You Are There!

- **Participation Exercise**—Form an interest group.

- **MicroCase Exercise**—"By the Numbers: Interest Groups."

- **Additional Resources**—All court cases, James H. Hammond, *Cotton Is King* (1858), United States Congress Lobby Acts of 1994, Regulation of Lobbying Act of 1964.

e-mocracy
Interests and the Internet

The Internet may have a strong equalizing effect in the world of lobbying and government influence. The first organizations to use electronic means to reach their constituents and drum up support for action were the large economic coalitions, including the Chamber of Commerce and the National Association of Manufacturers. Groups such as these, as well as those representing a single product such as tobacco, quickly realized that they could set up Web sites and mailing lists to provide information more rapidly to their members. Members could check the Web every day to see how legislation was developing in Congress or anywhere in the world. National associations could send e-mail to all of their members with one keystroke, mobilizing them to contact their representatives in Congress.

Logging On

Almost every interest group or association has its own Web site. To find one, use your favorite search engine (Lycos, Google, or another search engine) and search for the association by name. For a sense of the breadth of the kinds of interest groups that have Web sites, take a look at one or two of those listed here.

Gun control opponents may want to visit the National Rifle Association's site at

http://www.nra.org

If you are interested in human rights worldwide, you can go to the site of Human Rights Watch at

http://www.hrw.org

Information concerning environmental issues is available at a number of sites. The Environmental Defense Fund's site is

http://www.edf.org

You can also go to the National Resource Defense Council's site for information on environmental issues. Its URL is

http://www.nrdc.org

Using the Internet for Political Analysis

A great deal of information about how much money interest groups contribute to candidates for office is available to voters and the general public. Go to the Web site for the Center for Responsive Politics at http://www.opensecrets.org and look up the contributions to candidates from several states. How do the interest groups and PACs differ in their support of candidates? Do some candidates receive contributions from a wide range of groups and PACs? What does that mean? If you are interested in the overall record of contributions in current and past campaigns, continue your research at the Web site of the Federal Elections Commission at http://www.fec.gov.

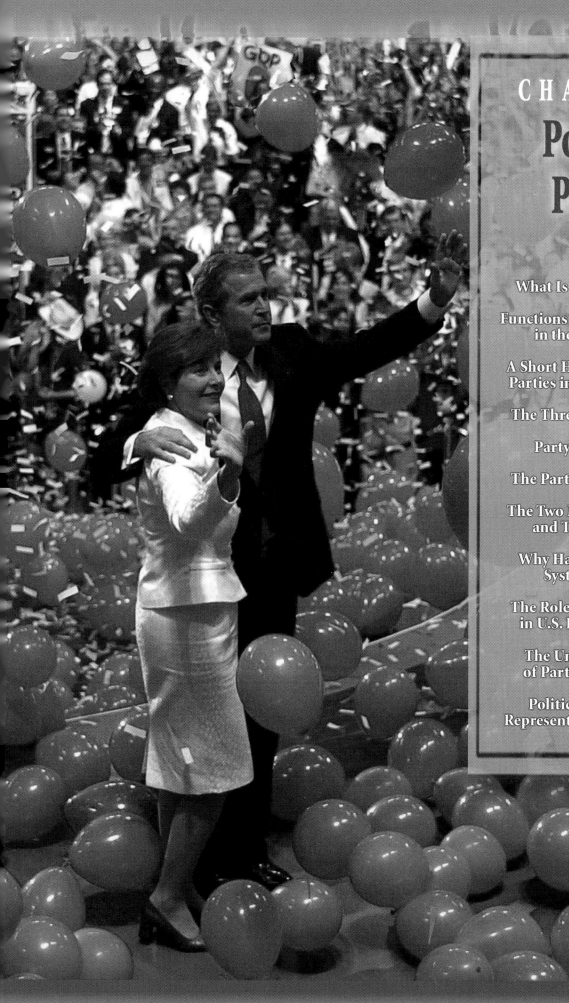

Political Parties

BACKGROUND

No provision in the Constitution requires that the party of the president also control Congress. When the two parties share the legislative and executive branches, this is divided government. Divided government has existed in the United States for much of its history, particularly since 1945. Only ten of the twenty-seven elections from 1945 through 2000 resulted in the same party being in control of the executive branch and both chambers of Congress.

Some argue that divided government in America creates gridlock—a situation in which party differences make government action difficult. If elections are to produce an effective government, then some argue that we should change our government so that an election can no longer result in the executive and legislative branches being divided between the parties.

WHAT IF THE LEGISLATIVE AND EXECUTIVE BRANCHES WERE ALWAYS CONTROLLED BY THE SAME PARTY?

The best way to discover what might happen in America if we required that the legislative and executive branches be controlled by the same party is to look at the British parliamentary system. In Britain, whichever party wins the most seats in the House of Commons (the equivalent of our House of Representatives) gets to elect the head of the government—the prime minister—who then chooses a cabinet to run the government. Thus, the British system is a form of majoritarian government.

THE MAKE-UP OF GOVERNMENT IN A PARLIAMENTARY SYSTEM

When people talk about the "national government" in America, it can be hard to know whether they mean the executive branch, Congress, or both. In the typical parliamentary system, however, references to the "national government" always mean the prime minister and her or his handpicked cabinet members. These cabinet members are usually long-time, experienced members of the parliament who are strong minded, independent, and committed to politics. A cabinet member who is dismissed by the prime minister can return to the parliament.

In the United States, the administration has a cabinet, and the secretaries are all beholden to the president. They are not part of the legislative body, however. Indeed, the separation of powers mandated by the Constitution means that a member of one branch of government cannot simultaneously be a member of another branch. Once out of the cabinet, U.S. cabinet members can return to politics, but most do not.

Compared with the cabinet members in a parliamentary system, U.S. cabinet members are usually less independent and less experienced in government. Even the president may be inexperienced in politics at the federal level. Such a situation is unlikely to occur in a parliamentary system. After all, the prime minister is a seasoned government official who has worked her or his way up through the party leadership in the parliament.

THE PEOPLE IN POWER COULD BE VOTED OUT BEFORE THE NEXT ELECTIONS

If the United States were to adopt a parliamentary system, it might opt for a "no-confidence" vote system. In such parliamentary systems, the parliament itself, not the people, can oust the prime minister by a no-confidence vote at any time, without having to wait for the next election cycle. As a result, the prime minister and his or her cabinet are held more immediately accountable for their actions, in notable contrast to the U.S. president. Only impeachment, death, or an incapacitating illness will prevent a president from continuing in office until the end of the presidential term.

FOR CRITICAL ANALYSIS

1. Some have argued in favor of a national referendum to censor a U.S. president's actions if they are "outrageous." How would this differ from a no-confidence vote in a parliamentary system?

2. Do you think a parliamentary system would eliminate gridlock in our national government?

Every two years, usually starting in early fall, the media concentrate on the state of the political parties. For example, near the end of the 2002 campaigns, the media offered continuous commentaries on how Democratic or Republican candidates were faring in the various races, including those for Congress and those for state legislatures and state governorships. As the elections drew near, the polls also concentrated on discovering to which political party each potential voter believes he or she "belongs." Prior to an election, a typical poll usually asks the following question: "Do you consider yourself to be a Republican, a Democrat, or an independent?" Generally, the responses indicate that Americans divide fairly evenly among these three choices, with nearly one-third identifying themselves as **independents.**

After the elections are over, the media publish the election results. Among other things, Americans will learn (in presidential election years) which party controls the presidency and how many Democrats and how many Republicans will be sitting in the House of Representatives and the Senate when the new Congress convenes. Americans will also learn whether we have a **divided government,** a term discussed in this chapter's opening *What If . . .* feature.

Notice that in the first paragraph, when discussing party membership, we put the word *belongs* in quotation marks. We did this because no one actually "belongs" to a political party in the sense of being a card-carrying member. To become a member of a political party, you do not have to pay dues, pass an examination, or swear an oath of allegiance. Therefore, at this point we can ask an obvious question: If it takes nothing to be a member of a political party, what, then, is a political party?

What Is a Political Party?

A **political party** might be formally defined as a group of political activists who organize to win elections, operate the government, and determine public policy. This definition explains the difference between an interest group and a political party. Interest groups do not want to operate the government, and they do not put forth political candidates—even though they support candidates who will promote their interests if elected or reelected. Another important distinction is that interest groups tend to sharpen issues, whereas American political parties tend to blur their issue positions to attract voters.

Political parties differ from **factions,** which are smaller groups that are trying to obtain certain benefits for themselves.[1] Factions generally preceded the formation of political parties in American history, and the term is still used to refer to groups within parties that follow a particular leader or share a regional identification or an ideological viewpoint. The Republican Party sometimes is seen as having a northeastern faction that holds more moderate positions than the dominant conservative majority of the party. Factions are subgroups within parties that may try to capture a nomination or get a position adopted by the party. The key difference between factions and parties is that factions do not have a permanent organization, whereas political parties do.

Functions of Political Parties in the United States

Political parties in the United States engage in a wide variety of activities, many of which are discussed in this chapter. Through these activities, parties perform a number of functions for the political system. These functions include the following:

1. *Recruiting candidates for public office.* Because it is the goal of parties to gain control of government, they must work to recruit candidates for all elective offices.

Independent
A voter or candidate who does not identify with a political party.

Divided Government
A situation in which one major political party controls the presidency and the other controls the chambers of Congress, or in which one party controls a state governorship and the other controls the state legislature.

Political Party
A group of political activists who organize to win elections, operate the government, and determine public policy.

Faction
A group or bloc in a legislature or political party acting together in pursuit of some special interest or position.

---

[1] See the comments on factions by James Madison in Chapter 2.

Supporters of George W. Bush and Dick Cheney lead the cheers for their presidential and vice presidential candidates during the 2000 Republican National Convention. (Touhig Sion/Corbis Sygma)

Often, this means recruiting candidates to run against powerful incumbents or for unpopular jobs. Yet if parties did not search out and encourage political hopefuls, far more offices would be uncontested, and voters would have limited choices.

2. *Organizing and running elections.* Although elections are a government activity, political parties actually organize the voter-registration drives, recruit the volunteers to work at the polls, provide most of the campaign activity to stimulate interest in the election, and work to increase voter participation.

3. *Presenting alternative policies to the electorate.* In contrast to factions, which are often centered on individual politicians, parties are focused on a set of political positions. The Democrats or Republicans in Congress who vote together do so because they represent constituencies that have similar expectations and demands.

4. *Accepting responsibility for operating the government.* When a party elects the president or governor and members of the legislature, it accepts the responsibility for running the government. This includes staffing the executive branch with loyal party supporters and developing linkages among the elected officials to gain support for policies and their implementation.

5. *Acting as the organized opposition to the party in power.* The "out" party, or the one that does not control the government, is expected to articulate its own policies and oppose the winning party when appropriate. By organizing the opposition to the "in" party, the opposition party forces debate on the policy alternatives.

The major functions of American political parties are carried out by a small, relatively loose-knit nucleus of party activists. This is quite a different arrangement from the more highly structured, mass-membership party organization typical of certain European working-class parties. American parties concentrate on winning elections rather than on signing up large numbers of deeply committed, dues-paying members who believe passionately in the party's program.

A Short History of Political Parties in the United States

Although it is difficult to imagine a political system in the United States with four, five, six, or seven major political parties, other democratic systems have three-party, four-party, or even ten-party systems. In some European nations, parties are clearly tied to ideological positions; parties that represent Marxist, socialist, liberal, conservative, and ultraconservative positions appear on the political continuum. Some nations have political parties that represent regions of the nation that have separate cultural identities, such as the French-speaking and German-speaking regions of Switzerland. Some parties are rooted in religious differences. In some Muslim nations, political parties are based on differences between factions of Islam. Parties also exist that represent specific economic interests—agricultural, maritime, or industrial—and some, such as monarchist parties, speak for alternative political systems.

Two-Party System
A political system in which only two parties have a reasonable chance of winning.

The United States has a **two-party system,** and that system has been around from about 1800 to the present (see Figure 9–1). The function and character of these political parties, as well as the emergence of the two-party system itself, have much to do

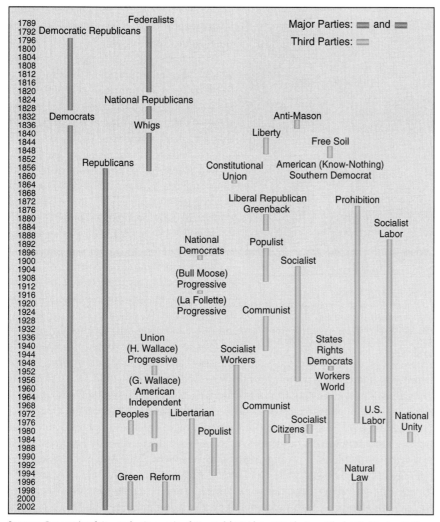

SOURCES: Congressional Quarterly, *Congressional Quarterly's Guide to U.S. Elections,* 2d ed. (Washington, D.C.: Congressional Quarterly Press, 1985), p. 224; *Congressional Quarterly Weekly Report* (1988), p. 3184; J. David Gillespie, *Politics at the Periphery* (Columbia, S.C.: University of South Carolina Press, 1993); and authors' update.

FIGURE 9-1

American Political Parties since 1789

The chart indicates the years that parties either ran presidential candidates or held national conventions. The life span for many political parties can only be approximated, because parties existed at the state or local level before they ran candidates in presidential elections, and parties continued to exist at local levels long after they ceased running presidential candidates. Not every party fielding a presidential candidate is represented in the chart.

with the unique historical forces operating from this country's beginning as an independent nation. Indeed, James Madison linked the emergence of political parties to the form of government created by our Constitution.

Generally, we can divide the evolution of our nation's political parties into six periods:

1. The creation of parties, from 1789 to 1812.
2. The era of one-party rule, or personal politics, from 1816 to 1828.
3. The period from Andrew Jackson's presidency to just prior to the Civil War, from 1828 to 1860.
4. The post–Civil War period, from 1864 to 1892.
5. The progressive period, from 1896 to 1928.
6. The modern period, from 1932 to the present.

The Formative Years: Federalists and Anti-Federalists

The first partisan political division in the United States occurred prior to the adoption of the Constitution. As you will recall from Chapter 2, the Federalists were

Thomas Jefferson, founder of the Democratic Republicans. His election to the presidency in 1800 was decided in the House of Representatives, because no candidate won a majority of the electoral votes. (Library of Congress)

those who pushed for the adoption of the Constitution, whereas the Anti-Federalists were against ratification.

In September 1796, George Washington, who had served as president for almost two full terms, decided not to run again. In his farewell address, he made a somber assessment of the nation's future. Washington felt that the country might be destroyed by the "baneful effects of the spirit of party." He viewed parties as a threat to both national unity and the concept of popular government. Early in his career, Thomas Jefferson did not like political parties either. In 1789, he stated, "If I could not go to heaven but with a party, I would not go there at all."[2]

What Americans found out during the first decade or so after the ratification of the Constitution was that not even a patriot-king such as George Washington could govern by consensus. During this period, it became obvious to many that something more permanent than a faction would be necessary to identify candidates for the growing number of citizens who would be participating in elections. Thus, according to many historians, the world's first democratic political parties were established in this country. The Federalists, who remained in power and solidified their identity as a political party, represented those with commercial interests, including merchants, shipowners, and manufacturers. The Federalists supported the principle of a strong national government. The Anti-Federalists, who gradually became known as the Democratic Republicans, represented artisans and farmers. They strongly supported states' rights. These interests were also fairly well split along geographic lines, with the Federalists dominant in the North and the Democratic Republicans dominant in the South. In 1800, when the Federalists lost the presidential election to the Democratic Republicans (also known as the Jeffersonian Republicans), one of the first peaceful transfers of power from one party to another was achieved.

The Era of Personal Politics

Era of Personal Politics
The years from 1816 to 1828, when attention centered on the character of individual candidates rather than on party identification.

From 1816 to 1828, a majority of U.S. voters regularly elected Democratic Republicans to the presidency and to Congress. Two-party competition did not really exist. This was the so-called **era of personal politics**, when attention centered on the character of individual candidates rather than on party identification. Although during elections the Democratic Republicans opposed the Federalists' call for a stronger, more active central government, they acquired the Louisiana Territory and Florida, established a national bank, enforced a higher tariff (tax on imports), and resisted European intrusion into the Western Hemisphere. Because there was no real political opposition to the dominant Democratic Republicans and thus little political debate, the administration of James Monroe (1817–1825) came to be known as the **era of good feeling**.

Era of Good Feeling
The years from 1817 to 1825, when James Monroe was president and there was, in effect, no political opposition.

---

[2]Letter to Francis Hopkinson written from Paris while Jefferson was minister to France. In John P. Foley, ed., *The Jeffersonian Cyclopedia* (New York: Russell & Russell, 1967), p. 677.

Andrew Jackson earned the name "Old Hickory" for his exploits during the War of 1812. In 1828, Jackson was elected president as the candidate of the new Democratic Party. (Corbis/Bettmann)

National Two-Party Rule: Democrats and Whigs

During the era of personal politics, one-party rule did not prevent the Democratic Republican factions from competing against each other. Indeed, there was quite a bit of intraparty rivalry. Finally, in 1824 and 1828, Democratic Republicans who belonged to the factions of Henry Clay and John Quincy Adams split with the rest of the party to oppose Andrew Jackson in those elections. Jackson's supporters and the Clay-Adams bloc formed separate parties, the **Democratic Party** and the **Whig Party**, respectively. That same Democratic Party is now the oldest continuing political party in the Western world.

The Whigs were those Democratic Republicans who were often called the "National Republicans." At the national level, the Whigs were able to elect two presidents— William Henry Harrison in 1840 and Zachary Taylor in 1848. The Whigs, however, were unable to maintain a common ideological base when the party became increasingly divided over the issue of slavery in the late 1840s. During the 1850s, the Whigs fell apart as a national party.

The Post–Civil War Period

The existing two-party system was disrupted by the election of 1860, in which there were four major candidates. Abraham Lincoln, the candidate of the newly formed **Republican Party**, was the victor with a majority of the electoral vote, although with only 39.9 percent of the popular vote. This newly formed Republican Party—not to be confused with the Democratic Republicans—was created in the mid-1850s from the various groups that sought to fill the vacuum left by the disintegration of the Whigs. It took the label of Grand Old Party, or GOP. Its first national convention was held in 1856, but its presidential candidate, John C. Frémont, lost.

After the end of the Civil War, the South became heavily Democratic (the Solid South), and the North became heavily Republican. This era of Republican dominance was highlighted by the election of 1896, when the Republicans, emphasizing economic development and modernization under William McKinley, resoundingly defeated the Democratic and Populist candidate, William Jennings Bryan. The Republicans' control was solidified by winning over the urban working-class vote in northern cities. From the election of Abraham Lincoln until the election of Franklin D. Roosevelt in 1932, the Republicans won all but four presidential elections.

The Progressive Movement

In 1912, a major schism occurred in the Republican Party when former Republican president Theodore Roosevelt campaigned for the presidency as a Progressive. Consequently, there were three significant contenders in that presidential contest. Woodrow Wilson was the Democratic candidate, William Howard Taft was the regular

INFOTRAC®
COLLEGE EDITION

To find out more about President Jackson, use the term "Andrew Jackson" in the Subject guide.

Democratic Party
One of the two major American political parties evolving out of the Democratic (Jeffersonian) Republican group supporting Thomas Jefferson.

Whig Party
One of the foremost political organizations in the United States during the first half of the nineteenth century, formally established in 1836. The Whig Party was dominated by the same anti-Jackson elements that organized the National Republican faction within the Democratic (Jeffersonian) Republicans and represented a variety of regional interests. It fell apart as a national party in the early 1850s.

Republican Party
One of the two major American political parties, which emerged in the 1850s as an antislavery party. It was created to fill the vacuum caused by the disintegration of the Whig Party.

William McKinley campaigns in 1896 on a platform draped with the flag. A century later, candidates were still using the same type of decorations. (The Smithsonian)

Republican candidate, and Roosevelt was the Progressive candidate. The Republican split allowed Wilson to be elected. The Wilson administration, although Democratic, ended up enacting much of the Progressive Party's platform. Left without any reason for opposition, the Progressive Party collapsed in 1921.[3]

Republican Warren Harding's victory in 1920 reasserted Republican domination of national politics until the Republicans' defeat by Franklin D. Roosevelt in 1932, in the depths of the Great Depression.

The Modern Era: From the New Deal to the Present

Franklin D. Roosevelt was elected in 1932 and reelected in 1936, 1940, and 1944. The impact of his successive Democratic administrations and the New Deal that he crafted is still with us today. Roosevelt used his enormous personal appeal to unify Democrats under his leadership, and he established direct communication between the president and the public through his radio fireside chats.[4]

1945 to 1968.   In April 1945, Roosevelt died; Vice President Harry Truman became president through succession and, in 1948, through election. The New Deal coalition, under Truman's revised theme of the Fair Deal, continued. Although Republican Dwight Eisenhower won the presidency in 1952 and was reelected in 1956, the Democrats regained control in 1960. Led first by John F. Kennedy and then by Lyndon B. Johnson, the Democrats held national power from 1960 through 1968.

---

[3] Although the Bull Moose Progressive Party fell apart in 1921, other state and local Progressive parties continued to be active, including the party led by Robert La Follette of Wisconsin, who won 17 percent of the vote for president in 1924 on the Progressive ticket.

[4] One of the warm, informal talks by Franklin D. Roosevelt to a few million of his intimate friends—via the radio (see Chapter 11). Roosevelt's fireside chats were so effective that succeeding presidents have been urged by their advisers to emulate him by giving more radio and television reports to the nation.

1968 to 1988. Republicans again gained control of the presidency with Richard Nixon's victory in 1968 and retained it in 1972, but they lost prestige and public support after the Watergate scandal forced Nixon's resignation on August 8, 1974. For this and other reasons, the Democrats were back in power after the presidential elections in 1976. But Democratic president Jimmy Carter was unable to win reelection against Ronald Reagan in 1980. The Republicans also gained control of the Senate in 1980 and retained it in the elections of 1982 and 1984. The 1984 reelection of Ronald Reagan appeared to some pollsters to signal the resurgence of the Republican Party as a competitive force in American politics as more people declared themselves to be Republicans than had done so in the previous several decades.

1988 to the Present. The election of George H. W. Bush in 1988 may have signaled the beginning of a true era of divided government. Republican Bush won the presidency, but his Republican Party lost seats in the House and Senate to Democrats. In 1992, Democrat Bill Clinton won the presidency, with Democratic control of the House and Senate, but his party actually lost congressional seats, presaging the Democrats' debacle in 1994 when the Republicans took control of both the House and the Senate. In 1996, Bill Clinton was reelected, but the voters returned Republicans to control in Congress. Republicans also controlled most of the governorships in the states. After the 2000 elections, divided government took on a new meaning. Although Republican George W. Bush won the presidency, Congress became almost evenly divided, with the Republicans holding a slim majority in the House and the Democrats holding an even narrower majority in the Senate. The Republicans succeeded in 2002 in holding on to the House and in regaining control of the Senate, but their majorities remained slim.

INFOTRAC®
COLLEGE EDITION

To find out more, use the term "divided government" in Keywords.

ELECTIONS 2002 Partisan Trends in the 2002 Elections

The losses by the Democrats in the 2002 midterm elections were attributed to their failure to make the economic downturn of 2001 and 2002 an election issue. President George W. Bush successfully focused media attention on the war on terrorism and on a potential showdown with Iraq over weapons inspections and disarmament. Bush campaigned aggressively for Republican candidates in forty states, including Georgia and South Dakota. In Georgia, the Republican challenger for Senate, Saxby Chambliss, characterized his opponent, incumbent Democrat Max Cleland, as soft on homeland security, despite the fact that Cleland is a decorated Vietnam War veteran. Chambliss consequently won, a surprising upset for Democrats.

The Three Faces of a Party

Although American parties are known by a single name and, in the public mind, have a common historical identity, each party really has three major components. The first component is the **party-in-the-electorate**. This phrase refers to all those individuals who claim an attachment to the political party. They need not be members in the sense that they pay dues or even participate in election campaigns. Rather, the party-in-the-electorate is the large number of Americans who feel some loyalty to the party or who use partisanship as a cue to decide who will earn their vote. Party membership is not really a rational choice; rather, it is an emotional tie somewhat analogous to identifying with a region or a baseball team. Although individuals may hold a deep loyalty to or identification with a political party, there is no need for members of the party-in-the-electorate to speak out publicly, to contribute to campaigns, or to vote

Party-in-the-Electorate
Those members of the general public who identify with a political party or who express a preference for one party over another.

a straight party ticket. Needless to say, the party leaders pay close attention to the affiliation of their members in the electorate.

The second component, the **party organization,** provides the structural framework for the political party by recruiting volunteers to become party leaders; identifying potential candidates; and organizing caucuses, conventions, and election campaigns for its candidates, as will be discussed in more detail shortly. It is the party organization and its active workers that keep the party functioning between elections, as well as make sure that the party puts forth electable candidates and clear positions in the elections. When individuals accept paid employment for a political party, they are considered party professionals. If the party-in-the-electorate declines in numbers and loyalty, the party organization must try to find a strategy to rebuild the grassroots following.

The **party-in-government** is the third component of American political parties. The party-in-government consists of those elected and appointed officials who identify with a political party. Generally, elected officials cannot also hold official party positions within the formal organization, although they often have the informal power to appoint party executives.

Party Organization

Each of the American political parties is often perceived as having a standard, pyramid-shaped organization, with the national chairperson and national committee at the top of the pyramid and the local precinct chairperson and committee on the bottom. This structure, however, does not accurately reflect the relative power and strengths of the individual parts of the party organization. If it did, the national chairperson of the Democratic Party or the Republican Party, along with the national committee, could simply dictate how the organization was to be run, just as if it were ExxonMobil Corporation or Ford Motor Company. In reality, the formal structure of political parties resembles a confederal arrangement, in which each unit has significant autonomy and is only loosely linked to the other units.

The National Party Organization

Each party has a national organization, the most clearly institutional part of which is the **national convention,** held every four years. The convention is used to nominate the presidential and vice presidential candidates. In addition, the **party platform** is written, ratified, and revised at the national convention. The platform sets forth the party's position on the issues and makes promises to initiate certain policies if the party wins the presidency.

After the convention, the platform frequently is neglected or ignored by party candidates who disagree with it. Because candidates are trying to win votes from a wide spectrum of voters, it is counterproductive to emphasize the fairly narrow and sometimes controversial goals set forth in the platform. The work of Gerald M. Pomper has shown, however, that once elected, the parties do try to carry out platform promises and that roughly three-fourths of the promises eventually become law.[5] Of course, some general goals, such as economic prosperity, are included in the platforms of both parties.

The party convention provides the most striking illustration of the difference between the ordinary members of a party, or party identifiers, and party activists. As a series of studies by the *New York Times* shows, delegates to the national party conventions are quite dissimilar from ordinary party identifiers. Delegates to the

Party Organization

The formal structure and leadership of a political party, including election committees; local, state, and national executives; and paid professional staff.

Party-in-Government

All of the elected and appointed officials who identify with a political party.

National Convention

The meeting held every four years by each major party to select presidential and vice presidential candidates, to write a platform, to choose a national committee, and to conduct party business. In theory, the national convention is at the top of a hierarchy of party conventions (the local and state conventions are below it) that consider candidates and issues.

Party Platform

A document drawn up by the platform committee at each national convention, outlining the policies, positions, and principles of the party; it is then submitted to the entire convention for approval.

---

[5] Gerald M. Pomper and Susan S. Lederman, *Elections in America: Control and Influence in Democratic Politics,* 2d ed. (New York: Longman, 1980).

Democratic National Convention, as shown in Table 9–1, are far more liberal than are ordinary Democratic voters. In the same fashion, Republican voters are not nearly as conservative as are delegates to the Republican National Convention. Why does this happen? In part, it is because a person, to become a delegate, must gather votes in a primary election from party members who care enough to vote in a primary or be appointed by party leaders. Furthermore, the primaries generally pit candidates against each other on intraparty issues. Delegates who are pledged to those candidates are also likely to hold positions on the issues that are far different from those of the other major party. Often, the most important activity for the convention is making peace between the delegates who support different candidates and helping them accept a party platform that will appeal to the general electorate.

TABLE 9–1

Convention Delegates and Voters: How Did They Compare on the Issues in 2000?

PERCENTAGE OF ...	DEMOCRATIC DELEGATES	DEMOCRATIC VOTERS	ALL VOTERS	REPUBLICAN VOTERS	REPUBLICAN DELEGATES
SCOPE OF GOVERNMENT					
Government should do more to ...					
... solve the nation's problems	73	44	33	21	4
... regulate the environmental and safety practices of businesses	60	61	50	37	8
SOCIAL ISSUES					
Abortion should be generally available	71	48	36	25	14
The penalty for murder should be death rather than life term	20	46	51	55	60
Favor programs to help minorities get ahead due to past discrimination	83	59	51	44	29
Favor child-safety locks on guns	94	81	84	76	48
CAMPAIGN FINANCE					
Favor limit on individual contributions to campaigns	58	39	37	36	34
Favor banning soft money for political parties	47	68	64	60	24
GOVERNMENT SPENDING					
Favor Medicare prescription benefit	58	39	37	36	34
Allow people to invest part of Social Security on own	23	44	53	61	89
IDEOLOGY					
Political ideology is ...					
... very liberal	14	6	4	1	<1
... somewhat liberal	20	28	19	10	1
... moderate	56	46	43	38	34
... somewhat conservative	2	12	19	28	27
... very conservative	2	4	12	21	30

SOURCE: *The New York Times,* August 14, 2000, p. A17.

National Committee
A standing committee of a national political party established to direct and coordinate party activities during the four-year period between national party conventions.

Choosing the National Committee. At the national convention, each of the parties formally chooses a national standing committee, elected by the individual state parties. This **national committee** is established to direct and coordinate party activities during the following four years. The Democrats include at least two members, a man and a woman, from each state, from the District of Columbia, and from the several territories. Governors, members of Congress, mayors, and other officials may be included as at-large members of the national committee. The Republicans, in addition, add state chairpersons from every state carried by the Republican Party in the preceding presidential, gubernatorial, or congressional elections. The selections of national committee members are ratified by the delegations to the national convention.

One of the jobs of the national committee is to ratify the presidential nominee's choice of a national chairperson, who in principle acts as the spokesperson for the party. Basically, the national chairperson and the national committee plan the next campaign and the next convention, obtain financial contributions, and publicize the national party.

Picking a National Chairperson. In general, the party's presidential candidate chooses the national chairperson. (If that candidate loses, however, the chairperson is often changed.) The major responsibility of the chairperson is to manage the national election campaign. In some cases, a strong national chairperson has considerable power over state and local party organizations. There is no formal mechanism for exercising direct control over subnational party structures, however. The national chairperson does such jobs as establish a national party headquarters, raise campaign funds and distribute them to state parties and to candidates, and appear in the media as a party spokesperson.

The national chairperson, along with the national committee, attempts basically to maintain some sort of liaison among the different levels of the party organization. The fact is that the real strength and power of a national party are at the state level.

The State Party Organization

There are fifty states in the Union, plus the District of Columbia and the territories, and an equal number of party organizations for each major party. Therefore, there

Terry McAuliffe (left), the national chairman of the Democratic National Committee, and Marc Racicot (right), the national chairman of the Republican National Committee. Is the function of a national party chairperson similar to the function of a chairperson of a corporate board of directors? (Left: AP Photo/Dimitrius Kambours—Fashion Wire Daily; Right: AP Photo/Great Falls Tribune)

are more than a hundred state parties (and even more, if we include local parties and minor parties). Because every state party is unique, it is impossible to describe what an "average" state political party is like. Nonetheless, state parties have several organizational features in common.

This commonality can be described in one sentence: each state party has a chairperson, a committee, and a number of local organizations. In theory, each **state central committee**—the principal organized structure of each political party within each state—has a similar role in the various states. The committee, usually composed of those members who represent congressional districts, state legislative districts, or counties, has responsibility for carrying out the policy decisions of the party's state convention, and in some states the state committee will direct the state chairperson with respect to policymaking.

Also, like the national committee, the state central committee has control over the use of party campaign funds during political campaigns. Usually, the state central committee has little, if any, influence on party candidates once they are elected. In fact, state parties are fundamentally loose alliances of local interests and coalitions of often bitterly opposed factions.

State parties are also important in national politics because of the **unit rule**, which awards electoral votes in presidential elections as an indivisible bloc (except in Maine and Nebraska). Presidential candidates concentrate their efforts in states in which voter preferences seem to be evenly divided or in which large numbers of electoral votes are at stake.

Local Party Machinery: The Grassroots

The lowest layer of party machinery is the local organization, supported by district leaders, precinct or ward captains, and party workers. Much of the work is coordinated by county committees and their chairpersons.

Patronage and City Machines.   At the end of the nineteenth century, the institution of **patronage**—rewarding the party faithful with government jobs or contracts—held the local organization together. For immigrants and the poor, the political machine often furnished important services and protections. The big-city machine was the archetypal example, and Tammany Hall, or the Tammany Society, which dominated New York City government for nearly two centuries, was perhaps the highest refinement of this political form.

The last big-city local political machine to exercise a great deal of power was run by Chicago's Mayor Richard J. Daley, who was also an important figure in national Democratic politics. Daley, as mayor, ran the Chicago Democratic machine from 1955 until his death in 1976. The Daley organization, largely Irish in candidate origin and voter support, was split by the successful candidacy of African American Democrat Harold Washington in the racially divisive 1983 mayoral election. The current mayor of Chicago, Richard M. Daley, son of the former mayor, today heads a party organization that includes many different groups in the electorate.

City machines are now dead, mostly because their function of providing social services (and reaping the reward of votes) has been taken over by state and national agencies. This trend began in the 1930s, when the social legislation of the New Deal established Social Security and unemployment insurance. The local party machine has little, if anything, to do with deciding who is eligible to receive these benefits.

Local Party Organizations Today.   Local political organizations, whether located in cities, in townships, or at the county level, still can contribute a great deal to local election campaigns. These organizations are able to provide the foot soldiers of politics—

State Central Committee
The principal organized structure of each political party within each state. This committee is responsible for carrying out policy decisions of the party's state convention.

Unit Rule
All of a state's electoral votes are cast for the presidential candidate receiving a plurality of the popular vote in that state.

Patronage
Rewarding faithful party workers and followers with government employment and contracts.

individuals who pass out literature and get out the vote on election day, which can be crucial in local elections. In many regions, local Democratic and Republican organizations still exercise some patronage, such as awarding courthouse jobs, contracts for street repair, and other lucrative construction contracts. The constitutionality of awarding—or not awarding—contracts on the basis of political affiliation has been subject to challenge, however. The Supreme Court has ruled that failing to hire or firing individuals because of their political affiliation is an infringement of the employees' First Amendment rights to free expression.[6] Local party organizations are also the most important vehicles for recruiting young adults into political work, because political involvement at the local level offers activists many opportunities to gain experience.

The Party-in-Government

After the election is over and the winners are announced, the focus of party activity shifts from getting out the vote to organizing and controlling the government. As you will see in Chapter 12, party membership plays an important role in the day-to-day operations of Congress, with partisanship determining everything from office space to committee assignments and power on Capitol Hill. For the president, the political party furnishes the pool of qualified applicants for political appointments to run the government. Although it is uncommon to do so, presidents can and occasionally do appoint executive personnel, such as cabinet secretaries, from the opposition party. As we note in Chapter 13, there are not as many of these appointed positions as presidents might like, and presidential power is limited by the permanent bureaucracy. Judicial appointments, however, offer a great opportunity to the winning party. For the most part, presidents are likely to appoint federal judges from their own party.

All of these party appointments suggest that the winning political party, whether at the national, state, or local level, has a great deal of control in the American system. Because of the checks and balances and the relative lack of cohesion in American parties, however, such control is an illusion. As we discuss in the chapter-opening *What If . . .* , for some time many Americans have seemed to prefer a "divided government," with the executive and legislative branches controlled by different parties. The trend toward **ticket splitting**—splitting votes between the president and members of Congress—has increased sharply since 1952. This practice may indicate a lack of trust in government or the relative weakness of party identification among many voters. Voters seem comfortable with having a president affiliated with one party and a Congress controlled by the other.

Ticket Splitting
Voting for candidates of two or more parties for different offices. For example, a voter splits her ticket if she votes for a Republican presidential candidate and for a Democratic congressional candidate.

The Two Major U.S. Parties and Their Members

The two major American political parties are often characterized as being too much like Tweedledee and Tweedledum, the twins in Lewis Carroll's *Through the Looking Glass.* When both parties nominate moderates for the presidency, the similarities between the parties seem to outweigh their differences. Yet the political parties do generate strong conflict for political offices throughout the United States, and there are significant differences between the parties, both in the characteristics of their members and in their platforms.

---

[6] *Rutan v. Republican Party of Illinois,* 497 U.S. 62 (1990).

The Parties' Core Constituents

Although Democrats and Republicans are not divided along religious or class lines to the extent that some European parties are, certain social groups are more likely to identify with each party. Since the New Deal of Franklin D. Roosevelt, the Democratic Party has appealed to the more disadvantaged groups in society. African American voters are far more likely to identify with the Democrats, as are members of union households, Jewish voters, and individuals who have less than a high school education. Republicans draw more of their support from college graduates, upper-income families, and professionals or businesspersons. In recent years, more women than men have tended to identify themselves as Democrats rather than as Republicans.

The coalition of minorities, the working class, and various ethnic groups has been the core of Democratic Party support since the presidency of Franklin D. Roosevelt. The social programs and increased government intervention in the economy that were the heart of Roosevelt's New Deal were intended to ease the strain of economic hard times on these groups. This goal remains important for many Democrats today. In general, Democratic identifiers are more likely to approve of social-welfare spending, to support government regulation of business, to approve of measures to improve the situation of minorities, and to support assistance to the elderly with their medical expenses. Republicans are more supportive of the private marketplace, and many Republicans feel that the federal government should be involved in fewer social programs.

Other Party Differences

Public opinion polls that ask the public which party they trust to handle certain issues reaffirm the loyalties of various groups. As shown in Figure 9–2, a majority of those polled think that Republicans would do a better job of protecting the country from future acts of terrorism, responding to foreign policy challenges in the Middle East, preventing corruption, managing the federal government, and (very marginally) getting the

ISSUE OR PROBLEM	REPUBLICANS	DEMOCRATS	ADVANTAGE
Protecting the country from future acts of terrorism	54%	21%	Republicans
Responding to foreign policy challenges in the Middle East	53%	30%	Republicans
Preventing corruption	39%	33%	Republicans
Managing the federal government	43%	38%	Republicans
Getting the country out of recession	43%	42%	Republicans
Representing your values	41%	47%	Democrats
Setting a tax policy that is fair to all Americans	35%	51%	Democrats
Ensuring the long-term strength of the Social Security system	34%	50%	Democrats
Improving the health-care system	31%	54%	Democrats

SOURCE: CNN/*USA Today*/Gallup poll, conducted April 5–7, 2002.

FIGURE 9–2

Which Party Is Better?

This public opinion poll asked respondents which political party they trusted more to handle certain issues facing the nation.

This handbill was used in the election campaign of 1860. Handbills served the same purpose as today's direct-mail advertisements, appealing directly to the voters with the candidate's message. (Corbis/Bettmann)

country out of the recession. Democrats are seen as having an advantage with respect to representing the respondents' values, setting a tax policy that is fair to all Americans, ensuring the long-term strength of the Social Security system, and improving the health-care system.

Note that in 1999, Democrats were seen as slightly more likely than Republicans to "ensure a strong economy." This is a bit of a reversal from the years of Ronald Reagan and George H. W. Bush, when Republicans were perceived to have an advantage on economic issues. The strong performance of the nation's economy during the Clinton presidency apparently increased voters' confidence in the ability of the Democratic Party to address economic issues effectively.

Why Has the Two-Party System Endured?

There are several reasons why two major parties have dominated the political landscape in the United States for almost two centuries. These reasons have to do with (1) the historical foundations of the system, (2) political socialization and party identification, (3) the commonality of views among Americans, (4) the winner-take-all electoral system, and (5) state and federal laws favoring the two-party system.

The Historical Foundations of the Two-Party System

As we have seen, the first two political parties in U.S. politics were the Federalists and the Democratic Republicans, who espoused many of the views expressed by the Anti-

"The euonymus likes partial shade and does equally well under Republican and Democratic Administrations."

Drawing by Steiner © 1994 The New Yorker Magazine, Inc.

Federalists. Each of these parties represented a distinct set of interests. Over time, political parties continued to represent different interests. During Andrew Jackson's time in power, eastern commercial interests were pitted against western and southern agricultural and frontier interests. Before the Civil War, the major split again became North versus South. The split was ideological (over the issue of slavery), as well as economic (the Northeast's industrial interests versus the agricultural interests of the South). After the Civil War, the Republicans found most of their strength in the Northeast, and the Democrats, among white voters in the Solid South. The period from the Civil War to the 1920s has been called one of **sectional politics.**

In the early 1970s, Kevin Phillips, a well-known commentator, predicted that migration from the North and the general conservative attitudes of southern white voters would lead to Republican control in the once solidly Democratic South. As the maps in Figure 9–3 show, the Republican Party now has control of the majority of southern governorships, Senate seats, and House seats. Only in the state legislatures are Democrats still in control. Republicans were able to capture the national offices first because the campaigns for these offices were often statewide (for the Senate) or covered larger areas (House seats). This meant that more of the newcomers to the region were included, and political conflicts were more national in nature. State legislatures often reflect very local interests as well as the power of local party organizations—which remain, to a great extent, Democratic in the southern states.

DID YOU KNOW . . .
That it takes about 700,000 signatures to qualify to be on the ballot as a presidential candidate in all fifty states **?**

Sectional Politics
The pursuit of interests that are of special concern to a region or section of the country.

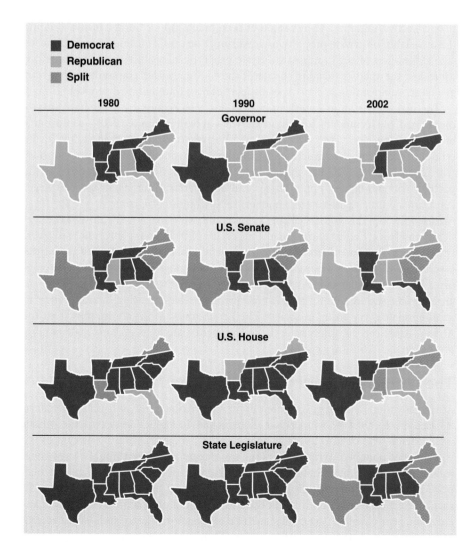

FIGURE 9–3

The Rise of the Republican South
In the years following the Civil War, the South, resentful of defeat by the Union, became solidly Democratic. As the figure shows, however, in recent years the "Solid South" has been giving way to a Republican South, except in state legislatures.

SOURCES: *The New York Times,* March 16, 1998; *The New York Times,* November 7, 2002.

National Politics
The pursuit of interests that are of concern to the nation as a whole.

Class Politics
Political preferences based on income level, social status, or both.

Today, sectional politics has largely given way to **national politics,** which focuses on the concerns of the nation as a whole. The contemporary period can also be described as one of **class politics,** with the Republicans generally finding support among groups of higher economic status and the Democrats appealing more to working-class constituencies and the poor.

Political Socialization and Party Identification

As we saw in Chapter 7, children are strongly influenced by their parents' political attitudes and preferences. Given that the majority of Americans identify with one of the two major political parties, it is not surprising that children learn at a fairly young age to think of themselves as either Democrats or Republicans. Relatively few are taught to think of themselves as Libertarians or Socialists or even independents. This generates a built-in mechanism to perpetuate a two-party system. Also, many politically oriented people who aspire to work for social change consider that the only realistic way to capture political power in this country is to be either a Republican or a Democrat.

The Political Culture of the United States

Another determining factor in the perpetuation of our two-party system is the commonality of goals among Americans. Most Americans want continuing material prosperity. They also believe that this goal should be achieved through individual, rather than collective, initiative. There has never been much support for the idea of limiting the ownership of private property or equalizing everyone's income. Most Americans take a dim view of such proposals. Private property is considered a basic American value, and the ability to acquire and use it the way one wishes commonly is regarded as a basic American right. Thus, socialist parties have found limited support.

The major division in American politics has been economic. As we have already mentioned, the Democrats have been known—at least since the 1920s—as the party of the working class. They have been in favor of government intervention in the economy and more government redistribution of income from the wealthy to those with lower incomes. The Republican Party has been known in modern times as the party of the middle and upper classes and commercial interests, in favor of fewer constraints on the market system and less redistribution of income.

Not only does the political culture support the two-party system, but also the parties themselves are adept at making the necessary shifts in their platforms or electoral appeal to gain new members. Because the general ideological structure of the parties is so broad, it has been relatively easy for them to change their respective platforms or to borrow popular policies from the opposing party or from minor parties to attract voter support. Both parties perceive themselves as being broad enough to accommodate every group in society. The Republicans try to gain support from the African American community, and the Democrats strive to make inroads among professional and business groups.

The Winner-Take-All Electoral System

Plurality
The total votes cast for a candidate who receives more votes than any other candidate but not necessarily a majority. Most national, state, and local electoral laws provide for winning elections by a plurality vote.

At virtually every level of government in the United States, the outcome of elections is based on the **plurality,** winner-take-all principle. In a plurality system, the winner is the person who obtains the most votes, even if a majority (over 50 percent of the votes) is not obtained. Whoever gets the most votes gets everything. Because most legislators in the United States are elected from single-member districts in which only one person represents the constituency, the candidate who finishes second in such an election receives nothing for the effort. For example, suppose that three candidates are running in a particular state for a congressional seat. Candidate A receives 36 percent of the votes, candidate B receives 32 percent of the votes, and candidate C receives another 32 percent of the votes. Candidate A wins, even though he or she did not win a *majority* (over 50 percent) of the votes.

Electoral College Voting. The winner-take-all system also operates in the **electoral college** (see Chapter 10). In virtually all of the states, the electors are pledged to presidential candidates chosen by their respective national party conventions. During the popular vote in November, in each of the fifty states and in the District of Columbia, the voters choose one slate of electors from those on the state ballot. If the slate of electors wins a plurality in a state, then usually *all* of the electors so chosen cast their ballots for the presidential and vice presidential candidates of the winning party. This means that if a particular candidate's slate of electors receives a plurality of, say, 40 percent of the votes in a state, that candidate will receive all of the state's electoral votes. Minor parties have a difficult time competing under such a system, even though they may influence the final outcome of the election. Because voters know that minor parties cannot succeed, they often will not vote for minor-party candidates, even though the candidates are ideologically in tune with them.

Run-off Elections. Not all countries, or even all states in the United States, use the plurality, winner-take-all electoral system. Some hold run-off elections until a candidate obtains at least one vote over 50 percent of the votes. Such a system also may be used in countries with multiple parties. Small parties hope to be able to obtain a sufficient number of votes at least to get into a run-off election. (See this chapter's *Which Side Are You On?* feature on the next page for a discussion of an instant run-off voting system that is being used in some parts of the country.)

Proportional Representation. Many other nations use a system of proportional representation with multimember districts. If, during the national election, party X obtains 12 percent of the vote, party Y gets 43 percent of the vote, and party Z gets the remaining 45 percent of the vote, then party X gets 12 percent of the seats in the legislature, party Y gets 43 percent of the seats, and party Z gets 45 percent of the seats. Because even a minor party may still obtain at least a few seats in the legislature, the smaller parties have a greater incentive to organize under such electoral systems than they do in the United States.

State and Federal Laws Favoring the Two Parties

Many state and federal election laws offer a clear advantage to the two major parties. In some states, the established major parties need to gather fewer signatures to place their candidates on the ballot than minor parties or independent candidates do. The criterion for determining how many signatures will be required is often based on the total party vote in the last general election, thus penalizing a new political party that did not compete in that election.

At the national level, minor parties face different obstacles. All of the rules and procedures of both houses of Congress divide committee seats, staff members, and other privileges on the basis of party membership. A legislator who is elected on a minor-party ticket, such as the Liberal Party of New York, must choose to be counted with one of the major parties to get a committee assignment. The Federal Election Commission (FEC) rules for campaign financing also place restrictions on minor-party candidates. Such candidates are not eligible for federal matching funds in either the primary or the general election. In the 1980 election, John Anderson, running for president as an independent, sued the FEC for campaign funds. The commission finally agreed to repay part of his campaign costs after the election in proportion to the votes he received. Since that time, the FEC has continued to give funds, after the election, to third-party candidates who gained a specified proportion of the vote.

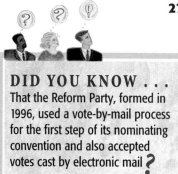

DID YOU KNOW . . .
That the Reform Party, formed in 1996, used a vote-by-mail process for the first step of its nominating convention and also accepted votes cast by electronic mail?

Electoral College
A group of persons called electors who are selected by the voters in each state. This group officially elects the president and the vice president of the United States. The number of electors in each state is equal to the number of each state's seats in both chambers of Congress.

Which Side Are You On?
Would Instant Run-off Elections Be Better?

As we pointed out, our "winner-take-all" system greatly favors the two major political parties. It is one of the reasons that third parties find it virtually impossible to become major parties. An alternative voting system, known as *instant run-off voting*, or *IRV*, is already being used in some areas, however. On March 5, 2002, San Francisco adopted IRV by passing Proposition A. Oakland, across the San Francisco Bay, passed a charter amendment that allows IRV to be used to fill a vacancy for mayor. The Utah Republican Party uses IRV to nominate congressional candidates at the state nominating convention.

THE MECHANICS OF INSTANT RUN-OFF VOTING

In an IRV system, instead of casting just one vote for one candidate, each voter ranks candidates in order of preference, indicating the first preference with the number 1, the second preference with the number 2, and so on. Then the votes are tallied. If no candidate receives more than 50 percent of the number 1 votes, then a process of elimination occurs. The candidate with the fewest number 1 votes is eliminated.

The ballot counters then look at the number 2 votes on the ballots of the candidate being eliminated. The votes for the first-choice candidate on these ballots are transferred to the second-choice candidates. The ballots are then recounted. Candidates are eliminated in this fashion until one winner emerges with a majority of the votes. Such a system avoids *plurality voting*, which is used throughout the United States for most elections. With plurality voting, a candidate can win without having a majority of the votes.

THE BENEFITS OF INSTANT RUN-OFF VOTING

According to its proponents, an IRV system would offer the following benefits:

- It may promote issue-based campaigns because candidates will seek second- and third-choice votes. IRV might also discourage negative campaigning, again because candidates will seek second- and third-choice votes.

- It minimizes "wasted" votes—that is, votes that do not help elect a winner.
- It may increase voter turnout because it gives voters more choices. In other words, IRV allows more candidates to be on the ballot, including independents and third-party candidates.
- It ensures majority rule, in contrast to plurality voting in which a candidate with less than 50 percent of the vote can win the election.

NOT EVERYONE FAVORS INSTANT RUN-OFF VOTING

Those who are not so sure about IRV point out that designing a computer system that would accurately tally multiple votes would be difficult and certainly not free of cost. Indeed, it might be quite expensive. There is also a constitutional issue to consider. Our electoral system is built on the principle of one person, one vote. That requires that you pick one candidate as your candidate and no other. If your candidate loses, you live with the consequences. IRV does not work within this existing constitutional framework. In other words, it gives voters more than one vote. Some critics of IRV contend that it is simply a way to enable supporters of a third-party candidate to vote for a long shot without having to worry that by doing so, they will "spoil" the chances of their favored major-party candidate.

WHAT'S YOUR POSITION?

If, as the opponents of IRV contend, such a system would be unconstitutional, would you be in favor of a constitutional amendment to allow for such a system? Why or why not?

GOING ONLINE

The Center for Democracy and Voting has a repository of articles on instant run-off voting. Go to **http://www.fairvote.org/irv**. To find out about efforts to implement instant run-off voting in your state, go to **http://www.instantrunoff.com/states.html**.

The Role of Minor Parties in U.S. Political History

For the reasons just discussed, minor parties have a difficult, if not impossible, time competing within the American two-party political system. Nonetheless, minor parties have played an important role in our political life. Frequently, dissatisfied groups have split from major parties and formed so-called **third parties**,[7] which have acted as barometers of changes in the political mood. Such barometric indicators have forced the major parties to recognize new issues or trends in the thinking of Americans. Political scientists also believe that third parties have acted as a safety valve for dissident political groups, perhaps preventing major confrontations and political unrest. Additionally, parties may be formed to represent a particular ethnic group, such as Hispanics, or groups such as gay men and lesbians.

Third Party
A political party other than the two major political parties (Republican and Democratic). Usually, third parties are composed of dissatisfied groups that have split from the major parties. They act as indicators of political trends and as safety valves for dissident groups.

Historically Important Minor Parties

Most minor parties that have endured have had a strong ideological foundation that is typically at odds with the majority mindset. Ideology has at least two functions. First, the members of the minor party regard themselves as outsiders and look to one another for support; ideology provides tremendous psychological cohesiveness. Second, because the rewards of ideological commitment are partly psychological, these minor parties do not think in terms of immediate electoral success. A poor showing at the polls therefore does not dissuade either the leadership or the grassroots participants from continuing their quest for change in American society. Some of the notable third parties in the modern era include the Libertarian Party, the Green Party, and the Reform Party.

The Libertarian Party supports a *laissez-faire* capitalist economic program, combined with a hands-off policy on regulating matters of moral conduct. The Reform Party, founded by H. Ross Perot in 1996, seeks to reform the political process and reduce the size of government. The Green Party began as a grassroots, environmentalist organization with affiliated political parties across North America and Western Europe. It was established in the United States as a national party in 1996 and nominated Ralph Nader to run for president in 2000.

Splinter Minor Parties

The most successful minor parties have been those that split from major parties. The impetus for these **splinter parties,** or factions, has usually been a situation in which a particular personality was at odds with the major party. The most famous spin-off was the Bull Moose Progressive Party, which split from the Republican Party in 1912 over the candidate chosen to run for president. Theodore Roosevelt rallied his forces and announced the formation of the Bull Moose Progressive Party, leaving the regular Republicans to support William Howard Taft. Although the party was not successful in winning the election for Roosevelt, it did succeed in splitting the Republican vote so that Democrat Woodrow Wilson won.

Among the Democrats, there have been three splinter third parties since the late 1940s: (1) the Dixiecrat (States' Rights) Party of 1948, (2) Henry Wallace's Progressive Party of 1948, and (3) the American Independent Party supporting George Wallace in 1968. The strategy employed by Wallace in the 1968 election was to attempt to deny Richard Nixon or Hubert Humphrey the necessary majority in the electoral college.

Splinter Party
A new party formed by a dissident faction within a major political party. Usually, splinter parties have emerged when a particular personality was at odds with the major party.

---

[7] The term *third party* is erroneous, because sometimes there have been third, fourth, fifth, and even sixth parties, and so on. Because it has endured, however, we will use the term here.

Theodore Roosevelt, president of the United States from 1901 to 1909, became president after William McKinley was assassinated. Roosevelt was reelected in 1904. In 1912, unable to gain the nomination of the Republican Party, Roosevelt formed a splinter group named the Bull Moose Progressive Party but was unsuccessful in his efforts to win the presidency. (The National Archives)

Many political scientists believe that Humphrey still would have lost to Nixon in 1968 even if Wallace had not run, because most Wallace voters would probably have given their votes to Nixon. The American Independent Party emphasized mostly racial issues and, to a lesser extent, foreign policy. Wallace received 9.9 million popular votes and forty-six electoral votes.

Other Minor Parties

Numerous minor parties have coalesced around specific issues or aims. The Free Soil Party, active from 1848 to 1852, was dedicated to preventing the spread of slavery. The goal of the Prohibition Party, started in 1869, was to ban the sale of liquor.

Some minor parties have had specific economic interests as their reason for being. When those interests are either met or made irrelevant by changing economic conditions, these minor parties disappear. Such was the case with the Greenback Party, which lasted from 1876 to 1884. It was one of the most prominent farmer-labor parties that favored government intervention in the economy. Similar to the Greenbacks, but with broader support, was the Populist Party, which lasted from about 1892 to 1908. Farmers were the backbone of this party, and agrarian reform was its goal. In 1892, it ran a presidential candidate, James Weaver, who received one million popular votes and twenty-two electoral votes. The Populists, for the most part, joined with the Democrats in 1896, when both parties endorsed the Democratic presidential candidate, William Jennings Bryan.

In 2000, the Green Party USA made a significant showing. Ralph Nader, its presidential candidate, campaigned against what he referred to as "corporate greed" and

Jill Stein, the Green Party candidate for governor of Massachusetts, meets supporters outside the first debate between gubernatorial candidates in 2002. Stein was not allowed to participate in the debate with the Democratic and Republican candidates. What criteria should be used to determine whether third-party candidates can participate in debates? (AP Photo/Steven Senne)

the increasing indifference of the major parties to a number of pressing issues, including universal health insurance and environmental concerns.[8]

The Impact of Minor Parties

Minor parties clearly have had an impact on American politics. What is more difficult to ascertain is how great that impact has been. Simply by showing that third-party issues were taken over some years later by a major party really does not prove that the third party instigated the major party's change. The case for the importance of minor parties may be strongest for the splinter parties. These parties do indeed force a major party to reassess its ideology and organization. There is general agreement that Teddy Roosevelt's Progressive Party in 1912 and Robert La Follette's Progressive Party in 1924 caused the major parties to take up business regulation as one of their major issues.

Minor parties can also have a serious impact on the outcomes of an election. In the 2000 presidential elections, the Green Party gathered 3 percent of the vote for its nominee, Ralph Nader, taking some votes away from Democrat Al Gore. Given the closeness of the vote in several crucial states, including Florida, the Green Party may have had an impact on the outcome. The Green Party was also successful in raising awareness of the role a third party might have in addressing issues and policies. In contrast, the Reform Party, which had won 8 percent of the vote in 1996, had little impact in 2000 because its nominee, Pat Buchanan, was too conservative for most of the party's members.

Calling the U.S. system a two-party system is an oversimplification. The nature and names of the major parties have changed over time, and smaller parties almost always have enjoyed a moderate degree of success. Whether they are splinters from the major parties or groups expressing social and economic issues not addressed adequately by factions within the major parties, the minor parties attest to the vitality and fluid nature of American politics.

INFOTRAC®
COLLEGE EDITION

To find out more on this topic, use the term "Green Party United States" in the Subject guide.

---

[8]Ralph Nader offers his own entertaining and detailed account of his run for the presidency in 2000 in *Crashing the Party: How to Tell the Truth and Still Run for President* (New York: St. Martin's Press, 2002).

Party Identification
Linking oneself to a particular political party.

I N F O T R A C ®
COLLEGE EDITION

To find out more, use the term "party identification" in Keywords.

The Uncertain Future of Party Identification

Figure 9–4 shows trends in **party identification**, as measured by standard polling techniques from 1937 to the present. What is evident is the rise of the independent voter combined with a relative strengthening of support for the Republican Party, so that the traditional Democratic advantage in party identification is relatively small today.

In the 1940s, only about 20 percent of voters classified themselves as independents. By 1975, this percentage had increased to about 33 percent, and more recent polls show it holding steady at about that level. At times, the Democrats have captured the loyalty of about half the electorate, and the Republicans, until 1960, had more than 30 percent support. By the 1990s, the Democrats could count on less than 40 percent of the electorate, and the Republicans could count on about 30 percent.

Not only have ties to the two major parties weakened in the last three decades, but also voters are less willing to vote a straight ticket—that is, to vote for all the candidates of one party. In the early twentieth century, straight-ticket voting was virtually universal. By mid-century, the percentage of voters who engaged in ticket splitting was 12 percent. In recent presidential elections, between 20 and 40 percent of the voters engaged in split-ticket voting. This trend, along with the increase in the number of voters who call themselves independents, suggests that parties have lost much of their hold on the loyalty of the voters.

Political Parties and Representative Government

You have learned about party organization and structure in this chapter. You have learned about which parties have controlled Congress and which parties have controlled the executive branch. An important question remains: Are today's political parties actually fulfilling the functions of a party as we have described them through-

---

FIGURE 9–4

Party Identification from 1937 to the Present

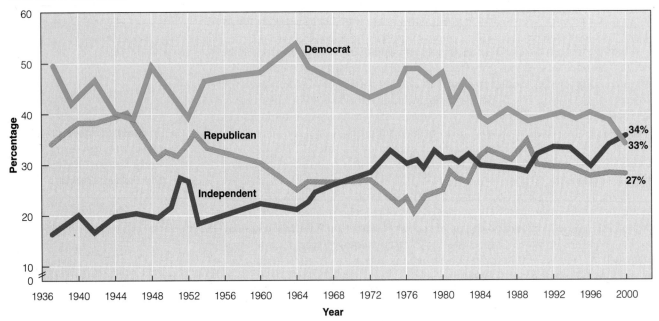

SOURCES: *Gallup Report,* August 1995; *New York Times*/CBS poll, June 1996; *Gallup Report,* February 1998; and authors' update.

out this chapter? An affirmative answer would mean that each of the two major political parties presents a clear alternative for voters. In that case, each political party would present clear and distinct policy proposals that contrast with the policies of the other party, and, if and when elected, that party would implement those proposed policies. (For a discussion of some of the difficulties facing the Democrats today with respect to fulfilling their "loyal opposition" function, see this chapter's *America's Security* feature.)

America's Security

Until 9/11, the Republican Party did not speak with a single voice. Many factions within the party wanted President George W. Bush to accomplish different things.

THE REPUBLICANS FIND THEIR VOICE

In the months immediately after 9/11, concerns over America's security took center stage. During times of crisis, voters tend to emphasize security—a concern that gives incumbents an advantage. This means that as long as Americans view security as America's most important problem, the Republican Party will hold the advantage.

WHAT HAPPENED TO THE LOYAL OPPOSITION?

Given the advantage that national security concerns gave the Republican Party, the Democrats had to ask the question: What could they oppose and still remain a loyal opposition? For some

Party Politics in the Aftermath of 9/11

time, whenever a Democrat criticized the way the Bush administration was running the war on terrorism, Republicans and even some of the media quickly lambasted that critic. The problem for the Democrats was to come up with alternative proposals for making America safe from terrorists.

The Democrats clearly faced a dilemma. They wanted to please anti-war liberals. At the same time, they did not want to alienate moderate voters and those rural districts and states on which control of Congress depends.

The political reality today is that partisanship has no place in a discussion of America's security, at least for most voters. This has made it difficult for Democrats to raise any complaints with respect to the war on terrorism.

FOR CRITICAL ANALYSIS

If the Democratic Party can never appear to be "weak" on America's security, does this mean that President Bush has absolute power in running the war on terrorism? What forces might stop his administration from expanding the war on terrorism too far?

The terrorist attacks of September 11, 2001, shocked and horrified the nation, regardless of party affiliation. Members of Congress put partisanship aside in many instances after the attacks. Here, members of Congress join hands during a ceremonial joint session in New York City one year after the attacks. (AP Photo/Ken Lambert)

The Reality of American Political Parties and Political Action

In America, the Democrats and the Republicans do represent somewhat different points of view. The parties differ with respect to certain social programs, the role that government should play in the economy, and so on. Nevertheless, American political parties are just too decentralized to actually take positions on important issues that differ distinctly from the positions of the other party and then—which is the key to understanding this point—implement such programs.

Consider how major laws are passed in Congress. Very rarely is a law passed by a vote strictly along party lines. Although most Democrats may be against a law, enough of them may vote for it so that, combined with the votes of Republicans who support the bill, the bill will pass. Although most Republicans may be against another law, enough of them may vote for it so that it will pass. This is not to say that Congress *never* votes along strict party lines. A notable example of such partisan voting occurred in the House of Representatives in 1998. The issue at hand was whether to impeach President Bill Clinton. Almost all votes were strictly along party lines— Democrats against, and Republicans for.

One reason that the political parties find it so hard to rally all of their members in Congress to vote along party lines is that parties in this country do not have a "boss system." In other words, the head of a political party in most instances cannot hand-pick candidates who share his or her views and will be beholden to that boss and to that party. In America, the candidates who win most elections largely do so on their own, without significant help from a political party. An individual generally gains a nomination through her or his own hard work and personal political organization. This means, though, that the parties have very little control over the candidates who run under the party labels. In fact, a candidate could run as a Democrat, for example, and be a rabid antigovernment anarchist. No one in the Democratic Party could stop this person from being nominated or even elected.

Party Polarization

Even though Republicans and Democrats do not take distinctly different positions on every issue, they do tend to disagree sharply on certain issues. One might have thought that after the terrorist attacks on September 11, 2001, the parties would have put partisanship aside out of concern for the national interest. After all, a common purpose and a known common enemy typically bring parties together. This has not happened, however. The war on terrorism continues, but Congress has other things to debate, such as economic policy. According to Senate majority leader Tom Daschle (D., S.D.), "There is nothing that divides our parties more, philosophically, than economic policy."[9] The major economic issues facing policymakers include regulatory relief, Social Security privatization, prescription-drug benefits for seniors, and business tax cuts. In each case, Republicans have accused the Democrats of being beholden to the unions, trial lawyers, and radical environmentalists. Democrats, in turn, have accused Republicans of favoring policies whose main purpose is to reward big business for supporting the Republican Party.

In the 2000 presidential races, candidate Ralph Nader claimed that his opponents had become "Republicrats." In fact, though, Democratic and Republican leaders perceive that they and their parties have vastly different ideas about economic issues. From that perspective, they are perhaps further apart than they have been since the early 1930s.[10] Some political scientists call this situation **hyperpartisanship.** They sug-

Hyperpartisanship
A situation in which members of the two major political parties are extremely party oriented in their choices.

---

[9] *Business Week,* January 14, 2002, p. 34.

[10] For some examples of, and some reasons for, partisan voting in Congress, see Derek Willis, "Pattern of Partnership Persists," *CQ Weekly,* Vol. 60, Issue 2 (January 12, 2002), pp. 114–116.

gest that hyperpartisanship may lead to increased public discontent because most Americans want moderate solutions to national problems.

Political Parties: Why Are They Important Today?

Although party machines no longer dominate local politics in our major cities, political parties remain important to you today. The party in power ends up with most of the important leadership positions in Congress. Therefore, a political party's electoral success may lead to new laws and regulations that affect your daily life. You may pay higher or lower taxes, face greater or fewer employment opportunities, or experience changes in the social environment around you—all depending on which political party dominated the last election.

With our two-party system, the political parties are also important because they impart stability to our government, a stability that is unknown in many parts of the world. While one party (the "in" party) governs, the other party (the "out" party) continues to present alternatives. The out party acts as the "loyal opposition," making sure that the party in power is unable to do something wildly out of line with what Americans want. Even if the Republicans controlled both chambers of Congress and the presidency, they would not be able to pass a new tax law eliminating taxes for the rich. Similarly, if the Democrats controlled both chambers of Congress and the presidency, they would not be able to pass a law imposing extraordinarily high taxes on the rich.

Finally, if you look back at Figure 9–1 on page 263, you will see that we have had numerous parties in this nation's history. Many of them have disappeared and been replaced with other parties. Although today's two major parties have endured for over a century and a half, significant numbers of voters do support third parties and their platforms at different times. History shows that one of the two major parties may lose an election, change its focus, or disappear entirely when threatened by a popular third party. Thus, the rise and fall of third parties also remain important to the political system today.

MAKING A DIFFERENCE | Electing Convention Delegates

The most exciting political party event, staged every four years, is the national convention. Surprising as it might seem, there are opportunities for the individual voter to become involved in nominating delegates to the national convention or to become such a delegate.

Participating in Conventions

For both the Republican and Democratic Parties, most delegates must be elected at the local level—either the congressional district or the state legislative district. These elections take place at the party primary election or at a neighborhood or precinct caucus level. If the delegates are elected in a primary, persons who want to run for these positions must file petitions with the board of elections in advance of the election. If you are interested in committing yourself to a particular presidential candidate and running for the delegate position, check with the local county committee or with the party's national committee about the rules you must follow.

Participating in Presidential Caucuses

It is even easier to get involved in the grassroots politics of presidential caucuses. In some states—Iowa being the earliest and most famous one—delegates are first nominated at the local precinct caucus. According to the rules of the Iowa caucuses, anyone can participate in a caucus if he or she is eighteen years old, a resident of the precinct, and registered as a party member. These caucuses, in addition to being the focus of national media attention in January or February, select delegates to the county conventions who are pledged to specific presidential candidates. This is the first step toward the national convention.

How to Get Involved

At both the county caucus and the convention levels, both parties try to find younger members to fill some of the seats. Contact the state or county political party to find out when the caucuses or primaries will be held. Then gather local supporters and friends, and prepare to join in an occasion during which political persuasion and debate are practiced at their best.

For further information about these opportunities (some states hold caucuses and state conventions in every election year), contact the state party office or your local state legislator for specific dates and regulations. Or write to the national committee for its informational brochures on how to become a delegate.

Republican National Committee
Republican National Headquarters
310 First St. S.E.
Washington, DC 20003
202-863-8500
http://www.rnc.org

Democratic National Committee
Democratic National Headquarters
430 Capital St. S.E.
Washington, DC 20003
202-863-8000
http://www.democrats.org/index.html

Key Terms

class politics 276	independent 261	party platform 268	third party 279
Democratic Party 265	national committee 270	patronage 271	ticket splitting 272
divided government 261	national convention 268	plurality 276	two-party system 262
electoral college 277	national politics 276	political party 261	unit rule 271
era of good feeling 264	party identification 282	Republican Party 265	Whig Party 265
era of personal politics 264	party-in-government 268	sectional politics 275	
faction 261	party-in-the-electorate 267	splinter party 279	
hyperpartisanship 284	party organization 268	state central committee 271	

Chapter Summary

1 A political party is a group of political activists who organize to win elections, operate the government, and determine public policy. Political parties perform a number of functions for the political system. These functions include recruiting candidates for public office, organizing and running elections, presenting alternative policies to the voters, assuming responsibility for operating the government, and acting as the opposition to the party in power.

2 The evolution of our nation's political parties can be divided into six periods: (a) the creation and formation of political parties, from 1789 to 1812; (b) the era of one-party rule, or personal politics, from 1816 to 1828; (c) the period from Andrew Jackson's presidency to the Civil War, from 1828 to 1860; (d) the post–Civil War period, from 1864 to 1892, ending with solid control by the modern Republican Party; (e) the progressive period, from 1896 to 1928; and (f) the modern period, from 1932 to the present.

3 A political party consists of three components: the party-in-the-electorate, the party organization, and the party-in-government. Each party component maintains linkages to the others to keep the party strong. Each level of the party—local, state, and national—has considerable autonomy. The national party organization is responsible for holding the national convention in presidential election years, writing the party platform, choosing the national committee, and conducting party business.

4 The party-in-government comprises all of the elected and appointed officeholders of a party. The linkage of party members is crucial to building support for programs among the branches and levels of government.

5 Although it may seem that the two major American political parties do not differ substantially on the issues, each has a different core group of supporters. The general shape of the parties' coalitions reflects the party divisions of Franklin D. Roosevelt's New Deal. It is clear, however, that party leaders are much further apart in their views than are the party followers.

6 Two major parties have dominated the political landscape in the United States for almost two centuries. The reasons for this include (a) the historical foundations of the system, (b) political socialization and party identification, (c) the commonality of views among Americans, (d) the winner-take-all electoral system, and (e) state and federal laws favoring the two-party system. For these reasons, minor parties have found it extremely difficult to win elections.

7 Minor parties have emerged from time to time, often as dissatisfied splinter groups from within major parties, and have acted as barometers of changes in the political mood. Splinter parties, or factions, usually have emerged when a particular personality was at odds with the major party, as when Teddy Roosevelt's differences with the Republican Party resulted in the formation of the Bull Moose Progressive Party. Numerous other minor parties, such as the Prohibition Party, have formed around single issues.

8 From 1937 to the present, independent voters have formed an increasing proportion of the electorate, with a consequent decline of strongly Democratic or strongly Republican voters. Minor parties have also had a serious impact on the outcome of elections. In 1998, a Reform Party candidate won the governorship in Minnesota. In 2000, Green Party candidate Ralph Nader took some of the votes that otherwise would have gone to Democratic candidate Al Gore.

9 An important question today is whether the parties are fulfilling the functions of political parties as outlined in this chapter. The Democrats have found it difficult to serve as the "loyal opposition" with respect to the war on terrorism. Party polarization, particularly with respect to economic issues, has led some to conclude that we are experiencing an era of hyperpartisanship that may lead to increasing public discontent with the parties.

Selected Print and Media Resources

SUGGESTED READINGS

Baer, Kenneth S. *Reinventing Democrats.* Lawrence, Kans.: University Press of Kansas, 2000. This book traces the movement of the Democratic Party to a more moderate, centrist position under the leadership of southern moderates such as Bill Clinton.

Cohen, Jeffrey E., Richard Fleisher, and Paul Kantor, eds. *American Political Parties.* Washington, D.C.: CQ Press, 2001. This collection of essays examines the elements of political parties, party changes through realignments and dealignments, and party responsibilities in a democratic government.

Feulner, Edwin J., Jr., ed. *Leadership for America: The Principles of Conservatism.* Dallas, Tex.: Spence Publishing Co., 2000. This collection of essays explores the major principles of conservatism and their importance for American political leadership and democratic government.

Horowitz, David. *The Art of Political War and Other Radical Pursuits.* Dallas, Tex.: Spence Publishing Co., 2000. The author, a former left-wing radical, contends that the Democratic Party's electoral dominance in recent years is due not to the issues that it supports or to its "theft" of Republican issues but to its greater mastery of "the art of political war."

Reynolds, David. *Democracy Unbound: Progressive Challenges to the Two Party System.* Boston: South End Press, 1997. The author explores the roots of discontent within the electorate that support the formation of political parties.

Sifry, Micah L. *Spoiling for a Fight: Third-Party Politics in America.* Florence, Ky.: Routledge, 2002. The author looks closely at Ralph Nader's run for the presidency in 2000 and at the importance and potential of alternative parties in American politics and government.

MEDIA RESOURCES

The American President—A 1995 film starring Michael Douglas as a president who must balance partisanship and friendship (Republicans in Congress promise to approve the president's crime bill only if he modifies an environmental plan sponsored by his liberal girlfriend).

The Best Man—A 1964 drama based on Gore Vidal's play of the same name. The film, which deals with political smear campaigns by presidential party nominees, focuses on political party power and ethics.

The Last Hurrah—A classic 1958 political film starring Spencer Tracy as a corrupt politician who seeks his fifth nomination for mayor of a city in New England.

A Third Choice—A film that examines America's experience with third parties and independent candidates throughout the nation's political history.

Your CD-ROM Resources

In addition to the chapter content containing hot links, the following resources are available on the CD-ROM:

- **Internet Activities**—Third parties in American politics.

- **Critical Thinking Exercises**—"Question Time," party platforms, Mayor Richard J. Daley.

- **Self-Check on Important Themes**—Can You Answer These?

- **Animated Figures**—Figure 9–4, "The Rise of the Republican South," Figure 9–5, "Party Identification from 1937 to the Present."

- **Video**—*Democrats in 1992, Republicans 2000.*

- **Public Opinion Data**—Find contrasting views on the possibility of a third party president and the "vote of no-confidence."

- **InfoTrac Exercise**—"It's Not Easy Being Green."

- **Simulation**—You Are There!

- **Participation Exercise**—Take an online quiz to determine which party is most compatible with your ideology.

- **MicroCase Exercise**—"By the Numbers: Who Are the Republicans and Democrats?"

- **Additional Resources**—Abraham Lincoln, *Letter to Henry L. Pierce and Others* (1859), Newt Gingrich, *The Contract with America* (1994).

e-mocracy

Political Parties and the Internet

Today's political parties all use the Internet to attract voters, organize campaigns, obtain campaign contributions, and the like. Voters, in turn, can go online to learn more about specific parties and their programs. Those who use the Internet for information on the parties, though, need to exercise some caution. Besides the parties' official sites, there are satirical sites mimicking the parties, sites distributing misleading information about the parties, and sites that are raising money for their own causes rather than for political parties.

Logging On

The Democratic Party is online at

http://www.democrats.org/index.html

The Republican National Committee is at

http://www.rnc.org

The Libertarian Party has a Web site at

http://www.lp.org

The Socialist Party in the United States can be found at

http://sp-usa.org

Politics1.com offers extensive information on U.S. political parties, including the major parties and fifty minor parties. Go to

http://www.politics1.com/parties.htm

The Pew Research Center for the People and the Press offers survey data online on how the parties fared during the most recent elections, voter typology, and numerous other issues. To access this site, go to

http://www.people-press.org

Using the Internet for Political Analysis

Access the home pages of both the Democratic and Republican Parties using the URLs given in the *Logging On*. List at least three major differences in the policies and approaches to government of the two parties. Then look at the home page for one of the other parties—such as the Libertarian, Socialist Workers', Green, or Populist Party—and compare the policy positions you find there with those of the major parties. What other kinds of information truly differentiate the major parties from the minor ones? To what extent do the two major parties manage to ignore or minimize the importance of any other parties? How do the goals of the major parties differ from those of the minor parties?

VOTER REGISTRATION

BACKGROUND

Voting mechanisms and ballots vary extensively from state to state in our federal system. Indeed, the physical act of voting varies from county to county within one state. Nationwide, one-third of the voters use punch-card devices. Another third use optical-scanning equipment. The remaining third use levered mechanical voting machines and mail-in ballots. Some voting systems appear to be better than others.

The Constitution does not give Congress any role in the conduct of federal elections. Consequently, we would have to pass a constitutional amendment before the federal government could establish a national uniform voting system.

WHAT IF WE HAD A NATIONAL ELECTION SYSTEM?

After the 2000 elections, the variation in voting systems around the country was widely publicized. Many systems, such as punch-card balloting, drew heavy criticism for being outdated and inefficient. As a result, the idea of a national election system, overseen by the federal government, found significant support among the public. According to a CBS News poll, 71 percent of respondents wanted the federal government to institute a uniform method of voting. According to an ABC News/*Washington Post* poll, 61 percent felt the same way.*

What would happen if the federal government was able to pass legislation requiring a uniform method of voting throughout all counties? Most likely, all mechanical-type voting machines would be replaced by optical-scanning equipment. Immediately, money would be an issue. In Florida alone, when such a bill was signed into law in 2001, the state had to set aside $25 million for counties to buy the new equipment.

THE ISSUE OF RECOUNTS

Every jurisdiction in America seems to have different rules for when a recount is required. Some jurisdictions require recounts when a candidate's margin of victory over her or his opponent is within 1 percent; others require recounts when the margin is less than 0.5 percent. A national election system might follow the most recent Florida election reform law, which requires a *machine* recount if the margin of victory is 0.5 percent or less. Florida also requires a *manual* recount of the overvotes and undervotes if the margin is 0.25 percent or less. Overvotes and under-

*These results are from a CBS News poll conducted on December 9–10, 2001, and an ABC News/*Washington Post* poll conducted on December 14, 2000.

votes occur when voting machines pick up multiple choices or no clear choices. Still left to be decided would be how manual recounters would make decisions regarding ambiguous ballots, such as those with partially erased choices.

TOWARD MORE EQUALITY IN VOTING

After the 2000 presidential elections, some critics argued that the voting systems used in a number of districts discriminated against certain voters. For example, poorer areas seemed to be using more outdated and inefficient voting equipment or techniques, such as punch-card ballots. Some potential voters claimed they were turned away from the polls because there was no record of their registrations. Other prospective voters claimed that they were denied physical access to the polls because of their race. Some contend that a national system in which all jurisdictions would use the same equipment with the same rules would curb such discrimination at the voting booth.

CONSTITUTIONAL ISSUES REMAIN

Constitutional scholars do not believe that the federal government can simply pass a uniform national voting system law. The Constitution not only left state elections to state officials but also put federal elections in state hands. Given this nation's long history of federalism in which the states have autonomy from the central government in certain areas, shifting all control over elections to the national government might prove to be a difficult task indeed.

FOR CRITICAL ANALYSIS

1. The cost of an electronic-type voting machine ranges from $4,000 to $7,000. Who would pay for the "upgrade" in our voting systems?
2. What are some of the costs involved in recounts?

The culmination of the democratic political process is the election in which the winner does take all. Prior to that election are many months during which the parties nominate their candidates and then those candidates conduct their campaigns. The nomination process differs depending on the office and even on the political party. In contrast, the campaign process has become more standardized—even though the messages may differ—as television has come to dominate that activity. The process of voting itself varies widely, as Americans found out, to their chagrin, in the hotly contested 2000 presidential elections. Indeed, some have called for a national voting system, as we pointed out in this chapter's *What If . . .* feature.

The demand for reform with respect to nominations, campaigns, and voting procedures has grown in the last several decades. Campaign reform bills have continuously been put before the state and federal legislatures. In 2002, one was even passed by Congress. Campaign costs continue to rise, however, and a large portion of campaign war chests goes toward political advertising on television. Although free air time for candidates has been proposed as a way to reduce the costs of campaigning, we probably will not see such reform in the near future. You will read about other proposed reforms later in this chapter.

The People Who Run for Office

For democracy to work, there must be candidates for office, and for voters to have a choice, there must be competing candidates for most offices. The presidential campaign provides the most colorful and exciting look at these candidates and how they prepare to compete for the highest office in the land. The men and women who wanted to be candidates in the 2000 presidential campaign faced a long and obstacle-filled

George W. Bush and wife Laura rally voters during the 2000 presidential campaign. Such large public events are carefully staged to gain maximum television exposure for a candidate while at the same time encouraging those in the audience to vote for the candidate. Why is television exposure so important today? (AP Photo/Eric Draper)

Presidential Primary
A statewide primary election of delegates to a political party's national convention to help a party determine its presidential nominee. Such delegates are either pledged to a particular candidate or unpledged.

path. First, they needed to raise enough money to tour the nation, particularly the states with early **presidential primaries**, to see if they had enough local supporters. They needed funds to create an organization, devise a plan to win primary votes, and win the party's nomination at the national convention. Finally, they needed funds to finance a successful campaign for president. Always, at every turn, was the question of whether they would have enough funds to wage a campaign.

Why They Run

People who choose to run for office can be divided into two groups—those who are "self-starters" and those who are recruited. The volunteers, or self-starters, get involved in political activities to further their careers, to carry out specific political programs, or in response to certain issues or events. The campaign of Senator Eugene McCarthy in 1968 to deny Lyndon Johnson's renomination grew out of McCarthy's opposition to the Vietnam War. H. Ross Perot's runs for the presidency in 1992 and in 1996 were a response to public alienation and discontent with the major parties' candidates. Ralph Nader's campaign for the presidency in 2000 was rooted in his belief that the two major parties were ignoring vital issues, such as environmental protection and the influence of corporate wealth on American politics.

Issues are important, but self-interest and personal goals—status, career objectives, prestige, and income—are central in motivating some candidates to enter political life. Political office is often seen as the steppingstone to achieving certain career goals. A lawyer or an insurance agent may run for office only once or twice and then return to private life with enhanced status. Other politicians may aspire to long-term political office—for example, county offices such as commissioner or sheriff sometimes offer attractive opportunities for power, status, and income and are in themselves career goals. Finally, we think of ambition as the desire for ever more important offices and higher status. Politicians who run for lower offices and then set their sights on Congress or a governorship may be said to have "progressive" ambitions.[1]

We tend to pay far more attention to the flamboyant politician or to the personal characteristics of those with presidential ambitions than to their colleagues who compete for lower offices. But it is important to note that there are far more oppor-

[1] See the discussion of this topic in Linda Fowler, *Candidates, Congress, and the American Democracy* (Ann Arbor, Mich.: University of Michigan Press, 1993), pp. 56–59.

Dwight D. Eisenhower campaigns for president in 1952. Why do few presidential candidates take the time to ride in parades today? (Minnesota Historical Society)

tunities to run for office than there are citizens eager to take advantage of them. To fill the slate of candidates for election to such offices as mosquito-abatement district commissioner, the political party must recruit individuals to run. The problem of finding candidates is compounded in states or cities where the majority party is so dominant that the minority-party candidates have virtually no chance of winning. In these situations, candidates are recruited by party leaders on the basis of loyalty to the organization and civic duty.

Who Is Eligible?

There are few constitutional restrictions on who can become a candidate in the United States. As detailed in the Constitution, the formal requirements for a national office are as follows:

1. *President.* Must be a natural-born citizen, have attained the age of thirty-five years, and be a resident of the country for fourteen years by the time of inauguration.
2. *Vice president.* Must be a natural-born citizen, have attained the age of thirty-five years, and not be a resident of the same state as the candidate for president.
3. *Senator.* Must be a citizen for at least nine years, have attained the age of thirty by the time of taking office, and be a resident of the state from which elected.
4. *Representative.* Must be a citizen for at least seven years, have attained the age of twenty-five by the time of taking office, and be a resident of the state from which elected. *& district.*

The qualifications for state legislators are set by the state constitutions and likewise relate to age, place of residence, and citizenship. (Usually, the requirements for the upper chamber of a legislature are somewhat higher than those for the lower chamber.) The legal qualifications for running for governor or other state office are similar.

Who Runs? In spite of these minimal legal qualifications for office at both the national and state levels, a quick look at the slate of candidates in any election—or at the current members of the U.S. House of Representatives—will reveal that not all

One of the many "firsts" of the 2000 elections was the campaign of a former First Lady for a seat in Congress. Hillary Rodham Clinton succeeded in garnering enough votes to win a contest in New York for one of that state's seats in the U.S. Senate. (AP Photo/Kathy Willens)

segments of the population take advantage of these opportunities. Holders of political office in the United States are overwhelmingly white and male. Until the twentieth century, politicians were also predominantly of northern European origin and predominantly Protestant. Laws enforcing segregation in the South and many border states, as well as laws that effectively denied voting rights, made it impossible to elect African American public officials in many areas in which African Americans constituted a significant portion of the population. As a result of the passage of major civil rights legislation in the last several decades, the number of African American public officials has increased throughout the United States.

Until recently, women generally were considered to be appropriate candidates only for lower-level offices, such as state legislator or school board member. The last ten years have seen a tremendous increase in the number of women who run for office, not only at the state level but for the U.S. Congress as well. Figure 10–1 shows the increase in female candidates. (In 2002, 135 women ran for Congress, and 62 were elected.) Whereas African Americans were restricted from running for office by both law and custom, women generally were excluded by the agencies of recruitment—parties and interest groups. Generally, women were not recruited because they had not worked their way up through the party organization or because they were thought to have no chance of winning. Women also had a more difficult time raising campaign funds. Today, it is clear that women are just as likely as men to participate in many political activities, and a majority of Americans say they would vote for a qualified woman or for an African American for president of the United States.

Professional Status.   Not only are candidates for office more likely to be male and white than female or African American, but they are also likely to be professionals, particularly lawyers. Political campaigning and officeholding are simply easier for some occupational and economic groups than for others, and political involvement can make a valuable contribution to certain careers. Lawyers, for example, have more flexible schedules than do other professionals, can take time off for campaigning, and

FIGURE 10–1

Women Running for Congress

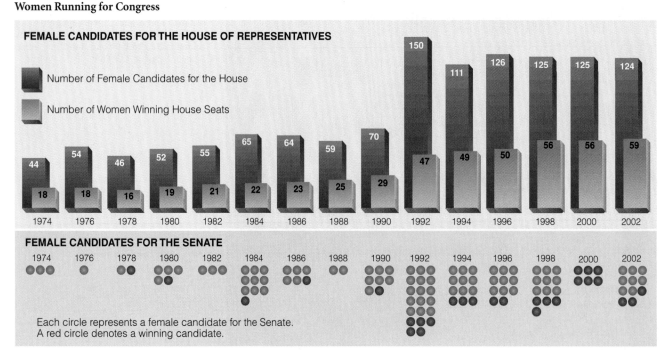

can leave their jobs to hold public office full-time. Furthermore, holding political office is good publicity for their professional practice, and they usually have partners or associates to keep the firm going while they are in office. Perhaps most important, many jobs that lawyers aspire to—federal or state judgeships, state attorney offices, or work in a federal agency—can be attained by political appointment. Such appointments most likely go to loyal partisans who have served their party by running for and holding office. Personal ambitions, then, are well served for certain groups by entering the political arena, whereas it could be a sacrifice for others whose careers demand full-time attention for many years.

The Modern Campaign Machine

American political campaigns are extravagant, year-long events that produce campaign buttons and posters for collectors, hours of film and sound to be relayed by the media, and, eventually, winning candidates who become the public officials of the nation. Campaigns are also enormously expensive; the total expenditures for 2002 were estimated to be several billion dollars for all congressional and local races in that year. Political campaigns exhaust candidates, their staff members, and the journalists covering the campaign—to say nothing of the public's patience.

The Changing Campaign

Campaigns seem to be getting longer and more excessive each year. The goal of the frantic activity is the same for all campaigns—to convince voters to choose a candidate or a slate of candidates for office. Part of the reason for the increased intensity of campaigns in the last decade is that they have changed from being centered on the party to being centered on the candidate. The candidate-centered campaign emerged in response to several developments: changes in the electoral system, the increased importance of television in campaigns, technological innovations such as computers, and the increased cost of campaigning.

INFOTRAC ®
COLLEGE EDITION

For updates on the 2002 elections, use the term "elections" in the Subject guide, and then go to subdivision "2002."

These campaign workers have volunteered their time to support the candidacy of Congresswoman Loretta Sanchez, a Democrat from California who was reelected to her fourth term in 2002. Political parties and candidates at all levels would have a difficult time conducting their campaigns without such volunteers. Volunteering for a campaign is one way to participate actively in the political process, to learn more about it, and to take advantage of one's rights as a citizen. (John Nourok/PhotoEdit)

A volunteer campaign worker uses the telephone to collect polling information from potential voters. (Bob Dammerich/Stock Boston)

Political Consultant
A paid professional hired to devise a campaign strategy and manage a campaign. Image building is the crucial task of the political consultant.

To run a successful and persuasive campaign, the candidate's organization must be able to raise funds for the effort, get coverage from the media, produce and pay for political commercials and advertising, schedule the candidate's time effectively with constituent groups and prospective supporters, convey the candidate's position on the issues, conduct research on the opposing candidate, and get the voters to go to the polls. When party identification was stronger among voters and before the advent of television campaigning, a strong party organization on the local, state, or national level could furnish most of the services and expertise that the candidate needed. Political parties provided the funds for campaigning until the 1970s. Parties used their precinct organizations to distribute literature, register voters, and get out the vote on election day. Less effort was spent on advertising for a single candidate's positions and character, because the party label communicated that information to many of the voters.

One of the reasons that campaigns no longer depend on parties is that fewer people identify with them (see Chapter 9), as is evident from the increased number of political independents. In 1952, about one-fifth of adults identified themselves as independents, whereas in 2002, about one-third classified themselves as independents. Political independents include not only adults who are well educated and issue oriented, but also many adults who are not very interested in politics or well informed about candidates or issues.

The Professional Campaign

Whether the candidate is running for the state legislature, for the governor's office, for the U.S. Congress, or for the presidency, every campaign has some fundamental tasks to accomplish. Today, most of these tasks are put into the hands of paid professionals rather than volunteers or amateur politicians.

The most sought-after and possibly the most criticized campaign expert is the **political consultant,** who, for a large fee, devises a campaign strategy, thinks up a campaign theme, and possibly chooses the campaign colors and candidate's portrait for all literature to be distributed. Political consultants began to displace volunteer campaign managers in the 1960s, about the same time that television became a force in campaigns. The paid consultant monitors the campaign's progress, plans all media appearances, and coaches the candidate for debates. The consultants and the firms they represent are not politically neutral; most will work only for candidates from one party or only for candidates of a particular ideological persuasion.

The Strategy of Winning

The goal of every political campaign is the same: to win the election. In the United States, unlike some European countries, there are no rewards for a candidate who comes in second; the winner takes all. The campaign organization must plan a strategy that maximizes the candidate's chances of winning. In American politics, candidates are guided by this basic wisdom: they seek to capture all the votes of their party members, to convince a majority of the independent voters to vote for them, and to gain a few votes from members of the other party. To accomplish these goals, candidates must consider their visibility, their message, and their campaign strategy.

Candidate Visibility and Appeal

One of the most important concerns is how well known the candidate is. If she or he is a highly visible incumbent, there may be little need for campaigning except to remind the voters of the officeholder's good deeds. If, however, the candidate is an unknown challenger or a largely unfamiliar character attacking a well-known public figure, the campaign must devise a strategy to get the candidate before the public.

In the case of the independent candidate or the candidate representing a minor party, the problem of name recognition is serious. There are usually a number of third-party candidates in each presidential election. Such candidates must present an overwhelming case for the voter to reject the major-party candidate. Both the Democratic and the Republican candidates use the strategic ploy of labeling third-party candidates as "not serious" and therefore not worth the voter's time.

The Use of Opinion Polls

One of the major sources of information for both the media and the candidates is opinion polls. Poll taking is widespread during the primaries. Presidential hopefuls have private polls taken to make sure that there is at least some chance they could be nominated and, if nominated, elected. Also, because the party nominees depend on polls to fine-tune their campaigns, during the presidential campaign itself continual polls are taken. Polls are taken not only by the regular pollsters—Roper, Harris, Gallup, and others—but also privately by each candidate's campaign organization. These private polls, as opposed to the independent public polls conducted by Gallup and others, are for the exclusive and secret use of the candidate and his or her campaign organization.

As the election approaches, many candidates use **tracking polls,** which are polls taken almost every day, to find out how well they are competing for votes. Tracking polls enable consultants to fine-tune the advertising and the candidate's speeches in the last days of the campaign.

Focus Groups

Another tactic is to use a **focus group** to gain insights into public perceptions of the candidate. Professional consultants organize a discussion of the candidate or of certain political issues among ten to fifteen ordinary citizens. The citizens are selected from certain target groups in the population—for example, working men, blue-collar men, senior citizens, or young voters. The group discusses personality traits of the candidate, political advertising, and other candidate-related issues. The conversation is videotaped (and often observed from behind a mirrored wall). Focus groups are expected to reveal more emotional responses to candidates or the deeper anxieties of voters—feelings that consultants believe often are not tapped by more impersonal telephone surveys. The campaign then can shape its messages to respond to these feelings and perceptions.

Financing the Campaign

In a book published in 1932 entitled *Money in Elections,* Louise Overacker had the following to say about campaign financing:

> The financing of elections in a democracy is a problem which is arousing increasing concern. Many are beginning to wonder if present-day methods of raising and spending campaign funds do not clog the wheels of our elaborately constructed mechanism of popular control, and if democracies do not inevitably become [governments ruled by small groups].[2]

Although writing more than seventy years ago, Overacker touched on a sensitive issue in American political campaigns—the connection between money and elections. It is estimated that over $3 billion was spent at all levels of campaigning in the 1999–2000 election cycle. At the federal level alone, a total of more than $500 million

George W. Bush attends a fund-raising event during the 2000 election campaign. (Rick Wilking/Getty Images)

Tracking Poll
A poll taken for the candidate on a nearly daily basis as election day approaches.

Focus Group
A small group of individuals who are led in discussion by a professional consultant to gather opinions on and responses to candidates and issues.

---

[2] Louise Overacker, *Money in Elections* (New York: Macmillan, 1932), p. vii.

Corrupt Practices Acts
A series of acts passed by Congress in an attempt to limit and regulate the size and sources of contributions and expenditures in political campaigns.

Hatch Act
An act passed in 1939 that prohibited a political group from spending more than $3 million in any campaign and limited individual contributions to a committee to $5,000. The act was designed to control political influence buying.

is estimated to have been spent in races for the House of Representatives, $300 million in senatorial races, and $800 million in the presidential campaign. Except for the presidential campaigns, all of the other money had to be provided by the candidates and their families, borrowed, or raised by contributions from individuals or political action committees (as discussed in Chapter 8). For the presidential campaigns, some of the money comes from the federal government.

Regulating Campaign Financing

The way in which campaigns are financed has changed dramatically in the last two and a half decades, and today candidates and political parties, when trying to increase their funding sources, must operate within the constraints imposed by complicated laws regulating campaign financing.

There have been a variety of federal **corrupt practices acts** designed to regulate campaign financing. The first, passed in 1925, limited primary and general election expenses for congressional candidates. In addition, it required disclosure of election expenses and, in principle, put controls on contributions by corporations. Numerous loopholes were found in the restrictions on contributions, and the acts proved to be ineffective.

The **Hatch Act** (Political Activities Act) of 1939 was passed in another attempt to control political influence buying. That act forbade a political group to spend more than $3 million in any campaign and limited individual contributions to a political group to $5,000. Of course, such restrictions were easily circumvented by creating additional political groups.

In the 1970s, Congress passed legislation that reshaped the nature of campaign financing. In 1971, it passed a law reforming the process. Then in 1974, in the wake of the Watergate scandal (see Chapter 7), Congress enacted further reforms.

The Federal Election Campaign Act

The Federal Election Campaign Act (FECA) of 1971, which became effective in 1972, essentially replaced all past laws and instituted a major reform. The act placed no limit on overall spending but restricted the amount that could be spent on mass-media advertising, including television. It limited the amount that candidates and their families could contribute to their own campaigns and required disclosure of all contributions and expenditures in excess of $100. In principle, the FECA limited the role of labor unions and corporations in political campaigns. It also provided for a voluntary $1 check-off on federal income tax returns for general campaign funds to be used by major-party presidential candidates (first applied in the 1976 campaign).

Further Reforms in 1974. For many, the 1971 act did not go far enough. Amendments to the FECA passed in 1974 did the following:

1. *Created the Federal Election Commission.* This commission consists of six nonpartisan administrators whose duties are to enforce compliance with the requirements of the act.
2. *Provided public financing for presidential primaries and general elections.* Any candidate running for president who is able to obtain sufficient contributions in at least twenty states can obtain a subsidy from the U.S. Treasury to help pay for primary campaigns. For example, each major party was given $15 million for its national convention in 2000. The major-party candidates have federal support for almost all of their expenses, provided they are willing to accept campaign-spending limits.
3. *Limited presidential campaign spending.* Any candidate accepting federal support has to agree to limit campaign expenditures to the amount prescribed by federal law.
4. *Limited contributions.* Under the 1974 amendments, citizens could contribute up to $1,000 to each candidate in each federal election or primary; the total limit on all

contributions from an individual to all candidates was $25,000 per year. Groups could contribute up to a maximum of $5,000 to a candidate in any election. (As you will read shortly, some of these limits were changed by the 2002 campaign reform legislation.)

5. *Required disclosure.* Each candidate must file periodic reports with the Federal Election Commission, listing who contributed, how much was spent, and for what the money was spent.

The 1976 Amendments. Further amendments to the FECA in 1976 allowed corporations, labor unions, and special interest groups to set up political action committees (PACs) to raise money for candidates. For a PAC to be legitimate, the money must be raised from at least fifty volunteer donors and must be given to at least five candidates in the federal election. Each corporation or each union is limited to one PAC. As you might imagine, corporate PACs obtain funds from executives, employees, and stockholders in their firms, and unions obtain PAC funds from their members.[3]

Buckley v. Valeo. The 1971 act had also limited the amount that each individual could spend on his or her own behalf. The Supreme Court declared the provision unconstitutional in 1976, in *Buckley v. Valeo*,[4] stating that it was unconstitutional to restrict in any way the amount congressional candidates or their immediate families could spend on their own behalf: "The candidate, no less than any other person, has a First Amendment right to engage in the discussion of public issues and vigorously and tirelessly to advocate his own election."

The *Buckley v. Valeo* decision, which has often been criticized, was directly countered by a 1997 Vermont law. The law, known as Act 64, imposed spending limits ranging from $2,000 to $300,000 (depending on the office sought) by candidates for

---

[3] See Paul Allen Beck, *Party Politics in America*, 8th ed. (New York: Longman Publishers, 1997), p. 285.
[4] 424 U.S. 1 (1976).

This photograph of George W. Bush was taken by an official White House photographer aboard Air Force One on September 11, 2001. It was later used by the Republican Party to raise campaign funds—the photo was offered by the Republican House and Senate campaign committees to anyone paying $150 to attend a party dinner. It has become common for such mementos of a presidency to be used in raising campaign funds. Do you think giving this photo to campaign donors is a legitimate technique for obtaining campaign contributions or an exploitation of the terrorist attacks, as many Democrats claimed later? (AP Photo/Eric Draper)

state offices in Vermont. A number of groups, including the American Civil Liberties Union and the Republican Party, challenged the act, claiming that it violated the First Amendment's guarantee of free speech. In landmark decision in August 2002, a federal appellate court disagreed and upheld the law. The court stated that Vermont has shown that, without spending limits, "the fundraising practices in Vermont will continue to impair the accessibility which is essential to any democratic political system. The race for campaign funds has compelled public officials to give preferred access to contributors, selling their time in order to raise campaign funds."[5]

The court's decision opened the door to further controversy over the Supreme Court's ruling in *Buckley v. Valeo*. Ultimately, the Supreme Court may have to revisit that ruling and re-evaluate the issue of whether spending limits violate the First Amendment.

Campaign Financing beyond the Limits

Within a few years after the establishment of the tight limits on contributions, new ways to finance campaigns were developed that skirted the reforms and made it possible for huge sums of money to be raised, especially by the major political parties.

Contributions to Political Parties.   As discussed in Chapter 8, candidates, PACs, and political parties have found ways to generate *soft money*—that is, campaign contributions to political parties that escaped the rigid limits of federal election law. Although the FECA limited contributions that would be spent on elections, there were no limits on contributions to political parties for party activities such as voter education or voter-registration drives. This loophole enabled the parties to raise millions of dollars from corporations and individuals. It was not unusual for some corporations to give more than a million dollars to the Democratic National Committee or to the Republican Party.[6] As shown in Table 10–1, nearly twice as much soft money was raised in the 1999–2000 presidential election cycle as in the previous (1995–1996) presidential election cycle. The parties then spent this money for their conventions, for registering voters, and for advertising to promote the general party position. The parties also sent a great deal of the money to state and local party organizations, which used it to support their own tickets.

Although soft money was outlawed after election day 2002 (as you will read shortly), political parties saw no contradiction in raising and spending as much soft money as possible during this election cycle. By October 2002, the parties together had raised more than $400 million in soft money, four times as much as they had raised eight years before. President George Bush raised even more money for his party than Bill Clinton had raised for the Democrats in prior election cycles.

[5] *Landell v. Vermont Public Interest Research Group*, 300 F.3d 129 (2d Cir. 2002).
[6] Beck, *Party Politics in America*, pp. 293–294.

TABLE 10–1

Soft Money Raised by Political Parties, 1994 to 2002

	1993–1994	1995–1996	1997–1998	1999–2000	2001–2002
Democratic Party	$ 45.6 million	$122.3 million	$ 92.8 million	$243.0 million	$199.6 million
Republican Party	59.5 million	141.2 million	131.6 million	244.4 million	221.7 million
Total	105.1 million	263.5 million	224.4 million	487.4 million	421.3 million

SOURCES: *Congressional Quarterly Weekly Report,* September 6, 1997, p. 2065; and authors' update.

Independent Expenditures. Business corporations, labor unions, and other interest groups discovered that it was legal to make **independent expenditures** in an election campaign so long as the expenditures were not coordinated with those of the candidate or political party. Hundreds of unique committees and organizations blossomed to take advantage of this campaign tactic. Although a 1990 United States Supreme Court decision, *Austin v. Michigan State Chamber of Commerce,*[7] upheld the right of the states and the federal government to limit independent, direct corporate expenditures (such as for advertisements) on behalf of *candidates,* the decision did not stop business and other types of groups from making independent expenditures on *issues.*

Indeed, issue advocacy—spending unregulated money on advertising that promotes positions on issues rather than candidates—has become a prevalent tactic in recent years. Interest groups routinely wage their own issue campaigns. For example, the Christian Coalition, which is incorporated, annually raises millions of dollars to produce and distribute voter guidelines and other direct-mail literature to describe candidates' positions on various issues and to promote its agenda. Although promoting issue positions is very close to promoting candidates who support those positions, the courts repeatedly have held, in accordance with the *Buckley v. Valeo* decision mentioned earlier, that interest groups have a First Amendment right to advocate their positions.

The Supreme Court clarified, in a 1996 decision,[8] that political parties may also make independent expenditures on behalf of candidates—as long as the parties do so *independently* of the candidates. In other words, the parties must not coordinate such expenditures with the candidates' campaigns or let the candidates know the specifics of how party funds are being spent.

Bundling. Yet another way to maximize contributions to a candidate or a party is through the practice of **bundling.** Bundling entails collecting the maximum individual contribution—$1,000 until 2002, when it was raised to $2,000—from a number of individuals in the same firm or family and then sending the quite large check to the candidate of choice. While this practice is in complete compliance with the law, it makes the candidate or party more aware of the source of the funding.

The effect of all of these strategies was to increase greatly the amount of money spent for campaigns and party activities. Critics of the system continued to wonder whether the voice of the individual voter or the small contributor was being drowned in the flood of big contributions. Although Congress considered reform measures every year, none was approved until 2002.

The Bipartisan Campaign Reform Act of 2002

Campaign reform had been in the air for so long that it was almost anticlimactic when President George W. Bush signed the Bipartisan Campaign Reform Act on March 27, 2002. This act, which amended the 1971 FECA, took effect on the day after the congressional elections were held on November 5, 2002.

Key Elements of the New Law. The 2002 law bans the large, unlimited contributions to national political parties that are known as soft money. It places curbs on, but does not entirely eliminate, the use of campaign ads by outside special interest groups advocating the election or defeat of specific candidates. Such ads are allowed up to sixty days before a general election and up to thirty days before a primary election.

In 1974, contributions by individuals to federal candidates were limited to $1,000 per individual. The 2002 act increased this limit to $2,000. In addition, the maximum

[7] 494 U.S. 652 (1990).
[8] *Colorado Republican Federal Campaign Committee v. Federal Election Commission,* 518 U.S. 604 (1996).

DID YOU KNOW...
That Abraham Lincoln sold pieces of fence rail that he had split as political souvenirs to finance his campaign?

Independent Expenditures
Nonregulated contributions from PACs, ideological organizations, and individuals. The groups may spend funds on advertising or other campaign activities so long as those expenditures are not coordinated with those of a candidate.

Bundling
The practice of adding together maximum individual campaign contributions to increase their impact on the candidate.

INFOTRAC®
COLLEGE EDITION

For updates and more information on this topic, use the term "campaign funds" in the Subject guide.

amount that an individual can give to all federal candidates was raised from $25,000 per year to $95,000 over a two-year election cycle.

The act did not ban soft money contributions to state and local parties. These parties can accept such contributions as long as they are limited to $10,000 per year per individual.

Consequences of the 2002 Act.   Certainly, one of the first consequences of the 2002 act will be constitutional challenges by groups negatively affected. Some observers believe that the Supreme Court will throw out the restrictions on campaign ads by special interest groups as limits on free speech.

In contrast, the regulation prohibiting the national parties from raising unregulated "soft dollars" will undoubtedly withstand all judicial challenges. This ban may have an unintended consequence, however. The two national parties have contributed to the stability of our political system by, in essence, usurping most minor parties and bringing almost everyone inside a "big tent." The strength of the Democrats and the Republicans has rested in part on their ability to raise large sums of money. Therefore, one unintended consequence of the 2002 campaign-financing reform law may be to undermine the stabilizing role of the two major parties. Without large amounts of soft money, the two major parties will no longer have the power they previously had to finance get-out-the-vote drives and phone banks. This task will fall to the state parties, which may not do such a good job.

Perhaps another unintended consequence of the campaign-financing reform bill will be that it benefits incumbents. We examine this issue in this chapter's *Politics and Campaigns* feature.

For updates and more information, use the term "campaign finance reform" in the Subject guide.

Running for President: The Longest Campaign

The American presidential election is the culmination of two different campaigns linked by the parties' national conventions. The presidential primary campaign lasts officially from January until June of the election year, and the final presidential campaign heats up around Labor Day.

Primary elections were first mandated in 1903 in Wisconsin. The purpose of the primary was to open the nomination process to ordinary party members and to weaken the influence of party bosses in the nomination process. Until 1968, however, there were fewer than twenty primary elections for the presidency. They were generally **"beauty contests"** in which the contending candidates for the nomination competed for popular votes, but the results had little or no impact on the selection of delegates to the national convention. National conventions were meetings of the party elite—legislators, mayors, county chairpersons, and loyal party workers—who were mostly appointed to their delegations. National conventions saw numerous trades and bargains among competing candidates, and the leaders of large blocs of delegate votes could direct their delegates to support a favorite candidate.

"Beauty Contest"
A presidential primary in which contending candidates compete for popular votes but the results have little or no impact on the selection of delegates to the national convention, which is made by the party elite.

Demonstrations outside the 1968 Democratic convention in Chicago. The demonstrations influenced the party to reform its delegate selection rules. (Paul Conklin/PhotoEdit)

Reforming the Primaries

In recent decades, the character of the primary process and the make-up of the national convention have changed dramatically. The mass public, rather than party elites, now generally controls the nomination process, owing to extraordinary changes in the party rules. After the disruptive riots outside the doors of the 1968 Democratic convention in Chicago, many party leaders pushed for serious reforms of the convention process. They saw the general dissatisfaction with the convention, and the riots in particular, as stemming from the inability of the average party member to influence the nomination system.

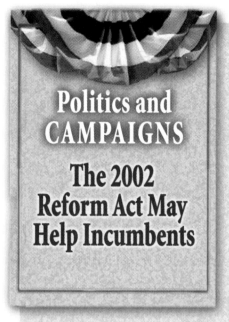

Politics and CAMPAIGNS

The 2002 Reform Act May Help Incumbents

When contributing soft money to political parties was legal, most of that money went into the campaigns that were the most competitive, or contested. Eliminating soft money may therefore make American elections less competitive.

HARD MONEY GOES TO INCUMBENTS

Most analyses show that "hard money," particularly campaign contri-butions made by PACs, goes to incumbents. In contrast, soft money typically has gone to credible challengers and sometimes vulnerable incumbents.[*] What this means is that the banning of soft money to the national parties will make it even more difficult for challengers in close races to succeed. Thus, in general, banning soft money will favor incumbents. Indeed, a number of journalists have referred to the law as the "Incumbent Protection Act."

BUSH IS A BENEFICIARY OF THE REFORM ACT

According to many political scientists, the biggest immediate beneficiary of the campaign-financing reform act will be President George W. Bush. In the last election, a group of Bush's back-ers, called the Pioneers, raised almost $115 million in private money. This was all hard money created by bun-dles of $1,000 individual contributions. Indeed, this was the most hard money ever raised in presidential campaign history. Now that the new law doubles the per-donor maximum to $2,000, the job of the Pioneers will become easier.

Bush will be able to maintain a large campaign fund while his Democratic opponent will have to spend considerable time and resources trying to match it. Why? The reason is that the Democratic Party will not have large amounts of soft money to support the Democratic presidential hopeful. Therefore, the Democratic nominee will have to seek more hard money—a difficult task because the Republicans have a larger hard-money donor base than the Democrats do.

FOR CRITICAL ANALYSIS

Does the end of soft-money contributions to the major political parties mean the end of political influence by special interest groups?

[*]Stephen Ansolabehere and J. N. Snyder, Jr., "Soft Money, Hard Money, Strong Parties," *Columbia Law Review,* Vol. 100 (April 2000), p. 610.

The Democratic National Committee appointed a special commission to study the problems of the primary system. Referred to as the McGovern-Fraser Commission, the group over the next several years formulated new rules for delegate selection that had to be followed by state Democratic Parties.

The reforms instituted by the Democratic Party, which were imitated in most states by the Republicans, revolutionized the nomination process for the presidency. The most important changes require that most convention delegates not be nomi-nated by the elites in either party; they must be elected by the voters in primary elec-tions, in **caucuses** held by local parties, or at state conventions. Delegates are mostly pledged to a particular candidate, although the pledge is not always formally binding at the convention. The delegation from each state must also include a proportion of women, younger party members, and representatives of the minority groups within the party. At first, virtually no special privileges were given to elected party officials, such as senators or governors. In 1984, however, many of these officials returned to the Democratic convention as **superdelegates.**

Types of Primaries

Not only do the states and state parties use different devices for nominations, but they also may hold different types of primary elections. Among the most common types are those discussed here.

Caucus
A closed meeting of party leaders to select party candidates or to decide on policy; also, a meeting of party members designed to select candidates and propose policies.

Superdelegate
A party leader or elected official who is given the right to vote at the party's national convention. Superdelegates are not elected at the state level.

Closed Primary. In a *closed primary,* the selection of a party's candidates in an election is limited to avowed or declared party members. In other words, voters must declare their party affiliation, either when they register to vote or at the primary election. A closed-primary system tries to make sure that registered voters cannot cross over into the other party's primary in order to nominate the weakest candidate of the opposing party or to affect the ideological direction of that party.

Open Primary. An *open primary* is a primary in which voters can vote in either party primary without disclosing their party affiliation. Basically, the voter makes the choice in the privacy of the voting booth. The voter must, however, choose one party's list from which to select candidates. Open primaries place no restrictions on independent voters.

Blanket Primary. A *blanket primary* is one in which the voter may vote for candidates of more than one party. Alaska, Louisiana, and Washington have blanket primaries. Blanket-primary campaigns may be much more costly because each candidate for every office is trying to influence all the voters, not just those in his or her party.

In 2000, the United States Supreme Court issued a decision that will alter significantly the use of the blanket primary. The case arose when political parties in California challenged the constitutionality of a 1996 ballot initiative authorizing the use of the blanket primary in that state. The parties contended that the blanket primary violated their First Amendment right of association. Because the nominees represent the party, they argued, party members—not the general electorate—should have the right to choose the party's nominee. The Supreme Court ruled in favor of the parties, holding that the blanket primary violated parties' First Amendment associational rights.[9]

The Court's ruling called into question the constitutional validity of blanket primaries in other states as well. The question before these states now is how to devise a primary election system that will comply with the Supreme Court's ruling yet offer independent voters a chance to participate in the primary elections.

Run-off Primary. Some states have a two-primary system. If no candidate receives a majority of the votes in the first primary, the top two candidates must compete in another primary, called a *run-off primary.*

Front-Loading the Primaries

As soon as politicians and potential presidential candidates realized that winning as many primary elections as possible guaranteed the party's nomination for president, their tactics changed dramatically. For example, candidates running in the 2000 primaries, such as John McCain, concentrated on building organizations in states that held early, important primary elections. Candidates realized that winning early primaries, such as the New Hampshire election in February, or finishing first in the Iowa caucus meant that the media instantly would label the winner as the **front-runner,** thus increasing the candidate's media exposure and escalating the pace of contributions to his or her campaign fund.

Front-Runner
The presidential candidate who appears to have the most momentum at a given time in the primary season.

The Rush to Be First. The states and state political parties began to see that early primaries had a much greater effect on the outcome of the presidential election and, accordingly, began to hold their primaries earlier in the season to secure that advantage. While New Hampshire held on to its claim as the "first" primary, other states moved to the next week. The southern states decided to hold their primaries on the

---

[9] *California Democratic Party v. Jones,* 530 U.S. 567 (2000).

same date, known as **Super Tuesday,** in the hopes of nominating a moderate south-erner at the Democratic convention. When California, which had held the last pri-mary (in June), moved its primary to March, the primary season was curtailed drastically. Due to this process of **front-loading** the primaries, in 2000 the presiden-tial nominating process was over in March, with both George W. Bush and Al Gore having enough convention delegate votes to win their respective nominations. This meant that the campaign was essentially without news until the conventions in August, a gap that did not appeal to the politicians or the media. Both parties dis-cussed whether more changes in the primary process were necessary.

Consequences of Early Primaries. Despite the apparent problems with the front-loaded primary season in 2000, the Democratic Party has decided to hold some of its primaries even earlier in the 2003–2004 presidential election cycle. For example, the Democratic Iowa caucus will be advanced to January 19, to be followed eight days later by the New Hampshire primary. The Democrats' goal in moving up their pri-maries is obvious: settle on a candidate early so that she or he will have a long time during which to raise money to unseat the incumbent president, George W. Bush. Critics of this front-loaded system point out, though, that it no longer provides for careful evaluation of potential presidential candidates. No longer will candidates for each party's nomination receive months of questioning about their ideas, ideol-ogy, and character.

Another consequence of front-loading the primaries is that the closer we come to a national primary, the more the advantage goes to the candidate with the most resources. Some political scientists contend that any potential candidate without at least $25 million in his or her campaign chest by January 2004 will not be a serious player.

A little-considered effect of advancing the Iowa caucus and the New Hampshire primary is that the results will not reflect the cultural, ethnic, and racial diversity of the nation. Iowa is 94 percent white, and New Hampshire 96 percent white. As one commentator put it, "Iowa and New Hampshire are about as ethnically diverse as a reunion of Mayflower descendants." Yet these two states will be the only ones in which voters will get to see a variety of presidential hopefuls campaign in person.

On to the National Convention

Presidential candidates have been nominated by the convention method in every election since 1832. The delegates are sent from each state and are apportioned on the basis of state representation. Extra delegates are allowed to attend from states that had voting majorities for the party in the preceding elections. Parties also accept del-egates from the District of Columbia, the territories, and certain overseas groups.

Seating the Delegates. At the convention, each political party uses a **credentials committee** to determine which delegates may participate. The credentials committee usually prepares a roll of all delegates entitled to be seated. Controversy may arise when rival groups claim to be the official party organization for a county, district, or state. The Mississippi Democratic Party split along racial lines in 1964 at the height of the civil rights movement in the Deep South. Separate all-white and mixed white and African American sets of delegates were selected, and both factions showed up at the national convention. After much debate on party rules, the committee decided to seat the pro–civil rights delegates and exclude those who represented the traditional "white" party.

Convention Activities. The typical convention lasts only a few days. The first day consists of speech making, usually against the opposing party. During the second day, there are committee reports, and during the third day, there is presidential balloting.

Super Tuesday
The date on which a number of presidential primaries are held, including those of most of the southern states.

Front-Loading
The practice of moving presidential primary elections to the early part of the campaign, to maximize the impact of certain states or regions on the nomination.

Credentials Committee
A committee used by political parties at their national conventions to determine which delegates may participate. The committee inspects the claim of each prospective delegate to be seated as a legitimate representative of his or her state.

Because delegates generally arrive at the convention committed to presidential candidates, no convention since 1952 has required more than one ballot to choose a nominee. Since 1972, candidates have usually come into the convention with enough committed delegates to win. On the fourth day, a vice presidential candidate is usually nominated, and the presidential nominee gives the acceptance speech.

In 2000, the outcome of the two conventions was so predictable that the national networks televised the convention proceedings for no more than two hours each evening. The convention planners concentrated on showing off the most important speeches during that prime-time period. Gavel-to-gavel coverage was available at several Internet sites, however.

The Electoral College

Elector

A person on the partisan slate that is selected early in the presidential election year according to state laws and the applicable political party apparatus. Electors cast ballots for president and vice president. The number of electors in each state is equal to that state's number of representatives in both chambers of Congress.

Most voters who vote for the president and vice president think that they are voting directly for a candidate. In actuality, they are voting for **electors** who will cast their ballots in the electoral college. Article II, Section 1, of the Constitution outlines in detail the number and choice of electors for president and vice president. The framers of the Constitution wanted to avoid the selection of president and vice president by the excitable masses. Rather, they wished the choice to be made by a few supposedly dispassionate, reasonable men (but not women).

The Choice of Electors

Each state's electors are selected during each presidential election year. The selection is governed by state laws and by the applicable party apparatus. After the national party convention, the electors are pledged to the candidates chosen. The total number of electors today is 538, equal to 100 senators, 435 members of the House, plus 3 electors for the District of Columbia (subsequent to the Twenty-third Amendment, ratified in 1961). Each state's number of electors equals that state's number of senators (two) plus its number of representatives. The graphic in Figure 10–2 shows how the electoral votes are apportioned by state.

FIGURE 10–2

State Electoral Votes in 2000

The map of the United States shown here is distorted to show the relative weight of the states in terms of electoral votes in 2000. Considering that a candidate must win 270 electoral votes to be elected, presidential candidates plan their visits around the nation to maximize their exposure in the most important states. As vice president, Al Gore visited California numerous times in anticipation of the 2000 elections.

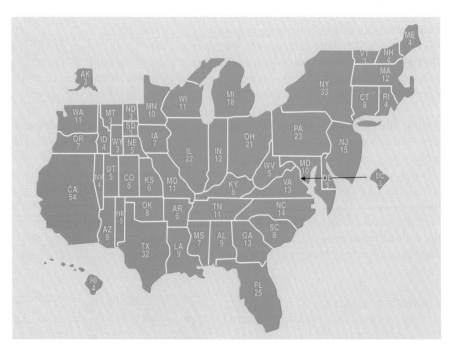

The Electors' Commitment

If a plurality of voters in a state chooses one slate of electors, then those electors are pledged to cast their ballots on the first Monday after the second Wednesday in December in the state capital for the presidential and vice presidential candidates of the winning party.[10] The Constitution does not, however, require the electors to cast their ballots for the candidates of their party.

The ballots are counted and certified before a joint session of Congress early in January. The candidates who receive a majority of the electoral votes (270) are certified as president-elect and vice president–elect. According to the Constitution, if no candidate receives a majority of the electoral votes, the election of the president is decided in the House from among the candidates with the three highest number of votes (decided by a plurality of each state delegation), each state having one vote. The selection of the vice president is determined by the Senate in a choice between the two highest candidates, each senator having one vote. Congress was required to choose the president and vice president in 1801 (Thomas Jefferson and Aaron Burr), and the House chose the president in 1825 (John Quincy Adams). The entire process is outlined in Figure 10–3.

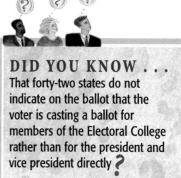

DID YOU KNOW . . .
That forty-two states do not indicate on the ballot that the voter is casting a ballot for members of the Electoral College rather than for the president and vice president directly **?**

---

[10] In Maine and Nebraska, electoral votes are based on congressional districts. Each district chooses one elector. The remaining two electors are chosen statewide.

FIGURE 10–3

How Presidents and Vice Presidents Are Chosen

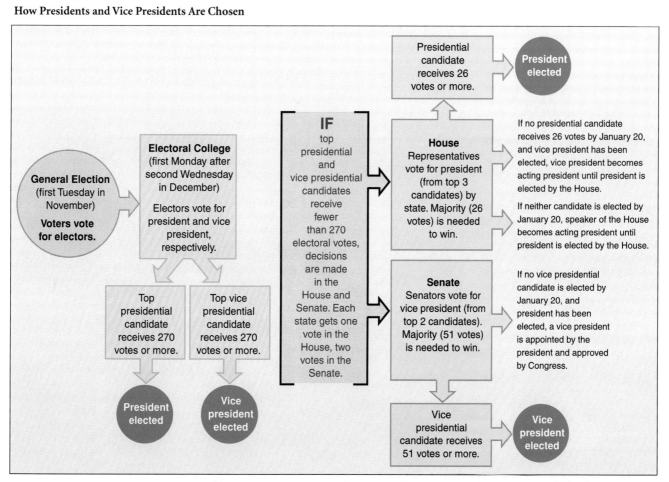

SOURCE: Adapted from Michael J. Glennon, *When No Majority Rules: The Electoral College and Presidential Succession* (Washington, D.C.: Congressional Quarterly Press, 1993), p. 20.

It is possible for a candidate to become president without obtaining a majority of the popular vote. There have been numerous minority presidents in our history, including Abraham Lincoln, Woodrow Wilson, Harry Truman, John F. Kennedy, Richard Nixon (in 1968), and Bill Clinton. Such an event can always occur when there are third-party candidates.

Perhaps more distressing is the possibility of a candidate's being elected when the opposing candidate receives a plurality of the popular vote. This has occurred on four occasions—in the elections of John Quincy Adams in 1824, Rutherford B. Hayes in 1876, Benjamin Harrison in 1888, and George W. Bush in 2000, all of whom won elections without obtaining a plurality of the popular vote.

Criticisms of the Electoral College

Besides the possibility of a candidate's becoming president even though his or her major opponent obtains more popular votes, there are other complaints about the electoral college. The idea of the Constitution's framers was to have electors use their own discretion to decide who would make the best president. But electors no longer perform the selecting function envisioned by the founders because they are committed to the candidate who has a plurality of popular votes in their state in the general election.[11]

One can also argue that the current system, which gives all of the electoral votes to the candidate who has a statewide plurality, is unfair to other candidates and their supporters. The current system of voting also means that presidential campaigning will be concentrated in those states that have the largest number of electoral votes and in those states in which the outcome is likely to be close. All of the other states generally get second-class treatment during the presidential campaign. It can also be argued that there is something of a less-populous-state bias in the electoral college, because including Senate seats in the electoral vote total partly offsets the edge of the

Members of Rhode Island's electoral college gathered on December 18, 2000, to vote for president. Although 32 percent of Rhode Island's popular vote went to George W. Bush and 6 percent to Ralph Nader, Rhode Island's four electors voted unanimously for Al Gore, who received 61 percent. Do you think the "winner-take-all" system in the electoral college is fair? How would you change it? (AP Photo/Victoria Arocho)

---

[11] Note, however, that there have been revolts by so-called *faithless electors*—in 1796, 1820, 1948, 1956, 1960, 1968, 1972, 1976, and 1988.

DID YOU KNOW...
That Texas's "LBJ Law" permits a U.S. senator to run for reelection to the Senate and run for president or vice president in the same election?

more populous states in the House. A state such as Alaska (with two senators and one representative) gets an electoral vote for roughly each 209,644 people (based on the 2000 census), whereas Iowa gets one vote for each 418,846 people, and New York has a vote for every 613,064 inhabitants.

Many proposals for reform of the electoral college system have been advanced, particularly after the turmoil resulting from the 2000 elections. The most obvious is to get rid of it completely and simply allow candidates to be elected on a popular-vote basis; in other words, have a direct election, by the people, for president and vice president. Because abolishing the electoral college would require a constitutional amendment, however, the chances of electing the president by a direct vote are remote.

The major parties are not in favor of eliminating the electoral college, fearing that it would give minor parties a more influential role. Also, less populous states are not in favor of direct election of the president because they feel they would be overwhelmed by the large urban vote.

How Are Elections Conducted?

The United States uses the **Australian ballot**—a secret ballot that is prepared, distributed, and counted by government officials at public expense. Since 1888, all states have used the Australian ballot. Before that, many states used the alternatives of oral voting and differently colored ballots prepared by the parties. Obviously, knowing which way a person was voting made it easy to apply pressure to change his or her vote, and vote buying was common.

Office-Block and Party-Column Ballots

Two types of Australian ballots are used in the United States in general elections. The first, called an **office-block ballot,** or sometimes a **Massachusetts ballot,** groups all the candidates for each elective office under the title of each office. Politicians dislike the office-block ballot because it places more emphasis on the office than on the party; it discourages straight-ticket voting and encourages split-ticket voting.

A **party-column ballot** is a form of general election ballot in which the candidates are arranged in one column under their respective party labels and symbols. It is also called the **Indiana ballot.** In some states, it allows voters to vote for all of a party's candidates for local, state, and national offices by simply marking a single "X" or by pulling a single lever. Most states use this type of ballot. As it encourages straight-ticket voting, the two major parties favor this form. When a party has an exceptionally strong presidential or gubernatorial candidate to head the ticket, the use of the party-column ballot increases the **coattail effect.**

Voting by Mail

Although voting by mail has been accepted for absentee ballots for many decades, particularly for those who are doing business away from home or for members of the armed forces, only recently have several states offered mail ballots to all of their voters. The rationale for going to the mail ballot is to make voting easier and more accessible to the voters. A startling result came in the spring 1996 special election in Oregon to replace Senator Bob Packwood: with the mail ballot, turnout in the election was 66 percent, and the state saved more than $1 million. In the 2000 presidential elections, in which Oregon voters were allowed to mail in their ballots, voter participation was over 80 percent. Although voters in a number of states now have the option of voting by mail, Oregon is the only state to have completely abandoned precinct polling places.

Australian Ballot
A secret ballot prepared, distributed, and tabulated by government officials at public expense. Since 1888, all states have used the Australian ballot rather than an open, public ballot.

Office-Block, or Massachusetts, Ballot
A form of general election ballot in which candidates for elective office are grouped together under the title of each office. It emphasizes voting for the office and the individual candidate, rather than for the party.

Party-Column, or Indiana, Ballot
A form of general election ballot in which candidates for elective office are arranged in one column under their respective party labels and symbols. It emphasizes voting for the party, rather than for the office or individual.

Coattail Effect
The influence of a popular candidate on the electoral success of other candidates on the same party ticket. The effect is increased by the party-column ballot, which encourages straight-ticket voting.

Norman Ornstein, an early critic of mail-in voting, has suggested that mail balloting subverts the whole process. In part, this is because the voter casts her or his ballot at any time, perhaps before any debates or other dialogues are held between candidates. Thus, the voter may be casting an uninformed ballot.[12] When voting methods came under scrutiny after the 2000 elections, the authors of three prominent national reports[13] also criticized mail-in voting for this reason, claiming that early voting deprives voters of a common base of knowledge. The reports also concluded that mail-in voting deprives voters of the secrecy guaranteed by polling-place voting, provides more opportunities for fraud, and represents the abandonment of an important civic rite of going to the polls on election day.

Others, however, see the mail ballot as the best way to increase voter participation at a time when many are too busy to vote or have little interest in the process. The next step in making voting easier may be Internet voting. (See this chapter's *Which Side Are You On?* feature for a discussion of this possibility.)

Vote Fraud

Vote fraud is something regularly suspected but seldom proved. Voting in the nineteenth century, when secret ballots were rare and people had a cavalier attitude toward the open buying of votes, was probably much more conducive to fraud than modern elections are. An investigation by Larry J. Sabato and Glenn R. Simpson, however, revealed that the potential for vote fraud is high in many states, particularly through the use of phony voter registrations and absentee ballots.[14]

In California, for example, it is very difficult to remove a name from the polling list even if the person has not cast a ballot for the prior two years. Thus, many persons are still on the rolls even though they no longer reside in California. Enterprising political

---

[12] Norman Ornstein, "Vote-by-Mail: Is It Good for Democracy?" *Campaigns and Elections*, May 1996, p. 47.
[13] These reports were based on studies conducted by a commission led by former presidents Gerald Ford and Jimmy Carter, by the Constitution Project at Georgetown University, and by a consortium at the Massachusetts Institute of Technology and the California Institute of Technology.
[14] Larry J. Sabato and Glenn R. Simpson, *Dirty Little Secrets: The Persistence of Corruption in American Politics* (New York: Random House, 1996).

The registration files of absentee ballots are verified at a counting facility in Fort Lauderdale, Florida, after the 2000 presidential election. Florida's election procedures came under scrutiny after the 2000 election as allegations of vote fraud and other voting irregularities threw the outcome of Florida's election into doubt. Is it possible to eliminate fraud entirely from the election process? (AP Photo/Wilfredo Lee)

Which Side Are You On?
Would Online Voting Be Better?

The lure of Internet voting has been around for at least half a decade, if not longer. Online voting would eliminate the necessity of walking, taking public transportation, or driving to the polls on election day. You could participate in the American political process from the comfort of your home. Some towns in the United Kingdom already allow voters to choose their local council members via the Internet. Would this be a good idea for America?

THERE WOULD BE BENEFITS TO ONLINE VOTING

Let there be no mistake, online voting would offer numerous benefits. It would cost less than the current voting system. It would allow for faster counting and perhaps reduce the possibility for human error. Online voting would also attract younger voters. Certainly, it would increase voter turnout because the individual time cost of voting would fall dramatically.

Consider that billions of dollars of transactions have been successfully managed on the Web. Why can't the Web handle voting as well?

Students at Broward Community College in Florida tested this online, touch-screen voting system, which is similar to an automatic-teller machine that prints a receipt after the voter has completed voting. Such voting systems have problems of their own, although perhaps fewer than those that occur with mechanical systems such as punch cards. (AP Photo/Alan Diaz)

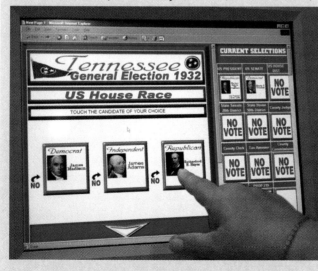

THE HIDDEN PITFALLS OF INTERNET VOTING

The major argument against online voting is the possibility of fraud. One of the reasons that financial transactions work so well over the Web is that the identities of the transactors are a well-known part of the transaction process. This fact alone allows for increased protection against fraud. Voting, however, is supposed to be anonymous. For individuals to be able to vote online without massive fraud, they would have to lose some of this anonymity. They would have to register and part with a certain amount of personal identifying information just as persons purchasing goods online must do.

Additionally, viruses routinely wreak havoc on the Internet. Why couldn't they do the same during election day while people were using their computers and Internet access to vote? There is a reason that security consultants advise their clients to update their antivirus programs at least once a day. Security remains a major issue on the Internet. Virus alerts occur frequently.

Then there is the problem of making sure that the online electronic voting system works. Internet financial transactions are carried out twenty-four hours a day, so any problems that arise are quickly handled. Given that we usually vote only once a year for certain elections, only once every two years for others, and only once every four years for president, who is to say that a large Internet voting system might not break down on the crucial day? Moreover, a system that is only used irregularly is much harder to make "fraud-proof" than one that is used regularly.

WHAT'S YOUR POSITION?

No voting system is perfect. The current systems in use have many faults. Does that mean that we should be willing to accept some level of insecurity with respect to an online voting system?

GOING ONLINE

The Brookings Institution has sponsored a series of reports on Internet voting. To view articles and resources on the topic, go to **http://www.brook.edu/dybdocroot/gs/ projects/iVoting.htm**. The Center for Technology and Society also includes a variety of articles on Internet voting at its Web site. Go to **http://www.tecsoc.org/govpol/ focusnetvote.htm**.

INFOTRAC®
COLLEGE EDITION

For more information on voting, use the term "voting" in the Subject guide.

Voter Turnout
The percentage of citizens taking part in the election process; the number of eligible voters that actually "turn out" on election day to cast their ballots.

activists can use these names for absentee ballots. Other states have registration laws that are meant to encourage easy registration and voting. Such laws can be taken advantage of by those who seek to vote more than once.

After the 2000 elections, Larry Sabato again emphasized the problem of voting fraud. "It's a silent scandal," said Sabato, "and the problem is getting worse with increases in absentee voting, which is the easiest way to commit fraud." He noted that in 2000, one-third of Florida's counties found that more than 1,200 votes were cast illegally by felons, and in one county alone nearly 500 votes were cast by unregistered voters. In two precincts, the number of ballots cast was greater than the number of people who voted.[15] As a result of the confusion generated by the 2000 elections, many states are now in the process of improving their voting systems and procedures. Some claim that certain reforms, such as requiring voters to show a voter-registration card or photo identification when they go to the polls, will help to curb voting fraud.

Voting in National, State, and Local Elections

In 2000, there were 200 million eligible voters. Of that number, 101 million actually went to the polls, or 50.7 percent of eligible voters. When only half of the eligible voters participate in elections, it means, among other things, that the winner of a close presidential election may be voted in by only about one-fourth of the voting-age population (see Table 10–2).

Figure 10–4 shows **voter turnout** for presidential and congressional elections from 1900 to 2002. The last "good" year of turnout for the presidential elections was 1960,

[15] As cited in "Blind to Voter Fraud," *The Wall Street Journal*, March 2, 2001, p. A10.

TABLE 10–2

Elected by a Majority?

Most presidents have won a majority of the votes cast in the election. We generally judge the extent of their victory by whether they have won more than 51 percent of the votes. Some presidential elections have been proclaimed *landslides*, meaning that the candidates won by an extraordinary majority of votes cast. As indicated below, however, no modern president has been elected by more than 38 percent of the total voting-age electorate.

YEAR—WINNER (PARTY)	PERCENTAGE OF TOTAL POPULAR VOTE	PERCENTAGE OF VOTING-AGE POPULATION
1932—Roosevelt (D)	57.4	30.1
1936—Roosevelt (D)	60.8	34.6
1940—Roosevelt (D)	54.7	32.2
1944—Roosevelt (D)	53.4	29.9
1948—Truman (D)	49.6	25.3
1952—Eisenhower (R)	55.1	34.0
1956—Eisenhower (R)	57.4	34.1
1960—Kennedy (D)	49.7	31.2
1964—Johnson (D)	61.1	37.8
1968—Nixon (R)	43.4	26.4
1972—Nixon (R)	60.7	33.5
1976—Carter (D)	50.1	26.8
1980—Reagan (R)	50.7	26.7
1984—Reagan (R)	58.8	31.2
1988—Bush (R)	53.4	26.8
1992—Clinton (D)	43.3	23.1
1996—Clinton (D)	49.2	23.2
2000—Bush (R)	47.8	24.9

SOURCES: *Congressional Quarterly Weekly Report*, January 31, 1989, p. 137; *The New York Times*, November 5, 1992; *The New York Times*, November 7, 1996; and *The New York Times*, November 12, 2000.

when almost 65 percent of the eligible voters actually voted. Each of the peaks in the figure represents voter turnout in a presidential election. Thus, we can also see that turnout for congressional elections is greatly influenced by whether there is a presidential election in the same year.

The same is true at the state level. When there is a race for governor, more voters participate both in the general election for governor and in the election for state representatives. Voter participation rates in gubernatorial elections are also greater in presidential election years. The average turnout in state elections is about 14 percentage points higher when a presidential election is held.

Now consider local elections. In races for mayor, city council, county auditor, and the like, it is fairly common for only 25 percent or less of the electorate to vote. Is something amiss here? It would seem obvious that people would be more likely to vote in elections that directly affect them. At the local level, each person's vote counts more (because there are fewer voters). Furthermore, the issues—crime control, school bonds, sewer bonds, and so on—touch the immediate interests of the voters. The facts, however, do not fit the theory. Potential voters are most interested in national elections, when a presidential choice is involved. Otherwise, voter participation in our representative government is very low (and, as we have seen, it is not overwhelmingly great even at the presidential level).

The Effect of Low Voter Turnout

There are two schools of thought concerning low voter turnout. Some view the decline in voter participation as a clear threat to our representative democratic government. Fewer and fewer individuals are deciding who wields political power in our society. Also, low voter participation presumably signals apathy about our political system in general. It also may signal that potential voters simply do not want to take the time to learn about the issues. When only a handful of people do take the time, it will be easier, say the alarmists, for an authoritarian figure to take over our government.

DID YOU KNOW...
That the Vietnamese government reported a 99 percent voter turnout in the May 2002 elections to elect a new National Assembly in that country (of course, in Communist Vietnam, voting is mandatory, there is only one political party, and supporting a multiparty system can lead to imprisonment)?

FIGURE 10–4

Voter Turnout for Presidential and Congressional Elections, 1900 to 2002

The peaks represent turnout in presidential election years; the troughs represent turnout in off-presidential-election years.

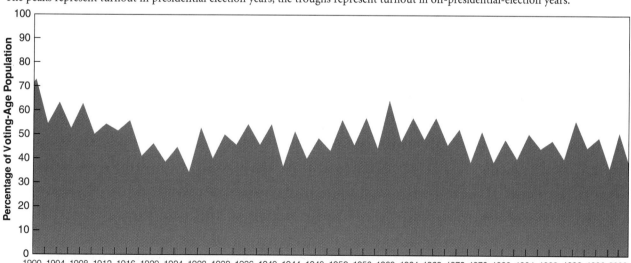

SOURCES: Historical Data Archive, Inter-university Consortium for Political and Social Research: U.S. Department of Commerce, *Statistical Abstract of the United States: 1980,* 101st ed. (Washington, D.C.: U.S. Government Printing Office, 1980), p. 515; William H. Flanigan and Nancy H. Zingale, *Political Behavior of the American Electorate,* 5th ed. (Boston: Allyn and Bacon, 1983), p. 20; *Congressional Quarterly,* various issues; and authors' update.

Poll workers in Nebraska wait for voters to turn out for a primary election in May 2002. Voter turnout was predicted to be low because most candidates were either unopposed or faced limited opposition. Is low voter participation a serious problem in elections today? What might the negative results be in our political system if low voter turnout continues? (AP Photo/Nati Harnik)

Others are less concerned about low voter participation. They believe that a decline in voter participation simply indicates more satisfaction with the status quo. Also, they believe that representative democracy is a reality even if a very small percentage of eligible voters vote. If everyone who does not vote believes that the outcome of the election will accord with his or her own desires, then representative democracy is working. The nonvoters are obtaining the type of government—with the type of people running it—that they want to have anyway.

Factors Influencing Who Votes

A clear association exists between voter participation and the following characteristics: age, educational attainment, minority status, income level, and the existence of two-party competition.

1. *Age.* Look at Table 10–3, which shows the breakdown of voter participation by age group for the 2000 presidential election. It would appear from these figures that age is a strong factor in determining voter turnout on election day. The reported turnout increases with older age groups. Greater participation with age is very likely due to the fact that older voters are more settled in their lives, are already registered, and have had more time to experience voting as an expected activity.

2. *Educational attainment.* Education also influences voter turnout. In general, the more education you have, the more likely you are to vote. This pattern is clearly evident in the 2000 election results, as you can see in Table 10–4. Reported turnout was over 30 percentage points higher for those who had some college education than it was for people who had never been to high school.

3. *Minority status.* Race and ethnicity are important, too, in determining the level of voter turnout. Non-Hispanic whites in 2000 voted at a 60.4 percent rate, whereas the non-Hispanic African American turnout rate was 54.1 percent. For Hispanics, the turnout rate was 27.5 percent, and for Asian Americans the rate was slightly lower, at 25.4 percent.

4. *Income level.* As you can see in Table 10–5, differences in income also correlate with differences in voter turnout. Wealthier people tend to be overrepresented in the electorate. In 2000, turnout varied from 28.2 percent for those with annual family

TABLE 10–3

Voting in the 2000 Presidential Elections by Age Group (in Percentages)

AGE	REPORTED TURNOUT
18–24	32.3
25–34	43.7
35–44	55.0
45–54	62.3
55–64	66.8
65–74	69.9
75 years and over	64.9

SOURCE: U.S. Bureau of the Census, February 27, 2002.

TABLE 10–4

Voting in the 2000 Presidential Elections by Education Level (in Percentages)

YEARS OF SCHOOL COMPLETED	REPORTED TURNOUT
Less than 9th grade	26.8
9th to 12th grade, no diploma	33.6
High school graduate	49.4
Some college or associate degree	60.3
Bachelor's degree	70.3
Advanced degree	75.5

SOURCE: U.S. Bureau of the Census, February 27, 2002.

TABLE 10–5

Voting in the 2000 Presidential Elections by Income (in Percentages)

INCOME	REPORTED TURNOUT
Under $5,000	28.2
$5,000 to $9,999	34.7
$10,000 to $14,999	37.7
$15,000 to $24,999	43.4
$25,000 to $34,999	51.0
$35,000 to $49,999	57.5
$50,000 to $74,999	65.2
$75,000 and over	71.5

SOURCE: U.S. Bureau of the Census, February 27, 2002.

incomes under $5,000 to about 71.5 percent for people with annual family incomes of $75,000 or more.

5. *Two-party competition.* Another factor in voter turnout is the extent to which elections are competitive within a state. More competitive states generally have higher turnout rates, and turnout increases considerably in states where there is a highly competitive race in a particular year. As the 1998 congressional elections showed, turnout can be increased through targeted get-out-the-vote drives among minority voters.

These statistics reinforce one another. White voters are likely to be wealthier than African American voters, who are also less likely to have obtained a college education.

Why People Do Not Vote

For many years, political scientists believed that one reason voter turnout in the United States was so much lower than in other Western nations was that it was so difficult to register to vote. In most states, registration required a special trip to a public office far in advance of elections. Many experts are now advancing other explanations for low U.S. voter turnout, however.

Uninformative Media Coverage and Negative Campaigning.   Some scholars contend that one of the reasons that some people do not vote has to do with media coverage of campaigns. Many researchers have shown that the news media tend to provide much more news about "the horse race," or which candidates are ahead in the polls, than about the actual policy positions of the candidates. Thus, voters are not given the kind of information that would provide an incentive to go to the polls on election day. Additionally, negative campaigning is thought to have an adverse effect on voter turnout. By the time citizens are ready to cast their ballots, most of the information they have heard about the candidates has been so negative that no candidate is appealing.

According to a year-long study conducted in 2000 by Harvard University's Center on the Press, Politics, and Public Policy, nonvoters and voters alike shared the same criticisms of the way the media cover campaigns: most thought the media treated campaigns like theater or entertainment. Nonvoters, however, were much more cynical about government and politicians than were voters. As the director of the study put it, "All the polls, the spin, the attack ads, the money and the negative news have soured Americans on the way we choose our president."[16]

The Rational Ignorance Effect.   Another explanation of low voter turnout suggests that citizens are making a logical choice in not voting. If citizens believe that their

---

[16] "The Vanishing Voter" study is online at **http://www.vanishingvoter.org**.

Rational Ignorance Effect

When people purposely and rationally decide not to become informed on an issue because they believe that their vote on the issue is not likely to be a deciding one; a lack of incentive to seek the necessary information to cast an intelligent vote.

votes will not affect the outcome of an election, then they have little incentive to seek the information they need to cast intelligent votes. The lack of incentive to obtain costly (in terms of time, attention, and so on) information about politicians and political issues has been called the **rational ignorance effect**. That term may seem contradictory, but it is not. Rational ignorance is a condition in which people purposely and rationally decide not to obtain information—to remain ignorant.

Why, then, do even one-third to one-half of U.S. citizens bother to show up at the polls? One explanation is that most citizens receive personal satisfaction from the act of voting. It makes them feel that they are good citizens and that they are doing something patriotic. Even among voters who are registered and who plan to vote, if the cost of voting goes up (in terms of time and inconvenience), the number of eligible voters who actually vote will fall. In particular, bad weather on election day means that, on average, a smaller percentage of eligible voters will go to the polls.

Plans for Improving Voter Turnout. Mail-in voting, Internet voting, registering to vote when you apply for a driver's license—these are all ideas that have been either suggested or implemented in the hope of improving voter turnout. Nonetheless, voter turnout remains low.

Two other ideas seemed promising. The first was to allow voters to visit the polls up to three weeks before election day. The second was to allow voters to vote by absentee ballot without having to give any particular reason for doing so. The Committee for the Study of the American Electorate discovered, however, that in areas that implemented these plans, neither plan increased voter turnout. Indeed, voter turnout actually fell in those jurisdictions. In other words, states that did *not* permit early voting or unrestricted absentee voting had *better* turnout rates than states that did. Apparently, these two innovations appeal mostly to people who already intended to vote.

What is left? One possibility is to declare election day a national holiday. In this way, more eligible voters will find it easier to go to the polls.

Legal Restrictions on Voting

Legal restrictions on voter registration have existed since the founding of the nation. Most groups in the United States have been concerned with the suffrage issue at one time or another.

Historical Restrictions

In colonial times, only white males who owned property with a certain minimum value were eligible to vote, leaving a far greater number of Americans ineligible than eligible to take part in the democratic process.

Property Requirements. Because many government functions concern property rights and the distribution of income and wealth, some of the founders of our nation felt it was appropriate that only people who had an interest in property should vote on these issues. The idea of extending the vote to all citizens was, according to South Carolina delegate Charles Pinckney, merely "theoretical nonsense."

The logic behind this restriction of voting rights to property owners was questioned seriously by Thomas Paine in his pamphlet *Common Sense:*

> Here is a man who today owns a jackass, and the jackass is worth $60. Today the man is a voter and goes to the polls and deposits his vote. Tomorrow the jackass dies. The next day the man comes to vote without his jackass and cannot vote at all. Now tell me, which was the voter, the man or the jackass?[17]

---

[17] Thomas Paine, *Common Sense* (London: H. D. Symonds, 1792), p. 28.

The writers of the Constitution allowed the states to decide who should vote. Thus, women were allowed to vote in Wyoming in 1870 but not in the entire nation until the Nineteenth Amendment was ratified in 1920. By about 1850, most white adult males in virtually all the states could vote without any property qualification. North Carolina was the last state to eliminate its property test for voting—in 1856.

Further Extensions of the Franchise. Extension of the franchise to black males occurred with the passage of the Fifteenth Amendment in 1870. This enfranchisement was short-lived, however, as the "redemption" of the South by white racists rolled back these gains by the end of the century. As discussed in Chapter 5, it was not until the 1960s that African Americans, both male and female, were able to participate in large numbers in the electoral process. Women received full national voting rights with the Nineteenth Amendment in 1920. The most recent extension of the franchise occurred when the voting age was reduced to eighteen by the Twenty-sixth Amendment in 1971. As Table 10–3 on page 316 showed, however, young people have a low turnout.

Current Eligibility and Registration Requirements

Voting requires **registration,** and to register, a person must satisfy the following voter qualifications, or legal requirements: (1) citizenship, (2) age (eighteen or older), and (3) residency—the duration varies widely from state to state and with types of elections. Since 1972, states cannot impose residency requirements of more than thirty days. In addition, most states disqualify people who are mentally incompetent, prison inmates, convicted felons, or election-law violators.

Each state has different qualifications for voting and registration. In 1993, Congress passed the "motor voter" bill, which requires that states provide voter-registration materials when people receive or renew driver's licenses, that all states allow voters to register by mail, and that voter-registration forms be made available at a wider variety of public places and agencies. In general, a person must register well in advance of an election, although voters in Maine, Minnesota, Oregon, and Wisconsin are allowed to register up to, and on, election day.

Some argue that registration requirements are responsible for much of the non-participation in our political process. Certainly, since their introduction in the late nineteenth century, registration laws have had the effect of reducing the voting participation of African Americans and immigrants. There also is a partisan dimension to the debate over registration and nonvoting. Republicans generally fear that an expanded electorate would help to elect more Democrats.

The question arises as to whether registration is really necessary. If it decreases participation in the political process, perhaps it should be dropped altogether. Still, as those in favor of registration requirements argue, such requirements may prevent fraudulent voting practices, such as multiple voting or voting by noncitizens.

Registration
The entry of a person's name onto the list of eligible voters for elections. To register, a person must meet certain legal requirements relating to age, citizenship, and residency.

Voter registration is an important part of our political process. These workers are helping a citizen register to vote in the next election. The requirements for voter registration vary across states. (Bob Dammrich/Stock Boston)

How Do Voters Decide?

Political scientists and survey researchers have collected much information about voting behavior. This information sheds some light on which people vote and why people decide to vote for particular candidates. We have already discussed factors influencing voter turnout. Generally, the factors that influence voting decisions can be divided into two groups: (1) socioeconomic and demographic factors and (2) psychological factors.

Socioeconomic and Demographic Factors

As Table 10–6 indicates, a number of socioeconomic and demographic factors appear to influence voting behavior, including (1) education, (2) income and **socioeconomic status,** (3) religion, (4) ethnic background, (5) gender, (6) age, and (7) geographic region. These influences all reflect the voter's personal background and place in society. Some factors have to do with the family into which a person is born: race, religion (for most people), and ethnic background. Others may be the result of choices made throughout an individual's life: place of residence, educational achievement, or profession. It is also clear that many of these factors are related. People who have more education are likely to have higher incomes and to hold professional jobs. Similarly, children born into wealthier families are far more likely to complete college than chil-

Socioeconomic Status

A category of people within a society who have similar levels of income and similar types of occupations.

TABLE 10–6

Vote by Groups in Presidential Elections since 1968 (in Percentages)

	1968			1972		1976			1980			1984	
	HUMPHREY (DEM.)	NIXON (REP.)	WALLACE (IND.)	McGOVERN (DEM.)	NIXON (REP.)	CARTER (DEM.)	FORD (REP.)	McCARTHY (IND.)	CARTER (DEM.)	REAGAN (REP.)	ANDERSON (IND.)	MONDALE (DEM.)	REAGAN (REP.)
NATIONAL	43.0	43.4	13.6	38	62	50	48	1	41	51	7	41	59
SEX													
Male	41	43	16	37	63	53	45	1	38	53	7	36	64
Female	45	43	12	38	62	48	51	*	44	49	6	45	55
RACE													
White	38	47	15	32	68	46	52	1	36	56	7	34	66
Nonwhite	85	12	3	87	13	85	15	*	86	10	2	87	13
EDUCATION													
College	37	54	9	37	63	42	55	2	35	53	10	39	61
High school	42	43	15	34	66	54	46	*	43	51	5	43	57
Grade school	52	33	15	49	51	58	41	1	54	42	3	51	49
OCCUPATION													
Professional	34	56	10	31	69	42	56	1	33	55	10	34	66
White collar	41	47	12	36	64	50	48	2	40	51	9	47	53
Manual	50	35	15	43	57	58	41	1	48	46	5	46	54
AGE (Years)													
Under 30	47	38	15	48	52	53	45	1	47	41	11	40	60
30–49	44	41	15	33	67	48	49	2	38	52	8	40	60
50 and older	41	47	12	36	64	52	48	*	41	54	4	41	59
RELIGION													
Protestants	35	49	16	30	70	46	53	*	39	54	6	39	61
Catholics	59	33	8	48	52	57	42	1	46	47	6	39	61
POLITICS													
Republicans	9	86	5	5	95	9	91	*	8	86	5	4	96
Democrats	74	12	14	67	33	82	18	*	69	26	4	79	21
Independents	31	44	25	31	69	38	57	4	29	55	14	33	67
REGION													
East	50	43	7	42	58	51	47	1	43	47	9	46	54
Midwest	44	47	9	40	60	48	50	1	41	51	7	42	58
South	31	36	33	29	71	54	45	*	44	52	3	37	63
West	44	49	7	41	59	46	51	1	35	54	9	40	60
MEMBERS OF LABOR UNION FAMILIES	56	29	15	46	54	63	36	1	50	43	5	52	48

*Less than 1 percent.

NOTE: Results do not include votes for all minor-party candidates.

dren from poorer families. Furthermore, some of these demographic factors relate to psychological factors—as we shall see.

Education. For some time, having a college education tended to be associated with voting for Republicans. This pattern began to change in 1992, as you can see in Table 10–6. In that year, 44 percent of college graduates voted for Democrat Bill Clinton, while only 39 percent voted for Republican George H. W. Bush. In the 2000 elections, voters with a college education split their votes evenly between Democrat Al Gore and Republican George W. Bush. As Table 10–6 also shows, a higher percentage of voters with only a high school education voted Republican in 2000, as compared to previous elections in which that group of voters tended to favor Democrats. Voters with only a grade school education have voted Democratic in nearly every election.

TABLE 10–6

Vote by Groups in Presidential Elections since 1968 (in Percentages)—continued

	1988		1992			1996			2000	
	DUKAKIS (DEM.)	BUSH (REP.)	CLINTON (DEM.)	BUSH (REP.)	PEROT (IND.)	CLINTON (DEM.)	DOLE (REP.)	PEROT (REF.)	GORE (DEM.)	BUSH (REP.)
NATIONAL	45	53	43	38	19	49	41	8	48	48
SEX										
Male	41	57	41	38	21	43	44	10	42	53
Female	49	50	46	37	17	54	38	7	54	43
RACE										
White	40	59	39	41	20	43	46	9	42	54
Nonwhite	86	12	NA	NA	NA	NA	NA	NA	NA	NA
EDUCATION										
College	43	56	44	39	18	44	46	8	48	48
High school	49	50	43	36	20	51	35	13	48	49
Grade school	56	43	56	28	NA	59	28	11	59	39
OCCUPATION										
Professional	40	59	NA	NA	NA	NA	NA	NA	NA	NA
White collar	42	57	NA	NA	NA	NA	NA	NA	NA	NA
Manual	50	49	NA	NA	NA	NA	NA	NA	NA	NA
AGE (Years)										
Under 30	47	52	44	34	22	54	34	10	48	46
30–49	45	54	42	38	20	48	41	9	NA	NA
50 and older	49	50	50	38	12	48	44	7	NA	NA
RELIGION										
Protestants	33	66	33	46	21	36	53	10	42	56
Catholics	47	52	44	36	20	53	37	9	50	47
POLITICS										
Republicans	8	91	10	73	17	13	80	6	8	91
Democrats	82	17	77	10	13	84	10	5	86	11
Independents	43	55	38	32	30	43	35	17	45	47
REGION										
East	49	50	47	35	NA	55	34	9	56	39
Midwest	47	52	42	37	NA	48	41	10	48	49
South	41	58	42	43	NA	46	46	7	43	55
West	46	52	44	34	NA	48	40	8	48	46
MEMBERS OF LABOR UNION FAMILIES	57	42	55	24	NA	59	30	9	59	37

*Less than 1 percent.

NOTE: Results do not include votes for all minor-party candidates.

SOURCES: *Gallup Report,* November 1984, p. 32; *The New York Times,* November 10, 1988, p. 18; *The New York Times,* November 15, 1992, p. B9; *The New York Times,* November 10, 1996, p. 16; *The New York Times,* November 12, 2000, Section 4, p. 4.

Signs in English and Spanish encourage voters to register for the next election. The Supreme Court has ruled that registration materials and ballots must be available in other languages if a specified proportion of the citizens speak a language other than English. (Mark Philips/ Photo Researchers)

Income and Socioeconomic Status.   Traditionally, the pattern has been that the higher the income, the more likely a person will vote Republican. Manual laborers, factory workers, and especially union members are more likely to vote Democratic (see Table 10–7). If socioeconomic status is measured by profession, then, traditionally, those of higher socioeconomic status—professionals and businesspersons, as well as white-collar workers—have tended to vote Republican. But there are no hard and fast rules. Indeed, recent research indicates that a realignment is occurring among those of higher socioeconomic status: professionals now tend to vote Democratic, while small-business owners, managers, and corporate executives tend to vote Republican.[18] Additionally, some very poor individuals are devoted Republicans, just as some extremely wealthy people support the Democratic Party.

Religion.   In the United States, Protestants have traditionally voted Republican, and Catholics and Jews have voted Democratic. Like the other patterns discussed, however, this one is somewhat fluid. Particularly notable in 2000 was the degree to which religious practices, particularly church attendance, rather than religious beliefs correlated with voting behavior. According to a postelection study conducted by the University of Akron, Ohio, voters who are more devout, regardless of their church affiliation, are voting Republican, while voters who are less devout are moving toward the Democrats.

In 2000, for example, devout Protestants who regularly attend church gave 84 percent of their votes to Bush, compared to 55 percent of those who attend church less often. Among Catholics, there was a similar pattern: a majority of Catholics who attend church regularly voted Republican, while a majority of those Catholics who are not regular churchgoers

[18]Thomas B. Edsall, "Voters Thinking Less with Their Wallets," *International Herald Tribune*, March 27, 2001, p. 3.

TABLE 10–7

How Democratic Are Labor Voters?

Although union members are more likely to identify themselves as Democrats than Republicans and labor organizations are far more likely to support Democratic candidates, the data below show that in seven of thirteen presidential elections, Republicans have captured at least 40 percent of the votes from union households.

UNION HOUSEHOLDS VOTING REPUBLICAN FOR PRESIDENT

YEAR	CANDIDATES	PERCENTAGE
1952	Eisenhower vs. Stevenson	44
1956	Eisenhower vs. Stevenson	57
1960	Kennedy vs. Nixon	36
1964	Johnson vs. Goldwater	17
1968	Nixon vs. Humphrey	44
1972	Nixon vs. McGovern	57
1976	Carter vs. Ford	36
1980	Reagan vs. Carter	45
1984	Reagan vs. Mondale	43
1988	Bush vs. Dukakis	41
1992	Clinton vs. Bush	32
1996	Clinton vs. Dole	30
2000	Gore vs. Bush	37

SOURCES: *CQ Researcher*, June 28, 1996, p. 560; *The New York Times*, November 10, 1996, p. 16; and authors' update.

voted for Al Gore. As one columnist put it, "It's reached the point where observant Catholics voted more heavily Republican than less devout [Protestants]."[19] There are two exceptions to this trend: African Americans of all religions and Jews remain strongly supportive of Democrats.

Ethnic Background. Traditionally, the Irish have voted for Democrats. So, too, have voters of Slavic, Polish, and Italian heritages. But Anglo-Saxon and northern European ethnic groups have voted for Republican presidential candidates. These patterns were disrupted in 1980, when Ronald Reagan obtained much of his support from several of the traditionally Democratic ethnic groups, with the help of fundamentalist religious groups.

African Americans voted principally for Republicans until Democrat Franklin Roosevelt's New Deal in the 1930s. Since then, they have largely identified with the Democratic Party. Indeed, Democratic presidential candidates have received, on average, more than 80 percent of the African American vote since 1956.

Gender. Until relatively recently, there seemed to be no fixed pattern of voter preference by gender in presidential elections. One year, more women than men would vote for the Democratic candidate; another year, more men than women would do so. In the last decade, however, it is clear that women have been shifting their preferences to Democratic candidates. A number of explanations for this trend have been offered, including the increase in the number of working women, feminism, and women's concerns over abortion rights and other social issues.

Two economists have reached a different conclusion, however. In their study of why women are politically moving to the left, Lena Edlund and Rohini Pande of Columbia University found no evidence that women's views on social and religious issues had any effect on the gender gap. Rather, the major factor has been the disparate economic impact on men and women of not being married. In the last three decades, men and women have tended to marry later in life or to stay single even after having children. The divorce rate has also risen dramatically. Edlund and Pande argue that this decline in marriage has tended to make men richer and women poorer. Consequently, support for Democrats is high among single women, particularly single mothers.[20] In any event, political strategists for both parties are increasingly concerned with finding ways to address the gender gap in voting behavior.

Age. Age clearly seems to relate to an individual's voting behavior. Younger voters have tended to vote Democratic, whereas older voters have tended to vote Republican. Only the voters under age thirty clearly favored Jimmy Carter during the Carter-Reagan election in 1980. This trend was reversed in 1984 and 1988, when voters under thirty voted heavily for Ronald Reagan and then for George H. W. Bush. In 1992, Bill Clinton won back the young voters by 10 percentage points, a margin that expanded to nearly 20 percentage points in 1996. In 2000, this margin decreased to only 2 percentage points; voters under the age of thirty split their votes almost evenly between Al Gore (48 percent) and George W. Bush (46 percent).

Geographic Region. As we noted in Chapter 9, the former Solid (Democratic) South has crumbled in national elections. As you can see in Table 10–6 on page 321, only 43 percent of the votes from the Southern states went to Democrat Al Gore in 2000, while 55 percent went to Republican George W. Bush.

---

[19] Ronald Brownstein, "Attendance, Not Affiliation, Key to Religious Voters," *The Los Angeles Times,* July 16, 2001, p. A10.

[20] Lena Edlund and Rohini Pande, "Why Have Women Become Left-Wing? The Political Gender Gap and the Decline in Marriage," *The Quarterly Journal of Economics,* Vol. 117, Issue 3 (August 2002), p. 917.

Democrats still draw much of their strength from large northern and eastern cities. Rural areas tend to be Republican (and conservative) throughout the country except in the South, where the rural vote still tends to be heavily Democratic. On average, the West has voted Republican in presidential elections. From 1956 until 1992, the Republicans held the edge in the western states in every presidential election, except for the 1964 election between Barry Goldwater and Lyndon Johnson. In 1992, however, Clinton captured the West; he did so again in 1996, and in 2000, for the third presidential election in a row, the majority of votes from the West went to the Democratic candidate.

Psychological Factors

In addition to socioeconomic and demographic explanations for the way people vote, at least three important psychological factors play a role in voter decision making. These factors, which are rooted in attitudes and beliefs held by voters, are (1) party identification, (2) perception of the candidates, and (3) issue preferences.

Party Identification.   With the possible exception of race, party identification has been the most important determinant of voting behavior in national elections. As we pointed out in Chapter 7, party affiliation is influenced by family and peer groups, by age, by the media, and by psychological attachment. During the 1950s, independent voters were a little more than 20 percent of the eligible electorate. In the middle to late 1960s, however, party identification began to weaken, and by the mid-1990s, independent voters constituted over 30 percent of all voters. In 2000, the estimated proportion of independent voters was between 26 and 33 percent. Independent voting seems to be concentrated among new voters, particularly among new young voters. Thus, we can still say that for established voters party identification is an important determinant in voter choice.

A number of factors determine how voters make decisions at the polling place. Aside from the many demographic influences that come into play, there are also psychological factors that help shape the way voters make decisions when they enter the voting booth.(AP Photo)

Perception of the Candidates. The image of the candidate also seems to be important in a voter's choice for president. To some extent, voter attitudes toward candidates are based on emotions (such as trust) rather than on any judgment about experience or policy. In 2000, voters seemed to be attracted to candidates of high integrity and honesty.

Issue Preferences. Issues make a difference in presidential and congressional elections. Although personality or image factors may be very persuasive, most voters have some notion of how the candidates differ on basic issues or at least know that the candidates want a change in the direction of government policy.

Historically, economic issues have the strongest influence on voters' choices. When the economy is doing well, it is very difficult for a challenger, particularly at the presidential level, to defeat the incumbent. In contrast, increasing inflation, rising unemployment, or high interest rates are likely to work to the disadvantage of the incumbent. Studies of how economic conditions affect the vote differ in their conclusions. Some indicate that people vote on the basis of their personal economic well-being, whereas other studies seem to show that people vote on the basis of the nation's overall economic health.

All candidates try to set themselves apart from their opposition on crucial issues in order to attract voters. What is difficult to ascertain is the extent to which issues overshadow partisan loyalty or personality factors in the voters' minds. It appears that some campaigns are much more issue oriented than others. Some research has shown that **issue voting** was most important in the presidential elections of 1964, 1968, and 1972, was moderately important in 1980, and was less important in the 1990s and early 2000s.

Issue Voting
Voting for a candidate based on how he or she stands on a particular issue.

Campaigns, Nominations, and Elections: Why Are They Important Today?

Campaigns and elections are not just for show. They perform a valuable function in a democracy. Without political campaigns, how would you learn about the candidates? How would you learn about the issues at stake in an upcoming election and which positions the candidates have taken on those issues? The culmination of all that campaigning, the election itself, is equally important. Who wins an election may determine how much you pay in taxes, whether more funds will be made available for education in your state, how much government aid you will receive if you become ill or lose your job, and the size of the Social Security check you will receive during your retirement years.

Because campaigns and elections are so important in our political system, it is critical to ensure that voting procedures and methods yield fair and accurate results. The need to improve the voting systems throughout the states became clear after the 2000 presidential elections, as discussed in this chapter's opening *What If . . .* feature. One of the biggest problems with campaigns is, of course, the high cost of running for a national or even a state political office. As long as the campaign process remains so expensive, numerous Americans who would like to run for office will not do so simply because they cannot raise the funds necessary to compete in the race.

During the next presidential election cycle, you will see how quickly the candidates in the presidential campaign withdraw from the race due to the early primaries. Will this lead to low voter turnout by the November elections? Will it lead to a low level of political knowledge in the electorate, perhaps due to boredom? These are some of the critical issues that affect you and every other American today.

MAKING A DIFFERENCE | Registering and Voting

In nearly every state, before you are allowed to cast a vote in an election, you must first register. Registration laws vary considerably from state to state, and, depending on how difficult a state's laws make it to register, some states have much higher rates of registration and voting participation than do others.

Residency and Age Requirements

What do you have to do to register and cast a vote? In general, you must be a citizen of the United States, at least eighteen years old on or before election day, and a resident of the state in which you intend to register. Most states require that you meet minimum-residency requirements. In other words, you must have lived in the state in which you plan to be registered for a specified period of time. You may retain your previous registration, if any, in another state, and you can cast an absentee vote if your previous state permits that. The minimum-residency requirement is very short in some states, such as one day in Alabama or ten days in New Hampshire and Wisconsin. No state requires more than thirty days. Other states with voter residency requirements have minimum-day requirements between these extremes. Twenty states do not have any minimum-residency requirement at all.

Time Limits

Nearly every state also specifies a closing date by which you must be registered before an election. In other words, even if you have met a residency requirement, you still may not be able to vote if you register too close to the day of the election. The closing date is different in certain states (Connecticut, Delaware, and Louisiana) for primary elections than for other elections. The closing date for registration varies from election day itself (Maine, Minnesota, Oregon, and Wisconsin) to thirty days before the election (Arizona). Delaware specifies the third Saturday in October as the closing date. In North Dakota, no registration is necessary.

In most states, your registration can be revoked if you do not vote within a certain number of years. This process of automatically "purging" the voter-registration lists of nonactive voters happens every two years in about a dozen states, every three years in Georgia, every four years in more than twenty other states, every five years in Maryland and Rhode Island, every eight years in North Carolina, and every ten years in Michigan. Ten states do not require this purging at all.

An Example

Using Iowa as an example, you normally would register through the local county auditor or when you obtain your driver's license (under the "motor voter" law of 1993). If you moved to a new address within the state, you would also have to change your registration to vote by contacting the auditor. Postcard registrations must be postmarked or delivered to the county auditor no later than the twenty-fifth day before an election. Party affiliation may be changed or declared when you register or reregister, or you may change or declare a party at the polls on election day. Postcard registration forms in Iowa are available at many public buildings, from labor unions, at political party headquarters, at the county auditors' offices, or from campus groups. Registrars who will accept registrations at other locations may be located by calling your party headquarters or your county auditor.

For more information on voting registration, contact your county or state officials, party headquarters, labor union, or local chapter of the League of Women Voters. The Web site for the League of Women Voters is **http://www.lwv.org**.

Key Terms

Chapter Summary

1 People may choose to run for political office to further their careers, to carry out specific political programs, or in response to certain issues or events. The legal qualifications for holding political office are minimal at both the state and local levels, but holders of political office still are predominantly white and male and are likely to be from the professional class.

2 American political campaigns are lengthy and extremely expensive. In the last decade, they have become more candidate centered rather than party centered in response to technological innovations and decreasing party identification. Candidates have begun to rely less on the party and more on paid professional consultants to perform the various tasks necessary to wage a political campaign. The crucial task of professional political consultants is image building. The campaign organization devises a campaign strategy to maximize the candidate's chances of winning. Candidates use public opinion polls and focus groups to gauge their popularity and to test the mood of the country.

3 The amount of money spent in financing campaigns is steadily increasing. A variety of corrupt practices acts have been passed to regulate campaign finance. The Federal Election Campaign Act of 1971 and its amendments in 1974 and 1976 instituted major reforms by limiting spending and contributions; the acts allowed corporations, labor unions, and interest groups to set up political action committees (PACs) to raise money for candidates. New techniques, including contributions to the parties, independent expenditures, and bundling, were subsequently used to raise money. The Bipartisan Campaign Reform Act of 2002 banned "soft money" contributions to the national parties, limited advertising by special interest groups, and increased the limits on individual contributions. Whether portions of the act will withstand constitutional challenges is not yet certain.

4 Following the Democratic convention of 1968, the McGovern-Fraser Commission was appointed to study the problems of the primary system. It formulated new rules, which were adopted by all Democrats and by Republicans in many states. These reforms opened up the nomination process for the presidency to all voters.

5 A presidential primary is a statewide election to help a political party determine its presidential nominee at the national convention. Some states use the caucus method of choosing convention delegates. The primary campaign recently has been shortened to the first few months of the election year.

6 In making a presidential choice on election day, the voter technically does not vote directly for a candidate but chooses between slates of presidential electors. The slate that wins the most popular votes throughout the state gets to cast all the electoral votes for the state. The candidate receiving a majority (270) of the electoral votes wins. Both the mechanics and the politics of the electoral college have been sharply criticized. There have been many proposed reforms, including a proposal that the president be elected on a popular-vote basis in a direct election.

7 The United States uses the Australian ballot, a secret ballot that is prepared, distributed, and counted by government officials. The office-block ballot groups candidates according to office. The party-column ballot groups candidates according to their party labels and symbols.

8 Voter participation in the United States is low (and generally declining) compared with that of other countries. Some view the decline in voter turnout as a threat to representative democracy, whereas others believe it simply indicates greater satisfaction with the status quo. There is an association between voting and a person's age, education, minority status, and income level. Another factor affecting voter turnout is the extent to which elections are competitive within a state.

9 In colonial times, only white males with a certain minimum amount of property were eligible to vote. The suffrage issue has concerned, at one time or another, most groups in the United States. Currently, to be eligible to vote, a person must satisfy registration, citizenship, and specified age and residency requirements. Each state has different qualifications. It is argued that these requirements are responsible for much of the nonparticipation in the political process in the United States.

10 Socioeconomic or demographic factors that influence voting decisions include (a) education, (b) income and socioeconomic status, (c) religion, (d) ethnic background, (e) gender, (f) age, and (g) geographic region. Psychological factors that influence voting decisions include (a) party identification, (b) perception of candidates, and (c) issue preferences.

Selected Print and Media Resources

SUGGESTED READINGS

Crouse, Timothy. *The Boys on the Bus.* New York: Random House, 1973. This classic book, which reads like a novel, is about political spin-doctoring in the 1972 Nixon/McGovern presidential campaigns, as seen by the press corps.

Niemi, Richard G., and Herbert F. Weisberg. *Controversies in Voting Behavior.* Washington, D.C.: CQ Press, 2001. The readings in this volume, all written by prominent scholars, provide important insights into U.S. politics, parties, elections, and voting behavior.

Rakove, Jack N., ed. *The Unfinished Election of 2000.* New York: Basic Books, 2001. This collection of essays by seven law professors addresses the many problems that surfaced during the 2000 elections. The authors contend that the election remains unfinished "for what it revealed about our politics, institutions, and perhaps even the Constitution itself."

Sabato, Larry J., ed. *Overtime! The Election 2000 Thriller.* Reading, Mass.: Addison Wesley Longman, 2001. This collection of essays offers firsthand accounts (including some by members of the presidential candidates' legal teams) of the political and legal drama that unfolded after the 2000 elections.

Witcover, Jules. *No Way to Pick a President.* New York: Farrar, Straus & Giroux, 2000. Witcover, a veteran Washington newspaper reporter, outlines the troubles that plague presidential elections—campaign financing, the electoral college, and voter alienation—and then proposes some changes.

MEDIA RESOURCES

Bulworth—A 1998 satirical film starring Warren Beatty and Halle Berry. Jay Bulworth, a senator who is fed up with politics and life in general, hires a hit man to carry out his own assassination. He then throws political caution to the wind in campaign appearances by telling the truth and behaving the way he really wants to behave.

The Candidate—A 1972 film, starring the young Robert Redford and produced by Warner Brothers, that effectively investigates and satirizes the decisions that a candidate for the U.S. Senate must make. It's a political classic.

Primary Colors—A 1998 film starring John Travolta as a southern governor who is plagued by a sex scandal during his run for the presidency.

The War Room—A 1993 documentary that uses video coverage taped throughout Bill Clinton's 1992 campaign for the presidency to show the strategic decisions behind the scenes in the campaign. Footage shows Clinton's strategists, including James Carville and George Stephanopoulos, pulling out all the stops for their candidate.

Your CD-ROM Resources

In addition to the chapter content containing hot links, the following resources are available on the CD-ROM:

- **Internet Activities**—Abolishing the electoral college, the controversy over voting-by-mail.

- **Critical Thinking Exercises**—Women and African American Politics, Campaign Reform Act of 2002, Election Day holiday.

- **Self-Check on Important Themes**—Can You Answer These?

- **Animated Figures**—Figure 10–1, "Female Candidates for the House of Representatives."

- **Videos**—*Young Voters, Soft Money.*

- **Public Opinion Data**—Find contrasting opinions on the ban on soft money and fining non-voters.

- **InfoTrac Exercise**—"How Does 2000 Stack Up?"

- **Simulation**—You Are There!

- **Participation Exercise**—Assume you are going to run for one of the two chambers of your state legislature.

- **MicroCase Exercise**—"By the Numbers: Who's Voting?"

- **Additional Resources**—All court cases, Hatch Act of 1939, Federal Election Campaign Act of 1971, Federal Election Campaign Acts of 1972 and 1974, *Bush v. Gore.*

e-mocracy
Elections and the Web

Today's voters have a significant advantage over those in past decades. It is now possible to obtain extensive information about candidates and issues simply by going online. Some sites present point-counterpoint articles about the candidates or issues in an upcoming election. Other sites are in favor of some candidates and positions and against others. The candidates themselves all now have Web sites that you can visit if you want to learn more about them and their positions. You can also obtain information online about election results by going to sites such as those listed in the *Logging On* section. While the Internet has proved to be a valuable vehicle for communicating information about elections, it is not clear whether it will be used for actual voting in national elections at some future time. Although Internet voting seems like a great idea, it also raises many concerns, particularly about security.

Logging On

For detailed information about current campaign-financing laws and for the latest filings of finance reports, see the site maintained by the Federal Election Commission at

http://www.fec.gov

To find excellent reports on where the money comes from and how it is spent in campaigns, be sure to view the site maintained by the Center for Responsive Politics at

http://www.opensecrets.org

You can learn about the impact of different voting systems on election strategies and outcomes at the Center for Voting and Democracy, which maintains the following Web site:

http://www.fairvote.org

Another excellent site for investigating voting records and campaign-financing information is that of Project Vote Smart. Go to

http://www.vote-smart.org

Using the Internet for Political Analysis

Point your browser at either the Federal Election Commission site (http://www.fec.org) or the Center for Responsive Politics site (http://www.opensecrets.org). Choose the campaign-financing records of at least three individual candidates or members of Congress. Print out those records, and then compare the types of donors that are listed. Can you find enough information about campaign donations to have some idea of what policy positions are held by the candidates? What does the donor list tell you about each person's role and importance in Congress?

The Internet Replaced Broadcast News ?

BACKGROUND

From the beginning of radio broadcasting until the development of cable television in the 1980s, the electronic media have been dominated by national networks. As television came to dominate the news industry, newspapers struggled to keep their readers. With the rise of cable television and the arrival of the Internet, many people now have multiple news outlets from which to choose.

Television networks and newspapers are trying to win back their former viewers and readers by establishing their own Web sites on the Internet. Unlike the evening network news, however, the Internet is accessible to users at any time, day or night. In addition, virtually anyone with a computer and telephone line can become a broadcaster and have his or her own newscast.

WHAT IF THE INTERNET REPLACED BROADCAST NEWS?

It took radio thirty-eight years to reach 50 million listeners. The Internet had more than that number of users in just four years. Given the rapid spread of Internet use among the public and the growth of high-speed connections for businesses and households, the Internet could easily replace broadcast news in the United States. Imagine everyone getting the headlines on her or his personal, hand-held device. Families would get the news via a permanently connected computer that could instantly retrieve the home page for a news source.

What would the news industry be like if the Internet supplanted television networks? The networks and cable companies would, of course, have their own Web sites. Users could also choose hundreds of alternative news sites. The cost of setting up an Internet site is so low that most towns and cities would offer many local sites, and thousands of newscasts would be available from third-party political groups or special interest groups, such as environmentalists.

What would happen to the news anchors and news-gathering organizations maintained by the networks? Although it would be possible to receive "video" of the news anchors over the Internet, "live broadcasts" would become obsolete. Why should users watch an old newscast on video when they can get breaking news from the Internet?

News gathering would become much more important because users want instant access to breaking stories. Instant access to breaking news, though, can result in inaccurate coverage. Today's major news organizations normally take the time to check sources and factual data before they broadcast or print news items. If news is posted on a Web site immediately, without these checks being undertaken, there is a danger that the news coverage may be inaccurate.

WOULD THE INTERNET BE BIASED?

The Internet has the potential to open the news to hundreds of different viewpoints. No longer could the public charge the media with bias toward either political party. Users could find virtually any political position or viewpoint on Internet broadcasts of news.

In addition, news broadcasts via the Internet could do a much better job of representing minority populations or other groups in the United States that have less access to the broadcast business. One would find Web sites hosted by African Americans, women, people with disabilities, Greek Americans, Turkish Americans, and so on. Internet journalists would cover worldwide events with digital cameras and post pictures on the Web instantly. Americans could see firsthand the oppression of people in some countries and learn about different cultures and political policies around the world.

Nonetheless, the Internet, by its nature, would be biased as a news source. Although Web sites provided by major news organizations would be edited for content and their news sources checked for accuracy, hundreds of Web sites would have no editing or checking of facts. Many individuals and groups would maintain Web sites to put forward their own views of the news and of public issues. Individual users would have to be much more critical of news sources to be sure of their accuracy. The Internet would provide many opportunities for hateful speech and the spreading of lies about individuals or specific groups.

FOR CRITICAL ANALYSIS

1. If all Americans had access to the Internet, would anyone want to watch network news? What would they want to see covered in such broadcasts?
2. How could people be assured that Internet news was factual and accurate?

The study of people and politics—of how people gain the information that they need to be able to choose between political candidates, to organize for their own interests, and to formulate opinions on the policies and decisions of the government—needs to take into account the role played by the media in the United States. Historically, the printed media played the most important role in informing public debate. The printed media developed, for the most part, our understanding of how news is to be reported. Today, however, more than 90 percent of Americans use television news as their primary source of information. In addition, the Internet has become a source for political communication and fund-raising. As Internet use grows, the system of gathering and sharing news and information is changing from one in which the media have a primary role to one in which the individual citizen may play a greater role. The chapter-opening *What If . . .* explores some of the possible consequences of such a change for the future. With that future in mind, it is important to analyze the current relationship between the media and politics.

The Media's Functions

The mass media perform a number of different functions in any country. In the United States, we can list at least six. Almost all of them can have political implications, and some are essential to the democratic process. These functions are as follows: (1) entertainment, (2) reporting the news, (3) identifying public problems, (4) socializing new generations, (5) providing a political forum, and (6) making profits.

Entertainment

By far the greatest number of radio and television hours are dedicated to entertaining the public. The battle for prime-time ratings indicates how important successful entertainment is to the survival of networks and individual stations.

Although there is no direct linkage between entertainment and politics, network dramas often introduce material that may be politically controversial and that may stimulate public discussion. Made-for-TV movies have focused on many controversial topics, including AIDS, incest, and wife battering.

President Bush is seen here through the windows of the Oval Office of the White House as he addresses the nation after the terrorist attacks of September 11, 2001. The president frequently addresses the nation in times of crisis, as in this instance, and also in seeking the public's support for his policies. The media are not required to air his remarks live, however. Indeed, on many occasions, the major television networks have refused to air presidential speeches live or in their entirety.
(AP Photo/Doug Mills)

Media Issues around the World

For all of our complaining about bias in the media and the superficiality of American news, the United States has more freedom of expression than many other nations.

Censorship of newspapers is still quite common around the world. The governments of Iraq and Iran routinely censor and shut down newspapers for political content, as does the government of China. Many nations censor television and movies for sexual content on the ground that it violates the mores of their societies. In virtually any nation that has an authoritarian government, newspapers are carefully watched and subjected to censorship if they express too much opposition to the government.

The Internet has provided a new and extremely useful tool for opposition groups throughout the world. Using just text or text and pictures, opposition media can transmit information about their political situation throughout the world. The Chinese government, for just that reason, has tightly controlled the Internet. Western citizens, in contrast, not only have unlimited access to news on the Internet but can even monitor government censorship through Web sites maintained by watchdog groups, such as MediaChannel (**http://www. mediachannel.org**).

FOR CRITICAL ANALYSIS

Why does the Internet pose such a threat to authoritarian governments?

Reporting the News

A primary function of the mass media in all their forms—newspapers and magazines, radio, television, cable, and online news services—is the reporting of news. The media convey words and pictures about events, facts, personalities, and ideas. The protections of the First Amendment are intended to keep the flow of news as free as possible, because it is an essential part of the democratic process. If citizens cannot get unbiased information about the state of their communities and their leaders' actions, how can they make voting decisions? Perhaps the most incisive comment about the importance of the media was made by James Madison, who said, "A people who mean to be their own governors must arm themselves with the power knowledge gives. A popular government without popular information or the means of acquiring it, is but a prologue to a farce or a tragedy or perhaps both." [1] Not all nations accept this premise of democratic thought, however, as explained in this chapter's *Global View.*

Identifying Public Problems

The power of information is important not only in revealing what the government is doing but also in determining what the government ought to do—in other words, in setting the **public agenda**. The mass media identify public issues, such as the placement of convicted sex offenders in new homes and neighborhoods. The media then influence the passage of legislation, such as "Megan's Law," which requires police to notify neighbors about the release and/or resettlement of certain offenders. American journalists also work in a long tradition of uncovering public wrongdoing, corruption, and bribery and of bringing such wrongdoing to the public's attention. Closely related to this investigative function is that of presenting policy alternatives. Public policy is often complex and difficult to make entertaining, but programs devoted to public policy increasingly are being scheduled for prime-time television. Most networks produce shows with a "news magazine" format that sometimes include segments on foreign policy and other issues.

Socializing New Generations

As mentioned in Chapter 7, the media, and particularly television, strongly influence the beliefs and opinions of all Americans. Because of this influence, the media play a significant role in the political socialization of the younger generation, as well as immigrants to this country. Through the transmission of historical information (sometimes fictionalized), the presentation of American culture, and the portrayal of the diverse regions and groups in the United States, the media teach young people and immigrants about what it means to be an American. TV talk shows, such as *Oprah*, sometimes focus on controversial issues (such as abortion or assisted suicide) that relate to basic American values (such as liberty). Many children's shows are designed not only to entertain young viewers but also to instruct them in the traditional moral values of American society. In recent years, the public has become increasingly concerned about the level of violence depicted on children's programs and on other shows during prime time.

Providing a Political Forum

As part of their news function, the media also provide a political forum for leaders and the public. Candidates for office use news reporting to sustain interest in their campaigns, whereas officeholders use the media to gain support for their policies or to present an image of leadership. Presidential trips abroad are an outstanding way for the chief executive to get colorful, positive, and exciting news coverage that makes

---

[1] As quoted in "Castro vs. (Some) Censorship," *The New York Times,* November 22, 1983, p. 24.

the president look "presidential." The media also offer ways for citizens to participate in public debate, through letters to the editor, televised editorials, or electronic mail. The question of whether more public access should be provided will be discussed later in this chapter.

Making Profits

Most of the news media in the United States are private, for-profit corporate enterprises. One of their goals is to make profits—for employee salaries, for expansion, and for dividends to the stockholders who own the companies. Profits are made, in general, by charging for advertising. Advertising revenues usually are related directly to circulation or to listener/viewer ratings.

Several well-known outlets are publicly owned—public television stations in many communities and National Public Radio. These operate without extensive commercials, are locally supported, and are often subsidized by the government and corporations.

Added up, these factors form the basis for a complex relationship among the media, the government, and the public. Throughout the rest of this chapter, we examine some of the many facets of this relationship. Our purpose is to set a foundation for understanding how the media influence the political process.

History of the Media in the United States

Many years ago Thomas Jefferson wrote, "Were it left to me to decide whether we should have a government without newspapers, or newspapers without a government, I should not hesitate a moment to prefer the latter."[2] Although the media have played

---

[2] As quoted in Richard M. Clurman, "The Media Learn a Lesson," *The New York Times,* December 2, 1983, p. A2.

DID YOU KNOW . . .
That there are approximately 1,250 full-time radio, TV, and newspaper correspondents in Washington, D.C.?

Public Agenda
Issues that commonly are perceived by members of the political community as meriting public attention and governmental action. The media play an important role in setting the public agenda by focusing attention on certain topics.

George W. Bush made an appearance on *The Tonight Show with Jay Leno* during the 2000 presidential campaign. Television and radio talk shows are an important forum for political candidates. They can reach a huge audience of potential voters without spending campaign funds. Late-night talk shows, such as this one, allow candidates to reach young voters, too. Is there any downside to a candidate appearing on a popular talk show? (AP Photo/Eric Draper)

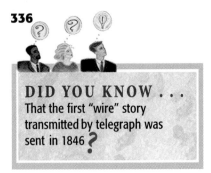

Managed News
Information generated and distributed by the government in such a way as to give government interests priority over candor.

a significant role in politics since the founding of this nation, they were not as overwhelmingly important in the past as they are today. For one thing, politics was controlled by a small elite who communicated personally. For another, during the early 1800s and before, news traveled slowly. If an important political event occurred in New York, it was not known until five days later in Philadelphia; ten days later in the capital cities of Connecticut, Maryland, and Virginia; and fifteen days later in Boston.

Roughly three thousand newspapers were being published by 1860. Some of these, such as the *New York Tribune,* were mainly sensation mongers that concentrated on crimes, scandals, and the like. The *New York Herald* specialized in self-improvement and what today would be called practical news. Although sensational and biased reporting often created political divisiveness (this was true particularly during the Civil War), many historians believe that the growth of the printed media played an important role in unifying the country.

The Rise of the Political Press

Americans may cherish the idea of an unbiased press, but in the early years of the nation's history, the number of politically sponsored newspapers was significant. The sole reason for the existence of such periodicals was to further the interests of the politicians who paid for their publication. As chief executive of our government during this period, George Washington has been called a "firm believer" in **managed news.** Although acknowledging that the public had a right to be informed, he felt that some matters should be kept secret and that news that might damage the image of the United States should be censored (not published). Washington, however, made no attempt to control the press. (In times of crisis, should the government be allowed to censor news articles in the interests of protecting the nation's security? For a discussion of this issue, see this chapter's *Which Side Are You On?* feature.)

The Development of Mass-Readership Newspapers

Two inventions in the nineteenth century led to the development of mass-readership newspapers. The first was the high-speed rotary press; the second was the telegraph. Faster presses meant lower per-unit costs and lower subscription prices. By 1848, the Associated Press had developed the telegraph into a nationwide apparatus for the dissemination of all types of information on a systematic basis.

" INTERESTING.....IT'S LIKE A PORTABLE 500K FILE and YOU DON'T HAVE TO WAIT FOR IT TO DOWNLOAD.... AND YOU SAY IT'S CALLED A NEWSPAPER ?"

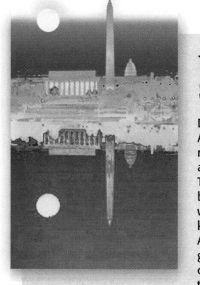

Which Side Are You On?
Should the Press Be Censored in Times of Crisis?

During periods of crisis, Americans have tended to rally around the president and other political leaders. The war on terrorism has been no different. But this war has presented new kinds of challenges for Americans and for their government. How do we defend ourselves against this new kind of enemy— one that is stateless, unpredictable, and at times intractable? To enable our security forces—including the Federal Bureau of Investigation, the Central Intelligence Agency, the police, and the armed forces—to do the best job possible, should the government prevent the media from publishing information that could harm those efforts? This would constitute a form of censorship, even if self-imposed by the media. Some people believe that no crisis is so great as to deny full freedom of the press. Others say that these times are truly different.

A DIVISIVE ISSUE

Americans are quite divided in their opinions about restricting the freedom of the press in the present crisis. A Pew Research Center poll taken after the terrorist attacks in September 2001 found that 53 percent of the respondents wanted the government to censor news that might threaten national security. A significant minority (almost 40 percent of the respondents), however, thought that the media should not refrain from reporting news that they believe to be in the national interest.

A similar split in opinion was reflected in another poll taken after 9/11 that asked the following question: Should Americans publicly criticize presidential decisions on military issues? According to the poll's results, 54 percent of the respondents thought that Americans should not criticize presidential decisions on these issues; 41 percent of the respondents, though, believed that it was all right to engage in such criticism.*

*CBS News poll, November 2001, as reported in *Public Perspective,* January/February 2002, p. 47.

A related issue concerns the degree to which the press should support the administration's position. The Pew Research Center poll mentioned above also asked that particular question. Almost three-fourths of those polled wanted news coverage that reflects all points of view. The American public wants a press that thinks independently and does not serve as a propaganda machine, even in times of crisis.

THE THORNY ISSUE OF NO PRIOR RESTRAINT

Since the ratification of the Bill of Rights, America has prided itself on its free press. Whenever the government has tried to prevent the publication of information that the media believed to be in the public interest, the courts have struck down such prior restraints. A key Supreme Court case on this issue was decided in 1971. The *New York Times* and the *Washington Post* were going to publish a secret history of the U.S. government's involvement in the war in Vietnam (1964–1975). The government attempted to prevent the publication of those documents, arguing that national security was threatened. The Supreme Court ruled in favor of the newspapers' right to publish.

WHAT'S YOUR POSITION?

In times of severe crisis, should the government be allowed to interfere with the media's attempts to publish information relating to America's security?

GOING ONLINE

For a perspective on the efforts of journalists to report the news in times of war and crisis, go to **http://www. newseum.org** and click on "Cyber Newseum" to see the latest exhibits. For a perspective on the current state of government censorship and self-censorship in war reporting, visit the MediaChannel and the part of its Web site devoted to that subject at **http://www.mediachannel. org/atissue/warpeace**.

Along with these technological changes came a growing population and increasing urbanization. A larger, more urban population could support daily newspapers, even if the price per paper was only a penny. Finally, the burgeoning, diversified economy encouraged the growth of advertising, which meant that newspapers could obtain additional revenues from merchants who seized the opportunity to promote their wares to a larger public.

The Popular Press and Yellow Journalism

Students of the history of journalism have ascertained a change, in the last half of the 1800s, not in the level of biased news reporting but in its origin. Whereas politically sponsored newspapers had expounded a particular political party's point of view, the post–Civil War mass-based newspapers expounded whatever political philosophy the owner of the newspaper happened to have.

Even if newspaper owners did not have a particular political axe to grind, they often allowed their editors to engage in sensationalism and what is known as **yellow journalism.** The questionable or simply personal activities of a prominent businessperson, politician, or socialite were front-page material. Newspapers, then as now, made their economic way by maximizing readership. As the *National Enquirer* demonstrates with its current circulation of more than five million, sensationalism is still rewarded by high levels of readership.

Yellow Journalism

A term for sensationalistic, irresponsible journalism. Reputedly, the term is short for "Yellow Kid Journalism," an allusion to the cartoon "The Yellow Kid" in the old *New York World,* a newspaper especially noted for its sensationalism.

In a cartoon attacking yellow journalism, William Randolph Hearst (left) and Joseph Pulitzer (right) are lampooned for emphasizing scandal and gossip in news coverage. (The Granger Collection)

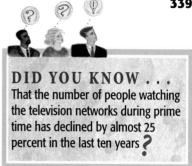

The Age of the Electromagnetic Signal

The first scheduled radio program in the United States featured politicians. On the night of November 2, 1920, KDKA–Pittsburgh transmitted the returns of the presidential-election race between Warren G. Harding and James M. Cox. The listeners were a few thousand people tuning in on very primitive, homemade sets.

By 1924, there were nearly 1,400 radio stations. But it wasn't until 8 P.M. on November 15, 1926, that the electronic media came into their own in the United States. On that night, the National Broadcasting Company (NBC) made its debut with a four-hour program broadcast by twenty-five stations in twenty-one cities. Network broadcasting had become a reality.

Even with the advent of national radio in the 1920s and television in the late 1940s, many politicians were slow to understand the significance of the **electronic media.** The 1952 presidential campaign was the first to involve a real role for television. Television coverage of the Republican convention helped Dwight Eisenhower win over delegates and secure the nomination. His vice presidential running mate, Richard Nixon, put the TV time to good use. Accused of hiding a secret slush fund, Nixon replied to his critics with his famous "Checkers" speech. He denied the attacks, cried real tears, and said that the only thing he ever received from a contributor for his personal use was his dog, Checkers. It was a highly effective performance.

Today, television dominates the campaign strategy of every would-be national politician, as well as that of every elected official. Politicians think of ways to continue to be newsworthy, thereby gaining access to the electronic media. Attacking the president's programs is one way of becoming newsworthy; other ways include holding highly visible hearings on controversial subjects, going on "fact-finding" trips, and employing gimmicks (such as taking a walking tour of a state).

The Revolution in the Electronic Media

Just as technological change was responsible for the end of politically sponsored periodicals, technology is increasing the number of alternative news sources today. The advent of pay TV, cable TV, subscription TV, satellite TV, and the Internet has completely

DID YOU KNOW . . .
That the number of people watching the television networks during prime time has declined by almost 25 percent in the last ten years ❓

Electronic Media
Communication channels that involve electronic transmissions, such as radio, television, and, to an increasing extent, the Internet.

In 1952, vice presidential nominee Richard Nixon used a television appearance to explain an $18,000 expense fund. It was known as his "Checkers" speech because of his reference to the family dog. Nixon's political career coincided with television's rise as the dominant political medium. Nixon participated in the first televised presidential debate with John Kennedy in 1960, and in 1974 Nixon announced his resignation as president in a televised speech to the nation. (AP Photo)

changed the electronic media landscape. When there were basically only three TV networks, it was indeed a "wasteland," as former Federal Communications Commission chairman Newton Minnow once claimed. But now, with hundreds, if not thousands, of potential outlets for specialized programs, the electronic media are becoming more and more like the printed media in catering to specialized tastes. This is sometimes referred to as **narrowcasting.** Both cable television and the Internet offer the public unparalleled access to specialized information on everything from gardening and home repair to sports and religion. Most viewers are able to choose among several sources for their favorite type of programming.

In recent years, narrowcasting has become increasingly prevalent. Consumers watch only those shows and channels that they like, and the networks' audiences are declining. Between 1982 and 2002, network television's share of the audience fell from 72 percent to 55 percent. At the same time, the percentage of households having access to the Internet grew from zero to more than 65 percent.

Talk-Show Politics and Internet Broadcasting

In the realm of politics, the multiple news outlets have given rise to literally thousands of talk shows, whether on television, radio, or the Internet. By 2003, there were more than two dozen national television talk shows; their hosts ranged from Jerry Springer, who is regarded as a sensationalist, to Larry King, whose show has become a political necessity for candidates. Ross Perot actually announced his candidacy for the presidency in the 1992 election on *Larry King Live.*

The real blossoming of "talk" has occurred on the radio. The number of radio stations that program only talk shows has increased from about 300 in 1989 to more than 1,200 today. The topics of talk shows range from business and investment, to psychology, to politics. There has been considerable criticism of the political talk shows, especially those hosted by Rush Limbaugh, G. Gordon Liddy, and other conservatives. Critics contend that such shows increase the level of intolerance and irrationality in American politics. The listeners to those shows are self-selected and tend to share the viewpoint of the host. Similarly, the Internet makes it possible for a Web

Narrowcasting
Broadcasting that is targeted to one small sector of the population.

To find out more on this subject, use the term "talk shows" in the Subject guide.

site to be highly ideological or partisan and to encourage online chat with others of the same persuasion. One of the potential hazards of narrowcasting of this kind is that people will be less open to dialogue with those whose opinions differ from their own, resulting in increased political extremism.

The Primacy of Television

Television is the most influential medium. It is also big business. National news TV personalities such as Peter Jennings may earn in excess of several million dollars per year from their TV news–reporting contracts alone. They are paid so much because they command large audiences, and large audiences command high prices for advertising on national news shows. Indeed, news *per se* has become a major factor in the profitability of TV stations.

The Increase in News-Type Programming

In 1963, the major networks—ABC, CBS, and NBC—devoted only eleven minutes daily to national news. By 2003, the amount of time on the networks devoted to news-type programming had increased to about three hours. In addition, a twenty-four-hour-a-day news cable channel—CNN—started operating in 1980. With the addition of CNN–Headline News, CNBC, MSNBC, the All-News Channel, and other news-format cable channels since the 1980s, the amount of news-type programming continues to increase. In recent years, all of the major networks have also added Internet sites to try to capture that market, but they face hundreds of competitors on the Internet.

Television's Influence on the Political Process

Television's influence on the political process today is recognized by all who engage in it. Its special characteristics are worthy of attention. Television news is often criticized for being superficial, particularly compared with the detailed coverage available in the *New York Times,* for example. In fact, television news is constrained by its peculiar technical characteristics, the most important being the limitations of time; stories must be reported in only a few minutes.

The most interesting aspect of television is, of course, the fact that it relies on pictures rather than words to attract the viewer's attention. Therefore, the videotapes or slides that are chosen for a particular political story have exaggerated importance. Viewers do not know what other photos may have been taken or events recorded—they note only those appearing on their screens. Television news can also be exploited for its drama by well-constructed stories. Some critics suggest that there is pressure to produce television news that has a "story line," like a novel or movie. The story should be short, with exciting pictures and a clear plot. In the extreme case, the news media are satisfied with a **sound bite,** a several-second comment selected or crafted for its immediate impact on the viewer.

It has been suggested that these formatting characteristics—or necessities—of television increase its influence on political events. (Newspapers and news magazines are also limited by their formats, but to a lesser extent.) As you are aware, real life is usually not dramatic, nor do all events have a neat or an easily understood plot. Political campaigns are continuing events, lasting perhaps as long as two years. The significance of their daily turns and twists is only apparent later. The "drama" of Congress, with its 535 players and dozens of important committees and meetings, is also difficult for the media to present. What television requires is dozens of daily three-minute stories.

INFOTRAC ®
COLLEGE EDITION

To find out more on this subject, use the term "television and politics" in the Subject guide.

Sound Bite
A brief, memorable comment that easily can be fit into news broadcasts.

The Media and Political Campaigns

All forms of the media—television, newspapers, radio, magazines, and online services—have an enormous political impact on American society. Media influence is most obvious during political campaigns. News coverage of a single event, such as the results of the Iowa caucuses or the New Hampshire primary, may be the most important factor in having a candidate be referred to in the media as the "front-runner" in presidential campaigns. It is not too much of an exaggeration to say that almost all national political figures, starting with the president, plan all public appearances and statements to snag media coverage.

Because television is the primary news source for the majority of Americans, candidates and their consultants spend much of their time devising strategies to use television to their benefit. Three types of TV coverage are generally used in campaigns for the presidency and other offices: advertising, management of news coverage, and campaign debates.

Advertising

Perhaps one of the most effective political ads of all time was a short, thirty-second spot created by President Lyndon Johnson's media adviser. In this ad, a little girl stood in a field of daisies. As she held a daisy, she pulled the petals off and quietly counted to herself. Suddenly, when she reached number ten, a deep bass voice cut in and began a

President Lyndon Johnson's "daisy girl" ad contrasted the innocence of childhood with the horror of an atomic attack.

VOTE FOR PRESIDENT JOHNSON
ON NOVEMBER 3.

countdown: "10, 9, 8, 7, 6 . . . ." When the voice intoned "zero," the unmistakable mushroom cloud of an atomic bomb began to fill the screen. Then President Johnson's voice was heard: "These are the stakes. To make a world in which all of God's children can live, or to go into the dark. We must either love each other or we must die." At the end of the commercial, the message read, "Vote for President Johnson on November 3."

To understand how effective this daisy girl commercial was, you must know that Johnson's opponent was Barry Goldwater, a Republican conservative candidate known for his expansive views on the role of the U.S. military. The ad's implication was that Goldwater would lead the United States into nuclear war. Although the ad was withdrawn within a few days, it has a place in political campaign history as the classic negative campaign announcement. The ad's producer, Tony Schwartz, describes the effect in this way: "It was comparable to a person going to a psychiatrist and seeing dirty pictures in a Rorschach pattern. The daisy commercial evoked Goldwater's pro-bomb statements. They were like dirty pictures in the audience's mind."[3]

Since the daisy girl advertisement, negative advertising has come into its own. Candidates vie with one another to produce "attack" ads and then to counterattack when the opponent responds. The public claims not to like negative advertising, but as one consultant put it, "Negative advertising works." Any advertising "works" when viewers or listeners remember an ad. It is clear that negative ads are more memorable than ads that praise the candidate's virtues. Negative advertising, which supporters and independents remember longer than positive advertising, works well. No vote gain is expected anyway from members of the other party or supporters of the candidate under attack.

As noted in Chapter 10, "advocacy ads," which argue for or against a policy or an issue (and, indirectly, for or against candidates who support that policy or issue), are another form of political advertising. These ads are very effective at conveying political messages to voters.

Management of News Coverage

Using political advertising to get a message across to the public is a very expensive tactic. Coverage by the news media, however, is free; it simply demands that the campaign ensure that coverage takes place. In recent years, campaign managers have shown increasing sophistication in creating newsworthy events for journalists to cover. As Doris Graber points out, "To keep a favorable image of their candidates in front of the public, campaign managers arrange newsworthy events to familiarize potential voters with their candidates' best aspects."[4]

To take advantage of the media's interest in campaign politics, whether at the presidential level or perhaps in a Senate race, the campaign staff uses several methods to try to influence the quantity and type of coverage the campaign receives. First, the campaign staff understands the technical aspects of media coverage—camera angles, necessary equipment, timing, and deadlines—and plans political events to accommodate the press. Second, the campaign organization is aware that political reporters and their sponsors—networks or newspapers—are in competition for the best stories and can be manipulated through the granting of favors, such as a personal interview with the candidate. Third, the scheduler in the campaign has the important task of planning events that will be photogenic and interesting enough for the evening news. A related goal, although one that is more difficult to attain, is to convince reporters that a particular interpretation of an event is correct.

Today, the art of putting the appropriate **spin** on a story or event is highly developed. Each presidential candidate's press advisers, often referred to as **spin doctors,**

DID YOU KNOW . . .
That the average length of a quote, or sound bite, for a candidate decreased from forty-nine seconds in 1968 to less than nine seconds today?

Spin
An interpretation of campaign events or election results that is most favorable to the candidate's campaign strategy.

Spin Doctor
A political campaign adviser who tries to convince journalists of the truth of a particular interpretation of events.

---

[3] As quoted in Kathleen Hall Jamieson, *Packaging the Presidency: A History and Criticism of Presidential Campaign Advertising,* 3d ed. (New York: Oxford University Press, 1996), p. 200.

[4] Doris Graber, *Mass Media and American Politics,* 5th ed. (Washington, D.C.: Congressional Quarterly Press, 1997), p. 59.

try to convince the journalists that their interpretations of the political events are correct. For example, in the 2000 primaries George W. Bush's camp played down his loss to John McCain in the Michigan primary by using the spin that Michigan independents who normally vote Democratic voted in the Republican primary to defeat Bush. Journalists began to report on the different spins and on how the candidates tried to manipulate campaign news coverage.

Going for the Knockout Punch—Presidential Debates

Perhaps of equal importance to political advertisements is the performance of the candidate in a televised presidential debate. After the first such debate in 1960, in which John Kennedy, the young senator from Massachusetts, took on the vice president of the United States, Richard Nixon, candidates became aware of the great potential of television for changing the momentum of a campaign. In general, challengers have much more to gain from debating than do incumbents. Challengers hope that the incumbent may make a mistake in the debate and undermine the "presidential" image. Incumbent presidents are loath to debate their challengers, because it puts their opponents on an equal footing with them.

After some negotiating about the structure and timing of debates, Vice President Al Gore and Governor George W. Bush met for three public debates prior to the 2000 presidential elections, and their respective vice presidential candidates met for one. The three presidential debates each featured a different format: one formal debate, one moderated discussion between them, and one "town meeting"–style debate. Vice President Gore was criticized for being too aggressive in one debate, and Governor Bush was criticized for either being too passive or being uninformative. The real issue was style—that is, whether a candidate could stay calm under pressure, be likable, and avoid any big mistakes. The debates were, in terms of voter influence, a draw.

Although debates are justified publicly as an opportunity for the voters to find out how candidates differ on the issues, what the candidates want is to capitalize on the power of television to project an image. They view the debate as a strategic opportu-

INFOTRAC®
COLLEGE EDITION

For updates and more information on debates, use the term "campaign debates" in the Subject guide.

A family watches the 1960 Kennedy-Nixon debates on television. After the debate, TV viewers thought Kennedy had won, whereas radio listeners thought Nixon had won. (The Library of Congress)

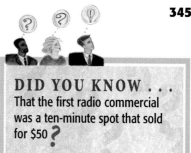

nity to improve their own images or to point out the failures of their opponents. Candidates also know that the morning-after interpretation of the debate by the news media may play a crucial role in what the public thinks. Regardless of the risks of debating, the potential for gaining votes is so great that candidates undoubtedly will continue to seek televised debates.

Political Campaigns and the Internet

Without a doubt, the Internet has become an important vehicle for campaign advertising and news coverage, as well as for soliciting campaign contributions. This was made clear during the 2000 presidential elections. A Pew Research Study poll conducted after the elections revealed that nearly one-fifth of the voters had gone online to obtain news about the elections—compared to only 4 percent who had done so in 1996. Of that one-fifth, nearly half claimed that their voting decisions had been influenced by the information that they accessed via the Internet.

Today, the campaign staff of virtually every candidate running for a significant political office includes an Internet campaign strategist—a professional hired to create and maintain the campaign Web site. The work of this strategist includes designing a user-friendly and attractive Web site for the candidate, managing the candidate's e-mail communications, tracking campaign contributions made via the site, and so on. Additionally, virtually all major interest groups in the United States now use the Internet to promote their causes. Prior to elections, various groups engage in issue advocacy from their Web sites. At little or no cost, they can promote certain positions taken by specific candidates and solicit contributions.

Only a few years ago, some speculated that the Internet would soon dominate political campaign advertising and news coverage. The traditional media—television, radio, and printed newspapers and magazines—would play a far less significant role than in the past. This, of course, has not happened. For example, during the 2000 presidential campaigns, the media devoted significant space to how the candidates were able to raise funds through online contributions. A Gallup poll, however, found that only 1 percent of the respondents who had access to the Internet said that they had made campaign contributions online.

The Media's Impact on the Voters

The question of how much influence the media have on voting behavior is difficult to answer. Generally, individuals watch television, read newspapers, or log on to a Web site with certain preconceived ideas about political issues and candidates. These attitudes and opinions act as a kind of perceptual screen that filters out information that makes people feel uncomfortable or that does not fit with their own ideas.

Voters watch campaign commercials and news about political campaigns with "selective attentiveness." That is, they tend to watch those commercials that support the candidates they favor and tend to pay attention to news stories about their own candidates. This selectivity also affects their perceptions of the content of the news story or commercial and whether it is remembered. Apparently, the media are most influential with those persons who have not formed an opinion about political candidates or issues. Studies have shown that the flurry of television commercials and debates immediately before election day has the most impact on those voters who are truly undecided. Few voters who have already formed their opinions change their minds under the influence of the media.

In 2000, as in prior years, the media focused on the "horse race" aspects of the presidential campaigns. While some media outlets did present careful analyses of the issues and critiques of the candidates' advertising spots, most of the television coverage focused on the ever-present polls. Both presidential candidates, Al Gore and George W. Bush, took advantage of every opportunity to be on prime-time television:

they visited with Oprah, David Letterman, and Larry King, among others. In fact, the news programs were shocked when a national poll indicated that some 20 percent of the voters said that they learned about politics from the late-night talk shows. The media's worst hour came on election night. All of the networks and cable news operations vied with each other to "call" the states for one or the other of the presidential candidates. Because the media were using data from exit polls rather than actual vote counts, a number of states were "too close to call," and several were called mistakenly and later changed. Whether the rush to declare the elections over had any impact on the outcome is uncertain.

ELECTIONS 2002 The Role of the Media in the 2002 Elections

The 2002 elections were the last to take place before the new Bipartisan Campaign Reform Act went into effect. This law is expected to influence dramatically the amount of money spent on campaign advertising. But in 2002, candidates, political parties, and interest groups still had plenty to spend. More than $336 million was spent on network television advertising on behalf of candidates for the House, Senate, and governorship in the last seven weeks of campaigning. And such spending yielded results: 95 percent of races for the House and 75 percent for the Senate were won by the candidate who spent the most money. Some observers argue that the barrage of political advertising on television in the final weeks of the campaign becomes simply "wallpaper," largely unnoticed by voters. Yet these same observers say television campaign ads will not disappear soon. Although a candidate may not win with the ads, he or she is even less likely to win without them.

The Media and the Government

The mass media not only wield considerable power when it comes to political campaigns, but they also, in one way or another, can wield power over the affairs of government and over government officials. For example, in November 2001 President George W. Bush issued an executive order establishing military tribunals for the prosecution of suspected terrorists. As initially proposed, these tribunals would have allowed defendants far fewer rights than military defendants facing courts-martial have. Over the next few months, numerous criticisms of the proposed tribunals appeared in both the printed and the electronic media. As mentioned in Chapter 4, this criticism effectively forced the government to revise the rules to allow more rights for the accused.

The Media and the Presidency

The relationship between the media and the president is most often reciprocal: each needs the other to thrive. Because of this co-dependency, both the media and the president work hard to exploit the other. The media need news to report, and the president may need coverage.

In the United States, the prominence of the president is accentuated by a **White House press corps** that is assigned full-time to cover the presidency. These reporters even have a lounge in the White House where they spend their days, waiting for a story to break. Most of the time, they simply wait for the daily or twice-daily briefing by the president's **press secretary**. Because of the press corps's physical proximity to the president, the chief executive cannot even take a brief stroll around the presidential swimming pool without its becoming news. Perhaps no other nation allows the press such access to its highest government official. Consequently, no other

White House Press Corps
A group of reporters assigned full-time to cover the presidency.

Press Secretary
The individual responsible for representing the White House before the media. The press secretary writes news releases, provides background information, sets up press conferences, and generally handles communication for the White House.

nation has its airwaves and print media so filled with absolute trivia regarding the personal lives of the chief executive and his family.

President Franklin D. Roosevelt brought new spirit to a demoralized country and led it through the Great Depression through his effective use of the media, particularly through his radio broadcasts. His radio "fireside chats" brought hope to millions. Roosevelt's speeches were masterful in their ability to forge a common emotional bond among his listeners. His decisive announcement in 1933 on the reorganization of the banks, for example, calmed a jittery nation and prevented the collapse of the banking industry, which was threatened by a run on banks, from which nervous depositors were withdrawing their assets. His famous Pearl Harbor speech, following the Japanese attack on the U.S. Pacific fleet on December 7, 1941 ("a day that will live in infamy"), mobilized the nation for the sacrifices and effort necessary to win World War II.

President Franklin D. Roosevelt, the first president to fully exploit the airwaves for his benefit, reported to the nation through radio "fireside chats." (Photo Researchers)

Setting the Public Agenda

Given that government officials have in front of them an array of problems with which they must deal, the process of setting the public agenda is constant. To be sure, what goes on the public agenda for discussion, debate, and, ultimately, policy action depends on many factors—not the least being each official's personal philosophy.

According to a number of studies, the media play an important part in setting the public agenda. Evidence is strong that whatever public problems receive the most media treatment will be cited by the public in contemporary surveys as the most important problems. Although the media do not make policy decisions, they do determine to a significant extent the policy issues that need to be decided—and this is an important part of the political process. Because those who control the media are not elected representatives of the people, the agenda-setting role of the media necessarily is a controversial one. The relationship of the media to agenda setting remains complex, though, because politicians are able to manipulate media coverage to control some of its effects, as well as to exploit the media to further their agendas with the public.

Government Regulation of the Media

The United States has perhaps the freest press in the world. Nonetheless, regulation of the media does exist, particularly of the electronic media. Many aspects of this regulation were discussed in Chapter 4, when we examined First Amendment rights and the press.

Controlling Ownership of the Media

The First Amendment does not mention electronic media, which did not exist when the Bill of Rights was written. For many reasons, the government has much greater control over the electronic media than it does over printed media. Through the Federal Communications Commission (FCC), which regulates communications by radio, television, wire, and cable, the number of radio stations has been controlled for many years, even though technologically we could have many more radio stations

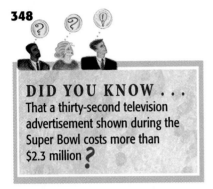

DID YOU KNOW ...
That a thirty-second television advertisement shown during the Super Bowl costs more than $2.3 million ❓

INFOTRAC®
COLLEGE EDITION

To find out more about the impact of this legislation, use the term "Telecommunications Act of 1996" in the Subject guide.

Media Access
The public's right of access to the media. The Federal Communications Commission and the courts gradually have taken the stance that citizens do have a right to media access.

than now exist. Also, the FCC created a situation in which the three major TV networks dominated the airwaves.

Most FCC rules have dealt with ownership of news media, such as how many stations a network can own. Recently, the FCC has decided to auction off hundreds of radio frequencies, allowing the expansion of cellular telephone applications.

In 1996, Congress passed legislation that has far-reaching implications for the communications industry—the Telecommunications Act. The act ended the rule that kept telephone companies from entering the cable business and other communications markets. What this means is that a single corporation—whether AT&T or Disney—can offer long-distance and local telephone services, cable television, satellite television, Internet services, and, of course, libraries of films and entertainment. The act opened the door to competition and led to more options for consumers, who now can choose among multiple competitors for all of these services delivered to the home. At the same time, it launched a race among competing companies to control media ownership. As discussed in the *Politics and the Media* feature, many media outlets are now owned by corporate conglomerates. A single entity may own a television network; the studios that produce shows, news, and movies; and the means to deliver that content to the home via cable, satellite, or the Internet. The question to be faced in the future is how to ensure competition in the delivery of news so that citizens have access to multiple points of view from the media.

Government Control of Content

In general, the broadcasting industry has avoided government regulation of content by establishing its own code. This code consists of a set of rules developed by the National Association of Broadcasters (the lobby for the TV and radio industry) that regulate the amount of sex, violence, nudity, profanity, and so forth that is allowed on the air. It should be noted that abiding by the code is voluntary on the part of networks and stations.

Since 1980, there has been continued public debate over whether the government should attempt to control polling and the "early calling" of presidential elections by the television networks. As discussed in Chapter 7, some legislators and citizens have called for a ban on exit polls or on releasing them before *all* polling places in the continental United States are closed. Others have called for a federal law establishing a uniform closing time for polling places so that voting would end at the same time all over the country, and thus exit polls could not be a factor. In any event, although turnout has been lower than expected in many western states, studies suggest that the early announcement of election results based on exit polls has little effect on election outcomes.

The Telecommunications Act of 1996 included two provisions that allow for some government control of the content of the media. One provision required that television manufacturers include a "V-chip" in each set. The V-chip allows parents to block programs that include violence or sexual conduct from being viewed on their televisions. The other provision, known as the Communications Decency Act, prohibited the transmission of indecent or patently offensive materials on the Internet in such a way that minors could access those materials. In 1997, the Supreme Court held that the provision restrained too much protected adult speech and was therefore unconstitutional. Further regulation of the Internet is obviously a matter of constitutional debate (see Chapter 4).

The Public's Right to Media Access

Does the public have a right to **media access**? Both the FCC and the courts gradually have taken the stance that citizens do have a right of access to the media, particularly the electronic media. The argument is that the airwaves are public, but because

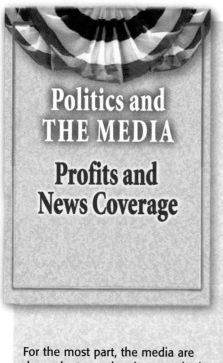

Politics and THE MEDIA
Profits and News Coverage

For the most part, the media are dependent on advertisers to obtain sufficient revenues to make profits. Those media outlets that do not succeed in generating sufficient revenues from advertising either go bankrupt or are sold. Consequently, individuals reporting the news often feel pressure from media owners and from advertisers.

SYNERGY AND THE MEDIA BUSINESS

Many a media owner also owns other companies. Within the past decade, all of the prime-time television networks have been purchased by major American corporations and have become part of corporate conglomerates. The Turner Broadcasting/CNN network was purchased by a major corporation, Time Warner. Later, Time Warner was acquired by America Online (AOL), a merger that combined the world's then-largest media company with the world's then-largest online company. Fox Television became a part of Rupert Murdoch's publishing and media empire. In addition to these mergers and acquisitions, many of these corporations have formed partnerships with computer software makers, such as Microsoft, for joint electronic publishing ventures.

Not surprisingly, media owners view their media outlets as places to promote their other businesses. They see nothing unethical about such a practice. In addition, media owners often take their cues from what advertisers want media outlets to do. If an important advertiser does not like the

political bent of a particular reporter, the reporter may be asked to alter his or her "style" of writing. The Project for Excellence in Journalism in 2001 discovered that 53 percent of local news directors said that advertisers try to tell them what to air and what not to air.*

BEHOLDEN TO ADVERTISERS

Advertisers have been known to pull ads from newspapers and TV stations whenever they read or view negative publicity about their own company or product. For example, when CBS ran a *60 Minutes* show about store security guards at Dillard's and other department stores using excessive force and racial profiling, the department-store chain Dillard's pulled its ads from CBS. This example can be multiplied many times over. It is an unpleasant fact in the media.

FOR CRITICAL ANALYSIS

How can a news organization remain independent of the pressure to generate ever-increasing profits via more ad revenues?

*Columbia Journalism Review, November/ December 2001.

---

they are used for private profit, the government has the right to dictate how they are used. It does so in many ways. Recall from Chapter 4 that in addition to the equal-time rule for candidates—under which broadcasters who sell airtime to political candidates must make equal time available to opposing candidates on equal terms—the FCC has also promulgated the personal attack rule. This rule allows individuals (or groups) airtime to reply to attacks that have previously been aired.

Technology is giving more citizens access to the electronic media and, in particular, to television. As more cable operators have more airtime to sell, some of that time will remain unused and will be available for public access. At the same time, the Internet makes media access by the public very easy, although not everyone has the resources to take advantage of it.

Bias in the Media

Many studies have been undertaken to try to identify the sources and direction of **bias** in the media, and these studies have reached different conclusions. Some claim that the press has a liberal bias. Others conclude that the press shows a conservative bias. Still others do not see any notable partisan bias.

Bias
An inclination or a preference that interferes with impartial judgment.

Do the Media Have a Partisan Bias?

In a classic study conducted in the 1980s, the researchers found that media producers, editors, and reporters (the "media elite") exhibited a notably liberal and "left-leaning"

INFOTRAC®
COLLEGE EDITION

To find out more, enter the term "media bias" in Keywords.

bias in their news coverage.[5] Since then, the contention that the media have a liberal bias has been repeated time and again. Joining the ranks of those who assert that the media has a liberal bias is Bernard Goldberg, a veteran CBS broadcaster. In his recently published book,[6] Goldberg argues that liberal bias is responsible for the declining number of viewers who watch network news. Goldberg claims that this liberal bias, which "comes naturally to most reporters," has given viewers less reason to trust the big news networks. Conservative journalist William McGowan also claims that the press exhibits a liberal bias. He maintains that most news reporters have liberal views on the issues they cover (he cites a survey of journalists in which over 80 percent of the respondents said that they were in favor of abortion rights) and that this bias prevents them from investigating and reporting on opposing viewpoints.[7]

According to Andrew Kohut, director of the Pew Research Center in Washington, D.C., however, the majority of those responding to Pew Research Center polls see no ideological or partisan pattern in media bias. Rather, what people mean when they say the press is biased in its political reporting is that it is biased toward its own self-interest—the need to gain higher ratings and thus more advertising revenues.

Interestingly, even though Bernard Goldberg, as just mentioned, argues that there is a liberal bias in the media, some of the examples he provides in his book would indicate that the bias in the press is more toward commercialism and elitism. For example, he states that during "sweeps" months (when ratings are important), the networks deliberately avoid featuring blacks, Hispanics, and poor or unattractive people on their prime-time news magazine shows. This, asserts Goldberg, is because such coverage might "turn off" the white, middle-class viewers that the networks want to attract so that they can build the ratings that advertisers want. (For a further discussion of how advertisers may affect news coverage, see this chapter's *Politics and the Media* feature on page 349.)

Other Theories of Media Bias

Others see the media as biased toward the "status quo," meaning that the media are biased toward supporting corporate America and its aims. This group believes that the press tends to downplay the complaints made by people who are seen as being on the fringes of the political spectrum, especially on the left.

Still others contend that the media are biased against "losers." For example, Kathleen Hall Jamieson, director of the Annenberg Public Policy Center at the University of Pennsylvania, concludes that if there is a bias in the press, it is not a partisan bias but a bias against losers. A candidate who falls behind in a race is immediately labeled a "loser," making it even more difficult for that candidate to regain favor in the voters' eyes.[8]

Calvin F. Exoo has offered yet another theory. In his study of politics in the media,[9] he concluded that journalists are constrained by both the pro-America bias of the media's owners and the journalists' own code of objectivity. Most are more interested in improving their career prospects by covering the winning candidate and pleasing their editors to get better assignments than they are in discussing public

[5] S. Robert Lichter, Stanley Rothman, and Linda S. Lichter, *The Media Elite* (New York: Adler and Adler, 1986).

[6] Bernard Goldberg, *Bias: A CBS Insider Exposes How the Media Distort the News* (Washington, D.C.: Regnery Publishing, 2001).

[7] William McGowan, *Coloring the News: How Crusading for Diversity Has Corrupted American Journalism* (San Francisco: Encounter Books, 2001).

[8] Kathleen Hall Jamieson, *Everything You Think You Know about Politics . . . and Why You're Wrong* (New York: Basic Books, 2000).

[9] Calvin F. Exoo, *The Politics of the Mass Media* (St. Paul: West, 1994).

policies. Thus, the bias in the media is toward not criticizing the American system and on producing "news" that will attract viewers and readers without threatening the American way of life. This analysis would support Thomas E. Patterson's view that the bias of the news media is to emphasize bad news and cynicism rather than any partisan position.[10]

The Media: Why Are They Important Today?

The media, particularly during elections, can influence your everyday life in many ways. The media are always present with political stories, issues, and debates. In the print media, you cannot avoid political discussions because they are regular features. When you watch the news on TV, there are political stories every day. If you listen to commercial radio, you hear political news at least once an hour. During campaigns you encounter paid political announcements on a regular basis in all media.

You may find the media annoying when they cover something you think is silly or insignificant. Nevertheless, the media remain important simply because they are the vehicles through which you obtain information about the current state of affairs both within and outside the United States. Certainly, in a world where security concerns have become paramount, you must be aware of what steps your government is taking to improve national security. If you do not, you may find that radical changes have been made—changes that may affect some of the basic freedoms that you take for granted.

Today, in addition to traditional news media, the Internet provides easy access to an expanded set of viewpoints. Not only can you access the Web sites of TV news shows, domestic newspapers and magazines, and a variety of sources of political commentary, but you can also access foreign newspapers. Foreign views of the United States are often very different from the views expressed in the U.S. media, particularly on issues relating to U.S. foreign policy. The Internet also provides access to the "alternative press," such as the *Nation,* the *Progressive,* and the *Washington Monthly.* Of course, the consumer of news publicized via the Internet must always be vigilant, must know what sources the news reporter used, and must be able to analyze news stories. We treat this topic further in this chapter's *Making a Difference* feature on the following page.

---

[10] Thomas E. Patterson, *Out of Order* (New York: Knopf, 1993).

MAKING A DIFFERENCE | Being a Critical Consumer of the News

Television and newspapers provide an enormous range of choice for Americans who want to stay informed. Still, critics of the media argue that a substantial amount of programming and print is colored either by the subjectivity of editors and producers or by the demands of profit making. Few Americans take the time to become critical consumers of the news, either in print or on the TV screen.

How to Be a Critical News Consumer

To become a critical news consumer, you must practice reading a newspaper with a critical eye toward editorial decisions. For example, ask yourself what stories are given prominence on the front page of the paper, and which ones merit a photograph. What is the editorial stance of the newspaper? Most American papers tend to have moderate to conservative editorial pages. Who are the columnists given space on the "op-ed" page, the page opposite the paper's own editorial page? For a contrast to most daily papers, occasionally pick up an outright political publication such as the *National Review* or the *New Republic* and take note of the editorial positions.

Watching the evening news can be far more rewarding if you look at how much the news depends on video effects. You will note that stories on the evening news tend to be no more than three minutes long, that stories with excellent videotape get more attention, and that considerable time is taken up with "happy talk" or human interest stories that tap the emotions of the audience.

Compare News Coverage

Another way to evaluate news coverage critically is to compare how the news is covered in different media. For example, you might compare the evening news with the daily paper on a given date. You will see that the paper is perhaps half a day behind television in reporting the news but that the printed story contains far more information.

You might also check out stories published in "alternative" news sources, such as those mentioned in the concluding section of this chapter. For example, explore some of the news reported in the *Nation* (go to **http://www.thenation.com**) and then compare what is said there with the stories about the same event in your local paper and on TV. Also, see if the *Nation* covers news that is not covered by your daily paper or by the TV network news stations.

Contact News Associations and Other Organizations

If you wish to obtain more information on the media and take an active role as a consumer of the news, you can contact one of the following organizations:

National Association of Broadcasters
1771 N St. N.W.
Washington, DC 20036
202-429-5300
http://www.nab.org

National Newspaper Association
129 Neff Annex
Columbia, MO 65211
1-800-829-4NNA
http://www.nna.org

Accuracy in Media
(a conservative group)
4455 Connecticut Ave. N.W.,
Suite 330
Washington, DC 20008
202-364-4401
http://www.aim.org

People for the American Way
(a liberal group)
2000 M St. N.W., Suite 400
Washington, DC 20036
202-467-4999
http://www.pfaw.org

Key Terms

bias 349	media access 348	public agenda 335	spin doctor 343
electronic media 339	narrowcasting 340	sound bite 341	White House press corps 346
managed news 336	press secretary 346	spin 343	yellow journalism 338

Chapter Summary

1 The media are enormously important in American politics today. They perform a number of functions, including (a) entertainment, (b) news reporting, (c) identifying public problems, (d) socializing new generations, (e) providing a political forum, and (f) making profits.

2 The media have always played a significant role in American politics. In the 1800s and earlier, however, news traveled slowly, and politics was controlled by a small group whose members communicated personally. The high-speed rotary press and the telegraph led to self-supported newspapers and mass readership.

3 Broadcast media (television and radio) have been important means of communication since the early twentieth century. New technologies, such as cable television and the Internet, are giving broadcasters the opportunity to air a greater number of specialized programs.

4 The media wield enormous political power during political campaigns and over the affairs of government and government officials by focusing attention on their actions. Today's political campaigns use political advertising and expert management of news coverage. Of equal importance for presidential candidates is how they appear in presidential debates.

5 The relationship between the media and the president is close; each has used the other—sometimes positively, sometimes negatively. The media play an important role in investigating the government, in getting government officials to understand better the needs and desires of American society, and in setting the public agenda.

6 The media in the United States, particularly the electronic media, are subject to government regulation, although many Americans believe that the United States has possibly the freest press in the world. Most Federal Communications Commission rules have dealt with ownership of TV and radio stations. Recent legislation has removed many rules about co-ownership of several forms of media.

7 Studies of bias in the media have reached different conclusions. Some claim that the media have a liberal bias; others contend that the press shows a conservative bias. Still others conclude that the press is biased toward its own self-interest—the need to gain higher ratings and thus more advertising revenues. Other studies have found other types of biases, such as a bias in favor of the status quo or a bias against losers.

Selected Print and Media Resources

SUGGESTED READINGS

Davis, Richard, and Diana Marie Owen. *New Media and American Politics*. New York: Oxford University Press, 1998. The authors critique many of the new media outlets, including e-zines, cable outlets, talk radio, and the Internet. They ask whether these new media actually do reflect the needs and desires of American voters.

Graber, Doris A. *Media Power in Politics*. Washington, D.C.: Congressional Quarterly Books, 2000. In this collection of essays, many of which are newly written, the author explores the mass media's ability to shape political agendas and the ways in which the mass media have profoundly changed American politics.

Herman, Edward S., and Noam Chomsky. *Manufacturing Consent: The Political Economy of the Mass Media*. New York: Pantheon Books, 2002. In this critical look at the U.S. media, the authors contend that media ownership, advertising, official sources, and other "filters" skew the way in which the news media report the news.

NBC, Marc Robinson, Tom Brokaw, *et al. Brought to You in Living Color: Seventy-five Years of Great Moments in Television and Radio from NBC*. Somerset, N.J.: Wiley, 2002. Although this book focuses on the history of NBC, it also provides an entertaining and informative history of network programming and entertainment over the past seventy-five years.

Wolfe, Tom. *Radical Chic & Mau-Mauing the Flak Catchers*. New York: Bantam Doubleday, 1999. This book chronicles a party that was held by composer/conductor (and liberal) Leonard Bernstein and his wife to raise money for the Black Panthers, a radical black group active in the 1960s. The book is still a good read about the ability of the rich and famous (and the media) to make radical politics "chic" and to turn political confrontation into a game.

MEDIA RESOURCES

All the President's Men—A film, produced by Warner Brothers in 1976, starring Dustin Hoffman and Robert Redford as the two *Washington Post* reporters, Bob Woodward and Carl Bernstein, who broke the story on the Watergate scandal. The film is an excellent portrayal of the *Washington Post* newsroom and the decisions that editors make in such situations.

Broadcast News—A 1987 film starring Holly Hunter, Albert Brooks, and William Hurt as the members of a television news team. The film examines the ways that news broadcasts are created and satirizes the role of the handsome news anchor.

Citizen Kane—A 1941 film, based on the life of William Randolph Hearst and directed by Orson Welles, that has been acclaimed as one of the best movies ever made. Welles himself stars as the newspaper tycoon. The film also stars Joseph Cotten and Alan Ladd.

The Insider—A 1999 film, starring Russell Crowe and Al Pacino, about the real-life drama that took place behind the scenes of the CBS news magazine *60 Minutes* when CBS corporate executives tried to pull the plug on a news story about a tobacco-industry whistleblower.

Your CD-ROM Resources

In addition to the chapter content containing hot links, the following resources are available on the CD-ROM:

- **Internet Activities**—Liberal bias in the media.

- **Critical Thinking Exercises**—Kennedy/Nixon debate, the Chinese Internet, compare media outlets for accuracy.

- **Self-Check on Important Themes**—Can You Answer These?

- **Video**—*Media Coverage of Conventions, Internet Voting.*

- **Public Opinion Data**—Find contrasting opinions on TV debates and banning exit polls.

- **Simulation**—You Are There!

- **InfoTrac Exercise**—"Machine Politics: How the Internet Is Really, Truly, Seriously! Going to Change Elections."

- **Participation Exercise**—Broadcast your political voice via local cable access television.

- **MicroCase Exercise**—"By the Numbers: Who's Keeping Up with the News?"

- **Additional Resources**—*The New York Times Company v. Sullivan* (1964), *The New York Times v. United States* (1971), *Zurcher v. Stanford Daily* (1978).

e-mocracy

The Media and the Internet

Today, the Internet offers a great opportunity to those who want to access the news. All of the major news organizations, including radio and television stations and newspapers, are now online. Most local newspapers include at least some of their news coverage and features on their Web sites, and all national newspapers are online. Even foreign newspapers can now be accessed online within a few seconds. Also available are purely Web-based news publications, including e-zines (online news magazines) such as *Slate, Salon,* and *Hotwired.* Because it is relatively simple for anyone or any organization to put up a home page or Web site, a wide variety of sites have appeared that critique the news media or give alternative interpretations of the news and the way it is presented.

Logging On

The Web site of the *American Journalism Review* includes features from the maga-

zine and original content created specifically for online reading. Go to

http://www.ajr.org

The *Drudge Report* home page, posted by Matt Drudge, provides a handy guide to the Web's best spots for news and opinions. Its mission is one-click access to breaking news and recent columns. It provides links to specific columnists and opinion pages for magazines and major daily newspapers. Go to

http://www.drudgereport.com

The American Review Web page critiques the media, promotes media activism, and calls for media reform. Its URL is

http://www.AmericanReview.us

To view *Slate,* the e-zine of politics and culture published by Microsoft, go to

http://Slate.msn.com

An AP–like system for college newspapers is Uwire, offered by Northwestern University and intended to provide college papers with a reliable source of information that directly affects their readers. You can access Uwire at

http://www.uwire.com

For an Internet site that provides links to news media around the world, including alternative media, go to

http://www.mediachannel.org

Using the Internet for Political Analysis

Compare the print version of a major national newspaper—such as the *New York Times, Los Angeles Times, Wall Street Journal, Washington Post,* or *USA Today*— with its online edition from the same day. How do the two versions differ? What decisions did the editors make in regard to picture choice, headlines, placement, and length of the stories that suggest a different audience for the online edition? How does the newspaper raise revenue from each of these editions? How does the way you read the paper vary between the two editions? Which format do you think is better for generating political dialogue, and why? If you could design your own online newspaper, what features would it include?

Political Institutions

Members of Congress Were Required to Spend Six Months Each Year in Their Districts?

BACKGROUND

Members of Congress spend far more time in Washington than they do at home. In fact, although incumbent members of Congress are very difficult to defeat, a few of them are challenged successfully each election by newcomers who point to the members' Washington town houses and heavy involvement with politics "inside the Beltway."

Some contend that congresspersons should spend more time in their home districts. After all, members of Congress are elected to represent the views of those who elected them—their constituents. How can members of Congress learn their constituents' views if those members are involved in Washington politics for most of the year?

WHAT IF MEMBERS OF CONGRESS WERE REQUIRED TO SPEND SIX MONTHS EACH YEAR IN THEIR DISTRICTS?

Requiring members of Congress to be in their districts for six months each year certainly would strengthen their relationship with the voters. The voters would have far more opportunities to meet with the members and express their views. It is likely that members would be even more immersed in problem solving for ordinary citizens than they are now. It is also very likely that local interests might be perceived as more powerful than they are now, and national lobbyists would have to compete with local demands. Having spent so much time listening to the concerns of local workers, for example, a member of Congress might be more aware of the impact of international trade on his or her constituents.

POSSIBLE EFFECTS ON PARTISANSHIP AND INCUMBENCY

Spending more time in the district could have the effect of reducing the legislator's tie to his or her political party. Strong state and regional interests would be likely to force the legislator to vote against the party's position if that position was contrary to constituent interests. If the legislator cultivated good constituency relations, the time spent at home probably would strengthen the power of incumbency. After all, it is much harder for voters to reject someone who has met with them and who may have helped their families or towns on an issue than it is to reject someone who is always in Washington, D.C. A new person often can get to Congress only by running for an open seat.

GETTING THE LEGISLATIVE WORK DONE

Could members of Congress complete the budget and all legislation in six months so they could go home? To be sure, most legislation could move faster than it does, particularly if members would be willing to delegate more power to committees or to the leadership. One of the problems of a speedier legislative process in Washington, D.C., however, is that not all issues might be raised or all interests considered in the process of writing legislation. Part of a representative democracy involves allowing all who have opinions to contribute to the legislative process. Shortening the time spent in Washington might reduce the amount of influence that the public has on the process. Furthermore, speeding up legislation could, in the long run, produce laws that soon would need to be reconsidered or amended. Time does allow difficult issues to be worked out.

Finally, sending members of Congress home for six months each year would transfer a great deal of power to the president and to the members of the executive branch to act without a counterbalance. While Americans might like their representatives to spend more time at home, they also are unlikely to place their trust in the executive branch for six months each year.

FOR CRITICAL ANALYSIS

1. Which local interests might receive stronger representation if members spent more time at home? Which interests would be unaffected?
2. Do you think that members of Congress could transact some of their business via electronic communications systems? Is face-to-face deliberation really necessary?

Most Americans spend little time thinking about the Congress of the United States, and when they do, their opinions are frequently unflattering. For many years, the public's approval rating of Congress as a whole was about 30 percent. During the late 1990s and early 2000s, Congress's approval ratings climbed to between 40 percent and 50 percent in most polls, however, and they have continued to be relatively high. Yet the majority of voters express even higher approval ratings (in the range of 60 percent to 70 percent) for the members of Congress from their districts. This is one of the paradoxes of the relationship between the people and Congress. Members of the public hold the institution in relatively low regard compared with the satisfaction they express with respect to their individual representatives.

Part of the explanation for these seemingly contradictory appraisals is that members of Congress spend considerable time and effort serving their **constituents.** If the federal bureaucracy makes a mistake, the senator's or representative's office tries to resolve the issue. What most Americans see of Congress, therefore, is the work of their own representatives in their home states. As suggested in this chapter's opening *What If . . .* feature, the tie between members of Congress and the voters might be even stronger if members were in their home states more of the time.

Constituent
One of the people represented by a legislator or other elected or appointed official.

Congress, however, was created to work not just for local constituents but also for the nation as a whole. Understanding the nature of the institution and the process of lawmaking is an important part of understanding how the policies that shape our lives are made.

Why Was Congress Created?

The founders of the American republic believed that the bulk of the power that would be exercised by a national government should be in the hands of the legislature. The leading role envisioned for Congress in the new government is apparent from its primacy in the Constitution. Article I deals with the structure, the powers, and the operation of Congress, beginning in Section 1 with an application of the basic principle of separation of powers: "All legislative Powers herein granted shall be vested in a Congress of the United States, which shall consist of a Senate and House of Representatives." These legislative powers are spelled out in detail in Article I and elsewhere.

The **bicameralism** of Congress—its division into two legislative houses—was in part an outgrowth of the Connecticut Compromise, which tried to balance the large-state population advantage, reflected in the House, and the small-state demand for equality in policymaking, which was satisfied in the Senate. Beyond that, the two chambers of Congress also reflected the social class biases of the founders. They wished to balance the interests and the numerical superiority of the common citizens with the property interests of the less numerous landowners, bankers, and merchants. This goal was achieved by providing in Sections 2 and 3 of Article I that members of the House of Representatives should be elected directly by "the People," whereas members of the Senate were to be chosen by the elected representatives sitting in state legislatures, who were more likely to be members of the elite. (The latter provision was changed in 1913 by the passage of the Seventeenth Amendment, which provides that senators also are to be elected directly by the people.)

Bicameralism
The division of a legislature into two separate assemblies.

The logic of separate constituencies and separate interests underlying the bicameral Congress was reinforced by differences in length of tenure. Members of the House are required to face the electorate every two years, whereas senators can serve for a much more secure term of six years—even longer than the four-year term provided for the president. Furthermore, the senators' terms are staggered so that only one-third of the senators face the electorate every two years, along with all of the House members.

360

The Powers of Congress

The Constitution is both highly specific and extremely vague about the powers that Congress may exercise. The first seventeen clauses of Article I, Section 8, specify most of the **enumerated powers** of Congress—that is, powers expressly given to that body.

Enumerated Powers

The enumerated, or expressed, powers of Congress include the right to impose taxes and import tariffs; borrow money; regulate interstate commerce and international trade; establish procedures for naturalizing citizens; make laws regulating bankruptcies; coin (and print) money and regulate its value; establish standards of weights and measures; punish counterfeiters; establish post offices and postal routes; regulate copyrights and patents; establish the federal court system; punish pirates and others committing illegal acts on the high seas; declare war; raise and regulate an army and a navy; call up and regulate the state militias to enforce laws, to suppress insurrections, and to repel invasions; and govern the District of Columbia.

The most important of the domestic powers of Congress, listed in Article I, Section 8, are the rights to collect taxes, to spend, and to regulate commerce, whereas the most important foreign policy power is the power to declare war. Other sections of the Constitution give Congress a wide range of further powers. Generally, Congress is also able to establish rules for its own members, to regulate the electoral college, and to override a presidential veto.

Some functions are restricted to only one chamber. Under Article II, Section 2, the Senate must advise on, and consent to, the ratification of treaties and must accept or reject presidential nominations of ambassadors, Supreme Court justices, and "all other Officers of the United States." But the Senate may delegate to the president, the courts, or department heads the power to make lesser appointments. Congress may regulate the extent of the Supreme Court's authority to review cases decided by the lower courts, regulate relations between states, and propose amendments to the Constitution.

The amendments to the Constitution provide for other congressional powers. Congress must certify the election of a president and a vice president or itself choose

Enumerated Power

A power specifically granted to the national government by the Constitution. The first seventeen clauses of Article I, Section 8, specify most of the enumerated powers of Congress.

Representative William Jefferson, a Democrat from Louisiana, shakes hands with a constituent during a visit to his home district. Jefferson represents the Second District in Louisiana, which includes most of the city of New Orleans. After a tough fight to win his seat in 1990, Jefferson has been reelected with ease. (Philip Gould/Corbis)

these officers if no candidate has a majority of the electoral vote (Twelfth Amendment). It may levy an income tax (Sixteenth Amendment) and determine who will be acting president in case of the death or incapacity of the president or vice president (Twentieth Amendment, Sections 3 and 4, and Twenty-fifth Amendment, Sections 2, 3, and 4). In addition, Congress explicitly is given the power to enforce, by appropriate legislation, the provisions of several other amendments.

The Necessary and Proper Clause

Beyond these numerous specific powers, Congress enjoys the right under Article I, Section 8 (the "elastic," or "necessary and proper," clause), "[t]o make all Laws which shall be necessary and proper for carrying into Execution the foregoing Powers [of Article I], and all other Powers vested by this Constitution in the Government of the United States, or in any Department or Officer thereof." As discussed in Chapter 3, this vague statement of congressional responsibilities set the stage for a greatly expanded role for the national government relative to the states. It also constitutes, at least in theory, a check on the expansion of presidential powers.

The Functions of Congress

The Constitution provides the foundation for congressional powers. Yet a complete understanding of the role that Congress plays requires a broader study of the functions that the national legislature performs for the American political system.

Congress, as an institution of government, is expected by its members, by the public, and by other centers of political power to perform a number of functions. Our perceptions of how good a job Congress is doing overall are tied closely to evaluations of whether and how it fulfills certain specific tasks. These tasks include lawmaking, service to constituents, representation, oversight, public education, and conflict resolution.

The Lawmaking Function

The principal and most obvious function of any legislature is **lawmaking**. Congress is the highest elected body in the country charged with making binding rules for all Americans. Lawmaking requires decisions about the size of the federal budget, about health-care reform and gun control, and about the long-term prospects for war or peace. This does not mean, however, that Congress initiates most of the ideas for legislation that it eventually considers. Most of the bills that Congress acts on originate in the executive branch, and many other bills are traceable to interest groups and political party organizations. Through the processes of compromise and **logrolling** (offering to support a fellow member's bill in exchange for that member's promise to support your bill in the future), as well as debate and discussion, backers of legislation attempt to fashion a winning majority coalition.

Lawmaking
The process of deciding the legal rules that govern society. Such laws may regulate minor affairs or establish broad national policies.

Logrolling
An arrangement in which two or more members of Congress agree in advance to support each other's bills.

Service to Constituents

Individual members of Congress are expected by their constituents to act as brokers between private citizens and the imposing, often faceless federal government. **Casework** is the usual form taken by this function of providing service to constituents. The legislator and her or his staff spend a considerable portion of their time in casework activity, such as tracking down a missing Social Security check, explaining the meaning of particular bills to people who may be affected by them, promoting a local business

Casework
Personal work for constituents by members of Congress.

Ombudsperson
A person who hears and investigates complaints by private individuals against public officials or agencies.

Representation
The function of members of Congress as elected officials in representing the views of their constituents.

Trustee
In regard to a legislator, one who acts according to her or his conscience and the broad interests of the entire society.

Instructed Delegate
A legislator who is an agent of the voters who elected him or her and who votes according to the views of constituents regardless of personal assessments.

Oversight
The responsibility Congress has for following up on laws it has enacted to ensure that they are being enforced and administered in the way Congress intended.

interest, or interceding with a regulatory agency on behalf of constituents who disagree with proposed agency regulations.

Legislators and many analysts of congressional behavior regard this **ombudsperson** role as an activity that strongly benefits the members of Congress. A government characterized by a large, confusing bureaucracy and complex public programs offers innumerable opportunities for legislators to come to the assistance of (usually) grateful constituents. Morris P. Fiorina once suggested, somewhat mischievously, that senators and representatives prefer to maintain bureaucratic confusion in order to maximize their opportunities for performing good deeds on behalf of their constituents:

> Some poor, aggrieved constituent becomes enmeshed in the tentacles of an evil bureaucracy and calls upon Congressman St. George to do battle with the dragon. . . . In dealing with the bureaucracy, the congressman is not merely one vote of 435. Rather, he is a nonpartisan power, someone whose phone call snaps an office to attention. He is not kept on hold. The constituent who receives aid believes that his congressman and his congressman alone got results.[1]

The Representation Function

If constituency service carries with it nothing but benefits for most members of Congress, the function of **representation** is less certain and even carries with it some danger that the legislator will lose his or her bid for reelection. Generally, representation means that the many competing interests in society should be represented in Congress. It follows that Congress should be a body acting slowly and deliberately and that its foremost concern should be to maintain a carefully crafted balance of power among competing interests.

How is representation to be achieved? There are basically two points of view on this issue.

The Trustee View of Representation. The first approach to the question of how representation should be achieved is that legislators should act as **trustees** of the broad interests of the entire society and that they should vote against the narrow interests of their constituents as their conscience and their perception of national needs dictate. For example, a number of Republican legislators supported strong laws regulating the tobacco industry in spite of the views of some of their constituents.

The Instructed-Delegate View of Representation. Directly opposed to the trustee view of representation is the notion that the members of Congress should behave as **instructed delegates;** that is, they should mirror the views of the majority of the constituents who elected them to power in the first place. On the surface, this approach is plausible and rewarding. For it to work, however, we must assume that constituents actually have well-formed views on the issues that are decided in Congress and, further, that they have clear-cut preferences about these issues. Neither condition is likely to be satisfied very often. Most people generally do not have well-articulated views on major issues.

Generally, most legislators hold neither a pure trustee view nor a pure instructed-delegate view. Typically, they combine both perspectives in a pragmatic mix.

The Oversight Function

Oversight of the bureaucracy is essential if the decisions made by Congress are to have any force. **Oversight** is the process by which Congress follows up on the laws it has enacted to ensure that they are being enforced and administered in the way

---

[1] Morris P. Fiorina, *Congress: Keystone of the Washington Establishment,* 2d ed. (New Haven, Conn.: Yale University Press, 1989), pp. 44, 47.

Congress intended. This is done by holding committee hearings and investigations, changing the size of an agency's budget, and cross-examining high-level presidential nominees to head major agencies. Also, until 1983, Congress could refuse to accede to proposed rules and regulations by resorting to the **legislative veto**. This allowed one or sometimes both chambers of Congress to prevent the enforcement of an executive rule by a simple majority vote against it within a specified period of time. The legislative veto was created by 1932 legislation that directed the president to restructure the executive branch. In 1983, however, the Supreme Court ruled that such a veto violated the separation of powers mandated by the Constitution, because the president had no power to veto the legislative action. Thus, the legislative veto was declared unconstitutional.[2]

Senators and representatives increasingly see their oversight function as a critically important part of their legislative activities. In part, oversight is related to the concept of constituency service, particularly when Congress investigates alleged arbitrariness or wrongdoing by bureaucratic agencies.

The Public-Education Function

Educating the public is a function that is exercised whenever Congress holds public hearings, exercises oversight over the bureaucracy, or engages in committee and floor debate on such major issues and topics as political assassinations, aging, illegal drugs, or the concerns of small businesses. In so doing, Congress presents a range of viewpoints on pressing national questions. Congress also decides what issues will come up for discussion and decision; **agenda setting** is a major facet of its public-education function.

The Conflict-Resolution Function

Congress is commonly seen as an institution for resolving conflicts within American society. Organized interest groups and representatives of different racial, religious, economic, and ideological interests look on Congress as an access point for airing their grievances and seeking help. This puts Congress in the role of trying to resolve the differences among competing points of view by passing laws to accommodate as many interested parties as possible. To the extent that Congress meets pluralist expectations in accommodating competing interests, it tends to build support for the entire political process by all branches of government.

House-Senate Differences

Congress is composed of two markedly different—but coequal—chambers. Although the Senate and the House of Representatives exist within the same legislative institution, each has developed certain distinctive features that clearly distinguish life on one end of Capitol Hill from conditions on the other (the Senate wing is on the north side of the Capitol building, and the House wing is on the south side). A summary of these differences is given in Table 12–1 on the next page.

Size and Rules

The central difference between the House and the Senate is simply that the House is much larger than the Senate. The House has 435 representatives, plus delegates from the District of Columbia, Puerto Rico, Guam, American Samoa, and the Virgin Islands, compared with just 100 senators. This size difference means that a greater

DID YOU KNOW . . .
That the Library of Congress's electronic information system is named THOMAS, for Thomas Jefferson?

Legislative Veto
A provision in a bill reserving to Congress or to a congressional committee the power to reject an action or regulation of a national agency by majority vote; declared unconstitutional by the Supreme Court in 1983.

Agenda Setting
Determining which public-policy questions will be debated or considered by Congress.

---

[2] *Immigration and Naturalization Service v. Chadha*, 454 U.S. 812 (1983).

TABLE 12–1

Differences between the House and the Senate

HOUSE*	SENATE*
Members chosen from local districts	Members chosen from an entire state
Two-year term	Six-year term
Originally elected by voters	Originally (until 1913) elected by state legislatures
May impeach (indict) federal officials	May convict federal officials of impeachable offenses
Larger (435 voting members)	Smaller (100 members)
More formal rules	Fewer rules and restrictions
Debate limited	Debate extended
Less prestige and less individual notice	More prestige and more media attention
Originates bills for raising revenues	Has power to advise the president on, and to consent to, presidential appointments and treaties
Local or narrow leadership	National leadership
More partisan	Less party loyalty

*Some of these differences, such as the term of office, are provided for in the Constitution. Others, such as debate rules, are not.

number of formal rules are needed to govern activity in the House, whereas correspondingly looser procedures can be followed in the less crowded Senate. This difference is most obvious in the rules governing debate on the floors of the two chambers.

The Senate normally permits extended debate on all issues that arise before it. In contrast, the House operates with an elaborate system in which its **Rules Committee** normally proposes time limitations on debate for any bill, and a majority of the entire body accepts or modifies those suggested time limits. As a consequence of its stricter time limits on debate, the House, despite its greater size, often is able to act on legislation more quickly than the Senate.

Debate and Filibustering

According to historians, the Senate tradition of unlimited debate, which is known as *filibustering* (see Chapter 5), dates back to 1790. In that year, a proposal to move the U.S. capital from New York to Philadelphia was stalled by such time-wasting tactics. This unlimited-debate tradition—which also existed in the House until 1811—is not absolute, however.

Under Senate Rule 22, debate may be ended by invoking *cloture*. Recall from Chapter 5 that cloture shuts off discussion on a bill. Amended in 1975 and 1979, Rule 22 states that debate may be closed off on a bill if sixteen senators sign a petition requesting it and if, after two days have elapsed, three-fifths of the entire membership (sixty votes, assuming no vacancies) vote for cloture. After cloture is invoked, each senator may speak on a bill for a maximum of one hour before a vote is taken.

In 1979, the Senate extended Rule 22 to provide that a final vote must take place within one hundred hours of debate after cloture has been imposed. It further limited the use of multiple amendments to stall postcloture final action on a bill.

Prestige

As a consequence of the greater size of the House, representatives generally cannot achieve as much individual recognition and public prestige as can members of the Senate. Senators, especially those who openly express presidential ambitions, are better able to gain media exposure and to establish careers as spokespersons for large national constituencies. To obtain recognition for his or her activities, a member of

Rules Committee

A standing committee of the House of Representatives that provides special rules under which specific bills can be debated, amended, and considered by the House.

INFOTRAC®
COLLEGE EDITION

To find out more about filibusters, use the term "filibuster" in Keywords.

the House generally must do one of two things. He or she might survive in office long enough to join the ranks of the leadership on committees or within the party. Alternatively, the representative could become an expert on some specialized aspect of legislative policy—such as tax laws, the environment, or education.

Congresspersons and the Citizenry: A Comparison

Government institutions are given life by the people who work in them and shape them as political structures. Who, then, are the members of Congress, and how are they elected?

Members of the U.S. Senate and the U.S. House of Representatives are not typical American citizens. Members of Congress are older than most Americans, partly because of constitutional age requirements and partly because a good deal of political experience normally is an advantage in running for national office. Members of Congress are also disproportionately white, male, Protestant, and trained in higher-status occupations. Lawyers are by far the largest occupational group among congresspersons, although the proportion of lawyers in the House is lower now than it was in the past. Increasingly, members of Congress are also much wealthier than the average citizen. Whereas fewer than 1 percent of Americans have assets exceeding $1 million, about one-third of the members of Congress are millionaires.

ELECTIONS 2002 Congressional Characteristics after the 2002 Elections

Several prominent conservatives in Congress retired in 2002, including Senators Jesse Helms of North Carolina and Strom Thurmond of South Carolina, and the majority leader in the House, Dick Armey of Texas. But the Republican party welcomed other longtime conservative voices into the 108th Congress, including former rivals for the 2000 presidential nomination, Elizabeth Dole of North Carolina and Lamar Alexander of Tennessee. The Democrats lost one of their most outspoken liberal voices, Senator Paul Wellstone of Minnesota, not by election or retirement but in a tragic plane crash just days before the election.

Aside from this shuffling among the figureheads of both parties, the characteristics of the 108th Congress may be described as "status quo." The number of women and minorities remained the same in both chambers—with African Americans and Hispanics still shut out of the Senate.

Congressional Elections

The process of electing members of Congress is decentralized. Congressional elections are operated by the individual state governments, which must conform to the rules established by the U.S. Constitution and by national statutes. The Constitution states that representatives are to be elected every second year by popular ballot, and the number of seats awarded to each state is to be determined by the results of the decennial census. Each state has at least one representative, with most congressional districts having about half a million residents. Senators are elected by popular vote (since the passage of the Seventeenth Amendment) every six years; approximately one-third of the seats are chosen every two years. Each state has two senators. Under Article I, Section 4, of the Constitution, state legislatures are given control over "[t]he Times, Places and Manner of holding Elections for Senators and Representatives"; however, "the Congress may at any time by Law make or alter such Regulations."

INFOTRAC®
COLLEGE EDITION

For updates and more information on congressional elections, use the term "United States Congress" in the Subject guide, and then go to subdivision "elections."

Candidates for Congressional Elections

Candidates for congressional seats may be self-selected, or, in districts where one party is very strong, they may be recruited by the local minority-party leadership.[3] Candidates may resemble the voters of the district in terms of ethnicity or religion, but they are also likely to be very successful individuals who have been active in politics before. Additionally, with respect to House seats, they are likely to have local ties to their districts. Candidates most likely choose to run because they believe they would enjoy the job and its accompanying status. They also may be thinking about a House seat as a steppingstone to future political office as a senator, governor, or presidential candidate.

Congressional campaigns have changed considerably in the past two decades. Like all other campaigns, they are much more expensive, with the average cost of a winning Senate campaign now being $5 million and a winning House campaign averaging more than $770,000. Campaign funds include direct contributions by individuals, contributions by political action committees (PACs), and "soft money" funneled through state party committees. As you read in Chapter 10, all of these contributions are regulated by law, including by the Federal Election Campaign Act of 1971, as amended, and most recently by the Bipartisan Campaign Reform Act of 2002. Once in office, legislators spend some time almost every day raising funds for their next campaign.

Most candidates for Congress must win the nomination through a **direct primary**, in which **party identifiers** vote for the candidate who will be on the party ticket in the general election. To win the primary, candidates may take more liberal or more conservative positions to get the votes of party identifiers. In the general election, they may moderate their views to attract the votes of independents and voters from the other party.

Presidential Effects.   Congressional candidates are always hopeful that a strong presidential candidate on the ticket will have "coattails" that will sweep in senators and representatives of the same party. In fact, coattail effects have been quite limited, appearing only in landslide elections such as Lyndon Johnson's victory over Barry Goldwater in 1964. Members of Congress who are from contested districts or who are in their first term are more likely to experience the effect of midterm elections, which are held in the even-numbered years in between presidential contests. In these years, voter turnout falls sharply, and the party controlling the White House normally loses seats in Congress. Additionally, voters in midterm elections often are responding to incumbency issues, because there is no presidential campaign. The result is a fragmentation of party authority and a loosening of ties between Congress and the president. Table 12–2 shows the pattern for midterm elections since 1942.

The Power of Incumbency

The power of incumbency in the outcome of congressional elections cannot be overemphasized. Table 12–3 shows that the overwhelming majority of representatives and a smaller proportion of senators who decide to run for reelection are successful. This conclusion holds for both presidential-year and midterm elections. David R. Mayhew argues that the pursuit of reelection is the strongest motivation behind the activities of members of Congress. The reelection goal is pursued in three major ways: by *advertising,* by *credit claiming,* and by *position taking.*[4] Advertising includes using the

Direct Primary

An intraparty election in which the voters select the candidates who will run on a party's ticket in the subsequent general election.

Party Identifier

A person who identifies with a political party.

TABLE 12–2

Midterm Gains and Losses by the Party of the President, 1942 to 2002

Seats Gained or Lost by the Party of the President in the House of Representatives	
1942	−45 (D.)
1946	−55 (D.)
1950	−29 (D.)
1954	−18 (R.)
1958	−47 (R.)
1962	−4 (D.)
1966	−47 (D.)
1970	−12 (R.)
1974	−48 (R.)
1978	−15 (D.)
1982	−26 (R.)
1986	−5 (R.)
1990	−8 (R.)
1994	−52 (D.)
1998	+5 (D.)
2002	+5 (R.)

---

[3] See the work of Gary Jacobson, *The Politics of Congressional Elections,* 5th ed. (New York: Addison Wesley, 2000).

[4] David R. Mayhew, *Congress: The Electoral Connection* (New Haven, Conn.: Yale University Press, 1974).

TABLE 12–3

The Power of Incumbency

	PRESIDENTIAL-YEAR ELECTIONS						MIDTERM ELECTIONS						
	1980	1984	1988	1992	1996	2000	1978	1982	1986	1990	1994	1998	2002
House													
Number of incumbent candidates	398	409	409	368	382	400	382	393	393	407	382	401	393
Reelected	361	390	402	325	359	394	358	352	385	391	347	394	383
Percentage of total	90.7	95.4	98.3	88.9	93.4	98.5	93.7	90.1	98.0	96.1	90.8	98.2	97.5
Defeated	37	19	7	43	23	6	24	39	8	16	35	8	10
In primary	6	3	1	19	2	0	5	10	2	1	1	1	3
In general election	31	16	6	24	21	6	19	29	6	15	34	7	7
Senate													
Number of incumbent candidates	29	29	27	28	21	29	25	30	28	32	26	29	28*
Reelected	16	26	23	23	19	23	15	28	21	31	24	26	24*
Percentage of total	55.2	89.6	85	82.1	90	82.7	60.0	93.3	75.0	96.9	92.3	89.6	85.7
Defeated	13	3	4	5	2	6	10	2	7	1	2	3	4
In primary	4	0	0	1	1	0	3	0	0	0	0	0	1
In general election	9	3	4	4	1	6	7	2	7	1	2	3	3

*In Louisiana, the Senate race was decided in a run-off election after this text went to print. The results of the run-off election might affect these numbers.

SOURCES: Norman Ornstein, Thomas E. Mann, and Michael J. Malbin, *Vital Statistics on Congress, 1993–1994* (Washington, D.C.: Congressional Quarterly Press, 1994), pp. 56–57; *Congressional Quarterly Weekly Report,* November 7, 1992, pp. 3551, 3576; and authors' update.

mass media, making personal appearances with constituents, and sending newsletters—all to produce a favorable image and to make the incumbent's name a household word. Members of Congress try to present themselves as informed, experienced, and responsive to people's needs. Credit claiming focuses on the things a legislator claims to have done to benefit his or her constituents—by fulfilling the congressional casework function or bringing money for mass transit to the district, for example. Position taking occurs when an incumbent explains her or his voting record on key issues; makes public statements of general support for presidential decisions; or indicates that she or he specifically supports positions on key issues, such as gun control or anti-inflation policies. Position taking carries with it certain risks, as the incumbent may lose support by disagreeing with the attitudes of a large number of constituents.

Divided Government after the 2000 Elections

As mentioned in Chapter 9, divided government—a government in which the president and the majority in Congress are from different political parties—took on new meaning after the 2000 elections. The Republicans lost seats in the House of Representatives, so their majority in that chamber was much slimmer than before. Initially, the Senate was evenly divided, with fifty Democrats and fifty Republicans. The Republicans had nominal control over the Senate, however, because when a vote is tied in the Senate, the vice president (meaning, after the 2000 elections, Republican Vice President Dick Cheney) can vote to break the tie.

In 2001, however, Senate control returned to the Democrats when James Jeffords, a Republican senator from Vermont, left the Republican Party. Jeffords declared that he was an independent but said that he would side with the Democrats for party organizational purposes.

Some contend that divided government has been responsible, at least in part, for some of the intense displays of partisanship that have been in evidence since the mid-1990s. For a further discussion of partisanship and its possible effects on our democracy, see this chapter's *Politics and Democracy* feature on the next page.

David Wellstone, the oldest son of Minnesota Senator Paul Wellstone, speaks during a public memorial service for his father, mother, and sister, who were killed in a plane crash on October 25, 2002. Political support for former Vice President Walter Mondale to take Senator Wellstone's place on the Minnesota ballot began to emerge even at the memorial service. Mondale agreed to run in Wellstone's place, with only five days to campaign before the election, in part to help Democrats keep control of the Senate. He lost to Republican Norm Coleman, however.
(AP Photo/Stacy Wescott, Pool)

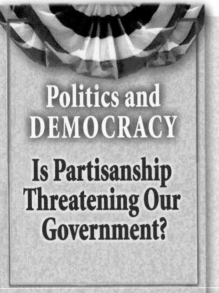

Politics and DEMOCRACY

Is Partisanship Threatening Our Government?

While the word *bipartisan*—with the support of both Democrats and Republicans—is a favorite one in Washington, D.C., the real world of politics is very partisan indeed. Democrats stick with Democrats; Republicans stick with Republicans.

EXAMPLES OF PARTISANSHIP

If you do not think this is so, just look at the Senate Judiciary Committee's hearings that were held to evaluate President George W. Bush's nominees for vacant federal judgeships. (As you will read in Chapter 15, all federal judges are nominated by the president and confirmed by the Senate.) For almost every nomination, the Judiciary Committee's ten Democrats voted against the nominee and the committee's nine Republicans voted for the nominee. Certainly, the impeachment

proceedings against President Bill Clinton in 1998 and 1999 demonstrated the extreme extent of partisanship. Whenever votes were taken, 99 percent of the voting was along clear partisan lines.

PARTISANSHIP AND ETHICS

Within Congress itself, minor ethical violations can create major partisan battles. Republicans drove former Speaker of the House James Wright out of office after accusing him of an ethics violation. Democrats succeeded in doing the same with prominent Republicans who had allegedly engaged in ethically questionable behavior. Partisanship leads congressional members to engage in

extremely inflammatory language against those of the opposite party whenever the smallest infraction occurs.

To be sure, democracy requires a healthy dose of disagreement and open political discourse. But does it require the blatantly partisan language and actions that are so prevalent today?

FOR CRITICAL ANALYSIS

Is partisanship in Congress good or bad for our democratic system? Are members of Congress taking strong stands supporting their beliefs when they vote in a partisan way, or are they simply following the "party line"?

The Senate Judiciary Committee has been accused of being particularly partisan in recent years. For example, President Bush's nominee to serve on the U.S. Court of Appeals for the Fifth Circuit, Texas Supreme Court Justice Priscilla Owen, shown here shaking the president's hand, was rejected by the committee along party lines. (AP Photo/J. Scott Applewhite)

ELECTIONS 2002   Party Control of Congress after the 2002 Elections

The Republican wins in the House and Senate in 2002 left the Democrats scrambling to find issues and leaders that would galvanize voters over the next two years. Two days after the elections, the Democratic minority leader in the House, Richard Gephardt, resigned that post, declaring that he would seek to lead his party in another capacity, possibly in a run for the White House in 2004. The Republicans also elected new leadership in the House with the resignation of the majority leader, Dick Armey, who did not seek reelection in 2002. Nonetheless, the Republicans emerged from the elections the stronger and more focused party, benefiting from the leadership shown by President Bush in the war on terrorism.

The Republican majority in Congress is slim, however. They have a twenty-two-seat majority in the House and only a one-seat majority in the Senate (with a few races still undecided for both chambers when this text was printed). These slim leads will force the Republicans to work in a bipartisan fashion on some issues. Many Democrats, however, came away from the 2002 elections believing that voters saw them as lacking vision and leadership. Consequently, Democrats may become more partisan over the next two years as they work to clarify their stand on the issues.

Congressional Reapportionment

By far the most complicated aspects of the mechanics of congressional elections are the issues of **reapportionment** (the allocation of seats in the House to each state after each census) and **redistricting** (the redrawing of the boundaries of the districts within each state).[5] In a landmark six-to-two vote in 1962, the Supreme Court made reapportionment a **justiciable** (that is, a reviewable) **question** in the Tennessee case of *Baker v. Carr*[6] by invoking the Fourteenth Amendment principle that no state can deny to any person "the equal protection of the laws." This principle was applied directly in the 1964 ruling in *Reynolds v. Sims*[7] when the Court held that *both* chambers of a state legislature must be apportioned with equal populations in each district. This "one person, one vote" principle was applied to congressional districts in the 1964 case of *Wesberry v. Sanders*,[8] based on Article I, Section 2, of the Constitution, which requires that congresspersons be chosen "by the People of the several States."

Severe malapportionment of congressional districts prior to *Wesberry* had resulted in some districts containing two or three times the populations of other districts in the same state, thereby diluting the effect of a vote cast in the more populous districts. This system generally had benefited the conservative populations of rural areas and small towns and harmed the interests of the more heavily populated and liberal urban areas. In fact, suburban areas have benefited the most from the *Wesberry* ruling, as suburbs account for an increasingly larger proportion of the nation's population, and cities include a correspondingly smaller segment of the population.

Gerrymandering

Although the general issue of reapportionment has been dealt with fairly successfully by the one person, one vote principle, the **gerrymandering** issue has not yet been resolved. This term refers to the legislative boundary-drawing tactics that were used by Elbridge Gerry, the governor of Massachusetts, in the 1812 elections (see Figure 12–1 on the following page). A district is said to have been gerrymandered when its shape is altered substantially by the dominant party in a state legislature to maximize its electoral strength at the expense of the minority party.

In 1986, the Supreme Court heard a case that challenged gerrymandered congressional districts in Indiana. The Court ruled for the first time that redistricting for the political benefit of one group could be challenged on constitutional grounds. In this specific case, *Davis v. Bandemer*,[9] however, the Court did not agree that the districts were drawn unfairly, because it could not be proved that a group of voters would consistently be deprived of influence at the polls as a result of the new districts.

Reapportionment
The allocation of seats in the House of Representatives to each state after each census.

Redistricting
The redrawing of the boundaries of the congressional districts within each state.

Justiciable Question
A question that may be raised and reviewed in court.

For more information on reapportionment, use the term "United States Congress" in the Subject guide, and then go to the subdivision "election districts."

Gerrymandering
The drawing of legislative district boundary lines for the purpose of obtaining partisan or factional advantage. A district is said to be gerrymandered when its shape is manipulated by the dominant party in the state legislature to maximize electoral strength at the expense of the minority party.

---

[5]For an excellent discussion of these issues, see *Congressional Districts in the 1990s* (Washington, D.C.: Congressional Quarterly Press, 1993).
[6]369 U.S. 186 (1962). The term *justiciable* is pronounced juhs-*tish*-a-buhl.
[7]377 U.S. 533 (1964).
[8]376 U.S. 1 (1964).
[9]478 U.S. 109 (1986).

FIGURE 12–1

The Original Gerrymander

The practice of "gerrymandering"—the excessive manipulation of the shape of a legislative district to benefit a certain incumbent or party—is probably as old as the republic, but the name originated in 1812. In that year, the Massachusetts legislature carved out of Essex County a district that historian John Fiske said had a "dragonlike contour." When the painter Gilbert Stuart saw the misshapen district, he penciled in a head, wings, and claws and exclaimed, "That will do for a salamander!" Editor Benjamin Russell replied, "Better say a Gerrymander" (after Elbridge Gerry, then governor of Massachusetts).

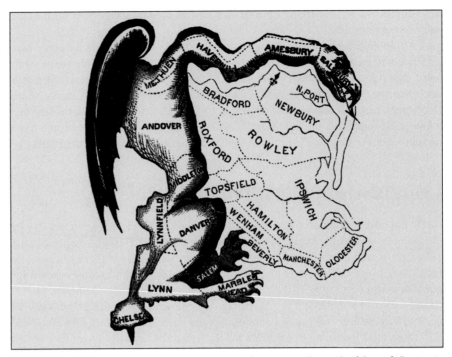

SOURCE: *Congressional Quarterly's Guide to Congress,* 3d ed. (Washington, D.C.: Congressional Quarterly Press, 1982), p. 695.

Redistricting after the 2000 Census

In the meantime, political gerrymandering continues. Certainly, it was evident in the redistricting that followed the 2000 census. Technically, state legislatures are responsible for redrawing legislative districts within their respective states. In fact, redistricting decisions are often made by a small group of political leaders within a state legislature. Typically, their goal is to shape voting districts in such a way as to maximize their party's chances of winning state legislative seats as well as seats in Congress. One of the techniques they use is called "packing and cracking." With the use of powerful computers and software, they pack voters supporting the opposing party into as few districts as possible or crack the opposing party's supporters into different districts. Consider that in Michigan, the Republicans who dominated redistricting efforts succeeded in packing six Democratic incumbents into only three congressional seats.

Clearly, partisan redistricting aids incumbents. The party that dominates a state's legislature will be making redistricting decisions. Through gerrymandering tactics such as packing and cracking, districts can be redrawn in such a way as to ensure that party's continued strength in the state legislature or Congress. Some estimated that only between 30 and 50 of the 435 seats in the House of Representatives were open for any real competition in the 2002 congressional elections. Perhaps, though, there is an alternative to partisan redistricting, a possibility that we examine in this chapter's *Which Side Are You On?* feature.

"Minority-Majority" Districts

In the early 1990s, the federal government encouraged a type of gerrymandering that made possible the election of a minority representative from a "minority-majority" area. Under the mandate of the Voting Rights Act of 1965, the Justice Department issued directives to states after the 1990 census instructing them to create congressional districts that would maximize the voting power of minority groups—that is, create dis-

Which Side Are You On?
Should Nonpartisan Commissions Take Charge of Redistricting?

As you have already learned, incumbents are routinely reelected to office. One of the reasons this is so is the partisan nature of the redistricting process each decade. Those in Congress enlist the help of party leaders in their states, who redistrict in such a way as to make congressional members' seats safe for reelection if they choose to run. According to one critic, "Those who draw the lines have become some of the most powerful people in America. They can reward legislators for good behavior and punish them for disloyalty." *

REDISTRICTING SHOULD NO LONGER BE PARTISAN

It used to be that on election day, Americans chose their representatives. Today, however, the opposite seems to be occurring—the representatives are choosing the voters through the political redistricting process. As mentioned, this gives incumbents an advantage—in addition to the many other advantages they enjoy. Simply as part of their job, for example, members of Congress appear in the news and enjoy free publicity on such programs as C-SPAN.

Some have suggested that the way redistricting is currently undertaken is shamefully biased. To ensure neutrality in redistricting, they propose that nonpartisan state commissions be established to make redistricting decisions. Iowa and Arizona have already used nonpartisan bodies to redistrict. Canada and Britain use this process, too, with great success. The boundaries are universally respected, and the legislative seats are more competitive.

*Stephen E. Gottlieb, "Incumbents Rule," *The National Law Journal*, February 25, 2002, p. A21.

"IF IT AIN'T BROKE, DON'T FIX IT"

Others contend that although partisanship may result in "packing" and "cracking" during redistricting, there is no truly neutral way to engage in this complicated activity every ten years. Indeed, when the Supreme Court looked at this issue in 1993 in *Shaw v. Reno*,[†] it found nothing wrong with traditional redistricting criteria or methods; that is to say, the Supreme Court accepted the current process as constitutional even though it often results in protecting the seats of incumbent legislators and improving their political advantages. If we were to pass a law that required all states to use nonpartisan commissions, that law might well be held unconstitutional.

One of the reasons the American democratic system has remained so stable is that we respect political tradition. The so-called faults of partisan redistricting have been part of that system for over two hundred years. Why should we change it if the end result has been a strong republic?

WHAT'S YOUR POSITION?

If you were on a nonpartisan redistricting commission, how might you go about redrawing congressional district boundaries after each census?

GOING ONLINE

The Center for Voting and Democracy has a page on its Web site devoted to the topic of redistricting, including the use of nonpartisan commissions. Visit **http://www.fairvote.org/redistricting**. The National Conference of State Legislatures also maintains a site on the process of redistricting, including the latest news on the topic. Go to **http://www.ncsl.org/public/issues.htm** and select "redistricting" from the pop-up menu.

[†]509 U.S. 630 (1993).

---

tricts in which minority voters were the majority. The result was a number of creatively drawn congressional districts—see, for example, the depiction of Illinois's Fourth Congressional District in Figure 12–2 on the following page.

Constitutional Challenges

Many of these "minority-majority" districts were challenged in court by citizens who claimed that to create districts based on race or ethnicity alone violates the equal protection clause of the Constitution. In 1995, the Supreme Court agreed with this argument when it declared that Georgia's new Eleventh District was unconstitutional.

FIGURE 12–2

The Fourth Congressional District of Illinois

This district, which is mostly within Chicago's city limits, was drawn to connect two Hispanic neighborhoods separated by an African American majority district.

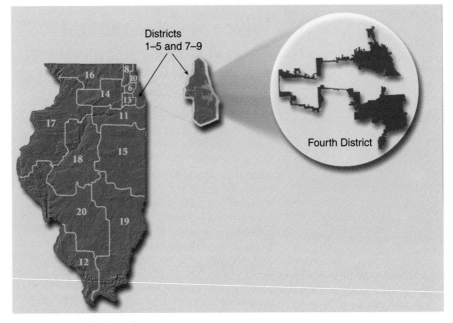

SOURCE: *The New York Times*, July 15, 2001, p. 16.

The district stretched from Atlanta to the Atlantic, splitting eight counties and five municipalities along the way. The Court referred to the district as a "monstrosity" linking "widely spaced urban centers that have absolutely nothing to do with each other." The Court went on to say that when a state assigns voters on the basis of race, "it engages in the offensive and demeaning assumption that voters of a particular race, because of their race, think alike, share the same political interests, and will prefer the same candidates at the polls." The Court also chastised the Justice Department for concluding that race-based districting was mandated under the Voting Rights Act of 1965: "When the Justice Department's interpretation of the Act compels race-based districting, it by definition raises a serious constitutional question."[10] In subsequent rulings, the Court affirmed its position that when race is the dominant factor in the drawing of congressional district lines, the districts are unconstitutional.

Changing Directions

In the early 2000s, the Supreme Court seemed to take a new direction with respect to racial redistricting challenges. In a 2000 case, the Court limited the federal government's authority to invalidate changes in state and local elections on the basis that the changes were discriminatory. The case involved a proposed school redistricting plan in Louisiana. The Court held that federal approval for the plan could not be withheld simply because the plan was discriminatory. Rather, the test was whether the plan left racial and ethnic minorities worse off than they were before.[11]

In 2001, the Supreme Court reviewed, for a second time, a case involving North Carolina's Twelfth District. The district was 165 miles long, following Interstate 85 for the most part. According to a local joke, the district was so narrow that a car traveling down the interstate highway with both doors open would kill most of the voters in the district. In 1996, the Supreme Court had held that the district was unconstitutional because race had been the dominant factor in drawing the district's

---

[10] *Miller v. Johnson*, 515 U.S. 900 (1995).

[11] *Reno v. Bossier Parish School Board*, 120 S.Ct. 886 (2000).

boundaries. Shortly thereafter, the boundaries were redrawn, but the district was again challenged as a racial gerrymander. A federal district court agreed and invalidated the new boundaries as unconstitutional. In 2001, however, the Supreme Court held that there was insufficient evidence for the lower court's conclusion that race had been the dominant factor when the boundaries were redrawn.[12]

Pay, Perks, and Privileges

Compared with the average American citizen, members of Congress are well paid. In 2002, annual congressional salaries were $150,000. Legislators also have many benefits that are not available to most workers.

Special Benefits

Members of Congress benefit in many ways from belonging to a select group. They have access to private Capitol Hill gymnasium facilities; receive free, close-in parking at the National and Dulles Airports near Washington; and get six free parking spaces per member in Capitol Hill garages—plus one free outdoor Capitol parking slot. They also avoid parking tickets because of their congressional license plates. They eat in a subsidized dining room and take advantage of free plants from the Botanical Gardens for their offices, free medical care, an inexpensive but generous pension plan, liberal travel allowances, and special tax considerations.

Members of Congress are also granted generous **franking** privileges that permit them to mail newsletters, surveys, and other letters to their constituents. The annual cost of congressional mail has risen from $11 million in 1971 to almost $60 million today. Typically, the costs for these mailings rise enormously during election years.

Franking
A policy that enables members of Congress to send material through the mail by substituting their facsimile signature (frank) for postage.

Permanent Professional Staffs

More than 35,000 people are employed in the Capitol Hill bureaucracy. About half of them are personal and committee staff members. The personal staff includes office clerks and secretaries; professionals who deal with media relations, draft legislation, and satisfy constituency requests for service; and staffers who maintain local offices in the member's home district or state.

The average Senate office on Capitol Hill employs about thirty staff members, and twice that number work on the personal staffs of senators from the most populous states. House office staffs typically are about half as large as those of the Senate. The number of staff members has increased dramatically since 1960. With the bulk of those increases coming in assistants to individual members, some scholars question whether staff members are really advising on legislation or are primarily aiding constituents and gaining votes in the next election.

Congress also benefits from the expertise of the professional staffs of agencies that were created to produce information for members of the House and Senate. For example, the Congressional Research Service, the General Accounting Office, and the Congressional Budget Office all provide reports, audits, and policy recommendations for review by members of Congress.

Privileges and Immunities under the Law

Members of Congress also benefit from a number of special constitutional protections. Under Article I, Section 6, of the Constitution, they "shall in all Cases, except

---

[12] *Easley v. Cromartie,* 532 U.S. 234 (2001).

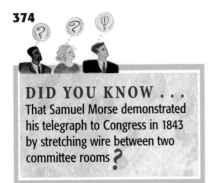

Discharge Petition
A procedure by which a bill in the House of Representatives may be forced out of a committee (discharged) that has refused to report it for consideration by the House. The discharge petition must be signed by an absolute majority (218) of representatives and is used only on rare occasions.

Standing Committee
A permanent committee in the House or Senate that considers bills within a certain subject area.

Congresswoman Connie Morella of Maryland sits at her desk while speaking with her staff in her Washington, D.C., office. Congressional staff members serve as researchers, help write speeches for their legislators, answer the mail, and assist constituents in getting their problems solved. Today, staff members spend more and more of their time answering e-mail and working on their legislators' Web sites. (Morella was defeated in the 2002 elections.) (Paul Conklin/PhotoEdit)

Treason, Felony and Breach of the Peace, be privileged from Arrest during their Attendance at the Session of their respective Houses, and in going to and returning from the same; and for any Speech or Debate in either House, they shall not be questioned in any other Place." The arrest immunity clause is not really an important provision today. The "speech or debate" clause, however, means that a member may make any allegations or other statements he or she wishes in connection with official duties and normally not be sued for libel or slander or otherwise be subject to legal action.

The Committee Structure

Most of the actual work of legislating is performed by the committees and subcommittees within Congress. Thousands of bills are introduced in every session of Congress, and no single member can possibly be adequately informed on all the issues that arise. The committee system is a way to provide for specialization, or a division of the legislative labor. Members of a committee can concentrate on just one area or topic—such as taxation or energy—and develop sufficient expertise to draft appropriate legislation when needed. The flow of legislation through both the House and the Senate is determined largely by the speed with which the members of these committees act on bills and resolutions.

The Power of Committees

Commonly known as "little legislatures," committees usually have the final say on pieces of legislation.[13] Committee actions may be overturned on the floor by the House or Senate, but this rarely happens. Legislators normally defer to the expertise of the chairperson and other members of the committee who speak on the floor in defense of a committee decision. Chairpersons of committees exercise control over the scheduling of hearings and formal action on a bill. They also decide which subcommittee will act on legislation falling within their committee's jurisdiction.

Committees only very rarely are deprived of control over a bill—although this kind of action is provided for in the rules of each chamber. In the House, if a bill has been considered by a standing committee for thirty days, the signatures of a majority (218) of the House membership on a **discharge petition** can pry a bill out of an uncooperative committee's hands. From 1909 to 2003, however, although over nine hundred such petitions were made, only slightly more than two dozen resulted in successful discharge efforts. Of those, twenty passed the House.[14]

Types of Congressional Committees

Over the past two centuries, Congress has created several different types of committees, each of which serves particular needs of the institution.

Standing Committees. By far the most important committees in Congress are the **standing committees**—permanent bodies that are established by the rules of each chamber of Congress and that continue from session to session. A list of the standing committees of the 108th Congress is presented in Table 12–4. In addition, most of the standing committees have created several subcommittees to carry out their work. In the 108th Congress, there were 68 subcommittees in the Senate and 88 in the House.[15]

---

[13] The term *little legislatures* is from Woodrow Wilson, *Congressional Government* (New York: Meridian Books, 1956 [first published in 1885]).

[14] Congressional Quarterly, Inc., *Guide to Congress,* 5th ed. (Washington, D.C.: CQ Press, 2000); and authors' update.

[15] *Congressional Directory* (Washington, D.C.: U.S. Government Printing Office, various editions).

Each standing committee is given a specific area of legislative policy jurisdiction, and almost all legislative measures are considered by the appropriate standing committees. Because of the importance of their work and the traditional influence of their members in Congress, certain committees are considered to be more prestigious than others. If a congressperson seeks to be influential, she or he will usually aspire to a seat on the Appropriations Committee in either chamber, the Ways and Means Committee in the House, the House Education and the Workforce Committee, or the Senate Foreign Relations Committee.

Each member of the House generally serves on two standing committees, except when the member sits on the Appropriations, Rules, or Ways and Means Committee—in which case he or she serves on only that one standing committee. Each senator may serve on two major committees and one minor committee (only the Rules and Administration Committee and the Veterans Affairs Committee are considered minor).

Select Committees.   A **select committee** normally is created for a limited period of time and for a specific legislative purpose. For example, a select committee may be formed to investigate a public problem, such as child nutrition or aging. Select committees are disbanded when they have reported to the chamber that created them. They rarely create original legislation.

Joint Committees.   A **joint committee** is formed by the concurrent action of both chambers of Congress and consists of members from each chamber. Joint committees, which may be permanent or temporary, have dealt with the economy, taxation, and the Library of Congress.

Conference Committees.   Special types of joint committees—**conference committees**—are formed for the purpose of achieving agreement between the House and the Senate on the exact wording of legislative acts when the two chambers pass legislative proposals in different forms. No bill can be sent to the White House to be signed into law unless it first passes both chambers in identical form. Sometimes called the "third house" of Congress, conference committees are in a position to make significant alterations in legislation and frequently become the focal point of policy debates.

DID YOU KNOW . . .
That the House members' gym has no locker room for female members, and women must call ahead to warn the men that they are coming to use the gym **?**

Select Committee
A temporary legislative committee established for a limited time period and for a special purpose.

Joint Committee
A legislative committee composed of members from both chambers of Congress.

Conference Committee
A special joint committee appointed to reconcile differences when bills pass the two chambers of Congress in different forms.

TABLE 12–4

Standing Committees of the 108th Congress, 2003–2005

HOUSE COMMITTEES	SENATE COMMITTEES
Agriculture	Agriculture, Nutrition, and Forestry
Appropriations	Appropriations
Armed Services	Armed Services
Budget	Banking, Housing, and Urban Affairs
Education and the Workforce	Budget
Energy and Commerce	Commerce, Science, and Transportation
Financial Services	Energy and Natural Resources
Government Reform	Environment and Public Works
House Administration	Finance
International Relations	Foreign Relations
Judiciary	Governmental Affairs
Resources	Health, Education, Labor, and Pensions
Rules	Judiciary
Science	Rules and Administration
Small Business	Small Business
Standards of Official Conduct	Veterans Affairs
Transportation and Infrastructure	
Veterans Affairs	
Ways and Means	

A committee hearing in Congress. Starting from the chair of the committee in the center, Democratic senators sit on the left in order of seniority, while Republicans take the seats on the right in order of seniority. (Dennis Brack/Black Star)

The House Rules Committee.   Because of its special "gatekeeping" power over the terms on which legislation will reach the floor of the House of Representatives, the House Rules Committee holds a uniquely powerful position. A special committee rule sets the time limit on debate and determines whether and how a bill may be amended. This practice dates back to 1883. The Rules Committee has the unusual power to meet while the House is in session, to have its resolutions considered immediately on the floor, and to initiate legislation on its own.

The Selection of Committee Members

In the House, representatives are appointed to standing committees by the Steering Committee of their party. Majority-party members with longer terms of continuous service on a standing committee are given preference when the committee chairperson—as well as holders of other significant posts in Congress—is selected. This is not a law but an informal, traditional process. The **seniority system**, although deliberately unequal, provides a predictable means of assigning positions of power within Congress.

The general pattern until the 1970s was that members of the House or Senate who represented **safe seats** would be reelected continually and eventually would accumulate enough years of continuous committee service to enable them to become the chairpersons of their committees.

In the 1970s, a number of reforms in the chairperson selection process somewhat modified the seniority system. The reforms introduced the use of a secret ballot in electing House committee chairpersons and established rules for the selection of subcommittee chairpersons that resulted in a greater dispersal of authority within the committees themselves. In 1995, Speaker Newt Gingrich introduced a set of reforms that restored power to committee chairpersons. In addition, the Republicans passed a rule limiting the term of a committee chairperson to six years.

The Formal Leadership

The limited amount of centralized power that exists in Congress is exercised through party-based mechanisms. Congress is organized by party. When the Democratic Party, for example, wins a majority of seats in either the House or the Senate,

Seniority System
  A custom followed in both chambers of Congress specifying that members with longer terms of continuous service will be given preference when committee chair-persons and holders of other significant posts are selected.

Safe Seat
  A district that returns the legislator with 55 percent of the vote or more.

Democrats control the official positions of power in that chamber, and every important committee has a Democratic chairperson and a majority of Democratic members. The same process holds when Republicans are in the majority.

We consider the formal leadership positions in the House and Senate separately, but you will note some broad similarities in the way leaders are selected and in the ways they exercise power in the two chambers.

Leadership in the House

The House leadership is made up of the Speaker, the majority and minority leaders, and the party whips.

The Speaker.   The foremost power holder in the House of Representatives is the **Speaker of the House.** The Speaker's position is technically a nonpartisan one, but in fact, for the better part of two centuries, the Speaker has been the official leader of the majority party in the House. When a new Congress convenes in January of odd-numbered years, each party nominates a candidate for Speaker. Ordinarily, all Democratic members of the House vote for their party's nominee, and all Republicans support their candidate.

The influence of modern-day Speakers is based primarily on their personal prestige, persuasive ability, and knowledge of the legislative process—plus the acquiescence or active support of other representatives. The major formal powers of the Speaker include the following:

1. Presiding over meetings of the House.
2. Appointing members of joint committees and conference committees.
3. Scheduling legislation for floor action.
4. Deciding points of order and interpreting the rules with the advice of the House parliamentarian.
5. Referring bills and resolutions to the appropriate standing committees of the House.

DID YOU KNOW . . .
That the Constitution does not require that the Speaker of the House of Representatives be an elected member of the House **?**

Speaker of the House
The presiding officer in the House of Representatives. The Speaker is always a member of the majority party and is the most powerful and influential member of the House.

INFOTRAC®
COLLEGE EDITION

For updates and more information, use the term "United States Congress House" in the Subject Guide, and then go to "Speaker."

Dennis Hastert, a Republican member of Congress from Illinois, became Speaker of the House in 1999 during the contentious impeachment process against President Bill Clinton. (AP Photo/Ron Edmonds)

A Speaker may take part in floor debate and vote, as can any other member of Congress, but recent Speakers usually have voted only to break a tie. Since 1975, the Speaker, when a Democrat, has also had the power to appoint the Democratic Steering Committee, which determines new committee assignments for House party members.

In general, the powers of the Speaker are related to his or her control over information and communications channels in the House. This is a significant power in a large, decentralized institution in which information is a very important resource. With this control, the Speaker attempts to ensure the smooth operation of the chamber and to integrate presidential and congressional policies.

Majority Leader of the House

A legislative position held by an important party member in the House of Representatives. The majority leader is selected by the majority party in caucus or conference to foster cohesion among party members and to act as spokesperson for the majority party in the House.

The Majority Leader.   The **majority leader of the House** is elected by a caucus of the majority party to foster cohesion among party members and to act as a spokesperson for the party. The majority leader influences the scheduling of debate and generally acts as the chief supporter of the Speaker. The majority leader cooperates with the Speaker and other party leaders, both inside and outside Congress, to formulate the party's legislative program and to guide that program through the legislative process in the House. The Democrats recruit future Speakers from that position.

Minority Leader of the House

The party leader elected by the minority party in the House.

The Minority Leader.   The **minority leader of the House** is the candidate nominated for Speaker by a caucus of the minority party. Like the majority leader, the leader of the minority party has as her or his primary responsibility the maintaining of cohesion within the party's ranks. The minority leader works for cohesion among the party's members and speaks on behalf of the president if the minority party controls the White House. In relations with the majority party, the minority leader consults with both the Speaker and the majority leader on recognizing members who wish to speak on the floor, on House rules and procedures, and on the scheduling of legislation. Minority leaders have no actual power in these areas, however.

Whip

An assistant who aids the majority or minority leader of the House or the Senate majority or minority floor leader.

Whips.   The formal leadership of each party includes assistants to the majority and minority leaders, who are known as **whips.** The whips assist the party leaders by passing information down from the leadership to party members and by ensuring that members show up for floor debate and cast their votes on important issues. Whips conduct polls among party members about the members' views on major pieces of legislation, inform the leaders about whose vote is doubtful and whose is certain, and may exert pressure on members to support the leaders' positions.

Leadership in the Senate

The Senate is less than one-fourth the size of the House. This fact alone probably explains why a formal, complex, and centralized leadership structure is less necessary in the Senate than it is in the House.

The two highest-ranking formal leadership positions in the Senate are essentially ceremonial in nature. Under the Constitution, the vice president of the United States is the president (that is, the presiding officer) of the Senate and may vote to break a tie. The vice president, however, only rarely is present for a meeting of the Senate. The Senate elects instead a **president *pro tempore*** ("pro tem") to preside over the Senate in the vice president's absence. Ordinarily, the president pro tem is the member of the majority party with the longest continuous term of service in the Senate. The president pro tem is mostly a ceremonial position. Junior senators take turns actually presiding over the sessions of the Senate.

President *Pro Tempore*

The temporary presiding officer of the Senate in the absence of the vice president.

Majority Floor Leader

The chief spokesperson of the majority party in the Senate, who directs the legislative program and party strategy.

Minority Floor Leader

The party officer in the Senate who commands the minority party's opposition to the policies of the majority party and directs the legislative program and strategy of his or her party.

The real leadership power in the Senate rests in the hands of the **majority floor leader,** the **minority floor leader,** and their respective whips. The Senate majority and minority leaders have the right to be recognized first in debate on the floor and generally exercise the same powers available to the House majority and minority leaders.

They control the scheduling of debate on the floor in conjunction with the majority party's Policy Committee, influence the allocation of committee assignments for new members or for senators attempting to transfer to a new committee, influence the selection of other party officials, and participate in selecting members of conference committees. The leaders are expected to mobilize support for partisan legislative initiatives or for the proposals of a president who belongs to the same party. The leaders act as liaisons with the White House when the president is of their party, try to obtain the cooperation of committee chairpersons, and seek to facilitate the smooth functioning of the Senate through the senators' unanimous consent. Floor leaders are elected by their respective party caucuses.

Senate party whips, like their House counterparts, maintain communication within the party on platform positions and try to ensure that party colleagues are present for floor debate and important votes. The Senate whip system is far less elaborate than its counterpart in the House, simply because there are fewer members to track.

A list of the formal party leaders of the 107th Congress is presented in Table 12–5. Party leaders are a major source of influence over the decisions about public issues that senators and representatives must make every day.

How Members of Congress Decide

Why congresspersons vote as they do is difficult to know with any certainty. One popular perception of the legislative decision-making process is that legislators take cues from other trusted or more senior colleagues. This model holds that because most members of Congress have neither the time nor the incentive to study the details of most pieces of legislation, they frequently arrive on the floor with no clear idea about what they are voting on or how they should vote. Their decision is simplified, according to the cue-taking model, by quickly checking how key colleagues have voted or intend to vote. More broadly, verbal and nonverbal cues can be taken from fellow committee members and chairpersons, party leaders, state delegation members, or the president.

TABLE 12–5

Party Leaders in the 107th Congress, 2001–2003

POSITION	INCUMBENT	PARTY/ STATE	LEADER SINCE
House			
Speaker	J. Dennis Hastert	R., Ill.	Jan. 1999
Majority leader	Dick Armey	R., Tex.	Jan. 1995
Majority whip	Tom DeLay	R., Tex.	Jan. 1995
Chairperson of the Republican Conference	J. C. Watts	R., Okla.	Jan. 1999
Minority leader	Richard Gephardt	D., Mo.	Jan. 1995
Minority whip	Nancy Pelosi	D., Calif.	Oct. 2001
Chairperson of the Democratic Caucus	Martin Frost	D., Tex.	Jan. 2001
Senate			
President *pro tempore*	Robert Byrd	D., W.V.	June 2001
Majority floor leader	Trent Lott	R., Miss.	June 1996
Assistant majority leader	Don Nickles	R., Okla.	June 1996
Secretary of the Republican Conference	Rick Santorum	R., Pa.	Jan. 2001
Minority floor leader	Tom Daschle	D., S.Dak.	Jan. 1995
Assistant floor leader	Harry Reid	D., Nev.	Jan. 1999
Secretary of the Democratic Conference	Barbara Mikulski	D., Md.	Jan. 1995

Conservative Coalition
An alliance of Republicans and southern Democrats that can form in the House or the Senate to oppose liberal legislation and support conservative legislation.

Most people who study the decision-making process in Congress agree that the single best predictor for how a member will vote is the member's party affiliation. Republicans tend to vote similarly on issues, as do Democrats. Of course, even though liberals predominate among the Democrats in Congress and conservatives predominate among the Republicans, the parties still may have internal disagreements about the proper direction that national policy should take. This was generally true for the civil rights legislation of the 1950s and 1960s, for example, when the greatest disagreement was between the conservative southern wing and the liberal northern wing of the Democratic Party.

Regional differences, especially between northern and southern Democrats, may overlap and reinforce basic ideological differences among members of the same party. One consequence of the North-South split among Democrats has been the **conservative coalition** policy alliance between southern Democrats and Republicans. This conservative, cross-party grouping formed regularly on votes during the Reagan years but has virtually disappeared since then, because many southern states and districts are now represented by conservative Republicans.

How a Bill Becomes Law

Each year, Congress and the president propose and approve many laws. Some are budget and appropriation laws that require extensive bargaining but must be passed for the government to continue to function. Other laws are relatively free of controversy and are passed with little dissension between the branches of government. Still other proposed legislation is extremely controversial and reaches to the roots of differences between Democrats and Republicans and between the executive and legislative branches. (In times of crisis, Congress may act quickly to pass legislation that later may not seem so necessary to many groups in the public. See, for example, the discussion of the controversial airline bailout bill in this chapter's *America's Security* feature on page 382.)

As detailed in Figure 12–3, each law begins as a bill, which must be introduced in either the House or the Senate. Often, similar bills are introduced in both chambers. If it is a "money bill," however, it must start in the House. In each chamber, the bill follows similar steps. It is referred to a committee and its subcommittees for study, discussion, hearings, and rewriting. When the bill is reported out to the full chamber, it must be scheduled for debate (by the Rules Committee in the House and by the leadership in the Senate). After the bill has been passed in each chamber, if it contains different provisions, a conference committee is formed to write a compromise bill, which must be approved by both chambers before it is sent to the president to sign or veto.

Another form of congressional action, the *joint resolution,* differs very little from a bill in how it is proposed or debated, and once it is approved by both chambers and signed by the president, it has the force of law.[16] A joint resolution to amend the Constitution, however, after it is approved by two-thirds of both chambers, is not sent to the president but to the states for ratification.

How Much Will the Government Spend?

The Constitution is extremely clear about where the power of the purse lies in the national government: all taxing or spending bills must originate in the House of Representatives. Today, much of the business of Congress is concerned with approving government expenditures through the budget process and with raising the revenues to pay for government programs.

---

[16] In contrast, *simple resolutions* and *concurrent resolutions* do not carry the force of law but rather are used by one or both chambers of Congress, respectively, to express facts, principles, or opinions. For example, a concurrent resolution is used to set the time when Congress will adjourn.

FIGURE 12-3

How a Bill Becomes Law

This illustration shows the most typical way in which proposed legislation is enacted into law. Most legislation begins as similar bills introduced into each chamber of Congress. The process is illustrated here with two hypothetical bills, House bill No. 100 (HR 100) and Senate bill No. 200 (S 200). The path of HR 100 is shown on the left, and that of S 200, on the right.

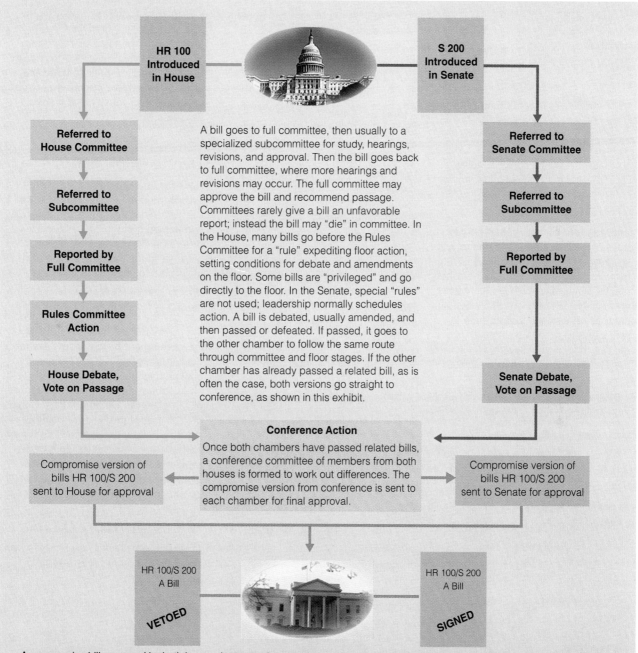

A compromise bill approved by both houses is sent to the president, who can sign it into law or veto it and return it to Congress. Congress may override a veto by a two-thirds majority vote in both houses; the bill then becomes law without the president s signature.

America's Security

Was the Airline Bailout Necessary?

After the terrorist acts in September 2001, American airline companies were severely weakened. In addition to the losses associated with the four crashed planes, significant revenues were lost immediately after the attacks when all airports were closed. Some, such as National Airport in Washington, D.C., did not reopen until several weeks after the attacks. Then the airlines suffered their worst decline in travel bookings ever, caused in part by new security fears. Additionally, many would-be flyers were deterred by real and imagined hassles during check-in.

THE AIR TRANSPORTATION SAFETY AND SYSTEM STABILIZATION ACT

A mere two weeks after 9/11, Congress passed the Air Transportation Safety and System Stabilization Act. In brief, this act provided up to $5 billion in payments to the airlines for the direct losses they incurred as a result of airport shutdowns immediately after the attacks. It also provided federal loans of up to $10 billion. In addition, it provided for expanded federally guaranteed aviation insurance, thereby limiting air carriers' liability for losses to no more than $100 million, taken together, for all claims arising because of an act of terrorism.

The justification given for these new subsidies to the airline industry was that the airlines play a crucial role in the nation's economy. The airlines, already in trouble before 9/11, saw their losses multiply two- and three-fold to literally billions of dollars in 2002. They also feared that their future would be filled with endless lawsuits for any new acts of terrorism. Congress and the president felt that America's security depended enough on the airline industry that it should be bailed out.

WHO SHOULD PAY THE CONSEQUENCES?

Not everyone agreed that the nation's security required the federal bailout of the airline industry. Critics of the legislation argued that the airlines themselves were partly responsible for the disasters because, in their efforts to cut costs, they failed to implement adequate security measures. According to this line of reasoning, the airlines should therefore pay the consequences. What would the consequences have been? Without the government bailout, some airlines would have gone bankrupt. Those bankrupt airlines would have been sold off to stronger airlines. Thus, the demise of some airlines would not have caused the collapse of the American airline industry. Rather, the strongest and most well managed airlines would have taken over the weaker and less well managed airlines. In the end, the airline industry might have been strengthened.

FOR CRITICAL ANALYSIS

To what extent should an industry be expected to pay for catastrophic disasters of any nature?

In 2001, Reagan National Airport in Washington, D.C., served 13.3 million passengers. The airport was closed completely from September 11 to October 4, 2001, after the terrorist attacks and reopened in phases between October 2001 and March 2002. On November 21, 2001, on what is traditionally the busiest travel day of the year (the Wednesday before the Thanksgiving holiday), the airport had nearly empty ticket counters, as seen here. (AP Photo/Hillery Smith Garrison)

From 1922, when Congress required the president to prepare and present to the legislature an **executive budget,** until 1974, the congressional budget process was so disjointed that it was difficult to visualize the total picture of government finances. The president presented the executive budget to Congress in January. It was broken down into thirteen or more appropriations bills. Some time later, after all of the bills were debated, amended, and passed, it was more or less possible to estimate total government spending for the next year.

Frustrated by the president's ability to impound funds and dissatisfied with the entire budget process, Congress passed the Budget and Impoundment Control Act of 1974 to regain some control over the nation's spending. The act required the president to spend the funds that Congress had appropriated, frustrating the president's ability to kill programs of which he or she disapproved by withholding funds. The other major accomplishment of the act was to force Congress to examine total national taxing and spending at least twice in each budget cycle.

The budget cycle of the federal government is described in the following subsections. (See Figure 12–4 for a graphic illustration of the budget cycle.)

Preparing the Budget

The federal government operates on a **fiscal year (FY)** cycle. The fiscal year runs from October through September, so that fiscal 2004, or FY04, runs from October 1, 2003, through September 30, 2004. Eighteen months before a fiscal year starts, the executive branch begins preparing the budget. The Office of Management and Budget (OMB) receives advice from the Council of Economic Advisers (CEA) and the Treasury Department. The OMB outlines the budget and then sends it to the various departments and agencies. Bargaining follows, in which—to use only two of many examples—the Department of Health and Human Services argues for more welfare spending, and the armed forces argue for fewer defense spending cuts.

Even though the OMB has only six hundred employees, it is known as one of the most powerful agencies in Washington. It assembles the budget documents and monitors the agencies throughout each year. Every year, it begins the budget process with a **spring review,** in which it requires all of the agencies to review their programs,

Executive Budget
The budget prepared and submitted by the president to Congress.

Fiscal Year (FY)
The twelve-month period that is used for bookkeeping, or accounting, purposes. Usually, the fiscal year does not coincide with the calendar year. For example, the federal government's fiscal year runs from October 1 through September 30.

Spring Review
The time every year when the Office of Management and Budget requires federal agencies to review their programs, activities, and goals and submit their requests for funding for the next fiscal year.

FIGURE 12–4

The Budget Cycle

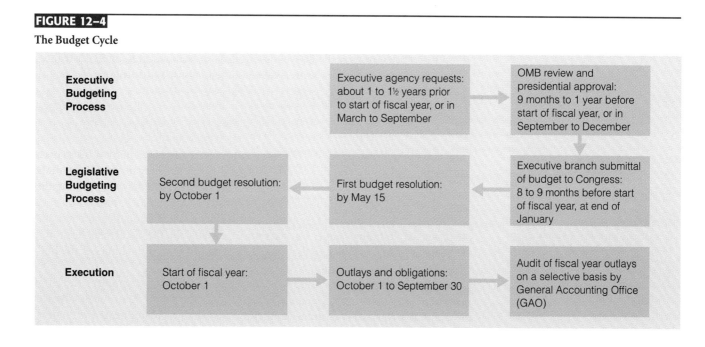

For more information on this topic, use the term "United States Office of Management and Budget" in the Subject guide.

Fall Review

The time every year when, after receiving formal federal agency requests for funding for the next fiscal year, the Office of Management and Budget reviews the requests, makes changes, and submits its recommendations to the president.

Authorization

A formal declaration by a legislative committee that a certain amount of funding may be available to an agency. Some authorizations terminate in a year; others are renewable automatically without further congressional action.

Appropriation

The passage, by Congress, of a spending bill, specifying the amount of authorized funds that actually will be allocated for an agency's use.

First Budget Resolution

A resolution passed by Congress in May that sets overall revenue and spending goals for the following fiscal year.

Second Budget Resolution

A resolution passed by Congress in September that sets "binding" limits on taxes and spending for the next fiscal year beginning October 1.

---

activities, and goals. At the beginning of each summer, the director of the OMB sends out a letter instructing agencies to submit their requests for funding for the next fiscal year. By the end of the summer, each agency must submit a formal request to the OMB.

In actuality, the "budget season" begins with the **fall review.** At this time, the OMB looks at budget requests and, in almost all cases, routinely cuts them back. Although the OMB works within guidelines established by the president, specific decisions often are left to the director and the director's associates. By the beginning of November, the director's review begins. The director meets with cabinet secretaries and budget officers. Time becomes crucial. The budget must be completed by January so that it can go to the printer to be included in the *Economic Report of the President.*

Congress Faces the Budget

In January, nine months before the fiscal year starts, the president takes the OMB's proposed budget, approves it, and submits it to Congress. Then the congressional budgeting process takes over. The budgeting process involves two steps. First, Congress must authorize funds to be spent. The **authorization** is a formal declaration by the appropriate congressional committee that a certain amount of funding may be available to an agency. Congressional committees and subcommittees look at the proposals from the executive branch and the Congressional Budget Office (CBO) in making the decision to authorize funds. After the funds are authorized, they must be appropriated by Congress. The appropriations committees of both the House and the Senate forward spending bills to their respective bodies. The **appropriation** of funds occurs when the final bill is passed.

The budget process involves large sums of money. For example, President George W. Bush's proposed budget for fiscal year 2003 called for expenditures of $2.13 trillion, or $2,130,000,000,000. Because of concerns over national security after the terrorist attacks of September 11, 2001, defense and homeland security consumed about 20 percent of the proposed budget. Close to 60 percent of the proposed expenditures were for Social Security, health care, and other social aid. The remaining outlays were for other government programs (12 percent) and interest on the national debt (9 percent).

When forming the budget for a given year, Congress and the president must take into account revenues, primarily in the form of taxes, as well as expenditures to balance the budget. If spending exceeds the amount brought in by taxes, the government runs a budget deficit (and increases the public debt—see Chapter 16). For example, President Bush's proposed FY03 budget called for expenditures of $2.13 trillion, although projected revenues from taxes amounted to only $2.05 trillion—leaving an $80 billion deficit.

Budget Resolutions

The **first budget resolution** by Congress is supposed to be passed in May. It sets overall revenue goals and spending targets. During the summer, bargaining among all the concerned parties takes place. Spending and tax laws that are drawn up during this period are supposed to be guided by the May congressional budget resolution.

By September, Congress is supposed to pass its **second budget resolution,** one that will set "binding" limits on taxes and spending for the fiscal year beginning October 1. Bills passed before that date that do not fit within the limits of the budget resolution are supposed to be changed.

In actuality, between 1978 and 1996, Congress did not pass a complete budget by October 1. In other words, generally, Congress does not follow its own rules. Budget resolutions are passed late, and when they are passed, they are not treated as binding. In each fiscal year that starts without a budget, every agency operates on the basis of

continuing resolutions, which enable the agencies to keep on doing whatever they were doing the previous year with the same amount of funding. Even continuing resolutions have not always been passed on time.

Continuing Resolution
A temporary law that Congress passes when an appropriations bill has not been decided by the beginning of the new fiscal year on October 1.

The Congress: Why Is It Important Today?

To many voters, the House and Senate seem like arcane institutions that spend too much time in political battles with each other and with the president. Many voters have the impression that too little legislation that matters to the people is produced by Congress, and too many members of Congress hold office just to satisfy their own ambitions. In addition, too much money seems to be spent in congressional campaigns. Despite the public's sometimes cynical attitude toward the institution, however, Congress affects our lives in immediate and profound ways.

One of the most important decisions Congress makes that affects our lives every day is how much the government spends. How much will the government spend to regulate job safety, the environment, or airline security? How much will be spent on intelligence gathering and military actions in the war on terrorism? How many guards will be paid to patrol our borders, protect our national infrastructure, or ride airplanes as air marshals? Congress makes these important decisions, and in turn, Congress decides how much we pay in taxes, which fund the government. Tax rates, deductions, and credits are all legislated by Congress. Although polls show that Americans give the president more credit than Congress for legislation that is enacted, members of Congress are more aware of the local needs of their states and districts than is the president, whose constituency is nationwide.

As you read in this chapter's opening *What If . . .* feature, members of Congress go home to their districts and, in most cases, build trusting relationships with their constituents. Voters have opportunities to meet their representatives, argue for or against legislation, and express their needs and concerns. Congress was created for just this purpose. Local and state interests are fully represented in our federal system of government through Congress. Just one representative from one district in one state has the power to influence how or whether a bill becomes a law.

MAKING A DIFFERENCE | Learn about Your Representatives

You can make a difference in our democracy simply by going to the polls on election day and voting for the candidates you would like to represent you in Congress. It goes without saying, though, that to cast an informed vote, you need to know how your congressional representatives stand on the issues and, if they are incumbents, how they have voted on bills that are important to you.

Contact Your Representatives

Many Web sites maintain an up-to-date list of congressional representatives and senators, their e-mail addresses, and their office addresses and phone numbers both in Washington, D.C., and in their home state or district. The best place to start is by going to the Web sites of the U.S. House of Representatives (at **http://www.house.gov**) and the U.S. Senate (at **http://www.senate.gov**). From these Web sites, you can search for your representative by state or zip code, send an e-mail to your representative directly from a form on the Web site, or link to your representative's own Web site.

In today's digital age, you can quickly and easily contact your congressional representatives. This ease of communication has drawbacks, however. Representatives and senators are now receiving large volumes of e-mail

from constituents, and they rarely read the e-mail themselves. They have staff members who read and respond to e-mail, instead. Many interest groups that encourage constituents to contact their representatives on an issue argue that U.S. mail, or even express mail or a phone call, is more likely to capture the attention of the representative than e-mail. You can contact your representatives directly at the Capitol using one of the following addresses or phone numbers:

United States House of
Representatives
Washington, DC 20515
202-224-3121

United States Senate
Washington, DC 20510
202-224-3121

Track Voting Records and Performance Evaluations

Interest groups also track the voting records of members of Congress and rate the members on how they perform on the issues. Project Vote Smart tracks the performance of over 13,000 political leaders, including their campaign finances, issue positions, and voting records. You can contact Project Vote Smart at the following address:

Project Vote Smart
One Common Ground
Philipsburg, MT 59858
Voter Hotline toll-free 1-888-VOTE-SMART (1-888-868-3762)
http://www.vote-smart.org/ce

You can also scroll down the Web page at Project Vote Smart and click on "Descriptions of the Groups Offering Performance Evaluations." This link will take you to a list of interest groups that rate members' performances on specific issues. To find out how a particular group evaluates members of Congress with respect to a certain issue, click on that group's name.

Know Where Your Representatives Get Their Money

Finally, if you want to know how your representatives funded their campaigns, contact the Center for Responsive Politics (CRP), a research group that tracks money in politics, campaign fund-raising, and similar issues. You can contact the CRP at the following address:

The Center for Responsive Politics
1101 14th St. N.W., Suite 1030
Washington, DC 20005
202-857-0044
http://www.opensecrets.org

Key Terms

Chapter Summary

1 The authors of the Constitution, believing that the bulk of national power should be in the legislature, set forth the structure, power, and operation of Congress. The Constitution states that Congress will consist of two chambers. Partly an outgrowth of the Connecticut Compromise, this bicameral structure established a balanced legislature, with the membership in the House of Representatives based on population and the membership in the Senate based on the equality of states.

2 The first seventeen clauses of Article I, Section 8, of the Constitution specify most of the enumerated, or expressed, powers of Congress, including the right to impose taxes, to borrow money, to regulate commerce, and to declare war. Besides its enumerated powers, Congress enjoys the right to "make all Laws which shall be necessary and proper for carrying into Execution the foregoing Powers, and all other Powers vested by this Constitution in the Government of the United States, or in any Department or Officer thereof." This is called the elastic, or necessary and proper, clause.

3 The functions of Congress include (a) lawmaking, (b) service to constituents, (c) representation, (d) oversight, (e) public education, and (f) conflict resolution.

4 There are 435 members in the House of Representatives and 100 members in the Senate. Owing to its larger size, the House has a greater number of formal rules. The Senate tradition of unlimited debate, or filibustering, dates back to 1790 and has been used over the years to frustrate the passage of bills. Under Senate Rule 22, cloture can be used to shut off debate on a bill.

5 Members of Congress are not typical American citizens. They are older and wealthier than most Americans; dispro-portionately white, male, and Protestant; and more likely to be trained in professional occupations.

6 Congressional elections are operated by the individual state governments, which must abide by rules established by the Constitution and national statutes. The process of nominating congressional candidates has shifted from party conventions to the direct primaries currently used in all states. The overwhelming majority of incumbent representatives and a smaller proportion of senators who run for reelection are successful. The most complicated aspect of the mechanics of congressional elections is reapportionment—the allocation of legislative seats to constituencies. The Supreme Court's "one person, one vote" rule has been applied to equalize the populations of state legislative and congressional districts.

7 Members of Congress are well paid and enjoy other benefits, including franking privileges. Members of Congress have personal and committee staff members available to them and also benefit from a number of legal privileges and immunities.

8 Most of the actual work of legislating is performed by committees and subcommittees within Congress. Legislation introduced into the House or Senate is assigned to the appropriate standing committees for review. Select committees are created for a limited period of time for a specific legislative purpose. Joint committees are formed by the concurrent action of both chambers and consist of members from each chamber. Conference committees are special joint committees set up to achieve agreement between the House and the Senate on the exact wording of legislative acts passed by both chambers in different forms. The seniority rule specifies that longer-serving members will be given preference when committee chairpersons and holders of other important posts are selected.

9 The foremost power holder in the House of Representatives is the Speaker of the House. Other leaders are the House majority leader, the House minority leader, and the majority and minority whips. Formally, the vice president is the presiding officer of the Senate, with the majority party choosing a senior member as the president *pro tempore* to preside when the vice president is absent. Actual leadership in the Senate rests with the majority floor leader, the minority floor leader, and their respective whips.

10 A bill becomes law by progressing through both chambers of Congress and their appropriate standing and joint committees to the president.

11 The budget process for a fiscal year begins with the preparation of an executive budget by the president. This is reviewed by the Office of Management and Budget and then sent to Congress, which is supposed to pass a final budget by the end of September. Since 1978, Congress has not followed its own time rules.

Selected Print and Media Resources

SUGGESTED READINGS

Barone, Michael, and Grant Ujifusa. *The Almanac of American Politics, 2000.* Washington, D.C.: National Journal, 1999. This book, which is published biannually, is a comprehensive summary of current political information on each member of Congress, his or her state or congressional district, recent congressional election results, key votes, ratings by various organizations, sources of campaign contributions, and records of campaign expenditures.

Clayton, Dewey M. *African Americans and the Politics of Congressional Redistricting (Race and Politics).* Hamden, Conn.: Garland Publishing, 2000. This book gives a detailed look at the role of race in the drawing of congressional districts from the Civil War to the present.

Cook, Rhodes. *How Congress Gets Elected.* Washington, D.C.: Congressional Quarterly Press, 1999. This is an authoritative source on the legal and political issues that affect the way congressional elections are conducted and the results of those elections. Topics include reapportionment, redistricting, and campaign financing, among others.

Davidson, Roger H., and Walter J. Oleszek. *Congress and Its Members,* 7th ed. Washington, D.C.: Congressional Quarterly Press, 2000. This updated classic looks carefully at the "two Congresses," the one in Washington and the role played by congresspersons at home.

Just, Ward S. *The Congressman Who Loved Flaubert.* New York: Carrol and Graf Publishers, 1990. This fictional account of a career politician was first published in 1973 and is still a favorite with students of political science. Ward Just is renowned for his political fiction, and particularly for his examination of character and motivation.

Tolchin, Susan, and Martin Tolchin. *Glass Houses: Congressional Ethics and the Politics of Venom.* Boulder, Colo.: Westview Press, 2001. The authors examine how ethics laws passed in the 1970s, after the Watergate scandal, became tools in partisan politics in the 1990s. They conclude that the obsessive scandalmongering of recent years has forced lawmakers to be "more honest and more ethical today than ever before" because they live in glass houses.

MEDIA SOURCES

Mr. Smith Goes to Washington—A 1939 film in which Jimmy Stewart plays the naïve congressman who is quickly educated in Washington. A true American political classic.

The Seduction of Joe Tynan—A 1979 film in which Alan Alda plays a young senator who must face serious decisions about his political role and his private life.

Your CD-ROM Resources

In addition to the chapter content containing hot links, the following resources are available on the CD-ROM:

* **Internet Activities**—Members of the House of Representatives, U.S. Senators.

* **Critical Thinking Exercises**—Filibustering, Senator James Jeffords.

* **Self-Check on Important Themes**—Can You Answer These?

* **Animated Figures**—Table 12–1, "Differences Between the House and Senate," Table 12–4, "Standing Committees of the 107th Congress 2001–2003," and Figure 12–3, "How a Bill Becomes a Law."

* **Videos**—*Congressional Oversight, The Cost of Congressional Campaigns.*

* **Public Opinion Data**—Find contrasting views on the airline industry bailout.

* **InfoTrac Exercise**—"The War on Terrorism."

* **Simulation**—You Are There!

* **Participation Exercise**—Participate in the newsgroup alt.politics.usa.congress that contains a wide variety of opinions about issues facing Congress.

* **MicroCase Exercise**—"By the Numbers: Backgrounds on the Members of the 106th Congress."

* **Additional Resources**—All court cases, *Federalist Paper* No. 55.

e-mocracy
Elections and the Web

With the Internet at your fingertips, it has never been easier to stay informed and involved in our political system. Virtually all senators and representatives now have Web sites that you can find simply by keying in their names in a search engine. As you read in this chapter's *Making a Difference* feature, you can easily learn the names of your congressional representatives by going to the Web site of the House or Senate (see the following *Logging On* section for the URLs for these sites). Once you know the names of your representatives, you can go to their Web sites to learn more about them and their positions on specific issues. You can also check the Web sites of the groups listed in the *Making a Difference* feature to track your representatives' voting records and discover the names of their campaign contributors.

Note that some members of Congress also provide important services to their constituents via their Web sites. Some sites, for example, allow constituents to apply for internships in Washington, D.C., apply for appointments to military academies, order flags, order tours of the Capitol, and register complaints electronically. Other sites may even provide forms from certain government agencies, such as the Social Security Administration, that their constituents can use to request assistance from those agencies or register complaints.

Logging On

To find out about the schedule of activities taking place in Congress, use the following Web sites:

http://www.senate.gov

http://www.house.gov

The Congressional Budget Office is online at

http://www.cbo.gov

The URL for the Government Printing Office is

http://www.access.gpo.gov

For the real inside facts on what's going on in Washington, D.C., you can look at the following resources:

RollCall, the newspaper of the Capitol:

http://www.rollcall.com

Congressional Quarterly, a publication that reports on Congress:

http://www.cq.com

The Hill, which investigates various activities of Congress:

http://www.hillnews.com

Using the Internet for Political Analysis

Point your browser to one of the general guides to Congress given at the following Web sites:

http://www.house.gov

http://www.senate.gov

Look up the Web pages of at least three different members of the House or the Senate. Try to pick members from each of the major parties. Compare the Web pages on the following issues:

1. Which page appears to provide the most assistance to constituents?

2. How much partisan information is included on the Web page?

3. To what extent is the member of Congress giving information about her or his policy stances?

4. To what extent is the member trying to build trust and loyalty through providing personal information and services?

BACKGROUND

When a U.S. president wishes to keep information secret, he or she can invoke *executive privilege*. Typically, administrations use executive privilege to safeguard national security secrets. Although there is no mention of executive privilege in the Constitution, presidents from George Washington to George W. Bush have invoked this privilege in response to encroachments on the executive branch by Congress and by the judiciary.

Nonetheless, Congress could pass a law prohibiting the executive branch from using executive privilege as a defense to requests for information. Alternatively, the Supreme Court could hold that executive privilege is an unconstitutional exercise of executive power.

WHAT IF THERE WERE NO EXECUTIVE PRIVILEGE?

If there were no executive privilege, a president would have to be aware that all of his or her words, documents, and actions could be made public. We know from twentieth-century history that when a president does not have full executive privilege to protect information, the results can be devastating. President Richard Nixon (1969–1974) had tape-recorded hundreds of hours of conversations in the Oval Office. During a scandal involving a cover-up (the Watergate scandal, as you will read later in this chapter), Congress requested those tapes. Nixon invoked executive privilege and refused to turn them over. Ultimately, the Supreme Court ordered him to do so, however, and the tapes provided damning information about Nixon's role in the purported cover-up of illegal activities. Rather than face impeachment, Nixon resigned the presidency.

Clearly, if executive privilege were eliminated, it is unlikely that conversations between the president and other members of the executive branch would be recorded or otherwise documented. As a result, we would have far fewer records of an administration's activities than we do today.

EXECUTIVE PRIVILEGE IN A WORLD FILLED WITH TERRORISM

Following the terrorist attacks on September 11, 2001, President George W. Bush instructed his administration to reassess government disclosure policies. One month later, Attorney General John Ashcroft advised federal agencies "to lean toward withholding information whenever possible." According to some administration critics, Bush has taken more steps against openness in government than any other modern president.

If executive privilege were eliminated, our current president would have a difficult time removing so much previously public information from the public records. Indeed, without executive privilege, the president might find it difficult to wage a war on terrorism. There would be nothing to stop Congress from requesting information (and, possibly, publishing it) from the executive branch about security matters.

PAST, PRESENT, AND FUTURE PRESIDENTIAL PAPERS

The White House is allowed to decide what is classified as top secret. Even if Congress requests top secret material, the White House does not have to release it. In general, not all transcripts of private conversations between past presidents and foreign heads of state are made available to congressional committees, for example.

If executive privilege were eliminated, the White House would have a difficult time regulating the flow of past presidential records into the public forum. Future presidents, of course, would know that virtually every word and act could be released to the public. The behavior of presidents and their administrations would certainly change. They might simply insist that there be no record of sensitive conversations. If so, future Americans would lose much of the historical background for America's domestic and international actions.

FOR CRITICAL ANALYSIS

1. The history of executive privilege dates back to 1796, when President George Washington refused a request by the House for certain documents. Given the changes that have taken place since that time, should executive privilege be eliminated? Or should it be retained as even more necessary today than it was at that time?

2. What would be the costs to the nation if executive privilege were eliminated?

Τhe writers of the Constitution created the presidency of the United States without any models on which to draw. Nowhere else in the world was there a democratically selected chief executive. What the founders did not want was a king. In fact, given their previous experience with royal governors in the colonies, many of the delegates to the Constitutional Convention wanted to create a very weak executive who could not veto legislation. Other delegates, especially those who had witnessed the need for a strong leader in the Revolutionary Army, believed a strong executive to be necessary for the republic. The delegates, after much debate, created a chief executive who had enough powers granted in the Constitution to balance those of Congress.[1]

The power exercised by each president who has held the office has been scrutinized and judged by historians, political scientists, the media, and the public. The executive privilege enjoyed by presidents has also been subject to scrutiny and debate, as you learned in the chapter-opening *What If . . .* feature. Indeed, it would seem that Americans are fascinated by presidential power and by the persons who hold the office. In this chapter, after looking at who can become president and at the process involved, we examine closely the nature and extent of the constitutional powers held by the president.

Who Can Become President?

The requirements for becoming president, as outlined in Article II, Section 1, of the Constitution, are not overwhelmingly stringent:

> No person except a natural born Citizen, or a Citizen of the United States, at the time of the Adoption of this Constitution, shall be eligible to the Office of President; neither shall any Person be eligible to that Office who shall not have attained to the Age of thirty-five Years, and been fourteen Years a Resident within the United States.

The only question that arises about these qualifications relates to the term "natural born Citizen." Does that mean only citizens born in the United States and its territories? What about a child born to a U.S. citizen (or to a couple who are U.S. citizens) visiting or living in another country? Although the question has not been dealt with directly by the Supreme Court, it is reasonable to expect that someone would be eligible if her or his parents were Americans. The first presidents, after all, were not even American citizens at birth, and others were born in areas that did not become part of the United States until later. These questions were debated when George Romney, who was born in Chihuahua, Mexico, made a serious bid for the Republican presidential nomination in the 1960s.[2]

The great American dream is symbolized by the statement that "anybody can become president of this country." It is true that in modern times, presidents have included a haberdasher (Harry Truman—for a short period of time), a peanut farmer (Jimmy Carter), and an actor (Ronald Reagan). But if you examine Appendix C, you will see that the most common previous occupation of presidents in this country has been the legal profession. Out of forty-three presidents, twenty-six have been lawyers, and many have been wealthy.

Although the Constitution states that the minimum-age requirement for the presidency is thirty-five years, most presidents have been much older than that when they assumed office. John F. Kennedy, at the age of forty-three, was the youngest elected president, and the oldest was Ronald Reagan, at age sixty-nine. The average age at inauguration has been fifty-four. There has clearly been a demographic bias in the selection of presidents. All have been male, white, and Protestant, except for John F. Kennedy, a Roman Catholic. Presidents have been men of great stature—such as

---

[1] Forrest McDonald, *The American Presidency: An Intellectual History* (Lawrence, Kans.: University Press of Kansas, 1994), p. 179.
[2] George Romney was governor of Michigan from 1963 to 1969. Romney was not nominated, and the issue remains unresolved.

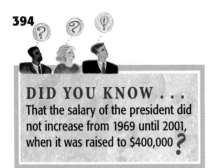

DID YOU KNOW...
That the salary of the president did not increase from 1969 until 2001, when it was raised to $400,000❓

George Washington—and men in whom leadership qualities were not so pronounced—such as Warren Harding (1921–1923).

The Process of Becoming President

Major and minor political parties nominate candidates for president and vice president at national conventions every four years. As discussed in Chapter 10, the nation's voters do not elect a president and vice president directly but rather cast ballots for presidential electors, who then vote for president and vice president in the electoral college.

Because the election is governed by a majority in the electoral college, it is conceivable that someone could be elected to the office of the presidency without having a plurality of the popular vote cast. Indeed, in four cases, candidates won elections even though their major opponents received more popular votes. One of those cases occurred in 2000, when George W. Bush won the electoral college vote and became president even though his opponent, Al Gore, won the popular vote. In elections when more than two candidates were running for office, many presidential candidates have won with less than 50 percent of the total popular votes cast for all candidates—including Abraham Lincoln, Woodrow Wilson, Harry Truman, John F. Kennedy, and Richard Nixon. In the 1992 election, Bill Clinton, with only 43 percent of the vote, defeated incumbent George H. W. Bush. Independent candidate Ross Perot garnered a surprising 19 percent of the vote. Remember from Chapter 10 that no president has won a majority of votes from the entire voting-age population.

On occasion, the electoral college has failed to give any candidate a majority. At this point, the election is thrown into the House of Representatives. The president is then chosen from among the three candidates having the most electoral college votes, as noted in Chapter 10. Only two times in our past has the House had to decide on a president. Thomas Jefferson and Aaron Burr tied in the electoral college in 1800. This happened because the Constitution had not been explicit in indicating which of the two electoral votes was for president and which was for vice president. In 1804, the **Twelfth Amendment** clarified the matter by requiring that the president and vice president be chosen separately. In 1824, the House again had to make a choice, this time among William H. Crawford, Andrew Jackson, and John Quincy Adams. It chose Adams, even though Jackson had more electoral and popular votes.

Twelfth Amendment
An amendment to the Constitution, adopted in 1804, that specifies the separate election of the president and vice president by the electoral college.

Chief of State
The role of the president as ceremonial head of the government.

The Many Roles of the President

The Constitution speaks briefly about the duties and obligations of the president. Based on a brief list of powers and the precedents of history, the presidency has grown into a very complicated job that requires balancing at least five constitutional roles. These are (1) chief of state, (2) chief executive, (3) commander in chief of the armed forces, (4) chief diplomat, and (5) chief legislator of the United States. Here we examine each of these significant presidential functions, or roles. It is worth noting that one person plays all these roles simultaneously and that the needs of these roles may at times come into conflict.

Chief of State

Every nation has at least one person who is the ceremonial head of state. In most democratic governments, the role of **chief of state** is given to someone other than the chief executive, who is the head of the executive branch of government. In Britain, for example, the chief of state is the queen. In France, the prime minister is the chief executive, and the chief of state is the president. But in the United States, the president is

From left to right, the first cabinet—Henry Knox, Thomas Jefferson, Edmund Randolph, Alexander Hamilton—and the first president, George Washington. (The Granger Collection)

both chief executive and chief of state. According to William Howard Taft, as chief of state the president symbolizes the "dignity and majesty" of the American people.

As chief of state, the president engages in a number of activities that are largely symbolic or ceremonial, such as the following:

- Decorating war heroes.
- Throwing out the first ball to open the baseball season.
- Dedicating parks and post offices.
- Receiving visiting chiefs of state at the White House.
- Going on official state visits to other countries.
- Making personal telephone calls to astronauts.
- Representing the nation at times of national mourning, such as after the terrorist attacks of September 11, 2001.

Many students of the American political system believe that having the president serve as both the chief executive and the chief of state drastically limits the time available to do "real" work. Not all presidents have agreed with this conclusion, however—particularly those presidents who have skillfully blended these two roles with their role as politician. Being chief of state gives the president tremendous public exposure, which can be an important asset in a campaign for reelection. When that exposure is positive, it helps the president deal with Congress over proposed legislation and increases the chances of being reelected—or getting the candidates of the president's party elected.

Chief Executive

According to the Constitution, "The executive Power shall be vested in a President of the United States of America. . . . [H]e may require the Opinion, in writing, of the principal Officer in each of the executive Departments, upon any Subject relating to the Duties of their respective Offices . . . and he shall nominate, and by and with the Advice and Consent of the Senate, shall appoint . . . Officers of the United States. . . . [H]e shall take Care that the Laws be faithfully executed."

As **chief executive,** the president is constitutionally bound to enforce the acts of Congress, the judgments of federal courts, and treaties signed by the United States. The duty to "faithfully execute" the laws has been a source of constitutional power for presidents. To assist in the various tasks of the chief executive, the president has a federal bureaucracy (see Chapter 14), which currently consists of about 2.7 million federal civilian employees.

Chief Executive
The role of the president as head of the executive branch of the government.

President George W. Bush is shown here working in the Oval Office. This oval-shaped office in the White House is often used to represent the power of the presidency and of the United States. Indeed, common references to "the Oval Office" mean specifically the president who is in power at that time. (AP Photo/Doug Mills)

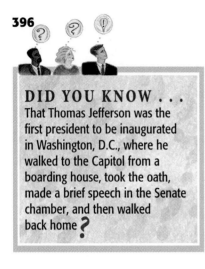

DID YOU KNOW . . .
That Thomas Jefferson was the first president to be inaugurated in Washington, D.C., where he walked to the Capitol from a boarding house, took the oath, made a brief speech in the Senate chamber, and then walked back home **?**

Civil Service
A collective term for the body of employees working for the government. Generally, civil service is understood to apply to all those who gain government employment through a merit system.

Appointment Power
The authority vested in the president to fill a government office or position. Positions filled by presidential appointment include those in the executive branch and the federal judiciary, commissioned officers in the armed forces, and members of the independent regulatory commissions.

The Powers of Appointment and Removal. You might think that the president, as head of the largest bureaucracy in the United States, wields enormous power. The president, however, only nominally runs the executive bureaucracy because most government positions are filled by **civil service** employees.[3] Therefore, even though the president has **appointment power**, it is not very extensive, being limited to cabinet and subcabinet jobs, federal judgeships, agency heads, and about two thousand lesser jobs. This means that most of the 2.7 million federal employees owe no political allegiance to the president. They are more likely to owe loyalty to congressional committees or to interest groups representing the sector of the society that they serve. Table 13–1 shows what percentage of the total employment in each executive department is available for political appointment by the president.

The president's power to remove from office those officials who are not doing a good job or who do not agree with the president is not explicitly granted by the Constitution and has been limited. In 1926, however, a Supreme Court decision prevented Congress from interfering with the president's ability to fire those executive-branch officials whom the president had appointed with Senate approval.[4] There are ten agencies whose directors the president can remove at any time. These agencies include the Arms Control and Disarmament Agency, the Commission on Civil Rights, the Environmental Protection Agency, the General Services Administration, and the Small Business Administration. In addition, the president can remove all heads of cabinet departments, all individuals in the Executive Office of the President, and all political appointees listed in Table 13–1.

Harry Truman spoke candidly of the difficulties a president faces in trying to control the executive bureaucracy. On leaving office, he referred to the problems that Dwight Eisenhower, as a former general of the army, was going to have: "He'll sit here and he'll say do this! do that! and nothing will happen. Poor Ike—it won't be a bit like the Army. He'll find it very frustrating."[5]

[3] See Chapter 14 for a discussion of the Civil Service Reform Act.
[4] *Meyers v. United States,* 272 U.S. 52 (1926).
[5] Quoted in Richard E. Neustadt, *Presidential Power: The Politics of Leadership* (New York: Wiley, 1960), p. 9.

TABLE 13–1

Total Civilian Employment in Cabinet Departments Available for Political Appointment by the President

EXECUTIVE DEPARTMENT	TOTAL NUMBER OF EMPLOYEES	POLITICAL APPOINTMENTS AVAILABLE	PERCENTAGE
Agriculture	100,084	439	0.43
Commerce	39,151	446	1.13
Defense	670,568	466	0.06
Education	4,581	186	4.06
Energy	15,689	433	2.75
Health and Human Services	63,323	391	0.61
Housing and Urban Development	10,154	156	1.53
Interior	72,982	240	0.32
Justice	126,711	501	0.39
Labor	16,016	188	1.17
State	28,054	1,066	3.79
Transportation	64,131	274	0.42
Treasury	159,274	231	0.14
Veterans Affairs	223,137	315	0.14
TOTAL	1,593,855	5,332	0.33

SOURCES: *Policy and Supporting Positions* (Washington, D.C.: Government Printing Office, 2000); U.S. Office of Personnel Management, 2002.

The Power to Grant Reprieves and Pardons. Section 2 of Article II of the Constitution gives the president the power to grant **reprieves** and **pardons** for offenses against the United States except in cases of impeachment. All pardons are administered by the Office of the Pardon Attorney in the Department of Justice. In principle, pardons are granted to remedy a mistake made in a conviction.

The Supreme Court upheld the president's power to grant reprieves and pardons in a 1925 case concerning the pardon granted by the president to an individual convicted of contempt of court. The judiciary had contended that only judges had the authority to convict individuals for contempt of court when court orders were violated and that the courts should be free from interference by the executive branch. The Supreme Court simply stated that the president could grant reprieves or pardons for all offenses "either before trial, during trial, or after trial, by individuals, or by classes, conditionally or absolutely, and this without modification or regulation by Congress."[6]

In a controversial decision, President Gerald Ford pardoned former president Richard Nixon for his role in the Watergate affair before any charges were brought in court. In 1999, President Clinton granted executive clemency to sixteen Puerto Rican nationalists who had been convicted of plotting terrorism. Just before George W. Bush's inauguration in 2001, Clinton announced pardons for more than one hundred persons.

Commander in Chief

The president, according to the Constitution, "shall be Commander in Chief of the Army and Navy of the United States, and of the Militia of the several States, when called into the actual Service of the United States." In other words, the armed forces are under civilian, rather than military, control.

Wartime Powers. Certainly, those who wrote the Constitution had George Washington in mind when they made the president the **commander in chief**. Although we no longer expect our president to lead the troops into battle, presidents

---

[6] *Ex parte Grossman,* 267 U.S. 87 (1925).

Reprieve
The presidential power to postpone the execution of a sentence imposed by a court of law; usually done for humanitarian reasons or to await new evidence.

Pardon
The granting of a release from the punishment or legal consequences of a crime; a pardon can be granted by the president before or after a conviction.

INFOTRAC®
COLLEGE EDITION

To find out more on pardons, use the term "Clinton pardons" in Keywords.

Commander in Chief
The role of the president as supreme commander of the military forces of the United States and of the state National Guard units when they are called into federal service.

As commander in chief of one of the most well-armed militaries in the world, the president wields enormous power. After September 11, 2001, President George W. Bush met frequently with his key military advisers, National Security Adviser Condoleeza Rice, left, and Defense Secretary Donald Rumsfeld, right. In 2002, President Bush's role as commander in chief was even more pronounced as he rallied domestic and international support for a war against Iraq. Does the president have too much power as commander in chief? How is that power checked in the American political system? (AP Photo/Doug Mills)

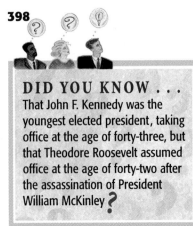

as commanders in chief have wielded dramatic power. Harry Truman made the awesome decision to drop atomic bombs on Hiroshima and Nagasaki in 1945 to force Japan to surrender and thus bring to an end World War II. Lyndon Johnson ordered bombing missions against North Vietnam in the 1960s, and he personally selected some of the targets. Richard Nixon decided to invade Cambodia in 1970. Ronald Reagan sent troops to Lebanon and Grenada in 1983 and ordered U.S. fighter planes to attack Libya in 1986. George H. W. Bush sent troops to Panama in 1989 and to the Middle East in 1990. Bill Clinton sent troops to Haiti in 1994 and to Bosnia in 1995, ordered missile attacks on alleged terrorist bases in 1998, and sent American planes to bomb Serbia in 1999.

The president is the ultimate decision maker in military matters. Everywhere he goes, so too goes the "football"—a briefcase filled with all the codes necessary to order a nuclear attack. Only the president has the power to order the use of nuclear force.

As commander in chief, the president has probably exercised more authority than in any other role. Constitutionally, Congress has the sole power to declare war, but the president can send the armed forces into a country in situations that are certainly the equivalent of war. When William McKinley ordered troops into Peking to help suppress the Boxer Rebellion in 1900, he was sending them into a combat situation. Harry Truman dispatched troops to Korea as part of a United Nations "police action" in 1950. Kennedy, Johnson, and Nixon waged an undeclared war in Southeast Asia, where more than 58,000 Americans were killed and 300,000 were wounded. In none of these situations did Congress declare war. (For a further discussion of the president's role in wartime, see this chapter's *America's Security* feature.)

The War Powers Resolution.   In an attempt to gain more control over such military activities, in 1973 Congress passed the **War Powers Resolution**—over President Nixon's veto—requiring that the president consult with Congress when sending American forces into action. Once they are sent, the president must report to Congress within forty-eight hours. Unless Congress approves the use of troops within sixty days or extends the sixty-day time limit, the forces must be withdrawn. The War Powers Resolution was tested in the fall of 1983, when Reagan requested that troops be left in Lebanon. The resulting compromise was a congressional resolution allowing troops to remain there for eighteen months. Shortly after the resolution was passed, however, more than 240 sailors and Marines were killed in the suicide bombing of a U.S. military housing compound in Beirut. That event provoked a furious congressional debate over the role American troops were playing in the Middle East, and all troops were withdrawn shortly thereafter.

In spite of the War Powers Resolution, the powers of the president as commander in chief are more extensive today than they were in the past. These powers are linked closely to the president's powers as chief diplomat, or chief crafter of foreign policy.

Chief Diplomat

The Constitution gives the president the power to recognize foreign governments; to make treaties, with the **advice and consent** of the Senate; and to make special agreements with other heads of state that do not require congressional approval. In addition, the president nominates ambassadors. As **chief diplomat,** the president dominates American foreign policy, a role that has been supported numerous times by the Supreme Court.

Diplomatic Recognition.   An important power of the president as chief diplomat is that of **diplomatic recognition,** or the power to recognize—or refuse to recognize—foreign governments. In the role of ceremonial head of state, the president has always received foreign diplomats. In modern times, the simple act of receiving a foreign diplomat has been equivalent to accrediting the diplomat and officially recognizing

War Powers Resolution
A law passed in 1973 spelling out the conditions under which the president can commit troops without congressional approval.

INFOTRAC®
COLLEGE EDITION

For more information on this topic, use the term "War Powers Resolution of 1973" in the Subject guide.

Advice and Consent
The power vested in the U.S. Senate by the Constitution (Article II, Section 2) to give its advice and consent to the president on treaties and presidential appointments.

Chief Diplomat
The role of the president in recognizing foreign governments, making treaties, and making executive agreements.

Diplomatic Recognition
The president's power, as chief diplomat, to acknowledge a foreign government as legitimate.

America's Security

The President's Role in Wartime

As we have pointed out before in this text, Americans look to their government, especially their president, to exercise leadership during times of crisis. Like previous presidents who were in office during wartime, President George W. Bush reacted vigorously to a crisis—the terrorist attacks of 9/11.

THE PRESIDENT ACTS

Soon after 9/11, President Bush took action. Note, though, that the actions he undertook were, to a great extent, unilateral—that is, as the executive, he ordered that certain actions be undertaken without waiting for congressional approval. He announced cuts in the U.S. nuclear arsenal, but did not put those cuts in a treaty, thus avoiding the requirement that the Senate ratify the

action. He also proposed reorganizing the Immigration and Naturalization Service without congressional action. The administration also expanded its power to monitor and detain terrorist suspects. Finally, as we have mentioned before (see Chapter 4), President Bush created military tribunals via executive order, again sidestepping Congress.

The White House also limited intelligence briefings to members of Congress to a much greater extent than in the past. In other words, the administration did not share with Congress the reasons for its actions with respect to the war on terrorism. Congress has, for better or for worse, acquiesced to what some have called the Bush administration's "power grab." Indeed, Congress gave the administration $40 billion to spend in response to 9/11. Virtually no strings were attached. Some argue that Bush's wartime powers rival those of President Franklin Roosevelt during World War II. As Tim Lynch, director of the Project on Criminal Justice at the Cato Institute, noted, "the power President Bush is wielding today is truly breathtaking."

WAR AND PRESIDENTIAL POPULARITY

Historically, presidents' approval ratings have soared when the United States enters wars. The use of American forces initially spurs a "rally 'round the flag" reaction. This positive effect lasts until

the number of casualties and the length of the engagement begin to wear on the public. During the Persian Gulf War at the beginning of the 1990s, then President George H. W. Bush saw his approval ratings jump when he sent troops to Saudi Arabia after Iraq's invasion of Kuwait. The day after the attack on Iraq, Bush's ratings went up to 82 percent, finally reaching 89 percent when it appeared that the war would be over soon. Less than a year later, Bush's ratings fell back to 50 percent, and he lost his bid for reelection against Bill Clinton in 1992.

President George W. Bush similarly saw his ratings skyrocket immediately after 9/11. They reached an unprecedented 90 percent during the successful war against the Taliban in Afghanistan and the al Qaeda network. Americans, though, seem to have relatively short memories. Bush's ratings started to slip to the 70 percent range by the spring of 2002. Unless there are continuing serious terrorist attacks on Americans abroad or on American soil, history tells us that America's security will not remain foremost in our thoughts forever.

FOR CRITICAL ANALYSIS

Never before has a U.S. president waged a war on terrorism. Should we allow President George W. Bush to exercise powers that are generally allowed only to wartime presidents?

his or her government. Such recognition of the legitimacy of another country's government is a prerequisite to diplomatic relations or negotiations between that country and the United States.

Deciding when to recognize a foreign power is not always simple. The United States, for example, did not recognize the Soviet Union until 1933—sixteen years after the Russian Revolution of 1917. It was only after all attempts to reverse the effects of that revolution—including military invasion of Russia and diplomatic isolation—had proved futile that Franklin Roosevelt extended recognition to the Soviet government. U.S. presidents faced a similar problem with the Chinese Communist revolution. In December 1978, long after the Communist victory in China in 1949, Jimmy Carter granted official recognition to the People's Republic of China.[7]

---

[7] The Nixon administration first encouraged new relations with the People's Republic of China by allowing a cultural exchange of ping-pong teams.

A diplomatic recognition issue that faced the Clinton administration involved recognizing a former enemy—the Republic of Vietnam. Many Americans, particularly those who believed that Vietnam had not been forthcoming in the efforts to find the remains of missing American soldiers or to find out about former prisoners of war, opposed any formal relationship with that nation. After the U.S. government had negotiated with the Vietnamese government for many years over the missing-in-action issue and engaged in limited diplomatic contacts for several years, President Clinton announced on July 11, 1995, that the United States would recognize the government of Vietnam and move to establish normal diplomatic relations.

Proposal and Ratification of Treaties.   The president has the sole power to negotiate treaties with other nations. These treaties must be presented to the Senate, where they may be modified and must be approved by a two-thirds vote. After ratification, the president can approve the senatorial version of the treaty. Approval poses a problem when the Senate has tacked on substantive amendments or reservations to a treaty, particularly when such changes may require reopening negotiations with the other signatory governments. Sometimes a president may decide to withdraw a treaty if the senatorial changes are too extensive—as Woodrow Wilson did with the Versailles Treaty in 1919. Wilson felt that the senatorial reservations would weaken the treaty so much that it would be ineffective. His refusal to accept the senatorial version of the treaty led to the eventual refusal of the United States to join the League of Nations.

President Carter was successful in lobbying for the treaties that provided for the return of the Panama Canal to Panama by the year 2000 and neutralizing the canal. President Bill Clinton won a major political and legislative victory in 1993 by persuading Congress to ratify the North American Free Trade Agreement (NAFTA). In so doing, he had to overcome opposition from Democrats and most of organized labor. In 1998, he worked closely with Senate Republicans to ensure Senate approval of a treaty governing the use of chemical weapons. In 2000, President Clinton won a major legislative victory when Congress voted to establish permanent trade relations with China.

In his roles of chief of state and chief diplomat, the U.S. president frequently visits or receives foreign diplomats and heads of state. Here, President George W. Bush talks with Egyptian President Hosni Mubarak at Camp David, Maryland, in 2002. How do the many roles of the president blend together during such visits with heads of state? (AP Photo/Kenneth Lambert)

Before September 11, 2001, President George W. Bush indicated his intention to steer the United States in a unilateral direction on foreign policy, citing the priority of domestic concerns over the need for international cooperation. He backed away from the Kyoto Agreement on global warming and proposed ending the 1972 Anti-Ballistic Missile (ABM) Treaty that was part of SALT I (see Chapter 17). After the terrorist attacks of 9/11, however, President Bush sought cooperation from U.S. allies in the war on terrorism. Bush's return to multilateralism was exemplified in the signing of a nuclear weapons reduction treaty with Russia in 2002. Nonetheless, his threats to invade Iraq and overthrow that country's government did not generate much international support.

Executive Agreements.   Presidential power in foreign affairs is enhanced greatly by the use of **executive agreements** made between the president and other heads of state. Such agreements do not require Senate approval, although the House and Senate may refuse to appropriate the funds necessary to implement them. Whereas treaties are binding on all succeeding administrations, executive agreements are not binding without each new president's consent.

Among the advantages of executive agreements are speed and secrecy. The former is essential during a crisis; the latter is important when the administration fears that open senatorial debate may be detrimental to the best interests of the United States or to the interests of the president.[8] There have been far more executive agreements (about 9,000) than treaties (about 1,300). Many executive agreements contain secret provisions calling for American military assistance or other support. For example, Franklin Roosevelt (1933–1945) used executive agreements to bypass congressional isolationists in trading American destroyers for British Caribbean naval bases and in arranging diplomatic and military affairs with Canada and Latin American nations.

Chief Legislator

Constitutionally, presidents must recommend to Congress legislation that they judge necessary and expedient. Not all presidents have wielded their powers as **chief legislator** in the same manner. President John Tyler was almost completely unsuccessful in getting his legislative programs implemented by Congress. Presidents Theodore Roosevelt, Franklin Roosevelt, and Lyndon Johnson, however, saw much of their proposed legislation put into effect.

In modern times, the president has played a dominant role in creating the congressional agenda. In the president's annual **State of the Union message,** which is required by the Constitution (Article II, Section 3) and is usually given in late January shortly after Congress reconvenes, the president as chief legislator presents his program. The message gives a broad, comprehensive view of what the president wishes the legislature to accomplish during its session. It is as much a message to the American people and to the world as it is to Congress. Its impact on public opinion can determine the way in which Congress responds to the president's agenda.

Getting Legislation Passed.   The president can propose legislation. Congress, however, is not required to pass any of the administration's bills. How, then, does the president get those proposals made into law? One way is by exercising the power of persuasion. The president writes to, telephones, and meets with various congressional leaders; makes public announcements to force the weight of public opinion

Executive Agreement
An international agreement made by the president, without senatorial ratification, with the head of a foreign state.

Chief Legislator
The role of the president in influencing the making of laws.

State of the Union Message
An annual message to Congress in which the president proposes a legislative program. The message is addressed not only to Congress but also to the American people and to the world. It offers the opportunity to dramatize policies and objectives and to gain public support.

---

[8] The Case Act of 1972 requires that all executive agreements be transmitted to Congress within sixty days after the agreement takes effect. Secret agreements are transmitted to the foreign relations committees as classified information.

Each year the president presents the State of the Union message, which is required by Article II, Section 3, of the Constitution and is usually given in late January, shortly after Congress reconvenes. Because the floor of the House of Representatives is so much larger than that of the Senate, the State of the Union speech is given there. Attendees include all members of Congress, plus usually the justices of the U.S. Supreme Court, the heads of most of the executive departments, and certain others, such as the chairman of the Federal Reserve Board of Governors. The press, of course, is in attendance, too. (AP Photo/ Doug Mills)

Veto Message
The president's formal explanation of a veto when legislation is returned to Congress.

Pocket Veto
A special veto power exercised by the chief executive after a legislative body has adjourned. Bills not signed by the chief executive die after a specified period of time. If Congress wishes to reconsider such a bill, it must be reintroduced in the following session of Congress.

onto Congress in favor of a legislative program; and, as head of the party, exercises legislative leadership through the congresspersons of the president's party.

To be sure, a president whose party holds a majority in both chambers of Congress may have an easier time getting legislation passed than does a president who faces a hostile Congress. But one of the ways in which a president who faces a hostile Congress still can wield power is through the ability to veto legislation.

Saying No to Legislation.   The president has the power to say no to legislation through use of the veto, by which the White House returns a bill unsigned to Congress with a **veto message** attached.[9] Because the Constitution requires that every bill passed by the House and the Senate be sent to the president before it becomes law, the president must act on each bill.

1. If the bill is signed, it becomes law.

2. If the bill is not sent back to Congress after ten congressional working days, it becomes law without the president's signature.

3. The president can reject the bill and send it back to Congress with a veto message setting forth objections. Congress then can change the bill, hoping to secure presidential approval and repass it. Or it can simply reject the president's objections by overriding the veto with a two-thirds roll-call vote of the members present in each house.

4. If the president refuses to sign the bill and Congress adjourns within ten working days after the bill has been submitted to the president, the bill is killed for that session of Congress. If Congress wishes the bill to be reconsidered, the bill must be reintroduced during the following session. This is called a **pocket veto**.

Presidents employed the veto power infrequently until the administration of Andrew Johnson, but it has been used with increasing vigor since then (see Table 13–2). The total number of vetoes from George Washington through George W. Bush's second year in office was 2,551, with about two-thirds of those vetoes being exercised by Grover Cleveland, Franklin Roosevelt, Harry Truman, and Dwight Eisenhower.

While campaigning for the presidency, George W. Bush pledged to restore cooperation with Congress. In the early period of his administration, he largely suc-

---

[9] *Veto* in Latin means "I forbid."

ceeded. Congress produced legislation that he was willing to sign. Bush nonetheless demonstrated a willingness to use his veto power while governor of Texas, and spoke during his 2000 campaign of numerous instances in which he would be willing to use the veto as president. He is also on record as supporting a revised version of the line-item veto that would correct the "constitutional flaw" in the Line Item Veto Act enacted in 1996—discussed next.

TABLE 13–2

Presidential Vetoes, 1789 to Present

Years	President	Regular Vetoes	Vetoes Overridden	Pocket Vetoes	Total Vetoes
1789–1797	Washington	2	0	0	2
1797–1801	J. Adams	0	0	0	0
1801–1809	Jefferson	0	0	0	0
1809–1817	Madison	5	0	2	7
1817–1825	Monroe	1	0	0	1
1825–1829	J. Q. Adams	0	0	0	0
1829–1837	Jackson	5	0	7	12
1837–1841	Van Buren	0	0	1	1
1841–1841	Harrison	0	0	0	0
1841–1845	Tyler	6	1	4	10
1845–1849	Polk	2	0	1	3
1849–1850	Taylor	0	0	0	0
1850–1853	Fillmore	0	0	0	0
1853–1857	Pierce	9	5	0	9
1857–1861	Buchanan	4	0	3	7
1861–1865	Lincoln	2	0	5	7
1865–1869	A. Johnson	21	15	8	29
1869–1877	Grant	45	4	48	93
1877–1881	Hayes	12	1	1	13
1881–1881	Garfield	0	0	0	0
1881–1885	Arthur	4	1	8	12
1885–1889	Cleveland	304	2	110	414
1889–1893	Harrison	19	1	25	44
1893–1897	Cleveland	42	5	128	170
1897–1901	McKinley	6	0	36	42
1901–1909	T. Roosevelt	42	1	40	82
1909–1913	Taft	30	1	9	39
1913–1921	Wilson	33	6	11	44
1921–1923	Harding	5	0	1	6
1923–1929	Coolidge	20	4	30	50
1929–1933	Hoover	21	3	16	37
1933–1945	F. Roosevelt	372	9	263	635
1945–1953	Truman	180	12	70	250
1953–1961	Eisenhower	73	2	108	181
1961–1963	Kennedy	12	0	9	21
1963–1969	L. Johnson	16	0	14	30
1969–1974	Nixon	26*	7	17	43
1974–1977	Ford	48	12	18	66
1977–1981	Carter	13	2	18	31
1981–1989	Reagan	39	9	39	78
1989–1993	G. H. W. Bush	29	1	15	44
1993–2001	Clinton	37†	2	1	38
2001–	G. W. Bush	0	0	0	0
TOTAL		1,485	106	1,066	2,551

*Two pocket vetoes by President Nixon, overruled in the courts, are counted here as regular vetoes.
†President Clinton's line-item vetoes are not included.

SOURCE: Office of the Clerk.

DID YOU KNOW . . .

That the expression "O.K.," which is used worldwide, was coined in the presidential campaign of 1840 in reference to Martin Van Buren, who was called "Old Kinderhook" after his birthplace (his New York supporters formed the "O.K." club and shouted the expression at political rallies and parades)

Line-Item Veto

The power of an executive to veto individual lines or items within a piece of legislation without vetoing the entire bill.

The Line-Item Veto. Ronald Reagan lobbied strenuously for Congress to give another tool to the president—the **line-item veto.** Reagan saw the ability to veto *specific* spending provisions of legislation that he was sent by Congress as the only way that the president could control overall congressional spending. In 1996, Congress passed the Line Item Veto Act, which provided for the line-item veto. Signed by President Clinton, the law granted the president the power to rescind any item in an appropriations bill unless Congress passed a resolution of disapproval. Of course, the congressional resolution could be, in turn, vetoed by the president. The law did not take effect until after the 1996 election.

President Clinton used the line-item veto on several occasions, beginning on August 11, 1997. While his early vetoes were of little consequence to the members of Congress, the next set of vetoes—of thirty-eight military construction projects—caused an uproar, and Congress passed a disapproval bill to rescind the vetoes. The act also was challenged in court as an unconstitutional delegation of legislative powers to the executive branch. In 1998, by a six-to-three vote, the United States Supreme Court agreed and overturned the act. The Court stated that "there is no provision in the Constitution that authorizes the president to enact, to amend or to repeal statutes."[10]

Congress's Power to Override Presidential Vetoes. A veto is a clear-cut indication of the president's dissatisfaction with congressional legislation. Congress, however, can override a presidential veto, although it rarely exercises this power. Consider that two-thirds of the members of each chamber who are present must vote to override the president's veto in a roll-call vote. This means that if only one-third plus one of the members voting in one of the chambers of Congress do not agree to override the veto, the veto holds. It was not until the administration of John Tyler that Congress overrode a presidential veto. In the first sixty-five years of American federal government history, out of thirty-three regular vetoes, Congress overrode only one, or about 3 percent. Overall, only about 7 percent of all vetoes have been overridden.

Other Presidential Powers

Constitutional Power

A power vested in the president by Article II of the Constitution.

Statutory Power

A power created for the president through laws enacted by Congress.

Expressed Power

A constitutional or statutory power of the president, which is expressly written into the Constitution or into statutory law.

Inherent Power

A power of the president derived from the loosely worded statement in the Constitution that "the executive Power shall be vested in a President" and that the president should "take Care that the Laws be faithfully executed"; defined through practice rather than through constitutional or statutory law.

The powers of the president just discussed are called **constitutional powers,** because their basis lies in the Constitution. In addition, Congress has established by law, or statute, numerous other presidential powers—such as the ability to declare national emergencies. These are called **statutory powers.** Both constitutional and statutory powers have been labeled the **expressed powers** of the president, because they are expressly written into the Constitution or into law.

Presidents also have what have come to be known as **inherent powers.** These depend on the loosely worded statement in the Constitution that "the executive Power shall be vested in a President" and that the president should "take Care that the Laws be faithfully executed." The most common example of inherent powers are those emergency powers invoked by the president during wartime. Franklin Roosevelt used his inherent powers to move the Japanese living in the United States into internment camps for the duration of World War II.

Clearly, modern U.S. presidents have numerous powers at their disposal. According to some critics, among the powers exercised by modern presidents are certain powers that rightfully belong to Congress but that Congress has yielded to the executive branch—see this chapter's *Which Side Are You On?* feature for a discussion of this issue.

---

[10] *Clinton v. City of New York*, 524 U.S. 417 (1998).

Which Side Are You On?
Is the President Becoming Too Powerful?

Our system of government is based on a system of checks and balances, with the three branches of government—executive, legislative, and judicial—supposedly serving as checks on one another. In recent years, some have argued that the executive branch has become too powerful. Indeed, some have described the presidency of George W. Bush as the "Imperial Presidency"—a phrase once used by presidential historian Arthur Schlesinger, Jr., to describe Richard Nixon's administration in 1973.

THE PRESIDENT HAS GONE TOO FAR

Critics of the current president's so-called power grab argue that a single individual is deciding questions that are extremely important for the nation and its citizens—such as whether the war on terrorism should be expanded to Iraq and how much privacy Americans are going to retain during the war on terrorism. Given that President Bush has stated that this war will be long, threats to privacy created by wartime measures will not go away anytime soon.

Even before the Bush administration, President Bill Clinton effectively used executive orders to skirt the need for congressional approval for his actions. For example, Clinton proclaimed that millions of acres in Utah that had been under federal management would be a national monument, thereby eliminating many future uses of this land.

The executive branch has also taken over lawmaking functions by issuing regulatory rules. Each year, administrative agency rules fill between 50,000 and 100,000 pages of the Federal Register, the government publication where such rules are initially published. All such agency rules are as legally binding as if they were laws passed by Congress, yet they are made not by elected congressional representatives but by administrative agencies within the executive branch.

Finally, presidents have effectively found various ways to get around the constitutional requirement that the Senate ratify treaties. President Clinton, for example, called treaties "founding acts" instead of "treaties" so that he could avoid the requirement. He also used such phrases as "political agreements" or "memorandums of understanding" to describe what were essentially treaties in order to avoid the need for the Senate to approve his actions.

PRESIDENTS DO WHAT THEY HAVE TO DO

Not everyone believes that the president has become too powerful. After all, since September 11, 2001, the United States has been in a crisis period. Without a strong, focused, and single-purposed executive branch, the United States might remain vulnerable to additional terrorist attacks. The White House itself has continually stressed that an increase in presidential powers is the correct prescription for a terrorist crisis. White House Press Secretary Ari Fleischer stated that "the way our nation is set up, and the way the Constitution is written, wartime powers rest fundamentally in the hands of the executive branch. It is not uncommon in time of war for a nation's eyes to focus on the executive branch and its ability to conduct the war with strength and speed."*

Another reason many Americans support increased presidential powers has to do with a difference between Congress and the president. Members of Congress tend to be elected on the basis of local issues. Although this is not always true, local issues do affect the popularity of congressional representatives and, to a lesser extent, senators. The president, in contrast, is the only elected official who is supposed to take the welfare of all Americans into account. Thus, goes the argument, the president should continue to expand the powers of the presidency so as to counteract Congress's more narrow focus on local issues and the desires of special interest groups.

WHAT'S YOUR POSITION?

Some say that everyone is in favor of broader presidential powers until the expansion of those powers affects the individual directly—say, by restricting his or her privacy. Do you believe that those who support increased presidential powers today do so naïvely? Explain your position.

GOING ONLINE

The Center for the Study of the Presidency maintains a publications and reference center with a wealth of information on the office of the presidency and the exercise of presidential power. Point your browser to **http://www.cspresidency.org/pubs/index.htm** and click on any of the numerous links there for more information. The Cato Institute, a libertarian public-policy research foundation, posts several articles on its Web site that view the presidency as too powerful. Go to **http://www.cato.org/research**, click on "Government and Politics (subtopics)," and then select "presidency."

*As quoted in Dana Milbank, "Bush's Wartime Powers Rival FDR's," International Herald Tribune, November 21, 2001, p. 1.

The President as Party Chief and Superpolitician

Presidents are by no means above political partisanship, and one of their many roles is that of chief of party. Although the Constitution says nothing about the function of the president within a political party (the mere concept of political parties was abhorrent to most of the authors of the Constitution), today presidents are the actual leaders of their parties.

The President as Chief of Party

As party leader, the president chooses the national committee chairperson and can try to discipline party members who fail to support presidential policies. One way of exerting political power within the party is by **patronage**—appointing individuals to government or public jobs. This power was more extensive in the past, before the establishment of the civil service in 1883 (see Chapter 14), but the president still retains impressive patronage power. As we noted earlier, the president can appoint several thousand individuals to jobs in the cabinet, the White House, and the federal regulatory agencies.

Presidents have a number of other ways of exerting influence as party chief. The president may make it known that a particular congressperson's choice for federal judge will not be appointed unless that member of Congress is more supportive of the president's legislative program.[11] The president may agree to campaign for a particular program or for a particular candidate. Presidents also reward loyal supporters in Congress with funding for local projects, tax breaks for regional industries, and other forms of "pork."

Constituencies and Public Approval

All politicians worry about their constituencies, and presidents are no exception. Presidents are also concerned with public approval ratings.

Presidential Constituencies.   Presidents have numerous constituencies. In principle, they are beholden to the entire electorate—the public of the United States—even to those who did not vote. They are certainly beholden to their party constituency, because its members helped to put them in office. The president's constituencies also include members of the opposing party whose cooperation the president needs. Finally, the president has to take into consideration a constituency that has come to be called the **Washington community**. This community consists of individuals who—whether in or out of political office—are intimately familiar with the workings of government, thrive on gossip, and measure on a daily basis the political power of the president.

Public Approval.   All of these constituencies are impressed by presidents who maintain a high level of public approval, partly because this is very difficult to accomplish. Presidential popularity, as measured by national polls, gives the president an extra political resource to use in persuading legislators or bureaucrats to pass legislation. After all, refusing to do so might be going against public sentiment. President Bill Clinton showed significant strength in the public opinion polls for a second-term chief executive, as Figure 13–1 indicates. President George W. Bush

Patronage
Rewarding faithful party workers and followers with government employment and contracts.

Washington Community
Individuals regularly involved with politics in Washington, D.C.

INFOTRAC®
COLLEGE EDITION

For updates on public approval, use the term "Bush approval" in Keywords.

---

[11] "Senatorial courtesy" (see Chapter 15) often puts the judicial appointment in the hands of the Senate, however.

*"I don't think you can distance yourself from the White House
on this one. After all, you are the President."*

received an unprecedented approval rating of 90 percent after the September 11, 2001, terrorist attacks. He maintained an approval rating of 80 percent or higher even after the first U.S. casualties were reported in the war in Afghanistan, which some analysts thought might cause his approval ratings to dip. Before the terrorist attacks, Bush's approval ratings hovered between 50 and 60 percent. This rally of public support behind the president allowed Bush to achieve legislative successes, such as an antiterrorism act in late 2001 and an education reform act in 2002.

FIGURE 13-1

Public Popularity of Modern Presidents

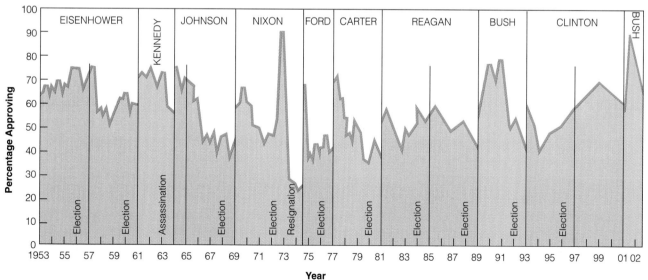

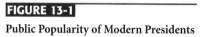

SOURCES: *Public Opinion,* February/March 1988, pp. 36–39; and Gallup polls, 1992 through 2002.

"Going Public."   The presidential preoccupation with public opinion has been criticized by at least one scholar as changing the balance of national politics. Since the early twentieth century, presidents have spoken more to the public and less to Congress. In the nineteenth century, only 7 percent of presidential speeches were addressed to the public; since 1900, 50 percent have been addressed to the public. Samuel Kernell has proposed that the style of presidential leadership has changed since World War II, owing partly to the influence of television.[12] Presidents frequently go over the heads of Congress and the political elites, taking their cases directly to the people. For example, in early 2001 President George W. Bush appealed directly to the public to support his proposed tax cut and budget. In a prime-time television speech, Bush urged Americans to send a message in favor of tax relief to their congressional representatives and senators. "After all," he said, "the surplus is your money."

This strategy, which Kernell dubbed "going public," gives the president additional power through the ability to persuade and manipulate public opinion. By identifying their own positions so clearly, presidents make compromises with Congress much more difficult and weaken the legislators' positions. Given the increasing importance of the media as the major source of political information for citizens and elites, presidents will continue to use public opinion as part of their arsenal of weapons to gain support from Congress and to achieve their policy goals.

Special Uses of Presidential Power

Presidents have at their disposal a variety of special powers and privileges not available in other branches of the U.S. government. These include (1) emergency powers, (2) executive orders, and (3) executive privilege.

Emergency Powers

If you were to read the Constitution, you would find no mention of the additional powers that the executive office may exercise during national emergencies. Indeed, the Supreme Court has indicated that an "emergency does not create power."[13] But it is clear that presidents have used their inherent powers during times of emergency, particularly in the realm of foreign affairs. The **emergency powers** of the president were first enunciated in the Supreme Court's decision in *United States v. Curtiss-Wright Export Corp.*[14] In that case, President Franklin Roosevelt, without authorization by Congress, ordered an embargo on the shipment of weapons to two warring South American countries. The Court recognized that the president may exercise inherent powers in foreign affairs and that the national government has primacy in foreign affairs.

Examples of emergency powers are abundant, coinciding with real or contrived crises in domestic and foreign affairs. Abraham Lincoln's suspension of civil liberties at the beginning of the Civil War (1861–1865), his calling of the state militias into national service, and his subsequent governance of conquered areas and even of areas of northern states were justified by claims that such actions were essential to preserve the Union. Franklin Roosevelt declared an "unlimited national emergency" following the fall of France in World War II (1939–1945) and mobilized the federal budget and the economy for war.

Emergency Power
An inherent power exercised by the president during a period of national crisis, particularly in foreign affairs.

---

[12] Samuel Kernell, *Going Public: New Strategies of Presidential Leadership*, 3d ed. (Washington, D.C.: Congressional Quarterly Press, 1997).

[13] *Home Building and Loan Association v. Blaisdell*, 290 U.S. 398 (1934).

[14] 299 U.S. 304 (1936).

President Harry Truman authorized the federal seizure of steel plants and their operation by the national government in 1952 during the Korean War. Truman claimed that he was using his inherent emergency power as chief executive and commander in chief to safeguard the nation's security, as the ongoing steel mill strike threatened the supply of weapons to the armed forces. The Supreme Court did not agree, holding that the president had no authority under the Constitution to seize private property or to legislate such action.[15] According to legal scholars, this was the first time a limit was placed on the exercise of the president's emergency powers.

Executive Orders

Congress allows the president (as well as administrative agencies) to issue **executive orders** that have the force of law. These executive orders can do the following: (1) enforce legislative statutes, (2) enforce the Constitution or treaties with foreign nations, and (3) establish or modify rules and practices of executive administrative agencies.

An executive order, then, represents the president's legislative power. The only apparent requirement is that under the Administrative Procedure Act of 1946, all executive orders must be published in the *Federal Register,* a daily publication of the U.S. government. Executive orders have been used to establish some procedures for appointing noncareer administrators, to implement national affirmative action regulations, to restructure the White House bureaucracy, to ration consumer goods and to administer wage and price controls under emergency conditions, to classify government information as secret, to regulate the export of restricted items, and to establish military tribunals for suspected terrorists.

Executive Privilege

Another inherent executive power that has been claimed by presidents concerns the ability of the president and the president's executive officials to refuse to appear before, or to withhold information from, Congress or the courts. This is called **executive privilege,** and it relies on the constitutional separation of powers for its basis.

As discussed in this chapter's *What If . . .* feature, presidents have frequently invoked executive privilege to avoid having to disclose information to Congress relating to actions of the executive branch. For example, President George W. Bush claimed executive privilege to keep the head of the newly established Office of Homeland Security, Tom Ridge, from testifying before Congress. The Bush administration also resisted attempts by the congressional General Accounting Office to obtain information about meetings and documents related to Vice President Dick Cheney's actions as chair of the administration's energy policy task force. Bush, like presidents before him, claimed that a certain degree of secrecy is essential to national security. Critics of executive privilege believe that it can be used to shield from public scrutiny actions of the executive branch that should be open to Congress and to the American public.

Limiting Executive Privilege. Limits to executive privilege went untested until the Watergate affair in the early 1970s. Five men had broken into the headquarters of the Democratic National Committee and were caught searching for documents that would damage the candidacy of the Democratic nominee, George McGovern. Later investigation showed that the break-in was planned by members of Richard Nixon's campaign committee and that Nixon and his closest advisers had devised a strategy for impeding the investigation of the crime, using the Central Intelligence Agency for illegal activities. After it became known that all of the conversations held in the Oval

---

[15] *Youngstown Sheet and Tube Co. v. Sawyer,* 343 U.S. 579 (1952).

DID YOU KNOW . . .
That President Jimmy Carter was the first president to hold a phone-in television broadcast, with Walter Cronkite as the moderator?

Executive Order
A rule or regulation issued by the president that has the effect of law. Executive orders can implement and give administrative effect to provisions in the Constitution, to treaties, and to statutes.

Federal Register
A publication of the executive branch of the U.S. government that prints executive orders, rules, and regulations.

Executive Privilege
The right of executive officials to refuse to appear before, or to withhold information from, a legislative committee. Executive privilege is enjoyed by the president and by those executive officials accorded that right by the president.

INFOTRAC®
COLLEGE EDITION

For more information on this subject, use the term "executive privilege" in the Subject guide.

Vice President Dick Cheney assembled a task force in 2001 to advise the president on his energy policy. The energy policy recommended the disbursement of millions of federal dollars to energy companies. The General Accounting Office, the investigative arm of Congress, sued Cheney for release of documents related to that energy task force. Cheney claimed that release of the information would affect the president's ability to get candid opinions from people outside government. Should all government meetings become public information? (AP Photo/John Todd)

Richard Nixon (right) leaves the White House after his resignation on August 9, 1974. Next to him are his wife, Pat, Betty Ford, and Gerald Ford, the new president. (Don Carl Steffan/Photo Researchers)

Office had been tape-recorded on a secret system, Nixon was ordered to turn over the tapes to the special prosecutor. As you read in this chapter's opening *What If . . .* feature, Nixon refused to do so, claiming executive privilege. He argued that "no president could function if the private papers of his office, prepared by his personal staff, were open to public scrutiny." In 1974, in one of the Supreme Court's most famous cases, *United States v. Nixon,*[16] the justices unanimously ruled that Nixon had to hand over the tapes to the Court. The Court held that executive privilege could not be used to prevent evidence from being heard in criminal proceedings.

Clinton's Attempted Use of Executive Privilege.   The claim of executive privilege was also raised by the Clinton administration as a defense against the aggressive investigation of Clinton's relationship with Monica Lewinsky by Independent Counsel Kenneth Starr. The Clinton administration claimed executive privilege for several presidential aides who might have discussed the situation with the president. In addition, President Clinton asserted that his White House counsel did not have to testify before the Starr grand jury due to attorney-client privilege. Finally, the Department of Justice claimed that members of the Secret Service who guard the president could not testify about his activities due to a "protective function privilege" inherent in their duties. The federal judge overseeing the case denied the claims of privilege, however, a decision that was upheld on appeal.

Abuses of Executive Power and Impeachment

Presidents normally leave office either because their first term has expired and they do not seek (or win) reelection or because, having served two full terms, they are not allowed to be elected for a third term (owing to the Twenty-second Amendment,

---

[16] 318 U.S. 683 (1974).

On December 19, 1998, the House of Representatives voted to impeach President Bill Clinton for perjury and obstruction of justice. That same day, Clinton addressed lawmakers and staff outside the Oval Office, surrounded by supporters. President Clinton was later acquitted by the Senate, but the events raised important issues about presidential privacy and ethics. To what extent should the president's personal life be the subject of public scrutiny while he or she is in office? (AP Photo/Doug Mills)

passed in 1951). Eight presidents have died in office. But there is still another way for a president to leave office—by **impeachment.** Articles I and II of the Constitution authorize the House and Senate to remove the president, the vice president, or other civil officers of the United States for committing "Treason, Bribery, or other high Crimes and Misdemeanors." Remember from Chapter 12 that according to the Constitution, the impeachment process begins in the House, which impeaches (accuses) the federal officer involved. If the House votes to impeach the officer, it draws up articles of impeachment and submits them to the Senate, which conducts the actual trial.

In the history of the United States, no president has ever been impeached and also convicted—and thus removed from office—by means of this process. President Andrew Johnson (1865–1869), who succeeded to the office after the assassination of Abraham Lincoln, was impeached by the House but acquitted by the Senate. More than a century later, the House Judiciary Committee approved articles of impeachment against President Richard Nixon for his involvement in the cover-up of the Watergate break-in of 1972. Convinced that he had little hope of surviving the trial in the Senate, Nixon resigned on August 9, 1974, before the full House voted on the articles.

The second president to be impeached by the House but not convicted by the Senate was President Bill Clinton. In September 1998, Independent Counsel Kenneth Starr sent the findings of his investigation of the president on the charges of perjury and obstruction of justice to Congress. After the 1998 elections, the House Judiciary Committee presented four charges to the House for consideration. The House approved two of the charges against Clinton: lying to the grand jury about his affair with Monica Lewinsky and obstruction of justice. The other two charges were rejected by the House. The articles of impeachment were then sent to the Senate, which conducted a trial and acquitted President Clinton.

The Executive Organization

Gone are the days when presidents answered their own mail, as George Washington did. It was not until 1857 that Congress authorized a private secretary for the president, to be paid by the federal government. Woodrow Wilson typed most of his correspondence, even though he did have several secretaries. At the beginning of

Impeachment

As authorized by Articles I and II of the Constitution, an action by the House of Representatives and the Senate to remove the president, vice president, or civil officers of the United States from office for committing "Treason, Bribery, or other high Crimes and Misdemeanors."

INFOTRAC®
COLLEGE EDITION

To find out more about the impeachment, use the term "Clinton impeachment" in Keywords.

Franklin Roosevelt's long tenure in the White House, the entire staff consisted of thirty-seven employees. It was not until the New Deal and World War II that the presidential staff became a sizable organization.

Today, the executive organization includes a White House Office staff of about 600, including some workers who are part-time employees and others who are detailed from their departments to the White House. Not all of these employees have equal access to the president, nor are all of them likely to be equally concerned about the administration's political success. The more than 350 employees who work in the White House Office itself are closest to the president. They often include many individuals who worked on the president's campaign. These assistants are most concerned with preserving the president's reputation. Also included in the president's staff are a number of councils and advisory organizations, such as the National Security Council. Although the individuals who hold staff positions in these offices are appointed by the president, they are really more concerned with their own areas than with the president's overall success. The group of appointees who perhaps are least helpful to the president is the cabinet, each member of which is the principal officer of a government department.

The Cabinet

Although the Constitution does not include the word *cabinet*, it does state that the president "may require the Opinion, in writing, of the principal Officer in each of the executive Departments." Since the time of George Washington, there has been an advisory group, or **cabinet,** to which the president turns for counsel.

Cabinet

An advisory group selected by the president to aid in making decisions. The cabinet currently numbers thirteen department secretaries and the attorney general. Depending on the president, the cabinet may be highly influential or relatively insignificant in its advisory role.

Members of the Cabinet.   Originally, the cabinet consisted of only four officials— the secretaries of state, treasury, and war, and the attorney general. Today, the cabinet numbers thirteen secretaries and the attorney general. (See Table 13–1 on page 396 for the names of the cabinet departments and Chapter 14 for a detailed discussion of these units.)

The cabinet may consist of more than the secretaries of the various departments. The president at his or her discretion can, for example, ascribe cabinet rank to the national security adviser, to the ambassador to the United Nations, or to others. Because neither the Constitution nor statutory law requires the president to consult with the cabinet, its use is purely discretionary.

President George W. Bush is seen here with Vice President Dick Cheney, the fourteen cabinet secretaries, and other key advisers. Soon there may be an additional cabinet position, that of secretary of homeland security. To whom do the cabinet members owe their allegiance? (AP Photo/White House, Paul Morse)

Often, a president will use a **kitchen cabinet** to replace the formal cabinet as a major source of advice. The term *kitchen cabinet* originated during the presidency of Andrew Jackson, who relied on the counsel of close friends who often met with him in the kitchen of the White House. A kitchen cabinet is a very informal group of advisers; usually, they are friends with whom the president worked before being elected.

Presidential Use of Cabinets.   Some presidents have relied on the counsel of their cabinets more than others. Dwight Eisenhower frequently turned to his cabinet for advice on a wide range of governmental policies—perhaps because he was used to the team approach to solving problems from his experience in the U.S. Army. Other presidents solicited the opinions of their cabinets and then did what they wanted to do anyway. Lincoln supposedly said—after a cabinet meeting in which a vote was seven nays against his one aye—"Seven nays and one aye, the ayes have it."

In general, few presidents have relied heavily on the advice of their cabinet members. Jimmy Carter thought he could put his cabinet to good use and held regular cabinet meetings for the first two years of his tenure. Then he fired three cabinet members and forced two others to resign, while reorganizing his "inner government." He rarely met with the members of his cabinet thereafter. In recent years, the growth of other parts of the executive branch, such as the White House Office, has rendered the cabinet less significant as an advisory board to the president.

It is not surprising that presidents meet with their cabinet heads only reluctantly. Often, the departmental heads are more responsive to the wishes of their own staffs or to their own political ambitions than they are to the president. They may be more concerned with obtaining resources for their departments than with helping presidents achieve their goals. So there is often a strong conflict of interest between presidents and their cabinet members. It is likely that formal cabinet meetings are held more out of respect for the cabinet tradition than for their problem-solving value.

The Executive Office of the President

When President Franklin Roosevelt appointed a special committee on administrative management, he knew that the committee would conclude that the president needed help. Indeed, the committee proposed a major reorganization of the executive branch. Congress did not approve the entire reorganization, but it did create the **Executive Office of the President (EOP)** to provide staff assistance for the chief executive and to help coordinate the executive bureaucracy. Since that time, a number of agencies have been created within the EOP to supply the president with advice and staff help. These agencies are as follows:

- White House Office (1939).
- Council of Economic Advisers (1946).
- National Security Council (1947).
- Office of the United States Trade Representative (1963).
- Council on Environmental Quality (1969).
- Office of Management and Budget (1970).
- Office of Science and Technology Policy (1976).
- Office of Administration (1977).
- Office of National Drug Control Policy (1988).
- Office of Policy Development (1993).
- Office of Homeland Security (2001).

Several of the offices within the EOP are especially important, including the White House Office, the Council of Economic Advisers, the Office of Management and Budget, and the National Security Council.

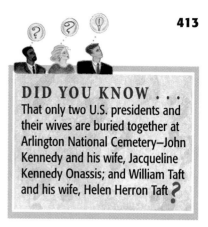

DID YOU KNOW...
That only two U.S. presidents and their wives are buried together at Arlington National Cemetery—John Kennedy and his wife, Jacqueline Kennedy Onassis; and William Taft and his wife, Helen Herron Taft **?**

Kitchen Cabinet
The informal advisers to the president.

Executive Office of the President (EOP)
Established by President Franklin D. Roosevelt by executive order under the Reorganization Act of 1939, the EOP currently consists of eleven staff agencies that assist the president in carrying out major duties.

White House Office

The personal office of the president, which tends to presidential political needs and manages the media.

Chief of Staff

The person who is named to direct the White House Office and advise the president.

Council of Economic Advisers (CEA)

A staff agency in the Executive Office of the President that advises the president on measures to maintain stability in the nation's economy; established in 1946.

Office of Management and Budget (OMB)

A division of the Executive Office of the President created by executive order in 1970 to replace the Bureau of the Budget. The OMB's main functions are to assist the president in preparing the annual budget, to clear and coordinate all departmental agency budgets, to help set fiscal policy, and to supervise the administration of the federal budget.

National Security Council (NSC)

A staff agency in the Executive Office of the President established by the National Security Act of 1947. The NSC advises the president on domestic and foreign matters involving national security.

The White House Office. One of the most important agencies within the EOP is the **White House Office,** which includes most of the key personal and political advisers to the president. Among the jobs held by these aides are those of legal counsel to the president, secretary, press secretary, and appointments secretary. Often, the individuals who hold these positions are recruited from the president's campaign staff. Their duties—mainly protecting the president's political interests—are similar to campaign functions. In all recent administrations, one member of the White House Office has been named **chief of staff.** This person, who is responsible for coordinating the office, is one of the president's chief advisers.

Employees of the White House Office have been both envied and criticized. The White House Office, according to most former staffers, grants its employees access and power. They are able to use the resources of the White House to contact virtually anyone in the world by telephone, cable, fax, or electronic mail as well as to use the influence of the White House to persuade legislators and citizens. Because of this influence, staffers are often criticized for overstepping the bounds of the office. It is the appointments secretary who is able to grant or deny senators, representatives, and cabinet secretaries access to the president. It is the press secretary who grants to the press and television journalists access to any information about the president. White House staff members are closest to the president and may have considerable influence over the administration's decisions. Often, when presidents are under fire for their decisions, the staff is accused of keeping the chief executive too isolated from criticism or help. Presidents insist that they will not allow the staff to become too powerful, but given the difficulty of the office, each president eventually turns to staff members for loyal assistance and protection.

The Council of Economic Advisers. The Employment Act of 1946 created a three-member **Council of Economic Advisers (CEA)** to advise the president on economic matters. The council's advice serves as the basis for the president's annual economic report to Congress. Each of the three members is appointed by the president and can be removed at will. In principle, the CEA was also created to advise the president on economic policy, but for the most part the function of the CEA has been to prepare the annual report.

The Office of Management and Budget. The **Office of Management and Budget (OMB)** was originally the Bureau of the Budget, which was created in 1921 within the Department of the Treasury. Recognizing the importance of this agency, Franklin Roosevelt moved it into the White House Office in 1939. Richard Nixon reorganized the Bureau of the Budget in 1970 and changed its name to reflect its new managerial function. It is headed by a director, who must make up the annual federal budget that the president presents to Congress each January for approval. In principle, the director of the OMB has broad fiscal powers in planning and estimating various parts of the federal budget, because all agencies must submit their proposed budget to the OMB for approval. In reality, it is not so clear that the OMB truly can affect the greater scope of the federal budget. The OMB may be more important as a clearinghouse for legislative proposals initiated in the executive agencies.

The National Security Council. The **National Security Council (NSC)** is a link between the president's key foreign and military advisers and the president. Its members consist of the president, the vice president, and the secretaries of state and defense, plus other informal members. The NSC has the resources of the National Security Agency (NSA) at its disposal in giving counsel to the president. (The NSA protects U.S. government communications and produces foreign intelligence information.) Included in the NSC is the president's special assistant for national security affairs. In 2001, Condoleezza Rice became the first woman to serve as the president's national security adviser.

The Vice Presidency

The Constitution does not give much power to the vice president. The only formal duty is to preside over the Senate—which is rarely necessary. This obligation is fulfilled when the Senate organizes and adopts its rules and when the vice president is needed to decide a tie vote. In all other cases, the president pro tem manages parliamentary procedures in the Senate. The vice president is expected to participate only informally in senatorial deliberations, if at all.

The Vice President's Job

Vice presidents have traditionally been chosen by presidential nominees to balance the ticket to attract groups of voters or appease party factions. If a presidential nominee is from the North, it is not a bad idea to have a vice presidential nominee who is from the South or the West. If the presidential nominee is from a rural state, perhaps someone with an urban background would be most suitable as a running mate. Presidential nominees who are strongly conservative or strongly liberal would do well to have vice presidential nominees who are more in the middle of the political road.

In recent presidential elections, vice presidents have been selected for other reasons. Bill Clinton picked Al Gore to be his running mate in 1992 even though both were southern and moderates. The ticket appealed to younger voters and moderates, both of whom were crucial to the election. In 2000, both vice presidential selections were intended to shore up the respective presidential candidates' "perceived weaknesses." Republican George W. Bush, who was subject to criticism for his lack of government experience and his "lightweight" personality, chose Dick Cheney, a former member of Congress who had also served as secretary of defense. Democrat Al Gore chose Senator Joe Lieberman of Connecticut, demonstrating his willingness to "take a chance" on a Jewish running mate.

The job of vice president is not extremely demanding, even when the president gives some specific task to the vice president. Typically, vice presidents spend their time supporting the president's activities. During the Clinton administration (1993–2001), however, Vice President Al Gore did much to strengthen the vice presidency position by his aggressive support for environmental-protection policies on a global basis. He also took a special interest in areas of emerging technology and was instrumental in providing subsidies to public schools for Internet use. Vice President Dick Cheney, as one of President George W. Bush's key advisers, clearly is an influential figure in the Bush administration. Of course, the vice presidency takes on even more significance if the president becomes disabled or dies in office—and the vice president becomes president.

Vice presidents infrequently have become elected presidents in their own right. John Adams and Thomas Jefferson were the first to do so. Then Martin Van Buren was elected president in 1836 after he had served as Andrew Jackson's vice president for the previous eight years. In 1988, George H. W. Bush was elected to the presidency after eight years as Ronald Reagan's vice president.

Presidential Succession

Eight vice presidents have become president because of the death of the president. John Tyler, the first to do so, took over William Henry Harrison's position after only one month. No one knew whether Tyler should simply be a caretaker until a new president could be elected three and a half years later or whether he actually should be president. Tyler assumed that he was supposed to be the chief executive and he acted as such—although he was commonly referred to as "His Accidency." On all occasions since then, vice presidents taking over the position of the presidency because of the incumbent's death have assumed all of the presidential powers.

An attempted assassination of Ronald Reagan occurred on March 31, 1981. In the foreground, two men bend over press secretary James Brady who lies seriously wounded. In the background, President Reagan is watched over by a U.S. secret service agent with an automatic weapon. A Washington, D.C., police officer, Thomas Delahanty, lies to the left after also being shot. (AP Photo/Ron Edmonds)

But what should a vice president do if a president becomes incapable of carrying out necessary duties while in office? When James Garfield was shot in 1881, he stayed alive for two and a half months. What was Vice President Chester Arthur's role?

This question was not addressed in the original Constitution. Article II, Section 1, says only that "[i]n Case of the Removal of the President from Office, or of his Death, Resignation, or Inability to discharge the Powers and Duties of the said Office, the same shall devolve on [the same powers shall be exercised by] the Vice President." There have been many instances of presidential disability. When Dwight Eisenhower became ill a second time in 1958, he entered into a pact with Richard Nixon that provided that the vice president could determine whether the president was incapable of carrying out his duties if the president could not communicate. John Kennedy and Lyndon Johnson entered into similar agreements with their vice presidents. Finally, in 1967, the **Twenty-fifth Amendment** was passed, establishing procedures in case of presidential incapacity.

Twenty-fifth Amendment
An amendment to the Constitution adopted in 1967 that establishes procedures for filling vacancies in the two top executive offices and that makes provisions for situations involving presidential disability.

The Twenty-fifth Amendment

According to the Twenty-fifth Amendment, when the president believes that he is incapable of performing the duties of his office, he must inform Congress in writing. Then the vice president serves as acting president until the president can resume his normal duties. When the president is unable to communicate, a majority of the cabinet, including the vice president, can declare that fact to Congress. Then the vice president serves as acting president until the president resumes his normal duties. If a dispute arises over the return of the president's ability to discharge his normal functions, a two-thirds vote of Congress is required to decide whether the vice president shall remain acting president or whether the president shall resume his duties.

In 2002, President George W. Bush formally invoked the Twenty-fifth Amendment for the first time by officially transferring presidential power to Vice President Dick Cheney while the president underwent a colonoscopy, a twenty-minute procedure. He commented that he undertook this transfer of power "because we're at war," referring to the war on terrorism. The only other time the provisions of the Twenty-fifth Amendment have been used was during President Reagan's colon surgery in 1985, although Reagan did not formally invoke the amendment.

When the Vice Presidency Becomes Vacant

The Twenty-fifth Amendment also addresses the issue of how the president should fill a vacant vice presidency. Section 2 of the amendment simply states, "Whenever there is a vacancy in the office of the Vice President, the President shall nominate a Vice President who shall take office upon confirmation by a majority vote of both Houses of Congress." This is exactly what occurred when Richard Nixon's vice president, Spiro Agnew, resigned in 1973 because of his alleged receipt of construction contract kickbacks during his tenure as governor of Maryland. Nixon turned to Gerald Ford as his choice for vice president. After extensive hearings, both chambers of Congress confirmed the appointment. Then, when Nixon resigned on August 9, 1974, Ford automatically became president and nominated as his vice president Nelson Rockefeller. Congress confirmed Ford's choice. For the first time in the history of the country, neither the president nor the vice president had been elected to their positions.

The question of who shall be president if both the president and vice president die is answered by the Succession Act of 1947. If the president and vice president die, resign, or are disabled, the Speaker of the House will act as president, after resigning from Congress. Next in line is the president pro tem of the Senate, followed by the cabinet officers in the order of the creation of their departments (see Table 13–3).

The Presidency: Why Is It Important Today?

Some suggest that the presidency is virtually "in your face" day in and day out in this country. Certainly, the media inundate us, often on a daily basis, with every single activity in which the president is involved. To be sure, most of the media coverage of the president provides entertainment value only. Yet it can generally be said that no other country puts its head of state under such a microscope.

Today, the powers of the U.S. president are more extensive than perhaps ever before, and these powers may significantly affect you, your family, or your friends. The president acts as chief legislator by submitting proposed legislation to Congress. The president can veto legislation. As commander in chief, the president can deploy troops even without the approval of Congress. The president also has the ability to act while Congress is not in session. For example, Lincoln suspended certain constitutional liberties, blockaded southern ports, and banned "treasonable correspondence" from the U.S. mails during a congressional recess.

President George W. Bush has certainly continued in the tradition of expanding presidential powers. He used an executive order—just one of 13,500 that have been issued in this nation's history—to create military tribunals to try foreigners accused of terrorism. (See Chapter 4 for a further discussion of this important issue.) He refused Congress's request for information relating to his administration's actions. As discussed in this chapter's opening *What If . . .* feature, he invoked executive privilege to avoid having to give such information to Congress.

Although President Bush entered the White House at a disadvantage, because he did not win the popular vote in the 2000 elections, today he stands front and center as a powerful president. We all know that much of this increased power has stemmed from the fact that the horrific terrorist acts on September 11, 2001, occurred while he was president. Bush's aggressive response to these events at home, throughout the world, and, in particular, in Afghanistan won widespread support among the American public. While it is anybody's guess whether Bush's popularity will continue, he has certainly shown how important the presidency is today.

Spiro Agnew was Richard Nixon's vice president from 1969 to 1973. Agnew resigned amid allegations of income tax evasion in connection with money he received when he was governor of Maryland. (Corbis/UPI/Bettmann)

TABLE 13–3

Line of Succession to the Presidency of the United States

1. Vice president
2. Speaker of the House of Representatives
3. Senate president *pro tempore*
4. Secretary of state
5. Secretary of the treasury
6. Secretary of defense
7. Attorney general
8. Secretary of the interior
9. Secretary of agriculture
10. Secretary of commerce
11. Secretary of labor
12. Secretary of health and human services
13. Secretary of housing and urban development
14. Secretary of transportation
15. Secretary of energy
16. Secretary of education
17. Secretary of veterans affairs

MAKING A DIFFERENCE | Communicating with the White House

Writing to the president of the United States has long been a way for citizens to express their political opinions. The most traditional form of communication is, of course, by letter. Letters to the president should be addressed to:

The President of the United States
The White House
1600 Pennsylvania Avenue N.W.
Washington, DC 20500

If you wish to write to the First Lady, letters may be sent to her at the same address. Will you get an answer? Almost certainly. The White House mail room is staffed by volunteers and paid employees who sort the mail for the president and tally the public's concerns. You may receive a standard response to your comments or a more personal, detailed response.

Telephone the White House

You can also call the White House on the telephone and leave a message for the president or First Lady. To call the switchboard, call 202-456-1414, a number publicized by former Secretary of State James Baker when he told the Israelis publicly, "When you're serious about peace, call us at . . . ." The switchboard received more than eight thousand calls in the next twenty-four hours.

The White House also has a round-the-clock comment line, which you can reach at 202-456-1111. When you call that number, an operator will take down your comments and forward them to the president's office. Again, the operators tally the calls to give the president a measurement of opinion on specific topics.

Use the Internet

In this electronic age, the White House has been aggressive in its use of the Internet and the World Wide Web. The home page for the White House is listed in the *Logging On* feature at the end of this chapter. It is always designed to be entertaining and to convey information about the president. You can, however, easily send your comments and ideas to the White House via e-mail. Send comments to the president to

President@whitehouse.gov

Address e-mail to the First Lady at

First.Lady@whitehouse.gov

You will receive an electronic response to your mail from the White House staff. Due to the extremely heavy e-mail load, you will receive only one response per day regardless of how many messages you send.

Key Terms

Chapter Summary

1 The office of the presidency in the United States, combining as it does the functions of chief of state and chief executive, is unique. The framers of the Constitution were divided over whether the president should be a weak executive controlled by the legislature or a strong executive.

2 The requirements for the office of the presidency are outlined in Article II, Section 1, of the Constitution. The president's roles include both formal and informal duties. The president is chief of state, chief executive, commander in chief, chief diplomat, chief legislator, and party chief.

3 As chief of state, the president is ceremonial head of the government. As chief executive, the president is bound to enforce the acts of Congress, the judgments of the federal courts, and treaties. The chief executive has the power of appointment and the power to grant reprieves and pardons.

4 As commander in chief, the president is the ultimate decision maker in military matters. As chief diplomat, the president recognizes foreign governments, negotiates treaties, signs agreements, and nominates and receives ambassadors.

5 The role of chief legislator includes recommending legislation to Congress, lobbying for the legislation, approving laws,

and exercising the veto power. Additionally, the president has statutory powers written into law by Congress. The president is also leader of his or her political party. Presidents use their power to persuade and their access to the media to fulfill this function.

6 Presidents have a variety of special powers not available to other branches of the government. These include emergency power, executive power, and executive privilege.

7 Abuses of executive power are dealt with by Articles I and II of the Constitution, which authorize the House and Senate to impeach and remove the president, vice president, or other officers of the federal government for committing "Treason, Bribery, or other high Crimes and Misdemeanors."

8 The president receives assistance from the cabinet and from the Executive Office of the President (including the White House Office).

9 The vice president is the constitutional officer assigned to preside over the Senate and to assume the presidency in case of the death, resignation, removal, or disability of the president. The Twenty-fifth Amendment, passed in 1967, established procedures to be followed in case of presidential incapacity and when filling a vacant vice presidency.

Selected Print and Media Resources

SUGGESTED READINGS

Greenfield, Meg. *Washington.* New York: Public Affairs, 2001. The author, a long-time *Washington Post* reporter, takes a candid look at Washington, D.C., politics and political players.

Greenstein, Fred I. *The Presidential Difference: Leadership Style from Roosevelt to Clinton.* Old Tappan, N.J.: Free Press, 2000. In this book, an eminent presidential scholar examines and discusses the leadership styles of eleven chief executives. Greenstein assesses each president in several categories including organization, skill, vision, and emotional intelligence.

Kennedy, Robert F. *Thirteen Days: A Memoir of the Cuban Missile Crisis.* New York: W. W. Norton and Co., 1999. Originally published in 1969, this is the ultimate insider's account of the Cuban missile crisis, told by one of the principal figures involved.

Kernell, Samuel. *Going Public: New Strategies of Presidential Leadership,* 3d ed. Washington, D.C.: Congressional Quarterly Press, 1997. This is a classic work on how presidents go "over the head of Congress" to the people and includes examples from the Clinton presidency.

Kunhardt, Peter W., and Philip B. Kunhardt III. *The American President.* New York: Riverhead Books, 1999. Although this book is aimed at a general readership, it contains hundreds of facts and interesting anecdotes about the presidents from Washington to Clinton.

Posner, Richard A. *An Affair of State: The Investigation, Impeachment, and Trial of President Clinton.* Cambridge, Mass.: Harvard University Press, 1999. The author, a federal judge, examines the investigation, impeachment, and trial of President Clinton from a careful legal point of view. He discusses a number of topics including whether a president can pardon himself and other fascinating nuances of the Clinton impeachment trial.

MEDIA RESOURCES

LBJ: A Biography—An acclaimed biography of Lyndon Johnson that covers his rise to power, his presidency, and the events of the Vietnam War, which ended his presidency; produced in 1991 as part of PBS's *The American Experience* series.

Nixon—An excellent 1995 film exposing the events of Richard Nixon's troubled presidency. Anthony Hopkins plays the embattled but brilliant chief executive.

Sunrise at Campobello—An excellent portrait of one of the greatest presidents, Franklin Delano Roosevelt; produced in 1960 and starring Ralph Bellamy.

Thirteen Days—A movie retelling the events of October 1962, when the Kennedy administration decided to blockade Cuba to force the Soviet Union to remove its missiles from Cuba. The 2001 film, starring Kevin Costner, Bruce Greenwood, and Steven Culp, gives an inside view of policymaking involving the president, his closest advisers, and the joint chiefs of staff.

Your CD-ROM Resources

In addition to the chapter content containing hot links, the following resources are available on the CD-ROM:

- **Internet Activities**—The War Powers Resolution, the current presidential cabinet.

- **Critical Thinking Exercises**—The factors of presidential greatness, presidential pardons, rallying around the flag.

- **Self-Check on Important Themes**—Can You Answer These?

- **Animated Figure**—Figure 13–1, "Public Popularity of Modern Presidents."

- **Video**—*Presidential Style, Clinton Style.*

- **Public Opinion Data**—Contrasting opinions on executive privilege and the impeachment of President Clinton.

- **InfoTrac Exercise**—"Monkey Do."

- **Simulation**—You Are There!

- **Participation Exercise**—Visit the Web site of the president and comment on one of the policies.

- **MicroCase Exercise**—"By the Numbers: Examine Trust and Confidence in the President over Time."

- **Additional Resources**—All court cases, Alexander Hamilton, *Federalist Paper* No. 70 (1788), Louis Fisher, *The Laws Congress Never Made* (1993), *William J. Clinton, President of the United States v. New York City* (1998), The Impeachment of William Jefferson Clinton (1998).

e-mocracy

The Presidency and the Internet

Today, the Internet has become such a normal part of most Americans' lives that it is almost hard to imagine what life was like without it. Certainly, accessing the latest press releases from the White House was much more difficult ten years ago than it is today. It was not until the Clinton administration (1993–2001) that access to the White House via the Internet became possible. President Bill Clinton supported making many White House documents available on the Web site for the White House. Correspondence with the president and the First Lady quickly moved from ordinary handwritten letters to e-mail. During the Clinton presidency, most agencies of the government, as well as congressional offices, also began to provide access and information on the Internet. Today, you can access the White House Web site (see the *Logging On* section) to find White House press releases, presidential State of the Union messages

and other speeches, historical data on the presidency, and much more.

Logging On

This site offers extensive information on the White House and the presidency:

http://www.whitehouse.gov

The Library of Congress Executive Branch page is a great source of information and has numerous presidency-related links. The URL is

http://www.loc.gov/global/ executive/fed.htm

Inaugural addresses of American presidents from George Washington to George W. Bush can be found at

http://www.bartleby.com/124

Using the Internet for Political Analysis

Take a look at the activities of the president of the United States by clicking on the White House at

http://www.whitehouse.gov

and the Government Documents site, SunSITE, at

http://www.ibiblio.org/govdocs.html

Try to find the president's schedule for a day or a week, or read at least two speeches he has given within the last few months. After you have read these documents, decide which role the president was playing when he engaged in certain activities or made certain statements: commander in chief, chief legislator, and so on.

You then might want to search a site such as that of the *Congressional Quarterly* at

http://www.cq.com

or AllPolitics at

http://www.cnn.com/ALLPOLITICS

and look at articles from the same date as the president's speech for an alternative view of what he was proposing.

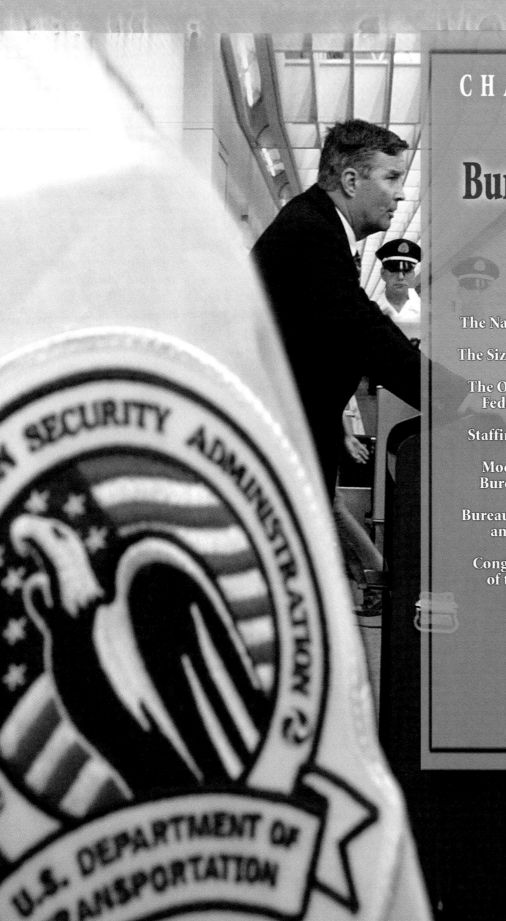

CHAPTER 14
The Bureaucracy

The Nature of Bureaucracy

•

The Size of the Bureaucracy

•

The Organization of the
Federal Bureaucracy

•

Staffing the Bureaucracy

•

Modern Attempts at
Bureaucratic Reform

•

Bureaucrats as Politicians
and Policymakers

•

Congressional Control
of the Bureaucracy

BACKGROUND

Bureaucrats have helped run the federal government from its inception. As you will learn in this chapter, until the passage of the Civil Service Reform Act of 1883, most new administrations fired bureaucrats in order to appoint their own supporters.

Since 1883, Congress has reformed the civil service on several occasions. In addition, each modern administration has claimed that it would change the federal bureaucracy to make bureaucrats more accountable. In spite of all efforts, however, bureaucrats are far from accountable to their bosses in the executive branch, to Congress, and, least of all, to the public—the taxpayers who pay their salaries.

WHAT IF BUREAUCRATS WERE REALLY HELD ACCOUNTABLE?

If bureaucrats in private businesses do not perform, their bosses simply fire them. If the entire bureaucracy within a business is not working well, the business either suffers losses or goes bankrupt. The business is held accountable to its customers and, if it is publicly traded, to its stockholders.

The federal bureaucracy, in contrast, is so well governed by rules and regulations about firing that virtually no one is ever fired. At most, a poorly performing bureaucrat might be transferred to another job.

Therefore, the first step in making bureaucrats really accountable would be to alter the civil service legislation that makes it so hard for government bureaucrats to be fired. Congress has the power to do this.

AVOIDING WASTE

If bureaucrats were truly held accountable, we might see less waste in government. A good example of the type of program that would be eliminated if federal bureaucrats were held accountable is the Creative Wellness Program. The Department of Housing and Urban Development (HUD) started this program in 1998 to reduce crime by curbing drug sales and use in urban areas. The bureaucrats in charge of that program claimed that if public housing residents felt better about themselves, they would be less likely to be involved with drugs, domestic violence, and crime. This multimillion-dollar program presented public housing tenants with information as to which gemstones, types of incense, and clothing colors they should utilize to improve their self-esteem! It turned out that an official at HUD had awarded this contract to a friend.

ENTER THE INSPECTOR GENERAL

The federal government already has a watchdog organization—the General Accounting Office (GAO), headed by an inspector general. The amount of waste and fraud discovered by this office already fills mountains of reports. Virtually no one ever receives any punishment for fraud or waste that is discovered, though. If bureaucrats were really held accountable for their actions, the federal government could fire them for their obviously inappropriate, inefficient, or fraudulent activities.

There are also numerous private groups that bring ridicule to the federal government by discovering laughable programs and actions by federal bureaucrats that virtually no one could justify. Again, if federal bureaucrats were held accountable and knew that they could be fired, fewer of them would dare to engage in such activities.

BUSH'S ACCOUNTABILITY BUDGET

The Bush administration has taken some steps to increase federal bureaucratic accountability. President George W. Bush's idea has been to create performance-based budgeting. In this plan, budgetary payouts are linked to specific performance criteria for each program. The problem, of course, is that it will have little impact on the incentives facing federal government bureaucrats. They will be only marginally more accountable than they are today—which is to say, not very accountable.

FOR CRITICAL ANALYSIS

1. Some argue that making it easier to fire federal bureaucrats will reduce the number of career civil servants. Do you agree? Explain your reasoning.
2. Some have argued that an alternative to making bureaucrats more accountable is simply to privatize more of the federal government's activities. Is this a good idea? What political forces would oppose such privatization?

Virtually every modern president, at one time or another, has proclaimed that his administration was going to "fix government," as discussed in this chapter's opening *What If . . .* feature. All modern presidents also have put forth plans to end government waste and inefficiency (see Table 14–1). Their success has been, in a word, underwhelming. Presidents have been generally powerless to affect significantly the structure and operation of the federal bureaucracy.

The bureaucracy has been called the "fourth branch of government," even though you will find no reference to the bureaucracy in the original Constitution or in the twenty-seven amendments that have been passed since 1787. But Article II, Section 2, of the Constitution gives the president the power to appoint "all other Officers of the United States, whose Appointments are not herein otherwise provided for." Article II, Section 3, states that the president "shall take Care that the Laws be faithfully executed, and shall Commission all the Officers of the United States." Constitutional scholars believe that the legal basis for the bureaucracy rests on these two sections in Article II.

The Nature of Bureaucracy

A **bureaucracy** is the name given to a large organization that is structured hierarchically to carry out specific functions. Generally, most bureaucracies are characterized by an organization chart. The units of the organization are divided according to the specialization and expertise of the employees.

Bureaucracy
A large organization that is structured hierarchically to carry out specific functions.

Public and Private Bureaucracies

We should not think of bureaucracy as unique to government. Any large corporation or university can be considered a bureaucratic organization. The fact is that the handling of complex problems requires a division of labor. Individuals must concentrate their skills on specific, well-defined aspects of a problem and depend on others to solve the rest of it.

Public or government bureaucracies differ from private organizations in some important ways, however. A private corporation, such as Microsoft, has a single set of leaders, its board of directors. Public bureaucracies, in contrast, do not have a single set of leaders. Although the president is the chief administrator of the federal system, all bureaucratic agencies are subject to the desires of Congress for their funding, staffing, and, indeed, their continued existence. Furthermore, public bureaucracies supposedly serve the citizen rather than the stockholder.

One other important difference between private corporations and government bureaucracies is that government bureaucracies are not organized to make a profit.

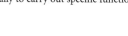

INFOTRAC®
COLLEGE EDITION

For more information about this topic, use the term "public administration" in the Subject guide.

TABLE 14–1

Selected Presidential Plans to End Government Inefficiency

PRESIDENT	NAME OF PLAN
Lyndon Johnson (1963–1969)	Programming, Planning, and Budgeting Systems
Richard Nixon (1969–1974)	Management by Objectives
Jimmy Carter (1977–1981)	Zero-Based Budgeting
Ronald Reagan (1981–1989)	President's Private Sector Survey on Cost Control (the Grace Commission)
George H. W. Bush (1989–1993)	Right-Sizing Government
Bill Clinton (1993–2001)	"From Red Tape to Results: Creating a Government That Works Better and Costs Less"
George W. Bush (2001–)	Performance-Based Budgeting

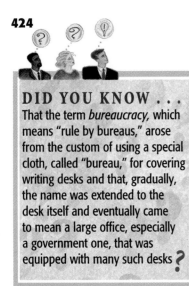

Weberian Model
A model of bureaucracy developed by the German sociologist Max Weber, who viewed bureaucracies as rational, hierarchical organizations in which power flows from the top downward and decisions are based on logical reasoning and data analysis.

Acquisitive Model
A model of bureaucracy that views top-level bureaucrats as seeking constantly to expand the size of their budgets and the staffs of their departments or agencies so as to gain greater power and influence in the public sector.

Monopolistic Model
A model of bureaucracy that compares bureaucracies to monopolistic business firms. Lack of competition within a bureaucracy leads to inefficient and costly operations. Because bureaucracies are not penalized for inefficiency, there is no incentive to reduce costs or use resources more productively.

Rather, they are supposed to perform their functions as efficiently as possible to conserve the taxpayers' dollars. Perhaps it is this aspect of government organization that makes citizens hostile toward government bureaucracy when they experience inefficiency and red tape.

These characteristics, together with the prevalence and size of the government bureaucracies, make them an important factor in American life.

Models of Bureaucracy

Several theories have been offered to help us better understand the ways in which bureaucracies function. Each of these theories focuses on specific features of bureaucracies.

Weberian Model.   The classic model, or **Weberian model,** of the modern bureaucracy was proposed by the German sociologist Max Weber.[1] He argued that the increasingly complex nature of modern life, coupled with the steadily growing demands placed on governments by their citizens, made the formation of bureaucracies inevitable. According to Weber, most bureaucracies—whether in the public or private sector—are hierarchically organized and governed by formal procedures. The power in a bureaucracy flows from the top downward. Decision-making processes in bureaucracies are shaped by detailed technical rules that promote similar decisions in similar situations. Bureaucrats are specialists who attempt to resolve problems through logical reasoning and data analysis instead of "gut feelings" and guesswork. Individual advancement in bureaucracies is supposed to be based on merit rather than political connections. Indeed, the modern bureaucracy, according to Weber, should be an apolitical organization.

Acquisitive Model.   Other theorists do not view bureaucracies in terms as benign as Weber's. Some believe that bureaucracies are acquisitive in nature. Proponents of the **acquisitive model** argue that top-level bureaucrats will always try to expand, or at least to avoid any reductions in, the size of their budgets. Although government bureaucracies are not-for-profit enterprises, bureaucrats want to maximize the size of their budgets and staffs, because these things are the most visible trappings of power in the public sector. These efforts are also prompted by the desire of bureaucrats to "sell" their products—national defense, public housing, agricultural subsidies, and so on—to both Congress and the public.

Monopolistic Model.   Because government bureaucracies seldom have competitors, some theorists have suggested that bureaucratic organizations may be explained best by using a **monopolistic model.** The analysis is similar to that used by economists to examine the behavior of monopolistic firms. Monopolistic bureaucracies—like monopolistic firms—essentially have no competitors and act accordingly. Because monopolistic bureaucracies usually are not penalized for chronic inefficiency, they have little reason to adopt cost-saving measures or to make more productive uses of their resources. Some economists have argued that such problems can be cured only by privatizing certain bureaucratic functions.

Bureaucracies Compared

The federal bureaucracy in the United States enjoys a greater degree of autonomy than do federal or national bureaucracies in most other countries. Much of the insu-

---

[1] Max Weber, *Theory of Social and Economic Organization,* ed. Talcott Parsons (New York: Oxford University Press, 1974).

The Department of Agriculture inspects meat-packing facilities throughout the United States, certifying the quality and condition of the meat to be sold. Why is it necessary for the U.S. government to have administrative agencies such as the Department of Agriculture? (David Frazier/PhotoResearchers)

larity that is commonly supposed to characterize the bureaucracy in this country may stem from the sheer size of the government organizations needed to implement a budget that exceeds $2 trillion. Because the lines of authority often are not well defined, some bureaucracies may be able to operate with a significant degree of autonomy.

The federal nature of the American government also means that national bureaucracies regularly provide financial assistance to their state counterparts. Both the Department of Education and the Department of Housing and Urban Development, for example, distribute funds to their counterparts at the state level. In contrast, most bureaucracies in European countries have a top-down command structure so that national programs may be implemented directly at the lower level. This is due not only to the small size of most European countries but also to the fact that public ownership of such business entities as telephone companies, airlines, railroads, and utilities is far more common in Europe than in the United States.

The fact that the U.S. government owns relatively few enterprises does not mean, however, that its bureaucracies are comparatively powerless. Indeed, there are numerous **administrative agencies** in the federal bureaucracy—such as the Environmental Protection Agency, the Nuclear Regulatory Commission, and the Securities and Exchange Commission—that extensively regulate private companies even though they virtually never have an ownership interest in those companies.

Administrative Agency
A federal, state, or local government unit established to perform a specific function. Administrative agencies are created and authorized by legislative bodies to administer and enforce specific laws.

The Size of the Bureaucracy

In 1789, the new government's bureaucracy was minuscule. There were three departments—State (with nine employees), War (with two employees), and Treasury (with thirty-nine employees)—and the Office of the Attorney General (which later became

FIGURE 14-1

Federal Agencies and Their Respective Numbers of Civilian Employees

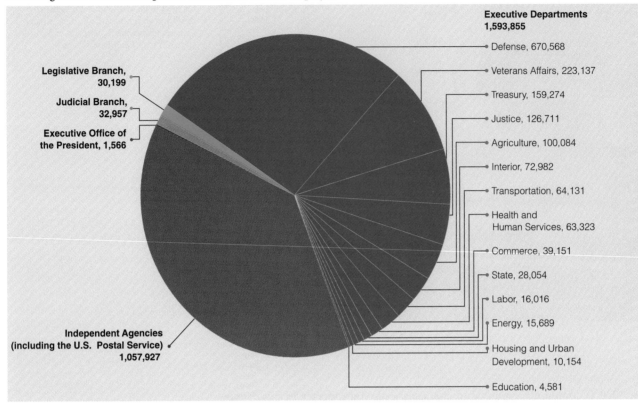

SOURCE: U.S. Office of Personnel Management, 2002.

FIGURE 14-2

Government Employment at the Federal, State, and Local Levels

There are more local government employees than federal and state employees combined.

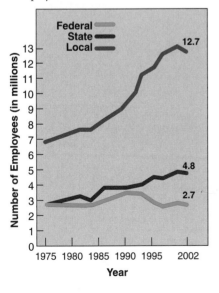

the Department of Justice). The bureaucracy was still small in 1798. At that time, the secretary of state had seven clerks and spent a total of $500 (about $6,100 in 2003 dollars) on stationery and printing. In that same year, the Appropriations Act allocated $1.4 million to the War Department (or $17.1 million in 2003 dollars).[2]

Times have changed, as we can see in Figure 14–1, which lists the various federal agencies and the number of civilian employees in each. Excluding the military, approximately 2.7 million government employees constitute the federal bureaucracy. That number has remained relatively stable for the last several decades. It is somewhat deceiving, however, because there are many other individuals working directly or indirectly for the federal government as subcontractors or consultants and in other capacities. In fact, according to some studies, the federal work force vastly exceeds the number of official federal workers.[3]

The figures for federal government employment are only part of the story. Figure 14–2 shows the growth in government employment at the federal, state, and local levels. Since 1970, this growth has been mainly at the state and local levels. If all government employees are counted, then, more than 15 percent of all civilian employment is accounted for by government.

The costs of the bureaucracy are commensurately high and growing. The share of the gross national product accounted for by all government spending was only 8.5 percent in 1929. Today, it exceeds 40 percent.

[2] Leonard D. White, *The Federalists: A Study in Administrative History, 1789–1801* (New York: Free Press, 1948).

[3] See, for example, Paul C. Light, *The True Size of Government* (Washington, D.C.: Brookings Institution Press, 1999).

The Organization of the Federal Bureaucracy

Within the federal bureaucracy are a number of different types of government agencies and organizations. Figure 14–3 outlines the several bureaucracies within the executive branch, as well as the separate organizations that provide services to Congress, to the courts, and directly to the president. In Chapter 13, we discussed those agencies that are considered to be part of the Executive Office of the President.

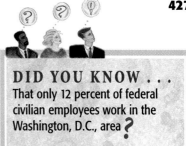

DID YOU KNOW . . .
That only 12 percent of federal civilian employees work in the Washington, D.C., area ?

FIGURE 14–3

Organization Chart of the Federal Government

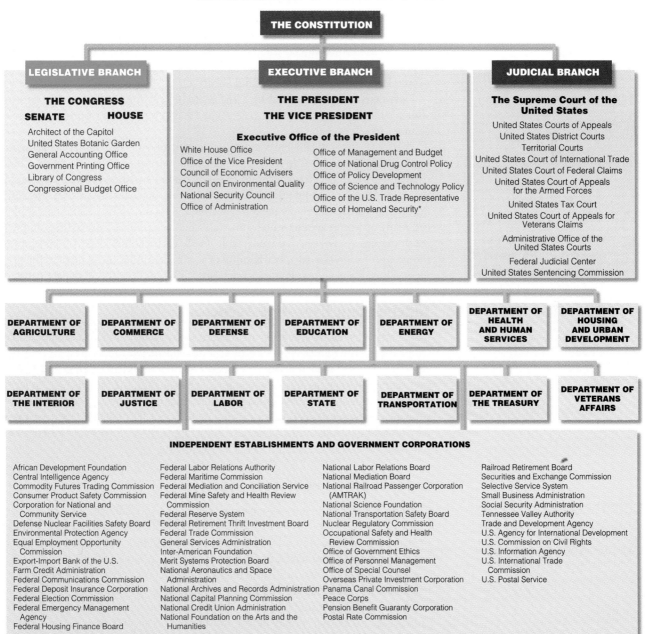

*By the time you read this, this office may have been elevated to a cabinet-level department.

SOURCE: *United States Government Manual, 2001/02* (Washington, D.C.: U.S. Government Printing Office, 2001), p. 22.

Cabinet Department
One of the fourteen departments of the executive branch (State, Treasury, Defense, Justice, Interior, Agriculture, Commerce, Labor, Health and Human Services, Housing and Urban Development, Education, Energy, Transportation, and Veterans Affairs).

Line Organization
With respect to the federal government, an administrative unit that is directly accountable to the president.

INFOTRAC ®
COLLEGE EDITION

For more information about the EPA, use the term "Environmental Protection Agency" in Keywords.

Independent Executive Agency
A federal agency that is not part of a cabinet department but reports directly to the president.

Independent Regulatory Agency
An agency outside the major executive departments charged with making and implementing rules and regulations to protect the public interest.

The executive branch, which employs most of the bureaucrats, has four major types of bureaucratic structures. They are (1) cabinet departments, (2) independent executive agencies, (3) independent regulatory agencies, and (4) government corporations. Each has a distinctive relationship to the president, and some have unusual internal structures, overall goals, and grants of power.

Cabinet Departments

The fourteen **cabinet departments** are the major service organizations of the federal government. They can also be described in management terms as **line organizations.** This means that they are directly accountable to the president and are responsible for performing government functions, such as printing money or training troops. These departments were created by Congress when the need for each department arose. The first department to be created was State, and the most recent one was Veterans Affairs, established in 1988. A president might ask that a new department be created or an old one abolished, but the president has no power to do so without legislative approval from Congress. (For example, by the time you read this, there may be a fifteenth department, that of Homeland Security.)

Each department is headed by a secretary (except for the Justice Department, which is headed by the attorney general) and has several levels of undersecretaries, assistant secretaries, and so on.

Presidents theoretically have considerable control over the cabinet departments, because presidents are able to appoint or fire all of the top officials. Even cabinet departments do not always respond to the president's wishes, though. One reason that presidents are frequently unhappy with their departments is that the entire bureaucratic structure below the top political levels is staffed by permanent employees, many of whom are committed to established programs or procedures and who resist change. As we can see from Table 14–2, each cabinet department employs thousands of individuals, only a handful of whom are under the control of the president. The table also describes the functions of each of the cabinet departments.

Independent Executive Agencies

Independent executive agencies are bureaucratic organizations that are not located within a department but report directly to the president, who appoints their chief officials. When a new federal agency is created—the Environmental Protection Agency, for example—Congress decides where it will be located in the bureaucracy. In recent decades, presidents often have asked that a new organization be kept separate or independent rather than added to an existing department, particularly if a department may in fact be hostile to the agency's creation. Table 14–3 on page 430 describes the functions of several selected independent executive agencies.

Independent Regulatory Agencies

The **independent regulatory agencies** are typically responsible for a specific type of public policy. Their function is to make and implement rules and regulations in a particular sector of the economy to protect the public interest. The earliest such agency was the Interstate Commerce Commission (ICC), which was established in 1887 when Americans began to seek some form of government control over the rapidly growing business and industrial sector. This new form of organization, the independent regulatory agency, was supposed to make technical, nonpolitical decisions about rates, profits, and rules that would be for the benefit of all and that did not require congressional legislation. In the years that followed the creation of the ICC, other agencies were formed to regulate communication (the Federal Communications

TABLE 14–2

Executive Departments*

DEPARTMENT AND YEAR ESTABLISHED	PRINCIPAL FUNCTIONS	MOST IMPORTANT SUBAGENCIES
State (1789) (28,054 employees)	Negotiates treaties; develops foreign policy; protects citizens abroad.	Passport Agency; Bureau of Diplomatic Security; Foreign Service; Bureau of Human Rights and Humanitarian Affairs; Bureau of Consular Affairs.
Treasury (1789) (159,274 employees)	Pays all federal bills; borrows money; collects federal taxes; mints coins and prints paper currency; operates the Secret Service; supervises national banks.	Internal Revenue Service; Bureau of Alcohol, Tobacco, and Firearms; U.S. Secret Service; U.S. Mint; Customs Service.
Interior (1849) (72,982 employees)	Supervises federally owned lands and parks; operates federal hydroelectric power facilities; supervises Native American affairs.	U.S. Fish and Wildlife Service; National Park Service; Bureau of Indian Affairs; Bureau of Land Management.
Justice (1870)[†] (126,711 employees)	Furnishes legal advice to the president; enforces federal criminal laws; supervises the federal corrections systems (prisons).	Federal Bureau of Investigation; Drug Enforcement Administration; Bureau of Prisons; Immigration and Naturalization Service.
Agriculture (1889) (100,084 employees)	Provides assistance to farmers and ranchers; conducts research to improve agricultural activity and to prevent plant disease; works to protect forests from fires and disease.	Soil Conservation Service; Agricultural Research Service; Food and Safety Inspection Service; Federal Crop Insurance Corporation; Farmers Home Administration.
Commerce (1913)[‡] (39,151 employees)	Grants patents and trademarks; conducts a national census; monitors the weather; protects the interests of businesses.	Bureau of the Census; Bureau of Economic Analysis; Minority Business Development Agency; Patent and Trademark Office; National Oceanic and Atmospheric Administration; U.S. Travel and Tourism Administration.
Labor (1913) (16,016 employees)	Administers federal labor laws; promotes the interests of workers.	Occupational Safety and Health Administration (OSHA); Bureau of Labor Statistics; Employment Standards Administration; Office of Labor-Management Standards.
Defense (1947)[§] (670,568 employees)	Manages the armed forces (army, navy, air force, and marines); operates military bases; is responsible for civil defense.	National Guard; National Security Agency; Joint Chiefs of Staff; Departments of the Air Force, Navy, Army.
Housing and Urban Development (1965) (10,154 employees)	Deals with the nation's housing needs; develops and rehabilitates urban communities; promotes improvement in city streets and parks.	Office of Block Grant Assistance; Emergency Shelter Grants Program; Office of Urban Development Action Grants; Office of Fair Housing and Equal Opportunity.
Transportation (1967) (64,131 employees)	Finances improvements in mass transit; develops and administers programs for highways, railroads, and aviation; is involved with offshore maritime safety.	Federal Aviation Administration; Federal Highway Administration; National Highway Traffic Safety Administration; U.S. Coast Guard; Federal Transit Administration.
Energy (1977) (15,689 employees)	Is involved in the conservation of energy and resources; analyzes energy data; conducts research and development.	Office of Civilian Radioactive Waste Management; Bonneville Power Administration; Office of Nuclear Energy; Energy Information Administration; Office of Conservation and Renewable Energy.
Health and Human Services (1979)[§§] (63,323 employees)	Promotes public health; enforces pure food and drug laws; is involved in health-related research.	Food and Drug Administration; Administration for Children and Families; Health Care Financing Administration; Public Health Service.
Education (1979)[§§] (4,581 employees)	Coordinates federal programs and policies for education; administers aid to education; promotes educational research.	Office of Special Education and Rehabilitation Service; Office of Elementary and Secondary Education; Office of Postsecondary Education; Office of Vocational and Adult Education.
Veterans Affairs (1988) (223,137 employees)	Promotes the welfare of veterans of the U.S. armed forces.	Veterans Health Administration; Veterans Benefits Administration; National Cemetery Systems.

*At the time of this writing, a new Department of Homeland Security was being debated in Congress.
[†]Formed from the Office of the Attorney General (created in 1789).
[‡]Formed from the Department of Commerce and Labor (created in 1903).
[§]Formed from the Department of War (created in 1789) and the Department of Navy (created in 1798).
[§§]Formed from the Department of Health, Education, and Welfare (created in 1953).

TABLE 14–3

Selected Independent Executive Agencies

NAME	DATE FORMED	PRINCIPAL FUNCTIONS
Central Intelligence Agency (CIA)*	1947	Gathers and analyzes political and military information about foreign countries so that the United States can improve its own political and military status; conducts activities outside the United States, with the goal of countering the work of intelligence services operated by other nations whose political philosophies are inconsistent with our own.
General Services Administration (GSA) (13,921 employees)	1949	Purchases and manages all property of the federal government; acts as the business arm of the federal government in overseeing federal government spending projects; discovers overcharges in government programs.
National Science Foundation (NSF) (1,204 employees)	1950	Promotes scientific research; provides grants to all levels of schools for instructional programs in the sciences.
Small Business Administration (SBA) (3,968 employees)	1953	Protects the interests of small businesses; provides low-cost loans and management information to small businesses.
National Aeronautics and Space Administration (NASA) (18,850 employees)	1958	Is responsible for the U.S. space program, including the building, testing, and operating of space vehicles.
Environmental Protection Agency (EPA) (17,968 employees)	1970	Undertakes programs aimed at reducing air and water pollution; works with state and local agencies to help fight environmental hazards.

*The CIA will not release information on the number of employees who work for this agency (because it is "classified information").

DID YOU KNOW . . .
That the federal government spends over $1 billion every five hours, every day of the year ?

Capture
The act of gaining direct or indirect control over agency personnel and decision makers by the industry that is being regulated.

Commission), nuclear power (the Nuclear Regulatory Commission), and so on. (The ICC was abolished on December 30, 1995.)

The Purpose and Nature of Regulatory Agencies

The regulatory agencies are administered independently of all three branches of government. They were set up because Congress felt it was unable to handle the complexities and technicalities required to carry out specific laws in the public interest. The regulatory commissions in fact combine some functions of all three branches of government—executive, legislative, and judicial. They are legislative in that they make rules that have the force of law. They are executive in that they provide for the enforcement of those rules. They are judicial in that they decide disputes involving the rules they have made.

Regulatory agency members are appointed by the president with the consent of the Senate, although they do not report to the president. By law, the members of regulatory agencies cannot all be from the same political party. Presidents can influence regulatory agency behavior by appointing people of their own parties or people who share their political views when vacancies occur, in particular when the chair is vacant. Members may be removed by the president only for causes specified in the law creating the agency. Table 14–4 describes the functions of selected independent regulatory agencies.

Agency Capture.   Over the last several decades, some observers have concluded that these agencies, although nominally independent, may in fact not always be so. They also contend that many independent regulatory agencies have been **captured** by the very industries and firms that they were supposed to regulate. The results have been less competition rather than more competition, higher prices rather than lower prices, and less choice rather than more choice for consumers.

Deregulation and Reregulation. During the presidency of Ronald Reagan (1981–1989), some significant deregulation (the removal of regulatory restraints—the opposite of regulation) occurred, much of which had started under President Jimmy Carter (1977–1981). For example, President Carter appointed a chairperson of the Civil Aeronautics Board (CAB) who gradually eliminated regulation of airline fares and routes. Then, under Reagan, the CAB was eliminated on January 1, 1985. During the first Bush administration, calls for reregulation of many businesses increased. Indeed, under President George H. W. Bush (1989–1993), the Americans with Disabilities Act of 1990, the Civil Rights Act of 1991, and the Clean Air Act Amendments of 1991, all of which increased or changed the regulation of many businesses, were passed. Additionally, the Cable Reregulation Act of 1992 was passed. Under President Bill Clinton (1993–2001), the Interstate Commerce Commission was eliminated, and there was deregulation of the banking and telecommunications industries, and many other sectors of the economy. At the same time, there was extensive regulation to protect the environment. Additionally, in the late 1990s and the early 2000s, major attempts to institute general regulatory reform were made in Congress. So far, no significant legislation of that nature has been passed.

Government Corporations

Another form of bureaucratic organization in the United States is the **government corporation.** Although the concept is borrowed from the world of business, distinct differences exist between public and private corporations.

A private corporation has shareholders (stockholders) who elect a board of directors, who in turn choose the corporate officers, such as president and vice president. When a private corporation makes a profit, it must pay taxes (unless it avoids them through various legal loopholes). It either distributes part or all of the after-tax profits to shareholders as dividends or plows the profits back into the corporation to make new investments.

DID YOU KNOW . . .
That the Commerce Department's U.S. Travel and Tourism Administration recently gave away $440,000 in so-called disaster relief to western ski resort operators because there hadn't been enough snow ?

INFOTRAC ®
COLLEGE EDITION

For more information about deregulation, use the term "deregulation" in the Subject guide.

Government Corporation
An agency of government that administers a quasi-business enterprise. These corporations are used when activities are primarily commercial. They produce revenue for their continued existence, and they require greater flexibility than is permitted for departments and agencies.

TABLE 14–4

Selected Independent Regulatory Agencies

NAME	DATE FORMED	PRINCIPAL FUNCTIONS
Federal Reserve System Board of Governors (Fed) (1,650 employees)	1913	Determines policy with respect to interest rates, credit availability, and the money supply.
Federal Trade Commission (FTC) (1,007 employees)	1914	Prevents businesses from engaging in unfair trade practices; stops the formation of monopolies in the business sector; protects consumer rights.
Securities and Exchange Commission (SEC) (2,946 employees)	1934	Regulates the nation's stock exchanges, in which shares of stocks are bought and sold; requires full disclosure of the financial profiles of companies that wish to sell stocks and bonds to the public.
Federal Communications Commission (FCC) (1,946 employees)	1934	Regulates all communications by telegraph, cable, telephone, radio, and television.
National Labor Relations Board (NLRB) (2,000 employees)	1935	Protects employees' rights to join unions and bargain collectively with employers; attempts to prevent unfair labor practices by both employers and unions.
Equal Employment Opportunity Commission (EEOC) (2,746 employees)	1964	Works to eliminate discrimination based on religion, gender, race, color, national origin, age, or disability; examines claims of discrimination.
Federal Election Commission (FEC) (347 employees)	1974	Ensures that candidates and states follow the rules established by the Federal Election Campaign Act.
Nuclear Regulatory Commission (NRC) (2,763 employees)	1974	Ensures that electricity-generating nuclear reactors in the United States are built and operated safely; regularly inspects the operations of such reactors.

A government corporation has a board of directors and managers, but it does not have any stockholders. We cannot buy shares of stock in a government corporation. If the government corporation makes a profit, it does not distribute the profit as dividends. Also, if it makes a profit, it does not have to pay taxes; the profits remain in the corporation. Table 14–5 describes the functions of selected government corporations.

Staffing the Bureaucracy

There are two categories of bureaucrats: political appointees and civil servants. As noted earlier, the president is able to make political appointments to most of the top jobs in the federal bureaucracy. The president also can appoint ambassadors to the most important foreign posts. All of the jobs that are considered "political plums" and that usually go to the politically well connected are listed in *Policy and Supporting Positions,* a book published by the Government Printing Office after each presidential election. This has been informally (and appropriately) called "The Plum Book." The rest of the individuals who work for the national government belong to the civil service and obtain their jobs through a much more formal process.

Political Appointees

To fill the positions listed in "The Plum Book," the president and the president's advisers solicit suggestions from politicians, businesspersons, and other prominent individuals. Appointments to these positions offer the president a way to pay off outstanding political debts. But the president must also take into consideration such things as the candidate's work experience, intelligence, political affiliations, and personal characteristics. Presidents have differed over the importance they attach to appointing women and minorities to plum positions. Presidents often use ambassadorships, however, to reward selected individuals for their campaign contributions.

The Aristocracy of the Federal Government. Political appointees are in some sense the aristocracy of the federal government. But their powers, although appearing formidable on paper, are often exaggerated. Like the president, a political appointee will

---

TABLE 14–5

Selected Government Corporations

NAME	DATE FORMED	PRINCIPAL FUNCTIONS
Tennessee Valley Authority (TVA) (13,488 employees)	1933	Operates a Tennessee River control system and generates power for a seven-state region and for the U.S. aeronautics and space programs; promotes the economic development of the Tennessee Valley region; controls floods and promotes the navigability of the Tennessee River.
Federal Deposit Insurance Corporation (FDIC) (6,532 employees)	1933	Insures individuals' bank deposits up to $100,000; oversees the business activities of banks.
Export-Import Bank of the United States (Ex-Im Bank) (426 employees)	1933	Promotes the sale of American-made goods abroad; grants loans to foreign purchasers of American products.
National Railroad Passenger Corporation (AMTRAK) (24,000 employees)	1970	Provides a balanced national and intercity rail passenger service network; controls 23,000 miles of track with 505 stations.
U.S. Postal Service* (856,550 employees)	1970	Delivers mail throughout the United States and its territories; is the largest government corporation.

*Formed from the Office of the Postmaster General in the Department of the Treasury (created in 1789).

occupy her or his position for a comparatively brief time. Political appointees often leave office before the president's term actually ends. In fact, the average term of service for political appointees is less than two years. As a result, most appointees have little background for their positions and may be mere figureheads. Often, they only respond to the paperwork that flows up from below. Additionally, the professional civil servants who make up the permanent civil service but serve under a normally temporary political appointee may not feel compelled to carry out their current boss's directives quickly, because they know that he or she will not be around for very long.

The Difficulty in Firing Civil Servants.   This inertia is compounded by the fact that it is extremely difficult to discharge civil servants, as mentioned in this chapter's opening *What If . . .* feature. In recent years, less than one-tenth of 1 percent of federal employees have been fired for incompetence. Because discharged employees may appeal their dismissals, many months or even years may pass before the issue is resolved conclusively. This occupational rigidity helps to ensure that most political appointees, no matter how competent or driven, will not be able to exert much meaningful influence over their subordinates, let alone implement dramatic changes in the bureaucracy itself. Of course, there are exceptions. Under the Civil Service Reform Act of 1978, for example, senior employees can be transferred within their departments

U.S. Postal Service employees sort the mail during the night shift at an Austin, Texas, post office. The postal service is the largest single employer in the United States. (Bob Daemmrich/Stock Boston)

and receive salary bonuses and other benefits as incentives for being productive and responsive to the goals and policy preferences of their politically appointed superiors.

History of the Federal Civil Service

When the federal government was formed in 1789, it had no career public servants but rather consisted of amateurs who were almost all Federalists. When Thomas Jefferson took over as president, he found that few in his party were holding federal administrative jobs, so he fired more than one hundred officials and replaced them with members of the so-called **natural aristocracy**—that is, with his own Jeffersonian (Democratic) Republicans. For the next twenty-five years, a growing body of federal administrators gained experience and expertise, becoming in the process professional public servants. These administrators stayed in office regardless of who was elected president. The bureaucracy had become a self-maintaining, long-term element within government.

To the Victor Belong the Spoils.   When Andrew Jackson took over the White House in 1828, he could not believe how many appointed officials (appointed before he became president, that is) were overtly hostile toward him and his Democratic Party. The bureaucracy—indeed an aristocracy—considered itself the only group fit to rule. But Jackson was a man of the people, and his policies were populist in nature. As the bureaucracy was reluctant to carry out his programs, Jackson did the obvious: he fired federal officials—more than had all his predecessors combined. The **spoils system**—an application of the principle that to the victor belong the spoils— reigned. The aristocrats were out, and the common folk were in. The spoils system was not, of course, a Jacksonian invention. Thomas Jefferson, too, had used this system of patronage in which the boss, or patron, rewards those who worked to get him or her elected.

The Civil Service Reform Act of 1883.   Jackson's spoils system survived for a number of years, but it became increasingly corrupt. Also, as the size of the bureaucracy increased by 300 percent between 1851 and 1881, the cry for civil service reform became louder. Reformers began to look to the example of several European countries, which had established a professional civil service that operated under a **merit system** in which job appointments were based on competitive examinations.

Natural Aristocracy
A small ruling clique of a society's "best" citizens, whose membership is based on birth, wealth, and ability. The Jeffersonian era emphasized government rule by such a group.

Spoils System
The awarding of government jobs to political supporters and friends; generally associated with President Andrew Jackson.

Merit System
The selection, retention, and promotion of government employees on the basis of competitive examinations.

On September 19, 1881, President James A. Garfield was assassinated by a disappointed office seeker, Charles J. Guiteau. The long-term effect of this event was to replace the spoils system with a permanent career civil service with the passage of the Pendleton Act in 1883, which established the Civil Service Commission. (Corbis/Bettmann)

In 1883, the **Pendleton Act**—or **Civil Service Reform Act**—was passed, bringing to a close the period of Jacksonian spoils. The act established the principle of employment on the basis of open, competitive examinations and created the **Civil Service Commission** to administer the personnel service. Only 10 percent of federal employees were initially covered by the merit system. Later laws, amendments, and executive orders, however, increased the coverage to more than 90 percent of the federal civil service. The effects of these reforms were felt at all levels of government, including city governments run by political machines.

The Supreme Court put an even heavier lid on the spoils system in *Elrod v. Burns*[4] in 1976 and *Branti v. Finkel*[5] in 1980. In those two cases, the Court used the First Amendment to forbid government officials from discharging or threatening to discharge public employees solely for not being supporters of the political party in power unless party affiliation is an appropriate requirement for the position. Additional curbs on political patronage were added in *Rutan v. Republican Party of Illinois*[6] in 1990. The Court's ruling effectively prevented the use of partisan political considerations as the basis for hiring, promoting, or transferring most public employees. An exception was permitted, however, for senior policymaking positions, which usually go to officials who will support the programs of the elected leaders.

The Civil Service Reform Act of 1978. In 1978, the Civil Service Reform Act abolished the Civil Service Commission and created two new federal agencies to perform its duties. To administer the civil service laws, rules, and regulations, the act created the Office of Personnel Management (OPM). The OPM is empowered to recruit, interview, and test potential government workers and determine who should be hired. The OPM makes recommendations to the individual agencies as to which persons meet the standards (typically, the top three applicants for a position), and the agencies generally decide whom to hire. To oversee promotions, employees' rights, and other employment matters, the act created the Merit Systems Protection Board (MSPB). The MSPB evaluates charges of wrongdoing, hears employee appeals from agency decisions, and can order corrective action against agencies and employees.

Federal Employees and Political Campaigns. In 1933, when President Franklin D. Roosevelt set up his New Deal, a virtual army of civil servants was hired to staff the numerous new agencies that were created. Because the individuals who worked in these agencies owed their jobs to the Democratic Party, it seemed natural for them to campaign for Democratic candidates. The Democrats controlling Congress in the mid-1930s did not object. But in 1938, a coalition of conservative Democrats and Republicans took control of Congress and forced through the **Hatch Act**—or **Political Activities Act**—of 1939. The act prohibited federal employees from actively participating in the political management of campaigns. It also forbade the use of federal authority to influence nominations and elections, and outlawed the use of bureaucratic rank to pressure federal employees to make political contributions.

The Hatch Act created a controversy that lasted for decades. Many contended that the act deprived federal employees of their First Amendment freedoms of speech and association. In 1972, a federal district court declared the act unconstitutional. The United States Supreme Court, however, reaffirmed the challenged portion of the act in 1973, stating that the government's interest in preserving a nonpartisan civil service was so great that the prohibitions should remain.[7] Twenty years later, Congress

Pendleton Act (Civil Service Reform Act)
The law, as amended over the years, that remains the basic statute regulating federal employment personnel policies. It established the principle of employment on the basis of merit and created the Civil Service Commission to administer the personnel service.

Civil Service Commission
The initial central personnel agency of the national government; created in 1883.

Hatch Act (Political Activities Act)
The act that prohibits the use of federal authority to influence nominations and elections or the use of rank to pressure federal employees to make political contributions. It also prohibits civil service employees from active involvement in political campaigns.

---

[4] 427 U.S. 347 (1976).
[5] 445 U.S. 507 (1980).
[6] 497 U.S. 62 (1990).
[7] *United States Civil Service Commission v. National Association of Letter Carriers*, 413 U.S. 548 (1973).

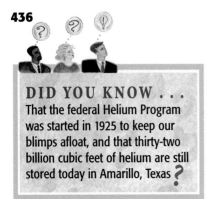

addressed the criticisms of the Hatch Act by passing the Federal Employees Political Activities Act of 1993. This act, which amended the Hatch Act, lessened the harshness of the 1939 act in several ways. Among other things, the 1993 act allowed federal employees to run for office in nonpartisan elections, participate in voter registration drives, make campaign contributions to political organizations, and campaign for candidates in partisan elections.

Modern Attempts at Bureaucratic Reform

As long as the federal bureaucracy exists, there will continue to be attempts to make it more open, efficient, and responsive to the needs of U.S. citizens. The most important actual and proposed reforms in the last several decades include sunshine and sunset laws, privatization, and more protection for so-called whistleblowers.

Sunshine Laws

Government in the Sunshine Act
A law that requires all multiheaded federal agencies to conduct their business regularly in public session.

In 1976, Congress enacted the **Government in the Sunshine Act.** It required for the first time that all multiheaded federal agencies—about fifty of them—hold their meetings regularly in public session. The bill defined *meetings* as almost any gathering, formal or informal, of agency members, including conference telephone calls. The only exceptions to this rule of openness are discussions of matters such as court proceedings or personnel problems, and these exceptions are specifically listed in the bill. Sunshine laws now exist at all levels of government.

Sunshine laws are consistent with the policy of information disclosure that has been supported by the government for decades. For example, beginning in the 1960s, a number of consumer protection laws have required that certain information be disclosed to consumers—when purchasing homes, borrowing funds, and so on. In 1966, the federal government passed the Freedom of Information Act, which required federal government agencies, with certain exceptions, to disclose to individuals, on their request, any information about them contained in government files. (You will learn more about this act in the *Making a Difference* feature at the end of this chapter.) Notably, since September 11, 2001, the trend toward government in the sunshine and information disclosure has been reversed at both the federal and state levels—see this chapter's *America's Security* feature for details on this development.

"Who do I see to get big government off my back?"

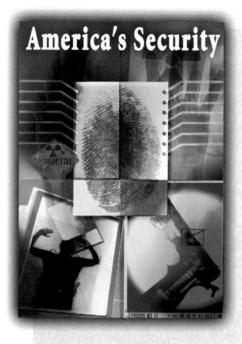

America's Security

Terrorists have put the country on guard. It is hard to know where or when they may strike next. They may attempt to poison water supplies, blow up nuclear power plants, cause dams to flood whole cities, and possibly commit a host of other atrocities. Terrorists need information to carry out such crimes, however. Much of the background information on the infrastructure in America is now readily available in libraries, government publications, and—to a growing extent—online. Since 9/11, however, a number of laws have been proposed, and some have been passed, in an effort to reduce the accessibility of such valuable information.

THE FEDERAL GOVERNMENT ACTS

Within weeks after September 11, 2001, numerous federal agencies removed hundreds, if not thousands, of documents from Internet sites, public libraries, and reading rooms found in various federal government departments. Information contained in some of the documents included diagrams of power plants and pipelines, structural details on dams, and safety plans for chemical plants. The military also immediately started

Placing Curbs on Information Disclosure

restricting information about its current and planned activities, as did the Federal Bureau of Investigation.

STATE AND LOCAL GOVERNMENTS REACT, TOO

There are over 87,000 separate centers of government in the United States. Many state and local governments control and supervise police forces, dams, electricity sources, and water supplies. Consequently, it is not surprising that many state and local governments followed in the footsteps of the federal government in curbing access to certain public records and information.

In early 2002, the Idaho legislature proposed a bill that would allow judges to close public records whenever that state's agencies were worried

Kate Martin is the director of the Center for National Security Studies in Washington, D.C. In October 2001, the Center filed a Freedom of Information Act request for release of information about people detained after the September 11 terrorist attacks. The request was denied. Martin called the arrests "frighteningly close to the practice of 'disappearing' people in Latin America." (AP Photo/Susan Walsh)

that such records might threaten the safety of the public or government officials. Additionally, the proposed bill would seal evacuation plans from the public. At about the same time, Florida's senate amended its rules so that it could hold closed meetings whenever the subject involved antiterrorism.

In general, such actions constitute a broad attempt by state and local governments to keep terrorists from learning about local emergency preparedness plans. While the public remains concerned about the threat of terrorist attacks, many of these proposed bills will become law. We can predict, however, that as soon as the public starts to believe that the threat has lessened, some groups will take state and local governments to court in an effort to increase public access to state and local records by reimposing the sunshine laws that were in effect before 9/11.

FOR CRITICAL ANALYSIS

The legislative council for the American Civil Liberties Union of Idaho argued that people need to know about how hazardous or nuclear materials are transported and stored so that they can protect themselves. How do you react to the counterargument—that the public can best be protected by preventing terrorists from accessing such information?

Sunset Laws

Sunset Legislation
A law requiring that an existing program be reviewed regularly for its effectiveness and be terminated unless specifically extended as a result of this review.

Potentially, the size and scope of the federal bureaucracy might be controlled through **sunset legislation,** which would place government programs on a definite schedule for congressional consideration. Unless Congress specifically reauthorized a particular federally operated program at the end of a designated period, it would be terminated automatically; that is, its sun would set.

The idea of sunset legislation—the first hint at the role of the bureaucracy in the legislative process—was initially suggested by Franklin D. Roosevelt when he created the plethora of New Deal agencies. His assistant, William O. Douglas, recommended that each agency's charter should include a provision allowing for its termination in ten years. Only an act of Congress could revitalize it. Obviously, the proposal was never adopted. It was not until 1976 that a state legislature—Colorado's—adopted sunset legislation for state regulatory commissions, giving them a life of six years before their suns set. Today, most states have some type of sunset law.

Privatization

Privatization
The replacement of government services with services provided by private firms.

Another approach to bureaucratic reform is **privatization,** which occurs when government services are replaced by services from the private sector. For example, the government might contract with private firms to operate prisons. Supporters of privatization argue that some services could be provided more efficiently by the private sector. Another scheme is to furnish vouchers to "clients" in lieu of services. For example, it has been proposed that instead of federally supported housing assistance, the government should offer vouchers that recipients could use to "pay" for housing in privately owned buildings.

The privatization, or contracting out, strategy has been most successful on the local level. Municipalities, for example, can form contracts with private companies for such things as trash collection. Such an approach is not a cure-all, however, as there are many functions, particularly on the national level, that cannot be contracted out in any meaningful way. For example, the federal government could not contract out all of the Defense Department's functions to private firms. Whether Social Security should be partially privatized is a topic currrently being debated—see Chapter 16 for a discussion of this issue.

INFOTRAC ®
COLLEGE EDITION

For more information about privatization, use the term "privatization" in the Subject guide.

Incentives for Efficiency and Productivity

An increasing number of state governments are beginning to experiment with a variety of schemes to run their operations more efficiently and capably. They focus on maximizing the efficiency and productivity of government workers by providing incentives for improved performance.[8] For example, many governors, mayors, and city administrators are considering ways in which government can be made more entrepreneurial. Some of the most promising measures have included such tactics as permitting agencies that do not spend their entire budgets to keep some of the difference and rewarding employees with performance-based bonuses.

Government Performance and Results Act.   At the federal level, the Government Performance and Results Act of 1997 was designed to improve efficiency in the federal work force. The act required that all government agencies (except the Central

---

[8] See, for example, David Osborne and Ted Gaebler, *Reinventing Government: How the Entrepreneurial Spirit Is Transforming the Public Sector* (Reading, Mass.: Addison-Wesley, 1992); and David Osborne and Peter Plastrik, *Banishing Bureaucracy: The Five Strategies for Reinventing Government* (Reading, Mass.: Addison-Wesley, 1997).

Intelligence Agency) describe their new goals and establish methods for determining whether those goals are met. Goals may be broadly crafted (for example, reducing the time it takes to test a new drug before allowing it to be marketed) or narrowly crafted (for example, reducing the number of times a telephone rings before it is answered).

Bureaucracy Changed Little, Though. Efforts to improve bureaucratic efficiency are supported by the assertion that although society and industry have changed enormously in the past century, the form of government used in Washington, D.C., and in most states has remained the same. Some observers believe that the nation's diverse economic base cannot be administered competently by traditional bureaucratic organizations. Consequently, government must become more responsive to cope with the increasing number of demands placed on it. Political scientists Joel Aberbach and Bert Rockman take issue with this contention. They argue that the bureaucracy has changed significantly over time in response to changes desired by various presidential administrations. In their opinion, many of the problems attributed to the bureaucracy are, in fact, a result of the political decision-making process. Therefore, attempts to "reinvent" government by reforming the bureaucracy are misguided.[9]

Other analysts have suggested that the problem lies not so much with traditional bureaucratic organizations as with the people who run them. According to policy specialist Taegan Goddard and journalist Christopher Riback, what needs to be "reinvented" is not the machinery of government but public officials. After each election, new appointees to bureaucratic positions may find themselves managing complex, multimillion-dollar enterprises, yet they often are untrained for their jobs. According to these authors, if we want to reform the bureaucracy, we should focus on preparing newcomers for the task of "doing" government.[10]

Saving Costs through E-Government. Many contend that the communications revolution brought about by the Internet has not only improved the efficiency with which government agencies deliver services to the public but also helped to reduce the cost of government. Agencies can now communicate with members of the public, as well as other agencies, via e-mail. Additionally, every federal agency now has a Web site to which citizens can go to find information about agency services instead of calling or appearing in person at a regional agency office. Since 2000, federal agencies have also been required to use electronic commerce whenever it is practical to do so and will save on costs. (In fact, the merits of e-government are so compelling that the tools of e-government are currently regarded as an effective form of aid to developing nations—see this chapter's *Global View* feature for a discussion of this program.)

Helping Out the Whistleblowers

The term **whistleblower** as applied to the federal bureaucracy has a special meaning: it is someone who blows the whistle on a gross governmental inefficiency or illegal action. Whistleblowers may be clerical workers, managers, or even specialists, such as scientists. The 1978 Civil Service Reform Act prohibits reprisals against whistleblowers by their superiors, and it set up the Merit Systems Protection Board as part of this protection. Many federal agencies also have toll-free hotlines that employees can use anonymously

Global View

E-Government as a New Type of Foreign Aid

While the United States forges ahead with its efforts to make government more accessible through the Internet, many foreign countries have not even conceived of how to do so. In terms of ease of access to government sites, Canada, Singapore, and the United States stand far above the rest of the world.

During a meeting of the Group of Seven (G-7) largest industrialized nations (plus Russia) in Genoa, Italy, there was much talk of the "digital divide" between rich and poor countries. At the behest of the head of the Italian government, the G-7 initiated the creation of new forms of aid for developing countries—e-government for development. Later, at a meeting of seventy-six countries, the developing countries launched a concrete program to help them reduce poverty and corruption by using the tools of e-government.

FOR CRITICAL ANALYSIS

Bill Gates, founder of Microsoft, once said that people who survive on a dollar a day need food and medicine, not computers. How does Gates's view relate to e-government as a foreign-aid tool?

Whistleblower
Someone who brings to public attention gross governmental inefficiency or an illegal action.

---

[9] Joel D. Aberbach and Bert A. Rockman, *In the Web of Politics: Three Decades of the U.S. Federal Executive* (Washington, D.C.: Brookings Institution Press, 2000).

[10] Taegan D. Goddard and Christopher Riback, *You Won—Now What? How Americans Can Make Democracy Work from City Hall to the White House* (New York: Scribner, 1998).

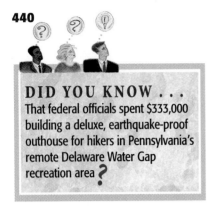

For more information about this topic, use the term "whistleblowing" in the Subject guide.

Enabling Legislation
A statute enacted by Congress that authorizes the creation of an administrative agency and specifies the name, purpose, composition, functions, and powers of the agency being created.

to report bureaucratic waste and inappropriate behavior. About 35 percent of all calls result in agency action or follow-up.

Further protection for whistleblowers was provided in 1989, when Congress passed the Whistle-Blower Protection Act. That act established an independent agency, the Office of Special Counsel (OSC), to investigate complaints brought by government employees who have been demoted, fired, or otherwise sanctioned for reporting government fraud or waste. There is little evidence, though, that potential whistleblowers truly have received more protection as a result of these endeavors. More than 40 percent of the employees who turned to the OSC for assistance in a recent three-year period stated that they were no longer employees of the government agencies on which they blew the whistle.

Some state and federal laws encourage employees to blow the whistle on their employers' wrongful actions by providing monetary incentives to the whistleblowers. At the federal level, for example, the False Claims Act of 1986 allows a whistleblower who has disclosed information relating to a fraud perpetrated against the U.S. government to receive a monetary award. If the government chooses to prosecute the case, the whistleblower receives between 15 and 25 percent of the proceeds. If the government declines to intervene, the whistleblower can bring suit on behalf of the government and will receive between 25 and 30 percent of the proceeds. (For a further discussion of this act and the controversy it has generated, see this chapter's *Politics and Ethics* feature.)

Bureaucrats as Politicians and Policymakers

Because Congress is unable to oversee the day-to-day administration of its programs, it must delegate certain powers to administrative agencies. Congress delegates the power to implement legislation to agencies through what is called **enabling legislation**. For example, the Federal Trade Commission was created by the Federal Trade Commission Act of 1914, the Equal Employment Opportunity Commission was created by the Civil Rights Act of 1964, and the Occupational Safety and Health Administration was created by the Occupational Safety and Health Act of 1970. The enabling legislation generally specifies the name, purpose, composition, functions, and powers of the agency.

In theory, the agencies should put into effect laws passed by Congress. Laws are often drafted in such vague and general terms, however, that they provide little guidance to agency administrators as to how the laws should be put into effect. This means that the agencies themselves must decide how best to carry out the wishes of Congress.

The discretion given to administrative agencies is not accidental. Congress has long realized that it lacks the technical expertise and the resources to monitor the implementation of its laws. Hence, the administrative agency is created to fill the gaps. This gap-filling role requires the agency to formulate administrative rules (regulations) to put flesh on the bones of the law. But it also forces the agency itself to become an unelected policymaker.

The Rulemaking Environment

Rulemaking does not occur in a vacuum. Suppose that Congress passes a new air-pollution law. The Environmental Protection Agency (EPA) might decide to implement the new law by a technical regulation relating to factory emissions. This proposed regulation would be published in the *Federal Register,* a daily government publication, so that interested parties would have an opportunity to comment on it. Individuals and companies that opposed parts or all of the rule might then try to

Politics and ETHICS

Rewards for Whistleblowers

Fraud against the federal government is nothing new, nor are attempts to curb the problem—as noted elsewhere in this chapter. Indeed, an early attempt by the government to deal with the problem dates back to the Civil War years. In 1863, as a result of investigations of the fraudulent use of federal funds, Congress passed the False Claims Act (FCA). As amended in 1986, the act provides that any person can sue an individual or a company for defrauding the government through false claims.

INCENTIVES FOR WHISTLEBLOWERS

A whistleblower who brings such a suit technically is acting on behalf of the U.S. government, which sometimes intervenes in the suit and always gets at least 70 percent of the proceeds of any settlement or verdict. The whistle-blower gets the rest, which usually amounts to between 15 and 25 percent of the recovered amount.

For example, in one case an employee of General Electric Company (GE) who blew the whistle on his employer's fraudulent use and embezzlement of government funds was awarded over $13 million—about 23 percent of the $59 million recovered in the suit against GE. Recently, an engineer who worked for FMC Corporation contended that FMC had defrauded the government of billions of dollars by producing a military machine (a vehicle that is part tank, part armored troop carrier) that was likely to fail in combat. The engineer's main accusation was that the machine, which was supposed to float, would sink. A jury believed him and levied a $310 million judgment against FMC, up to 30 percent ($93 million) of which will go to the engineer—and his lawyers—if the amount of damages is not reduced on appeal.

THE CONTROVERSY OVER THE FCA

Some consider the FCA to be a powerful weapon against fraud on the government. Others argue that the whistleblowers are merely bounty hunters and that a higher percentage of the amounts recovered should go to the government. Still others criticize the FCA's provisions on legal grounds. They contend that whistleblowers should not be able to bring such lawsuits because they do not have "standing to sue." As you will read in Chapter 15, standing to sue is a basic judicial requirement. To have standing, a person must have suffered a harm, or have been threatened by a harm, from the action about which he or she is complaining. Whistleblowers in cases brought under the FCA do not have standing if they have not suffered harm, or been threatened with harm, from their employers' fraud against the government.

The controversy over the standing issue was resolved in 2000 by the United States Supreme Court. The case was brought by Jonathan Stevens, a former state attorney who accused a Vermont agency of fraudulently filling out time cards for work done under a federal grant. A key issue before the Supreme Court was whether Stevens had standing to sue, given that he did not claim that he suffered any injury as a result of the fraud. The Supreme Court held that Stevens acquired standing because, technically, the government had "assigned" (transferred) to Stevens its right to sue Vermont for the fraud.*

FOR CRITICAL ANALYSIS

Since 1986, whistleblowers have received about $500 million in lawsuits brought under the FCA. Do you agree with some of the act's critics that more of these dollars should go into the federal treasury? Why or why not?

*Vermont Agency of Natural Resources v. United States ex rel. Stevens, 529 U.S. 765 (2000).

---

convince the EPA to revise or redraft the regulation. Some parties might try to persuade the agency to withdraw the proposed regulation altogether. In any event, the EPA would consider these comments in drafting the final version of the regulation following the expiration of the comment period.

Once the final regulation has been published in the *Federal Register*, there is a sixty-day waiting period before the rule can be enforced. During that period, businesses, individuals, and state and local governments can ask Congress to overturn the regulation rather than having to sue the agency after the rule takes effect. After that sixty-day period has lapsed, the regulation might still be challenged in court by a party having a direct interest in the rule, such as a company that could expect to incur significant costs in complying with it. The company could argue that the rule misinterprets the

applicable law or goes beyond the agency's statutory purview. An allegation by the company that the EPA made a mistake in judgment probably would not be enough to convince the court to throw out the rule. The company instead would have to demonstrate that the rule itself was "arbitrary and capricious." To meet this standard, the company would have to show that the rule reflected a serious flaw in the EPA's judgment—such as a steadfast refusal by the agency to consider reasonable alternatives to its rule.

How agencies implement, administer, and enforce certain legislation has resulted in controversy on a number of occasions. For example, decisions made by agencies charged with implementing and administering the Endangered Species Act have led to protests from farmers, ranchers, and others, particularly in the western states, whose economic interests have been harmed by agency decisions. For a recent controversy over this act's implementation, see this chapter's *Which Side Are You On?* feature.

Negotiated Rulemaking

Since the end of World War II (1939–1945), companies, environmentalists, and other special interest groups have challenged government regulations in court. In the 1980s, however, the sheer wastefulness of attempting to regulate through litigation became more and more apparent. Today, a growing number of federal agencies encourage businesses and public-interest groups to become directly involved in the drafting of regulations. Agencies hope that such participation may help to prevent later courtroom battles over the meaning, applicability, and legal effect of the regulations.

Congress formally approved such a process, which is called *negotiated rulemaking*, in the Negotiated Rulemaking Act of 1990. The act authorizes agencies to allow those who will be affected by a new rule to participate in the rule-drafting process. If an agency chooses to engage in negotiated rulemaking, it must publish in the *Federal Register* the subject and scope of the rule to be developed, the parties that will be affected significantly by the rule, and other information. Representatives of the affected groups and other interested parties then may apply to be members of the negotiating committee. The agency is represented on the committee, but a neutral third party (not the agency) presides over the proceedings. Once the committee members have reached agreement on the terms of the proposed rule, notice of the proposed rule is published in the *Federal Register,* followed by a period for comments by any person or organization interested in the proposed rule. Negotiated rulemaking often is conducted under the condition that the participants promise not to challenge in court the outcome of any agreement to which they were a party.

Bureaucrats Are Policymakers

Theories of public administration once assumed that bureaucrats do not make policy decisions but only implement the laws and policies promulgated by the president and legislative bodies. Many people continue to make this assumption. A more realistic view, which is now held by most bureaucrats and elected officials, is that the agencies and departments of government play important roles in policymaking. As we have seen, many government rules, regulations, and programs are in fact initiated by the bureaucracy, based on its expertise and scientific studies. How a law passed by Congress eventually is translated into concrete action—from the forms to be filled out to decisions about who gets the benefits—usually is determined within each agency or department. Even the evaluation of whether a policy has achieved its purpose usually is based on studies that are commissioned and interpreted by the agency administering the program.

The bureaucracy's policymaking role often has been depicted by what traditionally has been called the "iron triangle." Recently, the concept of an "issue network" has been viewed as a more accurate description of the policymaking process.

Which Side Are You On?
Does the Endangered Species Act Cause More Harm Than It Prevents?

Congress passed the Endangered Species Act (ESA) almost three decades ago. Both Republicans and Democrats supported the legislation. The ESA's goal was straightforward: to protect species that are on the brink of extinction. The two agencies most responsible for enforcing this act are the U.S. Fish and Wildlife Service and the National Marine Fisheries Service. Their combined budgets increased from $163 million in 1999 to over $400 million in 2003. Clearly, the federal government appears to be serious about helping endangered species.

SAVING SPECIES IS ALWAYS WORTH THE COST

Proponents of the ESA argue that we do not know the full benefits of keeping species extant. Stated in another way, the civilized world should do everything possible to maintain the existing fish, wildlife, and flora because we may discover additional uses for them in years to come. Although some humans may suffer harm—for example, by the loss of jobs—because of certain environmental regulations, that is simply the price we have to pay to guarantee the biodiversity we may need for the future. Biodiversity may allow us to develop lifesaving cures, thereby benefiting future generations.

The U.S. Fish and Wildlife Service designated this beach outside Coos Bay, Oregon, as a critical habitat for the snowy plover shore bird in 1999, thus restricting most recreational uses of the beach. Coos County Commissioner John Griffith, seen here, and others filed a suit in federal court in 2002 challenging this designation. What issues must the courts weigh in deciding a case such as this? (AP Photo/Jeff Barnard)

Already, only 0.02 percent of all of the species that have existed since the beginning of earth still remain. How low do we want that number to go? Some things on this earth are priceless. We have to treat endangered species as such so that our children, our grandchildren, and generations to come will be able to enjoy the same diversity of animal, insect, and plant life that we now enjoy.

COST MUST BE TAKEN INTO ACCOUNT

While no one can argue against the goals of the ESA, some people are unhappy with its implementation. These critics believe that its costs are greater than its benefits. In particular, they cite the most recent National Academy of Sciences (NAS) investigation of the government's decision to cut off the flow of irrigation water from Klamath Lake in Oregon in the summer of 2001. That action, which affected irrigation water for more than one thousand farms in southern Oregon and northern California, was undertaken to save endangered suckerfish and local salmon. It was felt that the lake's water level was so low that further use of the lake water for irrigation would harm these fish. The results of this decision were devastating for many farmers. The NAS report claimed that the government did not base its decision on scientific investigation. According to the report, the low water level never really threatened the suckerfish, and it may actually have helped the salmon population.

Critics of the ESA argue that all actions have costs and that those costs must be examined. If we decide to save a particular species, what are the benefits and the costs of so doing? If one hundred thousand people must lose their jobs to save an insect, plant, or animal, perhaps there should be a nationwide policy debate before such action is undertaken.

WHAT'S YOUR POSITION?

Is it possible to calculate the benefits of saving species? If not, then how can we compare the benefits of saving species with the costs? How should we decide when, where, and how to save species?

GOING ONLINE

The National Endangered Species Act Reform Coalition—a group of farmers, developers, energy companies, and others—seeks to reform the Endangered Species Act. To learn more about the lobbying efforts to change the act, go to the coalition's Web site at **http://www.nesarc.org**. The Endangered Species Coalition is dedicated to the preservation of the ESA, as well as the species it protects. Visit this coalition's Web site at **http://www.stopextinction.org**.

Iron Triangle
The three-way alliance among legislators, bureaucrats, and interest groups to make or preserve policies that benefit their respective interests.

Iron Triangles.   In the past, scholars often described the bureaucracy's role in the policymaking process by using the concept of an **iron triangle**—a three-way alliance among legislators in Congress, bureaucrats, and interest groups. The presumption was that policy was developed depending on how it would affect each component of the triangle.

Consider as an example the development of agricultural policy. Congress, as one component of the triangle, includes two major committees concerned with agricultural policy, the House Committee on Agriculture and the Senate Committee on Agriculture, Nutrition, and Forestry. The Department of Agriculture, the second component of the triangle, has over 100,000 employees, plus thousands of contractors and consultants. Agricultural interest groups, the third component of the iron triangle in agricultural policymaking, consist of large and powerful associations, including the American Farm Bureau Federation, the National Cattleman's Association, the Corn Growers Association, and many others. These three components of the iron triangle work together, formally or informally, to create policy.

For example, the various agricultural interest groups lobby Congress to develop policies that benefit their groups' interests. Members of Congress cannot afford to ignore the wishes of interest groups because those groups are potential sources of voter support and campaign contributions. The legislators in Congress also work closely with the Department of Agriculture, which, in implementing a policy, can develop rules that benefit—or are not adverse to—certain industries or groups. The Department of Agriculture, in turn, supports policies that enhance the department's budget and powers. In this way, according to theory, agricultural policy is created that benefits all three components of the iron triangle. In 2002, the result was the Farm Security and Rural Investment Act, the largest agricultural subsidy act in U.S. history.

Issue Networks.   To be sure, the preceding discussion presents a much simplified picture of how the iron triangle works. With the growth in the complexity of government, policymaking also has become more complex. The bureaucracy is larger, Congress has more committees and subcommittees, and interest groups are more powerful than ever. Although iron triangles still exist, often they are inadequate as descriptions of how policy is actually made. Frequently, different interest groups concerned about a certain area of policy have conflicting demands, which makes agency decision making difficult. Additionally, divided government in recent years has meant that departments are pressured by the president to take one approach and by Congress to take another.

Many scholars now use the term *issue network* to describe the policymaking process. An **issue network** consists of a group of individuals or organizations that support a particular policy position on the environment, taxation, consumer safety, or some other issue. Typically, an issue network includes legislators and/or their staff members, interest groups, bureaucrats, scholars and other experts, and representatives from the media. Members of a particular issue network work together to influence the president, members of Congress, administrative agencies, and the courts to change public policy on a specific issue. Each policy issue may involve conflicting positions taken by two or more issue networks.

Issue Network
A group of individuals or organizations—which may consist of legislators or legislative staff members, interest group leaders, bureaucrats, the media, scholars, and other experts—that supports a particular policy position on a given issue, such as one relating to the environment, taxation, or consumer safety.

Congressional Control of the Bureaucracy

Although Congress is the ultimate repository of political power under the Constitution, many political pundits doubt whether Congress can meaningfully control the federal bureaucracy. These commentators forget that Congress, as already mentioned, specifies in an agency's "enabling legislation" the powers of the agency and the parameters within

which it can operate. Additionally, Congress has the power of the purse and could, theoretically, refuse to authorize or appropriate funds for a particular agency (see the discussion of the budgeting process in Chapter 12). Whether Congress would actually take such a drastic measure would depend on the circumstances. It is clear, however, that Congress does have the legal authority to decide whether to fund or not to fund administrative agencies. Congress also can exercise oversight over agencies through investigations and hearings.

Congressional committees conduct investigations and hold hearings to oversee an agency's actions, reviewing them to ensure compliance with congressional intentions. The agency's officers and employees can be ordered to testify before a committee about the details of an action. Through these oversight activities, especially in the questioning and commenting by members of the House or Senate during the hearings, Congress indicates its positions on specific programs and issues. Congress can also ask the General Accounting Office (GAO) to investigate particular agency actions. The Congressional Budget Office (CBO) also conducts oversight studies. The results of a GAO or CBO study may encourage Congress to hold further hearings or make changes in the law. Even if a law is not changed explicitly by Congress, however, the views expressed in any investigations and hearings are taken seriously by agency officials, who often act on those views.

In 1996, Congress passed the Congressional Review Act. The act created special procedures that could be used to express congressional disapproval of particular agency actions. These procedures have rarely been used, however. Since the act's passage, the executive branch has issued over 15,000 regulations. Yet only eight resolutions of disapproval have been introduced, and none of these was passed by either chamber.

The Bureaucracy: Why Is It Important Today?

Federal bureaucrats have taken over an often-misunderstood policymaking function. They write rules and regulations that affect virtually every aspect of your life, including, among other things, the cars that you drive, the food that you eat, the education benefits that you receive, the way that you build your house, the places that you can go hiking, and the chemicals that are allowed in what you drink.

While everyone believes that Congress makes the laws, these laws are usually so vaguely worded that the federal bureaucracy must interpret them. Through their rulemaking functions, regulatory agencies staffed by bureaucrats create much of the "law" in the United States. Most of the body of environmental law, for example, consists of regulations issued by the Environmental Protection Agency. Some federal agencies have even levied taxes—a power that presumably only Congress can exercise. The federal bureaucracy has become so powerful and so pervasive in our everyday lives that some political scientists have called it the fourth branch of government.

As mentioned in the chapter's opening *What If . . .* feature, virtually every modern administration has proposed plans to reform the federal bureaucracy. Underlying each proposed reform is the goal of making the bureaucracy more efficient and more responsive to the American public. Have such reforms succeeded? Most objective observers of government believe that the bureaucracy has not changed much in the last one hundred years. If anything, the federal bureaucracy is more entrenched than ever. Unlike private employees, government employees cannot easily be fired. As long as this remains our reality, the federal bureaucracy will not change much.

DID YOU KNOW . . .
That a Defense Department purchasing system designed to save money produced millions of dollars of overpriced spare parts, including a $76 screw and a $714 electrical bell?

MAKING A DIFFERENCE | What the Government Knows about You

The federal government collects billions of pieces of information on tens of millions of Americans each year. These data are stored in files and gigantic computers and often are exchanged among agencies. You probably have at least several federal records (for example, those in the Social Security Administration; the Internal Revenue Service; and, if you are a male, the Selective Service).

The FOIA

The 1966 Freedom of Information Act (FOIA) requires that the federal government release, at your request, any identifiable information it has in the administrative agencies of the executive branch. This information can be about you or about any other subject. Ten categories of material are exempted, however (classified material, confidential material dealing with trade secrets, internal personnel rules, personal medical files, and the like). To request material, you must write directly to the Freedom of Information Act officer at the agency in question

(say, the Department of Education). You must also have a relatively specific idea about the document or information you wish to obtain.

The Privacy Act

A second law, the Privacy Act of 1974, gives you access specifically to information the government may have collected about you. This is a very important law, because it allows you to review your records on file with federal agencies (for example, with the Federal Bureau of Investigation) and to check those records for possible inaccuracies. Cases do exist in which the records of two people with similar or the same names have become confused. In some cases, innocent persons have had the criminal records of another person erroneously inserted into their files.

If you wish to look at any records or find out if an agency has a record on you, write to the agency head or Privacy Act officer, and address your letter to the specific agency. State that "under the provisions of the Privacy

Act of 1974, 5 U.S.C. 522a, I hereby request a copy of (or access to) _____." Then describe the record that you wish to investigate.

Contact the ACLU

The American Civil Liberties Union (ACLU) has published a manual, called *Your Right to Government Information,* that guides you through the steps of obtaining information from the federal government. The manual includes sample requests and appeal letters and addresses for sending requests. You can order it online by clicking on the link to the bookstore at the following Web site:

**http://www.aclu.org/
store/storemain.cfm**

Or you can order the manual from the ACLU at the following address:

ACLU Publications
P.O. Box 4713
Trenton, NJ 08650-4713
1-800-775-ACLU

Key Terms

acquisitive model 424

administrative agency 425

bureaucracy 423

cabinet department 428

capture 430

Civil Service Commission 435

enabling legislation 440

government corporation 431

Government in the Sunshine Act 436

Hatch Act (Political Activities Act) 435

independent executive agency 428

independent regulatory agency 428

iron triangle 444

issue network 444

line organization 428

merit system 434

monopolistic model 424

natural aristocracy 434

Pendleton Act (Civil Service Reform Act) 435

privatization 438

spoils system 434

sunset legislation 438

Weberian model 424

whistleblower 439

Chapter Summary

1 Presidents have long complained about their inability to control the federal bureaucracy. There is no reference to the bureaucracy itself in the Constitution, but Article II gives the president the power to appoint officials to execute the laws of the United States. Most scholars cite Article II as the constitutional basis for the federal bureaucracy.

2 Bureaucracies are rigid hierarchical organizations in which the tasks and powers of lower-level employees are defined clearly. Job specialties and extensive procedural rules set the standards for behavior. Bureaucracies are the primary form of organization of most major corporations and universities.

3 Several theories have been offered to explain bureaucracies. The Weberian model posits that bureaucracies have developed into centralized hierarchical structures in response to the increasing demands placed on governments by their citizens. The acquisitive model views top-level bureaucrats as pressing for ever-greater funding, staffs, and privileges to augment their own sense of power and security. The monopolistic model focuses on the environment in which most government bureaucracies operate, stating that bureaucracies are inefficient and excessively costly to operate because they often have no competitors.

4 Since the founding of the United States, the federal bureaucracy has grown from 50 to about 2.7 million employees (excluding the military). Federal, state, and local employees together make up over 15 percent of the nation's civilian labor force. The federal bureaucracy consists of fourteen cabinet departments, as well as numerous independent executive agencies, independent regulatory agencies, and government corporations. These entities enjoy varying degrees of autonomy, visibility, and political support.

5 A self-sustaining federal bureaucracy of career civil servants was formed during Thomas Jefferson's presidency.

Andrew Jackson implemented a spoils system through which he appointed his own political supporters. A civil service based on professionalism and merit was the goal of the Civil Service Reform Act of 1883. Concerns that the civil service be freed from the pressures of politics prompted the passage of the Hatch Act in 1939. Significant changes in the administration of the civil service were made by the Civil Service Reform Act of 1978.

6 There have been many attempts to make the federal bureaucracy more open, efficient, and responsive to the needs of U.S. citizens. The most important reforms have included sunshine and sunset laws, privatization, strategies to provide incentives for increased productivity and efficiency, and protection for whistle-blowers.

7 Congress delegates much of its authority to federal agencies when it creates new laws. The bureaucrats who run these agencies may become important policymakers, because Congress has neither the time nor the technical expertise to oversee the administration of its laws. In the agency rulemaking process, a proposed regulation is published. A comment period follows, during which interested parties may offer suggestions for changes. Because companies and other organizations have challenged many regulations in court, federal agencies now are authorized to allow parties that will be affected by new regulations to participate in the rule-drafting process.

8 Congress exerts ultimate control over all federal agencies, because it controls the federal government's purse strings. It also establishes the general guidelines by which regulatory agencies must abide. The appropriations process may also provide a way to send messages of approval or disapproval to particular agencies, as do congressional hearings and investigations relating to agency actions.

Selected Print and Media Resources

SUGGESTED READINGS

Bazerman, Max H., *et al.* *"You Can't Enlarge the Pie": The Psychology of Ineffective Government.* Cambridge, Mass.: Basic Books, 2001. The authors apply concepts about decision making taught in America's business schools to the world of government institutions, arguing that only when government leaders free themselves from specific psychological barriers will they make better policy choices.

Foerstel, Herbert N. *Freedom of Information and the Right to Know: The Origins and Applications of the Freedom of Information Act.* Westport, Conn.: Greenwood Publishing Group, 1999. The author, a strong advocate for freer access to information in the hands of the government, explores the origins of the American belief that citizens in a democracy have a right to know what their

government is doing. He looks closely at the Freedom of Information Act, its use, and the continuing impediments to the "right to know."

Heller, Joseph. *Catch 22.* New York: Simon & Schuster, 1961. Joseph Heller's classic novel is often considered an antiwar or anti-military novel, but its satirical humor is also directed at the culture, corruption, and contradictions of bureaucratic institutions generally. Its themes still resonate forty years after its first publication, and its title has entered the English language denoting a person trapped by at least two bad choices.

Jreisat, Jamil. *Comparative Public Administration.* Boulder Colo.: Westview Press, 2002. The author presents a comprehensive view of how globalism, information technology, and democratization are reshaping bureaucratic institutions around the world.

Reinhart, Bruce A. *In the Middle of a Muddle: How Not to Reinvent Government*. Washington, D.C.: Brookings Institution Press, 1999. The author offers an insider's perspective into the workings of the Department of Education. He also illustrates what can go wrong when political appointees try to restructure organizations that they do not understand.

Stivers, Camilla, ed. *Democracy, Bureaucracy, and the Study of Administration*. Boulder, Colo.: Westview Press, 2001. Should public institutions strive to be more effective or more efficient? The question may be unresolvable, but its exploration in this anthology leads to a better understanding of public administration.

MEDIA RESOURCES

Brazil (1985)—A 1985 film classic, directed by Terry Gilliam and starring Jonathan Pryce, about totalitarian bureaucracy. A quiet government clerk tries to correct an administrative error and in the process becomes an enemy of the state. It is a visually stunning portrayal of a future characterized by misery and wretchedness, punctuated by dark humor.

Men in Black—A 1997 science-fiction comedy about an unofficial government agency that regulates the immigration of aliens from outer space who are living on earth.

Missiles of October—A movie retelling the events of October 1962, when the Kennedy administration decided to blockade Cuba to force the Soviet Union to remove its missiles from Cuba. The 1974 film, starring William Devane and Ralph Bellamy, gives an excellent inside view of policymaking involving the State Department, the Defense Department, and the president.

1984—A 1984 adaptation of George Orwell's well-known novel about the bureaucratic world of the future, starring John Hurt and Richard Burton; a superb fable of government versus individual values.

Your CD-ROM Resources

In addition to the chapter content containing hot links, the following resources are available on the CD-ROM:

- **Internet Activities**—The Government Corporation: AMTRAK, the Government Regulatory Agency: OSHA.

- **Critical Thinking Exercises**—Whistleblowers, the Endangered Species Act.

- **Self-Check on Important Themes**—Can You Answer These?

- **Animated Figure**—Figure 14–2, "Government Employment at the Federal, State, and Local Levels."

- **Video**—*Congress and Bureaucratic Rulemaking.*

- **Public Opinion Data**—Find contrasting opinions on the "False Claims Act" and policies that would make it easier to fire civil servants.

- **InfoTrac Exercise**—"The Human Side of Public Administration."

- **Simulation**—You Are There!

- **Participation Exercise**—Pick a specific program of local, state, or national government to research.

- **MicroCase Exercise**—"By the Numbers: How Much Money Does the Public Think the Government Wastes?"

- **Additional Resources**—All court cases, the Pendleton Act.

e-mocracy

E-Government

As mentioned elsewhere, all federal government agencies (and virtually all state agencies as well) now have Web pages. Citizens can access these Web sites to find information and forms that, in the past, could normally be obtained only by going to a regional or local branch of the agency. For example, if you or a member of your family wants to learn about Social Security benefits available on retirement, you can simply access the Social Security Administration's Web site to find that information. A number of federal government agencies have also been active in discovering and prosecuting fraud perpetrated on citizens via the Internet.

Logging On

Numerous links to many federal agencies and information on the federal government can be found at the U.S. government's official Web site. Go to

http://www.firstgov.gov

The Federal Web Locator is an excellent site to access if you want to find information on the bureaucracy. Its URL is

http://www.infoctr.edu/fwl

You may want to examine two publications available from the federal government to learn more about the federal bureaucracy. The first is the *Federal Register*, which is the official publication for executive-branch documents. The second is the *United States Government Manual*, which describes the origins, purposes, and administrators of every federal department and agency. Both publications are available online at the following Web site:

http://www.access.gpo.gov/
su_docs/index.html

If you want to find telephone numbers for government agencies and personnel, you can go to

http://www.firstgov.gov/Agencies.shtml

"The Plum Book," which lists the bureaucratic positions that can be filled by presidential appointment, is online at

http://www.louisville.edu/library/ekstrom/
govpubs/federal/plum.html

Using the Internet for Political Analysis

Be a critical consumer of government information on the World Wide Web. Go to the Center for Information Law and Policy at

http://www.firstgov.gov

and compare the Web pages of at least three federal departments or agencies. Answer the following questions for each Web page:

1. Do you get the basic information about the department or agency, including its goals, locations, size, budget, and accessibility to citizens?

2. Can you tell from the page who the primary clients of the agency are? For example, are the agency's primary clients governments, ordinary citizens, businesses, or labor unions?

3. Is the page well designed, up to date, and easy for the average citizen to use?

4. What is the most valuable information on the page for you?

CHAPTER 15
The Judiciary

BACKGROUND

The nine justices who sit on the bench of the Supreme Court are not elected to their posts. Rather, they are appointed by the president (and confirmed by the Senate). They also hold their offices for life, barring gross misconduct. Nevertheless, these justices are among the most important "policymakers" of this nation because they have the final say on how the U.S. Constitution—the "supreme law of the Land"—should be interpreted.

In recent years, the Supreme Court has been strongly criticized by some for being too remote from the real world of politics and for making policy decisions on issues without regard for the practical consequences of those decisions. Would the justices act differently if they were elected and therefore had to campaign for their positions on the Court?

WHAT IF SUPREME COURT JUSTICES HAD TO CAMPAIGN?

Under the existing system, once approved by the Senate and seated on the high court's bench, a justice is free to decide cases as he or she wishes. Because they hold their offices for life, Supreme Court justices do not need to worry about job security. If, however, the justices were elected and had to campaign for election and reelection, the situation could change dramatically.

For one thing, very likely the justices would have to devote a substantial amount of their time to their campaigns, just as members of Congress do. This would take time away from their judicial work, and decisions might receive significantly less deliberation than under the current system. Additionally, if the justices had to run for reelection to maintain their seats on the high court, it is only natural that public opinion and particularly the wishes of major campaign contributors would come into play.

INTEREST GROUPS AND CAMPAIGN COSTS

If state judicial campaigns and elections can serve as a guide, it is likely that interest groups that made sizable contributions to the justices' campaigns would wield at least some influence over the justices' decisions. In the thirty-nine states where members of the judiciary are elected, judges increasingly are using their discretion in deciding cases to satisfy public opinion and campaign contributors. Typically, the largest donors to state judicial campaigns are attorneys, political parties, or interest groups involved in civil litigation before the judges they are helping to elect.

In a survey of Texas judges sponsored by that state's supreme court, 48 percent of the judges responded that campaign contributions were "fairly influential" or "very influential" in guiding their deci-sions. In fact, the degree to which elected state judges are influenced by their political and financial supporters has caused some to claim that justice is increasingly "for sale."

POLITICAL IDEOLOGY

Humorist Finley Peter Dunne once said that "th' Supreme Court follows th' iliction returns." In other words, Democratic presidents tend to appoint liberal judges and justices to federal benches, and Republican presidents tend to appoint conservative judges and justices. Ultimately, then, the federal judiciary, including the Supreme Court, does change in response to election returns, but this process takes time.

Justices on the nation's highest court, because they are at the top of the judicial career ladder, sometimes end up sitting on the Supreme Court for decades. If these justices were elected, the ideological complexion of the Court probably would change much more quickly. A voting bloc of liberal or conservative justices might be short-lived, with new alliances being formed after the next election. As a result, the decisions made by the Court, as the final interpreter of the Constitution, might not be very "final." If the next election brought in justices with different ideological views, the Court could overturn the precedents set by the Court during the previous term. Of course, staggered terms could be used, as in the Senate, to ensure more continuity in judicial decision making.

FOR CRITICAL ANALYSIS

1. Should Supreme Court justices be influenced by public opinion when making their decisions? Why or why not?
2. If Supreme Court justices were elected, would their decisions be less authoritative? Explain.

As indicated in this chapter's opening *What If . . .* feature, the justices of the Supreme Court are not elected but rather are appointed by the president and confirmed by the Senate. The same is true for all other federal court judges. This fact does not mean that the federal judiciary is apolitical, however. Indeed, our courts play a larger role in making public policy than courts in any other country in the world today.

As Alexis de Tocqueville, a nineteenth-century French commentator on American society, noted, "scarcely any political question arises in the United States that is not resolved, sooner or later, into a judicial question."[1] Our judiciary forms part of our political process. The instant that judges interpret the law, they become actors in the political arena—policymakers working within a political institution. As such, the most important political force within our judiciary is the United States Supreme Court.

How do courts make policy? Why do the federal courts play such an important role in American government? The answers to these questions lie, in part, in our colonial heritage. Most of American law is based on the English system, particularly the English common law tradition. In that tradition, the decisions made by judges constitute an important source of law.

The Common Law Tradition

In 1066, the Normans conquered England, and William the Conqueror and his successors began the process of unifying the country under their rule. One of the ways they did this was to establish the king's courts, or *curiae regis*. Before the conquest, disputes had been settled according to local custom. The king's courts sought to establish a common or uniform set of rules for the whole country. As the number of courts and cases increased, portions of the most important decisions of each year were gathered together and recorded in *Year Books*. Judges settling disputes similar to ones that had been decided before used the *Year Books* as the basis for their decisions. If a case was unique, judges had to create new laws, but they based their decisions on the general principles suggested by earlier cases. The body of judge-made law that developed under this system is still used today and is known as the **common law.**

The practice of deciding new cases with reference to former decisions—that is, according to **precedent**—became a cornerstone of the English and American judicial systems and is embodied in the doctrine of **stare decisis** (pronounced *ster*-ay dih-*si*-ses), a Latin phrase that means "to stand on decided cases." The doctrine of *stare decisis* obligates judges to follow the precedents set previously by their own courts or by higher courts that have authority over them.

For example, a lower state court in California would be obligated to follow a precedent set by the California Supreme Court. That lower court, however, would not be obligated to follow a precedent set by the supreme court of another state, because each state court system is independent. Of course, when the United States Supreme Court decides an issue, all of the nation's other courts are obligated to abide by the Court's decision—because the Supreme Court is the highest court in the land.

The doctrine of *stare decisis* provides a basis for judicial decision making in all countries that have common law systems. Today, the United States, Britain, and thirteen other countries have common law systems. Generally, those countries that were once colonies of Great Britain, including Australia, Canada, India, and New Zealand, have retained their English common law heritage since they achieved independence.

Common Law

Judge-made law that originated in England from decisions shaped according to prevailing custom. Decisions were applied to similar situations and gradually became common to the nation.

Precedent

A court rule bearing on subsequent legal decisions in similar cases. Judges rely on precedents in deciding cases.

Stare Decisis

To stand on decided cases; the judicial policy of following precedents established by past decisions.

---

[1] Alexis de Tocqueville, *Democracy in America* (New York: Harper & Row, 1966), p. 248.

Sources of American Law

The body of American law includes the federal and state constitutions, statutes passed by legislative bodies, administrative law, and case law—the legal principles expressed in court decisions.

Constitutions

The constitutions of the federal government and the states set forth the general organization, powers, and limits of government. The U.S. Constitution is the supreme law of the land. A law in violation of the Constitution, no matter what its source, may be declared unconstitutional and thereafter cannot be enforced. Similarly, the state constitutions are supreme within their respective borders (unless they conflict with the U.S. Constitution or federal laws and treaties made in accordance with it). The Constitution thus defines the political playing field on which state and federal powers are reconciled. The idea that the Constitution should be supreme in certain matters stemmed from widespread dissatisfaction with the weak federal government that had existed previously under the Articles of Confederation adopted in 1781.

Statutes and Administrative Regulations

Although the English common law provides the basis for both our civil and criminal legal systems, statutes (laws enacted by legislatures) increasingly have become important in defining the rights and obligations of individuals. Federal statutes may relate to any subject that is a concern of the federal government and may cover areas ranging from hazardous waste to federal taxation. State statutes include criminal codes, commercial laws, and laws relating to a variety of other matters. Cities, counties, and other local political bodies also pass statutes, which are called ordinances. These ordinances may deal with such issues as zoning proposals and public safety. Rules and regulations issued by administrative agencies are another source of law. Today, much of the work of the courts consists of interpreting these laws and regulations and applying them to circumstances in cases before the courts.

Case Law

Case Law
The rules and principles announced in court decisions. Case law includes judicial interpretations of common law principles and doctrines as well as interpretations of constitutional law, statutory law, and administrative law.

Because we have a common law tradition, in which the doctrine of *stare decisis* plays an important role, the decisions rendered by the courts also form an important body of law, collectively referred to as **case law.** Case law includes judicial interpretations of common law principles and doctrines as well as interpretations of the types of law just mentioned—constitutional provisions, statutes, and administrative agency regulations. As you learned in previous chapters, it is up to the courts, and particularly the Supreme Court, to decide what a constitutional provision or a statutory phrase means. In doing so, the courts, in effect, establish law. (We will discuss this policy-making function of the courts in more detail later in the chapter.)

The Federal Court System

The United States has a dual court system. There are state courts and federal courts. Each of the fifty states, as well as the District of Columbia, has its own fully developed, independent system of courts, which we will examine in Chapter 18. Here we focus on the federal courts. (For a discussion of additional federal courts, see this chapter's *America's Security* feature.)

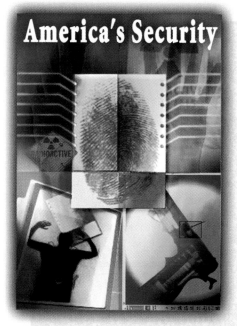

America's Security

Since the terrorist attacks on September 11, 2001, many Americans are rethinking their safety and what they need to do to protect it. The federal government, however, has been concerned with protecting the nation against terrorism for some time. Among other things, the government's

Does National Security Require Secret Courts?

efforts to curb terrorism have involved the establishment of "secret courts."

THE FISA COURT

The federal government created the first secret court in 1978. In that year, Congress passed the Foreign Intelligence Surveillance Act (FISA), which established a court to hear requests for warrants for the surveillance of suspected spies. The subjects might include people who have been released from custody or who are suspected of potential terrorist activity. Officials can request warrants without having to reveal to the suspect or to the public the information used to justify the warrant. Of the thousands of requests for warrants that officials have submitted to the FISA court, the court has approved almost all of them. There is no public access to the court's proceedings or records.

In the aftermath of the terrorist attacks on September 11, 2001, the Bush administration expanded the powers of the FISA court. Previously, the FISA allowed secret domestic surveillance only if "the purpose" was foreign intelligence. Recent amendments to the FISA changed this wording to "a significant purpose"—meaning that warrants may now be requested to obtain evidence that can be used in criminal trials. Additionally, the court has the authority to approve physical as well as electronic searches, which means that officials may search a suspect's property without obtaining a warrant in open court and without notifying the subject.

ALIEN "REMOVAL COURTS"

The FISA court is not the only court in which suspects have reduced rights. In response to the Oklahoma City bombing in 1996, Congress passed the Anti-Terrorism Act. The act included a provision creating an alien "removal court" to hear evidence against suspected "alien terrorists." The judges rule on whether there is probable cause for deportation. If so, a public deportation proceeding is held in a U.S. district court. The prosecution does not need to follow criminal procedures that normally apply in criminal cases. The defendant also does not have access to the evidence that the prosecution used to secure the hearing.

FOR CRITICAL ANALYSIS

Do you think that exceptions should be made to constitutional rights if it means greater national security?

Mazen Al-Najjar, a Palestinian academic who once taught at the University of South Florida, spent more than three years in federal prison on the basis of secret evidence. He was released in December 2000 but was arrested again in November 2001 and ordered deported because of alleged ties to terrorists, though he was never charged with a crime. Al-Najjar's case drew angry protests from other Arab Americans, as seen here. Do you think that the government should be able to deport noncitizens based on evidence to which the deportees have never had access? (AP Photo/Chris O'Meara)

Basic Judicial Requirements

In either court system, state or federal, before a case can be brought before a court, certain requirements must be met. Two important requirements relate to jurisdiction and standing to sue.

Jurisdiction

The authority of a court to decide certain cases. Not all courts have the authority to decide all cases. Where a case arises and what its subject matter is are two jurisdictional factors.

Federal Question

A question that pertains to the U.S. Constitution, acts of Congress, or treaties. A federal question provides a basis for federal jurisdiction.

Diversity of Citizenship

A basis for federal court jurisdiction over a lawsuit that involves citizens of different states or (more rarely) citizens of a U.S. state and citizens or subjects of a foreign country. The amount in controversy must be at least $75,000 before a federal court can take jurisdiction in such cases.

Jurisdiction.   A state court can exercise **jurisdiction** (the authority of the court to hear and decide a case) over the residents of a particular geographic area, such as a county or district. A state's highest court, or supreme court, has jurisdictional authority over all residents within the state. Because the Constitution established a federal government with limited powers, federal jurisdiction is also limited.

Article III, Section 1, of the U.S. Constitution limits the jurisdiction of the federal courts to cases that involve either a federal question or diversity of citizenship. A **federal question** arises when a case is based, at least in part, on the U.S. Constitution, a treaty, or a federal law. A person who claims that her or his rights under the Constitution, such as the right to free speech, have been violated could bring a case in a federal court. **Diversity of citizenship** exists when the parties to a lawsuit are from different states or (more rarely) when the suit involves a U.S. citizen and a government or citizen of a foreign country. The amount in controversy must be at least $75,000 before a federal court can take jurisdiction in a diversity case, however.

Standing to Sue.   Another basic judicial requirement is standing to sue, or a sufficient "stake" in a matter to justify bringing suit. The party bringing a lawsuit must have suffered a harm, or have been threatened by a harm, as a result of the action that led to the dispute in question. Standing to sue also requires that the controversy at issue be a justiciable controversy. As you learned in Chapter 12, a justiciable controversy is a controversy that is real and substantial, as opposed to hypothetical or academic. In other words, a court will not give advisory opinions on hypothetical questions.

Types of Federal Courts

As you can see in Figure 15–1, the federal court system is basically a three-tiered model consisting of (1) U.S. district courts and various specialized courts of limited

FIGURE 15–1

The Federal Court System

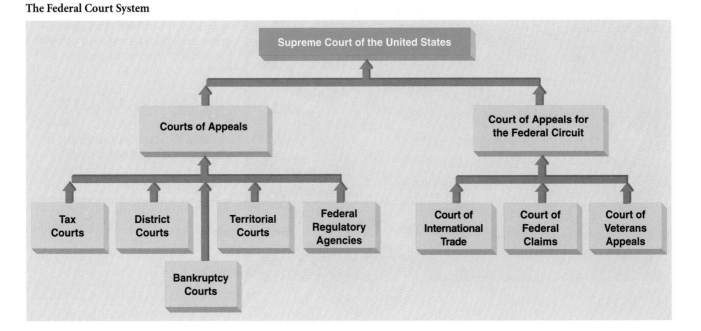

jurisdiction (not all of the latter are shown in the figure), (2) intermediate U.S. courts of appeals, and (3) the United States Supreme Court.

U.S. District Courts. The U.S. district courts are trial courts. **Trial courts** are what their name implies—courts in which trials are held and testimony is taken. The U.S. district courts are courts of **general jurisdiction,** meaning that they can hear cases involving a broad array of issues. Federal cases involving most matters typically are heard in district courts. (The other courts on the lower tier of the model shown in Figure 15–1 are courts of **limited jurisdiction,** meaning that they can try cases involving only certain types of claims, such as tax claims or bankruptcy petitions.)

There is at least one federal district court in every state. The number of judicial districts can vary over time, primarily owing to population changes and corresponding case loads. Currently, there are ninety-four federal judicial districts. A party who is dissatisfied with the decision of a district court judge can appeal the case to the appropriate U.S. court of appeals, or federal **appellate court.** Figure 15–2 shows the jurisdictional boundaries of the district courts (which are state boundaries, unless otherwise indicated by dotted lines within a state), as well as of the U.S. courts of appeals.

U.S. Courts of Appeals. There are thirteen U.S. courts of appeals—also referred to as U.S. circuit courts of appeals. Twelve of these courts, including the U.S. Court of Appeals for the District of Columbia, hear appeals from the federal district courts

Trial Court
The court in which most cases usually begin and in which questions of fact are examined.

General Jurisdiction
Exists when a court's authority to hear cases is not significantly restricted. A court of general jurisdiction normally can hear a broad range of cases.

Limited Jurisdiction
Exists when a court's authority to hear cases is restricted to certain types of claims, such as tax claims or bankruptcy petitions.

Appellate Court
A court having jurisdiction to review cases and issues that were originally tried in lower courts.

FIGURE 15–2

Geographic Boundaries of Federal District Courts and Circuit Courts of Appeals

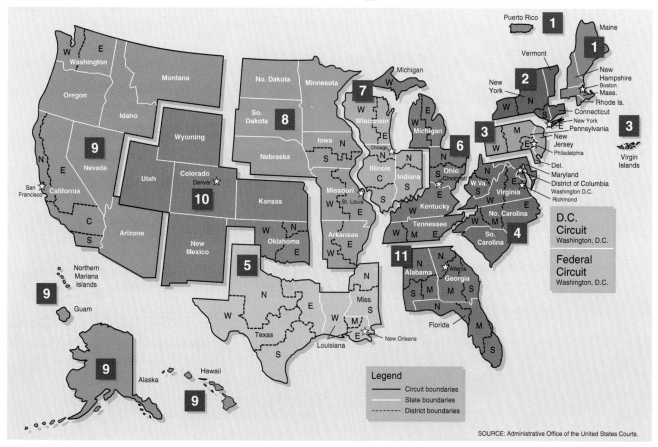

SOURCE: Administrative Office of the United States Courts.

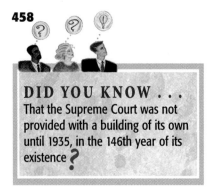

located within their respective judicial circuits (geographic areas over which they exercise jurisdiction). The Court of Appeals for the Thirteenth Circuit, called the Federal Circuit, has national appellate jurisdiction over certain types of cases, such as cases involving patent law and those in which the U.S. government is a defendant.

Note that when an appellate court reviews a case decided in a district court, the appellate court does not conduct another trial. Rather, a panel of three or more judges reviews the record of the case on appeal, which includes a transcript of the trial proceedings, and determines whether the trial court committed an error. Usually, appellate courts do not look at questions of *fact* (such as whether a party did, in fact, commit a certain action, such as burning a flag) but at questions of *law* (such as whether the act of flag burning is a form of speech protected by the First Amendment to the Constitution). An appellate court will challenge a trial court's finding of fact only when the finding is clearly contrary to the evidence presented at trial or when there is no evidence to support the finding.

A party can petition the United States Supreme Court to review an appellate court's decision. The likelihood that the Supreme Court will grant the petition is slim, however, because the Court reviews only a very few of the cases decided by the appellate courts. This means that decisions made by appellate judges usually are final.

The United States Supreme Court.   The highest level of the three-tiered model of the federal court system is the United States Supreme Court. When the Supreme Court came into existence in 1789, it had five justices. In the following years, more justices were added. At one point, in 1863, ten justices sat on the Supreme Court bench. Since 1869, however, there have been nine justices on the Court.

According to the language of Article III of the U.S. Constitution, there is only one national Supreme Court. All other courts in the federal system are considered "inferior." Congress is empowered to create other inferior courts as it deems necessary. The inferior courts that Congress has created include the district courts, the federal courts of appeals, and the federal courts of limited jurisdiction.

"Do you ever have one of those days when everything seems un-Constitutional?"

Although the Supreme Court can exercise original jurisdiction (that is, act as a trial court) in certain cases, such as those affecting foreign diplomats and those in which a state is a party, most of its work is as an appellate court. The Court hears appeals not only from the federal appellate courts but also from the highest state courts. Note, though, that the United States Supreme Court can review a state supreme court decision only if a federal question is involved. Because of its importance in the federal court system, we will look more closely at the Supreme Court in the next section.

Parties to Lawsuits

In most lawsuits, the parties are the plaintiff (the person or organization that initiates the lawsuit) and the defendant (the person or organization against whom the lawsuit is brought). There may be numerous plaintiffs and defendants in a single lawsuit. In the last several decades, many lawsuits have been brought by interest groups (see Chapter 8). Interest groups play an important role in our judicial system, because they **litigate**—bring to trial—or assist in litigating most cases of racial or gender-based discrimination, virtually all civil liberties cases, and more than one-third of the cases involving business matters. Interest groups also file *amicus curiae* (pronounced ah-*mee*-kous *kur*-ee-eye) **briefs**, or "friend of the court" briefs, in more than 50 percent of these kinds of cases.

Sometimes, interest groups or other plaintiffs will bring a **class-action suit**, in which whatever the court decides will affect all members of a class similarly situated (such as users of a particular product manufactured by the defendant in the lawsuit). The strategy of class-action lawsuits was pioneered by such groups as the National Association for the Advancement of Colored People (NAACP), the Legal Defense Fund, and the Sierra Club, whose members believed that the courts—rather than Congress—would offer the most sympathetic forum for their views.

Litigate
To engage in a legal proceeding or seek relief in a court of law; to carry on a lawsuit.

Amicus Curiae Brief
A brief (a document containing a legal argument supporting a desired outcome in a particular case) filed by a third party, or *amicus curiae* (Latin for "friend of the court"), who is not directly involved in the litigation but who has an interest in the outcome of the case.

Class-Action Suit
A lawsuit filed by an individual seeking damages for "all persons similarly situated."

Counsel questions a witness as the judge and jury look on. Most jury trials have between six and twelve jurors. Some trials are held without juries. (John Neubauer/PhotoEdit)

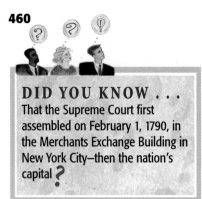

Procedural Rules

Both the federal and the state courts have established procedural rules that shape the litigation process. These rules are designed to protect the rights and interests of the parties, to ensure that the litigation proceeds in a fair and orderly manner, and to identify the issues that must be decided by the court—thus saving court time and costs. Court decisions may also apply to trial procedures. For example, the Supreme Court has held that the parties' attorneys cannot discriminate against prospective jurors on the basis of race or gender. Some lower courts have also held that people cannot be excluded from juries because of their sexual orientation or religion.

The parties must comply with procedural rules and with any orders given by the judge during the course of the litigation. When a party does not follow a court's order, the court can cite him or her for contempt. A party who commits *civil* contempt (failing to comply with a court's order for the benefit of another party to the proceeding) can be taken into custody, fined, or both, until the party complies with the court's order. A party who commits *criminal* contempt (obstructing the administration of justice or bringing the court into disrespect) also can be taken into custody and fined but cannot avoid punishment by complying with a previous order.

Throughout this text, you have read about how technology is affecting all areas of government. The judiciary is no exception. Today's courts are becoming increasingly "wired," and there is little doubt that in the future we will see more court proceedings being conducted via the Internet.

The Supreme Court at Work

The Supreme Court, by law, begins its regular annual term on the first Monday in October and usually adjourns in late June or early July of the next year. Special sessions may be held after the regular term is over, but only a few cases are decided in this way. More commonly, cases are carried over until the next regular session.

Of the total number of cases that are decided each year, those reviewed by the Supreme Court represent less than one-half of 1 percent. Included in these, however, are decisions that profoundly affect our lives. In recent years, the United States Supreme Court has decided issues involving capital punishment, affirmative action programs, religious freedom, assisted suicide, abortion, busing, term limits for congresspersons, sexual harassment, pornography, states' rights, limits on federal jurisdiction, and numerous other matters with significant consequences for the nation. Because the Supreme Court exercises a great deal of discretion over the types of cases it hears, it can influence the nation's policies by issuing decisions in some types of cases and refusing to hear appeals in others, thereby allowing lower court decisions to stand.

Which Cases Reach the Supreme Court?

Many people are surprised to learn that in a typical case, there is no absolute right of appeal to the United States Supreme Court. The Court's appellate jurisdiction is almost entirely discretionary—the Court can choose which cases it will decide. The justices never explain their reasons for hearing certain cases and not others, so it is difficult to predict which case or type of case the Court might select. Chief Justice William Rehnquist, in his description of the selection process in *The Supreme Court: How It Was, How It Is,*[2] said that the decision of whether or not to accept a case "strikes me as a rather subjective decision, made up in part of intuition and in part of legal judgment."

INFOTRAC ®
COLLEGE EDITION

For more information about the Supreme Court, use the term "United States Supreme Court" in the Subject guide.

---

[2] William H. Rehnquist, *The Supreme Court: How It Was, How It Is* (New York: Morrow, 1987).

Factors That Bear on the Decision.   Factors that bear on the decision include whether a legal question has been decided differently by various lower courts and needs resolution by the highest court, whether a lower court's decision conflicts with an existing Supreme Court ruling, and whether the issue could have significance beyond the parties to the dispute. In its 2002–2003 term, the Court decided to review cases involving such issues as whether antiabortion protesters can be charged with criminal extortion and racketeering and whether convicted felons who have served their time in prison can appeal to the courts to have the prohibition against possessing firearms lifted.

Another factor is whether the solicitor general is pressuring the Court to take a case. The solicitor general, a high-ranking presidential appointee within the Justice Department, represents the national government in the Supreme Court and promotes presidential policies in the federal courts. He or she decides what cases the government should ask the Supreme Court to review and what position the government

In her chambers, Justice Ruth Bader Ginsburg works on her case load with one of her law clerks. Each justice has four law clerks, who typically are culled from the "best and the brightest" graduates from U.S. law schools. Some critics of the Supreme Court's practices argue that the clerks have too much power and influence over the Court's decision making. (Paul Conklin/PhotoEdit)

should take in cases before the Court. The influence wielded by solicitors general over the Court's decision making has led some to refer to the solicitor general as the "Tenth Justice."

Granting Petitions for Review.   If the Court decides to grant a petition for review, it will issue a **writ of *certiorari*** (pronounced sur-shee-uh-*rah*-ree). The writ orders a lower court to send the Supreme Court a record of the case for review. More than 90 percent of the petitions for writs of *certiorari* are denied. A denial is not a decision on the merits of a case, nor does it indicate agreement with the lower court's opinion. (The judgment of the lower court remains in force, however.) Therefore, denial of the writ has no value as a precedent. The Court will not issue a writ unless at least four justices approve of it. This is called the **rule of four.**[3]

Deciding Cases

Once the Supreme Court grants *certiorari* in a particular case, the justices do extensive research on the legal issues and facts involved in the case. (Of course, some preliminary research was necessary before deciding to grant the petition for review.) Each justice is entitled to four law clerks, who undertake much of the research and preliminary drafting necessary for the justice to form an opinion.[4]

The Court normally does not hear any evidence, as is true with all appeals courts. The Court's consideration of a case is based on the abstracts, the record, and the briefs. The attorneys are permitted to present **oral arguments.** The Court hears oral arguments on Monday, Tuesday, Wednesday, and sometimes Thursday, usually for seven two-week sessions scattered from the first week in October to the end of April or the first week in May. All statements and the justices' questions are tape-recorded during these sessions. Unlike the practice in most courts, lawyers addressing the Supreme Court can be (and often are) questioned by the justices at any time during oral argument.

The justices meet to discuss and vote on cases in conferences held each Wednesday and Friday throughout the term. In these conferences, in addition to deciding cases currently before the Court, the justices decide which new petitions for *certiorari* to grant. These conferences take place in the oak-paneled chamber and are strictly private—no stenographers, tape recorders, or video cameras are allowed. Two pages used to be in attendance to wait on the justices while they were in conference, but fear of information leaks caused the Court to stop this practice.[5]

Decisions and Opinions

When the Court has reached a decision, its opinion is written. The **opinion** contains the Court's ruling on the issue or issues presented, the reasons for its decision, the rules of law that apply, and other information. In many cases, the decision of the lower court is **affirmed,** resulting in the enforcement of that court's judgment or decree. If the Supreme Court feels that a reversible error was committed during the trial or that the jury was instructed improperly, however, the decision will be **reversed.** Sometimes the case will be **remanded** (sent back to the court that originally heard the case) for a new trial or other proceeding. For example, a lower court

---

Writ of *Certiorari*

An order issued by a higher court to a lower court to send up the record of a case for review. It is the principal vehicle for United States Supreme Court review.

Rule of Four

A United States Supreme Court procedure requiring four affirmative votes to hear the case before the full Court.

Oral Arguments

The verbal arguments presented in person by attorneys to an appellate court. Each attorney presents reasons to the court why the court should rule in her or his client's favor.

Opinion

The statement by a judge or a court of the decision reached in a case tried or argued before it. The opinion sets forth the law that applies to the case and details the legal reasoning on which the ruling was based.

Affirm

To declare that a court ruling is valid and must stand.

Reverse

To annul or make void a court ruling on account of some error or irregularity.

Remand

To send a case back to the court that originally heard it.

---

[3] The "rule of four" is modified when seven or fewer justices participate, which occurs from time to time. When that happens, as few as three justices can grant *certiorari*.

[4] For a former Supreme Court law clerk's account of the role these clerks play in the high court's decision-making process, see Edward Lazarus, *Closed Chambers: The First Eyewitness Account of the Epic Struggles inside the Supreme Court* (New York: Times Books, 1998).

[5] It turned out that one supposed information leak came from lawyers making educated guesses.

might have held that a party was not entitled to bring a lawsuit under a particular law. If the Supreme Court holds to the contrary, it will remand (send back) the case to the trial court with instructions that the trial go forward.

The Court's written opinion sometimes is unsigned; this is called an opinion *per curiam* ("by the court"). Typically, the Court's opinion will be signed by all the justices who agree with it. When in the majority, the chief justice will assign the opinion and will often write it personally. Whenever the chief justice is in the minority, the senior justice on the majority side decides who writes the opinion.

When all justices unanimously agree on an opinion, the opinion is written for the entire Court (all the justices) and can be deemed a **unanimous opinion.** When there is not a unanimous opinion, a **majority opinion** is written, outlining the views of the majority of the justices involved in the particular case. Often, one or more justices who feel strongly about making or emphasizing a particular point that is not made or emphasized in the unanimous or majority written opinion will write a **concurring opinion.** That means the justice writing the concurring opinion agrees (concurs) with the conclusion given in the majority written opinion, but for different reasons. Finally, in other than unanimous opinions, one or more dissenting opinions are usually written by those justices who do not agree with the majority. The **dissenting opinion** is important because it often forms the basis of the arguments used years later that cause the Court to reverse the previous decision and establish a new precedent.

Shortly after the opinion is written, the Supreme Court announces its decision from the bench. At that time, the opinion is made available to the public at the office of the clerk of the Court. The clerk also releases the opinion for online publication. Ultimately, the opinion is published in the *United States Reports,* which is the official printed record of the Court's decisions.

The Selection of Federal Judges

All federal judges are appointed. The Constitution, in Article II, Section 2, states that the president appoints the justices of the Supreme Court with the advice and consent of the Senate. Congress has provided the same procedure for staffing other federal courts. This means that the Senate and the president jointly decide who shall be a federal judge, no matter what the level.

There are over 850 federal judgeships in the United States. Once appointed to such a judgeship, a person holds that job for life. Judges serve until they resign, retire voluntarily, or die. Federal judges who engage in blatantly illegal conduct may be removed through impeachment, although such action is extremely rare.

Judicial Appointments

Judicial candidates for federal judgeships are suggested to the president by the Department of Justice, senators, other judges, the candidates themselves, and lawyers' associations and other interest groups. In selecting a candidate to nominate for a judgeship, the president considers not only the person's competence but also other factors, including the person's political philosophy (as will be discussed shortly), ethnicity, and gender.

The nomination process—no matter how the nominees are obtained—always works the same way. The president makes the actual nomination, transmitting the name to the Senate. The Senate then either confirms or rejects the nomination. To reach a conclusion, the Senate Judiciary Committee (operating through subcommittees) invites testimony, both written and oral, at its various hearings. In the case of federal district court judgeships, a practice used in the Senate, called **senatorial courtesy,** is a constraint on the president's freedom to appoint whomever the administration

DID YOU KNOW . . .
That today, a single federal appellate judge will typically turn out fifty signed opinions each year, while the nine Supreme Court justices combined issue about seventy-five signed opinions per year **?**

Unanimous Opinion
A court opinion or determination on which all judges agree.

Majority Opinion
A court opinion reflecting the views of the majority of the judges.

Concurring Opinion
A separate opinion, prepared by a judge who supports the decision of the majority of the court but who wants to make or clarify a particular point or to voice disapproval of the grounds on which the decision was made.

Dissenting Opinion
A separate opinion in which a judge dissents from (disagrees with) the conclusion reached by the majority on the court and expounds his or her own views about the case.

Senatorial Courtesy
In regard to federal district court judgeship nominations, a Senate tradition allowing a senator of the president's political party to veto a judicial appointment in his or her state simply by indicating that the appointment is personally not acceptable. At that point, the Senate may reject the nomination, or the president may withdraw consideration of the nominee.

chooses. Senatorial courtesy allows a senator of the president's political party to veto a judicial appointment in her or his state.

Federal District Court Judgeship Nominations.   Although the president nominates federal judges, the nomination of federal district court judges typically originates with a senator or senators of the president's party from the state in which there is a vacancy. If the nominee is deemed unqualified, as a matter of political courtesy the president will discuss with the senator or senators who originated the nomination whether the nomination should be withdrawn. Also, when a nomination is unacceptable politically to the president, the president will consult with the appropriate senator or senators, indicate that the nomination is unacceptable, and work with the senator or senators to seek an alternative candidate.

Federal Courts of Appeals Appointments.   There are many fewer federal courts of appeals appointments than federal district court appointments, but they are more important. This is because federal appellate judges handle more important matters, at least from the point of view of the president, and therefore presidents take a keener interest in the nomination process for such judgeships. Also, appointments to the U.S. courts of appeals have become "steppingstones" to the Supreme Court. Typically, the president culls the Circuit Judge Nominating Commission's list of nominees for potential candidates. The president may also use this list to oppose senators' recommendations that may be unacceptable politically to the president.

Supreme Court Appointments.   As we have described, the president nominates Supreme Court justices.[6] As you can see in Table 15–1, which summarizes the background of all Supreme Court justices to 2003, the most common occupational background of the justices at the time of their appointments has been private legal

---

[6] For a discussion of the factors that may come into play during the process of nominating Supreme Court justices, see David A. Yalof, *Pursuit of Justices: Presidential Politics and the Selection of Supreme Court Nominees* (Chicago: University of Chicago Press, 1999).

"Before we begin today, may I say that both my client and I were astonished that Your Honor was not nominated for the Supreme Court?"

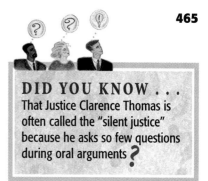

practice or state or federal judgeships. Those nine justices who were in federal executive posts at the time of their appointments held the high offices of secretary of state, comptroller of the treasury, secretary of the navy, postmaster general, secretary of the interior, chairman of the Securities and Exchange Commission, and secretary of labor. In the "Other" category under "Occupational Position before Appointment" in Table 15–1 are two justices who were professors of law (including William H. Taft, a former president) and one justice who was a North Carolina state employee with responsibility for organizing and revising the state's statutes.

 TABLE 15–1

Background of Supreme Court Justices to 2003

	NUMBER OF JUSTICES (108 = TOTAL)
Occupational Position before Appointment	
Private legal practice	25
State judgeship	21
Federal judgeship	28
U.S. attorney general	7
Deputy or assistant U.S. attorney general	2
U.S. solicitor general	2
U.S. senator	6
U.S. representative	2
State governor	3
Federal executive post	9
Other	3
Religious Background	
Protestant	83
Roman Catholic	11
Jewish	6
Unitarian	7
No religious affiliation	1
Age on Appointment	
Under 40	5
41–50	31
51–60	58
61–70	14
Political Party Affiliation	
Federalist (to 1835)	13
Democratic Republican (to 1828)	7
Whig (to 1861)	1
Democrat	44
Republican	42
Independent	1
Educational Background	
College graduate	92
Not a college graduate	16
Gender	
Male	106
Female	2
Race	
Caucasian	106
Other	2

SOURCES: Congressional Quarterly, *Congressional Quarterly's Guide to the U.S. Supreme Court* (Washington, D.C.: Congressional Quarterly Press, 1996); and authors' update.

**For updates and more
information on the subject,
use the term "Senate
Committee on the
Judiciary" in the Subject
guide.**

Partisanship and Judicial Appointments

Ideology plays an important role in the president's choices for judicial appointments. As a result, presidential appointments to the federal judiciary have had an extremely partisan distribution. The justices' partisan attachments have been mostly the same as those of the president who appointed them. There have been some exceptions, however. Nine nominal Democrats have been appointed by Republican presidents, three Republicans by Democratic presidents, and one Democrat by Whig president John Tyler.[7]

Presidents see their federal judiciary appointments as the one sure way to institutionalize their political views long after they have left office. By 1993, for example, Presidents Ronald Reagan and George H. W. Bush together had appointed nearly three-quarters of all federal court judges. This preponderance of Republican-appointed federal judges strengthened the legal moorings of the conservative social agenda on a variety of issues, ranging from abortion to civil rights. Nevertheless, President Bill Clinton had the opportunity to appoint about two hundred federal judges, thereby shifting the ideological make-up of the federal judiciary.

Following the 2000 elections, some observers speculated that one or more of the justices of the Supreme Court may retire during George W. Bush's tenure as president. Should this happen, Bush will be in a position to exercise considerable influence over the future ideological make-up of the Supreme Court. As many presidents have learned, however, there is no guarantee that once appointed to the bench, a justice's decisions will please the president.

The Senate's Role

Ideology also plays a large role in the Senate's confirmation hearings, and presidential nominees to the Supreme Court have not always been confirmed. In fact, almost 20 percent of presidential nominations to the Supreme Court have been either rejected or not acted on by the Senate. Numerous acrimonious battles over Supreme Court appointments have ensued when the Senate and the president have not seen eye to eye about political matters.

The U.S. Senate had a long record of refusing to confirm the president's judicial nominations from the beginning of Andrew Jackson's presidency in 1829 to the end of Ulysses Grant's presidency in 1877. During a fairly long period of relative acquiescence to presidential nominations on the part of the Senate, from 1894 until 1968, only three nominees were not confirmed. From 1968 through 1987, however, four presidential nominees to the highest court were rejected. One of the most controversial Supreme Court nominations was that of Clarence Thomas, who underwent an extremely volatile confirmation hearing in 1991, replete with charges of sexual harassment against him. He was ultimately confirmed by the Senate, however.

President Bill Clinton had little trouble gaining approval for both of his nominees to the Supreme Court: Ruth Bader Ginsburg and Stephen Breyer. Clinton found it more difficult, however, to secure Senate approval for his judicial nominations to the lower courts. In fact, during the late 1990s and early 2000s the duel between the Senate and the president aroused considerable concern about the consequences of the increasingly partisan and ideological tension over federal judicial appointments. As a result of Senate delays in confirming nominations, the number of judicial vacancies mounted, as did the backlog of cases pending in the federal courts.

---

[7] Actually, Tyler was a member of the Democratic Party who ran with William H. Harrison on the Whig ticket. When Harrison died, much to the surprise of the Whigs, Tyler—a Democrat—became president, although they tried to call him "acting president." Thus, some historians would quibble over the statement that Tyler was a Whig.

Policymaking and the Courts

The partisan battles over judicial appointments reflect an important reality in today's American government: the importance of the judiciary in national politics. Because appointments to the federal benches are for life, the ideology of judicial appointees can affect national policy for years to come. Although the primary function of judges in our system of government is to interpret and apply the laws, inevitably judges make policy when carrying out this task. One of the major policymaking tools of the federal courts is their power of judicial review.

Judicial Review

Remember from Chapter 2 that the power of the courts to determine whether a law or action by the other branches of government is constitutional is known as the power of *judicial review.* This power of the judiciary enables the judicial branch to act as a check on the other two branches of government, in line with the checks and balances system established by the U.S. Constitution.

The power of judicial review is not mentioned in the Constitution, however. Rather, it was established by the United States Supreme Court's decision in *Marbury v. Madison.*[8] In that case, in which the Court declared that a law passed by Congress violated the Constitution, the Court claimed such a power for the courts:

> It is emphatically the province and duty of the Judicial Department to say what the law is. Those who apply the rule to a particular case, must of necessity expound and interpret that rule. If two laws conflict with each other, the courts must decide on the operation of each.

If a federal court declares that a federal or state law or policy is unconstitutional, the court's decision affects the application of the law or policy only within that court's jurisdiction. For this reason, the higher the level of the court, the greater the impact of the decision on society. Because of the Supreme Court's national jurisdiction, its decisions can have a significant impact. For example, when the Supreme Court held that an Arkansas state constitutional amendment limiting the terms of congresspersons was unconstitutional, laws establishing term limits in twenty-three other states also were invalidated.[9]

Some claim that the power of judicial review gives unelected judges and justices on federal court benches too much influence over national policy. Despite continued attacks on the legitimacy of judicial review, courts continue to exercise the power. (Judicial review is also practiced by courts in other countries around the world—see this chapter's *Global View* feature on the next page for details.)

Judicial Activism and Judicial Restraint

Judicial scholars like to characterize different judges and justices as being either activist or restraintist. The doctrine of **judicial activism** rests on the conviction that the federal judiciary should take an active role in using its powers to check the activities of Congress, state legislatures, and administrative agencies when those government bodies exceed their authority. One of the Supreme Court's most activist eras was the period from 1953 to 1969 when the Court was headed by Chief Justice Earl Warren. The Warren Court propelled the civil rights movement forward by holding,

---

[8] 5 U.S. 137 (1803).
[9] *U.S. Term Limits v. Thornton,* 514 U.S. 779 (1995).

DID YOU KNOW . . .
That among the 108 persons who have served on the Supreme Court from 1789 to 2003, only two (Thurgood Marshall and Clarence Thomas) have been African American and only two (Sandra Day O'Connor and Ruth Bader Ginsburg) have been women **?**

INFOTRAC®
COLLEGE EDITION

For more information on judicial review, use the term "judicial review" in the Subject guide.

INFOTRAC®
COLLEGE EDITION

For more information on judicial activism, use the term "judicial activism" in the Subject guide.

Judicial Activism
A doctrine holding that the Supreme Court should take an active role in using its powers to check the activities of Congress, state legislatures, and administrative agencies when those government bodies exceed their authority.

Global View

Judicial Review

The concept of judicial review was pioneered by the United States. As noted elsewhere, the U.S. Constitution does not explicitly mention that the Supreme Court may deem actions of the other branches of government unconstitutional. Yet the Court's 1803 assertion in *Marbury v. Madison* that it had this power became widely accepted in this country. Some maintain that one of the reasons the doctrine was readily accepted was that it

fit in well with the checks and balances designed by the founders, who were as concerned about the tyranny of popular majorities as they were with giving the people a voice in government.

Judicial Review versus Popular Sovereignty

Ironically, judicial review was perceived in European countries as a force contrary to popular sovereignty. As representatives of the people, parliaments should not have their actions invalidated by unelected court judges. These attitudes later changed, however, with the rise of totalitarian governments in the 1920s and 1930s. It became clear that "popular" leaders, such as Adolf Hitler in Germany and Benito Mussolini in Italy, could be far more dangerous to individual liberty than any court. As a result, the courts came to be viewed, as in the United States, as protectors of civil rights and liberties.

Judicial Review across Nations

Today, all established constitutional democracies have some type of judicial review—the power to rule on the

constitutionality of laws—but its form varies from country to country. For example, Canada's Supreme Court can exercise judicial review only if a law does not include a provision explicitly prohibiting such review. France has a Constitutional Council that rules on the constitutionality of laws before the laws take effect. Prior review is also an option in Germany and Italy, if requested by the national or a regional government. In contrast, the United States Supreme Court does not give advisory opinions; rather, there must be an actual dispute concerning an issue before the Supreme Court can render a decision on the matter.

FOR CRITICAL ANALYSIS

In any country in which a constitution sets forth the basic powers and structure of government, some government branch or unit has to decide whether laws enacted by government are consistent with that constitution. Is this task best handled by the courts? Can you think of a better alternative?

DID YOU KNOW . . .

That in 1930, Justice Oliver Wendell Holmes, Jr., dissenting from the Supreme Court's majority opinion striking down economic legislation as violative of due process, wrote, "I see hardly any limit but the sky" to the Court's invalidation of statutes **?**

Judicial Restraint
A doctrine holding that the Supreme Court should defer to the decisions made by the elected representatives of the people in the legislative and executive branches.

among other things, that laws permitting racial segregation violated the equal protection clause.

In contrast, the doctrine of **judicial restraint** rests on the assumption that the courts should defer to the decisions made by the legislative and executive branches, because members of Congress and the president are elected by the people whereas members of the federal judiciary are not. Because administrative agency personnel normally have more expertise than the courts do in the areas regulated by the agencies, the courts likewise should defer to agency rules and decisions. In other words, under the doctrine of judicial restraint, the courts should not thwart the implementation of legislative acts and agency rules unless they are clearly unconstitutional.

Judicial activism sometimes is linked with liberalism, and judicial restraint with conservatism. In fact, a conservative judge can be activist, just as a liberal judge can be restraintist—and vice versa. In the 1950s and 1960s, the Supreme Court was activist and liberal. Some observers believe that the Rehnquist Court, with its conservative majority, has become increasingly activist since the 1990s. Some go even further and claim that the federal courts, including the Supreme Court, wield too much power in our democracy—see this chapter's *Which Side Are You On?* feature for an exploration of this issue.

Ideology and the Rehnquist Court

William H. Rehnquist became the sixteenth chief justice of the Supreme Court in 1986, after fifteen years as an associate justice. He was known as a strong anchor of

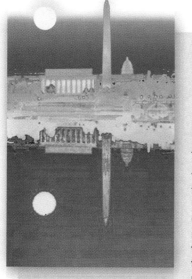

Which Side Are You On?
Is the Federal Judiciary Too Powerful?

Initially, there was only one court in the federal judiciary—the Supreme Court. In the early years of the nation, the Court had little stature or influence. Indeed, the first Supreme Court chief justice, John Jay, refused to serve a second term because he thought that the Court would never play an important role in American society. Today's Supreme Court bears little resemblance to the Court headed by John Jay. Indeed, the power and influence exercised by today's federal judiciary has led some to claim that the federal courts have too much power.

TOO MUCH POWER FOR UNELECTED JUSTICES AND JUDGES?

Many observers believe that justices and judges who are not elected by the people should not be allowed to influence public policy to the extent that they do today. Clearly, the courts' power of judicial review—the authority to determine whether actions taken by the executive or legislative branch are constitutional—allows them to determine policy with respect to a number of wide-ranging issues. This is particularly true of decisions rendered by the United States Supreme Court because those decisions apply throughout the country. In recent years, the Supreme Court has decided such issues as whether banning virtual child pornography on the Internet violates our constitutional right to free speech and whether the implementation of school vouchers violates the Constitution's establishment clause. It is the justices of the Supreme Court, not the elected members of Congress, who decide these and other important issues.

The decisions of federal appellate judges are also significant because, unless those decisions are overturned by the Supreme Court (and most of them are not), they are final. Consider just one example of how a federal appellate court can establish policy. In 1995, the U.S. Court of Appeals for the Fifth Circuit held that affirmative action in college recruiting violated the Fourteenth Amendment's equal protection clause. The Supreme Court declined to review the case, so the Fifth Circuit's decision stood. In effect, that means that affirmative action in college admissions is now banned in all of the states within that court's jurisdiction—Texas, Louisiana, and Mississippi.

THE COURTS GUARD OUR CONSTITUTIONAL RIGHTS AND LIBERTIES

Others argue that the powers exercised by the federal courts, particularly the power of judicial review, are necessary to protect our constitutional rights and liberties. Built into our federal form of government is a system of checks and balances. If the federal courts did not have the power of judicial review, there would be no governmental body to check Congress's lawmaking authority.

Furthermore, even though the Supreme Court has no enforcement powers, the Court's decisions carry significant weight. This is because Americans have a great respect for the Supreme Court and its rulings. Additionally, the Court rarely, if ever, overreaches its authority. Typically, Supreme Court justices show self-restraint when issuing opinions.

Federal courts are also limited in the laws and policy that they can affect. There must be an actual dispute before a court can hear a case or rule on the issue raised in the case. If the Supreme Court wants to clarify the law on a given issue, it must wait until a case involving that issue is appealed to the Court for review. Additionally, the courts, including the Supreme Court, normally follow precedents. Only rarely does the Supreme Court refuse to follow an earlier decision made by the Court. The practice of following precedent also hinders the federal courts' power to "legislate from the bench."

WHAT'S YOUR POSITION?

Do you think that unelected federal judges and justices wield too much power in our democracy? Why or why not?

GOING ONLINE

The Justice at Stake Campaign is a coalition of judicial, legal, and citizen groups organized to promote an independent judiciary. Visit their Web site at **http://www.justiceatstake.org**. *Policy Review*, once a publication of the Heritage Foundation and now a publication of the Hoover Institution of Stanford University, has included several articles on the power of the federal judiciary. Go to **http://www.policyreview.org** and type "federal judiciary" into the search box for a menu of relevant articles.

The Rehnquist Court

LIBERAL/MODERATE

John Paul Stevens

David Souter

Ruth Bader Ginsburg

Stephen Breyer

SWING VOTES

Sandra Day O'Connor   Anthony Kennedy

CONSERVATIVE

William Rehnquist   Antonin Scalia   Clarence Thomas

I N F O T R A C ®
COLLEGE EDITION

For more information on the chief justice, use the term "William Rehnquist" in the Subject guide.

the Court's conservative wing. With Rehnquist's appointment as chief justice, it seemed to observers that the Court necessarily would become more conservative.

This, in fact, has happened. The Court began to take a rightward shift shortly after Rehnquist became chief justice, and the Court's rightward movement continued as other conservative appointments to the bench were made during the Reagan and Bush administrations. Today, three of the justices (William Rehnquist, Antonin Scalia, and Clarence Thomas) are notably conservative in their views. Four of the justices (John Paul Stevens, David Souter, Ruth Bader Ginsburg, and Stephen Breyer) hold liberal-to-moderate views. The middle of the Court is now occupied by two moderate-to-conservative justices, Sandra Day O'Connor and Anthony Kennedy. O'Connor and Kennedy usually provide the "swing votes" on the Court in controversial cases. The ideological alignments on the Court vary, however, depending on the issues involved in particular cases.

Certainly, today's Supreme Court has moved far from the liberal positions taken by the Court under Earl Warren (1953–1969) and under Warren Burger (1969–1986). Since the mid-1990s, the Court has issued numerous conservative rulings, many of which you have already read about in this text.

Federalism.   Several of these rulings reflect a conservative approach to constitutional law with respect to states' rights and other federalist issues. For example, in 1995 the Court curbed—for the first time in sixty years—the national government's constitutional power under the commerce clause to regulate intrastate activities. The Court held that a federal law regulating the possession of guns in school zones had nothing to do with interstate commerce, and therefore Congress had overreached its powers by attempting to regulate this activity.[10] In 1997, the Court again upheld states' rights when it invalidated portions of the federal gun control law. The Court stated that the federal government lacked constitutional authority to require state officials to perform background checks on prospective gun purchasers.[11]

In 2000, the Court held that Congress had overreached its authority under the commerce clause when it included a federal remedy for gender-motivated violence, such as rape or stalking, in the Federal Violence against Women Act of 1994. The Court concluded that the effect of such violence on interstate commerce was not sufficient to justify national regulation of noneconomic, violent criminal conduct.[12]

In view of the Court's support for states' rights, many scholars were surprised when the Court involved itself in the dispute over the manual recounting of the Florida votes after the 2000 elections. Nonetheless, in a historic decision, the Court reversed the Florida Supreme Court's order to manually recount the votes in selected Florida counties—a decision that effectively handed the presidency to George W. Bush.[13]

---

[10] *United States v. Lopez,* 514 U.S. 549 (1995).
[11] *Printz v. United States,* 521 U.S. 898 (1997).
[12] *United States v. Morrison,* 529 U.S. 598 (2000).
[13] *Bush v. Gore,* 531 U.S. 98 (2000).

In December 2000, with the outcome of the presidential election still in doubt, the United States Supreme Court agreed to hear an appeal from George W. Bush to stop the manual recount of ballots in Florida. Many people considered the Court's involvement in the disputed election unwarranted. Do you think the Supreme Court wields too much political power? (AP Photo/Steve Helber)

Civil Rights.   In regard to civil rights issues, the Rehnquist Court's generally conservative ("strict") interpretation of the Constitution has had mixed results. In one decision, the Court refused to extend the constitutional right to privacy to include the right of terminally ill persons to end their lives through physician-assisted suicide. Therefore, a state law banning this practice did not violate the Constitution.[14] (Essentially, the Court left it up to the states to decide whether to ban—or to permit—assisted suicide; to date, only one state, Oregon, has passed a law permitting the practice.) In another decision, the Court held that a federal statute expanding religious liberties was an unconstitutional attempt by Congress to rewrite the Constitution.[15]

In early 2000, the Court rendered a decision in a case challenging the constitutionality of the federal Driver's Privacy Protection Act of 1994. The act restricted the sale of personal information gathered by states when they issue driver's licenses. Many thought that the key issue in the case was drivers' privacy and hoped that the decision might open the door to tighter federal laws protecting privacy rights. The Court, however, barely mentioned the privacy issue. Rather, it ruled that the act was constitutional because (1) drivers' personal data had become articles of interstate commerce and (2) the act did not "commandeer" states into enforcing federal law.[16]

What Checks Our Courts?

Our judicial system is probably the most independent in the world. But the courts do not have absolute independence, for they are part of the political process. Political checks limit the extent to which courts can exercise judicial review and engage in an activist policy. These checks are exercised by the executive branch, the legislature, the public, and, finally, the judiciary itself.

Executive Checks

President Andrew Jackson was once supposed to have said, after Chief Justice John Marshall made an unpopular decision, that "John Marshall has made his decision; now let him enforce it."[17] This purported remark goes to the heart of **judicial implementation**—the enforcement of judicial decisions in such a way that those decisions are translated into policy. The Supreme Court simply does not have any enforcement powers, and whether a decision will be implemented depends on the cooperation of the other two branches of government. Rarely, though, will a president refuse to enforce a Supreme Court decision, as President Jackson did. To take such an action could mean a significant loss of public support because of the Supreme Court's stature in the eyes of the nation.

More commonly, presidents exercise influence over the judiciary by appointing new judges and justices as federal judicial seats become vacant. Additionally, as mentioned earlier, the U.S. solicitor general plays a significant role in the federal court system, and the person holding this office is a presidential appointee.

Executives at the state level also may refuse to implement court decisions with which they disagree. A notable example of such a refusal occurred in Arkansas after the Supreme Court ordered schools to desegregate "with all deliberate speed" in 1955.[18] Arkansas governor Orval Faubus refused to cooperate with the decision and

Judicial Implementation
The way in which court decisions are translated into action.

---

[14] *Washington v. Glucksberg,* 521 U.S. 702 (1997).
[15] *City of Boerne v. Flores,* 521 U.S. 507 (1997).
[16] *Reno v. Condon,* 528 U.S. 141 (2000).
[17] The decision referred to was *Cherokee Nation v. Georgia,* 30 U.S. 1 (1831).
[18] *Brown v. Board of Education,* 349 U.S. 294 (1955)—the second *Brown* decision.

A handful of pro-prayer advocates show their support for student-led prayer before football games after the Supreme Court ruled that student-led prayer over a public address system is not allowed at sporting events in public schools. (AP Photo/Brett Coomer)

used the state's National Guard to block the integration of Central High School in Little Rock. Ultimately, President Dwight Eisenhower had to federalize the Arkansas National Guard and send federal troops to Little Rock to quell the violence that had erupted.

Legislative Checks

Courts may make rulings, but often the legislatures at local, state, and federal levels are required to appropriate funds to carry out the courts' rulings. A court, for example, may decide that prison conditions must be improved, but it is up to the legislature to authorize the funds necessary to carry out such a ruling. When such funds are not appropriated, the court that made the ruling, in effect, has been checked.

Courts' rulings can be overturned by constitutional amendments at both the federal and state levels. Many of the amendments to the U.S. Constitution (such as the Fourteenth, Fifteenth, and Twenty-sixth Amendments) check the state courts' ability to allow discrimination, for example. Proposed constitutional amendments that were created in an effort to reverse courts' decisions on school prayer and abortion have failed.

Finally, Congress or a state legislature can rewrite (amend) old laws or enact new ones to overturn a court's rulings if the legislature concludes that the court is interpreting laws or legislative intentions erroneously. For example, Congress passed the Civil Rights Act of 1991 in part to overturn a series of conservative rulings in employment-discrimination cases. In 1993, Congress enacted the Religious Freedom Restoration Act (RFRA), which broadened religious liberties, after Congress concluded that a 1990 Supreme Court ruling restricted religious freedom to an unacceptable extent.[19]

According to political scientist Walter Murphy, "A permanent feature of our constitutional landscape is the ongoing tug and pull between elected government and the courts."[20] Certainly, today's Supreme Court and the other two branches of government

---

[19] *Employment Division, Department of Human Resources of Oregon v. Smith*, 494 U.S. 872 (1990).

[20] As quoted in Neal Devins, "The Last Word Debate: How Social and Political Forces Shape Constitutional Values," *American Bar Association Journal*, October 1997, p. 48.

have been at odds on several occasions in the last decade. Consider the battle over religious rights and the RFRA. On signing the RFRA, President Clinton stated that the act was necessary to reverse the Court's erroneous interpretation of the Constitution in its 1990 decision. According to the president, the elected government's view of religious liberty was "far more consistent with the intent of the founders than [was] the Supreme Court." The Supreme Court responded in kind. In 1997, it invalidated the RFRA, declaring that the act represented an unconstitutional attempt by Congress to add new rights to the Constitution.[21] The Court proclaimed horror at the prospect that "[s]hifting legislative majorities could change the Constitution."

Public Opinion

Public opinion plays a significant role in shaping government policy, and certainly the judiciary is not excepted from this rule. For one thing, persons affected by a Supreme Court decision that is noticeably at odds with their views may simply ignore it. Prayers were banned in public schools in 1962, yet it was widely known that the ban was (and still is) ignored in many southern districts. What can the courts do in this situation? Unless someone complains about the prayers and initiates a lawsuit, the courts can do nothing.

The public also can pressure state and local government officials to refuse to enforce a certain decision. As already mentioned, judicial implementation requires the cooperation of government officials at all levels, and public opinion in various regions of the country will influence whether or not such cooperation is forthcoming.

Additionally, the courts themselves necessarily are influenced by public opinion to some extent. After all, judges are not "islands" in our society; their attitudes are influenced by social trends, just as the attitudes and beliefs of all persons are. Courts generally tend to avoid issuing decisions that they know will be noticeably at odds with public opinion. In part, this is because the judiciary, as a branch of the government, prefers to avoid creating divisiveness among the public. Also, a court—particularly the Supreme Court—may lose stature if it decides a case in a way that markedly diverges from public opinion. For example, in 2002 the Supreme Court ruled that the execution of mentally retarded criminals violates the Eighth Amendment's ban on cruel and unusual punishment. In its ruling, the Court did not hide the fact that public opinion influenced its decision, noting that there is "powerful evidence that today our society views mentally retarded offenders as categorically less culpable than the average criminal."[22]

Judicial Traditions and Doctrines

Supreme Court justices (and other federal judges) typically exercise self-restraint in fashioning their decisions. In part, this restraint stems from their knowledge that the other two branches of government and the public can exercise checks on the judiciary, as previously discussed. To a large extent, however, this restraint is mandated by various judicially established traditions and doctrines. For example, in exercising its discretion to hear appeals, the Supreme Court will not hear a meritless appeal just so it can rule on the issue. Also, when reviewing a case, the Supreme Court typically narrows its focus to just one issue or one aspect of an issue involved in the case. The Court rarely makes broad, sweeping decisions on issues. Furthermore, the doctrine of *stare decisis* acts as a restraint because it obligates the courts, including the Supreme Court,

---

[21] *City of Boerne v. Flores,* 521 U.S. 507 (1997).
[22] *Atkins v. Virginia,* 122 S.Ct. 2242 (2002).

to follow established precedents when deciding cases. Only rarely will courts overrule a precedent.

Other judicial doctrines and practices also act as restraints. As already mentioned, the courts will hear only what are called justiciable disputes—disputes that arise out of actual cases. In other words, a court will not hear a case that involves a merely hypothetical issue. Additionally, if a political question is involved, the Supreme Court often will exercise judicial restraint and refuse to rule on the matter. A **political question** is one that the Supreme Court declares should be decided by the elected branches of government—the executive branch, the legislative branch, or those two branches acting together. For example, the Supreme Court has refused to rule on the controversy regarding the rights of gay men and lesbians in the military, preferring instead to defer to the executive branch's decisions on the matter. Generally, fewer questions are deemed political questions by the Supreme Court today than in the past.

Political Question
An issue that a court believes should be decided by the executive or legislative branch.

Higher courts can reverse the decisions of lower courts. Lower courts can act as a check on higher courts, too. Lower courts can ignore—and have ignored—Supreme Court decisions. Usually, this is done indirectly. A lower court might conclude, for example, that the precedent set by the Supreme Court does not apply to the exact circumstances in the case before the court; or the lower court may decide that the Supreme Court's decision was ambiguous with respect to the issue before the lower court. The fact that the Supreme Court rarely makes broad and clear-cut statements on any issue facilitates different interpretations of the Court's decisions by the lower courts.

The Judiciary: Why Is It Important Today?

John Marshall, chief justice of the United States Supreme Court from 1801 to 1835, stated, "The Judicial Department comes home in its effects to every man's fireside: it passes on his property, his reputation, his life, his all." Whether it is a Supreme Court decision on prayer in the schools or a local court decision against a neighbor, what the courts say and do strongly influences American life and politics.

The federal judiciary is one of the most important institutions in American political life. Indeed, it would be hard to imagine what life in this country would be like if the judiciary was not an independent branch of government but was under the control, say, of Congress. As you learned in this chapter, there is an ongoing interplay among the judiciary, Congress, and the executive branch. Time and again, through the process of judicial review, the federal courts have checked attempts by Congress to pass laws that are not consistent with the U.S. Constitution. In turn, Congress at times has enacted legislation specifically to overturn Supreme Court decisions. On some occasions, the courts have also checked actions of the executive branch.

Because the United States Supreme Court is the highest court in the nation, its decisions must be followed by all other courts in the United States. Thus, Supreme Court decisions can directly affect the everyday lives of millions of Americans. Consider just one example—the Supreme Court's decision in *Brown v. Board of Education of Topeka* (1954). This decision, which outlawed segregation in public schools, dramatically changed the course of race relations throughout America. Furthermore, the Supreme Court has played a significant role in determining the nature and scope of our constitutional rights and liberties. For example, privacy rights were not specifically mentioned in the Constitution. The Supreme Court, however, has held that such rights can be inferred from other constitutional provisions.

MAKING A DIFFERENCE | Changing the Legal System

The U.S. legal system may seem all-powerful and too complex to be influenced by one individual, but its power nonetheless depends on our support. A hostile public has many ways of resisting, modifying, or overturning statutes and rulings of the courts. Sooner or later a determined majority will prevail. Even a determined minority can make a difference. As Alexander Hamilton suggested in *The Federalist Papers,* the people will always hold the scales of justice in their hands, and ultimately all constitutional government depends on their firmness and wisdom.

An Example—Mothers Against Drunk Driving

One example of the kind of pressure that can be exerted on the legal system began with a tragedy. On a spring afternoon in 1980, thirteen-year-old Cari Lightner was hit from behind and killed by a drunk driver while she was walking in a bicycle lane. The driver turned out to be a forty-seven-year-old man with two prior drunk-driving convictions. He was at that time out on bail for a third arrest. Cari's mother, Candy, quit her job as a real estate

agent to form Mothers Against Drunk Driving (MADD) and launched a personal campaign to stiffen penalties for drunk-driving convictions.

The organization now has three million members and supporters. Outraged by the thousands of lives lost every year because of drunk driving, the group not only seeks stiff penalties against drunk drivers but also urges police, prosecutors, and judges to crack down on such violators. MADD, by becoming involved, has gotten results. Owing to its efforts and the efforts of other citizen-activist groups, many states have responded with stiffer penalties and deterrents. If you feel strongly about this issue and want to get involved, contact the following organization:

> MADD
> P.O. Box 541688
> Dallas, TX 75354-1688
> 1-800-GET-MADD
> **http://www.madd.org**

Other Organizations

Several other organizations have been formed by people who want to change or influence the judicial system. A few of them follow:

HALT—An Organization of
   Americans for Legal Reform
1612 K St. N.W., Suite 510
Washington, DC 20006
1-800-FOR-HALT
http://www.halt.org

National Legal Center for
   the Public Interest
1600 K Street, N.W., Suite 800
Washington, DC 20006
202-466-9360
http://www.nlcpi.org/

Information about the Supreme Court

If you want information about the Supreme Court, contact the following by telephone or letter:

   Clerk of the Court
   The Supreme Court
      of the United States
   1 First St. N.E.
   Washington, DC 20543
   202-479-3000

You can access online information about the Supreme Court at the following site:

   http://oyez.nwu.edu

Key Terms

Chapter Summary

1 American law is rooted in the common law tradition, which is part of its legal heritage from England. The common law doctrine of *stare decisis* (which means "to stand on decided cases") obligates judges to follow precedents established previously by their own courts or by higher courts in their jurisdiction. Precedents established by the United States Supreme Court, the highest court in the land, are binding on all lower courts. Fundamental sources of American law include the U.S. Constitution and state constitutions, statutes enacted by legislative bodies, regulations issued by administrative agencies, and case law.

2 Article III, Section 1, of the U.S. Constitution limits the jurisdiction of the federal courts to cases involving (a) a federal question—which is a question based, at least in part, on the U.S. Constitution, a treaty, or a federal law; and (b) diversity of citizenship—which arises when a lawsuit is between parties of different states or involves a foreign citizen or government. The federal court system is basically a three-tiered model consisting of (a) U.S. district (trial) courts and various lower courts of limited jurisdiction; (b) U.S. courts of appeals; and (c) the United States Supreme Court. Cases may be appealed from the district courts to the appellate courts. In most cases, the decisions of the federal appellate courts are final because the Supreme Court hears relatively few cases.

3 The Supreme Court begins its annual term on the first Monday in October and usually adjourns in late June or early July of the next year. A special session may be held, but this rarely occurs. The Court's decision to review a case is influenced by many factors, including the significance of the parties and issues involved and whether the solicitor general is pressing the Court to take the case. After a case is accepted, the justices (a) undertake research (with the help of their law clerks) on the issues involved in the case, (b) hear oral argu-ments from the parties, (c) meet in conference to discuss and vote on the issue, and (d) announce the opinion, which is then released for publication.

4 Federal judges are nominated by the president and con-firmed by the Senate. Once appointed, they hold office for life, barring gross misconduct. The nomination and confirmation process, particularly for Supreme Court justices, is often extremely politicized. Democrats and Republicans alike real-ize that justices may occupy seats on the Court for decades and naturally want to have persons appointed who share their basic views. Nearly 20 percent of all Supreme Court appoint-ments have been either rejected or not acted on by the Senate.

5 In interpreting and applying the law, judges inevitably become policymakers. The most important policymaking tool of the federal courts is the power of judicial review. This power was not mentioned specifically in the Constitution, but John Marshall claimed the power for the Court in his 1803 decision in *Marbury v. Madison.* Judges who take an active role in checking the activities of the other branches of government sometimes are characterized as "activist" judges, and judges who defer to such activities sometimes are regarded as "restraintist" judges. The Warren Court of the 1950s and 1960s was activist in a liberal direction, whereas today's Rehnquist Court seems to be increasingly activist in a conservative direc-tion. Several politicians and scholars argue that judicial activism has gotten out of hand. A question being debated today is whether the policymaking powers of the federal courts should be curbed.

6 Checks on the powers of the federal courts include execu-tive checks, legislative checks, public opinion, and judicial tra-ditions and doctrines.

Selected Print and Media Resources

SUGGESTED READINGS

Bugliosi, Vincent. *The Betrayal of America: How the Supreme Court Undermined the Constitution and Chose Our President.* New York: Thunder's Mouth Press, 2001. The author strongly criticizes the Supreme Court's ruling in *Bush v. Gore,* which effectively decided the outcome of the 2000 presidential elections.

Irons, Peter, and Stephanie Guitton. *May It Please the Court.* New York: New Press, 1993. The book includes introductions and tran-scripts of twenty-three live recordings of influential cases argued before the Supreme Court since 1955. Also included is a cassette containing live recordings of the same cases with the actual voices of the attorneys and justices in oral argument and questioning.

Lazarus, Edward. *Closed Chambers: The First Eyewitness Account of the Epic Struggles inside the Supreme Court.* New York: Times Books, 1998. Lazarus, who served as a clerk to former Supreme Court Justice Harry Blackmun during the Court's 1988–1989 term, gives an eyewitness account of some of the significant ide-ological struggles waged within the Court, among both law clerks and the justices.

Segal, Jeffrey, and Harold J. Spaeth. *Majority Rule or Minority Will: Adherence to Precedent on the U.S. Supreme Court.* Cambridge, Mass.: Harvard University Press, 1999. These two constitutional scholars examine the influence of precedents (prior decisions on issues being considered by the Court) in Supreme Court deci-sion making. They conclude that although the justices cite precedents to support their legal reasoning, in fact, because there are always precedents to support either side of an issue, following precedent does not mean that the justices are influ-enced by precedent.

Tushnet, Mark. *Taking the Constitution Away from the Courts.* Princeton, N.J.: Princeton University Press, 1999. In this book, a serious constitutional scholar proposes that a constitutional amendment be adopted to overrule *Marbury v. Madison* (1803), in which the Supreme Court assumed the power of judicial review. The author believes that constitutional interpretation should be decided by the voters and their elected representatives rather than by judges.

MEDIA RESOURCES

Amistad—A 1997 movie, starring Anthony Hopkins, about a slave ship mutiny in 1839. Much of the story revolves around the prosecution, ending at the Supreme Court, of the slave who led the revolt.

Court TV—This TV channel covers high-profile trials, including those of O. J. Simpson, the Unabomber, British nanny Louise Woodward, and Timothy McVeigh. (You can learn how to access Court TV from your area at its Web site—see the *Logging On* section on the next page for its URL.)

Gideon's Trumpet—A 1980 film starring Henry Fonda as the small-time criminal James Earl Gideon, which makes clear the path that a case takes to the Supreme Court and the importance of cases decided there.

The Magnificent Yankee—A 1950 movie, starring Louis Calhern and Ann Harding, that traces the life and philosophy of Oliver Wendell Holmes, Jr., one of the Supreme Court's most brilliant justices.

Marbury v. Madison—A thirty-minute video on this famous 1803 case that established the principle of judicial review.

Your CD-ROM Resources

In addition to the chapter content containing hot links, the following resources are available on the CD-ROM:

- **Internet Activities**—The U.S. Supreme Court's current term, advocates of judicial restraint, filling judicial vacancies.

- **Critical Thinking Exercises**—The right of appeal, Senate questioning, judicial coalitions.

- **Self-Check on Important Themes**—Can You Answer These?

- **Animated Figures**—Figure 15–1, "The Federal Court System," and Table 15–1, "Background of Supreme Court Justices to 2003."

- **Videos**—*Justice Bork, Advise and Consent.*

- **Public Opinion Data**—Find contrasting views on judicial restraint, Bush administration nominations.

- **InfoTrac Exercise**—"Supreme Court Voting Patterns 1994–2001."

- **Simulation**—You Are There!

- **Participation Exercise**—Visit a courtroom and follow the course and resolution of a trial.

- **MicroCase Exercise**—"By the Numbers: Cases before the Court since 1940."

- **Additional Resources**—All court cases, The Judiciary Act of 1789, The Magna Carta, *Federalist Paper* No. 78.

e -mocracy

Courts on the Web

Most courts in the United States now have sites on the Web. Each site allows varying levels of accessibility. Some courts simply display contact information for court personnel. Others include recent judicial decisions along with court rules and forms. Many federal courts permit attorneys to file documents electronically in certain types of cases. The information available on these sites is continuing to grow as courts try to avoid being left behind in the information age. One day, courts may decide to implement *virtual courtrooms,* in which judicial proceedings take place totally via the Internet. The Internet may ultimately provide at least a partial solution to the twin problems of overloaded dockets and the high time and money costs of litigation.

Logging On

The home page of the federal courts is a good starting point if you are learning about the federal court system in general.

At this site, you can even follow the "path" of a case as it moves through the federal court system. Go to

http://www.uscourts.gov

To access the Supreme Court's official Web site, on which Supreme Court decisions are made available within hours of their release, go to

http://supremecourtus.gov

Several Web sites offer searchable databases of Supreme Court decisions. You can access Supreme Court cases since 1970 at FindLaw's site:

http://www.findlaw.com

The following Web site also offers an easily searchable index to Supreme Court opinions, including some important historic decisions:

http://supct.law.cornell.edu/supct

You can find information on the justices of the Supreme Court, as well as their decisions, at

http://oyez.nwu.edu

Court TV's Web site offers information ranging from its program schedule and how you can find Court TV in your area to famous cases and the wills of famous people. For each case it includes on the site, it gives a complete history as well as selected documents filed with the court and court transcripts. You can access this site at

http://www.courttv.com

Using the Internet for Political Analysis

Go to one of the sites on the Web that organizes the Supreme Court's cases, such as the federal courts site or the Cornell site given above. Then look up the list of Supreme Court decisions for a recent time period—say, three months. Select three cases, and read the summary of each case. Try to categorize the federal or constitutional issue that was decided in each case. To whom is the decision important? Does the decision change the relationship between the ordinary citizen and the government? What other kinds of information would make this site more useful to you?

BACKGROUND

Our Social Security system was created more than six decades ago when the Great Depression wiped out the savings of millions of Americans. The country turned to the federal government to create a safety net for the nation's elderly. Payroll taxes to fund Social Security payments started then.

In 1945, payroll taxes from forty-two workers supported one Social Security recipient. By 1960, only nine workers funded each retiree's Social Security benefits. Today, about three workers provide for each retiree's Social Security and Medicare benefits. If current trends continue, by 2030 only two workers will be available to pay the Social Security and Medicare benefits due each recipient. By then, if nothing changes, the payroll tax rate will rise to 40 percent from today's approximately 16 percent.

WHAT IF THERE WERE NO SOCIAL SECURITY?

Suppose that Congress abolished Social Security for all those, say, below the age of eighteen and those who will be born in years to come. Current beneficiaries of Social Security would not be affected, at least for a while. In time, though, Congress might be tempted to reduce Social Security benefits, or at least not increase them.

HOW WOULD PEOPLE PAY FOR RETIREMENT?

If there were no Social Security benefits, the way people would create their own retirement funds would depend largely on whether Congress also eliminated the payroll tax currently assessed. If Congress eliminated the tax, working Americans would have almost 16 percent more income. Presumably, Congress would also increase or add to current tax-free retirement savings programs that allow retirement funds to grow over time without the earnings being taxed.

The combination of tax-free private pension accounts and reduced (or eliminated) payroll taxes would certainly encourage many, if not most, working Americans to save more; that is to say, those workers entering the labor force after the change in law would have a double incentive to create their own private pension plans. Some political scientists and economists argue that this increased saving would provide more funds for increased investment, thereby leading to greater economic growth.

WHEN PROBLEMS MIGHT ARISE

The first hint of problems with such a system (or the lack of Social Security completely, as it were) would occur when today's teenagers would be retiring. So, in about forty-five years the nation might discover that an alarmingly large percentage of those who had been working had not provided adequately for their own retire-ments. Although a callous observer might contend that people's failure to save should be no one's problem but their own, compassionate Americans and their political representatives might think otherwise. Thus, elimination of Social Security for today's young people and for generations that follow might result in increased welfare payments.

As an alternative, the government might require that all workers put a certain percentage of their salaries into their own private pension plans. In essence, then, the government would be replacing Social Security with a forced-saving plan based wholly in the private sector.

DONT FORGET MEDICARE

Tightly linked to Social Security is our Medicare system. In fact, Medicare is paid for through Social Security taxes. If Medicare were also eliminated for young people today and for generations that follow, then all Americans aged eighteen and younger, as well as future generations, would have to plan to pay for private health insurance to cover medical expenses during their retirement years. Starting forty-five years from now, those Americans who choose not to spend money on health insurance during their retirement might become burdens on the state if they became ill. Again, it is possible that the federal and state governments might have to provide more welfare payments for these people.

As with the alternative of forced saving above, the government could eliminate Medicare but at the same time require that everyone purchase a medical insurance policy, just as most states require all drivers to carry automobile insurance.

FOR CRITICAL ANALYSIS

1. What groups in American society might be in favor of eliminating Social Security?
2. What political forces might prevent Social Security from ever being eliminated?

This chapter's opening *What If . . .* feature touched on an important federal government policy dilemma—how to handle the increasing demands placed on the Social Security system as our population ages. Whatever policy decision is made with respect to Social Security, some groups will be better off and some groups will be hurt. All economic policymaking generally involves such a dilemma.

Part of the public-policy debate in our nation involves domestic problems. **Domestic policy** can be defined as all of the laws, government planning, and government actions that affect each individual's daily life in the United States. Consequently, the span of such policies is enormous. Domestic policies range from relatively simple issues, such as what the speed limit should be on interstate highways, to more complex issues, such as how best to protect our environment. Many of our domestic policies are formulated and implemented by the federal government, but a number of others are the result of the combined efforts of federal, state, and local governments.

In this chapter, we look at domestic policy issues involving airline safety, poverty and welfare, crime, and the environment. We also examine national economic policies undertaken solely by the federal government. Before we start our analysis, we must look at how public policies are made.

Domestic Policy
Public plans or courses of action that concern issues of national importance, such as poverty, crime, and the environment.

The Policymaking Process

How does any issue get resolved? First, of course, the issue has to be identified as a problem. Often, policymakers simply have to open their local newspapers—or letters from their constituents—to discover that a problem is brewing. On rare occasions, a crisis, such as that brought about by the terrorist attacks of September 11, 2001, creates the need to formulate policy. Like most Americans, however, policymakers receive much of their information from the national media. Finally, different lobbying groups provide information to members of Congress.

A challenging issue after 9/11 was how to increase the safety of airline travel. In response to concerns over this issue, Congress passed the Aviation Security Act, which was signed by President George W. Bush in November 2001. This legislation provides a good example of the steps involved in the policymaking process.

No matter how simple or how complex the problem, those who make policy follow a number of steps. Based on observation, we can divide the process of policymaking into at least five steps: agenda building, policy formulation, policy adoption, policy implementation, and policy evaluation.

Agenda Building

First of all, the issue must get on the agenda. In other words, Congress must become aware that an issue requires congressional action. Agenda building may occur through a crisis, technological change, or mass media campaigns, as well as through the efforts of strong political personalities and effective lobbying groups.

With respect to aviation security, the crisis of 9/11 put that issue on the agenda immediately after the attacks. A number of groups pressured Congress to take immediate action, which Congress did by enacting the Aviation Transportation Act (more commonly known as the Aviation Security Act) of 2001.

Policy Formulation

During the next step in the policymaking process, various policy proposals are discussed among government officials and the public. Such discussions may take place in the printed media, on television, and in the halls of Congress. Congress holds hearings, the president voices the administration's views, and the topic may even become a campaign issue.

With respect to the Aviation Security Act, members of Congress worked closely with representatives from a number of groups and trade associations. Recall from the *America's Security* feature in Chapter 8, which looked at the lobbying surrounding the aviation security legislation, that these groups included representatives from the airline industry, pilots' associations, private security contractors, manufacturers of airport screening equipment, employees' unions, immigrant groups, and many others. Not surprisingly, the debates focused on the question of whether airport security should become the responsibility of the federal government.

Generally, the Senate thought that the federal government should assume this responsibility and that all airport screening personnel should become federal employees. Some groups, including those representing immigrants, objected to this idea because it would require existing airport screening employees to meet certain requirements, such as being a U.S. citizen and a high school graduate. (Again, recall from Chapter 8 that at the time this bill was being considered, about one-third of the existing airport screening personnel did not have a high school diploma and a number of others were not U.S. citizens.) Several members of the House of Representatives urged that airport security be left in the hands of private security contractors but subject to federal supervision and requirements.

Policy Adoption

The third step in the policymaking process involves choosing a specific strategy from among the proposals that have been discussed. The bill that finally passed the House and Senate was a compromise: airport security was federalized, but not necessarily permanently. For three years, all airport screening was to be under the supervision of the government. Screening personnel would have to be U.S. citizens and become federal employees. During this three-year period, five airports of differing sizes would be allowed to test various screening procedures in pilot programs. At the end of the period, airports could opt out of the federal worker program and use private security contractors—but under federal supervision.

House Republicans who had objected to the federalization of airport security were satisfied with the compromise and also with the final bill's inclusion of additional provisions proposed by the House. These provisions included steps that would increase security for caterers, checked baggage, and runways and other areas.

Policy Implementation

The fourth step in the policymaking process involves the implementation of the policy alternative chosen by Congress. Government action must be implemented by bureaucrats, the courts, police, and individual citizens. With respect to the Aviation Security Act, implementation began immediately. Airport screening workers who wanted to retain their jobs were required to apply to the federal government for employment. Full implementation of the act, of course, would take time. For example, the requirement that new equipment to detect explosives be installed in airports would take months or even years to put in place.

Policy Evaluation

After a policy has been implemented, it is evaluated. Groups inside and outside the government conduct studies to determine what actually happens after a policy has been implemented for a given period of time. Based on this "feedback" and the per-

ceived success or failure of the policy, a new round of policymaking initiatives will be undertaken to correct and hopefully improve on the effort. At this point, it is too early to know how effective the Aviation Security Act will be in providing greater aviation security. Within a few years, though, Congress will have received significant feedback on the results of the act's implementation.

Poverty and Welfare

Throughout the world, historically poverty has been accepted as inevitable. Even today, little has been done on an international level to eliminate worldwide poverty. The United States and other industrialized nations, however, have sustained enough economic growth in the past several hundred years to eliminate mass poverty. In fact, considering the wealth and high standard of living in the United States, the persistence of poverty here appears bizarre and anomalous. How can there still be so much poverty in a nation of so much abundance? And what can be done about it?

A traditional solution has been **income transfers.** These are methods of transferring income from relatively well-to-do to relatively poor groups in society, and as a nation, we have been using such methods for a long time. Today, a vast array of welfare programs exists for the sole purpose of redistributing income. We know, however, that these programs have not been entirely successful. Before we examine the problems posed by the welfare system, let's look at the concept of poverty in more detail and at the characteristics of the poor.

DID YOU KNOW . . .
That in the mid-1930s, during the Great Depression, Senator Huey P. Long of Louisiana proposed that the government confiscate all personal fortunes of more than $5 million and all incomes of over $1 million and use the money to give every American family a house, a car, and an annual income of $2,000 or more **?**

Income Transfer
A transfer of income from some individuals in the economy to other individuals. This is generally done by way of the government. It is a transfer in the sense that no current services are rendered by the recipients.

The 1996 welfare reform law limits to two years the eligibility of many families for federal assistance. Private organizations can sometimes pick up where government assistance leaves off. For example, Farm Share redistributes fruits and vegetables considered unsuitable for the retail market due to size or minor blemishes to needy people at distribution centers such as this one. (AP Photo/J. Pat Carter)

In-Kind Subsidy
A good or service—such as food stamps, housing, or medical care—provided by the government to lower-income groups.

For updates and more information on welfare reform, use the term "welfare reform" in the Subject guide.

FIGURE 16–1

The Official Number of Poor in the United States

The number of individuals classified as poor fell steadily from 1959 through 1969. From 1970 to 1981, the number stayed about the same. It then increased during the 1981–1982 recession. The number of poor then fell somewhat, until the early 1990s, when it began to increase. Since 1994, the number has fallen steadily.

The Low-Income Population

We can see in Figure 16–1 that the number of individuals classified as poor fell rather steadily from 1959 through 1969. Then, for about a decade, the number of poor leveled off, until the recession of 1981 to 1982. The number then fell somewhat until the early 1990s, when it began to increase—until 1994. Since then, it has fallen steadily.

Defining Poverty.   The threshold income level, which is used to determine who falls into the poverty category, was originally based on the cost of a nutritionally adequate food plan designed by the U.S. Department of Agriculture for emergency or temporary use. The threshold was determined by multiplying the food-plan cost times three, on the assumption that food expenses constitute approximately one-third of a poor family's expenditures. In 1969, a federal interagency committee examined the calculations of the threshold and decided to set new standards. Until then, annual revisions of the threshold level had been based only on price changes in the food budget. After 1969, the adjustments were made on the basis of changes in the consumer price index (CPI). The CPI is based on the average prices of a specified set of goods and services bought by wage earners in urban areas.

The low-income poverty threshold thus represents an absolute measure of income needed to maintain a specified standard of living as of 1963, with the constant-dollar value, or purchasing-power value, increased year by year in relation to the general increase in prices. For 2003, for example, the official poverty level for a family of four was about $18,300. It has gone up since then by the amount of the change in the CPI during the intervening period. (The poverty level varies with family size and location.)

Transfer Payments as Income.   The official poverty level is based on pretax income, including cash but not **in-kind subsidies**—food stamps, housing vouchers, and the like. If we correct poverty levels for such benefits, the percentage of the population that is below the poverty line drops dramatically. Some economists argue that the way in which the official poverty level is calculated makes no sense in a nation that annually redistributed over $900 billion in cash and noncash transfers in the past few years.

Welfare Reform

Welfare assistance to the poor traditionally has taken a variety of forms. Through a number of welfare programs, hundreds of billions of dollars have been transferred to the poor over the last several decades. With the passage in 1996 of the Personal Responsibility and Work Reconciliation Act, popularly known as the Welfare Reform

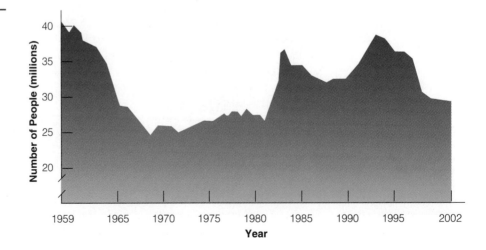

Act, Congress made significant changes in the nation's welfare system. Notably, the states gained more responsibility for establishing welfare rules and managing the welfare program.

Temporary Assistance to Needy Families.   Prior to the Welfare Reform Act of 1996, the basic welfare program in the United States was known as Aid to Families with Dependent Children (AFDC). This program provided aid for children who did not receive financial support from the father. The 1996 welfare reform legislation abolished the AFDC program and replaced it with a program called **Temporary Assistance to Needy Families (TANF).** Under the TANF program, the U.S. government turns over to the states, in the form of block grants (see Chapter 3), funds targeted for welfare assistance. The states, not the national government, now have to meet the costs of any increased welfare spending. For example, if a state wishes to increase the amount of TANF payments to individuals over what the national government gives it, the state has to pay for the additional costs.

One of the basic aims of the Welfare Reform Act was to reduce welfare spending by all governments in the long run. To do this, the act made two significant changes in the basic welfare program. One change involved limiting most welfare recipients to only two years of welfare assistance. After two years, welfare payments must be discontinued unless the recipient is working, either at a public service job or in the private sector. The bill also limited lifetime welfare assistance to five years. (The federally established five-year limit can be avoided by the states, however, if they use their own funds to pay for continued welfare benefits.)

Welfare Reform—A Success, but There Are Clouds on the Horizon.   A booming economy was responsible for part of the success of welfare reform. After all, it is a lot easier for former welfare recipients to get jobs when times are good. As the economy moved into a relatively mild recession in 2001 and 2002, though, those individuals forced off welfare due to the relatively new time limits had a harder time finding jobs. Additionally, more states experienced increased food-stamp usage during the latter half of 2000, during all of 2001, and during a good part of 2002.

One cannot deny the overall long-term benefits of the 1996 Welfare Reform Act, though. During the first five years of welfare reform, the number of families receiving welfare payments declined by 50 percent. Over the same period, the percentage of single mothers—the predominant group of welfare recipients—who were employed rose, from 63 percent to 73 percent. In addition, there has been a decline in teen-age motherhood, partly due to the new restrictions on welfare to this group of individuals.

Other Forms of Government Assistance

The **Supplemental Security Income (SSI)** program was established in 1974 to provide a nationwide minimum income for elderly persons and persons with disabilities who do not qualify for Social Security benefits. The SSI program is one of the fastest-growing programs in the United States. When it started, it cost less than $8 billion annually. Today, that figure is about $35 billion.

The government also issues **food stamps,** coupons that can be used to purchase food. Food stamps are available for low-income individuals and families. Recipients must prove that they qualify by showing that they do not have very much income (or no income at all). In 1964, about 367,000 Americans were receiving food stamps. In 2002, the number of those receiving food stamps was estimated at more than 28 million. The annual cost of funding food stamps jumped from $860,000 in 1964 to an estimated $30 billion in 2002. Workers on strike, and even some college students, are eligible to receive food stamps. The food-stamp program has become a major part of the welfare system in the United States, although it was started in 1964 mainly to

Temporary Assistance to Needy Families (TANF)
A state-administered program in which grants from the national government are given to the states, which use the funds to provide assistance to those eligible to receive welfare benefits. The TANF program was created by the Welfare Reform Act of 1996 and replaced the former AFDC program.

Supplemental Security Income (SSI)
A federal program established to provide assistance to elderly persons and disabled persons.

Food Stamps
Coupons issued by the federal government to low-income individuals to be used for the purchase of food.

Earned-Income Tax Credit (EITC) Program
A government program that helps low-income workers by giving back part or all of their Social Security taxes.

shore up the nation's agricultural sector by distributing surplus food through retail channels.

The **earned-income tax credit (EITC) program** was created in 1975 to help low-income workers by giving back part or all of their Social Security taxes. Since its creation, the EITC program has grown remarkably. Currently, more than 20 percent of all taxpayers claim an EITC, and an estimated $23 billion a year is rebated to taxpayers through the program. The EITC has generated controversy in recent years, however. Although it was designed to reward hard-working Americans who are employed full-time, in fact many part-time workers benefit from the program. According to the General Accounting Office (GAO), the average recipient of EITC rebates works only 1,300 hours per year, whereas the normal working year exceeds 2,000 hours. The GAO further claims that the EITC program has decreased the poverty rate by less than one percentage point. In addition, the Urban Institute released a study in 2001 showing that 35 percent of families eligible for the EITC have never heard of it.[1]

Homelessness—Still a Problem

The plight of the homeless remains a problem. Indeed, some observers argue that the Welfare Reform Act of 1996 has increased the number of homeless persons. There are no hard statistics on the homeless, but estimates of the number of people without a home on any given night in the United States range from a low of 230,000 to as many as 750,000 people.

It is difficult to estimate how many people are homeless because the number depends on how the homeless are defined. There are *street people*—those who sleep in bus stations, parks, and other areas. Many of these people are youthful runaways.

---

[1] Katherin Ross Phillips, "Who Knows about the Earned Income Tax Credit?" *New Federalism: National Survey of American Families* (Washington, D.C.: Urban Institute, January 2001).

Less than one hundred yards from the White House, a homeless man sleeps, with his head on a cart containing all of his possessions. What should (or can) the government do to help the homeless? (Jeff Lawrence/Stock Boston)

There are the so-called *sheltered homeless*—those who sleep in government-supported or privately funded shelters. Many of these individuals used to live with their families or friends. While street people are almost always single, the sheltered homeless include numerous families with children. Homeless families are the fastest-growing subgroup of the homeless population.

As a policy issue, how to handle the homeless problem pits liberals against conservatives. Conservatives argue that there are not really that many homeless and that most of them are alcoholics, drug users, or the mentally ill. Conservatives contend that these individuals should be dealt with by either the mental-health system or the criminal justice system. In contrast, many liberals argue that homelessness is caused by a reduction in welfare benefits and by excessively priced housing. They want more shelters to be built for the homeless.

Recently, cities have been attempting to "criminalize" homelessness. Many municipalities have outlawed sleeping on park benches and sidewalks, as well as panhandling and leaving personal property on public property. In some cities, police sweeps remove the homeless, who then become part of the criminal justice system.

Since 1993, the U.S. Department of Housing and Urban Development has spent nearly $5 billion on programs designed to combat homelessness. Yet because there is so much disagreement about the number of homeless persons, the reasons for homelessness, and the possible cures for the problem, there has been no consistent government policy. Whatever policies have been adopted usually have been attacked by one group or another.

DID YOU KNOW...
That a University of Southern California evaluation of a gang prevention program discovered that when the program lost funding, the gang broke up and the gang's crime rate declined **?**

INFOTRAC ®
COLLEGE EDITION

For more information on the homeless, use the term "homelessness" in the Subject guide.

Crime in the Twenty-first Century

The issue of crime has been on the national agenda for years now. Virtually all polls taken in the United States in the last decade show that crime is one of the major concerns of the public. Although crime rates have fallen, on average, in the last several years, the public's concern has not been misplaced. A related issue that has been on the domestic policy agenda for decades is controlling the use and sale of illegal drugs—activities that are often associated with crimes of violence. More recently, finding ways to deal with terrorism has become a priority for the nation's policymakers.

Crime in American History

In every period in the history of this nation, people have voiced their apprehension about crime. Some criminologists argue that crime was probably as frequent around the time of the American Revolution as it is currently. During the Civil War, mob violence and riots erupted in numerous cities. After the Civil War, people in San Francisco were told that "no decent man is in safety to walk the streets after dark; while at all hours, both night and day, his property is jeopardized by incendiarism [arson] and burglary."[2] In 1886, *Leslie's Weekly* reported, "Each day we see ghastly records of crime ... murder seems to have run riot and each citizen asks ... 'who is safe?'" From 1860 to 1890, the crime rate rose twice as fast as the population.[3] In 1910, one author stated that "crime, especially in its more violent forms and among the young, is increasing steadily and is threatening to bankrupt the Nation."[4]

---

[2] President's Commission on Law Enforcement and Administration of Justice, *Challenge of Crime in a Free Society* (Washington, D.C.: Government Printing Office, 1967), p. 19.

[3] Richard Shenkman, *Legends, Lies and Cherished Myths of American History* (New York: HarperCollins, 1988), p. 158.

[4] President's Commission, *Challenge of Crime*, p. 19.

From 1900 to the 1930s, social violence and crime increased dramatically. Labor union battles and racial violence were common. Only during the three-decade period from the mid-1930s to the early 1960s did the United States experience, for the first time in its history, stable or slightly declining overall crime rates.

What most Americans are worried about is violent crime. From the mid-1980s to 1994, its rate rose relentlessly. The murder rate per 100,000 people in 1964 was 4.9, whereas in 1994 it was estimated at 9.3, an almost 100 percent increase. Since 1995, however, violent crime rates have declined each year until 2001. Some argue that the cause of this decline in crime rates is the booming economy the United States has generally enjoyed since about 1993. Others claim that the $3 billion of additional funds the federal government has spent to curb crime in the last few years has led to less crime. Still others argue that an increase in the number of persons who are jailed or imprisoned is responsible for the reduction in crime.

Crimes Committed by Juveniles

A disturbing aspect of crime is the number of serious crimes committed by juveniles, although the number of such crimes is also dropping. The political response to this rise in serious juvenile crimes has been varied. Some cities have established juvenile curfews. Several states have begun to try more juveniles as adults, particularly juveniles who have been charged with homicides. Still other states are operating "boot camps" to try to "shape up" the less violent juvenile criminals. Additionally, victims of juvenile crime and victims' relatives are attempting to pry open the traditionally secret juvenile court system.[5]

Some worry that the decline in serious juvenile crimes is only temporary. The number of youths between the ages of fifteen and seventeen will rise from about nine million today to almost thirteen million in the year 2010. It is thus understandable that there is grave concern about preventing an even worse juvenile crime problem in the years to come.

Rehabilitation is an important goal at juvenile detention facilities. Society generally accepts that juveniles should have a "second chance" to lead a life without crime. This education group at Circleville Juvenile Detention Center in Ohio is designed to teach juvenile sex offenders mental exercises that will keep them from repeating their crimes after their release. Do you think rehabilitation is more likely to succeed for juvenile than for adult offenders? (AP Photo/Will Shilling)

[5] See Chapter 6 for details on the rights of juveniles in our legal system.

Federal Drug Policy

Illegal drugs are a major cause of crime in America. A rising percentage of arrests are for illegal drug use or drug trafficking. The violence that often accompanies the illegal drug trade occurs for several reasons. One is that drug dealers engage in "turf wars" over the territories in which drugs can be sold. Another is that when drug deals go bad, drug dealers cannot turn to the legal system for help, so they turn to violence. Finally, drug addicts who do not have the income to finance their habits often turn to a life of crime—assault, robbery, and sometimes murder.

The war on drugs and the increased spending on drug interdiction over the years have had virtually no effect on overall illegal drug consumption in the United States. In fact, there is more and higher-quality cocaine available today than at any other time in the history of this country. Mandatory sentences, which have been imposed by the federal government since the late 1980s for all federal offenses, including the sale or possession of illegal drugs, are also not an ideal solution. Indeed, many have concluded that mandatory sentences only lead to a further problem—overcrowded prisons. Furthermore, nearly 50 percent of the 1.6 million people arrested each year in the United States are arrested on marijuana charges—and most of that 50 percent are charged with possession only.

While the federal government has done little to modify its drug policy, state and local governments have been experimenting with new approaches to the problem. Many states now have special "drug courts" for those arrested for illegal drug use. In these courts, offenders typically are "sentenced" to a rehabilitation program. Although efforts in some states to legalize marijuana have failed, eight states have adopted laws that allow marijuana to be used for certain medical purposes. Inevitably, though, state initiatives to legalize the use of marijuana for any purpose run into problems because they conflict with federal drug policy. (For a further discussion of this issue, see this chapter's *Which Side Are You On?* feature on the next page.)

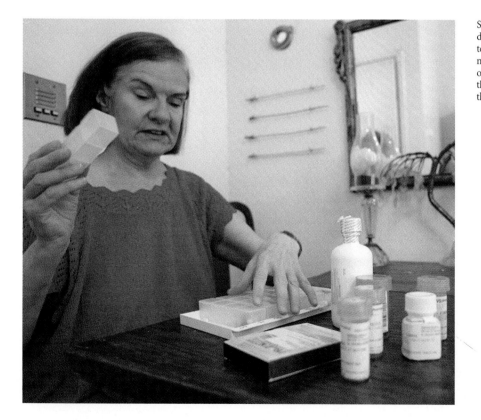

Sheila Doran, who suffers from muscular dystrophy, smokes marijuana to relieve pain and to stimulate her appetite. She is among a large number of Americans who favor the legalization of marijuana for medical purposes. How might the legalization of medical marijuana influence the war on drugs? (AP Photo/Michelle Poire)

Which Side Are You On?
The Debate over Marijuana

In the last decade, eight states—Alaska, Arizona, California, Colorado, Maine, Nevada, Oregon, and Washington—and Washington, D.C., have adopted laws legalizing marijuana, or cannabis, for medical use. Some other states, including Connecticut and Vermont, are considering the adoption of such laws as well. Typically, laws legalizing marijuana use for medical reasons allow physicians to prescribe marijuana only for patients who are suffering from terminal illnesses, such as cancer or AIDS.

The adoption of "medical marijuana" laws has triggered further debate over whether marijuana should be legalized for certain purposes. Because federal drug policy prohibits the use of marijuana for any purpose, the debate is framed, to a great extent, by the federal structure of our government. In other words, it concerns the general question of whether drug policy should be dictated by the federal government or left to the states to decide.

NATIONAL DRUG POLICY PREVAILS

State laws legalizing marijuana for medical purposes directly conflict with the federal Controlled Substances Act of 1970. This act defines marijuana as a substance subject to federal control, and those who possess marijuana are subject to federal criminal penalties. Recall from Chapter 3 that the Constitution states, in the supremacy clause, that the Constitution and federal laws and treaties are the supreme law of the land. Thus, if a state law conflicts with a federal law, the federal law takes priority. This means that state laws authorizing the use of marijuana for medical purposes, when challenged, may be invalidated by the courts. In one case challenging an Oakland, California, cooperative that distributed cannabis to those who wanted it for medical purposes, the United States Supreme Court held that the federal law prevailed. In response to the cooperative's argument that an exception to the federal act should be made for medical purposes, the Court stated that no such exception could be made.*

Many Americans believe that drug policy should be left in the hands of the federal government. This group argues that if each state could create its own laws on drugs, citizens would not have uniform protection against the prob-

*United States v. Oakland Cannabis Buyers' Coop, 532 U.S. 483 (2001).

lems stemming from drug use and abuse. After all, the use and sale of illegal drugs are nationwide problems; therefore, the national government should control drug policy. Furthermore, the national government has far greater resources available to fight the war on drugs.

LET THE STATES DECIDE

Proponents of medical marijuana argue that the federal government should respect the wishes of the majority of the voters in the states that have legalized marijuana use for medical purposes. If this means revising federal drug policy, then that should be done. They also point out that several other nations, including England and Canada, have legalized medical marijuana. Why shouldn't the United States do so as well?

Some supporters of medical marijuana go even further and contend that the mere possession of small amounts of marijuana for any purpose should be decriminalized. By definition, a *crime* is a wrong against society as a whole. If someone purchases and uses small doses of marijuana, what harm does that do to others—to society generally? This group argues that a wiser marijuana policy would be similar to that adopted in the Netherlands. There, although marijuana is illegal, Dutch police are not allowed to arrest someone for the sale or possession of fewer than five grams of cannabis. In addition, approximately 1,200 "coffee shops" are allowed to sell marijuana. The Dutch authorities believe that these coffee shops keep users off the streets and reduce the risk that they will move on to "harder" drugs, such as cocaine and heroin.

WHAT'S YOUR POSITION?

If an initiative to legalize the use of marijuana for medical purposes were placed on your state's ballot, how would you vote? Why?

GOING ONLINE

The Marijuana Policy Project seeks to minimize the harm associated with marijuana (the greatest harm being, in its opinion, imprisonment) by promoting the legalization of marijuana for certain purposes, including medical uses. Visit its Web site at **http://www.mpp.org** for its views as well as for information on recent developments in this area. The National Institute on Drug Abuse believes that more studies need to be undertaken before allowing marijuana to be prescribed for medical purposes. It offers information on marijuana and its effects at **http://www.nida.nih.gov/ MarijBroch/Marijintro.html**.

Confronting Terrorism

Of all of the different types of crimes, terrorism can be the most devastating. The victims of terrorist attacks can number in the hundreds—or even in the thousands, as was the case when hijacked airplanes crashed into the Pentagon and the World Trade Center on September 11, 2001. Additionally, locating the perpetrators is often extremely difficult. With respect to suicide bombings, the perpetrators have themselves been killed, so the search is not for the perpetrators but for others who might have conspired with them in planning the attack.

Terrorism is certainly not a new phenomenon in the world, but it is a relatively new occurrence on U.S. soil. And certainly, the 9/11 attacks made many Americans aware for the first time of the hatred for America harbored by foreigners—in this case, a network of religious fundamentalists in foreign countries. As you have read elsewhere in this text, immediately after 9/11 the U.S. government took numerous actions, including launching a war in Afghanistan, as part of a "war on terrorism." Congress quickly passed new legislation to fund these efforts, as well as a number of other acts, such as the Aviation Security Act discussed earlier in this chapter. Some of the actions taken in the wake of 9/11, such as the war in Afghanistan, were widely supported by the public. Others, such as the enactment of the USA Patriot Act (see Chapter 1) and President Bush's executive order establishing military tribunals (see Chapter 4), have been criticized for infringing too greatly on Americans' civil liberties. This war on terrorism will likely be ongoing for many years. As with all policies, the nation's policy with respect to terrorism will be evaluated—and perhaps modified—over time.

Ayman Gheith, right, and Omar Choudhary, left, were among three men detained by police on Interstate 75 in Florida on September 13, 2002. A woman reported to police that she overheard them making terrorist threats while dining at a restaurant in Georgia, which triggered a search for the men. The men, medical students on their way to Miami to begin hospital internships, were later cleared of any wrongdoing. The incident led to claims of racial profiling by Muslim Americans. Police defended their actions, saying any threat of terrorism would be taken seriously. (AP Photo/J. Pat Carter)

Environmental Policy

Human actions may create unwanted side effects—including the destruction of the environment and the ecology (the total pattern of environmental relationships). Every day, humans, through their actions, emit pollutants into the air and the water. Each year, the world atmosphere receives twenty million metric tons of sulfur dioxide, eighteen million metric tons of ozone pollutants, and sixty million metric tons of carbon monoxide.

The government has been responding to pollution problems since before the American Revolution, when the Massachusetts Bay Colony issued regulations to try to stop the pollution of Boston Harbor. In the nineteenth century, states passed laws controlling water pollution after scientists and medical researchers convinced most policymakers that dumping sewage into drinking and bathing water caused disease. At the national level, the Federal Water Pollution Control Act of 1948 provided research and assistance to the states for pollution-control efforts, but little was done. In 1952, the first state air-pollution law was passed in Oregon. The federal Air Pollution Control Act of 1955 gave some assistance to states and cities. Table 16–1 on page 496 describes the major environmental legislation in the United States.

Protesters in Central Point, Oregon, held signs during a visit to the area by President George W. Bush in 2002. Environmentalists vowed to fight Bush's proposal to increase logging in national forests. Who benefits and who loses by such logging? (AP Photo/Don Ryan, File)

Environmental Impact Statement (EIS)

As a requirement mandated by the National Environmental Policy Act, a report that must show the costs and benefits of major federal actions that could significantly affect the quality of the environment.

The National Environmental Policy Act

The year 1969 marked the start of the most concerted national government involvement in solving pollution problems. In that year, the conflict between oil exploration interests and environmental interests literally erupted when a Union Oil Company's oil well six miles off the coast of Santa Barbara, California, exploded, releasing 235,000 gallons of crude oil. The result was an oil slick, covering an area of eight hundred square miles, that washed up on the city's beaches and killed plant life, birds, and fish. Hearings in Congress revealed that the Interior Department did not know which way to go in the energy-environment trade-off. Congress did know, however, and passed the National Environmental Policy Act in 1969. This landmark legislation established, among other things, the Council on Environmental Quality. Also, it mandated that an **environmental impact statement (EIS)** be prepared for all major federal actions that could significantly affect the quality of the environment. The act gave citizens and public-interest groups concerned with the environment a weapon against the unnecessary and inappropriate use of natural resources by the government.

TABLE 16–1

Major Federal Environmental Legislation

1899 Refuse Act. Made it unlawful to dump refuse into navigable waters without a permit. A 1966 court decision made all industrial wastes subject to this act.

1948 Federal Water Pollution Control Act. Set standards for the treatment of municipal water waste before discharge. Revisions to this act were passed in 1965 and 1967.

1955 Air Pollution Control Act. Authorized federal research programs for air-pollution control.

1963 Clean Air Act. Assisted local and state governments in establishing control programs and coordinating research.

1965 Clean Air Act Amendments. Authorized the establishment of federal standards for automobile exhaust emissions, beginning with 1968 models.

1965 Solid Waste Disposal Act. Provided assistance to local and state governments for control programs and authorized research in this area.

1965 Water Quality Act. Authorized the setting of standards for discharges into waters.

1967 Air Quality Act. Established air-quality regions, with acceptable regional pollution levels. Required local and state governments to implement approved control programs or be subject to federal controls.

1969 National Environmental Policy Act. Established the Council on Environmental Quality (CEQ) for the purpose of coordinating all federal pollution-control programs. Authorized the establishment of the Environmental Protection Agency (EPA) to implement CEQ policies on a case-by-case basis.

1970 Clean Air Act Amendments. Authorized the Environmental Protection Agency to set national air-pollution standards and restricted the discharge of six major pollutants into the lower atmosphere. Automobile manufacturers were required to reduce nitrogen oxide, hydrocarbon, and carbon monoxide emissions by 90 percent (in addition to the 1965 requirements) during the 1970s.

1972 Clean Water Act (Federal Water Pollution Control Act Amendments). Set national water-quality goal of restoring polluted waters to swimmable, fishable waters by 1983.

1972 Federal Environmental Pesticide Control Act. Required that all pesticides used in interstate commerce be approved and certified as effective for their stated purpose. Required certification that they were harmless to humans, animal life, animal feed, and crops.

1974 Clean Water Act. Originally called the Safe Drinking Water Act, this law set (for the first time) federal standards for water suppliers serving more than twenty-five people, having more than fifteen service connections, or operating more than sixty days a year.

1976 Resource Conservation and Recovery Act. Encouraged the conservation and recovery of resources. Put hazardous waste under government control. Prohibited the opening of new dumping sites. Required that all existing open dumps be closed or upgraded to sanitary landfills by 1983. Set standards for providing technical, financial, and marketing assistance to encourage solid waste management.

1977 Clean Air Act Amendments. Postponed the deadline for automobile emission requirements.

1980 Comprehensive Environmental Response, Compensation, and Liability Act. Established a "Superfund" to clean up toxic waste dumps.

1990 Clean Air Act Amendments. Provided for precise formulas for new gasoline to be burned in the smoggiest cities, further reduction in carbon monoxide and other exhaust emissions in certain areas that still have dangerous ozone levels in the year 2003, and a cap on total emissions of sulfur dioxide from electricity plants. Placed new restrictions on toxic pollutants.

1990 Oil Pollution Act. Established liability for the cleanup of navigable waters after oil-spill disasters.

1996 Food Quality and Protection Act. Amended the Federal Food, Drug, and Cosmetic Act of 1938 to regulate the use of pesticides in the cultivation and marketing of food products.

1999 Chemical Safety Information, Site Security, and Fuels Regulatory Relief Act. Established new provisions to regulate risk management plans at certain chemical and fuel facilities to reduce the risk of chemical explosions and to lessen the vulnerability of these facilities to criminal and terrorist activities.

Curbing Air Pollution

The most comprehensive government attempt at cleaning up our environment occurred in 1990. After years of lobbying by environmentalists and counterlobbying by industry, the Clean Air Act of 1990 was passed. This act amended the 1963 Clean Air Act, which had also been amended in 1970 and 1977. The 1990 amendments required automobile manufacturers to cut new automobiles' exhaust emissions of nitrogen oxide by 60 percent and emissions of other pollutants by 35 percent. By 1998, all new automobiles had to meet this standard. Regulations that will go into effect beginning with 2004 model cars call for cutting nitrogen oxide tailpipe emissions by nearly 10 percent by 2007. For the first time, sport utility vehicles and light trucks were required to meet the same emission standards as automobiles.

Stationary sources of air pollution were also made subject to more regulation under the 1990 act. The act required 110 of the oldest coal-burning power plants in the United States to cut their emissions by 40 percent by the year 2001. Controls were placed on other factories and businesses in an attempt to reduce ground-level ozone pollution in ninety-six cities to healthful levels by 2005 (except in Los Angeles, which has until 2010 to meet the standards). The act also required that the production of chlorofluorocarbons (CFCs) be stopped completely by the year 2002. CFCs are thought to deplete the ozone layer and increase global warming. CFCs are used in air-conditioning and other refrigeration units.

In 1997, in light of evidence that very small particles (2.5 microns, or millionths of a meter) of soot might affect our health as significantly as larger particles, the Environmental Protection Agency (EPA) issued new particulate standards for motor vehicle exhaust systems and other sources of pollution. The EPA also established a more rigorous standard for ozone, which is formed when sunlight combines with pollutants from cars and other sources. Ozone is the basic ingredient of smog.

A curtain of smog shrouds the Los Angeles skyline. Strict air pollution standards for automobiles have been phased in over the past several years to curb such air pollution. How do policymakers measure the economic impact of clean air policies? (AP Photo/Nick Ut)

Water Pollution

One of the most important acts regulating water pollution is the Clean Water Act of 1972, which amended the Federal Water Pollution Control Act of 1948. The Clean Water Act established the following goals: (1) make waters safe for swimming, (2) protect fish and wildlife, and (3) eliminate the discharge of pollutants into the water. The act set specific time schedules, which were subsequently extended by further legislation. Under these schedules, the EPA establishes limits on discharges of types of pollutants based on the technology available for controlling them. The 1972 act also required municipal and industrial polluters to apply for permits before discharging wastes into navigable waters.

The Clean Water Act also prohibits the filling or dredging of wetlands unless a permit is obtained from the Army Corps of Engineers. The EPA defines *wetlands* as "those areas that are inundated or saturated by surface or ground water at a frequency and duration sufficient to support, and that under normal circumstances do support, a prevalence of vegetation typically adapted for life in saturated soil conditions." In recent years, the broad interpretation of what constitutes a wetland subject to the regulatory authority of the federal government has generated substantial controversy.

Perhaps one of the most controversial regulations concerning wetlands was the "migratory-bird rule" issued by the Army Corps of Engineers. Under this rule, any

INFOTRAC®
COLLEGE EDITION

For more information on air pollution, use the term "air pollution" in the Subject guide.

bodies of water that could affect interstate commerce, including seasonal ponds or waters "used or suitable for use by migratory birds" that fly over state borders, were "navigable waters" subject to federal regulation under the Clean Water Act as wetlands. In 2001, after years of controversy, the United States Supreme Court struck down the rule. The Court stated that it was not prepared to hold that isolated and seasonal ponds, puddles, and "prairie potholes" become "navigable waters of the United States" simply because they serve as a habitat for migratory birds.[6]

The Politics of Economic Decision Making

Nowhere are the principles of public policymaking more obvious than in the area of economic decisions undertaken by the federal government. The president and Congress (and to a growing extent, the judiciary) are faced constantly with questions concerning economic policy. Three economic policy areas of particular concern are taxes, Social Security, and monetary policy.

Each policy action with respect to these three areas carries with it costs and benefits, known as **policy trade-offs.** The costs are typically borne by one group and the benefits enjoyed by another group.

The Politics of Taxes and Subsidies

Taxes are not just given to us from above. Rather, they are voted on by members of Congress. Members of Congress also vote on *subsidies,* which are a type of negative taxes that benefit certain businesses and individuals. An examination of the Internal Revenue Code, encompassing thousands of pages, thousands of sections, and thousands of subsections, gives some indication that our tax system is not very simple.

We begin our analysis with the premise that in the world of taxes and subsidies, the following is always true: *For every action on the part of the government, there will be a reaction on the part of the public.* Eventually, the government will react with another action, followed by the public's further reaction. The **action-reaction syndrome** is a reality that has plagued government policymakers since the beginning of this nation.

Tax Rates and Tax Loopholes.   People are not assessed a lump-sum tax each year; each family does not just pay $1,000 or $10,000 or $20,000. Rather, individuals and businesses pay taxes based on tax rates. (Table 16–2 shows the 2002 tax rates for individuals and married couples.) The higher the tax rate—the action on the part

Policy Trade-Offs
The cost to the nation of undertaking any one policy in terms of all of the other policies that could have been undertaken. For example, an increase in the expenditures on one federal program means either a reduction in expenditures on another program or an increase in federal taxes (or the deficit).

Action-Reaction Syndrome
For every action on the part of government, there is a reaction on the part of the affected public. Then the government attempts to counter the reaction with another action, which starts the cycle all over again.

---

[6] *Solid Waste Agency of Northern Cook County v. U.S. Army Corps of Engineers,* 531 U.S. 159 (2001).

TABLE 16–2

2002 Tax Rates for Single Persons and Married Couples

SINGLE PERSONS		MARRIED COUPLES	
MARGINAL TAX BRACKET	MARGINAL TAX RATE	MARGINAL TAX BRACKET	MARGINAL TAX RATE
$ 0–$ 6,000	10.0%	$ 0–$ 12,000	10.0%
$ 6,000–$ 27,950	15.0%	$ 12,000–$ 46,700	15.0%
$ 27,950–$ 67,700	27.0%	$ 46,700–$112,850	27.0%
$ 67,700–$141,250	30.0%	$112,850–$171,950	30.0%
$141,250–$307,050	35.0%	$171,950–$307,050	35.0%
$307,050 and above	38.6%	$307,050 and above	38.6%

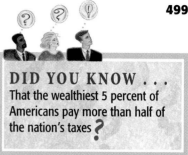

of the government—the greater the public's reaction to that tax rate. Again, it is all a matter of costs and benefits. If the highest tax rate you pay on the income you make is 15 percent, that means that any method you can use to reduce your taxable income by one dollar saves you fifteen cents in tax liabilities that you owe the federal government. Therefore, those individuals paying a 15 percent rate have a relatively small incentive to avoid paying taxes. But consider individuals who were faced with a tax rate of 94 percent in the 1940s. They had a tremendous incentive to find legal ways to reduce their taxable incomes. For every dollar of income that was somehow deemed nontaxable, these taxpayers would reduce tax liabilities by ninety-four cents.

So, individuals and corporations facing high tax rates will always react by making concerted attempts to get Congress to add **loopholes** to the tax law that allow them to reduce their taxable incomes. When the Internal Revenue Code imposed very high tax rates on high incomes, it also provided for more loopholes. Special provisions enabled investors in oil and gas wells to reduce their taxable incomes. Loopholes allowed people to shift income from one year to the next. Other loopholes allowed individuals to avoid some taxes completely by forming corporations outside the United States.

Loophole
A legal method by which individuals and businesses are allowed to reduce the tax liabilities owed to the government.

These same principles apply to other interest groups. As long as one group of taxpayers sees a specific benefit from getting the law changed and that benefit means a lot of money per individual, the interest group will aggressively support lobbying activities and the election and reelection of members of Congress who will push for special tax loopholes. In other words, if enough benefits are to be derived from influencing tax legislation, such influence will be exerted by the affected parties.

Why We Probably Will Never Have a Truly Simple Tax System. The federal government was running large deficits in the late 1980s, and these continued until the late 1990s and reoccurred starting in 2001. When faced with the prospect of having to cut the growth of federal government spending, Congress balked. Instead, it raised tax rates. This occurred under the first Bush administration in 1990 and under the Clinton administration in 1993. Indeed, at the upper end of income earners, the tax rate paid on each extra dollar earned went up from 28 percent in 1986 to 39.6 percent in 1993. That was an increase in the effective tax rate of 41.4 percent.

In response, the action-reaction syndrome went into effect. As tax rates went up, those who were affected spent more time and effort to get Congress to legislate special exceptions, exemptions, loopholes, and the like, so that the *full* impact of such tax-rate increases would not be felt by richer Americans. In 2001, President George W. Bush fulfilled a campaign pledge by persuading Congress to enact new legislation lowering tax rates. In an effort to prevent budget deficits, however, the new rates are being phased in over several years. As a result, the U.S. tax code became even more complicated than it was before.

In June 2001, President George W. Bush signed a $1.35 trillion tax-cut bill, fulfilling a campaign promise to return budget surpluses to taxpayers. By 2002, however, budget deficits had returned, and many lawmakers questioned the wisdom of the tax-cut bill. Does the fact that the tax cut is to take effect gradually over many years matter in this debate? (AP Photo/Ron Edmonds)

TAX RELIEF FOR AMERICA

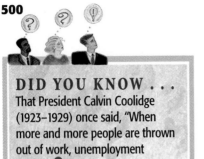

Social Security: How Long Will It Last?

Closely related to the question of taxes in the United States is the viability of the Social Security system. Social Security taxes came into existence when the Federal Insurance Contribution Act (FICA) was passed in 1935. In that year, the United States was beginning to recover from the Great Depression. The financial resources of many people had been demolished during the previous six years: jobs had been lost, stock prices had tumbled, and thousands of banks had failed, wiping out the accounts of their depositors. It was widely felt that recent retirees and those soon to retire faced destitution. Moreover, many people argued that the elderly should be protected from any similar disasters in the future. Hence, the decision was made to establish Social Security as a means of guaranteeing a minimum level of pension benefits to all persons. Today, many people regard Social Security as a kind of "social compact"—a national promise to successive generations that they will receive support in their old age.

When the FICA tax was first levied, it was 1 percent of earnings up to $3,000. By 1963, the percentage rate had increased to 3.625 percent. As of 2002, a 6.2 percent rate was imposed on each employee's wages up to a maximum of $84,900 to pay for Social Security. In addition, employers must pay in ("contribute") an equal percentage. Also, there is a combined employer/employee 2.9 percent tax rate assessed for Medicare on all wage income, with no upper limit. Medicare is a federal program, begun in 1965, that pays hospital and physicians' bills for persons over the age of sixty-five.

The Trust Fund That Isn't. During the early years of Social Security's existence, payroll taxes were collected, but no benefits were paid. The monies collected over this period were used to purchase bonds issued by the U.S. Treasury, and this accumulation of bonds was called the Social Security Trust Fund. (Medicare has a similar trust fund; because the basic principles apply to both funds, only Social Security's is discussed in detail.) Even today, Social Security tax collections continue to exceed ben-

efits, and so the Trust Fund has continued to grow. As the baby boomers move into retirement in a few years, benefit payments each year will exceed tax receipts, and the Social Security system will begin to sell the bonds in the Trust Fund to finance the difference. Eventually—estimates indicate around the year 2030 unless the current system is changed—all of the bonds in the Trust Fund will have been sold. Any further benefits will have to be *explicitly* financed out of current-day taxes.

The Grim Future of the Social Security System. If the current structure of the Social Security system is not changed, the continuing retirements of large numbers of baby boomers, born between the late 1940s and early 1960s, will leave today's college students, and their children, with a potentially staggering bill to pay. As the number of Americans aged sixty-five and older increases from about 35 million today to 45 million in the year 2010, and to 75 million in the year 2040, Medicare expenditures alone, as a percentage of total national income, are expected to grow dramatically—as you can see in Figure 16–2. For Social Security and Medicare to be maintained, the payroll tax rate may have to rise to 25 percent. And a payroll tax rate of 40 percent is not unlikely by 2050.

One way to think about the future bill that today's college students (and their successors) could face in the absence of fundamental changes in Social Security is to consider the number of workers available to support each retiree. The chapter-opening *What If . . .* feature described how that number has fallen. Today, as you can see in Figure 16–3, roughly three workers provide for each retiree's Social Security, *plus* his or her Medicare benefits. Unless the current system is changed, by 2030 only two workers will be available to pay the Social Security and Medicare benefits due each recipient. In this event, a working couple would find themselves responsible for supporting not only themselves and their family, but also someone outside the family who is receiving Social Security and Medicare benefits.

These stark figures illustrate why efforts to reform these programs have begun to dominate the nation's public agenda. What remains to be seen is how the government ultimately will resolve the problem.

What Will It Take to Salvage Social Security?

The United States now finds itself with a social compact—the Social Security system—that entails a flow of promised benefits that could exceed the inflow of taxes by as early as 2010. What, if anything, might be done about this? We look here at some of the options being considered today.

Raise Taxes. One option is to raise the Social Security payroll tax rate. A prominent proposal promises an $80 billion annual increase in contributions via a 2.2 percentage point hike in the payroll tax rate, to an overall rate of 17.5 percent. At best, however, such a tax increase would keep current taxes above current benefits only until 2020, after which the system would again technically be in "deficit." To cover Social Security's projected deficits through the remainder of this century, the payroll tax would have to be increased to more than 22 percent.

Another proposal is to eliminate the current cap on the level of wages to which the payroll tax is applied; this measure would also generate about $80 billion per year in additional tax revenues. Nevertheless, even a combined policy of eliminating the wage cap and implementing a 2.2 percentage point tax increase would not, by itself, keep tax collections above benefit payments over the long run.

Reduce Benefits Payouts. Proposals are also on the table to increase the age of full benefit eligibility, perhaps to as high as seventy. Another option is to cut benefits to

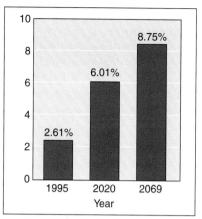

FIGURE 16–2

Medicare Expenditures as a Percentage of Total National Income

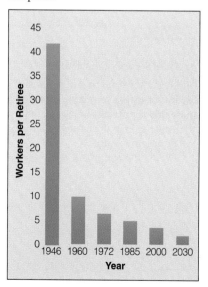

FIGURE 16–3

Workers per Retiree

The average number of workers per Social Security retiree has declined dramatically since the program's inception.

SOURCES: Social Security Administration and authors' estimates.

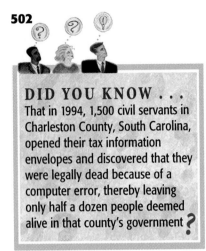

DID YOU KNOW...
That in 1994, 1,500 civil servants in Charleston County, South Carolina, opened their tax information envelopes and discovered that they were legally dead because of a computer error, thereby leaving only half a dozen people deemed alive in that county's government?

I N F O T R A C ®
COLLEGE EDITION

For more information on Social Security, use the term "Social Security reform" in the Subject guide.

nonworking spouses. A third proposal is to impose "means testing" on some or all Social Security benefits. As things stand now, all persons covered by the system collect benefits when they retire, regardless of their assets or other sources of retirement income. Under a system of means testing, individuals with substantial amounts of other retirement income would receive reduced Social Security benefits.

Reform Immigration Policies. Many experts believe that significant changes in U.S. immigration laws could offer the best hope of dealing with the tax burdens and workforce shrinkage of the future. Currently, however, more than 90 percent of new immigrants are admitted based on a selection system that has not changed since 1952. Under this system, immigration rights are tied to family status. Thus, most people admitted to the United States are the spouses, children, or siblings of earlier immigrants. Unless Congress changes the system to also give a preference to those with training or skills that are highly valued in the U.S. workplace, new legal immigrants are unlikely to relieve much of the pressure building due to our aging population.

Increase the Rate of Return on Social Security Contributions. The first Social Security taxes (called "contributions") were collected in 1937, but the first retirement benefits were not paid until 1940. For the average retiree of 1940, the Social Security system was more generous than any private investment plan anyone was likely to devise: after adjusting for inflation, the rate of return on contributions was an astounding 135 percent. (Roughly speaking, this means that every $100 of combined employer and employee contributions yielded $135 *per year* during each and every year of that person's retirement.) Ever since the early days of Social Security, however, the rate of return has decreased. As you can see in Figure 16–4, by 2000 the rate of return had dropped to 4 percent. Looking into the future, the situation appears grim. By 2020, the rate of return will be negative, and it will become increasingly negative in subsequent years.

One proposal being debated calls for the partial privatization of the Social Security system as a means of increasing the rate of return on individuals' retirement contributions. Privatization would allow workers to invest a specified portion of their Social Security payroll taxes in the stock market. Although such a solution would have been unthinkable in past decades, today there is some support for the

FIGURE 16–4

Private Rates of Return on Social Security Contributions

Although those who paid in to Social Security in earlier years got a good deal, those who are paying in now and those who will pay in in the future are facing low or negative returns.

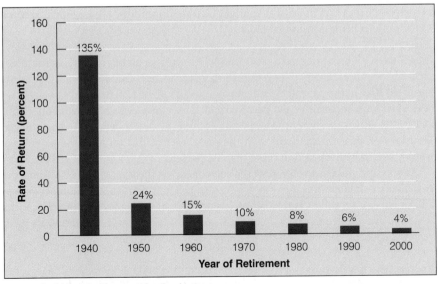

SOURCES: Social Security Trustees and authors' estimates.

idea of reaping greater returns on Social Security contributions through private investments. Indeed, President George W. Bush's proposal that Social Security be partially privatized in this way has drawn significant support.

A number of groups oppose the concept of partial privatization, however. These groups fear that the diversion of Social Security funds into individual stock portfolios could jeopardize the welfare of future retirees, who would be at the mercy of the volatile stock market. Opponents of partial privatization also worry that such a change could be a first step down the slippery slope toward full privatization—and no government guarantees with respect to Social Security.

Certainly, changing from a public system to a private system would face enormous political roadblocks in the United States. Yet, regardless of how the Social Security problem is solved, it must be solved—because there is no way to stop the aging of the population.

The Politics of Fiscal and Monetary Policy

Changes in the tax code sometimes form part of an overall fiscal policy change. **Fiscal policy** is defined as the use of changes in government expenditures and taxes to alter national economic variables, such as the rate of inflation, the rate of unemployment, the level of interest rates, and the rate of economic growth. The federal government also controls **monetary policy,** defined as the use of changes in the amount of money in circulation so as to affect interest rates, credit markets, the rate of inflation, and employment. Fiscal policy is the domain of Congress and the president. Monetary policy, as we shall see, is much less under the control of Congress and the president, because the monetary authority in the United States, the Federal Reserve System, or the Fed, is an independent agency not directly controlled by either Congress or the president.

Fiscal Policy: Theory and Reality. The theory behind fiscal policy changes is relatively straightforward: When the economy is going into a recession (a period of rising unemployment), the federal government should stimulate economic activity by increasing government expenditures, by decreasing taxes, or both. When the economy is becoming overheated with rapid increases in employment and rising prices

Fiscal Policy
The use of changes in government spending or taxation to alter national economic variables, such as the rate of unemployment.

Monetary Policy
The use of changes in the amount of money in circulation to alter credit markets, employment, and the rate of inflation.

Wall Street during the stock market crash of 1929. Another spectacular drop in the stock market occurred in October of 1987. Stock prices tumbled yet again in the fall of 1998 and also in the spring and summer of 2002. (AP Photo)

Keynesian Economics
An economic theory, named after English economist John Maynard Keynes, that gained prominence during the Great Depression of the 1930s. It is typically associated with the use of fiscal policy to alter national economic variables—for example, increased government spending during times of economic downturns.

Federal Open Market Committee (FOMC)
The most important body within the Federal Reserve System. The FOMC decides how monetary policy should be carried out by the Federal Reserve System.

Alan Greenspan, the chairman of the Federal Reserve. The Federal Reserve is responsible for our nation's monetary policy. Greenspan is often called to testify before various congressional committees. He frequently finds himself in the "hot seat" when the economy enters a recession. (AP Photo/Doug Mills)

(a condition of inflation), fiscal policy should become contractionary, reducing government expenditures and increasing taxes. That particular view of fiscal policy was first implemented in the 1930s and became popular again during the 1960s. It was an outgrowth of the economic theories of the English economist John Maynard Keynes. Keynes's ideas, published during the Great Depression of the 1930s, influenced the economic policymakers guiding President Franklin D. Roosevelt's New Deal.

Keynes believed that the forces of supply and demand operated too slowly in a serious recession and that government should step in to stimulate the economy. Such actions thus are guided by **Keynesian economics.** Keynesian (pronounced *kayn*-zeean) economists believe, for example, that the Great Depression resulted from a serious imbalance in the economy. The public was saving more than usual, and businesses were investing less than usual. According to Keynesian theory, at the beginning of the depression, the government should have filled the gap that was created when businesses began limiting their investments. The government could have done so by increasing government spending or cutting taxes.

Monetary Policy: Politics and Reality.   The theory behind monetary policy, like that behind fiscal policy, is relatively straightforward. In periods of recession and high unemployment, we should stimulate the economy by expanding the rate of growth of the money supply. (The money supply is defined loosely as checking account balances and currency.) An easy-money policy is supposed to lower interest rates and induce consumers to spend more and producers to invest more. With rising inflation, we should do the reverse: reduce the rate of growth of the amount of money in circulation. Interest rates should rise, choking off some consumer spending and some business investment. But the world is never so simple as the theory we use to explain it. If the nation experiences stagflation—rising inflation *and* rising unemployment—expansionary monetary policy (expanding the rate of growth of the money supply) will lead to even more inflation. Ultimately, the more money there is in circulation, the higher prices will be—there will be inflation.

The Monetary Authority—The Federal Reserve System.   Congress established our modern central bank, the Federal Reserve System, in 1913. It is governed by a board of governors consisting of seven members, including the very powerful chairperson. All of the governors, including the chairperson, are nominated by the president and approved by the Senate. Their appointments are for fourteen years.

Through the Federal Reserve System, called the Fed, and its **Federal Open Market Committee (FOMC),** decisions about monetary policy are made eight times a year. The Board of Governors of the Federal Reserve System is independent. The president can attempt to convince the board, and Congress can threaten to merge the Fed with the Treasury, but as long as the Fed retains its independence, its chairperson and governors can do what they please. Hence, talking about "the president's monetary policy" or "Congress's monetary policy" is inaccurate. To be sure, the Fed has, on occasion, yielded to presidential pressure, and for a while the Fed's chairperson felt constrained to follow a congressional resolution requiring him to report monetary targets over each six-month period. But now, more than ever before, the Fed remains one of the truly independent sources of economic power in the government.

Monetary Policy and Lags. Monetary policy does not suffer from the lengthy time lags that affect fiscal policy, because the Fed can, within a very short period, put its policy into effect. Nonetheless, researchers have estimated that it takes almost fourteen months for a change in monetary policy to become effective, measured from the time the economy either slows down or speeds up too much to the time the economy feels the policy change. This means that by the time monetary policy goes into effect, a different policy might be appropriate.

Budget Deficits and the Public Debt

Until the late 1990s, the federal government ran a deficit—spent more than it received—in every year except two since 1960. Every time a budget deficit occurred, the federal government issued debt instruments in the form of **U.S. Treasury bonds.** The sale of these bonds to corporations, private individuals, pension plans, foreign governments, foreign businesses, and foreign individuals added to the **public debt,** or **national debt,** defined as the total amount owed by the federal government. Thus, the relationship between the annual federal government budget deficit and the public debt is clear: if the public debt is, say, $4 trillion this year and the federal budget deficit is $150 billion during the year, then at the end of the year the public debt will be $4.15 trillion. Table 16–3 shows what has happened to the net public debt over time.

It would seem that until recently the nation increasingly was mortgaging its future. But this table does not take into account two important variables: inflation and increases in population. A better way to examine the relative importance of the public debt is to compare it to total national output. We do this in Figure 16–5. There you see that, as a percentage of total national output, the public debt reached its peak

For more information on the Federal Reserve, use the term "Alan Greenspan" in the Subject Guide.

U.S. Treasury Bond
Evidence of debt issued by the federal government; similar to corporate bonds but issued by the U.S. Treasury.

Public Debt, or National Debt
The total amount of debt carried by the federal government.

FIGURE 16–5

Net Public Debt as a Percentage of National Output

The public debt as a percentage of national output reached its peak during World War II and then dropped consistently until about 1975. It then grew steadily—until the mid-1990s, when it again started to fall, only to rise again in 2002.

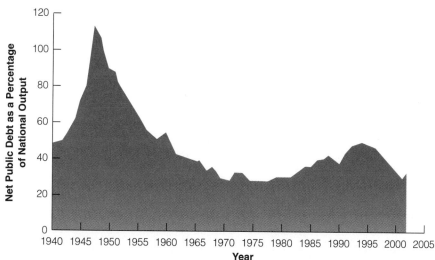

TABLE 16–3

Net Public Debt of the Federal Government

YEAR	TOTAL (BILLIONS OF CURRENT DOLLARS)
1940	$ 42.7
1945	235.2
1950	219.0
1960	237.2
1970	284.9
1980	709.3
1990	2,410.1
1992	2,998.6
1993	3,247.5
1994	3,432.1
1995	3,603.4
1996	3,747.1
1997	3,900.0
1998	3,870.0
1999	3,632.9
2000	3,448.6
2001	3,200.3
2002	3,528.7
2003	3,714.8*

*Estimate.

SOURCE: U.S. Office of Management and Budget.

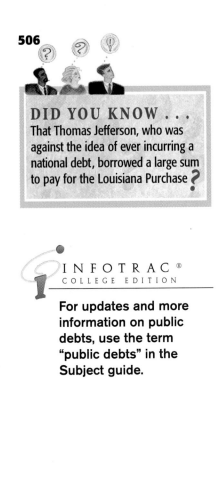

INFOTRAC®
COLLEGE EDITION

For updates and more information on public debts, use the term "public debts" in the Subject guide.

Public Debt Financing
The government's spending more than it receives in taxes and paying for the difference by issuing U.S. Treasury bonds, thereby adding to the public debt.

during World War II and fell steadily thereafter until the mid-1970s. Since then, except for a slight reduction in 1990, it rose until 1995, when it again started to fall, only to start rising again in 2002.

The New Reality of Federal Government Deficits

The economy had already gone into the beginnings of a recession in 2001 when terrorists attacked the Pentagon and the World Trade Center towers. The blow to the nation's economy kept it in a recession for many months to follow. Thus, federal government revenues from taxes did not rise as planned. At the same time, federal government expenditures increased rather dramatically because of the new war on terrorism. For example, Congress passed an emergency $40 billion funding bill for the war on terrorism.

Occasionally, Congress and the president used the war on terrorism as an excuse to fund all sorts of additional programs in the name of "security." One of those was a farm bill that even supporters of President Bush labeled "a blow to rationality in government spending." The farm bill added $73.5 billion over ten years to the $98.5 billion previously legislated to maintain current government agricultural subsidy programs. (For a further look at this issue, see this chapter's *America's Security* feature.)

In conclusion, we can expect to see federal government deficits, and therefore increases in the net public debt, for some years to come.

The Problem of "Crowding Out"

The prospect of an increasing public debt is worrisome to many economists. As we have seen, a large public debt is made up of a series of annual federal government budget deficits. Each time the federal government runs a deficit, we know that it must go into the financial marketplace to borrow the money. This process, in which the U.S. Treasury sells U.S. Treasury bonds, is called **public debt financing**. Public debt financing, in effect, "crowds out" private borrowing. Consider that to borrow, say, $100 billion, the federal government must bid for loanable funds in the marketplace, just as any business does. It bids for those loanable funds by offering to pay higher interest rates. Consequently, interest rates are increased when the federal government runs large deficits and borrows money to cover them. Higher interest rates can stifle or slow business investment, which reduces the rate of economic growth.

America and the Global Economy

At the close of World War II in 1945, the United States was clearly the most powerful and influential nation on earth. Japan, Europe, and the Soviet Union were all in shambles. From the end of the war through most of the 1960s, America retained its economic hegemony. Over the next twenty-five years, however, U.S. dominance in the global marketplace was challenged. Japan rose from its wartime defeat to become one of the top world economic powers. Some of its Pacific Rim neighbors—Taiwan, Hong Kong, Singapore, Malaysia, and Thailand—also started to catch up.

On the other side of the world, the fifteen countries of the former European Community (EC) became one consumer market—the European Union, or EU—on December 31, 1992. For the first time in more than a hundred years, the U.S. economy slipped to second place, behind the 360-million-consumer economy of the EU. Adding to the EU's formidable economic power is the untapped low-cost labor that is available from the former republics of the Soviet Union and from Eastern Europe. (For a discussion of how a common currency—the euro—may affect the economic strength of the EU, see this chapter's *Global View* feature on page 508.)

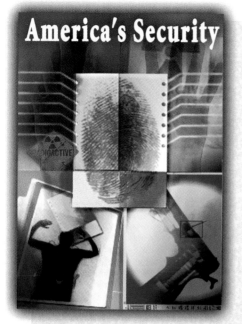

America's Security

Policymaking in the Face of Terrorism

Soon after 9/11, members of Congress and the American public reacted in a predictable way, demanding that government do more to fight the terrorist threat than it has in the past. "Doing more" usually means, in the world of politics, spending more. Certainly, no one at that time was against increased funding for the military, the FBI, the CIA, airport surveillance and security, and increased police protection. Not surprisingly, in addition, many interest groups tried to use America's security as a rationale for increased spending on their particular pet projects.

THE FARM SECURITY ACT OF 2002

One brazen example of linking straightforward subsidies—additional government spending—to the war on terrorism is the Farm Security Act of 2002. Since 1978, farmers' incomes have been increased by over $300 billion from the federal government, representing almost 10 percent of the nation's net public debt.

In 1996, Congress passed the Freedom to Farm bill, which was intended to phase out subsidies to farmers gradually. Not only have the subsidies increased since then, but also members of Congress from farm states have used the war on terrorism as a pretext to ask for even more. They included the word *security* in the title of the bill to link the insecurity that farmers are currently feeling about their future incomes to the insecurity that Americans in general are feeling in the wake of the terrorist attacks. Over the next ten years, the new subsidies added by the 2002 law, combined with existing federal subsidies, will cost American taxpayers about $175 billion.

THE AIRLINES, AGAIN

As we pointed out in Chapter 12, immediately after 9/11 the airlines received billions of dollars in direct aid and billions more in loan guarantees. Few people criticized this policy. Nonetheless, it looks as if the subsidies will have little long-term impact on the airline industry. At current rates of losses, many of today's major airlines will run out of money soon. Therefore, well-intentioned subsidies to a particularly vulnerable industry after 9/11 may have simply put off the day when the least-profitable airlines will have to merge with stronger airlines.

FOR CRITICAL ANALYSIS

Can you think of examples of the government "doing something" to improve America's security without spending more?

In 2002, Congress passed the Farm Security Act, providing huge subsidies to farm states, such as that of Senator Tom Harkin of Iowa, seen here in the foreground. The bill ends the phase-out of farm subsidies intended by the 1996 farm bill. Some claim that it was the single biggest giveaway in history. (AP Photo/Dennis Cook)

It was very fashionable in the 1980s and even for much of the 1990s to argue that America had lost its competitive edge in the world economy. Numerous reports showed that we were lagging behind European countries and particularly Asian countries—such as Japan, Indonesia, Malaysia, Thailand, Hong Kong, South Korea, and Taiwan. Today, one rarely reads anything about problems with America's global competitiveness. Why? The reason is that the Asian economies went into near collapse in

Will Europe Rival the United States Now That They Both Have Common Currencies?

Until 2002, all of the nations in Europe had their own currencies—francs, deutsche marks, pesetas, lira, and so on. Today, you can travel among twelve European nations with only one currency—the euro. Americans have always been able to travel throughout the fifty states with one currency—the dollar. Some argue that Europe's adoption of a common currency will allow Europe to catch up with America's single-market economic power.

Today, the euro is the world's second-largest currency in terms of the total size of the economies that use it. If the European Union decides to add new countries and if some countries, such as England, which have so far refrained from adopting the euro decide to adopt it, then the euro could represent the largest world currency in terms of the combined economic powers of the countries using it.

The dollar's dominance in world financial markets is not about to go away, but the euro definitely represents a serious threat.

FOR CRITICAL ANALYSIS

What might have happened to America had the different states each been allowed to have their own currencies?

the late 1990s, and Europe has been stagnating. At the same time, the U.S. economy, at least until recently, was booming—millions of jobs were added every year, the unemployment rate dropped to low levels, and there was little inflation. The economy was so strong that the United States had to import skilled laborers from other countries, particularly for the information-technology sector.

Clearly, the United States remains the premier world economic power, although this position should not be taken for granted. Many countries have been economic powerhouses, only to find themselves years later way down on the ladder of developed countries.

Domestic and Economic Policy: Why Is It Important Today?

Whether policy is made by the president or by Congress, policymaking affects you perhaps more than any other aspect of government. Certainly, if you fly, you saw how policymaking affected the ease, or lack thereof, of getting on a plane after new security measures were implemented following 9/11. If you have attempted to fill out your own income tax forms recently, you discovered that due to complicated policy decisions by Congress and the Internal Revenue Service, it is harder and harder to understand how to fill out those forms, which are due on April 15 every year.

As we pointed out in the last chapter, much domestic policymaking is carried out by nonelected appointees to government agencies. One of the most powerful appointees is the chair of the U.S. Federal Reserve System. That person and his or her staff can determine how much you pay in interest when you decide to buy a car or a house. The Federal Reserve, through its monetary policies, ultimately determines the value, in terms of purchasing power, of the dollars you have in your wallet and checking account. Therefore, as long as we use money, monetary policy will directly affect you.

The major issues facing you and the nation today are, for the most part, domestic policy issues. They include domestic security, Social Security, welfare, health care, and Medicare. We already talked about what might happen if Social Security and Medicare were eliminated in our chapter-opening *What If . . .* feature.

Though policymaking may seem far removed from you as an average citizen, you can influence policymaking in many ways. The first one, obviously, is to vote for candidates who share your views on policy issues. The two major parties have rather different views on some major policy issues. Second, you can let your elected representatives at all levels of government know your opinions on specific policy matters. Third, you can help shape public opinion by writing letters to the editor to publicize your views. Finally, you can join interest groups that support your views on a specific domestic policy or policies.

MAKING A DIFFERENCE | Working for a Cleaner Environment

Energy undoubtedly will be among the most important domestic issues in the coming decades. Ultimately, every energy policy involves environmental questions. Not only is this issue central to our everyday lives, but also, it is argued, the fate of the planet may hang in the balance as today's policymakers construct decisions about energy production and environmental protection. To make things more complicated, these parallel struggles of coping with energy problems and preserving our environment tend to work at cross-purposes. In the pursuit of secure and abundant energy, the interests of clean air, water, and land—as well as people—sometimes are sacrificed.

When objectives clash, difficult political trade-offs must be made. To a large group of environmentalists in this country, the choice is clear: if we want to improve or even preserve our quality of life, we must stop environmental degradation.

Environmental groups work on a host of issues, ranging from solar power to mass transit and from wildlife preservation to population control. If you feel strongly about these or other environmental issues and want to get involved, contact the following groups:

Environmental Defense Fund
257 Park Ave. South
New York, NY 10010
800-684-3322
http://www.edf.org

National Environmental Policy Institute
1401 K St. N.W., Suite M-103
Washington, DC 20005
202-857-4784
http://www.nepi.org

Friends of the Earth
1025 Vermont Ave. N.W., Suite 300
Washington, DC 20005
877-843-8687
http://www.foe.org

Greenpeace USA
702 H St. N.W., Suite 300
Washington, DC 20001
800-326-0959
http://www.greenpeaceusa.org

League of Conservation Voters
1920 L St. N.W., Suite 800
Washington, DC 20036
202-785-8683
http://www.lcv.org

National Audubon Society
700 Broadway
New York, NY 10003
212-979-3000
http://www.audubon.org/nas

National Parks Conservation
  Association
1300 Nineteenth St. N.W., Suite 300
Washington, DC 20036
800-628-7275
http://www.npca.org

National Wildlife Federation
11100 Wildlife Center Drive
Reston, VA 20190
800-822-9919
http://www.nwf.org

Natural Resources Defense Council
40 West 20th St.
New York, NY 10011
212-727-2700
http://www.nrdc.org

Sierra Club
85 Second St., 2nd Floor
San Francisco, CA 94105
415-977-5500
http://www.sierraclub.org

Wilderness Society
1615 M. St., N.W.
Washington, DC 20036
1-800-THE-WILD
http://www.wilderness.org

Key Terms

action-reaction syndrome 498

domestic policy 485

earned-income tax credit
  (EITC) program 490

environmental impact
  statement (EIS) 496

Federal Open Market
  Committee (FOMC) 504

fiscal policy 503

food stamps 489

income transfer 487

in-kind subsidy 488

Keynesian economics 504

loophole 499

monetary policy 503

policy trade-offs 498

public debt, or
  national debt 505

public debt financing 506

Supplemental Security Income
  (SSI) 489

Temporary Assistance to
  Needy Families (TANF) 489

U.S. Treasury bond 505

Chapter Summary

1 Domestic policy consists of all of the laws, government planning, and government actions that affect the lives of American citizens. Policies are created in response to public problems or public demand for government action. Major policy problems now facing this nation include aviation security, poverty and welfare, crime, the environment, and Social Security.

2 The policymaking process is initiated when policymakers become aware—through the media or from their constituents—of a problem that needs to be addressed by the legislature and the president. The process of policymaking includes five steps: agenda building, policy formulation, policy adoption, policy implementation, and policy evaluation. All policy actions necessarily result in both costs and benefits for society.

3 In spite of the wealth of the United States, a significant number of Americans live in poverty or are homeless. The low-income poverty threshold represents an absolute measure of income needed to maintain a specified standard of living as of 1963, with the constant-dollar, or purchasing-power, value increased year by year in relation to the general increase in prices. The official poverty level is based on pretax income, including cash, and does not take into consideration in-kind subsidies (food stamps, housing vouchers, and so on).

4 The 1996 Welfare Reform Act transferred more control over welfare programs to the states, limited the number of years people can receive welfare assistance, and imposed work requirements on welfare recipients. The reform act succeeded in reducing the number of welfare recipients in the United States by at least 50 percent.

5 There is widespread concern in this country about violent crime, particularly the large number of crimes that are committed by juveniles. The overall rate of violent crime, including crimes committed by juveniles, has been declining since 1995, however. Crimes associated with illegal drug sales and use have also challenged policymakers. A controversial issue today is whether federal drug policy, as reflected in the Controlled Substances Act of 1970, should take priority over conflicting state laws that legalize the use of marijuana for certain medical purposes. A pressing issue facing Americans and their government today, of course, is terrorism—one of the most devastating forms of crime. Government attempts to curb terrorism will no doubt continue for some time to come.

6 Pollution problems continue to plague the United States and the world. Since the nineteenth century, a number of significant federal acts have been passed in an attempt to curb the pollution of our environment. The National Environmental Policy Act of 1969 established the Council on Environmental Quality. That act also mandated that environmental impact statements be pre-pared for all legislation or major federal actions that might significantly affect the quality of the environment. The Clean Water Act of 1972 and the Clean Air Act amendments of 1990 constituted the most significant government attempts at cleaning up our environment.

7 In the area of taxes and subsidies (negative taxes), policymakers have long had to contend with what is known as the action-reaction syndrome. For every action on the part of the government, there will be a reaction on the part of the public, to which the government will react with another action, to which the public will again react, and so on. In regard to taxes, as a general rule, individuals and corporations that pay the highest tax rates will react to those rates by pressuring Congress into creating exceptions and tax loopholes (loopholes allow high-income earners to reduce their taxable incomes). This action on the part of Congress results in a reaction from another interest group—consisting of those who want the rich to pay more taxes. In response, higher tax rates are imposed on the rich, and so the cycle continues.

8 Closely related to the question of taxes is the viability of the Social Security system. As the number of people who are working relative to the number of people who are retiring declines, those who work will have to pay more Social Security taxes to pay for the benefits of those who retire. Proposed solutions to the Social Security problem include raising taxes, reducing benefits payouts, reforming immigration policies, and allowing partial privatization of the Social Security system to obtain higher rates of return on contributions.

9 Fiscal policy is the use of changes in government expenditures and taxes to alter national economic variables, such as the rate of inflation or unemployment. Monetary policy is defined as the use of changes in the amount of money in circulation so as to affect interest rates, credit markets, the rate of inflation, and employment. Fiscal policy economics usually means increasing government spending during recessionary periods and increasing taxes during inflationary boom periods. The problem with fiscal policy and monetary policy is the lag between the time a problem occurs in the economy and the time when policy changes are actually felt in the economy.

10 Whenever the federal government spends more than it receives, it runs a deficit. The deficit is met by U.S. Treasury borrowing. This adds to the public debt of the federal government. Those who oppose large increases in government spending argue that one effect of the federal deficit is the crowding out of private investment. Although the federal budget deficit had virtually disappeared by 1998, by 2002 it appeared likely that Americans would once again see budget deficits, and thus increases in the net public debt, for years to come.

Selected Print and Media Resources

SUGGESTED READINGS

Friedman, Milton, and Walter Heller. *Monetary versus Fiscal Policy.* New York: Norton, 1969. This is a classic presentation of the pros and cons of monetary and fiscal policy given by a noninterventionist (Friedman) and an advocate of federal government intervention in the economy (Heller).

Miller, Roger LeRoy, *et al. The Economics of Public Issues,* 12th ed. Reading, Mass.: Addison-Wesley, 2001. Chapters 4, 12, 15–17, 22, 26, 28, and 29–31 are especially useful. The authors use short essays of three to seven pages to explain the purely economic aspects of numerous social problems, including health care, the environment, and poverty.

Peterson, Peter G. *Gray Dawn: How the Coming Age Wave Will Transform America—and the World.* New York: Times Books, 1999. As populations age and decline, will economies decline as well? The author explores this question and its ramifications for policymakers and suggests possible solutions to the "gray dawn" of the twenty-first century.

President's Council of Economic Advisers. *Economic Report of the President.* Washington, D.C.: U.S. Government Printing Office, published annually. This volume contains a wealth of details concerning current monetary and fiscal policy and what is happening to the economy.

Rosenbaum, Walter A. *Environmental Politics and Policy,* 5th ed. Washington, D.C.: CQ Press, 2002. The author examines U.S. environmental policy since 1970, including issues such as nuclear waste, air and water pollution, the battle for public lands, and global environmentalism.

MEDIA RESOURCES

America's Promise: Who's Entitled to What?—A four-part series that examines the current state of welfare reform and its impact on immigrant and other populations.

Crimes and Punishments: A History—A controversial documentary that traces the often brutal history of criminal punishment from the medieval era through today.

Rollover—A 1981 film starring Jane Fonda as a former film star who inherits a multimillion-dollar empire when her husband is mysteriously murdered and Kris Kristofferson as a financial troubleshooter who helps her try to save the company. The film offers an insider's view of the politics of currency crises.

Traffic—A 2001 film, starring Michael Douglas and Benicio Del Toro, that offers compelling insights into the consequences of failed drug policies. (*Authors' note:* Be aware that this film contains material of a violent and sexual nature that may be offensive.)

Young Criminals, Adult Punishment—An ABC program that examines the issue of whether the harsh sentences given out to adult criminals, including capital punishment, should also be applied to young violent offenders.

Your CD-ROM Resources

In addition to the chapter content containing hot links, the following resources are available on the CD-ROM:

- **Internet Activities**—Abolishing the federal income tax, the future of social security.

- **Critical Thinking Exercises**—American crime, Bush's environmental policies, Bush's social security plan.

- **Self-Check on Important Themes**—Can You Answer These?

- **Animated Figures**—Figure 16–1, "The Official Number of Poor in the United States," Figure 16–4, "Workers per Retiree."

- **Video**—*How Rules Are Made.*

- **Public Opinion Data**—Find contrasting opinions on the best way to treat the homeless and on medical marijuana.

- **InfoTrac Exercise**—"What Monetary Policy Can and Cannot Do: Knowing Economic Limitations."

- **Simulation**—You Are There!

- **Participation Exercise**—Research an interest group that focuses on economic issues.

- **MicroCase Exercise**—"By the Numbers: Which State's Citizens Pay the Most in Federal Income Taxes?"

- **Additional Resources**—Aviation Transportation Act (2001), Welfare Reform Act (1996), Clean Air Act (1990), General Agreement on Tariffs and Trade (1994), Eisenhower Farewell Address (1961), Reagan Address to Congress (1981), North American Free Trade Agreement (1994), Clinton State of the Union Address (1994).

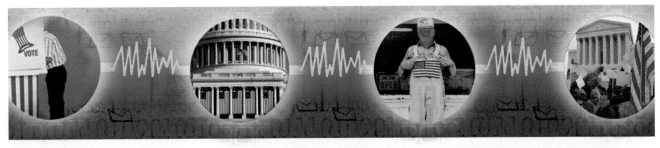

e-mocracy

E-Commerce and Economic Policy

The age of e-commerce has brought with it several challenges for economic policy-makers. Indeed, more than five hundred technology-related bills were introduced in the 107th Congress. One challenging issue for policymakers has to do with whether Internet transactions should be taxed. In 1998, Congress passed a law providing for a three-year moratorium (which has since been extended) to allow Congress time to study the potential consequences of Internet taxation.

Another economic policy issue has to do with electronic money, or *e-money,* which includes a number of alternatives to traditional means of payment. In one type of e-money, a balance of funds is recorded on a magnetic stripe on a card; each time the card is used, a computer terminal debits funds from the balance. Another type uses a microprocessor chip embedded in a so-called *smart card.* A smart card can be encrypted to protect the value on the card from theft. E-money is sometimes referred to as *e-cash* because it can be used like cash, meaning that no personally identifiable records are created. The problem for policymakers is that e-cash moves about completely outside the network of banks, checks, and paper currency. With the growth of e-cash, the traditional definition of money will certainly no longer hold. And the Federal Reserve will have even less ability to control the money supply.

Logging On

You can find further information on most of the issues discussed in this chapter at Project Vote Smart's Web site. Go to

http://www.vote-smart.org/issues

For current statistics on poverty in the United States, go to

http://www.census.gov

The National Governors Association offers information on the current status of welfare reform among the various states at

http://www.nga.org

The Federal Bureau of Investigation offers information about crime rates at its Web site:

http://www.fbi.gov

You can also find statistics and other information on crime in the United States at the Web site of the Bureau of Justice Statistics. Go to

http://www.ojp.usdoj.gov/bjs

To find more information on poverty in the United States and the latest research on this topic, go to the site of the Institute for Research on Poverty at

http://www.ssc.wisc.edu/irp

You can keep up with actions taken by the Federal Reserve by checking the home page of the Federal Reserve Bank of San Francisco at

http://www.frbsf.org

For further information on Social Security, access the Social Security Administration's home page at

http://www.ssa.gov

For information on the 2003 budgets of the U.S. government, go to

http://w3.access.gpo.gov/usbudget

Using the Internet for Political Analysis

Take your turn at proposing a federal budget, balanced or not. Go to the budget explorer at the following Web site:

http://www.kowaldesign.com/budget

Allocate the federal budget according to how you believe federal dollars should be spent. The budget explorer will then give you feedback on how your numbers compare to the actual federal budget.

To investigate how the federal government makes budget decisions, visit the Web site of the Office of Management and Budget (OMB) at

http://www.whitehouse.gov/omb

Click on "Budget Information" and read through some of the documents available at the site to learn about budget priorities and constraints.

CHAPTER 17
Foreign and Defense Policy

BACKGROUND

Since World War II (1939–1945), the United States has frequently sent military forces to defend other nations from attack. The Korean War (1950–1953), the Vietnam War (1964–1975), and the Persian Gulf War (1991) are examples of such actions.

The United States is not often called upon to fulfill its obligations to the North Atlantic Treaty Organization (NATO) or to other alliance partners or international organizations to which it belongs, such as the United Nations. Nonetheless, this does happen occasionally, as with the Korean and Gulf Wars. Because of its treaty obligations, the United States maintains military bases around the world and spends huge sums on military preparedness. Yet all of this capability did not prevent the terrorist attacks on September 11, 2001.

WHAT IF THE UNITED STATES DEFENDED ONLY ITSELF?

For more than 150 years, the United States approached global affairs from an isolationist perspective, avoiding any mutual defense alliances. What if the United States returned to that sort of posture, maintaining military forces only to defend U.S. soil and U.S. citizens?

With an isolationist policy, organizing the U.S. military effort would be much simpler and cheaper. American airbases and naval bases around the world would be closed, and the hundreds of thousands of Americans stationed overseas would be brought home. Expenditures for military weapons would probably concentrate on missile defenses, coastal defenses, and homeland security, utilizing high technology instead of massive numbers of military personnel. Much of the U.S. defense effort would probably be carried out by the National Guard and reserve contingents, because a large standing army would not be necessary. The president's chief reason to use troops would be to protect the United States against attacks at home.

WOULD WARS BREAK OUT AROUND THE GLOBE?

If the United States returned to a "fortress America" posture, it is possible that a number of wars might break out around the globe. One of the reasons for NATO and other mutual defense pacts, as well as for the United Nations, is that they raise the stakes for an aggressor nation. Any nation that starts a war must plan for massive retaliation by a group of nations bound in a defensive alliance. If the United States were to pull out of its alliances, many of them might fall apart.

Another real possibility would be an increase in terrorist attacks, threats by rogue nations, and civil wars. After September 11, the United States declared war against terrorists and expressed a willingness to assist other nations in that effort. The United States could choose to provide only technical assistance, however, not military force.

In that event, other nations might become the world's leaders in the pursuit of peace. Or, possibly, the United Nations could become a truly powerful force for peace, uniting its many members to enforce the peace as it was founded to do.

HOW COULD THE UNITED STATES PULL OUT OF ITS COMMITMENTS?

If the United States decided to follow an isolationist policy, it would have to renounce its commitments to treaties, such as the NATO alliance, probably by vote of Congress. The United States could be pressured to relinquish its seat on the United Nations Security Council and might, to be safe, give up membership in the United Nations altogether. If the United States did not withdraw, it might be subject to sanctions or other actions for failing to follow through on commitments made by the United Nations. Given the increased desire of Americans to protect their own shores, however, such a return to isolationism might meet with popular approval.

FOR CRITICAL ANALYSIS

1. Do you think that U.S. interests could be sufficiently protected if the United States decided to defend only U.S. soil and U.S. citizens against aggression?
2. If the military takes on a greater role in defending U.S. soil, is it possible that the military might abuse its power?

On September 11, 2001, Americans were forced to change their view of national security and of our relations with the rest of the world—literally overnight. No longer could citizens of the United States believe that national security issues involved only threats overseas or that the American homeland could not be attacked. No longer could Americans believe that regional conflicts in other parts of the world had no impact on the United States.

On the day of the attacks on the World Trade Center towers and the Pentagon, Americans quickly realized that these were acts of war perpetrated not by a nation but by terrorists. Within a few days, it became known that the attacks were planned and carried out by a terrorist network named al Qaeda that was funded and directed by the radical Islamic leader Osama Bin Laden. The network was closely linked to the Taliban government of Afghanistan, which had ruled that nation since 1996.

As a symbol of American military power, the Pentagon building became a target of terrorists on September 11, 2001. (Department of Defense photo)

Americans were shocked by the complexity and the success of the attacks. They wondered how our airport security systems could have failed so drastically. How could the Pentagon, the heart of the nation's defense, have been successfully attacked? Shouldn't our intelligence community have known about and defended against this network? And, finally, how could our foreign policy have been so blind to the anger voiced by Islamic groups throughout the world?

In this chapter, the tools of foreign policy and national security policy will be examined in the light of the many challenges facing the United States today. As suggested by the *What If . . .* feature opening this chapter, the United States might think about defending only itself; but would that strategy really serve the vital interests of our nation?

Facing the World: Foreign and Defense Policy

The United States is only one nation in a world with more than one hundred independent countries, many located in regions where armed conflict is ongoing. What tools does our nation have to deal with the many challenges to its peace and prosperity? One tool is the set of policies and positions that we refer to as **foreign policy**. By this term, we mean both the goals the government wants to achieve in the world and the techniques and strategies to achieve them. For example, if one national goal is to achieve stability in Eastern Europe and to encourage the formation of pro-American governments there, U.S. foreign policy in that area may be carried out using various techniques, including **diplomacy, economic aid, technical assistance,** or military intervention. Sometimes foreign policies are restricted to statements of goals or ideas, such as helping to end world poverty, whereas at other times foreign policies are comprehensive efforts to achieve particular objectives.

In the United States, the **foreign policy process** usually originates with the president and those agencies that provide advice on foreign policy matters. Foreign policy formulation often is affected by congressional action and national public debate.

National Security Policy

As one aspect of overall foreign policy, **national security policy** is designed primarily to protect the independence and the political integrity of the United States. It concerns itself with the defense of the United States against actual or potential (real or imagined) enemies, domestic or foreign.

Foreign Policy
A nation's external goals and the techniques and strategies used to achieve them.

Diplomacy
The total process by which states carry on political relations with each other; settling conflicts among nations by peaceful means.

Economic Aid
Assistance to other nations in the form of grants, loans, or credits to buy the assisting nation's products.

Technical Assistance
The sending of experts with technical skills in such areas as agriculture, engineering, or business to aid other nations.

Foreign Policy Process
The steps by which external goals are decided and acted on.

National Security Policy
Foreign and domestic policy designed to protect the independence and political and economic integrity of the United States; policy that is concerned with the safety and defense of the nation.

For more information on the NSC, use the term "United States National Security Council" in the Subject guide.

National Security Council (NSC)
A board created by the 1947 National Security Act to advise the president on matters of national security.

Defense Policy
A subset of national security policy that generally refers to the set of policies that direct the scale and size of the U.S. armed forces.

U.S. national security policy is based on determinations made by the Department of Defense, the Department of State, and a number of other federal agencies, including the **National Security Council (NSC)**. The NSC acts as an advisory body to the president, but it has increasingly become a rival to the State Department in influencing the foreign policy process.

Defense policy is a subset of national security policy. Generally, defense policy refers to the set of policies that direct the scale and size of the U.S. armed forces. Among the questions defense policymakers must consider is the number of major wars the United States should be prepared to fight simultaneously. Defense policy also considers the types of armed forces units we need to have, such as Rapid Defense Forces or Marine Expeditionary Forces, and the types of weaponry that should be developed and maintained for the nation's security. Defense policies are proposed by the leaders of the nation's military forces and the secretary of defense and are greatly influenced by congressional decision makers.

Diplomacy

Diplomacy is another aspect of foreign policy. Diplomacy includes all of a nation's external relationships, from routine diplomatic communications to summit meetings among heads of state. More specifically, diplomacy refers to the settling of disputes and conflicts among nations by peaceful methods. Diplomacy is the set of negotiating techniques by which a nation attempts to carry out its foreign policy.

Diplomacy may or may not be successful, depending on the willingness of the parties to negotiate. For example, in 1993, after years of refusing to negotiate or even recognize each other's existence, Israel and representatives of the Palestine Liberation Organization (the PLO) reached an agreement under which Israel returned control of Jericho and part of the West Bank to the Palestinians. By 2003, however, relations between Israel and the Palestinians continued to erupt in conflict, with the United States, together with the leaders of the European Union, using diplomatic tools to try to get the parties to resume peace negotiations.

Morality versus Reality in Foreign Policy

From the earliest years of the republic, Americans have felt that their nation had a special destiny. The American experiment in democratic government and capitalism, it was thought, would provide the best possible life for men and women and be a model for other nations. As the United States assumed greater status as a power in world politics, Americans came to believe that the nation's actions on the world stage should be guided by American political and moral principles. As Harry Truman stated, "The United States should take the lead in running the world in the way that it ought to be run."

Moral Idealism

Moral Idealism
A philosophy that sees all nations as willing to cooperate and agree on moral standards for conduct.

This view of America's mission has led to the adoption of many foreign policy initiatives that are rooted in **moral idealism**, a philosophy that sees the world as fundamentally benign and other nations as willing to cooperate for the good of all.[1] In this perspective, nations should come together and agree to keep the peace, as President Woodrow Wilson (1913–1921) proposed for the League of Nations. Nations should

---

[1] Charles W. Kegley, Jr., and Eugene Wittkopf, *American Foreign Policy, Pattern and Process,* 3d ed. (New York: St. Martin's Press, 1987), p. 73.

see the wrong in violating the human rights of ethnic or religious minorities and should work to end such injustice. Many of the foreign policy initiatives taken by the United States have been based on this idealistic view of the world, but few of these actions have been very successful. The Peace Corps, however, which was created by President John Kennedy in 1961, is one example of an effort to spread American goodwill and technology that has achieved some of its goals.

Political Realism

In opposition to the moral perspective is **political realism**. Realists see the world as a dangerous place in which each nation strives for its own survival and interests. Foreign policy decisions must be based on a cold calculation of what is best for the United States without regard for morality. Realists believe that the United States must be prepared militarily to defend itself, because all other nations are, by definition, out to improve their own situations. A strong defense will show the world that the United States is willing to protect its interests. The practice of political realism in foreign policy allows the United States to sell weapons to military dictators who will support its policies, to support American business around the globe, and to repel terrorism through the use of force. Political realism leads, for example, to a policy of not negotiating with terrorists who take hostages, because such negotiations simply will lead to the taking of more hostages.

Raquib Jamal is a business volunteer in Ghana helping farmers develop and run tourism businesses. Her work is an example of the moral idealism that is an important component of American foreign policy. (Peace Corps photo)

Political Realism
A philosophy that sees each nation acting principally in its own interest.

American Foreign Policy—A Mixture of Both

It is important to note that the United States never has been guided by only one of these principles. Instead, both moral idealism and political realism affect foreign policy-making. President George W. Bush drew on the tradition of morality in foreign policy when he declared that the al Qaeda network of Osama Bin Laden was "evil" and that fighting terrorism was fighting evil. To actually wage war on the Taliban in Afghanistan, however, U.S. forces needed the right to use the airspace of India and Pakistan, neighbors of Afghanistan. The United States had previously criticized both of these South Asian nations because they had developed and tested nuclear weapons. In addition, the United States had taken the moral stand that it would not deliver certain fighter aircraft to Pakistan as long as it continued with its weapons program. When it became absolutely necessary to work with India and Pakistan, the United States switched to a realist policy, promising aid and support to both regimes in return for their assistance in the war on terrorism.

Challenges in World Politics

The foreign policy of the United States, whether moralist, realist, or both, must be formulated to deal with world conditions. Early in its history, the United States was a weak, new nation facing older nations well equipped for world domination. In the twenty-first century, the United States faces different challenges. Now it must devise foreign and defense policies that will enable it to survive in a world with almost no recognized order. To be sure, the United States is the global superpower and has no equal. Nevertheless, the absence of a recognized balance of power among nations makes it difficult to formulate an effective foreign policy, particularly because many of the challenges facing the United States involve religious, regional, and ethnic conflicts.

Terrorism

Dissident groups, rebels, and other revolutionaries always have engaged in some sort of terrorism to gain attention and to force their enemies to the bargaining table. Over the last two decades, terrorism has continued to threaten world peace and the lives of ordinary citizens.

Terrorism and Civil Strife.   Terrorism can be a weapon of choice in domestic or civil strife. The conflict in the Middle East between Israel and the Arab states is an example. Until recently, the conflict had been lessened by a series of painfully negotiated agreements between Israel and some of the Arab states. Those opposed to the peace process, however, have continued to disrupt the negotiations through assassinations, mass murders, and bomb blasts in the streets of major cities within Israel. At this point, most of the terrorist attacks are carried out by groups (either Israeli or Arab) that reject the peace process. Similar "domestic" terrorist acts were used to disrupt talks between Britain and Ireland over the fate of Northern Ireland. The terrorist acts did not stop the peace process in Ireland, however, which culminated in a vote supporting the agreement in 1998. Terrorist acts by rebels or separatist groups have also occurred in Sri Lanka (the Tamils), Paris (Algerian extremists), Russia (Chechen rebels), and Japan (secret cults).

Terrorist Attacks against Foreign Civilians.   In other cases, terrorist acts are planned against the civilians of foreign nations to make an international statement and to frighten the citizens of a faraway land. One of the most striking of these attacks was that launched by Palestinian terrorists against Israeli athletes at the Munich

Terrorist bombings have become increasingly destructive in recent decades. In the Palestinian-Israeli conflict, Palestinian suicide bombers target crowded public places, such as bus stops, as depicted in the photo directly below. (AP Photo/ZOOM 77) On the bottom right, Palestinians carry sacks of food through the remains of a market in Bethlehem, destroyed after a stand-off between Israeli troops and Palestinians in the fall of 2002. (AP Photo/Achmad Ibrahim) In the photo on the upper right, the bombing of a popular nightclub on the island of Bali in Indonesia horrified much of the world in the fall of 2002. Over 180 foreign tourists were killed, most of whom were Australian. A wing of al Qaeda was blamed for that bombing. (AP Photo/David Guttenfelder)

Olympics in 1972, during which eleven were killed. Other attacks have included ship and airplane hijackings, as well as bombings of government facilities abroad, such as embassies or military bases. For example, in the 1990s, several attacks were targeted at Americans abroad. In 1996, radical elements in Saudi Arabia bombed an American military compound there, killing a number of American military personnel. In 1998, terrorist bombings of two American embassies in Africa killed 257 people, including 12 Americans, and injured over 5,500 others. In 2000, terrorists bombed the USS *Cole* while it was at port on the Arabian peninsula, killing seventeen American sailors.

September 11. In 2001, terrorism came home to the United States in ways that no American had ever imagined. In a well-coordinated, well-financed attack, nineteen terrorists hijacked four airplanes and crashed three of them into buildings—two into the World Trade Center towers in New York City and one into the Pentagon in Washington, D.C. The fourth airplane crashed in a field in Pennsylvania, probably because the passengers tried to fight the hijackers. Why did the al Qaeda network plan and launch attacks on the United States? Apparently, the leaders of the network, including Osama Bin Laden, were angered by the presence of U.S. troops on the soil of Saudi Arabia, which they regard as sacred. They also saw the United States as the primary defender of Israel against the Palestinians and as the defender of the royal

A satellite image of lower Manhattan shows the devastation after the collapse of the World Trade Center towers on September 11, 2001. Terrorists crashed two commercial airplanes into the twin towers. Three thousand people were killed in the terrorist attacks. How do you think this horrible event changed American foreign policy? (Department of Defense photo)

As part of the war on terrorism, the United States destroyed al Qaeda training camps in Afghanistan and the Taliban regime that allowed terrorists to train and flourish in that country. Here, an F-18 Hornet is launched from the aircraft carrier USS *Carl Vinson*. A fleet of aircraft carrier battle groups allow the U.S. military to launch bombing raids against almost any country in the world. In the case of Afghanistan, a landlocked country, the United States needed permission to fly over the airspace of Pakistan. How do you think that limitation affected the conduct of the war in Afghanistan? (Department of Defense photo by Petty Officer First Class Greg Messier, U.S. Navy)

For updates and more information on terrorism, use the term "terrorism" in the Subject guide.

family that governs Saudi Arabia. The attacks were intended to frighten and demoralize the American people, thus convincing their leaders to withdraw American troops from the Middle East.

The Bush administration responded to the attacks by declaring war on terrorism, with the military effort first directed at the al Qaeda camps in Afghanistan. After building a coalition of allies and supporters, the United States defeated the Taliban regime, which had ruled Afghanistan since 1996, and supported the creation of an interim government that did not back terrorism.

What can nations do to prevent terrorism? Besides taking a clear stand about the consequences of such acts and punishing the perpetrators either militarily or economically, a nation's best defense is to be vigilant. This includes stronger security measures to protect its facilities and personnel abroad, a commitment to intelligence gathering, and enhanced measures to protect homeland security. After 9/11, the Bush administration sought and received congressional support for heightened airport security, new laws allowing greater domestic surveillance of potential terrorists, and new funding for the military. A democracy that upholds liberty for its citizens, however, must balance the needs of increased surveillance for criminals against the rights of citizens to be free of police spying and record keeping.

Nuclear Proliferation

More than 32,000 nuclear warheads are known to be in stock worldwide, although the exact number is uncertain because some countries do not reveal the extent of their nuclear stockpiles. Although the United States and Russia have dismantled some of their nuclear warheads and delivery systems since the end of the Cold War and the dissolution of the Soviet Union in 1991 (discussed later in this chapter), both still retain sizable nuclear arsenals. Even more problematic is the recent nuclear proliferation as several countries, including India and Pakistan, have developed nuclear weapons, and several other countries are suspected of having a nuclear program or are considered capable of developing one. In 1999, the U.S. Senate rejected the Comprehensive Nuclear Test Ban Treaty, which had been presented to it for ratification by the Clinton administration. For a discussion of this action and the threat of nuclear proliferation to terrorists, see this chapter's *America's Security* feature.

America's Security

Nuclear Proliferation and Terrorists

In 1945, the United States was the only nation to possess nuclear weapons. Several nations quickly joined the "nuclear club," however, including the Soviet Union in 1949, Great Britain in 1952, France in 1960, and China in 1964. Few nations have made public their nuclear weapons programs since China's successful test of nuclear weapons in 1964. India and Pakistan were the most recent nations to do so, detonating nuclear devices within a few weeks of each other in 1998. Nonetheless, many nations are suspected of possessing nuclear weapons or the capability to produce them in a short time.

TERRORISTS COULD OBTAIN NUCLEAR WEAPONS

Among the nations suspected of having nuclear weapons programs are Algeria, Iran, Iraq, Libya, North Korea, and Syria. All of these nations are described by the United States as "states of concern," "terrorist regimes," or "rogue states." In addition, Israel is believed to possess one hundred nuclear warheads, and Argentina, Brazil, South Korea, South Africa, and Taiwan are all believed to have the scientific and industrial base to develop nuclear weapons. Since the dissolution of the Soviet Union in 1991, the security of its

nuclear arsenal has declined. There have been reported thefts, smugglings, and illicit sales of nuclear material from the former Soviet Union in the past decade.[*]

With nuclear weapons, materials, and technology available worldwide, it is conceivable that terrorists could develop a nuclear device and use it in a terrorist act. In fact, a U.S. federal indictment filed in 1998, after the attack on the American embassies in Kenya and Tanzania, charges Osama Bin Laden and his associates with trying to buy nuclear bomb-making components "at various times" since 1992.

[*]Rensselaer Lee, *Smuggling Armageddon: The Nuclear Black Market in the Former Soviet Union and Europe* (New York: St. Martin's Press, 2000).

With the collapse of the Soviet Union, Moscow's Kurchatov Institute, home to ten tons of bomb-grade uranium, was protected by a single guard at a lobby desk who waved scientists through. With the assistance of a U.S. delegation, security checkpoints were established at the Kurchatov Institute, including this "man trap" entrance, surveillance video, and radiation detectors. (AP Photo/Mikhail Metzel)

EFFORTS TO HALT NUCLEAR PROLIFERATION

In the 1980s and 1990s, the United States and the Soviet Union negotiated several treaties aimed at reducing the threat that their nuclear arsenals pose to the world. In addition, the United States has attempted to influence late arrivals to the "nuclear club" through a combination of rewards and punishments. In some cases, the United States has promised aid to a nation to gain cooperation. In other cases, such as those of India and Pakistan, it has imposed economic sanctions as a punishment for carrying out nuclear tests.

In 1999, President Clinton presented the Comprehensive Nuclear Test Ban Treaty to the Senate for ratification. The treaty, formed in 1996, prohibits all nuclear test explosions worldwide and provides for the establishment of a global network of monitoring stations. Ninety-three nations have ratified the treaty. Among those that had not ratified it by 2002 were China, Israel, India, and Pakistan. In a defeat for the Clinton administration, the U.S. Senate rejected the treaty in 1999.

Has the defeat of the treaty increased the nuclear threat? It is possible that pressure from nations that had ratified the treaty would be instrumental in influencing other nations to stop nuclear testing. Perhaps the next step, after ratifying the test-ban treaty, could have been imposing greater security measures on existing weapons materials and technology. In any case, the United States, clearly the strongest "influencer" in halting the proliferation of nuclear weapons, lost its moral authority to lobby other nations to do the same when it failed to ratify the test-ban treaty.

FOR CRITICAL ANALYSIS

What methods could the United States or other countries use to prevent the spread of nuclear technology to terrorists?

The New Power: China

Since Richard Nixon's visit to China in 1972, American policy has been to gradually engage the Chinese in diplomatic and economic relationships in the hope of turning the nation toward a more pro-Western and capitalistic system. In 1989, however, when Chinese students engaged in extraordinary demonstrations against the government, the Chinese government crushed the demonstrations, killing a number of students and protesters and imprisoning others for political crimes.

China's Economic Power.   Nevertheless, the Clinton administration continued the policy of diplomatic outreach to the Chinese, in part because China had allowed free enterprise in many regions of the country and had the potential to be a major trading partner of the United States. China was granted **most-favored-nation status** for tariffs and trade policy on a year-to-year basis. In 2000, over objections from organized labor and human rights groups, Congress approved a permanent grant of most-favored-nation status to China.

In 1997, China seemed to be conscious of Western concerns when it took over the government of Hong Kong in ceremonies that promised a continuation of the previous government and economic system in the former British colony. Although the new government did impose an appointed assembly, it was careful to preserve the free enterprise system of Hong Kong.

China's Tense Relationship with the United States.   The Chinese-American connection eventually reached domestic politics in the United States when campaign-finance investigations showed that a number of Chinese Americans had made large contributions to the 1996 Clinton reelection campaign. Some of the contributions were illegal and were returned by the Democratic Party. Although there were allegations that the Chinese government had been able to purchase advanced technology that could be used for weapons contrary to American policy, the Clinton administration (1993–2001) continued to support economic ties with China.

In early 2001, an American spy plane flying in international airspace collided with a Chinese fighter jet. The damaged American plane was forced to land on Hainan Island, and a standoff developed between the two nations. The United States demanded the return of the aircraft and its crew while the Chinese demanded an

Most-Favored-Nation Status
A status granted by an international treaty by which each member nation must treat other members at least as well as it treats the country that receives its most favorable treatment.

After an eleven-week stand-off between Chinese and U.S. officials over the fate of a U.S. spy plane forced to land on Hainan Island in China, the fuselage of the plane is prepared for shipment back to the United States. The crew of twenty-four Americans had returned to the United States nine weeks earlier. (AP Photo/Lockheed Martin Aeronautics Co.)

apology for intrusion into their airspace. After several weeks of tense negotiation, the crew was released, the United States issued a statement of concern, and, eventually, the airplane was brought home. Six months later, after the September 11 attacks, China offered its full support to the United States in the war on terrorism and, for the first time ever, supplied intelligence to the United States about terrorist activities.

The Global Economy

Although the United States derives only about 10 percent of its total national income from world trade, it is deeply dependent on the world economy. A serious stock market crash in 1987 showed how closely other markets watch the economic situation of the United States and, conversely, how U.S. markets follow those of London and Japan. In 1997 and 1998, when several Asian countries experienced serious economic problems, the American economy, now dependent on Asian markets for materials, products, and customers, showed some signs of weakness, at least for a short period of time. The Asian countries—among them South Korea and Thailand—received aid from the International Monetary Fund on the condition that they impose severe restrictions on their economies and people. In Indonesia, the failing economy brought down President Suharto, who had held that office for thirty years, and led to increased cries for reform among that nation's people.

Furthermore, since the 1980s, the United States has become a debtor nation, meaning that we owe more to foreigners than foreigners owe to us. The reason for this is a large trade deficit and the willingness of foreign individuals and nations to finance part of the U.S. national debt by purchasing U.S. government securities. Because the United States imports more goods and services than it exports, it has a net trade deficit. These imports include BMWs, Sonys, Toshibas, and Guccis, as well as cheaper products such as shoes manufactured in Brazil and clothes from Taiwan.

No one can predict how a unified Europe will affect world trade. With the European Union having become one economic "nation" on December 31, 1992, some expect Europe will gradually close some markets to outside economic powers. By 2002, the European Union remained a major trading partner of the United States, however.

This sign in downtown Moscow displays the exchange rates between the U.S. dollar and the Russian ruble and between the euro and the ruble. Virtually all countries are interconnected today in a global economy. (AP Photo/ Maxim Marmur)

Regional Conflicts

The United States has played a role—sometimes alone, sometimes in conjunction with other powers—in many regional conflicts. During the 1990s, the United States became involved in conflicts in countries and regions around the globe.

Haiti. The Caribbean nation of Haiti became a focal point of U.S. policy in the 1990s. The repressive military regime there ousted the democratically elected president Jean-Bertrand Aristide in 1992. The Clinton administration announced that it would support sanctions and other measures to reinstate Aristide in office. At the same time, the administration tried to stem the tide of refugees who attempted to reach Florida by sea from the island nation by returning them to their native land. By 1994, however, the administration announced that the United States would at least listen to pleas for political asylum if refugees could reach Jamaica or other Caribbean islands. The administration also increased the sanctions on Haiti in 1994 and then sent troops to Haiti to assist in the reinstatement of President Aristide. The troops were withdrawn in 1999, leaving Haiti as poor and politically corrupt as before.

Cuba. The United States continued to face problems with Cuba. In the last days of the summer of 1994, Fidel Castro threatened to "swamp" the United States with Cuban refugees. True to his word, he allowed thousands to leave the island on anything that would float. President Clinton was forced to rescind the U.S. open-door policy for Cuban refugees. He ordered the Coast Guard to return all refugees picked up at sea to the U.S. naval base at Guantánamo in Cuba. Then U.S. and Cuban authorities reached an agreement under which the United States would accept 20,000 legal Cuban immigrants a year. In exchange, Castro agreed to police Cuba's shores to prevent an exodus of Cuban refugees.

In 1996, another incident occurred. Cuban military aircraft shot down two planes flown by anti-Castro American residents who were searching for Cubans escaping by

Former President Jimmy Carter, center, made a historic visit to Cuba in May 2002 and met with Cuban President Fidel Castro, right. Carter's work as a diplomat and humanitarian after leaving office earned him the Nobel Peace Prize in 2002. (AP Photo/Gregory Bull)

sea. The United States, refusing to accept Cuba's explanation that the two planes were over Cuban territorial waters, retaliated by passing the Helms-Burton Act. Among other things, the act punished owners of foreign firms (and their family members) for investing in formerly American-owned business firms that had been nationalized by Cuba by barring those persons from the United States. The act sparked international opposition.

Tensions between the United States and Cuba increased tremendously in late 1999 and 2000 after a little boy, Elian Gonzalez, survived a boat wreck in which his mother died. They had been crossing from Cuba to join Miami relatives. With his mother dead, Elian became the prize in a political tug of war between Castro and the Cuban American population in Miami until the Clinton administration returned the young boy to his family in Cuba. Cuban-American relations continue to be politically important because the Cuban American population can influence American election outcomes in Florida, a state that all presidential candidates try to win.

The Middle East.   The United States has also played a role in the Middle East. As a longtime supporter of Israel, the United States has undertaken to persuade the Israelis to negotiate with the Palestinians who live in the territories occupied by the state of Israel. The conflict, which began in 1948, has been extremely hard to resolve. One reason is that it requires all the Arab states in the region to recognize Israel's right to exist. Another reason is that resolution of the conflict would require Israel to make some settlement with the Palestine Liberation Organization (PLO), which has launched attacks on Israel from within and outside its borders and which Israel has regarded as a terrorist organization. In December 1988, the United States began talking directly to the PLO, and in 1991, under great pressure from the United States, the Israelis opened talks with representatives of the Palestinians and other Arab states.

In 1993, the Israeli-Palestinian peace talks reached a breakthrough, with both parties agreeing to set up Palestinian territories in the West Bank and Gaza. The historic agreement, signed in Cairo on May 4, 1994, put in place a process by which the Palestinians would assume self-rule in the Gaza Strip and in the town of Jericho. In the months that followed, Israeli troops withdrew from much of the occupied territory, Palestinians assumed police duties, and many Palestinian prisoners were freed by the Israelis. During an election campaign speech in 1995, however, Israeli prime minister Yitzhak Rabin, a key figure in the negotiations for peace, was assassinated by a right-wing Israeli student who opposed the peace process. Although negotiations between the Israelis and the Palestinian Authority resulted in more agreements in Oslo, Norway, in 2000, the agreements were rejected by Palestinian radicals who began a campaign of suicide bombings in Israeli cities. In 2002, the Israeli government responded by moving tanks and troops into Palestinian towns to kill or capture the terrorists. The crisis seemed to doom all further peace agreements.

The Persian Gulf.   On August 2, 1990, the Persian Gulf became the setting for a major challenge to the authority of the United States and its ability to buy oil from its allies there. President Saddam Hussein of Iraq sent troops into the neighboring oil sheikdom of Kuwait, occupying the entire nation. At the formal request of the king of Saudi Arabia, American troops were dispatched to set up a defensive line at the Kuwaiti border. After the United Nations approved a resolution authorizing the use of force if Saddam Hussein did not respond to sanctions, the U.S. Congress reluctantly also approved such an authorization. On January 17, 1991, two days after the deadline for President Hussein to withdraw, the coalition forces launched a massive air attack on Iraq. After several weeks of almost unopposed aerial bombardment, the ground offensive began. Iraqi troops retreated from Kuwait a few days later, and the war ended, although many Americans criticized President George H. W. Bush for not sending troops to Baghdad and deposing Saddam Hussein.

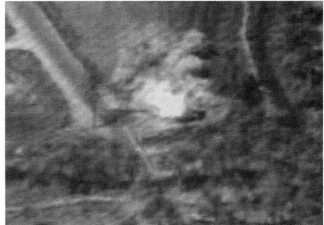

In 2002, Iraq became the focus of the war on terrorism. The U.S. secretary of defense used these photographs showing a truck-mounted, surface-to-air missile being fired at U.S. aircraft to make the case that Iraqi President Saddam Hussein continues to violate UN resolutions signed at the end of the Gulf War. The U.S. presented evidence throughout 2002 that the Iraqi leader was a danger not only to his own people, but to the rest of the world. (Department of Defense photo)

As part of the official cease-fire that ended the Gulf War, Iraq agreed to abide by all United Nations resolutions, including allowing UN weapons inspectors to oversee the destruction of its medium-range missiles and all chemical- and nuclear-weapons research facilities. Economic sanctions would continue to be imposed on Iraq until the weapons inspectors finished their jobs. In 1999, however, Iraq successfully barred further weapons inspectors from entering the country and established economic ties with many Middle Eastern and European nations. The United States continued to support economic sanctions on Iraq, however (see this chapter's *Which Side Are You On?* feature for a discussion of the use of sanctions as a tool of foreign policy).

After the terrorist attacks on the United States on September 11, 2001, the United States made it clear that it considered Iraq and Saddam Hussein terrorists. In 2002, President George W. Bush called for a "regime change" in Iraq and began assembling an international coalition that might support further military action in Iraq.

Eastern Europe.   After the end of the Cold War, Eastern Europe, a region that had been extremely stable while under Soviet domination, suddenly became an unknown quantity in U.S. policy. With the decision of the Soviet Union to allow free elections and non-Marxist governments in Eastern Europe in the late 1980s, these nations took separate paths to becoming self-governing states with mixed or market-oriented economies. Some nations immediately held elections; some struggled first to repair damaged economies; and still others attempted to deal with ethnic tensions within their populations.

It is difficult to overestimate the potential for civil disorder in these nations, particularly with regard to ethnic differences. The world watched in 1991 as Yugoslavia split into a number of independent states. As former provinces of Yugoslavia—Slovenia, Croatia, and Bosnia and Herzegovina—tried to declare independence, Serbian military and government leaders launched attacks on their neighbors. The fighting was caused by historic conflicts and by strong ethnic and religious differences.

The fighting was fiercest in the former province of Bosnia, where Serbs and Muslims launched attacks on each other's villages and cities. News reports suggested that many women were raped and that the men were sent to camps to force their families to leave their homes. The United States and European nations required the Serbs to withdraw their weapons from the province and to begin a process for permanent disengagement. With guarantees from the United States and other NATO allies, the warring parties began the process of establishing separate ethnic provinces and returning to their home villages. Troops from the United States and other

Which Side Are You On?
Should the United States Impose Sanctions?

Today, a hotly debated issue has to do with whether the United States and other nations should use economic sanctions to attempt to achieve their foreign policy goals. Are sanctions a viable weapon against rogue nations that engage in or support terrorist activities or against nations that attack their neighbors, destabilizing a region of the world? Should sanctions be used against nations that defy world opinion by keeping brutal dictators in power or engaging in genocide against part of their own citizenry?

THE USE OF SANCTIONS

The use of sanctions as a tool of foreign policy became popular after multilateral sanctions applied against South Africa helped to force the nation's white-controlled government to negotiate with the opposition African National Congress and end officially sanctioned racial segregation (apartheid) in 1992. Sanctions came to be seen as a way for the United States, alone or in coalition with other nations, to try to force a nation to change its ways without resorting to the use of force. In some cases, sanctions are imposed to encourage people of a nation to demand political change from their government.

In other situations, the sanctions are intended to force a government to comply with some aspect of international law; for example, sanctions have been imposed on Iraq to force it to comply with the agreements it made after the 1991 Persian Gulf War. In addition to South Africa and Iraq, sanctions have been imposed against Myanmar (formerly Burma) for its political repression and against Libya for engaging in terrorism. Because sanctions are a nonmilitary tool, they remain popular.

THE COST OF SANCTIONS

Economic sanctions are intended to put political pressure on a regime by denying a nation critical materials and access to very important trading partners. Sanctions that restrict trade with a nation can be extremely costly in terms of trade opportunities lost, however. A study by the Institute for International Economics found that sanctions cost U.S. businesses between $15 billion and $20 billion in a recent year and affected more than 200,000 American workers.

ARE SANCTIONS EFFECTIVE?

Because of the incredible changes that have taken place in South Africa—a peaceful end to civil strife, the end of apartheid, and the installation of a new, multiethnic regime—there is a tendency to see sanctions as being effective. In other cases, it is less clear that sanctions have had the intended results, however. In the case of Libya, the United States recently lifted sanctions imposed because of that nation's terrorist activity. The leader of Libya, Muammar Qaddafi, is still in control of the country.

The Iraqi situation has proved even more troublesome. Human rights observers report that thousands of Iraqi children have died from malnutrition and from diseases for which the nation lacks medicine. Not only has the ruler, Saddam Hussein, stayed in office, but he and his family have grown even more wealthy. They control much of the black market in goods smuggled into Iraq in defiance of the embargo. They sell the goods at inflated prices to those who have money while other sectors of Iraqi society suffer from the impact of the sanctions. Furthermore, several of the allies of the United States in the Persian Gulf War believe that sanctions have done as much as they can to influence Hussein and should be lifted. These nations are suffering economic losses from the sanctions as well.

WHAT'S YOUR POSITION?

Should the United States continue to use sanctions as a foreign policy tool even though they may cost Americans economic opportunities or bring starvation and deprivation to the people of the nations that are sanctioned?

GOING ONLINE

To find out more about the debate over sanctions, try the Web site **http://www.policy.com**. For the U.S. government's position on sanctions, go to the site of the State Department, **http://www.state.gov**. Position papers on sanctions are also available at the Brookings Institution's site, **http://www.brookings.edu**.

Nine thousand U.S. troops were still stationed in the Balkans in 2001 when the war in Afghanistan began. Here, President George W. Bush greets soldiers stationed at Camp Bondsteel in Kosovo. With so many U.S. forces deployed in peacekeeping missions, such as in Kosovo and Bosnia, redeploying troops for the war in Afghanistan or a war in Iraq is a serious concern. Can the United States fulfill all of its military obligations around the world and fight the war against terrorism at the same time? (Department of Defence photo by Staff Sgt. Clinton J. Evans, U.S. Army)

European nations patrolled the new borders and assisted in the process. Prospects for a lasting peace after the troops leave are not great due to the degree of ethnic hatred in this region.

By 1998, the situation in the Balkans had again become violent as ethnic Albanians sought independence for the Kosovo region of Serbia. The United States and several European powers launched a bombing campaign against Serbia to force an end to the Serbs' war against the ethnic Albanians in Kosovo.

Africa. The continent of Africa witnessed both great strides for freedom and savage civil strife during the mid-1990s and early 2000s. In South Africa, the first all-race elections were held in 1994—mostly in an orderly and peaceful manner—and Nelson Mandela was elected as the first president under a new constitution. Most South African constituencies took part in the election and seemed ready to support the new black-majority regime. The economic sanctions applied by the United States had helped bring the white South African government to a position of economic hardship and led, in part, to its negotiations with Mandela and his African National Congress Party.

In central Africa, another situation arose that seemed to be totally beyond the influence of the United States, Europe, or the United Nations. After a plane crash that killed the presidents of Rwanda and of neighboring Burundi, civil war erupted in Rwanda. The political war between the government and the rebel forces was complicated by a terrible ethnic struggle between the Hutu and Tutsi tribes. Observers estimated that more than half a million people were killed within a few weeks, with many bodies dumped in the rivers. About 250,000 refugees arrived in Uganda, setting up a small city in less than a week. Over a million others fled into neighboring Zaire. The United Nations called for troops to assist in relief efforts, but only France responded (and pulled out shortly thereafter). The United States played virtually no part in this situation until small military and civilian contingents were sent to assist with the refugee crisis.

Perhaps an even greater threat to world stability, however, comes from disease, especially AIDS (acquired immune deficiency syndrome). The disease infects one-fourth of the populations in Botswana and Zimbabwe in sub-Saharan Africa. Millions of adults die from AIDS, leaving orphaned children. Millions of children are also infected by the disease and will die at an early age. The epidemic is taking a huge economic toll on African nations, both because of the cost of caring for patients and because the work force is shrinking. Poor nations may soon find themselves embroiled in civil war or at the mercy of aggressive neighbors. A report released by the U.S. Central Intelligence Agency suggests that the deaths of the educated elites in many of these nations will lead to a vacuum in leadership, one that could be filled by military coups and other nondemocratic forms of leadership.

Who Makes Foreign Policy?

Given the vast array of challenges in the world, developing a comprehensive U.S. foreign policy is a demanding task. Does this responsibility fall to the president, to Congress, or to the executive and congressional branches of government jointly? There is no easy answer to this question, because, as constitutional authority Edwin S. Corwin once observed, the U.S. Constitution created an "invitation to struggle" between the president and Congress for control over the foreign policy process. Let us look first at the powers given to the president by the Constitution.

Constitutional Powers of the President

The Constitution confers on the president broad powers that are either explicit or implied in key constitutional provisions. Article II vests the executive power of the government in the president. The presidential oath of office given in Article II, Section 1, requires that the president "solemnly swear" to "preserve, protect and defend the Constitution of the United States."

In October 2002, President George W. Bush signed a joint resolution from Congress authorizing the use of military force against Iraq to dismantle all of Iraq's weapons of mass destruction. Although the president is the commander in chief, the Constitution does not give him or her the authority to declare war. That authority rests solely with Congress. (AP Photo/Ron Edmonds)

In addition, and perhaps more important, Article II, Section 2, designates the president as "Commander in Chief of the Army and Navy of the United States." Starting with Abraham Lincoln, all presidents have interpreted this authority dynamically and broadly. Indeed, since George Washington's administration, the United States has been involved in at least 125 undeclared wars that were conducted under presidential authority. For example, Harry Truman ordered U.S. armed forces in the Pacific to enter into North Korea's conflict with South Korea. Dwight Eisenhower threatened China and North Korea with nuclear weapons if the Korean peace talks were not successfully concluded. Bill Clinton sent troops to Haiti and Bosnia.

Article II, Section 2, of the Constitution also gives the president the power to make treaties, provided that two-thirds of the senators present concur. Presidents usually have been successful in getting treaties through the Senate. In addition to this formal treaty-making power, the president makes use of executive agreements (discussed in Chapter 13). Since World War II (1939–1945), executive agreements have accounted for almost 95 percent of the understandings reached between the United States and other nations.

Executive agreements have a long and important history. Significant in their long-term effects were the several agreements Franklin Roosevelt reached with the Soviet Union and other countries, especially at Yalta, during World War II. Also important were the series of executive agreements in which the United States promised support to the government of South Vietnam, particularly under Dwight Eisenhower, John Kennedy, and Lyndon Johnson. In all, since 1946 over eight thousand executive agreements with foreign countries have been made. There is no way to get an accurate count, because perhaps as many as several hundred of these agreements have been secret.

An additional power conferred on the president in Article II, Section 2, is the right to appoint ambassadors, other public ministers, and consuls. In Section 3 of that article, the president is given the power to recognize foreign governments through receiving their ambassadors.

Informal Techniques of Presidential Leadership

Other broad sources of presidential power in the U.S. foreign policy process are tradition, precedent, and the president's personality. The president can employ a host of informal techniques that give the White House overwhelming superiority within the government in foreign policy leadership.

First, the president has access to information. More information is available to the president from the Central Intelligence Agency (CIA), the State Department, and the Defense Department than to any other governmental official. This information carries with it the ability to make quick decisions—and that ability is used often. Second, the president is a legislative leader who can influence the amount of funds that are allocated for different programs. Third, the president can influence public opinion. President Theodore Roosevelt once made the following statement:

> People used to say to me that I was an astonishingly good politician and divined what the people are going to think. . . . I did not "divine" how the people were going to think; I simply made up my mind what they ought to think and then did my best to get them to think it.[2]

Presidents are without equal with respect to influencing public opinion, partly because of their ability to command the media. Depending on their skill in appealing to patriotic sentiment (and sometimes fear), they can make people think that their course in foreign affairs is right and necessary. Public opinion often seems to be impressed by the president's decision to make a national commitment abroad. President George W. Bush's speech to Congress shortly after the September 11 attacks

---

[2] Sidney Warren, *The President as World Leader* (New York: McGraw-Hill, 1964), p. 23.

rallied the nation and brought new respect for his leadership. It is worth noting that presidents normally, although certainly not always, receive the immediate support of the American people when reacting to (or creating) a foreign policy crisis.

Finally, the president can commit the nation morally to a course of action in foreign affairs. Because the president is the head of state and the leader of one of the most powerful nations on earth, once the president has made a commitment for the United States, it is difficult for Congress or anyone else to back down on that commitment.

Other Sources of Foreign Policymaking

There are at least four foreign policymaking sources within the executive branch, in addition to the president. These are (1) the Department of State, (2) the National Security Council, (3) the intelligence community and informational programs, and (4) the Department of Defense.

The Department of State. In principle, the State Department is the executive agency that is most directly concerned with foreign affairs. It supervises U.S. relations with the nearly two hundred independent nations around the world and with the United Nations and other multinational groups, such as the Organization of American States. It staffs embassies and consulates throughout the world. It has more than 31,000 employees. This number may sound impressive, but it is small compared with, say, the Department of Health and Human Services with its more than 61,000 employees. Also, the State Department had an annual operating budget of only $7.7 billion in fiscal year 2003, one of the smallest budgets of the cabinet departments.

Newly elected presidents usually tell the American public that the new secretary of state is the nation's chief foreign policy adviser. Nonetheless, the State Department's preeminence in foreign policy has declined dramatically since World War II. The State Department's image within the White House Executive Office and Congress (and even foreign governments) is quite poor—a slow, plodding, bureaucratic maze of inefficient, indecisive individuals. There is even a story about how Premier Nikita Khrushchev of the Soviet Union urged President John Kennedy to formulate his own views rather than to rely on State Department officials who, according to Khrushchev, "specialized in why something had not worked forty years ago."[3] In any event, since the days of Franklin Roosevelt, the State Department sometimes has been bypassed and often has been ignored when crucial decisions are made.

It is not surprising that the State Department has been overshadowed in foreign policy. It has no natural domestic constituency as does, for example, the Department of Defense, which can call on defense contractors for support. Instead, the State Department has what might be called **negative constituents**—U.S. citizens who openly oppose American foreign policy. One of the State Department's major functions, administering foreign aid, often elicits criticisms. Also, within Congress, the State Department is often looked on as an advocate of unpopular and costly foreign involvement. It is often called "the Department of Bad News."

Negative Constituents
Citizens who openly oppose government foreign policies.

The National Security Council. The job of the National Security Council (NSC), created by the National Security Act of 1947, is to advise the president on the integration of "domestic, foreign, and military policies relating to the national security." Its larger purpose is to provide policy continuity from one administration to the next. As it has turned out, the NSC—consisting of the president, the vice president, the secretaries of state and defense, the director of emergency planning, and often the chairperson of the joint chiefs of staff and the director of the CIA—is used in just about any way the president wants to use it.

---

[3] Theodore C. Sorensen, *Kennedy* (New York: Harper & Row, 1965), pp. 554–555.

Intelligence Community
The government agencies that are involved in gathering information about the capabilities and intentions of foreign governments and that engage in activities to further U.S. foreign policy aims.

INFOTRAC®
COLLEGE EDITION

For updates and more information on the CIA, use the term "Central Intelligence Agency" in the Subject guide.

The role of national security adviser to the president seems to adjust to fit the player. Some advisers have come into conflict with heads of the State Department. Henry A. Kissinger, Nixon's flamboyant and aggressive national security adviser, rapidly gained ascendancy over William Rogers, the secretary of state, in foreign policy. When Jimmy Carter became president, he appointed Zbigniew Brzezinski as national security adviser. Brzezinski competed openly with Secretary of State Cyrus Vance (who apparently had little power). Although there were rumors of divisions over policy within George W. Bush's national security team, Secretary of State Colin Powell, National Security Adviser Condoleezza Rice, and Secretary of Defense Donald Rumsfeld all became important players and spokespersons for the administration.

The Intelligence Community. No discussion of foreign policy would be complete without some mention of the **intelligence community.** This consists of the forty or more government agencies or bureaus that are involved in intelligence activities, informational and otherwise. On January 24, 1978, President Carter issued Executive Order 12036, in which he formally defined the official major members of the intelligence community. They are as follows:

1. Central Intelligence Agency (CIA).
2. National Security Agency (NSA).
3. Defense Intelligence Agency (DIA).
4. Offices within the Department of Defense.
5. Bureau of Intelligence and Research in the Department of State.
6. Federal Bureau of Investigation (FBI).
7. Army intelligence.
8. Air Force intelligence.
9. Department of the Treasury.
10. Drug Enforcement Administration (DEA).
11. Department of Energy.

The CIA was created as part of the National Security Act of 1947. The National Security Agency and the Defense Intelligence Agency were created by executive order. Until recently, Congress voted billions of dollars for intelligence activities with little knowledge of how the funds were being used.

Covert Actions. Intelligence activities consist mostly of overt information gathering, but covert actions also are undertaken. Covert actions, as the name implies, are done secretly, and rarely does the American public find out about them. In the late 1940s and early 1950s, the CIA covertly subsidized anti-Communist labor unions in Western Europe. The CIA covertly aided in the overthrow of the Mossadegh regime in Iran, which allowed the restoration of the shah in 1953. The CIA also helped to overthrow the Arbenz government of Guatemala in 1954 and apparently was instrumental in destabilizing the Allende government in Chile from 1970 to 1973.

During the mid-1970s, the "dark side" of the CIA was at least partly uncovered when the Senate undertook an investigation of its activities. One of the major findings of the Senate Select Committee on Intelligence was that the CIA had routinely spied on American citizens domestically—supposedly, a strictly prohibited activity. Consequently, the CIA came under the scrutiny of six, and later eight, oversight committees within Congress, which restricted the scope of its activity. By 1980, however, the CIA had regained much of its lost power to engage in covert activities. In the early 1990s, as relationships with the states of the former Soviet Union eased, the attention of the CIA and other agencies began to turn from military to economic intelligence.

By 2001, the agency came under fire for a number of intelligence lapses, including the conviction of one of its own agents for spying, the failure to detect Pakistan's nuclear arsenal, and, finally, the failure to have any advance knowledge about the terrorist attack on the United States on September 11. With the rise of terrorism as a threat to the nation, the intelligence agencies have received more funding and enhanced surveillance powers, but these moves have also aroused fear that the agencies are being given too much power to spy on citizens and legal residents of the United States.

The Department of Defense.   The Department of Defense (DOD) was created in 1947 to bring all of the various activities of the American military establishment under the jurisdiction of a single department headed by a civilian secretary of defense. At the same time, the joint chiefs of staff, consisting of the commanders of each of the military branches and a chairperson, was created to formulate a unified military strategy.

Although the Department of Defense is larger than any other federal department, it declined in size after the fall of the Soviet Union in 1991. In the last ten years, the total number of civilian employees was reduced by about 400,000, to the current number of about 670,000. Military personnel were also reduced from 2.1 million in 1985 to about 1.4 million today. Until 2002, the defense budget had remained relatively flat in recent years, but with the advent of the war on terrorism, funding is being increased again. Given the reduced budget and the cut in uniformed personnel in the 1990s, it has been difficult for the Defense Department to maintain a high level of readiness.

The Department of Defense is the largest federal department. Its role is to work with the commanders of each branch of the military, known as the joint chiefs of staff, to develop military strategy. Here, Defense Secretary Donald Rumsfeld, left, and Chairman of the Joint Chiefs General Richard B. Myers, right, speak to members of the media. (Department of Defense photo by R. D. Ward)

Congress Balances the Presidency

A new interest in the balance of power between Congress and the president on foreign policy questions developed during the Vietnam War (1964–1975). Sensitive to public frustration over the long and costly war and angry at Richard Nixon for some of his other actions as president, Congress attempted to establish some limits on the power of the president in setting foreign and defense policy. In 1973, Congress passed the War Powers Resolution over President Nixon's veto. The act limited the president's use of troops in military action without congressional approval (see Chapter 12). Most presidents, however, have not interpreted the "consultation" provisions of the act as meaning that Congress should be consulted before military action is taken. Instead, Presidents Ford, Carter, Reagan, Bush, and Clinton ordered troop movements and then informed congressional leaders. Critics note that it is quite possible for a president to commit troops to a situation from which the nation could not withdraw without incurring heavy losses, whether or not Congress is consulted.

Congress has also exerted its authority to limit or deny the president's requests for military assistance to Angolan rebels and to the government of El Salvador, as well as requests for new weapons, such as the B-1 bomber. In general, Congress has been far more cautious in supporting the president in situations in which military involvement of American troops is possible.

At times, Congress can take the initiative in foreign policy. In 1986, Congress initiated and passed a bill instituting economic sanctions against South Africa to pressure that nation into ending its policy of racial segregation (apartheid). President Ronald Reagan vetoed the bill, but the veto was overridden by large majorities in both the House and the Senate.

Domestic Sources of Foreign Policy

The making of foreign policy is often viewed as a presidential prerogative because of the president's constitutional power in that area and the resources of the executive branch that the president controls. Foreign policymaking is also influenced by a number of other sources, however, including elite and mass opinion and the military-industrial complex.

DID YOU KNOW ...
That the Pentagon's stockpile of strategic materials includes 1.5 million pounds of quartz crystals used in pre–Great Depression radios and 150,000 tons of tannin used in tanning cavalry saddles **?**

Attentive Public
That portion of the general public that pays attention to policy issues.

Military-Industrial Complex
The mutually beneficial relationship between the armed forces and defense contractors.

I N F O T R A C ®
COLLEGE EDITION

For more information on the military-industrial complex, use the term "military-industrial complex" in the Subject guide.

Elite and Mass Opinion

Public opinion influences the making of U.S. foreign policy through a number of channels. Elites in American business, education, communications, labor, and religion try to influence presidential decision making through several strategies. A number of elite organizations, such as the Council on Foreign Relations and the Trilateral Commission, work to increase international cooperation and to influence foreign policy through conferences, publications, and research.

The members of the American elite establishment also exert influence on foreign policy through the general public by encouraging debate over foreign policy positions, publicizing the issues, and using the media. Generally, the efforts of the president and the elites are most successful with the segment of the population called the **attentive public.** This sector of the mass public, which probably constitutes 10 to 20 percent of all citizens, is more interested in foreign affairs than are most other Americans, and they are likely to transmit their opinions to the less interested members of the public through conversation and local leadership.

The Military-Industrial Complex

Civilian fear of the relationship between the defense establishment and arms manufacturers (the **military-industrial complex**) dates back many years. During President Eisenhower's eight years in office, the former five-star general of the army experienced firsthand the kind of pressure that could be brought against him and other policymakers by arms manufacturers. Eisenhower decided to give the country a solemn and, as he saw it, necessary warning of the consequences of this influence. On January 17, 1961, in his last official speech, he said,

> In the councils of government, we must guard against the acquisition of unwarranted influence, whether sought or unsought, by the military-industrial complex. The potential for the disastrous rise of misplaced power exists and will persist. . . . Only an alert and knowledgeable citizenry can compel the proper meshing of the huge industrial and military machinery of defense with our peaceful methods and goals, so that security and liberty may prosper together.[4]

The Pentagon has supported a large sector of our economy through defense contracts. It also has supplied retired army officers as key executives to large defense-contracting firms. Perhaps the Pentagon's strongest allies have been members of Congress whose districts or states benefited from the economic power of military bases or contracts. After the Cold War ended in the late 1980s, the defense industry looked abroad for new customers. Sales of some military equipment to China raised serious issues for the Clinton administration. The war on terrorism provoked a new debate about what types of weaponry would be needed to safeguard the nation in the future. When President George W. Bush proposed legislation in 2002 to increase the Defense Department's budget substantially, weapons manufacturers looked forward to increased sales and increased profits.

The Major Foreign Policy Themes

Although some observers might suggest that U.S. foreign policy is inconsistent and changes with the current occupant of the White House, the long view of American diplomatic ventures reveals some major themes underlying foreign policy. In the early years of the nation, presidents and the people generally agreed that the United States should avoid foreign entanglements and concentrate instead on its own devel-

---

[4] *Congressional Almanac* (Washington, D.C.: Congressional Quarterly Press, 1961), pp. 938–939.

opment. From the beginning of the twentieth century until today, however, a major theme has been increasing global involvement, with the United States taking an active role in assisting the development of other nations, dominating the world economy, and, in some cases, acting as a peacemaker. The major theme of the post–World War II years was the containment of communism. In the following brief review of American diplomatic history, these three themes predominate. The theme for the twenty-first century, now that there are multiple strong nations and only one superpower, has not yet emerged. Some have suggested, however, that the theme may well be the containment of terrorism.

The Formative Years: Avoiding Entanglements

Foreign policy was largely nonexistent during the formative years of the United States. Remember that the new nation was operating under the Articles of Confederation. The national government had no right to levy and collect taxes, no control over commerce, no right to make commercial treaties, and no power to raise an army (the Revolutionary army was disbanded in 1783). The government's lack of international power was made clear when Barbary pirates seized American hostages in the Mediterranean. The United States was unable to rescue the hostages and ignominiously had to purchase them in a treaty with Morocco.

The founders of this nation had a basic mistrust of corrupt European governments. George Washington said it was the U.S. policy "to steer clear of permanent alliances," and Thomas Jefferson echoed this sentiment when he said America wanted peace with all nations but "entangling alliances with none." This was also a logical position at a time when the United States was so weak militarily that it could not influence European development directly. Moreover, being protected by oceans that took weeks to traverse certainly allowed the nation to avoid entangling alliances. During the 1700s and 1800s, the United States generally stayed out of European conflicts and politics.

The Monroe Doctrine.   President James Monroe, in his message to Congress on December 2, 1823, stated that this country would not accept foreign intervention in the Western Hemisphere. In return, the United States would not meddle in European affairs. The **Monroe Doctrine** was the underpinning of the U.S. **isolationist foreign policy** toward Europe, which continued throughout the nineteenth century.

Monroe Doctrine
The policy statement included in President James Monroe's 1823 annual message to Congress, which set out three principles: (1) European nations should not establish new colonies in the Western Hemisphere, (2) European nations should not intervene in the affairs of independent nations of the Western Hemisphere, and (3) the United States would not interfere in the affairs of European nations.

Isolationist Foreign Policy
Abstaining from an active role in international affairs or alliances, which characterized U.S. foreign policy toward Europe during most of the nineteenth century.

This painting shows President James Monroe explaining the Monroe Doctrine to a group of government officials. Essentially, the Monroe Doctrine made the Western Hemisphere the concern of the United States. (Library of Congress photo)

A lone U.S. soldier stands in a trench in France during World War I. On June 28, 1914, Archduke Franz Ferdinand of Austria and his wife were assassinated in Sarajevo, Bosnia. As a result, Germany declared war on Russia on August 1, 1914, with England and Belgium entering the war days later. Under President Woodrow Wilson, the United States declared war on April 6, 1917, to make the world "safe for democracy." More than nine million people died before Armistice Day, November 11, 1918. (National Archives photo)

The atomic bomb explodes over Nagasaki, Japan, on August 9, 1945. (U.S. Air Force photo)

In this hemisphere, however, the United States pursued an actively expansionist policy. The nation purchased Louisiana in 1803, annexed Texas in 1845, gained half of Mexico's territory in the 1840s, purchased Alaska in 1867, and annexed Hawaii in 1898.

The Spanish-American War and World War I.   The end of the isolationist policy started with the Spanish-American War in 1898. Winning that war gave the United States possession of Guam, Puerto Rico, and the Philippines (which gained independence in 1946). On the heels of that war came World War I (1914–1918). In his reelection campaign of 1916, President Woodrow Wilson ran on the slogan "He kept us out of war." Nonetheless, on April 6, 1917, the United States declared war on Germany. It was evident to Wilson that without help, the Allies would be defeated, and American property and lives, already under attack, increasingly would be endangered. In the 1920s, the United States did indeed go "back to normalcy," as President Warren G. Harding urged it to do. U.S. military forces were largely disbanded, defense spending dropped to about 1 percent of total annual national income, and the nation entered a period of isolationism.

The Era of Internationalism

Isolationism was permanently shattered and relegated to its place in history by the bombing of the U.S. naval base at Pearl Harbor, Hawaii, on December 7, 1941. The surprise attack by the Japanese resulted in the deaths of 2,403 American servicemen and the wounding of 1,143 others. Eighteen warships were sunk or seriously damaged, and 188 planes were destroyed at the airfields. The American public was outraged. President Franklin Roosevelt asked Congress to declare war on Japan immediately, and the United States entered World War II. This unequivocal response was certainly due to the nature of the provocation. American soil had not been attacked by a foreign power since the burning of Washington, D.C., by the British in 1814.

The United States was the only major participating country to emerge from World War II with its economy intact, and even strengthened. The Soviet Union, Japan, Italy, France, Germany, Britain, and a number of minor participants in the war were all economically devastated. The United States was also the only country to have control over operational nuclear weapons. President Harry Truman had personally made the decision to use two atomic bombs, on August 6 and August 9, 1945, to end the

British Prime Minister Winston Churchill, U.S. President Franklin Roosevelt, and Soviet leader Joseph Stalin met at Yalta from February 4 to 11, 1945, to resolve their differences over the shape that the international community would take after World War II. (Corbis/Bettmann)

war with Japan. (Historians still dispute the necessity of this action, which ultimately killed more than 100,000 Japanese civilians and left an equal number permanently injured.) The United States truly had become the world's superpower.

The Cold War.   The United States had become an uncomfortable ally of the Soviet Union after Adolf Hitler's invasion of Soviet territory. Soon after World War II ended, relations between the Soviet Union and the West deteriorated. The Soviet Union wanted a weakened Germany, and to achieve this, it insisted that the country be divided in two, with East Germany becoming a buffer against the West. Little by little, the Soviet Union helped to install Communist governments in Eastern European countries, which began to be referred to collectively as the **Soviet bloc.** In response, the United States encouraged the rearming of Western Europe. The **Cold War** had begun.[5]

In Fulton, Missouri, on March 5, 1946, Winston Churchill, in a striking metaphor, declared that from the Baltic to the Adriatic Sea "an iron curtain has descended across the [European] continent." The term **iron curtain** became even more appropriate when Soviet-dominated East Germany built a wall separating East Berlin from West Berlin in August 1961.

Containment Policy.   In 1947, a remarkable article was published in *Foreign Affairs.* The article was signed by "X." The actual author was George F. Kennan, chief of the policy-planning staff for the State Department. The doctrine of **containment** set forth in the article became—according to many—the Bible of Western foreign policy. "X" argued that whenever and wherever the Soviet Union could successfully challenge

---

[5] See John Lewis Gaddis, *The United Nations and the Origins of the Cold War* (New York: Columbia University Press, 1972).

INFOTRAC®
COLLEGE EDITION

For more information on the Cold War, use the term "Cold War" in the Subject guide.

Soviet Bloc
The Eastern European countries that installed Communist regimes after World War II.

Cold War
The ideological, political, and economic impasse that existed between the United States and the Soviet Union following World War II.

Iron Curtain
The term used to describe the division of Europe between the Soviet Union and the West; popularized by Winston Churchill in a speech portraying Europe as being divided by an iron curtain, with the nations of Eastern Europe behind the curtain and increasingly under Soviet control.

Containment
A U.S. diplomatic policy adopted by the Truman administration to "build situations of strength" around the globe to contain Communist power within its existing boundaries.

Truman Doctrine
The policy adopted by President Harry Truman in 1947 to halt Communist expansion in southeastern Europe.

For more information on George F. Kennan, use the term "George Kennan" in the Subject guide.

Western institutions, it would do so. He recommended that our policy toward the Soviet Union be "firm and vigilant containment of Russian expansive tendencies."[6]

The containment theory was expressed clearly in the **Truman Doctrine**, which was enunciated by President Harry Truman in his historic address to Congress on March 12, 1947. In that address, he announced that the United States must help countries in which a Communist takeover seemed likely. Later that year, he backed the Marshall Plan, an economic assistance plan for Europe that was intended to prevent the expansion of Communist influence there. By 1950, the United States had entered into a military alliance with the European nations called the North Atlantic Treaty Organization, or NATO. The combined military power of the United States and the European nations worked to contain Soviet influence to Eastern Europe and to maintain a credible threat to any Soviet military attack on the European continent.

Superpower Relations

During the Cold War, there was never any direct military confrontation between the United States and the Soviet Union. Rather, confrontations among "client" nations were used to carry out the policies of the superpowers. Only on occasion did the United States directly enter a conflict in a significant way. Two such occasions were in Korea and Vietnam.

In 1950, North Korean troops were embroiled in a war with South Korea. President Truman asked for and received a Security Council order from the United Nations (UN) for the North Koreans to withdraw their troops. The Soviet Union was absent from the council on that day, protesting the exclusion of the People's Republic of China from the UN, and did not participate in the discussion. Truman then authorized the use of American forces in support of the South Koreans. For the next three years, American troops were engaged in a land war in Asia, a war that became a stalemate and a political liability to President Truman. One of Dwight Eisenhower's major 1952 campaign promises was to end the Korean War—which he did. An armistice was signed on July 27, 1953. (American troops have been stationed in South Korea ever since, however.)

U.S. involvement in Vietnam began shortly after the end of the Korean conflict. When the French army in Indochina was defeated by the Communist forces of Ho Chi Minh and the two Vietnams were created in 1954, the United States assumed the role of supporting the South Vietnamese government against North Vietnam. President John Kennedy sent 16,000 "advisers" to help South Vietnam, and after Kennedy's death in 1963, President Lyndon Johnson greatly increased the scope of that support. American forces in Vietnam at the height of the U.S. involvement totaled more than 500,000 troops. More than 58,000 Americans were killed, and 300,000 were wounded, in the conflict. The debate over U.S. involvement in Vietnam divided the American electorate and, as mentioned previously, spurred congressional efforts to limit the ability of the president to commit forces to armed combat.

The Cuban Missile Crisis.   With the two superpowers having enough nuclear bombs to destroy the world, a direct confrontation between the United States and the Soviet Union was unthinkable. Perhaps the closest the two nations came to such a confrontation was the Cuban missile crisis in 1962. The Soviets placed missiles in Cuba, ninety miles off the U.S. coast, in response to Cuban fears of an American invasion and to try to balance the American nuclear advantage. President Kennedy and his advisers rejected the possibility of armed intervention, setting up a naval blockade around the island instead. When Soviet vessels, apparently carrying nuclear

---

[6]X, "The Sources of Soviet Conduct," *Foreign Affairs,* July 1947, p. 575.

warheads, appeared near Cuban waters, the tension reached its height. After intense negotiations between Washington and Moscow, the Soviet ships turned around on October 25, and on October 28 the Soviet Union announced the withdrawal of its missile operations from Cuba. In exchange, the United States agreed not to invade Cuba and to remove some of its own missiles that were located near the Soviet border in Turkey.

A Period of Détente.   The French word **détente** means a relaxation of tensions. By the end of the 1960s, it was clear that some efforts had to be made to reduce the threat of nuclear war between the United States and the Soviet Union. The Soviet Union gradually had begun to catch up in the building of strategic nuclear delivery vehicles in the form of bombers and missiles, thus balancing the nuclear scales. Each nation acquired the military capacity to destroy the other with nuclear weapons.

As the result of protracted negotiations, in May 1972, the United States and the Soviet Union signed the **Strategic Arms Limitation Treaty (SALT I).** That treaty "permanently" limited the development and deployment of antiballistic missiles (ABMs), and it limited for five years the number of offensive missiles each country could deploy. To further reduce tensions, under the policy of Secretary of State Henry Kissinger and President Nixon, new scientific and cultural exchanges were arranged with the Soviets, as well as new opportunities for Jewish emigration out of the Soviet Union.

DID YOU KNOW . . .
That the United States invaded and occupied part of Russia in 1919 **?**

Détente
A French word meaning a relaxation of tensions. The term characterizes U.S.–Soviet policy as it developed under President Richard Nixon and Secretary of State Henry Kissinger. Détente stressed direct cooperative dealings with Cold War rivals but avoided ideological accommodation.

Strategic Arms Limitation Treaty (SALT I)
A treaty between the United States and the Soviet Union to stabilize the nuclear arms competition between the two countries. SALT I talks began in 1969, and agreements were signed on May 26, 1972.

President Richard Nixon signs SALT I, a Cold War agreement with the Soviet Union, in 1972. The Soviet Union dissolved in late December 1991. Consequently, do you think that the member republics of the former Soviet Union should have to abide by the SALT I agreement? (AP Photo)

The policy of détente was not limited to U.S. relationships with the Soviet Union. Seeing an opportunity to capitalize on increasing friction between the Soviet Union and the People's Republic of China, Kissinger secretly began negotiations to establish a new relationship with that nation. President Nixon eventually visited the People's Republic of China in 1972 and set the stage for the formal diplomatic recognition of that country, which occurred during the Carter administration (1977–1981).

The Reagan-Bush Years. President Ronald Reagan took a hard line against the Soviet Union during his first term, proposing the strategic defense initiative (SDI), or "Star Wars," in 1983. SDI was designed to serve as a space-stationed defense against enemy missiles. Reagan and others in his administration argued that the program would deter nuclear war by shifting the emphasis of defense strategy from offensive to defensive weapons systems.

In November 1985, President Reagan and Mikhail Gorbachev, the Soviet leader, held summit talks in Geneva. The two men agreed to reestablish cultural and scientific exchanges and to continue the arms control negotiations. Progress toward an agreement was slow, however.

In 1987, representatives of the United States and the Soviet Union continued work on an arms reduction agreement. Although there were setbacks throughout the year, the negotiations resulted in a historic agreement signed by Reagan and Gorbachev in Washington, D.C., on December 8, 1987. The terms of the Intermediate-Range Nuclear Force (INF) Treaty, which was ratified by the Senate, required the superpowers to dismantle a total of four thousand intermediate-range missiles within the first three years of the agreement.

Beginning in 1989, President George H. W. Bush continued the negotiations with the Soviet Union to reduce the number of nuclear weapons and the number of armed troops in Europe. Subsequent events, including developments in Eastern Europe, the unification of Germany, and the dissolution of the Soviet Union (in December 1991), made the process much more complex, however. American strategists worried as much about who now controlled the Soviet nuclear arsenal as about completing the treaty process. In 1992, the United States signed the Strategic Arms Reduction Treaty (START) with four former Soviet republics—Russia, Ukraine, Belarus, and Kazakhstan—to reduce the number of long-range nuclear weapons. President George W. Bush changed directions in 2001, announcing that the United States was withdrawing from the 1972 ABM treaty. Six months later, Bush and Russian President Vladimir Putin signed an agreement greatly reducing the number of nuclear weapons on each side over the next few years.

The Dissolution of the Soviet Union. After the fall of the Berlin Wall in 1989, it was clear that the Soviet Union had relinquished much of its political and military control over the states of Eastern Europe that formerly had been part of the Soviet bloc. No one expected the Soviet Union to dissolve into separate states as quickly as it did, however. Though Gorbachev tried to adjust the Soviet constitution and political system to allow greater autonomy for the republics within the union, demands for political, ethnic, and religious autonomy grew. In August 1991, the Soviet military tried to slow the process by arresting Gorbachev. These efforts to preserve the Soviet state were thwarted by the Russian people and parliament under the leadership of Boris Yeltsin, then president of Russia.

Instead of restoring the Soviet state, the military leaders' attempt to gain control hastened the process of creating an independent Russian state led by Yeltsin. On the day after Christmas in 1991, the Soviet Union was officially dissolved. A few months later, a majority of the former republics had joined a loose federation called the Commonwealth of Independent States, although a few of the larger republics, including Georgia and Ukraine, refused to join. Another uprising in Russia, this time led by anti-Yeltsin members of the new parliament who wanted to restore the Soviet Union immediately, failed in 1993.

In 2000, Yeltsin resigned due to poor health. He named Vladimir Putin, architect of the Russian military effort against the breakaway ethnic movement in the province of Chechnya, as acting president. A few months later, Putin won the presidency in a national election. As the United States launched its war on terrorism, Putin stood by President George W. Bush's side as an ally. Of course, Russia had suffered from terrorism within its own borders, and the Russian economy had much to gain from selling oil to the United States if the Arab states cut their oil production.

Foreign and Defense Policy: Why Is It Important Today?

The tremendous changes in the political system of the Soviet Union and its successor states, including Russia, ended the world order created by World War II. By the end of the twentieth century, the United States was recognized as the sole global superpower. Although many Americans believe that other nations in Europe and Asia should help solve problems around the world, those nations and their peoples are turning to the United States for leadership in resolving conflicts that might lead to larger wars.

No president or secretary of state can predict the future of world politics. There is simply no way of knowing whether the states of the former Soviet Union will be a source of future conflicts, whether ethnic tensions will erupt in more nations, or whether the United Nations will be able to assemble an effective peacekeeping force. Nonetheless, it is necessary for U.S. leaders to try to plan for the future. The United States needs to devise a strategy for self-defense rather than a strategy for confronting Russia.

The terrorist attacks on the United States on September 11, 2001, made clear that how the United States conducts its foreign and defense policy has an immediate and serious effect on Americans' domestic security. A generation of terrorists has been nurtured by dissatisfaction with existing governments. Because the United States wields so much power around the world, many terrorists have become convinced that an attack on the United States will somehow aid their cause. This is a consideration in the development of foreign policy that U.S. policymakers have not considered as seriously in the past as they do today.

Other issues that need to be resolved include the role that the United States sees for the United Nations, the degree to which the United States must keep a vital intelligence service, the strategies for supporting American interests in the Western Hemisphere and throughout the world, and the degree to which the United States will play an active role in the world. Without the structure of the Cold War, it is likely that foreign policy for the United States, as well as for other leading nations, will need to be much more flexible than it has been in the past to deal with changing conditions and complex situations.

MAKING A DIFFERENCE | Working for Human Rights

In many countries throughout the world, human rights are not protected to the extent that they are in the United States. In some nations, people are imprisoned, tortured, or killed because they oppose the current regime. In other nations, certain ethnic or racial groups are oppressed by the majority population. In nations such as Somalia, where civil war has caused starvation among millions of people, international efforts to send food relief to the refugee camps were hampered by the fighting among rival factions that raged within that country.

Joining an Organization

What can you do to work for the improvement of human rights in other nations? One way is to join one of the national and international organizations listed to the right that attempt to keep watch over human rights violations. By publicizing human rights violations, these organizations try to pressure nations into changing their tactics. Sometimes, such organizations are able to apply enough pressure and cause enough embarrassment that some victims may be freed from prison or allowed to emigrate.

Keeping Informed

Another way to work for human rights is to keep informed about the state of affairs in other nations and to write personally to those governments or to their embassies, asking them to cease these violations. Again, the organizations listed in the next column have newsletters or other publications to keep you aware of developments in other nations.

If you want to receive general information about the position of the United States on human rights violations, you could begin by contacting the State Department:

U.S. Department of State
Bureau of Democracy,
Human Rights, and Labor
2201 C St. N.W.
Washington, DC 20520
202-647-4000
http://www.state.gov/g/drl/hr

You can also contact the United Nations:

United Nations
777 United Nations Plaza
New York, NY 10017
212-963-1234
http://www.un.org

The following organizations are well known for their watchdog efforts in countries that violate human rights for political reasons:

Amnesty International U.S.A.
322 Eighth Ave., Fl. 10
New York, NY 10001
212-807-8400
http://www.amnestyusa.org

American Friends Service Committee
1501 Cherry St.
Philadelphia, PA 19102
215-241-7000
http://www.afsc.org

Key Terms

attentive public 534
Cold War 537
containment 537
defense policy 516
détente 539
diplomacy 515
economic aid 515

foreign policy 515
foreign policy process 515
intelligence community 532
iron curtain 537
isolationist foreign policy 535
military-industrial complex 534

Monroe Doctrine 535
moral idealism 516
most-favored-nation status 522
National Security Council (NSC) 516
national security policy 515

negative constituents 531
political realism 517
Soviet bloc 537
Strategic Arms Limitation Treaty (SALT I) 539
technical assistance 515
Truman Doctrine 538

Chapter Summary

1 Foreign policy includes national goals and the techniques used to achieve them. National security policy, which is one aspect of foreign policy, is designed to protect the independence and the political and economic integrity of the United States. Diplomacy involves the nation's external relationships and is an attempt to resolve conflict without resort to arms. Sometimes U.S. foreign policy is based on moral idealism. At other times, U.S. policies stem from political realism.

2 Terrorism has become a major challenge facing the United States and other nations. Terrorist networks foment civil war and revolution in nations across the globe. The United States waged war on terrorism after the September 11 attacks, but it is extremely difficult to eradicate the root causes of terrorist movements.

3 Nuclear proliferation continues to be an issue due to the breakup of the Soviet Union and the loss of control over its nuclear arsenal, along with the continued efforts of other nations to gain nuclear warheads. The number of warheads is known to be more than thirty-two thousand.

4 The United States is dependent on the world economy, as shown by the vulnerability of its stock market to world forces, its status as a debtor nation, and its significant trade deficit. The effects of a unified Europe on world trade are yet to be fully realized.

5 Ethnic tensions and political instability in many regions of the world provide challenges to the United States. The nations of Central America and the Caribbean, including Haiti, require American attention because of their proximity. Negotiations have brought agreement in South Africa, but civil wars have torn apart Rwanda and Yugoslavia. The Middle East continues to be a hotbed of conflict despite efforts to continue the peace process.

6 The formal power of the president to make foreign policy derives from the U.S. Constitution, which makes the president responsible for the preservation of national security and designates the president as commander in chief of the army and navy. Presidents have interpreted this authority broadly. They also have the power to make treaties and executive agreements. In principle, the State Department is the executive agency most directly involved with foreign affairs. The National Security Council (NSC) advises the president on the integration of "domestic, foreign, and military policies relating to the national security." The intelligence community consists of forty or more government agencies engaged in intelligence activities varying from information gathering to covert actions. In response to presidential actions in the Vietnam War, Congress attempted to establish some limits on the power of the president in foreign policy by passing the War Powers Resolution in 1973.

7 Three major themes have guided U.S. foreign policy. In the early years of the nation, isolationism was the primary focus. With the start of the twentieth century, this view gave way to global involvement. From the end of World War II through the 1980s, the major goal was to contain communism and the influence of the Soviet Union.

8 During the 1700s and 1800s, the United States had little international power and generally stayed out of European conflicts and politics. The nineteenth century has been called the period of isolationism. The Monroe Doctrine of 1823 stated that the United States would not accept foreign intervention in the Western Hemisphere and would not meddle in European affairs. The United States pursued an actively expansionist policy in the Americas and the Pacific area during the nineteenth century, however.

9 The end of the policy of isolationism toward Europe started with the Spanish-American War of 1898. U.S. entanglement in European politics became more extensive when the United States entered World War I on April 6, 1917. World War II marked a lasting change in American foreign policy. The United States was the only major country to emerge from the war with its economy intact and the only country with operating nuclear weapons.

10 Soon after the close of World War II, the uncomfortable alliance between the United States and the Soviet Union ended, and the Cold War began. A policy of containment, which assumed an expansionist Soviet Union, was enunciated in the Truman Doctrine. Following the frustrations of the Vietnam War and the apparent arms equality of the United States and the Soviet Union, the United States was ready for détente. Although President Ronald Reagan took a tough stance toward the Soviet Union in the first term of his administration, the second term saw serious negotiations toward arms reduction, culminating with the signing of the Intermediate-Range Nuclear Force Treaty in 1987 and the Strategic Arms Reduction Treaty in 1992. After the fall of the Soviet Union, Russia emerged as a less threatening state. The United States and Russia have forged agreements on some issues in recent years, such as the fight against terrorism.

Selected Print and Media Resources

SUGGESTED READINGS

Friedman, Thomas L. *The Lexus and the Olive Tree: Understanding Globalization.* Des Plaines, Ill.: Bantam Doubleday, 2000. Written by a *New York Times* reporter, this book examines the trend toward globalization. The author focuses on the difference in goals between nations that seek material wealth and those that seek less tangible assets.

Fromkin, David. *Kosovo Crossing: American Ideals Meet Reality on the Balkan Battlefields.* New York: The Free Press, 2000. In this discussion of the U.S. intervention in Kosovo, the author argues that sometimes vital national interests may suggest that intervention is a mistake. He looks at the military and humanitarian options in these situations.

Hoge, James F., Jr., and Gideon Rose. *How Did This Happen? Terrorism and the New War.* New York: Public Affairs, 2001. Compiled after the September 11 attacks, this book of essays discusses the causes of terrorism and the foreign policy and defense initiatives that must be taken to confront it.

Lewis, Bernard. *What Went Wrong? Western Impact and Middle Eastern Response.* Oxford: Oxford University Press, 2002. Lewis, an outstanding scholar of the Middle East, provides a brief history of how the West and the Middle East have taken different paths in the last few centuries and how those choices bring them to conflict.

Miller, Judith, Stephen Engelberg, and William Broad. *Germs: Biological Weapons and America's Secret War.* New York: Simon & Schuster, 2001. The authors describe the biological weapons programs of several nations and the attempts by the United States to stop those programs.

Rashid, Ahmed. *Taliban: Militant Islam, Oil and Fundamentalism in Central Asia.* New Haven, Conn.: Yale University Press, 2001. Written by a reporter who spent twenty-one years in Afghanistan, this book examines the causes of Islamic radicalism and of the anger against the United States expressed by the Taliban.

MEDIA RESOURCES

Black Hawk Down—This 2002 film recounts the American siege of Mogadishu, Somalia, in October 1993, during which two Black Hawk helicopters of the U.S. Rangers were shot down. The film, which is based on reporter Mark Bowden's best-selling book by the same name, contains graphic scenes of terrifying urban warfare.

Dr. Strangelove or How I Learned to Stop Worrying and Love the Bomb—A classic portrayal of a crazed general who is trying to start a nuclear war, produced in 1964 and starring Peter Sellers, who plays three roles. The film also stars George C. Scott and James Earl Jones.

The Mouse That Roared—An outrageous 1959 comedy that satirizes how Americans treat nations that they defeat. Peter Sellers leads the army of a very tiny nation that invades the United States in order to be defeated but ends up winning the war.

On the Beach—A film starring Gregory Peck, Ava Gardner, and Anthony Perkins that examines the lives of survivors of a nuclear holocaust living in Australia, the only nation to escape the blast.

Your CD-ROM Resources

In addition to the chapter content containing hot links, the following resources are available on the CD-ROM:

- **Internet Activities**—The U.S. State Department, learning more about Iraq's "weapons of mass destruction" threat.
- **Critical Thinking Exercises**—Mass and attentive public, the Cuban missile crisis, the new Russia.
- **Self-Check on Important Themes**—Can You Answer These?
- **Public Opinion Data**—Should the United States stand alone in the war on terrorism? Should immigration policy ban foreign students from nations harboring or sponsoring terrorists?

- **Simulation**—You Are There!
- **Participation Exercise**—Research a current foreign or defense policy issue involving the United States that is of great interest to you.
- **MicroCase Exercise**—"By the Numbers: How Important Is Foreign Policy to Americans?"
- **Additional Resources**—The Monroe Doctrine (1823), The Truman Doctrine (1947), Washington's Farewell Address (1796), Lyndon Johnson's Tonkin Gulf Speech and the Tonkin Gulf Resolution (1964).

e -mocracy

Attacking Government Computer Systems

Although the incidents frequently are not reported in the media, attacks on the government's computer systems occur often and are sometimes extremely successful. During the Persian Gulf War (1991), European computer hackers were able to access U.S. military computers at several dozen sites and gain information. In 1996, hackers caused mischief at the computers of the Central Intelligence Agency and the Justice Department and destroyed the Air Force's home page. In early 1998, computer hackers accessed a whole series of nonclassified sites, caused major university and National Aeronautics and Space Administration computers to crash, and defaced military base home pages. It is clear from these episodes that the electronic network used by the U.S. military and intelligence organizations is quite susceptible to access by amateurs, criminals, and spies.

Military and defense sites are not the only ones targeted by hackers: perhaps even more damage could be caused by interruptions to the global economic and banking system. During 1997, a survey of banks, universities, and companies showed that more than 60 percent had been accessed "illegitimately" during that year alone. In 2000, a series of computer viruses crippled businesses around the world. One of the most destructive, the "I Love You" virus, was eventually traced to a graduate student in the Philippines whose thesis had been rejected.

The potential consequences of successful attacks on government or business computer systems are almost too great to contemplate. Among the networks that, if impaired or destroyed, could bring down the nation's activities are those that connect the military services; guide satellites for communications and defense; launch missiles; guide submarines; and control all air traffic, credit-card transactions, interbank transactions, utility grids throughout the nation, and generally all telecommunications. The collapse of the World Trade Center towers in 2001 damaged telecommunications and Internet communications for all of lower Manhattan. Repairs to those systems took months to complete.

Logging On

Our government and the governments of other nations maintain hundreds of Web sites about foreign and defense policy. If you are interested in information about visas, passports, and data about individual countries, you can access the site maintained by the Department of State at

http://www.state.gov

For information about human rights, national security, and other issues from a European point of view, check the Web site maintained by the Swiss government, the International Relations and Security Network, at

http://www.fsk.ethz.ch

The Brookings Institution, a Washington, D.C., think tank, provides access to its research reports at the following Web site:

http://www.brook.edu

The Global Affairs Agenda, an interest group that promotes a progressive or liberal foreign policy, provides information about many topics at

http://www.foreignpolicy-infocus.org

For information about the intelligence community, go to the Web site of the Central Intelligence Agency at

http://www.cia.gov

Freedom House, an organization that promotes its vision of democracy around the world, rates all nations on their democratic practices at

http://www.freedomhouse.org

Using the Internet for Political Analysis

Go to the home page maintained by the Center for Defense Information, a nonpartisan and independent research group, at

http://www.cdi.org

Go to the "Select a Research Topic" button and choose one of the topics, such as nuclear weapons or arms trade. Read several of the articles on the topic and then try to propose a foreign policy position for the United States to meet that challenge. If you then want to see what the government has proposed, look at the Web site for the State Department, given above, or for the Department of Defense at

http://www.defense.gov

How close was your policy to that being pursued by the government?

PART SIX

State and Local Politics

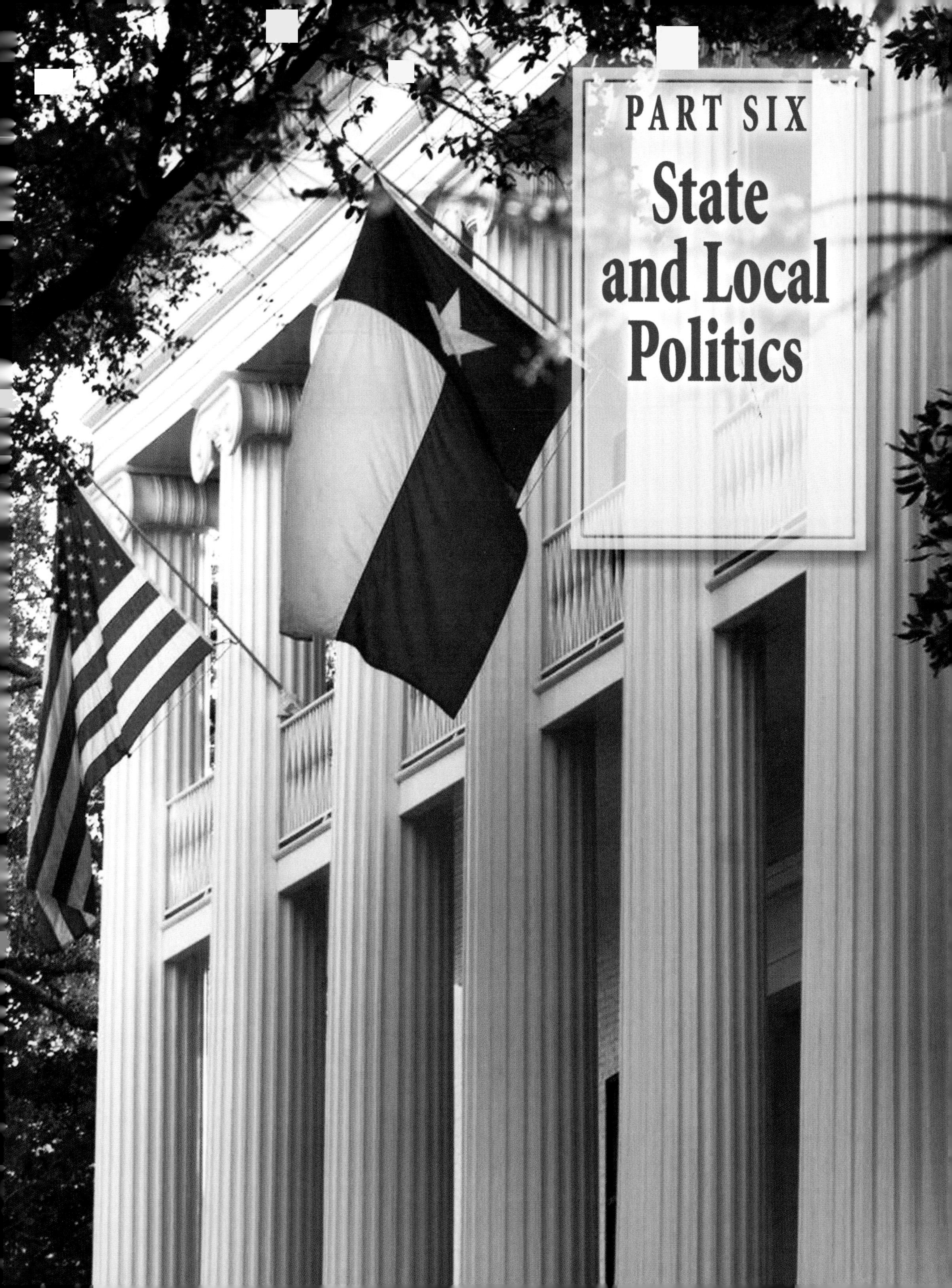

BACKGROUND

There is a growing sense in this country that our educational system is declining. Routinely, U.S. students test poorly in achievement, particularly in math and science, compared to students in such countries as Japan, Russia, and Germany.

Not surprisingly, many observers of the educational scene believe that the fault lies in our public school system. They argue that change is needed and that the easiest way to improve the system is to allow school choice. Currently, parents normally are required to send their children to a public school in the particular district where the family's physical residence is located. Generally, only families that wish to spend from $3,000 to $10,000 a year for tuition at private schools (in addition to the property taxes they pay to support their local public school district) have a choice.

WHAT IF ALL STATES ALLOWED SCHOOL CHOICE?

The concept of school choice sometimes involves open districts, meaning that parents can choose to send their children to public schools outside their districts. The aspect of school choice that generates substantial controversy, however, usually involves giving families vouchers, representing state funds, that can be used at any school, public or private. In other words, a voucher would be worth some specified amount of money, such as $5,000, but only if it were redeemed by a bona fide public or private school.

Under such a system, parents would determine where their children went to school. The children could attend the same local public school, a public school in another district, or a private school anywhere. Private schools might accept the vouchers as full payment for tuition fees or request that additional fees be paid.

COMPETITION WOULD BECOME EVIDENT

Certainly, competition for students would develop. Public schools would have to compete not only among themselves (which they currently do in areas that have open districts) but also with private schools. Private schools would have to compete with all schools, including new competitors in the educational marketplace.

Some critics of school choice, particularly public school teachers and administrators, are uncomfortable with treating public education like a business. Because of the competitive environment that would be created by school choice, some public schools might not be able to keep and attract enough students to survive. These schools, unless further subsidized by state and local governments, would "go bankrupt" and disappear.

THE CONSTITUTIONAL ISSUE

Other critics of school vouchers claim that such programs are unconstitutional because they allow state funds to be used to pay for education at religious schools. For example, in a voucher program set up in Cleveland, Ohio, children from low-income families received state funds, in the form of vouchers, to attend the school of their choice. Most of the four thousand children in the program left public schools to attend Catholic educational institutions.

According to those who challenged the program, the use of tax dollars to support religious education violated the establishment clause of the First Amendment to the Constitution, which requires the separation of church and state (see Chapter 4). An Ohio court agreed and invalidated the program, but in 2002 the Supreme Court held that the voucher program was constitutional. The Court's majority reasoned that because families theoretically could use the vouchers to send their children not only to religious schools but also to secular private academies, suburban public schools, or charter schools, the program did not unconstitutionally entangle church and state.

FOR CRITICAL ANALYSIS

1. Why are teachers' unions, such as the National Education Association, so adamantly against school choice?
2. Given that the goal of our public school system is universal education, do you see school choice as hurting or helping students from low-income families? Explain.

As you read in this chapter's *What If . . .* feature, it is up to the individual states to determine whether to allow school choice. There is no federal law that determines the issue, at least not yet. Within each state, even if a law allowing school choice were passed, local governments, particularly school boards, no doubt would have a large say in determining exactly how school choice would be made available in their particular areas.

This is true with respect to many state—and federal—policies. Typically, it is the local governing units in this country that give a human face to particular policies, such as welfare reform, and that deal directly with the people affected by those policies. Indeed, many people, when they think of government, think of local agencies or sets of individuals—such as city councils, city or county commissioners, school boards, libraries, zoning boards, fire and police departments, and so on—and not their state government or the federal government. Because they shape the environments in which all Americans live, the more than 87,000 local governmental units in the United States play a vital role in our federal system.

From a practical point of view, it is impossible to understand American politics and government today without a knowledge of how state and local governments operate—the topic of this chapter. We begin by examining the constitutional powers of the states as set forth by the founders in the U.S. Constitution. As you will see, local governments were not mentioned in the Constitution. The founders left their existence in the hands of state government.

The U.S. Constitution and the State Governments

Public education is a service that is largely controlled and funded by state and local governments, not by the federal government. This often creates conflict over specific education reforms, such as the use of school vouchers. Here, Reverend Timothy McDonald addresses a rally in Atlanta, Georgia, opposing school vouchers. What arguments do opponents of school vouchers use to defend their position? (AP Photo/Rick Bowmer)

Police Power
Authority to promote and safeguard the health, morals, safety, and welfare of the people.

We live in a federal system in which there are fifty separate state governments and one national government. The U.S. Constitution reserves a broad range of powers for state governments. It also prohibits state governments from engaging in certain activities. The U.S. Constitution does not say explicitly what the states actually may do. Rather, state powers are simply reserved, or residual: states may do anything that is not prohibited by the Constitution or anything that is not expressly within the realm of the national government.

The major reserved powers of the states are the powers to tax, spend, and regulate intrastate commerce, or commerce within a given state. The states also have general **police power,** meaning that they can impose their will on their citizens in the areas of safety (through, say, traffic laws), health (immunizations), welfare (child-abuse laws), and morals (regulation of pornographic materials).

Restrictions on state and local governmental activity are implied by the Constitution in Article VI, Clause 2:

> This Constitution, and the Laws of the United States which shall be made in Pursuance thereof; and all Treaties made, or which shall be made, under the Authority of the United States, shall be the supreme Law of the Land; and the Judges in every State shall be bound thereby, any Thing in the Constitution or Laws of any State to the Contrary notwithstanding.

DID YOU KNOW . . .
That Texas's constitution declares that banks may use automated teller machines and that New York's constitution specifies the width of ski trails?

For more information on state constitutions, use the term "state constitutions" in the Subject guide.

Alabama's constitution has been amended almost six hundred times. It is the longest and most amended of any state constitution. Here, Governor Don Seigelman of Alabama speaks to a gathering of people in favor of adopting an entirely new constitution for the state. Why has the federal Constitution remained so short, with only twenty-seven amendments? (AP Photo/Kevin Glackmeyer)

In other words, it is the U.S. Constitution that is the supreme law of the land. No state or local law can be in conflict with the Constitution, with laws made by the national Congress, or with treaties entered into by the national government. Judicially, the United States Supreme Court has been the final arbiter of conflicts arising between the national government and state governments.

State Constitutions

The U.S. Constitution is a model of brevity, although at the cost of specificity. State constitutions, however, typically are excessively long and detailed. The U.S. Constitution has endured for two hundred years and has been amended only twenty-seven times. State constitutions are another matter. Louisiana has had eleven constitutions; Georgia, ten; South Carolina, seven; and Alabama, Florida, and Virginia, six. The number of amendments that have been submitted to voters borders on the absurd. For example, the citizens of Alabama have adopted nearly six hundred amendments to their state constitution.

Why Are State Constitutions So Long?

According to historians, the length and mass of detail of many state constitutions reflect the loss of popular confidence in state legislatures between the end of the Civil War and the early 1900s. During that period, forty-two states adopted or revised their constitutions. Those constitutions adopted before or after that period are shorter and contain fewer restrictions on the powers of state legislatures. Another equally important reason for the length and detail of state constitutions is that state constitution makers apparently have had a difficult time distinguishing between constitutional and statutory law. Does the Louisiana constitution need an amendment to declare Huey Long's birthday a legal holiday? Is it necessary for the constitution of South Dakota to authorize a cordage and twine plant at the state penitentiary? Does the California constitution need to discuss the tax-exempt status of the Huntington Library and Art Gallery? The U.S. Constitution contains no such details. It leaves to the legislature the nuts-and-bolts activity of making specific statutory laws.

In all fairness to the states, their courts do not interpret their constitutions as freely as the United States Supreme Court interprets the U.S. Constitution.

Therefore, the states feel compelled to be more specific in their own constitutions. Additionally, the framers of state constitutions may feel obliged to fill in the gaps left by the very brief federal constitution.

The Constitutional Convention and the Constitutional Initiative

Two of the several ways to effect constitutional changes are the state constitutional convention and the constitutional initiative. As of 2003, over 230 state constitutional conventions had been used to write an entirely new constitution or to attempt to amend an existing one. In eighteen states, the constitution can be amended by **constitutional initiatives**.[1] An initiative allows citizens to place a proposed amendment on the ballot without calling a constitutional convention. The number of signatures required to get a constitutional initiative on the ballot varies from state to state; it is usually between 5 and 10 percent of the total number of votes cast for governor in the last election. The initiative process has been used most frequently in California and Oregon. Relatively few initiative amendments are approved by the electorate.

The State Executive Branch

All state governments in the United States have executive, legislative, and judicial branches. Here the similarity with the federal government ends. State governments do not always have strong executive branches.

A Weak Executive

During the colonial period, governors were appointed by the Crown and had the power to call the colonial assembly (the colonial legislative body) into session, recommend legislation, exercise veto power, and dissolve the assembly. The colonial governor acted as commander in chief of the colony's military forces and was also the head of the judiciary.

Not surprisingly, the colonies' revolt against British rule centered on the all-powerful colonial governors. When the first states were formed after the Declaration of Independence, hostility toward the governor's office ensured a weak executive branch and an extremely strong legislative branch. By the 1830s, however, the state executive office had become more important. Since Andrew Jackson's presidency, all governors (except in South Carolina) have been elected directly by the people. Simultaneously, there was an effort to democratize state government by popularly electing other state government officials as well.

Under the tenets of Jacksonian democracy, the more public officials who are elected (and not appointed), the more democratic (and better) the system will be. Even today, some states have numerous state offices with independently elected officials. The direct election of so many executive officials makes it likely that no one will have much power, because each official is working to secure his or her own political support. Only if the elected officials happen to be able to work together cohesively can they get much done.

A slight majority of the states require that the candidates for governor and lieutenant governor run for election as a team. In some states where this is not required, however, the voters have at times chosen a governor from one political party and a

Constitutional Initiative
An electoral device whereby citizens can propose a constitutional amendment through petitions signed by the required number of registered voters.

---

[1] These states are Arizona, Arkansas, California, Colorado, Florida, Illinois, Massachusetts, Michigan, Mississippi, Missouri, Montana, Nebraska, Nevada, North Dakota, Ohio, Oklahoma, Oregon, and South Dakota.

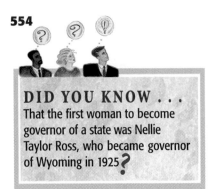

lieutenant governor from another. As a result, the governor may be unwilling to leave the state in order to prevent the lieutenant governor from exerting power during the governor's travels.

Reforming the System

Most states follow the practice of electing numerous executive officials. Nonetheless, governors have exercised the authority of their office with increasing frequency in recent years. Governors have become a significant force in legislative policymaking. The governor, in theory, enjoys the same advantage that the president has over Congress in his or her ability to make policy decisions and to embody these in a program on which the state legislative body can act. How the governor exercises this ability often depends on her or his powers of persuasion. A strong personality can make for a strong executive office. Personal skill, the strength of political parties and special interest groups, and the governor's use of the media can affect how much actual power she or he has.

Reorganization of the state executive branch to achieve greater efficiency has been attempted numerous times and in many states. There are some obstacles to reorganizing state executive branches, however. Voters do not want to lose their ability to influence politics directly. Both the voters and the legislators fear that reorganization will concentrate too much authority in the hands of the governor. Finally, many believe that numerous governmental functions, such as control of the highway program, should remain administrative rather than political.

Despite the fragmentation of executive power and doubts about the concentration of power in an executive's hands, the trend toward modernization has increased

The National Governors Association is one of the most influential lobbying organizations in the country. It has also been an important source in providing governors with reports on a variety of innovative state programs. Here, Kentucky Governor Paul Patton, left, and Michigan Governor John Engler, right, speak at the association's annual meeting. (AP Photo/Troy Maben)

the powers of many of the states' highest executives. Based on a governor's ability to make major appointments, formulate a state budget, veto legislation, and exercise other powers, the National Governors Association ranks the governors of at least twenty-five states as powerful or very powerful executives. Only eleven states are assessed as giving their executives little or very little power.

Moreover, state governors—as well as legislators—are playing increasingly important roles as the states assume more authority over programs, such as welfare, that for decades have been controlled by the national government. The trend towards states' rights during the 1990s and early 2000s has allowed governors to become models of leadership on a number of issues affecting national politics, including crime, welfare, and education. A state governorship also may be a steppingstone to the U.S. presidency. Seventeen of the nation's forty-three presidents (39 percent), including several recent presidents (Jimmy Carter, Ronald Reagan, Bill Clinton, and George W. Bush), served as state governors before assuming the presidential office. For these reasons, elections to state governorships tend to receive more national attention than in the past.

The Governor's Veto Power

The veto power gives the president of the United States immense leverage. Simply the threat of a presidential veto often means that legislation will not be passed by Congress. In some states, governors have strong veto power, but in other states,

DID YOU KNOW...
That Missouri state legislators approved a five-pound, 1,012-page bill aimed at reducing state paperwork?

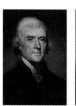 

Thomas Jefferson
Virginia
1779–1781

James Monroe
Virginia
1799–1802

Martin Van Buren
New York
1828–1829

John Tyler
Virginia
1825–1827

James Polk
Tennessee
1839–1841

Andrew Johnson
Tennessee
1853–1857

Rutherford B. Hayes
Ohio
1867–1871,
1875–1877

Grover Cleveland
New York
1882–1884

William McKinley
Ohio
1892–1896

Theodore Roosevelt
New York
1898–1900

Woodrow Wilson
New Jersey
1911–1912

Calvin Coolidge
Massachusetts
1918–1920

Franklin D. Roosevelt
New York
1929–1933

Jimmy Carter
Georgia
1971–1975

Ronald Reagan
California
1967–1975

Bill Clinton
Arkansas
1979–1981,
1983–1992

George W. Bush
Texas
1994–2000

The seventeen presidents who served as state governors before assuming the presidential office.

Item Veto
The power exercised by the governors of most states to veto particular sections or items of an appropriations bill, while signing the remainder of the bill into law.

governors have no veto power at all. Some states give the governor veto power but allow only five days in which to exercise it. Thirteen states give the governor pocket veto power (see Chapter 13).

In forty-three states, the governor has some form of **item veto** power on appropriations. If the governor in such a state does not particularly like one item, or line, in an appropriations bill, he or she can veto that item. In twelve states, the governor can reduce the amount of the appropriation but cannot reduce it to zero. Nineteen states give governors the ability to use the item veto on more than just appropriations.

The State Legislature

Although there has been a move in recent years to increase the power of governors, state legislatures are still an important force in state politics and state governmental decision making. The task of these assemblies is to legislate on such matters as taxes and the regulation of business and commerce, highways, school systems and the funding of education, and welfare payments. Allocation of funds and program priorities are vital issues to local residents and communities, and conflicts between regions within the state or between the cities and the rural areas are common.

State legislatures have been criticized for being unprofessional and less than effective. It is true that state legislatures sometimes spend their time considering trivial legislation (such as the official state pie in Florida), and lobbyists often have too much influence in state capitals. At the same time, state legislators are often given few resources with which to work. In many states, legislatures are limited to meeting only part of the year, and in some the pay is a disincentive to real service. In a number of states, state legislators are paid less than $10,000 per year. A complete list of state legislators' salaries, as well as other characteristics of state legislatures, is given in Table 18–1.

We have seen earlier how a bill becomes a law in the U.S. Congress. A similar process occurs at the state level. Figure 18–1 on page 558 traces how an idea becomes a law in the Florida legislature. Similar steps are followed in other states (note that Nebraska has a unicameral legislature, however, so there is no second chamber process).

Legislative Apportionment

Drawing up legislative districts—state as well as federal—has long been subject to gerrymandering—creative cartography designed to guarantee that one political party maintains control of a particular voting district. Malapportionment is the skewed distribution of voters in a state's legislative districts. The United States Supreme Court ruled in 1962 that malapportioned state legislatures violate the equal protection clause of the Fourteenth Amendment.[2] In a series of cases that followed, the Court held that legislative districts must be as nearly equal as possible in terms of population, and the grossest examples of state legislative malapportionment were eliminated.[3] The Supreme Court, however, allowed "benevolent, bipartisan gerrymandering" in certain states. Indeed, in 1977, the Supreme Court held that a state had an obligation under the 1965 Voting Rights Act to draw district boundaries to maximize minority legislative representation.[4] Thus, each decade, state and federal legislative districts must be redrawn to ensure that every person's vote is roughly equal and that minorities are represented adequately.

By the mid-1990s, however, the Supreme Court had reversed its position on what has been called "racial gerrymandering." In a series of cases, the Court held that voting districts that are redrawn with the goal of maximizing the electoral strength and

[2] *Baker v. Carr,* 369 U.S. 186 (1962).
[3] *Reynolds v. Sims,* 377 U.S. 533 (1964); and other cases.
[4] *United Jewish Organizations of Williamsburg v. Cary,* 430 U.S. 144 (1977).

TABLE 18–1

Characteristics of State Legislatures

	Seats in Senate	Length of Term	Seats in House	Length of Term	Years Sessions Are Held	Salary*
Alabama	35	4	105	4	Annual	$10(d)†
Alaska	20	4	40	2	Annual	24,012†
Arizona	30	2	60	2	Annual	24,000
Arkansas	35	4	100	2	Odd	12,796†
California	40	4	80	2	Even	99,000†
Colorado	35	4	65	2	Annual	30,000†
Connecticut	36	2	151	2	Annual	28,000
Delaware	21	4	41	2	Annual	33,400
Florida	40	4	120	2	Annual	27,900†
Georgia	56	2	180	2	Annual	16,200†
Hawaii	25	4	51	2	Annual	32,000†
Idaho	35	2	70	2	Annual	15,646†
Illinois	59	‡	118	2	Annual	55,788†
Indiana	50	4	100	2	Annual	11,600†
Iowa	50	4	100	2	Annual	20,758†
Kansas	40	4	125	2	Annual	76(d)†
Kentucky	38	4	100	2	Annual	158(d)†
Louisiana	39	4	105	4	Annual	16,800†
Maine	35	2	151	2	Even	10,815§
Maryland	47	4	141	4	Annual	31,591†
Massachusetts	40	2	160	2	Annual	50,123†
Michigan	38	4	110	2	Annual	77,400†
Minnesota	67	4	134	2	Odd	31,140†
Mississippi	52	4	122	4	Annual	10,000†
Missouri	34	4	163	2	Annual	31,561†
Montana	50	4	100	2	Odd	72(d)†
Nebraska"	49	4	—	—	Annual	12,000†
Nevada	21	4	42	2	Odd	130(d)†
New Hampshire	24	2	400	2	Annual	200(b)
New Jersey	40	4	80	2	Annual	35,000
New Mexico	42	4	70	2	Annual	—†
New York	61	2	150	2	Annual	79,500†
North Carolina	50	2	120	2	Odd	13,951†
North Dakota	49	4	98	4	Odd	111(d)†
Ohio	33	4	99	2	Annual	51,674
Oklahoma	48	4	101	2	Annual	38,400†
Oregon	30	4	60	2	Odd	15,396†
Pennsylvania	50	4	203	2	Annual	61,889†
Rhode Island	50	2	100	2	Annual	11,236
South Carolina	46	4	124	2	Annual	10,400†
South Dakota	35	2	70	2	Annual	12,000#
Tennessee	33	4	99	2	Annual	16,500†
Texas	31	4	150	2	Odd	7,200†
Utah	29	4	75	2	Annual	120(d)†
Vermont	30	2	150	2	Odd	536(w)†
Virginia	40	4	100	2	Annual	18,000†
Washington	49	4	98	2	Annual	32,064†
West Virginia	34	4	100	2	Annual	15,000†
Wisconsin	33	4	99	2	Annual	44,333†
Wyoming	30	4	60	2	Annual	125(d)†

*Salaries annual unless otherwise noted as (d)—per day, (b)—biennium, or (w)—per week.
†Plus *per diem* living expenses.
‡Terms vary from two to four years.
§For odd year; $7,500 for even year.
"Unicameral legislature.
#For 2 years.

Source: Adapted from Council of State Governments, *Book of the States, 2002–2003.*

representation of minority groups violate the equal protection clause.[5] (See Chapter 12 for a more detailed discussion of this issue.)

Term Limits for State Legislators

For more than a decade, a number of states have agreed that a legislator's tenure should be limited. Although the restrictions vary, seventeen states currently have laws restricting the number of terms a legislator can serve. In three other states—Oregon, Washington, and Massachusetts—term limits laws were thrown out by the respective state supreme courts, while Idaho's legislature repealed its voter-approved term limits law.

Advocates of term limits argue that lawmakers who have not spent years in public office will best represent the interests of voters. Special interest groups will have less chance to influence a politician who does not have a future campaign to finance. Opponents of term limits argue that the same inexperienced lawmakers who are less likely to be swayed by special interests are also more likely to lack the experience that is required to understand state policy. Such opponents, ironically, include current politicians who once voted for term limits but are now subject to its consequences.

Direct Democracy: The Initiative, Referendum, and Recall

There is a major difference between the legislative process as outlined in the U.S. Constitution and the legislative process as outlined in the various state constitutions.

---

[5] *Miller v. Johnson,* 515 U.S. 900 (1995); *Shaw v. Hunt,* 517 U.S. 899 (1996); and *Bush v. Vera,* 517 U.S. 952 (1996).

FIGURE 18-1

How an Idea Becomes a Law

HOUSE OF REPRESENTATIVES

CONCERNED CITIZEN group, organization, or legislator suggests legislation → REPRESENTATIVE authors bill → BILL FILED WITH CLERK numbered, printed → BILL READ FIRST TIME Speaker assigns to committee → COMMITTEE HEARINGS Bill reported 1. Favorably 2. Favorably, with amendment 3. Favorably, with committee substitute 4. Unfavorably (killed) → SECOND READING bill read for amendment → THIRD READING bill debated, roll call vote on passage, if passed → Deliver to SENATE DESK

BILL READ FIRST TIME President assigns to committee ← COMMITTEE HEARINGS Bill reported 1. Favorably 2. Favorably, with amendment 3. Unfavorably (killed) ← SECOND READING bill read for amendment ← THIRD READING bill debated, roll call vote on passage, if passed ← RETURNED TO HOUSE without amendments / with amendments

SENATE

HOUSE concurs / HOUSE refuses to concur → CONFERENCE COMMITTEE HOUSE members SENATE members → TO ENROLLMENT (as act) → TO GOVERNOR → signs act / approves without signature / vetoes → TO SECRETARY OF STATE → BECOMES EFFECTIVE on 60th day after adjournment *sine die** or on specified date

HOUSE and SENATE adopt conference report, pass bill

two-thirds vote in each house overrides veto

OFFICE OF THE CLERK HOUSE OF REPRESENTATIVES

A simplified chart showing the route a bill takes through the Florida legislature. Bills may originate in either house. This bill originated in the House of Representatives.

Sine die means "without assigning a day for a further meeting."
SOURCE: Allen Morris and Joan Perry Morris, compilers, *The Florida Handbook, 1999–2000,* 27th ed. (Tallahassee, Fla.: Peninsular Publishing Co., 2000).

Many states exercise a type of direct democracy through the initiative, the referendum, and the recall—procedures that allow voters to control the government directly.

The Initiative.   One technique lets citizens bypass legislatures by proposing new statutes or changes in government for citizen approval. Most states that permit the citizen **legislative initiative** require that the initiative's backers circulate a petition to place the issue on the ballot and that a certain percentage of the registered voters in the last gubernatorial election sign the petition. Twenty-four states use the legislative initiative, typically those states in which political parties are relatively weak and non-partisan groups are strong. Legislative initiatives have involved a range of issues, including crime victims' rights, campaign contributions, corporate spending on ballot questions, affirmative action, physician-assisted suicide, and the medical use of marijuana. In some cases, voters have passed state initiatives that are contrary to federal policy. For example, several states have passed initiatives legalizing the use of marijuana for medical purposes, a policy that conflicts with federal law.

The Referendum.   The **referendum** is similar to the initiative, except that the issue (or constitutional change) is proposed first by the legislature and then directed to the voters for their approval. The referendum is most often used for approval of local school bond issues and for amendments to state constitutions. In a number of states that provide for the referendum, a bill passed by the legislature may be suspended by obtaining the required number of voters' signatures on petitions. A statewide referendum election is then held. If a majority of the voters disapprove of the bill, it is no longer valid.

DID YOU KNOW . . .
That by 2003, at least twenty-three state legislatures had enacted some form of law making English the official language of those states **?**

Legislative Initiative
A procedure by which voters can propose a change in state or local laws by gathering signatures on a petition and placing a proposed law on the ballot for the voters' approval.

Referendum
An electoral device whereby legislative or constitutional measures are referred by the legislature to the voters for approval or disapproval.

In September 2002, the federal Drug Enforcement Agency (DEA) confiscated the marijuana supplies of an organization in Santa Cruz, California, that grows and distributes marijuana to terminally ill patients. The distribution of medical marijuana is legal under a local ordinance. The Santa Cruz City Council allowed the organization to pass out marijuana to patients on the steps of city hall after the DEA raid, as seen here. Which side will normally prevail when state or local ordinances conflict with those of the federal government? (AP Photo/Mike Fiala)

For more information on the referendum, use the term "referendum" in the Subject guide.

Recall
A procedure enabling voters to remove an elected official from office before his or her term has expired.

The referendum was not initially intended for regular use, and indeed it was used infrequently in the past. Its opponents argue that it is an unnecessary check on representative government and that it weakens legislative responsibility. In recent years, the referendum has become increasingly popular as citizens have attempted to control their state and local governments. Interest groups have been active in sponsoring the petition drives necessary to force a referendum. Over two-thirds of the states provide for the referendum.

The Recall.   The right of citizens to recall, or remove, elected officials is not exercised frequently. **Recall** is a provision written into the constitutions of fifteen states. It allows voters to remove elected state officials, including the governor, before the expiration of their terms of office. In the case of judges, the recall can terminate a lifetime appointment.

Citizens begin the recall process by circulating petitions demanding a statewide vote to remove the offending officeholder. The number of signatures required to bring about the election ranges from 10 to 40 percent of the last vote for the office in question. If the required number of signatures is obtained, the question of whether to remove the incumbent is decided in a general election.

The recall and the initiative are examples of "pure democracy," in which the people as a whole vote directly on important issues. Such measures are distinct in theory and in practice from the norms of "representative democracy," in which the people govern only indirectly, through their elected representatives. (For a discussion of the initiative process and the controversy it has engendered, see this chapter's *Which Side Are You On?* feature.)

The State Judiciary

Each of the fifty states, as well as the District of Columbia, has its own separate court system (which is in addition to the federal courts—see Chapter 15). Figure 18–2 on page 562 shows a sample state court system. Like the federal court system, it has several tiers, including trial courts, intermediate courts of appeal, and a supreme court.

Trial Courts

All states have major trial courts, commonly called circuit courts, district courts, or superior courts. The number of judges and their terms in office vary widely. As in the federal court system, the trial courts are of two types: those having limited jurisdiction and those having general jurisdiction.[6] Cases heard before these courts can be appealed to the state appellate court and ultimately to the state supreme court.

Appellate Courts

About three-fourths of the states have intermediate appellate courts between the trial courts of original jurisdiction and the highest state appellate court, or the supreme court. These are usually called courts of appeals. Salaries of state judges vary widely, but higher pay is given to appellate and supreme court members.

The highest state appellate courts are usually called simply supreme courts, although they are also labeled the supreme judicial court (Maine and Massachusetts), the court of appeals (Maryland and New York), the court of criminal appeals (Oklahoma and Texas, which also have separate supreme courts for appeals in noncriminal cases), or the supreme court of appeals (West Virginia). The decisions of each state's highest court on all questions of state law are final. Only when issues of

---

[6] See Chapter 15 for a definition of these terms.

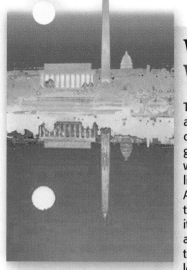

Which Side Are You On?
Will of the People or Dollar Democracy?

The voter initiative has been around since the nineteenth century—it is a product of the grassroots politicking that was characteristic of an earlier era in American politics. According to some, such initiatives represent politics at its best—citizens proposing and voting on laws tailored to the needs of their state or local region. Twenty-four states permit voter initiatives, and they are particularly popular in the western states, such as Arizona, California, Oregon, and Washington.

THE USE OF INITIATIVES

California first used the voter initiative in 1911, but it became widely popular in that state only after 1978, when Californians voted in favor of a controversial initiative referred to as Proposition 13. This proposition capped local property tax rates and cut $5 billion in taxes statewide—something that California politicians said could not be done. Since Proposition 13, some of the state's most significant legislation has come about through the initiative process. In 1994, Californians voted to deny social benefits, such as education, to illegal immigrants. (This law was eventually invalidated by the courts.) Two years later, an initiative was passed outlawing affirmative action. In 1998, a ballot initiative was used to repeal bilingual education, and in 2000 voters approved Proposition 22, which denies equal marital rights to same-sex couples.

Similarly, other states (and cities) are using voter initatives to settle controversial issues. For example, Oregon citizens passed an initiative legalizing physician-assisted suicide, and Arizona citizens supported a measure to make English the official language of the state.

THE CONTROVERSY OVER
THE INITIATIVE PROCESS

Those who favor ballot initiatives see them as a backlash against a political system that does not represent the will of the people. It is no coincidence, say supporters, that the popularity of initiatives has risen as the percentage of Americans who vote in local and national elections has dropped. Many citizens, the argument goes, mistrust what they see as an impossibly complex lawmaking system that favors wealthy special interests and denies them a voice.

Critics of ballot initiatives claim that it is naïve to think that the initiative process represents the triumph of grassroots politicking. On the contrary, the process has come to

California voters have used the ballot initiative many times to change the law in their state. Here, supporters of Proposition 22, which prohibits California from recognizing same-sex marriages from other states, celebrate its passage. What are some potential problems with the initiative process? (AP Photo/Rich Pedroncelli)

be dominated by large, often national interest groups that funnel millions of dollars into advertising the merits (or faults) of particular initiatives. In California, it costs approximately $1 million just to gather the signatures necessary to get an initiative on the ballot. Furthermore, note the critics, the process bypasses the traditional research and deliberation that legislators undertake before enacting new laws. Instead, initiatives often call for radical departures from existing law without exploring the consequences. Some commentators, for example, contend that Proposition 13 shifted the property tax burden from corporations to individual homeowners, hardly the intent of most of those who voted for it.

WHAT'S YOUR POSITION?

Should it matter whether state initiatives are financed by national interest groups? Why or why not?

GOING ONLINE

To access opposing viewpoints on the initiative process in the context of California's Proposition 209 concerning affirmative action, go to **http://www.thirteen.org/federalist/opinion-prop.html**. To visit the home page of the Ballot Initiative Strategy Center, go to **http://www.ballot.org**.

federal law are involved can a decision made by a state's highest court be overruled by the United States Supreme Court.

Judicial Elections and Appointments

State court judges are either elected or appointed, depending on the state and (often) on the level of court involved—the procedures vary widely from state to state. In some states, including Delaware, the procedure is similar to the way federal judges are appointed—the judges are appointed by the governor and confirmed by the upper chamber of the legislature. In other states, all state court judges are elected, either on a partisan ballot (as in Arkansas) or on a nonpartisan ballot (as in Kentucky). In several states, judges in some of the lower courts are elected, while those in the appellate courts are appointed. Additionally, depending on the state, judges who are appointed may have to run for reelection if they wish to serve a second term.

FIGURE 18–2

A Sample State Court System

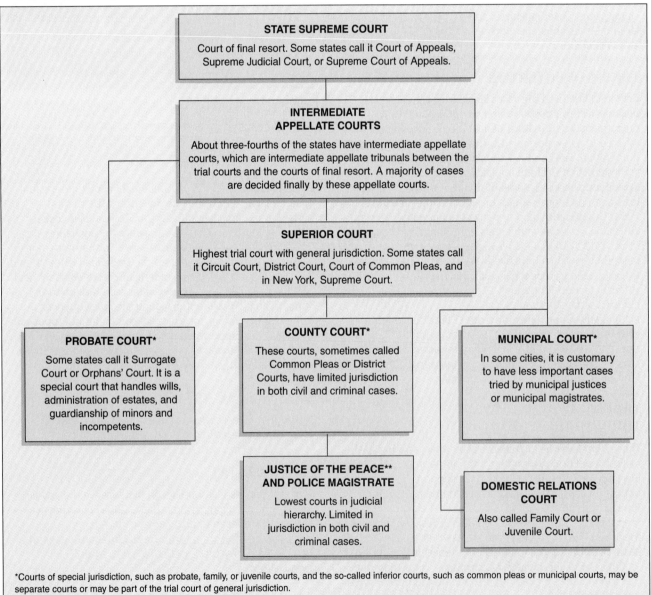

STATE SUPREME COURT

Court of final resort. Some states call it Court of Appeals, Supreme Judicial Court, or Supreme Court of Appeals.

INTERMEDIATE APPELLATE COURTS

About three-fourths of the states have intermediate appellate courts, which are intermediate appellate tribunals between the trial courts and the courts of final resort. A majority of cases are decided finally by these appellate courts.

SUPERIOR COURT

Highest trial court with general jurisdiction. Some states call it Circuit Court, District Court, Court of Common Pleas, and in New York, Supreme Court.

PROBATE COURT*

Some states call it Surrogate Court or Orphans' Court. It is a special court that handles wills, administration of estates, and guardianship of minors and incompetents.

COUNTY COURT*

These courts, sometimes called Common Pleas or District Courts, have limited jurisdiction in both civil and criminal cases.

MUNICIPAL COURT*

In some cities, it is customary to have less important cases tried by municipal justices or municipal magistrates.

JUSTICE OF THE PEACE AND POLICE MAGISTRATE**

Lowest courts in judicial hierarchy. Limited in jurisdiction in both civil and criminal cases.

DOMESTIC RELATIONS COURT

Also called Family Court or Juvenile Court.

*Courts of special jurisdiction, such as probate, family, or juvenile courts, and the so-called inferior courts, such as common pleas or municipal courts, may be separate courts or may be part of the trial court of general jurisdiction.
**Justices of the peace do not exist in all states. Their jurisdiction varies greatly from state to state when they do exist.

SOURCE: William P. Statsky, *Introduction to Paralegalism,* 5th ed. (St. Paul: West, 1997), p. 329.

How Local Government Operates

Local governments are difficult to describe because of their great dissimilarities and because, if we include municipalities, counties, towns, townships, and special districts, there are so many of them. We limit the discussion here to the most important types and features of local governments.

The Legal Existence of Local Government

As mentioned earlier, the U.S. Constitution makes no mention of local governments. Article IV, Section 4, states that "[t]he United States shall guarantee to every State in this Union a Republican Form of Government." Actually, then, the states do not even have to have local governments. Consequently, every local government is a creature of the state. The state can create a local government, and the state can terminate the right of a local government to exist. Indeed, states often have abolished entire counties, school districts, cities, and special districts. Since World War II (1939–1945), almost twenty thousand school districts have gone out of existence as they were consolidated with other school districts.

Because the local government is the legal creation of the state, does that mean the state can dictate everything the local government does? For many years that seemed to be the case. The narrowest possible view of the legal status of local governments follows **Dillon's rule,** outlined by Judge John F. Dillon in his *Commentaries on the Law of Municipal Corporations* in 1872. He stated that municipal corporations may possess only powers "granted in express words . . . [that are] necessarily or fairly implied in or incident to the powers expressly granted."[7] Cities governed under Dillon's rule have sometimes been dominated by the state legislatures, depending on the extent of the authority granted to the cities by the legislatures. Those communities wishing to obtain the status of a municipal corporation have simply petitioned the state legislature for a **charter.**

In a revolt against state legislative power over municipalities, the home rule movement began. It was based on **Cooley's rule,** derived from an 1871 decision by Michigan judge Thomas Cooley stating that cities should be able to govern themselves.[8] Since 1900, about four-fifths of the states have allowed **municipal home rule,** but only with respect to local concerns for which no statewide interests are involved. A municipality must choose to become a **home rule city;** otherwise, it operates as a **general law city.** In the latter case, the state makes certain general laws relating to cities of different sizes, which are designated as first-class cities, second-class cities, or towns. Once a city, by virtue of its population, receives such a ranking, it follows the general law put down by the state. Only if it chooses to be a home rule city can it avoid such state government restrictions. In most states, only cities with populations of 2,500 or more can choose home rule.

Local Governmental Units

There are four major types of local governmental units: municipalities, counties, towns and townships, and special districts.

Municipalities.   A municipality is a political entity created by the people of a city or town to govern themselves locally. Currently, there are over nineteen thousand municipalities within the fifty states. Almost all municipalities are fairly small cities. Only about two hundred cities have populations over one hundred thousand, and only ten

For more information on local government, use the term "local government" in the Subject guide.

Dillon's Rule
The narrowest possible interpretation of the legal status of local governments, outlined by Judge John F. Dillon, who in 1872 stated that a municipal corporation can exercise only those powers expressly granted by state law.

Charter
A document issued by a government that grants to a person, a group of persons, or a corporation the right to carry on one or more specific activities. A state government can grant a charter to a municipality allowing that group of persons to carry on specific activities.

Cooley's Rule
The view that cities should be able to govern themselves, presented in an 1871 Michigan decision by Judge Thomas Cooley.

Municipal Home Rule
The power vested in a local unit of government to draft or change its own charter and to manage its own affairs.

Home Rule City
A city with a charter allowing local voters to frame, adopt, and amend their own charter.

General Law City
A city operating under general state laws that apply to all local governmental units of a similar type.

---

[7] John F. Dillon, *Commentaries on the Law of Municipal Corporations,* 5th ed. (Boston: Little, Brown, 1911), Vol. 1, Sec. 237.
[8] *People v. Hurlbut,* 24 Mich. 44 (1871).

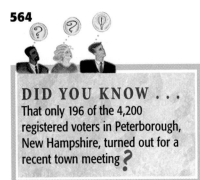

County
The chief governmental unit set up by the state to administer state law and business at the local level. Counties are drawn up by area, rather than by rural or urban criteria.

New England Town
A governmental unit in the New England states that combines the roles of city and county in one unit.

Town Meeting
The governing authority of a New England town. Qualified voters may participate in the election of officers and in the passage of legislation.

Town Manager System
A form of city government in which voters elect three selectpersons, who then appoint a professional town manager, who in turn appoints other officials.

Selectperson
A member of the governing group of a town.

Township
A rural unit of government based on federal land surveys of the American frontier in the 1780s. Townships have declined significantly in importance.

cities (Chicago, Dallas, Detroit, Houston, Los Angeles, New York, Philadelphia, Phoenix, San Antonio, and San Diego) have populations over a million. City expenditures are primarily for water supply and other utilities, police and fire protection, and education. About three-fourths of municipal tax revenues come from property taxes. Municipalities rely very heavily on financial assistance from both the federal and state governments.

Counties. The difference between a **county** and a municipality is that a county may not be created at the behest of its inhabitants. The state sets up counties on its own initiative to serve as political extensions of the state government. Counties apply state law and administer state business at the local level.

Counties, of which there are over three thousand within the United States, vary greatly in both size and population. San Bernardino County in California is the largest geographically, with 20,102 square miles. New York County in New York is the smallest, with less than 22 square miles. County populations range from millions of residents, as in Los Angeles County, to fewer than a hundred residents, as in Kalawao County, Hawaii.

County governments' responsibilities include zoning, building regulations, health, hospitals, parks, recreation, highways, public safety, justice, and record keeping. Typically, when a municipality is established within a county, the county withdraws most of its services from the municipality; for example, the municipal police force takes over from the county police force. County governments are extremely complex entities, a product of the era of Jacksonian democracy and its effort to bring government closer to the people. There is no easy way to describe their operation in summary form. Indeed, the county has been called by one scholar "the dark continent of American politics."[9]

Towns and Townships. A unique governmental creation in the New England states is the **New England town**—not to be confused with the word *town* when used as just another name for a city. In Maine, Massachusetts, New Hampshire, Vermont, and Connecticut, the unit called the town combines the roles of city and county in one governing unit. A New England town typically consists of one or more urban settlements and the surrounding rural areas. Consequently, counties have little importance in New England. In Connecticut, for example, they are simply geographic units.

From the New England town is derived the tradition of the **town meeting**, an annual meeting at which direct democracy was—and continues to be—practiced. Each resident of a town is summoned to the annual meeting at the town hall. Those who attend levy taxes, pass laws, elect town officers, and appropriate money for different activities.

Normally, few residents show up for town meetings today unless an item of high interest is on the agenda or unless family members want to be elected to office. The town meeting takes a day or more, and few citizens are able to set aside such a large amount of time. Because of the declining interest in town meetings, many New England towns have adopted a **town manager system**: the voters simply elect three **selectpersons**, who then appoint a professional town manager. The town manager in turn appoints other officials.

Townships operate somewhat like counties. Where they exist, there may be several dozen within a county. They perform the same functions that the county would otherwise perform. Indiana, Iowa, Kansas, Michigan, Minnesota, New Jersey, New York, Ohio, Pennsylvania, and Wisconsin all have numerous townships. A township is not the same thing as a New England town, because it is meant to be a rural government

---

[9]Henry S. Gilbertson, *The County, the "Dark Continent of American Politics"* (New York: National Short Ballot Association, 1917).

rather than a city government. Moreover, it is never the principal unit of local government, as are New England towns. The boundaries of most townships are based on federal land surveys that began in the 1780s, mapping the land into six-mile squares called townships. They were then subdivided into thirty-six blocks of one square mile each, called sections. Along the boundaries of each section, a road was built.

Although townships have few functions left to perform in many parts of the nation, they are still politically important in others. In some metropolitan areas, townships are the political unit that provides most public services to residents who live in suburban **unincorporated areas.**

Special Districts and School Districts. The most numerous local government units are special districts. Currently, there are more than thirty-five thousand special districts (see Table 18–2). Special districts are one-function governments that usually are created by the state legislature and governed by a board of directors. Special districts may be called authorities, boards, corporations—or simply districts.

One important feature of special districts is that they cut across geographic and governmental boundaries. Sometimes special districts even cut across state lines. For example, the Port of New York Authority was established by an interstate compact between New Jersey and New York in 1921 to develop and operate the harbor facilities in the area. A mosquito control district may cut across both municipal and county lines. A metropolitan transit district may provide bus service to dozens of municipalities and to several counties.

School districts, although listed separately in Table 18–2, are essentially a type of special district. Except for school districts, the typical citizen is not very aware of most special districts. Indeed, most citizens do not know who furnishes their weed control, mosquito control, water, or sewage control. Part of the reason for the low profile of special districts is that most special district administrators are appointed, not elected, and therefore receive little public attention.

Consolidation of Governments

With over eighty thousand separate and often overlapping governmental units within the United States, the trend toward consolidation in recent years is understandable. **Consolidation** is the union of two or more governmental units to form a

TABLE 18–2

Local Governments in the United States

Counties	3,034
Municipalities (mainly cities and towns)	19,431
Townships (less extensive powers)	16,506
Special districts (water supply, fire protection, hospitals, libraries, parks and recreation, highways, sewers, and so on)	35,356
School districts	13,522
Total	**87,849**

SOURCE: U.S. Census Bureau, *Preliminary Report, 2002 Census of Governments.*

Unincorporated Area

An area not located within the boundary of a municipality.

Consolidation

The union of two or more governmental units to form a single unit.

A billboard in Blue Earth, Minnesota, supports a referendum to increase taxes to pay for a new school. There are over 13,000 school districts in the United States today. (Photo courtesy of John Anderson)

Functional Consolidation
The cooperation of two or more units of local government in providing services to their inhabitants.

Council of Government (COG)
A voluntary organization of counties and municipalities concerned with areawide problems.

single unit. Typically, a state constitution or a state statute will designate consolidation procedures.

Consolidation is often recommended for metropolitan-area problems, but to date there have been few consolidations within metropolitan areas. The most successful consolidations have been **functional consolidations**—particularly of city and county police, health, and welfare departments. In some cases, functional consolidation is a satisfactory alternative to the complete consolidation of governmental units. The most successful form of functional consolidation was started in 1957 in Dade County, Florida. The county government, now called Miami-Dade, is a union of twenty-six municipalities. Each municipality has its own governmental entity, but the county government has the authority to furnish water, planning, mass transit, and police services and to set minimum standards of performance. The governing body of Miami-Dade is an elected board of county commissioners, which appoints an executive mayor.

A special type of consolidation is the **council of government (COG)**, a voluntary organization of counties and municipalities that attempts to tackle areawide problems. More than two hundred COGs have been established, mainly since 1966. The impetus for their establishment was, and continues to be, federal government grants. COGs are an alternative means of treating major regional problems that various communities are unwilling to tackle on a consolidated basis either by true consolidation of governmental units or by functional consolidation.

The power of COGs is advisory only. Each member unit simply selects its council representatives, who report back to the unit after COG meetings. Nonetheless, today several COGs have begun to have considerable influence on regional policy. These include the Metropolitan Washington Council of Governments, the Supervisors' Inter-County Commission in Detroit, and the Association of Bay Area Governments in San Francisco.

How Municipalities Are Governed

We can divide municipal representative governments into four general types of plans: (1) the commission plan, (2) the council-manager plan, (3) the mayor-administrator plan, and (4) the mayor-council plan.

The Commission Plan.   The commission form of municipal government consists of a commission of three to nine members who have both legislative and executive powers. The salient aspects of the commission plan are as follows:

1. Executive and legislative powers are concentrated in a small group of individuals, who are elected at large on a (normally) nonpartisan ballot.
2. Each commissioner is individually responsible for heading a particular municipal department, such as the department of public safety.
3. The commission is collectively responsible for passing ordinances and controlling spending.
4. The mayor (an office that is only ceremonial) is selected from the members of the commission.

The commission plan, originating in Galveston, Texas, in 1901, had its greatest popularity during the first twenty years of the twentieth century. It appealed to municipal government reformers. They looked on it as a type of business organization that would eliminate the problems they believed to be inherent in the long ballot and in partisan municipal politics. Unfortunately, vesting both legislative and executive power in the hands of a small group of individuals means that there are no checks and balances on administration and spending. Also, because the mayoral office is ceremonial, there is no provision for strong leadership. Not surprisingly, only about one hundred cities today use the commission plan—Tulsa, Salt Lake City, Mobile, Topeka, and Atlantic City are a few of them.

The Council-Manager Plan. In the council-manager form of municipal government, a city council appoints a professional manager, who acts as the chief executive. He or she typically is called the city manager. In principle, the manager is there simply to see that the general directions of the city council are carried out. The important features of the council-manager plan are as follows:

1. A professional, trained manager can hire and fire subordinates and is responsible to the council.
2. The council or commission consists of five to seven members, elected at large on a nonpartisan ballot.
3. The mayor may be chosen from within the council or from outside, but he or she has no executive function. As with the commission plan, the mayor's job is largely ceremonial. The city manager works for the council, not the mayor (unless, of course, the mayor is part of the council).

Today, about two thousand cities use the council-manager plan. About one-third of the cities with populations of more than 5,000 and about one-half of the cities with populations of more than 25,000 operate with this type of plan. Only four large cities with populations of more than 500,000—Cincinnati, Dallas, San Antonio, and San Diego—have adopted this plan.

The major defect of the council-manager scheme, as with the commission plan, is that there is no single, strong political executive leader. It is therefore not surprising that large cities rarely use such a plan.

The Mayor-Administrator Plan. The mayor-administrator plan is often used in large cities where there is a strong mayor. It is similar to the council-manager plan except that the political leadership is vested in the mayor. The mayor is an elected chief executive. She or he appoints an administrative officer, whose function is to free the mayor from routine administrative tasks, such as personnel direction and budget supervision.

DID YOU KNOW . . .
That because Texas was the only state to enter the Union after having sovereign status, it is the only state that can fly its state flag at the same height as the U.S. flag **?**

A citizen addresses the city council of Gloucester, Massachusetts. What are some of the problems facing city governments today? (Nancy Sheehan, PhotoEdit)

Patronage
Rewarding faithful party workers and followers with government employment and contracts.

The Mayor-Council Plan.   The mayor-council form of municipal government is the oldest and most widely used. The mayor is an elected chief executive, and the council is the legislative body. Virtually all councils are unicameral except in Everett, Massachusetts. The council typically has five to nine members, except in very large cities, such as Chicago, where the council has fifty members. Council members are popularly elected for terms as long as six, but normally four, years.

The mayor-council plan can either be a strong-mayor type or a weak-mayor type. In the *strong mayor–council plan,* the mayor is the chief executive and has virtually complete control over hiring and firing employees, as well as preparing the budget. The mayor exercises strong and positive leadership in the formation of city policies. The *weak mayor–council plan* separates executive and legislative functions completely. The mayor is elected as chief executive officer; the council is elected as the legislative body. This traditional division of powers allows for checks and balances on spending and administration.

About 50 percent of American cities use some form of the mayor-council plan. Most recently, the mayor-council plan has lost ground to the council-manager plan in small and middle-sized cities.

Machine versus Reform in City Politics

For much of the late nineteenth and early twentieth centuries, many major cities were run by "the machine." The machine was an integrated political organization. Each city block within the municipality had an organizer, each neighborhood had a political club, each district had a leader, and all of these parts of the machine had a boss—such as William Tweed in New York, Richard Daley in Chicago, Edward Crump in Memphis, or Tom Pendergast in Kansas City. The machine became a popular form of city political organization in the 1840s, when the first waves of European immigrants came to the United States to work in urban factories. Those individuals, often lacking the ability to communicate in English, needed help; and the machine was created to help them.[10] The urban machine drew on the support of the dominant ethnic groups to forge a strong political institution that was able to keep the boss (usually the mayor) in office year after year. The machine was oiled by **patronage**—rewarding faithful party workers and followers with government employment and contracts. The party in power was often referred to as the patronage party.[11]

According to sociologist Robert Merton, the machine offered personalized assistance to the needy, helped to establish local businesses, opened avenues of upward social mobility for the underprivileged, and afforded a locus of strong political authority and responsibility.[12] Others, however, viewed party machines and the behind-the-scenes government that they often involved as contrary to our principles of government. In their classic work on city politics, Edward Banfield and James Q. Wilson also gave a critical appraisal of machine politics:

> [M]achine government is, essentially, a system of organized bribery. The destruction of machines . . . permit[s] government on the basis of appropriate motives, that is, public-regarding ones. In fact it has other highly desirable consequences—especially greater honesty, impartiality, and (in routine matters) efficiency.[13]

When the last of the big-city bosses, Mayor Richard Daley of Chicago, died in December 1976, with him died an era. The big-city machine began to be in serious trouble in the 1960s, when community activists organized to work for a more professional

[10] See Harvey W. Zorbaugh, *The Gold Coast and the Slum: A Sociological Study of Chicago's Near North Side* (Chicago: University of Chicago Press, 1929).

[11] See, for example, Harold F. Gosnell, *Machine Politics: Chicago Model* (Chicago: University of Chicago Press, 1937).

[12] Robert Merton, *Social Theory and Social Structure* (Glencoe, Ill.: Free Press, 1957), pp. 71–81.

[13] Edward C. Banfield and James Q. Wilson, *City Politics* (New York: Vintage Books, 1963), p. 12.

and efficient municipal government. Soon, a government of administrators rather than politicians began to appear. Fewer offices were elective; more were appointive.

Switching from a political to an administrative form of urban government was a way to break up the centralized urban political machine. In some cities, the results have been beneficial to most citizens. In others, decentralization has gone so far that there is no strong leader who can pull together discordant factions to create and follow a coherent policy. Consequently, in cities with a greatly decentralized government typified by numerous independent commissions and boards, a lot that should be done does not get done, particularly when an areawide problem is involved. This is an especially severe problem for less economically privileged people, who used to be able to rely on machine-sponsored activities and on the machine's political clout to help them compete against wealthier citizens for a share of the city's services. Reform is in some ways a middle-class preoccupation, whereas the less advantaged may find themselves better served by machine politics.

Governing Metropolitan Areas

Large cities are often faced with problems that develop in part from a shrinking employment base. When employers move out of a city, there is a smaller tax base, and more people are out of work. Less tax revenue means less money to pay for schools and to meet other municipal obligations, including fighting crime and assisting those who are unemployed. These developments feed on themselves, leading to more crime, more poverty, an even smaller job base, and other problems.

But crime, as well as such problems as traffic congestion and pollution, is not contained within municipal political boundaries. For this reason, solutions are sometimes sought by governing a metropolitan area as a whole. Annexation by a city of the surrounding suburbs is one solution; consolidation of city and county governments into one government is another. People who live in the suburbs often oppose such measures, however, particularly when they and the residents of a city are of different races or social classes, or have different political agendas.

DID YOU KNOW . . .
That the first African American mayors of big cities were Richard G. Hatcher of Gary, Indiana, and Carl B. Stokes of Cleveland, Ohio, both elected in 1967 ?

Concerned citizens meet with police and city council members regarding crime, drugs, and gang violence in Austin, Texas.
(Bob Daemmrich, Stock Boston)

A third possible solution to problems that spread beyond limited political boundaries is to set up a system of metropolitan government. With this method, a single entity, such as a county, concerns itself with the problems of an entire metropolitan area, and smaller entities, such as individual city governments, concern themselves with local matters. People who live in the suburbs often oppose this solution, however, for the same reasons that they oppose other measures: they want to preserve their communities and lifestyles as they are.

A fourth solution is the creation of special districts, each of which is concerned with a specific service—an area's water supply or public transportation system, for example. Special districts are more popular than the other solutions, in part because they can deal with a single matter relatively more efficiently without concern for social issues or class conflict.

Paying for State and Local Government

Examining the spending habits of a household often gives relevant information about the personalities and priorities of the household members. Examination of the expenditure patterns of state and local governments likewise can be illuminating.

State and Local Government Expenditures

Table 18–3 shows state expenditures, expressed in percentages, for the latest fiscal year for which data are available. Table 18–4 shows the same data for local governments. There is a clear-cut pattern. State and city expenditures are concentrated in the areas of education, public welfare, highways, health, and police protection.

Education is the biggest category of expenditure, particularly at the local level. Contrast this expenditure pattern with that of the federal government, which allocates only about 4 percent of its budget to education. In 2003, state and local expenditures exceeded $1 trillion. Despite these expenditures, state and local governments are finding that their educational programs are not always producing the desired outcome—well-educated students. As mentioned in the chapter-opening *What If . . .* feature, several states have been implementing various education reforms, such as school choice. For another example of how states are trying to improve educational achievement, see this chapter's *Politics and Education* feature.

INFOTRAC ®
COLLEGE EDITION

For updates and more information on school choice, use the term "school choice" in the Subject guide.

TABLE 18–3	
State Expenditures (in percentages)	
EXPENDITURE	**PERCENTAGE**
Education	31.7
Public welfare	22.4
Insurance trust	9.8
Health and hospitals	6.9
Highways	6.8
Corrections	3.3
Governmental administration	3.3
Interest on general debt	2.9
Natural resources	1.5
Utilities	.9
Police	.9
Parks and recreation	.5
Liquor stores	.3
Other	8.8

SOURCE: U.S. Bureau of the Census, 2000.

TABLE 18–4	
Local Expenditures (in percentages)	
EXPENDITURE	**PERCENTAGE**
Education	41.9
Health and hospitals	8.6
Governmental administration	5.4
Police	5.4
Public welfare	5.1
Interest on general debt	5.0
Highways	4.5
Sewerage	3.2
Housing and community development	2.8
Fire protection	2.6
Parks and recreation	2.2
Solid waste management	2.0
Corrections	1.7
Natural resources	0.4
Other	9.2

SOURCE: U.S. Bureau of the Census, 2000.

Politics and EDUCATION

The Controversy over Standardized Tests

On January 8, 2002, President George W. Bush signed into law the "No Child Left Behind Act," as it is officially called. The bill, which won bipartisan support in Congress, requires in part that students in the third through eighth grades be tested in reading and math each year to monitor their progress. Bush is certainly not the first person to see the need to jump-start the learning process in our public schools. California, for instance, developed its own standardized test to combat its low achievement levels. That state tied for last place in the nation for student reading skills in 1995. According to estimates, by 2003, students in twenty-six states will be required to pass at least one standardized test to graduate, and all fifty states now have some statewide testing policies in place.

OPPOSITION TO STANDARDIZED TESTS

Many politicians applaud the president for his initiative and dedication to education reform. Yet a number of those who are "in the trenches"—teachers, administrators, and students alike—believe that the president's emphasis on standardized tests is a step backwards in evaluating student achievement. In February 2000, at least two hundred Illinois students boycotted new state English and math exams. In April 2002, hundreds of Massachusetts students boycotted the first of eleven days of standardized testing. In Ohio, parents and teachers are working through a referendum to amend or repeal the state's testing laws. So, why are so many education providers and recipients disgruntled with standardized tests?

According to opponents of mandatory testing, the need for students to pass one standardized test forces teachers to prepare their classes to take that one test, and little else. Critics believe that learning tools such

Although public education is generally the responsibility of state and local governments, the federal government has recently intervened with a variety of reform efforts. Here, President George W. Bush signs legislation requiring students in third through eighth grades to pass tests in reading and math each year. (White House photo by Paul Morse)

as class discussion, critical thinking, and group projects will be abandoned as teachers focus on teaching the best way to answer a set of multiple-choice questions.

Opponents of standardized tests also say that minorities will be among those hurt the most by mandatory testing. In Massachusetts, 80 percent of African Americans and 83 percent of Latinos failed the tenth-grade MCAS (Massachusetts Comprehensive Assessment System), compared to 45 percent of whites.

SOMETHING HAS TO BE DONE

Those who support standardized testing believe that the system of evaluating achievement has been broken for many years. To the argument that higher percentages of minorities have done poorly on recent standardized tests, proponents of the tests respond that such discrepancies result from the lack of proper testing in the past. The achievement gap will shrink with the requirement of standardized testing, they say. Standardized tests will force states to publicly report their progress in improving student achievement. Statewide test data will be separated by race, income, and other criteria to show whether the gap is narrowing, and states where the gap remains the same or gets worse will be forced to amend their systems.

FOR CRITICAL ANALYSIS

Do you think that the increase in standardized testing will widen or narrow the achievement gap? Why?

State and Local Government Revenues

State and local expenditures have to be paid for somehow. Until the twentieth century, almost all state and local expenditures were paid for by state and local revenues raised within state borders. Starting in the twentieth century, however, federal grants to state and local governmental units began to pay some of these costs.

Figure 18–3 on the next page shows the percentages of revenues in various categories received by state and local governments. By far the most important tax at the

FIGURE 18–3

State and Local Government Revenues

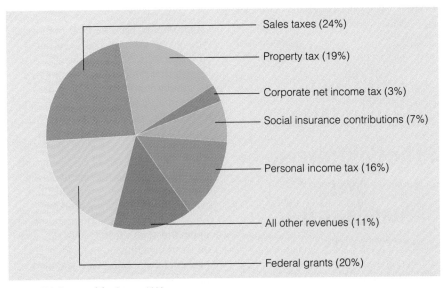

- Sales taxes (24%)
- Property tax (19%)
- Corporate net income tax (3%)
- Social insurance contributions (7%)
- Personal income tax (16%)
- All other revenues (11%)
- Federal grants (20%)

SOURCE: U.S. Bureau of the Census, 2000.

General Sales Tax

A tax levied as a proportion of the retail price of a commodity at the point of sale.

Property Tax

A tax on the value of real estate. This tax is limited to state and local governments and is a particularly important source of revenue for local governments.

state level is the **general sales tax**. Whereas the federal government obtains about 45 percent of its total revenues from the personal income tax, states obtain only about 16 percent in this way. By 2003, seven states still did not have a personal income tax. Other taxes assessed by states include corporate income taxes and fees, permits, and licenses at both the state and local governmental level, as well as inheritance and gift taxes at the state level. At the local level, the most important tax is the **property tax**. About 90 percent of property tax revenues are raised by local governments. Generally, the types of taxes that states levy vary widely from state to state.

A tremendous amount of variation also exists in the total amounts of state and local taxes collected. Among the states receiving the highest amounts in tax revenues are California and New York. Those levying the lowest taxes are North Dakota, South Dakota, and Wyoming.

Nontax revenue includes federal grants to state and local governments. Today, federal grants to state and local governments total about $235 billion annually and provide about 20 percent of state government income. The grants are not always without "strings," however. Federal programs in such areas as education, highway construction, health care, and law enforcement may dispense cash subject to certain conditions. For example, the funds may be used only for a specific purpose or only if matching funds are contributed (see Chapter 3).

Profits generated by publicly operated businesses are another source of revenue for state and local governments. Publicly operated businesses include toll roads and bridges, as well as water, electric power, and mass transportation systems. More than a third of the states sell liquor through state-operated stores that earn profits. Other state-operated businesses include Washington's ferries and North Dakota's commercial banks. Some states receive lease payments for public lands, and some cities rent space in publicly owned buildings.

Other nontax revenue sources include court fines and interest on loans and investments. In the 1980s, state-run lotteries became an increasingly popular way to raise money. By 2003, nearly three-fourths of the states and the District of Columbia sponsored lotteries. It is expected that the rest of the states will soon follow.

Fiscal Policy Lessons

In the 1980s, when state budgets more than doubled, most states tried to close the gap between state income and spending by raising taxes. Many of these states continued

this policy into the early 1990s. The states that approved the largest tax increases in the early 1990s, however, also approved the greatest increases in spending.

By 1999, it became clear that states' attempts to reduce their budget deficits by increasing taxes were not especially successful at lowering those deficits. In fact, many states actually harmed, rather than helped, their economies. This was the lesson learned by such states as California, Connecticut, New Jersey, Pennsylvania, and Rhode Island.

At the same time, states such as Massachusetts, Michigan, Mississippi, and Virginia attempted to balance their budgets by cutting spending instead of raising taxes. This policy proved more successful, resulting in balanced budgets and improved state economies. By the mid-1990s, many of these states were proposing state tax cuts to encourage the development of business and further improve their local economies.

By 2000, a number of states—including Arizona, California, Indiana, Minnesota, North Carolina, South Carolina, Texas, and Washington—experienced budget surpluses of half a billion dollars or more. Not surprisingly, cries for state tax cuts were heard throughout the nation. Significant state tax cuts were enacted in over one-third of the states. While the tax cuts generally did not represent major reductions in general state revenues, they did indicate a change in the trend toward ever-increasing taxes.

In many states, however, the economic downturn that began in 2001 put an end to the surpluses, forcing the states to deal with increasingly tighter budgets. Many states did not prepare by setting aside "rainy day" funds and now face serious decisions of whether to increase taxes or cut spending.

State and Local Government: Why Is It Important Today?

While the federal government often helps state and local governments with the costs of providing certain programs, many of the services you and your neighbors rely on most are implemented, maintained, and funded by state and local governments.

In recent years, the federal government has transferred many of the programs previously under its control to the states, with more likely to come. Currently, the states are responsible for making and monitoring welfare distributions to their poor residents. At the beginning of 2002, President George W. Bush signed a bill into law giving each state the responsibility to test its students yearly in reading and math. States already have some responsibility, and will soon have more, for environmental control and cleanup within their borders. Although the federal government typically offers at least some financial support for such ventures, states often have to dip into their own tight budgets to pay some or all of the costs of providing government services.

Though we often think of "government" in terms of the federal government, your state and local governments affect much of your daily life. The state where you live can make a significant difference with respect to the amount of money allocated for education and the curriculum being taught. As state budgets shrink, public schools often must be closed or suffer cutbacks in funding. Everything from school funding to the annoying pothole in your town square and the number of local police officers is under the jurisdiction of your state or local government. When you want that pothole fixed or the number of police officers increased, you do not call your representative in the U.S. Congress. You call your neighbor down the street who happens to be on the city council. State and local governments are as important, if not more so, as the federal government when it comes to providing for the everyday wants and needs of citizens.

MAKING A DIFFERENCE | Learning about Local Politics and Government in Your Community

What government does or fails to do in the areas of education, health, employment, and crime affects you, your family, and your friends. Your sense of adventure, concern, curiosity, or injustice may urge you to take an active part in the government of a society with which you might not be particularly content. Yet getting involved on the national level may seem complicated, and national issues may not be of immediate concern. You may not even know exactly where you stand on many of those issues.

Every week, however, decisions are being made in your community that directly affect your local environment, transportation, education, health, employment, rents, schools, utility rates, freedom from crime, and overall quality of life. The local level is a good place to begin discovering who you are politically.

Local Meetings

Many neighborhoods have formed neighborhood associations for the purposes of protecting their interests. One way to learn about issues that directly affect you (such as whether a street in your neighborhood should be widened or a park created) is to attend a local neighborhood association meeting. Another way to familiarize yourself with local political issues is to attend a city council meeting. Think about the issues being discussed. How do these issues and their outcomes concern you as an individual? What is your position on each issue?

If you are interested in education and educational reform, you can attend a school board meeting. Typically, the board will devote a substantial amount of time to budgetary

decisions. Pay close attention to how the board feels school funds should be allocated. What are the board's primary concerns and priorities? Do you agree with the board's views? Find out if the school district is considering proposals to implement innovative educational programs.

Environmental Groups

Virtually all communities have groups that are working to improve the environment at the state or local level. At the local level, environmental issues may concern efforts to beautify the city (by restricting billboards or yard signs, for example) or to implement recycling programs to control waste. State environmental organizations may need volunteers to go door-to-door in your community to distribute information on their lobbying efforts before the state legislature, to gather signatures for petitions, and the like. If you look in the Yellow Pages under "Environment" or "Environmental," you probably will find a listing of several local and state organizations to contact.

State and Local Campaigns

Getting involved in a campaign for a local or state office is another way to learn about political issues that affect your community or your state. You also can participate at the local level in campaigns by candidates seeking national

A recycling program in Portland, Oregon, is an example of a local government's successful effort in tackling a policy problem. (David Weintraub, Photo Researchers)

office, such as candidates running for Congress. Working at the "grassroots" level for a political candidate gives you firsthand knowledge of how the politics of democracy actually works.

Local Court Proceedings

Finally, to observe the judicial branch of government at work, you can watch the proceedings in your local courts. An important court at the local level is the small claims court. Small claims courts hear disputes involving claims under a certain amount, such as $2,500 or $5,000 (the amount varies from state to state). Lawyers are not required, and many small claims courts do not permit lawyers. Other local courts are described in Figure 18–2 on page 562. For information on your local courts and on when you can attend court proceedings, call the courthouse clerk.

Key Terms

charter 563

consolidation 565

constitutional initiative 553

Cooley's rule 563

council of government (COG) 566

county 564

Dillon's rule 563

functional consolidation 566

general law city 563

general sales tax 572

home rule city 563

item veto 556

legislative initiative 559

municipal home rule 563

New England town 564

patronage 568

police power 551

property tax 572

recall 560

referendum 559

selectperson 564

town manager system 564

town meeting 564

township 564

unincorporated area 565

Chapter Summary

1 The United States has more than 87,000 separate governmental units. State and local governments perform a wide variety of highly visible functions, such as education, police and fire protection, and so on.

2 Under the U.S. Constitution, powers not delegated expressly to the federal government are reserved to the states. The states may exercise taxing, spending, and general police powers. State constitutions are often very long, owing to the desire of their framers to include much of what we would consider statutory law because of a loss of popular confidence in state legislatures at the end of the nineteenth century. Other reasons include state courts' reluctance to interpret state constitutions as freely as the United States Supreme Court interprets the U.S. Constitution.

3 In colonial America, the governors of the colonies were vested with extensive powers. Following the Revolutionary War, most states established forms of government in which the governor was given extremely limited powers. After Andrew Jackson's presidency, however, all governors (except in South Carolina) were elected directly by the people. Most governors have the right to exercise some sort of veto power; some enjoy item veto power.

4 State legislatures deal with matters such as taxes, schools, highways, and welfare. They also must redraw state and federal legislative districts each decade to ensure that every person's vote is roughly equal to that of others and that minorities are adequately represented in both the state legislature and Congress. Voters may exercise some direct control over state government through the use of the initiative, referendum, and recall. Every state has its own court system. Most such systems have several levels of courts—including trial courts, intermediate courts of appeal, and a supreme court.

5 There are over 19,000 municipalities in the United States, most of which are small cities. The more than three thousand counties in this country are merely extensions of state authority and apply state laws at the local level. Many of the functions of municipalities and counties are combined in towns or townships, particularly in the New England area. Municipalities may be governed by a commission consisting of members with executive and legislative powers, or they may be administered according to a council-manager, mayor-administrator, or mayor-council plan. Most major cities used to be run by political machines, which freely dispensed favors to supporters. In recent decades, however, machine politics has fallen into disfavor, particularly among the middle class.

6 State and local government spending is concentrated in the areas of education, public welfare, highways, health, and police protection. State services are funded primarily by sales taxes, whereas local services are financed by property taxes.

Selected Print and Media Resources

SUGGESTED READINGS

Bartlett, Randall. *The Crisis of America's Cities.* New York: M. E. Sharpe, 1999. This book offers a colorful overview of America's urban history and the crises facing metropolitan areas today. The author predicts that cities will continue to lose jobs, population, and economic activity to suburbs and "edge cities" on their peripheries.

Coppa, Frank J. *County Government: A Guide to Efficient and Accountable Government.* Westport, Conn.: Praeger, 2000. The author gives an excellent review of the historical foundations of county government in the United States. In addition, he shows how charter reform can address the issues that face local governments.

Sabato, Larry. *Dangerous Democracy?* Lanham, Md.: Rowman & Littlefield Publishing, 2001. This book analyzes the significant effects of initiatives on the democratic process through a collection of essays by leading scholars, journalists, and political consultants. Included are discussions on the growth of initiatives and the wealth of funding to support these causes.

Solamine, Michael E., and James L. Walker. *Respecting State Courts: The Inevitability of Judicial Federalism.* Westport, Conn.: Greenwood Press, 1999. The authors make a case for the value of judicial federalism—the division of judicial power between the federal and state court systems. They emphasize the important role played by state courts in implementing federal civil rights, interpreting their own state constitutions, and dealing with special problems, such as the death penalty.

MEDIA RESOURCES

Can the States Do It Better?—A program examining devolution—shifting federal powers back to the states—and what this means for the states with respect to, among other things, school reform.

City Hall—A 1996 drama about corruption at City Hall in New York and a mayor, played by Al Pacino, who is willing to break the law to fulfill his presidential aspirations.

The Last Hurrah—A film based, in part, on the career of James Curley (1874–1958) of Massachusetts, who played a leading role in creating and running Boston's political machine in the first half of the twentieth century. When Curley was convicted of mail fraud and sent to prison in 1947, he refused to resign as mayor and maintained his office while in jail.

Our Town—A 1980 film based on Thornton Wilder's play about day-to-day life and politics in a small, picturesque community—Peterborough ("Grover's Corners" in the play) in New Hampshire.

Your CD-ROM Resources

In addition to the chapter content containing hot links, the following resources are available on the CD-ROM:

- **Internet Activities**—NCSL and the term limits survey; the role state governors play in homeland security.

- **Critical Thinking Exercises**—Voter initiative, effectiveness of your local government, state lotteries.

- **Animated Figures**—Figure 18–2, "A Sample State Court System," Tables 18–3 and 18–4, "State Expenditures" and "Local Expenditures," and Figure 18–3, "State and Local Government Revenues."

- **Video**—*The Drinking Age.*

- **Public Opinion Data**—Find contrasting opinions on solving America's drug problem and on school vouchers.

- **Simulation**—You Are There!

- **Participation Exercise**—What are some examples of the different types of commissions in your region? How does one become a member of that commission?

- **MicroCase Exercise**—"By the Numbers: Diversity of the States."

e-mocracy

Public Access to Information on the Internet Is Growing

Individuals conduct only a tiny fraction—less than 1 percent—of their fund transactions with federal, state, and local governments over the Internet each year. This percentage should increase sharply over the next decade as activities such as voting, paying fines, and registering automobiles become more accessible on the Internet.

The type of information one can access on the Internet is also growing and is certainly not limited to government resources. Now, the places where that information can be accessed are growing as well. Children are becoming more exposed to cyberspace as public schools add computers to their classroom tools. Community centers, public libraries, and other local organizations or entities often have computers that can be used by patrons who otherwise would not have the means to obtain such access or information. Shoppers at a mall in Medford, Oregon, can use computers in an office space run by the Oregon Department of Employment to look for available job opportunities. As a result of these innovations, standing in long lines at the post office to file taxes or at the employment office to apply for a job might one day become a thing of the past.

Logging On

If you are interested in state law codes (statutes) and state court cases, go to

> http://www.findlaw.com/
> casecode/state.html

Information on state governments, including their constitutional powers, education, and finances, can be accessed online at

> http://www.vote-smart.org/
> reference/primer

Another excellent source for information on state governments is the following Web site:

> http://www.statesnews.org

You can access the *Book of the States,* a biennial publication of the Council of State Governments, from the preceding site, or access it directly at

> http://www.statesnews.org/
> publications/bos.html

The National Governors Association offers a wide variety of information on issues and data relating to state governments at

> http://www.nga.org

The National Conference of State Legislators is a good source for state information as well. Its URL is

> http://www.ncsl.org

You can find a wealth of data on state and local governments at the "Map Stats" site of the U.S. Census Bureau by simply clicking on states and counties on the maps. Go to

> http://www.census.gov/
> datamap/www/index.html

Piper Resources offers a Web site with numerous links to state and local government resources. You can access this site at

> http://www.piperinfo.com/index.cfm

Using the Internet for Political Analysis

As you are aware, each state has its own approach to taxation, government, and the work force. Go to the home pages of several different states, and then try to find their departments of economic development. Compare how states describe their tax advantages and other virtues to try to "sell" themselves to businesses that are relocating. Seek out the sales pitches that the states make for new businesses and then compare these marketing efforts across states. Which state do you think would be most favorable to business? Which states are able to offer the best business climate? Which states have few advantages for business? How does the political climate in a state influence its business climate? Do the states make a serious effort to attract workers or those with other, nonbusiness interests?

APPENDIX A
The Declaration of Independence

In Congress, July 4, 1776

A Declaration by the Representatives of the United States of America, in General Congress assembled. When in the Course of human Events, it becomes necessary for one People to dissolve the Political Bands which have connected them with another, and to assume among the Powers of the Earth, the separate and equal Station to which the Laws of Nature and of Nature's God entitle them, a decent Respect to the Opinions of Mankind requires that they should declare the causes which impel them to the Separation.

We hold these Truths to be self-evident, that all Men are created equal, that they are endowed by their Creator with certain unalienable Rights, that among these are Life, Liberty, and the Pursuit of Happiness—That to secure these Rights, Governments are instituted among Men, deriving their just Powers from the Consent of the Governed, that whenever any Form of Government becomes destructive of these Ends, it is the Right of the People to alter or to abolish it, and to institute new Government, laying its Foundation on such Principles, and organizing its Powers in such Forms, as to them shall seem most likely to effect their Safety and Happiness. Prudence, indeed, will dictate that Governments long established should not be changed for light and transient Causes; and accordingly all Experience hath shewn, that Mankind are more disposed to suffer, while Evils are sufferable, than to right themselves by abolishing the Forms to which they are accustomed. But when a long Train of Abuses and Usurpations, pursuing invariably the same Object, evinces a Design to reduce them under absolute Despotism, it is their Right, it is their Duty, to throw off such Government, and to provide new Guards for their future Security. Such has been the patient Sufferance of these Colonies; and such is now the Necessity which constrains them to alter their former Systems of Government. The History of the present King of Great-Britain is a History of repeated Injuries and Usurpations, all having in direct Object the Establishment of an absolute Tyranny over these States. To prove this, let Facts be submitted to a candid World.

He has refused his Assent to Laws, the most wholesome and necessary for the public Good.

He has forbidden his Governors to pass Laws of immediate and pressing Importance, unless suspended in their Operation till his Assent should be obtained; and when so suspended, he has utterly neglected to attend to them.

He has refused to pass other Laws for the Accommodation of large Districts of People, unless those People would relinquish the Right of Representation in the Legislature, a Right inestimable to them, and formidable to Tyrants only.

He has called together Legislative Bodies at Places unusual, uncomfortable, and distant from the Depository of their Public Records, for the sole Purpose of fatiguing them into Compliance with his Measures.

He has dissolved Representative Houses repeatedly, for opposing with manly Firmness his Invasions on the Rights of the People.

He has refused for a long Time, after such Dissolutions, to cause others to be elected; whereby the Legislative Powers, incapable of Annihilation, have returned to the People at large for their exercise; the State remaining in the mean time exposed to all the Dangers of Invasion from without, and Convulsions within.

He has endeavoured to prevent the Population of these States; for that Purpose obstructing the Laws for Naturalization of Foreigners; refusing to pass others to encourage their Migrations hither, and raising the Conditions of new Appropriations of Lands.

He has obstructed the Administration of Justice, by refusing his Assent to Laws for establishing Judiciary Powers.

He has made Judges dependent on his Will alone, for the Tenure of their offices, and the Amount and payment of their Salaries.

He has erected a Multitude of new Offices, and sent hither Swarms of Officers to harrass our People, and eat out their Substance.

He has kept among us, in Times of Peace, Standing Armies, without the consent of our Legislatures.

He has affected to render the Military independent of, and superior to the Civil Power.

He has combined with others to subject us to a Jurisdiction foreign to our Constitution, and unacknowledged by our Laws; giving his Assent to their Acts of pretended Legislation:

For quartering large Bodies of Armed Troops among us:

For protecting them, by a mock Trial, from Punishment for any Murders which they should commit on the Inhabitants of these States:

For cutting off our Trade with all Parts of the World:

For imposing Taxes on us without our Consent:

For depriving us, in many cases, of the Benefits of Trial by Jury:

For transporting us beyond Seas to be tried for pretended Offences:

For abolishing the free System of English Laws in a neighbouring Province, establishing therein an arbitrary Government, and enlarging its Boundaries, so as to render it at once an Example and fit Instrument for introducing the same absolute Rule into these Colonies:

For taking away our Charters, abolishing our most valuable Laws, and altering fundamentally the Forms of our Governments:

For suspending our own Legislatures, and declaring themselves invested with Power to legislate for us in all Cases whatsoever.

He has abdicated Government here, by declaring us out of his Protection and waging War against us.

He has plundered our Seas, ravaged our Coasts, burnt our towns, and destroyed the Lives of our People.

He is, at this Time, transporting large Armies of foreign Mercenaries to compleat the works of Death, Desolation, and Tyranny, already begun with circumstances of Cruelty and Perfidy, scarcely paralleled in the most barbarous Ages, and totally unworthy the Head of a civilized Nation.

He has constrained our fellow Citizens taken Captive on the high Seas to bear Arms against their Country, to become the Executioners of their Friends and Brethren, or to fall themselves by their Hands.

He has excited domestic Insurrections amongst us, and has endeavoured to bring on the Inhabitants of our Frontiers, the merciless Indian Savages, whose known Rule of Warfare, is an undistinguished Destruction, of all Ages, Sexes and Conditions.

In every state of these Oppressions we have Petitioned for Redress in the most humble Terms: Our repeated Petitions have been answered only by repeated Injury. A Prince, whose Character is thus marked by every act which may define a Tyrant, is unfit to be the Ruler of a free People.

Nor have we been wanting in Attentions to our British Brethren. We have warned them from Time to Time of Attempts by their Legislature to extend an unwarrantable Jurisdiction over us. We have reminded them of the Circumstances of our Emigration and Settlement here. We have appealed to their native Justice and Magnanimity, and we have conjured them by the Ties of our common Kindred to disavow these Usurpations, which, would inevitably interrupt our Connections and Correspondence. They too have been deaf to the Voice of Justice and of Consanguinity. We must, therefore, acquiesce in the Necessity, which denounces our Separation, and hold them, as we hold the rest of Mankind, Enemies in War, in Peace, Friends.

We, therefore, the Representatives of the UNITED STATES OF AMERICA, in General Congress Assembled, appealing to the Supreme Judge of the World for the Rectitude of our Intentions, do, in the Name, and by the Authority of the good People of these Colonies, solemnly Publish and Declare, That these United Colonies are, and of Right ought to be, Free and Independent States; that they are absolved from all Allegiance to the British Crown, and that all political Connection between them and the State of Great-Britain, is and ought to be totally dissolved; and that as Free and Independent States, they have full Power to levy War, conclude Peace, contract Alliances, establish Commerce, and to do all other Acts and Things which Independent States may of right do. And for the support of this declaration, with a firm Reliance on the Protection of divine Providence, we mutually pledge to each other our lives, our Fortunes, and our sacred Honor.

Many important court cases are discussed in references in footnotes throughout this book. Court decisions are recorded and published. When a court case is mentioned, the notation that is used to refer to, or to cite, the case denotes where the published decision can be found.

State courts of appeals decisions are usually published in two places, the state reports of that particular state and the more widely used *National Reporter System* published by West Publishing Company. Some states no longer publish their own reports. The *National Reporter System* divides the states into the following geographic areas: Atlantic (A. or A.2d, where *2d* refers to *Second Series*), South Eastern (S.E. or S.E.2d), South Western (S.W., S.W.2d, or S.W.3d), North Western (N.W. or N.W.2d), North Eastern (N.E. or N.E.2d), Southern (So. or So.2d), and Pacific (P., P.2d, or P.3d).

Federal trial court decisions are published unofficially in *West's Federal Supplement* (F.Supp.), and opinions from the circuit courts of appeals are reported unofficially in West's *Federal Reporter* (F., F.2d, or F.3d). Opinions from the United States Supreme Court are reported in the *United States Reports* (U.S.), the *Lawyers' Edition of the Supreme Court Reports* (L.Ed.), West's *Supreme Court Reporter* (S.Ct.), and other publications. The *United States Reports* is the official publication of United States Supreme Court decisions. It is published by the federal government. Many early decisions are missing from these volumes. The citations of the early volumes of the *U.S. Reports* include the names of the actual reporters, such as Dallas, Cranch, or Wheaton. *McCulloch v. Maryland,* for example, is cited as 17 U.S. (4 Wheat.) 316. Only after 1874 did the present citation system, in which cases are cited based solely on their volume and page numbers in the *United States Reports,* come into being. The *Lawyers' Edition of the Supreme Court Reports* is an unofficial and more complete edition of Supreme Court decisions. West's *Supreme Court Reporter* is an unofficial edition of decisions dating from October 1882. These volumes contain headnotes and numerous brief editorial statements of the law involved in the case.

State courts of appeals decisions are cited by giving the name of the case; the volume, name, and page number of the state's official report (if the state publishes its own reports); the volume, unit, and page number of the *National Reporter;* and the volume, name, and page number of any other selected reporter. Federal court citations are also listed by giving the name of the case and the volume, name, and page number of the reports. In addition to the citation, this textbook lists the year of the decision in parentheses. Consider, for example, the case *United States v. Curtiss-Wright Export Co.,* 299 U.S. 304 (1936). The Supreme Court's decision of this case may be found in volume 299 of the *United States Reports* on page 304. The case was decided in 1936.

Today, many courts, including the United States Supreme Court, publish their opinions online. This makes it much easier for students to find and read cases, or summaries of cases, that have significant consequences for American government and politics. To access cases via the Internet, use the URLs given in the *Logging On* section at the end of Chapter 15.

	TERM OF SERVICE	AGE AT INAUGURATION	POLITICAL PARTY	COLLEGE OR UNIVERSITY	OCCUPATION OR PROFESSION
1. George Washington	1789–1797	57	None		Planter
2. John Adams	1797–1801	61	Federalist	Harvard	Lawyer
3. Thomas Jefferson	1801–1809	57	Democratic-Republican	William and Mary	Planter, Lawyer
4. James Madison	1809–1817	57	Democratic-Republican	Princeton	Lawyer
5. James Monroe	1817–1825	58	Democratic-Republican	William and Mary	Lawyer
6. John Quincy Adams	1825–1829	57	Democratic-Republican	Harvard	Lawyer
7. Andrew Jackson	1829–1837	61	Democrat		Lawyer
8. Martin Van Buren	1837–1841	54	Democrat		Lawyer
9. William H. Harrison	1841	68	Whig	Hampden-Sydney	Soldier
10. John Tyler	1841–1845	51	Whig	William and Mary	Lawyer
11. James K. Polk	1845–1849	49	Democrat	U. of N. Carolina	Lawyer
12. Zachary Taylor	1849–1850	64	Whig		Soldier
13. Millard Fillmore	1850–1853	50	Whig		Lawyer
14. Franklin Pierce	1853–1857	48	Democrat	Bowdoin	Lawyer
15. James Buchanan	1857–1861	65	Democrat	Dickinson	Lawyer
16. Abraham Lincoln	1861–1865	52	Republican		Lawyer
17. Andrew Johnson	1865–1869	56	Nat/l. Union†		Tailor
18. Ulysses S. Grant	1869–1877	46	Republican	U.S. Mil. Academy	Soldier
19. Rutherford B. Hayes	1877–1881	54	Republican	Kenyon	Lawyer
20. James A. Garfield	1881	49	Republican	Williams	Lawyer
21. Chester A. Arthur	1881–1885	51	Republican	Union	Lawyer
22. Grover Cleveland	1885–1889	47	Democrat		Lawyer
23. Benjamin Harrison	1889–1893	55	Republican	Miami	Lawyer
24. Grover Cleveland	1893–1897	55	Democrat		Lawyer
25. William McKinley	1897–1901	54	Republican	Allegheny College	Lawyer
26. Theodore Roosevelt	1901–1909	42	Republican	Harvard	Author
27. William H. Taft	1909–1913	51	Republican	Yale	Lawyer
28. Woodrow Wilson	1913–1921	56	Democrat	Princeton	Educator
29. Warren G. Harding	1921–1923	55	Republican		Editor
30. Calvin Coolidge	1923–1929	51	Republican	Amherst	Lawyer
31. Herbert C. Hoover	1929–1933	54	Republican	Stanford	Engineer
32. Franklin D. Roosevelt	1933–1945	51	Democrat	Harvard	Lawyer
33. Harry Truman	1945–1953	60	Democrat		Businessman
34. Dwight D. Eisenhower	1953–1961	62	Republican	U.S. Mil. Academy	Soldier
35. John F. Kennedy	1961–1963	43	Democrat	Harvard	Author
36. Lyndon B. Johnson	1963–1969	55	Democrat	Southwest Texas State	Teacher
37. Richard M. Nixon	1969–1974	56	Republican	Whittier	Lawyer
38. Gerald R. Ford‡	1974–1977	61	Republican	Michigan	Lawyer
39. James E. Carter, Jr.	1977–1981	52	Democrat	U.S. Naval Academy	Businessman
40. Ronald W. Reagan	1981–1989	69	Republican	Eureka College	Actor
41. George H. W. Bush	1989–1993	64	Republican	Yale	Businessman
42. William Jefferson Clinton	1993–2001	46	Democrat	Georgetown	Lawyer
43. George W. Bush	2001–	54	Republican	Harvard	Businessman

*Church preference; never joined any church.

†The National Union Party consisted of Republicans and War Democrats. Johnson was a Democrat.

**Inaugurated Dec. 6, 1973, to replace Agnew, who resigned Oct. 10, 1973.

‡Inaugurated Aug. 9, 1974, to replace Nixon, who resigned that same day.

§Inaugurated Dec. 19, 1974, to replace Ford, who became president Aug. 9, 1974.

	RELIGION	BORN	DIED	AGE AT DEATH	VICE PRESIDENT	
1.	Episcopalian	Feb. 22, 1732	Dec. 14, 1799	67	John Adams	(1789–1797)
2.	Unitarian	Oct. 30, 1735	July 4, 1826	90	Thomas Jefferson	(1797–1801)
3.	Unitarian*	Apr. 13, 1743	July 4, 1826	83	Aaron Burr	(1801–1805)
					George Clinton	(1805–1809)
4.	Episcopalian	Mar. 16, 1751	June 28, 1836	85	George Clinton	(1809–1812)
					Elbridge Gerry	(1813–1814)
5.	Episcopalian	Apr. 28, 1758	July 4, 1831	73	Daniel D. Tompkins	(1817–1825)
6.	Unitarian	July 11, 1767	Feb. 23, 1848	80	John C. Calhoun	(1825–1829)
7.	Presbyterian	Mar. 15, 1767	June 8, 1845	78	John C. Calhoun	(1829–1832)
					Martin Van Buren	(1833–1837)
8.	Dutch Reformed	Dec. 5, 1782	July 24, 1862	79	Richard M. Johnson	(1837–1841)
9.	Episcopalian	Feb. 9, 1773	Apr. 4, 1841	68	John Tyler	(1841)
10.	Episcopalian	Mar. 29, 1790	Jan. 18, 1862	71		
11.	Methodist	Nov. 2, 1795	June 15, 1849	53	George M. Dallas	(1845–1849)
12.	Episcopalian	Nov. 24, 1784	July 9, 1850	65	Millard Fillmore	(1849–1850)
13.	Unitarian	Jan. 7, 1800	Mar. 8, 1874	74		
14.	Episcopalian	Nov. 23, 1804	Oct. 8, 1869	64	William R. King	(1853)
15.	Presbyterian	Apr. 23, 1791	June 1, 1868	77	John C. Breckinridge	(1857–1861)
16.	Presbyterian*	Feb. 12, 1809	Apr. 15, 1865	56	Hannibal Hamlin	(1861–1865)
					Andrew Johnson	(1865)
17.	Methodist*	Dec. 29, 1808	July 31, 1875	66		
18.	Methodist	Apr. 27, 1822	July 23, 1885	63	Schuyler Colfax	(1869–1873)
					Henry Wilson	(1873–1875)
19.	Methodist*	Oct. 4, 1822	Jan. 17, 1893	70	William A. Wheeler	(1877–1881)
20.	Disciples of Christ	Nov. 19, 1831	Sept. 19, 1881	49	Chester A. Arthur	(1881)
21.	Episcopalian	Oct. 5, 1829	Nov. 18, 1886	57		
22.	Presbyterian	Mar. 18, 1837	June 24, 1908	71	Thomas A. Hendricks	(1885)
23.	Presbyterian	Aug. 20, 1833	Mar. 13, 1901	67	Levi P. Morton	(1889–1893)
24.	Presbyterian	Mar. 18, 1837	June 24, 1908	71	Adlai E. Stevenson	(1893–1897)
25.	Methodist	Jan. 29, 1843	Sept. 14, 1901	58	Garret A. Hobart	(1897–1899)
					Theodore Roosevelt	(1901)
26.	Dutch Reformed	Oct. 27, 1858	Jan. 6, 1919	60	Charles W. Fairbanks	(1905–1909)
27.	Unitarian	Sept. 15, 1857	Mar. 8, 1930	72	James S. Sherman	(1909–1912)
28.	Presbyterian	Dec. 29, 1856	Feb. 3, 1924	67	Thomas R. Marshall	(1913–1921)
29.	Baptist	Nov. 2, 1865	Aug. 2, 1923	57	Calvin Coolidge	(1921–1923)
30.	Congregationalist	July 4, 1872	Jan. 5, 1933	60	Charles G. Dawes	(1925–1929)
31.	Friend (Quaker)	Aug. 10, 1874	Oct. 20, 1964	90	Charles Curtis	(1929–1933)
32.	Episcopalian	Jan. 30, 1882	Apr. 12, 1945	63	John N. Garner	(1933–1941)
					Henry A. Wallace	(1941–1945)
					Harry Truman	(1945)
33.	Baptist	May 8, 1884	Dec. 26, 1972	88	Alben W. Barkley	(1949–1953)
34.	Presbyterian	Oct. 14, 1890	Mar. 28, 1969	78	Richard M. Nixon	(1953–1961)
35.	Roman Catholic	May 29, 1917	Nov. 22, 1963	46	Lyndon B. Johnson	(1961–1963)
36.	Disciples of Christ	Aug. 27, 1908	Jan. 22, 1973	64	Hubert H. Humphrey	(1965–1969)
37.	Friend (Quaker)	Jan. 9, 1913	Apr. 22, 1994	81	Spiro T. Agnew	(1969–1973)
					Gerald R. Ford**	(1973–1974)
38.	Episcopalian	July 14, 1913			Nelson A. Rockefeller§	(1974–1977)
39.	Baptist	Oct. 1, 1924			Walter F. Mondale	(1977–1981)
40.	Disciples of Christ	Feb. 6, 1911			George H. W. Bush	(1981–1989)
41.	Episcopalian	June 12, 1924			J. Danforth Quayle	(1989–1993)
42.	Baptist	Aug. 19, 1946			Albert A. Gore	(1993–2001)
43.	Methodist	July 6, 1946			Dick Cheney	(2001–)

In 1787, after the newly drafted U.S. Constitution was submitted to the thirteen states for ratification, a major political debate ensued between the Federalists (who favored ratification) and the Anti-Federalists (who opposed ratification). Anti-Federalists in New York were particularly critical of the Constitution, and in response to their objections, Federalists Alexander Hamilton, James Madison, and John Jay wrote a series of eighty-five essays in defense of the Constitution. The essays were published in New York newspapers and reprinted in other newspapers throughout the country.

For students of American government, the essays, collectively known as The Federalist Papers, *are particularly important because they provide a glimpse of the founders' political philosophy and intentions in designing the Constitution—and, consequently, in shaping the American philosophy of government.*

We have included in this appendix three of these essays: Federalist Papers *No. 10, No. 51, and No. 78. Each essay has been annotated by the authors to indicate its importance in American political thought and to clarify the meaning of particular passages.*

Federalist Paper **No. 10**

Federalist Paper No. 10, *penned by James Madison, has often been singled out as a key document in American political thought. In this essay, Madison attacks the Anti-Federalists' fear that a republican form of government will inevitably give rise to "factions"—small political parties or groups united by a common interest—that will control the government. Factions will be harmful to the country because they will implement policies beneficial to their own interests but adverse to other people's rights and to the public good. In this essay, Madison attempts to lay to rest this fear by explaining how, in a large republic such as the United States, there will be so many different factions, held together by regional or local interests, that no single one of them will dominate national politics.*

Madison opens his essay with a paragraph discussing how important it is to devise a plan of government that can control the "instability, injustice, and confusion" brought about by factions.

Among the numerous advantages promised by a well-constructed Union, none deserves to be more accurately developed than its tendency to break and control the violence of faction. The friend of popular governments never finds himself so much alarmed for their character and fate as when he contemplates their propensity to this dangerous vice. He will not fail, therefore, to set a due value on any plan which, without violating the principles to which he is attached, provides a proper cure for it. The instability, injustice, and confusion introduced into the public councils have, in truth, been the mortal diseases under which popular governments have everywhere perished, as they continue to be the favorite and fruitful topics from which the adversaries to liberty derive their most specious declamations. The valuable improvements made by the American constitutions on the popular models, both ancient and modern, cannot certainly be too much admired; but it would be an unwarrantable partiality to contend that they have as effectually obviated the danger on this side, as was wished and expected. Complaints are everywhere heard from our most considerate and virtuous citizens, equally the friends of public and private faith and of public and personal liberty, that our governments are too unstable, that the public good is disregarded in the conflicts of rival parties, and that measures are too often decided, not according to the rules of justice and the rights of the minor party, but by the superior force of an interested and overbearing majority. However anxiously we may wish that these complaints had no foundation, the evidence of known facts will not permit us to deny that they are in some degree true. It will be found, indeed, on a candid review of our situation, that some of the distresses under which we labor have been erroneously charged on the operation of our governments; but it will be found, at the same time, that other causes will not alone account for many of our heaviest misfortunes; and, particularly, for that prevailing and increasing distrust of public engagements and alarm for private rights which are echoed from one end of the continent to the other. These must be chiefly, if not wholly, effects of the unsteadiness and injustice with which a factious spirit has tainted our public administration.

Madison now defines what he means by the term faction.

By a faction I understand a number of citizens, whether amounting to a majority or minority of the whole, who are united and actuated by some common impulse of passion, or of interest, adverse to the rights of other citizens, or the permanent and aggregate interests of the community.

Madison next contends that there are two methods by which the "mischiefs of faction" can be cured: by removing the causes of faction or by controlling their effects. In the following paragraphs, Madison explains how liberty itself nourishes factions. Therefore, to abolish factions would involve abolishing liberty—a cure "worse than the disease."

There are two methods of curing the mischiefs of faction: the one, by removing its causes; the other, by controlling its effects.

There are again two methods of removing the causes of faction: the one, by destroying the liberty which is essential to its existence; the other, by giving to every citizen the same opinions, the same passions, and the same interests.

It could never be more truly said than of the first remedy that it was worse than the disease. Liberty is to faction what air is to fire, an aliment without which it instantly expires. But it could not be a less folly to abolish liberty, which is essential to political life, because it nourishes faction than it would be to wish the annihilation of air, which is essential to animal life, because it imparts to fire its destructive agency.

The second expedient is as impracticable as the first would be unwise. As long as the reason of man continues fallible, and his is at liberty to exercise it, different opinions will be formed. As long as the connection subsists between his reason and his self-love, his opinions and his passions will have a reciprocal influence on each other; and the former will be objects to which the latter will attach themselves. The diversity in the faculties of men, from which the rights of property originate, is not less an insuperable obstacle to a uniformity of interests. The protection of these faculties is the first object of government. From the protection of different and unequal faculties of acquiring property, the possession of different degrees and kinds of property immediately results; and from the influence of these on the sentiments and views of the respective proprietors ensues a division of the society into different interests and parties.

The latent causes of faction are thus sown in the nature of man; and we see them everywhere brought into different degrees of activity, according to the different circumstances of civil society. A zeal for different opinions concerning religion, concerning government, and many other points, as well of speculation as of practice; an attachment to different leaders ambitiously contending for pre-eminence and power; or to persons of other descriptions whose fortunes have been interesting to the human passions, have, in turn, divided mankind into parties, inflamed them with mutual animosity, and rendered them much more disposed to vex and oppress each other than to co-operate for their common good. So strong is this propensity of mankind to fall into mutual animosities that where no substantial occasion presents itself the most frivolous and fanciful distinctions have been sufficient to kindle their unfriendly passions and excite their most violent conflicts. But the most common and durable source of factions has been the various and unequal distribution of property. Those who hold and those who are without property have ever formed distinct interests in society. Those who are creditors, and those who are debtors, fall under a like discrimination. A landed interest, a manufacturing interest, a mercantile interest, a moneyed interest, with many lesser interests, grow up of necessity in civilized nations, and divide them into different classes, actuated by different sentiments and views. The regulation of these various and interfering interests forms the principal task of modern legislation and involves the spirit of party and faction in the necessary and ordinary operations of government.

No man is allowed to be a judge in his own cause, because his interest would certainly bias his judgment, and, not improbably, corrupt his integrity. With equal, nay with greater reason, a body of men are unfit to be both judges and parties at the same time; yet what are many of the most important acts of legislation but so many judicial determinations, not indeed concerning the rights of single persons, but concerning the rights of large bodies of citizens? And what are the different classes of legislators but advocates and parties to the causes which they determine? Is a law proposed concerning private debts? It is a question to which the creditors are parties on one side and the debtors on the other. Justice ought to hold the balance between them. Yet the parties are, and must be, themselves the judges; and the most numerous party, or in other words, the most powerful faction must be expected to prevail. Shall domestic manufacturers be encouraged, and in what degree, by restrictions on foreign manufacturers? Are questions which would be differently decided by the landed and the manufacturing classes, and probably by neither with a sole regard to justice and the public good. The apportionment of taxes on the various descriptions of property is an act which seems to require the most exact impartiality; yet there is, perhaps, no legislative act in which greater opportunity and temptation are given to a predominant party to trample on the rules of justice. Every shilling with which they overburden the inferior number is a shilling saved to their own pockets.

It is in vain to say that enlightened statesmen will be able to adjust these clashing interests and render them all subservient to the public good. Enlightened statesmen will not always be at the helm. Nor, in many cases, can such an adjustment be made at all without taking into view indirect and remote considerations, which will rarely prevail over the immediate interest which one party may find in disregarding the rights of another or the good of the whole.

The inference to which we are brought is that the *causes* of faction cannot be removed and that relief is only to be sought in the means of controlling its *effects*.

Having concluded that "the causes of faction cannot be removed," Madison now looks in some detail at the other method by which factions can be cured—by controlling their effects. This is the heart of his essay. He begins by positing a significant question: How can you have self-government without risking the possibility that a ruling faction, particularly a majority faction, might tyrannize over the rights of others?

If a faction consists of less than a majority, relief is supplied by the republican principle, which enables the majority to defeat its sinister views by regular vote. It may clog the administration, it may convulse the society; but it will be unable to execute and mask its violence under the forms of the Constitution. When a majority is included in a faction, the form of popular government, on the other hand, enables it to sacrifice to its ruling passion or interest both the public good and the rights of other citizens. To secure the public good and private rights against the danger of such a faction, and at the same time to preserve the spirit and the form of popular government, is then the great object to which our inquiries are directed. Let me add that it is the great desideratum by which alone this form of government can be rescued from the opprobrium under which it has so long labored and be recommended to the esteem and adoption of mankind.

Madison now sets forth the idea that one way to control the effects of factions is to ensure that the majority is rendered incapable of acting in concert in order to "carry into effect schemes of oppression." He goes on to state that in a democracy, in which all citizens participate personally in government decision making, there is no way to prevent the majority from communicating with each other and, as a result, acting in concert.

By what means is this object attainable? Evidently by one of two only. Either the existence of the same passion or interest in a majority at the same time must be prevented, or the majority, having such coexistent passion or interest, must be rendered, by their number and local situation, unable to concert and carry into effect schemes of oppression. If the impulse and the opportunity be suffered to coincide, we well know that neither moral nor religious motives can be relied on as an adequate control. They are not found to be such on the injustice and violence of individuals, and lose their efficacy in proportion to the number combined together, that is, in proportion as their efficacy becomes needful.

From this view of the subject it may be concluded that a pure democracy, by which I mean a society consisting of a small number of citizens, who assemble and administer the government in person, can admit of no cure for the mischiefs of faction. A common passion or interest will, in almost every case, be felt by a majority of the whole; a communication and concert results from the form of government itself; and there is nothing to check the inducements to sacrifice the weaker party or an obnoxious individual. Hence it is that such democracies have ever been spectacles of turbulence and contention; have ever been found incompatible with personal security or the rights of property; and have in general been as short in their lives as they have been violent in their deaths. Theoretic politicians, who have patronized this species of government, have erroneously supposed that by reducing mankind to a perfect equality in their political rights, they would at the same time be perfectly equalized and assimilated in their possessions, their opinions, and their passions.

Madison now moves on to discuss the benefits of a republic with respect to controlling the effects of factions. He begins by defining a republic and then pointing out the "two great points of difference" between a republic and a democracy: a republic is governed by a small body of elected representatives, not by the people directly; and a republic can extend over a much larger territory and embrace more citizens than a democracy can.

A republic, by which I mean a government in which the scheme of representation takes place, opens a different prospect and promises the cure for which we are seeking. Let us examine the points in which it varies from pure democracy, and we shall comprehend both the nature of the cure and the efficacy which it must derive from the Union.

The two great points of difference between a democracy and a republic are: first, the delegation of the government, in the latter, to a small number of citizens elected by the rest; secondly, the greater number of citizens and greater sphere of country over which the latter may be extended.

In the following four paragraphs, Madison explains how in a republic, particularly a large republic, the delegation of authority to elected representatives will increase the likelihood that those who govern will be "fit" for their positions and that a proper balance will be achieved between local (factional) interests and national interests. Note how he stresses that the new federal Constitution, by dividing powers between state governments and the national government, provides a "happy combination in this respect."

The effect of the first difference is, on the one hand, to refine and enlarge the public views by passing them through the medium of a chosen body of citizens, whose wisdom may best discern the true interest of their country and whose patriotism and love of justice will be least likely to sacrifice it to temporary or partial considerations. Under such a regulation it may well happen that the public voice, pronounced by the representatives of the people, will be more consonant to the public good than if pronounced by the people themselves, convened for the purpose. On the other hand, the effect may be inverted. Men of factious tempers, of local prejudices, or of sinister designs, may, by intrigue, by corruption, or by other means, first obtain the suffrages, and then betray the interests of the people. The question resulting is, whether small or extensive republics are most favorable to the election of proper guardians of the public weal; and it is clearly decided in favor of the latter by two obvious considerations.

In the first place it is to be remarked that however small the republic may be the representatives must be raised to a certain number in order to guard against the cabals of a few; and that however large it may be they must be limited to a certain number in order to guard against the confusion of a multitude. Hence, the number of representatives in the two cases not being in proportion to that of the constituents, and being proportionally greatest in the small republic, it follows that if the proportion of fit characters be not less in the large than in the small republic, the former will present a greater option, and consequently a greater probability of a fit choice.

In the next place, as each representative will be chosen by a greater number of citizens in the large than in the small republic, it will be more difficult for unworthy candidates to practice with success the vicious arts by which elections are too often carried; and the suffrages of the people being more free, will be more likely to center on men who possess the most attractive merit and the most diffusive and established characters.

It must be confessed that in this, as in most other cases, there is a mean, on both sides of which inconveniencies will be found to lie. By enlarging too much the number of electors, you render the representative too little acquainted with all their local circumstances and lesser interests; as by reducing it too much, you render him unduly attached to these, and too little fit to comprehend and pursue great and national objects. The federal Constitution forms a happy combination in this respect; the great and aggregate interests being referred to the national, the local and particular to the State legislatures.

Madison now looks more closely at the other difference between a republic and a democracy—namely, that a republic can encompass a larger territory and more citizens than a democracy can. In the remaining paragraphs of his essay, Madison concludes that in a large republic, it will be difficult for factions to act in concert. Although a factious group—religious, political, economic, or otherwise—may control a local or regional government, it will have little chance of gathering a national following. This is because in a large republic, there will be numerous other factions whose work will offset the work of any one particular faction ("sect"). As Madison phrases it, these numerous factions will "secure the national councils against any danger from that source."

The other point of difference is the greater number of citizens and extent of territory which may be brought within the compass of republican than of democratic government; and it is this circumstance principally which renders factious combinations less to be dreaded in the former than in the latter. The smaller the society, the fewer probably will be the distinct parties and interests composing it; the fewer the distinct parties and interests, the more frequently will a majority be found of the same party; and the smaller the number of individuals composing a majority, and the smaller the compass within which they are placed, the more easily will they concert and execute their plans of oppression. Extend the sphere and you take in a greater variety of parties and interests; you make it less probable that a majority of the whole will have a common motive to invade the rights of other citizens; or if such a common motive exists, it will be more difficult for all who feel it to discover their own strength and to act in unison with each other. Besides other impediments, it may be remarked that, where there is a consciousness of unjust or dishonorable purposes, communication is always checked by distrust in proportion to the number whose concurrence is necessary.

Hence, it clearly appears that the same advantage which a republic has over a democracy in controlling the effects of faction is enjoyed by a large over a small republic—is enjoyed by the Union over the States composing it. Does this advantage consist in the substitution of representatives whose enlightened views and virtuous sentiments render them superior to local prejudices and to schemes of injustice? It will not be denied that the representation of the Union will be most likely to possess these requisite endowments. Does it consist in the greater security afforded by a greater variety of parties, against the event of any one party being able to outnumber and oppress the rest? In an equal degree does the increased variety of parties comprised within the Union increase this security. Does it, in fine, consist in the greater obstacles opposed to the concert and accomplishment of the secret wishes of an unjust and interested majority? Here again the extent of the Union gives it the most palpable advantage.

The influence of factious leaders may kindle a flame within their particular States but will be unable to spread a general conflagration through the other States. A religious sect may degenerate into a political faction in a part of the Confederacy; but the variety of sects dispersed over the entire face of it must secure the national councils against any danger from that source. A rage for paper money, for an abolition of debts, for an equal division of property, or for any other improper or wicked project, will be less apt to pervade the whole body of the Union than a particular member of it, in the same proportion as such a malady is more likely to taint a particular county or district than an entire State.

In the extent and proper structure of the Union, therefore, we behold a republican remedy for the diseases most incident to republican government. And according to the degree of pleasure and pride we feel in being republicans ought to be our zeal in cherishing the spirit and supporting the character of federalists.

Publius
(James Madison)

Federalist Paper **No. 51**

Federalist Paper No. 51, also authored by James Madison, is another classic in American political theory. Although the Federalists wanted a strong national government, they had not abandoned the traditional American view, particularly notable during the revolutionary era, that those holding powerful government positions could not be trusted to put national interests and the common good above their own personal interests. In this essay, Madison explains why the separation of the national government's powers into three branches—executive, legislative, and judicial—and a federal structure of government offer the best protection against tyranny.

To what expedient, then, shall we finally resort, for maintaining in practice the necessary partition of power among the several departments as laid down in the Constitution? The only answer that can be given is that as all these exterior provisions are found to be inadequate the defect must be supplied, by so contriving the interior structure of the government as that its several constituent parts may, by their mutual relations, be the means of keeping each other in their proper places. Without presuming to undertake a full development of this important idea I will hazard a few general observations which may perhaps place it in a clearer light, and enable us to form a more correct judgment of the principles and structure of the government planned by the convention.

In the next two paragraphs, Madison stresses that for the powers of the different branches (departments) of government to be truly separated, the personnel in one branch should not be dependent on another branch for their appointment or for the "emoluments" (compensation) attached to their offices.

In order to lay a due foundation for that separate and distinct exercise of the different powers of government, which to a certain extent is admitted on all hands to be essential to the preservation of liberty, it is evident that each department should have a will of its own; and consequently should be so constituted that the members of each should have as little agency as possible in the appointment of the members of the others. Were this principle rigorously adhered to, it would require that all the appointments for the supreme executive, legislative, and judiciary magistracies should be drawn from the same fountain of authority, the people, through channels having no communication whatever with one another. Perhaps such a plan of constructing the several departments would be less difficult in practice than it may in contemplation appear. Some difficulties, however, and some additional expense would attend the execution of it. Some deviations, therefore, from the principle must be admitted. In the constitution of the judiciary department in particular, it might be inexpedient to insist rigorously on the principle: first, because peculiar qualifications being essential in the members, the primary consideration ought to be to select that mode of choice which best secures these qualifications; second, because the permanent tenure by which the appointments are held in that department

must soon destroy all sense of dependence on the authority conferring them.

It is equally evident that the members of each department should be as little dependent as possible on those of the others for the emoluments annexed to their offices. Were the executive magistrate, or the judges, not independent of the legislature in this particular, their independence in every other would be merely nominal.

In the following passages, which are among the most widely quoted of Madison's writings, he explains how the separation of the powers of government into three branches helps to counter the effects of personal ambition on government. The separation of powers allows personal motives to be linked to the constitutional rights of a branch of government. In effect, rivaling personal interests in each branch will help to keep the powers of the three government branches separate and, in so doing, will help to guard the public interest.

But the great security against a gradual concentration of the several powers in the same department consists in giving to those who administer each department the necessary constitutional means and personal motives to resist encroachments of the others. The provision for defense must in this, as in all other cases, be made commensurate to the danger of attack. Ambition must be made to counteract ambition. The interest of the man must be connected with the constitutional rights of the place. It may be a reflection on human nature that such devices should be necessary to control the abuses of government. But what is government itself but the greatest of all reflections on human nature? If men were angels, no government would be necessary. If angels were to govern men, neither external nor internal controls on government would be necessary. In framing a government which is to be administered by men over men, the great difficulty lies in this: you must first enable the government to control the governed; and in the next place oblige it to control itself. A dependence on the people is, no doubt, the primary control on the government; but experience has taught mankind the necessity of auxiliary precautions.

This policy of supplying, by opposite and rival interests, the defect of better motives, might be traced through the whole system of human affairs, private as well as public. We see it particularly displayed in all the subordinate distributions of power, where the constant aim is to divide and arrange the several offices in such a manner as that each may be a check on the other—that the private interest of every individual may be a sentinel over the public rights. These inventions of prudence cannot be less requisite in the distribution of the supreme powers of the State.

Madison now addresses the issue of equality between the branches of government. The legislature will necessarily predominate, but if the executive is given an "absolute negative" (absolute veto power) over legislative actions, this also could lead to an abuse of power. Madison concludes that the division of the legislature into two "branches" (parts, or chambers) will act as a check on the legislature's powers.

But it is not possible to give to each department an equal power of self-defense. In republican government, the legislative authority necessarily predominates. The remedy for this inconveniency is to divide the legislature into different branches; and to render them, by different modes of election and different principles of action, as little connected with each other as the nature of their common functions and their common dependence on the society will admit. It may even be necessary to guard against dangerous encroachments by still further precautions. As the weight of the legislative authority requires that it should be thus divided, the weakness of the executive may require, on the other hand, that it should be fortified. An absolute negative on the legislature appears, at first view, to be the natural defense with which the executive magistrate should be armed. But perhaps it would be neither altogether safe nor alone sufficient. On ordinary occasions it might not be exerted with the requisite firmness, and on extraordinary occasions it might be perfidiously abused. May not this defect of an absolute negative be supplied by some qualified connection between this weaker department and the weaker branch of the stronger department, by which the latter may be led to support the constitutional rights of the former, without being too much detached from the rights of its own department?

If the principles on which these observations are founded be just, as I persuade myself they are, and they be applied as a criterion to the several State constitutions, and to the federal Constitution, it will be found that if the latter does not perfectly correspond with them, the former are infinitely less able to bear such a test.

In the remainder of the essay, Madison discusses how a federal system of government, in which powers are divided between the states and the national government, offers "double security" against tyranny.

There are, moreover, two considerations particularly applicable to the federal system of America, which place that system in a very interesting point of view.

First. In a single republic, all the power surrendered by the people is submitted to the administration of a single government; and the usurpations are guarded against by a division of the government into distinct and separate departments. In the compound republic of America, the power surrendered by the people is first divided between two distinct governments, and then the portion allotted to each subdivided among distinct and separate departments. Hence a double security arises to the rights of the people. The different governments will control each other, at the same time that each will be controlled by itself.

Second. It is of great importance in a republic not only to guard the society against the oppression of its rulers, but to guard one part of the society against the injustice of the other part. Different interests necessarily exist in different classes of citizens. If a majority be united by a common interest, the rights of the minority will be insecure. There are but two methods of providing against this evil: the one by creating a will in the community independent of the majority—that is, of the society itself; the other, by comprehending in the society so many separate descriptions of citizens as will render an unjust combination of a majority of the whole very improbable, if not impracticable. The first method prevails in all governments possessing an hereditary or self-appointed authority. This, at best, is but a precarious security; because a power independent of the society may as well espouse the unjust views of the major as the rightful interests of the minor party, and may possibly be turned against both parties. The second method will be exemplified in the federal republic of the United States. Whilst all authority in it will be derived from and dependent on the society, the society itself will be broken into so many parts, interests and classes of citizens, that the rights of individuals, or of the minority, will be in little danger from interested combinations of the majority. In a free government the security for civil rights must be the same as that for religious rights. It consists in the one case in the multiplicity of interests, and in the other in the multiplicity of sects. The degree of security in both cases will depend on the number of interests and sects; and this may be presumed to depend on the extent of country and number of people comprehended under the same government. This view of the subject must particularly recommend a proper federal system to all the sincere and considerate friends of republican government, since it shows that in exact proportion as the territory of the Union may be formed into more circumscribed Confederacies, or States, oppressive combinations of a majority will be facilitated; the best security, under the republican forms, for the rights of every class of citizen, will be diminished; and consequently the stability and independence of some member of the government, the only other security, must be proportionally increased. Justice is the end of government. It is the end of civil society. It ever has been and ever will be pursued until it be obtained, or until liberty be lost in the pursuit. In a society under the forms of which the stronger faction can readily unite and oppress the weaker, anarchy may as truly be said to reign as in a state of nature, where the weaker individual is not secured against the violence of the stronger; and as, in the latter state, even the stronger individuals are prompted, by the uncertainty of their condition, to submit to a government which may protect the weak as well as themselves; so, in the former state, will the more powerful factions or parties be gradually induced, by a like motive, to wish for a government which will protect all parties, the weaker as well as the more powerful. It can be little doubted that if the State of Rhode Island was separated from the Confederacy and left to itself, the insecurity of rights under the popular form of government within such narrow limits would be displayed by such reiterated oppressions of factious majorities that some power altogether independent of the people would soon be called for by the voice of the very factions whose misrule had proved the necessity of it. In the extended republic of the United States, and among the great variety of interests, parties, and sects which it embraces, a coalition of a majority of the whole society could seldom take place on any other principles than those of justice and the general good; whilst there being thus less danger to a minor from the will of a major party, there must be less pretext, also, to provide for the security of the former, by introducing into the government a will not dependent on the latter, or, in other words, a will independent of the society itself. It is no less certain than it is important, notwithstanding the contrary opinions which have been entertained, that the larger the society, provided it lie within a practicable sphere, the more duly capable it will be of self-government. And happily for the republican cause, the practicable sphere may be carried to a very great extent by a judicious modification and mixture of the *federal principle*.

Publius
(James Madison)

Federalist Paper **No. 78**

In this essay, Alexander Hamilton looks at the role of the judicial branch (the courts) in the new government fashioned by the Constitution's framers. The essay is historically significant because, among other things, it provides a basis for the courts' power of judicial review, which was not explicitly set forth in the Constitution (see Chapters 3 and 15).

After some brief introductory remarks, Hamilton explains why the founders decided that federal judges should be appointed and given lifetime tenure. Note how he describes the judiciary as the "weakest" and "least dangerous" branch of government. Because of this, claims Hamilton, "all possible care" is required to enable the judiciary to defend itself against attacks by the other two branches of government. Above all, the independence of the judicial branch should be secured, because if judicial powers were combined with legislative or executive powers, there would be no liberty.

WE PROCEED now to an examination of the judiciary department of the proposed government.

In unfolding the defects of the existing Confederation, the utility and necessity of a federal judicature have been clearly pointed out. It is the less necessary to recapitulate the considerations there urged, as the propriety of the institution in the abstract is not disputed; the only questions which have been raised being relative to the manner of constituting it, and to its extent. To these points, therefore, our observations shall be confined.

The manner of constituting it seems to embrace these several objects: 1st. The mode of appointing the judges. 2d. The tenure by which they are to hold their places. 3d. The partition of the judiciary authority between different courts, and their relations to each other.

First. As to the mode of appointing the judges; this is the same with that of appointing the officers of the Union in general, and has been so fully discussed in the last two numbers, that nothing can be said here which would not be useless repetition.

Second. As to the tenure by which the judges are to hold their places; this chiefly concerns their duration in office; the provisions for their support; the precautions for their responsibility.

According to the plan of the convention, all judges who may be appointed by the United States are to hold their offices during good behavior; which is conformable to the most approved of the State constitutions and among the rest, to that of this State. Its propriety having been drawn into question by the adversaries of that plan, is no light symptom of the rage for objection, which disorders their imaginations and judgments. The standard of good behavior for the continuance in office of the judicial magistracy, is certainly one of the most valuable of the modern improvements in the practice of government. In a monarchy it is an excellent barrier to the despotism of the prince; in a republic it is a no less excellent barrier to the encroachments and oppressions of the representative body. And it is the best expedient which can be devised in any government, to secure a steady, upright, and impartial administration of the laws.

Whoever attentively considers the different departments of power must perceive, that, in a government in which they are separated from each other, the judiciary, from the nature of its functions, will always be the least dangerous to the political rights of the Constitution; because it will be least in a capacity to annoy or injure them. The Executive not only dispenses the honors, but holds the sword of the community. The legislature not only commands the purse, but prescribes the rules by which the duties and rights of every citizen are to be regulated. The judiciary, on the contrary, has no influence over either the sword or the purse; no direction either of the strength or of the wealth of the society; and can take no active resolution whatever. It may truly be said to have neither force nor will, but merely judgment; and must ultimately depend upon the aid of the executive arm even for the efficacy of its judgments.

This simple view of the matter suggests several important consequences. It proves incontestably, that the judiciary is beyond comparison the weakest of the three departments of power; that it can never attack with success either of the other two; and that all possible care is requisite to enable it to defend itself against their attacks. It equally proves, that though individual oppression may now and then proceed from the courts of justice, the general liberty of the people can never be endangered from that quarter; I mean so long as the judiciary remains truly distinct from both the legislature and the Executive. For I agree, that "there is no liberty, if the power of judging is not separated from the legislative and executive powers." And it proves, in the last place, that as liberty can have nothing to fear from the judiciary alone, but would have everything to fear from its union with either of the other departments; that as all the effects of such a union must ensue from a dependence of the former on the latter, notwithstanding a nominal and apparent separation; that as, from the natural feebleness of the judiciary, it is in continual jeopardy of being overpowered, awed, or influenced by its co-ordinate branches; and that as nothing can contribute so much to its firmness and independence as permanency in office, this quality may therefore be justly regarded as an indispensable ingredient in its constitution, and, in a great measure, as the citadel of the public justice and the public security.

Hamilton now stresses that the "complete independence of the courts" is essential in a limited government, because it is up to the courts to interpret the laws. Just as a federal court can decide which of two conflicting statutes should take priority, so can that court decide whether a statute conflicts with the Constitution. Essentially, Hamilton sets forth here the theory of judicial review—the power of the courts to decide whether actions of the other branches of government are (or are not) consistent with the Constitution. Hamilton points out that this "exercise of judicial discretion, in determining between two contradictory laws," does not mean that the judicial branch is superior to the legislative branch. Rather, it "supposes" that the power of the people (as declared in the Constitution) is superior to both the judiciary and the legislature.

The complete independence of the courts of justice is peculiarly essential in a limited Constitution. By a limited Constitution, I understand one which contains certain specified exceptions to the legislative authority; such, for instance, as that it shall pass no bills of attainder, no ex-post-facto laws, and the like. Limitations of this kind can be preserved in practice no other way than through the medium of courts of justice, whose duty it must be to declare all acts contrary to the manifest tenor of the Constitution void. Without this, all the reservations of particular rights or privileges would amount to nothing. Some perplexity respecting the rights of the courts to pronounce legislative acts void, because contrary to the Constitution, has arisen from an imagination that the doctrine would imply a superiority of the judiciary to the legislative power. It is urged that the authority which can declare the acts of another void, must necessarily be superior to the one whose acts may be declared void. As this doctrine is of great importance in all the American constitutions, a brief discussion of the ground on which it rests cannot be unacceptable.

There is no position which depends on clearer principles, than that every act of a delegated authority, contrary to the tenor of the commission under which it is exercised, is void. No legislative act, therefore, contrary to the Constitution, can be valid. To deny this, would be to affirm, that the deputy is greater than his principal; that the servant is above his master; that the representatives of the people are superior to the people themselves; that men acting by virtue of powers, may do not only what their powers do not authorize, but what they forbid.

If it be said that the legislative body are themselves the constitutional judges of their own powers, and that the construction they put upon them is conclusive upon the other departments, it may be answered, that this cannot be the natural presumption, where it is not to be collected from any particular provisions in the Constitution. It is not otherwise to be supposed, that the Constitution could intend to enable the representatives of the people to substitute their will to that of their constituents. It is far more rational to suppose, that the courts were designed to be an intermediate body between the people and the legislature, in order, among other things, to keep the latter within the limits assigned to their authority. The interpretation of the laws is the proper and peculiar province of the courts. A constitution is, in fact, and must be regarded by the judges, as a fundamental law. It therefore belongs to them to ascertain its meaning, as well as the meaning of any particular act proceeding from the legislative body. If there should happen to be an irreconcilable variance between the two, that which has the superior obligation and validity ought, of course, to be preferred; or, in other words, the Constitution ought to be preferred to the statute, the intention of the people to the intention of their agents.

Nor does this conclusion by any means suppose a superiority of the judicial to the legislative power. It only supposes that the power of the people is superior to both; and that where the will of the legislature, declared in its statutes, stands in opposition to that of the people, declared in the Constitution, the judges ought to be governed by the latter rather than the former. They ought to regulate their decisions by the fundamental laws, rather than by those which are not fundamental.

This exercise of judicial discretion, in determining between two contradictory laws, is exemplified in a familiar instance. It not uncommonly happens, that there are two statutes existing at one time, clashing in whole or in part with each other, and neither of them containing any repealing clause or expression. In such a case, it is the province of the courts to liquidate and fix their meaning and operation. So far as they can, by any fair construction, be reconciled to each other, reason and law conspire to dictate that this should be done; where this is impractical, it becomes a matter of necessity to give effect to one, in exclusion of the other. The rule which has obtained in the courts for determining their relative validity is, that the last in order of time shall be preferred to the first. But this is a mere rule of construction, not derived from any positive law, but from the nature and reason of the thing. It is a rule not enjoined upon the courts by legislative provision, but adopted by themselves, as consonant to truth the propriety, for the direction of their conduct as interpreters of the law. They thought it reasonable, that between the interfering acts of an equal authority, that which was the last indication of its will should have the preference.

But in regard to the interfering acts of a superior and subordinate authority, of an original and derivative power, the nature and reason of the thing indicate the converse of that rule as proper to be followed. They teach us that the prior act of a superior ought to be preferred to the subsequent act of an inferior and subordinate authority; and that accordingly, whenever a particular statute contravenes the Constitution, it will be the duty of the judicial tribunals to adhere to the latter and disregard the former.

It can be of no weight to say that the courts, on the pretense of a repugnancy, may substitute their own pleasure to the constitutional intentions of the legislature. This might as well happen in the case of two contradictory statutes; or it might as well happen in every adjudication upon any single statute. The courts must declare the sense of the law; and if they should be disposed to exercise will instead of judgment, the consequence would equally be the substitution of their pleasure to that of the legislative body. The observation, if it prove anything, would prove that there ought to be no judges distinct from that body.

If, then, the courts of justice are to be considered as the bulwarks of a limited Constitution against legislative encroachments, this consideration will afford a strong argument for the permanent tenure of judicial offices, since nothing will contribute so much as this to that independent spirit in the judges which must be essential to the faithful performance of so arduous a duty.

The independence of the judges is equally requisite to guard the Constitution and the rights of individuals from the effects of those ill humors, which the arts of designing men, or the influence of particular conjunctures, sometimes disseminate among the people themselves, and which, though they speedily give place to better information, and more deliberate reflection, have a tendency, in the meantime, to occasion dangerous innovations in the government, and serious oppressions of the minor party in the community. Though I trust the friends of the proposed Constitution will never concur with its enemies, in questioning that fundamental principle of republican government, which admits the right of the people to alter or abolish the established Constitution, whenever they find it inconsistent with their happiness, yet it is not to be inferred from this principle, that the representatives of the people, whenever a momentary inclination happens to lay hold of a majority of their constituents, incompatible with the provisions of the existing Constitution, would, on that account, be justifiable in a violation of those provisions; or that the courts would be under a greater obligation to connive at infractions in this shape, than when they had proceeded wholly from the cabals of the representative body. Until the people have, by some solemn and authoritative act, annulled or changed the established form, it is binding upon themselves collectively, as well as individually; and no presumption, or even knowledge, of their sentiments, can warrant their representatives in a

departure from it, prior to such an act. But it is easy to see, that it would require an uncommon portion of fortitude in the judges to do their duty as faithful guardians of the Constitution, where legislative invasions of it had been instigated by the major voice of the community.

But it is not with a view to infractions of the Constitution only, that the independence of the judges may be an essential safeguard against the effects of occasional ill humors in the society. These sometimes extend no farther than to the injury of the private rights of particular classes of citizens, by unjust and partial laws. Here also the firmness of the judicial magistracy is of vast importance in mitigating the severity and confining the operation of such laws. It not only serves to moderate the immediate mischiefs of those which may have been passed, but it operates as a check upon the legislative body in passing them; who, perceiving that obstacles to the success of iniquitous intention are to be expected from the scruples of the courts, are in a manner compelled, by the very motives of the injustice they meditate, to qualify their attempts. This is a circumstance calculated to have more influence upon the character of our governments, than but few may be aware of. The benefits of the integrity and moderation of the judiciary have already been felt in more States than one; and though they may have displeased those whose sinister expectations they may have disappointed, they must have commanded the esteem and applause of all the virtuous and disinterested. Considerate men, of every description, ought to prize whatever will tend to beget or fortify that temper in the courts; as no man can be sure that he may not be to-morrow the victim of a spirit of injustice, by which he may be a gainer to-day. Any every man must now feel, that the inevitable tendency of such a spirit is to sap the foundations of public and private confidence, and to introduce in its stead universal distrust and distress.

That inflexible and uniform adherence to the rights of the Constitution, and of individuals, which we perceive to be indispensable in the courts of justice, can certainly not be expected from judges who hold their offices by a temporary commission. Periodical appointments, however regulated, or by whomsoever made, would, in some way or other, be fatal to their necessary independence. If the power of making them was committed either to the Executive or legislature, there would be danger of an improper complaisance to the branch which possessed it; if to both, there would be an unwillingness to hazard the displeasure of either; if to the people, or to persons chosen by them for the special purpose, there would be too great a disposition to consult popularity, to justify a reliance that nothing would be consulted but the Constitution and the laws.

Hamilton points to yet another reason why lifetime tenure for federal judges will benefit the public: effective judgments rest on a knowledge of judicial precedents and the law, and such knowledge can only be obtained through experience on the bench. A "temporary duration of office," according to Hamilton, would "discourage individuals [of 'fit character'] from quitting a lucrative practice to serve on the bench" and ultimately would "throw the administration of justice into the hands of the less able, and less well qualified."

There is yet a further and a weightier reason for the permanency of the judicial offices, which is deducible from the nature of the qualifications they require. It has been frequently remarked, with great propriety, that a voluminous code of laws is one of the inconveniences necessarily connected with the advantages of a free government. To avoid an arbitrary discretion in the courts, it is indispensable that they should be bound down by strict rules and precedents, which serve to define and point out their duty in every particular case that comes before them; and it will readily be conceived from the variety of controversies which grow out of the folly and wickedness of mankind, that the records of those precedents must unavoidably swell to a very considerable bulk, and must demand long and laborious study to acquire a competent knowledge of them. Hence it is, that there can be but few men in the society who will have sufficient skill in the laws to qualify them for the stations of judges. And making the proper deductions for the ordinary depravity of human nature, the number must be still smaller of those who unite the requisite integrity with the requisite knowledge. These considerations apprise us, that the government can have no great option between fit character; and that a temporary duration in office, which would naturally discourage such characters from quitting a lucrative line of practice to accept a seat on the bench, would have a tendency to throw the administration of justice into hands less able, and less well qualified, to conduct it with utility and dignity. In the present circumstances of this country, and in those in which it is likely to be for a long time to come, the disadvantages on this score would be greater than they may at first sight appear; but it must be confessed, that they are far inferior to those which present themselves under other aspects of the subject.

Upon the whole, there can be no room to doubt that the convention acted wisely in copying from the models of those constitutions which have established good behavior as the tenure of their judicial offices, in point of duration; and that so far from being blamable on this account, their plan would have been inexcusably defective, if it had wanted this important feature of good government. The experience of Great Britain affords an illustrious comment on the excellence of the institution.

Publius
(Alexander Hamilton)

APPENDIX E
Justices of the U.S. Supreme Court since 1900

Chief Justices

NAME	YEARS OF SERVICE	STATE APP'T FROM	APPOINTING PRESIDENT	AGE APP'T	POLITICAL AFFILIATION	EDUCATIONAL BACKGROUND*
Fuller, Melville Weston	1888–1910	Illinois	Cleveland	55	Democrat	Bowdoin College; studied at Harvard Law School
White, Edward Douglass	1910–1921	Louisiana	Taft	65	Democrat	Mount St. Mary's College; Georgetown College (now University)
Taft, William Howard	1921–1930	Connecticut	Harding	64	Republican	Yale; Cincinnati Law School
Hughes, Charles Evans	1930–1941	New York	Hoover	68	Republican	Colgate University; Brown; Columbia Law School
Stone, Harlan Fiske	1941–1946	New York	Roosevelt, F.	69	Republican	Amherst College; Columbia
Vinson, Frederick Moore	1946–1953	Kentucky	Truman	56	Democrat	Centre College
Warren, Earl	1953–1969	California	Eisenhower	62	Republican	University of California, Berkeley
Burger, Warren Earl	1969–1986	Virginia	Nixon	62	Republican	University of Minnesota; St. Paul College of Law (Mitchell College)
Rehnquist, William Hubbs	1986–	Virginia	Reagan	62	Republican	Stanford; Harvard; Stanford University Law School

*SOURCE: Educational background information derived from Elder Witt, *Guide to the U.S. Supreme Court,* 2d ed. (Washington, D.C.: Congressional Quarterly Press, Inc., 1990). Reprinted with the permission of the publisher.

Associate Justices

NAME	YEARS OF SERVICE	STATE APP'T FROM	APPOINTING PRESIDENT	AGE APP'T	POLITICAL AFFILIATION	EDUCATIONAL BACKGROUND*
Harlan, John Marshall	1877–1911	Kentucky	Hayes	61	Republican	Centre College; studied law at Transylvania University
Gray, Horace	1882–1902	Massachusetts	Arthur	54	Republican	Harvard College; Harvard Law School
Brewer, David Josiah	1890–1910	Kansas	Harrison	53	Republican	Wesleyan University; Yale; Albany Law School
Brown, Henry Billings	1891–1906	Michigan	Harrison	55	Republican	Yale; studied at Yale Law School and Harvard Law School
Shiras, George, Jr.	1892–1903	Pennsylvania	Harrison	61	Republican	Ohio University; Yale; studied law at Yale and privately
White, Edward Douglass	1894–1910	Louisiana	Cleveland	49	Democrat	Mount St. Mary's College; Georgetown College (now University)

Associate Justices (continued)

Name	Years of Service	State App't From	Appointing President	Age App't	Political Affiliation	Educational Background*
Peckham, Rufus Wheeler	1896–1909	New York	Cleveland	58	Democrat	Read law in father's firm
McKenna, Joseph	1898–1925	California	McKinley	55	Republican	Benicia Collegiate Institute, Law Dept.
Holmes, Oliver Wendell, Jr.	1902–1932	Massachusetts	Roosevelt, T.	61	Republican	Harvard College; studied law at Harvard Law School
Day, William Rufus	1903–1922	Ohio	Roosevelt, T.	54	Republican	University of Michigan; University of Michigan Law School
Moody, William Henry	1906–1910	Massachusetts	Roosevelt, T.	53	Republican	Harvard; Harvard Law School
Lurton, Horace Harmon	1910–1914	Tennessee	Taft	66	Democrat	University of Chicago; Cumberland Law School
Hughes, Charles Evans	1910–1916	New York	Taft	48	Republican	Colgate University; Brown University; Columbia Law School
Van Devanter, Willis	1911–1937	Wyoming	Taft	52	Republican	Indiana Asbury University; University of Cincinnati Law School
Lamar, Joseph Rucker	1911–1916	Georgia	Taft	54	Democrat	University of Georgia; Bethany College; Washington and Lee University
Pitney, Mahlon	1912–1922	New Jersey	Taft	54	Republican	College of New Jersey (Princeton); read law under father
McReynolds, James Clark	1914–1941	Tennessee	Wilson	52	Democrat	Vanderbilt University; University of Virginia
Brandeis, Louis Dembitz	1916–1939	Massachusetts	Wilson	60	Democrat	Harvard Law School
Clarke, John Hessin	1916–1922	Ohio	Wilson	59	Democrat	Western Reserve University; read law under father
Sutherland, George	1922–1938	Utah	Harding	60	Republican	Brigham Young Academy; one year at University of Michigan Law School
Butler, Pierce	1923–1939	Minnesota	Harding	57	Democrat	Carleton College
Sanford, Edward Terry	1923–1930	Tennessee	Harding	58	Republican	University of Tennessee; Harvard; Harvard Law School
Stone, Harlan Fiske	1925–1941	New York	Coolidge	53	Republican	Amherst College; Columbia University Law School
Roberts, Owen Josephus	1930–1945	Pennsylvania	Hoover	55	Republican	University of Pennsylvania; University of Pennsylvania Law School
Cardozo, Benjamin Nathan	1932–1938	New York	Hoover	62	Democrat	Columbia University; two years at Columbia Law School
Black, Hugo Lafayette	1937–1971	Alabama	Roosevelt, F.	51	Democrat	Birmingham Medical College; University of Alabama Law School
Reed, Stanley Forman	1938–1957	Kentucky	Roosevelt, F.	54	Democrat	Kentucky Wesleyan University; Foreman Yale; studied law at University of Virginia and Columbia University; University of Paris
Frankfurter, Felix	1939–1962	Massachusetts	Roosevelt, F.	57	Independent	College of the City of New York; Harvard Law School
Douglas, William Orville	1939–1975	Connecticut	Roosevelt, F.	41	Democrat	Whitman College; Columbia University Law School

Associate Justices (continued)

NAME	YEARS OF SERVICE	STATE APP'T FROM	APPOINTING PRESIDENT	AGE APP'T	POLITICAL AFFILIATION	EDUCATIONAL BACKGROUND*
Murphy, Frank	1940–1949	Michigan	Roosevelt, F.	50	Democrat	University of Michigan; Lincoln's Inn, London; Trinity College
Byrnes, James Francis	1941–1942	South Carolina	Roosevelt, F.	62	Democrat	Read law privately
Jackson, Robert Houghwout	1941–1954	New York	Roosevelt, F.	49	Democrat	Albany Law School
Rutledge, Wiley Blount	1943–1949	Iowa	Roosevelt, F.	49	Democrat	University of Wisconsin; University of Colorado
Burton, Harold Hitz	1945–1958	Ohio	Truman	57	Republican	Bowdoin College; Harvard University Law School
Clark, Thomas Campbell	1949–1967	Texas	Truman	50	Democrat	University of Texas
Minton, Sherman	1949–1956	Indiana	Truman	59	Democrat	Indiana University College of Law; Yale Law School
Harlan, John Marshall	1955–1971	New York	Eisenhower	56	Republican	Princeton; Oxford University; New York Law School
Brennan, William J., Jr.	1956–1990	New Jersey	Eisenhower	50	Democrat	University of Pennsylvania; Harvard Law School
Whittaker, Charles Evans	1957–1962	Missouri	Eisenhower	56	Republican	University of Kansas City Law School
Stewart, Potter	1958–1981	Ohio	Eisenhower	43	Republican	Yale; Yale Law School
White, Byron Raymond	1962–1993	Colorado	Kennedy	45	Democrat	University of Colorado; Oxford University; Yale Law School
Goldberg, Arthur Joseph	1962–1965	Illinois	Kennedy	54	Democrat	Northwestern University
Fortas, Abe	1965–1969	Tennessee	Johnson, L.	55	Democrat	Southwestern College; Yale Law School
Marshall, Thurgood	1967–1991	New York	Johnson, L.	59	Democrat	Lincoln University; Howard University Law School
Blackmun, Harry A.	1970–1994	Minnesota	Nixon	62	Republican	Harvard; Harvard Law School
Powell, Lewis F., Jr.	1972–1987	Virginia	Nixon	65	Democrat	Washington and Lee University; Washington and Lee University Law School; Harvard Law School
Rehnquist, William H.	1972–1986	Arizona	Nixon	48	Republican	Stanford; Harvard; Stanford University Law School
Stevens, John Paul	1975–	Illinois	Ford	55	Republican	University of Colorado; Northwestern University Law School
O'Connor, Sandra Day	1981–	Arizona	Reagan	51	Republican	Stanford; Stanford University Law School
Scalia, Antonin	1986–	Virginia	Reagan	50	Republican	Georgetown University; Harvard Law School
Kennedy, Anthony M.	1988–	California	Reagan	52	Republican	Stanford; London School of Economics; Harvard Law School
Souter, David Hackett	1990–	New Hampshire	Bush	51	Republican	Harvard; Oxford University
Thomas, Clarence	1991–	District of Columbia	Bush	43	Republican	Holy Cross College; Yale Law School
Ginsburg, Ruth Bader	1993–	District of Columbia	Clinton	60	Democrat	Cornell University; Columbia Law School
Breyer, Stephen, G.	1994–	Massachusetts	Clinton	55	Democrat	Stanford University; Oxford University; Harvard Law School

CONGRESS	YEARS	PRESIDENT	MAJORITY PARTY IN HOUSE	MAJORITY PARTY IN SENATE
57th	1901–1903	T. Roosevelt	Republican	Republican
58th	1903–1905	T. Roosevelt	Republican	Republican
59th	1905–1907	T. Roosevelt	Republican	Republican
60th	1907–1909	T. Roosevelt	Republican	Republican
61st	1909–1911	Taft	Republican	Republican
62d	1911–1913	Taft	Democratic	Republican
63d	1913–1915	Wilson	Democratic	Democratic
64th	1915–1917	Wilson	Democratic	Democratic
65th	1917–1919	Wilson	Democratic	Democratic
66th	1919–1921	Wilson	Republican	Republican
67th	1921–1923	Harding	Republican	Republican
68th	1923–1925	Coolidge	Republican	Republican
69th	1925–1927	Coolidge	Republican	Republican
70th	1927–1929	Coolidge	Republican	Republican
71st	1929–1931	Hoover	Republican	Republican
72d	1931–1933	Hoover	Democratic	Republican
73d	1933–1935	F. Roosevelt	Democratic	Democratic
74th	1935–1937	F. Roosevelt	Democratic	Democratic
75th	1937–1939	F. Roosevelt	Democratic	Democratic
76th	1939–1941	F. Roosevelt	Democratic	Democratic
77th	1941–1943	F. Roosevelt	Democratic	Democratic
78th	1943–1945	F. Roosevelt	Democratic	Democratic
79th	1945–1947	Truman	Democratic	Democratic
80th	1947–1949	Truman	Republican	Democratic
81st	1949–1951	Truman	Democratic	Democratic
82d	1951–1953	Truman	Democratic	Democratic
83d	1953–1955	Eisenhower	Republican	Republican
84th	1955–1957	Eisenhower	Democratic	Democratic
85th	1957–1959	Eisenhower	Democratic	Democratic
86th	1959–1961	Eisenhower	Democratic	Democratic
87th	1961–1963	Kennedy	Democratic	Democratic
88th	1963–1965	Kennedy/Johnson	Democratic	Democratic
89th	1965–1967	Johnson	Democratic	Democratic
90th	1967–1969	Johnson	Democratic	Democratic
91st	1969–1971	Nixon	Democratic	Democratic
92d	1971–1973	Nixon	Democratic	Democratic
93d	1973–1975	Nixon/Ford	Democratic	Democratic
94th	1975–1977	Ford	Democratic	Democratic
95th	1977–1979	Carter	Democratic	Democratic
96th	1979–1981	Carter	Democratic	Democratic
97th	1981–1983	Reagan	Democratic	Republican
98th	1983–1985	Reagan	Democratic	Republican
99th	1985–1987	Reagan	Democratic	Republican
100th	1987–1989	Reagan	Democratic	Democratic
101st	1989–1991	G. H. W. Bush	Democratic	Democratic
102d	1991–1993	G. H. W. Bush	Democratic	Democratic
103d	1993–1995	Clinton	Democratic	Democratic
104th	1995–1997	Clinton	Republican	Republican
105th	1997–1999	Clinton	Republican	Republican
106th	1999–2001	Clinton	Republican	Republican
107th	2001–2003	G. W. Bush	Republican	Democratic
108th	2003–2005	G. W. Bush	Republican	Republican

APPENDIX G
Spanish Equivalents for Important Terms in American Government

Acid Rain: Lluvia Acida
Acquisitive Model: Modelo Adquisitivo
Actionable: Procesable, Enjuiciable
Action-reaction
Syndrome: Sídrome de Acción y Reacción
Actual Malice: Malicia Expresa
Administrative Agency: Agencia Administrativa
Advice and Consent: Consejo y Consentimiento
Affirmative Action: Acción Afirmativa
Affirm: Afirmar
Agenda Setting: Agenda Establecida
Aid to Families with Dependent Children (AFDC): Ayuda para Familias con Niños Dependientes
Amicus Curiae **Brief:** Tercer persona o grupo no involucrado en el caso, admitido en un juicio para hacer valer el intéres público o el de un grupo social importante.
Anarchy: Anarquía
Anti-Federalists: Anti-Federalistas
Appellate Court: Corte de Apelación
Appointment Power: Poder de Apuntamiento
Appropriation: Apropiación
Aristocracy: Aristocracia
Attentive Public: Público Atento
Australian Ballot: Voto Australiano
Authority: Autoridad
Authorization: Autorización

Bad-Tendency Rule: Regla de Tendencia-mala
"Beauty Contest": Concurso de Belleza
Bicameralism: Bicameralismo
Bicameral Legislature: Legislatura Bicameral
Bill of Rights: Declaración de Derechos
Blanket Primary: Primaria Comprensiva
Block Grants: Concesiones de Bloque
Bureaucracy: Burocracia
Busing: Transporte público

Cabinet: Gabinete, Consejo de Ministros
Cabinet Department: Departamento del Gabinete
Cadre: El núcleo de activistas de partidos políticos encargados de cumplir las funciones importantes de los partidos políticos americanos.
Canvassing Board: Consejo encargado con la encuesta de una violación.
Capture: Captura, toma
Casework: Trabajo de Caso
Categorical Grants-in-Aid: Concesiones Categóricas de Ayuda
Caucus: Reunión de Dirigentes
Challenge: Reto
Checks and Balances: Chequeos y Equilibrio
Chief Diplomat: Jefe Diplomático

Chief Executive: Jefe Ejecutivo
Chief Legislator: Jefe Legislador
Chief of Staff: Jefe de Personal
Chief of State: Jefe de Estado
Civil Law: Derecho Civil
Civil Liberties: Libertades Civiles
Civil Rights: Derechos Civiles
Civil Service: Servicio Civil
Civil Service Commission: Comisión de Servicio Civil
Class-action Suit: Demanda en representación de un grupo o clase.
Class Politics: Política de Clase
Clear and Present Danger Test: Prueba de Peligro Claro y Presente
Climate Control: Control de Clima
Closed Primary: Primaria Cerrada
Cloture: Cierre al voto
Coattail Effect: Effecto de Cola de Chaqueta
Cold War: Guerra Fría
Commander in Chief: Comandante en Jefe
Commerce Clause: Clausula de Comercio
Commercial Speech: Discurso Comercial
Common Law: Ley Común, Derecho Consuetudinario
Comparable Worth: Valor Comparable
Compliance: De acuerdo
Concurrent Majority: Mayoría Concurrente
Concurring Opinion: Opinión Concurrente

Confederal System: Sistema Confederal
Confederation: Confederación
Conference Committee: Comité de Conferencia
Consensus: Concenso
Consent of the People: Consentimiento de la Gente
Conservatism: Calidad de Conservador
Conservative Coalition: Coalición Conservadora
Consolidation: Consolidación
Constant Dollars: Dólares Constantes
Constitutional Initiative: Iniciativa Constitucional
Constitutional Power: Poder Constitucional
Containment: Contenimiento
Continuing Resolution: Resolució Contínua
Cooley's Rule: Régla de Cooley
Cooperative Federalism: Federalismo Cooperativo
Corrupt Practices Acts: Leyes Contra Acciones Corruptas
Council of Economic Advisers (CEA): Consejo de Asesores Económicos
Council of Government (COG): Consejo de Gobierno
County: Condado
Credentials Committee: Comité de Credenciales
Criminal Law: Ley Criminal

De Facto **Segregation:** Segregación de Hecho
De Jure **Segregation:** Segregación Cotidiana
Defamation of Character: Defamación de Carácter
Democracy: Democracia
Democratic Party: Partido Democratico
Dillon's Rule: Régla de Dillon
Diplomacy: Diplomácia
Direct Democracy: Democracia Directa
Direct Primary: Primaria Directa
Direct Technique: Técnica Directa
Discharge Petition: Petición de Descargo

Dissenting Opinion: Opinión Disidente
Divisive Opinion: Opinión Divisiva
Domestic Policy: Principio Político Doméstico
Dual Citizenship: Ciudadanía Dual
Dual Federalism: Federalismo Dual
Détente: No Spanish equivalent.

Economic Aid: Ayuda Económica
Economic Regulation: Regulación Económica
Elastic Clause, or Necessary and Proper Clause: Cláusula Flexible o Cláusula Propia Necesaria
Elector: Elector
Electoral College: Colegio Electoral
Electronic Media: Media Electronica
Elite: Elite (el selecto)
Elite Theory: Teoría Elitista (de lo selecto)
Emergency Power: Poder de Emergencia
Enumerated Power: Poder Enumerado
Environmental Impact Statement (EIS): Afirmación de Impacto Ambiental
Equality: Igualdad
Equalization: Igualación
Equal Employment Opportunity Commission (EEOC): Comisión de Igualdad de Oportunidad en el Empleo
Era of Good Feeling: Era de Buen Sentimiento
Era of Personal Politics: Era de Política Personal
Establishment Clause: Cláusula de Establecimiento
Euthanasia: Eutanasia
Exclusionary Rule: Regla de Exclusión
Executive Agreement: Acuerdo Ejecutivo
Executive Budget: Presupuesto Ejecutivo
Executive Office of the President (EOP): Oficina Ejecutiva del Presidente
Executive Order: Orden Ejecutivo
Executive Privilege: Privilegio Ejecutivo

Expressed Power: Poder Expresado
Extradite: Entregar por Extradición

Faction: Facción
Fairness Doctrine: Doctrina de Justicia
Fall Review: Revision de Otoño
Federalist: Federalista
Federal Mandate: Mandato Federal
Federal Open Market Committee (FOMC): Comité Federal de Libre Mercado
Federal Register: Registro Federal
Federal System: Sistema Federal
Federalists: Federalistas
Fighting Words: Palabras de Provocación
Filibuster: Obstrucción de iniciativas de ley
Fireside Chat: Charla de Hogar
First Budget Resolution: Resolució Primera Presupuesta
First Continental Congress: Primér Congreso Continental
Fiscal Policy: Politico Fiscal
Fiscal Year (FY): Año Fiscal
Fluidity: Fluidez
Food Stamps: Estampillas para Comida
Foreign Policy: Politica Extranjera
Foreign Policy Process: Proceso de Politica Extranjera
Franking: Franqueando
Fraternity: Fraternidad
Free Exercise Clause: Cláusula de Ejercicio Libre
Full Faith and Credit Clause: Cláusula de Completa Fé y Crédito
Functional Consolidation: Consolidación Funcional
Gag Order: Orden de Silencio
Garbage Can Model: Modelo Bote de Basura
Gender Gap: Brecha de Género
General Law City: Regla General Urbana
General Sales Tax: Impuesto General de Ventas
Generational Effect: Efecto Generacional
Gerrymandering: División arbitraria de los distritos electorales con fines políticos.
Government: Gobierno

Government Corporation: Corporación Gubernamental

Government in the Sunshine Act: Gobierno en la acta: Luz del Sol

Grandfather Clause: Clausula del Abuelo

Grand Jury: Gran Jurado

Great Compromise: Grán Acuerdo de Negociación

Hatch Act (Political Activities Act): Acta Hatch (acta de actividades politicas)

Hecklers' Veto: Veto de Abuchamiento

Home Rule City: Regla Urbana

Horizontal Federalism: Federalismo Horizontal

Hyperpluralism: Hiperpluralismo

Ideologue: Ideólogo

Ideology: Ideología

Image Building: Construcción de Imágen

Impeachment: Acción Penal Contra un Funcionario Público

Inalienable Rights: Derechos Inalienables

Income Transfer: Transferencia de Ingresos

Incorporation Theory: Teoría de Incorporación

Independent: Independiente

Independent Candidate: Candidato Independiente

Independent Executive Agency: Agencia Ejecutiva Independiente

Independent Regulatory Agency: Agencia Regulatoria Independiente

Indirect Technique: Técnica Indirecta

Inherent Power: Poder Inherente

Initiative: Iniciativa

Injunction: Injunción, Prohibición Judicial

Institution: Institución

Instructed Delegate: Delegado con Instrucciones

Intelligence Community: Comunidad de Inteligencia

Intensity: Intensidad

Interest Group: Grupo de Interés

Interposition: Interposición

Interstate Compact: Compacto Interestatal

In-kind Subsidy: Subsidio de Clase

Iron Curtain: Cortina de Acero

Iron Triangle: Triágulo de Acero

Isolationist Foreign Policy: Politica Extranjera de Aislamiento

Issue Voting: Voto Temático

Item Veto: Artículo de Veto

Jim Crow Laws: No Spanish equivalent.

Joint Committee: Comité Mancomunado

Judicial Activism: Activismo Judicial

Judicial Implementation: Implementacion Judicial

Judicial Restraint: Restricción Judicial

Judicial Review: Revisión Judicial

Jurisdiction: Jurisdicción

Justiciable Dispute: Disputa Judiciaria

Justiciable Question: Pregunta Justiciable

Keynesian Economics: Economía Keynesiana

Kitchen Cabinet: Gabinete de Cocina

Labor Movement: Movimiento Laboral

Latent Public Opinion: Opinión Pública Latente

Lawmaking: Hacedores de Ley

Legislative History: Historia Legislativa

Legislative Initiative: Iniciativa de legislación

Legislative Veto: Veto Legislativo

Legislature: Legislatura

Legitimacy: Legitimidad

Libel: Libelo, Difamación Escrita

Liberalism: Liberalismo

Liberty: Libertad

Limited Government: Gobierno Limitado

Line Organization: Organización de Linea

Literacy Test: Exámen de alfabetización

Litigate: Litigar

Lobbying: Cabildeo

Logrolling: Práctica legislativa que consiste en incluir en un mismo proyecto de ley temas de diversa ídole.

Loophole: Hueco Legal, escapatoria

Madisonian Model: Modelo Madisónico

Majority: Mayoría

Majority Floor Leader: Líder Mayoritario de Piso

Majority Leader of the House: Líder Mayoritario de la Casa

Majority Opinion: Opinión Mayoritaria

Majority Rule: Regla de Mayoría

Managed News: Noticias Manipuladas

Mandatory Retirement: Retiro Mandatorio

Matching Funds: Fondos Combinados

Material Incentive: Incentivo Material

Media: Media

Media Access: Acceso de Media

Merit System: Sistema de Mérito

Military-Industrial Complex: Complejo Industriomilitar

Minority Floor Leader: Líder Minoritario de Piso

Minority Leader of the House: Líder Minorial del Cuerpo Legislativo

Monetary Policy: Politica Monetaria

Monopolistic Model: Modelo Monopólico

Monroe Doctrine: Doctrina Monroe

Moral Idealism: Idealismo Moral

Municipal Home Rule: Regla Municipal

Narrow Casting: Mensaje Dirigído

National Committee: Comité Nacional

National Convention: Convención Nacional

National Politics: Politica Nacional

National Security Council (NSC): Concilio de Seguridad Nacional

National Security Policy: Politica de Seguridad Nacional

Natural Aristocracy: Aristocracia Natural

Natural Rights: Derechos Naturales

Necessaries: Necesidades

Negative Constituents: Constituyentes Negativos

New England Town: Pueblo de Nueva Inglaterra

New Federalism: Federalismo Nuevo
Nullification: Nulidad, Anulación

Office-Block, or Massachusetts, Ballot: Cuadro-Oficina, o Massachusetts, Voto
Office of Management and Budget (OMB): Oficina de Administració y Presupuesto
Oligarchy: Oligarquía
Ombudsman: Funcionario que representa al ciudadano ante el gobierno.
Open Primary: Primaria Abierta
Opinion: Opinión
Opinion Leader: Líder de Opinión
Opinion Poll: Encuesta, Conjunto de Opinión
Oral Arguments: Argumentos Orales
Oversight: Inadvertencia, Omisión

Paid-for-Political Announcement: Anuncios Politicos Pagados
Pardon: Perdón
Party-Column, or Indiana, Ballot: Partido-Columna, o Indiana, Voto
Party Identification: Identificación de Partido
Party Identifier: Identificador de Partido
Party-in-Electorate: Partido Electoral
Party-in-Government: Partido en Gobierno
Party Organization: Organización de Partido
Party Platform: Plataforma de Partido
Patronage: Patrocinio
Peer Group: Grupo de Contemporáneos
Pendleton Act (Civil Service Reform Act): Acta Pendleton (Acta de Reforma al Servicio Civil)
Personal Attack Rule: Regla de Ataque Personal
Petit Jury: Jurado Ordinario
Pluralism: Pluralismo
Plurality: Pluralidad
Pocket Veto: Veto de Bolsillo
Police Power: Poder Policiaco
Policy Trade-offs: Intercambio de Politicas

Political Action Committee (PAC): Comité de Acción Política
Political Consultant: Consultante Político
Political Culture: Cultura Politica
Political Party: Partido Político
Political Question: Pregunta Politica
Political Realism: Realismo Político
Political Socialization: Socialización Politica
Political Tolerance: Tolerancia Política
Political Trust: Confianza Política
Politico: Político
Politics: Politica
Poll Tax: Impuesto sobre el sufragio
Poll Watcher: Observador de Encuesta
Popular Sovereignty: Soberanía Popular
Power: Poder
Precedent: Precedente
Preferred-Position Test: Prueba de Posición Preferida
Presidential Primary: Primaria Presidencial
President Pro Tempore: Presidente Provisoriamente
Press Secretary: Secretaría de Prensa
Prior Restraint: Restricción Anterior
Privileges and Immunities: Privilégios e Imunidades
Privitization, or Contracting Out: Privatización
Property: Propiedad
Property Tax: Impuesto de Propiedad
Public Agenda: Agenda Pública
Public Debt Financing: Financiamiento de Deuda Pública
Public Debt, or National Debt: Deuda Pública o Nacional
Public Interest: Interes Público
Public Opinion: Opinión Pública
Purposive Incentive: Incentivo de Propósito

Ratification: Ratificación
Rational Ignorance Effect: Effecto de Ignorancia Racional
Reapportionment: Redistribución
Recall: Suspender
Recognition Power: Poder de Reconocimiento

Recycling: Reciclaje
Redistricting: Redistrictificación
Referendum: Referédum
Registration: Registración
Regressive Tax: Impuestos Regresivos
Relevance: Pertinencia
Remand: Reenviar
Representation: Representación
Representative Assembly: Asamblea Representativa
Representative Democracy: Democracia Representativa
Reprieve: Trequa, Suspensión
Republic: República
Republican Party: Partido Republicano
Resulting Powers: Poderes Resultados
Reverse: Cambiarse a lo contrario
Reverse Discrimination: Discriminación Reversiva
Rules Committee: Comité Regulador
Rule of Four: Regla de Cuatro
Run-off Primary: Primaria Residual

Safe Seat: Asiento Seguro
Sampling Error: Error de Encuesta
Secession: Secesión
Second Budget Resolution: Resolución Segunda Presupuestal
Second Continental Congress: Segundo Congreso Continental
Sectional Politics: Política Seccional
Segregation: Segregación
Selectperson: Persona Selecta
Select Committee: Comité Selecto
Senatorial Courtesy: Cortesia Senatorial
Seniority System: Sistema Señiorial
Separate-but-Equal Doctrine: Separados pero iguales
Separation of Powers: Separación de Poderes
Service Sector: Sector de Servicio
Sexual Harassment: Acosamiento Sexual
Sex Discrimination: Discriminacion Sexual
Slander: Difamación Oral, Calumnia
Sliding-Scale Test: Prueba Escalonada
Social Movement: Movimiento Social

Social Security: Seguridad Social
Socioeconomic Status: Estado Socioeconómico
Solidary Incentive: Incentivo de Solideridad
Solid South: Súr Sólido
Sound Bite: Mordida de Sonido
Soviet Bloc: Bloque Soviético
Speaker of the House: Vocero de la Casa
Spin: Girar/Giro
Spin Doctor: Doctor en Giro
Spin-off Party: Partido Estático
Spoils System: Sistema de Despojos
Spring Review: Revisión de Primavera
Stare Decisis: El principio característico del ley comú por el cual los precedentes jurisprudenciales tienen fuerza obligatoria, no sólo entre las partes, sino tambien para casos sucesivos análogos.
Stability: Estabilidad
Standing Committee: Comité de Sostenimiento
State Central Committee: Comité Central del Estado
State: Estado
State of the Union Message: Mensaje Sobre el Estado de la Unión
Statutory Power: Poder Estatorial
Strategic Arms Limitation Treaty (SALT I): Tratado de Limitación de Armas Estratégicas
Subpoena: Orden de Testificación
Subsidy: Subsidio
Suffrage: Sufrágio
Sunset Legislation: Legislación Sunset
Superdelegate: Líder de partido o oficial elegido quien tiene el derecho de votar.

Supplemental Security Income (SSI): Ingresos de Seguridad Suplementaria
Supremacy Clause: Cláusula de Supremacia
Supremacy Doctrine: Doctrina de Supremacia
Symbolic Speech: Discurso Simbólico

Technical Assistance: Asistencia Técnica
Third Party: Tercer Partido
Third-party Candidate: Candidato de Tercer Partido
Ticket Splitting: División de Boletos
Totalitarian Regime: Régimen Totalitario
Town Manager System: Sistema de Administrador Municipal
Town Meeting: Junta Municipal
Township: Municipio
Tracking Poll: Seguimiento de Encuesta
Trial Court: Tribunal de Primera
Truman Doctrine: Doctrina Truman
Trustee: Depositario
Twelfth Amendment: Doceava Enmienda
Twenty-fifth Amendment: Veinticincoava Enmienda
Two-Party System: Sistema de Dos Partidos

Unanimous Opinion: Opinión Unánime
Underground Economy: Economía Subterráea
Unicameral Legislature: Legislatura Unicameral
Unincorporated Area: Area no Incorporada
Unit Rule: Regla de Unidad
Unitary System: Sistema Unitario

Universal Suffrage: Sufragio Universal
U.S. Treasury Bond: Bono de la Tesoreria de E.U.A.

Veto Message: Comunicado de Veto
Voter Turnout: Renaimiento de Votantes

War Powers Act: Acta de Poderes de Guerra
Washington Community: Comunidad de Washington
Weberian Model: Modelo Weberiano
Whip: Látigo
Whistleblower: Privatización o Contratista
White House Office: Oficina de la Casa Blanca
White House Press Corps: Cuerpo de Prensa de la Casa Blanca
White Primary: Sufragio en Elección Primaria/Blancos Solamente
Writ of Certiorari: Prueba de certeza; orden emitida por el tribunal de apelaciones para que el tribunal inferior dé lugar a la apelación.
Writ of Habeas Corpus: Prueba de Evidencia Concreta
Writ of Mandamus: Un mandato por la corte para que un acto se lleve a cabo.

Yellow Journalism: Amarillismo Periodístico

Glossary

A

Acquisitive Model   A model of bureaucracy that views top-level bureaucrats as seeking constantly to expand the size of their budgets and the staffs of their departments or agencies so as to gain greater power and influence in the public sector.

Action-Reaction Syndrome   For every action on the part of government, there is a reaction on the part of the affected public. Then the government attempts to counter the reaction with another action, which starts the cycle all over again.

Actual Malice   Actual malice in libel cases generally consists of intentionally publishing any written or printed statement that is injurious to the character of another with either knowledge of the statement's falsity or a reckless disregard for the truth.

Administrative Agency   A federal, state, or local government unit established to perform a specific function. Administrative agencies are created and authorized by legislative bodies to administer and enforce specific laws.

Advice and Consent   The power vested in the U.S. Senate by the Constitution (Article II, Section 2) to give its advice and consent to the president on treaties and presidential appointments.

Affirm   To declare that a court ruling is valid and must stand.

Affirmative Action   A policy in educational admissions or job hiring that gives special consideration or compensatory treatment to traditionally disadvantaged groups in an effort to overcome present effects of past discrimination.

Agenda Setting   Determining which public-policy questions will be debated or considered by Congress.

Amicus Curiae Brief   A brief (a document containing a legal argument supporting a desired outcome in a particular case) filed by a third party, or amicus curiae (Latin for "friend of the court"), who is not directly involved in the litigation but who has an interest in the outcome of the case.

Anarchy   The condition of having no government and no laws. Each member of the society governs himself or herself.

Anti-Federalist   An individual who opposed the ratification of the new Constitution in 1787. The Anti-Federalists were opposed to a strong central government.

Appellate Court   A court having jurisdiction to review cases and issues that were originally tried in lower courts.

Appointment Power   The authority vested in the president to fill a government office or position. Positions filled by presidential appointment include those in the executive branch and the federal judiciary, commissioned officers in the armed forces, and members of the independent regulatory commissions.

Appropriation   The passage, by Congress, of a spending bill, specifying the amount of authorized funds that actually will be allocated for an agency's use.

Aristocracy   Rule by the best suited, through virtue, talent, or education; in later usage, rule by the upper class.

Attentive Public   That portion of the general public that pays attention to policy issues.

Australian Ballot   A secret ballot prepared, distributed, and tabulated by government officials at public expense. Since 1888, all states have used the Australian ballot rather than an open, public ballot.

Authority   The features of a leader or an institution that compel obedience, usually because of ascribed legitimacy. For most societies, government is the ultimate authority.

Authorization   A formal declaration by a legislative committee that a certain amount of funding may be available to an agency. Some authorizations terminate in a year; others are renewable automatically without further congressional action.

B

Bad-Tendency Rule   A rule stating that speech or other First Amendment freedoms may be curtailed if there is a possibility that such expression might lead to some "evil."

"Beauty Contest"   A presidential primary in which contending candidates compete for popular votes but the results have little or no impact on the selection of delegates to the national convention, which is made by the party elite.

Bias   An inclination or a preference that interferes with impartial judgment.

Bicameral Legislature   A legislature made up of two chambers, or parts. The U.S. Congress, composed of the House of Representatives and the Senate, is a bicameral legislature.

Bicameralism   The division of a legislature into two separate assemblies.

Block Grants   Federal programs that provide funds to state and local governments for general functional areas, such as criminal justice or mental-health programs.

Bundling   The practice of adding together maximum individual campaign contributions to increase their impact on the candidate.

Bureaucracy   A large organization that is structured hierarchically to carry out specific functions.

Busing   The transportation of public school students from areas where they live to schools in other areas to eliminate school segregation based on residential patterns.

C

Cabinet   An advisory group selected by the president to aid in making decisions. The cabinet currently numbers thirteen department secretaries and the attorney general. Depending on the president, the cabinet may be highly influential or relatively insignificant in its advisory role.

Cabinet Department   One of the fourteen departments of the executive branch (State, Treasury, Defense, Justice, Interior, Agriculture, Commerce,

Labor, Health and Human Services, Housing and Urban Development, Education, Energy, Transportation, and Veterans Affairs).

Capture   The act of gaining direct or indirect control over agency personnel and decision makers by the industry that is being regulated.

Case Law   The rules and principles announced in court decisions. Case law includes judicial interpretations of common law principles and doctrines as well as interpretations of constitutional law, statutory law, and administrative law.

Casework   Personal work for constituents by members of Congress.

Categorical Grants-in-Aid   Federal grants-in-aid to states or local governments that are for very specific programs or projects.

Caucus   A closed meeting of party leaders to select party candidates or to decide on policy; also, a meeting of party members designed to select candidates and propose policies.

Charter   A document issued by a government that grants to a person, a group of persons, or a corporation the right to carry on one or more specific activities. A state government can grant a charter to a municipality allowing that group of persons to carry on specific activities.

Checks and Balances   A major principle of the American government system whereby each branch of the government exercises a check on the actions of the others.

Chief Diplomat   The role of the president in recognizing foreign governments, making treaties, and making executive agreements.

Chief Executive   The role of the president as head of the executive branch of the government.

Chief Legislator   The role of the president in influencing the making of laws.

Chief of Staff   The person who is named to direct the White House Office and advise the president.

Chief of State   The role of the president as ceremonial head of the government.

Civil Law   The law regulating conduct between private persons over noncriminal matters. Under civil law, the government provides the forum for the settlement of disputes between private parties in such matters as contracts, domestic relations, and business relations.

Civil Liberties   Those personal freedoms that are protected for all individuals and that generally deal with individual freedom. Civil liberties typically involve restraining the government's actions against individuals.

Civil Rights   Generally, all rights rooted in the Fourteenth Amendment's guarantee of equal protection under the law.

Civil Service   A collective term for the body of employees working for the government. Generally, civil service is understood to apply to all those who gain government employment through a merit system.

Civil Service Commission   The initial central personnel agency of the national government; created in 1883.

Class Politics   Political preferences based on income level, social status, or both.

Class-Action Suit   A lawsuit filed by an individual seeking damages for "all persons similarly situated."

Clear and Present Danger Test   The test proposed by Justice Holmes for determining when government may restrict free speech. Restrictions are permissible, he argued, only when speech presents a "clear and present danger" to the public order.

Climate Control   The use of public relations techniques to create favorable public opinion toward an interest group, industry, or corporation.

Cloture   A method invoked to close off debate and to bring the matter under consideration to a vote in the Senate.

Coattail Effect   The influence of a popular candidate on the electoral success of other candidates on the same party ticket. The effect is increased by the party-column ballot, which encourages straight-ticket voting.

Cold War   The ideological, political, and economic impasse that existed between the United States and the Soviet Union following World War II.

Commander in Chief   The role of the president as supreme commander of the military forces of the United States and of the state National Guard units when they are called into federal service.

Commerce Clause   The section of the Constitution in which Congress is given the power to regulate trade among the states and with foreign countries.

Commercial Speech   Advertising statements, which increasingly have been given First Amendment protection.

Common Law   Judge-made law that originated in England from decisions shaped according to prevailing customs. Decisions were applied to similar situations and thus gradually became common to the nation.

Compliance   The act of accepting and carrying out authorities' decisions.

Concurrent Powers   Powers held jointly by the national and state governments.

Concurring Opinion   A separate opinion, prepared by a judge who supports the decision of the majority of the court but who wants to make or clarify a particular point or to voice disapproval of the grounds on which the decision was made.

Confederal System   A system of government consisting of a league of independent states, each having essentially sovereign powers. The central government created by such a league has only limited powers over the states.

Confederation   A political system in which states or regional governments retain ultimate authority except for those powers they expressly delegate to a central government. A voluntary association of independent states, in which the member states agree to limited restraints on their freedom of action.

Conference Committee   A special joint committee appointed to reconcile differences when bills pass the two chambers of Congress in different forms.

Consensus   General agreement among the citizenry on an issue.

Consent of the People   The idea that governments and laws derive their legitimacy from the consent of the governed.

Conservatism   A set of beliefs that includes a limited role for the national government in helping individuals, support for traditional values and lifestyles, and a cautious response to change.

Conservative Coalition   An alliance of Republicans and southern Democrats that can form in the House or the Senate to oppose liberal legislation and support conservative legislation.

Consolidation   The union of two or more governmental units to form a single unit.

Constituent   One of the people represented by a legislator or other elected or appointed official.

Constitutional Initiative   An electoral device whereby citizens can propose a constitutional amendment through petitions signed by the required number of registered voters.

Constitutional Power   A power vested in the president by Article II of the Constitution.

Containment   A U.S. diplomatic policy adopted by the Truman administration to "build situations of strength" around the globe to contain Communist power within its existing boundaries.

Continuing Resolution   A temporary law that Congress passes when an appropriations bill has not been decided by the beginning of the new fiscal year on October 1.

Cooley's Rule   The view that cities should be able to govern themselves, presented in an 1871 Michigan decision by Judge Thomas Cooley.

Cooperative Federalism   The theory that the states and the national government should cooperate in solving problems.

Corrupt Practices Acts   A series of acts passed by Congress in an attempt to limit and regulate the size and sources of contributions and expenditures in political campaigns.

Council of Economic Advisers (CEA)   A staff agency in the Executive Office of the President that advises the president on measures to maintain stability in the nation's economy; established in 1946.

Council of Government (COG)   A voluntary organization of counties and municipalities concerned with areawide problems.

County   The chief governmental unit set up by the state to administer state law and business at the local level. Counties are drawn up by area, rather than by rural or urban criteria.

Credentials Committee   A committee used by political parties at their national conventions to determine which delegates may participate. The committee inspects the claim of each prospective delegate to be seated as a legitimate representative of his or her state.

Criminal Law   The law that defines crimes and provides punishment for violations. In criminal cases, the government is the prosecutor because crimes are against the public order.

D

***De Facto* Segregation**   Racial segregation that occurs because of past social and economic conditions and residential patterns.

***De Jure* Segregation**   Racial segregation that occurs because of laws or administrative decisions by public agencies.

Defamation of Character   Wrongfully hurting a person's good reputation. The law has imposed a general duty on all persons to refrain from making false, defamatory statements about others.

Defense Policy   A subset of national security policy that generally refers to the set of policies that direct the scale and size of the U.S. armed forces.

Democracy   A system of government in which ultimate political authority is vested in the people. Derived from the Greek words *demos* ("the people") and *kratos* ("authority").

Democratic Party   One of the two major American political parties evolving out of the Democratic (Jeffersonian) Republican group supporting Thomas Jefferson.

Détente   A French word meaning a relaxation of tensions. The term characterizes U.S.–Soviet policy as it developed under President Richard Nixon and Secretary of State Henry Kissinger. Détente stressed direct cooperative dealings with Cold War rivals but avoided ideological accommodation.

Dillon's Rule   The narrowest possible interpretation of the legal status of local governments, outlined by Judge John F. Dillon, who in 1872 stated that a municipal corporation can exercise only those powers expressly granted by state law.

Diplomacy   The total process by which states carry on political relations with each other; settling conflicts among nations by peaceful means.

Diplomatic Recognition   The president's power, as chief diplomat, to acknowledge a foreign government as legitimate.

Direct Democracy   A system of government in which political decisions are made by the people directly, rather than by their elected representatives; probably possible only in small political communities.

Direct Primary   An intraparty election in which the voters select the candidates who will run on a party's ticket in the subsequent general election.

Direct Technique   An interest group activity that involves interaction with government officials to further the group's goals.

Discharge Petition   A procedure by which a bill in the House of Representatives may be forced out of a committee (discharged) that has refused to report it for consideration by the House. The discharge petition must be signed by an absolute majority (218) of representatives and is used only on rare occasions.

Dissenting Opinion   A separate opinion in which a judge dissents from (disagrees with) the conclusion reached by the majority on the court and expounds his or her own views about the case.

Diversity of Citizenship   A basis for federal court jurisdiction over a lawsuit that involves citizens of different states or (more rarely) citizens of a U.S. state and citizens or subjects of a foreign country. The amount in controversy must be at least $75,000 before a federal court can take jurisdiction in such cases.

Divided Government   A situation in which one major political party controls the presidency and the other controls the chambers of Congress, or in which one party controls a state governorship and the other controls the state legislature.

Divisive Opinion   Public opinion that is polarized between two quite different positions.

Domestic Policy   Public plans or courses of action that concern issues of national importance, such as poverty, crime, and the environment.

Dominant Culture   The values, customs, language, and ideals established by the group or groups in a society that traditionally have controlled politics and government institutions in that society.

Dual Federalism   A system of government in which the states and the national government each remain supreme within their own spheres. The doctrine looks on nation and state as coequal sovereign powers. It holds that acts of states within their reserved powers are legitimate limitations on the powers of the national government.

E

Earned-Income Tax Credit (EITC) Program   A government program that helps low-income workers by giving back part or all of their Social Security taxes.

Economic Aid   Assistance to other nations in the form of grants, loans, or credits to buy the assisting nation's products.

Elastic Clause, or Necessary and Proper Clause   The clause in Article I, Section 8, that grants Congress the power to do whatever is necessary to execute its specifically delegated powers.

Elector   A person on the partisan slate that is selected early in the presidential election year according to state laws and the applicable political party apparatus. Electors cast ballots for president and vice president. The number of electors in each state is equal to that state's number of representatives in both chambers of Congress.

Electoral College   A group of persons called electors selected by the voters in each state and Washington, D.C.; this group officially elects the president and vice president of the United States. The number of electors in each state is equal to the number of each state's representatives in both chambers of Congress. The Twenty-third Amendment to the Constitution permits Washington, D.C., to have as many electors as a state of comparable population.

Electronic Media   Communication channels that involve electronic transmissions, such as radio, television, and, to an increasing extent, the Internet.

Elite   An upper socioeconomic class that controls political and economic affairs.

Elite Theory   A perspective holding that society is ruled by a small number of people who exercise power in their self-interest.

Emergency Power   An inherent power exercised by the president during a period of national crisis, particularly in foreign affairs.

Enabling Legislation   A statute enacted by Congress that authorizes the creation of an administrative agency and specifies the name, purpose, composition, functions, and powers of the agency being created.

Enumerated Power   A power specifically granted to the national government by the Constitution. The first seventeen clauses of Article I, Section 8, specify most of the enumerated powers of Congress.

Environmental Impact Statement (EIS)   As a requirement mandated by the National Environmental Policy Act, a report that must show the costs and benefits of major federal actions that could significantly affect the quality of the environment.

Equal Employment Opportunity Commission (EEOC)   A commission established by the 1964 Civil Rights Act to (1) end discrimination based on race, color, religion, gender, or national origin in conditions of employment and (2) promote voluntary action programs by employers, unions, and community organizations to foster equal job opportunities.

Equal Time Rule   A Federal Communications Commission regulation that requires broadcasting stations that give or sell air time to political candidates to make equal amounts of time available to all competing candidates.

Equality   A concept that all people are of equal worth.

Era of Good Feeling   The years from 1817 to 1825, when James Monroe was president and there was, in effect, no political opposition.

Era of Personal Politics   The years from 1816 to 1828, when attention centered on the character of individual candidates rather than on party identification.

Establishment Clause   The part of the First Amendment prohibiting the establishment of a church officially supported by the national government. It is applied to questions of state and local government aid to religious organizations and schools, questions of the legality of allowing or requiring school prayers, and questions of the teaching of evolution versus fundamentalist theories of creation.

Exclusionary Rule   A policy forbidding the admission at trial of illegally seized evidence.

Executive Agreement   An international agreement made by the president, without senatorial ratification, with the head of a foreign state.

Executive Budget   The budget prepared and submitted by the president to Congress.

Executive Office of the President (EOP)   Established by President Franklin D. Roosevelt by executive order under the Reorganization Act of 1939, the EOP currently consists of eleven staff agencies that assist the president in carrying out major duties.

Executive Order   A rule or regulation issued by the president that has the effect of law. Executive orders can implement and give administrative effect to provisions in the Constitution, to treaties, and to statutes.

Executive Privilege   The right of executive officials to refuse to appear before, or to withhold information from, a legislative committee. Executive privilege is enjoyed by the president and by those executive officials accorded that right by the president.

Expressed Power A constitutional or statutory power of the president, which is expressly written into the Constitution or into statutory law.

F

Faction A group or bloc in a legislature or political party acting together in pursuit of some special interest or position.

Fall Review The time every year when, after receiving formal federal agency requests for funding for the next fiscal year, the Office of Management and Budget reviews the requests, makes changes, and submits its recommendations to the president.

Federal Mandate A requirement in federal legislation that forces states and municipalities to comply with certain rules.

Federal Open Market Committee (FOMC) The most important body within the Federal Reserve System. The FOMC decides how monetary policy should be carried out by the Federal Reserve System.

Federal Question A question that pertains to the U.S. Constitution, acts of Congress, or treaties. A federal question provides a basis for federal jurisdiction.

Federal Register A publication of the executive branch of the U.S. government that prints executive orders, rules, and regulations.

Federal System A system of government in which power is divided by a written constitution between a central government and regional, or subdivisional, governments. Each level must have some domain in which its policies are dominant and some genuine political or constitutional guarantee of its authority.

Federalist The name given to one who was in favor of the adoption of the U.S. Constitution and the creation of a federal union with a strong central government.

Feminism The movement that supports political, economic, and social equality for women.

Fighting Words Words that, when uttered by a public speaker, are so inflammatory that they could provoke the average listener to violence; the words are usually of a racial, religious, or ethnic type.

Filibuster In the Senate, unlimited debate to halt action on a particular bill.

First Budget Resolution A resolution passed by Congress in May that sets overall revenue and spending goals for the following fiscal year.

First Continental Congress The first gathering of delegates from twelve of the thirteen colonies, held in 1774.

Fiscal Policy The use of changes in government spending or taxation to alter national economic variables, such as the rate of unemployment.

Fiscal Year (FY) The twelve-month period that is used for bookkeeping, or accounting, purposes. Usually, the fiscal year does not coincide with the calendar year. For example, the federal government's fiscal year runs from October 1 through September 30.

Focus Group A small group of individuals who are led in discussion by a professional consultant to gather opinions on and responses to candidates and issues.

Food Stamps Coupons issued by the federal government to low-income individuals to be used for the purchase of food.

Foreign Policy A nation's external goals and the techniques and strategies used to achieve them.

Foreign Policy Process The steps by which external goals are decided and acted on.

Franking A policy that enables members of Congress to send material through the mail by substituting their facsimile signature (frank) for postage.

Free Exercise Clause The provision of the First Amendment guaranteeing the free exercise of religion.

Free Rider Problem The difficulty interest groups face in recruiting members when the benefits they achieve can be gained without joining the group.

Front-Loading The practice of moving presidential primary elections to the early part of the campaign, to maximize the impact of certain states or regions on the nomination.

Front-Runner The presidential candidate who appears to have the most momentum at a given time in the primary season.

Functional Consolidation The cooperation of two or more units of local government in providing services to their inhabitants.

G

Gag Order An order issued by a judge restricting the publication of news about a trial in progress or a pretrial hearing in order to protect the accused's right to a fair trial.

Gender Discrimination Any practice, policy, or procedure that denies equality of treatment to an individual or to a group because of gender.

Gender Gap A term most often used to describe the difference between the percentage of votes a candidate receives from women and the percentage of votes the candidate receives from men. The term came into use after the 1980 presidential elections.

General Jurisdiction Exists when a court's authority to hear cases is not significantly restricted. A court of general jurisdiction normally can hear a broad range of cases.

General Law City A city operating under general state laws that apply to all local governmental units of a similar type.

General Sales Tax A tax levied as a proportion of the retail price of a commodity at the point of sale.

Generational Effect A long-lasting effect of events of a particular time period on the political opinions or preferences of those who came of political age at that time.

Gerrymandering The drawing of legislative district boundary lines for the purpose of obtaining partisan or factional advantage. A district is said to be gerrymandered when its shape is manipulated by the dominant party in the state legislature to maximize electoral strength at the expense of the minority party.

Government The institutions, or permanent structures, that have the power to enforce rules that impose order and stability on society.

Government Corporation An agency of government that administers a quasi-business enterprise. These corporations are used when activities are primarily commercial. They produce revenue for their continued existence, and they require greater flexibility than is permitted for departments and agencies.

Government in the Sunshine Act A law that requires all multiheaded federal agencies to conduct their business regularly in public session.

Grandfather Clause A device used by southern states to exempt whites from state taxes and literacy laws originally intended to disenfranchise African American voters. It restricted the voting franchise to those who could prove that their grandfathers had voted before 1867.

Great Compromise The compromise between the New Jersey and the Virginia plans that created one chamber of Congress based on population and one chamber representing each state equally; also called the Connecticut Compromise.

H

Hatch Act An act passed in 1939 that prohibited a political group from spending more than $3 million in any campaign and limited individual contributions to a committee to $5,000. The act was designed to control political influence buying.

Hecklers' Veto Boisterous and generally disruptive behavior by listeners to public speakers that, in effect, vetoes the public speakers' right to speak.

Home Rule City A city with a charter allowing local voters to frame, adopt, and amend their own charter.

Horizontal Federalism Activities, problems, and policies that require state governments to interact with one another.

Hyperpartisanship A situation in which members of the two major political parties are extremely party oriented in their choices.

Hyperpluralism A situation that arises when interest groups become so powerful that they dominate the political decision-making structures, rendering any consideration of the greater public interest impossible.

I

Ideology A comprehensive and logically ordered set of beliefs about the nature of people and about the institutions and role of government.

Impeachment As authorized by Articles I and II of the Constitution, an action by the House of Representatives and the Senate to remove the president, vice president, or civil officers of the United States from office for committing "Treason, Bribery, or other high Crimes and Misdemeanors."

Income Transfer A transfer of income from some individuals in the economy to other individuals. This is generally done by way of the government. It is a transfer in the sense that no current services are rendered by the recipients.

Incorporation Theory The view that most of the protections of the Bill of Rights are applied against state governments through the Fourteenth Amendment's due process clause.

Independent A voter or candidate who does not identify with a political party.

Independent Executive Agency A federal agency that is not part of a cabinet department but reports directly to the president.

Independent Expenditures Nonregulated contributions from PACs, ideological organizations, and individuals. The groups may spend funds on advertising or other campaign activities so long as those expenditures are not coordinated with those of a candidate.

Independent Regulatory Agency An agency outside the major executive departments charged with making and implementing rules and regulations to protect the public interest.

Indirect Technique A strategy employed by interest groups that uses third parties to influence government officials.

Inherent Power A power of the president derived from the loosely worded statement in the Constitution that "the executive Power shall be vested in a President" and that the president should "take Care that the Laws be faithfully executed"; defined through practice rather than through constitutional or statutory law.

Initiative A procedure by which voters can propose a law or a constitutional amendment.

In-Kind Subsidy A good or service—such as food stamps, housing, or medical care—provided by the government to lower-income groups.

Institution A long-standing, identifiable structure or association that performs certain functions for society.

Instructed Delegate A legislator who is an agent of the voters who elected him or her and who votes according to the views of constituents regardless of personal assessments.

Intelligence Community The government agencies that are involved in gathering information about the capabilities and intentions of foreign governments and that engage in activities to further U.S. foreign policy aims.

Interest Group An organized group of individuals sharing common objectives who actively attempt to influence policymakers in all three branches of the government and at all levels.

Interstate Compact An agreement between two or more states. Agreements on minor matters are made without congressional consent, but any compact that tends to increase the power of the contracting states relative to other states or relative to the national government generally requires the consent of Congress. Such compacts serve as a means by which states can solve regional problems.

Iron Curtain The term used to describe the division of Europe between the Soviet Union and the West; popularized by Winston Churchill in a speech portraying Europe as being divided by an iron curtain, with the nations of Eastern Europe behind the curtain and increasingly under Soviet control.

Iron Triangle The three-way alliance among legislators, bureaucrats, and interest groups to make or preserve policies that benefit their respective interests.

Isolationist Foreign Policy Abstaining from an active role in international affairs or alliances, which characterized U.S. foreign policy toward Europe during most of the nineteenth century.

Issue Advocacy Advertising Advertising paid for by interest groups that supports or opposes a candidate or candidate's position on an issue without mentioning voting or elections.

Issue Network A group of individuals or organizations—which may consist of legislators or legislative staff members, interest group leaders, bureaucrats, the media, scholars, and other experts—that supports a particular policy position on a given issue, such as one relating to the environment, taxation, or consumer safety.

Issue Voting Voting for a candidate based on how he or she stands on a particular issue.

Item Veto The power exercised by the governors of most states to veto particular sections or items of an appropriations bill, while signing the remainder of the bill into law.

J

Joint Committee A legislative committee composed of members from both chambers of Congress.

Judicial Activism A doctrine holding that the Supreme Court should take an active role in using its powers to check the activities of Congress, state legislatures, and administrative agencies when those government bodies exceed their authority.

Judicial Implementation The way in which court decisions are translated into action.

Judicial Restraint A doctrine holding that the Supreme Court should defer to the decisions made by the elected representatives of the people in the legislative and executive branches.

Judicial Review The power of the Supreme Court or any court to declare unconstitutional federal or state laws and other acts of government.

Jurisdiction The authority of a court to decide certain cases. Not all courts have the authority to decide all cases. Where a case arises and what its subject matter is are two jurisdictional factors.

Justiciable Question A question that may be raised and reviewed in court.

K

Keynesian Economics An economic theory, named after English economist John Maynard Keynes, that gained prominence during the Great Depression of the 1930s. It is typically associated with the use of fiscal policy to alter national economic variables—for example, increased government spending during times of economic downturns.

Kitchen Cabinet The informal advisers to the president.

L

Labor Movement Generally, the full range of economic and political expression of working-class interests; politically, the organization of working-class interests.

Latent Interests Public-policy interests that are not recognized or addressed by a group at a particular time.

Lawmaking The process of deciding the legal rules that govern society. Such laws may regulate minor affairs or establish broad national policies.

Legislative Initiative A procedure by which voters can propose a change in state or local laws by gathering signatures on a petition and placing a proposed law on the ballot for the voters' approval.

Legislative Veto A provision in a bill reserving to Congress or to a congressional committee the power to reject an action or regulation of a national agency by majority vote; declared unconstitutional by the Supreme Court in 1983.

Legislature A governmental body primarily responsible for the making of laws.

Legitimacy A status conferred by the people on the government's officials, acts, and institutions through their belief that the government's actions are an appropriate use of power by a legally constituted governmental authority following correct decision-making policies. These actions are regarded as rightful and entitled to compliance and obedience on the part of citizens.

Libel A written defamation of a person's character, reputation, business, or property rights. To a limited degree, the First Amendment protects the press from libel actions.

Liberalism A set of beliefs that includes the advocacy of positive government action to improve the welfare of individuals, support for civil rights, and tolerance for political and social change.

Liberty The greatest freedom of individuals that is consistent with the freedom of other individuals in the society.

Limited Government A form of government based on the principle that the powers of government should be clearly limited either through a written document or through wide public understanding; characterized by institutional checks to ensure that government serves the public rather than private interests.

Limited Jurisdiction Exists when a court's authority to hear cases is restricted to certain types of claims, such as tax claims or bankruptcy petitions.

Line Organization   With respect to the federal government, an administrative unit that is directly accountable to the president.

Line-Item Veto   The power of an executive to veto individual lines or items within a piece of legislation without vetoing the entire bill.

Literacy Test   A test administered as a precondition for voting, often used to prevent African Americans from exercising their right to vote.

Litigate   To engage in a legal proceeding or seek relief in a court of law; to carry on a lawsuit.

Lobbyist   An organization or individual who attempts to influence the passage, defeat, or contents of legislation and the administrative decisions of government.

Logrolling   An arrangement in which two or more members of Congress agree in advance to support each other's bills.

Loophole   A legal method by which individuals and businesses are allowed to reduce the tax liabilities owed to the government.

M

Madisonian Model   A structure of government proposed by James Madison in which the powers of the government are separated into three branches: executive, legislative, and judicial.

Majority   1) More than 50 percent; 2) Full age; the age at which a person is entitled by law to the right to manage her or his own affairs and to the full enjoyment of civil rights.

Majority Floor Leader   The chief spokesperson of the majority party in the Senate, who directs the legislative program and party strategy.

Majority Leader of the House   A legislative position held by an important party member in the House of Representatives. The majority leader is selected by the majority party in caucus or conference to foster cohesion among party members and to act as spokesperson for the majority party in the House.

Majority Opinion   A court opinion reflecting the views of the majority of the judges.

Majority Rule   A basic principle of democracy asserting that the greatest number of citizens in any political unit should select officials and determine policies.

Managed News   Information generated and distributed by the government in such a way as to give government interests priority over candor.

Mandatory Retirement   Forced retirement when a person reaches a certain age.

Material Incentive   A reason or motive having to do with economic benefits or opportunities.

Media   The technical means of communication with mass audiences.

Media Access   The public's right of access to the media. The Federal Communications Commission and the courts gradually have taken the stance that citizens do have a right to media access.

Merit System   The selection, retention, and promotion of government employees on the basis of competitive examinations.

Military-Industrial Complex   The mutually beneficial relationship between the armed forces and defense contractors.

Minority Floor Leader   The party officer in the Senate who commands the minority party's opposition to the policies of the majority party and directs the legislative program and strategy of his or her party.

Minority Leader of the House   The party leader elected by the minority party in the House.

Monetary Policy   The use of changes in the amount of money in circulation to alter credit markets, employment, and the rate of inflation.

Monopolistic Model   A model of bureaucracy that compares bureaucracies to monopolistic business firms. Lack of competition within a bureaucracy leads to inefficient and costly operations. Because bureaucracies are not penalized for inefficiency, there is no incentive to reduce costs or use resources more productively.

Monroe Doctrine   The policy statement included in President James Monroe's 1823 annual message to Congress, which set out three principles: (1) European nations should not establish new colonies in the Western Hemisphere, (2) European nations should not intervene in the affairs of independent nations of the Western Hemisphere, and (3) the United States would not interfere in the affairs of European nations.

Moral Idealism   A philosophy that sees all nations as willing to cooperate and agree on moral standards for conduct.

Most-Favored-Nation Status   A status granted by an international treaty by which each member nation must treat other members at least as well as it treats the country that receives its most favorable treatment.

Municipal Home Rule   The power vested in a local unit of government to draft or change its own charter and to manage its own affairs.

N

Narrowcasting   Broadcasting that is targeted to one small sector of the population.

National Committee   A standing committee of a national political party established to direct and coordinate party activities during the four-year period between national party conventions.

National Convention   The meeting held every four years by each major party to select presidential and vice presidential candidates, to write a platform, to choose a national committee, and to conduct party business. In theory, the national convention is at the top of a hierarchy of party conventions (the local and state conventions are below it) that consider candidates and issues.

National Politics   The pursuit of interests that are of concern to the nation as a whole.

National Security Council (NSC)   A staff agency in the Executive Office of the President established by the National Security Act of 1947. The NSC advises the president on domestic and foreign matters involving national security.

National Security Policy   Foreign and domestic policy designed to protect the independence and political and economic integrity of the United States; policy that is concerned with the safety and defense of the nation.

Natural Aristocracy   A small ruling clique of a society's "best" citizens, whose membership is based on birth, wealth, and ability. The Jeffersonian era emphasized government rule by such a group.

Natural Rights   Rights held to be inherent in natural law, not dependent on governments. John Locke stated that natural law, being superior to human law, specifies certain rights of "life, liberty, and property." These rights, altered to become "life, liberty, and the pursuit of happiness," are asserted in the Declaration of Independence.

Necessaries   In contract law, necessaries include whatever is reasonably necessary for suitable subsistence as measured by age, state, condition in life, and so on.

Negative Constituents   Citizens who openly oppose government foreign policies.

New England Town   A governmental unit in the New England states that combines the roles of city and county in one unit.

O

Office of Management and Budget (OMB)   A division of the Executive Office of the President created by executive order in 1970 to replace the Bureau of the Budget. The OMB's main functions are to assist the president in preparing the annual budget, to clear and coordinate all departmental agency budgets, to help set fiscal policy, and to supervise the administration of the federal budget.

Office-Block, or Massachusetts, Ballot   A form of general election ballot in which candidates for elective office are grouped together under the title of each office. It emphasizes voting for the office and the individual candidate, rather than for the party.

Oligarchy   Rule by a few members of the elite, who generally make decisions to benefit their own group.

Ombudsperson   A person who hears and investigates complaints by private individuals against public officials or agencies.

Opinion   The statement by a judge or a court of the decision reached in a case tried or argued before it. The opinion sets forth the law that applies to the case and details the legal reasoning on which the ruling was based.

Opinion Leader   One who is able to influence the opinions of others because of position, expertise, or personality. Such leaders help to shape public opinion.

Opinion Poll   A method of systematically questioning a small, selected sample of respondents who are deemed representative of the total population. Opinion polls are widely used by government, business, university scholars, political candidates, and voluntary groups to provide reasonably accurate data on public attitudes, beliefs, expectations, and behavior.

Oral Arguments   The verbal arguments presented in person by attorneys to an appellate court. Each attorney presents reasons to the court why the court should rule in her or his client's favor.

Oversight   The responsibility Congress has for following up on laws it has enacted to ensure that they are being enforced and administered in the way Congress intended.

P

Pardon   The granting of a release from the punishment or legal consequences of a crime; a pardon can be granted by the president before or after a conviction.

Party Identification   Linking oneself to a particular political party.

Party Identifier   A person who identifies with a political party.

Party Organization   The formal structure and leadership of a political party, including election committees; local, state, and national executives; and paid professional staff.

Party Platform   A document drawn up by the platform committee at each national convention, outlining the policies, positions, and principles of the party; it is then submitted to the entire convention for approval.

Party-Column, or Indiana, Ballot   A form of general election ballot in which candidates for elective office are arranged in one column under their respective party labels and symbols. It emphasizes voting for the party, rather than for the office or individual.

Party-in-Government   All of the elected and appointed officials who identify with a political party.

Party-in-the-Electorate   Those members of the general public who identify with a political party or who express a preference for one party over another.

Patronage   Rewarding faithful party workers and followers with government employment and contracts.

Peer Group   A group consisting of members sharing common relevant social characteristics. These groups play an important part in the socialization process, helping to shape attitudes and beliefs.

Pendleton Act (Civil Service Reform Act)   The law, as amended over the years, that remains the basic statute regulating federal employment personnel policies. It established the principle of employment on the basis of merit and created the Civil Service Commission to administer the personnel service.

Personal Attack Rule   A Federal Communications Commission regulation that requires broadcasting stations, if the stations are used to attack the honesty or integrity of persons, to allow the persons attacked the fullest opportunity to respond.

Picket-Fence Federalism   A model of federalism in which specific programs and policies (depicted as vertical pickets in a picket fence) involve all levels of government—national, state, and local (depicted by the horizontal boards in a picket fence).

Pluralism   A theory that views politics as a conflict among interest groups. Political decision making is characterized by bargaining and compromise.

Plurality   The total votes cast for a candidate who receives more votes than any other candidate but not necessarily a majority. Most national, state, and local electoral laws provide for winning elections by a plurality vote.

Pocket Veto   A special veto power exercised by the chief executive after a legislative body has adjourned. Bills not signed by the chief executive die after a specified period of time. If Congress wishes to reconsider such a bill, it must be reintroduced in the following session of Congress.

Police Power   The authority to legislate for the protection of the health, morals, safety, and welfare of the people. In the United States, most police power is a reserved power of the states.

Policy Trade-Offs   The cost to the nation of undertaking any one policy in terms of all of the other policies that could have been undertaken. For example, an increase in the expenditures on one federal program means either a reduction in expenditures on another program or an increase in federal taxes (or the deficit).

Political Action Committee (PAC)   A committee set up by and representing a corporation, labor union, or special interest group. PACs raise and give campaign donations on behalf of the organizations or groups they represent.

Political Consultant   A paid professional hired to devise a campaign strategy and manage a campaign. Image building is the crucial task of the political consultant.

Political Culture   The collection of beliefs and attitudes toward government and the political process held by a community or nation.

Political Party   A group of political activists who organize to win elections, operate the government, and determine public policy.

Political Question   An issue that a court believes should be decided by the executive or legislative branch.

Political Realism   A philosophy that sees each nation acting principally in its own interest.

Political Socialization   The process through which individuals learn a set of political attitudes and form opinions about social issues. The family and the educational system are two of the most important forces in the political socialization process.

Political Trust   The degree to which individuals express trust in the government and political institutions, usually measured through a specific series of survey questions.

Politics   A process that regulates conflict within a society; according to Harold Lasswell, "who gets what, when, and how" in a society.

Poll Tax   A special tax that must be paid as a qualification for voting. The Twenty-fourth Amendment to the Constitution outlawed the poll tax in national elections, and in 1966 the Supreme Court declared it unconstitutional in all elections.

Power   The ability to cause others to modify their behavior and to conform to what the power holder wants.

Precedent   A court rule bearing on subsequent legal decisions in similar cases. Judges rely on precedents in deciding cases.

President *Pro Tempore*   The temporary presiding officer of the Senate in the absence of the vice president.

Presidential Primary   A statewide primary election of delegates to a political party's national convention to help a party determine its presidential nominee. Such delegates are either pledged to a particular candidate or unpledged.

Press Secretary   The individual responsible for representing the White House before the media. The press secretary writes news releases, provides background information, sets up press conferences, and generally handles communication for the White House.

Prior Restraint   Restraining an action before the activity has actually occurred. It involves censorship, as opposed to subsequent punishment.

Privatization   The replacement of government services with services provided by private firms.

Property   Anything that is or may be subject to ownership. As conceived by the political philosopher John Locke, the right to property is a natural right superior to human law (laws made by government).

Property Tax   A tax on the value of real estate. This tax is limited to state and local governments and is a particularly important source of revenue for local governments.

Public Agenda   Issues that commonly are perceived by members of the political community as meriting public attention and governmental action. The media play an important role in setting the public agenda by focusing attention on certain topics.

Public Debt Financing   The government's spending more than it receives in taxes and paying for the difference by issuing U.S. Treasury bonds, thereby adding to the public debt.

Public Debt, or National Debt   The total amount of debt carried by the federal government.

Public Figures   Public officials, movie stars, and generally all persons who become known to the public because of their positions or activities.

Public Interest   The best interests of the collective, overall community; the national good, rather than the narrow interests of a self-serving group.

Public Opinion   The aggregate of individual attitudes or beliefs shared by some portion of the adult population. There is no one public opinion, because there are many different "publics."

Purposive Incentive   A reason or motive having to do with ethical beliefs or ideological principles.

R

Ratification   Formal approval.

Rational Ignorance Effect   When people purposely and rationally decide not to become informed on an issue because they believe that their vote on the issue is not likely to be a deciding one; a lack of incentive to seek the necessary information to cast an intelligent vote.

Reapportionment   The allocation of seats in the House of Representatives to each state after each census.

Recall   A procedure allowing the people to vote to dismiss an elected official from state office before his or her term has expired.

Redistricting   The redrawing of the boundaries of the congressional districts within each state.

Referendum   An electoral device whereby legislative or constitutional measures are referred by the legislature to the voters for approval or disapproval.

Registration   The entry of a person's name onto the list of eligible voters for elections. To register, a person must meet certain legal requirements relating to age, citizenship, and residency.

Remand   To send a case back to the court that originally heard it.

Representation   The function of members of Congress as elected officials in representing the views of their constituents.

Representative Assembly   A legislature composed of individuals who represent the population.

Representative Democracy   A form of government in which representatives elected by the people make and enforce laws and policies.

Reprieve   The presidential power to postpone the execution of a sentence imposed by a court of law; usually done for humanitarian reasons or to await new evidence.

Republic   A form of government in which sovereignty rests with the people, who elect agents to represent them in lawmaking and other decisions.

Republican Party   One of the two major American political parties, which emerged in the 1850s as an antislavery party. It was created to fill the vacuum caused by the disintegration of the Whig Party.

Reverse   To annul or make void a court ruling on account of some error or irregularity.

Reverse Discrimination   The charge that affirmative action programs requiring preferential treatment or quotas discriminate against those who do not have minority status.

Rule of Four   A United States Supreme Court procedure requiring four affirmative votes to hear a case before the full Court.

Rules Committee   A standing committee of the House of Representatives that provides special rules under which specific bills can be debated, amended, and considered by the House.

S

Safe Seat   A district that returns the legislator with 55 percent of the vote or more.

Sampling Error   The difference between a sample's results and the true result if the entire population had been interviewed.

Second Budget Resolution   A resolution passed by Congress in September that sets "binding" limits on taxes and spending for the next fiscal year beginning October 1.

Second Continental Congress   The 1775 congress of the colonies that established an army.

Sectional Politics   The pursuit of interests that are of special concern to a region or section of the country.

Select Committee   A temporary legislative committee established for a limited time period and for a special purpose.

Selectperson   A member of the governing group of a town.

Senatorial Courtesy   In regard to federal district court judgeship nominations, a Senate tradition allowing a senator of the president's political party to veto a judicial appointment in his or her state simply by indicating that the appointment is personally not acceptable. At that point, the Senate may reject the nomination, or the president may withdraw consideration of the nominee.

Seniority System   A custom followed in both chambers of Congress specifying that members with longer terms of continuous service will be given preference when committee chairpersons and holders of other significant posts are selected.

Separate-but-Equal Doctrine   The doctrine holding that segregation in schools and public accommodations does not imply that one race is superior to another, and that separate-but-equal facilities do not violate the equal protection clause.

Separation of Powers   The principle of dividing governmental powers among the executive, the legislative, and the judicial branches of government.

Service Sector   The sector of the economy that provides services—such as food services, insurance, and education—in contrast to the sector of the economy that produces goods.

Sexual Harassment   Unwanted physical or verbal conduct or abuse of a sexual nature that interferes with a recipient's job performance, creates a hostile environment, or carries with it an implicit or explicit threat of adverse employment consequences.

Slander   The public uttering of a false statement that harms the good reputation of another. The statement must be made to, or within the hearing of, persons other than the defamed party.

Social Contract   A voluntary agreement among individuals to secure their rights and welfare by creating a government and abiding by its rules.

Social Movement   A movement that represents the demands of a large segment of the public for political, economic, or social change.

Socioeconomic Status   A category of people within a society who have similar levels of income and similar types of occupations.

Soft Money   Campaign contributions that evade contribution limits by being given to parties and party committees to help fund general party activities.

Solidary Incentive   A reason or motive having to do with the desire to associate with others and to share with others a particular interest or hobby.

Sound Bite   A brief, memorable comment that easily can be fit into news broadcasts.

Soviet Bloc   The Eastern European countries that installed Communist regimes after World War II.

Speaker of the House   The presiding officer in the House of Representatives. The Speaker is always a member of the majority party and is the most powerful and influential member of the House.

Spin   An interpretation of campaign events or election results that is most favorable to the candidate's campaign strategy.

Spin Doctor   A political campaign adviser who tries to convince journalists of the truth of a particular interpretation of events.

Splinter Party   A new party formed by a dissident faction within a major political party. Usually, splinter parties have emerged when a particular personality was at odds with the major party.

Spoils System   The awarding of government jobs to political supporters and friends; generally associated with President Andrew Jackson.

Spring Review   The time every year when the Office of Management and Budget requires federal agencies to review their programs, activities, and goals and submit their requests for funding for the next fiscal year.

Standing Committee   A permanent committee in the House or Senate that considers bills within a certain subject area.

Stare Decisis   To stand on decided cases; the judicial policy of following precedents established by past decisions.

State   A group of people occupying a specific area and organized under one government; may be either a nation or a subunit of a nation.

State Central Committee   The principal organized structure of each political party within each state. This committee is responsible for carrying out policy decisions of the party's state convention.

State of the Union Message   An annual message to Congress in which the president proposes a legislative program. The message is addressed not only to Congress but also to the American people and to the world. It offers the opportunity to dramatize policies and objectives and to gain public support.

Statutory Power A power created for the president through laws enacted by Congress.

Strategic Arms Limitation Treaty (SALT I) A treaty between the United States and the Soviet Union to stabilize the nuclear arms competition between the two countries. SALT I talks began in 1969, and agreements were signed on May 26, 1972.

Subpoena A legal writ requiring a person's appearance in court to give testimony.

Suffrage The right to vote; the franchise.

Sunset Legislation A law requiring that an existing program be reviewed regularly for its effectiveness and be terminated unless specifically extended as a result of this review.

Super Tuesday The date on which a number of presidential primaries are held, including those of most of the southern states.

Superdelegate A party leader or elected official who is given the right to vote at the party's national convention. Superdelegates are not elected at the state level.

Supplemental Security Income (SSI) A federal program established to provide assistance to elderly persons and disabled persons.

Supremacy Clause The constitutional provision that makes the Constitution and federal laws superior to all conflicting state and local laws.

Supremacy Doctrine A doctrine that asserts the superiority of national law over state or regional laws. This principle is rooted in Article VI of the Constitution, which provides that the Constitution, the laws passed by the national government under its constitutional powers, and all treaties constitute the supreme law of the land.

Symbolic Speech Nonverbal expression of beliefs, which is given substantial protection by the courts.

T

Technical Assistance The sending of experts with technical skills in such areas as agriculture, engineering, or business to aid other nations.

Temporary Assistance to Needy Families (TANF) A state-administered program in which grants from the national government are given to the states, which use the funds to provide assistance to those eligible to receive welfare benefits. The TANF program was created by the Welfare Reform Act of 1996 and replaced the former AFDC program.

Third Party A political party other than the two major political parties (Republican and Democratic). Usually, third parties are composed of dissatisfied groups that have split from the major parties. They act as indicators of political trends and as safety valves for dissident groups.

Ticket Splitting Voting for candidates of two or more parties for different offices. For example, a voter splits her ticket if she votes for a Republican presidential candidate and for a Democratic congressional candidate.

Totalitarian Regime A form of government that controls all aspects of the political and social life of a nation. All power resides with the government. The citizens have no power to choose the leadership or policies of the country.

Town Manager System A form of city government in which voters elect three selectpersons, who then appoint a professional town manager, who in turn appoints other officials.

Town Meeting The governing authority of a New England town. Qualified voters may participate in the election of officers and in the passage of legislation.

Township A rural unit of government based on federal land surveys of the American frontier in the 1780s. Townships have declined significantly in importance.

Tracking Poll A poll taken for the candidate on a nearly daily basis as election day approaches.

Trial Court The court in which most cases usually begin and in which questions of fact are examined.

Truman Doctrine The policy adopted by President Harry Truman in 1947 to halt Communist expansion in southeastern Europe.

Trustee In regard to a legislator, one who acts according to her or his conscience and the broad interests of the entire society.

Twelfth Amendment An amendment to the Constitution, adopted in 1804, that specifies the separate election of the president and vice president by the electoral college.

Twenty-fifth Amendment An amendment to the Constitution adopted in 1967 that establishes procedures for filling vacancies in the two top executive offices and that makes provisions for situations involving presidential disability.

Two-Party System A political system in which only two parties have a reasonable chance of winning.

U

U.S. Treasury Bond Evidence of debt issued by the federal government; similar to corporate bonds but issued by the U.S. Treasury.

Unanimous Opinion A court opinion or determination on which all judges agree.

Unicameral Legislature A legislature with only one legislative body, as compared with a bicameral (two-house) legislature, such as the U.S. Congress. Nebraska is the only state in the Union with a unicameral legislature.

Unincorporated Area An area not located within the boundary of a municipality.

Unit Rule All of a state's electoral votes are cast for the presidential candidate receiving a plurality of the popular vote in that state.

Unitary System A centralized governmental system in which local or subdivisional governments exercise only those powers given to them by the central government.

Universal Suffrage The right of all adults to vote for their representatives.

V

Veto Message The president's formal explanation of a veto when legislation is returned to Congress.

Voter Turnout The percentage of citizens taking part in the election process; the number of eligible voters that actually "turn out" on election day to cast their ballots.

W

War Powers Resolution A law passed in 1973 spelling out the conditions under which the president can commit troops without congressional approval.

Washington Community Individuals regularly involved with politics in Washington, D.C.

Watergate Break-in The 1972 illegal entry into the Democratic National Committee offices by participants in President Richard Nixon's reelection campaign.

Weberian Model A model of bureaucracy developed by the German sociologist Max Weber, who viewed bureaucracies as rational, hierarchical organizations in which power flows from the top downward and decisions are based on logical reasoning and data analysis.

Whig Party One of the foremost political organizations in the United States during the first half of the nineteenth century, formally established in 1836. The Whig Party was dominated by the same anti-Jackson elements that organized the National Republican faction within the Democratic (Jeffersonian) Republicans and represented a variety of regional interests. It fell apart as a national party in the early 1850s.

Whip An assistant who aids the majority or minority leader of the House or the Senate majority or minority floor leader.

Whistleblower Someone who brings to public attention gross governmental inefficiency or an illegal action.

White House Office The personal office of the president, which tends to presidential political needs and manages the media.

White House Press Corps A group of reporters assigned full-time to cover the presidency.

White Primary   A state primary election that restricts voting to whites only; outlawed by the Supreme Court in 1944.

Writ of *Certiorari*   An order issued by a higher court to a lower court to send up the record of a case for review. It is the principal vehicle for United States Supreme Court review.

Writ of *Habeas Corpus*   *Habeas corpus* means, literally, "you have the body." A writ of *habeas corpus* is an order that requires jailers to bring a person before a court or judge and explain why the person is being held in prison.

Y

Yellow Journalism   A term for sensationalistic, irresponsible journalism. Reputedly, the term is short for "Yellow Kid Journalism," an allusion to the cartoon "The Yellow Kid" in the old *New York World*, a newspaper especially noted for its sensationalism.

Index

A

AARP
  accomplishments of, 243, 244
  material incentives to join, 235
  membership of, 243
  power of, 186, 235, 243
ABC News, 213, 341
ABC News/*Washington Post* poll, 292
Aberbach, Joel, 439
Abington School District v. Schempp, 114
Abortion(s), 32, 59
  "partial-birth," 130
  privacy rights and, 32, 128–130
  Roe v. Wade and, 129, 130
  special interest groups and, 242
Absentee ballots, 312, 314
Accidental sample, 224
Accommodation(s)
  reasonable, for persons with disabilities,
    186–187
    "undue hardship" versus, 186, 187
  of religious conduct, 117
Accuracy in Media, 352
Accused, rights of
  extending, 133–136
  reduced, 134
  rights of society versus, 131–138
Achievement tests, 550, 571
ACLU. *See* American Civil Liberties Union
Acquired immune deficiency syndrome. *See*
  AIDS
Acquisitive model of bureaucracy, 424
Action-reaction syndrome, 498
Actual malice, 125
ADA (Americans for Democratic Action),
  246
ADA (Americans with Disabilities
  Act)(1990), 186–188, 197, 431

Adams, Abigail, 163
Adams, John, 91, 163, 415
Adams, John Quincy, 265, 309, 310, 394
Adams, Samuel, 50
Adarand Constructors, Inc. v. Peña, 180
ADEA (Age Discrimination in Employment
  Act)(1967), 185
Administrative agency(ies)
  defined, 425
  federal, civilian employees of, number of,
    426
  independent executive. *See* Independent
    executive agency(ies)
  independent regulatory. *See* Independent
    regulatory agency(ies)
  regulations of, as source of law, 454
Administrative Procedure Act (1946), 409
Adoption, gay males and lesbians and, 190,
  191, 192, 193
Advertising
  advocacy, 248, 250, 251–252, 303, 343
  "attack," 343
  "daisy girl," 342–343
  for elections of 2002, 346
  First Amendment protection and, 120
  handbills and, 274
  negative, 317, 342–343
    low voter turnout and, 317
  political, 343, 346
  reelection goal of incumbent pursued by,
    366–367
  television, during Super Bowl and, 348
Advice and consent, 360, 398, 463
Advocacy ads, 248, 250, 251–252, 303, 343
AFDC (Aid to Families with Dependent
  Children), 489
Affirmation of judgment, 462
Affirmative action, 179–181
  California Proposition 209 and, 178, 180

college admissions and, 178, 179–180, 469
defined, 179
further limitations on, 180, 469
future of, 181, 197
Afghanistan
  al Qaeda network in, 5, 9, 25, 223, 399,
    515, 520
  Taliban government in. *See* Taliban
    government
  war in, against al Qaeda and Taliban, 5,
    25, 399, 517, 520
    American public's support for, 213,
      399, 406–407, 417, 495
  women's rights in, 168
AFL (American Federation of Labor), 239
AFL-CIO, 239, 244
  budget of, 240
  Committee on Public Education (COPE)
    of, 239
  Democratic Party candidates endorsed by,
    246
  formation of, 239
  Public Employee Department of, 240
Africa
  AIDS epidemic in, 529
  regional conflicts in, 528–529
  United States embassies in, bombing of,
    519, 521
African American(s). *See also* Affirmative
  action; Race(s)
  Black Muslims and, 156
  Black power and, 156–157
  civil rights movement and, 154–157, 232,
    307
  Civil War service and, 152
  college admissions and, 178
  in Congress, 150, 159, 365
  consequences of slavery and, 147–154. *See
    also* Slaves/slavery

Monroe Doctrine, 535
Montesquieu, Baron de, 46–47, 50
Montgomery Voters' League, 155
Moral idealism, 516–517
Morales, Dan, 159
Morella, Connie, 374
Morison, Samuel Eliot, 35
Morocco, Barbary pirates and, 535
Morris, Gouverneur, 42
Morrison, United States v., 98
Morse, Samuel, 374
Mossadegh, Mohammad, 532
Most-favored-nation status, 522
Mothers Against Drunk Driving (MADD), 476
"Motor-voter" law (1993), 319
Mott, Lucretia, 163
Mountain States Legal Defense Foundation, 242
MSNBC, 341
MSPB (Merit Systems Protection Board), 435, 439
Mubarak, Hosni, 400
Muir, John, 241
Municipal home rule, 563
Municipalities, 563–564
   defined, 563
   government of, 566–568
Murphy, Walter, 473
Muslim Americans, racial profiling and, 495
Mussolini, Benito, 468
Myanmar (Burma), sanctions against, 527
Myers, Richard B., 533

N

NAACP (National Association for the Advancement of Colored People), 151, 155, 232, 459
Nader, Ralph, 242, 279, 280–281, 284, 294, 310
NAFTA (North American Free Trade Agreement), 246, 400
Narrowcasting, 340
NASA (National Aeronautics and Space Administration), 430
Nast, Thomas, 568
Nation, 351, 352
National Abortion Rights Action League, 59, 242
National Academy of Sciences, 443
National Aeronautics and Space Administration (NASA), 430
National American Woman Suffrage Association, 164
National Archives, 55
National Association for the Advancement of Colored People (NAACP), 151, 155, 232, 459

National Association of Automobile Dealers, 235
National Association of Broadcasters, 348, 352
National Association of Manufacturers, 238, 254
National Audubon Society, 234–235, 239, 241, 509
National Broadcasting Company. *See* NBC, 339
National Cattleman's Association, 444
National chairperson, 270
National Coalition to Ban Handguns, 255
National convention(s), 307–308
   activities at, 307–308
   amending the United States Constitution and, 56
   defined, 268
   delegates to, 268–269
      compared to voters, on issues, 269
      credentials committee and, 307
      election of, 286
      seating, 307
      superdelegates and, 305
      women as, 270
National debt. *See* Public debt
National Defense Act (1916), 80
National Education Association (NEA), 233, 240, 246
National Education for Women's Leadership (the NEW Leadership), 166
National Endangered Species Act Reform Coalition, 443
National Enquirer, 338
National Environmental Policy Act (1969), 496
National Environmental Policy Institute, 509
National Farmers' Union (NFU), 238
National Federation of Business and Professional Women's Clubs, 165
National Gay and Lesbian Task Force, 189
National government
   aristocracy of, 432–433
   budget of
      budget cycle and, 383
      deficit and, 505–506
      preparation process and, 383–385
   building codes and, 85
   bureaucracy of
      civil service and. *See* Civil service
      congressional control of, 444–445
      organization of, 427–432
   illustrated, 427
   checks and balances system and. *See* Checks and balances
   civil service and. *See* Civil service
   courts of. *See* Court(s); Federal court system; Judiciary

deficit and, 505–506
employees of, number of, 426
executive branch of. *See* President(s)
growth of, Civil War and, 92
inefficiency in, presidential plans to end, 423
information about private citizens and, 128, 446
laws of, making of. *See* Congress, lawmaking process of
partisanship and, 368
powers of. *See also* Congress, powers of; President(s), powers of
   commerce clause and. *See* Commerce clause
   concurrent, 87
   division of, between powers of state governments and, continuing dispute over, 92–97
   enumerated, 85
   inherent, 86
   to levy taxes, 87
   limitation on, 14, 109, 147
   prohibited, 87
   separation of, 46–47, 207
   preemption by, 88
   public debt of. *See* Public debt
   skyscraper building codes and, 85
   spending by, 380, 383–385
      on Medicare and Social Security, 186, 384
      shift toward, illustrated, 95
National Governors Association, 554, 555
National Guard, 18, 80, 514
   federalized by President Eisenhower, 88, 152, 472–473
   of the United States, 80
National identification card, 108
National Institute of Standards and Technology, 85
National Intelligence Council, 9
National Labor Relations Board (NLRB), 431
National Marine Fisheries Service, 443
National Network for Immigrant and Refugee Rights, 172
National Newspaper Association, 352
National Opinion Research Center, 207
National Organization for Women (NOW), 165, 232
National origin, discrimination on basis of, 158, 159, 179, 186, 197
National Parks Conservation Association, 509
National politics, 276
National Public Radio, 335
National Railroad Passenger Corporation (AMTRAK), 432
National Retired Teachers' Association, 186

Photo Credits